CARTRIDGES
OF THE WORLD

**A COMPLETE AND ILLUSTRATED
REFERENCE FOR MORE THAN
1,500 CARTRIDGES**

FRANK C. BARNES
Edited by W. TODD WOODARD

Published by

Gun Digest® Books, an imprint of F+W Media, Inc.
Krause Publications • 700 East State Street • Iola, WI 54990-0001
715-445-2214 • 888-457-2873
www.krausebooks.com

To order books or other products call toll-free 1-800-258-0929
or visit us online at www.gundigeststore.com

ISBN-13: 978-1-4402-4642-5
ISBN-10: 1-4402-4642-4

Cover Design by Tom Nelsen
Interior Design by Sandi Carpenter and Kevin Ulrich
Edited by W. Todd Woodard
Managing Editor: Corey Graff

Printed in the United States of America

10 9 8 7 6 5 4 3 2 1

About the Covers

The cover of this 15th Edition of *Cartridges of the World* features some truly outstanding new ammunition offerings from Hornady Manufacturing. An industry leader when it comes to innovation in cartridge performance and reloading, Hornady continues to push the envelope for rifle and handgun hunters, long-range competitors and the self-defense market. To learn more check out their website at www.hornady.com.

Gracing the cover of this edition is Hornady's new Precision Hunter rifle ammo, featuring best-in-class ballistic coefficient ELD-X™ bullet with Heat Shield™ tip, a game-changer for shooters, which has been tested and confirmed via Doppler radar to retain its shape better through the flight curve by resisting deformation from air friction heat. The result is down-range accuracy previously thought impossible. But the bullet isn't just a tack-driver for paper targets — upon impact on game its tip plows rearward to start what can only be described as devastating expansion, while the bullet's thick jacket retains up to 85-90 percent weight for excellent penetration and wound channel characteristics. Indeed, it merges match-grade accuracy with a tough hunting bullet you can count on to take the trophy of a lifetime.

On the back cover is Hornady's American Gunner line of ammo, which features the tried-and-true XTP® (eXtreme Terminal Performance) bullet. American Gunner is equally adept at target shooting for fun or practice, or going after your chosen game animal. It's available in a wide array of handgun and rifle chamberings, from .380 Auto, .40 S&W, 9mm and .45 ACP to rifle offerings in .223 Rem., 6.8mm SPC, 300 Blackout, and .308 Win.

Foreword

Sportsmen and firearms enthusiasts in general are fond of indulging in a timeless, endless discussion that usually begins something like this: "If you had the opportunity to hunt all over the world, but due to space-weight limitations could carry only one gun, what would it be?" This simple assumption is good for hours or even days of lively debate. Also, on occasion, a few fist fights. This is mentioned, not to engage in any phase of this classic argument, but because it is apropos to a summary of this book.

Let me put it this way, if you were traveling to Mars or some other planet by rocket ship, and because of space-weight limitations could carry only one book on cartridges, what would it be? We sincerely hope it would be this one, because it contains more usable information per pound than any other single book on the subject.

As of this writing, there is no record of any copies of *Cartridges of the World* having been carried to other worlds, although the effort did get off the ground here on earth. The many letters received by the author and editors indicate that we certainly followed the right path in our treatment of the many known cartridges. The word used most often in describing this book is "useful." We consider this a high compliment, because it describes our original objective—to publish a useful cartridge book. We sincerely believe the buyer of this edition will also find it so. —*Frank C. Barnes*

Dedications

To my parents, Clifford and Margaret Barnes, whose encouragement of my boyhood dreams and ambitions made all that came later possible, this book is wholeheartedly dedicated. — F.C.B.

This 15th Edition is dedicated the wide-ranging interests of shooters everywhere, and their entertaining attempts to solve problems with lead, brass, copper and powder. When I poke around in the brass at the range these days, I constantly check headstamps to see what wonderful and unique arm the fellow at the next bench had been using. I see a single piece of .338 Lapua brass on the ground, bright and shiny, and I know it came from the fellow who had three long, camoflauge-clad rifles fitted with silencers, and whose groups were little cloverleafs downrange. A single piece of brass can raise so many questions. — W. Todd Woodard

Acknowledgments

For this and past editions of *Cartridges of the World*, we wish to give special thanks to the following people and organizations for their contributions toward the various improvements and additions:

Bill Ball, freelance journalist
Randy Brooks, CEO, Barnes Bullets
Steve Comus, Publications Director, Safari Club International
Michael Cyrus, Cross Outdoors / Lehigh Defense
Chris Ellis, Ellis Communications
Kevin Howard, President, Howard Communications
Hornady Manufacturing, Inc.
Tim Janzen, Chief Ballistician, Barnes Bullets
J.D. Jones, President, SSK Industries
Mike Jordan, Senior Account Executive, Howard Communications
Dave Kiff, Pacific Tool & Gauge
Dr. Ken Oehler, Oehler Research, Inc.
Christer Larsson, Norma
Jeff Patterson, Swanson Russell Agency
Rick Patterson, SAAMI
Carroll Pilant, Ballistician, Sierra Bullets
Gary Reeder, Reeder Custom Guns

Contents

Features

Cartridge Information

Introduction

The original philosophy worked out by myself and the late John T. Amber (the original editor) was to assemble a practical and useful book that would appeal to as broad a spectrum of the shooting fraternity as possible. The sales record of the book through the years indicates that this was the proper approach. This edition carries on in the same tradition as the previous editions in offering both something new, as well as retaining old data that is either useful or of general interest. There is really not much that can be done in the area of, say, obsolete cartridges, because nothing changes except that occasionally one or two of the old-timers will be reintroduced. This requires moving such cartridges back into the chapter covering modern cartridges, or, on the other hand, some commercially loaded number will be discontinued and relegated to the obsolete designation. Such changes are updated in this next edition. We have retained the encyclopedic reference format and are continuing to present the information from a shooter's and hunter's point of view.

Included is information covering handgun, rifle, shotgun, obsolete black powder, European, British, military, wildcat, and proprietary cartridges, along with data on the guns that shoot these cartridges, something for everyone. The information was obtained from many sources, including textbooks, new and old catalogs, periodicals, and individuals. Amber supplied many out-of-print and rare cartridge catalogs from his extensive library. Much information is from the author's and editors' files, as well as other original sources, and will not be found elsewhere. Practical experience also weighs heavily in the balance. I had more than 50 years of hunting, shooting, reloading and collecting experience. Amber was a gun collector with extensive hunting experience in North America, Europe, and Africa. Ken Warner, successor to Amber and former editor of *Gun Digest*, is also a collector, hunter, and shooter with many years of experience. This collective experience is reflected in the pages of this book.

The book is divided into chapters based on each category of ammunition: Current American Rifle, Obsolete American Rifle, Handgun, Military, etc. Ballistics and basic loading data have been included with each cartridge listing if possible. Extensive dimensional charts and tables are found at the end of each chapter. Dimensional data is presented in this manner, rather than with the individual cartridges, in order to simplify the identification of unknown cartridges. Cartridges are listed in the order of increasing bullet diameter, or, if caliber is the same, by length or power. One of the more difficult facts to establish with certainty is the date of origin for older obsolete cartridges. This is a matter of some importance to historians and, occasionally, archaeologists digging into our recent past when they find spent cases or cartridges in graves or on old battlefields. It can be useful when attempting to determine the caliber of certain guns or the relationship between firearms, ammunition and historical events. Those who write western novels or make similar movies might be well served if they would peruse the pages of this book, so that they would not constantly be placing the wrong guns in the wrong time period. It might surprise them to discover that the U.S. Cavalry in the 1870s did not carry either Model 1892 or 1894 Winchester lever-action carbines. These guns were unavailable then, and none of the cartridges those rifles chambered were ever adopted by the military.

Many law-enforcement agencies and military organizations have found *Cartridges of the World* to be a worthwhile reference source. It is also used as a basic text in colleges and universities for firearms identification courses. Firearms identification involves working with cartridges as much as working with firearms. *Cartridges of the World* even made it into television when it showed up in one episode of the once-popular cop show, *Miami Vice*.

Under the heading "General Comments," an effort has been made to rate the various cartridges for hunting purposes. Admittedly, any such ratings are highly subjective, since there is no quantitative formula for determining what cartridge is suitable for what game. Evidence (or lack thereof), observations in the hunting field, and personal opinion inevitably enter this process. If the reader takes issue with the author or editor regarding the efficacy of a particular cartridge for some specific purpose, it doesn't necessarily follow that someone is wrong. Rather, the problem is evaluated from different points of view. I remember reading several years ago about a fellow in Africa who fired a .22 Long Rifle at an elephant in an effort to scare it away from his garden. Unfortunately, he hit the poor beast and dropped it in its tracks with a single, misplaced round, and then really had a hell of a time getting it out. I hardly think that this qualifies the .22 Long Rifle as an elephant round, although some might think so. Also, many years ago, I ran into an old-time trapper in the Yukon Territory who had a much-used Savage Model 99 lever-action rifle chambered for the .303 Savage. He handloaded all his ammunition with hand-cast 190-grain bullets at a muzzle velocity of about 1950 fps, insisting this .30-30-class combination was more than adequate for moose, grizzly bear, or anything else—and with his experience as a woodsman, trapper, and hunter, it was. But not many present-day gun writers would agree. So ideas about what's good for what in the world of hunting cartridges depends a good deal on personal experience, skill, and opinion.

Finally we come to the subject of which cartridges should or should not be included within the pages of *Cartridges of the World*. Obviously, this book does not include every known cartridge in the world. If it did, it would have to be divided into many volumes. From time to time, certain readers write rather irate letters wondering why such-and-such a cartridge has not been included (or why we bothered to include certain cartridges). Admittedly, there must be hundreds of cartridges and variations that have been excluded. There are several reasons for this. First, editorial constraints on the number of pages don't leave sufficient room to include everything in one volume. The book has to be kept in balance to appeal to a general, rather than a specific, audience. Second, while most gun nuts are casual cartridge collectors, only a few shooters are avid cartridge collectors. There are already a large number of excellent books aimed specifically at the cartridge collector per se, such as those written by Charles Suydam, Herschel Logan, Fred Datig, and others. The criteria used in this book to determine what cartridges to include are based largely on what the author and editor perceive as being of greatest general interest, what has historical significance, or is of unusual interest. In all, the author and the editors have tried to please as many potential readers as possible, but remember, as in the biblical parable of the man and his donkey, it is impossible to please everybody.
—*Frank C. Barnes*

NOTE: In this edition, we have expanded the proprietary and wildcat cartridge chapters, and others have new additions, as well. In fact, we included more than 50 new cartridges, easily identified with "NEW."

DISCLAIMER: Any and all loading data found in this book or previous editions is to be taken as reference material *only*. The publishers, editors, authors, contributors, and their entities bear no responsibility for the use by others of the data included in this book or the editions that came before it.

WARNING: For any modern firearm, it is essential that you adhere to the loading recommendations put forth in the reloading manuals of today's components manufacturers, as well as to the owners manual of the maker of your individual firearm (some of today's firearms are so specialized that they will chamber and function reliably only within a very narrow set of criteria in a given caliber range). The potential for things to go wrong is exacerbated in guns long out of production, those chambering obsolete cartridges, and those using cartridges containing black powder or cordite. As a separate caution, you must *never* fire any cartridge in any gun just because it looks similar to, or has a similar designation to, the cartridge the gun is chambered for. This can be *extremely* dangerous. Almost is not good enough, so if you are at all uncertain about the proper cartridge, have a competent gunsmith check the bullet diameter and case dimensions and firearms chamber and headspace.

About the Author

It is not given to many of us in the bookish trades to create perennials, books that go on and on. Fellow named Webster did it with dictionaries and a woman named Irma Rombauer hit a good lick with *Joy of Cooking,* and Frank C. Barnes made the grade with this very book, *Cartridges of the World.*

Actually, Barnes was not, at the beginning, very deeply into bookish stuff. He was more of a doer. However, *COTW* caught him well and truly and held him, one edition after another, for decades.

Barnes died in 1992 and was sick a while before that. It was then he handed over the job, sure that the book would go on for decades.

He was born June 25, 1918, in Chicago, Ill. He began collecting cartridge data about age 12, which would be about 1930.

Before he began to write of guns and ammunition, he made a living as a geologist-engineer and spent a lot of time in the field in the West and Southwest. He did not "go hunting," he said many times, because he was already there. This experience made Barnes a practical hunter-rifleman, entitled to his opinions on rifles and shotguns and their cartridges. Barnes came to the same sort of competence with handguns even earlier — his father was a police officer who let his son shoot his sidearms if he kept them clean.

The net result was a practical sort of fellow, and his principal creation, *Cartridges of the World,* is a practical sort of book. He decided it should cover all the cartridges that count, that it should be a great guide to all of those and not get lost in the esoteric worlds of headstamps and variations. It proved a good plan.

Barnes was a pilot and raced sports cars and rode motorcycles. Eventually he received a Master's Degree in Justice, and taught law enforcement matters at the college level.

And he designed cartridges, too, becoming a respected wildcatter. When he generated the 458 American by cutting ½ inch off the redoubtable .458 Winchester Magnum, Barnes put it into a practical rifle. His shortened big bore fit very nicely into a short-actioned 722 Remington, stocked to the muzzle.

Barnes' last project, his last wildcat, was another practical sort of thing. It involved a .416 on the .45-70 case fitted into the Marlin Model 1895 lever-action rifle. This one was not to be, however — he just didn't get it finished. He did finish enough in his 74 years, however. If he's remembered as long as his book lasts, that's a lot longer than the rest of us ever count on.

About the Editor

Todd Woodard is Texan through and through. Born in San Angelo, he lived in various West Texas towns growing up, including Sweetwater, Odessa, and Midland. But most of his childhood years he spent in the small town of Crane, located about 30 miles south of Odessa. There, he could take his BB gun and walk two blocks to the west, slip between a couple of strands of barbed wire, and roam miles of hardscrabble dirt and mesquite in search of birds, lizards, and snakes. He became involved in 4-H, and as a youngster, handled his first Anschutz bolt action 22 LR, a loaner from the club. He won a state 4-H shooting championship with a Winchester 52D International and Canjar trigger.

Then in college at Texas A&M, he won four varsity letters with a Walther LGR air rifle and GX-1 three-position rifle, and was the first Aggie to participate in the NCAA Air Rifle Championships. At 56, he finally understands why old guys prefer to shoot prone.

Professionally, he's had bylines in *American Rifleman,* the *New York Times, Popular Mechanix,* and a variety of shooting and outdoors magazines. He has been a staffer at *Field & Stream,* editor of *Texas Fisherman* magazine, and has been editor of *Gun Tests* magazine since 1998. Under editor Ken Ramage, he updated the new-gun section in the *Gun Digest* annual for four years, and produced the *14th Edition of Cartridges of the World,* and before that, the *Shooter's Bible Guide to Cartridges,* and the *Brownells Guide to 101 Gun Gadgets.*

He enjoys sub-gauge shotgun shooting with his wife Tracey, son J.T., and daughter Cara in and around Houston.

Preface

The *15th Edition of Cartridges of the World* is an ongoing historical record of ingenuity and metalcraft that's impossible to absorb in one sitting. I imagine it's sitting on coffee tables, shop shelves, and in offices or other spaces wherever shooters have a minute to navel-gaze or scratch an intellectual itch. Over and over during the creation of new entries for this edition, I have wound up going down the rabbit hole, an allusion to *Alice's Adventures in Wonderland* by Lewis Caroll.

If you'll recall, Carroll's book opens with a young girl (Alice) strolling aimlessly through a meadow. She sees a white rabbit boasting a waistcoat, and then the rabbit "[takes] a watch out of its waistcoat-pocket, and [looks] at it." Alice realizes that "She had never before seen a rabbit with either a waistcoat-pocket, or a watch to take out of it, and, burning with curiosity, she ran [through] the field after it." Further, Alice decides to follow the rabbit, and she catches up with it "just in time to see it pop down a large rabbit-hole under the hedge. In another moment down went Alice after it, never once considering how in the world she was to get out again."

Thus, going down the rabbit-hole represents a new opportunity that leads to discovery and adventure. Even though Alice isn't sure where "chasing" this rabbit will lead, she's enthralled about the ability to embark on an adventure. Our trips down the COTW rabbit hole are not as fanciful as Alice's, but they are compelling nonetheless. If you start to pull the string on cartridges and their histories, you find adventure, intrigue, and innovation. That such innovation continues unabated — folks continue to search for the better mousetrap — becomes clear when you examine the new entries in this edition:

In Chapter 1, you'll find that for the first time in decades, Weatherby rolled out a new cartridge in 2016, the 6.5-300 Weatherby Magnum. But this cartridge isn't "new" new; Roy Weatherby himself built a 6.5-300 in the early 1950s, the proof being an old Mauser-action rifle in the company's historical collection. We learned that on June 27, 2016 SAAMI accepted the standards for the 6.5-300 Weatherby.

Other companies are jumping on the 6.5 bandwagon, as you'll see elsewhere in Chapters 1, 3, and 4. In Chapter 1, the 6.5x47 Lapua case has a base diameter and loading length similar to the .308 Win., allowing it to accept the same bolt heads and fit into similar actions and magazines. In the field, the performance of the 6.5x47 Lapua closely resembles the .260 Remington, and I think of the 6.5x47 to be a shortened and improved .260 Remington, with a sharper shoulder and a longer neck.

The 6.5mm SAUM (or RSAUM) is a necked-down case made from a 7mm Remington Short Action Ultra Magnum (7mm SAUM) or a 300 SAUM case. The SAUM cases are short, fat, and unbelted and are designed to work in short-action rifles. The 6.5mm SAUM may be able to displace the need for magnums for long-range hunting and competition when they are loaded with high-BC, long bullets.

The 6.5 MPC (Multi Purpose Cartridge) by SSK Industries is based on the 5.56 cartridge shortened and opened to 6.5mm, with the same OAL as the 5.56. Like the similar 6.8 SPC, the 6.5 MPC is superior to the 5.56 NATO downrange, but the 6.5 MPC offers some benefits over and above the 6.8 SPC. The 6.8 round requires conversion of barrels, bolts and caliber-specific magazines. In M16/AR-15 rifles, the 6.5 MPC utilizes the 5.56 bolt and magazines as well as all other parts, except for the barrel.

Obviously, 6.5's are attempts by companies and wildcatters to offer ballistic solutions to various problems in the field, as are the extensive lineup of proprietary rounds put forth by B&M Rifles and Cartridges, in Chapter 4. Two hunters, William V. Bruton and Michael McCourry (thus the B&M), didn't want to carry heavy, long-action rifles on safari, so they began building a lineup of shorter cartridges that were optimized for handy bolt actions and lever actions – mainly, Winchester M70 WSM bolt-actions with barrels of 18 or 20 inches. Rounds include the 9.3 B&M, 375 B&M, 416 B&M, 458 B&M, 475 B&M, and 50 B&M, and then variations on those, including the 458 B&M and 475 B&M Super Shorts, the 50 B&M Alaskan, and others that are in development as wildcats in Chapter 3.

Then there's a developer who went the other way — a whole line of massive cartridges that can only be fired in 20-pound-plus firearms that don't have a lot of applications outside the "can this be done?" window. Ed Hubel is the wildcatter's name, and his creations include the 12 Gauge from Hell shotshell-based rifle cartridge in Chapter 3. Then there is the even bigger 4 Bore Hubel in Chapter 10, and then other Hubels back in Chapter 3, including the .499 Hubel Express No. 2, .585 Hubel Express, and .700 Hubel Express.

As you see, it's easy to spend hours bouncing around in the rabbit hole, so let's follow Alice and dive right in. — *W. Todd Woodard*

Cartridge Nomenclature

It is difficult or impossible for the novice to follow the action without some knowledge of cartridge caliber designation. Even the individual experienced with standard American ammunition may be ignorant of British, European, and obsolete American cartridge nomenclature. The subject, regrettably, is full of inconsistencies and confusion.

With the majority of American, British, or European (metric) cartridges, the caliber (indicating bore land diameter in 1/100-inch), is the first figure given. However, there are exceptions that will be pointed out later. Caliber may be given in terms of bullet or bore diameter (the later in either land or groove), and is neither accurate nor consistent. For example, we have the .307 Winchester cartridge, which uses the same .308-inch diameter bullet as the .308 Winchester. Then there is the .458 Winchester Magnum and the .460 Weatherby Magnum, both of which are loaded with the same .458-inch diameter bullet. In the latter example, the Weatherby people didn't want anyone to get their round mixed up with the Winchester design, so they changed the figures a little. That is one reason some cartridges do not follow in normal caliber designation in the dimensional tables. There are others.

The second figure, if there is one, is usually some distinguishing feature such as case length or powder charge. Cartridges of European origin are, almost without exception, designated in metric units by caliber and case length. Obsolete American cartridges or any that have a black-powder origin are designated by caliber and powder charge weight, or caliber/powder charge/bullet weight (the last two in grain weight). Smokeless powder charges vary so widely with the powder type and grain structure that this system is no longer used. However, there are, again, such exceptions as the .30-30 Winchester and .30-40 Krag. Here, the second figure represents the original smokeless powder charge, although it no longer has anything to do with it. With black-powder cartridges, the designation ".45-70 Springfield" means a .45-caliber bullet with 70 grains of black powder. The designation ".45-70-405" spells out the same cartridge, but with a 405-grain bullet to distinguish it from such other bullet loadings as the .45-70-500. And then there was the .45-56-405 carbine load — in the same case!

The truth of the matter is the American "system" of cartridge nomenclature really hasn't any system at all to it, and what there is can only be learned through reading and experience. Otherwise, you simply never know what is meant. For example, take the .30-06, a very popular military and sporting round. Here, the first figure shows the caliber, while the last two numbers are the date of origin. In other words, a .30-caliber cartridge — model of 1906. Or, again, the .250-3000 Savage (".25-3000" simply lacked that special "ring" the advertising folks wanted). This translates out as a .25-caliber cartridge firing a bullet at 3,000 fps muzzle velocity. Yet the bullet diameter is actually .257-inch and muzzle velocity varies with bullet weight from 2,800 to over 3,000 fps. Some of the older black-powder cartridges included the case length and type, thus, the .44-90 Sharps 2⅝-inch Necked or .45-120 Sharps 3¼-inch Straight. As you can see, cartridge nomenclature isn't a system at all — it's a *code*.

The British, to a large extent, follow the same "system" as we do. However, they add to the general confusion with such cartridges as the .577/.450 or .500/.465. Here, the second figure gives the approximate bullet diameter in 1/1,000-inch, and what is meant is that the .577 case is necked to .450-caliber, while the .500 case is necked to .465-caliber. The British may also add the case length. At this point, it is necessary to point out that some American wildcat (i.e., non-commercial), cartridges dreamed up by individual experimenters are designated by a similar, though opposite, system. Here, we have such cartridges as the 8mm-06, .30-338, and .25-06. These work out as an 8mm based on the .30-06 case, a .30-caliber based on the .338 Winchester case, and a .25-caliber based on the .30-06 case.

The Europeans have evolved the only real system of cartridge designation that is consistent and somewhat meaningful. Dimensions are in millimeters, including bore land diameter, case length, and type. The 7x57mm Mauser is a cartridge, for example, for use with a 7mm bore land size (7.21mm groove size), with a 57mm rimless case. The 9.3x74Rmm is a 9.3mm caliber with a 74mm rimmed case. The "R" denotes the rimmed type, while its absence indicates a rimless case. The name of the originator or manufacturer may follow. This is a relatively simple and straightforward system, but, unfortunately, it isn't perfect, either. The Germans used two rim types in some of their older cartridges, and this resulted in duplicate designations of cartridges that differ only in the rim (9.05x36.4R, 10.85x24.9R, etc.), and there must be at least three 9.3x72mm cartridges that differ only in case configuration. This is all something of a mess and probably too late to change. *Editor's Note: The late Frank Barnes, the original author of* Cartridges of the World, *in an effort to straighten things out (or, perhaps, add to the confusion), developed two wildcat cartridges that he designated as the .308x1½-inch and .458x2-inch.*

To further elucidate, the reader needs to know that there are two major classifications of cartridges — centerfire and rimfire. The former is fired by a primer located in the center of the case head, the latter by priming compound distributed throughout the entire inside of the rim's outer diameter. The modern centerfire cartridge primer is removable and replaceable, so that the case can be reloaded after it is fired. It is possible, but not practical, to reload rimfire cases after they have been fired. Centerfire cartridges are subdivided into two types based on the primer, Berdan and Boxer. The Berdan-primed case has the anvil as a separate protrusion or teat in the bottom of the primer pocket. The Boxer primer is completely self-contained, its anvil a part of the primer. All American-made ammunition is normally Boxer-primed, whereas much British and European ammunition is Berdan-primed. Most foreign-made ammunition manufactured for the American market has the Boxer-type primer.

Rim Types

There are four common types of centerfire cartridge cases based on rim type. These are rimmed, rimless, semi-rimmed, and belted. The British equivalents are flanged, rimless, semi-flanged, and belted. There is a fifth type, not widely used, which is the rebated rimless, in which the rim is of smaller diameter than the base of the case. Examples of cartridges with rebated rims would be the .284 Winchester and .30 Remington AR. The .41 Action Express pistol cartridge is also rebated. The purpose of the rebated rim is to allow the use of a standard diameter bolt with a larger diameter cartridge. In the past, there have been a few rimless cases without the usual extractor groove.

Both centerfire and rimfire cartridges may be of straight or necked type. Contrary to popular opinion, the necked case was *not* designed to provide greater velocity for smokeless powder cartridges. It evolved back in black-powder days, as a means of getting the same powder charge in a shorter case, thus allowing the repeating actions of the day to handle cartridges of the same power as the single-shots with their long, straight cartridges. Some of the very early rimfire cartridges were of the necked type.

The latest fad in cartridges is the caseless, or combustible type, an idea not really all that very new, as it actually dates back to the early 1800s or before. The original design used a nitrated paper or cloth container for the powder charge and, sometimes, the bullet. The entire package was loaded into the gun, and the powder and its container were consumed in firing. During World War II, the Germans began an intense research and development program to perfect caseless ammunition and design weapons to shoot it. The principal motivating factor at the time was the severe shortage of brass and other metal for cartridge cases. The Germans are known to have had at least partial success with caseless cartridges, and some insist complete success. United States military ordnance facilities, as well as private industry, have been working on the problem of caseless ammunition for the past 50 years or more. There has been considerable success in developing caseless and partially caseless artillery rounds, but there are still many problems in the small arms field. Obturation is a big problem, as is ejecting a misfired round from the chamber of a repeating action. Modern caseless ammunition usually consists of compressed powder grains fastened to the base of the bullet, or the powder may be encased in a plastic case made of the same material as the propellant. Ignition may be percussion or electrical, and there is, in some types, a booster charge extending through the center of the powder charge.

Cartridge Collectors

Though this book is not a collectors' manual, it nonetheless includes considerable material of use and interest to collectors and any serious student of cartridges and related weapons. The tables of dimensions are organized to facilitate cartridge identification. The key to reading these tables lies in the bullet diameter and case type. The reader must understand that, in measuring cartridge dimensions, certain manufacturing tolerances must be allowed, and these can affect the last, or even the second, decimal figure. Dimensional tolerances can be rather considerable with old black-powder cartridges and the modern bottlenecked numbers. Also, the true diameter of the obsolete paper-patched bullet should include the patch, not just the lead slug protruding from it. Minor variations in dimensions should not be mistaken for errors or the existence of an unknown caliber.

The dimensional tables can also be used to identify the caliber of a gun, if the chamber dimensions are known. This can best be determined by a chamber casting. The means of doing this are explained in Chapter 3. If you own an obsolete or foreign gun for which ammunition is not available, the tables of dimensions will assist in determining whether ammunition can be made by reforming some similar, existing case.

Metallic Cartridge Development

The self-contained metallic cartridge is a fairly modern development, one perfected only about 1850. The use of black powder as a propellant in guns in the Western world goes back something like 650 years, and the knowledge of gunpowder more than 700 years. The Chinese knew about gunpowder 500 or 600 years before it was introduced to Europeans, although they used it as fireworks and not as a propellant any earlier than the Europeans.

The centerfire cartridge, a necessary prerequisite to our modern ammunition, evolved during the 1860s and '70s. Smokeless powder and high-velocity cartridges date back only to the 1890s. Improvements since the turn of the century have been more in the area of improved ignition, powder chemistry, and bullet construction, rather than cartridge design. Charles Newton designed cartridges back around 1910 that, had modern powders been available, would have equaled the performance of present-day high-velocity developments of similar caliber and type. Smokeless powder military cartridges designed between 1888 and 1915 were so good that improvement was possible only after more advanced powders became available, and many of these cartridges were still in use through World War II. As the result of this situation, many modern innovations in the gun and cartridge field turn out, after a little investigation, to be a reintroduction of something really quite old.

A few examples of the not-really-very-new among modern cartridges are worth pointing out. The .244 Remington (6mm) makes a good case with which to start. Introduced in 1955, it is based on the .257 Roberts case necked down, which, in turn, is the 7x57mm Mauser slightly modified. Back in 1895, or thereabout, the Germans had a 6x57mm, made by necking down the 7x57mm Mauser. With the exception of a slight (insignificant) difference in the shoulder angle, the .244 Remington is a carbon copy of this much older cartridge.

The 7mm Remington Magnum is another brilliant "design" that is really just a modification of a much older cartridge. It is very similar to the .275 Holland & Holland Magnum introduced around 1912 or 1913. However, the H&H round didn't have a good American smokeless powder of later development to bring out its full potential. On the other hand, there are a number of wildcat 7mm short-belted magnums practically identical to the 7mm Remington Magnum that pre-date it by quite a few years and are identical in performance.

Yet another Remington innovation is the .280 Remington, a rimless cartridge based on the .30-06 case necked down. This is a dead ringer for the 7x64mm Brenneke, introduced in 1917. It is also practically identical to the wildcat 7mm-06 developed around 1928, so there is nothing very original here. It should be noted that none of these cartridges are interchangeable.

The commercial manufacturers are not alone in their design duplication. Many individuals have inadvertently done the same thing. One of the most popular wildcat cartridges anyone has thought up is the .35 Whelen, introduced about 1922 and adopted as a commercial standard by Remington, in 1987. This is simply the .30-06 case necked-up to .35-caliber. It was originated by the late Col. Townsend Whelen, but it is a very close copy of the German 9x63mm, which dates back to about 1905. As a matter of fact, a number of wildcat cartridges are nothing more than a duplication of some much older British or European designs. In fairness, it must be stated that the originator of the wildcat version probably was completely unaware of the existence of a parallel cartridge at the time.

Some companies and wildcatters go to considerable trouble to complete the circle, often coming up with something that duplicates a long-forgotten cartridge. If they were more familiar with the history of cartridge development, they could save a lot of time. The .444 Marlin, introduced during 1964, is a good case in point. To begin with, it is a poorly disguised copy of the wildcat .44 Van Houten Super that pre-dates it by at least three years. According to Parker Ackley, in his Handbook for Shooters and Reloaders, the .44 VHS is made by necking up the .30-40 Krag case, trimming it to two inches, and turning down the rim. When this is done, we end up with a near carbon copy of the 10.3x65Rmm Swiss cartridge (DWM 237A) that originated around 1900 or earlier. The only difference is in the fact that the 10.3mm case is .3-inch longer than the .44 VHS or .2-inch longer than the .444 Marlin. However, that's not all there is to the story, because 10.3x65Rmm cartridge is based on the brass .410

shotgun shell loaded with a conical bullet and fired in a rifled barrel. It is possible to make the .444 Marlin from brass .410 cases, and the new originators could have done the same thing in the beginning.

Cartridges don't just happen; they evolve in response to some need or use requirement. Our Western frontier dictated American cartridge development for 50 years or more. Its influence is still an important factor in directing the imagination of the modern hunter. British rifle cartridges, in the main, were designed for conditions existing in other parts of the world, such as Africa and India, rather than the home island. European cartridges were developed on one hand because of hunting conditions and available game on the European continent, and on the other to compete with American and British innovations. Since the end of World War II, there has been considerable blending and standardization of the various worldwide cartridge designs. More British and European rifles and cartridges are used by American gun buffs than ever before, and they, in turn, have adopted many of our ideas.

Modern Ammunition

The most important factor influencing the ammunition available at any given time is economics. The ammunition manufacturers are willing to produce anything that will sell, but, obviously, are most reluctant to tool up and turn out something for which there is little or no demand. Military developments, as illustrated by the .30 Carbine, .30-06, 7.62mm NATO (.308 Winchester), 5.56mm (.223 Remington), .45 ACP, and that old standby, the .45-70, have almost always provided a good long-term sales record, when introduced in sporting version. For this reason, the ammunition companies have usually been quick to adopt these. They have not been quite so enthusiastic in their attitude toward cartridges developed by individuals or wildcatters. However, Remington has been the leader in introducing commercial versions of what were originally wildcat cartridges. It initiated the trend with the .257 Roberts, back in 1934, and, since 1945, have added a number of others, including the .17 Remington, .22-250 Remington, 6mm Remington, .25-06 Remington, 7mm-08, 7mm Remington Magnum, and the 8mm Remington Magnum, to name most of them. Actually, we must recognize that Winchester adopted the .22 Hornet (an original wildcat development), in 1930. Also, the .300 Winchester Magnum and possibly the .358 Winchester were around in wildcat versions before the company decided to develop something similar. The .444 Marlin is another cartridge based on a wildcat innovation. Since most of these have had good sales records, it would not be surprising to see some of the other more popular wildcats introduced in commercial version as time goes on. This is a healthy trend, and we hope it will continue.

Nostalgia is another factor that is now exerting considerable influence on ammunition and firearms trends. Shooting muzzleloading and black-powder cartridge guns of all types is a solidly established facet of the shooting game. Although there have always been a few muzzleloading clubs and a small core of black-powder devotees, the current popularity of this sport has given birth to a whole new industry specializing in the manufacture of replica arms. Muzzleloading clubs with several hundred members are now common, and most states have special muzzleloading big-game hunting seasons. As an example of the magnitude of this development, Colt once again sold its cap-and-ball revolvers, Harrington & Richardson offered replicas of the U.S. 1873 Trapdoor cavalry carbine, Shiloh Rifle Mfg. will sell you 1874 Sharps carbines and rifles, and one can buy any number of Hawken-type muzzleloading replicas. What is mentioned here is only a very small portion of what is available to black-powder shooters. If you are interested in the full extent of the offerings in this field, I suggest you buy the latest edition of *Gun Digest* (from the same publishers that produce this book) and look in the manufacturer's web directory in the back of the book.

How does all this affect modern cartridges? The nostalgia syndrome is responsible for the reappearance of a number of long-obsolete cartridges, or at least new reloadable cases, although, admittedly, this is as yet on a rather limited or custom basis for most of the old-timers. Dixie Gun Works, for example, is offering new, reloadable cases in the old .50-70 Government caliber and has recently brought in the .41 Rimfire. The development of modern cartridges is a dynamic, rather than a static, process, although it does move in starts and stops, depending on the fads and trends of any given time. These, then, are the factors that shape our modern ammunition, and this includes some very exciting innovations (some old and some new) since the first edition of *Cartridges of the World*.

Cartridge Loading Data

Basic loading data has been furnished as part of the general information on each cartridge when available and if test rifles or cartridges were obtainable. Insofar as possible, the loads listed are for those powders that provide the most efficient velocity and energy for the caliber and bullet weight involved. With old black-powder cartridges or obsolete smokeless powder numbers, the objective has been to supply data that more or less duplicates the original factory performance figures. The cartridge loading data has been gathered from various published sources and the extensive experience of the original author and various editors. The data selected for inclusion in COTW provides a good starting point for the handloader, but there are many more good powders available for loading each cartridge than can possibly be presented here. It is, therefore, recommended that the serious reloader obtain one or more of the very fine reloading manuals published by Lyman, Speer, Hornady, Hodgdon, Sierra, Nosler, P.O. Ackley, and others. Loading data listed here does not necessarily agree with that published elsewhere, regarding the velocity obtainable with a given charge of powder, because the test conditions and equipment are not the same. There is no such thing as absolute loading data, and all published loads reflect the conditions of test firing, which include a number of important variables such as barrel length, chamber configuration, temperature, components used, test equipment, etc.

All loading data, wherever published, should be used with caution and common sense. If you are not sure or don't know what you are doing, *don't do it!* Since neither the author, editors, nor publisher has any control over the components, assembly of the ammunition, arms they are to be fired in, the degree of reloading knowledge involved, or how the resulting ammunition might be used, no responsibility, either implied or expressed, is assumed for the use of any of the cartridge loading data in this or any previous edition of *COTW*.

Cartridge Dimensional Data

The reader should understand that the cartridge schematics and the table of cartridge dimensional data at the end of this book are based either on actual cartridge measurements, SAAMI specs, or other drawings. In some instances, data is based on measurement of a single specimen. In others, it may be an average taken from several cartridges of different manufacture. The table is intended primarily to assist the reader in identifying cartridges, and its use for the purpose of chambering rifles is not recommended unless checked carefully against manufacturers' chamber dimensions. The reason? There are far greater differences in cartridge dimensions between makes and production lots than most people realize. There are differences in the third decimal place even within most 20-round boxes, in fact.

This brings up another point. From time to time, the editors will receive letters from readers complaining that their measurement of some cartridge dimension does not agree with ours and, therefore, we must be wrong. We have, for example, two letters before us — one claiming a certain figure is too high, the other stating that the very same figure is too low. The differences are all in the third decimal place. This is not a matter of anyone being wrong, but rather variances in manufacturing tolerance.

As a more specific example of the tolerance factor, I acquired a box of 10mm pistol ammunition for the Bren 10 and other semi-autos and, in measuring several rounds, found some discrepancy in the rim diameters. Just to see what the minimum and maximum figures were, I measured the entire 20-round box. It turned out that the minimum rim diameter was .419-inch and the maximum was .426-inch, or a difference of .007-inch. Is that a sufficient range to cause the pistol to malfunction? I hardly think so.

All of this is just to get the subject of cartridge dimensions into proper perspective. In any event, if your measurements don't match someone else's by a few thousandths of an inch, don't get excited and don't get the idea you may have discovered a new and heretofore unknown cartridge. You may be dealing with maximum and the other guy with minimum dimensions.—*Frank C. Barnes*

Cartridge
Identification BY Frank C. Barnes

Cartridge identification is important to anyone who works with cartridges, whatever the reason. It is of particular consequence to those involved in forensic firearms identification, military intelligence, or serious collecting. In addition to the information presented here, the collector of old, obsolete cartridges has special problems involving ignition systems and types not manufactured for 100 years or more. Much of this is beyond the scope of this book, but the basic procedures are still the same.

In teaching classes in firearms identification, I always tell my students that the easiest way to identify a cartridge is to look at the headstamp, if there is one, because in many instances that will tell you exactly what it is. Unfortunately, it isn't always that simple, since some cartridges don't have headstamps, or if it is a military or foreign round, the headstamp may not be readily decipherable. Additionally, the headstamp may be misleading. You might be dealing with a wildcat cartridge, something made by necking an original case up or down or otherwise changing the configuration. For example, the .30-06 case is used as the basis for a variety of wildcats using both military and commercial cases, so the headstamp would only indicate the original case, not the actual cartridge. Cartridge identification may range from a simple determination of caliber to the more complex ascertainment of the country of origin, date of origin, place of manufacture, and type of gun involved.

The various factors and problems involved in cartridge identification can be summarized as follows:

1. What is the caliber and/or other designation of the cartridge? For example, .38 Special, 9mm Luger, .250 Savage, 7.62x39mm (M43) Russian, .303 British, etc.
2. What type of cartridge is it: handgun, rifle, sporting, or military? Is it modern or obsolete?
3. What is the country of origin, who made it, and when was it made? The headstamp is usually the clue to these answers, but it may not do for all of them.
4. What is the functional character of the cartridge — ball, tracer, incendiary, explosive, sporting, match, etc.?
5. Is the cartridge functional? This usually requires actual testing and is important primarily to those in the forensic field. Obviously, one does not test-fire rare and valuable collectors cartridges.

Cartridges are classified on the basis of ignition type, case shape, and rim type. Combustion of the propellant charge is initiated by the primer. If the priming compound is distributed around the rim of the cartridge, it is a rimfire. If the priming compound is contained in a separate cup in the center of the case head, it is a centerfire. Until the advent of Remington's EtronX® ammunition and rifle system featuring electronic ignition in 2000, all small arms cartridges are percussion-fired. That is, the primer is detonated by the blow or impact of a hammer or firing pin. However, some military ammunition, usually of a size 20mm or greater, is electrically fired. There are two types of centerfire primers currently in general use, Boxer and Berdan. The Boxer primer is entirely self-contained with the anvil as a part of the primer. The Berdan type lacks the anvil that is produced as a small "teat" or protrusion in the primer pocket. Boxer-primed cases have a single flash hole in the center of the primer pocket, whereas Berdan-primed cases have two or more flash holes surrounding the anvil. The Boxer-type primer is used almost exclusively in the United States at the present time, although some Berdan-primed cartridges were manufactured here in the 1800s and early 1900s. The Berdan type is preferred by many European manufacturers and is usually an indication of such origin.

The cartridge base and rim type are important identifying features. These also serve an important functional purpose in feeding and extraction of the cartridge within the gun mechanism. There are five rim types: rimmed, semi-rimmed, rimless, belted and rebated.

Rimmed cartridges have a rim or extractor flange of larger diameter than the case base, often with a grooved or undercut area immediately ahead of the rim. Semi-rimmed cartridges have a rim that is only slightly larger in diameter than the base, and usually also a distinct undercut area between the rim and case base. It is

Cartridge Identification

sometimes difficult to recognize a semi-rimmed cartridge without actually measuring rim and base diameter, and these can easily be mistaken for a rimless case. Rimless cartridges have a rim and base of the same diameter, although the rim may actually be .001 or .002 inch larger than the base. These are the most common type of military cartridges. Belted cartridges have a distinct belt or flange at the base, just forward of the rim, and an extractor groove between the rim and the belt. Rebated cartridges have a rim of significantly smaller diameter than the case body at the base, plus a definite extractor groove between rim and base or belt. Only a few rebated cartridges have been

commercialized with success, and those are usually easy to identify. In several rebated rim designs, the rim is only very slightly smaller than the case head. The .404 Jeffery and its derivatives (chiefly the Imperial and Canadian Magnums) are the best examples. These can be difficult to identify without taking careful measurements. Also, note that naming a case design "semi-rimmed" versus "rimmed" is strictly a subjective call — there is no specified difference in base diameter and rim diameter that automatically separates these two styles. However, cases described as semi-rimmed are usually visually distinguishable from similar rimless cases.

The shape or configuration of the car-

tridge case is also an important identifying characteristic. Cartridges can be divided into the following 12 case types, with their corresponding letter designation used in the cartridge dimensional tables at the end of each chapter:

A. Rimmed bottleneck
B. Rimmed straight
C. Rimless bottleneck
D. Rimless straight
E. Belted bottleneck
F. Belted straight
G. Semi-rimmed bottleneck
H. Semi-rimmed straight
I. Rebated bottleneck
J. Rebated straight
K. Rebated belted bottleneck
L. Rebated belted straight

It will be important to note when referencing these letter designations that some cases described and lettered as straight are actually often tapered; case diameter can be considerably larger at the base, compared to the neck.

The bullet or projectile also provides a clue to the identity of a cartridge, its functional use, and the gun it is fired in. Based on the material or construction, bullets are divided into two major types, lead and jacketed. Lead bullets are used for low-velocity guns, such as handguns or black-powder arms. However, these may also be used for target practice in more powerful guns. Training cartridges may have wooden, fiber, composition or plastic bullets. The shape of the projectile is also important and can be round-nose, flat-nose, conical or spitzer (sharp pointed). Because of the Hague Convention, military bullets do not have lead exposed at the point and are restricted to full-metal-jacket types. Sporting ammunition or that intended for civilian use can have a variety of bullet tips with varying degrees of lead exposed, hollowpoint, plastic tips and bronze or other metal tips, to control expansion in the target.

Bullets for military use can also be classified in terms of special functional design, such as ball; tracer (T); armor-piercing (AP); incendiary (I); high explosive (HE); and observation/ranging, or spotter-tracer types. There can also be two or more of these combined in the same bullet, such as APT, API-T, HEI, or HE-T. Not all types are made in every cartridge, since their function is developed to fulfill a specific military requirement. In addition, makeup depends, to some extent,

CASE TYPES

on the gun for which each is loaded. In general, ball or full metal jacket (FMJ) bullets are intended for use against personnel or unarmored vehicles. These usually have a lead core covered by a cupronickel jacket, or a mild steel jacket plated with some copper alloy. These can be easily identified with a magnet. At one time, the French 8mm Lebel military bullet was made of solid bronze. Tracer bullets are used for fire correction or target designation. These cannot be distinguished from ball, unless some identifying marking, such as a colored tip (usually, but not always, red), is included. Armor-piercing bullets are also similar to ball except they have a hardened steel or tungsten alloy core. They may or may not have a colored tip. Incendiary bullets contain an incendiary mixture that ignites on impact; visual identification depends on the color-coding system used. High-explosive bullets are uncommon, but do exist. These are made to explode on impact and can only be recognized by the color-coding. Observation and ranging bullets are intended to produce a flash and/or a puff of smoke to mark the point of impact. Again, these are recognizable only when color-coded. One should handle any ammunition with a colored bullet tip with great care, as appropriate.

The headstamp is the stamped markings on the head of the cartridge. Information that can be obtained from the headstamp is extremely varied and depends on the intended purpose or use of the cartridge and who manufactured it.

Headstamps consist of one or more parts or information elements. Cartridges intended for sporting or civilian use usually have two elements. One identifies the specific chambering, the other identifies the manufacturer. Military cartridges can have from one to five elements, including cartridge, date and place of manufacture, plus other identifying markings. Some headstamps are segmented. That is, these have one or more segment lines that divide the head into two to four equal parts. This usually indicates an older cartridge, since most countries discontinued segment lines shortly after World War I. The location of the elements is most conveniently indicated by its clock-face orientation, with 12 o'clock at the top, three o'clock at the right, six o'clock at the bottom, and nine o'clock at the left. The basic U.S. military headstamp before World War II had two elements, with the factory code

at 12 o'clock and the date at six o'clock. Rapid expansion of ammunition manufacturing facilities as the result of the war introduced many new designs without any effort at standardization. Some used three elements spaced equidistant from each other while others adopted a four-element system located at 12, three, six, and nine o'clock. Also, the location of the factory code was changed, in some instances, to six o'clock or another location.

Worldwide, there are more than 800 military headstamps in existence plus some 400 or more commercial headstamps that have existed at various times. Obviously, this is a complex and highly specialized field. Several volumes have been published on headstamps, including at least three by various U.S. governmental agencies. In addition, some books for cartridge collectors include headstamp data on obsolete cartridges. Since it would require another whole book to adequately cover the subject, it is quite impossible to include more than a few basics here. However, we have listed several sources for such data to assist those readers who find a need for it.

The procedure for identifying a cartridge, using the tables in *Cartridges of the World*, are as follows:

1. First look at the headstamp and see what, if any, information is provided there.
2. Look at the cartridge and determine what type it is: straight, necked, rimmed, rimless, etc.
3. Measure the dimensions of the cartridge and make up a table as follows:
   Type (A, B, C, D, etc., as shown in the tables)
   Bullet Diameter
   Neck Diameter
   Shoulder Diameter (if there is one)
   Base Diameter
   Rim Diameter
   Case Length
   Cartridge Length

Now go to the cartridge measurement tables in Chapter 12 or at the end of each group chapter and compare your data with the dimensional data. Check bullet diameters under the proper type, and then compare case length and, finally, other dimensions with your measurements. The

type of cartridge case, caliber, and case length are the key elements to start with. For practice, two examples are shown below. See if you can identify the cartridges.

Example #1
Type: C

Bullet Diameter:	.308"
Neck Diameter:	.340"
Shoulder Diameter:	.441"
Base Diameter:	.470"
Rim Diameter:	.473"
Case Length:	2.490"
Cartridge Length:	3.340"

Example #2
Type: B

Bullet Diameter:	.410"
Neck Diameter:	.432"
Shoulder Diameter:	n/a
Base Diameter:	.433"
Rim Diameter:	.488"
Case Length:	1.280"
Cartridge Length:	1.580"

Bear in mind that there is a certain amount of manufacturing tolerance to be allowed for and your measurements may vary .001- to .002-inch plus or minus from some dimensions in the table. The cartridge in Example 1 will be found in the chapter on modern rifle cartridges; Example 2 is in the chapter on handgun cartridges. Not every known cartridge is listed in *Cartridges of the World,* particularly the more obscure black-powder types. However, practically all modern sporting and military are included, so most readers will not have any difficulty. The idea here is to help you to determine what the cartridge is rather than where it originated or when.

In trying to identify cartridges, there are a couple things the reader should know. For one thing, the major ammunition manufacturers have, from time to time, made up batches of ammunition on special order with the purchaser's headstamp. Anyone can do this if your order is large enough and you have the money. Then there is the matter of commercial reloading firms that turn out ammunition for police departments and others using recycled cases of varying make and loaded with powder and bullets never used by the original company. Last, but not least, you have the individual handloader whose imagination is unbounded and who may turn out a few wondrous and non-standard products.

Cartridge Identification

Headstamp Markings of the Principal American Ammunition Manufacturers

Federal Cartridge Co.
Rimfire, AL EP, G or G, HP, F, XL, XR and WM Centerfire, FC

General Electric Co.
GE plus date (military)

Newton Arms Co.
NA plus caliber (Made by Rem.)

Peters Cartridge Co.
Rimfire, P or PETERSHV Centerfire, P, PC, P.C., PCCO,

PETERS E. Remington & Sons
E REMINGTON & SONS (1870-1890)

Remington Arms Co.
U, UMC, REM, REM*, UMC, R-P, RAH

Robin Hood Ammunition Co.
R, RHA, R.H.A. Co.

Savage Arms Co.
S.A. Co. (made by U.S. Cartridge Co.)

Savage Repeating Arms Co.
S.A. Co., S.R.A.C.O.

Richard Speer Manufacturing Co.
SPEER WEATHERBY

Union Metallic Cartridge Co.
U, UMC or R B (Purchased by Remington in 1911)

United States Cartridge Co.
US, U.S., *U.S. CARTRIDGE CO*,U.S.C. CO. or RL (1869 to 1936)

Western Cartridge Co.
SUPER X, SUPER-X, W, WCC, W.C. Co. WESTERN

Winchester
W, H, SUPER SPEED, W.C. Co.

Winchester-Western
W-W, super speed

There were about 15 other companies that manufactured ammunition at various times, particularly during the 1860-1900 period. Also a number of private firms manufactured military ammunition during World War I and II.

United States Arsenal Headstamp Markings

Alleghany Ordnance Plant	KS plus date
Denver Ordnance Plant	DEN plus date
Des Moines Ordnance Plant	DM plus date
Eau Claire Ordnance Plant	EW plus date
Evansville Ordnance Plant	ECS plus date
Frankford Arsenal	CF plus date (45-70) F plus date FA plus date
Lake City Arsenal	LC plus date
Lowell Ordnance Plant	LM plus date
Milwaukee Ordnance Plant	M plus date
Saint Louis Ordnance Plant	SL plus date
Twin Cities Ordnance Plant	TW plus date
Utah Ordnance Plant	U plus date UT plus date

U.S. Small Arms Ammunition Color Codes

Bullet Tip Marking	Functional Type
Black	Armor piercing (AP)
Red	Tracer
White	Tracer, aircraft type
Blue	Incendiary

Bibliography of Cartridge Identification Publications

Jane's Directory of Military Small Arms Ammunition, by Ian V. Hogg. Jane's Publications, Inc., N.Y., N.Y., 1988.

Cartridges For Collectors, by Fred A. Datig. The Fadco Publishing Co., Vol. I, 1956 and Vol. 2, 1958.

Cartridges For Collectors, by Fred A. Datig. Borden Publishing Co., Los Angeles, Calif., Vol. 3, 1967.

Handbuch der Pistolen und Revolver Patronen, Vol. 1, by Hans A. Erlmeier und Jakob H. Brandt. E. Schwend GmbH, West Germany, 1967.

History of Modern U.S. Military Small Arms and Ammunition, by F.W. Hackley, W.H. Woodin, and E.L. Scranton. The Macmillan Co., N.Y., N.Y., 1967.

Cartridges, by Herschel C. Logan. The Stackpole Co., Harrisburg, PA, 1959.

Cartridge Guide 11/71, by Dr. Manfred R. Rosenberger, and Lilla E. Rosenberger. Sporting Goods GmbH, Bremen, West Germany, 1971.

The American Cartridge, by Charles R. Suydam. G. Robert Lawrence, Santa Ana, CA, 1960.

Centerfire Metric Pistol and Revolver Cartridges, Volume 1 of Cartridge Identification, H.P. White and B.D. Mundhall. The Infantry Journal Press, Washington, DC, 1948.

Centerfire American and British Pistol and Revolver Cartridges, Volume 2 of Cartridge Identification, by H.P. White and B.D. Munhall. The Combat Force Press, Washington, DC, 1950.

Cartridge Headstamp Guide, by H.P. White and B.D. Munhall. H.P. White Laboratory, Bel Air, MD, 1963.

Small-Caliber Ammunition Identification Guide, Volume 1 & 2; Army Material Development and Readiness Command, DST-1160G-514-78-Vol. I & II.

Recognition Guide of Ammunition Available to, or Used by, The Viet Cong; Dept. of the Army Pamphlet #381-12, 1966.

Small Arms Ammunition Identification Guide; U.S. Army Foreign Science Technology Center, FSTC-CW-7-68, Washington, DC 20315.

EXAMPLES OF HEADSTAMP STYLES

SINGLE ELEMENT
6 O'CLOCK

DOUBLE ELEMENT
6 & 12 O'CLOCK

TRIPLE ELEMENT
2, 10 & 6 O'CLOCK

RIMFIRE
FEDERAL CART. CO.

QUADRUPLE ELEMENT
3, 6, 9 & 12 O'CLOCK

DOUBLE SEGMENTED
3 & 9 O'CLOCK

QUADRANGLE SEGMENTED
FOUR ELEMENTS
2, 4, 8 & 10 O'CLOCK

MILITARY
DENVER ORDNANCE
PLANT 1943

COMMERCIAL
REMINGTON

COMMERCIAL
WESTERN CART. CO.

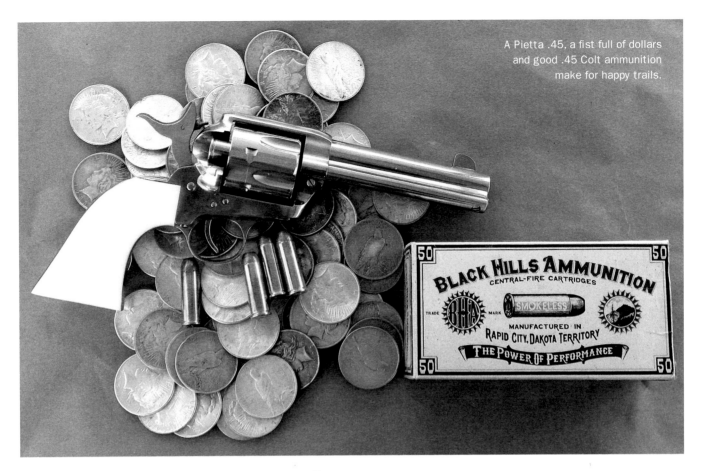

A Pietta .45, a fist full of dollars and good .45 Colt ammunition make for happy trails.

Cowboy Calibers

Some of the cowboy calibers are timeless cartridges, offering excellent performance. Others are less desirable for a modern shooter.

BY BOB CAMPBELL

Cowboy action shooting has been one of the greatest developments in the shooting sports. As a fan of Western operas, I didn't need cowboy action to spark my interest, but it has made replica guns, holsters and even ammunition much easier to find. The fun and challenge of the shooting sports with a single-action revolver and lever-action rifle is awfully appealing. I have my favorites, including examples from Colt, Pietta, Uberti and Winchester. Anyone who takes firearms design seriously will appreciate the exquisite appeal of a Colt Single Action Army or Winchester 1892 rifle.

Quite a bit of shooting occurs during a cowboy action match. This means the accuracy and economy of the caliber are important. Yes, in modern times, light recoil and economy might be more important when the target doesn't shoot back. But some of us like traditional firearms for carry on the trail and even hunting small and medium game. What they did years ago they will do

Cowboy calibers can be quite versatile. Left to right, here's a .32-20 with a hard cast bullet, a .32-20 with a rifle-only JHP load, a .38 Special Winchester Cowboy load, a .44 Special Critical Defense, .a 44-40 Hornady, .a 44-40 hard cast, a .45 Colt Winchester SXT and a Black Hills Ammunition .45 Colt Cowboy load.

Cowboy Calibers

The traditional SAA action features a firing pin in the hammer, but the transfer-bar action has a frame-mounted firing pin. Make your choice, and then check caliber availability.

The ready availability of affordable .38 Special loads edged out the other calibers for cowboy action use.

This shoulder holster by Rock K Saddlery (rockingksaddlery. com) is difficult to make and superbly authentic. The author often carries the .357 Mag. under his coat when hiking or traveling during winter.

again. And although I won't press the issue with the tactically minded, more than a few homeowners keep a cowboy gun at ready for home defense. The lever-action rifle in particular — sometimes called the cowboy assault rifle or Brooklyn special — is a great choice for home defense.

In this report, I'll look at cowboy cartridges from all angles, including competition, hunting and personal defense. If you're going to begin cowboy action shooting, some choices are better than others. Some folks, like me, searched for a period firearm and ended up with what was available or affordable. You should avoid these calibers. And when you are choosing a caliber, you're doing so for two distinctly different firearms. If you're going to shoot cowboy action, the handgun and rifle should be chambered for the same cartridge. For a casual shooter, this isn't as important, but the combination can be beneficial.

Caliber Choices

You have two basic considerations: original calibers and calibers chambered in replicas. The originals are what they are. Modern firearms are chambered for most of the cowboy calibers and also modern calibers. Availability is important. If you run short on ammunition, you cannot run into most shops and pick up a supply of .44-40 WCF. If the store has ammunition, it will probably be .38 Special, so that's one consideration.

The caliber is tied to firearms choice. For example, many modern shooters like a single-action revolver with the transfer-bar system. The original revolvers demand that the revolver be carried hammer down on an empty chamber. You load one, skip one, load four, cock the hammer and then lower the hammer on an empty chamber. Modern transfer-bar systems are safer. If you

The most versatile cowboy action caliber is easily the .357 Mag. when you consider use with .357 Mag. and .38 Special ammunition.

You cannot get an original rifle in stainless steel. The Rossi has advantages.

The new Rossi .357 Mag., top, is more practical. The appeal of the Winchester 1892 in .32-20 is undeniable. Note the Lyman tang sight, a recent addition.

Cowboy Calibers

These modern lever-action replicas are great all-around rifles. The Rossi, top, is far more practical than the Uberti Henry rifle, lower, but the Uberti wins on the cool factor. They're chambered in .357 Mag. and .44-40, respectively.

believe the original action is more crisp, adhere to safety, and keep five beans under the wheel. Even so, when gifting the children or wife with a SAA, I always choose a transfer-bar action.

The original SAA calibers are .32-20 WCF, .38-40 WCF and .44-40 WCF. You'll also find the .45 Colt and a few other calibers in this handgun, but the .45 Colt was not originally chambered in lever-action rifles. Smith & Wesson cowboy gun calibers include the .44 S&W American, .44 Russian, and .45 Schofield. The latter two cartridges are available from Black Hills Ammunition. A high-volume cowboy action shooter will obtain a set of loading dies, a steady supply of brass from Starline and a good supply of cast bullets. A recreational shooter might have a different perspective.

I regard the .45 Colt as the greatest handgun caliber based on man-stopping ability and the .44-40 WCF as the superior rifle cartridge. But a stage at cowboy action might change my mind. Further, a cowboy action shooter needs two revolvers in competition. So, we really need three firearms chambered in the same caliber for cowboy matches. Light recoil and economy are important.

Cowboy action loads are pretty light, and light recoil and the .44-40 are not mutually exclusive. A 200-grain flat-point .44 at 800 fps doesn't kick very much. One caliber we need to discuss is the .41 Colt. The collector's market for SAA revolvers isn't the shooter's market. If you find an affordable Colt SAA in .41 Colt, or .455 Eley and such, it's best to avoid this relic, unless you're willing to rebarrel the piece and add a cylinder in a more useful caliber. It's terribly expensive to obtain and difficult to load. The .32-20 WCF is the baseline, and I admit affection for this cartridge. The .32-30 is readily available from Black Hills Ammunition; 115 grains at 780 fps from the pistol and 1,100 fps from the rifle. If you're looking for low recoil, this is it. If you

It's possible to load the Barnes X bullet in many cowboy calibers. At moderate ranges, this is an effective combination. The .45 Colt responds well to a careful loader.

handload, the dinky little brass is a bit hard to handle, and you will crush an occasional case mouth. In a lever-action rifle, this is a great small-game round. A Hornady 85 grain XTP at 1,800 fps is a good coyote load.

The .38-40 is the midsize WCF. I have little experience with this. Black Hills offers a good load, and I have fired it in vintage Colts. In a good, strong smokeless-powder Colt, you can stroke a 200-grain bullet to about 1,000 fps. It's similar to the 10mm

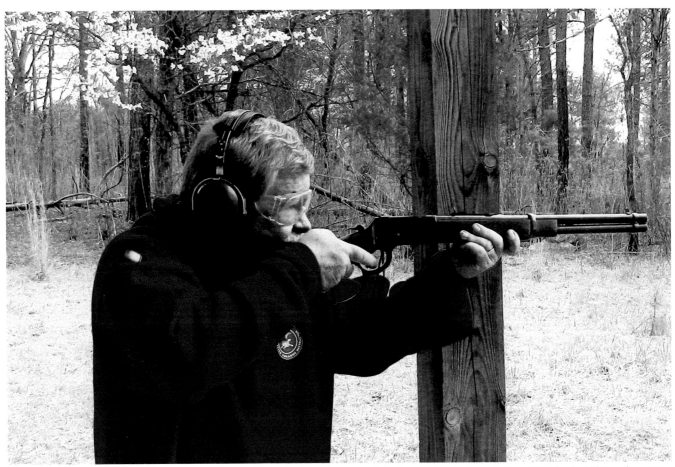

The short throw of the pistol-caliber lever-action allows for fast shooting. Note the cartridge case at the author's shoulder as he gets back on target with the Rossi .45 Colt.

but not quite as strong. If you own a vintage pair of Colt and Winchester firearms, you have fine guns, but those would not be my first choice. The .44-40 WCF is more readily available. Starline produces excellent brass for WCF cartridges. The Black Hills Ammunition .44-40 load is brilliantly accurate in revolvers and rifles. My Uberti replica Henry rifle is chambered for .44-40, which is a great choice for convenience. Not many of us wish to chase down the .44 Rimfire. This rifle cannot be loaded higher than cowboy action pressure, and the Black Hills Ammunition load is ideal. With cast bullets, the .44-40 is economical. It's reasonably effective for personal defense, even with cast bullet CAS loads, and with proper loading, a Winchester '92 is a great game rifle.

The .45 Colt is an odd man out because original rifles were not chambered in this caliber. A caution on the original firearms: Chamber dimensions were not always consistent. The bullets, usually 20 parts lead to 1 part tin, were soft enough to slug up and deliver good accuracy. Hard cast bullets are not always best in period firearms.

Modern Calibers

Modern calibers useful for cowboy action shooting include the .32 H&R Mag., .38 Special, .357 Mag., .44 Special, .44 Mag. and .45 Colt.

Let's get the obvious misfit out of the way first. The .45 Colt is included in modern calibers because it was not chambered in lever-action rifles on the frontier. Many marshals carried a .45 Colt revolver and .44-40 WCF rifle. The .45 Colt is the least economical of the cowboy cartridges because it's big. The cartridge cases are large, and the bullets are heavy. Just the same, this straight-walled case is easy to load and handle. In lever-action rifles, I've never found the .45 Colt as accurate as the .44-40. On the other hand, when hiking or during days when a SAA just feels right on the belt, there is no SAA caliber I have more confidence in than the .45 Colt. Loaded with a 250-grain SWC at 950 fps on the trail or a Hornady Critical Defense JHP around home, this is a potent combination.

The greatest cowboy caliber might not be the best for competition shooting. The .32 H&R Mag. is a neat cartridge

This Pietta features factory engraving and a transfer-bar ignition, and is chambered for .357 Mag. It doesn't get any better.

This long-barreled Rossi with an octagon barrel is brilliantly and even surprisingly accurate in .357 Mag.

that's easier to handload than the .32-20, although not quite as strong or authentic. Further, it's easily the most economical of all cowboy guns. The Marlin 1894 CB in .32 Mag. is more accurate than Winchester clones, on average. For field use, the Hornady 85-grain XTP over a stout charge of H110 works well, if you're so inclined. Black Hills Ammunition offers a cowboy load.

When you consider the .38 Special and .357 Mag. combination, I recommend the .38 Special for cowboy action shooting. Most SAA revolvers are available in .357 Mag. It's fine to use .38 Special in these handguns. In the lever-action rifle, the shorter .38 Colt does not feed well, so use .38 Special brass. This combination is recommended for cowboy action shooting. The .38 Special is widely available, accurate, economical and useful for small-game hunting. Recoil with mild loads is practically indistinguishable from the .32s. Black Hills Ammunition offers a 158-grain load that travels just slower than 800 fps. The only .38 Special load likely to be more accurate is the 148-grain match load from the same maker. The caliber is more than accurate enough for cowboy action matches. As for the magnum, if I learned anything in 20 years behind a badge, it's that you cannot always have the best cards. The .357 Mag. might stack the deck in your favor. For personal defense and firing at 100 yards or farther in the rifle, the .357 Mag. is easily the most accurate of the possible combinations for cowboy action shooting. My faith is strong in the .45 Colt, but much of it is hearsay, and my experience with the magnum is personal. For home defense, the .357 Mag. and Hornady 125-grain Critical Defense are ideal. In the

rifle, a Hornady 140-grain LEVERevolution or a handload with the 1,800-grain XTP are excellent choices for close-range deer. Unless you just love the smell of black-powder smoke and the cowboy ideal, the .38/.357 combo is at the top of the heap.

The .44 Special is a grand old cartridge. When used in cowboy action shooting, it's accurate and mild shooting. It's easier to handload than the .44-40 because of the Special's straight-walled cartridge case. All factory loads are rather light, but the Black Hills Cowboy load is accurate and affordable in 50-round boxes. Economy is good. When handloaded, it will outpace the .44-40 with heavier bullets. The SAA revolvers are usually chambered in .44 Special, the rifles in .44 Mag. A .44 Mag. rifle kicks a bit but is deadly on big boar hogs. I've never seen anything die so quickly as a large hog hit with a 240-grain XTP. So, this combination has much merit and is superior in every way to traditional cowboy loads.

Summary

I used the logic ladder and surprised myself with my conclusions. However, a demonstration of positive science is always better than myth. The modern .357 Mag. cartridge is the best all-around choice not only for cowboy action shooting — even if that's the only task of the firearms — but also for hunting and home defense. Close behind comes the .44 Special/Mag. combination. It's kind of like putting a modern Chevy engine in a '37 Chevy truck. Looks and tradition are cool, but practical everyday use wins out.

The .45 Colt:
A Wheelgun Classic

Everyone loves this classic cartridge, and it's still relevant after almost 150 years.

BY PHILLIP MASSARO

1873 was a notable year in American history. The Indian Wars and westward expansion were underway, and the stock market crash that autumn started the first financial depression. Our nation was still reeling from the effects of the Civil War, and the firearms and cartridges that fought that terrible conflict were changing rapidly and radically. Muzzleloading rifles and cap-and-ball pistols were fading quickly and being replaced by lever-action repeating rifles and centerfire revolvers. Among the numerous designs, a cartridge was developed and adopted by the U.S. Army that would change firearms history: the .45 Colt.

Although the .44-40 took a large portion of the nostalgic Western spotlight, the .45 Colt was, and still is, a terrific cartridge. Hell, .45 Colt — and only the .45 Colt — was dubbed "The Peacemaker." It can be equally at home in a Colt Single Action Army revolver or a modern lever-action rifle, making for a sensible short-range woods gun. In the hands of soldiers, the .45 made a formidable weapon, and although its tenure as the official sidearm of the U.S Army was brief compared to John M. Browning's fabled .45 ACP, it left an indelible mark on military cartridge design. In the late 19th century, the U.S. military's pursuit of lighter and potentially more effective cartridges (think of the transition from .45-70 Gov. to .30-40 Krag) led to .45-caliber sidearms being replaced by the .38 Long Colt. However, the Philippines insurrection demonstrated the weaknesses of the .38 and superiority of .45-caliber cartridges.

The original incarnation of the .45 Colt was a 255-grain lead bullet over a charge of 40 grains of black powder, generating a muzzle velocity of about 900 fps from the 7½-inch barrel of the Colt Single Army revolver. That load was slightly reduced to a velocity of 850 fps, and made the cartridge famous. Mild enough to be handled effectively yet potent enough to end an argument quickly, the .45 Colt was an instant success. Its immediate competitor was the .45 S&W, better known as the .45 Schofield. The Colt case is a bit longer than the Schofield's, and the Colt cham-

The .45 Colt, center, can use bullets made for the .45 ACP, left. As with any straight-wall cartridge for a revolver, it requires a good roll crimp on the finished cartridge to keep the bullet in place. The same goes for the .454 Casull, right.

ber can handle the Schofield cartridge, yet the reverse is not true. The bullet diameter of modern jacketed bullets for the .45 Colt is 0.452 inch, though some of the earlier pistols had wide variation of cylinder and throat diameters. This has been resolved in modern firearms, resulting in cartridges and reloading dies that will give proper bullet tension with lead and jacketed bullets.

The case length of the .45 Colt is the source of the addition of the Long moniker, indicating the difference between it and the shorter Smith & Wesson Schofield case. The addition of the word Long irritates many shooters, but whatever label the shooting world wants to put on the cartridge, it's obvious it was a favorite of gunfighters, pioneers, lawmen, career criminals, American Indians and Indian fighters. It's the only cartridge I can name that has had a Major League Baseball team named in honor of it (OK, maybe it was the pistol that earned the name, but I like to think the cartridge was honored). Also, a 1950 Western starring Randolph Scott and Lloyd Bridges honored the Colt .45.

Since 1873, many new pistol cartridges have come and gone. Some are classics — such as the .44 Rem. Mag. and .357 Rem. Mag. — and some remain proprietary, such as the .375 JDJ. But

Most ammunition manufacturers still offer an original load of a round-nose or flat-point lead bullet of 250 to 255 grains, at a muzzle velocity about 800 fps, and that formula works as well as it did in 1873. Today's single-action revolver hunter might want more oomph behind a modern bullet design, such as these 300-grain Sierra hollow-points.

velocities in modern SAA clones, such as the Ruger Blackhawk I love so much. The .45 Colt can be an excellent cartridge for sending paper banditos to Boot Hill (in cowboy action shooting) and neatly dispatching big game at sensible ranges. In a modern handgun, the .45 Colt can also be very accurate. My pistol, a Ruger New Model Blackhawk, has adjustable sights that give me an accuracy edge compared to the fixed sights of the SAA clones. I can keep a full cylinder of shots within a 3-inch group at 45 yards, which is more than acceptable to me with my mid-40s eyes. The Blackhawk has a 7½-inch barrel, generating a bit more velocity, but more important to me, giving me a longer sighting radius. My gun performs better with heavier bullets, and I'm fine with that. Anything heavier than 250 grains provides at least acceptable accuracy, with a few heavy slugs being exceptional.

The variation of bullet weights is another desirable feature of the .45 Colt. It can be loaded to purr like a kitten, and those mild loads are excellent for training a new shooter or for fun plinking days. Yet in my Blackhawk, it can launch slugs weighing up to 360 grains for serious big-game work.

Most ammunition manufacturers still offer the original load of a round-nose or flat-point lead bullet of 250 to 255 grains, with a muzzle velocity of about 800 fps, and that formula works as well as it did in 1873. Yet folks who hunt big game with the

despite being a veteran of the post-Civil War era, the .45 Colt isn't going anywhere soon. In fact, the .45 Colt is the basis for the .454 Casull. The latter is simply an elongated version of the Colt cartridge loaded to a much higher pressure. The .460 S&W takes the same rim and body diameter yet uses an even longer case — 1.800 inch for the .460 versus 1.285 for the Colt — to obtain its unprecedented velocities. The Casull and .460 Smith have a heavier recoil level that takes some getting used to in order to place your shots accurately. However, both guns can fire .45 Colt ammunition as a low-recoiling alternative to the high-pressure hunting ammunition. The .45 is no wallflower, though, as I'll demonstrate later.

Still Valid After All These Years

The .45 Colt has hung on for years for several reasons. The cartridge has a sound design: a semi-rimmed configuration — that small rim has been criticized through the decades but has never posed a problem in my gun — that has enough case capacity to drive the .452-inch-diameter bullets to respectable velocities in older Single Action Army revolvers and even higher

The author's Blackhawk likes a Hornady 300-grain XTP-Mag bullet seated over 16.5 grains of Accurate Arms No. 9 powder. The recoil is considerably more than what cowboy loads produce, but it's manageable in the 7½-inch-barreled revolver.

The .45 Colt is a semi-rimmed configuration that has enough case capacity to drive .452-inch-diameter bullets to safe velocities in older Single Action Army revolvers and to higher velocities in the Ruger Blackhawk. The variation of bullet weights is another desirable feature of the .45 Colt. The .45 Colt runs on a standard large pistol primer, and the primers need to be seated flush with the case head or slightly recessed.

old cartridge can find plenty of factory ammunition options, provided you have a pistol or rifle designed to handle the higher pressures. CorBon offers a 335-grain hard-cast lead flat-point in the +P designation, which leaves the muzzle at 1,025 fps and produces 820 foot-pounds of energy. If that's not heavy enough for you, DoubleTap ammunition produces a 360-grain hard-cast wide flat-point, which produces 1,200 fps from the muzzle for 1,150 foot-pounds. In a 16-inch-barreled rifle, that will leave the muzzle at just slower than 1,500 fps for more than 1,700 foot-pounds. That load, in a carbine, is approaching the performance of some lighter .45-70 Gov. loads and would handle about all North American game at close ranges.

There have been many modern upgrades to ammunition for the older wheelguns and lever-action rifles in the past decade, and the .45 Colt is no exception. The most popular is the Hornady LEVERevolution line, which includes the company's proprietary FTX, or Flex Tip eXpanding, bullet, which uses a flexible polymer tip to allow the use of spitzer bullets in a tubu-

lar magazine of a lever-action rifle. At 225 grains, the Hornady LEVERevolution load will leave the rifle's muzzle at 900 fps, and provides a much flatter trajectory than the round-nose and flat-point bullets. That configuration adds quite a bit of versatility to traditional lever guns and makes a perfect choice for folks who hunt deer and bear in the thickly forested Northeast, as I do.

On the Defensive

The .45 Colt is not just a hunting tool, though. Although the rifles and pistols are not the traditional choice of a defensive weapon — especially with today's plethora of Model 1911 and AR-15 style firearms — they will save your bacon just as well now as they did in 1873. Many newer handgun bullets designed for autoloaders will function well in the .45 Colt revolvers. My gun loves the Hornady XTP in 250 and 300 grains, as well as the Speer Gold Dot 300-grain slug. Both of those have an impeccable reputation as a defensive bullet (they also make fantastic big-game bullets, but that's not the point), and they shoot very well from most .45 Colts I've shot.

On the other end of the spectrum, Cutting Edge Bullets makes a 150-grain Handgun Raptor bullet that can achieve very high velocities (upward of 1,600 fps) in the .45 Colt case. These modern projectiles have mono-metal construction and use a deep hollow-point for rapid expansion. The wall of the hollow-point breaks into small blades for initial impact trauma, and the base of the copper bullet remains at caliber dimension for deep penetration. The bullets make a good choice for home defense — at least for me.

There was a reason I chose that Ruger New Model Blackhawk as my first handgun: Although the pistol was always securely stored, the transfer-bar design of the Ruger revolver seemed to present the most accident-resistant package I could find. In the hands of an educated shooter, the pistol would operate fine, but if the hammer was cocked and the pistol accidentally dropped, the transfer bar would prevent accidental discharge. The same goes for trigger pull: The trigger must remain depressed throughout the firing sequence for the gun to fire. Any light touch on the trigger would result in a click rather than a fired cartridge. I also appreciated the nostalgia of the .45 Colt over more modern cartridges — namely the .44 Rem. Mag. — so that combination of traditional appearance and modern safety features made for a package I couldn't resist. My good buddy Donnie Thorne, better known as Col. Le Frogg, has a brace of Ruger Vaqueros in .45 Colt, with the classic 5½-inch barrels, that are nickel plated and have the actions slicked up. They are possibly the most accurate .45s I've shot, and those pistols have a special affinity for my 255-grain lead-bullet handloads, sitting over a mild charge of Alliant's Unique powder. The Vaquero is set up with the same transfer bar as my Blackhawk, so you can carry it confidently with a full cylinder. However, I was trained to always carry a single-action revolver on an empty chamber, and old habits die hard. Le Frogg and I thought long and hard about the cartridge choice for our revolvers, and though we bounced back and forth between classics — .44-40, .44 Mag. and .45 Colt — you know what we ultimately chose.

Compare and Contrast

Let's address the classic comparison between the .44 Mag. and .45 Colt. On paper, you'd think the .44 Mag. would be the hands-down choice in a hunting revolver. I mean, the .44 Mag. was developed by Elmer Keith (please pause for a moment of silence) and made famous by detective Harry Callahan, so it had the cool factor. But the .45 Colt has appeared in countless Western movies and was carried across Europe by some dude with a bunch of stars on his uniform named Patton. Famed lawman Bat Masterson ordered a Colt .45 directly from Samuel Colt. The great controversy around Wyatt Earp's Buntline Special will continue to rage, but if it existed, it was chambered in .45 Colt (tongue planted firmly in cheek). Needless to say, the .45 Colt's cool factor rivaled that of the .44 Mag. The fact that Keith (cue angelic music) sang the praises of the .45 Colt, relating tales of mad cows being neatly dispatched and mean broncs having to be put down quickly as they tried to stomp him into the ground, sealed the deal for me.

The .44 Mag. is a fantastic hunting round, fully capable for big game. It can push bullets of similar weight, albeit at a higher pressure and with a bit more recoil. The better sectional density of the .429-inch bullets might penetrate a bit farther, when of the same weight, but a couple of features of the .45 Colt really appealed to me. First, the .45 Colt can use the many component bullets for the uber-popular .45 ACP, and that's good. The vast amount of .45-caliber FMJ projectiles manufactured each year make the .45 Colt a wise decision from an economic standpoint as well as availability. The stout hunting bullets in .452-inch caliber also let the Colt shine as a hunting round. Second, although the .44 Mag. and .45 Colt can produce performance so similar that no animal could tell the difference, the Colt can do so at a much lower pressure. That translates into easier case extraction, longer case life and less recoil, all of which are important to me. So, being a handloader who appreciates the points of the cartridge, I couldn't wait to start the loading process and find those sweet combinations that make a cartridge shine.

At the Reloading Bench

The .45 Colt isn't a difficult cartridge to load. You'll need a good set of reloading dies, with the best roll crimp you can get. As with any straight-wall cartridge for a revolver, you'll need a good roll crimp on your finished cartridge to keep the bullet in place and prevent it from extending out of the case during recoil. Especially in the hard-kicking cartridges — such as the full-house .45 Colt loads, as well as the .454 Casull and .44 Mag. — this is very important, as the bullet can pull out of the case and

prevent the cylinder from rotating, as well as pose a dangerous situation if the bullet isn't properly aligned to the bore, which could result in catastrophe or death. I like the Redding Profile Crimp die, as it has produced the most uniform roll crimp I've experienced. I also like the Redding Dual Carbide Sizing dies, as they give the exact dimension I want for proper bullet tension yet don't overwork the body of the case, extending case life. Carbide dies don't require lubrication during resizing and won't allow the case to stick in the die, which is a nice feature when you consider the smaller rim of the Colt case.

The .45 Colt runs on a standard large pistol primer, and I prefer the Federal GM150M for its consistency and reliability. Be sure your primers are seated exactly flush with the case head or slightly recessed to prevent malfunctions and to let the cylinder rotate properly.

Although the .45 Colt has been criticized for having a thin case wall, especially in comparison to the younger magnum pistol cartridges such as the .44 Mag. and .454 Casull, I've never had a problem working with the .45 Colt. I try not to excessively flare the case mouth, giving just enough to allow the bullet to seat properly yet not overworking the brass.

In respect to load data, the .45 Colt is really three cartridges in one, and if you intend to reload it, you must be aware of the differences. Look at it this way: There is one set of data for the Colt Single Action Army revolver and its clones, held to a lower

Left to right are three stout wheelgun cartridges: The .460 S&W, .454 Casull and venerable .45 Colt. The .45 Colt is sometimes called the .45 Long Colt, indicating the difference between it and the shorter Smith & Wesson Schofield case. The addition of the word Long irritates some shooters, but ammo companies use both names interchangeably. The .45 Colt is the basis for the .454 Casull, the latter being an elongated version of the Colt cartridge loaded to a much higher pressure. The .460 S&W takes the same rim and body diameter yet uses an even longer case — 1.800 inch for the .460 versus 1.285 for the Colt.

velocity and pressure limit. Then, there's the data for the stronger revolvers and single-shot pistols, which allow the pressures to climb much higher while still performing safely. Last, there's the data developed for the lever guns — an entirely different animal.

For SAA-class loads, I invariably prefer Alliant's Unique powder. It burns a bit dirty but has given me fantastic accuracy with many types of cast lead bullets. My favorite combination in this class is the Falcon Bullets Co.'s 230-grain round-nose Fal-Coated lead bullet over 8.0 grains of Unique. It's an affordable bullet and plenty accurate for plinking and smaller game.

For my Blackhawk, as a hunting/defense load, I like the Hornady 300-grain XTP-Mag bullet seated over 16.5 grains of Accurate Arms No. 9 powder, at 1,120 fps. This is my favorite load for early-season black bears, because that Hornady bullet will provide consistent expansion and penetration. The recoil is considerably more than the cowboy loads described earlier, but it's more than manageable in the 7½-inch-barreled revolver and has proven to be the most accurate of the hunting loads I've developed. I limit my distances to 35 to 40 yards, and although Mr. Bruin and I haven't met when I've carried the Blackhawk, I'm confident the venerable cartridge will get the job done.

For lever guns, I like the Hornady FTX bullet. It requires some special treatment from a reloader's point of view, because the tapered ogive of the FTX bullet demands that the brass case of the .45 Colt be trimmed from 1.285 inch to 1.215 inch so the case mouth aligns with the shank of the projectile rather than sitting upon the ogive. Load that shorter case with 11½ grains of Alliant's Blue Dot powder, and you'll have an even 1,100 fps out of your rifle.

Conclusion

The face of cartridge development is ever changing. There's no denying that. Projectiles continue to be made stronger, cases are modified to produce faster velocities and powders are developed to provide the most uniform results possible. Many hunters and shooters will flock to embrace the newest technologies, yet others are content with their grandfathers' cartridges, embracing the nostalgia and romance of yesteryear. I tend to float between the worlds, enjoying the classic combinations that have wonderful reputations but not afraid to put a modern spin on a classic. The .45 Colt epitomizes that idea for me, and I'm happy to have carried one for more than a decade.

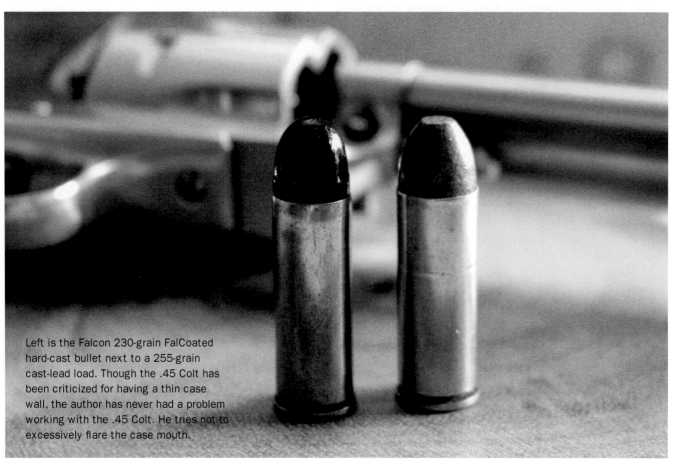

Left is the Falcon 230-grain FalCoated hard-cast bullet next to a 255-grain cast-lead load. Though the .45 Colt has been criticized for having a thin case wall, the author has never had a problem working with the .45 Colt. He tries not to excessively flare the case mouth.

7mm Mauser: Military Cartridge Decommissioned to an All-Around Sporting Round

This cartridge broke ground in the military and remains a top hunting choice.

BY ROBERT SADOWSKI

The 7mm Mauser — also known as the 7x57mm Mauser, 7mm Spanish Mauser and .275 Rigby — was originally designed as a military cartridge and chambered in the then-new Mauser Model 1892 and Model 1893 rifles. Armies found the round was accurate at long range with moderate recoil. Hunters discovered the round offered good killing power with deep penetration and minimal recoil in lightweight rifles.

By today's standards, the 7x57mm Mauser is in the same league, albeit slightly less powerful than the .270 Win., .280 Rem., 7mm-08, and .284 Win. Sure, the 7mm Mauser is an old-timer, but this older round can keep up with newer ones. Even though this cartridge is 124 years old, there's no question the 7mm Mauser makes an excellent all-around big-game round for all except big bears and perhaps moose. But as has been demonstrated, the round has been used quite effectively on the biggest game animals — elephants. For handloaders, manufacturers make a wide variety of excellent 7mm bullets, allowing it to be loaded with bullets weights from 120 to 175 grains.

The 7x57mm Mauser was a game changer in military and hunting cartridges. America's first exposure to the 7x57mm Mauser was in Cuba in 1898, during the brief Spanish-American War. It was brutally clear that Spanish forces were better equipped than American soldiers. More than 15,000 U.S. troops attacked about 760 entrenched Spanish forces in Santiago de Cuba. San Juan heights protected the city. The only way to the city was up two hills American troops called San Juan Hill and Kettle Hill. In the tropical heat on July 1, American troops attacked. About 200 U.S. soldiers were killed and more than 1,000 wounded from the fire laid down by the Spanish troops with their Mauser 1893 rifles chambered in 7x57mm Mauser. Spanish losses were minimal considering the size of the attacking American force. About 115 soldiers were killed and 366 wounded. The Spanish troops' 1893 Spanish Mauser rifles gave them an edge. Not only was the Mauser quicker to reload via a stripper clip, but the 7x57mm cartridge had a farther effective range and was more accurate. The U.S. Model 1898 Krag-Jorgenson rifle was no match. The slow-loading Krag rifle and its caliber, .30-40

7mm Mauser

As a hunting round, the 7mm Mauser excels for deer, black bear and wild pigs. W.D.M. "Karamojo" Bell used the 7mm surgically to take down elephants in the early 1900s.

Krag, were outclassed. In the aftermath of the Spanish-American War, the United States quickly developed a better bolt-action rifle and caliber so it wouldn't be caught flat-footed again. The rifle was a modified Mauser rifle called the M1903 Springfield, chambered in .30-06. The 7mm Spanish Mauser really pushed U.S. military commanders to re-evaluate the country's weapon and caliber at the time.

The 7x57mm cartridge was developed by Paul Mauser in 1892, and subsequently adopted as a military cartridge by Spain in 1893 for the M1892 Mauser rifle and the new M1893 rifle, which soon replaced the '92. That's why the cartridge is sometimes called the 7mm Spanish Mauser. Other European and Latin-American countries — Brazil, Uruguay, Colombia and others — also adopted the cartridge and rifle for military use. It was a turning point in modern cartridge design. The 7x57mm was cutting edge at the time and used new (in the late 19th century) smokeless powder. The original military bullet was a round-nose,

173-grain full-metal jacket. The case measured 57 millimeters long, which is why the cartridge is also called the 7x57mm. That original military bullet fired from the M1893's 29.1-inch barrel with a 1:8.6-inch twist rate had a muzzle velocity of about 2,296 fps and a muzzle energy of 2,025 foot-pounds. At the time, those ballistics were impressive. The round was also fairly flat shooting, and offered excellent penetration and modest felt recoil. Part of the success of the cartridge was the long, heavy bullets used. They have a high sectional density. Sectional density, according to the Hornady Handbook of Cartridge Reloading, is "the ratio of a bullet's weight in pounds to the square of its diameter in inches. Bullets of the same shape but with more weight in relation to their diameter retain their velocity and energy better." The longer bullets in the 7mm Mauser gave the round its long-range capabilities and good penetration.

The 7x57mmR is similar to the 7x57mm Mauser. It's a rimmed cartridge developed from the 7x57mm Mauser soon af-

The Mauser M1893 was chambered in the 7mm Mauser and adopted by Spain, Mexico and countries in South America. It proved a decisive weapon during the Spanish-American War.

ter its debut for use in break-action rifles and combination guns such as drillings and other multiple-barrel hunting guns. Suffice to say, the 7x57mmR is rare today and is mainly encountered in European break-action guns. The only modern guns I know that are chambered for the 7x57mmR are the Blaser K95, B95/97, BD14 and D99 break-action, single-shot or combination guns.

The accuracy and effectiveness of the 7x57mm Mauser was further proven in South Africa during the Second Boer War from Oct. 1, 1899, to May 31, 1902. The British were armed with the .303 British cartridge, which still used cordite as a propellant. They were overwhelmed by the Boer sharpshooters' long-range ability with Mauser M1895 rifles chambered in 7x57mm. Maximum effective range on paper was farther than 3,500 yards, but actual use was closer. Boer sharpshooters could easily hit man-sized targets in the 700- to 1,000-yard range effectively using open sights. Remember, at that time, optics were rare on military and sporting guns. W.D.M. "Karamojo" Bell joined the Canadian Mounted Rifles and took part in the Boer War. After the war, in the early part of the 20th century, Bell went on to use the 7mm Mauser to kill literally tons of elephants in Africa, building his fame as a big-game and ivory hunter.

The effectiveness of the round was not lost on hunters. Sportsman discovered the 7mm Mauser made an excellent over-all hunting cartridge. At the time, Mauser rifles ruled the roost with military forces, and Mausers for hunting, with lighter-taper barrels and more graceful cut-down sporter stocks, were the darlings of hunters in Europe and Africa. Starting in 1899, prominent British rifle maker John Rigby had the importing license for Mauser rifles and crafted exquisite sporting rifles, chambering some in 7x57mm Mauser but renaming the round .275 Rigby. The dimension of a 7mm rifle bore measures .275 inches across the lands, so the caliber was given the .275 Rigby moniker. The name change helped sell rifles to English hunters.

Bell used a Rigby-Mauser Model 98 when hunting for ivory. His tally of elephants was 1,011. Of that total, about 800 were killed using the Rigby-Mauser chambered in .275 Rigby with 173-grain round-nose military ammunition. The caliber is hardly considered a dangerous-game round, but Bell was surgical with the 7mm. It was also the most reliable cartridge at the time. When hunting elephants, Bell wanted the cartridge to fire when he pulled the trigger. The 7mm Mauser round was also light to

carry and less expensive than traditional dangerous-game ammunition. Shot placement was the key to Bell's success. On average, it took him 1.5 shots to kill an elephant. Bell took extensive notes and collected data on his kills, so he knew the details. A quick, accurate shot to an elephant's brain stopped the beast while not alarming a herd. His elephant kill count for one day was 19. He also shot elephants from relatively close range — 30 to 40 yards — and developed what is known as "the Bell shot," a rear-angled shot through the neck muscles into the brain. The 7mm Mauser suited him quite well. It recoiled less than traditional dangerous-game rounds, so flinch did not hinder accuracy. Another famous big-game hunter also used the cartridge with effect. James Edward "Jim" Corbett, who tracked down infamous man-eating tigers and leopards, used a .275 Rigby-Mauser rifle to put down the man-eating Leopard of Rudraprayag in May of 1926. Other hunters across the pond also liked the performance of the 7mm Mauser. American hunter and writer Jack O'Connor liked the 7x57mm, and in fact, his wife used the caliber ex-

Famed ivory hunter W.D.M. Bell, shown here in the 1950s, used a Rigby modified Mauser bolt-action in .275 Rigby to kill about 800 elephants with 173-grain military grade ammunition.

This is Charge of the 24th and 25th Colored Infantry, July 2nd, 1898, depicting the Battle of San Juan Hill, from an 1899 lithograph by Chicago printers Kurz and Allison.

tensively. O'Connor's enthusiasm for the .270 Win., however, overshadowed his affection for the 7mm Mauser.

By 1913, the 7mm Mauser increased its range and effectiveness with the introduction of spitzer-style bullets. The French and German armies had been experimenting and adopted pointed-tip, or spitzer, bullets, which greatly reduced air drag on the bullet compared to the more common flat-nose or round-nose bullets used by militaries at the time. The performance of the 7mm Mauser shifted into high gear with the new spitzer bullets, which weighed 139 to 173 grains. The 139-grain bullet, the military load for Brazil and Columbia, had a muzzle velocity of 2,950 fps and a muzzle energy of 2,580 foot-pounds from a typical 23-inch military bolt-action rifle of the time. Maximum effective range was slightly farther than 4,000 yards.

At one time, numerous surplus Mauser rifles and surplus 7mm Mauser ammunition were abundant. Pallets of rifles from South American countries were available at low cost to shooters. In the United States, the round was fairly common east and west of the Mississippi River. Many surplus Mausers became sporters. American firearms manufacturers also produced rifles in the caliber. Around 1897, Remington chambered its single-shot Rolling Block rifle and the Remington-Lee M1899 sporting rifles in 7mm Mauser. Between World War I and World War II, Remington also chambered the Model 30 in 7mm Mauser. The Model 30 was a sporting rifle based on the military P14/

M1917 Enfield rifle action, which Remington manufactured for the British and American governments during World War I. With bolt-action rifles becoming more popular with American hunters, the Winchester Model 54 debuted. The Model 54 was a new rifle design made specifically for the sporting market and is considered the first successful production bolt-action rifle for civilians. It was also available in 7mm Mauser. Today, 7mm Mauser rifles are produced in limited runs, but ammunition is quite common and easily obtained.

All of the big four U.S. ammo factories load the cartridge. Hornady, Federal, Remington and Winchester produced 7mm Mauser ammo. Most U.S.-made 7mm Mauser ammunition is loaded with bullets in the 139- to 145-grain range. European ammo uses 139- to 175-grain bullets. Hornady loads a 139-grain GMX or SST bullet in its Superformance line, which has a velocity of slightly faster than 2,700 fps — more velocity than other 7mm Mauser factory ammo. I have had excellent results with this ammo. Winchester loads a 145-grain Power Point bullet in its Super X line of hunting ammo with a muzzle velocity of 2,600 fps. Remington loads its rock-solid Core-Lokt in 140-grain bullets to a 2,660 fps muzzle velocity. Federal loads three bullets under its Vital-Shok and Power-Shok lines: a 175-grain soft-point round-nose at 2,390 fps, a 140-grain Speer Hot-Cor soft-point and a 140-grain Nosler Partition. Both the 140-grain loads have a muzzle velocity of 2,660 fps. Nosler also

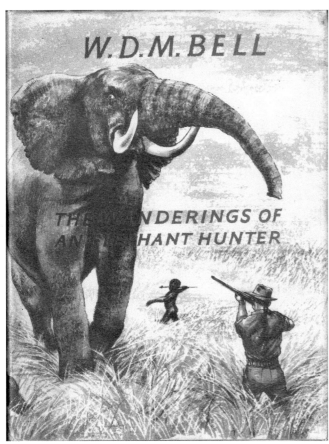

W.D.M. Bell's book, The Wanderings of an Elephant Hunter, was published in 1915, recounting his hunting adventures in Africa from 1897 to 1922. Using mostly small-caliber rifles — the 7mm Mauser in particular — he killed more than 1,000 elephants.

All major ammunition manufacturers produce the 7mm Mauser, though foreign-made ammo typically has more bullet weight and type selections.

offers a 140-grain with an AccuBond bullet that clocks 2,700 fps at the muzzle. European ammunition manufacturers such as PPU Prvi Partizan in Serbia load a 139-grain soft-point at 2,657 fps. Czech-made Seller & Bellot offers a 139-grain soft-point, 140-grain full metal jacket and a 173-grain soft-point cutting edge. The 139- and 140-grain bullets have a muzzle velocity slight faster than 2,600 fps. The 173-grain soft-point cutting-edge bullet has a muzzle velocity of 2,379 fps and leaves crisply cut holes in paper, like you fired a wad cutter, because of the cut-through edge built into the bullet's jacket. I have also had excellent results with PPU and Sellier & Bellot ammunition. Plus, it's typically less expensive than U.S.-made ammo.

The ballistic coefficient of the 7x57mm Mauser is high, which means it's more efficient when flying through air. BC is a measure of a bullet's slipperiness or air drag. In essence, it's the ratio of the bullet's sectional density to its coefficient of form. The bigger the BC number, the more easily the bullet flies through the air. The 7mm Mauser is slick when it flies, so it has a flatter trajectory. When comparing the 7mm Mauser to other

more modern cartridges — such as the 7mm-08, .270 Win., .280 Rem. and .284 Win. — in similar bullet weights, you'll see the 7mm Mauser lags behind the newer cartridges by a few hundred fps and foot-pounds. (Of course, those cartridges aren't really new. The .270 Win. was developed in 1925, the 7mm-08 in 1980, the 284. Win. in 1963 and the .280 Rem. in 1957.). The 7mm Mauser is most like the 7mm-08 of those compared, and it would be fair to say the 7mm Mauser paved the way for 7mm-08 and all the other 7mm cartridges developed by Remington and Winchester. For me, there's a bit of nostalgia firing the 7mm Mauser. Deer don't seem to notice a difference, nor would, I think, wild pigs, black bear, speed goats and the rest. For moose and elk, take a cue from Bell. A surgical shot from a 7mm Mauser means you'll be processing meat.

You can still find Winchester Model 70 and Ruger M77 rifles, older European sporters that range from a few hundred dollars to

On the Ruger No. 1 International, the caliber 7mm Mauser is signified by 7x57. The 7mm Mauser has numerous names, such as 7x57mm Mauser, 7mm Spanish Mauser and .275 Rigby.

a king's ransom depending on the rifle manufacturer, and older surplus military rifles from Brazil, Chile and other South American countries. You can also find many older Model 98 Mausers in 7mm Mauser sporterized and trimmed up for hunting. I use the round in a Ruger No. 1, and it's a sweet rifle/cartridge combination for deer.

My Ruger No. 1 International is basically a standard No. 1 with shortened barrel and full-length Mannlicher-style stock. The falling-block action is Ruger's modified version of the Farqharson-style action with an internal hammer and has been around since 1967. Ruger and Lipsey's usually come out with unique calibers yearly in the rifle. I snapped up a 7mm Mauser when I had the chance and have always regretted it. I should have bought two.

A lever that locks into the trigger guard is pressed down to drop the stainless-steel block and load the rifle. Rounds easily slide into the chamber, and when the muzzle is pointed to the ground, gravity accelerates the process, and the chamber is accessible even when a scope is mounted. The action comes from the factory set to eject cartridges, but you can remove the forearm and back-off on the ejector spring strut so cartridges extract instead. The barrel and receiver are deeply blued, and Ruger's proprietary quarter rib and rings allows mounting of a scope. The rear sight is also mounted on the rib and folds down to accommodate large objectives. The front sight is a tiny gold-colored bead. The barrel is free-floated along the Mannlicher forearm through the steel end cap. The wood has nice figuring, and the checkering is crisp and neat, with a plastic grip cap and a gold Ruger logo. The solid yet soft recoil pad is mated nicely to the stock. It's nice to handle a traditional wood and blued-steel rifle. Traditional, for sure. This Ruger, because of the type of action, is also very compact even with a 20-inch barrel, making the little rifle feel lively in hand. I mounted a Leupold VX-3 3.5-10x40mm on my No. 1 International for hunting, which seems to suit it fine. When a friend wanted to buy the scope, I obliged him and never replaced it. The open sights are adequate, and most of my shots are 100 yards or closer in the brush I hunt. It's also a dream in the confined space of a tree stand or ground blind.

Knowing the barrel on my No.1 International was not the length used to collect factory data, I wanted to see what, if any, velocity was siphoned off because of the missing 4 inches of barrel. I found on average about 100 fps is lost in the little Ruger Mannlicher compared to factory data. Not surprising. Shooting the 7mm at 100 yards was a real chip shot. The cartridge has minimal recoil, making it ideal for beginning shooters or those of petite and small statures. The little Mannlicher is also easy to

carry. And not that I like sharing my ammo with hunting buddies, but I also don't have pals asking to borrow a few rounds. Unique calibers make good hunting companions.

The 7mm Mauser takes well to reloading. There's a slew of 7mm bullets in all weights and types available. Bullet weights from 120 to 175 grains are effective in the 7mm Mauser. Bullet types from ballistic tip boat-tails to inexpensive round-nose bullets are available. Powders with a medium to slow burn rate — such as Win 760, Hogdon H414, Varget and IMR 4064 — yield good accuracy. I keep it simple and load 139-grain or 140-grain bullets and load to just past 2,600 fps. The Ruger No.1 action is strong, so at times I've also loaded up to 2,700 fps. I have found the round performs well at 2,600 to 2,700 fps. In surplus Mauser rifles, I would keep velocity at 2,600 fps. It's not that those older Mauser are not strong. You just don't know how they've been treated through the years.

The 7x57mm Mauser, by whatever name you want to call it, was an excellent, ground-breaking military round, and as an all-around hunting round, it's superb.

BALLISTICS COMPARISON

	BULLET WEIGHT/TYPE	BALLISTIC COEFFICIENT	AVERAGE VELOCITY	MUZZLE ENERGY
7x57mm Mauser	140-grain/Nosler Partition	0.434	2,660 fps	2,199 ft.-lbs.
.270 Win.	130-grain/Soft Point	0.372	3,060 fps	2,703 ft-lbs.
7mm-08 Rem.	140-grain/Trophy Bonded Tip	0.43	2,800 fps	2,437 ft-lbs.
.280 Rem.	140-grain/Nosler Ballistic Tip	0.485	2,990 fps	2,779 ft-lbs.
.284 Win.	150-grain/Power Point	0.364	2,860 fps	2,724 ft-lbs.

Factory ballistic data was collected from a 24-inch barrel.

RSI-1 RUGER, NO. 1 INTERNATIONAL ACCURACY DATA

	AVERAGE VELOCITY	MUZZLE ENERGY	SMALLEST GROUP	LARGEST GROUP	AVERAGE GROUP
Hornady 7x57mm, 139-grain SST Superformance	2,666 fps	2,194 ft.-lbs.	1.2 in.	2.0 in.	1.6 in.
Winchester Super-X 7x57mm, 145-grain Power Point	2,406 fps	1,864 ft-lbs.	1.9 in.	2.8 in.	2.6 in.
Federal Premium Vital-Shok 7x57mm, 140-grain Nosler Partition	2560 fps	2,038 ft-lbs.	1.5 in.	2.3 in.	1.9 in.

Accuracy data was collected from three-shot groups at 100 yards using a bench rest.
Velocities were recorded using a ProChrono digital chronograph set 15 feet from the muzzle.

Lead Versus Steel: Texas Study Compares Dove Loads

A recent comparison of hunting shotshells sheds light on the effectiveness of each and highlights the need for further research.

BY RALPH WININGHAM

Dove hunters in the know are looking at the horizon with a tinge of apprehension as they face the possibility of a federal mandate requiring non-lead shot for mourning and white-wing doves.

There has been no definitive decision about the issue, but the potential for a steel-only mandate looms large over a hunting community still reeling from the federal requirement forcing waterfowl hunters to abandon lead shot. With Texas leading the nation in the number of dove hunters (about 250,000 to 300,000 annually), who bring down about 30 percent of the country's annual harvest (about 5 million mourning doves

and 1.4 million white-winged doves), it has a huge stake in any potential federal no-lead mandate.

Carter Smith, executive director of Texas Parks and Wildlife Department, said, "Texas is the 800-pound gorilla in the room" whenever lead versus steel shot for doves is the subject. So, TPW biologists and a noted

All eyes are on a dove being shot by Tom Roster as Texas Parks and Wildlife Department biologists undergo training before engaging in a study comparing the effectiveness of steel versus lead shot in three 12-gauge loads.

shotgun ammunition ballistics expert participated in a two-year study during 2008 and 2009 that's apparently the only examination delving into the difference in field performance between 12-gauge loads on mourning doves. The cost of the study, published in the March 2015 The Wildlife Society Bulletin, was about $500,000. Funding was provided thorough migratory game bird and Texas white-winged dove stamp revenue.

A TPW press release said the "study is the first on the lethality of lead versus non-toxic shot under typical hunting conditions for mourning dove to be published in a scientific journal," citing The Wildlife Society Bulletin, a peer-reviewed scientific publication containing papers related to ethics, economics, philosophy, administration, wildlife management, conservation education, conservation law enforcement and contemporary resource problems.

During the 2008 and 2009 dove seasons, under the watch of trained observers, 53 volunteer hunters of average shooting ability fired 5,094 shots to kill 1,146 mourning doves while wounding 739 and missing 3,209. The field collection phase of the study was conducted in Brown, Coleman and McCulloch counties in the Texas Hill Country, with Tom Roster, noted

shotshell ballistics authority, leading the effort. He trained and tested observers to meet his requirements for data collection on hunter success, shooting range and other information concerning test loads.

The study examined three 12 gauge 2¾-inch loads made by Polywad Inc., a shotshell developer and manufacturer in Roberta, Ga., with the stipulation that the loads mirror the ballistics of ammunition most commonly used by Texas dove hunters. Several other ammunition manufacturers declined to participate, apparently concerned about becoming engaged in the controversial issue.

Ammunition used in the test included a 1-1/8-ounce load of No. 7½ high-density (6 percent antimony) lead pellets, and two steel shot loads featuring high-quality pellets used for bead blasting. The steel loads — 1 ounce of No. 6 shot and 1 ounce of No. 7 shot — were selected because their ballistics are comparable to the lead loads.

The double-blind testing prevented hunters and their observers from using the appearance of ammunition to determine whether lead or steel shot was being fired. Observers were ran-

Brian Pierce, a biologist with the Institute of Renewable Natural Resources at Texas A&M University, examines some of the 12-gauge shells to be used during a study of the effectiveness of lead versus steel shot. The shells were manufactured to be indistinguishable.

Lead Versus Steel

Hunters should conduct their own shotshell testing and review data from informed sources.

He pointed out that the limited study, with shooters of average ability using three specific loads in their own shotguns, reflects only a tiny fraction of the estimated 100 million shots fired at mourning doves each year. In addition, he said study results should not be extrapolated to include the larger, stronger white-winged doves, which are also popular wing-shooting targets. Roster said he would "absolutely" expect different results if more shooters of various skill levels shot several loads through different chokes at several types of doves. (Hunters only shot mourning doves during the study, not the larger white-winged or Eurasian collared doves.) No one conducted lead-versus-steel field studies on ducks and geese before federal officials decreed in the late 1980s that waterfowl hunters could only use non-toxic shot. The mandate was based on wildlife biologist and environmentalist assertions that many ducks and geese were dying from ingesting lead shotgun pellets. Biologists have never produced any physical evidence of substantial number of waterfowl deaths from lead ingestion.

The federal ban on lead shot has been cited as a factor in a sharp decrease in waterfowl hunters. Some have predicted similar results if dove hunters are placed under a non-toxic shot requirement. Waterfowl hunters commonly complain about non-toxic shot's lackluster performance in killing ducks and geese and the high price and low availability of non-lead ammunition — particularly in sub-gauge loads.

That lack of confidence in performance and concerns about the potential economic impact of a non-toxic shot requirement are well documented in the dove hunting community. A national dove hunter survey released in July 2014 indicated that more than 50 percent of respondents believe steel and other substitutes do not perform as well as lead for dove hunting. Of the 12,631 hunters who returned surveys (a response rate of about 41.6 percent), 36 percent said they would "probably quit hunting doves if required to use non-lead shot." About 50 percent said they thought requiring non-lead shot would limit their time afield while also reducing the number of young people recruited to hunting.

In addition, although about 85 percent "mostly" or "always" used lead shot to hunt doves, nearly half of those surveyed said they didn't know if ingesting lead pellets would be fatal to doves. The same percentage of respondents cited concerns that lost bird rates from doves wounded with steel shot were higher than with lead shot. About 40 percent said doves have such a brief lifespan (an average of 18 months) that possible exposure or ingestion of lead shot would have limited effects on the dove population.

Roster and TPW officials have stressed the informational aspects of the lead-versus-steel comparison, with the ultimate goal of providing useful data to help Texas hunters make informed decisions on the loads for dove hunting.

"Hunters want proof that their lead shot is causing a problem, and we don't have that yet," Roster said. "There is no reason a hunter should be required to shoot (any specific type of shot) until we have more information."

domly assigned to hunters, and ammunition lots were randomly issued to the observer-hunter pairs before each field test. The observers dispensed ammunition, recorded data, tagged harvested birds taken with one shot, retrieved spent shells and completed post-hunt opinion surveys. Of the 1,146 birds retrieved, 1,110 underwent necropsies, and observers carefully recorded and compiled all wounds. Birds were excluded from necropsies if they had been struck by more than one load, hit at an angle indicating a second strike or were missing body parts.

That data was assimilated with the observers' records of the number of missed or hit birds, the kill-to-wounding ratio, the distance at which each shot was taken (57.6 percent of attempts were at birds closer than 32 yards) and various other observations. The results?

"Researchers determined no statistical significant difference in harvest efficiencies between the three loads tested, regardless of distance," TPW officials said in a press release. "Success afield should not change with the type of shot used." However, Roster said he was somewhat hesitant to make such a broad-brush statement about the study findings.

"This was a tiny test, and we have to be very humble about the study results," he said. "This is not an end-all, tell-all study. I would have liked to have seen 20,000 to 30,000 shots fired as part of the study, but that was considered too expensive."

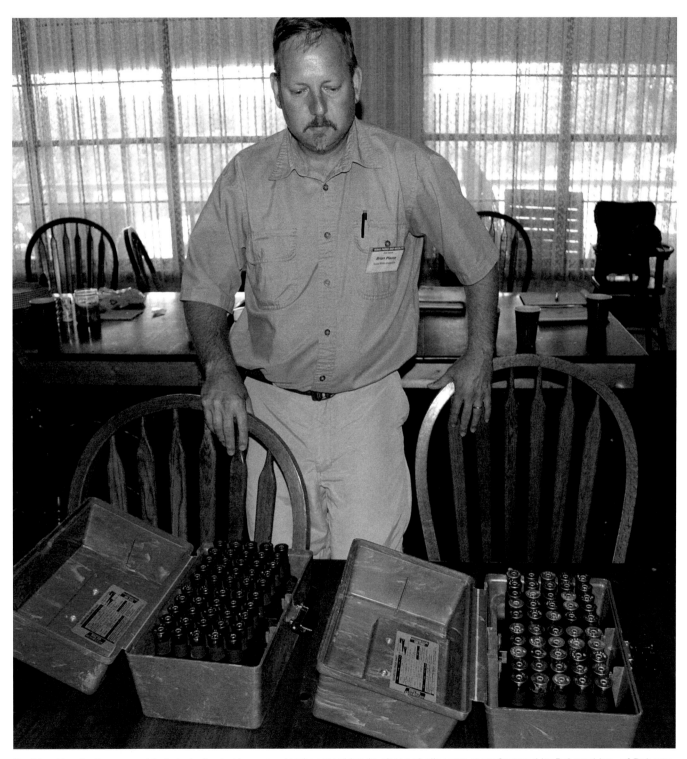

Designed to display no markings to indicate they were lead or steel loads, these shells were manufactured by Polywad Inc. of Roberta, Ga., for use in the Texas steel-versus-lead study.

Lead Versus Steel

He said hunters should consider testing various lead and steel loads in their guns before deciding which shells to take afield. With more dove hunters switching to sub-gauge shotguns because of reduced recoil and lighter carry weights, such experimentation becomes even more important.

"We absolutely believe in hunter choice, and we also want hunters to be as informed as possible on matters affecting their outdoor pursuits," Smith said in the TPW press release issued before publication of the study.

"Doves are a shared international resource, and the question about whether or not lead shot should be banned for dove hunting is not something Texas is prepared to make independent of other jurisdictions and based solely on the findings of this study. This research offers an important data point in the larger discussion, but there are many other factors to consider."

Collecting previously unavailable data on how steel shot compares with lead afield was necessary to keep in front of possible national wildlife policy considerations or decisions, Smith said. He explained that Texas officials were particularly concerned about getting caught up in an uncomfortable position with the state's hunting population should a non-toxic shot mandate be issued by federal officials.

Smith said that about the same time as the state was planning the study, officials in other states and even at the national level were discussing a possible lead shot ban for dove hunters, similar to the non-toxic shot mandate for waterfowl. In addition, wildlife biologists and game-bird managers were expressing concerns about a slight down-trend in dove populations. That downward trend has reversed itself, with the national mourning dove population increasing slightly in recent years.

As the Texas study was considered and formulated, wild-life biologists in other states released findings that indicated they believed about 2 to 6.5 percent of the nation's 450 million mourning doves might have ingested one or more lead shot pellets deposited on the ground in hunting areas. Biologists have theorized that as few as one or two ingested pellets might result in fatal lead poisoning for a mourning dove.

One study, "Ingested Shot and Tissue Lead Concentration In Mourning Doves," was conducted by biologists from 1998 through 2000, with findings published in 2009. It evaluated the lead exposure in 4,884 hunter-harvested mourning doves during a two-year period in Arizona, Georgia, Missouri, Oklahoma, Pennsylvania, Tennessee and South Carolina. The frequency of ingested lead pellets in gizzards of doves killed at hunting areas that allowed lead shot was about 2.5 percent.

Another examination of the issue, "Lead Shot Ingestion by Mourning Doves on a Disked Field," was conducted in 2008 with wild mourning doves collected at the campus of Southern

For the number crunchers in the crowd, the following are some of the details of the two-year study of six field sessions by 53 volunteers who participated in the Texas Parks & Wildlife Department study of the effectiveness of one type of lead shot versus two sizes of steel shot.

The graphic below concerns the lethality of the different shot types and the ranges at which doves were shot. Bagged birds were those doves that were dead or died within 30 seconds of being retrieved; the hit/bagged numbers are those collected doves that were mobile for more than 30 seconds after being retrieved; the hit/lost category is wounded birds that were hit and got away; missed birds gave no indication of being hit; and the mean distance is how far away the dove was flying when a shot was attempted (listed in meters).

SHOT LOAD	SHOT ATTEMPTS	BAGGED BIRDS	HIT/ BAGGED BIRDS	HIT/ LOST BIRDS	MISSED BIRDS	MEAN DISTANCE
Lead 7½	1,683	303	49	237	1,094	29.57
Steel 7	1,727	346	69	268	1,044	28.71
Steel 6	1,684	316	63	234	1,071	29.31

Concerning the frequency of shot outcomes with the three loads, the following is the breakdown from the study (distances are in meters):

SHOT LOAD	OUTCOME	>28.3	>28.3
Lead 7½	Bagged	218	134
	Wounded	104	133
	Missed	514	580
Steel 7	Bagged	255	160
	Wounded	135	133
	Missed	480	564
Steel 6	Bagged	248	131
	Wounded	115	119
	Missed	469	602

Illinois University at Carbondale, Ill. That study was published in 2011. In each of three treatment groups of 80 birds, 35 birds were exposed to low-density lead shot concentrations, 35 others were exposed to high-density lead shot concentrations and 10 served as controls with no lead shot exposure. Lead shot and mixed seed was scattered on loosely packed soil in the cages containing birds, and after four days of exposure, 2.9 percent of the doves had voluntarily ingested at least one lead shot pellet.

"Assuming that 10 percent of the 450 million mourning dove population feeds in high-risk areas, such as managed dove fields, and annually 2.9 percent of those birds ingest shot, 1.31 million birds are at risk of lead shot ingestion," researchers concluded. "However, if the proportion of birds that ingest shot is 4.9 percent, then 2.21 million birds are at risk; and if 75 percent of these birds die from direct effects of lead shot ingestion or lead toxicity-induced increased susceptibility to predation, 1.66 million mourning doves could die from lead shot ingestion each year."

Although 1.66 million is a large number, putting the biologists' worst-case scenario into perspective means lead poisoning might potentially cause the loss of .35 percent of the nation's mourning doves annually — less than one half of 1 percent of the total population. In addition, as noted by state and national officials after the release of the Texas study, the nation's dove population has been on an upward trend the past several years, with no indication of any impact from lead ingestion among birds in the wild. There also have been no documented reports of anyone finding wild mourning doves suffering from or having been killed by lead ingestion in hunting or non-hunted areas.

"The purpose of our study is to replace perception with facts,'" said Corey Mason, who helped lead the lethality study while serving as dove program director for TPW. "It is not our intention to force a change in anyone's beliefs.

"When we started out, we realized we could only do so much at one time. We think we have provided some very valuable information that can be used by hunters, should they choose to use it."

Roster said he would recommend much larger studies be conducted with additional variables to obtain a better picture of the effectiveness of steel versus lead shot on mourning doves and other migratory birds. Factors should include the increased use of sub-gauge shotguns, a wider variety of available ammunition, hunters of different skill levels and shooting ability, additional testing at ranges beyond 40 yards and other variables.

"Some would have you believe that dove hunters are the world's worst shooters based on the number of shells fired at birds every year," he said. "I have seen figures that show the average harvest is two birds per hunter.

"One of the issues that should be addressed is hunter skill level. I was surprised at the success of the shooters in this study, which was about 4.5 shells per downed bird. That is actually pretty good."

According to ammunition manufacturers, the average hunter fires about seven to nine shots for every dove killed.

Roster said that given the limitations and restrictions of the 2008-2009 study, he was satisfied the findings were true and accurate for that group of hunters and loads.

"Hunters were unable to distinguish the ammunition type being used in the field, and we detected no relationship between ammunition type and level of hunter satisfaction," the study's abstract said.

"Field analyses detected no differences in doves bagged per shot, wounded per shot, bagged per hit or wounded per hit among the three ammunition types. Necropsy analyses detected no difference in the proportion of birds with through-body strikes, mean penetration depth of through-body strikes or mean embedded pellet depth among ammunition types.

"Our results indicated that pellet density is but one factor influencing ammunition performance. Further, the forensic evaluation of shotshell ammunition is a complicated subject, and will require more testing if we (the public, industry, state and federal agencies) are to define the ballistic factors (internal, external and terminal) responsible for differences in field performance among ammunition types (a large combination of different hulls, shot, wads, primers and powders).

"Because necropsy metrics reveal subtle differences in terminal ballistic behavior that are unobtainable through other means, and provide an effective means for comparing ammunition performances, they should be included in all further lethality studies." In summarizing, the study said: "We caution readers that our results may provide limited inference to other loads.

"Therefore managers and hunters should evaluate ammunition carefully, referencing creditable lethality tables for selecting shot size, minimum load weights and choke constriction; in conjunction with pattern testing at applicable ranges."

Observations recorded by Texas Parks and Wildlife Department biologist David Butler during a training session conducted by Tom Roster are graded and examined to obtain accurate data on the effectiveness of steel versus lead shot for dove hunting.

This old Colt has seen a lot of use. It's shown here with an original DH Lawrence holster. The New Service works well with .45 ACP and .45 AR cartridges.

The Three .45s

These .45-caliber cartridges are excellent choices in the handguns for which they were designed.

BY BOB CAMPBELL

Handgun and handgun cartridge evolution is always interesting. For example, the .44 Smith & Wesson American was basically a centerfire .44 Henry that advanced to the .44 S&W American, then the .44 Russian and finally the .44 Special. The Special is the parent of the .44 Mag.

And consider the three .45s: the .45 Automatic Colt Pistol, .45 Colt and .45 Auto Rim. The .45 automatic cartridge spun off the .451 Detonics, .460 Rowland, .45 GAP and a few others, including the .400 CorBon and .38-45. The .45 Colt birthed the .454 Casull and .460 S&W but remains the most popular

The author fires his 1917 Smith & Wesson. This is a great defensive revolver.

The author's three favorite .45s are much loved and much used.

This is a brand-new nickel Colt Single Action Army .45. It just doesn't get any better than this for handling and eye appeal.

cartridge by a considerable margin. The .45 Auto Rim is not nearly as popular as the other .45s but serves a real purpose. The .45 Colt was the first with the most, and the .45 ACP was designed to mimic the performance of the Colt. This is one of the few cases in which the primogenitor remains in production and popular.

All the .45 cartridges can be improved through judicious handloading, but they're proven workhorses in factory form. You might argue that each offers similar performance in a different firing platform. These calibers are an American institution.

My experience mirrors the positive results enjoyed by others in wartime and personal defense. Unlike small bores, the .45s are effective for personal defense with non-expanding ammunition. And although they're not magnums, they have each proven effec-

tive against medium-size game and useful in defense — even against bears. The .45 ACP's 230-grain full-metal-jacketed bullet and the .45 Colt's 255-grain conical load are among the most respected defense cartridges with folks who have participated in battle and not simply read fiction and junk science. Plus, the cartridges can be controlled by average shooters using standard-size handguns. Modest powder charges and cast bullets allow each to be fired with economy. And each .45 operates at low pressure, resulting in modest wear.

The First .45

The voluminous .45 Colt case was intended for black powder. The original cartridge case was drawn copper and expanded when fired. As a result, the .45 Colt is sometimes difficult to get a handle on with modern powders. You get smoky loads and gas blow-by when experimenting. As such, you should stick with 250-grain bullets and moderate burning powders, such as WW 231. The button-ejecting single-action revolver works fine with the .45 Colt, but double-action revolvers and star ejectors sometimes don't mate well with the .45 Colt's thin case rim. The .45 Auto Rim might be a better choice as a pure combat cartridge.

The .45 Colt served American lawmen well for many years and also served the Army. It's often overlooked, but from the time the .45 was rushed to the Philippines after the disastrous failure of the .38 Colt, the Single Action Army or Colt New Service in the same caliber was the preferred sidearm of soldiers until replaced by the Colt 1911. That's a lot of combat. The Mexican revolution gave the Colt SAA an extra decade of battle. The .45 Colt was prized for its effect on men and horses. In battles against the Apache, Cheyenne and Comanche, more horses than men became casualties.

Left to right, we see three powerhouse cartridges: the .45 Colt, .45 ACP and .45 Auto Rim, all with cast bullets and Starline Brass.

The Three .45s

Note the differences in case rims. First, the thin .45 Colt, next the .45 Auto Rim and finally the extractor-grooved .45 ACP.

The excellent hand fit and modest recoil of the 1911 and SAA make for pleasant shooting with heavy loads.

The .45 ACP is efficient even in short barrels. These short-barrel .45s are excellent defensive handguns.

The Smith & Wesson 1917, top, sports Hogue grips and a special front sight. The Smith and Wesson 1911 target model, lower, is match-grade accurate.

In the author's opinion, this stainless Colt Rail Gun .45 is the finest service handgun ever made.

Bob Campbell

The bottom line is power, and the .45 Colt edges the .45 ACP in that regard and has the reputation as the most reliable stopper of men and killer of game. A 250-grain hard-cast SWC at 950 fps has plenty of knock-down power for game at moderate ranges. I see the .45 Colt as a powerhouse for outdoorsmen, modern cowboys and people traveling in country inhabited by dangerous game.

Loading the .45 Colt with lighter jacketed bullets doesn't necessarily produce the desired velocity for expansion and might raise ignition issues, with larger charges of powder behind a light bullet with less bullet pull. I have used the 250-grain Hornady XTP in the .45 Colt with excellent results. For practice, I use the mild Black Hills Ammunition cowboy load, an accurate and affordable combination. When wearing the SAA— and I do so often — the revolver is loaded with handloads.

(Because we're discussing practical everyday packing pistols, I won't get into Ruger-only handloads and the heavy revolvers.)

The .45 ACP

The .45 ACP was designed as a self-loading version of the .45 Colt. Modern smokeless powder allowed good velocity with a modest powder charge. The Colt immediately proved itself in action. The punitive expedition into Mexico and then World War 1 gave the 1911 a fine reputation. Other wars large and small only solidified that.

You can realize excellent ballistic efficiency with the .45 ACP. A 230-grain load exhibits a full powder burn with little muzzle signature. Black Hills Ammunition's 230-grain JHP is my usual carry load. Handloads using the 200-grain Hornady XTP have proven accurate, and this bullet has enough penetration for any chore. The .45 ACP is a wonderful cartridge for reloaders, offering economy, power and accuracy with modest pressure.

My 1911s are an important part of my life. Although it's true the 1911 is best suited for personal defense and the .45 Colt is best suited to hunting, I have used each in the opposite pursuit

The author often carries his Colt in this shark-skin rig from DM Bullard. The 1911 is flat enough for excellent concealment.

at times. The .45 Colt is a good defense cartridge with a trained shooter, and the .45 ACP will take game in the proper environment. But it's best to use each where they shine.

Pushing Too Much

Many shooters have attempted to obtain results comparable to the .45 Colt by handloading 255-grain SWC bullets in a .45 ACP case. Accuracy is not always good, and battering results. Frames have been cracked, and otherwise good Colt 1911s were

Here's the Model 1917 carry gun with Captech JHP loads. It doesn't get better in a revolver for personal defense.

A .45 will take a lot of shooting. The cartridge pressure is low, and the handguns are well designed. This Springfield has passed the 20,000-round mark.

ruined. An outdoorsman using a 1911 might handload a hard-cast 200-grain bullet to 1,100 fps with good results. The .45 Colt is better served with a 255-grain SWC at 950 fps. Each is on the ideal end of effectiveness. You'll have a good cartridge with excellent knockdown and not too much kick in your palm. When it comes to pure big-bore performance, the .45 ACP and .45 Colt are the ideal choices.

The Odd Man Out

The story of the Smith & Wesson and Colt revolvers chambered for the .45 ACP cartridge is a thrice-told tale. They were an important addition to the war effort in 1917 and 1918. The moon-clipped revolver has many advantages as a pure combat revolver, including the fastest and surest reload of any double-action revolver type. But civilians didn't wish to fool with moon clips for casual shooting. The .45 Auto Rim cartridge was created after World War 1 to solve the problem of using a .45 ACP revolver in the normal fashion.

The .45 Auto Rim is more than a rimmed .45 ACP. The head design is stronger than the .45 ACP. A careful handloader might load the .45 AR to .45 Colt levels: a 255-grain SWC and 900 fps. You can use a full crimp in this revolver case. The .45 AR is more economical than the .45 Colt for powder and lead use. When using my custom 1917 revolver for personal defense, I usually carry it loaded with full moon clips and the Black Hills 230-grain JHP. A spare moon clip takes up little space in my jacket pocket. For field use, I often carry a handload using the Hornady 200-grain XTP at 1,050 fps in the .45 Auto Rim case. This revolver is versatile and relatively light — a go-anywhere, do-anything handgun. For those who don't handload, Captech International (Captechintl.com) offers .45 AR ammunition and other hard-to-find cartridges. This is an excellent resource for the .45 AR. Starline offers new brass.

The Three .45s

Three Beauties

These cartridges are ideal in the respective handguns for which they were designed: single-action revolvers, self-loading pistols and double-action revolvers. In my opinion, they are the best big-bore cartridges in the world, and they are all .45s.

If you plan to carry the 1917 revolver for personal defense, a couple of moon clips provide a good backup.

The .300 Win. Mag.: The Answer to Most Hunting Questions

BY PHILLIP MASSARO

The temperature soared higher than 100 degrees, and the wind blowing through the rooibos trees was beginning to swirl, making our tracking job that much more difficult. Professional hunter Nick Prinsloo pointed down at the heart-shaped kudu bull tracks, and I could tell the direction the bull was heading would be quickly contaminated by our scent.

"Let's back off him and let these winds settle," Nick said.

We headed back toward where we believed we had left the cruiser, with the late-October sun pounding down on our shoulders. I was looking forward to a late-morning drink from the coolbox. Then, just as quickly as we had called the hunt off, one flick of a kudu cow's ear started the game again. One, two, four, six cows, and at the rear of the herd was the kudu I've dreamed of for 12 years and six safaris: a kudu bull with immense, spiraling, perfect horns, replete with ivory tips glowing in the late-morning spring sun. The Legendary Arms Works Professional rifle came to shoulder in an easy, fluid motion, and when Nick spread the shooting sticks, I heard two of my favorite words: "Shoot him."

He was running straight away with that loping kudu gait you won't soon forget if you've seen it, yet when the trigger broke and the rifle barked, the kudu fell out of the scope. After the euphoria that ensued, realizing that a quest had been fulfilled and a curse broken, I glanced down at the rifle and reflected on the merits of the cartridge I had chosen for this safari: the .300 Win. Mag.

Brought to us in 1963, eight years before I was born, the .300 Win. was the fourth cartridge in a series of belted magnums designed to fit in a standard long (.30-'06 length) action. The .458, .338 and .264 were based on the same case — the .375

The .300 Win. is well-suited for hunting 95 percent of the world's game, partly because of the selection of .30-caliber bullets available today. This is Norma's 180-grain Oryx load.

The .300 Win. Mag.

H&H Mag. — and shared the same shortened case length — 2.500 inch — to maintain a cartridge overall length of 3.340 inch. When Winchester announced the .300 Win. Mag., almost everyone expected the cartridge to be the .338 necked down to hold .308-inch bullets; essentially the .30-338 or very close to the .308 Norma Mag. What they saw was a different design. The COL of 3.340 inch was held, but the case was elongated to 2.620 inch, and the neck length shortened to 0.264 inch. The result was a belted cartridge that fits in a long-action rifle and is the ballistic equivalent of the venerable .300 H&H, which requires the longer, magnum-length receiver.

Author Phil Massaro used a .300 Win. Mag. to take this big kudu bull. The .300 Win. Mag. splits the difference between the .30-'06 Springfield and .300 Weatherby Mag. It works best in a rifle with a barrel at least 24 inches long. The author used a handloaded 150-grain Cutting Edge Bullets Copper Raptor bullet, a monumental hollow-point with a polymer tip. The new Enduron line of powder, IMR 4451, pushed the Raptor to a muzzle velocity of 3,340 fps.

It was less, in length and velocity, than the .300 Weatherby Mag., yet it was enough. The initial loading bettered the velocities of the cornerstone American cartridge, the .30-'06 Springfield, by 250 fps or so, giving a decided advantage in kinetic energy values as well. The many fantastic choices among the already existing and field-proven .30-caliber bullets made for a versatile cartridge. Winchester used the same 25-degree shoulder for the .300 Win. that it used for the .338 and .264, but the added case capacity gave the Winchester cartridge an advantage over the Norma and the .30/338 wildcat. The resulting case holds 81 to 85 grains of water, depending on brand, when filled to the base of the neck.

Detractors immediately criticized the short neck, as it's generally preferable to have a bottleneck cartridge use a neck dimension of at least one caliber in length. It had no negative effect. I have found there's plenty of neck tension to keep things in place, even with the longest bullets, and among the myriad rifle cartridges I've loaded, the .300 Win. Mag., is among the most accurate. Not unlike the .222 Rem. and .308 Win., there is something inherently accurate about the design of the .300 Win. — something lovers of ballistics cannot explain scientifically. To use the vernacular, the .300 Winnie just shoots.

Unlike the .308 Win., which will perform just fine in a rifle sporting a 20-inch barrel, the .300 Win. works best with a barrel of at least 24 inches to fully use the powder capacity of the case. I have two .300s. My Legendary Arms Works Professional has a 24-inch barrel, and my Winchester Model 70 Classic Stainless sports a 26-inch pipe. Neither rifle has ever been a handicap to me while hunting, regardless of how close the shots were or how thick the flora. As they're hunting rifles I use across the world, I've tried to set them up with riflescopes that can handle a variety of situations, from the prairie of Wyoming, to the tioga of Quebec to black bear in the inky hemlock and spruce thickets of the Catskill and Adirondack mountains of New York. The Model 70 wears a Leupold VX-6 2-12x44 with a 30mm tube, which can focus up close to shoot a bear trying to dine on your lower extremities to caribou or elk at the edge of my self-imposed hunting limits. The Professional wears a Bushnell Elite 4500 2.5-10x40, a trim, bright piece of glass that's lighter than most and matches the rifle well. Both of these riflescopes are reminiscent of the .300 Win.; capable of getting the job done no matter the range.

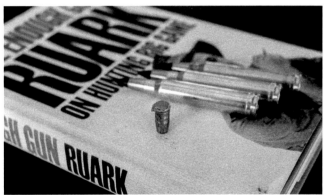

Much like the iconic .30-'06 Springfield, the .300 Win. is well-suited for hunting 95 percent of the world's game. This is, in fact, partly because of the fabulous selection of .30-caliber bullets we have today. Although the recoil is rather severe to make it a good choice for varmint work, I've loaded some 125-grain Nosler Ballistic Tips that have printed rather impressive groups, cruising along at a muzzle velocity of 3,400 fps. Let's just say the varmints didn't stand a chance.

As a big-game round, however, the .300 Win. shines. From deer and hogs, to distant pronghorn antelope, to moose and elk, and the ungulates of Africa, I really like the .300 Win. as an all-around choice. The bullet choices for big game, with a handful of exceptions, run from 150 to 220 grains, and man, there are some wonderful choices. I have used many of them in various applications. For most of my hunting with a .300 Winnie, I have found the 180-grain slugs give the best balance of trajectory, energy and accuracy. The lighter bullet choices will work, if of stout construction and if velocities are allowed to slow down a bit. Whitetails hit with a standard cup-and-core 150-grain bullet at less than 100 yards from full-house .300 Win. ammunition have an exorbitant amount of blood-shot meat, and penetration can be poor because of violent expansion, brought on by impact velocities greater than 3,200 fps. The standard 165-grain bullets are a bit better and are a perfect choice if you use a premium

bullet. Heavyweight projectiles — 200- and 220-grain bullets — are good choices for the largest deer and antelope you would hunt with a .30-caliber, as well as for the bears and other game that can even the score in a hurry.

Most ammunition companies offer a few hunting loads in .300 Win. Mag., and many are very well constructed. The Federal Premium load featuring the 180-grain Trophy Copper Tipped bullet has provided more than satisfactory results from my rifles, and the solid copper construction ensures that premature bullet break-up is no issue. ABM ammo makes a great long-range .300 Win. load built around the Berger 185-grain, which leaves the

The .300 Win. Mag.

The author's Winchester Model 70 Classic Stainless sports a 26-inch barrel and a Leupold VX-6 2-12x44 with the 30mm tube. There is something inherently accurate about the design of the round. The .300 Winnie just shoots.

barrel at 3,080 fps and still delivers 2,365 foot-pounds of energy at 400 yards. The .300 Win. has attained the status most rifle calibers dream of: You can find ammunition, of one variety or another, in most back-country gun shops and almost all the box stores that sell ammunition and hunting supplies. It has become that universal.

But, in my opinion, handloading lets you see the true genius of the .300 Win. Mag. design as a hunting cartridge. I've received many comments and questions to this effect: "Why would I choose to use the magnum cartridge when there are so many fantastic rifles available in .308 Win. and .30-'06? What is the advantage, when so many of hunting shots are inside 200 yards?" My answer is: First, I shoot my .300 Wins. very well. They are good rifles; accurate and well-fitted, and that's very important. Second, I can, via handloading, create ammunition for my .300 Win. that will mimic the performance of the .308 Win. and/or .30-'06, but I can't get my .308s and '06s to give me .300 Win. performance. When I'm on a hunt in unfamiliar territory, where I have the possibility of multiple species and/or distant shots, I'm much happier carrying a .300 and taking a close shot rather than one of the slower cartridges.

Through the years, I've developed a collection of pet loads that have given me reliable field performance on two continents and in many hunting situations. The .300 Win. Mag. is best served by a large rifle magnum primer. For most of my loads, I prefer Federal's Gold Medal Match GM215M. The hotter spark gives a more uniform result, and the deviation of velocities tends to be very low. The .300 Win. can be fueled by powders that range from the medium burning IMR4064 and Hodgdon's VARGET to the slowest burning powders, such as IMR7828 and 7977 to Alliant's Reloder 25. I like Norma brass and Federal GM215M primers to spark the large powder charges. For an all-around big-game load, I like two bullets: the 180-grain Sierra Game King for a standard bullet and the 180-grain Swift Scirocco II for a bonded-core choice. Both are boat-tail spitzer bullets, the Sierra being a standard cup-and-core, and the Swift a thick jacket, bonded-core polymer-tip design. The Sierra accounted for my first caribou, taken across a frozen lake in Quebec at minus 15, and the Scirocco accounted for my best pronghorn, taken in Wyoming at the end of September, when the country there is as pretty as any place I've seen. Both loads have accompanied me on many local deer hunts in my native

New York, and they have worked just fine. These bullets like the same powder charges. I go back and forth between 68.5 grains of IMR453 and 73.0 grains of Alliant's Reloder-19, as both have given me three-shot groups of less than ½ MOA, and both produce a velocity of about 2,960 fps, depending on the rifle and temperature. Although these bullets are rather long, there's no problem seating them in the .300 Win. case and maintaining the SAAMI specified COL.

For my first African safari, I packed a .300 Win. as my light rifle, nicely complementing my .375 H&H Mag. Because kudu and eland were on the shopping list, I wanted a bullet that would not only deliver a decent trajectory but be strong enough to deliver the bone-smashing power that an antelope weighing almost a ton can demand. I chose the 200-grain Swift A-Frame for this hunt, fueled by 75.0 grains of the slow-burning Reloder-25, for a muzzle velocity of 2,710 fps. This load, which printed 1-inch groups at 100 yards, accounted for my first head of African game: a heavy-horned gemsbok bull that holds a place of honor among my hunting trophies. That combination, with that strong A-Frame bullet, which retains more than 90 percent of its

weight, would easily handle interior grizzly bear and just about any creature shy of cape buffalo and elephant.

New York has a healthy population of black bears, which, although not particularly tough in comparison to grizzlies, can attain weights of 600 pounds or more. When an animal has claws and teeth that can rearrange your anatomy, I prefer to carry a rifle that ends an argument quickly. I was reading some classic hunting literature in which the author waxed poetically about the virtues of the .30-'06 Springfield and the classic 220-grain round-nose load at 2,400 fps. I figured I could get the .300, with a bit of creative handloading, to perform the same. It didn't take long to obtain a box of good Hornady Interlocks and some old data from an aged reloading manual. I used 53.0 grains of IMR 4064 to achieve a muzzle velocity of 2,425 fps; perfect for whitetail and black bears. That load prints at 1 MOA, and has accounted for a New York black bear and my best local whitetail: an 11-point buck that proudly resides on the wall of my dining room.

The kudu bull I mentioned earlier was taken with a special load, built around the 150-grain Cutting Edge Bullets Copper Raptor bullet. The Raptor is a monometal hollow-point with a

The .300 Win. Mag.

This puts the 300 Win. Mag. in perspective with some other well-known cartridges. Left to right are the 308 Win., 30-'06 Springfield, 300 Win. Mag., 300 WSM and 300 RUM.

The 300 Win. Mag., left, was the fourth cartridge in a series of belted magnums designed to fit in a standard long action. The other Winchester magnums are, from left to right, the .264, .338 and .458, all based on the .375 H&H Mag. case.

polymer tip. Upon impact, the skived walls of the hollow-point section break off into small blades for serious impact trauma, and the rear portion of the bullet remains at caliber dimension for deep penetration. I know, a 150-grain seems awfully light for an animal the size of a kudu, which are often comparable to elk, but my previous experiences with these bullets engendered a bunch of confidence, and my theory that they would handle kudu and the like was proven correct. That bull dropped in his tracks. That load also accounted for a big waterbuck bull at 215 yards a couple of days later. I used the new Enduron line of powder — IMR 4451 — to arrive at ¾ MOA accuracy and a muzzle velocity of 3,340 fps. According to Chris Hodgdon, president of the Hodgdon Powder Co., which now produces the IMR line, that marked the first use of IMR4451 in Africa. The only bullet base I recovered was from the kudu bull. All the other shots passed through, at ranges from 70 to 215 yards. All in all, it proved to be a thoroughly dependable load with very little recoil.

Among the hunting rounds, there are more powerful .30s on the market. The .300 Weatherby Mag., .300 Rem. Ultra Mag. and the behemoth .30-378 Weatherby will produce higher muzzle velocities and flatter trajectories than the .300 Win., yet that comes at the price of a considerable increase in recoil and barrel wear. As an example, my dad's favorite .30-caliber magnum is the .300 RUM, which will drive a 180-grain slug at faster than 3,350 fps but requires just shy of 100 grains of slow-burning powder to do so. My .300 Win. will push the same bullet at 3,050 fps but with

fewer than 80 grains of powder, with much more comfortable and manageable recoil. Let's also compare the trajectory of the two. Using a 200-yard zero and the same 180-grain projectile, the .300 Win. will be 6 inches low at 300 yards and 18 inches low at 400 yards. The .300 RUM will be just less than 4 inches low at 300 yards and 12 inches low at 400. Although the RUM has an appreciable difference in long-range trajectory, the added case length, longer receiver and significant increase in recoil of the .300 RUM give the edge to the .300 Win., in my opinion. Based on my shooting experiences, off the bench doing load development and in real-world hunting situations, I feel comfortable saying the .300 Win. has a power level the average shooter can accurately shoot without beginning to think about a muzzle brake. Everyone has a different level of recoil tolerance, but I know many shooters who insist on using a .300 Weatherby or bigger caliber and develop a nasty flinch, resulting in poor targets and wounded game. No matter how big the case is, a .30-caliber bullet placed improperly will not kill game. I believe that among the choices for magnum cartridges, the .300 Win. Mag. (and its ballistic twin, the .300 H&H Mag.) makes the most logical and practical choice for sportsmen.

The .300 Win. is not only a hunting cartridge, though. It's comfortable on the bench-rest circuit and has been adopted by the U.S. Marine Corps in sniper rifles. Paper-punchers can find many wonderful match-grade bullets that will print tiny cloverleaf groups. With a 1:10-inch twist rate, the .300 Win. has the horsepower to push the heaviest target bullets, such as the

230-grain Berger Match Hybrid Target, at muzzle velocity of faster than 2,800 fps. With a G1 ballistic coefficient of 0.717, this combination offers the long-range target shooter all sorts of wind resistance — perfect for the 1,000-yard range. The 168 and 180-grain Sierra Match Kings will also make fantastic choices for accurate target work. Although the recoil of a .300 Win. can be a bit much for extended shooting sessions, in a rifle with sufficient weight, it can be more than tolerable.

When it comes to the actual construction of the case, the belt is unnecessary. Unlike the .375 H&H, .300 H&H and .458 Win., the .300 headspaces off that well-pronounced shoulder. Those other cartridges can exhibit long-term case stretching just in front of the belt, but this effect seems to be minimized in the .300 Win. The case feeds just fine, unlike some of the feeding issues associated with the Winchester Short Magnum series, and because it shares the same action length as the .30-'06, it's quite easy to convert a rifle of .30-'06 length action to the .300 Win. Mag. Among the .30-caliber magnums, the .300 H&H owns the nostalgia category, and the .300 RUM wears the horsepower crown among commonly produced rifles, but you can take my word for it: The .300 Win. will hold its title of King Versatile for generations.

How does a .300 Win. compare to other calibers with a similar case capacity? Is it anemic when compared to the .338 Win. Mag.? Does the 7mm Rem. Mag. make a mockery of the .300 in the trajectory department? The answer to both questions is an emphatic no. The difference between the 7mm Rem. Mag. and the .300 is so slight that I believe the larger frontal diameter of the .300 — as well as the better selection of bullet weights — gives a definite edge to the .300 Win. Although the .338 has an even larger diameter, the recoil begins to ramp up significantly. Even though the .338 can use bullets weighing 165 to 250 grains, the .300 can use bullets from 100 to 250 grains. Yes, that's right; a 250-grain .30-caliber bullet. The 250-grain Barnes Original, which looks about as long as a golf pencil, will attain velocities of 2,500 fps — only 150 fps behind the .338 with the same bullet weight — and group rather accurately. Grab some Cutting Edge Bullets 100-grain Raptors for your .300 Win., and you've got as fine a coyote-killing machine as was ever invented.

There have been several cartridges that tried to usurp the .30-caliber magnum crown — such as the .300 Win. Short Mag. — but the .300 Win. still reigns supreme. The blend of flat trajectory, striking power and manageable recoil will ensure its position at the top of the heap. Will it ever replace the king of all cartridges, the .30-'06 Springfield? Probably not. But although I've had some great hunting and shooting experiences with the ought-six, to me the .300 Win. represents a cartridge that delivers just a bit more, and although some folks reading this might deem that velocity advantage unnecessary, for me it engenders confidence in the rifle. I firmly believe that confidence is a huge part of good marksmanship.

Here are the .300 Win. Mag, right, and the .30-338, the latter being a .338 Win. Mag case necked down to hold .308-inch bullets, something very close to the .308 Norma Mag.

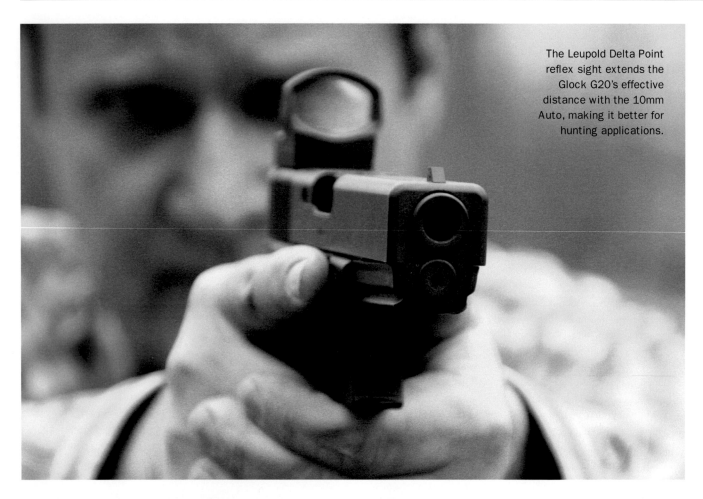

The Leupold Delta Point reflex sight extends the Glock G20's effective distance with the 10mm Auto, making it better for hunting applications.

The 10mm Automatic — Cooper's Big Bore

After a rough start, this powerful beast has found its way into the hearts of many shooters.

BY ROBERT SADOWSKI

The 10mm Auto, or just plain 10mm, is an example of a cartridge that was a good idea but had a rough start. Designed to best the external ballistics of the .45 ACP, the 10mm easily surpasses the venerable round and the .357 Mag. and closes in on the power of the .41 Mag., and does so in a service-sized semi-automatic pistol.

Initial 10mm pistols were plagued with production delays and malfunctions. The round loaded as originally intended produced 44,440 psi, which is enough to shake the blueing off any pistol. The round battered pistols, which yielded poor accuracy, shadowing the 10mm early on. If not for a disastrous FBI gunfight, the 10mm might have faded from memory. That shootout and the fans of the cartridge did not allow the round to

The Bren Ten was the first production handgun chambered in 10mm Auto. It was adapted from the CZ-75f and manufactured by Dornaus & Dixon Enterprises Inc.

die. In fact, Glock and SIG have recently debuted new pistols chambered in 10mm Auto, and ammunition manufacturers such as SIG Sauer, Buffalo Bore and Double Tap are loading the cartridge as it should be — to its full potential. The 10mm Auto is going through a renaissance of sorts. There is no doubt the 10mm Auto is a powerful round with substantial recoil, and it's well suited for hunting and combat scenarios.

Jeff Cooper is considered the father and the creator of the modern technique of handgun shooting. His tool of choice was the 1911 platform chambered in .45 ACP. If Cooper's chosen tool had a weakness, it was the .45 ACP's external ballistics. The heavy bullet pushed at a slow velocity rapidly sheds power across distance. Cooper envisioned a combat pistol round that had more power. From 1982 to 1983, Cooper and his cohorts — John Adams, Whit Collins and Irving Stone — designed a round and used a .30 Remington case cut down to .992 inch and loaded

The Rock Island Armory TAC Ultra FS is chambered in 10mm Auto. Expect excellent accuracy in this tricked-out 1911 platform.

with a .40 caliber bullet like the ones used in the .38-40 WCF cartridge. The ammunition manufacturer, Norma, ironed out the cartridge design and was the first ammo maker to produce the 10mm Auto. The initial load debuted in 1983 and used a 200-grain full-jacketed truncated-cone bullet. The bullet was similar to 9mm and .45 ACP bullets of that time. The muzzle velocity was 1,200 fps, with 635 foot-pounds muzzle energy. This load had a mean working pressure of 37,000 psi with a maximum pressure of 44,400 psi. For comparison, the 9mm has a maximum pressure of 35,001 psi, and the .45 ACP has a maximum pressure of 21,000 psi. The .357 Mag. and .41 Mag. have a max of 35,000 psi. Even the .44 Mag. pressure at 36,000 psi is less than the 10mm. It's safe to say the initial 10mm Auto was hot. But remember, the 10mm Auto was designed to be a hot, powerful cartridge. At that point, the missing piece to the 10mm Auto cartridge was a pistol.

In 1979, a separate group of similar-thinking firearm enthusiasts, Thomas Dornaus and Michael Dixon of Dornaus & Dixon Enterprises Inc., began developing a semi-automatic pistol to address the power gap between magnum revolvers and semi-automatic pistols. They made contact with Cooper in about 1980 and found he and his group were working on a new cartridge design. They threw in together to develop the pistol and cartridge, and the result was the Bren Ten pistol. Although the Bren Ten was adapted from the CZ-75, it's highly modified, meaning it was beefed up to hold up to the pressure the 10mm Auto unleashed.

The Bren Ten was a semi-automatic pistol that used a selective double-action trigger system. It had a 5-inch barrel, high-profile visible sights, an 11-round magazine and a stainless frame and slide. The pistols were produced from 1984 to 1986, and perhaps about 1,500 total were made. Issues arose with the magazine, and the recoil caused the pistols to not function properly. It seemed the only time the pistol functioned properly was when Sonny Crockett, the lead character on the TV show Miami Vice, fired his trademark Bren Ten. The show helped elevated the gun into cult status, but in reality, the pistol was released too soon. More testing should have been done. Dornaus & Dixon Enterprises filed for bankruptcy, and it appeared the 10mm was dead. Obviously, popularity of the round and the defective pistols began to wane with law enforcement and civilian shooters. The aforementioned gunfight in Florida changed perceptions.

In 1986, the FBI was involved in a shootout in Miami-Dade County. The battle involved eight FBI agents and two suspected bank robbers. The event lasted less than five minutes, and although agents outnumbered the suspects, who were ex-military, and even though the suspects were hit numerous times, they returned fire and pinned down law enforcement. The agents were armed with 12-gauge shotguns, 9mm

The 10mm Automatic — Cooper's Big Bore

semi-automatic pistols and .38 Special and .357 Mag. revolvers. One suspect was hit six times, and the other was shot 12 times. About 145 shots were exchanged. In the aftermath, two FBI agents were killed, along with the two suspected bank robbers. An ensuing investigation by the FBI placed partial blame on the death of its agents on the lack of stopping power of the agents' service handguns. Soon after the shootout, in 1987, the FBI tested 9mm and .45 ACP ammo and found both calibers lacking.

Cartridges loaded with 180-grain JHP bullets make an excellent defensive round. The Federal 180-grain Hydra-Shok are loaded to a lower velocity — about 1,030 fps depending on the barrel length — compared to the SIG Sauer 180-grain JHP, which is loaded to a hot 1,250 fps. The Buffalo Bore load clocks at 1,350 fps.

The author's 10mm hunting setup includes a Glock G20 Gen4 SF with a 6-inch barrel and Leupold Delta Point reflex sight.

The agency began studying wound ballistics and concluded that a bullet that penetrated vital organs creating a larger wound channel would be most effective — a conclusion that seems obvious today. By 1988, the FBI had developed a protocol for testing ammunition for penetration on soft targets through various barriers.

Tests are conducted at set distances with a block of 10 percent ordnance-grade ballistic gel, which simulates human flesh. According to the protocol, a cartridge has a minimum requirement to meet, which includes a minimum penetration into ballistic gelatin of 12 to 18 inches, expansion of the bullet to at least 1.5 times original diameter and 100 percent weight retention of expanded bullet. Bullets are fired through various barriers, including steel, wallboard, plywood, heavy clothing and automotive glass at 10 feet and 20 yards. The 10mm Auto excelled in the tests and offered a compromise between a larger caliber and low magazine capacity, such as the .45 ACP, and the high magazine capacity of a less powerful round such as the 9mm.

The FBI approved adoption of the 10mm Auto cartridge in 1989 but needed a pistol. An RFP was issued, and pistol manufactures such as Colt and Smith & Wesson submitted guns for testing. Smith & Wesson was awarded the contract for about 9,500 Model 1076 semi-automatic pistols. Colt offered a 1911 pistol in 10mm, but the RFP specs for the new 10mm pistol design were detailed, and some requirements excluded a 1911-style pistol, such as the requirement for a DA/SA trigger and 11+1 magazine capacity. Besides, early on, when the 1911 was chambered in 10mm, it performed like it was off its meds. The classic platform needed tweaking. The Model 1076 was a full-sized stainless-steel pistol built to take the abuse the 10mm doled out, with a 4.25-inch barrel, no manual safety, a bobbed hammer, a nine-round single-stack magazine and a frame-mounted decocker like SIG-Sauer pistols. Extended magazines of 11 and 15 rounds were also part of the FBI's new pistol requirements. The FBI went all in on the 10mm and also chambered some ancient Thompson Model 1928 submachine guns in the cartridge. It also contracted with Heckler & Koch for its MP5 submachine in 10mm, calling it the MP5/10. The issue then was recoil.

Many agents could not control the 10mm Auto, even in the heavy Model 1076 pistols. The term used was "unmanageable recoil." The FBI then decided to continue testing, with a 180-grain Sierra JHP bullet to a muzzle velocity of 980 fps. This load reduced recoil enough for agents to tolerate it. The FBI requested Federal ammunition to duplicate that reduced load, which became known as the "FBI-lite" round. Other ammunition manufacturers followed the light loading, and some shooters found their 10mm pistols did not function properly with the reduced-power load. The light load also defeated the purpose of the 10mm, which was meant to offer better penetration and more power. It was a similar experience the .41 Mag. received when it was offered to law enforcement as an alternative to the .38 Special and .357 Mag — too much recoil.

Because there was extra space in the 10mm Auto cartridge case because of the light load, Smith & Wesson cut the case from .992 inch to .850 inch to create the .40 S&W. The .40 S&W is essentially the 10mm Auto light load in a more compact cartridge. The .40 S&W debuted in 1990 and was immediately popular with law-enforcement agencies because it could be chambered in 9mm-sized guns and had ballistics that nearly matched the 10mm Auto light load. Plus, recoil was much more controllable. It would seem the 10mm Auto was again in its death throes, but die-hard fans of the caliber remained.

Even before the .40 S&W hit the scene, other firearms manufacturers saw potential in the 10mm Auto. Again, the powerful round experienced fits and starts. In 1987, Colt debuted the Colt Delta Elite, a 1911-style platform chambered in 10mm Auto. The Delta Elite pistols were well made, but again, more testing with the round should have been conducted. The 10mm beat up the 1911 design. The flaw in the Colt 10mm was the recoil system. A shock-buffer was needed to lessen the battering the pistol received from the round. Some receivers cracked as a result. Colt redesigned the recoil assembly to better withstand the recoil and added a slot cut into the receiver or frame to alleviate stress. Current Delta Elites function flawlessly.

Issues with the Bren Ten and early Colt Delta Elites did not endear the 10mm to accuracy. In fact, the round was thought of as inaccurate. Not so with current guns. Glock offered a full size striker-fire pistol the G20 in 1990 in 10mm Auto. Subsequently, compact, sub-compact and long-barrel Glocks were offered in 10mm. In 2015, SIG redesigned the legendary P220 to handle

Initially, the 10mm was not considered an accurate round. Here is an eight-shot group fired from 25 yards out of the Rock Island Armory Tac Ultra FS, a 1911-style platform.

the round. Probably the heir apparent to the Bren Ten is the full-sized Tanfoglio Witness, built in Italy and imported by EAA Corp. Like the Bren Ten, the Witness is based off the CZ-75 and is a heavy-duty version with features such as an SA/DA trigger, extended beavertail frame and exposed knurled hammer. Kimber, Para, Dan Wesson and custom 1911-platform builders such as STI also chamber pistols in the caliber. In 1990, Smith & Wesson even chambered a revolver in the 10mm: the Model 610, a six-shot N-frame. It used moon clips to fire the rimless 10mm round and could also fire the .40 S&W cartridge.

Handgun hunters have found a lot to like with the caliber, and that's the section where my seat is in the 10mm fan club. I have liked the round since the Colt Delta Elites hit dealer shelves, and I tend to like it even more every time I fire the round out of various platforms, such as the Glock and SIG. For a serious hunting semi-automatic pistol, nothing really comes close to the 10mm Auto. There are three platforms I tend to lean toward: Glock, 1911 and SIG — and that's in no specific order.

If you think 1911 pistols can't hunt, you haven't fired the 10mm through one. Buffalo Bore and Double Tap push 200-grain wide flat-nose hard-cast bullets at speeds of 1,300 fps with about 750 foot-pounds of muzzle energy — big medicine in such a handy-sized pistol.

The 10mm offers good penetration when you need to collapse a wild pig quick or fill the freezer with venison. All the

The Delta Elite was Colt's first pistol chambered in 10mm Auto. Initial models suffered from cracked receivers.

major ammo manufacturers offer loads, but specialty manufacturers such as Buffalo Bore and Double Tap load the cartridge to its maximum potential. These 200- and 220-grain hard-cast bullets are made to punch holes through flesh and bones with ease. I keep my shots at less than 50 yards when hunting pigs and deer, though I'm sure others have pushed the round much farther. I'm sure the rounds would do well from tree stand on a black bear with a sweet tooth.

I've achieved my best accuracy with the 1911 platform, which I attribute to the pistol and my comfort with shooting it. A few years ago, I had the pleasure of running an RIA TAC Ultra FS in 10mm. I'm still running it. This is an inexpensive 1911-style pistol that shoots like a tight-fitting custom pistol. The TAC Ultra FS uses a Series 70 system along with a one-piece guide rod and bull-barrel design that dispenses with the traditional barrel bushing. This setup aids accuracy. The flared bull barrel locks up tight at the muzzle. The barrel is stainless steel with a feed ramp, like a Clark Custom barrel. The integral ramp fully supports the case, so there's no gap between the frame and barrel for bullet noses to snag on. The weight from an extra-long dust cover helps a bit with recoil, as do the serrations on the front strap and the checkered polymer main-spring housing. All aid in gripping and controlling this beast.

In the case of the Glock, the polymer frame makes recoil feel lighter. It flexes when the pistol is fired, so it absorbs some of the felt recoil. I've set up a Glock G20 FS Gen4 with a 6-inch hunting barrel and a Leupold DeltaPoint reflex sight especially for boar and deer. The longer barrel helps squeeze out more velocity and, therefore, energy, and the red-dot increases my effective distance with the pistol. With 180-grain JHP loaded heavy by Buffalo Bore, I averaged 1,161 fps velocity with 539 foot-pounds of energy. The G40 Gen4 MOS is set up like mine, except it doesn't have an inch or so of barrel sticking out of the business end of the slide. The Glock 10mm pistols, in my opinion, are the softest shooting of the 10mm Autos I've fired. At first, I was prepared for the Delta Point reflex sight to fly off, but it has not — addi-

The SIG Sauer P220 Match Elite takes SIG's legendary P220 frame and slide re-engineered for the 10mm Auto. Accurate and smooth, reliable operation is the result with the 10mm.

tional proof modern pistol designs have tamed the 10mm.

The iconic P220 has recently been re-chambered in 10mm, similar to how custom gun builder Gray Guns has been doing it for years. With Bruce Gray's success at converting P220s to 10mm Auto, SIG approached him when it decided to go big bore with the P220.

"The 10mm creates an enormous volume of high pressure and a really fast acceleration rate of the bullet," Gray said. "Lock-up systems take a beating like what was experienced initially with 1911 platforms chambered in the round."

The frame of the SIG P220 pistol is very durable, and through some engineering, SIG used a combination of slide mass and recoil-spring system to tame the round. The P220 10mm pistol uses a multi-wire, stranded cable-style recoil spring to manage slide movement. Glock employs a flat spring configuration in its 10mm pistols. The Colt Delta Elite 1911 uses a double-nested spring system to manage the recoil. Firing the 10mm out of a P220 Elite Match with its DA/SA trigger system, along with the grip shape and texture, allowed me to get back on target fast without the pistol shifting in my grip during recoil. It's about time SIG chambered its P220 with a serious caliber.

Whether choosing the 10mm Auto for hunting, concealed carry or combat situations, remember to choose an appropriate load. As a concealed-carry pistol, it makes sense to load rounds that have less penetration. Remember, you are responsible for the bullets you fire. You do not want to defeat your assailant only to have the bullet pass though to accidentally kill a bystander. Then again, if you like to go fly-fishing and share the stream with the locals, meaning bears, the 10mm Auto offers a lot of negotiating power in an easy-to-tote package.

The 10mm Auto (center) is flanked by the .357 Mag. (left) and .41 Mag. (right). The 10mm Auto exceeds .357 Magnum ballistics and has nearly the same ballistics of the .41 Mag.

The 180-grain FMJ are good all-around training rounds or if you need extra penetration on your target. A variety of ammunition makers produce this go-to load.

Because the .40 S&W caliber is so popular — thanks in part to the 10mm — there are numerous bullet weights and styles from which to choose. For a reloader, the sweet spot for bullet weight is a 180-grain or 200-grain bullet, though lighter bullets work, too. These weights prove to be most accurate, along with a powder that has a fast to fast-medium burn rate, such as Alliant Blue Dot, Accurate Arms No. 7, Accurate Arms No. 9 and Winchester 231. Your .40 S&W dies will load 10mm Auto, so there really is no reason not to have a 10mm. The history of the .40 S&W and 10mm Auto can't be pried apart. The two cartridges will forever be entwined.

The rough start for the 10mm proved to make it a better round. Die-hard 10mm fans have numerous pistol platforms to choose from, and the round is being loaded to suit the use: full potential or "lite." One of those fans is Ted Nugent, who uses the round to hunt and for concealed carry. He Tweeted a while ago, "10mm is the best damn pistol cal, period. If ya ain't got 1 get 2 asap." Listen to Uncle Ted, who is not too particular on the platform as long as it fires 10mm Auto. Who knows, perhaps the Bren Ten and 10mm will be resurrected. In 2010 to 2011, Vitor Mfg. started to manufacture the Bren Ten, but it also ran into issues with the pistol. But why wait when there are plenty of SIG, Glock and 1911-platform pistols available for the 10mm Auto beast?

The 10mm Auto is a beast of a round with substantial recoil. Here the SIG P220 Elite Match is captured in full recoil. All 10mms exhibit similar recoil.

BALLISTICS COMPARISON

	MUZZLE VELOCITY	MUZZLE ENERGY
10mm Automatic 180-grain Hydra-Shok JHP (FBI "lite-load")*	1,030 fps	424 ft-lbs.
10mm Automatic 180-grain Trophy Bonded JSP**	1,275 fps	650 ft-lbs.
9mm 115-grain GDHP***	1,210 fps	374 ft-lbs.
.38 Special +P 135-grain GDHP***	945 fps	208 ft-lbs.
.357 Magnum 125-grain GDHP***	1,450 fps	584 ft-lbs.
.45 ACP 230-grain HST***	890 fps	404 ft-lbs.

*Federal Premium Law Enforcement factory data
**Federal Premium factory data
***Speer LE factory data.

BALLISTICS COMPARISON:
10mm Auto vs. .40 S&W

	MUZZLE VELOCITY	MUZZLE ENERGY	MAXIMUM PRESSURE (SAAMI)
10mm Automatic 180-grain JHP	1,250 fps	524 ft-lbs.	37,500 psi
.40 S&W 180-grain JHP	985 fps	388 ft-lbs.	35,000 psi

Sauer Elite Performance factory data.

BALLISTICS COMPARISON:
10mm Auto Hunting Loads vs. 10mm Auto

	MUZZLE VELOCITY	MUZZLE ENERGY
Buffalo Bore Heavy 10mm Outdoorsman 220-grain Hard Cast FN*	1,200 fps	703 ft-lbs.
Double Tap 220-grain Hard Cast FN*	1,300 fps	750 ft-lbs.
Federal Premium Vital-Shok 180-grains Trophy Bonded JSP*	1,275 fps	650 ft-lbs.

*Buffalo Bore and Federal Premium factory data from 5-inch barrel
**Double Tap factory data from 4.6-inch barrel.

BALLISTICS COMPARISON:
10mm Auto vs. Magnum Revolvers

	MUZZLE VELOCITY	MUZZLE ENERGY
10mm Automatic 220-grain Hard Cast FN*	1,200 fps	703 ft-lbs.
.357 Magnum 158-grain XTP**	1,250 fps	548 ft-lbs.
.41 Magnum 240-grains Platinum Tip HP***	1,250 fps	833 ft-lbs.

*Buffalo Bore factory data
**Hornady factory data
***Winchester factory data.

PERFORMANCE:
Glock 20 Gen4 SF 10mm Automatic

	MUZZLE VELOCITY	MUZZLE ENERGY	ACCURACY AVERAGE
Buffalo Bore 180-grain JHP*	1,367 fps	747 ft-lbs.	1.9 in.
Buffalo Bore 180-grain JHP**	1,332 fps	709 ft-lbs.	1.8 in.
Hornady 165-grain FTX*	1,250 fps	573 ft-lbs.	2.1 in.
Hornady 165-grain FTX**	1,224 fps	549 ft-lbs.	2.0
PMC 200-grain FMJ-TC*	1,085 fps	532 ft-lbs.	2.0
PMC 200-grain FMJ-TC**	1,050 fps	490 ft-lbs.	1.8

Muzzle velocity was collected 15 feet from the muzzle by a ProChrono digital chronograph; average accuracy of three five-shot groups at 25 yards; *6-inch barrel; **4.6-inch barrel.

PERFORMANCE:
SIG Sauer P220-10 Match Elite 10mm Automatic

	MUZZLE VELOCITY	MUZZLE ENERGY	ACCURACY AVERAGE
American Eagle 180-grain FMJ	1,078 fps	465 ft-lbs.	1.9 in.
SIG Sauer V-Crown 180-grain JHP	1,332 fps	606 ft-lbs.	2.1 in.
SIG Sauer 180 FMJ	1,222 fps	597 ft-lbs.	1.9 in.
Federal Premium Personal Defense 180-grain Hydra-Shok JHP	983 fps	386 ft-lbs.	1.8 in.

Muzzle velocity was collected 15 feet from the muzzle by a ProChrono digital chronograph; average accuracy of three five-shot groups at 25 yards. 5.03-inch barrel.

PERFORMANCE:
Rock Island Armory TAC Ultra FS 10mm Automatic

	MUZZLE VELOCITY	MUZZLE ENERGY	ACCURACY AVERAGE
American Eagle 180-grain FMJ	1,058 fps	447 ft-lbs.	1.2 in.
PMC 200-grain FMJ-TC	1,023 fps	465 ft-lbs.	2.2 in.
Federal Premium Personal Defense 180-grain Hydra-Shok JHP	1,012 fps	409 ft-lbs.	1.5 in.

Muzzle velocity was collected 15 feet from the muzzle by a ProChrono digital chronograph; average accuracy of three, five-shot groups at 25 yards; 5-inch barrel.

Current American Sporting Cartridges

(Centerfire Rifle)

CHAPTER 1

The criterion used to determine which cartridges should be included in this chapter is the requirement that the cartridge be currently manufactured and available to the American sportsman through local dealers, either on an over-the-counter basis or by special order, since no gun store carries every single item of ammunition that is manufactured.

The cartridges listed here include not only the most modern developments, but also some that are ancient and obsolete by any standard. The characteristic they share is that they are manufactured on a commercial basis, still used, and rifles are available chambered for the round, although perhaps not made by the major American arms companies. Two of the oldest American centerfire cartridges included in this group are the .44-40 Winchester and the .45-70 Government, both of which originated in 1873 and have been in continuous use since. Several replica rifles are now chambered for the .44-40, and the .45-70 has staged a remarkable comeback. Both modern and replica rifles are being chambered for the .45-70. The popularity of this grand old military and sporting cartridge continues to increase.

One thing that can be said about many cartridges in Chapter 1 is that they have stood the test of time and include among their numbers the best and most useful designs available to the American shooter. Interestingly, nostalgia is in the process of moving a few of these formerly obsolete rounds back into Chapter 1.

For many years, the new trend in cartridge and rifle design has been toward high velocity and flat trajectory, often at the expense of almost any other consideration. It appears to be the fashionable thing, in some circles, to show up on a big-game hunt with the largest caliber or most powerful rifle in the crowd. This odd psychosis is partly responsible for the success of the Weatherby line of rifles and cartridges, although prestige and owning a perceived superior product also enter into this. The major gun manufacturers in the United States were slow in recognizing this as a fact of life, but have since closed the gap. Modern high-velocity magnum cartridges can cancel out some small measure of poor judgment in estimating range or lead, if the shooter can handle the added recoil and muzzle blast without flinching.

The editors, at various times, owned and shot most of the modern magnum rifles and handguns and have a very high regard for their capabilities, but also have reservations as to any real need for the larger calibers under normal North American hunting conditions. A great deal depends, of course, on what is to be hunted and under what conditions. Is there any actual advantage, for example, in owning a .300 Magnum, if your hunting area is confined to, say, southern California? What game would one encounter there so large or so dangerous that would require all that extra power? Yes, I understand the magnum might provide an extra 100-yard sure-hit range, but, with a little practice in range estimation, wouldn't something like the .257 Roberts, .270 Winchester, or the .30-06 do just as well? Be that as it may, one should never disparage a man's wife, his automobile, or his favorite hunting rifle. Therefore, far be it for me to make enemies by casting aspersions on those who favor the magnum cartridges for whatever reason. My only point is that one doesn't need a magnum to kill a mouse, not that there is anything wrong with doing so. In any event, if you are looking for the latest and the most powerful, it will be found in Chapter 1.

The reader who is trying to determine which of the current American rifle cartridges best suits his hunting needs should first determine what game animals he intends to hunt. Second, he should decide which type of rifle action is preferred: bolt, lever, semi-auto, pump, or single-shot. Next, sit down with a copy of the annual *Gun Digest* book, the *Gun Digest* semi-monthly magazine, or a variety of gun catalogs to see what calibers are available for the different actions. Finally, give some careful and realistic thought as to how the gun is to be used, type of cover, average range, and the variety of game animals to be legally hunted. Once you have all these factors in hand, check through the cartridges listed in this chapter and pick the one that matches your particular needs and situation. Don't select the most powerful or the one with the highest velocity in the ballistics tables, unless this actually offers some real advantage to you. Bear in mind that high velocity and flat trajectory offer no advantage if the bulk of your hunting is confined to brush or heavy timber with ranges that average only 50 yards or so. On the other hand, a big, heavy, slow bullet won't put meat in the freezer, if you are shooting antelope at 300 yards and beyond. Always bear in mind that the 20 foot-pounds of recoil energy produced by cartridges in the .30-06 class is about all the average person can stand without flinching badly. In other words, use a little common sense and be realistic in your choice of hunting calibers. All the velocity, energy, and killing power in the world is of no value if you can't hit anything with the rifle.—*F.C.B.*

15th Edition Update

This is an unusual version of Chapter 1 because it contains five additions to the rolls of factory-manufactured rounds, including the first from Weatherby in decades. The 6.5-300 Weatherby Magnum is an idea whose recognition has been a long time coming, but which promises to make quite a bang among long-distance shooters. "This is now the fastest production 6.5mm cartridge in the world," said Adam Weatherby, executive vice president and chief operating officer of Weatherby, Inc. "The speed and energy of this cartridge is unprecedented and worthy of carrying the Weatherby name, all while exhibiting very manageable recoil."

Also introduced in 2016, Nosler rolled out the newest member of its cartridge family, the 30 Nosler. The 30 Nosler meets the velocity of the 300 Weatherby and fits in the same standard-length action of a 300 Winchester Magnum. It is a SAAMI-standardized cartridge, and Nosler will be supporting this new cartridge with Nosler brass, Trophy Grade ammunition, and a full line of M48 rifles in 26-inch barrel configurations.

Nosler created its new 28 Nosler in 2015 by necking up the 26 Nosler case, itself a derivative of the 7mm RUM case, which descended from the .404 Jeffery. It is amazing how an existing case such as the .404 Jeffery can propel so many variations.

It is only a matter of time before the 6.5×47mm Lapua (or 6.5×47mm), jointly developed by Finnish ammunition maker Nammo Lapua Oy and the Swiss rifle manufacturer Grünig & Elmiger AG in 2005, will break out of its intended use — 300- to 1000-meter competition shooting — and find wider acceptance. Some case designs are more accurate than others, and, as you've heard, only accurate rifles are interesting. This class of cartridges with 6.5 in their names may finally overcome the market resistance American shooters have put up for decades. One of my favorite cartridges growing up as a kid was the now-defunct 6.5 Remington Magnum. The .264 Win. Mag. puts up great performance but it ate barrels. The .260 Remington continues to hang around, but it's not setting the world on fire. Makers are seeing something with the 6.5 diameters, and perhaps shooters will eventually join in and love the bullets for their accurate, range, and soft-shooting characteristics.

The 7.62x40 WT is another sign that manufacturers want to offer a 30-caliber round that fits in an AR-15-length magazine, because customers want more power than the 5.56mm NATO can muster. The .300 AAC Blackout is already there, of course, but folks want something more, or they don't know enough about the .300 BLK to appreciate it. — *W.T.W*

.17 Hornet

Historical Notes: With the introduction of the .17 HMR rimfire cartridge, in 2002, interest in .17-caliber cartridges has been rejuvenated. Hornady's .17 Hornet is the latest centerfire .17-caliber offering. The .17 Hornet uses the .22 Hornet as a parent case. The shoulder angle is increased from 5 to 25 degrees, and the shoulder diameter is increased, as well. The result is more powder capacity. Balli ically, the .17 Hornet duplicates the performance of the 60-year-old .17 Ackley Hornet developed by P.O. Ackley. The major difference between the two is the 38-degree shoulder angle of the Ackley wildcat.

General Comments: Hornady wisely worked with Ruger to launch the .17 Hornet. Ruger's fine little 77/22 Hornet bolt-action rifle only needs a new barrel to be compatible with the .17 Hornet. Initially, Hornady will be offering a single load, a 20-grain V-Max with a muzzle velocity of 3650 fps. This is about 600 fps slower than the two other popular .17-caliber centerfire cartridges, the .17 Remington Fireball, or the .17 Remington. The .17 Hornet should show less barrel fouling and wear than either of these faster .17s. Out to about 400 yards, the trajectory of the .17 Hornet is very similar to a .223 Remington loaded with a 55-grain bullet. The .17 Hornet should prove to be a fine rifle for gophers or prairie dogs and even larger varmints inside 200 yards.

.17 Hornet Loading Data and Factory Ballistics

Bullet (grains/type)	Powder	Grains	Velocity	Energy	Source
20 V-Max	AA 1680	10.7	3,650	591	Hornady
20 V-Max	FL		3,650	591	Hornady Factory Load

.17 Remington

Historical Notes: The .17 Remington was introduced, in 1971, as a new caliber for Remington's 700 series bolt-action rifles. It is the smallest caliber centerfire rifle cartridge offered on a commercial basis to date. The case is based on the .223 Remington necked-down to .17-caliber, with the shoulder moved back .087-inch to lengthen the neck while retaining the same shoulder angle. The .17 Remington is similar but not identical to the .17-223 wildcat developed about 1965. Experiments with .17-caliber rifles go back to 1944, when P.O. Ackley, the well-known gunsmith and experimenter, developed the .17 Ackley Bee based on necking down the Improved .218 Bee case. There are a number of other .17-caliber wildcat cartridges made by necking down .22-caliber centerfire cases, such as the .221 Remington Fireball, .222 Remington, etc. Remington, Ultra Light Arms, Wichita, and Sako offer rifles in this caliber.

General Comments: The .17 Remington has had a steady, though unspectacular, sales record since its introduction. Its greatest drawback is that it is a special-purpose cartridge suited almost exclusively for varmint shooting. For the sportsman who wants a rifle only for that purpose, this is not a disadvantage, but those requiring a rifle for both varmint and deer hunting would be better served with some other caliber.

With the 25-grain hollow-point bullet loaded by Remington and similar bullets available for handloading by Hornady, the .17 Remington must be rated as a short-range varmint cartridge. On the other hand, it has certain advantages such as minimal recoil and ricochet probability, and a very flat trajectory due to the high initial velocity of over 4000 fps. Disadvantages include: rapid barrel fouling, extreme sensitivity to slight charge weight variation, and limited component availability. Factory loaded ammunition is available only from Remington. (New advances, such as moly-plated bullets and cleaner-burning powders, could eliminate the rapid fouling problem.)

.17 Remington Loading Data and Factory Ballistics

Bullet (grains/type)	Powder	Grains	Velocity	Energy	Source/Comments
25 HP	IMR-4064	22.5	3,800	801	Hornady
25 HP	IMR-4320	24.7	4,000	888	Hornady
25 HP	IMR-4895	23.8	3,900	845	Hornady
25 HP	IMR-3031	21.6	3,800	801	Hornady
25 HP	N135	22.8	4,040	906	Vihtavuori
20 AccuTip	FL		4,250	802	Remington factory load
25 HP	FL		4,040	906	Remington factory load

Note: Remington cases and Remington No. 7½ primers used in all loads.

.17 Remington Fireball

Historical Notes: One of many wildcats dreamed up by P.O. Ackley through the years was the .17/221 Fireball, which is the .221 Remington Fireball case necked down for bullets measuring .172-inch in diameter. When Las Vegas gunsmith Vern O'Brien started building custom rifles around the small Sako L461 action, he obtained permission from Ackley to chamber them for the .17/221 but decided to rename it the .17 Mach IV. O'Brien offered the same chambering in custom single-shot pistols built on the XP-100 action, but called it the .17 Mach III, due to lower velocities from their shorter barrels. As is commonly seen in more than one wildcat, dimensions can vary slightly among makers of chamber reamers which means that even though at first glance the .17 Remington Fireball appears to be the old .17 Mach IV with a different name, a closer inspection may reveal minor dimensional differences. For this reason, Remington discourages the firing of .17 Fireball ammunition in rifles chambered to .17 Mach IV and vice versa.

General Comments: Even though case dimensions of the .17 Fireball can differ a bit from those of the .17 Mach IV, the two cartridges are virtually identical in powder capacity and for this reason their velocity potential is the same. Capable of accelerating a 20-grain bullet along at over 4000 fps, the trajectory of the .17 Fireball is quite flat, and mild recoil makes the little cartridge lots of fun to shoot. Contrary to what has been written about the .17 Mach IV in the past and will likely be written about the .17 Fireball in the future, neither cartridge is capable of matching the velocities of the .17 Remington which is on a modified version of the more capacious .223 Remington case. It has also been written that bullet jacket fouling builds up more rapidly in a rifle chambered for the .17 Remington, but the original author of this book found this to be untrue when the three cartridges are used in barrels having bores of equal quality and smoothness.

.17 Remington Fireball Loading Data and Factory Ballistics

Bullet (grains/type)	Powder	Grains	Velocity	Energy	Source
20 Hornady V-Max	H4198	17.3	4,037	722	Hodgdon
20 Hornady V-Max	H335	20.5	4,027	719	Hodgdon
25 Hornady HP	Benchmark	19.0	3,745	778	Hodgdon
25 Hornady HP	IMR-4198	16.2	3,692	756	Hodgdon
30 Berger HP	H322	18.0	3,533	831	Hodgdon
30 Berger HP	Benchmark	18.7	3,569	848	Hodgdon
20 AccuTip-V	FL		4,250	802	Remington
25 HP	FL		3,850	823	Remington

4.6x30 HK

Historical Notes: This cartridge was designed for the Heckler & Koch MP7 Personal Defense Weapon (PDW). The intent was to offer high-volume fire in a lightweight, low-recoiling firearm capable of defeating body armor. Typically, this cartridge is loaded with a steel core, brass-jacketed bullet. So loaded, this cartridge is capable of penetrating a 1.6mm titanium plate and 20 layers of Kevlar at 200 meters. Due to the limited availability of sporting bullets, as of now, this cartridge is almost entirely a military, law enforcement, or self-defense proposition.

General Comments: Due to the extreme small size of this cartridge, a solider or law enforcement officer can carry much more ammunition than he can if he was armed with a 5.56 NATO type weapon. Due to the lightweight bullet, recoil is minimal, and this offers fast follow-up shots or repetitive hits during automatic fire. While this cartridge does a tremendous job of defeating body armor, it does have limited wounding capacity, due its small caliber bullet. Also, due to the cartridge's limited application and the lack of adoption by any major military force, it looks to be headed to obsolescence in the near future.

14th Edition Update: A check of Heckler & Koch's website lists the current submachine gun chambered for this cartridge as the model MP7A1. The website also claims that the firearm and round have been adopted by "several of the world's leading special operation units." A little more research says the gun and round are being used by the U.S. Navy S.E.A.L.s, but we didn't find much information beyond one blog post to confirm this. What we did turn up, just as this book was going through its first edit, was that H&K is apparently introducing a civilian version of the MP7A1, a pistol designated at the HK97 (no shoulder stock is included as with the submachine gun version). However, beyond the shooting test report we read, there's nothing, zilch, nada on this gun. Heckler & Koch's website doesn't list it, and even Google wasn't any help beyond finding the blog post where the HK97 was being tested. Beyond that, there's not much chatter about the gun or the ammo, but there may be life ahead if H&K is indeed making a civilian-ready gun available in this special round.

4.6 X 30 Factory Ballistics

Bullet (grains/type)	Powder	Grains	Velocity	Energy	Source/Comments
26 Steel AP	FL		2,380	330	RUAG
31 Steel AP	FL		2,272	351	RUAG
42 FMJ	FL		2,000	401	RUAG

.204 Ruger

Historical Notes: Introduced in 2004 as a joint Hornady-Ruger project for varmint and target shooting, the .204 Ruger became the first .20-caliber cartridge to be produced on a large commercial scale. Remarkably, it also offers excellent barrel life. After shooting approximately 500 prairie dogs with the Ruger and Dakota rifles chambered for the .204 Ruger, a former contributing editor to this book found it to be an accurate, low-recoil round, superbly suited for long-range varminting. The .204 Ruger received the Academy of Excellence 2004 Cartridge of the Year Award.

General Comments: The .204 Ruger uses the 47mm-long .222 Remington Magnum as its parent case, necking it down to accept .204 bullets and changing the shoulder angle to 30 degrees. It performs best with 26-inch barrels using a 1:12 rifling twist. The cartridge is available in Ruger, Dakota, Remington, and Savage bolt-action rifles, Thompson/Center and SSK Industries Contender single-shot rifles, and AR-15 style rifles. Hornady, Remington, and Winchester offer loaded ammunition.

.204 Ruger Loading Data and Factory Ballistics

Bullet (grains/type)	Powder	Grains	Velocity	Energy	Source/Comments
32 V-Max	FL		4,225	1,268	Hornady
40 V-Max	FL		3,900	1,351	Hornady
32 V-Max	BL-C(2)	30.7	4,081	1,183	Hodgdon
32 V-Max	Benchmark	28.0	4,047	1,163	Hodgdon
40 V-Max	BL-C(2)	30.0	3,774	1,264	Hodgdon

.22 Hornet (5.6X36Rmm)

Historical Notes: The .22 Hornet, based on the black-powder .22 WCF, was developed during the late 1920s by a group of experimenters at Springfield Armory, including Col. Townsend Whelen, Captain G. L. Wotkyns, and others. Winchester produced the first commercial ammunition, in 1930. Within a few years, the Hornet had been standardized by all American manufacturers. The original rifles were based on Springfield M1903 military and Martini single-shot actions. Winchester announced its Model 54 bolt action in .22 Hornet caliber in 1932, but rifles didn't actually reach the market until early 1933. Savage Model 23-D bolt-action rifles were available in .22 Hornet by August 1932. The Stevens single-shot Model 417 "Walnut Hill" target and 417½ sporting rifles were advertised in .22 Hornet caliber, in 1933. During World War II, military survival rifles were made for the Hornet. At present, Anschütz, Ruger, and Meacham chamber rifles for the Hornet, and Thompson/Center has the Contender in the caliber. In Europe, the Hornet is known by the metric designation 5.6x35Rmm.

General Comments: The .22 Hornet was the pioneer high-velocity smallbore cartridge marketed in the United States primarily for varmint and small-game shooting. It has never been commercially available in anything but bolt-action and single-shot rifles. For this reason, it quickly established a reputation for superb accuracy. No other cartridge of this type has ever caught on so fast or achieved such wide popularity.

Although not quite as powerful as the .218 Bee, it is a perfectly adequate small-game and varmint cartridge. It remains popular, but suffers in comparison with the .223 Remington and the .22-250. It remains a fine choice for economical shooting at ranges between 100 and 150 yards. Due to its reduced powder capacity, the Hornet won't do as well with heavier bullets of 50 or 55 grains, as will the .218 Bee. It is a good cartridge for use in settled areas, because of the light report and low incidence of ricochet. Early rifles had bores requiring bullets of .223-inch diameter. Sierra still offers such bullets. Later rifles had normal bores for .224-inch diameter bullets. Most bullet manufacturers offer special bullets for loading the Hornet. The Improved "K" Hornet is among the best-known wildcats based on the Hornet and the most common of all Improved chamberings. Loaded ammunition is available from Remington, Winchester, and Norma.

.22 Hornet Loading Data and Factory Ballistics

Bullet (grains/type)	Powder	Grains	Velocity	Energy	Source/Comments
35 V-Max	FL		3,200	795	Hornady factory load
35 V-Max	H-110	11.2	3,060	725	Hodgdon
40 SP	2400	10	2,700	648	Sierra
40 SP	IMR 4227	11.4	2,700	648	Speer, Sierra
45 SP	2400	9.2	2,500	725	Hornady, Sierra
45 SP	IMR 4227	11	2,600	678	Nosler, Hornady, Sierra
50 SP	2400	9	2,400	640	Sierra, Hornady, Nosler
50 SP	IMR 4227	11	2,550	694	Hornady, Nosler, Sierra
55 SP	IMR 4227	10.8	2,400	704	Sierra, Hornady
55 SP	IMR 4198	12	2,400	704	Sierra
45 SP	FL		2,690	723	Factory load

.218 Bee

Historical Notes: The .218 Bee, introduced by Winchester, in 1938, was originally chambered in the Model 65 lever-action rifle, a modernized version of the Model 1892. Considerable enthusiasm greeted the announcement of this cartridge, and many magazine articles were devoted to comparing its superior killing power and range to the .22 Hornet. Although criticized as inaccurate, some Model 65s were capable of minute-of-angle accuracy. After WWII, Winchester brought out the Model 43 bolt-action rifle in .218 Bee. Mechanical troubles developed in some early models, and the rifle was discontinued. For a time, one or two European manufacturers, such as Sako and Krico, furnished small Mauser-type rifles in .218 Bee. The .218 Bee is based on the .32-20 case necked down to .22-caliber. Cases can be made by necking down .25-20 or .32-20 cases, and then fire-forming.

General Comments: The .218 Bee has a larger case and somewhat greater powder capacity than the .22 Hornet. It provides higher velocity and a greater effective range than the Hornet, and, in a good single-shot or bolt-action rifle, is just as accurate. It is one of the most economical small-game or varmint cartridges available. On small varmints, it can be counted on out to 200 yards, but on coyote, bobcat, or the like, it cannot be depended on for one-shot kills farther than 150 yards. On rabbits or other edible game, it is necessary to use full jacketed bullets or reduced loads, otherwise it ruins much of the meat.

The Bee is easy to reload, and one can duplicate anything from the .22 Short up to and exceeding the .22 Hornet. With modern powders, the factory performance can be improved safely. By using heavier bullets of 50 or 55 grains, its killing power and range can be increased.

Although still a fine cartridge and useful for many purposes, the .218 Bee has been largely displaced by the .223 Remington and .22-250 Remington. The .218 Bee, like the .22 Hornet, has a relatively mild report compared to the more powerful .22 centerfires and can be used under circumstances in which the larger cartridges would not be acceptable. It is a better performer than the .22 Hornet, and its lack of popularity has always been something of a mystery.

The Bee is the basis of several useful wildcats. Ackley's version approximately equals .222 Remington performance. The .17 Bee Improved offers impressive short-barrel performance. Factory loaded ammunition is available from Winchester.

.218 Bee Loading Data and Factory Ballistics

Bullet (grains/type)	Powder	Grains	Velocity	Energy	Source/Comments
40 HP	2400	12	2,800	697	Sierra
40 HP	IMR-4227	11.7	2,600	601	Hornady, Sierra
45 SP	2400	11.6	2,700	729	Sierra
45 SP	IMR-4227	13	2,800	784	Nosler, Sierra
50 SP	2400	10.5	2,500	694	Sierra, Nosler
50 SP	IMR-4227	12	2,700	810	Hornady, Sierra
55 SP	2400	10	2,300	646	Sierra
55 SP	IMR-4198	14	2,500	763	Sierra
55 SP	IMR-4227	12.5	2,500	763	Sierra
46 SP	FL		2,760	778	Winchester

.22 PPC

Historical Notes: The .22 PPC was developed in 1974 by Dr. Louis Palmisano and Ferris Pindell, primarily for use as a benchrest cartridge. Although originally a wildcat, Sako of Finland introduced commercial rifles and ammunition late in 1987. Norma followed suit in 1993 with loaded ammunition. Since it is an American development, it is listed here as a current American rifle cartridge, rather than as a European cartridge. The cartridge is based on the .220 Russian case, which is a necked-down version of the 7.62x39mm Soviet military cartridge. The Wichita Engineering and Supply Co. made the first rifles for both the .22 and 6mm

PPC cartridges. Many custom rifles have been turned out in this caliber. In 1993, Ruger announced its No. 1V and M77 varmint rifles in this caliber.

General Comments: The originators altered the .220 Russian case by giving it a 10-degree body taper and 30-degree shoulder angle, as well as expanding the neck to accept the standard .224-inch diameter bullet used in the U.S. The cartridge cases are made in Finland by Sako, or in Sweden by Norma, and use Small Rifle primers. Although the .22 PPC is a short, rather stubby case only 1.51 inches long, it nevertheless develops ballistics superior to some larger, longer cartridges such as the .222 and .223 Remington. The 52-grain bullet can be pushed out of the muzzle at over 3500 fps, and this definitely places the .22 PPC in the varmint and small-game class. A 1:14 twist has become pretty much standard for these rifles, although a 1:12 twist will sometimes be found.

.22 PPC Loading Data and Factory Ballistics

Bullet (grains/type)	Powder	Grains	Velocity	Energy	Source/Comments
40 Nos BT	Varget	29.5	3,560	1,125	Hodgdon
52 HP	BL-C2	28.3	3,400	1,335	Speer
52 HP	W748	28.0	3,300	1,258	Speer, Nosler, Hornady
55 SP	H-335	27.0	3,200	1,251	Speer, Nosler
55 SP	W748	28.0	3,200	1,251	Hornady, Nosler, Speer
52 HP	FL		3,400	1,335	Sako factory load

.224 Weatherby Magnum

Historical Notes: The Weatherby line of proprietary cartridges was somewhat incomplete for lack of an ultra-velocity .22. The previous .220 Weatherby Rocket was actually an Improved wildcat based on the .220 Swift case, and Weatherby never manufactured ammunition of this caliber. The .224 Varmintmaster was introduced in 1963, but, according to the late Roy Weatherby, development work went back 10 years prior to that. Introduction of the cartridge was delayed because of lack of a suitable action. The caliber was offered in a reduced-size version of the Weatherby Mark V rifle, but the gun is no longer available. Weatherby continues to sell the ammunition.

General Comments: The .224 Weatherby lies ballistically between the .223 Remington and the .220 Swift. It is a belted case with the advantages and disadvantages inherent in this type of construction. For the handloader, it mitigates certain headspace and case-stretch problems and should provide maximum case life. It is an excellent long-range varmint cartridge with performance similar to the .22-250 Remington. Its popularity was determined largely by economic factors. One could buy a Remington, Ruger or Winchester bolt-action in .22-250 caliber for much less than a .224 Weatherby. It was the smallest belted case manufactured commercially.

.224 Weatherby Magnum Loading Data and Factory Ballistics

Bullet (grains/type)	Powder	Grains	Velocity	Energy	Source/Comments
40 HP	IMR 4198	28.5	4,100	1,493	Sierra
45 SP	IMR 4198	28	3,900	1,520	Sierra
50 SP	IMR 4064	32.8	3,800	1,604	Hornady, Sierra
50 SP	IMR 4895	33	3,800	1,604	Hornady
53 HP	IMR 4064	32	3,600	1,526	Hornady, Sierra
55 SP	IMR 4064	32	3,600	1,583	Sierra, Hornady
55 SP	IMR 4895	32	3,600	1,583	Hornady

Bullet (grains/type)	Powder	Grains	Velocity	Energy	Source/Comments
55 SP	FL		3,650	1,627	Factory load
60 HP	IMR 4895	31.5	3,500	1,632	Hornady

.223 Remington (5.56X45mm)

Historical Notes: The .223 Remington first appeared in 1957 as an experimental military cartridge for the Armalite AR-15 assault rifle. In 1964, it was officially adopted by the U.S. Army as the 5.56mm ball cartridge M193. It is used in the selective-fire M16 rifle, which is based on the original AR-15 design. The cartridge was the work of Robert Hutton, who was technical editor of Guns & Ammo magazine and had a rifle range in Topanga Canyon, California. One of the requirements for the cartridge was that the projectile have a retained velocity in excess of the speed of sound (about 1080 fps at sea level) at 500 yards, something that could not be achieved with the .222 Remington. Working with Gene Stoner of Armalite, Hutton designed a case slightly longer than the .222 and had Sierra make a 55-grain boat-tail bullet. This combination met the design requirements. All this was documented in the 1971 issue of the *Guns & Ammo Annual.*

Originally an alternative military cartridge, the .223 (5.56x45mm) is now the official U.S. and NATO military round; additional information will be found in Chapter 6 covering military cartridges. We should note here that NATO forces, including the United States, have standardized a new 5.56X45mm round with a heavy bullet, and the M193 is no longer standard.

Shortly after the military adopted this cartridge, Remington brought out the sporting version, which has largely replaced both the .222 Remington and Remington Magnum in popularity. Practically every manufacturer of bolt-action rifles has at least one model chambered for the .223. In addition, there are a large number of military-type semi-auto rifles available in this caliber. At one time, the Remington Model 760 pump-action was available in .223.

General Comments: The .223 Remington is nearly identical to the .222 Remington Magnum, the only difference being that the .223 has a slightly shorter case. The two are not interchangeable, although the .223 will chamber in a .222 Magnum rifle. The result, though, creates a gross headspace condition, and the .223 case can rupture if fired in the .222 Magnum chamber.

The .223 has proven to be an effective military cartridge for fighting in jungle or forested areas and for close-in fire support, and has been improved lately by NATO with heavier (SS109 designed by FN of Belgium) bullets fired through fast-twist (1:7) barrels. As a sporting round, it is just as accurate as any of the other long-range, centerfire .22s. Military brass cases are sometimes heavier than commercial cases, so maximum loads in military brass should be reduced by at least 10 percent and approached cautiously. That is because the reduced case capacity results in a higher loading density and increased pressure with the same powder charge. The .223 Remington can be classed as an excellent medium-range varmint cartridge at ranges out to 250 yards.

Update: In 1965, when the text above was originally composed by author Frank Barnes, it was considered foolish by most hunters to use a .22-caliber centerfire on deer or similarly sized game. Things have changed. Nosler now offers a .224-caliber, 60-grain version of the famous Partition bullet, Barnes offers several different weight Triple Shock bullets, and Swift has the excellent 75-grain Sirocco bullet. Any of these bullets are totally adequate for use on animals that weigh up to 250 pounds or so, as long as impact velocities are high enough to insure complete expansion—about 2300 fps or so. However, these bullets are often too long to work with standard twist rates common with older .223 Remington rifles, so, to find acceptable accuracy, a new barrel with a faster twist rate or a more modern rifle with a faster twist rate is often needed.

There has also been a great deal of confusion as to the interchangeability of the .223 Remington cartridge and 5.56x45mm NATO ammunition. Dimensionally, these two cartridge cases are identical. However, 5.56 NATO ammo is generally loaded to a higher pressure than commercial .223 Remington ammunition. In 1979, SAAMI cautioned shooters that 5.56x45mm military chambers and throats differ from .223 Remington sporting rifle chambers. Therefore, military ball ammo may produce high chamber pressures in sporting rifles. In a bolt-action rifle of quality manufacturer, this is a non-issue, but, in a semi-auto rifle, problems can be experienced. These can be as minor as reliability issues and as unsafe as blown primers and even firearm damage and shooter injury. The difference between these two cartridges is pressure and the difference in the rifles is the way the lead—the section of the chamber in front of the cartridge case—is cut into the barrel; 5.56 NATO chambers have a longer lead. Maybe the simplest way to explain the difference is to say that the 5.56 NATO round is a +P version of the .223 Remington. Exercise the necessary caution and sort your ammunition accordingly.

.223 Remington Loading Data and Factory Ballistics

Bullet (grains/type)	Powder	Grains	Velocity	Energy	Source/Comments
40 SP	IMR 3031	25	3,300	1,140	Sierra, Speer
40 SP	IMR 4198	22	3,200	995	Sierra, Speer
40 Nos BT	Varget	28.0	3,674	1,195	Hodgdon
45 SP	IMR 3031	25	3,300	1,162	Hornady, Sierra
45 SP	IMR 4198	22	3,200	965	Hornady, Sierra, Speer
50 SP	IMR 3031	25.2	3,250	1,250	Sierra, Nosler, Hornady, Speer
50 SP	IMR 4198	21.5	3,200	1,155	Nosler, Hornady, Speer, Sierra
55 SP	IMR 3031	24.5	3,200	1,330	Hornady, Nosler, Sierra
55 SP	W748	25	3,000	1,110	Hornady, Nosler, Sierra
55	Varget	27.5	3,384	1,395	Hodgdon
60 HP	IMR 3031	24	3,100	1,130	Hornady, Sierra
80	Varget	25.0	2,869	1,460	Hodgdon
55 SP	FL		3,240	1,280	Factory load
55 FMJBT	FL		3,250	1,290	Military load
40 HP	FL		3,650	1,185	Federal factory load
62 Fusion	FL		3,000	1,239	Fusion Factory Load
60 Nosler Partition	FL		3,160	1,330	Federal Factory Load
75 BTHP	FL		2,930	1,429	Hornady Superformance

.222 Remington

Historical Notes: The .222 Remington was introduced by Remington in 1950 for the 722 bolt-action rifle, which was later superseded by the current 700 series. For a short time, the Remington Model 760 pump-action repeater was also available in this caliber. Much of the credit for the .222 is due to Mike Walker, a longtime Remington employee. The cartridge became very popular with benchrest competitors in the 1970s, and varmint hunters also found its performance excellent. But, by the early 1990s, the .222 Remington had lost much of its popularity to the .223 Remington.

General Comments: The .222 Remington is in about the same class as the older .219 Zipper, but is rimless and adapted to modern bolt-action rifles. It is not based on any older case necked down, but is of original design. It is a more or less scaled-down version of the .30-06 and fills the gap between the .218 Bee and the .220 Swift. It is well suited to the needs of the average person who desires a high-velocity .22. A great many benchrest matches have been won with the .222 Remington, and it has a reputation for superb accuracy. It is an excellent 200-yard cartridge for the full range of varmint and small-game animals up to, but not including, deer. It has been outlawed for big game in many of the 50 states because, like the .220 Swift, you can't always depend on it to kill large animals humanely. I [Frank Barnes] have seen several deer and antelope killed very cleanly with the .222 handloaded with heavier-jacketed 55- and 60-grain bullets. Range was about 125 yards. This caliber is offered by all large domestic ammunition manufacturers and several foreign companies.

Update: When Frank Barnes wrote the general comments on this cartridge (everything above this paragraph), in 1965, it was considered foolish by most hunters to use a .22-caliber centerfire on deer or similarly sized game. Things have changed. Nosler now offers a .224-caliber, 60-grain version of the famous Partition bullet, Barnes offers several different weight Triple Shock bullets, and Swift has the excellent 75-grain Sirocco bullet. Any of these are totally adequate for use on animals that weigh up to 250 pounds or so, as long as impact velocities are high enough to ensure complete expansion, about 2300 fps or so. However, these bullets are often too long to work with standard twist rates common to the .222 Remington cartridge, so to find acceptable accuracy, a new barrel with a faster twist rate is often needed. Also, with regards to the statement, "It has been outlawed for deer hunting in many of the 50 states," as of 2012, 38 states currently allow the hunting of deer with a centerfire .22-caliber round.

.222 Remington Loading Data and Factory Ballistics

Bullet (grains/type)	Powder	Grains	Velocity	Energy	Source/Comments
35 V-Max	H4198	22.0	3,591	1,000	Hodgdon
40 HP	IMR 4198	20	3,300	967	Speer, Sierra
40 HP	W748	26.3	3,400	1,027	Speer, Sierra
45 SP	H335	24.5	3,100	960	Hornady, Speer
45 SP	IMR 4198	21	3,300	1,088	Hornady, Speer, Sierra, Nosler
50 SP	W748	25.8	3,100	1,067	Speer, Sierra, Hornady
50 SP	RE 7	20.9	3,150	1,102	Hornady, Speer, Sierra
50 SP	IMR 4198	20	3,200	1,132	Speer, Hornady, Sierra
55 SP	H335	24	3,200	1,174	Sierra, Speer, Hornady, Nosler
55 SP	IMR 4320	25	3,000	1,099	Hornady, Speer
55 SP	IMR 4895	24.5	3,000	1,099	Speer, Hornady, Sierra
55	Varget	25.0	2,095	1,170	Hodgdon
60 HP	IMR 4895	23	2,900	1,121	Nosler, Hornady, Speer
50 SP	FL		3,140	1,094	Factory load
55 FMJ	FL		3,020	1,114	Factory load

.22-250 Remington
(.22 Varminter, .22 Wotkyns,
Original Swift)

Historical Notes: The .22-250 Remington was adopted early in 1965, as one of the calibers for the Remington 700 series bolt-action rifles and also for the Model 40XB match rifle. Browning bolt-action rifles were offered in .22-250 two years earlier. This is not a factory design, but rather a popular wildcat that has been around for many years and made good. However, Remington's adoption of the round moved it into the commercial classification.

There is some confusion regarding date of origin of the .22-250, which is based on the .250-3000 Savage case necked to .22-caliber. Its moniker is derived from the caliber (.22) and the parent case name (.250). The parent cartridge was introduced in 1915, and a .22 version may have been made up experimentally shortly thereafter. Harvey Donaldson, Grosvenor Wotkyns, J.E. Gebby, J.B. Smith, and John Sweany all worked on versions of the .22-250 between 1934 and 1937. Gebby and Smith are usually credited with having developed the present configuration, in 1937. However, there are different versions of this cartridge, and much depends on which one is referred to. The Gebby version was named the .22 Varminter, and he obtained a copyright on the name. Other gunsmiths renamed it the .22-250. The Wotkyns version was the forerunner of the .220 Swift, although Winchester ended up using the 6mm Lee Navy case, rather than the .250 Savage.

At the present time, all major American and European rifle makers furnish bolt-action rifles in .22-250 chambering. In addition, the Ruger, Thompson/Center, and other single-shots are available in this caliber.

General Comments: The .22-250 is one of the best balanced and most flexible of the high-powered .22 centerfires. It is also the most popular of the long-range .22 varmint cartridges, effective to ranges of 400 yards or more. The .22-250 also has a reputation for outstanding accuracy and has been used with some success for benchrest shooting. Many individuals who have had experience with both the .22-250 and the .220 Swift report that the former gives significantly longer case life with full loads than the latter. The .22-250, as with most of the other high-powered .22s, is not recommended for use on deer or other medium game. The reason, of course, is that the light varmint bullets are made to expand quickly and will not offer sufficient penetration on a large animal. This is one of the best all-round, long-range .22 varmint cartridge available today.

In a 2000 press release, Remington announced the availability of electronic ignition .22-250 ammunition for use in its new (and now defunct) EtronX rifle. The initial loading used a 50-grain Hornady V-Max, polymer-tipped bullet. Owing to the unique primer, this ammunition will not work in a conventional rifle (just as conventional ammunition will not work in the EtronX rifle). Except for the primer, this ammunition uses conventional components.

Update: When the .22-250 was introduced in 1965 there were no .22-caliber bullets truly suitable for use on medium-sized game. Things have changed a great deal in the last 47 years. Nosler now offers a 60-grain version of the famous Partition bullet, Barnes offers several different weight Triple Shock bullets, and Swift has the excellent 75-grain Sirocco bullet. Any of these bullets are totally adequate for use on animals that weigh up to 250 pounds or so, as long as impact velocities are high enough to ensure complete expansion—about 2300 fps or so. As a matter of fact, in Texas, the .22-250 and other .22-caliber centerfire rifles have become very popular for deer hunting.

.22-250 Remington Loading Data and Factory Ballistics

Bullet (grains/type)	Powder	Grains	Velocity	Energy	Source/Comments
40 HP	IMR 4895	36	3,900	1,345	Speer, Sierra
40 HP	IMR 3031	35	3,900	1,345	Sierra, Speer
40	Varget	39.5	4,135	1,515	Hodgdon
45 SP	IMR 4064	37	3,900	1,520	Speer, Sierra
45 SP	IMR 3031	32	3,500	1,224	Hornady, Speer
50 SP	IMR 4064	36	3,700	1,520	Hornady, Speer, Sierra
50 SP	IMR 3031	34.5	3,700	1,520	Speer, Hornady, Sierra
55 SP	IMR 4064	35	3,600	1,580	Hornady, Speer, Sierra
55 SP	RL-7	29	3,500	1,496	Sierra
55 SP	IMR 4320	35	3,500	1,496	Nosler, Hornady, Sierra
60 HP	RL-7	28	3,300	1,451	Sierra
60 HP	IMR 4320	34	3,500	1,630	Hornady, Nosler, Sierra
70 SP	IMR 4064	33	3,300	1,690	Speer
70 SP	N205	41	3,300	1,690	NA
40 HP	FL		4,000	1,420	Federal factory load
55 SP	FL		3,680	1,655	Factory load

.223 Winchester Super Short Magnum (.223 WSSM)

Historical Notes: Announced in 2002, the .223 WSSM is intended to deliver a new level of long-range performance and accuracy to the .223 family of chamberings. Cartridge overall length is 2.36 inches, a half-inch shorter than the 2.8-inch length of existing short-action cartridges. The .223 WSSM will be chambered in super short rifle actions, which should improve receiver stiffness and accuracy. A new Browning bolt-action rifle, the Super Short Magnum A-Bolt, weights six pounds and uses a shorter action for the 2.36-inch cartridge. Winchester Firearms also plans a shorter-action rifle for this round, the Winchester Super Short Magnum Model 70.

General Comments: The .223 WSSM case does not employ a belt; it headspaces on the case shoulder. For efficient and consistent powder burning, it retains the short-fat cartridge case geometry of the Winchester Short Magnum line. Cartridges will be available in three bullet types: 55-grain Ballistic Silvertip and Pointed Soft Point, and 64-grain Power-Point. WSSM velocities are targeted at roughly 200 fps faster than the .22-250 Remington offerings. It is suitable for long-range varmint shooting and for light thin-skinned game, a good combination cartridge with light recoil.

Currently, Winchester is the only major ammunition manufacturer loading ammunition for the .223 WSSM. The cartridge and all its siblings became embroiled in a legal battle, and the end result was a less than enthusiastic appeal on the part of other manufacturers to offer rifles and/or ammunition for sale.

The .223 WSSM is a fine cartridge, and the most accurate rifle the editor of the 13th Edition says he ever fired was chambered for this cartridge. It looks, however, that all of the Super Short Winchester Magnum cartridges have peaked in terms of interest and availability.

.223 Winchester Super Short Magnum (WSSM) Load Data/Factory Ballistics

Bullet (grains/type)	Powder	Grains	Velocity	Energy	Source
40 Nosler Ballistic Tip	H414	50.5	4,301	1,641	Hodgdon
45 Barnes X	IMR-4895	44.6	4,194	1,756	Hodgdon
50 Barnes XLC	BL-C(2)	46.0	4,058	1,826	Hodgdon
52 Speer HPBT	IMR-4064	43.3	3,970	1,818	Hodgdon
55 Hornady V-Max	H414	46.8	3,886	1,842	Hodgdon
60 Nosler Partition	IMR-4350	46.0	3,707	1,829	Hodgdon
69 Sierra HPBT	H4831	46.5	3,489	1,863	Hodgdon
77 Sierra HPBT	IMR-4831	44.8	3,360	1,928	Hodgdon
55 BST	FL		3,850	1,810	Winchester/Olin
55 PSP	FL		3,850	1,810	Winchester/Olin
64 PP	FL		3,600	1,841	Winchester/Olin

.225 Winchester

Historical Notes: The .225 Winchester was officially announced in June 1964. Both the standard and a heavier-barreled varmint version of the Model 70 bolt-action were offered for this round. The .225 replaced the older .220 Swift in the Winchester lineup. It is a semi-rimmed case with an unusually large rim for this type of cartridge. The .220 Swift never achieved great popularity, and neither did its replacement, the .225. The last Winchester catalog to list the cartridge as a caliber available for the Model 70 rifle was in 1972. No other manufacturer picked it up as a standard chambering, because the already popular .22-250 was standardized by Remington in 1965, and it was just common sense to adopt the .22-250 instead. Winchester still loads .225 ammunition, but this cartridge did not have a very long life, being semi-obsolete in only eight years.

General Comments: The .225 is a fine varmint cartridge with performance similar to the .224 Weatherby or the .22-250. But the .22-250 was already established as a popular wildcat with an outstanding reputation, and it was inevitable that it would dominate the field. Those who purchased .225 Winchester rifles have no need to feel bad or trade them off for anything else, because the .225 cartridge is just as accurate and will do anything that the more popular .22-250 will do. It simply turned out to be a design or idea whose time had not yet arrived. As a matter of fact, it might be wise to hang on to your .225, because not a great many were sold and eventually some gun writer will rediscover it as the greatest .22 varmint cartridge conceived by the mind of man—and, at that point, all your shooting friends will wish they had one, too. The .225 has an edge over both the .222 and the .223 Remington for long-range varmint shooting, because of the increased muzzle velocity. At one time, Winchester was supposed to furnish a 50-grain loading at 3800 fps and a 60-grain at 3500 fps, along with the standard 55-grain at 3650 fps (now reduced to 3570 fps), but these loads never materialized. For handloaders, this cartridge is nothing more than a slightly modified .30-30. Neck down the .30-30 to .22-caliber, shorten the case slightly, turn the rim to '06 dimensions and slightly Improve, and you have the .225 Winchester.

.225 Winchester Loading Data and Factory Ballistics

Bullet (grains/type)	Powder	Grains	Velocity	Energy	Source/Comments
40 Speer SP	BL-C(2)	36.0	4,020	1,435	Hodgdon
40 HP	IMR 4064	31.5	3,400	1,027	Speer, Sierra
45 SP	IMR 4064	33	3,600	1,295	Hornady, Speer
50 SP	IMR 3031	31	3,400	1,284	Speer, Nosler, Hornady

.225 Winchester Loading Data and Factory Ballistics

Bullet (grains/type)	Powder	Grains	Velocity	Energy	Source/Comments
50 SP	IMR 4895	33	3,600	1,439	Sierra
55 SP	IMR 4320	34.5	3,700	1,672	Hornady
60 HP	IMR 4064	31.8	3,500	1,632	Hornady
70 SP	IMR 4350	34.5	3,000	1,399	Speer
55 SP	FL		3,570	1,556	Winchester factory load

.220 Swift

Historical Notes: The .220 Swift was developed by Winchester and introduced in 1935 as a new caliber for the Model 54 bolt-action rifle. When the Model 70 Winchester bolt-action was first issued, in 1936, the .220 Swift was one of the standard calibers offered and continued to be until it was discontinued, in 1964. Now, the Savage Model 112V, the Ruger Model 77, and the Ruger No. 1V single-shot are offered in the .220 Swift chambering. The Model 70 Winchester is no longer made in this caliber. Norma of Sweden lists the .220 Swift with a 50-grain bullet at 4110 fps, and it also sells unprimed brass cases for reloading. Hornady/Frontier offer 55-grain SP and 60-grain HP loadings.

The prototype for the .220 Swift was developed in 1934-'35 by Grosvenor Wotkyns, who necked down the .250-3000 Savage as a means of achieving very high velocities. However, the final commercial version developed by Winchester is based on the old 6mm Lee Navy cartridge necked down. It is a semi-rimmed case.

General Comments: The .220 Swift was and still is the fastest commercial cartridge in the world. It is also one of the most accurate super-velocity .22 cartridges ever developed. Its popularity has been somewhat retarded by the fact that ammunition in this caliber is expensive. Swift barrels have never been noted for long life, but this factor has been negated to a large degree by development of modern, erosion-resistant barrel steels since World War II. Factory ammunition has always featured the 48-grain and 50-grain bullets, but the Swift will handle the 55-grain or heavier bullets quite well at slightly reduced maximum velocity. The .220 Swift is considered adequate on all animals up to deer size. There is certainly plenty of field evidence to demonstrate that, on occasion, it will give fantastic one-shot kills on deer and antelope. However, the .220 Swift tends to be erratic in its performance on large animals, and most states will not permit its use on big game of any kind. Properly constructed bullets would almost certainly solve this problem on animals to mule deer size. In any case, factory bullets are designed for quick expansion on light animals. Most varmint hunters agree that the .220 Swift is the best varmint cartridge made. It remains sufficiently popular that various manufacturers occasionally chamber it.

In a 2000 press release, Remington announced the availability of electronic ignition 220 Swift ammunition for use in its new (and now defunct) EtronX rifle. The initial loading uses a 50-grain Hornady V-Max, polymer-tipped bullet. Owing to the unique primer, this ammunition will not work in a conventional rifle (just as conventional ammunition will not work in the EtronX rifle). Except for the primer, this ammunition uses conventional components.

.220 Swift Loading Data and Factory Ballistics (Note: *Discontinued loading.)

Bullet (grains/type)	Powder	Grains	Velocity	Energy	Source/Comments
40 HP	IMR 4064	39	4,000	1,421	Speer, Sierra
40	Varget	40.5	4,113	1,500	Hodgdon
45 HP	IMR 4350	41.5	3,600	1,295	Hornady, Speer, Sierra
45 SP	IMR 3031	37	4,000	1,599	Hornady, Speer, Sierra
45 SP	IMR 4895	38.5	3,900	1,520	Sierra
45 SP	H-380	43	3,850	1,481	Speer, Sierra
50 SP	IMR 4320	39	4,400	1,689	Sierra

.220 Swift Loading Data and Factory Ballistics (Note: *Discontinued loading.)

Bullet (grains/type)	Powder	Grains	Velocity	Energy	Source/Comments
50 SP	IMR 3031	37	4,000	1,777	Sierra
55 SP	IMR 4350	44	3,800	1,764	Speer, Hornady
55 SP	IMR 4320	40	3,000	1,955	Sierra
55 SP	H-380	42	3,800	1,764	Nosler, Sierra, Speer
60 HP	IMR 4895	33	3,400	1,541	Hornady, Sierra
*48 SP	FL		4,110	1,800	Factory Load
50 SP	FL		4,110	1,877	Norma factory load
55 SP	FL		3,650	1,627	Hornady/Frontier factory load
40 SP	FL		4,250	1,603	Federal
60 HP	FL		3,600	1,727	Hornady/Frontier factory load

6mm PPC

Historical Notes: The 6mm PPC is an outgrowth of the .22 PPC and based on the same case configuration with the neck expanded to take 6mm (.243-inch) bullets. This cartridge was also developed by Dr. Louis Palmisano and Ferris Pindell and based on the .220 Russian case, which is a variation of the 7.62X39mm (M43) Soviet military cartridge. The original rifles were made by Wichita Engineering and Supply Co., in 1975. Many custom rifles have been made up in this caliber in both sporter and benchrest types. Although the 6mm PPC was originally a benchrest wildcat, Sako of Finland began turning out commercial bolt-action rifles and supplying loaded ammunition late in 1987. In 1993, Ruger announced that its M77 Varmint and No. 1 Varmint rifles would be offered in this caliber, and, at the same time, Norma announced factory-loaded ammunition. The 6mm PPC is one of the top competitive benchrest cartridges. In addition to loaded ammunition and factory cases, many handloaders make their own cases by fireforming .220 Russian cases or necking-down and reforming 7.62x39mm brass.

General Comments: Chronograph tests by various individuals have demonstrated that the 6mm PPC gives very uniform velocity readings, which accounts for its fine accuracy. On the other hand, practically all rifles chambered for the cartridge are heavy-barrel accuracy jobs, and that must also be a factor. Rifles for match shooting usually have a 1:14 twist, although a few are turned out with a 1:12 twist. The 6mm PPC is not only an outstanding benchrest cartridge, but gives very good results on small game and varmints. It is only slightly less powerful than the .243 Winchester, despite the much smaller case. It should also do well on deer or antelope at moderate ranges. The velocity with the 90-grain bullet is only some 100 to 150 fps less than the .243 Winchester. Popularity of this caliber is growing beyond benchrest shooting, as varmint hunters are now also taking it up. Look for continued growth here.

6mm PPC Loading Data and Factory Ballistics

Bullet (grains/type)	Powder	Grains	Velocity	Energy	Source/Comments
60 Sierra HP	H-4895	29.0	3,218	1,375	Hodgdon
60 HP	H-322	28.4	3,200	1,365	Sierra
70 HP	H-335	29	3,100	1,494	Hornady, Sierra
75 HP	H-322	26.7	3,100	1,601	Hornady, Speer, Sierra
80 SP	W748	29	2,800	1,393	Speer
85 SP	H-335	28.0	3,000	1,699	Speer
90 SP	H-335	29	3,000	1,799	Speer
70 SP	FL		3,140	1,535	Sako factory load

6XC Tubb

Historical Notes: The 6XC is a development of well-known rifle competitor David Tubb. It is intended for the AR-10 rifle, as well as bolt-action rifles, such as the Tubb 2000, that utilize the AR-10 magazine. The .243 Winchester will also work in those rifles, but when extremely long bullets weighing over 100 grains are seated to an overall cartridge length compatible with the AR-180 magazine, the mouth of the case is, depending on the particular bullet, positioned over the ogive of the bullet rather than on its full-diameter shank. Using a shorter case with a gross capacity only seven grains less than the .243 Winchester case solved that problem. The 6XC case is in improved version of the 6mm International, a cartridge created during the early 1960s by avid benchrest shooter Mike Walker. Walker worked for Remington at the time, and the 40X target rifle built in the custom shop of that company has long been chambered for his cartridge. Whereas the 6mm International is the .250 Savage case necked down with no other change, the 6XC is the same case necked down and blown out to the Improved configuration with .015-inch of body taper and a 30-degree shoulder angle. Cases made by Norma are available from Superior Shooting Systems of Canadian, Texas, and they can also be made by fireforming .250 Savage or .22-250 cases in a rifle chambered for the 6XC. Loaded ammunition is also available from SSS.

General Comments: As this section was written, in late 2008, David Tubb has won 11 NRA National High Power Rifle championship titles at Camp Perry. He has also won close to 30 open, individual national championship titles in all four rifle categories of NRA Silhouette competition, along with seven Sportsmen's Team Challenge championships. In other words, if anyone is qualified to develop a cartridge for consistently winning matches at distances as great as 1,000 yards, it is Tubb. When loaded with match-grade bullets of extremely high ballistic coefficients, such as the 105-grain Berger, 107-grain Sierra MatchKing, and 115-grain DETAC, the 6XC bucks wind as well as cartridges of larger caliber, but its lower level of recoil makes it easier to shoot accurately. Since it pretty much duplicates the velocity of the .243 Winchester with a case of less capacity, it is commonly loaded to slightly higher chamber pressures than that cartridge. Currently, only CorBon and Norma offer loaded ammunition for the 6XC Tubb.

6XC Loading Data and Factory Ballistics

Bullet (grains/type)	Powder	Grains	Velocity	Energy	Source
115 DETAC HPBT	H4350	39.5	2,950	2,220	David Tubb
115 DETAC HPBT	H4350	43.5	2,950	2,220	David Tubb
105 Berger DLBT	FL		3,020	2,124	Norma Precision

.240 Weatherby Magnum

Historical Notes: The .240 Weatherby was added to round out the Weatherby proprietary magnum line, in 1968. It differs from other 6mms in having a belted case with somewhat greater powder capacity. It is very similar to the .240 Belted Rimless Nitro-Express introduced by Holland & Holland around 1923. Thus far, it is available only in the Weatherby Mark V bolt-action rifle or through custom gunsmiths. It is an excellent cartridge and will push the 100-grain 6mm bullet with about 200 fps greater muzzle velocity than the 6mm Remington, and around 300 fps faster than the .243 Winchester. However, a considerable portion of this ballistic advantage results from increased barrel length and loading pressure. It is important to allow plenty of barrel cooling time with this and all high-intensity cartridges. The principal detraction regarding the .240 Weatherby Magnum is that ammunition is expensive and difficult to find. The .240 case has about the same capacity as the .30-06, and rim diameter is also the same.

General Comments: The .240 Weatherby is among the most powerful of the 6mm cartridges. It represents the maximum performance that one can squeeze through a 6mm tube with modern powders. The .244 H&H Belted Rimless Magnum, based on necking-down the .375 H&H Magnum case, will hold more powder, but doesn't produce any improvement in ballistics. The late Roy Weatherby built a successful proprietary gun business on the basis of a good product plus the all-important element of ballistic one-upmanship. The Weatherby magnum cartridges have traditionally offered higher velocity and energy than their standard factory counterparts. The .240 was born of this same tradition. Of course, Remington, Winchester, Norma, etc., have their own magnum lines in various calibers, and Winchester offered the .300 and .375 H&H Magnums before World War II. However, Roy Weatherby was the first to really popularize this British innovation in the United States, convincing the American shooters that it was something they truly needed.

.240 Weatherby Magnum Loading Data and Factory Ballistics

Bullet (grains/type)	Powder	Grains	Velocity	Energy	Source/Comments
60 HP	IMR 4350	53	3,800	1,924	Sierra
70 HP	IMR 4350	52	3,700	2,128	Hornady, Nosler
75 HP	IMR 4320	50.5	3,800	2,405	Hornady
80 SP	IMR 4831	52.5	3,500	2,177	Hornady, Speer
85 SP	IMR 4350	51	3,450	2,247	Nosler, Speer, Sierra
90 SP	IMR 4831	52	3,400	2,311	Speer, Hornady, Sierra
95 SP	IMR 4350	47	3,050	1,963	Nosler
100 SP	IMR 4831	52	3,300	2,419	Hornady
105 SP	IMR 4831	49.5	3,150	2,314	Speer
70 HP	FL		3,850	2,304	Weatherby factory load
87 SP	FL		3,500	2,366	Weatherby factory load
100 SP	FL		3,395	2,559	Weatherby factory load

6mm Norma BR

Historical Notes: In February 1996, Norma introduced this "new" cartridge. While case dimensions are identical to the 6mm BR Remington, chambering specifications differ. Remington perceived this cartridge as a traditional benchrest number. Therefore, it designed chambering specifications around bullets of about 70 grains. Conversely, with considerable prodding from the late Roger Johnston, Norma recognized the long-range target potential of this basic case. That company standardized a chambering specification appropriate for very low drag (VLD) bullets exceeding 100 grains. Therefore, the Norma chamber has a much longer neck. While there are no case differences, CIP (the European counterpart to SAAMI) requires a new designation for any cartridge or chambering differing in any way from any previous version. Therefore, Norma was required to apply a new name.

General Comments: While the 6mm BR Remington has failed to become a world-beater in traditional benchrest, with heavy VLD bullets, Norma's version has established itself as a force to be reckoned with in the long-range game. It is also a superior long-range varminting choice. Given a 28-inch barrel and loaded with any of the better 95- to 115-grain VLD moly-plated bullets, this cartridge can achieve sufficient velocity for 1,000-yard benchrest shooting. Owing to the high BCs of these bullets, 1,000-yard retained velocity is surprisingly high—often exceeding 1400 fps.

For cartridges of this genre, such loads generate unusually light recoil, which contributes to precise shooting. However, unless conditions are unusually good, those using larger-bored rifles usually fare better. While those rifles generate more recoil, which effectively reduces intrinsic accuracy, the longer bullets exhibit less wind drift and, therefore, reduce the error associated with imperfections in the shooter's ability to properly dope the wind.

6mm Norma BR Loading Data

Bullet (grains/type)	Powder	Grains	Velocity	Energy	Source/Comments
68 Berger Match	N202	32.0	3,393	1,735	Norma (26-inch Bbl)
80 Hornady	N203	32.1	3,232	1,855	Norma (26-inch Bbl)
95 Nosler	N203	30.1	2,914	1,790	Norma (26-inch Bbl)

.25-20 Winchester (.25-20 WCF)

Historical Notes: The .25-20 Winchester Center Fire was developed for the short action of the Winchester Model 1892 lever-action rifle. The case is based on the .32-20 necked down. Opinions differ as to when it was actually introduced. Some authorities say 1893, others 1895. In any event, it was quickly adopted by a majority of the gun manufacturers and achieved considerable popularity. The Winchester lever-action 1892 and modernized Model 65, Remington pump-action Model 25, Marlin pump-action 27 and lever-action Model 94, and the Savage bolt-action repeater Model 23 were all available in .25-20 WCF. Marlin reintroduced the .25-20 WCF in its Model 1894CL lever-action. Winchester also loaded this chambering with a slightly different bullet shape and headstamped it .25-20 Marlin.

General Comments: Prior to the .22 Hornet and the .218 Bee, the .25-20 WCF was one of the most popular small-game and varmint cartridges around. It was also advertised as being suitable for deer and similar animals. No doubt it has killed plenty of deer, but it is not a satisfactory big-game cartridge by any standard. Today, it is universally outlawed for big-game hunting. On smaller animals, the 60-grain bullet is quite effective for 100- to 150-yard varmint shooting. The 86-grain soft-point or lead bullet does a fine job on rabbit or turkey to 125 yards. A great many rifles were made in this caliber and are still in use by trappers, ranchers, and farmers. Under certain conditions, the .25-20 repeater is still a useful small-game number. It will probably be around for a good many more years. With the growing popularity of cowboy action shooting, the .25-20 is destined for renewed popularity.

The .25-20 is another old-timer the original author of this book played around with at various times. His ownership of a Winchester Model 1892 lever-action and later a Winchester Low Wall single-shot in this caliber allowed ample opportunity to test its potential for small game and varmint hunting. It will do the job, but has serious range limitations due in part to bullet design. The 60-grain high-velocity load achieves its maximum expansion at a range of between 50 and 70 yards. Beyond that, good bullet placement is essential for quick kills. At ranges out to 50 yards, bullet expansion will ruin most of the edible meat on small game. The 86-grain bullet is a better load for meat hunting, although the lower velocity requires good distance judgment at ranges much beyond 75 yards.

On the other hand, the .25-20 is one of those cartridges that can be improved to a satisfying degree by handloading. The 86-grain bullet can be loaded to deliver around 1700 fps, but the 60-grain bullet can't be improved much over the factory load. The .25-20 is also capable of very good accuracy when fired in a single-shot or bolt-action rifle. Both Winchester and Remington continue to offer this caliber only with the 86-grain bullet.

.25-20 Winchester (.25-20 WCF) Loading Data and Factory Ballistics

Bullet (grains/type)	Powder	Grains	Velocity	Energy	Source/Comments
60 Win OPE	680	13.0	2,300	700	Hodgdon
60 SP	2400	9.6	2,200	645	Hornady
60 SP	H-4227	11	2,200	645	Hornady
60 SP	FL		2,250	675	Factory load
86 SP	FL		1,460	407	Factory load

.243 Winchester

Historical Notes: The .243 Winchester was introduced by Winchester in 1955 for its Model 70 bolt-action and Model 88 lever-action rifles. The .243 was quickly adopted by Savage for its Model 99 lever- and Model 110 bolt-action rifles. All the British and European manufacturers soon began chambering bolt-action rifles for this round. In fact, even Remington, which developed its own 6mm, had to recognize the popularity of the .243 and start chambering its rifles for it. The .243 (6mm) Winchester is nothing more than the .308 Winchester case necked down. Original development and publicity was due largely to the efforts of one gun writer, the late Warren Page, who, along with other wildcatters, worked out a similar version before Winchester. The .243 is probably chambered in more different rifles than any other cartridge, except possibly the .30-06 Springfield. All other manufacturers of rifles offer this caliber.

General Comments: The .243 Winchester represents a successful effort to develop a light deer rifle caliber that could hold its own with the high-velocity .22s for long-range use on small targets and still be adequate for larger animals. The .243 does this job well. It eliminates the need to own two different rifles for anything from small game and pests up to and including deer and antelope. The 80-grain bullet is intended primarily for varmint and small game and the 100-grain bullet for deer-size animals. The .257 Roberts and the .250-3000 Savage are supposed to cover the same range and certainly do. All major domestic and overseas manufacturers of commercial ammunition offer this caliber. Its popularity as a deer caliber has prevailed over its varmint capabilities.

(Editor's note: The .243 has garnered a reputation among ballisticians for erratic performance. Handloaders should keep this firmly in mind.)

In a 2000 press release, Remington announced the availability of electronic ignition .243 Winchester ammunition for use in its new (and now defunct) EtronX rifle. The initial loading uses a 90-grain Nosler Ballistic Tip bullet. Owing to the unique primer, this ammunition will not work in a conventional rifle (just as conventional ammunition will not work in the EtronX rifle). Except for the primer, this ammunition uses conventional components.

Update: The recent introduction of all-copper, mono-metal bullets such as the Barnes Triple Shock and Tipped Triple Shock, the Hornady GMX, and Lapua Naturalis allow the .243 Winchester, as well as other 6mm cartridges that produce the same or higher velocities, to be very effective on big game while using a faster and lighter bullet. Additionally, Frank Barnes mentioned the erratic performance handloaders could expect when working with the .243 Winchester; while this has become an ever-persistent warning with this cartridge, I have been handloading the .243 Winchester for 20-plus years and find it as easy to work with as any other cartridge.—*R.A.M, editor, 13th Edition*

.243 Winchester Loading Data and Factory Ballistics

Bullet (grains/type)	Powder	Grains	Velocity	Energy	Source/Comments
55 Nos BT	H4895	44.5	4,058	2,010	Hodgdon
75 HP	IMR 4064	40	3,300	1,814	Hornady, Speer
80 SP	IMR 4320	38	3,000	1,599	Speer, Hornady
85 SP	H-380	38.5	3,100	1,814	Sierra
90 SP	IMR 4831	44	3,000	1,799	Speer, Sierra
95 SP	IMR 3031	35	2,900	1,775	Nosler
100 SP	IMR 4350	42	2,900	1,868	Sierra, Hornady
80 SP	FL		3,550	1,993	Factory load
85 SP	FL		3,320	2,080	Factory load
100 SP	FL		2,960	1,945	Factory load
105 SP	FL		3,100	2,133	Factory load

6mm Remington
(.244 Remington)

Historical Notes: The 6mm Remington has exactly the same case dimensions as the .244 Remington. They differ only in the fact that the 6mm Remington is loaded with bullets of up to 100 grains, whereas the .244 Remington was never loaded with bullets of more than 90 grains. Ammunition marked .244 Remington can be fired in 6mm Remington chambers and vice versa. However, rifles marked .244 Remington will not always stabilize the 100-grain bullet. The difference in the two is that .244 rifles (if manufactured by Remington) have a 1:12 rifling twist, and rifles marked 6mm have a 1:9 twist. When Remington introduced the .244, in 1955, it selected the 1:12 twist as best suited to long-range accuracy with bullets of 75 to 90 grains. That was correct, except that most shooters wanted to be able to use bullets of 100 to 105 grains to cover the range of game from varmints through deer with the same rifle. To correct this misjudgment,

Remington renamed the cartridge 6mm Remington and changed to a 1:9 twist. To have retained the .244 designation and simply changed the twist would have brought on complaints from purchasers of the original .244s with the slower twist, when they tried to use the new 100-grain load. The change in cartridge nomenclature to 6mm and the faster twist occurred in 1963. The Remington 700 series and 788 bolt-action rifles, as well as the firm's autoloaders and the slide-actions, have been available in 6mm.

General Comments: The original 6mm Remington was loaded only with the 100-grain bullet. However, it is now available with 80-, 90-, and 100-grain bullets, which greatly extends its flexibility. Although the older .244 lost out to the .243 Winchester, the 6mm Remington with faster twist barrels is gradually picking up a following. It is an excellent choice for the varmint hunter who also wants to use his rifle for deer and antelope. Although the 6mm has a slightly larger powder capacity than the .243, the difference in performance is negligible as far as killing power is concerned. Nevertheless, this small advance in ballistics appeals to some people and so does the longer neck of the 6mm case, which many handloaders consider desirable. This caliber is commercially loaded by Federal and Winchester, as well as Remington.

6mm (.244) Remington Loading Data and Factory Ballistics

Bullet (grains/type)	Powder	Grains	Velocity	Energy	Source/Comments
55 Nos BT	H4895	45.5	4,115	2,065	Hodgdon
60 HP	H-335	42	3,700	1,824	Sierra
70 SP	IMR 4350	47	3,400	1,797	Sierra, Hornady
75 HP	IMR 4064	41	3,500	2,041	Speer, Nosler
75 HP	IMR 4350	47	3,450	1,983	Nosler, Speer, Sierra
80 SP	IMR 4350	45	3,200	1,820	Hornady
80 SP	IMR 4831	47	3,200	1,820	Hornady, Speer
90 HP	IMR 4350	45	3,200	2,047	Speer, Sierra
90 HP	IMR 4831	45	3,100	1,921	Speer, Sierra
100 SP	IMR 4350	42	2,900	1,868	Hornady, Speer, Sierra, Nosler
100 SP	IMR 4831	44	2,900	1,868	Speer, Sierra, Hornady
100	H1000	51.0	3,111	2,145	Hodgdon
105 SP	IMR 4350	42	2,950	2,030	Speer
105 SP	IMR 4064	37	2,900	1,961	Speer
80 SP	FL		3,470	2,139	Factory load
90 SP	FL		3,190	2,133	Factory load
100 SP	FL		3,100	2,133	Factory load

.243 Winchester Super Short Magnum (.243 WSSM)

Historical Notes: Announced in 2002, the .243 WSSM is intended to deliver a new level of long-range performance and accuracy to the .243 family of chamberings. Cartridge overall length is 2.36 inches, a half-inch shorter than the 2.8-inch length of existing short-action cartridges. The .243 WSSM will be chambered in super-short rifle actions, which should improve receiver stiffness and accuracy. A new Browning bolt-action rifle, the Super Short Magnum A-Bolt, weighs six pounds and uses a shorter action for the 2.36 length cartridge. Winchester Firearms also plans a shorter-action rifle for this round, the Winchester Super Short Magnum Model 70.

General Comments: The .243 WSSM case does not employ a belt; it headspaces on the case shoulder. For efficient and consistent powder burning, it retains the short-fat cartridge case geometry of the Winchester Short Magnum line. Cartridges will be available in three bullet types: 55-grain Ballistic Silvertip, 95-grain Ballistic Silvertip, and 100-grain Power Point. The .243 WSSM shares the same basic cartridge case with the .223 WSSM, also announced in 2002. Like its small-diameter brother, it is suitable for long-range varmint shooting and for light, thin-skinned game—a good combination cartridge with light recoil.

Currently, Winchester is the only major ammunition manufacturer loading ammunition for the .243 WSSM. The cartridge and all its siblings become embroiled in a legal battle and the end result was a less than enthusiastic appeal on the part of manufacturers to offer rifles and/or ammunition for sale. The .243 WSSM is a fine cartridge, but it appears that all of the Super Short Winchester Magnum cartridges have peaked in terms of interest and availability.

.243 Winchester Super Short Magnum Load Data/Factory Ballistics

Bullet (grains/type)	Powder	Grains	Velocity	Energy	Source/Comments
58 Hornady V-Max	BL-C(2)	49.2	4,068	2,129	Hodgdon
70 Nosler Ballistic Tip	IMR-4320	45.0	3,663	2,083	Hodgdon
80 Sierra SBT	H414	48.0	3,514	2,191	Hodgdon
90 Swift Scirocco	IMR-7828	48.5	3,280	2,148	Hodgdon
100 Speer BTXP	Supreme 780	50.0	3,117	2,155	Hodgdon
55 BST	FL		4,060	2,013	Winchester/Olin
95 BST	FL		3,250	2,258	Winchester/Olin
100 PP	FL		3,110	2,147	Winchester/Olin

.25-35 Winchester (.25-35 WCF)

Historical Notes: The .25-35 was developed by Winchester and introduced, in 1895, for the Model 94 lever-action rifle. Along with the .30-30, it was one of the first small-bore, smokeless powder sporting cartridges developed in the United States. Winchester, Marlin, and Savage all chambered repeating lever-action rifles for this cartridge. Quite a few single-shot rifles also chambered the .25-35 and, in Europe, it was used in combination-type arms. No American rifles have been made for the .25-35 since the end of World War II.

General Comments: The .25-35 is one of the most accurate cartridges available in the older lever-action rifles. In a good, solid-frame single-shot, it will shoot about as accurately as any .25 ever developed. It does not have sufficient velocity for long-range shooting. It has never been noted for great stopping power on deer or similar animals. In fact, it is illegal for this purpose in many states. There are still a large number of .25-35 rifles in use, but it is more or less obsolete. It is not nearly as effective as the .250-3000 Savage, .257 Roberts, or any of the more modern 6mm cartridges. However, it does have moderate recoil and will do a good job on small game and varmints at medium ranges. Modern powders would allow significant ballistic improvement if loads were at the same pressure as the current .30-30 factory ammunition. Loaded thusly, this cartridge might not appear to be quite so anemic and would be better suited to deer hunting. Ackley's Improved version provides impressive performance. Winchester is the only remaining manufacturer of this ammunition.

.25-35 Winchester (.25-35 WCF) Loading Data and Factory Ballistics

Bullet (grains/type)	Powder	Grains	Velocity	Energy	Source/Comments
60 SP	IMR 4064	30.5	2,800	1,045	Hornady
60 SP	IMR 4320	32	2,900	1,120	Hornady
117 SP	IMR 3031	25.5	2,300	1,375	Hornady
117 SP	IMR 4320	27	2,200	1,258	Hornady
117 SP	FL		2,230	1,292	Winchester factory load

.25-45 Sharps

Historical Notes: The .25-45 Sharps cartridge was developed by Michael H. Blank of the Sharps Rifle Company (SRC). SRC is not to be confused with Shilo Rifles, which builds historically accurate, black-powder Sharps rifles. The modern Sharps Rifle Company specializes in AR-15 styles of rifles, and that is the platform the .25-45 Sharps was developed for. The goal was to provide an optimum of ballistic performance from the .233 Remington (5.56 NATO) case. Blank felt the best all-around option was a .25-caliber bullet of 100 grains or less and ultimately settled on a .223 Remington case necked up to .25-caliber with a case length of 45mm and a shoulder angle of 23 degrees. The goal was to duplicate as closely as possible .250-3000 (.250 Savage) ballistics with an 87-grain bullet.

General Comments: An interesting side note to the .25-45 Sharps cartridge is the name. The .250 Sharps, .257 Sharps, and .25x45mm were considered. Ultimately, .25-45 Sharps was settled on, because it accurately depicted the caliber and case length. It should be noted that original Sharps cartridges were identified by two numbers as well, but, with those cartridges, the first number signified the caliber and the second the amount of black powder that was used in the load. The .25-45 Sharps continues this two-number naming tradition, but the second number now indicates case length. According to Blank, Federal will be manufacturing a factory load for the .25-45 Sharps, under the Sharps name. The cartridge does have merit, and not only in the AR-15 platform. Although velocities fall just a tad short of what can be obtained with a .250 Savage and an 87-grain bullet, the performance is close to that of the 6.5 Grendel with a similar weigh bullet, the main difference being that the Grendel requires a new bolt face and magazine for the AR-15, while the .25-45 Sharps can use both the existing magazine and bolt face for any AR-15 currently chambered for the .223 Remington/5.56 NATO. Those looking to up the performance of a lightweight .223 bolt-action, like the CZ 527 or Mossberg's new MVP Predator, will only need to install a new barrel. With modern, lightweight, mono-metal bullets, like the Barnes 80-grain Tipped TSX on the .25-45 Sharps should be a very effective deer and hog cartridge that offers very mild recoil from a bolt rifle or an AR-15.

.25-45 Sharps Factory Ballistics

Bullet (grains/type)	Powder	Grains	Velocity	Energy	Source
87 Speer Hot Core	FL		2,950	1,671	Sharps Rifle Company

.257 Weatherby Magnum

Historical Notes: This cartridge was designed by Roy Weatherby in 1944, a year before he went into the commercial gun business. Like most other Weatherby cartridges, it is based on the necked-down and blown-out .300 H&H case. Commercial ammunition under the Weatherby name has been available since 1948. These have been based on Norma components since 1951. There are a number of wildcat versions of the .300 H&H Magnum necked down to .25-caliber, but the Weatherby cartridge has largely displaced these.

General Comments: The .257 Weatherby Magnum was one of the first modern, ultra-velocity, small-bore rifle cartridges to be produced on a commercial basis that developed and retained a degree of popularity. It is accurate and well-suited for long-range varmint shooting, but also delivers sufficient velocity and energy to take on almost any North American big game. A superb deer, antelope, sheep, goat, or black bear cartridge, it has also been used successfully on elk, moose, brown bear, lion, buffalo, and zebra. Many authorities insist that it is much too light for heavy game, but high-velocity advocates insist that, with proper bullets, it is adequate for anything except the largest game in close cover. However, like most of its ilk, this cartridge can be extremely hard on its barrel, especially if insufficient time is allowed between shots for the barrel to cool or if the barrel has not been cleaned adequately. And, like all high-intensity chamberings, it loses a great deal of velocity with barrels shorter than 26 inches. It is in its element for long-range plains or mountain hunting. The original author of this book used a custom Model 70 Winchester and, later, a Weatherby Mark V in this caliber, and it was dynamite on deer-size animals. For long-range varmint shooting, it can only be described as spectacular.

.257 Weatherby Magnum Loading Data and Factory Ballistics

Bullet (grains/type)	Powder	Grains	Velocity	Energy	Source/Comments
75 HP	IMR 4350	66.5	3,800	2,405	Hornady
87 SP	IMR 4831	71	3,700	2,645	Speer
100 SP	IMR 4831	66.5	3,400	2,568	Sierra, Speer, Nosler
117 SP	IMR 4831	61.5	3,100	2,497	Hornady, Sierra
120 SP	IMR 4350	59	3,200	2,729	Hornady
87 SP	FL		3,825	2,827	Weatherby factory load
100 SP	FL		3,602	2,882	Weatherby factory load
120 SP	FL		3,305	2,911	Weatherby factory load

.250 Savage (.250-3000)

Historical Notes: Designed by Charles Newton, the .250 Savage was introduced by the Savage Arms Co. as a high-velocity round for the Model 99 lever-action rifle. The original loading used an 87-grain bullet at 3000 fps muzzle velocity, and Savage named it the .250-3000. One suspects the 87-grain bullet was chosen because it could be safely driven at 3000 fps with the powders then available. This allowed Savage to introduce it with the ever-so-sexy name .250-3000. Remember, in 1915, when this cartridge was introduced, riflemen were still marveling at cartridges achieving 2000 fps. About 1932, the 100-grain bullet load was marketed by Peters Cartridge Co., and later the velocity of the 87-grain bullet was slightly increased. Now it is simply called the .250 Savage. The Savage Model 20 and 40 bolt-action rifles also chambered the round, as did the Winchester Model 54 and 70 bolt-actions. Late in 1971, Savage announced that the Model 99 would again be available in this caliber. Others, such as Ruger and Remington, have made rifles in this caliber, also.

General Comments: Flat trajectory, outstanding accuracy, and good killing power on anything up to and including deer are established characteristics of the .250 Savage. It was, and is, excellent on varmints through deer. In the past few years, it has been edged out by the .257 Roberts and the new 6mm cartridges. It is far superior as a deer cartridge to the .30-30 or anything in that class, regardless of what some .30-30 addicts claim. Because of its light recoil, it is an excellent choice for youths and women. The .250-3000 is the basis of one of Ackley's best wildcats, the .250 Ackley Improved. Both Remington and Winchester continue to load this caliber. However, the 87-grain and 120-grain bullets are no longer factory loaded.

.250 Savage (.250-3000) Loading Data and Factory Ballistics

Bullet (grains/type)	Powder	Grains	Velocity	Energy	Source/Comments
60 Hdy SP	H4895	40.0	3,667	1,790	Hodgdon
60 SP	IMR 4064	39	3,500	1,632	Hornady
87 SP	IMR 4895	36.5	3,200	1,979	Sierra
87 SP	IMR 4064	35	3,100	1,857	Sierra
100 SP	IMR 4320	36	2,800	1,741	Nosler
117 SP	IMR 4064	32.5	2,700	1,894	Hornady
87 SP	FL		3,030	1,770	Factory load
100 SP	FL		2,820	1,765	Factory load

Bullet (grains/type)	Powder	Grains	Velocity	Energy	Source/Comments
120 SP	FL		2,645	1,865	Factory load

.25-06 Remington

Historical Notes: The .25-06, originally a wildcat cartridge, was picked up by Remington and added to its commercial line, late in 1969. The wildcat version dates back to 1920, when it was introduced by A.O. Niedner. Remington has stuck to his original configuration of simply necking down the .30-06 case. The Remington Model 700 series bolt-action rifles were the first to be offered in the newly adopted caliber. At the present time, Remington, Interarms, Ruger, Savage, Winchester, Weatherby, Sako, and almost every other manufacturer of bolt-action rifles offer at least one version in .25-06. In addition, the Ruger single-shot is available in this caliber. This round became a very popular number, but that has waned recently.

General Comments: The .25-06 is a fine .25-caliber wildcat. Its emergence as a standardized factory load was welcomed by many. As a varmint cartridge with the 87-grain bullet, some have claimed it is unsurpassed. However, a comparison of factory ballistics and a little chronographing can be most informative. Comparing factory data, we see that as a varmint cartridge, both the 6mm Remington and .270 Winchester beat anything the .25-06 can offer in every category that matters. Amazingly, in spite of its much smaller case, the 6mm Remington 100-grain load is only marginally behind the .25-06 120-grain load in retained energy at long range. There really isn't any comparison between hunting loads in the .25-06 and the .270 Win. Chronograph results suggest that factory data is equally representative of what each can realistically do. So, just exactly what does the .25-06 offer? Evidently something, because many laud the .25-06 as among the best. Federal, Winchester, and Remington offer this cartridge in several bullet weights.

.25-06 Remington Loading Data and Factory Ballistics

Bullet (grains/type)	Powder	Grains	Velocity	Energy	Source/Comments
75 Hdy V-Max	H4350	62.0	3,700	2275	Hodgdon
75 HP	IMR 4350	55	3,500	2,041	Hornady, Sierra
87 SP	IMR 4831	57	3,500	2,367	Hornady
100 SP	IMR 4831	54.5	3,300	2,419	Sierra, Speer
120 SP	IMR 4064	44	3,000	2,399	Hornady
120 SP	IMR 4831	50	3,000	2,399	Nosler, Speer
87 SP	FL		3,500	2,370	Factory load
90 SP	FL		3,440	2,364	Factory load
100 SP	FL		3,230	2,316	Factory load
117 SP	FL		2,990	2,320	Factory load
120 SP	FL		2,940	2,382	Factory load

.257 Roberts (.257 Roberts +P)

Historical Notes: The commercial version of the .257 Roberts was released by Remington in 1934, chambered in its Model 30 bolt-action rifle. It was quickly picked up by Winchester for its Model 54 and the later Model 70. The

Remington 722 bolt-action and the 760 pump-action models were also available in .257-caliber. In recent years, many American manufacturers have discontinued it, although Ruger continues to offer it in the Model 77 bolt-action. The original cartridge was designed by N.H. Roberts (a well-known experimenter and gun writer during the 1920s and '30s), and is based on the 7x57mm Mauser necked down. Remington changed the Roberts' shoulder angle from 15 to 20 degrees. The name of the cartridge was adopted to honor its original developer. Custom rifles in this caliber were made by the Niedner Rifle Co. as early as 1928.

General Comments: The .257 Roberts has often been referred to as the "most useful rifle cartridge ever developed." That is not very far wrong. It is suitable for a wide range of hunting under a variety of conditions. As a long-range varmint cartridge, it is as good as they come, being only slightly inferior to the newer 6mms. On deer, antelope, black bear, sheep, or goat, it is as good as any other cartridge available. Naturally, it is not as powerful as the .270 Winchester or .30-06, but it has ample power for the game mentioned at all practical ranges.

The .257 was underloaded by ammunition companies. However, in the late 1980s, higher pressure +P loads were introduced, which enabled factory-loaded .257 Roberts ammunition to reach full potential. With modern powders, the handloader can improve performance safely in all bullet weights. With 117- or 120-grain boat-tail bullets at velocities of around 2800 fps, the .257 can be used successfully on elk and caribou. It is at this end of the scale that it has an advantage over the 6mms. The original author of this book used it for many years, and it was one of his favorite calibers for Western hunting.

Ackley's Improved version of the .257 Roberts practically duplicates the ballistics of the longer .25-06. Winchester, Federal, and Remington all offer this cartridge. The 87- and 100-grain bullets are no longer factory loaded.

.257 Roberts (.257 Roberts +P) Loading Data and Factory Ballistics

Bullet (grains/type)	Powder	Grains	Velocity	Energy	Source/Comments
60 Hdy SP	H335	46.0	3,885	2,010	Hodgdon
60 SP	IMR 4064	44	3,600	1,727	Hornady
75 HP	IMR 4064	42	3,300	1,814	Sierra
75 Hdy HP	H4895	44.0	3,561	2,110	Hodgdon
87 SP	IMR 4320	37.5	3,000	1,739	Hornady
87 SP	H-380	46	3,200	1,979	Sierra, Hornady
100 SP*	IMR 4831	45.5	3,100	2,134	Nosler, Speer
100 SP	IMR 3031	34	2,800	1,741	Hornady, Sierra
117 SP	IMR 4320	36	2,600	1,757	Sierra
117 SP	IMR 4064	34.5	2,600	1,757	Hornady, Sierra
120 SP*	IMR 4831	42.5	2,800	2,091	Nosler
120 SP	IMR 4350	38.5	2,600	1,802	Hornady
87 SP	FL		3,200	1,980	+P factory load
100 SP	FL		3,000	1,998	+P factory load
117 SP	FL		2,780	2,009	+P factory load
120 SP	FL		2,645	1,865	Factory load

.25 Winchester Super Short Magnum

Historical Notes: Tailored for use in a shorter-action rifles, the .25 WSSM uses a short and fat cartridge case to equal .25-06 ballistics with 14 percent less powder and less perceived recoil. Winchester significantly re-directed the shape of magnum cartridges through the 2000 introduction of the Winchester short magnums and, later, the Winchester super short magnum families. Introduced in 2005, the .25 WSSM is intended as a versatile, dual purpose (varmint and medium game) hunting cartridge.

General Comments: The WSSM case is a half-inch shorter than the Winchester Short Magnum cases used for the .300, 7mm, and .270 WSM cartridges. The short and fat design improves interior ballistics of the .25 WSSM cartridge. Exposing more propellant surface area to the primer results in more consistent ignition. The beltless cartridge case headspaces off the shoulder to provide better centering of the bullet in the chamber. Winchester and Browning super-short rifle actions for this cartridge are stiffer, reducing accuracy-inhibiting vibrations. Winchester offers .25 WSSM unprimed cartridge cases for reloaders.

Currently, Winchester is the only major ammunition manufacturer loading ammunition for the .25 WSSM. The cartridge and all its siblings become embroiled in a legal battle and the end result was a less than enthusiastic appeal on the part of manufacturers to offer rifles and/or ammunition for sale. The .25 WSSM is a fine cartridge, but it appears that all of the Super Short Winchester Magnum cartridges have peaked in terms of interest and availability.

.25 Winchester Super Short Magnum Loading Data and Factory Ballistics

Bullet (grains/type)	Powder	Grains	Velocity	Energy	Source/Comments
85 BST	FL		3,470	2,273	Winchester
120 AccuBond	FL		3,100	2,347	Winchester
115 BST	FL		3,060	2,392	Winchester
120 PEP	FL		2,990	2,383	Winchester
75 V-Max	BL-C(2)	49.3	3,775	2,372	Hodgdon
85 Nos BT	BL-C(2)	47.5	3,547	2,374	Hodgdon
100 Spr BT	H4350	48.5C	3,233	2,320	Hodgdon
120 SP	H414	44.7	2,985	2,373	Hodgdon

6.5 Grendel

Historical Notes: The 6.5 Grendel cartridge underwent three years of development, before Bill Alexander (Alexander Arms) released it in 2003 as a long-range cartridge specifically intended for the AR-15 family of rifles and carbines. The 6.5 Grendel transforms the military 7.62x39 parent case by necking it down to 6.5mm, blowing out the shoulder, and changing to a Small Rifle primer and flash hole. As a close relative of the benchrest-proven 6.5mm PPC, the 6.5 Grendel is the ideal length to seat long-ogive 120-grain and 130-grain bullets within the AR-15 magazine length constrictions.

General Comments: Accuracy in the 6.5 Grendel, in suitably barreled AR-15 rifles, readily attains sub-MOA, making it a great choice for long-range deer and varmint hunting. The 6.5 Grendel accommodates lightweight varmint bullets in the 90-grain class, which offer superb accuracy for competition and small-game shooting, mid-weight 108- or 120-grain competition bullets, and 130- or 140-grain game bullets for long shots on medium-sized game. Seventeen 6.5 Grendel cartridges will fit into an Alexander Arms-supplied magazine dimensioned to fit into the magazine well of an AR-15's lower receiver. The cartridge performs well in a 24-inch barrel using a 1:9 twist. Factory loads do not exceed 50,000 psi. Alexander Arms (www.alexanderarms.com) supplies rifles, magazines, ammunition, reloading dies, and brass.

Alexander Arms relinquished its trademark claim on the 6.5 Grendel as the 13th edition of this book went to print, which led to SAAMI standardization. Hornady and Wolf are now factory loading this round.

6.5 Grendel Loading Data

Bullet (grains/type)	Powder	Grains	Velocity	Energy	Source/Comments
90 Speer TNT	FL		3,030		Alexander Arms
120 Nosler BT	FL		2,580		Alexander Arms
123 Lapua Scenar	FL		2,650		Alexander Arms
129 Hornady SST	FL		2,450		Alexander Arms

.260 Remington/6.5-08 A-Square

Historical Notes: Inclusion of this cartridge presents us with a bit of a problem. Along about 1996, A-Square—a bona fide member of SAAMI—submitted drawings, chambering specifications, chambering reamers, sample cartridges, and all other necessary materials and data describing a new factory chambering to be adopted into the SAAMI fold. A-Square requested that the chambering be named "6.5-08 A-Square," as specified on the sample cartridge headstamp. Many months later, Remington submitted a memo to SAAMI, wherein it mentioned that it intended to eventually standardize a 6.5mm version of the .308 Winchester as the .260 Remington. Since SAAMI subsequently chose to christen this chambering as ".260 Remington," a disinterested observer would have to conclude that something was a bit rank somewhere.

General Comments: This cartridge has precisely two things to recommend it. First, it is a superior choice for long-range target shooting, particularly in the NRA High Power game, where reduced recoil with lighter bullets is valuable for the shorter-range events and where barrel life is an issue—a serious competitor can wear out several barrels each year. Second, for those who want or need a very light hunting rifle and are honest enough to admit that they cannot tolerate much recoil, this chambering is a superior choice.

Hunting load ballistics far exceed what the .243 Winchester can produce, but are not insurmountably far behind the 7mm-08 Remington. Nevertheless, this would seem to be a minimal chambering for use on any North American big game. Those intending to use this cartridge for elk hunting should consider only the best premium bullets, such as bonded core and partition designs and the 100-grain Barnes X.

.260 Remington Load Data/Factory Ballistics

Bullet (grains/type)	Powder	Grains	Velocity	Energy	Source/Comments
85 Sierra HP	RL-15	46.1	3,500	2,310	Sierra
100 Sierra HP	BigGame	46.2	3,200	2,271	Sierra
107 Sierra MatchKing	Varget	42.1	3,100	2,281	Sierra
120 Sierra MatchKing	V-N540	42.0	3,000	2,395	Sierra
140 Sierra MatchKing	RL-19	44.5	2,700	2,264	Sierra
120 Nosler BT	FL		2,890	2,226	Remington factory load
125 Nosler Partition	FL		2,875	2,294	Remington factory load
140 PSP Core-Lokt	FL		2,750	2,351	Remington factory load

6.5x55 Swedish Mauser

Historical Notes: Jointly developed by Norway and Sweden, this cartridge was adopted by both countries as an official military chambering, in 1894. Originally, both countries loaded and used essentially identical ammunition. Later, the Swedes modified dimensions and loaded to a higher pressure for use in their Mauser rifles, while the Norwegians kept the original version for use in the Krag rifle. In 1990, the National Rifle Associations of Denmark, Norway, and Sweden agreed on a standardized set of drawings and specifications, renaming the cartridge 6.5x55 SKAN. This cartridge remained in active Swedish military service until quite recently. It is quite popular throughout Scandinavia for hunting all types of game, including moose. It is also a popular choice for 300-meter target shooting and other forms of rifle competition.

Prior to World War II, the 6.5x55 Swedish was almost unknown in the United States. After the war, Canadian and U.S. sportsmen became acquainted with this chambering through the thousands of surplus Swedish Mauser rifles sold in North America. Canadian sportsmen were first to appreciate the virtues of this cartridge in the 1950s and 1960s. U.S. sportsmen arrived at the same conclusions in the 1970s and 1980s. Other than imported rifles from Scandinavian countries, few sporting rifles in this chambering were available in the U.S. until the 1990s. This has changed, as Winchester has offered its Featherweight M70 rifle and Ruger its M77 rifle in this chambering.

General Comments: The 6.5x55 is one of the few 6.5mm calibers ever to catch on in the United States. For many years, Norma of Sweden was the only manufacturer of this cartridge, until 1991-'92, when Federal Cartridge Co. added this cartridge to its Premium product line. This cartridge continues to gain popularity, as surplus Swedish Mauser rifles are still being imported. Two reasons for its growth in popularity are low recoil and superb accuracy. It is an excellent deer and antelope cartridge and is also suitable for bear and elk under good conditions at moderate ranges. Because of its flat trajectory, it is an outstanding choice in lightweight rifles for hunting sheep and goat in mountainous terrain.

Lack of suitable bullets and handload data handicapped the full potential of this cartridge for many years. This has changed, as good bullets and reloading data are now available from most component manufacturers. The 140-grain bullets are best for most types of hunting and are also the most accurate. The 6.5x55 Swedish Mauser case is not related to typical Mauser cartridge cases.

6.5x55mm Swedish Mauser Loading Data and Factory Ballistics

Bullet (grains/type)	Powder	Grains	Velocity	Energy	Source/Comments
85 Sierra HP	H4895	44.0	3,370	2,140	Hodgdon
85 HP	IMR 4320	47	3,100	1,814	Sierra
100 HP	H-380	43.5	3,000	1,999	Hornady
120 SP	H-4350	47	3,000	2,399	Nosler, Barnes
129 SP	H-380	43.5	2,800	2,246	Hornady
140 SP	IMR 4831	47	2,600	2,102	Speer, Barnes
140 Speer SP	H1000	51.5	2,651	2,185	Hodgdon
160 SP	H-4831	44	2,600	2,402	Speer
140 SP	FL		2,550	2,020	Federal factory load

6.5 Creedmoor

Historical Notes: Cartridges of 6.5mm-caliber have never really caught on among American hunters, but some have gained a good bit of ground with long-range target shooters. The 6.5-284 Norma and .260 Remington are excellent examples. The .260 Remington has become popular not only among those who use bolt-action rifles, but among those who shoot AR-10 rifles. In that rifle, the .260 works fine with most hunting bullets, but when loaded with extremely long match bullets, such as the Sierra 140-grain MatchKing and Hornady 140-grain A-Max, they have to be seated quite deeply in the case in order to keep overall cartridge length compatible with its magazine. Engineers at Hornady solved that problem by developing a shorter cartridge called the 6.5 Creedmoor. Maximum length of the case is 1.915 inches, compared to 2.036 inches for the .260 Remington, but since the 6.5 Creedmoor case has a bit less body taper combined with a sharper shoulder angle, its gross capacity is only about five percent less.

General Comments: As competitors who shoot at great distances have proven, the .260 Remington is capable of delivering excellent accuracy and there is no reason to believe the same does not hold true for the 6.5 Creedmoor. The Remington cartridge will probably continue to be more popular among bolt-gun shooters, simply because its slightly greater powder capacity allows it to be loaded to slightly higher velocities. It also has the advantage of being easily formed by simply necking down the .308 Winchester case. Chances are good the 6.5 Creedmoor will crowd the .260 from the trough among those who shoot AR rifles in competition. As big-game cartridges, both are in the same class as the excellent 6.5x55mm Swedish.

6.5 Creedmoor Loading Data and Factory Ballistics

Bullet (grains/type)	Powder	Grains	Velocity	Energy	Source
120 A-MAX	FL		3,050	2,476	Hornady
140 A-MAX	FL		2,820	2,469	Hornady

6.5x47 Lapua — *NEW*

Historical Notes: The 6.5×47mm Lapua (or 6.5×47mm) was jointly developed by Finnish ammunition maker Nammo Lapua Oy and the Swiss rifle manufacturer Grünig & Elmiger AG in 2005 for 300- to 1,000-meter competition shooting. The 6mm BR Norma currently dominates 300-meter shooting because of its excellent accuracy, good ballistics and low recoil, but after 2,500 rounds, top accuracy begins to erode, and it was hoped the 6.5x47 would maintain the 6mm BR's performance without the erosion problems.

General Comments: The 6.5x47 Lapua case has base diameter and loading length similar to the .308 Win., allowing it to accept the same bolt heads and fit into similar actions and magazines. In the field, the performance of the 6.5x47 Lapua closely resembles the .260 Rem., and it's not out of line to consider the 6.5x47 to be a shortened and improved .260 Rem., with a sharper shoulder and a longer neck. Factory 6.5x47 Lapua ammunition runs about 100 to 150 fps slower than the same bullets in .260 Rem.

For reloaders, powders such as RL15, H4350, Varget and N550 generally produce excellent accuracy with 123-grain and 139-grain Lapua Scenars and 130-grain Berger VLDs. Factory competition 6.5x47 Lapua loads (26-inch barrel) shoot the 123-grain Scenar at 2,790 fps and the 139-grain Lapua Scenar at 2,690 fps. A hunting load with the 140-grain Naturalis round-nose bullet takes off at 2,592 fps.

6.5x47 Lapua Factory Ballistics

Bullet (grains/type)	Powder	Grains	Velocity	Energy	Source/Comments
120 Scenar-L	NA	NA	2,772	2,053	Factory Load 4316017
123 Scenar	NA	NA	2,790	2,134	Factory Load 4316011
139 Scenar	NA	NA	2,690	2,231	Factory Load 4316012
140 Naturalis	NA	NA	2,592	2,094	Factory Load N316301

6.5-284 Norma

Historical Notes: Hornady now produces cases and will produce ammunition (depending upon rifle manufacturing) for this long-popular wildcat chambering. Originally, this version of the .284 Winchester was designed to offer a shorter hunting cartridge that approximates 6.5-06 ballistics; the long-range accuracy potential was recognized much later. This chambering has been used extensively in NRA High Power and elsewhere, where accuracy and barrel life are important. Peak pressure specification for this thoroughly modern cartridge is comparatively high.

General Comments: A 28-inch barrel loaded with any of the better VLD (Very Low Drag) moly-plated bullets between 130 and 155 grains in this cartridge easily achieves sufficient velocities for accurate 1,000-yard benchrest shooting. These combinations generate much less recoil than any effective .30- or .33-caliber 1,000-yard match combination. This contributes to precise shooting. However, unless conditions are unusually good, those using larger-bored rifles usually fare better. While those rifles generate more recoil, which effectively reduces intrinsic accuracy, the longer bullets those bigger bores can accurately fire exhibit less wind drift and, therefore, reduce the error associated with imperfections in the shooter's ability to properly dope the wind.

Owing to a relatively high working pressure, ballistic potential is not too different from that of the .270 Winchester, making this a fine hunting cartridge and one that will function in medium-length actions. One only hopes that current gun writers treat the 6.5-284 Norma more fairly than their forebears did its progenitor.

6.5-284 Norma Loading Data (Note: *Accuracy load; **Favorite deer and pronghorn load)

Bullet (grains/type)	Powder	Grains	Velocity	Energy	Source/Comments
120 Sierra/Nosler	RL-25	59.4	3,217	2,755	Norma (26-inch Bbl)

6.5-284 Norma Loading Data (Note: *Accuracy load; **Favorite deer and pronghorn load)

Bullet (grains/type)	Powder	Grains	Velocity	Energy	Source/Comments
120 Sierra MatchKing	IMR-4350	44.8	2,900*	2,238	Sierra
125 Nosler Partition	RL-22	54.5	3,137**	2,728	Layne Simpson
130 Swift Scirocco	RL-22	54.0	3,122**	2,810	Layne Simpson
140 Match	RL-25	57.4	3,028	2,850	Norma (26-inch Bbl)
140 Nosler Partition	RL-22	52.5	2,925	2,657	Nosler
140 Sierra MatchKing	RL-22	47.5	2,827*	2,482	Layne Simpson
142 Sierra MatchKing	RL-22	47.5	2,834*	2,530	Layne Simpson

.26 Nosler

Historical Notes: The .26 Nosler is a new cartridge submitted for approval to SAAMI in June 2013. The round's formal launch took place at the 2014 SHOT Show. The .26 Nosler, the first cartridge to bear the Nosler family's name, was designed to take advantage of the inherently accurate and high-BC 6.5mm (.264-caliber) bullets. Based on a shortened .404 Jeffery case, the .26 Nosler case is non-belted, thus, it headspaces off of the shoulder to further enhance accuracy. The .26 utilizes a standard .30-06-length action and likes a 1:9-twist barrel. Bob Nosler, CEO/president of Nosler, Inc., said this is a quintessential deer, antelope, and long-range target cartridge.

General Comments: The case is necked down to 6.5mm with a 40-degree shoulder. The rim is rebated to .532-inch, so a belted magnum bolt face requires no alteration. The Trophy Grade Ammunition load No. 60110 fires a Nosler 129-grain AccuBond Long Range bullet at 3,400 fps out of the muzzle. Zeroed at 350 yards, the .26 Nosler has a point-blank range of zero to 415 yards. Loaded with the 129-grain ABLR, the .26 Nosler retains as much velocity at 400 yards as the .260 Remington produces at the muzzle.

.26 Nosler Loading Data and Factory Ballistics

Bullet (grains/type)	Powder	Grains	Velocity	Energy	Source/Comments
129 AccuBond LR	FL		3,400	3,310	Nosler Factory Load
140 AccuBond	FL		3,300	3,119	Nosler Factory Load

6.5-300 Weatherby Magnum —
NEW

Historical Notes: For the first time in decades, Weatherby unleashed a new cartridge in 2016, this one based on a necked-down .300 Weatherby Magnum: the 6.5-300 Weatherby Magnum.

This cartridge isn't exactly new, even though Weatherby is billing it that way. Roy Weatherby built a 6.5-300 in the early 1950s, as evidenced by an old Mauser-action rifle in the company's collection. Also, in the early 1970s, a group of benchrest wildcatters built rifles chambered for the 6.5-300 WWH (Weatherby Wright Hoyer), a 6.5mm cartridge using the .300 Weatherby as the parent case.

"This is now the fastest production 6.5mm cartridge in the world," said Adam Weatherby, executive vice president and chief operating officer of Weatherby Inc. "The speed and energy of this cartridge is unprecedented and worthy of carrying the Weatherby name, all while exhibiting very manageable recoil."

General Comments: The three loads are a 127-grain Barnes LRX running at 3,531 fps, a 130-grain Swift Scirocco shooting at 3,475 fps and a 140-grain Swift A-Frame scooting along at 3,395 fps. The ammunition is $95 for a box of 20 rounds. The 6.5-300 Weatherby Magnum was chambered in the New Mark V family of rifles and offered in the Accumark, Accumark RC and Ultra Lightweight models for 2016. All the rifles have 26-inch barrels (the Ultra Lightweight also has a 2-inch muzzle brake) with 1-in-8-inch twists. Factory-supplied ballistics show that with a 300-yard zero, the 127-grain Barnes drops 7.12 inches at 400 yards and 18.99 inches at 500 yards. The drop figures for the 130-grain Swift are 7.2 inches and 19.0 inches at 400 and 500 yards, respectively. Drops for the 140-grain A-Frame are 8.6 and 23.3 at 400 and 500 yards, respectively.

6.5-300 Weatherby Magnum Factory Ballistics

Bullet (grains/type)	Powder	Grains	Velocity	Energy	Source/Comments
127 Barnes LRX	NA	NA	3,531	3,516	Factory Load
130 Swift Scirocco	NA	NA	3,475	3,487	Factory Load
140 Swift A-Frame	NA	NA	3,395	3,583	Factory Load

.264 Winchester Magnum

Historical Notes: This cartridge was officially announced by Winchester in 1958. The .264 Magnum is one of a series of cartridges based on the original Winchester .458 belted case, necked down. It is historically significant, as it is the first American 6.5mm cartridge since the long-defunct .256 Newton was announced back in 1913. It was originally available only in the Winchester bolt-action Model 70 Westerner with a 26-inch stainless steel barrel. For a time, the Remington 700 Series was offered in .264-caliber, as was the Ruger M77.

General Comments: The .264 Winchester is a fine, ultra-velocity cartridge with excellent long-range capabilities and ballistics superior to the time-tried .270 Winchester. Its development may well have been suggested by the .257 Weatherby Magnum, for the two are quite similar. The .264 is able to equal the .257 Weatherby Magnum, but with the added advantage of the heavier 140-grain bullet for larger species of big game. The 100-grain bullet is intended for animals in the deer and antelope class, the 140-grain for elk and larger game. The rifling twist used by Winchester is not quick enough to stabilize spitzer bullets of more than 140 grains. The handloader has a wide choice of bullets ranging from 87 to 160 grains.

All things considered, the .264 Magnum is adequate for any North American big game. It is a plains and mountain cartridge. Like most of its ilk, this cartridge can be extremely hard on its barrel, especially with either careless shooting, inadequate barrel cooling between shots, or inadequate cleaning. (Joyce Hornady said the company went through three barrels for this chambering just trying to work up the data for three bullets with a few powders each. They were tipped off to a problem, when the maximum charge for the 140-grain bullet turned out to be quite a bit higher than the maximum charge for the 120-grain bullet with the same powder.) Like all high-intensity chamberings, it loses a great deal of velocity with barrels shorter than 26 inches. To quantify this, the best-possible safe .264 Winchester Magnum loads from 22-inch barrels produce less energy than best-possible .270 Winchester loads from a 22-inch barrel, with equal-weight bullets. Both Remington and Winchester still offer this loading. However, only the 140-grain bullet is available.

.264 Winchester Magnum Loading Data and Factory Ballistics

(Note: loads shown are for the factory 26-inch barrel, using Winchester-Western cases.

Bullet (grains/type)	Powder	Grains	Velocity	Energy	Source/Comments
85 Sierra HP	H4831	78.0	3,812	2,740	Hodgdon
85 SP	IMR 4895	57	3,700	2,585	Sierra
100 SP	IMR 4831	65	3,500	2,721	Hornady
120 SP	IMR 4350	60	3,200	2,729	Nosler, Sierra
129 SP	IMR 4350	57	3,100	2,753	Hornady
140 SP	IMR 4831	61	3,100	2,988	Hornady
140 Nosler Part.	H870	73.0	3,163	3,110	Hodgdon
160 SP	IMR 4831	54.5	2,700	2,591	Hornady
140 SP	FL		3,030	2,854	Factory load

.270 Weatherby Magnum

Historical Notes: Most shooting enthusiasts think that the .270 Weatherby was developed to satisfy a demand for this caliber after the popularity of the .300 Weatherby Magnum had been established. As a matter of fact, the .270 was the first of the line developed by Roy Weatherby on the necked-down .300 H&H case. This was in 1943, after experiments with an improved .220 Swift that Weatherby called the .220 Rocket. It was largely actual hunting experience with the .270 WM that started Weatherby on the high-velocity trail. This culminated in his starting a commercial gun business in September 1945.

General Comments: The popularity of the .270 Winchester made it almost mandatory for Roy Weatherby to include this caliber in his line of commercial magnum rifle cartridges. The .270 Weatherby Magnum has been used extensively, and successfully, on all species of North American big game. It has also achieved notable success on African plains game. Those who have used it claim the .270 Weatherby provides flat trajectory, excellent long-range stopping power on all thin-skinned game, and noticeably less recoil than the famous .300 Weatherby Magnum. As an added attraction, the .270 Weatherby Magnum is not impractical for varmint shooting. The 100-grain bullet is excellent for this purpose, thus making the .270 Weatherby Magnum a very versatile all-round caliber. However, it is important to allow plenty of barrel-cooling time with this and all high-intensity cartridges. The .270 Weatherby Magnum is easy and economical to reload, and empty cases are available for it. Like the other large-capacity magnum cases, it does not lend itself to reduced loads and is at its best with full or nearly full charges. It is a very fine choice for the hunter who wants to include varmint hunting potential in a big-game rifle. It has been one of the most popular calibers that Weatherby offers.

.270 Weatherby Magnum Loading Data and Factory Ballistics

Bullet (grains/type)	Powder	Grains	Velocity	Energy	Source/Comments
90 HP	IMR 4350	73	3,800	2,886	Sierra
100 SP	IMR 4350	71	3,600	2,878	Speer
100 SP	H-4831	76.5	3,500	2,721	Hornady
130 SP	IMR 4350	68	3,300	3,144	Speer, Sierra, Nosler
130 SP	IMR 4831	70	3,300	3,144	Sierra, Speer
140 SP	IMR 4350	66.5	3,100	2,988	Nosler
150 SP	IMR 4350	66	3,000	2,998	Hornady, Speer
150 SP	IMR 4831	67	3,000	2,998	Nosler, Sierra
160 SP	IMR 4831	65	2,900	2,989	Nosler
100 SP	FL		3,760	3,139	Weatherby factory load
130 SP	FL		3,375	3,283	Weatherby factory load
150 SP	FL		3,245	3,501	Weatherby factory load

6.8mm Special Purpose Cartridge (6.8 SPC)

Historical Notes: Anecdotal reports from U.S. forces involved in combat in Iraq and Afghanistan in recent years indicate the six decade-old 7.62x39 cartridge and AK47 rifle may be more effective in combat than the U.S. M4 carbines firing the 5.56x45 cartridge. In 2003, Steve Holland and Cris Murray, individuals associated with special forces and marksmanship units, developed a special-purpose cartridge to improve combat effectiveness in short-barreled (16.5-inch) M4 carbines used for special operations. The resulting 6.8 SPC (Special Purpose Cartridge) achieved favorable results in actual usage, but has not been officially adopted by the U.S. Army, as of 2005. The cartridge is under review by the U.S. Marine Corps and FBI.

General Comments: Intended to launch heavier bullets than the standard U.S. 5.56 round, the 6.8 SPC uses the 1906-vintage .30 Remington cartridge shortened and necked down to accept a .270-caliber (6.8mm) bullet. Holland and Murray selected the .30 Remington as a parent case for two reasons. First, bolts for the M-16 family of rifles and carbines can readily be manufactured to accept the .30 Remington's case head diameter (.420). Second, standard 20-round and 30-round M-16 magazines can accept the 6.8 SPC without change. After extensive test firings into ordnance gel blocks, and on military firing ranges with the .30 Remington cases sized for .30, 7mm, .270, 6.5mm, and 6mm bullets, .270-caliber bullets delivered the best balance of velocity, accuracy, and terminal performance. Hornady and Remington offer loaded 6.8 SPC ammunition. The cartridge is chambered by Barrett, DPMS, and PRI in AR15 rifles; by both SSK Industries and Thompson/Center in Contender, G2, and Encore single-shot actions; by Remington in bolt-action rifles; and by custom gunsmiths on CZ-527 bolt-actions. It is a good whitetail deer cartridge.

6.8mm Special Purpose Cartridge (6.8 SPC) Loading Data and Factory Ballistics

Bullet (grains/type)	Powder	Grains	Velocity	Energy	Source/Comments
110 V-Max	FL		2,550	1,588	Hornady
115 MC	FL		2,800	2,002	Remington
90 Spr HP	H4198	28.6C	3,012	1,812	Hodgdon
110 V-Max	Benchmark	27.0	2,518	1,548	Hodgdon
115 Sierra HPBT	H322	28.2C	2,608	1,736	Hodgdon

.270 Winchester

Historical Notes: Designed by Winchester in 1925 for its Model 54 bolt-action rifle, the .270 caused quite a stir in shooting circles. It has remained somewhat controversial ever since. At the time of introduction, it offered better long-range performance than any big-game cartridge available on the American market. It has now been adopted by practically every manufacturer of standard bolt-action, high-powered sporting rifles in the world. The Remington pump-action and Remington and Browning semi-autos are also available in .270-caliber. The cartridge is based on the .30-06 case necked down to .277-inch. (It is just possible that Winchester chose a .277-inch bullet to avoid paralleling anything European or British, and they could possibly have been inspired by a Chinese cartridge that used a .277-inch bullet. We will likely never know.) The case neck is .050-inch longer but, except for the neck and headstamp, the .270 Winchester is otherwise identical to the .30-06. This cartridge was a long-time favorite of the late, well-known gun writer Jack O'Connor, who probably contributed more to popularizing the .270 than any other individual. Today, the .270 Winchester is one of the most popular calibers on the market.

General Comments: Along with the .30-06, this is one of the most accurate and effective all-round American big-game cartridges. Its reputation and popularity have increased steadily since its introduction. Although not intended as a varmint cartridge, the .270 will serve very well in that capacity when loaded with bullets of 90 to 110 grains. It is generally conceded to be a better long-range varmint cartridge than its parent, the .30-06. The 130-grain bullet at 3,100 fps muzzle velocity is considered adequate by many experienced hunters for any North American big game. When first introduced, some deer hunters complained that the 130-grain bullet had such an explosive effect that it ruined too much meat. To satisfy the demand for a deer load, Winchester brought out a 150-grain bullet at a reduced velocity of 2,675 fps. However, it was short-lived, because the people who demanded it wouldn't buy it. The present 150-grain bullet at 2,860 fps is intended for maximum penetration on heavier animals such as elk, moose, or bear. Some disagree, but current evidence reinforces the conclusion that the .270 is adequate for any North American big game and some African plains game, as well.

Assuming the hunter uses the proper bullet for the job at hand, the .270 will deliver reliable performance. In any comparison of the .270 with the .30-06, much depends on intended use and hunting conditions. For some reason, many individuals shoot better with the .270 than the .30-06. The .270 is flatter shooting than the .30-06 and, thus, makes a better varmint/big-game rifle where this is a consideration. The .30-06, with its 180-, 200-, and 220-grain bullets, must be conceded as a better heavy-game cartridge. In accuracy and general performance, there isn't a great deal to argue about. Anyone trying to make a big case for one against the other is beating a pretty dead horse. The .270 Winchester is commercially loaded by all large domestic and most foreign ammunition manufacturers.

.270 Winchester Loading Data and Factory Ballistics

Bullet (grains/type)	Powder	Grains	Velocity	Energy	Source/Comments
90 Sierra HP	H4350	62.0	3,603	2,590	Hodgdon
100 Speer SP	RL-19	64.0	3,510	2,735	Hodgdon
110 Hornady HP	H4350	57.0	3,267	2,605	Hodgdon
130 Speer SP	RL-19	60.0	3,160	2,880	Hodgdon
135 Sierra SPBT	H1000	63.0	3,011	2,715	Hodgdon
140 Swift SP	H1000	63.0	2,979	2,755	Hodgdon
150 SP	IMR 4831	54	2,800	2,612	Speer, Sierra, Hornady
150 Sierra SPBT	RL-22	58.5	3,010	3,020	Hodgdon
160 Nosler Part.	H1000	59.0	2,765	2,715	Hodgdon
180 Barnes JRN	RL-22	53.0	2,762	3,045	Barnes
100 SP	FL		3,480	2,612	Factory load
130 SP	FL		3,060	2,702	Factory load
150 SP	FL		2,850	2,705	Factory load

.270 Winchester Short Magnum (.270 WSM)

Historical Notes: Introduced in 2001 and intended for riflemen preferring the .270 family of cartridges, the .270 WSM is crafted from the instantly popular .300 WSM case, necked down to accept .277-inch diameter bullets. Compared to the long-popular .270 Winchester the late Jack O'Connor held in high esteem, the .270 WSM is a modern magnum upgrade, suitable for short-action rifles and offering higher performance—that approaching .270 Weatherby Magnum velocity levels with similar weight bullets. SSK Industries also re-barrels the AR-10 self-loading rifle for .270 WSM.

General Comments: For efficient and consistent powder burning, the .270 WSM continues the short-fat cartridge case geometry Winchester first popularized in the .300 WSM, a benchrest-proven concept for nearly three decades. Retaining the 35-degree shoulder of the parent .300 WSM case, the .270 WSM headspaces on the shoulder, which should provide for tighter headspacing tolerances and improved accuracy potential.

This cartridge and all its Winchester Short Magnum siblings became embroiled in a legal battle, and the end result was a less than enthusiastic appeal on the part of other manufacturers to offer rifles and/or ammunition for sale. However, unlike the Winchester Super Short Magnums that are collecting dust on the shelves or in shooters' gun racks, the WSM line still enjoys moderate appeal, especially the .270 and .300 offerings.

.270 Winchester Short Magnum Loading Data and Factory Ballistics

Bullet (grains/type)	Powder	Grains	Velocity	Energy	Source/Comments
130 BST	FL		3,275	3,096	Winchester
140 Fail Safe	FL		3,175	3,035	Winchester
150 XP3	FL		3120	3,242	Winchester
140 Nosler Ballistic Tip	Magnum	71.0	3,200	3,182	Nosler
150 Nosler Ballistic Tip	Magpro	68.0	3,187	3,382	Nosler

7-30 Waters

Historical Notes: The 7-30 Waters was introduced in 1984 for the U.S. Repeating Arms Model 94XTR Angle Eject rifle and carbine. The cartridge was the work of Ken Waters, a well-known gun writer and ballistics expert. He began planning the cartridge, in 1976, as a high-velocity, flat-trajectory round for short, handy, lever-action carbines.

There are many problems to be overcome by those who would improve on the performance of the .30-30 cartridge class in lever-action rifles. Severe restrictions are imposed by tubular magazines, the length of the action, and permissible working pressures. However, by 1982, Ken had developed a cartridge that would push the 139-grain 7mm bullet at 2,600 fps. At this point, U.S. Repeating Arms Co. became interested in the project and decided in 1983 to produce Model 94 lever-action rifles in this new cartridge. Federal Cartridge Co. then completed the final version of the cartridge by making various dimensional changes and opting for a lighter 120-grain bullet to achieve higher velocity at less pressure. The current commercial loading uses a 120-grain Nosler Partition bullet that develops a muzzle velocity of 2,700 fps when fired from a 24-inch barrel.

General Comments: The 7-30 Waters does offer improved performance for those who like lever-action carbines or rifles. This should make a good deer and black bear-class cartridge. However, the majority of .30-30 lever-action shooters prefer the short carbine, since most are woods hunters. The 7-30, with its light 120-grain bullet, is unlikely to best the .30-30, .32 Special, .38-55, etc., with shots at close range. Also, it is not going to be the answer for the long-range plains or mountain hunter. When fired from a 20-inch barrel, its performance is considerably reduced. So, anyone interested in this cartridge will be better served if they buy the rifle rather than the carbine. The light recoil of this cartridge makes it an excellent choice for a woman, boy, or anyone who is recoil sensitive. The 7-30 is at its best in broken country, with shots varying from patches of brush and trees to open areas with shots ranging from 75 to 175 yards.

7-30 Waters Loading Data and Factory Ballistics

Bullet (grains/type)	Powder	Grains	Velocity	Energy	Source/Comments
120 Nosler FP Part.	H414	42.0	2,757	2,025	Hodgdon
120 SP	H-335	28.5	2,500	1,666	Nosler
130 SP	H-335	33	2,600	1,952	Speer
139 Hornady FP	RL-15	34.7	2,540	1,990	Hodgdon
140 SP	W748	35	2,500	1,943	Hornady
140 SP	H-335	34	2,600	2,102	Hornady
145 SP	748	34	2,400	1,855	Speer
154 Hornady NR	H414	37.0	2,347	1,835	Hodgdon
120 SP	FL		2,700	1,940	Federal factory load

28 Nosler — *NEW*

Historical Notes: In 2015, Nosler created its new 28 Nosler by necking up the 26 Nosler case, itself a derivative of the 7mm RUM case, which descended from the .404 Jeffery. Nosler supports this new cartridge with Nosler brass, Trophy Grade ammunition and M48 rifles in 26-inch barrel configurations.

The 28 Nosler is the only cartridge in the family (26, 27, 28, 30, 33, 35 and 36) that shares all of the 26 Nosler case dimensions, with the exception of being necked up. The 27 Nosler was changed from the 26 as well. The case might be the same length, but the shoulder datum was brought back to a shorter dimension. Nosler said there were two main reasons these features were changed between cartridges: Designers wanted to stay within a 3.340 maximum COAL and had to design around the longest-ogive Nosler bullets in each caliber. Getting up to .30-caliber and larger sizes necessitates shortening the brass and therefore moving the shoulder accordingly to preserve adequate neck length. The most important reason the shoulder and length dimensions were changed is to prevent cross-caliber chambering. For example, bullet and neck diameter alone is not enough to guarantee someone can't force a 28 Nosler shell into a 27 Nosler chamber. By bringing the shoulder back on the 27, it can prevent serious injury if a shooter inadvertently chambers and fires a larger-caliber shell in the smaller chamber.

General Comments: The fat case creates powder space, with a water capacity of 93.8 grains when loaded with a 150-grain AccuBond Long Range Spitzer, according to Nosler specs. The rebated-rim centerfire rifle cartridge shares the same overall cartridge length (3.340) as the 26 Nosler, which allows it to be chambered in standard-length actions. Likewise, the .284-caliber (7mm) centerfire .28 Nosler has the same 3.340-inch maximum cartridge overall length as the .30-06, but the case length is 2.590 inches with a 35-degree shoulder. Accordingly, the 28 Nosler cartridge case can be formed by necking-up a 26 Nosler case to 7mm (.284 inch) diameter.

Slower-burning powders and high load densities generally yield the best loads. Some of the best are with Norma 217 and RL 33, but other propellants of similar speed give excellent results as well. For family bragging rights, the 26 Nosler is capable of firing a 129-grain AccuBond-LR bullet at a muzzle velocity of 3,400 fps, but the 28 Nosler launches a 160-grain AccuBond at 3,300 fps, and the 30 Nosler fires a 180-grain AccuBond at 3,200 fps.

28 Nosler Loading Data and Factory Ballistics

Bullet (grains/type)	Powder	Grains	Velocity	Energy	Source/Comments
150 Ballistic Tip	IMR 7828 SSC	74.0	3,227	3,467	81% Load Density*
150 CT Ballistic Tip	RL 33	90	3,320	3,670	98%, Most Accurate*
160 AccuBond	NA	NA	3,300	3,883	Factory Load
175 AccuBond LR	NA	NA	3,125	3,806	Factory Load

*Nosler Reloading Guide 8 data

.280 Ackley Improved

Historical Notes: In addition to being a famous gunsmith, a barrel maker, and a college professor, P.O. Ackley absolutely ruled the roost when it came to creating wildcat and improved cartridges. One of his earliest was the 7mm-06 Improved, which was formed by necking down the .30-06 case and fire-forming it to less body taper and a 40-degree shoulder angle. Years later, and not long after the .280 Remington was introduced, reloading equipment maker Fred Huntington reformed its case to the Improved configuration with minimum body taper and a 35-degree shoulder angle and called it the .280 RCBS. Since cases for Huntington's cartridge could be formed by firing .280 Remington ammo in a rifle chambered for it, Ackley abandoned his 7mm-06 Improved and started chambering rifles for the .280 RCBS, but rather than staying with its 35-degree shoulder angle, he changed it to 40 degrees. And so was born a cartridge we know today as the .280 Ackley Improved. After close to a half-century of being something only handloaders could love, the .280 Ackley Improved became a factory number, when Nosler registered it with SAAMI, started loading the ammunition, and began chambering rifles for it, in 2007.

General Comments: We are tempted to say the .280 Ackley Improved is more accurate than the .280 Remington, but doing so would be unfair, since all of the rifles Frank Barnes tried it in were rather expensive custom jobs, while all he tested chambered for the standard .280 Remington were off-the-shelf factory rifles. The Ackley version is a fine old cartridge and, when loaded with the right bullet, is big enough medicine for game up to elk and moose. Even so, the .280 Ackley Improved is not as fast as the 7mm Remington Magnum, as a few of that cartridge's avid supporters would have us believe. All things including barrel length and the chamber pressure to which the two are loaded being equal, the .280 Ackley Improved is about 100 fps faster with all bullet weights than the standard .280 Remington. Cases are easily formed by firing .280 Remington factory ammo in a rifle properly chambered for the .280 Ackley Improved.

.280 Ackley Improved Loading Data and Factory Ballistics

Bullet (grains/type)	Powder	Grains	Velocity	Energy	Source
120 Nosler Ballistic Tip	H4831	65.0	3,240	2,794	Hodgdon
130 Sierra HPBT	IMR-4831	58.3	3,128	2,821	Hodgdon
140 Nosler Ballistic Tip	H4350	55.5	3,012	2,817	Hodgdon
150 Barnes TSX	IMR-4831	54.5	2,881	2,762	Hodgdon
160 Nosler AccuBond	IMR-4831	55.5	2,847	2,877	Hodgdon
175 Speer Grand Slam	IMR-4831	55.0	2,702	2,834	Hodgdon
140 Nosler AccuBond	FL	FL	3,050	2,889	Nosler

7mm Weatherby Magnum

Historical Notes: The 7mm Weatherby Magnum was developed, in 1944, as one of a series of cartridges based on the necked-down .300 H&H case (it is the .270 WM necked up .007-inch, although it does use a longer overall cartridge length). There are several similar wildcat versions, but Weatherby's design is the most popular, due to the availability of commercial ammunition.

General Comments: The 7mm (or .284-caliber) has long been popular in the United States in various wildcat cartridges, yet the original 7mm Mauser never generated any great enthusiasm. The 7mm Weatherby Magnum, offered as a maximum-performance cartridge, is probably the best known and widely used of the current 7mm Magnums, with the single exception of the 7mm Remington Magnum. This is due in part to the availability of factory loaded ammunition having a good selection of bullet weights. The 7mm Weatherby has a slight edge over the .270 Weatherby on tough or dangerous game, because it can use heavier bullets and churns up greater energy. However, if long-range varmint shooting is on the agenda, the .270 is the better choice. The 7mm Weatherby Magnum is adequate for any North American big game and all thin-skinned African game. The 7mm Weatherby Magnum has, to a large extent, lost popularity to the 7mm Remington Magnum, because the Remington version is available in a wider variety of rifles that are generally less expensive than the Weatherbys. Like most high-intensity cartridges, the 7mm WM can be somewhat hard on its barrel, especially with either careless shooting, inadequate barrel cooling between shots, or inadequate barrel cleaning. And, like all similar chamberings, it loses significant velocity with barrels shorter than 24 inches. Ammunition in this caliber is now available from Remington and PMC, as well as Weatherby. For many years now, Norma has loaded Weatherby ammunition in all calibers under the Weatherby brand name. In 1992, Norma began offering Weatherby calibers under the Norma brand name. Norma ammunition is distributed in the United States by Dynamit Nobel.

7mm Weatherby Magnum Loading Data and Factory Ballistics

Bullet (grains/type)	Powder	Grains	Velocity	Energy	Source/Comments
100 HP	IMR 4350	73.5	3,600	2,878	Hornady
115 HP	IMR 4831	76	3,600	3,310	Speer
120 SP	IMR 4350	70	3,400	3,081	Sierra, Nosler, Hornady
130 SP	IMR 4320	63	3,300	3,144	Speer
139 SP	IMR 4350	68	3,200	3,161	Sierra, Nosler, Hornady
154 SP	IMR 4350	67	3,100	3,287	Hornady
160 SP	IMR 4350	65	3,000	3,198	Sierra, Speer
175 SP	IMR 4350	65	2,800	3,047	Speer, Hornady
195 SP	IMR 7828	61	2,500	2,707	Speer
139 SP	FL		3,340	3,443	Weatherby factory load
154 SP	FL		3,260	3,633	Weatherby factory load

Bullet (grains/type)	Powder	Grains	Velocity	Energy	Source/Comments
175 SP	FL		3,070	3,662	Weatherby factory load

.280 Remington/ 7mm Express Remington

Historical Notes: The .280 Remington was introduced by that company in 1957. Initially it was chambered in the Remington Model 740 autoloader, later in the 760 pump-action and the 721 and 725 bolt-actions. The Remington 700 series bolt-action rifles originally included the .280 chambering. In an effort to increase sales, from 1979 to 1980 Remington cataloged the .280 as the 7mm Express Remington. But too much confusion resulted, and Remington went back to the original .280 moniker. The .280 Remington, actually a 7mm with a bullet diameter of .284-inch, is based on the .30-06 case necked down. It is very similar to the wildcat 7mm-06, which has been around for a good many years. In 1979, Remington introduced a new 150-grain loading.

General Comments: This is a .30-06 case necked down and with the shoulder moved forward .050-inch to prevent it from being chambered in .270 Winchester rifles. Had this been possible, the oversized neck might not have had room to open enough to free the bullet, and the results could have been extremely dangerous—yet, by moving the shoulder forward, Remington created an even more dangerous situation. The .270 Winchester cartridge, which is visually almost indistinguishable from the .280, chambers effortlessly in .280 Remington rifles. Should the extractor catch the case during loading and then allow it to slip forward when the firing pin strikes the primer, or should the striker reach the primer of a load that was chambered ahead of the extractor, the results would be a .050-inch headspace problem with almost certain head separation and the resulting flood of 50,000-psi gas in one's face. Not a pretty thought. Remington could have solved the original problem and eliminated the one it created by simply enlarging the case at the shoulder or increasing the shoulder angle.

The .280 Remington is slightly more powerful than the .270 Winchester. It would be stretching a point to say that the .280 is better than the .270 Winchester, although it is probably a little more versatile, due to the wider variety of factory bullets available. If you are a handloader, any difference would be one of personal preference. The .280 is certainly adequate for any North American big game and would also lend itself for use on large varmints. It is another case of a good wildcat cartridge finally emerging in a commercial version. It has picked up a modest following among 7mm fans since its introduction. Loaded with the 120-grain or new 100-grain varmint bullets, the .280 becomes an excellent varmint cartridge. The 150-grain bullet at 2970 fps brings out some of the latent potential of this cartridge, which is truly an excellent long-range big-game cartridge. Both Remington and Winchester commercially load this cartridge.

.280 Remington Loading Data and Factory Ballistics

Bullet (grains/type)	Powder	Grains	Velocity	Energy	Source/Comments
100 Sierra HP	VarGet	51.3	3,433	2,615	Hodgdon
120 Barnes XFB	H4350	56.0	3,114	2,580	Hodgdon
130 SP	IMR 4350	57	3,100	2775	Speer
140 Nosler Part.	H4831	58.5	2,927	2,660	Hodgdon
150 SP	IMR 4831	48	2,900	2,802	Sierra, Nosler
160 Sierra SPBT	RL-22	55.7	2,795	2,775	Hodgdon
175 SP	IMR 4350	52	2,650	2,730	Speer, Hornady
120 SP	FL		3,150	2,643	Factory load
150 SP	FL		2,890	2,781	Factory load
165 SP	FL		2,820	2,913	Factory load
140 SP	FL		3,050	2,799	Factory load

7mm-08 Remington

Historical Notes: Remington introduced this medium-capacity rifle cartridge to the marketplace in 1980. It is based on the .308 Winchester case necked down to 7mm and was loaded with a 140-grain bullet at 2860 fps. Remington advertised this cartridge as the "... first modern 7mm round designed for use in short-action rifles." This is an interesting claim, in view of the fact that the .284 Winchester, designed for the same purpose, arrived on the scene in 1963. Furthermore, the 7mm-08 is a direct copy of the 7mm/.308 wildcat dating back to 1958 and earlier. This is not meant to denigrate a fine cartridge, but to demonstrate that there really sometimes isn't much new under the sun, despite advertising claims. The 7mm-08 is chambered in exactly the same actions as the .284 Winchester, but cannot equal .284 ballistics.

Original rifles chambered for the 7mm-08 were the Remington Model 788 and 700BDL Varmint Special bolt actions. Current Remington catalogs list the 700 series and Model Seven bolt-actions as available in this chambering. Other makers have also chambered it.

Remington has hung its hat on the 7mm caliber, and with considerable success. It now offers six chamberings: 7mm BR, 7mm-08, 7x57mm Mauser, 7mm Express (.280 Remington), 7mm Remington Magnum, and 7 STW. The 7mm BR originated as something of a semi-wildcat based on the .308x1.5-inch necked down. Remington has contributed more than any other company to the belated recognition of the ballistic advantages of the 7mm caliber by U.S. shooters.

General Comments: Owing partly to a more pointed bullet shape, the 7mm-08 140-grain load surpasses the .308 Winchester 150-grain load downrange, according to Remington tests from a 24-inch barrel. This appears to be true. At 500 yards, the 7mm-08 bullet has an edge of 238 fps and 750 ft-lbs of energy over the .308 bullet. This would make quite a difference in potential killing power and also help in better bullet placement at unknown distances. There is not sufficient difference to cause owners of .308-caliber rifles to rush down and trade them off for 7mm-08s, but it does illustrate the ballistic advantages of the smaller caliber loaded with more streamlined bullets.

The 7mm-08 is a great favorite with many metallic silhouette shooters, and there are many glowing reports regarding its accuracy on the range, particularly with handloads. It is also building a good reputation as a long-range deer and antelope cartridge. When handloaded with bullets heavier than 140 grains, it is also suitable for heavier game, such as elk. Unfortunately, the two factory bullet weights do not make for a very flexible big-game cartridge. On the other hand, by handloading, this cartridge can be adapted to anything from varmint shooting through elk.

Case capacity of the 7mm-08 is slightly less than the 7x57mm Mauser, and performance with the heavier bullets of around 175 grains is about 100 to 150 fps less, which is not anything to get really excited about. The fact of the matter is that the 7mm-08 is adequate for most North American hunting, though handicapped by only two commercial bullet loadings. Remington has been joined by Federal in offering factory loaded ammunition in this caliber.

7mm-08 Remington Loading Data and Factory Ballistics

Bullet (grains/type)	Powder	Grains	Velocity	Energy	Source/Comments
100 HP	H-335	40.5	3,000	1,999	Hornady
120 SP	IMR 4320	41	2,700	1,943	Hornady, Sierra, Nosler
130 SP	IMR 4064	45	3,000	2,599	Speer
140 SP	IMR 4895	44	2,900	2,615	Sierra
150 SP	IMR 4320	38	2,400	1,919	Hornady, Sierra
160 SP	IMR 4350	44	2,650	2,496	Nosler, Sierra, Speer
175 SP	IMR 4350	44	2,600	2,627	Speer
120 SP	FL		3,000	2,398	Factory load
140 SP	FL		2,860	2,542	Factory load

7mm Remington Magnum

Historical Notes: Introduced by Remington during 1962, the 7mm Remington Magnum was brought out at the same time as the improved bolt-action 700-series rifles, which replaced the earlier Models 721, 722, and 725. Most other manufacturers have since added this popular caliber to their lines. It took American firearms manufacturers nearly 40 years to realize that the .275 Holland & Holland (made long ago by Western Cartridge Co.) is a first-rate, medium-game, long-range cartridge. The long line of 7mm wildcats is much like the old .275 H&H, which came out in 1912. Remington chose to ignore the classic 7mm bullet—160-grain spitzer—in its 7mm Magnum loads.

General Comments: The 7mm Remington Magnum is a fine long-range, big-game cartridge. There is a good selection of factory loaded 7mm bullets available, and the handloader could make it do just about anything. It has ample power for any North American big game and most thin-skinned African varieties. However, it is an open-country plains or mountain cartridge, rather than a woods or brush number. Many will compare it with the 7mm Weatherby Magnum or the 7x61mm Sharpe & Hart Super. Bitter arguments will ensue as to which is the best or most powerful. This will be akin to the ancient Greek pastime of discussing how many spirits can dance on the head of a pin. However, any difference in these cartridges will be strictly a matter of opinion or imagination. They all have nearly the same case capacity, and none will do anything the others can't duplicate. In fact, the 7mm Remington is hardly a new or brilliant design, rather, it is largely a commercial version of several short-bellied wildcat 7mm magnums (Ackley, Luft, Mashburn, etc.).

The principal advantage to the 7mm Remington Magnum lies in the fact that it is a standard factory product that is widely distributed and available in well-made, moderately priced rifles. Come to think of it, that's quite a bit to a lot of people. However, don't trade off your present 7mm Magnum with the idea that the Remington round is going to provide some mysterious extra margin of power or knockdown. The 7mm Rem. Mag. can be somewhat hard on barrels, especially with either careless shooting, inadequate barrel cooling between shots, or inadequate cleaning. And, like all similar chamberings, it loses significant velocity with barrels shorter than 24 inches. Actual ballistics may be closer to the 7mm Weatherby Magnum than factory data suggests. Ammunition in 7mm Remington Magnum caliber is available in a wide variety from all domestic and most foreign ammunition manufacturers.

7mm Remington Magnum Loading Data and Factory Ballistics

Bullet (grains/type)	Powder	Grains	Velocity	Energy	Source/Comments
100 HP	IMR 4831	71.5	3,500	2,721	Hornady
115 HP	IMR 4831	71	3,400	2,953	Speer
120 SP	IMR 4350	66	3,350	2,991	Sierra, Nosler
130 SP	IMR 4350	63	3,200	2,957	Speer
140 SP	IMR 4350	64	3,100	2,988	Nosler, Sierra, Hornady
150 SP	IMR 4831	62	3,000	2,998	Nosler, Sierra
160 SP	IMR 4831	62.5	3,000	3,198	Sierra, Nosler, Speer
175 SP	H-450	64.5	2,900	3,269	Sierra
140 SP	FL		3,175	3,133	Factory load
150 SP	FL		3,110	3,221	Factory load
160 SP	FL		2,950	3,090	Factory load
165 SP	FL		2,900	3,081	Factory load
175 SP	FL		2,860	3,178	Factory load

7mm Shooting Times Westerner (7mm STW)

Historical Notes: The 7mm Shooting Times Westerner (STW) was created around 1981 by firearms writer Layne Simpson and introduced in the May 1988 edition of *Shooting Times* magazine. Simpson initially called it the 7mm Remington Maximum, but later changed its name to 7mm Shooting Times Westerner as his way of dedicating it to his readers. It is simply the 8mm Remington Magnum case necked down, with no other change. Like other cartridges on the full-length Holland & Holland belted case, its length requires the use of a long-action rifle, such as the Remington Model 700, Winchester Model 70, and Weatherby Mark V. The first factory-built rifles chambered for the 7mm STW (actually while the round was still a wildcat), were Winchester Model 70s built by the U.S. Repeating Arms custom shop, and rifles built around the 1917 Enfield action by A-Square. The latter company was also first to offer the ammunition. In 1997, Remington registered the cartridge with SAAMI and began to load the ammunition and chamber Model 700 rifles for it. In a ceremony held during the 1997 NRA Annual Meetings, Simpson was presented with the very first production Model 700 built in 7mm STW, along with the first box of 140-grain Core-Lokt ammunition to come off the production line. Twelve months hence, Remington had sold just over 600,000 rounds of 7mm STW ammo.

General Comments: The hunting world was obviously ready for the 7mm STW, as few wildcats have been adopted by major ammunition and rifle manufacturers as quickly. Remington later introduced its own 7mm Ultra Mag., and while ballistics charts published by the company show it as being slightly faster, those who have compared the two in barrels of the same length know otherwise. The 7mm STW shoots extremely flat while delivering levels of energy adequate for taking game up to the size of elk and moose at long range, and yet its recoil is considerably milder than magnum cartridges of larger calibers. High performance comes at a price, and while barrel accuracy life is shorter than for a smaller cartridge such as the 7mm-08 Remington, a good barrel properly maintained and not heated excessively by a great deal of rapid-fire shooting should still be delivering long-range hunting accuracy at the 2,000-round mark and possibly beyond.

7mm Shooting Times Westerner (7mm STW) Loading Data and Factory Ballistics

Bullet (grains/type)	Powder	Grains	Velocity	Energy	Source
120 TSX/BT	RL-19	83.5	3,625	3,409	Barnes
140 TSX/BT	RL-22	82.0	3,405	3,600	Barnes
140 Nosler BT	RL-22	79.0	3,410	3,615	A-Square
150 SBT	IMR-7828	77.7	3,300	3,623	Sierra
160 SBT	RL-25	78.5	3,250	3,748	Sierra
175 SBT	H870	86.3	3,100	3,730	Sierra
140 Nosler BT	FL		3,450	3,700	A-Square
140 Swift S-Frame	FL		3,325	3,436	Remington
150 Nosler BT	FL		3,180	3,370	Federal
160 Nosler AccuBond	FL		3,100	3,415	Federal
160 Sierra SBT	FL		3,250	3,750	A-Square

7mm Mauser (7x57mm)

Historical Notes: Developed by Mauser as a military cartridge, the 7x57mm was introduced in 1892. Shortly afterward, this caliber was adopted by the Spanish government and chambered in a limited quantity of Model 92 Mauser bolt-action rifles. In 1893, Spain adopted a new model Mauser rifle in this same cartridge. This rifle has been called the Spanish Mauser ever since, although it was also adopted by Mexico and a number of South American countries. Remington chambered its rolling block and Lee rifles for the 7mm about 1897, and later the Model 30. The Winchester Model 54 and 70 also chambered it. Recently, the Ruger Model 77 and Winchester Featherweight bolt-action, plus the Ruger No. 1 single-shot, offer the 7mm as standard.

Also, most European-made bolt-action rifles and combination guns chamber the 7mm Mauser, as do many custom-made rifles each year.

General Comments: Although originally a military cartridge, the 7x57mm Mauser has proven to be one of the best all-round sporting rounds ever developed. It is particularly useful in lightweight rifles, because it delivers good killing power with moderate recoil. It has been used successfully on every species of big game on earth. However, it is no dangerous-game cartridge in the true sense of the term. Its success in the field is due largely to the ability of the hunters who have used it. Ballistically, it is only slightly less powerful than the .270 Winchester or .280 Remington. It is adequate for most American big game, but is perhaps on the light side for large bear or moose. The 7mm Mauser was once discontinued by American gun manufacturers (about 1940) due to lack of popularity. Since the end of World War II, it has become increasingly common, due to the influx of surplus 7mm military rifles. The wide selection of 7mm bullets now available for handloading has also contributed to an increase in popularity. The 7x57mm Mauser is commercially loaded by all domestic and most foreign ammunition manufacturers.

7mm Mauser (7x57mm) Loading Data and Factory Ballistics

Bullet (grains/type)	Powder	Grains	Velocity	Energy	Source/Comments
100 HP	W748	52.6	3,300	2,419	Hornady
115 SP	IMR 3031	46	3,000	2,299	Speer
120 SP	IMR 4064	46	2,900	2,241	Hornady
130 SP	IMR 4350	52	2,850	2,345	Speer
139 SP	IMR 4064	45	2,800	2,420	Hornady
150 SP	IMR 4064	41.5	2,700	2,429	Sierra, Nosler, Hornady
160 Sierra SPBT	RL-22	50.0	2,690	2,570	Hodgdon
175 SP	IMR 4895	42	2,500	2,430	Hornady
175 SP	IMR 4064	39	2,450	2,333	Nosler, Sierra
140 SP	FL		2,660	2,199	Factory load
145 SP	FL		2,690	2,334	Factory load
154 SP	FL		2,690	2,475	Factory load
175 SP	FL		2,440	2,313	Factory load

.284 Winchester

Historical Notes: The .284 was introduced by Winchester, in 1963, for its Model 88 lever-action and Model 100 semi-auto rifles. Both have since been discontinued. This is the first American commercial cartridge to have a rebated, or undercut, rim of smaller diameter than the body of the case, though British and European designers used this type of case years ago. For a short time, the Savage Model 99 lever-action and Browning's BLR were available in .284. No major gun makers now offer this chambering.

General Comments: The .284 Winchester has the rim diameter of the .30-06 and the body diameter of the belted magnums. This provides increased case capacity in a relatively short case. The cartridge is designed for short actions and will increase the performance of these short, light rifles. Ballistics are practically identical to the .280 Remington. There is no difference in killing power, range, or capability between the two (except in some gun writers' imaginations!). The .284 Winchester should be a good long-range cartridge for any North American big game. It could also be adapted for varmint shooting. This cartridge has recently staged a well-deserved comeback and continues to prosper, particularly as a basis for short-action wildcats.

.284 Winchester Loading Data and Factory Ballistics

Bullet (grains/type)	Powder	Grains	Velocity	Energy	Source/Comments
100 HP	IMR 4350	60.5	3,200	2,274	Sierra

Bullet (grains/type)	Powder	Grains	Velocity	Energy	Source/Comments
120 Hornady SP	RL-19	60.5	3,265	2,840	Hodgdon
130 SP	IMR 4350	58	3,100	2,775	Speer
140 SP	IMR 4350	55	3,000	2,799	Hornady
140 SP	IMR 4895	46	2,800	2,438	Sierra
145 Speer SP	RL-19	55.0	2,940	2,780	Hodgdon
150 SP	IMR 4350	53.5	2,800	2,612	Sierra
160 Sierra SPBT	RL-19	54.0	2,885	2,955	Hodgdon
175 SP	IMR 4350	50	2,600	2,627	Hornady, Sierra, Speer
150 SP	FL		2,860	2,724	Winchester factory load

7mm Remington Short Action Ultra Mag

Historical Notes: In 2001, Remington introduced the 7mm Remington Short Action Ultra Mag cartridge as a competitor to Winchester's 7mm Winchester Short Magnum. Ballistic performance of the Remington and Winchester offerings is similar. The 7mm Remington Short Action Ultra Magnum easily exceeds or equals 7mm Remington Magnum performance, while fitting into easy-carrying, fast-handling rifles such as the short-action Remington Model 7.

General Comments: Based on a shortened .300 Ultra Magnum case, which is itself derived from a slightly modified .404 Jeffery cartridge of African fame, the 7mm Remington Short Action Ultra Magnum is slightly shorter and smaller in diameter than its Winchester counterpart. Short, fat cases burn powder very efficiently, since the primer's flash ignites a larger area of the packed gunpowder. The case is unbelted and headspaces on the shoulder for improved shoulder tolerances. Remington barrels for this cartridge use a twist rate of 1:9¼. Shooters are cautioned never to fire a 7mm Remington Short Action Ultra Magnum in a 7mm WSM-chambered rifle, as the headspace would be excessive, leading to possible injury or firearms damage.

7mm Remington Short Action Ultra Mag Loading Data and Factory Ballistics

Bullet (grains/type)	Powder	Grains	Velocity	Energy	Source/Comments
120 Nosler Ballistic Tip	H414	64.5	3,424	3,120	Nosler
140 Nosler Partition	RL-19	62.0	3,147	3,075	Nosler
Nosler 150 Partition	IMR-4350	58.5	3,047	3,089	Nosler
Nosler 160 AccuBond	RL-22	59.0	2,942	3,072	Nosler
Nosler 175 Partition	RL-22	59.0	2,851	3,155	Nosler
140 PSP	FL		3,175	3,133	Remington factory load
150 PSP	FL		3,110	3,221	Remington factory load
160 Nosler Partition	FL		2,960	3,112	Remington factory load

7mm Winchester Short Magnum (7mm WSM)

Historical Notes: Introduced in 2001 and intended for ranks of riflemen preferring 7mm calibers, the 7mm WSM is crafted from the instantly popular .300 WSM case, necked down to accept .284-inch diameter bullets. Also, the 7mm WSM shoulder was lengthened by .038-inch to prevent any possibility of chambering in a .270

WSM rifle. The 7mm WSM is the modern short-action equivalent of the 7mm Remington Magnum, a cartridge that showed untold numbers of hunters just how effective a flat-shooting, highly efficient .284 cartridge could be for North American and large African plains game. SSK Industries also rebarrels the AR-10 self-loading rifle for 7mm WSM.

General Comments: For efficient and consistent powder burning, the 7mm WSM continues the short-fat cartridge case geometry Winchester first popularized in the .300 WSM, a benchrest-proven concept for nearly three decades. Omitting a belt on the case, the 7mm WSM headspaces on the shoulder, which should provide for tighter headspacing tolerances and bettered accuracy potential. Shooters are cautioned never to fire the slightly shorter, physically similar 7mm Remington Short Action Ultra Magnum in a .270 WSM- or 7mm WSM-chambered rifles, as the .270 bore is smaller and the headspace would be excessive, leading to possible injury or firearms damage.

This cartridge and all its Winchester Short Magnum siblings become embroiled in a legal battle, and the end result was a less than enthusiastic appeal on the part of other manufacturers to offer rifles and/or ammunition for sale. However, unlike the Winchester Super Short Magnums that are collecting dust on the shelves or in shooters' gun racks, the WSM line still enjoys moderate appeal, especially the .270 and .300 offerings.

7mm Winchester Short Magnum Loading Data and Factory Ballistics

Bullet (grains/type)	Powder	Grains	Velocity	Energy	Source/Comments
140 BST	FL		3,225	3,233	Winchester/Olin
150 P Pt	FL		3,200	3,410	Winchester/Olin
160 Fail Safe	FL		2,990	3,176	Winchester/Olin
140 BST	WXR	70.0	3,200	3,184	Winchester/Olin 61,500 psi
140 SP	WXR	66.5	3,220	3,224	Winchester/Olin 63,900 psi
150 SP	WXR	68.0	3,145	3,295	Winchester/Olin 61,600 psi
160 BST	WXR	60.5	2,915	3,020	Winchester/Olin 61,700 psi

7mm Remington Ultra Mag

Historical Notes: The 7mm Remington Ultra Mag draws upon a large-capacity case to become a serious contender for the title of flattest-shooting factory big-game cartridge on the planet. The performance-driven popularity of the .300 Remington Ultra Magnum cartridge, following its 1999 introduction, led Remington to offer a family of cartridges based on this beltless, magnum-sized case. Shooting flatter than the 7mm STW, the 7mm Ultra Mag. delivers a flatter trajectory with a 140-grain bullet than a .22-250 does with a 55-grain bullet. At 300 yards, it produces 24 percent more energy than the standard 7mm Remington Magnum, and 12 percent greater energy than the 7mm STW.

General Comments: In suitably equipped rifles, such as the Remington 700, and in the hands of a skillful hunter, the 7mm Ultra Magnum is a superb choice for long-range antelope, deer, and sheep. Except for bullet diameter, the technical details of this cartridge are identical to the .300 Remington Ultra Mag cartridges.

7 mm Remington Ultra Mag Load Data/Factory Ballistics

Bullet (grains/type)	Powder	Grains	Velocity	Energy	Source/Comments
120 Nosler Ballistic Tip	RL-25	95.5	3,639	3,525	Nosler
140 Nosler Partition	Retumbo	96.0	3,485	3,771	Nosler
150 Nosler Partition	Retumbo	94.0	3,368	3,774	Nosler
160 Nosler AccuBond	RL-25	88.0	3,261	3,774	Nosler
175 Nosler Partition	Retumbo	92.0	3,164	3,885	Nosler
140 PSP	FL		3,425	3,646	Remington factory load

Bullet (grains/type)	Powder	Grains	Velocity	Energy	Source/Comments
140 Nosler Partition	FL		3,425	3,646	Remington factory load
160 Nosler Partition	FL		3,200	3,637	Remington factory load

.30-30 Winchester
(.30-30 WCF/.30 Winchester)

Historical Notes: The .30-30, or .30 WCF, was the first American small-bore, smokeless powder sporting cartridge. It was designed by Winchester and first marketed in early 1895 as one of the chamberings available for the Model 1894 lever-action rifle. The original loading used a 160-grain soft-point bullet and 30 grains of smokeless powder, thus the name .30-30 for a .30-caliber bullet and 30 grains of powder. This is really an older way of describing a caliber based on black-powder usage. Muzzle velocity was 1,970 fps.

It was adapted to the Winchester Model 54 bolt-action, as well as various versions of the original 1894 action, such as the models 55 and 64. Marlin chambered it in the Model 1893 lever-action, the improved Model 36, and the Model 336. At one time, the Savage Model 99 lever-action was made in .30-30, and Savage also chambered the old Model 40 bolt-action for it, as well as the Model 340. The Remington rolling block and Winchester single-shot were also at one time available in this caliber. In Europe, the .30-30 is known as the 7.62x51R and is popular in single-shot and combination guns. Modern factory loads in this caliber are assembled with 150- or 170-grain bullets. Despite the designation, .308-inch diameter bullets are used.

General Comments: The .30-30 has long been the standard American deer cartridge, and it is still the yardstick by which the performance of all others is compared. To say that a cartridge is in the .30-30 class means that it is suitable for game up to and including deer and black bear at moderate ranges. Its popularity is due to the fact that this cartridge has always been available in short, light rifles or carbines. It is extremely popular in Mexico and Latin America, so much so that, in many backcountry areas, the treinta-treinta, it is the only high-powered cartridge anyone knows or has heard of. It was, and to a large extent still is, the most popular small-bore sporting cartridge.

Despite this popularity, the .30-30 is no wonder cartridge, with regard to accuracy or killing power. For larger deer, the 170-grain bullet is a good choice, and the 170-grain Nosler Partition or the Barnes 150-grain XPF are the best choices for those who wish to tackle elk. For smaller species, 125- to 150-grain bullets give adequate penetration with reduced recoil. In no case is it suited for shots beyond about 200 yards. Although sometimes reloaded with bullets of 80 to 110 grains, it has neither the velocity nor the accuracy (in most rifles) to make a very good varmint round. Despite its faults, it is a perfectly adequate deer cartridge if properly used by a good shot. Frank Barnes' first modern high-powered rifle was a .30-30 Model 1894 Winchester carbine, and it served for many useful and game-filled years. All major domestic ammunition companies offer this cartridge.

Several attempts to increase the terminal performance and external ballistics of a lever gun in .30-30 Winchester have been attempted. Examples would be the 7x30 Waters, the .307 Winchester and the .308 Marlin Express. However, none have been as successful as Hornady's LEVERevoultion line of ammunition for the .30-30 Winchester. Using a special powder formulated by Hodgdon and high BC bullets with a soft rubber tip, this line of factory loaded ammunition has brought about the single largest advancement in lever-action rifles in more than a century.

.30-30 Winchester Loading Data and Factory Ballistics

Bullet (grains/type)	Powder	Grains	Velocity	Energy	Source/Comments
100 SP	IMR 3031	33	2,600	1,394	Speer
110 Speer FP	H335	38.0	2,684	1,755	Hodgdon
125 Sierra JFP	RL-7	30.0	2,630	1,920	Hodgdon
150 Sierra JFP	RL-15	36.0	2,450	1,995	Hodgdon

.30-30 Winchester Loading Data and Factory Ballistics

Bullet (grains/type)	Powder	Grains	Velocity	Energy	Source/Comments
170 Hornady JFP	RL-15	34.1	2,330	2,045	Hodgdon
150 SP	FL		2,390	1,902	Factory load
170 SP	FL		2,200	1,827	Factory load
55 Accelerator	FL		3,400	1,412	Remington Factory Load
140 Mono-Flex	FL		2,465	1,889	Hornady Factory Load

With the exception of Hornady FTX and Mono-Flex bullets, always use round- or flat-pointed bullets in tubular magazine rifles; sharp-pointed bullets might set off other cartridges in the magazine.

.30-378 Weatherby

Historical Notes: The .30-378 Weatherby Magnum is the .378 Weatherby Magnum case necked to .30-caliber. It was created by Roy Weatherby during the 1950s, upon request by the U.S. government for determination of the resistance of various types of armor plating to penetration by high-speed projectiles. Using special lightweight bullets made by Speer Bullet Company, Weatherby managed to exceed a muzzle velocity of 6000 fps during his tests. Years later, while still a wildcat, the .30-378 became popular among members of the Original 1,000-Yard Rifle Club, in Pennsylvania, where it was used to shoot the world's record group at that distance. After several years of coaxing by firearms writer Layne Simpson, Roy's son, Ed Weatherby, decided to add the cartridge to the Weatherby lineup, in 1996. During that year, Norma started loading the ammunition for Weatherby, and Weatherby began to offer its Mark V rifle in that chambering. The first rifle was auctioned off with the proceeds going to Ed Weatherby's favorite charity, while the second rifle was presented to Layne Simpson. Much to the surprise of everyone (except Simpson), the .30-378 went on to become the best-selling cartridge in the Mark V rifle for several years and continues to sell at a steady pace.

General Comments: The .30-378 case can hold more than 120 grains of powder, compared to about 90 grains for the .300 Weatherby. With the advent of new slower-burning powders, increased capacity promises a useful advantage to the handloader. (Recent availability of 250-grain match-grade bullets served to increase potential benefit and demand for a chambering with increased powder capacity.) The .30-378 Weatherby certainly delivers on this promise. It is a simple matter to load 250-grain Sierra MatchKing bullets to produce almost 3000 fps muzzle velocity, without exceeding .30-06 pressure levels—from a 26-inch barrel! Lighter bullets can be driven faster, but with those this chambering offer less advantage over standard .300 Magnum chamberings. When bullets lighter than 200 grains are fired from a 26-inch barrel, this cartridge is only marginally superior to the .300 Weatherby. Recently, tests have demonstrated that lighter bullet (150- to 180-grain) ballistics are markedly improved by use of slower rifling twist (1:13 to 1:15 works well), compared to the factory 1:10 twist. However, with 30-inch barrels installed, ballistic difference is significant with all bullet weights.

Those looking for the ultimate long-range hunting rifle for smaller species might give this chambering a hard look. A single-shot rifle equipped with a 30-inch tube offers reasonable handling ease and, if chambered for this cartridge, would deliver huge doses of energy to a distant target with the flattest trajectory available. Accurate Arms data shows the 250-grain MatchKing generating the same muzzle energy as the .458 Winchester Magnum, when loaded to about the same pressure! So long as a good barrel is properly cleaned and not subjected to excessive rapid-fire shooting, its accuracy can remain good enough up to 2,000 rounds for long-range target shooting, and perhaps 2,500 to 3,000 rounds for big-game hunting.

.30-378 Weatherby Loading Data/Factory Ballistics (26-inch barrel)

Bullet (grains/type)	Powder	Grains	Velocity	Energy	Source/Comments
180 Barnes-X	AA 8700	118.0	3,283	4,310	Accurate
200 Nosler Partition	AA 8700	117.0	3,208	4,570	Accurate

Bullet (grains/type)	Powder	Grains	Velocity	Energy	Source/Comments
200 Sierra HPBT	AA 8700	117.0	3,163	4,440	Accurate
220 Sierra HPBT	AA 8700	115.0	3,050	4,545	Accurate
250 Sierra HPBT	AA 8700	111.0	2,954	4,840	Accurate
165 Ballistic Tip	FL		3,500	4,483	Weatherby
180-gr. AccuBond	FL		3,400	4,619	Weatherby
200-gr. Partition	FL		3,160	4,434	Weatherby

.300 AAC Blackout

Historical Notes: The intent behind the .300 AAC Blackout was to offer a .30-caliber cartridge that would function in AR-15 rifles without a reduction in magazine capacity, that was also compatible with the standard bolt, and that would offer both supersonic and subsonic performance. The .300 AAC Blackout was developed by Advanced Armament Corporation (AAC), a subsidiary of the Freedom Group, and is almost identical to the .300 Whisper that was originally developed by J.D. Jones. Another way of looking at the .300 AAC Blackout is as a standardization of the .300/.221 Wildcat cartridge. AAC standardized the case dimensions and submitted the cartridge to SAAMI, which has established the cartridge with a maximum average operating pressure of 55,000 psi.

General Comments: From a supersonic standpoint, the .300 AAC Blackout offers performance similar to the 7.62x39 Soviet cartridge. Hunters can expect performance on game to be similar to the 7.62x39 or the .30-30 Winchester. One thing hunters should recognize is that heavy match bullets at subsonic velocities will not expand in game animals. However, LeHigh Defense, working with J.D. Jones, has developed a subsonic bullet load that does offer expansion and good terminal performance at subsonic velocities.

Much of the appeal of this cartridge is its subsonic performance, but there is some contention that optimum performance from an AR-15 is unattainable with either supersonic or subsonic suppressed loads. It is also arguable that a single twist rate offers optimal stabilization with both a 125-grain bullet at 2200 fps and a 220-grain bullet at 1050 fps. AAC suggests that a 1:8 twist be used, and most commercially offered rifles will come so equipped. DPMS and Bushmaster will offer AR-15 rifles in .300 AAC Blackout, and Remington will offer three factory loads. All three of these companies are sister companies to AAC under the Freedom Group banner. AAC is offering both Remington 700 .300 AAC Blackout replacement barrels and loading dies.

300 AAC Blackout Loading Data and Factory Ballistics

Bullet (grains/type)	Powder	Grains	Velocity	Energy	Source/Comments
110 V-Max	IMR 4227	19.5C	2,130	1,107	Hodgdon
115 Berger TGT FB	H110	20.0	2,348	1,407	Hodgdon
125 Nosler BT	Lil'Gun	20.5	2,393	1,598	Hodgdon
135 Sierra HPBT	Lil'Gun	18.0	2,127	1,355	Hodgdon
220 Sierra HPBT	IMR 4198	11.5	1,036	524	Hodgdon
220 Sierra HPBT	AA1680	11.2	1,010	498	AAC

300 AAC Blackout Loading Data and Factory Ballistics

Bullet (grains/type)	Powder	Grains	Velocity	Energy	Source/Comments
220 Sierra HPBT	W 296	9.9	1,050	538	Hodgdon
125 Match	FL		2,220	1,367	Remington Factory Load
125 Accutip	FL		2,230	1,380	Remington Factory Load
220 OTM	FL		1,010	498	Remington factory Load

.300 Winchester Magnum

Historical Notes: This cartridge was introduced in 1963 for the Winchester Model 70 bolt-action rifle. Rifles chambered for the .300 Winchester Magnum have since been introduced by most domestic and European manufacturers.

General Comments: Arrival of the .300 Winchester Magnum was rather anti-climatic, because everyone had been predicting it from the day the .338 Winchester Magnum was brought out in 1958. The .30-338 wildcat quickly followed. The newer .300 Winchester Magnum has a slightly longer body (by about .12-inch), and a shorter neck than its predecessors. This short neck is considered a poor feature, as it means the heavy bullets have to seat back into the powder space quite a bit. The .308 Norma Magnum, introduced in 1960, is nearly identical to the .338 Winchester Magnum necked down. If that chambering had not been offered before Winchester was ready to produce its own .30-caliber magnum, it is possible the company would simply have necked the .338 to 30-caliber. In any event, the .300 Winchester Magnum is a fine long-range, big-game cartridge in the same class as the .300 Weatherby and suitable for any North American species. Actual factory-load ballistics may be closer to .300 Weatherby Magnum ballistics than published data suggests. With cartridges in this class and above, recoil becomes a factor for many shooters. It is loaded by all domestic and many foreign ammunition manufacturers.

.300 Winchester Magnum Loading Data and Factory Ballistics

Bullet (grains/type)	Powder	Grains	Velocity	Energy	Source/Comments
110 HP	IMR 4350	80	3,600	3,166	Hornady, Sierra
125 SP	IMR 4350	77	3,400	3,209	Sierra
130 SP	IMR 4064	66	3,300	3,144	Speer, Hornady
150 SP	IMR 4350	76	3,300	3,628	Sierra
150 SP	IMR 4895	62	3,150	3,306	Speer, Sierra
150 SP	IMR 4350	76	3,200	3,412	Speer, Sierra
165 SP	IMR 4831	76	3,200	3,753	Speer, Sierra
180 SP	IMR 4350	71	3,000	3,598	Sierra
190 SP	IMR 4831	74	3,150	4,187	Speer
200 SP	IMR 4350	68	2,950	3,866	Nosler
220 SP	IMR 4350	60	2,500	3,054	Hornady, Sierra
150 SP	FL		3,290	3,605	Factory load
180 SP	FL		2,960	3,501	Factory load
200 SP	FL		2,825	3,544	Factory load
220 SP	FL		2,680	3,508	Factory load

.30 Carbine (.30 M1 Carbine)

Historical Notes: In 1940, the U.S. Ordnance Department concluded that a light carbine would have advantages over the .45-caliber pistol in many combat situations. Various designs were submitted by a number of private manufacturers and, in the end, Winchester's offering was selected. The semi-auto .30 M1 Carbine was officially adopted, in 1941. The cartridge, a modification of the .32 Winchester Self-Loading round of 1906, was hardly a revolutionary new design, but it served the purpose. About the same time, the Germans developed their StG 44 assault rifle and the 7.92mm Kurz cartridge. The M1 Carbine is not an assault rifle. The military insists it was designed to fulfill a different purpose.

For a few years, starting in 1966, the Marlin Model 62 Levermatic was available in .30 Carbine. Iver Johnson, Plainfield, and others manufactured several versions of the M1 Carbine for the sporting trade. Federal, Remington, and Winchester load soft-point sporting ammunition. One version of the Ruger Blackhawk single-action revolver is available in .30 Carbine.

General Comments: In mid-1963, the government began releasing .30-caliber M1 Carbines for sale to civilians through the National Rifle Association at the moderate price of around $20. Thousands of these guns are, as a result, used for sporting purposes. The .30 Carbine cartridge is in the same class as the .32-20 WCF. It is wholly a small-game and varmint number, despite contrary claims by those who love the short, light, handy M1 Carbine. The accuracy of the carbine, combined with the ballistics of the cartridge, limit the effective sporting accuracy range to about 150 yards maximum.

This book's original author used an M1 Carbine to hunt small game and deer as early as 1943, before most people could get their hands on one, so he had a pretty good idea of the capability of the cartridge. Remember that the .32 Winchester Self-Loading round became obsolete, in 1920, because it was more or less useless for sporting purposes; the .30 Carbine was derived from it and shares the same shortcomings. Because of inadequate energy, the .30 Carbine is illegal for deer hunting in most states. It is, however, effective against the smaller deer species, when shots are at short range. It is ideal for hunting smaller game, such as peccary. Had the military chosen to adopt this round with a modern, full-pressure standard, performance would have been about 40-percent better, and we might have a different opinion.

.30 Carbine Loading Data and Factory Ballistics

Bullet (grains/type)	Powder	Grains	Velocity	Energy	Source/Comments
85 Sierra RN	H110	17.5	2,458	1,140	Hodgdon
100	H-110	14.5	1,950	845	Speer
100	H-110	16.5	2,200	1,075	Hornady
110 SP	H-110	14	1,900	882	Hornady, Speer
110 FMJ	FL		1,900	882	Military load
110 SP	FL		1,990	967	Factory load

.300 Weatherby Magnum

Historical Notes: The .300 Weatherby Magnum is the most popular and well-known cartridge of the Weatherby line. At the same time, it is one of the most controversial. It was developed in 1944. Commercial ammunition has been available since 1948, under the Weatherby label. Weatherby brand ammunition is loaded by Norma of Sweden. The Weatherbys were the only U.S. rifles chambered for this round on a commercial basis, but it is a popular caliber among custom rifle makers. In 1989, Remington offered the Model 700 Classic in .300 Weatherby, and other makers have since followed suit. Recently, several ammo manufacturers have begun offering ammunition in this caliber.

General Comments: Until the advent of the .30-378 Weatherby, the .300 Weatherby Magnum was the biggest of the commercial .300 belted magnums. Barrel life can be short, some might classify recoil as severe, and ballistics suffer greatly when shorter barrels are tried. None of these limitations matter to many who use it strictly for big-game hunting and seldom fire the round more than a few dozen times a year. It can be adapted to long-range varmint shooting, if one can develop an accurate enough load, but it is not very flexible in that regard. For the hunter who wants one rifle suitable for any species of non-dangerous big game worldwide, the .300 Weatherby Magnum is an excellent choice. However, because of caliber restrictions, local game laws may prohibit its use, even against non-dangerous species. This is another case of archaic regulations, where the law might allow one to use an entirely inappropriate loading from a much less powerful big-bore, when, given the right choice of bullets, the .300 WM would be much more effective and humane.

.300 Weatherby Magnum Loading Data and Factory Ballistics

Bullet (grains/type)	Powder	Grains	Velocity	Energy	Source/Comments
110 HP	IMR 4064	79.5	3,800	3,528	Hornady, Sierra
125 SP	IMR 4831	87.5	3,500	3,401	Sierra
150 SP	H-380	77	3,300	3,628	Sierra
150 SP	IMR 4350	80.5	3,200	3,412	Hornady, Speer
165 SP	IMR 4831	82	3,200	3,753	Speer, Sierra
180 SP	IMR 4350	76.5	3,000	3,598	Hornady, Speer, Nosler, Sierra
180 SP	MRP	84	3,100	3,842	Speer
200 SP	IMR 4350	75	2,900	3,736	Speer, Sierra
220 SP	H-450	77	2,800	3,831	Hornady
250 SP	IMR 7828	69	2,350	3,066	Barnes
150 SP	FL		3,600	4,316	Factory load
165 SPBT	FL		3,450	4,360	Factory load
180 SP	FL		3,300	4,352	Factory load
190 SPBT	FL		3,030	3,873	Factory load
220 SP	FL		2,905	4,122	Factory load

30 Nosler — *NEW*

Historical Notes:	In 2016, Nosler rolled out the newest member of its cartridge family, the 30 Nosler. The 30 Nosler meets the velocity of the .300 Weatherby, headspaces on the shoulder like a .300 RUM, has an efficient powder column like the .300 WSM and fits in the same standard-length action of a .300 Win. Mag. The 30 Nosler is a SAAMI-standardized cartridge, and Nosler will be supporting this new cartridge with Nosler brass, Trophy Grade ammunition and the full line of M48 rifles in 26-inch barrel configurations.
	Designed with a maximum COAL of 3.340 inches, the .308-caliber, rebated-rim centerfire rifle cartridge has a case capacity of 88 grains of water. All three of Nosler's name-brand cartridges — the 26 Nosler, 28 Nosler and 30 Nosler — are based on the same .404 Jeffrey parent case. Although the 26 and 28 Nosler share the same cartridge case dimensions, the 30 Nosler has a slightly shorter shoulder length dimension than the 26 and 28.
General Comments:	Initial offerings in Nosler's Trophy Grade Ammunition line were 180-grain AccuBonds and 210-grain AccuBond LRs (Long Range). When fired out of a 26-inch barrel, the company claimed of muzzle velocity of 3,200 fps for the former and 3,000 fps for the latter. For 180-grain bullets in Nosler loadings, that's better than the muzzle velocities of the .300 Weatherby Magnum (3,175 fps), the .300 Win. Mag. (2,950 fps) and the .300 H&H Mag. (2,950 fps), and just behind the .300 RUM (3,250 fps).
	The 30 Nosler is well behaved with nearly all powders of proper burn rate for the bullet being loaded. Anything from Retumbo up to H4831 will work well, with IMR 7828 and RL 22 being a couple of the best. As a tip, adjust your sizing die to just barely bump the shoulder back between firings, and case life can be extended significantly.

Bullet (grains/type)	Powder	Grains	Velocity	Energy	Source/Comments
180 AccuBond	NA	NA	3,200	4,092	Factory Load
210 AccuBond LR	NA	NA	3,000	4,196	Factory Load

.30-40 Krag (.30 Army)

Historical Notes: The .30 U.S. Army, or .30-40 Krag—the first United States small-bore military cartridge—was adopted in 1892. (The first smokeless sporting cartridge, the .30-30, did not arrive until three years later, in 1895.)

The Winchester high-wall single-shot was the first commercial rifle in the United States produced for a small-bore, smokeless-powder cartridge. This happened when the .30-40 Krag was added to the available calibers, in 1893. The Remington-Lee bolt-action, Remington rolling block, and Winchester Model 95 lever-action and high-wall single-shot were the first commercial sporting rifles to offer this chambering. No commercial rifles used the cartridge from 1936 to 1973. From 1973 until 1977, the Ruger No. 3 single-shot was chambered for the .30-40 Krag, thus stimulating a renewed interest in the cartridge. A rimless version headstamped as .30 USA and loaded by United Metallic Cartridge was offered for use in the Blake rifle.

General Comments: The .30-40 Krag—.30-caliber/40 grains of the original smokeless powder load—holds the unusual distinction of being the cartridge used to take what was, until recently, the world's record Rocky Mountain elk, in 1899. This cartridge has retained its popularity, primarily because large numbers of fine sporting conversions of the Krag military rifles and carbines chambered for it are still in use. This speaks highly for both cartridge and gun.

Although not quite as powerful as either the .30-06 or the .308 Winchester, the .30-40 is well suited for use against North American big game. Just as with any cartridge, marksmanship and bullet choice are important, especially when going after the biggest and the meanest species on this continent. The Krag earned its reputation with the 220-grain loading, but it can be loaded to great advantage with lighter bullets for smaller species.

Interestingly, most authorities consider the 1895 Winchester chambering to be safe with loads at a somewhat higher pressure than the Krag rifle. However, both actions have limitations, and one should be particularly circumspect in this regard. Bountiful loading data can be found in current manuals. The .30-40 is the basis of an entire genre of powerful Ackley Improved chamberings particularly suited to strong single-shot rifles. Winchester is the only remaining manufacturer of this ammunition. Only the 180-grain bullet is still offered.

.30-40 Krag Loading Data and Factory Ballistics

Bullet (grains/type)	Powder	Grains	Velocity	Energy	Source/Comments
100 SP	H-322	45	3,000	1,999	Speer
110 SP	IMR 4320	47	2,700	1,781	Sierra, Speer
125 SP	IMR 4895	44.5	2,600	1,877	Sierra
130 SP	IMR 4064	45.5	2,900	2,428	Hornady, Speer
150 SP	IMR 4895	40	2,400	1,919	Nosler, Sierra
165 SP	IMR 4350	47	2,500	2,290	Hornady, Nosler, Sierra
180 SP	IMR 4350	46	2,450	2,400	Nosler, Sierra, Speer
180 SP	IMR 4895	39	2,200	1,935	Sierra
200 SP	IMR 3031	34	2,100	1,959	Nosler, Speer, Sierra
220 SP	IMR 4350	42	2,100	2,155	Hornady, Speer, Nosler
180 SP	FL		2,430	2,360	Factory load

Bullet (grains/type)	Powder	Grains	Velocity	Energy	Source/Comments
220 SP	FL		2,200	2,360	Factory load

.300 Holland & Holland Magnum (.300 H&H Super)

Historical Notes: The .300 H&H Magnum was introduced in 1925, by the British firm of Holland & Holland as "Holland's Super 30." The Western Cartridge Co., the first American company to load this round commercially, offered it here, in 1925. No American-made commercial rifles were chambered for the .300 H&H until 12 years after its introduction. However, Griffin & Howe and other custom rifle makers turned out rifles for it almost as soon as the British. In 1935, Ben Comfort won the 1,000-yard Wimbledon Cup Match with this cartridge and, overnight, it became a sensation. The Model 70 Winchester was chambered for the .300 H&H in 1937, and the Model 721 and succeeding Model 700 Remingtons were also available in this chambering. Most European bolt-action rifles chambered it as standard.

General Comments: Since 1935, the .300 H&H has enjoyed a limited popularity in the United States. Many shooters consider it the best all-round .30-caliber available to the American hunter. Others insist it is hardly better than the .30-06. Regardless of which side one favors, this is an accurate cartridge and adequate for any North American big game. Its most useful range is for elk on up, but it is also a very fine long-range cartridge for antelope, sheep, or goats. It is popular in Africa as an all-round caliber for plains game. Lately, its popularity has suffered considerably from competition with the .300 Weatherby and .300 Winchester Magnums. It is no longer used for match competition. Derived from the earlier .375 H&H, the .300 H&H is the direct progenitor of an entire family of belted magnums. With modern powders and best handloads, the .300 H&H is very close ballistically to even the biggest .300 Magnums. Winchester, Remington, and Federal all load this cartridge.

.300 Holland & Holland Magnum Loading Data and Factory Ballistics

Bullet (grains/type)	Powder	Grains	Velocity	Energy	Source/Comments
110 HP	IMR 4350	76	3,600	3,166	Sierra, Hornady
130 SP	IMR 4320	64	3,400	3,338	Hornady
150 SP	IMR 4831	73	3,300	3,628	Nosler, Sierra, Speer
165 SP	IMR 4350	69	3,100	3,522	Sierra, Speer, Hornady
180 SP	IMR 4831	68	2,900	3,362	Sierra, Speer
190 SP	H-380	65.5	3,000	3,798	Hornady
200 SP	IMR 4831	67.5	2,800	3,483	Sierra, Speer
220 SP	IMR 4350	63	2,700	3,562	Hornady, Sierra
150	FL		3,190	3,390	Factory load
180	FL		2,880	3,315	Factory load
220	FL		2,620	3,350	Factory load

.300 Savage

Historical Notes: Developed and introduced by Savage Arms Co. for the Model 99 lever-action rifle in 1920, the .300 Savage was later chambered in the Savage Models 20 and 40 bolt-actions. The .300 Savage was intended as a cartridge that would work through medium-length actions and deliver ballistics similar to the .30-06. Remington chambered it in the Model 81 autoloader, 760 pump-action, and 722 bolt-action. The cartridge achieved considerable popularity, but has since lost out to the superior .308 Winchester.

General Comments: The .300 Savage provided lever-, pump-action, and semi-auto fans with performance close enough to the .30-06 to make rifles of this type useful for most American big game. The original factory load used a 150-grain bullet and matched the original .30-06 sporting load at 2700 fps. If loaded to original factory pressure levels with IMR-4064, it can significantly but safely exceed that velocity. It is not fully adequate for moose or brown bear, but it is a fine deer and elk cartridge; it is a better choice than the .30-30 for deer under any conditions. The .308 Winchester fulfills the same function as a short-action cartridge and has somewhat more power, so it has gradually replaced the .300 Savage. However, many thousands of .300 Savage-caliber rifles are still in use, so the cartridge will continue to be loaded for many more years. In a bolt-action rifle, it is as accurate as any other .30-caliber. All the major domestic ammunition companies offer this ammunition.

.300 Savage Loading Data and Factory Ballistics

Bullet (grains/type)	Powder	Grains	Velocity	Energy	Source/Comments
100 SP	IMR 4064	46	3,000	1,999	Speer
110 SP	IMR 4895	43	2,800	1,915	Speer, Sierra
110 SP	BL-C2	42	2,800	1,915	Hornady, Speer, Sierra
125 SP	IMR 4895	43.5	2,800	2,177	Sierra
130 SP	IMR 4064	43	2,700	2,105	Speer, Hornady
150 SP	IMR 4064	41.5	2,600	2,252	Sierra, Hornady, Speer
150 SP	IMR 4895	40.5	2,600	2,252	Sierra
150 SP	IMR 4064	44.0	2,800	2,610	Hornady
165 SP	IMR 3031	37.8	2,500	2,290	Hornady, Sierra
180 SP	IMR 4350	46	2,400	2,303	Hornady, Speer
180 SP	IMR 4895	39.5	2,400	2,303	Sierra
150 SP	FL		2,630	2,303	Factory load
180 SP	FL		2,350	2,207	Factory load

.30-06 Springfield
(7.62x63mm/.30 Government M'06)

Historical Notes: The .30-06 Springfield is a United States military cartridge adapted from the .30-03 by employing a lighter, streamlined bullet and making other minor changes. In this it parallels other military cartridge developments of the era, with French and German developments leading the way. It was adopted, in 1906, for the Model 1903 Springfield service rifle, which was based on the Mauser bolt-action system. The Winchester Model 1895 lever-action appears to have been the first sporting rifle chambered for the .30-06. The cartridge was added to the line in 1908. The Remington bolt-action Model 30, introduced in 1921, and the Winchester bolt-action Model 54, brought out in 1925, both offered the .30-06, among other chamberings. The Savage bolt-action Model 40 and 45 Super-Sporter rifles were also so chambered, when introduced in 1928. At present, in addition to the many bolt-action rifles, the Remington Model 7600 pump-action and 7400 semi-auto, as well as the Browning semi-auto, include the .30-06 as standard chamberings. The Ruger No. 1 single-shot rifle is also offered in .30-06. A number of British and

European side-by-side or over/under double rifles can be ordered in this chambering, and so can some European rifle-shotgun combination guns.

General Comments: The .30-06 is undoubtedly the most flexible, useful, all-round big-game cartridge available to the American hunter. For many years, it has been the standard by which all other big-game cartridges have been measured. To say that a cartridge is in the .30-06 class means it is suitable for any game in North America. The secret to success, when using this cartridge, is to select the right bullet for the game and hunting conditions at hand. Lighter bullets of 100 to 130 grains should be used only for varmint and small-game hunting. While these bullets can be driven at impressive velocities (well over 3000 fps), they are designed to expand rapidly on small game and will not penetrate properly on large game. For deer, antelope, goats, sheep, or black or brown bear under most hunting conditions, the 150- or 165-grain bullet is proper and a good compromise for those seeking one load for medium to heavy game. For heavier game, such as elk, moose, or large brown bear, the 165-, 180-, 200-, or 220-grain bullets are the best choice. The '06 performs impressively with handloads using 250-grain bullets. Many experienced hunters consider the 180-grain bullet the most satisfactory all-round loading for the .30-06, because it can be used effectively on anything from deer to the heaviest game under almost any hunting conditions. As a matter of fact, the .30-06 will give a good account on all but the heaviest or most dangerous African or Asiatic species, under average hunting conditions. The 220-grain bullet is generally recommended for African game, although the 180-grain also has a good reputation. With the proper bullet, this cartridge can be adapted to any game or hunting situation in North or South America, whether in the mountains, plains, woods, or jungles. Few other cartridges can claim equal versatility.

.30-06 Springfield Loading Data and Factory Ballistics

Bullet (grains/type)	Powder	Grains	Velocity	Energy	Source/Comments
100 SP	IMR 4064	59	3,400	2,568	Speer
110 SP	IMR 4064	54.5	3,300	2,660	Sierra, Hornady
110 SP	H-380	56	3,300	2,660	Sierra
125 SP	IMR 3031	50	3,100	2,668	Sierra
130 SP	IMR 4350	58	3,000	2,599	Hornady, Speer
150 SP	IMR 4350	59	3,000	2,998	Nosler, Speer, Sierra, Hornady
150 SP	IMR 4895	51	2,900	2,802	Nosler
165 SP	IMR 4320	50.5	2,800	2,873	Sierra
180 SP	IMR 4320	48.5	2,700	2,910	Sierra, Nosler
180 SP	IMR 4831	57	2,750	3,023	Speer, Nosler, Sierra
190 SP	IMR 4350	54	2,700	3,076	Hornady, Speer, Sierra
200 SP	IMR 4320	47	2,400	2,559	Nosler, Sierra
220 SP	IMR 4350	50.5	2,400	2,854	Hornady, Sierra, Barnes
220 SP	IMR 4831	54	2,500	3,054	Hornady, Sierra
250 SP	IMR 4831	47	2,100	2,499	Barnes
55 SP	FL (Accelerator)		4,080	2033	Remington factory load
125 SP	FL		3,140	2,736	Factory load
150 SP	FL		2,920	2,839	Factory load
165 SP	FL		2,800	2,873	Factory load
168 HPBT	FL		2,700	2,720	Factory load
180 SP	FL		2,700	2,913	Factory load
220 SP	FL		2,410	2,837	Factory load

.30 Remington AR

Historical Notes: The .30 Remington AR was designed by Remington as a big-game cartridge specifically for the company's R-15 rifle. It was introduced in 2009. Remington engineers started with the .450 Bushmaster case and went from there. A pointed .30-caliber bullet of reasonable weight is longer than a blunt-nosed .45-caliber bullet, so, to keep overall cartridge length compatible with the standard AR-15 magazine, the case was shortened to 1.525 inches from the original 1.7 inches of the Bushmaster design. Back at its base, the .30 AR case starts with a diameter of .500 inch, and from there it tapers to .488 inch at the juncture of the body and shoulder. Neck diameter is .341 inch, and the case has a shoulder angle of 25 degrees.

The AR-15 rifle in .450 Bushmaster utilizes the standard .223 Remington bolt, modified by increasing its bolt face diameter to a nominal .473-inch (same as the .308 Winchester). When this is done, the counter-bore wall or shroud of the bolt becomes rather thin. This is considered a safe modification for that cartridge, because it operates at a maximum chamber pressure level of 38,000 psi (same as the .30-30 Winchester). But, since the .30 AR is loaded to 55,000 psi, Remington opted for additional case rim support. This was accomplished by modifying the larger-diameter AR-10 bolt to fit the AR-15 upper. The face of that bolt is commonly sized for the .473-inch rim diameter of the .308 Winchester, but Remington went one step further by opening it up a bit and increasing the rim diameter of the .30 AR case to .492-inch. By the time the job was done, the only thing the .30 AR case had in common with the .450 Bushmaster case was a base diameter of .500-inch. Remington went with a case rim diameter larger than that for the .450 Bushmaster to prevent a bolt built for that cartridge from being used in an R-15 upper with a .30 AR barrel.

General Comments: With a length of .305-inch, the neck of the .30 Remington AR is capable of exerting plenty of tension on the bullet, a good thing to have on a cartridge designed to survive the rather violent trip it must take from the magazine to the chamber of an autoloading rifle. The short, fat case of rebated rim design has a gross capacity of 44 grains, about 10 grains less than for the .308 Winchester case, or approximately the same as for the .30-30 Winchester case. But, since the .30 AR is loaded to higher chamber pressures than the .30-30, it exceeds the maximum velocity of that cartridge. When the 125-grain Core-Lokt factory load is zeroed three inches high at 100 yards, it will strike about two inches above point of aim at 200 yards and approximately seven inches low at 300, where it is still packing upwards of 1000 ft-lbs of energy. The .30 AR comes close to duplicating the performance of the .300 Savage when both are loaded with a 125-grain or 150 grain bullet.

The true allure of this cartridge is the fact that it turns the AR-15 platform into a true big-game rifle capable of terminal performance identical to that of the .300 Savage with bullets weighing 150 grains or less. It is suitable for deer, black bear, and similarly sized game out to around 300 yards. It is a true gem of a rifle in a compact bolt-action like the model 20 Short from New Ultra Light Arms, and it is suspected that wildcatters will soon neck the .30 Remington AR case up and down, further increasing the versatility of the AR 15 platform.

.30 Remington AR Loading Data and Factory Ballistics

Bullet (grains/type)	Powder	Grains	Velocity	Energy	Source
123 Remington FMJ	FL		2,800	2,141	Remington
125 Remington Core-Lokt	FL		2,800	2,176	Remington
125 Remington Accutip	FL		2,800	2,176	Remington
150 Remington Core-Lokt	FL		2,450	1,998	Remington

.30 Remington AR Loading Data and Factory Ballistics

Bullet (grains/type)	Powder	Grains	Velocity	Energy	Source
110 Barnes Tipped Triple Shock	AA 2200	39.2	3,115	2,369	Accurate Powder
110 Hornady SP	Xterminator	41.7	3,058	2,283	Ramshot Powder
125 Nosler Ballistic Tip	H 335	40.0	2,880	2,301	Richard Mann
150 Nosler Accubond	AA 2200	35.2	2,600	2,251	Richard Mann

.30 T/C (Thompson/Center)

Historical Notes: The .30 T/C was developed by Hornady for Thompson/Center and introduced in that company's Icon rifle. Basically a shortened version of the .308 Winchester case with a sharper 30-degree shoulder angle, it has less powder capacity than that cartridge and yet, due to the utilization of Light Magnum technology previously developed by Hornady for other cartridges, it exceeds in performance standard loadings of the .308 Winchester and equals the performance of the .30-06 Springfield when the three cartridges are loaded with a 150-grain bullet. As of early 2009, only the T/C Icon rifle was chambered for the .30 TC, and only Hornady loads the ammunition.

General Comments: Despite impressive velocities for its size, the .30 T/C is rather an odd duck, to say the least, and this has raised questions about its existence among hunters and shooters. The Icon rifle was introduced with a short action, and had the action been too short to handle the .308 Winchester, the .30 TC would have made sense—but this was not the case. Not only is the short version of the Icon action long enough to handle the .308 Winchester, but that was one of the first chamberings offered in the Icon rifle. And, while it is true that, in its factory loading, the .30 TC delivers higher velocity than standard loadings of the .308 Winchester, it is also true that Light Magnum loadings of the .308 Winchester from Hornady are just as fast. When both are handloaded with bullets of the same weight and to the same chamber pressure, velocity will be a bit lower with the .30 T/C, due to the smaller case capacity.

.30 Thompson/Center Data and Factory Ballistics

Bullet (grains/type)	Powder	Grains	Velocity	Energy	Source
135 Sierra HPBT	H335	47.0	3,127	2,928	Hodgdon
150 Hornady IB	IMR-3031	42.5	2,856	2,714	Hodgdon
165 Barnes TSX	W748	46.0	2,748	2,764	Hodgdon
180 Hornady SP	H335	42.0	2,580	2,658	Hodgdon
150 Hornady SST	FL		3,000	2,994	Hornady

.308 Marlin Express

Historical Notes: In 1982, Winchester introduced rimmed versions of the .308 Winchester and .358 Winchester and called them the .307 Winchester and .356 Winchester, respectively. They became available in a special version of the Winchester Model 94 lever-action rifle, with the receiver sidewalls reinforced to handle higher chamber pressures than are common for the .30-30 Winchester and other cartridges for which that rifle was originally designed. Two loadings of the .307 Winchester were available: a 150-grain deer load at 2760 fps and a 180-grain moose load at 2510 fps. Despite the fact that the new cartridge delivered the same level of energy at 200 yards as the .30-30 at 100 yards, it failed to win the hearts of America's deer hunters and was eventually dropped from the Model 94 rifle.

Many hunting seasons later, those clever chaps at Hornady developed a bullet with a pointed tip soft enough to make it safe to use in lever-action rifles with tubular magazines. Other cartridges such as the .30-30 Winchester, .35 Remington, and .444 Marlin were first to receive the new bullet design, but Hornady eventually got around to the .307 Winchester. In fact, I have a box of .307 Winchester ammunition loaded by Hornady with the new 160-grain Flex-Tip bullet. But all was not perfect with that particular idea. When both weigh the same, a pointed bullet is longer than one with a flat or round nose, and, when the 160-grain FTX bullet was loaded in the .307 Winchester to an overall cartridge length short enough to feed through lever actions such as the Marlin Model 336 and Winchester Model 94, the mouth of the case almost extended out onto the ogive of the bullet. This prompted Hornady technicians to come up with a shortened version of the .307 Winchester called the .308 Marlin Express. And, as its name implies, the new cartridge was introduced in the Marlin Model 336 rifle.

General Comments: Hunters who have used the .307 Winchester on deer, black bear, moose, and other game have often described it as the most effective cartridge to ever become available in the Winchester Model 94 and Marlin Model 336. The .308 Marlin Express is an even better cartridge—at the muzzle of a rifle, the .307 Winchester pretty much duplicates the performance of the fine old .300 Savage cartridge, but its flat-nosed bullet sheds velocity rather quickly and, by the time it reaches 100 yards, the .300 Savage is beginning to pull away in the race. Due to the more streamlined shape of its bullet, the .308 Marlin equals the performance of the .300 Savage at any distance. This is saying a lot, when you consider that there was a time long ago when many hunters considered the .300 Savage plenty of cartridge for use on any game animal in North America, including the grizzly bear. The .308 Marlin will never become as popular in lever-action rifles as the .30-30 Winchester, but, when we gaze into our crystal ball, we see it winning over far more hunters than the .307 Winchester ever did.

.308 Marlin Express Loading Data and Factory Ballistics

Bullet (grains/type)	Powder	Grains	Velocity	Energy	Source
125 Sierra HP/FN	Varget	42.3	2,700	2,021	Hodgdon
130 Speer FN	H335	41.5	2,772	2,216	Hodgdon
150 Hornady RN	H4895	40.5	2,607	2,262	Hodgdon
170 Hornady FN	IMR-4064	39.3	2,416	2,201	Hodgdon
160 Hornady FTX	FL		2,660	2,511	Hornady
140 Hornady Mono-Flex	FL		2,800	2,437	Hornady

7.62x40 WT (Wilson Tactical) —

Historical Notes: Kurt Buchert originated this round as the 7.62x40 USA. Introduced commercially in 2011 by Wilson Combat, the 7.62×40mm Wilson Tactical is a centerfire rifle cartridge that's an accurate, low-recoil .30-caliber round that can be used in AR-15/M4 rifles with minimal changes beyond swapping the barrel. All other standard AR-platform 5.56-caliber components are compatible. The 7.62x40 WT will function reliably with standard unmodified Lancer L5 magazines if downloaded to 17 or 24 rounds. Wilson also has modified Lancer L5 AWM magazines with 18/19 or 28/29 round capacity available.

General Comments: The 7.62x40 WT is based on the 5.56x45 NATO cartridge case, which is shortened to 1.560 inches and then re-sized (single operation) in a standard 7.62x40 WT sizing die. Result: A formed 7.62x40 WT case with a finished overall case length of 1.565 inches. The cartridge is designed for 110- to 150-grain .308-diameter bullets loaded to supersonic velocities, but if chambered in a 1:8 twist barrel, it can also fire heavy bullets at subsonic speeds for suppressed use. After a 7.62x40 WT case has been fired once, it will be fire-formed and provide about 1 grain of additional powder capacity and the potential for another 25 to 50 fps more velocity at comparable pressure levels.

Fired from a 16-inch barrel, the 7.62x40 WT fires a factory 110-grain bullet at 2,534 fps muzzle velocity and a 125-grain bullet at 2,463 fps. A 7.62x39 round with a 123-grain bullet develops 2,320 fps muzzle velocity, a 6.8 SPC 110-grain runs 2,550 fps muzzle velocity, and the 300 Blackout 125-grain load goes 2,275 fps at the muzzle.

Wilson Combat offers complete rifles, upper receivers, barrels and five factory loads for the 7.62x40 WT, but not many other makers have followed suit. U.S. Machine Gun Armory in Utah has begun offering a conversion kit for the Mk 46/M249 in 7.62 WT.

7.62x40 WT Factory Ballistics

Bullet (grains/type)	Powder	Grains	Velocity	Energy	Source/Comments
110 Barnes TTSX	NA	NA	2,400*	1,407	Factory Load
125 Nosler Ballistic Tip	NA	NA	2,350*	1,533	Factory Load
*16-inch barrel					

.308 Winchester (7.62x51mm NATO)

Historical Notes: Introduced by Winchester as a new sporting cartridge in 1952, the .308 is nothing more than the NATO 7.62x51mm military round. This was a very smart move, to tack the Winchester name onto what was sure to become a popular sporting number. Practically every manufacturer of high-powered sporting rifles chambers the .308, since it will work through medium- or standard-length actions. The Model 70 bolt-action and 88 lever-action Winchesters were the first American sporting rifles so chambered. It was adopted as the official U.S. military rifle cartridge in 1954, although guns for it were not ready until 1957.

General Comments: In power, the .308 Winchester is superior to the .300 Savage and almost equal to the .30-06. It delivers about 100 fps less muzzle velocity than the larger .30-06 with any given bullet weight. Most authorities consider the .308 suitable for most North American big game, although it's on the light side for moose or brown bear. This chambering is a favorite of target shooters and has a reputation for excellent accuracy. It is the basis for a number of wildcat cartridges that have been adopted as factory chamberings: .243 Winchester, 6.5-08, 7mm-08 Remington, .358 Winchester, and the rimmed versions of the .307 Winchester and .356 Winchester. All major domestic and foreign ammunition companies offer this cartridge.

.308 Winchester Loading Data and Factory Ballistics

Bullet (grains/type)	Powder	Grains	Velocity	Energy	Source/Comments
110 SP	IMR 4064	50	3,200	2,502	Sierra
110 SP	IMR 4895	48	3,200	2,502	Hornady, Sierra
125 SP	W748	51.5	3,100	2,668	Sierra, Nosler
150 SP	IMR 4064	46	2,800	2,612	Nosler, Sierra, Speer
150 SP	IMR 4895	44	2,700	2,429	Nosler, Speer, Sierra
165 SP	IMR 4064	43	2,600	2,477	Sierra, Speer, Nosler, Hornady
180 SP	IMR 3031	41	2,500	2,499	Nosler
180 SP	IMR 4064	41.5	2,500	2,499	Nosler, Sierra, Hornady
190 SP	IMR 4064	41.5	2,500	2,637	Hornady, Speer, Sierra
200 SP	IMR 4064	41.5	2,400	2,559	Sierra
150 SP	FL		2,820	2,648	Factory load
168 HPBT	FL		2,600	2,180	Factory load
180 SP	FL		2,620	2,743	Factory load

.307 Winchester

Historical Notes: The development of the rimmed .307 Winchester began in 1980, with the first public announcement in December 1982. However, the cartridge and the Model 94 XTR Angle Eject carbine chambered for it were not available until early 1983. The Marlin Model 336ER in .307 chambering introduced at the same time is no longer offered. The Angle Eject feature is a design modification of the beefed-up Model 94 XTR that ejects spent cartridge cases to the side, rather than straight up, the same as earlier Model 94 actions. This was accomplished by changing the position of the extractor and ejector and lowering the receiver's right sidewall.

The .307-caliber designation is to avoid confusing this cartridge with the other .30-calibers. It actually uses standard .308-inch bullets. The .307 Winchester is essentially a rimmed .308 Winchester, although there is a difference in the overall cartridge length. Original factory loadings had 150- and 180-grain bullets.

General Comments: The popular Model 1894 Winchester lever-action has always suffered from two major deficiencies. The design didn't allow center mounting of a scope sight, and the tubular magazine required the use of flat-point bullets to prevent one cartridge from setting off others in the magazine under recoil. These factors combined to relegate the Model 1894 to largely short-range use. The new XTR Angle Eject redesign eliminates the scope-mounting problem and modernizes an old but popular action.

The .307 Winchester can enhance the range and power of lever-action rifles so chambered. It is, based on factory ballistics, faster than the .30-30 by 375 fps in muzzle velocity. Although the .307 Winchester has the same general configuration as the rimless .308 Winchester, there are slight differences that prevent it from achieving .308 full power. For one, the bullet is seated slightly deeper, to maintain an overall length compatible with the length of the Model 1894 action; for any given barrel length and the same bullet weight, the .308 will deliver about 60 to 110 fps more muzzle velocity. Also, with its pointed bullet, the .308 will lose velocity at a slower rate than the flat-point .307.

It is possible to chamber and fire .308 cartridges in some .307 rifles. However, for various reasons, this is an unsafe practice that could result in damage to the rifle and possible injury to the shooter.

The .307 has slightly less velocity at 200 yards than the .30-30 has at 100 yards. If the .30-30 is an adequate 100-yard-plus deer cartridge, then the .307 is certainly a 200-yard deer cartridge. It is not likely to replace the .30-30 as America's favorite deer cartridge, but it is a more versatile cartridge and certainly takes the Model 94 carbine out of the woods, bush, and short-range class. Although it has been reported that the .307 Winchester has thicker case walls and, therefore, reduced internal volume, measurements do not verify this. Winchester is the only manufacturer of ammunition in this caliber. Only the 180-grain bullet is still offered.

.307 Winchester Loading Data and Factory Ballistics (Note: In tubular magazine rifles, load only flat-point bullets.)

Bullet (grains/type)	Powder	Grains	Velocity	Energy	Source/Comments
110 Sierra HP	H322	44.0	3,000	2,195	Hodgdon
130 Speer FP	H4895	43.0	2,762	2,200	Hodgdon
150 Hornady RN	H4895	42.0	2,604	2,255	Hodgdon
170 Hornady FP	BI-C (2)	44.0	2,535	2,425	Hodgdon
170 SP	IMR4064	41.0	2,500	2,360	Hornady
150 SP	FL		2,760	2,538	Factory load
180 SP	FL		2,510	2,519	Factory load

.300 Ruger Compact Magnum (.300 RCM)

Historical Notes: The tail end of the twentieth century will go down in shooting history as the era of short, fat cartridges of true magnum performance. First out of the starting gate from the major ammunition manufacturers was Winchester's .300 WSM and other calibers on the same case. As rumor had it, Remington actually had the first in its family of Short Action Ultra Mag cartridges ready for launching sometime before Winchester was ready to unveil its WSM family, but chose to introduce the .300 Ultra Mag first, with plans to introduce the .300 Short Action Ultra Mag the following year. That allowed Winchester to beat Remington to the punch and, as everyone knows, when it comes to introducing cartridges of the same caliber and similar performance, the first one to exit the starting gate usually wins the popularity race among hunters and shooters. The .300 WSM went on to become at least mildly popular, while the .300 SAUM has been a commercial failure. Whereas the Winchester and Remington cartridges are basically shortened and necked-down versions of the old .404 Jeffrey case, the .300 Ruger Compact Magnum is basically a shortened and necked-down version of the .375 Ruger case. And, while the length of the .300 RCM case is the same as that of the .300 WSM, body diameter is a bit smaller. For this reason, its powder capacity is less. According to my measurements, gross capacity of the .300 RCM case is 8 percent less than that of the .300 WSM and about 1 percent greater than that of the .300 SAUM.

General Comments: In its factory loading, the .300 RCM pretty much duplicates the performance of the .300 SAUM. Unless the Light Magnum loading technology used by Hornady in loading this cartridge eventually becomes available to handloaders, those who load their own will be unable to greatly exceed .30-06 velocities with 180-grain bullets. Some claim short, fat cartridges are inherently more accurate than long, slim cartridges, but they have yet to come up with proof in rifles light enough to use for hunting. Most benchrest shooters will tell you that, when it comes to match-winning accuracy, a short, fat cartridge (with the 6mm PPC being a classic example), is the way to go. While this might be true in the world of benchrest competition where, in order to win, a rifle must be capable of consistently shooting five bullets inside .250-inch at 100 yards, the new breed of short magnums has proven to be no more accurate than longer and slimmer cartridges when all are fired in big-game rifles. In other words, if a gunsmith who specializes in building super-accurate hunting rifles were to build five in the .300 WSM, .300 SAUM, .300 RCM, .300 Winchester Magnum, .300 H&H Magnum, and .300 Weatherby Magnum, their accuracy would likely be the same. The one advantage a short cartridge has over a long cartridge is that it works in a short action weighing a few ounces less than a long action, and this is important to those who are in need of the lightest rifle possible.

.300 RCM Loading Data and Factory Ballistics

Bullet (grains/type)	Powder	Grains	Velocity	Energy	Source
150 Hornady IB	IMR-4895	56.0	3,081	3,158	Hodgdon
165 Barnes TSX	H414	59.5	2,958	3,202	Hodgdon
180 Hornady SP	H414	58.2	2,813	3,159	Hodgdon
150 Hornady SST	FL		3,200	3,410	Hornady
165 Hornady SST	FL		3,140	3,612	Hornady
180 Hornady SST	FL		3,000	3,597	Hornady

.300 Remington Ultra Mag

Historical Notes: When it debuted the .300 Remington Ultra Mag cartridge in 1999, Remington joined an increasingly popular trend toward big, beltless rounds. Popular from the onset, the .300 Remington Ultra Mag launched a whole family of non-belted, high-performance magnums, which includes the 7mm, .338, and .375 Remington Ultra Mags. When tested by Remington at 200 yards, the .300 Ultra Mag delivered nearly 18 percent greater retained energy than the .300 Weatherby Mag. and almost 27-percent greater retained energy than the .300 Winchester Magnum.

General Comments: The velocity and energy performance of Remington Ultra Mag cartridges comes from an innovative case design. Modifying the .404 Jeffery case with a rebated rim to fit Model 700 rifle bolt faces (for magnum cartridges), increased body taper, and a .30-caliber-sized neck, Remington's resulting case allows about 13 percent more internal capacity than the .300 Weatherby. It offers a similarly sized ballistic advantage. The result is a "non-belted magnum" with a larger case diameter, which allows for dramatically increased powder capacity. Headspacing on the shoulder of the case, rather than the use of a belt, promotes better accuracy, due to precise bore alignment.

.300 Remington Ultra Mag Load Data/Factory Ballistics

Bullet (grains/type)	Powder	Grains	Velocity	Energy	Source/Comments
150 Sierra SBT	RL-25	99.3	3,500	4,076	Sierra
165 Sierra SBT	Magnum	100.8	3,450	4,356	Sierra

Bullet (grains/type)	Powder	Grains	Velocity	Energy	Source/Comments
180 Sierra SBT	Retumbo	97.3	3,250	4,217	Sierra
190 Sierra MatchKing	RL-25	93.1	3,200	4,315	Sierra
150 Scirocco	FL		3,450	3,964	Remington factory load
180 PSP	FL		3,250	4,221	Remington factory load
180 Nosler Partition	FL		3,250	4,221	Remington factory load
180 Scirocco	FL		3,250	4,221	Remington factory load
200 Nosler Partition	FL		3,025	4,063	Remington factory load

.300 Remington Short Action Ultra Mag (SAUM)

Historical Notes: In 2001, Remington introduced the .300 Remington Short Action Ultra Mag cartridge as a competitor to Winchester's .300 Winchester Short Magnum. Ballistic performance of the Remington and Winchester offerings is similar.

General Comments: Based on a shortened .300 Ultra Mag case, which is itself derived from a slightly modified .404 Jeffery cartridge of African fame, the .300 Remington Short Action Ultra Mag is slightly shorter and smaller in diameter than its Winchester counterpart. Short, fat cases burn powder very efficiently, since the primer's flash ignites a larger area of the packed gunpowder. The case is unbelted and headspaces on the shoulder for improved shoulder tolerances. Remington barrels for this cartridge use a twist rate of 1:10. Shooters are cautioned never to fire a .300 Remington Short Action Ultra Magnum in a .300 WSM-chambered rifle, as the headspace would be excessive, leading to possible injury or firearms damage.

.300 Remington Short Action Ultra Mag Loading Data and Factory Ballistics

Bullet (grains/type)	Powder	Grains	Velocity	Energy	Source/Comments
150 PSP	FL		3,200	3,410	Remington factory load
165 PSP	FL		3,075	3,464	Remington factory load
180 Nosler Partition	FL		2,960	3,501	Remington factory load
180 Scirocco	FL		3,250	4,221	Remington factory load

.300 Winchester Short Magnum (.300 WSM)

Historical Notes: At the start of the twenty-first century, cartridge designs diverged. One direction was longer, fatter cartridges chambered in long-action rifles. Winchester took another path, with new, chubby, stubby cartridges sized to fit the more rigid short-action rifles. Introduced in 2000 and chambered in short, light Browning and Winchester rifles, the .300 Winchester Short Magnum demonstrated a remarkably accurate ability to duplicate .300 Winchester Magnum velocities, while consuming about 10 percent less powder. SSK Industries also re-barrels the AR-10 self-loading rifle for .300 WSM.

General Comments: The .300 WSM, an original Winchester cartridge case design, fits handily into bolt-actions sized for a cartridge length of 2.860 inches. Officially a rimless cartridge, the case rim is slightly rebated by .02-inch, and the case rim is sized to fit existing magnum bolt face dimensions. For highly efficient and consistent powder burning, the .300 WSM employs a short-fat powder column geometry, a concept revered by accuracy obsessed benchrest shooters for nearly three decades. Eschewing a belt on the case, the .300

WSM headspaces on the 35-degree shoulder, which should provide tighter headspacing tolerances and improved accuracy potential. Shooters are cautioned never to fire the slightly shorter, physically similar .300 Remington Short Action Ultra Magnum in a .300 WSM-chambered rifle, as the headspace would be excessive, leading to possible injury or firearms damage.

This cartridge and all its Winchester Short Magnum siblings became embroiled in a legal battle and the end result was a less than enthusiastic appeal on the part of other manufacturers to offer rifles and/or ammunition for sale. However, unlike the Winchester Super Short Magnums that are collecting dust on the shelves or in shooters' gun racks, the WSM line still enjoys moderate appeal, especially the .270 and .300 offerings.

.300 Winchester Short Magnum Loading Data and Factory Ballistics

Bullet (grains/type)	Powder	Grains	Velocity	Energy	Source/Comments
150 BST	FL		3,300	3,628	Winchester/Olin factory load
180 Fail Safe	FL		2,970	3,526	Winchester/Olin factory load
180 P Pt	FL		2,970	3,526	Winchester/Olin factory load
110 Hornady V-Max	Big Game	71.8	3,600	3,162	Hornady
130 Hornady SP	W760	71.4	3,400	3,333	Hornady
150 Hornady IB	H4350	70.9	3,250	3,514	Hornady
150 BST	WW760	71.0	3,250	3,519	Winchester/Olin 60,000 psi
165 Fail Safe	WW760	68.5	3,130	3,590	Winchester/Olin 63,300 psi
165 Hornady IB	W760	69.1	3,150	3,631	Hornady
168 BST	WW760	69.8	3,090	3,563	Winchester/Olin 0,300 psi
180 Hornady SST	V-N560	71.3	3,000	3,593	Hornady
180 SP	WW760	66.9	2,960	3,503	Winchester/Olin 60,500 psi
180 Fail Safe	WW760	68.0	2,940	3,456	Winchester/Olin 60,200 psi

.303 British

Historical Notes:	The .303 British was the official military rifle cartridge of England and the British Empire from its adoption in 1888 until the 7.62 NATO came along in the 1950s. The original loading was a 215-grain bullet and a compressed charge of black powder—cordite became the propellant in 1892. Manufacture in the United States began about 1897. Remington chambered its Lee bolt-action magazine rifle for this cartridge, and Winchester did likewise in its Model 95 lever-action. No American rifle has chambered the .303 British since 1936. However, Winchester, Federal, and Remington continue to load this popular cartridge.
General Comments:	The .303 British has always been popular in Canada and other parts of the British Empire. In the United States, it has not been as widely used, because of its performance similarity to the .30-40 Krag. However, since the end of World War II, the importation of large numbers of British Lee-Enfield military rifles has altered this situation. At the present time, the .303 is more popular than the .30-40 Krag. Norma imports 130- and 180-grain loads that greatly increase the flexibility and usefulness of this cartridge for the American hunter. The 215-grain bullet has always had a good reputation for deep penetration and is a favorite for moose and caribou in the Canadian backwoods. The .303 is suitable for anything the .30-40 Krag is in the way of game. In Australia, a number of popular sporting cartridges are based on necking down and/or reforming the .303 case.

Note: Although often classed with the .30-40 Krag, this cartridge is loaded to higher pressures and delivers superior ballistics. Foreign factory loads place it very close ballistically to the .308 Winchester and measurably above any factory .30-40 load, though handloads for the .30-40 in the Model 95 Winchester can match the .303 British.

.303 British Loading Data and Factory Ballistics

Bullet (grains/type)	Powder	Grains	Velocity	Energy	Source/Comments
123 Hornady SP	RL-15	49.8	3,015	2,480	Hodgdon
150 SP	IMR 4064	43	2,600	2,252	Speer, Hornady
150 SP	IMR 4895	42	2,400	1,919	Sierra, Speer
150 SP	IMR 4064	43	2,600	2,252	Speer, Sierra
150 Speer SP	RL-15	46.2	2,755	2,525	Hodgdon
180 SP	IMR 4895	42	2,400	2,303	Sierra
180 SP	IMR 4350	46	2,400	2,303	Speer, Hornady
180 Sako SP	N140	41.7	2,540	2,575	VihtaVuori
130 SP	FL		2,789	2,246	Factory load
150 SP	FL		2,690	2,400	Factory load
180 SP	FL		2,460	2,420	Factory load
215 SP	FL		2,180	2,270	Factory load

7.62X39mm
(7.62X39mm Soviet M43)

Historical Notes: This "assault rifle" cartridge was adopted by Russia, in 1943. It did not come into general use until after World War II, but the Russians now use it as their principal infantry small-arms cartridge. Original use was in the SKS semi-automatic carbine, later replaced by the AK-47 selective-fire assault rifle. The RPD light machine gun also uses the M43 cartridge. Finland, and those ex-satellite countries in the Soviet bloc, use the M43 cartridge in arms furnished by Russia or of their own design. This cartridge was adopted as the result of Russian military experience against German assault rifles chambered for the 7.92mm Kurz. Ruger introduced its Mini-30 semi-automatic rifle chambered for the 7.62x39mm, in 1987, and the bolt-action M77 Mark II rifle, in 1991. Most military ammunition has a steel case and corrosive Berdan primer, but reloadable cases are now readily available.

General Comments: The M43 is a ¼-inch longer than the German 7.92mm Kurz and will give substantially better performance with newer powders. This cartridge has been loaded commercially by Federal, Winchester, Remington, and Black Hills with Boxer-primed reloadable cases. Better handloads and factory ammunition using soft-point bullets up to about 150 grains place this cartridge far ahead of any reasonable .30-30 load, in terms of delivered energy beyond 100 yards.

This cartridge has become very popular and is now well-known enough, used in enough sporting rifles, and loaded by enough American ammunition companies to warrant its inclusion in this chapter.

7.62X39mm Soviet Loading Data and Factory Ballistics

Bullet (grains/type)	Powder	Grains	Velocity	Energy	Source/Comments
110 SP	IMR 4727	42	2,500	1,527	Speer
125 SP	RL-7	26.5	2,400	1,599	Hornady, Sierra
125 Speer SP	H335	31.5	2,408	1,605	Hodgdon
135 SP	IMR 4227	22.5	2,200	1,451	Sierra
150 SP	IMR 4198	22	2,100	1,469	Hornady
150 Hornady SP	H322	28.5	2,192	1,600	Hodgdon
123 SP	FL		2,300	1,445	Federal factory load
123 SP	FL		2,365	1,527	Winchester factory load
125 SP	FL		2,365	1,552	Remington factory load

7.62X39mm Soviet Loading Data and Factory Ballistics

Bullet (grains/type)	Powder	Grains	Velocity	Energy	Source/Comments
110 Sierra HP	AA 1680	27.5	2,547	1,580	Accurate Arms, Maximum load (.308")
125 Sierra SP	AA 1680	25.5	2,368	1,555	Accurate Arms, Maximum load (.311")
150 Sierra SP	AA 2015	26.0	2,072	1,430	Accurate Arms, Maximum load (.311")
122 Ball	ML		2,329	1,470	Military load
123 SP	FL		2,300	1,440	Black Hills factory load
150 SP	FL		2,200	1,610	Black Hills factory load

.32-20 Winchester (.32-20 WCF)

Historical Notes: Introduced by Winchester, in 1882, for the Model 73 lever-action rifle, the .32-20 quickly attained considerable popularity as a medium-power cartridge in both rifle and revolver. Practically all American makers have chambered rifles for the .32-20 in lever-, pump-, or bolt-action, and most single-shot rifles have also chambered it. Colt's, Smith & Wesson, and Bayard made revolvers in this caliber. Marlin reintroduced the cartridge for its Model 94CL lever action, in 1988. Winchester once offered a lighter 100-grain bullet black-powder load for the .32 Colt Lightning magazine rifle, headstamped .32 C.L.M.R. A similar 100-grain loading specifically for Marlin rifles was headstamped .32-20. Both Remington and Winchester still offer factory-loaded ammunition.

General Comments: Although recently semi-obsolete, the .32-20 still enjoys modest popularity with farmers, ranchers, trappers and meat hunters. It can be reloaded easily and at moderate cost. In addition, it delivers good killing power on small and medium game at ranges out to 100 yards, without destroying all the edible meat.

Winchester once advertised it as a combination small-game and deer cartridge. However, it is much too underpowered for deer-size animals. It is, nonetheless, a useful small-game and varmint cartridge at short ranges, and it is quite accurate in a bolt-action or solid-frame single-shot.

Frank Barnes had considerable personal experience with the old .32-20, having owned and hunted with several rifles of this caliber. These included (in chronological order) a Winchester Model 1892 lever-action, Savage Model 23C bolt-action, Remington Model 25A slide-action, and a rechambered Greener single-shot Cadet rifle. The Savage bolt-action with a scope sight would shoot very consistently into 1 to 1¼ inches at 100 yards. This was a very nice little varmint and small-game combination at ranges of 100 to 125 yards. Frank used this in the immediate post-World War II era, when nothing else was available, and it worked out very well within its range limitations. Frank also used the .25-20, but always considered the .32-20 a better all-around cartridge in this class. It's a better killer on just about anything at practical ranges.

In a strong single-action revolver, the .32-20 can be loaded to 1050 to 1100 fps from a six-inch barrel, which makes a very effective field gun. Trouble is, the cartridge is too long for most modern revolver cylinders. The .32 H&R Magnum is shorter and will serve to fill the requirement for a high-performance .32-caliber handgun round. The .357 Magnum revolver cartridge chambering in a rifle will out-perform the .32-20 by a substantial margin. The advent of cowboy action shooting has given this round a new lease on life. The .32-20 is the basis for the .25-20 and the .218 Bee.

.32-20 Winchester Loading Data and Factory Ballistics

Bullet (grains/type)	Powder	Grains	Velocity	Energy	Source/Comments
85 SP	2400	12.5	2,100	833	Rifle only — Hornady
85 SP	IMR 4227	17	2,300	999	Rifle only — Hornady
85 SP	H-110	14	2,100	833	Rifle only — Hornady
110 SP	IMR 4227	15	2,000	977	Rifle only — Hornady

Bullet (grains/type)	Powder	Grains	Velocity	Energy	Source/Comments
110 SP	H-110	15.5	2,100	1,077	Rifle only — Hornady
110 SP	2400	10.5	1,700	706	Rifle only — Hornady
80 SP	FL		2,100	780	Factory load
100 SP	FL		1,210	325	Factory load
WARNING: Do not use rifle loads in revolvers. Pressures develop beyond what the average handgun is designed to withstand.					

.32 Winchester Special (.32 WS)

Historical Notes: Introduced in 1902 for the Winchester Model 1894 lever-action, the .32 Winchester Special was an original smokeless powder design. Because it is a rimmed shell, it has never been used in anything but lever-action and single-shot rifles. Remington brought out a rimless version to function in its bolt and semi-auto rifles. Winchester and Marlin were the principal American companies to chamber the .32 Special. Federal, Remington, and Winchester continued to offer factory loaded ammunition until quite recently.

General Comments: In the 1916 catalog, Winchester had this to say about the 32 Special: "The .32 Winchester Special, which we have perfected, is offered to meet the demands of many sportsmen for a smokeless powder cartridge of larger caliber than the .30 Winchester and yet not so powerful as the .30 Army." It goes on to explain that the .32 Special meets these requirements, and the 1916 ballistics chart shows it generating 10.6 percent more energy than the .30-30 at the muzzle, retaining an edge to any reasonable hunting range.

Today, it is still loaded to higher velocity and, if loaded to equal pressure, it easily beats the .30-30 by over 100 fps. However, bullet selection is limited. Speer's 170-grain flat-point, the most streamlined available, actually has a higher ballistic coefficient than most 170-grain .30-30 bullets. For those whose .32 Special rifle has a truly shot-out barrel, Hornady's 170-grain round-nose .323-inch bullet works wonderfully.

There has been a mountain of bunk written about the .32 Special answering the demand of handloaders who wanted to use black powder. Since the same rifle was originally chambered for the .32-40 at about one-half the price of the nickel-steel .32 Special version, this seems highly unrealistic. Those writers would have us believe that the man wanting to save money on ammunition would for no reason spend the price of two rifles for the privilege. The fact that black powder can be used successfully in the .32 Special, and the fact that Winchester once provided a black-powder-height rear sight for the rifle, certainly do not prove that the cartridge was invented to allow folks to do what they could already do with the much cheaper .32-40 Model 94.

Much ink has also been spilled, claiming the .32 Special just wouldn't shoot straight after the barrel got a bit of wear. Frank Barnes experimented with two .32 Special carbines, a very early Winchester and a 1936 Marlin. With bullets that fit, both shot inside three inches at 100 yards with open sights. The Winchester had been so abused that its rifling hardly showed until it was thoroughly cleaned. The bore was pitted, but the gun shot just fine.

Several attempts to increase the terminal performance and external ballistics of a lever-action rifles have been attempted. However, none have been as successful as Hornady's LEVERevoultion line of ammunition. Using a special powder formulated by Hodgdon and high BC bullets with a soft rubber tip, this line of factory loaded ammunition has brought about the single largest advancement in lever-action rifles in more than a century.

.32 Winchester Special Loading Data and Factory Ballistics

Bullet (grains/type)	Powder	Grains	Velocity	Energy	Source/Comments
170 SP	RL7	31.0	2,283	1,965	Lyman
170 SP	W748	36.2	2,240	1,890	Winchester
170 SP	FL		2,250	1,910	Factory load

Bullet (grains/type)	Powder	Grains	Velocity	Energy	Source/Comments
165	FL		2,410	2,128	Hornady Factory Load

8mm Mauser (7.92mm Mauser/mJ/8x57mmI/8x57mmS/8x57JS)

Historical Notes: The 8mm or 7.92 Mauser was the German military rifle cartridge through both World Wars. It was officially adopted, in 1888, with a bullet diameter of .318 inch. In 1905, the bullet diameter was increased to .323 inch. In Europe, the 8mm Mauser and several other 8mm cartridges are available in both sizes. The larger size is always designated as "S" or "JS" bore. In the United States, ammunition companies load only the .323-inch diameter or "S" bullet. The 8mm Mauser is widely chambered in European sporting rifles, but American gunmakers have not adopted it as a standard sporting caliber. The "J" or "I" in the name denotes infantry ammunition. The German capital "I" was mistaken for a capital "J" by U.S. military interpreters after World War I, and the "J" misnomer came into common use here and even in Europe thereafter!

General Comments: The 8mm Mauser had not been very popular in the United States prior to World War II. However, the large number of obsolete, surplus 8mm military rifles sold here since the end of the war has increased its use substantially. American cartridge companies only put out one loading, the 170-grain bullet at 2360 fps or so. As loaded by Norma and by other European companies, such as RWS, it is in the same class as our .30-06. It is adequate for any North American big game if the proper bullets and full loadings are used. A large variety of good .323-inch bullets is now available for the individual handloader, and this has increased the usefulness of the 8mm Mauser for the American shooter.

8mm Mauser (8x57mm JS) Loading Data and Factory Ballistics

Bullet (grains/type)	Powder	Grains	Velocity	Energy	Source/Comments
125 SP	H-4198	44	3,100	2,668	Hornady
125 SP	IMR 3031	49	3,100	2,668	Hornady
150 SP	IMR 4320	53.5	2,900	2,802	Hornady
150 SP	IMR 3031	49	2,750	2,519	Speer
175 SP	IMR 3031	45.5	2,600	2,627	Sierra
200 SP	IMR 4831	54	2,400	2,559	Speer
220 SP	IMR 4831		2,200	2,365	Hornady
159 SP	FL		2,723	2,618	European factory load
170 SP	FL		2,360	2,100	U.S. factory load
196 SP	FL		2,526	2,778	European factory load
198 SP	FL		2,625	3,031	European factory load
200 SP	FL		2,320	2,390	European factory load
227 SP	FL		2,330	2,737	European factory load

WARNING! Many J-bore (.318-inch) rifles still exist and will fire S-bore (.323-inch) cartridges, creating dangerous pressures. When in doubt, check bore diameter carefully!

.325 Winchester Short Magnum (.325 WSM)

Historical Notes: After introducing its Short Magnum family of cartridges in 2000, Winchester recognized the need for another cartridge capable of launching 200-grain bullets (and heavier) with high inherent accuracy, energy capable of stopping the largest North American game, and lower perceived recoil. After considering different calibers, Winchester engineers determined the .325-caliber provided the best performance using the Short Magnum case. Released in 2005, the new .325 WSM cartridge delivers similar energies as the .338 Winchester Magnum, while using a smaller case.

General Comments: In addition to delivering excellent ballistics, the .325 WSM also exhibits exceptional accuracy. Initially, Winchester fielded three loads for the .325 WSM; a 200-grain Nosler Accubond CT, a Winchester 220-grain Power-Point bullet, and a 180-grain Ballistic Silvertip. Hunters can expect delayed, controlled expansion and deep penetration through thick, tough skin and heavy muscle tissue and bone, with ballistic coefficients ranging up to .477 for the 200-grain Nosler bullet. The .325 WSM is well suited for elk, bear, moose, or other large and dangerous game, where a lightweight short magnum rifle is desired.

.325 Winchester Short Magnum Load Data/Factory Ballistics

Bullet (grains/type)	Powder	Grains	Velocity	Energy	Source/Comments
150 Hornady SP	H414	70.0	3,200	3,407	Hornady
180 Barnes TSX	W760	69.0	3,119	3,884	Barnes
195 Hornady SP	RL-19	70.6	2,850	3,513	Hornady
200 Barnes TSX	W760	67.0	2,951	3,863	Barnes
200 Nosler Partition	RL-19	69.0	2,964	3,897	Nosler
180 BST	FL		3,060	3,743	Winchester
200 Nos AccuBond	FL		2,950	3,866	Winchester
220 Win PP	FL		2,840	3,941	Winchester

8mm Remington Magnum

Historical Notes: This cartridge was a Remington development, announced in 1978 for the Model 700 BDL bolt-action rifle. The 8mm Magnum is something of a departure from the usual belted, short magnum configuration favored by Remington in the past (a design that will work through the standard-length bolt-action). The 8mm Magnum is based on the full-length .375 H&H case blown out, thus requiring a .375-inch longer bolt travel than the standard .30-06.

Again, this is not an entirely original design, since it was preceded by similar developments in years past. The 8x68mm (S) Magnum, for example, originated in Germany around 1940, and a number of 8mm wildcat magnums such as the 8mm Ernst, 8x62 Durham, .323 Hollis, 8mm PMM, etc., date back to the late 1950s and early 1960s. However, this is the first commercial 8mm magnum cartridge introduced by an American company. Remington originally offered two loadings, a 185-grain bullet at a muzzle velocity of 3080 fps, and a 220-grain at 2830 fps. The 220-grain load has since been dropped. There is a good selection of 8mm (.323-inch diameter) bullets available for handloading this cartridge.

General Comments: Comparing either handloaded or factory ballistics for the .338 Winchester Magnum and the 8mm Remington Magnum, one can easily see why the latter failed to garner any great following. Any minuscule ballistic advantage it might have just didn't justify the increased cartridge length and recoil resulting from a heavier powder charge. Add to that a more limited bullet selection, and the 8mm Remington Magnum dims even further. With lighter recoil and potentially flatter trajectories, the various .300 Magnums have it beaten on that side, and, with heavier bullets shooting almost as flat and delivering more energy, the .338 Winchester Magnum and the .340 Weatherby Magnum have it beaten on the other. This is a classic example of a cartridge that fails to fill any useful niche. Due to its large powder capacity, this cartridge is another that is particularly sensitive to barrel length.

8mm Remington Magnum Loading Data and Factory Ballistics

Bullet (grains/type)	Powder	Grains	Velocity	Energy	Source/Comments
125 SP	IMR 4064/76		3,600	3,598	Hornady
150 SP	IMR 4350/	79.5	3,300	3,628	Speer, Hornady, Sierra
175 SP	IMR 4831	80	3,100	3,735	Speer, Sierra, Hornady
200 SP	IMR 4831	78	3,050	4,132	Nosler, Speer
220 SP	IMR 4831	76	2,800	3,831	Sierra, Hornady
250 SP	IMR 7828	72	2,550	3,611	Barnes
185 SP	FL		3,080	3,896	Remington factory load
220 SP	FL		2,830	3,912	Remington factory load

.340 Weatherby Magnum

Historical Notes: The growing popularity of the .338 Winchester Magnum for elk and larger game undoubtedly influenced the development of the .340 Weatherby. First announcement of the new caliber came in 1962. John Amber had one of the first .340 Weatherby Magnum rifles and reported 100-yard groups of two inches or less—quite good for such a heavy-caliber hunting rifle of that era.

General Comments: With its larger case, the .340 Weatherby develops higher velocities with any given bullet weight than does the .338 Winchester. Velocities of 3260 fps with the 200-grain bullet and 2980 with the 250-grain are impressive; this means around 4700 ft-lbs of energy with either bullet. This should be quite effective on African game. A 210-grain Nosler bullet loading is also available with a muzzle velocity of 3250 fps (all from 26-inch barrels). The cartridge is suitable for all North American big game and most African species, as well. Weatherby ammunition is loaded by Norma of Sweden. Handloaders will find that case life with older Weatherby (Norma) cases is very limited with top handloads, because of soft case heads. This problem can be eliminated by reforming 8mm Remington Magnum cases, but these require a significant reduction in charge because of the resulting much-reduced capacity. Nevertheless, such loads can surpass any safe load in older Norma cases, because Remington cases can safely withstand somewhat higher pressures and because the lost powder space wasn't necessary anyway. Ballistics are greatly handicapped if shorter barrels are used.

.340 Weatherby Magnum Loading Data and Factory Ballistics

Bullet (grains/type)	Powder	Grains	Velocity	Energy	Source/Comments
175 SP	IMR 4350	85.5	3,250	4,105	Barnes
200 SP	IMR 4350	82	3,000	3,998	Speer, Hornady
200 SP	IMR 4350	84	3,200	4,549	Hornady
210 SP	IMR 4350	83.5	3,200	4,776	Nosler
225 SP	IMR 4831	83	3,000	4,498	Hornady
250 SP	IMR 4350	77	2,800	4,353	Sierra, Speer, Hornady
250 SP	IMR 4831	80	2,800	4,353	Sierra, Hornady, Speer
275 SP	IMR 4350	76	2,600	4,129	Speer
275 SP	IMR 7828	88	2,750	4,619	Speer
300 SP	IMR 7828	77.5	2,550	4,333	Barnes
200 SP	FL		3,260	4,719	Weatherby factory load
210 SP	FL		3,250	4,924	Weatherby factory load

Bullet (grains/type)	Powder	Grains	Velocity	Energy	Source/Comments
250 SP	FL		2,980	4,931	Weatherby factory load

Federal 215 primers used in all cases.

.338 Federal

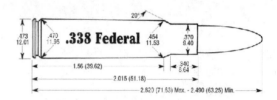

Historical Notes: In collaboration with Sako Rifles, Federal Cartridge's engineers and ballisticians have developed the .338 Federal, which necks up the proven .308 Winchester case to accept a .338-caliber bullet. This design, which is the first to bear the name "Federal" on the headstamp, is intended to provide big-bore wallop with moderate recoil for today's lightweight, short, bolt-action rifles. The .338 Federal was available in 2006 in Federal's Premium line of ammunition.

General Comments: The .338 Federal bears more than a passing resemblance to the .358 Winchester cartridge, which was introduced in 1955. Like the .358 Winchester, the .338 Federal offers excellent performance on big game without magnum recoil. Its muzzle energy exceeds the .30-06 with a similar weight bullet, equaling the muzzle energy of the 7mm Remington Magnum. Its muzzle velocity ranges to approximately 200 fps greater than its parent .308 Winchester with similar weight bullets. Leaving nothing to chance, Federal offers three loads for the .338 Federal, each tipped with a premium-grade bullet proven to deliver devastating results on game ranging from deer to elk to bear.

The .358 Winchester, having been introduced in a time when ever-higher velocities were the craze, now languishes in obscurity. Given the current interest in lightweight rifles and efficient cartridge designs, one hopes that the .338 Federal will fare better with the shooting public.

.338 Federal Load Data/Factory Ballistics

Bullet (grains/type)	Powder	Grains	Velocity	Energy	Source/Comments
180 Nosler AccuBond	Varget	48.0	2,706	2,923	Nosler
185 Barnes TSX	Benchmark	45.5	2,709	3,011	Barnes
200 Nosler AccuBond	W748	47.0	2,529	2,837	Nosler
210 Barnes TSX	AA-2230	46.0	2,570	3,076	Barnes
225 Barnes TSX	Benchmark	41.5	2,360	2,780	Barnes
180 Nos AccuBond	FL		2,830	3,200	Federal
185 Barnes TSX	FL		2,750	3,106	Federal
210 Nos Part	FL		2,630	3,225	Federal

.338 Winchester Magnum

Historical Notes: Announced in 1958, the .338 is another of the series based on the .458 Winchester necked down. Initially available only in the Winchester Model 70 Alaskan bolt-action rifle, Remington adopted it for the 700 Series bolt-action. Some of the European rifle makers also chamber it, as does Ruger for the Model 77 and No. 1 rifles, as well as many custom and semi-custom rifles. Browning's autoloader, lever-, and pump-action rifles also chamber it.

General Comments: With proper bullets, the .338 Winchester Magnum shoots almost as flat across 500 yards as similar loads in the various .30-caliber magnums—the difference amounts to only a few inches more drop. Designed to handle the heaviest North American big game, the .338 has also done well in Africa on the larger varieties of plains game. Although slightly less powerful than the .375 H&H Magnum, the .338 is better suited for North American hunting conditions and game. It is a well-balanced cartridge for anything from elk through moose and grizzly bear, under almost any situation. It could also serve very well for deer or antelope, even though it is overly powerful for this class. Like the .300 WM, the .338 Winchester would make an excellent one-gun cartridge for the worldwide hunter who has to travel light, though the .338 is automatically barred in some African countries in which the .375 is the minimum caliber. Lately, the .338 has enjoyed a renewed and well-deserved popularity. Winchester, Remington, and Federal all load this ammunition.

.338 Winchester Magnum Loading Data and Factory Ballistics

Bullet (grains/type)	Powder	Grains	Velocity	Energy	Source/Comments
175 SP	IMR 4895	67.5	3,200	3,980	Barnes
180 Nosler BT	H4350	74.5	3,157	3,980	Hodgdon
200 SP	IMR 4350	71.5	2,900	4,048	Speer, Hornady
210 SP	IMR 4350	73	2,900	3,923	Nosler
225 Hornady SP	RL-19	75.3	2,865	4,100	Hodgdon
250 SP	IMR 4831	71	2,700	4,048	Speer, Sierra
250 SP	IMR 4350	70	2,700	4,048	Sierra
275 SP	IMR 4831	68	2,500	3,817	Speer
275 SP	IMR 4064	58	2,400	3,518	Speer
300 SP	IMR 7828	70	2,500	4,164	Barnes
200 SP	FL		2,960	3,890	Factory load
225 SP	FL		2,780	3,860	Factory load
250 SP	FL		2,660	3,921	Factory load

.338-378 Weatherby

Historical Notes: In response to special requests from close friends, Roy Weatherby chambered a few rifles for a cartridge in which the case was formed by necking down his .378 Magnum case to .338 caliber. This took place as early as the 1970s, but it wasn't added to the Weatherby lineup of loaded cartridges and rifle chamberings until 1999. The .338-378 Weatherby Magnum is sometimes confused with the earlier .338-378 Keith-Thompson wildcat, but since the K-T version is on the shortened .378 Magnum case, loading data are not interchangeable between the two.

General Comments: The .338-378 Weatherby Magnum is in the same performance league as the .338 Remington Ultra Mag and .338 Lapua, and, from a practical point of view, that's not saying a whole lot. The smaller .340 Weatherby Magnum generates considerably less recoil, and yet Weatherby rates it only 100 fps slower than the .338-378 Magnum and at about the same speed as the .338 Remington Ultra Mag., when the three cartridges are loaded with 250-grain bullets.

.338-378 Weatherby Load Data/Factory Ballistics

Bullet (grains/type)	Powder	Grains	Velocity	Energy	Source
180 Barnes TSX	RL-25	113.0	3,373	4,542	Barnes
210 Barnes TSX	RL-25	108.5	3,183	4,719	Barnes
225 Barnes TSX	RL-25	105.0	3,066	4,691	Barnes

Bullet (grains/type)	Powder	Grains	Velocity	Energy	Source
250 Barnes TSX	RL-25	102.5	2,906	4,683	Barnes
200 Nosler AccuBond	FL		3,380	5,075	Weatherby
225 Barnes TSX	FL		3,180	5,052	Weatherby
250 Nosler Partition	FL		3,060	5,197	Weatherby

.338-06 A-Square/.338-06

Historical Notes: During 1945 to 1946, Charles O'Neil, Elmer Keith, and Don Hopkins developed a cartridge they named the .333 OKH, which was based on the .30-06 case necked up to .333-caliber. It was a very good big-game cartridge, but today it suffers from the lack of good, readily available .333-inch diameter bullets. When the .338 Winchester Magnum was introduced, in 1958, it was followed immediately by a variety of commercial .338-inch diameter bullets. Shortly thereafter, several individuals at different places conceived the idea of either altering the .333 OKH or necking up the .30-06 to accept .338-inch diameter bullets. Any difference in performance between the .333 OKH and the .338-06 is purely academic and almost invisible. The latter uses a commercial bullet of standard diameter, which has the advantage of being readily available through handloading supply dealers. The two cartridges are so nearly alike that one can use loading data from the .333 OKH in the .338-06 with virtually the same results. A-Square standardized the .338-06 as a factory round, in 1998, and, about 2001, Weatherby began chambering rifles in .338-06. With typical Weatherby honesty, their catalogs list the cartridge as the .338-06 A-Square.

General Comments: The .30-06 case is necked up to accept .338-diameter bullets, and retains the original 17.5-degree shoulder. The .338-06 delivers about 85 percent of the performance of the .338-caliber magnum cartridges, but without the recoil, cigar-sized cases, or magnum-length actions. Most .30-06 bolt-action rifles can be rebarreled to the .338-06, and the wide range of available bullets makes the .338-06 a flexible hunting alternative to its ballistic near-twin, the .35 Whelen. Weatherby uses Norma brass and powders, matching them with bullets well suited for the intended purpose. The Weatherby catalog lists just one bullet for the .338-06, the Nosler Partition. Weatherby offers Mark V Super Big Game Master and Ultra Lightweight rifles in .338-06 A-Square, both well suited for North American game.

.338-06 A-Square Loading Data and Factory Ballistics

Bullet (grains/type)	Powder	Grains	Velocity	Energy	Source/Comments
200 SP	IMR 3031	48.0	2,465	2,700	NA
200 SP	IMR 4320	54.0	2,610	3,020	NA
250 SP	IMR 4064	56.0	2,585	3,730	NA
250 SP	IMR 3031	47.0	2,370	3,130	NA
275 SP	IMR 4350	55.0	2,305	3,250	NA
275 SP	IMR 4895	50.0	2,275	3,165	NA
210 Nosler Partition	FL		2,750	3,527	Weatherby factory load

.338 Marlin Express

Historical Notes: In 1982, Winchester introduced rimmed versions of the .308 Winchester and .358 Winchester cartridges and called them the .307 Winchester and 356 Winchester. They became available in a special version of the Winchester Model 94 lever-action rifle, with its receiver sidewalls reinforced to handle higher chamber pressures than is common for the .30-30 Winchester and other cartridges for which that rifle was originally designed. Two loadings of the .356 Winchester were available, a 200-grain deer load at 2460 fps, and a 250-grain moose load at 2160 fps. Despite the fact that the new cartridge delivered the same level of energy at 200 yards as the .30-30 at 100 yards, it failed to win the hearts of America's deer hunters and was eventually dropped from the Model 94 rifle. Marlin also built a few Model 336 rifles in .356 Winchester.

Many hunting seasons later, those clever chaps at Hornady developed the Flex-Tip bullet with a pointed tip soft enough to make it safe to use in lever-action rifles with tubular magazines. Other cartridges such as the .30-30 Winchester, .35 Remington, 444 Marlin, and .45-70 Government were first to receive the new bullet design, but Hornady eventually got around to a couple new rimmed cartridges called .308 Marlin Express and .338 Marlin Express, the rounds introduced in the Marlin Model 336 rifle. Whereas Winchester had previously simply necked up the .307 Winchester case to produce the .356 Winchester cartridge, Hornady came up with a case of greater capacity for the new .338-caliber cartridge than it had for the .308 Marlin Express. The rim of the case is a rather odd diameter, a bit smaller than the rim of the .45-70 Government cases and considerably smaller than the rim of the .30-30 Winchester case. As rim diameters of various rifle cartridges of American design go, the closest we could find to it is a long-obsolete cartridge called the .40-63 Ballard.

General Comments: A past editor's favorite lever-action rifle had long been the old Winchester Model 71 in .348 Winchester, the only cartridge it was chambered for on a production basis. Even though the .348 Winchester case is longer than the .338 Marlin case, the Hornady factory load equals its velocity when both cartridges are loaded with a 200-grain bullet. But, since the Hornady Flex-Tip bullet is pointed, it sheds velocity more slowly, giving it a slightly flatter trajectory and allowing it to deliver more energy to a target downrange. When digging a wounded bear out of an alder thicket, the availability of 250-grain bullets that can be handloaded in the .348 Winchester gives an edge in effectiveness, although the 200-grain bullet of the .338 Marlin Express should be plenty of medicine for broadside, behind-the-shoulder shots on game as large as elk and moose.

.338 Marlin Express Loading Data and Factory Ballistics

Bullet (grains/type)	Powder	Grains	Velocity	Energy	Source
200 Hornady FTX	FL		2,565	2,919	Hornady

.338 Ruger Compact Magnum (.338 RCM)

Historical Notes: The tail end of the twentieth century will go down in shooting history as the era of short, fat cartridges of true magnum performance. First out of the starting gate from the major ammunition manufacturers was Winchester's .300 WSM, and other calibers such as .323 (8mm), .270, and 7mm on the same case. As rumor had it, Remington actually had the first in its family of Short Action Ultra Mag cartridges ready for launching sometime before Winchester was ready to unveil its WSM family, but chose to introduce the .300 Ultra Mag first with plans to introduce the .300 Short Action Ultra Mag the following year. That allowed Winchester to beat Remington to the punch and, as everyone knows, when it comes to introducing cartridges of the same caliber and similar performance, the first one to exit the starting gate is usually the winner. The .300 WSM went on to become at least mildly popular, while the .300 SAUM has been a commercial failure. Whereas the Winchester and Remington cartridges are basically shortened and necked-down versions of the old .404 Jeffery case, the .338 Ruger Compact Magnum is basically a shortened and necked-down version of the .375 Ruger case. As short and fat magnums go, the .338 RCM is similar in performance to the .325 WSM. And while the length of the .338 RCM case is the same as that of the .325 WSM case, body diameter is a bit smaller. For this reason, its powder capacity is less. According to our measurements, gross capacity of the .338 RCM case is eight-percent less than that of the .325 WSM.

General Comments: Performance of the .338 RCM falls somewhere between the .338-06 A-Square on the slower side and the .338 Winchester Magnum on the faster side. It makes a lot more sense than the .325 WSM, simply because cartridges of .338-caliber are at least mildly popular among big-game American hunters, whereas those of 8mm caliber (which is what the .325 WSM is), have never been and probably never will be. Its biggest shortcoming as this is written in early 2009 is availability only in rifles built by Ruger, plus the fact that only Hornady loads it. Nothing wrong with either Ruger rifles or Hornady ammunition, but everyone does not hunt with Ruger rifles and not every gun shop stocks Hornady ammo. If other rifle manufacturers start chambering for the .338 RCM, and if other ammunition manufacturers start offering the ammo, it will surely become more successful than the .325 WSM, which has yet to find a place in the hearts of American hunters.

.338 RCM Loading Data and Factory Ballistics

Bullet (grains/type)	Powder	Grains	Velocity	Energy	Source
185 Barnes TSX	W748	59.5	2,937	3,540	Hodgdon
200 Hornady SP	BL-C(2)	61.0	2,870	3,654	Hodgdon
210 Swift Scirocco	BL-C(2)	57.0	2,739	3,494	Hodgdon
225 Hornady IB	W748	56.0	2,654	3,515	Hodgdon
200 Hornady SST	FL		2,950	3,865	Hornady
225 Hornady SST	FL		2,775	3,847	Hornady

.338 Lapua Magnum 8.58x71mm (Finland)

Historical Notes: In 1983, Research Armament Co. in the U.S.,began development of a new, long-range sniper cartridge capable of firing a 250-grain, .338-inch diameter bullet at 3000 fps. After preliminary experiments, a .416 Rigby case necked down to .338-inch was selected. Brass Extrusion Labs Ltd. (then of Bensenville, Illinois), made the cases, Hornady produced bullets, and Research Armament built the gun under contract for the U.S. Navy. Subsequently, Lapua and Norma have put this cartridge into production. It is now a CIP standard chambering; since CIP and SAAMI have reciprocal agreements in place (at least in theory), that makes this a standard SAAMI chambering, as well.

General Comments: You have to burn a lot of powder to launch a 250-grain bullet at 3000 fps. The .338 Lapua Magnum, as it is known commercially, or the 8.58x71mm, does just that. The full metal jacket, boat-tail military bullet is reportedly very effective at 1500 meters. The commercial soft-point bullet is intended for hunting very heavy game. Cartridge cases are brass with Boxer primers. Guns for this cartridge are bolt-actions, but at least one gas-operated M-16-style rifle has been developed (RND Manufacturing, 14399 Mead Street, Longmont, CO 80504; (970) 535-4458).

.338 Lapua Magnum Factory Ballistics

Bullet (grains/type)	Powder	Grains	Velocity	Energy	Source/Comments
250 FMJ-BT Ball	FL		2,950	4,830	Military load
250 SP			2,855	4,525	Factory load

.338 Remington Ultra Mag

Historical Notes: The .338 Remington Ultra Mag is one of the most powerful .338-caliber rounds available, delivering 25 percent greater muzzle energy than the .338 Winchester Magnum and retaining a flatter trajectory all the way out to 500 yards. Remington introduced this cartridge in 2002 as a member of the Ultra Mag family of cartridges.

General Comments: In suitably equipped rifles, such as the Remington 700, and in the hands of a skillful hunter, the .338 Ultra Mag is an excellent choice for bear, elk, and moose. Except for bullet diameter and a slightly shorter case length, technical details of this cartridge are identical to the .300 Remington Ultra Mag.

.338 Remington Ultra Mag Factory Ballistics

Bullet (grains/type)	Powder	Grains	Velocity	Energy	Source/Comments
250 PSP	FL		2860	4540	Remington
250 Swift A-Frame	FL		2860	4540	Remington

.348 Winchester

Historical Notes: The .348 was developed by Winchester for the Model 71 lever-action rifle and introduced in 1936. No other rifle has ever been commercially available for this cartridge, and the Model 71 was discontinued in 1958. In 1987, Browning marketed a limited number of reproduction Model 71s that were made in Japan. At this writing, only Winchester still loads the .348, and the 200-grain bullet load is the lone survivor. The Model 71 was the smoothest lever-action ever built.

General Comments: One of the more powerful rimmed cartridges available for the lever-action rifle, the .348 was supposedly made obsolete by the newer .358 Winchester and the more modern Model 88 lever-action rifle (now also discontinued). The .348 is an excellent cartridge for any North American big game at close range. Due to the flat-point bullets required for use in the tubular magazine of the Model 71 rifle, it is not a particularly good long-range cartridge. The 150-grain bullet has very poor ballistic properties, due to its short, flat shape, and the 200- or 250-grain bullets are preferred for anything beyond 100 yards. Winchester dropped the 150-grain and 250-grain loads in 1962 but still offers the 200-grain loading. Remington no longer loads the round. The .348 is the basis for an entire list of Improved cartridges. Perhaps the best of these, a somewhat Improved .45-caliber version—which is very close to .458 Winchester Magnum performance—is still prized as among the best combination ever invented for use in Alaska, against heavy game in close quarters.

.348 Winchester Reloading Data and Factory Ballistics

Bullet (grains/type)	Powder	Grains	Velocity	Energy	Source/Comments
200 SP	H-4895	53	2,500	2,776	Hornady
200 SP	IMR 4350	60.5	2,500	2,776	Hornady
200 SP	IMR 4064	51	2,400	2,559	Hornady
250 SP	IMR 4350	55	2,300	2,937	Barnes
150 SP	FL		2,890	2,780	Factory load
200 SP	FL		2,520	2,820	Winchester factory load
250 SP	FL		2,350	3,060	Factory load

.35 Remington

Historical Notes: Introduced with the Remington Model 8 semi-automatic rifle, in 1906, the .35 Remington was later also chambered in the Remington models 14 and 141 pump-actions, the Model 81 semi-auto, Model 30 bolt-action, and, for a short time, in the Winchester bolt-action Model 70. At one time, the Marlin 336 lever-, Mossberg 479 lever-, and Savage 170 pump-action rifles were offered in .35 Remington. Currently, only the Marlin 336 rifle is still available; Remington's XP-100 was and Thompson/Center's handgun is still chambered for the .35 Remington.

General Comments: The .35 Remington is the only one of the Remington rimless line of medium-powered cartridges still alive. It has proven itself over the years as a reliable short-range woods cartridge on deer or black bear. It has far better knockdown power than the .30-30 under any conditions and at any range. The velocity and energy figures are not very different from the .30-30, but the larger, heavier bullet has greater shock and makes a more severe wound. The .35 Remington, with its moderate recoil, is a good cartridge for light rifles or carbines at short ranges (150 yards or less). It was originally the Remington counter to the much more powerful .35 Winchester. Remington, Winchester, Hornady, and Federal offer this ammunition.

Hornady now offers a LEVERevolution load with improved external ballistics, with about a 200 fps velocity advantage over standard factory loads. Buffalo Bore also offers a "heavy" .35 Remington load utilizing the excellent 220-grain Speer FP. Several bolt-action rifles have been chambered for the .35 Remington. My first custom bolt-action rifle was a .35 Remington built by Melvin Forbes' New Ultra Light Arms. Factory .35 Remington ammunition is held to a maximum average pressure of 33,500 psi, but, in a modern bolt-action, these is no reason this cartridge cannot be loaded to pressures (that's pressures, not velocities) similar to that of the more modern .358 Winchester. When chambered in a strong bolt-action like the Remington Model 7 available from the Remington custom shop as the Model 7 MS, a handloaded .35 Remington can push a 200-grain bullet to 2,400 fps with ease. Additionally, Indiana hunters looking for a cartridge that meets the newer .35-caliber and 1.8-inch case restriction would be wise to consider trimming a .35 Remington case by .12-inch.

.35 Remington Loading Data and Factory Ballistics

Bullet (grains/type)	Powder	Grains	Velocity	Energy	Source/Comments
200 Remington PSP	AA 2015	43.5	2,400	2,557	Richard Mann
125 SP	W680	32	2,400	1,599	Speer
140 HP	RL-7	40	2,500	1,943	Speer
158 SP	IMR 3031	37	2,200	1,698	Hornady, Speer
180 Speer FP	H4895	39.0	2,232	1,990	Hodgdon
200 Hornady RN	VarGet	39.5	2,139	2,030	Hodgdon
220 Speer FP	H4895	36.3	2,010	1,970	Hodgdon
150 SP	FL		2,300	1,762	Factory load
200 SP	FL		2,080	1,921	Factory load
220 Speer FP	FL		2,200	2,364	Buffalo Bore Factory Load

For light loads for small-game or varmint shooting at short range, use any 150- to 160-grain lead, gascheck, or half-jacketed .38 revolver bullet and 15 grains of 2400. Muzzle velocity will be about 2200 fps.

.35 Whelen

Historical Notes: Facts uncovered in recent research suggest that Col. Townsend Whelen may, after all, have been intimately involved in the creation of this cartridge, which has generally been heretofore attributed to James Howe of Griffin & Howe, of whom it was said developed and named it after the famous writer, hunter, and gun authority. The .35 Whelen is simply the .30-06 case necked up without any other change. Ackley championed an Improved version, which features less body taper and a sharper shoulder. The Improved version has two significant advantages. First it has about 10 percent more usable capacity, providing a similar increase in ballistics. The second is the more distinct shoulder, which completely solves the poor headspacing problem, resulting from a too narrow, steeply sloping shoulder, that .35 Whelen rifles have. One is hard pressed to explain why Remington chose to standardize the inferior version, when it adopted the .35 Whelen as a factory chambering in 1987.

General Comments: Remington has been active in adding popular wildcats to its line of commercial cartridges. The .35 Whelen is just one example. Previous editors for this book have had considerable past experience with the .35 Whelen, and it is an excellent cartridge for any North American big game, and most African species, as well. A pump-action rifle chambered for .35 Whelen makes a good combination. The .35 Whelen is one of the best balanced and most flexible medium bores for North American big game. There is a large variety of .35-caliber bullets available to the handloader, ranging from 110 to 300 grains in weight. The popularity of this round has waxed and waned over the years, reaching a peak during the 1920s and again shortly after World War II. Only Remington manufactures this ammunition.

.35 Whelen Loading Data and Factory Ballistics

Bullet (grains/type)	Powder	Grains	Velocity	Energy	Source/Comments
180 SP	IMR 4895	59	2,700	2,914	Hornady
180 SP	IMR 4320	56	2,700	2,914	Nosler
200 SP	IMR 4064	58.5	2,600	3,003	Hornady
225 SP	IMR 4320	56	2,500	3,123	Sierra
250 SP	IMR 4895	52.5	2,500	3,470	Hornady
250 SP	IMR 4064	54.5	2,400	3,198	Hornady
250 SP	RL-15	55	2,400	3,198	Hornady
200 SP	FL		2,675	3,177	Remington factory load
250 SP	FL		2,400	3,197	Remington factory load

.356 Winchester

Historical Notes: The .356 Winchester is a rimmed cartridge developed concurrently with the .307 Winchester for the Winchester Model 94 XTR Angle Eject lever-action carbine. Development of both cartridges began in 1980. Guns and ammunition were sold early in 1983. Marlin introduced the lever-action Model 336ER in .356-caliber about the same time the Winchester hit the market. The Winchester Model 94 XTR is a beefed-up version of the original Model 94 lever-action to allow the use of higher-pressure cartridges. The angle-eject feature is an additional modification to eject spent cartridge cases to the side instead of straight up. This feature allows center mounting of a scope sight, something not possible with the original 1894 action. This was accomplished by repositioning the extractor and ejector and lowering the right sidewall of the receiver slightly.

The .356-caliber designation was used to avoid confusion with the rimless .358 Winchester. In fact, the .356 is little more than a rimmed .358 and uses the same diameter bullets. The .356 and the .358 are not identical, since the .356 not only has a rim, but also the bullet is seated deeper to reduce overall length. It's possible to chamber .358 cartridges in .356 rifles, but firing them is an unsafe practice that could damage the gun and cause serious injury to the shooter.

General Comments: The ballistics of the .356 are slightly below the older rimless .358. Although it has been reported that the .356 Winchester and .307 have thicker case walls than the corresponding rimless .308 and .358 cartridges (and therefore reduced internal volume), measurements do not verify this. However, the .356 delivers performance superior to the .35 Remington by a significant margin. Factory published ballistics data show that the .35 Remington 200-grain bullet has a muzzle velocity of 2080 fps, whereas the .356 Winchester delivers 2,460 fps with the same bullet weight, both from a 24-inch barrel.

While the .35 Remington is largely a short-range cartridge for deer or black bear, the .356 Winchester would be adequate for larger game up to elk at longer ranges. One should consider, though, that both the Winchester and Marlin lever-action carbines, with their short 20-inch barrels, are intended primarily as light, handy guns for use in heavy cover. A hunter armed with one of the .356 carbines could probably take on just about anything likely to be encountered in the continental United States at short to moderate ranges. The .358 Winchester never achieved great popularity, and the .356 does not appear to be doing much better. Winchester is the only commercial manufacturer of this cartridge.

.356 Winchester Loading Data and Factory Ballistics

(Note: In tubular-magazine rifles, load only flat-point bullets.)

Bullet (grains/type)	Powder	Grains	Velocity	Energy	Source/Comments
158 SP	H-322	49	2,600	2,372	Speer
180 SP	H-322	48	2,600	2,703	Speer

.356 Winchester Loading Data and Factory Ballistics

(Note: In tubular-magazine rifles, load only flat-point bullets.)

Bullet (grains/type)	Powder	Grains	Velocity	Energy	Source/Comments
180 Speer FP	H4198	43.0	2,600	2,700	Hodgdon
220 SP	IMR 4064	46	2,300	2,585	Speer
250 Hornady RN	BL-C(2)	48.0	2,163	2,595	Hodgdon
200 SP	FL		2,460	2,688	Factory load
250 SP	FL		2,160	2,591	Factory load

.358 Winchester

Historical Notes: Introduced in 1955 by Winchester for its Model 70 Lightweight bolt-action and Model 88 lever-action rifles, the .358 Winchester is based on the .308 Winchester case necked up. It is known in Europe as the 8.8x51mm. Many European rifle makers chamber the round. In the United States, only the Browning BLR lever-action is currently chambered for this cartridge. The Model 99 Savage was also once available in .358.

General Comments: The .358 Winchester is one of the best commercial (non-magnum) .35-caliber cartridges turned out by any American manufacturer. It is a big improvement over the .35 Remington, slightly more powerful than the old .35 Winchester, and more useful than the .348 Winchester. As the 308 Winchester is a shortened version of the .30-06, by the same token the .358 is a shortened .35 Whelen. With its spitzer-pointed bullets, the .358 is a good medium- to long-range cartridge with capabilities out to 250 yards on big game. Although a good woods number, it is definitely beyond the short-range, deer-only class. In fact, the .358 is adequate for any North American big game. With the 250-grain bullet, it is better than the .30-06 on heavy game at close ranges. The .358 in a bolt-action rifle with a good scope is as accurate as any hunting cartridge available. Performance can be improved by handloading. Winchester is the only remaining manufacturer of this ammunition.

.358 Winchester Loading Data and Factory Ballistics

Bullet (grains/type)	Powder	Grains	Velocity	Energy	Source/Comments
158 SP	RL-7	48	2,850	2,850	Speer
180 SP	IMR 3031	51	2,700	2,914	Speer
200 SP	IMR 4320	50.5	2,500	2,776	Hornady, Sierra
200 SP	H-4198	40.5	2,500	2,776	Hornady
220 SP	BL-C2	49	2,500	3,054	Speer
250 SP	IMR 3031	41.5	2,200	2,687	Hornady, Speer
250 SP	IMR 4064	44	2,250	2,811	Speer
300 SP	IMR 4895	43	2,200	3,225	Barnes
200 SP	FL		2,490	2,753	Factory load
250 SP	FL		2,250	2,810	Factory load

.350 Remington Magnum

Historical Notes: Remington reintroduced the .350 Remington Magnum in 2002, chambered in its new Model 673 bolt-action rifle. The cartridge first appeared in the 1965 Remington catalog, concurrently with the Model 600

Magnum bolt-action carbine that chambered it. The original carbine had an 18-inch barrel, but, in 1968, this was lengthened to 20 inches in the Model 660 Magnum carbine. By 1971, the Model 600 and 660 Magnum carbines had been discontinued, but the .350 Magnum was continued as a standard chambering for the Model 700 bolt-action rifle until 1974. For a short time, the Ruger Model 77 bolt-action rifle was available in .350 Magnum. Currently, Remington offers the .350 Remington Magnum in the Model 673 Guide Rifle, which is a near lookalike M600 and based on the Model Seven action. The cartridge is unique in having a somewhat short, fat, belted case with somewhat more capacity than the .30-06. This allows for its use in short-action rifles that can be made a bit lighter and handier than those based on the standard-length bolt action.

General Comments: With bullets of moderate weight, the .350 Remington Magnum can nearly duplicate .35 Whelen ballistics in a much shorter barrel, and it can be chambered in short bolt-action rifles. This is a significant advantage for those preferring a light, handy rifle with plenty of punch. Also, many find the short-throw bolt to be much easier to use and master. For those preferring heavier bullets, the round-nose design doesn't take up so much of the powder space and, therefore, can safely develop better muzzle energy. For use where shots will not be long, these may be the best choice. For those with .350 Remington Magnum rifles in full-length actions, heavy spitzers can sometimes safely be seated to exceed the nominal 2.80-inch length for the cartridge, and increased muzzle energy can be achieved. Here, though, it is hard to see much advantage over the .35 Whelen, which generally feeds more smoothly from a magazine holding two additional cartridges. The .350 Remington Magnum is adequate for any North American big game at short to medium ranges.

.350 Remington Magnum Loading Data and Factory Ballistics

Bullet (grains/type)	Powder	Grains	Velocity	Energy	Source/Comments
125 HP	IMR 4895	60	2,850	2,255	Speer
158 SP	IMR 3031	58	2,850	2,850	Speer
180 SP	IMR 4064	62	2,900	3,362	Speer
200 SP	IMR 4320	60	2,700	3,238	Hornady, Sierra
220 SP	IMR 4895	60	2,650	3,431	Speer
250 SP	IMR 4895	53	2,350	3,066	Speer, Nosler
300 SP	IMR 4064	52	2,300	3,525	Barnes
200 SP	FL		2,710	3,261	Factory load

9.3x62mm Mauser

Historical Notes: Developed about 1905, by Otto Bock, a well-known Berlin gunmaker, this chambering was introduced to give the farmers and hunters in the German colonies of Africa an adequate cartridge. The story goes that, when many African countries were in the process of adopting restrictive laws specifying minimum chamberings for dangerous game hunting, most ruled for a minimum bore size of .40-caliber. Almost universally, the 9.3x62mm Mauser was exempted from the banned classification. It was soon used in Europe on wild boar and red deer. Mauser sporters were sold in the United States in this chambering until 1940. It is listed in late RWS and Norma catalogs. Browning and other rifles are available in Europe for this cartridge, and Steyr-Mannlicher rifles are currently so chambered.

General Comments: The 9.3x62mm is a powerful big-game cartridge, with a good reputation in Africa and Asia. It is sufficiently powerful for any North American big game and would be a good number for Alaskan bear. At one time, it was one of the most widely used, general-purpose medium bores in Africa. This was due partly to good performance, and partly to the fine, moderately priced bolt-action rifles that chambered it. A-Square and Norma produce ammunition and offer components, while Speer also makes appropriate bullets. A previous editor of this book used the listed 232-grain Norma Oryx load (bonded-core bullet) to dispatch his first moose. Bullet performance was flawless; at the shot, the bull dropped in his tracks and never so much as wiggled. This type of performance is the basis of the superior reputation this cartridge has earned worldwide.

14th Edition Update: In the last several years, due in part to the work of gun writers such as John Barsness, many American hunters are starting to warm up to this cartridge. It is starting to be chambered in factory new American rifles and several ammunition companies are now loading ammo for it. Previously listed in Chapter 8

("European Sporting Cartridges"), this newfound American appreciation of the 9.3x62mm cartridge warrants its movement to this chapter.

9.3x62mm Mauser Loading Data and Factory Ballistics

Bullet (grains/type)	Powder	Grains	Velocity	Energy	Source/Comments
250 SP	IMR 4350	63.0	2,606	3,754	Barnes (optimistic)
270 SP	IMR 4350	64.0	2,550	3,899	Speer (optimistic)
286 SP	H414	57.0	2,500	3,970	Barnes (optimistic)
232 Oryx	FL		2,624	3,548	Norma factory load
256 SP	FL		2,560	3,726	RWS factory load (optimistic)
286 SP	FL		2,360	3,544	Norma factory load
293 SP	FL		2,430	3,842	RWS factory load (optimistic)

.370 Sako Magnum
9.3x66mm Sako Magnum

Historical Notes: Few hunters who own rifles built by the Finnish firm of Sako realize the company started manufacturing ammunition during World War II, several years prior to building its first rifle. Sako rifles were introduced to the United States market during the early 1950s, but, with the exception of the .22 PPC and 6mm PPC, the ammunition has never been readily available here. Sako also makes big-game bullets of its own design, but also imports bullets from Sierra, Nosler, and Barnes for some cartridge loadings.

Around 2002, Sako introduced a new cartridge to the European market called the 9.3x66mm Sako. Lengthen the .30-06 case by three millimeters, expand its neck to accept a bullet of 9.3mm (or .366-inch) diameter and you've got it. Sako factory ammunition loaded with 250- and 286-grain bullets is rated at 2750 and 2550 fps, respectively. Worldwide, Sako exports more sporting rifles to the United States than any other country, and, since the 9.3x66mm Sako cartridge had quickly gained acceptance among Scandinavian hunters, the company decided to offer it to American hunters, as well. However, it saw a big, fat fly swimming around in that particular bowl of soup: historically, American hunters have pretty much ignored to death any cartridge with a metric designation. So, in an effort to make the cartridge more appealing to American hunters, its name was changed to .370 Sako Magnum. Since Sako doesn't import ammunition to the United States, the company chose Federal to make the ammo. This, by the way, was the second time those two companies have collaborated to bring us a new cartridge (the .338 Federal was first).

General Comments: While its slightly greater powder capacity allows the 9.3x66mm Sako Magnum to push all bullet weights about 100 fps faster than the considerably older 9.3x62mm Mauser, the two cartridge are still in the same performance class. When all are loaded with 250-grain bullets, the .35 Whelen also belongs here, although the slightly larger diameter of 9.3mm bullets, along with the fact that they are available in heavier weights, may give the two metric cartridges a bit of an edge, when used on the larger game animals. One of the biggest things the 9.3 Sako Magnum has going for it is any rifle chambered for any member of the .30-06 family of cartridges can be converted to it with rebarreling, and that being the only modification necessary. As factory cartridges of its caliber go, only the 9.3x64mm Brenneke is more powerful, and not by a lot at that. Quality Cartridge (www.qual-cart.com) currently lists brass for this round.

.370 Sako Magnum Loading Data and Factory Ballistics

Bullet (grains/type)	Powder	Grains	Velocity	Energy	Source
286 Nosler Partition		FL	2,550	4,125	Federal
286 Barnes TSX/FB		FL	2,550	4,125	Federal

9.3x66mm Sako Magnum Factory Ballistics

Bullet (grains/type)	Powder	Grains	Velocity	Energy	Source/Comments
250 Nosler BT	FL		2,756	4,210	Sako factory load
286 RN Hammerhead	FL		2,559	4,147	Sako factory load
286 Barnes X-Bullet	FL		2,543	4,093	Sako factory load
286 Barnes Solid	FL		2,559	4,147	Sako factory load

.376 Steyr

Historical Notes: Hornady and Steyr announced this chambering at the 2000 SHOT Show. Jeff Cooper has long heralded the "scout rifle" concept. Basically, this is a short, lightweight, bolt-action rifle that is essentially designed to be equipped with a forward-mounted, compact, long eye relief scope of low magnification. Hence, the Scout Rifle is a package deal. Cooper wanted a chambering for his creation that would do in a pinch for stopping practically any game on earth. The specific critter of his actual concern was the Cape buffalo, long noted for bad temper, tenacity, and terminally effective retaliation. From this backdrop grew the .376 Steyr. Using bullets up to 300-grains and easily generating as much as 4000 ft-lbs of muzzle energy, it would seem that the .376 Steyr should fulfill Jeff's wishes.

General Comments: This case, while an essentially new design, shares characteristics with several earlier numbers. Base diameter, at .500-inch, is just about the same as the .284 Winchester (nominally .496-inch) or the 9.3x64mm Brenneke (nominally .504-inch). The rim, at .494-inch, is sufficiently smaller than the case body, so as to qualify this as a (slightly) rebated rim design. Shoulder angle is quite shallow, to facilitate smooth feeding from the magazine. Case and cartridge length (2.35-inch and 3.075, respectively), are both intermediate between traditional short-action and long-action numbers. Capacity and maximum pressure specification are sufficient to accommodate substantial performance. With the ready availability of a wide selection of bullets of various quality levels and weights, this should be a very versatile chambering. We predict that it will also form the basis of an entire genre of new wildcat cartridges. To establish precedence, one of the former editor's of this book took the opportunity to declare his intentions to adjust neck diameter and length on the .376 Steyr case to produce cartridges appropriate to both 2.8-inch and 3.2-inch actions in every feasible bore size from 6mm to .41-caliber.

For those who prefer the style, the Scout Rifle is a very fine design for hunting dangerous game. However, with the proposed Steyr rifle weighing in at far under 8 pounds—making it significantly heavier would seem to defeat Cooper's design intent—recoil is no small matter.

The .376 Steyr drew a moderate amount of attention, when it was introduced. This was probably due to the fact it was available in the Steyr Scout Rifle. However, the cartridge has failed to catch on, very likely because no American firearms manufacturer offers rifles chambered for this cartridge. Some also predicted the case would become the basis for a wide range of wildcat cartridges. These, if any at all have been created, are getting no attention. However, it could be argued that the .30 Remington AR is loosely based on the .376 Steyr case.

.376 Steyr Factory Ballistics

Bullet (grains/type)	Powder	Grains	Velocity	Energy	Source/Comments
225 Hornady SP	FL		2,560	3,325	Hornady, Steyr Specified Loading
270 Hornady SP	FL		2,560	3,990	Hornady
250 Sierra SP	H 4895	65.0	2,732	4,142	Hodgdon
300 Swift SP	Varget	62.5C	2,560	3,325	Hodgdon
225 Hornady SP	FL		2,560	3,325	Hornady Factory Load
270 Hornady SP	FL		2,560	3,990	Hornady Factory Load

.378 Weatherby Magnum

Historical Notes: Another development by the late Roy Weatherby, this one dating back to 1953, this is an original design not based on any existing cartridge, although it is hard to miss the similarity in all critical dimensions to the .416 Rigby. It was first field-tested in the spring of 1953 by Weatherby, who downed an elephant with one shot. The Federal Cartridge Co.'s No. 215 Magnum Large Rifle primer was originally developed for this cartridge, as existing primers did not properly ignite the large quantity of powder used. Only the Weatherby line of rifles is commercially chambered for this round.

General Comments: According to the Weatherby catalog, the .378 WM was designed for deep penetration on heavy, thick-skinned game. It is also intended to furnish an extra margin of insurance when facing dangerous game such as rhino, Cape buffalo, elephant, or lion in thick cover. Field reports indicate that it lives up to these expectations. However, for proper performance at the velocities developed, it is necessary to use bullets with a very heavy jacket. Although considerably overpowered for any North American big game, it is nonetheless a fine cartridge for the hunter who requires optimum stopping power. Recoil of these cartridges is extremely heavy, so one should be sure such power is really needed before selecting anything in this class.

.378 Weatherby Magnum Loading Data and Factory Ballistics

Bullet (grains/type)	Powder	Grains	Velocity	Energy	Source/Comments
235 SP	H-4831	115	3,200	5,345	Barnes
250 SP	H-4831	113	3,050	5,165	Barnes
270 SP	IMR 4350	108	3,100	5,763	Hornady
300 SP	H-4831	112	2,900	5,604	Sierra, Nosler
350 SP	H-4831	102	2,650	5,459	Barnes
270 SP	FL		3,180	6,062	Weatherby factory load
300 SP	FL		2,925	5,701	Weatherby factory load

.375 Winchester

Historical Notes: Developed by Winchester, the .375 was announced in 1978 as a new cartridge for the Model 94 Big Bore lever-action carbine. The gun is a strengthened version of the standard Model 94 action and can be distinguished by the beefed-up rear quarter of the receiver, as opposed to the flat sides of the regular Model 94. The cartridge is based on a shortened (about 1/10-inch) .38-55 case, although .375 Winchester cases are heavier and stronger than those of the .38-55. Two carbines were initially available in this caliber, the Winchester Model 94 Big Bore and the Ruger No. 3 single-shot. This is a rimmed case and not well-suited to Mauser-type bolt-actions. Two bullet weights are offered, a 200-grain at 2200 fps muzzle velocity, and a 250-grain at 1900 fps, as advertised by Winchester.

General Comments: The .375 Winchester fills a gap in the line of cartridges available for the popular Winchester Model 1894 lever-action series. Many hunters who hunt in heavy cover prefer large- or medium-caliber rifles firing heavy bullets as the best combination for their particular hunting environment. Such a combination was not available for the Winchester Model 1894. The .375 offers competition to lever-actions chambered for the .35 Remington and .444 Marlin. Comparisons will be made between this .375 and the other popular woods cartridges, such as the .35 Remington, .44 Magnum, .444 Marlin, and .45-70. Ballistically, the .444 Marlin, with its 240-grain bullet and 2400 fps muzzle velocity, has the edge on all the others in the group. However, all these cartridges have one common failing: They are used in lever-action rifles with tubular magazines. This requires a flat-pointed bullet so that, under recoil, one cartridge won't set off the one ahead of it in the magazine. These blunt bullets offer high air resistance. No matter what the initial velocity, they all slow down quite rapidly. The result is that, at 200 yards or less, they all end up with about the same energy, which varies from 1000 to 1100 ft-lbs. All these brush cartridges, then, are at their best at ranges of 150 yards or less.

Certainly the .375 Winchester is a fine deer or black bear cartridge and would probably also do well on heavier game such as moose or brown bear. Within its range limitations, it would also serve as a good meat-getter on thin-skinned African species. The .375 cartridge can be chambered in .38-55 rifles, but must never be fired in any rifle except those specifically marked for it, because it develops much higher pressure than the older .38-55. To fire it in any of the old black-powder rifles would almost certainly result in a wrecked gun and serious injury to the shooter. Winchester is the only commercial manufacturer of this ammunition.

.375 Winchester Loading Data and Factory Ballistics

Bullet (grains/type)	Powder	Grains	Velocity	Energy	Source/Comments
200 Sierra JFP	H4198	38.0	2,480	2,730	Hodgdon
220 Hornady JFP	RL-7	36.0	2,260	2,495	Hodgdon
220 SP	RL-7	38	2,200	2,365	Hornady
235 SP	IMR 4198	32	2,000	2,088	Speer
235 SP	RL-7	35	1,950	1,985	Speer
255 SP	IMR 3031	36	1,900	20,45	Barnes
200 SP	FL		2,200	2,150	Winchester factory load
250 SP	FL		1,900	2,005	Winchester factory load

.375 Holland & Holland Magnum (.375 H&H Magnum)

Historical Notes: Originated by the British firm Holland & Holland in 1912, this is one of the original belted, rimless, magnum-type cartridges. It has been used as the basis for numerous wildcats and most of the Weatherby cartridges. H&H furnished it in a magnum Mauser action, and Griffin & Howe chambered rifles for it, beginning about 1926. The Western Cartridge Co. first offered it in 1925. At present, Federal, Remington, and Winchester load the .375. The first commercial rifle of American make to chamber the round was the Model 70 Winchester, in 1937. Weatherby rifles were at one time available in .375 H&H, as was the Remington Model 725 Kodiak. At present, several American manufacturers list the .375 H&H as standard including Ruger, Winchester, and Remington.

General Comments: Long considered the best all-round African caliber, the .375 H&H is overpowered for North American big game. However, many Alaskan hunters and guides prefer it for moose and grizzly bear. It isn't a very flexible cartridge for the American hunter, unless one expects to hunt the heaviest species and spend time in Africa or Asia. John Taylor, in his 1948 book *African Rifles and Cartridges*, rates the .375 as the best of the medium bores for African hunting. It is his candidate for the most effective all-round cartridge. This cartridge was the basis for H&H's latter .300 H&H Magnum and is therefore the great-grandfather of almost all modern belted magnum chamberings. It can certainly be said that it inspired the entire genre.

.375 Holland & Holland Magnum Loading Data and Factory Ballistics

Bullet (grains/type)	Powder	Grains	Velocity	Energy	Source/Comments
200 SP	IMR 4064	80	3,200	4,549	Sierra
220 SP	SR4759	42	2,300	2,585	Hornady
235 SP	IMR 4064	77	3,000	4,697	Speer
270 SP	RL-15	74	2,700	4,372	Hornady
270 SP	IMR 4064	70	2,600	4,054	Hornady
285 SP	IMR 4831	85	2,700	4,615	Speer
300 SP	IMR 4064	68	2,500	4,164	Hornady
300 SP	IMR 4350	77	2,600	4,504	Sierra, Hornady

Bullet (grains/type)	Powder	Grains	Velocity	Energy	Source/Comments
350 SP	IMR 4320	65.5	2,400	4,478	Barnes
270 SP	FL		2,690	4,340	Factory load
300 SP	FL		2,530	4,265	Factory load

.375 Weatherby Magnum

Historical Notes: The .375 Weatherby Magnum was developed by the late Roy Weatherby, between 1944 and 1945, and was chambered only in Weatherby rifles. There are several similar wildcat versions, such as the .375 Ackley Improved Magnum, but the .375 Weatherby had the advantage of commercial ammunition loaded by Weatherby using Norma cases. Its popularity lasted until the more powerful, harder-recoiling .378 Weatherby displaced it, about 1953, but returned to the Weatherby line when many hunters demanded something that recoiled less than the .378 Weatherby, but had more power than the .375 H&H.

General Comments: The .375 WM is a full-length, blown-out, and Improved cartridge based on the .375 H&H case. It holds more powder and delivers higher velocities with the same bullets, compared to the parent cartridge. It is really overpowered for North American big game. On African game, it will qualify for just about anything and is considered a fine all-round cartridge, particularly for dangerous game. The 270-grain bullet approximates .30-06 trajectories and is a fine long-range load for large North American game and for thin-skinned African animals. Commercial chambers are free-bored in the Weatherby tradition, and this increases the charge required to achieve any given pressure and velocity.

Out of production for several decades, the .375 Weatherby was reintroduced in 2001 and is available in Weatherby's Mark V Dangerous Game Rifle and Fibermark composite rifles. Some factory .375 H&H rifles can be rechambered to the .375 Weatherby.

.375 Weatherby Magnum Loading Data and Factory Ballistics

Bullet (grains/type)	Powder	Grains	Velocity	Energy	Source/Comments
235 SP	IMR 4064	84.0	3,015	4,745	Ackley
270 SP	IMR 4064	80.0	2,795	4,685	Ackley
300 SP	IMR 4350	86.0	2,675	4,770	Ackley
270 SP	FL		2,940	5,181	Weatherby factory load
300 SP	FL		2,800	5,223	Weatherby factory load
300 Nosler Partition	FL		2,800	5,224	Weatherby factory load

.375 Ruger

Historical Notes: The actions of popular rifles such as the Remington Model 700, Weatherby Mark V, and Winchester Model 70 are long enough to handle full-length belted magnums such as the .300 Weatherby Magnum and .375 Holland & Holland Magnum, but, with the exception of the rather expensive "Magnum" variation of the Ruger Model 77, the actions of Ruger bolt-action rifles are too short to handle them. So, rather than creating a more affordable version of the Magnum action, Ruger officials made the decision to team up with Hornady and introduce a magnum-performance chambering short enough for the company's standard action.

Maximum overall length of the .375 Ruger is 3.340 inches, which is the same as for medium-length belted cartridges such as the 7mm Remington Magnum and .300 Winchester Magnum. Rim diameter of the case is also the same as for those cartridges, but its powder capacity is greater, due to a body diameter close to that of the .375 Remington Ultra Mag.

General Comments: With a case capacity slightly greater than that of the .375 H&H Magnum, the .375 Ruger is about 100 fps faster than that cartridge, pretty much duplicating the performance of the .375 Dakota and treading closely on the heels of the .375 Weatherby Magnum. As any big-game hunter of experience knows, that puts it in very good company. As readily available factory cartridges of the same caliber go, only the .378 Weatherby Magnum and the .375 Remington Ultra Mag. are faster. Capable of pushing a 300-grain bullet along at 2600 fps, the .375 Ruger is plenty of cartridge for use on any game animal anywhere in the world, with the possible exception of the really big stuff, such as African elephant. Also in its favor is the fact that many excellent bullets of .375-caliber in both solid and expanding styles are available. Only time will tell if companies other than Hornady offer the ammunition.

.375 Ruger Loading Data and Factory Ballistics

Bullet (grains/type)	Powder	Grains	Velocity	Energy	Source
235 Barnes TSX/FB	H380	79.5	2,907	4,405	Hodgdon
260 Nosler Partition	RL-15	76.0	2,883	4,493	Nosler
300 Barnes TSX/FB	W760	78.5	2,642	4,645	Barnes
300 Nosler Partition	RL-15	72.0	2,619	4,564	Nosler
300 Hornady RN	H414	79.5	2,642	4,645	Hodgdon
300 Hornady DGX	FL		2,660	4,708	Hornady

.375 Remington Ultra Mag

Historical Notes: With the flat trajectory of a 150-grain .270 Winchester load, the .375 Remington Ultra Mag is one of the hardest-hitting .375 chamberings available. Introduced in 2002 and based on Remington's Ultra Mag cartridge family, the .375 Ultra Mag has 23 percent more energy at the muzzle than the .375 H&H and delivers more energy at 200 yards than does the .375 H&H at 100 yards.

General Comments: In suitably equipped rifles, such as the Remington 700, and in the hands of a skillful hunter, the .375 Ultra Magnum is an excellent choice for African and Alaskan game noted for their fangs, teeth, claws, and attitude. Except for bullet diameter, technical details of this cartridge are identical to the .300 Remington Ultra Magnum. (See separate listing.)

.375 Remington Ultra Magnum Load Data/Factory Ballistics

Bullet (grains/type)	Powder	Grains	Velocity	Energy	Source/Comments
Bullet (grains/type)	Powder	Grains	Velocity	Energy	Source
235 Barnes TSX	RL-19	107.0	3,191	5,307	Barnes
260 Nosler Partition	IMR-4350	96.0	3,026	5,280	Nosler
270 Barnes TSX	RL-19	102.5	3,019	5,458	Barnes
300 Nosler Partition	IMR-7828	96.0	3,026	6,093	Nosler
270 SP	FL		2,900	5,041	Remington factory load
300 Swift A-Frame	FL		2,760	5,073	Remington factory load

.38-55 Winchester (.38-55 Ballard)

Historical Notes: Like the smaller .32-40, the .38-55 was originally a Ballard-developed target cartridge. The present commercial version was introduced, in 1884, as one of the cartridges for the Ballard Perfection No. 4, which was originally chambered for the .38-50 Everlasting. According to Satterlee, in his *Catalog of Firearms, 2nd Ed.* (Detroit, 1939), the Union Hill Nos. 8 and 9 were also chambered for the .38-55 Ballard, in 1884. The external dimensions of the .38-55 Everlasting and the .38-55 Winchester & Ballard are nearly identical, but the heavier, thicker Everlasting version was a handloading proposition. The implication in Satterlee's book is that the original Everlasting case was introduced when Marlin Fire Arms Co. took over Ballard, in 1881. The .38-55 Everlasting is nothing more than a 1/10-inch longer case than the .38-50 that Ballard introduced in 1876.

The Marlin Model 93 and Winchester 94 lever-action repeaters were available in .38-55, as was the Remington-Lee bolt-action, Colt's New Lightning pump-action, Stevens, Remington, and Winchester single-shot rifles, and also the Savage Model 99. No commercial rifles were available after Winchester dropped the .38-55 from the Model 94 list of calibers, in 1940. However, Winchester has reintroduced the cartridge in several versions of the Model 94 in recent years, and it also has been offered in the H&R Handi-Rifle and others. The .225 Winchester, .22 Savage High Power, .25-35 Winchester, .32-40 Winchester, .30-30 Winchester, .32 Winchester Special, .375 Winchester, and a host of wildcat cartridges are based on this case.

General Comments: The .38-55 built up a reputation for fine accuracy at ranges out to 200 yards, and the growing popularity of cowboy action shooting has breathed new life into this fine old cartridge. It also developed a modest popularity with deer and black bear hunters. It gave good knockdown on deer-size animals with the 255-grain bullet at velocities of over 1500 fps. At one time, factory-loaded cartridges were available with the 255-grain bullet at a muzzle velocity of 1700 fps. At these higher velocities, it is a better deer cartridge than the .30-30. Present factory loadings more or less duplicate black-powder ballistics. In old Ballard and Stevens single-shot rifles, it is not safe to use loads developing velocities over 1500 fps. Discontinued in 1970, the .38-55 is again listed in Winchester ammunition catalogs. Proper bullet diameter for cast bullets is .379-inch.

.38-55 Winchester & Ballard Loading Data and Factory Ballistics

Bullet (grains/type)	Powder	Grains	Velocity	Energy	Source/Comments
200 FN	XMP5744	25.5	1,853	1,525	Accurate Arms
220 SP	RL-7	31	1,600	1,257	Hornady
220 SP	IMR 3031	33	1,600	1,251	Hornady
220 SP	IMR 3031	34.5	1,700	1,412	Hornady
220 SP	IMR 4198	26	1,600	1,251	Hornady
220 SP	RL-7	29.5	1,400	958	Hornady
240 Lead	XMP5744	22.0	1,601	1,365	Accurate
222 FN	XMP5744	23.5	1,648	1,325	Accurate
255 SP	H-4895	35	1,700	1,637	Barnes
255 SP	FL		1,320	987	Winchester factory load
255 JFN	FL		1,980	2,153	Buffalo Bore Factory Load

.38-40 Winchester (.38-40 WCF)

Historical Notes: The .38-40 was developed by Winchester as a companion cartridge to its .44-40 and introduced in 1874. It is based on the .44-40 case necked down to what is actually .40-caliber (.401-inch). It was originally a black-powder cartridge chambered in the Winchester Model 73 lever-action. About 1878, Colt's began chambering revolvers for it. It was later offered in the Remington Model 14½ pump-action, Winchester

92 and Marlin 94 lever-actions, plus a number of single-shot rifles. No rifles have been chambered for the .38-40 since 1937. Winchester loaded a slightly different version especially for the Colt Lightning Magazine Rifle, headstamped .38 C.L.M.R. Another version was loaded with the same 180-grain bullet as the .38 Winchester, but with 40 grains of black powder instead of Winchester's standard load of 38 grains and was headstamped .38-40 instead of .38 W.C.F. This raises the intriguing possibility that the name we now use, .38-40, came from 38 grains of black powder and a .40-caliber bore.

General Comments: The .38-40 was, at one time, a popular medium-power cartridge. Winchester used to load a high-velocity rifle version with a 180-grain bullet at 1775 fps. This was considered a pretty good short-range deer number, but was not intended for old black-powder rifles or revolvers. It was discontinued because it caused a lot of trouble for people who never read labels. The present factory loading is strictly for revolvers, and it is necessary to handload in order to realize the full potential in a rifle. With proper load and bullets, the .38-40 can be used on small game, varmints, medium-size game, or even deer at short range. Rifle loads should not be used in revolvers, as these loads develop pressures beyond safe limits.

Frank Barnes' experience with the .38-40 was limited to one Remington Model 14½R pump-action carbine that was used for several years before being traded off for something more useful. Although it was a nice, handy little rifle, he was not particularly impressed with the cartridge. The .38-40 is a bit much for most varmint and small-game shooting and really not adequate for deer-size animals. In any event, it is quite limited in its effective range on whatever you happen to be using it for. This lack of enthusiasm notwithstanding, the .38-40 enjoyed a certain popularity from its inception until about 1920, after which it declined in sales volume. It was finally discontinued in 1937. Actually, there is no great difference in performance between the .38-40 and the .44-40, although some considered the .38-40 a better cartridge for a woman or young boy because it had less recoil. Honestly, neither one has any great recoil, and Frank could never tell much difference between the two in that regard.

The .38-40 made a better revolver cartridge than it did a rifle cartridge. The present factory load with the 180-grain bullet at 1160 fps (Winchester) cannot be considered adequate for deer, and only by handloading can one achieve acceptable performance for much of anything except self-defense, for which it is formidable.

.38-40 Winchester Loading Data and Factory Ballistics

Bullet (grains/type)	Powder	Grains	Velocity	Energy	Source/Comments
155 SP	2400	15	1,200	496	Hornady
155 SP	IMR 4227	19.5	1,200	496	Hornady
180 HP	2400	14.5	1,100	484	Hornady
180 HP	Unique	9	1,100	484	Hornady
180 HP	IMR 4227	18.5	1,100	484	Hornady
200 HP	Unique	8.4	1,000	444	Hornady
200 HP	2400	13.5	1,050	490	Hornady
180 SP	FL		1,160	538	Winchester factory load

.416 Weatherby Magnum

Historical Notes: There has been a moderate, but persistent, interest in .40-caliber dangerous-game cartridges for a good many years. The demand has been filled by several wildcat cartridges, but the call for a factory .40-caliber intensified in the 1980s. Remington was the first to exploit this potential market with its .416 Remington Magnum, in 1988. This was followed by the .416 Weatherby Magnum (which is based on the .378 Weatherby Magnum), in 1989. In the game of cartridge one-upmanship, the Weatherby version was bound to be somewhat more powerful than an "ordinary" .416.

General Comments: The .416 Weatherby Magnum offers 300 fps more initial velocity than the .416 Remington Magnum with the same bullet weight. How useful this will be in the field is difficult to assess, because both cartridges are adequate for the intended purpose, which is to dispatch large and/or dangerous game with a minimum of fuss. On the other hand, Weatherby rifles carry a certain prestige, and there is nothing wrong with having a little extra power when the crucial moment arrives. The choice between the two will probably be a matter of personal preference. However, recoil is rather brisk with any such chambering, and more powder pushing the same bullet faster translates into more recoil.

.416 Weatherby Loading Data and Factory Ballistics

Bullet (grains/type)	Powder	Grains	Velocity	Energy	Source/Comments
300 SP	IMR 4831	115	3,000	5,997	Barnes
350 SP	IMR 4831	110	2,800	6,095	Barnes
400 SP	IMR 4831	110.5	2,700	6,477	Hornady
400 SP	H-450	119	2,700	6,477	Hornady
400 SP	IMR 7828	117	2,600	6,006	Hornady
400 SP	FL		2,700	6,474	Weatherby factory load

.416 Ruger

Historical Notes: The actions of popular rifles such as the Remington Model 700, Weatherby Mark V, and Winchester Model 70 are long enough to handle full-length belted magnums such as the .375 Holland & Holland Magnum and .416 Remington Magnum, but with the exception of the rather expensive "Magnum" variation of the Ruger Model 77, the actions of Ruger bolt-action rifles are too short to handle them. So, rather than coming up with a more affordable version of the Magnum action, Ruger officials made the decision to team up with Hornady and introduce a magnum-performance chambering short enough for the company's standard action. Maximum overall length of the .416 Ruger is 3.240 inches, which is the same as for medium-length belted cartridges such as the 7mm Remington Magnum and .300 Winchester Magnum. Rim diameter of the case is also the same as for those cartridges, but its powder capacity is greater, due to a body diameter close to that of the .375 Remington Ultra Mag.

General Comments: With a case capacity only slightly less than that of the .416 Remington Magnum, the .416 Ruger comes close to duplicating the performance of that cartridge, and it exceeds standard loadings of the .416 Rigby. As any big-game hunter who has used the Remington and Rigby cartridges on game knows, this puts the Ruger cartridge in very good company. As readily available factory cartridges of the same caliber go, only the .416 Weatherby Magnum is faster. Capable of easily pushing a 400-grain bullet along at 2400 to 2500 fps, the .416 Ruger is plenty of cartridge for use on any game animal anywhere in the world, when loaded with the proper bullets. Also in its favor is the fact that many excellent bullets of .416-caliber in both solid and expanding styles are available.

.416 Ruger Loading Data and Factory Ballistics

Bullet (grains/type)	Powder	Grains	Velocity	Energy	Source
400 Hornady DGX	FL		2,500	5,545	Hornady

.416 Rigby

Historical Notes: Introduced by John Rigby of London, the .416 Rigby is a good example of a sound design that refuses to die. Until quite recently, fewer than 10,000 rifles in this caliber had been made. However, most of the older rifles in that chambering are still in use. In 1992, Ruger added this cartridge to its rifle product line. Ruger thus increased the total number of guns in this chambering by 10 percent in one year. The company continues to produce it. In 1989, Federal Cartridge Co. added the .416 Rigby to its Premium product line. In so doing, Federal became the first major American manufacturer to offer this classic African cartridge.

By their actions, both Ruger and Federal took away much of the momentum from the new .416 Remington Magnum cartridge. Their efforts in reintroducing the .416 Rigby have been successful, and sales remain brisk. This only goes to show that not all new product success stories use totally new products.

General Comments: The .416 Rigby is today a great favorite of African game wardens and professional hunters alike. It is an excellent choice for the hunter who wishes to take only one rifle to Africa. Federal ballistics are identical to previous British loads, so the point of impact with express sights will be the same. Breech pressures of the .416 are only about 40,000 CUP, in order to avoid sticky extraction exhibited by high pressures on very hot days. This is strictly good sense, based on many years of African experience. Remington has chosen to load the .416 Remington Magnum to pressure levels of 50,000 CUP, which makes one wonder if extraction at very high temperatures has been adequately tested, and handloaders should resist the urge to improve the .416 Rigby ballistics for this reason. Bullets and brass for handloading are available from Huntington (www.huntingtonsports.com).

.416 Rigby Loading Data and Factory Ballistics

Bullet (grains/type)	Powder	Grains	Velocity	Energy	Source/Comments
300 Barnes XFB	RL-22	103.0	2,590	4,470	Hodgdon
350 Barnes XFB	H4350	102.0	2,518	4,925	Hodgdon
400 Hornady FMJNR	H4831	106.0	2,422	5,210	Hodgdon
410 SP/FMJ	FL		2,370	5,115	Federal factory load

.416 Remington Magnum

Historical Notes: Officially announced in November 1988, the .416 Remington Magnum was the first American cartridge designed for use on African game to be introduced since the .458 Winchester Magnum in 1956, and the .460 Weatherby Magnum back in 1958. The .416 is based on the 8mm Remington Magnum necked up to .416-caliber. It was initially available with either a 400-grain pointed soft-point or a 400-grain solid bullet loaded to a muzzle velocity of 2400 fps and a muzzle energy of 5115 ft-lbs. The company says that the 400-grain solid is exactly that, turned from solid brass and not a lead core with a heavy jacket. The cartridge was available in the Remington Model 700 Safari bolt-action rifle. Other rifle manufacturers have picked up the .416 Remington. It is available in a variety of bolt-action and single-shot rifles, including those from Ruger. It has proven to be a fairly popular cartridge.

General Comments: There has been a persistent call, by those who hunt dangerous game, for a cartridge to fill the gap between the .375 Holland & Holland Magnum and the .458 Winchester Magnum. The .416 Rigby accomplished this rather well, but both rifles and ammunition became increasingly difficult to obtain, until Federal began offering that cartridge in the late 1980s. This problem was then solved, to some extent, by a number of wildcat cartridges such as the .416 Taylor, .416 Hoffman, and the .425 Express. These cartridges all more or less duplicated the performance of the .416 Rigby, and the .416 Remington does pretty much the same thing. However, the Remington version has one great advantage in that it is available as a commercial loading in a proven commercial rifle. The combination will be much easier and less expensive to come by than a custom rifle for wildcat or proprietary cartridges.

Although the .416 bullet is 100 grains lighter than that of the .458 Winchester, it starts out with an almost 300 fps higher velocity. That, combined with better sectional density and a superior aerodynamic shape, gives it certain ballistic advantages. It not only has a higher initial velocity, it also increases its retained velocity over the .458 as the range increases. According to the factory figures, it has an 11 percent advantage in muzzle energy, and this increases to 18 percent at 100 yards and 30 percent at 200 yards.

The .416 Remington should be ideal for dangerous game, including Cape buffalo, elephant, lion, and brown bear. It would also do well on moose and elk. The .416 Remington has a trajectory very similar to the .375 H&H and is a better long-range cartridge than the .458 Winchester for use against thin-skinned game. For the man who has to travel light, the .416 would be a good one-gun cartridge choice for use in Africa. To date, only Remington loads ammunition in this caliber.

Bullet (grains/type)	Powder	Grains	Velocity	Energy	Source/Comments
300 SP	H-4895	78	2,850	5,412	Barnes
350 SP	H-4895	80	2,700	5,667	Barnes
400 SP	IMR 4064	78	2,400	5,117	Hornady
400 SP	IMR 4895	76.5	2,400	5,117	Hornady
300 SP	FL		2,530	4,262	Remington factory load
350 SP	FL		2,520	4,935	Remington factory load
400 SP	FL		2,400	5,115	Remington factory load

.44-40 Winchester
(.44 WCF, .44 Winchester)

Historical Notes: This was the original cartridge of the famous Winchester Model 1873 lever-action repeating rifle. By 1878, Colt's began offering revolvers in .44-40-caliber. At one time or another, just about every American arms manufacturer has offered some kind of gun chambered for this cartridge. The Colt-Burgess lever-action rifle of 1883 was made for the .44-40, and so was the 1885 Colt Lightning pump-action rifle. The Remington Model 14½ pump-action used it, as did the Winchester 92 and Marlin 94, both lever-action repeaters. Most of the single-shot rifles made in the United States had a .44-40 model at one time or another. In Spain, there was a copy of the Winchester Model 92 in .44-40 caliber manufactured for police and civil guard use. No American-made rifles have chambered the round since 1937, but Colt's revolvers retained it until 1942. Several foreign-made replicas of the Henry Carbine and the Winchester Model 66 and 73 are currently available in .44-40, as are new revolvers.

Winchester once loaded a 217-grain bullet in two separate headstamps: .44 C.L.M.R. for the Colt Lightning Magazine Rifle, and .44-40 for Marlin rifles. It also offered a 34-grain black powder load behind a 115-grain bullet for the Marble Game Getter rifle, which was headstamped .44 G.G.

General Comments: The .44-40 is one of the all-time great American cartridges. It is said that it has killed more game, large and small, and more people, good and bad, than any other commercial cartridge ever developed. In its original black-powder loading, it was the first effective combination cartridge that could be used interchangeably in rifle or revolver, and was a great favorite in the early days of the American West.

With proper handloads used in strong rifles, the .44-40 can safely propel the 200-grain jacketed bullet at 1800 fps. Compared to the standard .30-30 load with a 170-grain bullet at about 2100 fps, this is a superior combination against deer at short range. It was once offered in a high-velocity loading specifically designed to take advantage of the Model 92 Winchester's strength. As with many other high-velocity loadings of yesteryear, it had to be discontinued, because certain folks just insisted on chambering anything that would fit in whatever gun was at hand. The .44-40 became obsolete in the revolver with the advent of the .357 and .44 Magnums, and in the rifle by the .30-30 and similar cartridges that have a flatter trajectory at ranges beyond 100 yards. Present factory loads by Remington and Winchester are intended for revolvers, and it is necessary to handload in order to get top performance from the rifle. Many .44-40 rifles have been rebarreled for the .44 Magnum. The rise of cowboy action shooting has rekindled the .44-40's popularity.

.44-40 Winchester Loading Data and Factory Ballistics

Bullet (grains/type)	Powder	Grains	Velocity	Energy	Source/Comments
180 SP	2400	18	1,250	625	Hornady
180 SP	SR4756	11	1,150	529	Hornady
180 SP	2400	16.5	1,000	400	Hornady
180 SP	Unique	10.4	1,150	529	Hornady
200 SP	IMR 4227	20	1,100	537	Hornady

Bullet (grains/type)	Powder	Grains	Velocity	Energy	Source/Comments
200 SP	2400	15.3	1,000	444	Hornady
200 SP	Unique	9.5	1,050	490	Hornady
200 SP	FL		1,190	629	Factory load

.444 Marlin

Historical Notes: News and data on the .444 Marlin round was released to the public in June 1964. The cartridge was designed for the Marlin Model 336 lever-action rifle. Initially, the rifle was manufactured with a 24-inch Micro-Groove barrel, two-thirds length magazine, and recoil pad. The straight-grip stock had a Monte Carlo cheekpiece. Original ammunition was made by Remington.

The .444 Marlin is somewhat similar to the .44 Van Houten Super. The .44 VH was developed by E.B. Van Houten and "Lucky" Wade of Phoenix, Ariz. It was made by necking up .30-40 Krag brass, trimming it to two inches, and turning down the rims slightly. It was designed for the 336 Marlin or 94 Winchester actions. It pre-dates the Marlin round by at least three years. Ballistics of the two rounds are nearly identical.

General Comments: The .44 Magnum revolver cartridge achieved popularity as a rifle round. However, anyone using it discovers quite quickly that it has a rainbow-like trajectory, and its killing power on heavier game such as elk and moose is adequate only at close range. Consequently, there was need for a somewhat more powerful option. The .444 Marlin extends both the effective range and killing power inherent in the .44 Magnum. This round fires the same 240-grain soft-point bullet at 2330 fps, as compared to 1850 fps for the average .44 Magnum rifle. The .444 Marlin is substantially more powerful than the old .30-30 or the .35 Remington at short ranges. It develops about the same energy as the .348 Winchester and slightly more than the later .358 Winchester. However, with its larger diameter bullet, it should provide better knockdown power. It is a short- to medium-range cartridge and should be adequate for any North American big game and effective on most thin-skinned African game, (non-dangerous). Its advantage over the above-named cartridges is at ranges out to 150 yards. Beyond that, due to better bullet shape and sectional density, those all catch up to and finally surpass the .444 in retained velocity and energy. The .444 Marlin was formerly available as a superb all-round hunting load with a 265-grain bullet. Remington, Hornady, and Buffalo Bore offer ammunition.

.444 Marlin Loading Data and Factory Ballistics

Bullet (grains/type)	Powder	Grains	Velocity	Energy	Source/Comments
180 HP	IMR 4198	51	2,500	2,499	Sierra
220 SP	IMR 4198	49	2,350	2,698	Sierra
240 HP	IMR 4198	46.5	2,300	2,820	Hornady, Sierra
240 HP	H-322	53	2,300	2,820	Hornady, Sierra
250 SP	IMR 4198	47	2,250	2,811	Sierra
265 Hornady JFP	H-4198	47.0	2,273	3,040	Hodgdon
275 SP	RL-7	47	2,250	3,092	Barnes
280 Swift HP	H322	49.5	2,120	2,790	Hodgdon
300 SP	RL-7	46	2,150	3,080	Barnes
300 Swift HP	H4198	42.5	2,082	2,885	Hodgdon
240 SP	FL		2,330	2,942	Remington factory load

.45-70 Government (.45-70-330/.45-70-350/ .45-70-405/.45-70-500)

Historical Notes: Adopted by the U.S. military in 1873 with the single-shot "Trapdoor" Springfield rifle, this continued as the official service cartridge for 19 years. It was replaced in 1892 by the .30-40 Krag. The .45-70 Government was also a popular cartridge for sporting use, and many repeating and single-shot rifles were chambered for it, including the Remington rolling block, Remington-Keene, Remington-Lee, Marlin Model 81, Winchester Model 86, and Hotchkiss, plus many others. Though the Krag officially replaced the .45-70, in 1892, all volunteer Spanish-American War regiments—with the reported sole exception being Teddy Roosevelt's Rough Riders—were equipped with the Trapdoor .45-70. Many state militias were armed with the .45-70 Springfields well beyond 1900.

American companies dropped the .45-70 as a rifle chambering in the early 1930s. However, it has staged a major comeback in popularity, and currently Marlin, Ruger, and Browning chamber rifles for the .45-70. Winchester once loaded many versions of the basic .45-70 case with different bullet weights, shapes, and black-powder charges. It also loaded one variant of the .45-70-405 Winchester load expressly for the Marlin 1881 lever-action rifle. That load featured a differently shaped 405-grain bullet and was headstamped .45-70 Mar.

General Comments: "Old soldiers never die," and apparently neither do old military cartridges. The .45-70 has been with us for more than 125 years and is still very much alive. As a short-range cartridge for anything from deer to grizzly bear, the .45-70 will hold its own with most of our more modern developments. Its greatest fault is the curved trajectory that makes it difficult to place shots beyond 150 yards with any certainty.

Unfortunately, the U.S. Springfield and most of the other black-powder rifles won't stand pressures over 25,000 psi or so. This prevents using heavy loads of smokeless powder. In late-Model 86 Winchesters or other smokeless powder rifles, the .45-70 can be loaded to deliver very impressive performance on the heaviest species of big game. Winchester, Remington, Federal, CorBon, and Buffalo Bore offer .45-70 ammunition.

.45-70 U.S. Government Loading Data and Factory Ballistics

Bullet (grains/type)	Powder	Grains	Velocity	Energy	Source/Comments
300 HP	IMR 4198	34	1,400	1,306	Hornady, Sierra
300 HP	IMR 4227	29	1,400	1,306	Hornady, Sierra
300 HP	IMR 3031	43	1,400	1,306	Hornady
300 HP	SR 4759	27	1,400	1,306	Hornady

Loads for Modern Smokeless Powder Rifles Only

Bullet (grains/type)	Powder	Grains	Velocity	Energy	Source/Comments
300 HP	IMR 4198	46	2,000	2,665	Hornady
300 HP	IMR 4227	43	2,100	2,938	Sierra
350 Hornady JFP	H4198	54.0	2,191	3,730	Hodgdon
400 SP	H4198	50.5	2,002	3,555	Hodgdon
400 SP	IMR 3031	54	1,800	2,878	Speer
300 SP	FL		1,880	2,355	Factory load
405 SP	FL		1,330	1,590	Factory load
350 JFN	FL		2,100	3,427	Buffalo Bore Factory Load
325 FTX	FL		2,050	3,032	Hornady Factory Load

.458 Winchester Magnum

Historical Notes: The .458 Winchester Magnum was introduced,in 1956 for a dressed-up version of the Model 70 rifle called the African. The Remington 700 Safari is available in .458, and so are many other American- and European-made rifles, such as the A-Square, Dakota 76, BRNO, and the Ruger 77. The .458 has become a world standard, and many factories and individual makers provide hunting arms for it. Ruger also chambers the .458 in its No. 1 single-shot rifle.

General Comments: With an increasing number of American sportsmen making the trek to Africa, and with the Weatherby Magnum line of cartridges selling rather well, Winchester decided to get into the act. The result is the fine .458, a cartridge suitable for any of the most dangerous game in the world. This cartridge has been tested thoroughly in Africa and has proven itself adequate for the toughest game found there. It is as powerful as most of the oversized English big-bore elephant cartridges. Although overpowered for North American big game, it has nonetheless found favor with many hunters as a woods and brush cartridge, when reloaded with lighter-than-standard factory bullets. With the 300-, 350-, or 405-grain bullets, it can be loaded to duplicate the .45-70 at any level and to cover a wide range of game and hunting conditions. As a factory load, it isn't good for anything but the biggest and toughest. But, then, that is what it was intended for. Federal, Winchester, and Remington offer ammunition.

.458 Winchester Loading Data and Factory Ballistics

Bullet (grains/type)	Powder	Grains	Velocity	Energy	Source/Comments
300 SP	RL-7	58	2,100	2,938	Hornady
300 SP	IMR 4198	49	2,100	2,938	Hornady, Sierra
350 SP	IMR 4198	70.5	2,500	4,859	Hornady
400 SP	IMR 4198	64	2,250	4,498	Speer
400 SP	IMR 4320	77	2,200	4,300	Speer
500 SP	IMR 3031	70	2,100	4,897	Hornady
350 SP	FL		2,470	4,740	Factory load
400 SP	FL		2,380	5,031	Factory load
500 FMJ	FL		2,040	4,620	Factory load
510 SP	FL		2,040	4,712	Factory load

.450 Bushmaster

Historical Notes: The .450 Bushmaster (parent cartridge is the .45 Professional) rifle/cartridge conversion, was developed by Tim LeGendre, of LeMag Firearms LLC, and licensed to Bushmaster Firearms International for production and distribution. LeGendre still retains ownership. The .450 Bushmaster is designed to be used in the standard M-16/AR-15 platform, using five-round magazines.

Bushmaster asked Hornady to produce the .45 Professional ammunition for this project, and Hornady agreed. Hornady wanted the .45 Professional shortened to accommodate its 250-grain pointed SST bullet. Hornady asked Bushmaster for the change (1.771-inch to the now standard 1.7-inch), and Bushmaster asked LeGendre to sign off on that change. He did. Bushmaster eventually wanted a name change, and LeGendre agreed to that, too, and that is what has now become the popular .450 Bushmaster.

Based on a concept by Col. Jeff "Thumper" Cooper, the goal was to provide guaranteed one-shot kills on big-game animals at 250 yards, with a large-bore semi-auto (.44-caliber or larger). Cooper, upon being presented with the early .45 Professional, stated, "This is Thumper Senior … . I can now own an AR-15." A .45 Pro was indeed built for Col. Cooper, which was remarkable, considering his disdain for the AR-15 in 5.56 NATO. Hornady, with its extreme expertise, busted the Cooper 250-yard limit. The result is the .450 Bushmaster, a semi-auto rifle/cartridge combination that absolutely provides more than enough stopping power to adequately kill all big game in North America.

General Comments: While the two cartridges have nothing in common dimensionally, the appearance of the .450 Bushmaster is remindful of the old .401 Winchester, which was designed for another autoloading rifle, the Winchester Model 1910. The .401 Winchester is capable of pushing a .40-caliber 250-grain bullet along at 1900 fps, while the .450 Bushmaster pushes a .45-caliber bullet of the same weight along at 2200 fps. But, due to its higher velocity, along with the more streamlined shape of the Hornady FTX bullet, the newer cartridge delivers a deadlier blow downrange. Out to about 225 yards, it retains a sufficient level of energy to handle game as large as moose and elk.

.450 Bushmaster Loading Data and Factory Ballistics

Bullet (grains/type)	Powder	Grains	Velocity	Energy	Source
250 Hornady FTX	FL		2,200	2,686	Hornady

.457 WWG

Historical Notes: Wild West Guns out of Alaska, and now Las Vegas, Nev., has been building custom lever guns for a long time. Many are chambered for the .47-70 and will endure potent high-pressure loads not available in standard SAAMI-spec ammunition. CorBon has been supplying Wild West Guns with hot-loaded .45-70 ammo for these exquisite lever guns, but the concern always existed that someone would stuff one of these high pressure loads in an older and not so strong rifle. This led Jim West, the man behind Wild West Guns, to develop his own hot-rod .45-caliber lever gun cartridge that he calls the .457 WWG. Originally a proprietary design on its own unique case, the cartridge has been chambered in many Wild West Guns. As of the publication of the *13th Edition of Cartridges of the World*, the .457 WWWG has been submitted to SAAMI and is pending approval. One of the most unique things about lever guns chambered for this cartridge is that they can still function and fire .45-70 ammunition. The .457 WWG has an operating pressure of 43,500 psi, as compared to 28,000 psi for the .45-70.

General Comments: The most popular rifle available from Wild West Guns is its Co-Pilot model, which is a compact, take-down lever gun designed to offer bush pilots or anyone else existing in big bear country a compact rifle capable of stopping any critter that might decide to do them harm. Pushing a 405-grain bullet to almost 2000 fps, this cartridge lives up to that claim. It is suspected that, once it's SAAMI approved, you will see firearms from other manufacturers offered in this chambering, as well as ammunition from CorBon, The Hunting Shack, and maybe even other ammo manufacturers.

.457 WWG Loading Data and Factory Ballistics

Bullet (grains/type)	Powder	Grains	Velocity	Energy	Source/Comments
350 A Frame	FL		2,300	4,112	Cor-Bon Factory Load
405 Hard Cast	FL		1,950	3,420	Cor-Bon Factory Load

.450 Marlin

Historical Notes: Hornady and Marlin announced the .450 Marlin at the 2000 SHOT Show. This is the first new chambering from Marlin since the introduction of the .444 Marlin, in mid-1964. The motivation for this cartridge is simple. Handloaders have been souping up .45-70 loads for use in Marlin's modern 1895 since the day that gun was introduced. Owing to the many weaker .45-70 rifles still in use, Marlin could not condone this practice, nor could it stop it. Something had to give. Some have asked why Marlin didn't simply lengthen the .45-70 case and standardize a new higher-pressure cartridge. That alternative wasn't tenable, because such a cartridge would have chambered in older (potentially weaker) rifles designed for the .45-90, .45-110, etc.

General Comments: When one considers a simple approach that could have been taken, this cartridge design is a poor, second-best choice for chambering in the new M-1895 Marlin. The simple adoption of an Ackley Improved version of the .45-70 would have provided a superior case design with a cartridge that would function better through the Marlin rifle and would not chamber in any older factory rifle. In any case, the .450 Marlin offers lever-action fans a factory chambering with significant ballistic potential. Shooters in this country have a long history of fascination with large-bore lever-action rifles. Except for caliber, Marlin's new number is quite reminiscent of Winchester's circa-1903 .50-110 Winchester High Velocity load, which originated for the same reason; muzzle energy is essentially identical. This cartridge and rifle make a fine and versatile combination for those who hunt dangerous game under the worst possible conditions. Given correct bullet choice and shot placement, this is a capable performer for any task.

Interestingly, Lewis Potter, proprietor of Potter & Walker (Evasham, Worcestershire, UK), reports that, around the time the .450 Marlin was being introduced, he—quite coincidentally—successfully shortened and reformed .375 H&H Magnum cases to something quite similar to the new Marlin number, for use in a client's modified Ruger No. 1. Potter's wildcat, the performance of which fell somewhere between that of a high-end .45-70 and the .450 Marlin, was playfully christened the .45-70 Nitro Express.

.450 Marlin Load Data and Factory Ballistics

Bullet (grains/type)	Powder	Grains	Velocity	Energy	Source/Comments
250 Barnes TSX/FN	H4198	54.0	2,493	3,446	Barnes
300 Nosler PPP	H335	67.0	2,282	3,465	Nosler
350 Hornady FP	RL-7	51.5	2,000	3,105	Hornady
400 Speer JFP	H335	55.0	1,953	3,383	Hodgdon
350 Hornady FP	FL		2,100	3,427	Hornady factory load

.458 Lott

Historical Notes: When a twice-shot African buffalo energetically squashed Jack Lott, dissatisfaction with his .458 Winchester's performance led to the creation, in 1971, of a more capable .458 cartridge, the .458 Lott. By using a case 2.8 inches long, the .458 Lott was able to achieve 2150 fps with a 500-grain bullet. The genius of the late Lott's design is that .458 Lott rifles also chambered and fired .458 Winchester Magnum ammo. On the downside, the wildcat .458 Lott was strictly a handloading and custom rifle proposition. Then, in 2002, Hornady decided to produce factory ammunition, and Ruger chambered its Model 77 MKII in .458 Lott.

General Comments: The .458 Winchester is advertised as developing 2040 fps with the 500-grain bullet when fired from a 24-inch barrel. In reality, poorly constructed factory loads often produce little more than 1900 fps in 22-inch barreled rifles. The .458 Lott will do an honest 2,300-plus fps from a 22-inch barrel. It has been field-tested in Africa, and it has chalked up an impressive number of one-shot kills on elephants and buffalo. It is similar to the .450 Watts, which is also based on the full-length .375 H&H case expanded to .458-caliber, but is shorter. Rifles chambered for the .458 Lott will also safely shoot .458 Winchester ammo. Since Hornady has adopted this cartridge as a factory loading, availability of ammo and brass should improve markedly. Numerous bullet makers make bullets suitable for the .458 Lott, with weights ranging from 350 grains to 600 grains. With factory ammo and production rifles now readily available, the .458 Lott continues to be a superb choice for virtually any dangerous game worldwide.

.458 Lott Loading Data and Factory Ballistics

Bullet (grains/type)	Powder	Grains	Velocity	Energy	Source/Comments
500 SP	IMR 4320	85.0	2,330	6,020	NA
500 SP	IMR 4064	79.0	2,230	5,520	NA
500 RN	FL		2,300	5,873	Factory load

.460 Weatherby Magnum

Historical Notes: This big, potent caliber was brought out, in 1958, for the avowed purpose of providing the world's most powerful commercial rifle cartridge. It was developed by necking the .378 Weatherby case up to .45-caliber. Rifles and ammunition are available only through Weatherby on a commercial basis, but custom-made rifles based on Mauser-type bolt actions are occasionally chambered for this round.

General Comments: Until the advent of the .700 Nitro Express, which is just barely in the ranks of commercial cartridges, the .460 Weatherby Magnum was among the most powerful available. Recent factory ballistics have been toned down a bit, but it still delivers better than 7500 ft-lbs of muzzle energy, which far exceeds most dangerous game loads. The big .460 is overly powerful for any North American big game, but it does provide that ultimate bit of insurance against the dangerous African or Asiatic varieties under adverse conditions—it would, of course, be preferable to be caught slightly overgunned than to be eaten by a lion or trampled by an elephant. Two wildcat cartridges, the .450 and .475 Ackley, are in the same class as the .460 Weatherby insofar as energy is concerned. The .475 A&M Magnum reportedly develops a muzzle energy of some 10,000 ft-lbs. However, none of these are commercial cartridges. Recently, many new A-Square and proprietary numbers have exceeded the .460 Weatherby.

.460 Weatherby Magnum Loading Data and Factory Ballistics

Bullet (grains/type)	Powder	Grains	Velocity	Energy	Source/Comments
300 SP	IMR 4320	112	3,000	5,997	Barnes
350 SP	IMR 4064	111	2,900	6,538	Hornady
500 SP	IMR 4350	123.5	2,650	7,799	Hornady
500 SP	IMR 4320	108	2,550	7,221	Hornady
500 SP	IMR 3031	99	2,500	6,941	Hornady
500 SP	H-4831	125	2,650	7,799	Barnes
500 SP/FMJ	FL		2,600	7,507	Weatherby factory load

.470 Nitro Express (.470 NE)

Historical Notes: Since its introduction in 1907, the .470 Nitro Express has proven to be one of the most popular and long lived of the British Nitro Express cartridges. Guns in this chambering are not excessively heavy, and recoil, while stout, is acceptable. This makes a good combination for the hunter who wants to use one cartridge for all African game, without fear of being under-gunned. For this reason, most guns in this cartridge are the tried-and-true double rifles, such as the English-made H&H, Purdey, J. Rigby & Co., Westley Richards, Powell, and a few others. Production of such rifles is also abundant in Europe, with Beretta of Italy, Francotte of Belgium, and Heym of Germany offering models priced from $10,000 on up.

The 5130 ft-lbs of muzzle energy generated by the 500-grain, steel-jacketed solid bullet is the stuff from which myths are made in the hot-stove league.

General Comments: In 1989, Federal Cartridge Co. added this caliber to its Premium product line, making it the first British Nitro Express caliber offered by a major American manufacturer. The .470 is generally too powerful for most North American game, but works well on medium to large game worldwide. Many .470 shooters reload the cartridge, because of the high cost of factory ammo. Federal's factory loads can provide cases, and Barnes offers bullets.

.470 Nitro Express Loading Data and Factory Ballistics

Bullet (grains/type)	Powder	Grains	Velocity	Energy	Source/Comments
500 Barnes SP	H4831	119.0	2,159	5,175	Hodgdon
600 Barnes SP	H4831	105.0	1,941	5,020	Hodgdon
500 SP/FMJ	FL		2,150	5,130	Federal factory load

.50 Browning Machine Gun (.50 BMG)

Historical Notes: The .50 BMG was invented by its namesake and adopted into United States military service, in 1918, for John M. Browning's famous heavy machine gun. Browning's attentions in this area were prompted by a battlefield need recognized during World War I. There have been other developments, and at least once the Pentagon considered dropping the .50 BMG in favor of more modern and generally bigger chamberings. However, the .50 BMG has remained. The advent of saboted loads generating 4500 fps muzzle velocities and having devastating armor-penetration capabilities, and its performance in the Gulf War have seemed to cement its continued existence as a stable part of NATO's arsenal.

Battlefield use is against light-armored vehicles to ranges of a mile or more, and used against the unprotected, it is effective to several times that range.

General Comments: There has long been interest in the .50 BMG as a quasi-sporting round. Today, the most significant sporting use for this chambering is long-range accuracy shooting, with some competitions exceeding one mile. The 1,000-yard .50-caliber record, as of this writing, is a five-shot group of just under three inches on centers. Several bolt-action rifles are currently available for the Big 50. The .50 BMG easily launches the 750-grain bullets available for it at 2700 fps. The lighter 647-grain bullets available can be launched at 3000 fps. For obvious reasons, sporting rifles chambered for the Big 50 uniformly feature muzzle brakes and weigh 20 pounds or more. Recoil is a bit harsh until the rifle's weight approaches 30 pounds.

Commercial ammunition is available for the .50 BMG from PMC and Hornady, among others that are loading both once-fired and new brass and calling their offerings "factory new." Components and specialized tools and equipment to handload this cartridge are available to the advanced reloader.

.50 Browning Machine Gun Loading Data and Factory Ballistics

Bullet (grains/type)	Powder	Grains	Velocity	Energy	Source/Comments
750	H870	225.0	2,769	12,775	Barnes
800	AA8700	215.0	2,675	12,720	Barnes
660	FL		3,080	13,910	PMC factory load

Dimensional Data (SAAMI Maximum Cartridge Data)

Cartridge	Case	Bullet Dia.	Neck Dia.	Shoulder Dia.	Base Dia.	Rim Dia.	Rim Thick.	Case Length	Ctge. Length	Primer	Page
.17 Hornet	A	.172	.194	.294	.298	.345	.050	1.350	1.72	S	66
.17 Remington	C	.172	.198	.355	.374	.377	.041	1.79	1.86	S	66
.17 Remington Fireball	C	.172	.204	.3655	.3759	.332	.045	1.410	1.83	S	67
4.6x30 HK	C	.183	.209	.305	.316	.315	.043	1.201	1.516	S	68
.204 Ruger	C	.204	.229	.360	.373	.375	.045	1.850	2.260	S	68
.22 Hornet	A	.223	.242	.274	.294	.345	.060	1.40	1.72	S	69
.218 Bee	A	.224	.241	.331	.349	.408	.060	1.35	1.68	S	70
.22 PPC	C	.224	.245	.430	.440	.441	.050	1.52	1.96	S	70
.224 Weatherby Magnum	E	.224	.247	.405	.413	.425	.045	1.92	2.44	L	71
.223 Remington	C	.224	.249	.349	.373	.375	.041	1.76	2.10	S	72
.222 Remington	C	.224	.253	.355	.375	.375	.041	1.70	2.15	S	73
.22-250 Remington	C	.224	.254	.412	.466	.470	.045	1.91	2.33	L	74
.223 WSSM	C	.224	.254	.544	.555	.535	.040	1.670	2.360	L	75
.225 Winchester	A	.224	.260	.406	.422	.473	.045	1.93	2.50	L	76
.220 Swift	G	.224	.260	.402	.443	.472	.045	2.20	2.68	L	77
6mm PPC	C	.243	.260	.430	.441	.442	.050	1.50	2.12	S	78
6XC Tubb	C	.243	.271	.450	.466	.468	.049	1.898	2.808	L	79
.240 Weatherby Magnum	E	.243	.271	.432	.453	.473	.045	2.50	3.06	L	79
6mm Norma BR	C	.243	.271	.458	.469	.470	.051	1.56	2.44	S	80
.25-20 Winchester (WCF)	A	.257	.274	.329	.349	.405	.060	1.33	1.60	S	81
.243 Winchester	C	.243	.276	.454	.470	.470	.049	2.05	2.71	L	81
6mm Remington	C	.243	.276	.454	.470	.472	.045	2.23	2.91	L	82
.243 WSSM	I	.243	.287	.544	.555	.535	.054	1.67	2.06 (2.36)	L	83
.25-35 Winchester (WCF)	A	.257	.280	.355	.420	.500 (.506)	.059	2.04	2.53	L	84
.25-45 Sharps	C	.257	.284	.353	.376	.378	.045	1.76	2.135	S	85
.257 Weatherby Magnum	E	.257	.285	.490	.511	.530	.048	2.55	3.25	L	85
.250 Savage (.250-3000)	C	.257	.286	.413	.468	.470	.045	1.91	2.52 (2.515)	L	86
.25-06 Remington	C	.257	.287	.441	.470	.471	.045	2.49	3.00	L	87
.257 Roberts (257 Roberts +P)	C	.257	.290	.430	.468	.473	.045	2.23	2.74	L	87
.25 WSSM	C	.257	.299	.544	.555	.535	.040	1.670	3.260	L	88
6.5 Grendel	C	.264	.293	.428	.439	.441	.059	1.526		SR	89
.260 Remington	C	0.264	0.297	0.454	0.470	0.473	0.054	2.035	2.800	L	90
6.5x55 Swedish Mauser	C	.264	.297	.435	.480 (.477)	.480 (.479)	.050	2.16	3.15	L	90
6.5 Creedmoor	C	.264	.297	.458	.467	.468	.054	1.915	2.720	L	91
6.5x47 Lapua	I	0.264	0.292	0.454	0.470	0.473	0.054	1.900	2.740	S	92
6.5-284 Norma	I	.264	.297	.475	.500	.470	.051	2.17	3.23	S	92
.26 Nosler	C	.264	.297	.5275	.55	.532	.05	2.59	3.34	L	93
6.5-300 Weatherby Magnum	E	0.264	0.297	0.495	0.513	0.530	0.048	2.820	3.560	L	93
.264 (6.5mm) Win. Magnum	E	.264	.289	.490	.515 (.5127)	.532	.047	2.52	3.29	L	94
.270 Weatherby Magnum	E	.277	.305	.490	.511	.530	.048	2.55	3.25	L	95
6.8 Special Purpose Cartridge (SPC)	C	.277	.306	.401	.421	.417	.049	1.686	2.260	L	95
.270 Winchester	C	.277	.307	.440	.468	.470	.045	2.54	3.28	L	96
.270 WSM	A	.277	.314	.5381	.555	.535	.054	2.10	2.86	L	97
7-30 Waters	A	.284	.306	.399	.422 (.4215)	.506	.058	2.04	2.52	L	98
28 Nosler	I	0.284	0.320	0.528	0.550	0.534	0.050	2.590	3.340	LRM	98
.280 Ackley Improved	C	.284	.311	.454	.470	.472	.049	2.525	3.330	L	99
7mm Weatherby Magnum	E	.284	.312	.490	.511	.530	.048	2.55	3.25	L	100
.280 Remington (7mm Express Remington)	C	.284	.315	.441	.470	.472	.045	2.54	3.33	L	101
7mm-08 Remington	C	.284	.315	.454	.470	.473	.050	2.04 (2.035)	2.80	L	102
7mm Remington Magnum	E	.284	.315	.490	.511	.525	.047	2.50	3.24	L	103
7mm STW	E	.284	.316	.487	.513	.532	.048	2.85	3.65	L	104
7mm Mauser (7x57mm)	C	.284	.320	.420 (.4294)	.470	.474	.046	2.24 (2.235)	3.06	L	104
.284 Winchester	I	.284	.320	.465 (.4748)	.495 (.500)	.470	.049	2.17	2.75	L	105
7mm Remington SAUM	I	.284	.320	.534	.550	.534	.050	2.035	2.45 (2.86)	L	106

Dimensional Data (SAAMI Maximum Cartridge Data)

Cartridge	Case	Bullet Dia.	Neck Dia.	Shoulder Dia.	Base Dia.	Rim Dia.	Rim Thick.	Case Length	Ctge. Length	Primer	Page
7mm WSM	I	.284	.321	.538	.555	.535	.054	2.10	2.56 (2.86)	L	106
7mm Remington Ultra Mag	I	.284	.322	.525	.550	.534	.050	2.85	3.45 (3.60)	L	107
.30-30 Winchester	A	.308	.328	.402	.422 (.4215)	.502	.058	2.03 (2.039)	2.53	L	108
.30-378 Weatherby Magnum	K	.308	.330	.560	.589	.603/.580∂	.060	2.90	3.865	L	109
.300 AAC Blackout	C	.308	.334	.361	.375	.375	.045	1.368	1.78	S	110
.300 Winchester Magnum	E	.308	.334	.4891	.5126	.530	.046	2.60 (2.62)	3.30	L	111
.30 Carbine	D	.308	.335	.355	.3567	.3598	.05	1.29	1.679	SR	112
.300 Weatherby Magnum	E	.308	.337	.495	.513 (.5117)	.530	.048	2.82 (2.825)	3.56	L	112
30 Nosler	I	0.308	0.340	0.528	0.550	0.534	0.050	2.556	3.340	LRM	113
.30-40 Krag	A	.308	.338	.415 (.419)	.457 (.4577)	.540	.059	2.31	3.10 (3.089)	L	114
.300 H&H Magnum	E	.308	.338	.447	.513	.530	.048	2.85	3.60	L	115
.300 Savage	C	.308	.339	.443 (.4466)	.470	.470	.045	1.87	2.62	L	116
.30-06 Springfield	C	.308	.340	.441	.470	.473	.045	2.49	3.34	L	116
.30 Remington AR	I	.308	.341	.488	.500	.492	.054	1.525	2.260	S	118
.30 T/C	C	.308	.343	.464	.470	.473	.054	1.920	2.645	L	119
.308 Marlin Express	A	.308	.344	.448	.463	.502	.049	1.910	2.585	L	119
7.62x40 WT	C	0.308	0.325	0.365	0.376	0.375	0.041	1.565	2.260	Bx	120
.308 Winchester	C	.308	.344	.454	.470	.470	.049	2.01 (2.015)	2.75	L	121
.307 Winchester	G	.308	.344	.454	.470	.506	.059	2.02 (2.015)	2.60 (2.56)	L	121
.300 Ruger Compact Magnum	C	.308	.344	.515	.532	.532	.040	2.100	2.825	L	122
.300 Remington Ultra Mag	I	.308	.344	.525	.550	.532	.050	2.845	3.60	L	123
.300 Remington SAUM	I	.308	.344	.534	.550	.534	.050	2.015	2.450 (2.825)	L	124
.300 WSM	I	.308	.344	.538	.555	.535	.054 (2.860)	2.10	2.560	L	124
.303 British	A	.311	.338	.401	.458	.530	.062	2.21 (2.222)	3.05 (3.075)	L	125
7.62x39mm Soviet	C	.311	.340 (.337)	.344 (.396)	.438 (.433)	.440	.053	1.52 (1.528)	2.20	S	126
.32-20 Winchester	A	.312	.326	.338 (.3424)	.353	.405	.058	1.32 (1.315)	1 59	S	127
.32 Winchester Special	A	.321	.343	.396 (.4014)	.422 (.4219)	.506	.058	2.04	2.55 (2.565)	L	128
8X57 Mauser	C/A	.323	.350	.435	.470	.473/.526	.043/.048	2.24/2.25	3.17/3.55	5603/366D1	129
.325 WSM	C	.323	.358	.538	.555	.535	.054	2.10	2.560	L	130
8mm Remington Magnum	E	.323	.351 (.3541)	.485 (.4868)	.509 (.5126)	.530	.047	2.85	3.57 (3.600)	L	130
.340 Weatherby Magnum	E	.338	.366	.495	.513	.530	.048	2.82	3.60	L	131
.338 Federal	C	.338	.369	.454	.470	.473	.049	.201	2.75	L	132
.338 Winchester Magnum	E	.338	.369	.480 (.491)	.515 (.5127)	.530	.047	2.49 (2.50)	3.30 (3.34)	L	132
.338-378 Weatherby Magnum	E	.338	.369	.561	.581	.579	.063	2.193	3.638	L	133
.338-06 A-Square	C	.338	.370	.441	.470	.473	.049	2.494	3.24 (3.44)	L	134
.338 Marlin Express	A	.338	.370	.493	.506	.553	.055	1.890	2.585	L	134
.338 Ruger Compact Magnum	C	.338	.370	.515	.532	.532	.040	2.100	2.825	L	135
.338 Lapua Magnum	C	.338	.370	.540	.590	.590	.060	2.72	3.60		136
.338 Remington Ultra Mag	I	.338	.371	.526	.550	.532	.050	2.76	3.60	L	136
.348 Winchester	A	.348	.379 (.3757)	.485	.553	.610	.062	2.26 (2.255)	2.80 (2.795)	L	137
.35 Remington	C	.358	.384	.419 (.4259)	.458 (.4574)	.460	.046	1.92	2.52	L	137
.35 Whelen	C	.358	.388	.441	.470	.473	.045	2.50 (2.494)	3.34	L	138
.356 Winchester	G	.358	.388	.454	.4703	.508	.058	2.02 (2.015)	2.56	L	139
.358 Winchester	C	.358	.388	.454	.4703	.473	.048	2.01 (2.015)	2.78	L	140
.350 Remington Magnum	E	.358	.388	.495	.5126	.532	.046	2.17	2.8	L	140
9.3x62mm Mauser	C	.365	.388	.447	.473	.470	.044	2.42	3.29	5603/474	141
.370 Sako Magnum/9.3x66 Sako	C	.366	.405	.450	.477	.470	.047	2.598	3.346	L	142
.376 Steyr	I	.375	.398	.472	.501	.494	.048	2.35	3.075	L	143
.378 Weatherby Magnum	E	.375	.399	.560	.582	.579	.063	2.913	3.65	L	144
.375 Winchester	B	.375	.400	.415 (.4198)	.502	.046	.063	2.56	12	L	144
.375 H&H Magnum	E	.375	.402	.440 (.4478)	.521	.530	.046	2.85	3.60	L	145
.375 Weatherby Magnum	E	.375	.402	.492	.512	.531	.051	2.85	3.54 (3.80)	L	146
.375 Ruger	C	.375	.405	.515	.532	.532	.050	2.580	3.340	L	146
.375 Remington Ultra Mag	I	.375	.405	.525	.550	.534	.050	2.85	3.54 (3.60)	L	147

Dimensional Data (SAAMI Maximum Cartridge Data)

Cartridge	Case	Bullet Dia.	Neck Dia.	Shoulder Dia.	Base Dia.	Rim Dia.	Rim Thick.	Case Length	Ctge. Length	Primer	Page
.38-55 Winchester (.38-55 Ballard)	B	.379	.392	.3938	.422	.506	.058	2.12 (2.085)	2.51	L	148
.38-40 Winchester (WCF)	A	.401	.416	.438 (.4543)	.465	.520	.058	1.30	1.59	L	148
.416 Weatherby Magnum	K	.416	.444	.561	.584	.603/.580∂	.062	2.915	3.75	L	149
.416 Ruger	C	.416	.445	.515	.532	.532	.050	2.580	3.240	L	150
.416 Rigby	C	.416	.445 (.4461)	.539 (.5402)	.589	.586	.058	2.90	3.75	L	150
.416 Remington Magnum	E	.416	.447	.487	.509	.530	.046	2.85	3.60	L	151
.44-40 Winchester (WCF)	A	.427/ .429	.443	.4568	.471	.525	.058	1.31	1.92	LP	152
.444 Marlin	B	.429	.453	.4549	.469	.514	.058	2.16 (2.225)	2.57	L	153
.45-70 Government	B	.458	.475 (.480)	.4813	.500	.600 (.608)	.065	2.105	2.55	L	154
.458 Winchester Magnum	F	.458	.478 (.4811)	.4825	.513	.532	.046	2.50	3.34	L	155
.450 Bushmaster	J	.458	.480	–	.500	.473	.050	1.700	2.260	L	155
.457 WWG	B	.458	.480	-	.5039	.605	.07	2.21	2.49	L	156
.450 Marlin	F	.458	.480	.511	.532	.47	.047	2.55	2.2	L	157
.458 Lott	F	.458	.481		.513	.532	.048	2.80	3.60	L	157
.460 Weatherby Magnum	K	.458	.485	.560	.584	.603/.580∂	.062	2.91	3.75	L	158
.470 Nitro Express	A	.475	.504	.528 (.5322)	.5728	.655	.037	3.25	3.98	L	158
.50 BMG	C	.510/ .511	.560	.714	.804	.804	.080	3.91	5.545	50 BMG	159

Case Type: A = Rimmed, bottleneck. B = Rimmed, straight. C = Rimless, bottleneck. D = Rimless, straight. E = Belted, bottleneck. F = Belted, straight. G = Semi-rimmed, bottleneck. H = Semi-rimmed, straight. I = Rebated, bottleneck. J = Rebated, straight. K = Rebated, belted bottleneck. L = Rebated, belted straight.

Primer Type: S = Small rifle (0.175"). SP = Small pistol (0.175"). L = Large rifle (0.210"). LP = Large pistol (0.210"). 50 BMG = CCI-35/VihtaVuori-110/RWS-8212. B-1 = Berdan #1. B-2 = Berdan #2.

Other Codes: Belt/Rim Diameter. Unless otherwise noted, all dimensions in inches. Twist (factory) is given as inches of barrel length per complete revolution, e.g., 12 = 1 turn in 12", etc. Unless otherwise noted, all dimensions are in inches. Data in parenthesis represents SAAMI maximum specifications. Bullet upset performance of the 264 Winchester Magnum 140 gr. Power Point at ranges of 100, 200, 300, 400 and 500 yards.

Obsolete American Rifle Cartridges

(Centerfire Sporting – Black-Powder and Smokeless)

Chapter 2 covers obsolete rifle cartridges, those no longer loaded by American ammunition manufacturers and those no longer chambered in commercially available rifles. Sometimes such ammunition is still available out of dealers' old stocks. Both smokeless powder and black-powder cartridges are included in this section, and the total number of old black-powder sporting cartridge types is quite large. Many of those are now collectors' items.

Some authorities are bound to disagree with a few of the cartridges placed in the obsolete category. For example, wildcat experimenters have kept the Newton cartridge line alive over the years, and it might be argued that those belong in that classification. A wildcat cartridge is usually defined as one that is not loaded, chambered, or available on a commercial basis. Strictly speaking, this would make wildcats of almost all the cartridges listed in this chapter. However, the rounds listed here have one common, differentiating characteristic—all were, at one time, available as true commercial cartridges. Furthermore, used rifles and ammunition out of old stock are sometimes still available for the majority of smokeless powder types. These are also listed in old catalogs and ballistics tables, and it might create confusion to call these wildcats.

The cartridges in Chapter 2 can be considered as commercial innovations that have not stood the test of time. This is as true of the Newton cartridges as the others, but, in addition, the Newton designs must be recognized as too advanced for their day. If Charles Newton were alive and his cartridges introduced today, they would be hailed as brilliant and modern in every respect. Unfortunately, modern powders and entirely suitable actions were not available back around 1910, nor was the sporting world quite ready to accept high-intensity cartridges. The general big-game hunting conditions at that time made the benefits of these developments of doubtful value.

The trouble with being ahead of the times is that people do not appreciate your genius during your lifetime. Posthumous recognition must be of precious little comfort to the individual involved. The late Roy Weatherby, on the other hand, arrived on the scene at the right time. He was also a far better promoter and businessman than Newton. Result? Ultra-velocity Weatherby rifles are a commercial success and Weatherby's ideas are accepted the world over by all but a few die-hards. Still, there are a couple of Weatherby rounds included in this chapter.

The principal importance of obsolete commercial cartridges to today's sportsmen is that rifles for many of these are still floating around, particularly the smokeless powder types. It is well to be aware of their existences and disadvantages before some sharpy unloads an obsolete rifle on you. Obtaining ammunition for any of these chamberings is going to be an ever-increasing problem. Of course, certain handloaders like to play around with obsolete cartridges, just to be different or to try to improve performance. If you belong to this group, well and good, you probably know what you are doing. However, cartridges in Chapter 1 will serve the average sportsman better.

Up to this point, we have aimed most of these remarks toward obsolete smokeless powder cartridges. The true black-powder types are a different story. Many of the old black-powder rifles are now quite valuable, and from time to time there's a resurgence in the use of these old rifles for target shooting, hunting, and the sport of cowboy action shooting.

Cartridge Development

Black-powder cartridges discussed in this chapter cover arms development from about 1868 to 1895. Ideas and experiments of this interval were a necessary prerequisite to perfection of modern, high-powered rifles and ammunition. This was also one of the most romantic periods of American history, that being the consolidation and settling of the Western frontier.

The first successful, self-contained metallic cartridge produced on a commercial basis in the United States was the .22 Short rimfire, introduced by Smith & Wesson for its small, tip-up revolver, in 1857. Commercial cartridge production from then until after the close of the Civil War was mostly in the rimfire field. Patents issued to George W. Morse, in 1856 and 1858, covered the essential features of the modern centerfire cartridge. His design incorporated an anvil, formed out of a wire and soldered inside the case. A perforated rubber disc held at the base of the case by this wire supported the primer (or "cap," as was the common name at that time).

American Col. Hiram Berdan perfected his priming system, with the anvil formed in the bottom of the primer pocket, during 1866. British Col. Edward Boxer developed his self-contained primer and anvil, in 1867. (Oddly, European manufacturers use the Berdan type extensively, while American manufacturers use the Boxer primer almost exclusively.) Frankford Arsenal initiated experiments to develop a satisfactory centerfire system, as early as 1858. The Union Metallic Cartridge Co. (now Remington), began manufacturing Berdan centerfire cartridges in 1868, about a year after formation of the company. The first of the American outside-primed, Berdan-type cartridges were probably the .50-70 Government and .50 Remington Navy rounds.

After 1870, development and introduction of improved centerfire cartridges was quite rapid. In 1885, the French chemist Paul Marie Eugène Vieille developed the first practical smokeless powder, and, in 1886, the French adapted this to the new 8mm Lebel military cartridge. The United States military adopted its first smokeless powder small-bore cartridge, in 1892, for the Krag bolt-action rifle. Winchester developed the first smokeless powder sporting round, the .30 Winchester Center Fire (now known as the .30-30 Winchester), during 1895.

The popularity of black-powder cartridges did not begin a serious decline in the United States until after about 1910. Even then, both Remington and Winchester were still loading black powder in some of the old cartridges as late as 1936 or 1937. Many black-powder centerfire cartridges, such as the .32-20, .32-40, .38-55, .38-40, .44-40, .45 Colt, and .45-70, survived the change to smokeless powder. Several manufacturers load one or more of these, but now with smokeless powder. (CorBon offers a limited production of black-powder Cowboy Action loads in .45 Colt and .45-70.) We cover those early rounds still produced in other chapters, as appropriate.

Cartridge Designation Confusion

There are two great sources of confusion with black-powder sporting cartridges. The first is the method of nomenclature, the second is the manufacturer's habit of sticking its name on any cartridge it manufactured or for which that company chambered guns. Two or three numbers were normally used to designate a particular cartridge and loading, e.g., .45-70 Gov't. or the .45-70-500 Gov't. The first numeral represents the caliber (approximate bullet diameter in hundredths of an inch); the second numeral signifies the black powder charge (in grains); the third numeral specifies bullet weight (in grains). The manufacturer often tacked on its name after the final numeral. Worse, sometimes, a manufacturer would offer several interchangeable cartridges, but with differing and distinct names. For example, Winchester offered two essentially identical .45-70 loadings. One was called .45-70-350 WCF, while the other, offered for Marlin rifles, was called .45-70-300 Marlin. As a matter of confusing fact, the Sharps Rifle Co. designated this same .45-70 Gov't. round as the .45/2.1-inch Sharps. As another example, Winchester introduced the tapered-case .40-65 WCF, while, for its rifle, Marlin loaded the same case with 60 grains of black powder and called the resulting round the .40-60 Marlin. Despite the distinct names, these two cartridges are nearly identical and are fully interchangeable. But then, Winchester also introduced its own .40-60 WCF, which had a shorter and entirely different case than the .40-60 Marlin. Finally, consider the following trio: .50-100, .50-105, and .50-110 Winchester. Some references have listed these as different cartridges, but these are, in reality, just different loadings of the same case, which Winchester originally offered as the .50-110-300 WCF. Confusing indeed!

To add a bit more difficulty to this mess, consider the Everlasting, a heavy, reloadable-type case that was popular for many years. These cases were often so thick and heavy that the original powder charge wouldn't fit! Manufacturers solved this problem by making the case slightly longer than standard. This practice gave rise to all manner of different cartridges, which are simply a slightly lengthened version of something else. Trying to tie the standard original and the longer reloadable version together is often difficult. We have attempted to unravel this confusion as much as possible.

Most cartridge-book authors list bullet diameter based upon that portion of the projectile protruding from the case mouth. This is okay for identification purposes, but not much help to the handloader. Bullet diameter, as given here, is that recommended for loading and shooting and is based upon average groove diameter. We obtained this by measuring bullets removed from factory ammunition or from old Ideal catalogs or manufacturers' specifications. Ideal catalogs had a reference table listing various cartridges and the loading tool and standard bullet furnished. This is a good index for bullet diameter in any given cartridge, but old rifle bores exhibited considerable variation. It is a good idea to measure bore diameter before you order a mold, just to be on the safe side.

If you cannot figure out the chambering of your rifle, have it checked by a gunsmith or make a chamber cast and measure it. A comparison of chamber dimensions with the cartridge dimensions in Chapter 12 should allow you to determine chambering of almost any rifle. These cartridge dimensions will also assist in making up ammunition for the old-timers or determining the proper name of unmarked cases.

Chamber Casting

In making chamber castings, one can use sulphur, a low melting point bismuth alloy, or paraffin wax. Lead alloy can also be used, but it is not recommended. Flowers of sulphur (obtainable on www.Amazon.com, pretty much like anything else these days), is satisfactory. However, sulphur casts are extremely brittle and prone to breakage during removal from the chamber or during later handling. The tinker must heat a sulphur solution (four ounces of sulphur, a pinch of lampblack, and about a teaspoon of camphor), very slowly, with continuous stirring. As soon as this becomes fully molten, it is ready for pouring into the chamber. It should be poured quickly and allowed to cool thoroughly, before attempting to remove the cast. The chamber must be thoroughly cleaned and lightly oiled before pouring. The bore should be plugged just forward of the chamber, thus also giving you a cast of the bore for measurement. A good method is to drive a piece of wire through a bore-fitting cork and leave this wire extending from the breech. A finger loop on the end of this wire mandrel aids in removing the cast.

For a less precise, but nonetheless perfectly useful, casting, simply prepare the chamber the same way, then plug the bore with a paper wad or other similar device and fill the chamber with molten paraffin. After thorough cooling, this casting will easily come free from the chamber. This provides a very good casting, but will always shrink a few thousandths of an inch in every dimension. Nevertheless, this will usually be adequate to distinguish correct chambering designation.

The most satisfactory and durable chamber casts are accomplished with chamber cast metal available from gunsmith supply houses (such as Brownells, (800) 741-0015; www.brownells.com). These are bismuth alloys. The user can repeatedly re-melt and reuse casts made from this material. Lightly oil the chamber and throat as above. One of the typical bismuth alloys used for chamber castings is Cerrosafe. This alloy has a pouring temperature of 190 degrees Fahrenheit, significantly below the boiling point of water. You should be cautious to avoid overheating this material, as doing so will destroy its reusability. Cerrosafe shrinks slightly for a few minutes after it hardens, which simplifies removal of large or long castings. Measurements made approximately one hour after removal give truest dimensions. Surfaces of bismuth alloy casts are very smooth, unlike those of lead alloy, which often wrinkle badly.

Black-Powder Loads and Shooting

Although considerable differences in terminal performance exist among black-powder sporting cartridges, little variation in effective range exists. Stories abound about market-era buffalo hunters killing game at ranges of a half-mile or more and, no doubt, this sometimes happened. Competitors used some of the big-bore match cartridges for 1,000- and even 1,400-yard target shooting, and buffalo hunters were generally professionals who had spent years in the field and must have developed a keen ability for estimating distances. Of course, on the target range, distance was known and the rifle sighted-in before the match started. Many people cannot tell 100 feet from 100 yards in the field, and that is why black-powder rifles, with their rainbow-like trajectories, are restricted to an effective game range of not much beyond 150 yards. An experienced hunter, someone with an accurate rangefinder, or anyone who has practiced with his rifle and knows how to judge distance with reasonable accuracy can, of course, do better.

Black-powder cartridges below about .38-caliber are mostly for small or medium game. Larger calibers include many good short- to medium-range deer and black bear cartridges. The big and long .45- to .50-caliber numbers would knock the stuffing out of the largest moose or grizzly bear that ever lived. All you have to do is place the shot correctly.

Loading ammunition for black-powder rifles requires caution, if you intend to use smokeless powder. As a matter of safety, velocity and pressure must be kept at the original level in most rifles. Jacketed bullets and high velocity are out of the question, unless you have a modern action and a steel barrel designed for use with smokeless powder loads. While a few of the old actions are strong enough to be re-barreled to modern chamberings, most are not. Among the strongest are the Peabody-Martini, Remington rolling blocks and Hepburns, Sharps-Borchardt, Stevens 44½, and the Winchester single-shot. Late models of these are as strong as many modern actions, but early models do not have the improved "smokeless powder steel," and caut ion is advisable. The weakest of the lot are the U.S. 1866 and 1873 Springfields, Kennedys, Whitneys, and Winchester Models 1873s and 1876s. In these, use black powder or very light smokeless powder loads. Do not use a smokeless powder charge given for one bullet weight when switching to a heavier bullet, as this will raise pressures, perhaps beyond safe limits. Old cartridge cases are often of the folded-head (balloon) type, which are not particularly strong.

Remember that, since black powder residue is corrosive to brass, you'll need to inspect your cases very carefully. It is safer to use modern-made cases in original or reformed sizes, when possible. Non-corrosive primers do not leave chloride salts in the bore, hence, they reduce that corrosion. However, these can also raise pressures—a fact to bear in mind when working up loads. Shooting black-powder rifles and cartridges is lots of fun, and doing so can be just as safe as shooting modern rifles. At the same time, it requires common sense and education. If in doubt, don't do it! Ask a good gunsmith and follow his advice—in the end, that practice will be cheaper.

Shooting old black-powder rifles has become such a popular pastime that furnishing ammunition for these obsolete guns is a growing business. As a further aid in obtaining ammunition, get a copy of the book *Cartridge Conversions* by the late Maj. George C. Nonte, Jr. This will tell you how to make, via re-forming, most of the non-existent black-powder cartridges. An article by Nonte in the 1962 16th Edition of *Gun Digest* introduces this subject. The *Lyman Reloaders Handbook* and the *NRA's Illustrated Reloading Handbook* (out of print) also have much valuable information on making and loading obsolete cartridges.

It is not surprising to find reproductions (identical in every important way to the originals), and replicas (dimensionally and functionally similar to the originals), of some of the more popular black-powder cartridge rifles being manufactured. This follows the success of percussion replica arms. Many supplies for loading both these rifles and the origials can be obtained from Huntington's (www.huntingtonsports.com) or The Old Western Scrounger (www.ows-ammo.com).— *F.C.B.*

.219 Zipper

Historical Notes:	The .219 Zipper was brought out in 1937 by Winchester for its Model 64 lever-action rifle, which was a modernization of the Model 94. This combination (as with the .218 Bee in the Model 65), did not prove sufficiently accurate for long-range shooting on small targets and, in addition, did not allow the proper mounting of telescopic sights. Winchester discontinued the Model 64 after World War II. The last commercial rifle chambered for this cartridge was Marlin's Model 336 lever-action, discontinued in this chambering in 1961. A number of custom-made single-shot and Krag-Jorgensen rifles have been made for the .219 Zipper. It is not and never has been very popular. It is based on the necked-down .25-35 WCF case. Winchester dropped the .219 Zipper in 1962, and Remington followed shortly thereafter.
General Comments:	In a good, solid-frame single-shot or bolt-action rifle, the .219 Zipper is just as accurate as any other high-velocity .22 in its class. Since it was designed for tubular magazines, all factory-loaded ammunition is furnished with flat- or round-nosed bullets, and this causes rapid velocity loss. Although overshadowed by the .222 Remington, it is still an entirely satisfactory small-game, varmint, or target cartridge. Given carefully prepared ammunition in a carefully prepared lever-action, performance of this cartridge and rifle combination is limited more by the necessary use of blunt bullets than by intrinsic accuracy constraints. Such a combination is certainly capable of 200-yard shots on vermin, which is stretching what most shooters can do with iron sights anyway; beyond that range, velocity drops off so fast that trajectory limits usefulness, even given a telescopic sight. This is one of the few American cartridges that functions well through the British Lee-Enfield action. Some of these rifles have been rebarreled and altered to handle the Zipper. Anecdotal information from several serious shooters who have bothered to wring out the cartridge's accuracy in the Model 64 suggests that Winchester should have spent more effort on ammunition quality.

.219 Zipper Loading Data and Factory Ballistics

Bullet (grains/type)	Powder	Grains	Velocity	Energy	Source/Comments
45 SP	IMR 4320	30.0	3,600	1,295	Hornady
45 SP	BL-C	27.0	3,400	1,152	Hornady
45 SP	H380	30.5	3,500	1,224	Sierra
50 SP	IMR 3031	26.0	3,400	1,284	Sierra
50 SP	H380	31.0	3,500	1,360	Sierra, Hornady
55 SP	IMR 4320	29.0	3,300	1,330	Hornady, Sierra
55 SP	H380	30.0	3,300	1,330	Hornady, Sierra
55 SP	IMR 4320	27.0	3,300	1,330	Sierra
60 SP	IMR 4064	28.0	3,300	1,451	Hornady
60 SP	H380	31.0	3,300	1,451	Hornady
55 SP	FL		3,110	1,200	Factory load

.222 Remington Magnum

Historical Notes: The .222 Remington Magnum was originally developed as an experimental military cartridge in a cooperative effort between Remington and Springfield Arsenal. Since it was never adopted by the military, Remington introduced it as a sporting round in 1958, as one of the calibers for its Model 722 bolt-action rifle, and also, for a time, in the later 700 series bolt-action rifles. At present, no Remington rifles are available in this caliber. None of the other major American sporting arms manufacturing companies currently offer the .222 Remington Magnum.

General Comments: In comparison to the standard .222 Remington, the Magnum version has about 20-percent greater case capacity and consequently delivers 100 or so fps higher muzzle velocity and an effective range of between 50 and 75 yards greater than the .222. Though its case capacity is 4 to 5 percent greater than the .223 Remington, the performance of these two is indistinguishable because the .222 Remington Magnum is factory loaded to a lower maximum pressure. The .222 Magnum is nearly 1/10-inch longer than the .223 in overall case length, and it is also slightly longer in body length. As a result, the two are not interchangeable, and though the .223 can be chambered and fired in a .222 Magnum rifle, a dangerous headspace condition exists and case rupture is almost certain to occur when the round is fired. The .222 Remington Magnum is probably every bit as accurate as the standard .222 or the .223 and is certainly adequate for anything up to, but not including, deer. It never achieved the popularity of the standard .222 and has been largely superseded by the .223 Remington. It is, nevertheless, a very fine long-range varmint cartridge.

.222 Remington Magnum Loading Data and Factory Ballistics

Bullet (grains/type)	Powder	Grains	Velocity	Energy	Source/Comments
40 Sierra SP	BL-C(2)	30.0	3,818	1,290	Hodgdon
45 SP	H-380	29.5	3,400	1,125	Hornady
45 SP	BL-C2	27	3,400	1,236	Hornady, Sierra
45 SP	IMR 4895	27	3,400	1,082	Speer, Hornady
50 SP	H-380	30	3,400	1,180	Hornady
50 SP	BL-C2	26	3,300	1,190	Nosler, Hornady, Speer
50 SP	IMR 3031	26	3,300	1,204	Speer
55 SP	H-380	29	3,200	1,234	Hornady
55 SP	RL-7	22	3,200	1,170	Sierra
55 SP	IMR 3031	26	3,300	1,332	Speer
55 SP	IMR 4064	26	3,300	1,340	Hornady
60 HP	IMR 4895	25	3,000	1,242	Nosler, Hornady
55 SP	FL		3,240	1,282	Remington factory load

.22 Accelerator

Historical Notes: The .22 Accelerator is not a new cartridge, but rather a special loading of .30-30, and .30-06 cartridges using a sub-caliber .224-inch diameter bullet held in a discarding .30-caliber plastic sabot. These loadings were introduced by Remington; the .30-06 in 1977 and the .30-30 and the .308 in subsequent years. The .308 version has subsequently been dropped. All versions employ a 55-grain .224-caliber soft-point bullet retained in a 7-grain, six-fingered, plastic sabot with a hollow base. According to the 1979 Remington catalog, the rifling of the barrel imparts spin, which, combined with air resistance, causes the bullet and sabot to separate approximately 14 inches from the muzzle. The .30-30-224 Accelerator has a muzzle velocity of 3400 fps, and the .30-06-224 the impressive muzzle velocity of 4080 fps. The existence of two different .30-caliber Accelerator rounds seems to indicate commercial success. Remington originally intended to offer other Accelerator calibers, but these never materialized.

General Comments Frank Barnes' experience shooting Accelerator cartridges indicated that accuracy is not as good as when the same 55-grain bullet is fired in one of the high-velocity centerfire .22 rifles, such as the .222 Remington, .22-250, etc. Most of these rifles, when properly tuned, will deliver minute-of-angle groups or better. Shooting at 100 yards and using various rifles, I was unable to print any groups with the 30-30 Accelerator that ran under 2½ inches or under two inches with the .30-06 (five-shot groups). Actually, the Accelerator cartridges appear to group about the same as the standard .30-caliber cartridge does in the same rifle. This is just what the factory says it will do. In other words, if your rifle ordinarily makes three-inch five-shot groups at 100 yards, it isn't going to do any better with the Accelerator. However, from a practical point of view, the Accelerator loads will allow one to use a regular .30-30 or .30-06 big-game rifle for varmint shooting. The lack of MOA accuracy might restrict effective range to 200 yards or less, but this will vary greatly with individual rifles. The Accelerator concept is of greater usefulness to the shooter who does not reload than to the fellow who can cook up his own varmint loads with light 110-grain .30-caliber bullets. After firing, the plastic sabots are usually found anywhere from 40 to 100 feet in front of the muzzle. Remington has applied an old principle to modern sporting ammunition and come up with a very useful innovation.

Sabotted military loads, both as new loadings for old chamberings and for sabot-specific guns, are most effective. Likely, sabot-specific sporting guns could be accurate enough for sporting purposes and external ballistics could be most impressive. Though obsolete now, sabots for handloading Accelerator rounds are available from several Web sources.

.22 Accelerator Loading Data and Factory Ballistics

Bullet (grains/type)	Powder	Grains	Velocity	Energy	Source/Comments
30-30 Accelerator	FL	55 SP	3,400	1,412	Remington factory load
30-06 Accelerator	FL	55 SP	4,080	2,033	Remington factory load
.308 Accelerator	FL	55 SP			Remington factory load
.30-30 Accelerator	FL	55 SP			Remington factory load

.228 Weatherby Magnum

Historical Notes: There was a time when cartridges loaded with .22-caliber bullets were considered quite suitable for use on big game. The first of this breed to be introduced commercially in America was the .22 Savage High-Power. Rather than using a bullet of .224-inch diameter, as is common today with cartridges such as the .223 Remington and .22-250, the Savage cartridge was loaded with a bullet measuring a nominal .227- to .228-inch in diameter. The same also held true of deer cartridges of European design, with the 5.6x61mm Von Hofe Super Express a classic example. That bullet diameter also appeared in a few wildcat cartridges of American design, and the most popular was probably the .228 Ackley Magnum. It is also the bullet diameter chosen by Roy Weatherby for use in his .228 Weatherby Magnum. With the exception of the .220 Rocket and .224 Magnum, all of Weatherby's cartridges below his .378 Magnum in caliber are on the Holland & Holland belted case, and this includes the .228 Magnum.

Not a lot is known about this cartridge, but its photo in the 1947-1948 Weatherby catalog shows it on the shortened Holland & Holland belted case with a case length about the same as that of the .257 Weatherby Magnum. In the Weatherby archives are two samples of the .228 Magnum, one identified as "unformed", the other identified as "fireformed." The cartridge shown in the catalog has more body taper than the .257 Magnum, so that photo is obviously of the .228 Magnum before the case was fireformed to its final shape. The photo above shows the cartridge in its final, fireformed shape. Interestingly enough, the .228 Magnum case does not have the double-radius shoulder Roy Weatherby was so fond of. The introduction of the .243 Winchester and .244 Remington, in 1955, spelled doom for deer cartridges of smaller caliber, and this explains why the .228 Weatherby Magnum did not hang around for very long.

General Comments: The .228 Magnum was probably not a bad open-country cartridge for use on game such as whitetail deer and pronghorn antelope, but the .240 Magnum, introduced by Roy Weatherby in 1968 is even better, due to its ability to handle heavier bullets. As Weatherby rifles go, one chambered in .228 Magnum has to be the rarest of them all, simply because very few are thought to have been built. This was long before Weatherby introduced his Mark V action, and, in those days, he built rifles on whatever actions he could get his hands on, including the Winchester Model 70, Winchester Model 54, Remington Model 30, 1903 Springfield, 1917 Enfield, and 1898 Mauser.

.228 Weatherby Magnum Loading Data and Factory Ballistics

Bullet (grains/type)	Powder	Grains	Velocity	Energy	Source
70 PSN	IMR-4064	58.0	3,844	2,292	Roy Weatherby
70 PSN	IMR-4320	58.0	3,835	2,291	Roy Weatherby
70 PSN	IMR-4350	62.0	3,705	2,128	Roy Weatherby

.22-15-60 Stevens

Historical Notes: One of a number of cartridges for the Stevens 44 or 44½ series of single-shot rifles, this cartridge was introduced by Stevens in 1896. Actual design is credited to Charles H. Herrick, of Winchester, Mass. It did not enjoy a particularly long life, as most shooters preferred the 25-21 or some of the larger calibers. Many shooters claimed the .22-15 Stevens gave better accuracy than the .22 WCF.

General Comments: This is an improved centerfire .22 of substantially better killing power than other .22s of its day. With the heavy 60-grain bullet, it would shoot relatively flat for 125 yards or so. As a target or match cartridge, most of the black-powder .22s fouled the bore badly and required frequent cleaning. Most shooters preferred the larger calibers of .25 on up. The .22-15-60 was displaced by the .22 WCF and smokeless powder developments in the rimfire group. Original primer was the 1½ size, the same as our modern Small Rifle or Pistol primer of .175-inch diameter. Charge was 15 grains of FFFFg or FFFg. Lyman No. 22636 or 22637 in 54- to 60-grain weight is the proper bullet. Therefore, if you should have one of these old rifles in shooting condition, you can still shoot it—if you can find cases.

.22-15-60 Stevens Loading Data and Factory Ballistics

Bullet (grains/type)	Powder	Grains	Velocity	Energy	Source/Comments
60 Lead	Unique	3.4	1,070*	152	Lyman No. 22636
60 Lead	black powder (FFg)	15.0	1,150	176	Factory load
*Estimated					

.22 Winchester Centerfire (.22 WCF)

Historical Notes: The .22 WCF was introduced in 1885 as one of the original cartridges for the famous Winchester single-shot rifle, first manufactured that year. It was also chambered in the Remington No. 7 rolling block rifle, in 1904. It was actually too long for most of the short repeating actions of the day, although Winchester once cataloged it for the Model 1873, so its use was confined mostly to single-shot rifles. It is the predecessor of the .22 Hornet.

General Comments: The .22 WCF enjoyed considerable popularity as a target, small-game, and varmint cartridge, until 1925. Winchester advertised it as a 200-yard cartridge, but, with its mid-range trajectory of some 13.5 inches, it was more of a 100- to 125-yard number. Although originally a black-powder cartridge, it was loaded in a smokeless powder version with identical ballistics. In Europe, it was stepped up to about 1700 to 1800 fps and used in drillings or other combination guns. The .22 WCF was discontinued in 1936.

.22 Winchester Centerfire Loading Data and Factory Ballistics

Bullet (grains/type)	Powder	Grains	Velocity	Energy	Source/Comments
45 SP	Unique	4.0	1,500	226	
45 SP	2400	6.0	1,650	273	
45 Cast	black powder (FFg)	13.0	1,560	244	Lyman No. 228151

Bullet (grains/type)	Powder	Grains	Velocity	Energy	Source/Comments
45 Lead	black powder (FFFg)	13.0	1,540	240	Factory load

.22 Extra Long Centerfire (Maynard)

Historical Notes:	The .22 Extra Long Centerfire is one of a series of cartridges for the Model 1882 Maynard single-shot hunting and gallery rifles. It is, in effect, a centerfire version of the .22 Extra Long rimfire. It originally used the small No. 0 primer, which has not been manufactured for many years. It was replaced by the longer .22 centerfires and the 22 WCF. Ballard and Stevens rifles were also available in this caliber.
General Comments:	Powder charge varied from eight to 10 grains of FFFg or FFFFg black powder or semi-smokeless powder. Case lengths of 115/32 inches to 1¼ inches will be encountered. Three or four grains of IMR 4756 shotgun powder makes a satisfactory load. Lyman's No. 228151 (45-grain) bullet is proper for this cartridge.

.22 Extra Long Centerfire (Maynard) Factory Ballistics

Bullet (grains/type)	Powder	Grains	Velocity	Energy	Source/Comments
45 Lead	black powder (FFFg)	8.0-10.0	1,100	122	Factory load

.22 Savage High-Power (.22 High-Power/.22 Imp) 5.6x52Rmm

Historical Notes:	Designed by Charles Newton, this cartridge was introduced as a commercial cartridge by the Savage Arms Co., in its Model 99 lever-action rifle, about 1912. The cartridge was first called the "Imp." In the United States, only Savage produced a commercial rifle in this chambering, although a great many custom rifles were chambered for it. In England, the BSA Martini single-shot was chambered for it, about 1912. In Europe, it is known as the 5.6x52Rmm and has been chambered in various drillings or combination rifle and shotgun arms. The .22 Savage is based on the .25-35 case necked down. It has been obsolete in the U.S. since the 1930s. Norma still manufactures this ammunition.
General Comments:	The .22 Savage High-Power enjoyed considerable popularity through the early 1900s. However, accuracy was often marginal for small game and the bullets sometimes failed to penetrate adequately on larger game. No doubt, considering the general quality of jacketed bullets of that era, the Imp was greatly handicapped by poor bullet quality. Nonetheless, the .22 Savage was used in Africa and Asia on such unlikely beasts as lion and tiger, with some glowing reports on its effectiveness. It is a perfectly adequate small-game and varmint cartridge, but no big-game number by any standard. It has been rendered obsolete by new and much improved modern cartridges, such as the .222 Remington. For single-shot rifles, most modern shooters prefer the .225 Winchester, because of the availability of ammunition and cases, plus the fact that the .225 uses standard .224-inch diameter bullets, as opposed to the .228-inch bullets of the .22 Savage High-Power.

.22 Savage High-Power Loading Data and Factory Ballistics

Bullet (grains/type)	Powder	Grains	Velocity	Energy	Source/Comments
55 SP	IMR 4895	27.0	2,870	1,106	
55 SP	IMR 3031	30.0	3,260	1,291	
55 SP	H380	29.0	3,200	1,249	

Bullet (grains/type)	Powder	Grains	Velocity	Energy	Source/Comments
70 SP	RI-7	23.0	2,900	1,308	Hornady
70 SP	IMR 4198	23.0	3,000	1,399	Hornady
70 SP	IMR 3031	27.0	3,100	1,494	Hornady
71 SP	FL		2,790	1,228	Norma factory load

6mm Bench Rest Remington (6mm BR Remington)

Historical Notes: The 6mm BR Remington is one of eight cartridges based on the .308x1½-inch case necked either up or down. It is impossible to determine who first came up with the 6mm version, because a number of individuals claim the honor, dating back to 1962 and 1963, shortly after the original author of this book introduced the .308x1½-inch. However, Mike Walker, of Remington Arms, deserves credit for standardizing dimensions and the configuration in 1978. This allowed the cartridge to be adopted as a standard commercial cartridge. In late 1988, Remington announced that the 6mm BR would be produced as loaded factory ammunition. Prior to that, it was a sort of factory wildcat. Cases had to be formed from Remington BR brass, which is actually a modified .308 Winchester with a Small Rifle primer pocket, comparatively thin walls, and annealing to facilitate reforming. The factory load has a 100-grain bullet with a muzzle velocity of 2550 fps and muzzle energy of 1444 ft-lbs. The 6mm BR was intended primarily as a benchrest cartridge, but it also makes a good varmint number. It was available as one of the chamberings for the Remington XP-100 single-shot pistol. (Editor's note: Since the 6mm BR was in use before it was a factory round, there will be some chamber confusion. The original chambers were mostly intended for cases with turned necks.)

General Comments: The 6mm BR is similar to the 6mm PPC, except that the case is of larger diameter and has about 10 percent greater capacity. The 6mm PPC is loaded somewhat hotter than the 6mm BR, with some loading manuals listing the 90-grain bullet around 3000 fps. There is no reason why the 6mm BR can't do anything the 6mm PPC can, and the availability of factory ammunition should increase its popularity. This will also help overcome one of the problems with the 6mm PPC—the matter of obtaining suitable brass on an over-the-counter basis and at a reasonable price. Remington was the only manufacturer to take up commercial production of this caliber, and that briefly.

6mm BR Remington Loading Data and Factory Ballistics

Bullet (grains/type)	Powder	Grains	Velocity	Energy	Source/Comments
60 Sierra HP	H322	32.0	3,481	1,610	Hodgdon
70 SP	W748	32	3,200	1,592	Hornady
75 HP	W748	33	3,200	1,706	Hornady
80 SP	W748	31.5	3,100	1,708	Hornady
80 SP	RL-7	24	2,900	1,494	Hornady
80	Varget	32.5	3,159	1,740	Hodgdon
87 SP	W748	31	3,000	1,739	Hornady
87 SP	H-322	25.5	2,800	1,515	Hornady
100 SP	FL		2,550	1,444	Remington factory load

.244 Remington
(.243 Rockchucker)

Historical Notes: The .244 Remington was introduced by Remington in 1955 in its Model 722 bolt-action rifle. The cartridge is based on the .257 Roberts necked down to 6mm. It was actually originated as a wildcat by Fred Huntington of Oroville, Calif. The wildcat version preceded the factory design by several years and was called the .243 Rockchucker. Only Remington chambered the .244 among American manufacturers, but several European-made bolt-action rifles were available in this chambering.

General Comments: The .244 Remington is ballistically almost identical to the .243 Winchester. The only notable difference is that Remington made its 6mm rifles with a 1:12 twist, whereas Winchester adopted a 1:10 twist for its 6mm. The faster twist rate of the Winchester enabled use of 100-grain spitzer bullets, whereas the slower twist of the Remington did not. The net result is that the .244 Remington will not stabilize spitzer bullets heavier than about 90 grains in weight, while the .243 Winchester does very well with all 100- and even 105-grain bullets. Remington looked on the 6mm as largely a varmint and small-game development and concluded that anything beyond the 90-grain bullet was unnecessary. Winchester, on the other hand, decided the 6mm was very much a big-game cartridge and, therefore, heavier bullets would be highly desirable. Who was right? It appears as if something like 10 .243 Winchester-chambered rifles were sold for each .244 Remington-chambered gun. Remington changed to a 1:9 twist at the last, but too late to rescue the .244 from oblivion. What Remington did to extricate itself from this dilemma was to change the name of the .244 to the 6mm Remington and make all such rifles with a 1:9 twist. (Since, with lighter bullets, the 6mm Remington is interchangeable with the .244 Remington, then, strictly speaking, only the headstamp is obsolete.)

.244 Remington Loading Data and Factory Ballistics

Bullet (grains/type)	Powder	Grains	Velocity	Energy	Source/Comments
75 HP	IMR 4831	48.0	3,300	1,814	Speer, Hornady
75 HP	IMR 4350	47.0	3,400	1,926	Nosler, Sierra
75 HP	H380	42.0	3,150	1,653	Hornady
90 SP	IMR 4831	47.0	3,200	2,047	Speer, Sierra, Hornady
90 SP	IMR 4350	44.5	3,100	1,921	Sierra, Speer, Hornady
90 SP	H380	39.0	3,000	1,799	Sierra, Speer
90 SP	IMR 3031	36.6	3,000	1,799	Sierra
75 SP	FL		3,500	2,040	Remington factory load
90 SP	FL		3,200	2,050	Remington factory load

6mm Lee Navy
(.236 Navy)

Historical Notes: The 6mm Lee cartridge (also known as the .236 Navy) was used in the 1895 Lee Straight Pull bolt-action military rifle manufactured by Winchester for the United States Navy. About 15,000 of these rifles were made and used by the Navy on a trial basis. Winchester, Remington, and Blake also chambered sporting rifles for this cartridge. No factory-loaded ammunition has been available since 1935.

General Comments: The .244-caliber, or 6mm, was revived in two cartridges introduced by Remington and Winchester in 1955, the .244 (now the 6mm Remington) and the .243, respectively. The 6mm Lee cartridge died out mainly because it was too far ahead of its time. The powders available in 1895 were not suitable to a caliber this small. A few shooters who have old rifles for this round reload and use it for hunting. It is a good varmint, medium-game, deer, black bear, and antelope cartridge at moderate ranges. It is not as powerful as the 6mm Remington or the .243 Winchester. By increasing the rim to fit the standard Mauser bolt face and necking the case to accept .224-inch bullets, Winchester created the .220 Swift.

Bullet (grains/type)	Powder	Grains	Velocity	Energy	Source/Comments
75 SP	IMR 3031	37.0	3,300	1,809	Ackley
95 Cast	Unique	5.0	1,200	305	Lyman No. 244203
100 SP	IMR 4895	34.0	2,680	1,595	
112 SP	IMR 3031	30.0	2,650	1,895	Ackley
112 SP	IMR 4895	34.0	2,670	1,946	
112 SP	FL		2,560	1,635	Factory load

.25-20 Marlin

Historical Notes: This cartridge was loaded for the Marlin repeating rifle Model 1894. Winchester loaded the .25-20 Marlin, beginning at the turn of the century and until about World War I. It is nothing more than a special version of the .25-20 Winchester, except perhaps for the bullet nose shape, seating depth, and the .25-20 Marlin headstamp. It is otherwise identical to the current .25-20 Winchester. In 1916, Winchester offered five versions of this cartridge: lead, black powder (86 grains, 17 grains); soft-point, smokeless powder; full-patch, smokeless powder; high-velocity, soft-point; and high-velocity, full-patch.

General Comments: Sales of Marlin's Model 1894 rifles evidently generated sufficient demand for special-cartridge versions of the rifle's typical chamberings or, perhaps, cartridges with slightly different bullet shapes or loading lengths were found to function better in it. There must have been some good reason, for Winchester's 1916 catalog shows separate cartridge loadings with the following names: .25-20 Marlin, .32-20 Marlin, .38-40 Marlin, and .44-40 Marlin. It is possible the .25-20 Marlin was somehow unique from the .25-20 Winchester, because the catalog does not specify adaptation to Winchester rifles, as it does with the others. In addition, Winchester showed the same black-powder load and bullet weight for both the .25-20 Winchester and the .25-20 Marlin. The .32-20, .38-40, and .44-40 were unique loadings.

.25-20 Single Shot

Historical Notes: Designed by J. Francis Rabbeth—a gun writer at the turn of the century who used the pen name of J. Francis—the .25-20 Single Shot first appeared about 1882 and was one of the first .25-caliber centerfire wildcats. The first commercial cartridges were loaded by Remington (UMC) and, shortly thereafter, Maynard, Remington, Stevens, and Winchester chambered single-shot rifles for the round. No commercial rifles have been available in this chambering since the late 1920s, and manufacturers stopped loading this number in the mid '30s. Buffalo Arms (www.buffaloarms.com) shows this as an available cartridge in its vast lineup of antique and obsolete loadings.

General Comments: The .25-20 Single Shot was too long to work through the action of the Winchester Model 1892, so Winchester designed the .25-20 WCF, or Repeater, version with a shorter, more bottlenecked case. The .25-20 SS is quite accurate and was used almost entirely in single-shot rifles. As a varmint or small-game cartridge, it is in the same class as the .25-20 WCF. At one time there was a good deal of leftover ammunition on dealer shelves, but, as this cartridge is the base for forming the once-popular 2R Lovell wildcat, most of this was bought up by 2R fans. Most rifles for this cartridge have been rechambered for the still-available .25-20 WCF.

.25-20 Single Shot Loading Data and Factory Ballistics

Bullet (grains/type)	Powder	Grains	Velocity	Energy	Source/Comments
60 SP	2400	8.0	1,535	310	Ackley
65 Cast	2400	8.0	1,620	380	Lyman No. 257420

Bullet (grains/type)	Powder	Grains	Velocity	Energy	Source/Comments
86 SP	IMR 4227	8.5	1,400	370	Ackley
86 SP	FL		1,410	380	Factory load

.25-21 Stevens

Historical Notes: The .25-21 Stevens was developed about 1897 as a shortened version of the slightly older .25-25. First introduced for the Stevens 44 rifles and later available in the 44½ series, it was designed by Capt. W.L. Carpenter of the 9th U.S. Infantry, the man who also designed the .25-25 Stevens. The Remington-Hepburn was available in various models for the .25-21, and it was a popular target and small-game number. Many shooters of the period disliked the bottlenecked case, and the .25-21 was intended as a straight-case version of the .25-20 SS.

General Comments: The .25-21 was noted as a very accurate cartridge, reportedly capable of ½-inch, 100-yard groups. It gave about the same performance as the .25-20 SS, but was much too long for the standard repeating actions. It is easy to reload and quite pleasant to shoot. Use Lyman No. 25720 flat-point or No. 25727 hollow-point cast bullets. The former weighs 86 grains, the latter 75 grains. Twenty to 23 grains of FFFg black powder or the light smokeless powder loads listed below can be used.

.25-21 Stevens Loading Data

Bullet (grains/type)	Powder	Grains	Velocity	Energy	Source/Comments
86 Lead	2400	9.0	1,610	498	NA
86 Lead	Unique	5.0	1,500	434	NA
88 Cast	Unique	5.5	1,440	406	Lyman No. 257231

.25 Remington

Historical Notes: The .25 Remington is one of a series of rimless cartridges developed for the Remington Model 8 Autoloading rifle and later used in other Remington rifles. It was introduced in 1906. The Remington Model 14 pump-action and Model 30 bolt-action and the Stevens Model 425 lever-action also used the .25 Remington. No rifles have chambered this cartridge since 1942, and the ammunition companies stopped loading it about 1950.

General Comments: The .25 Remington is nothing more than a rimless version of the .25-35, but it differs slightly in shape. The two are not interchangeable. Since the Remington line of rifles, particularly the Model 30 bolt-action, would stand higher pressures than the lever-action, it is possible to get slightly better performance out of the .25 Remington. However, the difference is not sufficient to make the rimless version anything but a barely adequate deer cartridge. It will do for varmints and small to medium game quite well, and deer in a pinch, provided the hunter is a good shot. The .30-30 is a better cartridge for anything, and the .25 Remington is hardly in the same class as the .250 Savage or the .257 Roberts.

.25 Remington Loading Data and Factory Ballistics

Bullet (grains/type)	Powder	Grains	Velocity	Energy	Source/Comments
60 SP	H4895	31.0	2,900	1,121	Hornady
60 SP	IMR 4320	32.0	2,900	1,121	Hornady
117 SP	H4895	26.5	2,200	1,258	Hornady

Bullet (grains/type)	Powder	Grains	Velocity	Energy	Source/Comments
117 SP	IMR 3031	25.5	2,300	1,375	Hornady
100 SP	FL		2,330	1,216	Factory load
117 SP	FL		2,125	1,175	Factory load

.25-36 Marlin

Historical Notes: This cartridge, adopted by Marlin in 1895 for its lever-action Model 93 rifle, was designed by William V. Lowe a year or so prior and originally called the .25-37. It was probably inspired by the .25-35 Winchester. The two are very similar, but not interchangeable, although the .25-35 can be fired in the slightly longer .25-36 chamber. The .25-36 Marlin was loaded in a smokeless powder version and survived until the early 1920s.

General Comments: The .25-36 and the .25-35 WCF are similar; however, many rifles for the Marlin cartridge were not strong enough to withstand maximum loads safely. In general, one should not exceed 2000 fps velocity with the .25-36. It is not an adequate deer cartridge, and its use should be confined to small or medium game. It did not acquire a reputation for outstanding accuracy.

.25-36 Marlin Loading Data and Factory Ballistics

Bullet (grains/type)	Powder	Grains	Velocity	Energy	Source/Comments
87 SP	IMR 3031	20.0	2,010	770	NA
117 SP	IMR 3031	20.0	1,800	845	NA
117 SP	FL		1,855	893	Factory load

.25-25 Stevens

Historical Notes: The .25-25 was the first straight case manufactured for Stevens. Designed by Capt. Carpenter, in 1895, Stevens introduced it for its Model 44 single-shot rifles and for the 44½ series after this action was marketed, in 1903. It was also a standard chambering for some of the Remington-Hepburn target rifles. It was somewhat popular, but the shorter .25-21 developed practically the same performance and was a little cleaner shooting.

General Comments: A very freakish-appearing cartridge, with its excessive length-to-diameter ratio, it is the .25-21 with about a half-inch added to its overall length. The late Phil Sharpe wrote (*The Rifle in America*, 1938) that the .25-25 caused much extraction trouble, and that is why the shorter .25-21 was developed. However, modern users say this is not so, although the .25-25 fouls the bore a little more than the .25-21. It is highly probable the .25-21 was developed because it was found that 20 or 21 grains of powder gave practically the same ballistics as the extra four grains or so. You can use any cast .257-inch diameter bullet of 60- to 86-grain weight; the gascheck type is preferable with smokeless powder.

.25-25 Stevens Loading Data and Factory Ballistics

Bullet (grains/type)	Powder	Grains	Velocity	Energy	Source/Comments
86 Lead	Unique	5.5	1,525	448	NA
86 Lead	IMR 4198	10.2	1,520	446	NA
86 Lead	FL		1,500	434	Factory load

.256 Winchester Magnum

Historical Notes: The .256 Winchester Magnum was announced in 1960 as a new handgun cartridge. However, the only handgun that chambered it was the single-shot, enclosed-breech Ruger Hawkeye, introduced in late 1961. The .256 Winchester Magnum is listed as a rifle cartridge, because Marlin produced its Model 62 lever-action rifle in this chambering, and Universal Firearms made the semi-auto Ferret on the M-1 Carbine action. The Marlin rifle was available about a year after the Ruger Hawkeye, and both were discontinued after a relatively short production life. The Thompson/Center Contender, a single-shot pistol, was also available for this round. The cartridge is based on the necked-down .357 Magnum revolver case.

General Comments: As a rifle cartridge, the .256 is considerably more potent than the .25-20 and several jumps ahead of the .22 Hornet or the .218 Bee. The factory-loaded 60-grain bullet develops over 2760 fps muzzle velocity when fired from a 24-inch rifle barrel. This offers 1015 ft-lbs of muzzle energy, which is well above the Hornet or Bee. The .256 Magnum is an effective varmint cartridge out to ranges of 200 yards. It can be handloaded with heavier 75- or 87-grain bullets to velocities of 2500 and 2230 fps, respectively. Although a good varmint and small-game chambering, it is not an adequate deer cartridge, and most states will not allow its use for this purpose. Winchester was the only commercial manufacturer to offer the .256 Winchester Magnum. It was discontinued in the early 1990s.

.256 Winchester Magnum Loading Data and Factory Ballistics

Bullet (grains/type)	Powder	Grains	Velocity	Energy	Source/Comments
60 SP	H4227	14.0	2,500	833	Hornady
60 SP	H4227	16.0	2,800	1,045	Hornady
60 SP	2400	14.0	2,600	901	Hornady
75 HP	H4227	14.0	2,400	958	Hornady
75 HP	IMR 4227	15.5	2,500	1,041	Sierra
87 SP	IMR 4227	14.0	2,200	935	Sierra
87 SP	H4227	14.0	2,200	935	Hornady
60 SP	FL		2,760	1,015	Winchester factory load

.256 Newton

Historical Notes: One of several high-velocity rimless cartridges designed by Charles Newton for his bolt-action rifles, the .256 Newton was introduced in 1913 by the Western Cartridge Co. Until the .264 Winchester Magnum came along, in 1958, this was the only American-designed 6.5mm to be offered on a commercial basis. The last of the Newton rifle companies failed in the early 1920s, and Western quit loading Newton cartridges in 1938. The .256 Newton is based on the .30-06 case necked down.

General Comments: The .256 Newton has hung on as a wildcat cartridge and, occasionally, custom rifles are made for it. Cases can be made by necking down, reforming, and shortening .30-06 brass. This is a good cartridge and adequate for practically all North American big game, but it is not as effective as the .270 Winchester. With modern, slow-burning powders, its performance can be improved over original factory ballistics.

.256 Newton Loading Data and Factory Ballistics

Bullet (grains/type)	Powder	Grains	Velocity	Energy	Source/Comments
120 SP	IMR 4350	55.0	2,980	2,362	NA
130 SP	IMR 4895	46.0	2,900	2,425	NA

Bullet (grains/type)	Powder	Grains	Velocity	Energy	Source/Comments
140 SP	IMR 4831	57.0	2,890	2,598	NA
129 SP	FL		2,760	2,180	Western factory load

6.5mm Remington Magnum

Historical Notes: The 6.5mm is a Remington innovation, introduced in 1966 for its Model 600 carbine. The 6.5mm Remington Magnum is based on the .350 Remington Magnum case necked down to 6.5mm (.264-inch). The Remington Model 600 carbine had an 18½-inch barrel, and the later 660 carbine a 20-inch barrel. Neither of these carbines allowed the cartridge to develop its full velocity potential and both were discontinued. By 1971, only the Remington Model 700 and 40-XB target rifle with 24-inch barrels were cataloged as available in 6.5mm Magnum chambering. For a short time, the Ruger Model 77 was offered in this chambering. All of the rifles referred to are bolt-actions. Currently, no one offers rifles chambered for the 6.5mm Remington Magnum.

General Comments: The 6.5mm Remington Magnum has greater case capacity and develops higher velocities than any of the European military 6.5s. It is an excellent cartridge for North American big game and can double as a varmint cartridge by handloading the lighter bullets. Probably one reason it never achieved great popularity was that the chambering's rifles had short magazines, which required deep seating of heavier bullets, with a consequent loss in powder capacity and performance. Combined with the short barrels of the Remington Model 600 and 660 carbines, this added up to ballistics well below the .30-06 class of cartridges. In a standard long action that will allow seating heavier bullets farther out, one can approach the performance of the .270 Winchester. With the proper bullet, the 6.5mm Magnum is adequate for North American big game at moderate ranges under normal hunting conditions. Unfortunately, this is another case of a good cartridge that did not catch on. At one time, Remington offered two bullet weights, a 100-grain bullet at an advertised muzzle velocity of 3450 fps, and a 120-grain bullet at 3220 fps. The older 6.5mm cartridges gained its reputation with heavier bullets of 140 to 160 grains; the lack of such a factory load is very likely another reason for the demise of the Remington version. Early factory-advertised ballistics were based on a longer-than-standard barrel and were, therefore, unrealistic.

6.5mm Remington Magnum Loading Data and Factory Ballistics

Bullet (grains/type)	Powder	Grains	Velocity	Energy	Source/Comments
85 SP	IMR 4350	57.0	3,100	1,814	Sierra
100 SP	H4831	56.2	3,200	2,274	Hornady
100 SP	H380	51.5	3,100	2,134	Sierra
120 SP	IMR 4831	55.0	3,000	2,399	Speer
129 SP	H4831	54.0	3,000	2,579	Hornady
140 SP	IMR 4831	52.0	2,750	2,352	Speer
160 SP	H4831	54.5	2,800	2,786	Hornady
120 SP	FL		3,210	2,745	Remington factory load

7x61mm Sharpe & Hart Super (7x61mm S&H Super)

Historical Notes: The 7x61mm was developed in the United States by Philip B. Sharpe and Richard F. Hart. Its design was originally based on a rimless, experimental French 7mm semi-auto military cartridge. It was copyrighted and made available on a commercial basis in the Schultz & Larsen rifle, in 1953. Ammunition was loaded and imported by Norma. The final version had a belted case with "Super" added to its name. Ammunition loaded with a 154-grain bullet (instead of the original 160-grain), was recently offered by Norma.

General Comments: The 7x61mm Sharpe & Hart (now listed as the S&H Super), is very similar to the .275 H&H Magnum, a belted case cartridge that was chambered and loaded in England. It is in the short 7mm magnum class, and its performance is the same as a number of other wildcat cartridges based on the blown out and shortened .300 H&H Magnum case. However, the Sharpe & Hart case has a slightly larger base diameter than the .300 H&H. This cartridge is quite popular in Canada, but its popularity in the United States was limited by competition from the 7mm Weatherby Magnum, the 7mm Remington Magnum, and various wildcats. The 7mm S&H is, nonetheless, a fine cartridge for any North American game and most African plains game.

Like any of this ilk, this number can be somewhat hard on its barrel, especially with careless shooting, not allowing plenty of time between shots for barrel cooling, or inadequate cleaning. Moreover, like all similar chamberings, it loses significant velocity with barrels shorter than 24 inches. Actual ballistics may be closer to the 7mm Weatherby than factory data suggests.

7x61mm Sharpe & Hart Super Loading Data and Factory Ballistics

Bullet (grains/type)	Powder	Grains	Velocity	Energy	Source/Comments
120 SP	IMR 4350	64.0	3,300	2,902	Sierra
140 SP	IMR 4831	63.0	3,100	2,988	Sierra
140 SP	IMR 4350	62.5	3,200	3,184	Hornady, Sierra
150 SP	IMR 4831	64.5	3,100	3,202	Sierra
160 SP	IMR 4350	58.0	2,900	2,989	Hornady, Sierra
175 SP	IMR 4350	60.5	2,900	3,269	Hornady
154 SP	FL		3,060	3,200	Norma factory load (latest)
160 SP	FL		3,100	3,410	Norma factory load (original)

.275 Holland & Holland Magnum

Historical Notes: First loaded in Great Britain about 1912, this cartridge was introduced in the United States by Western Cartridge Co., in 1926. Western Cartridge loaded this cartridge with only the 175-grain bullet, until production was discontinued in 1939.

General Comments: The .275 H&H was never particularly popular in this country. It resembled the .280 Ross, but did not give the velocity of the Ross. Its chief advantage over other 7mm cartridges was its ability to handle a 175-grain bullet at increased velocity. The Western Cartridge loading, with a 175-grain soft-point boat-tail bullet, gave a muzzle velocity of 2690 fps, a muzzle energy of 2810 ft-lbs, and a mid-range (iron-sight) trajectory at 100 yards of .7-inch. Impressive performance, considering the powders then available. See Chapter 7 for additional information.

.275 H&H Magnum Loading Data

Bullet (grains/type)	Powder	Grains	Velocity	Energy	Source/Comments
140	IMR 4064	48.0	2,810	2,455	Ackley

.275 H&H Magnum Loading Data

Bullet (grains/type)	Powder	Grains	Velocity	Energy	Source/Comments
160	IMR 4350	59.0	3,050	3,305	Ackley
180	IMR 4350	58.0	2,850	3,245	Ackley
195	IMR 4350	52.0	2,671	3,090	Ackley

.28-30-120 Stevens

Historical Notes: The .28-30-120 was probably the first American-designed, commercial 7mm cartridge. Introduced by the J. Stevens Arms & Tool Co. in 1900, it was designed by Charles H. Herrick of Winchester, Massachusetts. Both 44 and 44½ Stevens rifles were chambered for the round. It was an early favorite of Harry M. Pope, who made and fitted barrels to a variety of single-shot actions in this chambering. As a match cartridge, it established a reputation for exceptional accuracy.

General Comments: Remington made the first factory loads for the .28-30, and these used the 120-grain bullet and 30 grains of Fg black powder. By 1918, it was no longer listed in the Remington catalog. Some match shooters who used the .28-30 considered it superior to the .32-40 out to 300 yards. It makes a good 150-yard small-game or varmint cartridge. Lyman No. 285222 or 285228 is the proper cast bullet, but one can use any standard cast 7mm bullet up to 180 grains. Do not use jacketed bullets in the old black-powder barrels, as they will wear the bore excessively and the fine accuracy may be destroyed within a few hundred rounds. Gas-checked bullets are okay.

.28-30-120 Loading Data and Factory Ballistics

Bullet (grains/type)	Powder	Grains	Velocity	Energy	Source/Comments
135 Lead	black powder (Fg)	28.0	1,410	602	
135 Lead	IMR 4198	17.0	1,500	605	
120 Lead	FL		1,500	605	Factory load

.30 Remington

Historical Notes: A rimless version of the .30-30 Winchester, the .30 Remington was introduced by Remington in 1906 for its Model 8 autoloader. When the Model 14 pump-action came out, in 1912, it was also chambered for the .30 Remington, as was the Model 30 bolt-action, introduced in 1921. The Stevens lever-action Model 425 and the Standard gas-operated rifle also used the .30 Remington. No new rifles have chambered this round since immediately after World War II. Some domestic ammunition companies continued to load it, until recently. There are a large number of rifles for this caliber still in use. The original rifles were marked ".30-30 Remington."

Editor's note: Imagine the confusion that must have arisen when Remington originally called this cartridge the ".30-30 Remington." One wonders how many hunters found themselves in the wilderness with a box of Remington-brand .30-30 Winchester ammunition and a Model 8 rifle the rounds would not fit into. The simple request to "Give me a box of Remington .30-30s" was bound to lead to this problem.

General Comments: Identical to the .30-30 Winchester in performance, the .30 Remington is strictly in the small-, medium-, and deer-size game class. Its advantages are in the nature of the guns that chambered it. It is possible to use spitzer bullets in most .30 Remington rifles, which help retain velocity at longer ranges. The .30 Remington can be reloaded to better performance than the .30-30 Winchester. Interestingly, handloading data has seldom, if ever, reflected this possibility. Similarly, factory ammunition has uniformly downplayed the Remington rimless series, with loads rated a full 100 fps slower than their rimmed counterparts. However, the difference is not great enough to take the .30 Remington out of the .30-30 class. Note: The nominal bullet diameter is given as .307-inch.

.30 Remington Loading Data and Factory Ballistics

Bullet (grains/type)	Powder	Grains	Velocity	Energy	Source/Comments
150 SP	IMR 4895	35.5	2,350	1,840	Lyman
150 SP	IMR 4320	36.0	2,320	1,794	Lyman
170 SP	IMR 3031	30.0	2,115	1,690	Lyman
170 SP	IMR 4895	33.0	2,145	1,735	Lyman
170 SP	FL		2,120	1,696	Remington factory load

.30-30 Wesson

Historical Notes:	The .30-30 Wesson was used in rifles designed and marketed by Frank Wesson, of Worcester, Massachusetts, who operated from the 1860s into the late 1880s. During the Civil War, the government purchased about 150 Wesson military carbines in caliber .44 rimfire. Some of the state militias also purchased Wesson carbines. His sporting rifles were marketed, in rimfire types, as early as 1861. As near as can be determined, the .30-30 Wesson was probably developed sometime around 1880. Frank Wesson was a brother of Daniel B. Wesson, co-founder of Smith & Wesson. Both Remington and Winchester made bullets and cases for this cartridge, and U.S. Cartridge Co. catalogs listed it. Usable cases can probably be fabricated from .357 Maximum cases.
General Comments:	The most common Wesson rifle was a single-shot with a double trigger arrangement. The forward trigger unlatched the breech, allowing the barrel to be tipped up for loading and unloading. Several models were marketed, including sporting and target types. There were, in addition, under-lever falling-block solid-frame types that quite scarce, as are the Wesson cartridges themselves. The .30-30 Wesson is not the same as the .30-30 Winchester, and there is nothing to indicate that it had any influence on the design of the .30-30. Smokeless powder loads would not be advisable in this rifle.

.30-30 Wesson Loading Data and Factory Ballistics

Bullet (grains/type)	Powder	Grains	Velocity	Energy	Source/Comments
165 Lead	black powder (Fg)	30.0	1,250	1,010	Factory load

.30 USA/.30-40 Rimless

Historical Notes:	We have little information on this cartridge. It was used in the Blake rifle, and ammunition was produced by United Metallic Cartridge for a time. No doubt, considerable confusion ensued in that era of rapid development and the nascent exposure of U.S. shooters to rimless chamberings. We include this number here to demonstrate that Europeans were not the only ones to muddy up the water with rimless and rimmed versions of otherwise identical or nearly identical cartridges.

.30-03 Springfield/
.30-03 Government

Historical Notes: In 1903, the U.S. Government adopted a new military loading to replace the .30 Army (.30-40 Krag), which had been adopted in 1892. Like the .30-40 Krag, this new (.30-Caliber, Model of 1903) cartridge featured a 220-grain round-nosed, full metal jacket bullet. However, the '03 increased muzzle velocity by about 100 fps, even though the M1903 rifle featured a significantly shorter barrel. The rimless cartridge design, generously borrowed from Mauser, was also an improvement, as it featured superior feeding from a box magazine. Nevertheless, as seems to have been typical in that era, the U.S. Army was slow to the task of modernizing. As the .30-03 was standardized, all other world powers were in the process of adopting spitzer-bullet military loadings; the brand new .30-03 became instantly obsolete. A crash program was instituted and, in 1906, a modified version of this basic cartridge was adopted as the .30 Caliber, Model of 1906. That loading featured a lighter spitzer bullet and a shorter case neck. The spitzer bullets had a much shorter bearing surface, so the existing rifles were modified by turning back the barrels two threads and recutting the chambers.

General Comments: Despite its short life, this cartridge, like the .30-06, found application in John M. Browning's Winchester Model 1895. Considering the ambitious pressure levels common in the early days of these chamberings, that was perhaps not such a good idea. For the handloader, case life could be extremely limited, owing to case stretching because of the rear lockup on those rifles. Compared to the .30-06, the .30-03 offers no advantage as a sporting round. Ammunition was available at least until World War I. By today's standards, that is remarkable, for there were very few sporting rifles chambered for this cartridge and, very soon after 1906, virtually all 1903 Springfields had been converted to .30-06.

.30 Newton
.30 Adolph Express

Historical Notes: The .30 Newton was originally designed for Fred Adolph and was called the "Adolph Express," when introduced in 1913. It was not until several years later that Charles Newton produced rifles for his own brainchild and the cartridge received the gun inventor's name. The Western Cartridge Co. produced the .30 Newton cartridge. No commercial rifle other than the Newton ever chambered it. Production of rifles ceased in the early 1920s, and Western dropped the cartridge, about 1938.

General Comments: The .30 Newton is a rimless, magnum-type cartridge similar to the .30-06, but larger in diameter. Neither ammunition nor cases are readily available, since it has been obsolete for more than 50 years. However, brass can be readily formed from RWS 8x68mm. A limited quantity of new cases was manufactured right after World War II, by Richard Speer. The .30 Newton is powerful enough for any North American big game. The .300 H&H Magnum and .300 Weatherby Magnum outperform it, although its performance can be improved by handloading with modern powders.

.30 Newton Loading Data and Factory Ballistics

Bullet (grains/type)	Powder	Grains	Velocity	Energy	Source/Comments
150 SP	IMR 4320	67.0	3,175	3,361	NA
150 SP	IMR 4831	76.0	3,100	3,206	NA
180 SP	IMR 4320	62.0	2,840	3,235	NA
180 SP	IMR 4831	73.0	2,890	3,350	NA
200 SP	IMR 4350	66.0	2,730	3,318	NA
180 SP	FL		2,860	3,270	Western factory load

.32-40 Remington/
.32-40-150 (2⅛-inch)
Remington

Historical Notes:	The .32-40-150 (2-1/8-inch) Remington was one of the cartridges for the single-shot, rolling block Sporting Rifle No. 1, introduced in 1870. This cartridge appears to have been introduced shortly after the rifle, about 1871 to '72. The .32-40 Remington was also one of the cartridges for the No. 3 Hepburn and some of the Farrow single-shot rifles. Other than this, no one else seems to have adopted it. Remington quit loading it in 1910.
General Comments:	This is a very odd-looking cartridge, with a long tapered shoulder that merges imperceptibly with an elongated neck. It is usually listed as a straight case, but it is not straight and is not exactly necked. It might best be described as a taper-necked case. On the dimensional chart, it is shown as type "A," or rimmed, bottleneck, but this is not totally correct, either. The shoulder diameter is arbitrary, since it is difficult to decide just where the shoulder begins. Although called a .32-caliber, true bullet diameter is .308- or .309-inch; hence, it is really a .30-caliber. It was both a hunting and target round of limited popularity. It lost out to the .32-40 Ballard, which was available in both single-shot and repeating rifles. It was a small- to medium-game cartridge, but was probably also used to some extent for hunting deer-size animals. Usable cases might be formed from either .30-40 Krag or .303 British cases.

.32-40 Remington Loading Data and Factory Ballistics

Bullet (grains/type)	Powder	Grains	Velocity	Energy	Source/Comments
150 Lead	IMR 4198	14.5	1,350	607	Lyman No. 308156
150 Lead	FL125		1,350	607	Factory load

.303 Savage
.301 Savage

Historical Notes:	Originally developed as a potential military cartridge, in 1895, the .303 Savage was later introduced commercially as one of several chamberings for the popular Savage Model 1899 lever-action. Savage discontinued this chambering, when rifle production was resumed after World War II. In England, it is known as the .301 Savage. No new rifles are chambered for this round at present.
General Comments:	Dogma holds that the .303 Savage is not a true .303 but, instead, uses standard .308-inch bullets. However, current SAAMI specifications call for a bullet of .311-inch. Measurements of bullets on three lots of each of two makes of World War II-era factory loads yielded mixed results. Some were .308-inch-plus, others .310-inch-plus. The .303 is similar to the .30-30 in size, shape, and performance, but the two are not interchangeable. With its 190-grain bullet, many old woods hunters swore by it. With the relatively heavy bullet at moderate velocity, it gave good penetration on deer-sized animals. However, it is ballistically no more powerful than the .30-30, so its use should be restricted to deer at short ranges. Unfortunately, Savage never took advantage of the fact that the 99 rifle is particularly suited to the use of spitzer bullets. Proper loadings of 150-grain spitzers in the .303 could have moved it completely out of the .30-30 class and might have gone a long way toward increasing its popularity. As it has always been loaded, it is effective only at close range. This need not have been the case. Many handloaders still use the .303 Savage with 150-grain spitzer bullets loaded to about 2500 fps. It is still no long-range wonder, but such a load gives it a decided edge over any other .30-30-class chambering.

.303 Savage Loading Data and Factory Ballistics

Bullet (grains/type)	Powder	Grains	Velocity	Energy	Source/Comments
150 SP	IMR 4064	36	2,400	1,919	Lyman
170 SP	IMR 3031	31	2,170	1,778	Lyman

Bullet (grains/type)	Powder	Grains	Velocity	Energy	Source/Comments
180 SP	FL		2,140	1,830	Factory load
190 SP	FL		1,890	1,507	Winchester factory load

.32-20 Marlin
.32-20-100 Marlin Safety

Historical Notes: This cartridge was loaded for the Marlin 1894 repeating rifle. Winchester loaded this cartridge, beginning around the turn of the century and until about World War I. It is nothing more than a special version of the .32 WCF (.32-20 Winchester). Compared to the Winchester round, it was loaded with a lighter bullet of 100 grains versus 117 grains. With the exceptions of perhaps bullet nose shape, seating depth, and headstamp, this loading appears to have been otherwise identical to the .32-20 Winchester. In 1916, Winchester offered three versions of this cartridge: lead and black powder (100 grains, 20 grains); soft-point (117 grains) and smokeless powder; and full-patch (117 grains) and smokeless powder. High-velocity loadings were not offered.

General Comments: Evidently, sales of Marlin's Model 1894 rifle generated sufficient demand for special versions of the cartridges for which that rifle was nominally chambered. Perhaps cartridges with slightly different bullet shapes or loading lengths were found to function better in it. Whatever the reason, the 1916 catalog shows separate cartridge loadings with these names: .25-20 Marlin, .32-30 Marlin, .38-40 Marlin, and .44-40 Marlin. Winchester says this cartridge was adapted to both Winchester and Marlin rifles, as were the .38-40 and .44-40 Marlin cartridges.

.32-30 Remington

Historical Notes: This bottleneck cartridge, similar to the .32-20 WCF, was one of the chamberings available for the Remington-Hepburn No. 3 series single-shot rifle, introduced in 1880. The cartridge was first made in November of 1884. Not a true .32, bullet diameter is .312-inch.

General Comments: The Remington-Hepburn was billed as a "long-range hunting and target rifle," but the .32-30 is hardly a long-range cartridge. It is only a notch or so above the .32-20 WCF. It was not a popular cartridge and died out in 1912. Like most other single-shot cartridges, this one was too long for the short repeating actions, such as the Model 92 Winchester. These were, in addition, too small for the larger actions. This in-between position eliminated these, as the repeater gained popularity. Rifles for the .32-30 are comparatively rare today. Ammunition can be made by reforming .357 Magnum or .357 Maximum cases.

.32-30 Remington Loading Data and Factory Ballistics

Bullet (grains/type)	Powder	Grains	Velocity	Energy	Source/Comments
111 Lead	IMR 4198	14.0	1,650	676	Lyman No. 311316
115 Lead	black powder (FFg)	35.0	1,430	528	NA
125 Lead	FL		1,380	535	Factory load

.32-35 Stevens & Maynard

Historical Notes: A match cartridge, introduced by J. Stevens Arms & Tool Co. in the mid-1880s, this was one of the chamberings available for the New Model Range Rifle Nos. 9 and 10, which first appeared in 1886. These were on a tip-up, single-shot action, and some of the earlier models might have chambered the .32-35. Later rifles based on the 44 and 44½ under-lever single-shot actions were available in .32-35.

General Comments: This was one of the most accurate of the Stevens target cartridges, and many records were established with it. The .32-40 was responsible for the .32-35's gradual obsolescence. Best accuracy usually was obtained by seating the bullet in the chamber 1/16 inch or so ahead of the case; the case, full of powder and with a wad to prevent powder spillage, was then inserted in the chamber behind the bullet. Lyman's No. 3117 bullet of 153 grains was popular with many riflemen. The correct charge of black powder was 35 grains of Fg or FFg.

.32-35 Stevens & Maynard Loading Data and Factory Ballistics

Bullet (grains/type)	Powder	Grains	Velocity	Energy	Source/Comments
153 Lead	IMR 4198	14.0	1,410	683	NA
165 Lead	IMR 4227	11.0	1,380	696	NA
165 Lead	FL		1,400	683	Factory load

.32-40 Bullard

Historical Notes: This is the smallest cartridge of a series designed for the Bullard single-shot and repeating rifles. Bullard patents were granted in 1881, and manufacture of its rifles is believed to have started during 1882 or 1883. Exact date of introduction of the individual cartridges is difficult to establish, but all were available by 1887.

General Comments: The Bullard lever-action repeating rifle resembled the Winchester, but employed a different rack-and-pinion mechanism. The loading port in the magazine was located on the bottom, unlike the Winchester's side port. The single-shot was of the under-lever type and quite strong. Although Bullard rifles and cartridges were as good as any of contemporary manufacture, they did not endure beyond 1900. Some Bullard cartridges were made by Remington and Winchester. Performance of the .32-40 Bullard is the same as the .32-40 Winchester and Marlin. Both are scarce items. Usable cases can be easily formed from .357 Remington Maximum cases.

.32-40 Bullard Loading Data and Factory Ballistics

Bullet (grains/type)	Powder	Grains	Velocity	Energy	Source/Comments
150 Lead	IMR 4198	15.0	1,470	719	Lyman No. 311241
155 Lead	2400	13.0	1,400	674	NA
150 Lead	FL		1,492	750	Factory load

.32 Long (Center Fire)

Historical Notes: This centerfire, reloadable version of the .32 Long rimfire with an outside-lubricated bullet was introduced, in 1875, in a variety of light-frame single-shot rifles and the Marlin Models of 1891 and 1892. Some of these were constructed so that both rimfire and centerfire ammunition could be used by changing the firing pin or hammer.

General Comments: The .32 Long was not a satisfactory or effective cartridge. A longer case called the "Extra Long" was soon employed, in order to increase range and killing power on small game. Eventually the .32 Long was replaced by such numbers as the .32-20 WCF, .32 Ideal, and the .32-35 Stevens. It is very similar to the .32 Colt revolver cartridge. The standard load consisted of 13 grains of FFFg black powder and an 80- to 85-grain bullet. Muzzle velocity was only about 800 to 900 fps, depending on load and barrel length. The .32 S&W Long or .32 Long Colt will work in most old rifles in this chambering. These cartridges are now collector's items.

.32 Long (CF) Loading Data and Factory Ballistics

Bullet (grains/type)	Powder	Grains	Velocity	Energy	Source/Comments
85 Lead	FL		850	136	Factory load

.32 Ballard Extra Long

Historical Notes: The .32 Extra Long is an elongated version of the .32 Long centerfire, the latter being one of the chamberings available for the J.M. Marlin 1876 Ballard No. 2 Sporting Rifle. The .32 Extra Long cartridge appeared in 1879. This was after Marlin Fire Arms Co. began manufacturing Ballard rifles. Marlin introduced (or continued) the Sporting Rifle No. 2, in 1881. Stevens, Remington, Wurfflein, and other single-shot rifles were also available in this chambering. It was popular, but lost out to the .32-20 WCF. Most companies stopped loading it by 1920. Rifles chambered for this cartridge will usually chamber and fire both the .32 S&W Long and .32 Long Colt.

General Comments: This is essentially a centerfire version of the .32 Extra Long rimfire, and ballistics are practically identical. It was used as a target and small-game cartridge throughout the late 1800s. It is very similar in performance to the black powder loading of the .32-20 WCF. Most of the old rifles for this cartridge will not safely withstand heavy loads of modern smokeless powder. An outside-lubricated bullet of the same diameter as the case neck was first used.

.32 Ballard Extra Long Loading Data and Factory Ballistics

Bullet (grains/type)	Powder	Grains	Velocity	Energy	Source/Comments
115 Lead	IMR 4198	9.0	1,360	473	NA
115 Lead	black powder (FFg)	20.0	1,200	372	Factory load

.32-40 (.32-40 Ballard/ .32-40 Winchester)

Historical Notes: Originally developed as a black-powder match or target cartridge for the single-shot Ballard Union Hill Rifle Nos. 8 and 9, the .32-40 was introduced, in 1884, loaded with a 165-grain lead bullet in front of 40 grains of Fg black powder. It established a reputation for fine accuracy, and Winchester and Marlin added it to their lines of lever-action repeating and single-shot rifles late in 1886. The late Harry Pope's favorite cartridges were the .32-40 and his own variant, the .33-40. Ammunition has been discontinued by major companies. However, in the early 1980s, Winchester loaded this cartridge to boost sales of its John Wayne Commemorative rifle.

General Comments: In a good, solid-frame rifle, the .32-40 will shoot as well as any modern high-powered match cartridge out to 200 or 300 yards. It was a popular hunting cartridge for medium game and deer and, while it has certainly killed its share of deer, the factory loading barely qualifies in that class. However, in a strong action, it can be handloaded to equal the .30-30. For small to medium game or varmints, it will do very well at moderate ranges. Do not use high-velocity loadings in the old Ballard or Stevens 44 rifles. A number of modern copies of old Sharps single-shot rifles and a special commemorative M1894 Winchester have been chambered for the .32-40 in recent years. Usable cases can easily be formed from .30-30, .32 Special, or .38-55 cases.

.32-40 Loading Data and Factory Ballistics

Bullet (grains/type)	Powder	Grains	Velocity	Energy	Source/Comments
155 Lead	2400	13.0	1,460	786	
165 Lead	H4895	16.0	1,410	729	OK for old rifles – Hodgdon
165 Lead	H4198	14.0	1,340	658	OK for old rifles – Hodgdon
165 Lead	H4895	22.0	1,865	1275	Not for old rifles – Hodgdon
165 Lead	H335	23.0	1,890	1309	Not for old rifles – Hodgdon
170 Lead	AA 5744	20.0	1,802	1226	Accurate Arms
165 SP	FL		1,440	760	Winchester factory load
165 SP	FL		1,752	1125	Winchester factory load high velocity

.32 Winchester Self-Loading (.32 WSL)

Historical Notes: This is the second of two cartridges developed for the Winchester Model '05 self-loading rifle, which was introduced in 1905-1906. It became obsolete, when the rifle was discontinued in 1920. The case is of the semi-rimmed type similar to the 35 SL, which was the original cartridge for the Model '05 rifle. The .32 Winchester SL was probably the prototype of the .30 U.S. Carbine cartridge. The two are very similar, except for bullet diameter and the fact that the .30 Carbine cartridge is rimless.

General Comments: The .32 Winchester SL cartridge is in the same class as the .32-20 Winchester, strictly a small- to medium-game number at close range. However, it is not nearly as flexible as the .32-20, because of the semi-automatic rifle in which it was used. This was never a very popular cartridge. Not only was the cost of ammunition relatively high, the cartridge is not well-suited to reloading, even if you could find the empty cases after being ejected from the action. Some might consider this cartridge the best candidate for the title "World's Most Useless Centerfire Rifle Cartridge."

.32 Winchester Self-Loading Loading Data and Factory Ballistics

Bullet (grains/type)	Powder	Grains	Velocity	Energy	Source/Comments
155 Cast	2400	9.5	1,270	556	Lyman No. 321298
165 SP	2400	12.0	1,450	775	NA
165 SP	IMR 4227	12.5	1,440	760	NA
165 SP	FL		1,400	760	Winchester factory load

.32 Remington

Historical Notes: Another of the Remington rimless line of medium high-power rifle cartridges, this one is a rimless version of the .32 Winchester Special. Introduced in 1906, it was originally chambered in the Model 8 autoloader and later available in Remington pump-action and bolt-action rifles. The ammunition companies discontinued it many years ago.

General Comments: Remington felt some need to counter the popular series of rimmed cartridges chambered in Winchester's Model 94 lever-action. The incentive was great enough to persuade Remington to invent substitutions for Winchester's rimmed .25-, .30-, and .32-caliber cartridges. It could be argued that the .35 Remington was an answer to Winchester's .38-55., but a bit of reflection suggests the folks at Remington were confused. It was not the cartridges that made Browning's invention successful, it was Browning's invention that made the cartridges successful. The .32 Remington is, nonetheless, perfectly adequate for any task to which the .30-30 or .32 Special are suited.

.32 Remington Loading Data and Factory Ballistics

Bullet (grains/type)	Powder	Grains	Velocity	Energy	Source/Comments
170 SP	IMR 4895	33.0	2,070	1,578	Lyman
170 SP	IMR 3031	30.0	2,020	1,546	NA
170 SP	IMR 4198	26.0	1,992	1,718	NA
170 SP	FL		2,220	1,860	Remington factory load

.32 Ideal/.32-25-100

Historical Notes: One of the chamberings available for the single-shot Stevens 44 and 44½ rifles, as well as for other single-shot rifles, this cartridge was introduced in 1903 and was quite popular for 20 years or so.

General Comments: The .32 Ideal is an improvement over the older .32 Extra Long Ballard in having inside lubrication and better performance. It is cleaner to handle and easier to reload. It was also quite accurate and an adequate 150-yard small- or medium-game number. Use of bullets lighter than standard provides room for more powder and gives higher velocity. Sometimes called the .32-25-150, the .32 Ideal uses a bullet diameter of .323-inch and, as pointed out in early Ideal handbooks, it offered new life, via reboring and re-rifling, to "thousands of .32-caliber, Short, Long and Extra Long, Rim and Center Fire rifles that have been shot out or rusted … ."

.32 Ideal Loading Data and Factory Ballistics

Bullet (grains/type)	Powder	Grains	Velocity	Energy	Source/Comments
115 Lead	black powder (FFg)	38.0	1,425	524	Lyman No. 32359
150 Lead	black powder (Fg)	25.0	1,250	526	Lyman No. 32360
150 Lead	IMR 4198	12.0	1,330	596	NA
150 Lead	black powder (FFg)	25.0	1,250	526	Factory load

.33 Winchester

Historical Notes:	Introduced in 1902 for the Winchester Model 86 lever-action rifle and discontinued, along with the rifle, in 1936, it was replaced by the .348 Winchester developed for an updated version of its '86, the Model 71 rifle. It was also chambered in Marlin's Model 95 lever-action and in the Winchester Model of 1885 single-shot. This round was dropped in 1940.
General Comments:	The .33 Winchester earned a good reputation as a deer, black bear, and elk cartridge, when used in the woods at moderate ranges. Its paper ballistics are no better than the .35 Remington rimless, but it uses a smaller diameter bullet with better sectional density than the 200-grain .35-caliber. It gave good penetration and satisfactory killing power, when properly used. It is still a good cartridge for anything up to and including elk, and it can be improved safely with modern powders. In any case, it is not quite as powerful as the .348 Winchester, and early Model 86 actions are not quite as strong as the Model 71's. Cases can be formed from .45-70 brass.

.33 Winchester Loading Data and Factory Ballistics

Bullet (grains/type)	Powder	Grains	Velocity	Energy	Source/Comments
200 SP	H4895	45.0	2,200	2,150	Hornady
200 SP	IMR 3031	40.0	2,100	1,959	Hornady
200 SP			2,200	2,150	Winchester factory load

.35 Winchester Self-Loading (.35 WSL)

Historical Notes:	The .35 SL was the original cartridge for the Winchester Model '05 semi-auto rifle, introduced in 1905. The Model '05 was the only rifle that ever chambered it, and the cartridge was such a poor one that it was discontinued by 1920.
General Comments:	The .35 SL cartridge was unsuitable for anything but small to medium game at very close ranges. However, it was too expensive for such shooting. It is too underpowered for deer and ranks right along with the .32 SL as a rather useless cartridge. It is semi-rimless and can be fired in the .38 Special or .357 Magnum revolver if reloaded with .357-inch diameter lead bullets. Just what value this might have is difficult to imagine, but it is an interesting fact.

.35 Winchester Self-Loading Loading Data and Factory Ballistics

Bullet (grains/type)	Powder	Grains	Velocity	Energy	Source/Comments
180 SP	IMR 4227	13.5	1,440	834	NA
180 SP	2400	13.0	1,430	823	NA
165 Lead	2400	8.0	920	312	NA
180 SP	FL		1,452	842	Winchester factory load

.351 Winchester Self-Loading (.351 WSL)

Historical Notes: Introduced in 1907 to replace the underpowered .35 SL, the .351 Self-Loading is a more powerful round for the improved Model 1907 Winchester autoloading rifle. This cartridge was used to a very limited extent by the French, in both World War I and II, as a military cartridge. The rifle was discontinued in 1957.

General Comments: The .351 SL does not have much to offer, although it is an improvement over the older .35. It does not qualify as a suitable deer cartridge, although it has been used for that purpose. It is a good medium-game cartridge for coyote, mountain lion, or other animals in that class, but is too powerful for small game; it is expensive, not accurate enough, and too limited in range for varmint shooting. Nevertheless, it far surpasses even the best .357 Magnum rifle loads and comes very close to duplicating the .357 Remington Maximum. It has been popular for Latin American jungle hunting because, at the short ranges involved, it has sufficient power for the game encountered there. Here in the United States, the .351 WSL and the handy Model 1907 semi-automatic rifle in which it was introduced were used extensively by prison guards. The rifle is notorious for being one of the guns used in the killings of Bonnie and Clyde, and it has been used from low-flying light aircraft, in the western United States, for pest control. Like the .35, the .351 SL is semi-rimmed. The principal differences are a .24-inch longer case used in the .351 and higher loading pressures. Winchester was the last company to offer ammunition.

.351 Winchester Self-Loading Loading Data and Factory Ballistics

Bullet (grains/type)	Powder	Grains	Velocity	Energy	Source/Comments
177 Cast	IMR 4227	16.0	1,550	947	Lyman No. 351319
180	2400	19.0	1,793	1,280	Medium game only; Lyman
180	IMR 4227	19.5	1,751	1,225	NA
180	FL		1,850	1,370	Factory load

.350 Griffin & Howe Magnum

Historical Notes: The .350 G&H Magnum was developed by Griffin & Howe in the early 1930s. It is also known as the .350 Holland & Holland Magnum, since that company chambered it in its rifles for a number of years. In the United States, ammunition was loaded by Western Cartridge Co. It is based on the .375 H&H case necked down and is similar to a number of .35-caliber wildcats that came along years later. It did not achieve popularity and died out by the end of the 1930s. Today, it is largely a collector's item.

General Comments: The .350 G&H Magnum used standard .357-inch-diameter bullets and, so, could be handloaded with a variety of weights and types. It is a good big-game cartridge for either North American or African hunting. However, it is obsolete, and the 358 Norma Magnum or one of the .35-caliber short magnums would be a better choice. Cases are easy to make, and plenty of good bullets are available.

.350 Griffin & Howe Loading Data and Factory Ballistics

Bullet (grains/type)	Powder	Grains	Velocity	Energy	Source/Comments
220 SP	IMR 4350	88.0	3,120	4,762	NA
250 SP	IMR 4831	93.0	2,950	4,848	NA
250 SP	FL		2,700	4,055	Western factory load

.35 Winchester

Historical Notes: Developed by Winchester for its Model 1895 lever-action rifle, the .35 Winchester was introduced in 1903. The Remington-Lee bolt-action rifle also chambered this round. It was discontinued in 1936, along with the Model 95 rifle. It was listed in the 1962 British Kynoch ammunition catalogs.

General Comments: The .35 Winchester is a more powerful cartridge than the .33 Winchester, but is not as potent as the .348 or the .358 Winchester. It had a good reputation as a short-range number for elk, moose, or brown bear. It is certainly powerful enough for any North American big game, but has little to offer when compared to more modern cartridges. It can be improved by using modern powders, but pressures in the old 1895 lever-action should be kept to about 45,000 psi. This cartridge, like the .405 Winchester, is based on the same basic case as the .30-40 Krag. Here, by moving headspace control to the case shoulder, it is feasible to form perfectly useful cases from .30-40 Krag cases. The case neck will be somewhat shorter than with original cases, but this poses no problem, because it is not necessary to crimp the case mouth in cartridges used in the M-95.

.35 Winchester Loading Data and Factory Ballistics

Bullet (grains/type)	Powder	Grains	Velocity	Energy	Source/Comments
200 SP	IMR 4895	52.0	2,480	2,738	NA
200 SP	IMR 4064	45.0	2,220	2,182	NA
204	IMR 4227	18.0	1,550	1,091	Lyman No. 358315
250 SP	IMR 4895	50.0	2,290	2,920	NA
250 SP	IMR 4320	48.0	2,190	2,670	NA
250 SP	FL		2,195	2,670	Winchester factory load

.35 Newton

Historical Notes: The .35 Newton was listed in the 1915 Newton Rifle Co. catalog, which presumably was the year it was introduced. It is the .30 Newton case necked up to .35-caliber. The Western Cartridge Co. listed it until 1936, but no commercial rifles other than the Newtons chambered this round.

General Comments: The .35 Newton is more powerful, in some loadings, than the .375 H&H Magnum. The factory load listed below was the last one offered by the Western Cartridge Co. but, at one time, other loads were available. This cartridge is somewhat overpowered for most North American big game. It has been used in Africa with considerable success, although the Newton rifle was much too light and poorly stocked for such a powerful cartridge. Cases can be readily formed from RWS 8x68mm brass or by necking up the .30 Newton, itself a scarce item. Performance is similar to the later .358 Norma Magnum, which would be a far better choice, because ammunition has been recently offered and handloading is easier through a simple conversion of readily available cases.

.35 Newton Loading Data and Factory Ballistics

Bullet (grains/type)	Powder	Grains	Velocity	Energy	Source/Comments
200 SP	IMR 3031	78.0	3,030	4,100	NA
250 SP	IMR 4064	70.0	2,650	3,918	NA
250 SP	IMR 4320	75.0	2,815	4,410	NA
250 SP	FL		2,660	3,930	Western factory load

Bullet (grains/type)	Powder	Grains	Velocity	Energy	Source/Comments
250 SP	FL		2,975	4,925	Western factory load

.38-45 Stevens

Historical Notes: One of the special Stevens "Everlasting" cartridges, this one was introduced with the 1875 tip-up models. It was not very popular and was discontinued within a few years. Today, it is one of the rarer Stevens cartridges.

General Comments: Another of the .38-40 class cartridges, the .38-45 used a heavier bullet, but ballistics are similar. The .38-40 and .38-55 made most of these in-between cartridges obsolete. Original loadings called for 45 to 50 grains of Fg black powder and a bullet of 210 to 255 grains. It should be possible to convert .303 British cases to work in these rifles.

.38-45 Stevens Loading Data and Factory Ballistics

Bullet (grains/type)	Powder	Grains	Velocity	Energy	Source/Comments
210 Lead	IMR 4198	16.0	1,340	845	Lyman No. 36275
210 Lead	FL		1,420	947	Factory load

.35-30 Maynard (1882)

Historical Notes: The .35-30 was one of a series of cartridges designed for and introduced with the Model 1882 Maynard single-shot rifle. The Improved Hunters Rifle Nos. 7 and 9, along with the Target & Hunting No. 10 and Improved Target No. 16, were available in this chambering.

General Comments: Maynard rifles were used during the Civil War. After the war, the company manufactured sporting rifles. The Maynard rifle used a tip-up breech linked to an under-lever. These were smooth operating, safe, and possessed excellent accuracy. Ammunition for the .35-30 can be made from .38-55 cases. Nominal .358-inch case bullets can usually be used as cast (without sizing). Lyman's 165-grain No. 358429 bullet usually works well. A version with an unusually wide rim was also made. Such cases are available from Ballard Rifle & Cartridge Co.: (307) 587-4914; www.ballardrifles.com.

.35-30 Maynard 1882 Loading Data and Factory Ballistics

Bullet (grains/type)	Powder	Grains	Velocity	Energy	Source/Comments
165 Lead	IMR 4198	16.0	1,320	645	Lyman No. 350293
165 Lead	2400	13.0	1,450	787	Lyman No. 350293
250 Lead	FL		1,280	918	Factory load

.35-40 Maynard (1882)

Historical Notes: This an elongated version of the .35-30 and used in the Model 1882 Maynard rifles.

General Comments: The .35-40 provides greater powder capacity than the shorter .35-30. The case dimensions are not identical, but cases can be made from .38-55 cases, just as with the .35-30. The long case is probably superior for hunting, but, since both are strictly small- to medium-game numbers, any advantage would be a matter of opinion. Any cast .358-inch rifle or revolver bullet can be sized to work. The Lyman No. 358429 (165 grains) would be a good choice.

.35-40 Maynard Loading Data and Factory Ballistics

Bullet (grains/type)	Powder	Grains	Velocity	Energy	Source/Comments
165 Lead	IMR 4198	18.0	1,400	725	Lyman No. 358429
250 Lead	FL		1,355	1,018	Factory load

.35-30 Maynard (1865)

Historical Notes: This unusual, externally ignited "cartridge" was chambered in the Model of 1865 Maynard rifle. This was a forerunner to all centerfire cartridges, because it featured a central flash hole in the base of the case. This was also forerunner to the .35-30 Maynard cartridge used in Model 1873 and 1882 rifles. While Maynard rifles saw Civil War usage, this particular combination came along quite late in that conflict.

General Comments: This rifle combines what appears to be a more-or-less conventional cartridge case with external priming. The base of the case has a centered, small-diameter flash hole. This hole carries the flash from a conventional cap into the charge. Conceptually, it is a very small step from this design to one combining the cap and the case into one unit.

One could argue that this "cartridge" falls outside the purview of this book, because it does not incorporate a self-contained primer and is, therefore, not a complete cartridge in the modern sense. It is, however, much closer to the modern cartridge than its forerunners, the paper-cased "cartridge." Therefore, since this rifle and cartridge represent a significant step toward perfection of the self-contained cartridge, we feel that this number is worthy of mention here. Fully functional .35-30 Maynard pinfire cases are available from Ballard Rifle & Cartridge Co. (307-587-4914; www.ballardrifle.com).

.38-40 Remington-Hepburn

Historical Notes: Although listed as the .38-40 Remington-Hepburn, this cartridge was available in the No. 1 Sporting Model rolling block rifle that preceded the Hepburn action by 10 years. The No. 1 rifle was also chambered for the .38-40 WCF shortly after Winchester introduced it, during 1873 and 1874. It is likely this cartridge was intended as a straight-case version of the bottlenecked Winchester round. The .38-40 Remington-Hepburn appeared about 1875.

General Comments: Rifle and ammunition manufacturers went all out to please every segment of the trade during the 1800s. Some riflemen didn't cotton to bottlenecked cases, so all kinds of straight, tapered, and bottleneck designs appeared in the same calibers and with the same powder charge. This may have provided a great lift to the men using these, but it is very confusing. The .38-40 Remington and .38-40 Winchester are a case in point. Neither could do anything the other would not, but the Winchester round won out in company with the repeating rifle. The Remington cartridge is a good target or small- to medium-game number. The original bullet is slightly heavier than the .38 WCF, but loading data for one will give similar results in the other. It is possible to convert .30-40 Krag cases to load this cartridge.

.38-40 Remington-Hepburn Loading Data and Factory Ballistics

Bullet (grains/type)	Powder	Grains	Velocity	Energy	Source/Comments
190 Lead	IMR 4198	16.0	1,427	865	Lyman No. 373164
250 Lead	2400	15.0	1,300	937	NA
245 Lead			1,200	790	Remington factory load

.38-45 Bullard

Historical Notes: This is another of the special cartridges for the Bullard lever-action, single-shot, and repeating rifles. It was introduced approximately 1887. Remington once loaded this round, but it was never very popular.

General Comments: Very few rifles in this chambering still exist. Ballistically, it is similar to the .38-40 WCF. It was an accurate cartridge, suitable primarily for small or medium game at close ranges. These cartridges are now collector's items. It should be possible to convert .44 Remington Magnum cases to work in these rifles.

.38-45 Bullard Loading Data and Factory Ballistics

Bullet (grains/type)	Powder	Grains	Velocity	Energy	Source/Comments
175 Lead	2400	16.0	1,480	883	Lyman No. 37582
250 Lead	Unique	10.0	1,200	797	NA
190 Lead	FL		1,388	822	Remington factory load

.38 Long, Centerfire (.38 Long, CF)

Historical Notes: The .38 Long, Centerfire is another old-timer designed to replace a similar rimfire cartridge. It was introduced in 1875-'76 and used in a number of single-shot rifles, including the Ballard, Stevens, Remington, and others. It was obsolete by 1900. Oddly, the original rimfire version outlived the centerfire.

General Comments: The .38 Long, Centerfire, like the .32 and .44, was not very effective and had a short life. It was an alternative to the rimfire, and many of the old rifles could, by a simple adjustment, fire either. The .38 Long Colt or .38 S&W Special can be used to make ammunition. The standard load was 20 to 25 grains of black powder and a 140- to 150-grain bullet.

.38 Long, Centerfire Loading Data and Factory Ballistics

Bullet (grains/type)	Powder	Grains	Velocity	Energy	Source/Comments
145 Lead	FL		950	291	Factory load

.38 Ballard Extra Long

Historical Notes: This centerfire version of the .38 Ballard Extra Long rimfire was introduced in 1885-'86 as one of the chamberings for the Ballard No. 2 Sporting Model. It also was used by many other companies. It had the old No. 1 primer that now has not been made for many years. Some of these rifles were furnished with a changeable firing pin or hammer arrangement, so they could fire the rimfire or centerfire version with only a minor adjustment.

General Comments: The .38 Ballard Extra Long was designed to furnish a reloadable case to those who favored the .38 Extra Long rimfire ballistics. It was a nice little plinking, small-game, or target cartridge for those who wanted economy. Any .358-inch bullet of suitable weight can be used. Using Lyman No. 358161 (145 grains) and 31 grains of FFg black powder will work fine. The .357 Remington Maximum case can be converted to work in the .38 Ballard Extra Long chamber.

.38 Ballard Extra Long Loading Data and Factory Ballistics

Bullet (grains/type)	Powder	Grains	Velocity	Energy	Source/Comments
150 Lead	Unique	6.0	1,160	450	Lyman No. 358160
146 Lead	FL		1,275	533	Factory load

.38-35 Stevens

Historical Notes: Introduced, in 1875, for the Stevens tip-up single-shot rifles, this was one of the special Stevens "Everlasting" cartridges. It was not very popular, so it was dropped after a few years. In its original form, it is occasionally referred to as the .38-33.

General Comments: Stevens "Everlasting" shells were sold as separate components; the older, less popular numbers are seldom encountered as loaded rounds. These cases, intended to give very long reloading life, were necessarily thick and heavy. About six of these special chamberings survived. Loadings were not standard, and they may be found with a variety of bullet weights in both grooved and paper-patched form. A load of 35 grains or so of Fg black powder and any bullet of 180 to 255 grains can be used in this cartridge. It should be possible to chamber and safely shoot either .41 Short Colt or the .41 Long Colt lead bullet loads in these rifles. The softer oversize bullet will safely swage down to bore diameter.

.38-35 Stevens Loading Data and Factory Ballistics

Bullet (grains/type)	Powder	Grains	Velocity	Energy	Source/Comments
180 Lead	black powder (Fg)	35.0	1,350*	729	NA
215 Lead	black powder (Fg)	35.0	1,255	758	Factory load
* Estimated					

.38-50 Maynard (1882)

Historical Notes: The .38-50 Maynard is practically identical to the .38-55 Ballard and Winchester and uses a bullet of similar diameter. It was not popular because it was so similar to the Winchester number.

General Comments: To reload the .38-50, one can make cases by resizing and trimming .38-55 cases and loading .38-caliber cast rifle bullets sized to correct diameter. The .38-55 would only hold 48 to 50 grains of black powder, after the ammunition companies began using heavier, solid-head cases. For all practical purposes, there is no performance difference between the .38-50 Maynard and the .38-55.

.38-50 Maynard Loading Data and Factory Ballistics

Bullet (grains/type)	Powder	Grains	Velocity	Energy	Source/Comments
149 Lead	IMR 4198	10.0	1,100	420	Lyman No. 37583
250 Lead	IMR 4198	16.0	1,320	974	Lyman No. 375248
255 Lead	FL		1,325	990	Factory load

.38-50 Remington-Hepburn

Historical Notes: Introduced in 1883 as one of the chamberings for the Remington-Hepburn match rifles, this was too similar to the popular .38-55 to gain much of a following and was discontinued after a few years.

General Comments: Loading data for the .38-55 Winchester and Marlin can be applied to this cartridge. There is no difference in usefulness or performance. It should be possible to convert .303 British or .30-40 Krag cases to work in these rifles.

.38-50 Remington-Hepburn Loading Data and Factory Ballistics

Bullet (grains/type)	Powder	Grains	Velocity	Energy	Source/Comments
255 Lead	IMR 4198	23.0	1,580	1,421	NA
250 Lead	Unique	10.0	1,200	797	NA
255 Lead	FL		1,320	989	Factory load

.38-50 Ballard Everlasting

Historical Notes: This cartridge was the forerunner of the .38-55. It was introduced, in 1876, for the Ballard Perfection No. 4 and Pacific No. 5 rifles, but was also available in other models. It is an Everlasting-type case, heavier than the standard .38-55 and 3/16-inch shorter. It was replaced by the .38-55, when that cartridge was introduced in 1884.

General Comments: Standard bullet diameter for most .38-caliber rifles was .375-inch, but many had a groove diameter of .379-inch, requiring a larger bullet. It is wise to measure the bore diameter before ordering a bullet mould for these old rifles. Lyman moulds are available in a variety of .38 rifle bullets, from 150 grains to more than 300 grains. Modern .38-55 cases can be used in .38-50 rifles by shortening the case to the proper length. Performance and usefulness are on a par with the .38-55.

The so-called "Everlasting," or reloadable case, was popular with hunters and target shooters during the 1880-'90 period. These heavy cases could be reused repeatedly. In fact, they were made so heavy that powder capacity was often reduced by five or 10 grains. To get around this, the Everlasting case was often made longer than the standard.

.38-50 Ballard Loading Data and Factory Ballistics

Bullet (grains/type)	Powder	Grains	Velocity	Energy	Source/Comments
145 Lead	IMR 4198	14.0	1,300	550	Lyman No. 37583
250 Lead	IMR 4198	17.0	1,350	1,020	Lyman No. 375248

Bullet (grains/type)	Powder	Grains	Velocity	Energy	Source/Comments
255 Lead	FL		1,321	989	Factory load

.38-90 Winchester Express Single Shot (.38 Express)

Historical Notes: Introduced in 1886 as one of many chamberings for the successful Winchester Model 1885 single-shot, this was not a popular cartridge and, by 1904, it had been discontinued.

General Comments: This is a long, bottlenecked case with a light bullet for cartridges in this class. Since it is designated an "Express" cartridge, it was probably intended to develop superior velocity for a .38-caliber rifle. Old Ideal catalogs list bullet No. 375248 as standard with the No. 3 loading tool for this cartridge, but any of the lighter .38-55 bullets can be used. A charge of 90 grains of Fg black powder was the original factory loading.

.38-90 Winchester Express Loading Data and Factory Ballistics

Bullet (grains/type)	Powder	Grains	Velocity	Energy	Source/Comments
218 Lead	IMR 4198	21.0	1,350	886	Lyman No. 37584
218 Lead	IMR 4198	23.0	1,470	1,045	Lyman No. 37584
217 Lead	FL		1,595	1,227	Winchester factory load

.38-56 Winchester

Historical Notes: Introduced in 1887 for the Model 1886 Winchester repeater, this cartridge was also used in the single-shot and the 1895 Marlin. The .38-56 made the transition into the smokeless powder era and was loaded until about 1936. The Colt New Lightning pump-action magazine rifles also used this cartridge.

General Comments: Design of this cartridge was intended to develop increased velocity without lengthening the case. It is a sort of super .38-55 in conception, but not in fact. With smokeless powder and within allowable pressures, there isn't any real performance difference. It is a bottlenecked case and will not interchange with others of similar designation. Although advertised as a powerful big-game number, it is little more than a deer or black bear cartridge. With maximum handloads, it might do okay for elk at short range. Cases can be made from .45-70 cases.

.38-56 Winchester Loading Data and Factory Ballistics

Bullet (grains/type)	Powder	Grains	Velocity	Energy	Source/Comments
255 Lead	IMR 3031	36.0	1,830	1,908	NA
265 Lead	IMR 4198	25.0	1,600	1,512	Lyman No. 375296 gas checked
255 SP	FL		1,395	1,105	Factory load

.38-72 Winchester

Historical Notes:	This round was designed for and introduced with the Model 1895 Winchester lever-action box magazine repeater. Both gun and cartridge were obsolete by 1936. The .38-72 was only moderately popular.
General Comments:	This is a nearly straight case with a very slight neck. Some cases have a pronounced groove around the neck to prevent the bullet from receding under recoil. This tends to obscure the slight neck. This is another .38-caliber cartridge touted as being very powerful when, in fact, it is nearly the same as the .38-55. The .38-72 case has the same basic body as the .30-40 Krag, but, because headspacing is on the rim, it may not be possible to safely use that case to make the .38-72, except for very low-pressure loads.

.38-72 Winchester Loading Data and Factory Ballistics

Bullet (grains/type)	Powder	Grains	Velocity	Energy	Source/Comments
255 Lead	IMR 3031	33.0	1,735	1,715	NA
275 Lead	IMR 4198	27.0	1,350	1,120	Lyman No. 375167
275 Cast	black powder (Fg)	72.0			Lyman No. 357167
275 SP	FL		1,475	1,330	Winchester factory load

.40-70 Sharps (Straight)
.40-65 Sharps (1876)

Historical Notes:	This is the .40-2½-inch straight case, introduced in 1876. It is sometimes referred to as the .40-65, because, with heavy, reloadable cases, that is all the powder it would hold, unless a lighter bullet was used. Remington and Winchester single-shots also chambered this round.
General Comments:	This is another cartridge with ballistics similar to a half-dozen others of different make or origin. There are actually more than a dozen .40-caliber cartridges with powder charges of around 40 to 70 grains, but none offer any stupendous advantage over the others. Like other .40 Sharps numbers, this one used a .403-inch bullet weighing 330 or 370 grains. These chambers were cut to use bore-diameter bullets (often paper-patched). Groove diameter is typically .408-inch to .411-inch. A number of Lyman bullet moulds are available in this size. Although longer, this case has the same basic body as the .30-40 Krag. However, because headspacing is on the rim, it may not be possible to safely use that case to make the .40-70, except for very low-pressure loads.

.40-70 Sharps (Straight) Loading Data and Factory Ballistics

Bullet (grains/type)	Powder	Grains	Velocity	Energy	Source/Comments
330 Lead	IMR 4198	23.0	1,250	1,150	Lyman No. 403149
330 Lead	FL		1,258	1,160	Factory load

.38-70 Winchester

Historical Notes:	Introduced in 1894 for the Model 1886 Winchester lever-action repeater, the .38-70 did not catch on and was discontinued within a few years.

General Comments: This cartridge offers little if any improvement over the .38-55. It is of bottlenecked design, but is not the same as the .38-56 or the .38-72 Winchester. The older Lyman catalogs indicated it used the standard .38-55 bullet of .379-inch. Although the .38-70 case is longer than that of the .45-70, usable, short-necked cases could be made from the .45-70. However, the basic .45 cases now available will make perfect replacement cases.

.38-70 Winchester Loading Data and Factory Ballistics

Bullet (grains/type)	Powder	Grains	Velocity	Energy	Source/Comments
250 Lead	IMR 4198	26.0	1,710	1,625	NA
265 Lead	IMR 3031	41.0	1,700	1,698	NA
255 Lead	FL		1,490	1,257	Factory load

.40-50 Sharps (Straight)
.40-1⁷⁄₈-inch Sharps

Historical Notes: Introduced in 1879, this is the smallest of the Sharps cartridges. There is a similar necked version. In addition to Sharps rifles, the Winchester single-shot was available in this chambering, as was the Remington rolling block. This is also known as the .40-1 -inch Sharps.

General Comments: Although listed as the .40-50, this cartridge was actually loaded with 40 or 45 grains of powder and was identical in performance to the .40-40 Maynard and other similar rounds. Standard diameter of most .40-caliber rifle bullets is .403-inch, and almost any bullet of that diameter can be used. These chambers were cut to use bore-diameter paper-patch bullets; groove diameter is typically .408 inch to .411 inch. It should be possible to convert the .30-40 Krag case to work in these rifles. However, the rim is .010-inch too thin, so only very light loads should be used. Better to get the correct case from Buffalo Arms Co.: (208) 263-6953; www.buffaloarms.com.

.40-50 Sharps (Straight) Loading Data and Factory Ballistics

Bullet (grains/type)	Powder	Grains	Velocity	Energy	Source/Comments
260 Lead	IMR 4198	21.0	1,450	1,220	Lyman No. 403169
265 Lead	FL		1,410	1,168	Factory load

.40-50 Sharps (Necked)
.40-1¹¹⁄₁₆-inch Sharps

Historical Notes: Also known as the .40-111/16-inch, this cartridge was introduced, in 1869, for that model of Sharps Sporting rifle. It was available with several bullet weights, including 265, 285, and 296 grains. The Remington rolling block and other single-shot rifles also chambered this cartridge.

General Comments: The .40-50 bottlenecked cartridge is shorter than the straight version, but there is little difference in ballistics. The .40-50 Sharps (Straight) and .40-50 Sharps (Necked) are not interchangeable. Proper bullet diameter is .403-inch, and several Lyman bullet moulds are available in this size. These chambers were cut to use bore-diameter paper-patch bullets; groove diameter is typically .408 inch to .411 inch. This is largely a medium-game, deer, or intermediate-range target cartridge. It should be possible to convert .45-70 cases to work in these rifles.

Bullet (grains/type)	Powder	Grains	Velocity	Energy	Source/Comments
260 Lead	IMR 4198	21.0	1,500	1,308	Lyman No. 403169
265 Lead	FL		1,460	1,262	Factory load

.40-85 Ballard Everlasting
.40-90 Ballard Everlasting

Historical Notes: The .40-85 and the .40-90 Ballard Everlastings are the same case with different loadings. L.D. Satterlee lists the .40-90 Everlasting with the J.M. Marlin Ballard Pacific No. 5 and Sporting No. 4½ (introduced in 1878). He shows the .40-85 chambering for the Pacific No. 5, after the Marlin Fire Arms Co. took over manufacture in 1881.

General Comments: The 4.0-90 Ballard Everlasting case is heavier and about -inch longer than the regular .40-90 or .40-85 case. Many of the .40-90 Everlasting cases were nickel-plated. This is a hunting cartridge very similar to the .40-90 Sharps (Straight). The same loading data can be used for both, though they are not interchangeable. Although the case of the .40-85 Ballard Everlasting is longer, it has the same basic body as the .444 Marlin case. It should be possible to make usable, albeit shorter, cases from those. These rifles had chambers designed to use a .403-inch (bore-diameter), paper-patched bullet. Groove diameter typically ran .408 inch to .411 inch.

The so-called "Everlasting," or reloadable case, was popular with hunters and target shooters during the 1880-'90 period. These heavy cases could be reused repeatedly. In fact, they were made so heavy that powder capacity was often reduced by five or 10 grains. To get around this, the Everlasting case was often made longer than the standard.

Bullet (grains/type)	Powder	Grains	Velocity	Energy	Source/Comments
370 Lead	IMR 4198	28.0	1,400	1,615	Lyman No. 40395
370 Lead	FL		1,427	1,672	Factory load

.40-60 Marlin

Historical Notes: The .40-60 is one of the chamberings for Marlin 1881 and 1895 lever-action repeaters. The 1895 uses the same basic system as the 1893 and 1894 models, but is larger and longer. This appears to be the same case as the .40-65 Winchester, but with a slightly different loading. The pump-action Colt New Lightning rifles also used the Marlin loading of this cartridge.

General Comments: During the late 1800s, the same cartridge often went under various names, depending on who loaded it or whose rifle it was used in. It was also common practice to change the name if you furnished more than one load or bullet in the same case; that is what happened here. The .40-60 Marlin and the .40-65 Winchester are interchangeable and either can be used in the same gun. However, the old Ideal catalog states the .40-60 Marlin "must not be confused with the .40-60 Winchester, as they are not the same." This, of course, is true. If the reader is not thoroughly confused by now, he should be. Go ahead. Read it through a few more times and it will clear up. Converting .45-70 cases into .40-60 Marlin cases is easily done. Marlin .40-caliber rifles often have significantly oversized bores. Groove diameters as large as .414-inch are noted.

.40-60 Marlin Loading Data and Factory Ballistics

Bullet (grains/type)	Powder	Grains	Velocity	Energy	Source/Comments
260 Lead	IMR 4198	23.0	1,500	1,308	Lyman No. 403170
260 Lead	IMR 3031	35.0	1,480	1,263	NA
260 Lead	FL		1,385	1,115	Factory load

.40-60 Colt

Historical Notes: At a casual glance, this cartridge appears to be identical to both the .40-60 Marlin and the .40-65 Winchester (except bullet diameter). However, this cartridge includes a definitive shoulder, while the other two are true tapered designs. The value or need for a cartridge so similar to the .40-60 Marlin seems moot. Almost certainly, the Marlin round would chamber and fire normally in the Colt's rifles.

General Comments: It seems that this version must have been created in response to a request from Colt's for a cartridge that was specifically intended for use in its rifle. Winchester displayed this number for at least one year on its product advertisement board, but it was not found in any catalog listing between 1879 and 1910 or in the 1916 catalog. Therefore, it seems unlikely that it was ever actually offered for sale—at least not directly from Winchester. We present it here in an effort to try to demonstrate just how confusing such research can become. Unless this number was loaded with a different bullet weight, which seems unlikely, ballistics would have been identical to the .40-60 Marlin (see ballistics table).

.40-90 Sharps (Straight)

Historical Notes: Sharps catalogs do not list this cartridge, although Sharps rifles and others chambered for it are known. It was introduced about 1885. The Remington-Hepburn No. 3 single-shot was advertised in this chambering, and UMC and Winchester manufactured cases and ammunition.

General Comments: The so-called Everlasting, or reloadable, case was popular with hunters and target shooters during the 1880-'90 period. These heavy cases could be reused repeatedly. In fact, they were made so heavy that powder capacity was often reduced by five or 10 grains. To get around this, the Everlasting case was often made longer than the standard. UMC cases of the .40-3¼-inch are usually of very heavy, reloadable construction.

The reason for mentioning this is that it might have a bearing on the origin of this cartridge. Physical measurements of the so-called .40-90 Sharps Straight are practically identical to the .40-90 Ballard Everlasting, except for the length. It is possible that the design of the .40-90 Sharps Straight is based on lengthening the Ballard cartridge to create an Everlasting version with the same capacity and ballistics. Anyway, the idea would probably occur to anyone who compared the two. Although longer, this case has the same basic body as the .444 Marlin. It should be possible to make usable, albeit much shorter, cases from those. These rifles had a chamber cut to use a bore-diameter (.403-inch), paper-patched bullet; groove diameter was .408 inch to .411 inch.

.40-90 Sharps (Straight) Loading Data and Factory Ballistics

Bullet (grains/type)	Powder	Grains	Velocity	Energy	Source/Comments
370 Lead	IMR 4198	30.0	1,400	1,612	Lyman No. 403171
370 Lead	FL		1,387	1,582	Factory load

.40-65 Ballard Everlasting

Historical Notes: The .40-65 Ballard Everlasting was introduced, in 1876, as one of the original chamberings for the Perfection No. 4 and Pacific No. 5 rifles and, in 1879, it was added to the Hunter No. 1½. These were all the same basic under-lever, single-shot action. This cartridge was used in the J.M. Marlin Ballards. After the Marlin Fire Arms Co. took over, it was altered to the .40-70 and .40-63.

General Comments: The .40-70 or .40-63 Ballard can be chambered in the older .40-65 rifles, but the .40-65 case will not fit the other chamber. Note that firing the smaller diameter cases could result in a case wall rupture, so this is *not* a good idea. It is a much heavier case of slightly larger diameter, although all have the same length. Ballistics of all are the same for practical purposes, and the loading data shown for the .40-63 will give the same results in any of the cases. The .40-65 Everlasting is one of the rarer Ballard cartridges and is seldom encountered. It should be possible to convert .444 Marlin cases to work in these rifles.

.40-90 Sharps (Necked)
.40-100 Sharps (Necked)

Historical Notes: The .40-90 Sharps was introduced in 1873 for the Sharps side-hammer model rifles. There was also another loading, referred to as the .40-100 Sharps, which used a 190-grain hollow-point bullet on the same 2-inch long case.

General Comments: This became one of the more popular Sharps cartridges. The hollow-point Express bullets made by Sharps were designed to accept a .22 rimfire blank, which was supposed to provide explosive expansion and better knockdown power. The original author of this book experimented with bullets of this type, and they did not work as they were intended. An ordinary hollow-point or a properly constructed soft-point will do as much damage. Perfect cases can be made from the .45 Basic case

.40-90 Sharps (Necked) Loading Data and Factory Ballistics

Bullet (grains/type)	Powder	Grains	Velocity	Energy	Source/Comments
370 Lead	IMR 4198	28.0	1,450	1,735	Lyman No. 403171
370 Lead	FL		1,475	1,800	Factory load

.40-70 Sharps (Necked)

Historical Notes: This is the .40-2¼-inch bottlenecked Sharps that was brought out in 1871 for the Model 1871 Sporting rifle. It was used in other single-shot rifles, also.

General Comments: The .40-70 necked cartridge had a reputation for fine accuracy and was popular as a match cartridge, as much as for hunting. While many people regard the Sharps rifles as strictly buffalo guns, Sharps also made match rifles that gained worldwide respect on the range—hence the name "Sharps-shooter." The best marksmen were given Sharps rifles in a special squad, and its notoriety grew until the single word "sharpshooter" was synonymous with accurate rifle fire.

It should be possible to convert the .45-70 case to work in these rifles, but the neck would be very short. The .45 Basic will make perfect cases. These rifles have chambers that were cut to use a bore-diameter (.403-inch), paper-patched bullet. Groove diameter is typically .408 inch to .411 inch.

.40-70 Sharps (Necked) Loading Data and Factory Ballistics

Bullet (grains/type)	Powder	Grains	Velocity	Energy	Source/Comments
330 Lead	IMR 4759	26.0	1,510	1,671	NA
330 Lead	IMR 4198	27.0	1,450	1,542	Lyman No. 403139
330 Lead	FL		1,420	1,482	Factory load

.40-110 Winchester Express (.40 Express)

Historical Notes: Designed for the Winchester single-shot rifle and introduced in 1886, the .40-110 was intended to compete with the big Sharps cartridges.

General Comments: In its original form, the .40-110 used a copper-tubed bullet. The Ideal catalog lists bullet No. 403169 (260 grains) as proper for reloading. The .50 Basic will make perfect cases.

.40-110 Winchester Express Loading Data and Factory Ballistics

Bullet (grains/type)	Powder	Grains	Velocity	Energy	Source/Comments
260 Lead	FG	110.0	1,617	1,509	NA
260 Lead	IMR 4198	32.0	1,650	1,580	Lyman No. 403169
260 SP	FL		1,617	1,509	Winchester factory load

.40-63 Ballard Everlasting
.40-70 Ballard Everlasting

Historical Notes: These two cartridges have identical length and outside dimensions, so they are listed together. The .40-63 is actually just a heavier-cased version of the .40-70 factory cartridge. Both are, in turn, an outgrowth of the original .40-65 Ballard Everlasting case, which had to be handloaded. The .40-63 and .40-70 were first listed for the Ballard Perfection No. 4 and Pacific No. 5, after the Marlin Fire Arms Co. took over manufacture of these rifles, in 1881.

General Comments: This was a popular cartridge among Ballard rifle fans and was as good as similar cartridges offered by Winchester and others. However, cartridges designed for repeating rifles tended to survive longer than those intended for single-shots. These were used more as match cartridges than anything else, but these also made good deer, black bear, or elk numbers. Their performance is identical to the .40-70 Sharps Straight or the .40-72 Winchester. The .444 Marlin case should work in these rifles. However, the rim is generally too small to properly engage the extractor. These chambers were cut to use bore-diameter (.403-inch), paper-patch bullets; groove diameter is typically .408-inch to .411-inch.

The so-called Everlasting, or reloadable case, was popular with hunters and target shooters during the 1880-'90 period. These heavy cases could be reused repeatedly. In fact, they were made so heavy that powder capacity was often reduced by five or 10 grains. To get around this, the Everlasting case was often made longer than the standard.

.40-63 Ballard Everlasting/.40-70 Ballard Everlasting Loading Data and Factory Ballistics

Bullet (grains/type)	Powder	Grains	Velocity	Energy	Source/Comments
330 Lead	IMR 4198	22.0	1,310	1,260	Lyman No. 403149 — 1/20 or 1/30 tin-lead
330 Lead	FL		1,335	1,318	Factory load

.40-60 Winchester

Historical Notes: The .40-60 Winchester is a sharply tapered, slightly necked cartridge made for the Model 1876 Winchester rifle, which is a heavier version of the lever-action Model 1873 and designed to handle more powerful cartridges. Rifle and cartridge were marketed from 1876 until 1897. This was a popular cartridge, and Winchester continued to load it up to 1934.

General Comments: The big, powerful cartridges available for the Sharps and other single-shot rifles forced Winchester to bring out a more potent line of rounds for its repeaters. The cartridges for the Centennial Model marked the beginning of such a trend. This is not the same as the .40-60 Marlin. It is a better hunting choice than the old .44-40 WCF. The .45-70 case can be easily converted to make .40-60 Winchester cases.

.40-60 Winchester Loading Data and Factory Ballistics

Bullet (grains/type)	Powder	Grains	Velocity	Energy	Source/Comments
210 Lead	IMR 4198	21.0	1,520	1,083	Lyman No. 403168
210 Lead	FL		1,562	1,138	Winchester factory load

.40-70 Winchester

Historical Notes: This cartridge was developed for the Model 1886 Winchester repeater and was used in the Winchester single-shot. It was introduced in 1894, but never became popular or widely used. The Marlin Model 1895 repeating rifle was also available in this chambering.

General Comments: This is a bottlenecked case generally similar to the .38-70 Winchester. It provides a larger, heavier bullet in a cartridge suitable to the same action as the .38-caliber. This case is not the same as that of the .40-72 Winchester. However, the ballistics are nearly identical. It should be possible to convert .45-70 cases to work in these rifles, but the neck would be short. The .45 Basic will make perfect cases. Although groove diameter was typically .408-inch, original bullets were .406-inch diameter.

.40-70 Winchester Loading Data and Factory Ballistics

Bullet (grains/type)	Powder	Grains	Velocity	Energy	Source/Comments
330 Lead	IMR 4759	26.0	1,540	1,738	
330 Lead	IMR 4198	25.0	1,380	1,050	Lyman No. 406150
330 Lead	FL		1,383	1,333	Factory load

.40-70 Remington

Historical Notes: Although listed as the .40-70 Remington, this cartridge is really Remington's version of the .40-70 Sharps necked. The Remington rolling block No. 1 Sporting Model chambered it, and so did the Hepburn No. 3. It was added to the Remington line in 1880.

General Comments: Two versions of this cartridge were available, one with a regular brass case, the other with a special reloading case having a brass body and steel head. The steel head fastened to the brass body with an inside screw, which served as a primer anvil and had a flash hole drilled through it. Steel head cases—in 1880! There really is nothing new under the sun. The .40-70 was used more for match shooting than for hunting. It should be possible to convert .45-70 cases to work in these rifles, but the neck would be very short. The .45 Basic will make perfect cases.

.40-70 Remington Loading Data and Factory Ballistics

Bullet (grains/type)	Powder	Grains	Velocity	Energy	Source/Comments
330 Lead	IMR 4198	27.0	1,450	1,542	Lyman No. 403139
330 Lead	FL		1,420	1,482	Remington factory load

.40-65 Winchester
.40-65 Winchester & Marlin

Historical Notes: The .40-65 Winchester (also known as the .40-65 Winchester & Marlin) was introduced in 1887 for the Model 1886 Winchester rifle. The Winchester single-shot also chambered it, as did the Marlin Model 1895. The .40-65 Winchester was loaded in both black-powder and smokeless powder versions, and Winchester catalogs listed it to 1935.

General Comments: The .40-65 was a further effort to put more steam in the repeating rifles' cartridges so they would be competitive with similar single-shot cartridges. This one, reasonably popular, continued for almost 50 years. Rifles in this chambering are common and ammunition can be made by reforming .45-70 cases. Although groove diameter was typically .408 inch, original load bullets were .406-inch diameter.

.40-65 Winchester Loading Data and Factory Ballistics

Bullet (grains/type)	Powder	Grains	Velocity	Energy	Source/Comments
260 Lead	IMR 4198	23.0	1,500	1,308	Lyman No. 403169
260 Lead	IMR 3031	44.0	1,720	1,708	NA
260 Lead	AA 5744	26.0	1,651	1,573	Accurate Arms
300 Lead	AA 5744	24.0	1,515	1,528	Accurate Arms
260 Lead	FL		1,420	1,165	Factory load

.40-72 Winchester

Historical Notes: Introduced for and with the Winchester Model 1895 lever-action box-magazine repeater, the .40-72 was not very popular, but was loaded until 1936.

General Comments: This cartridge uses a smaller diameter but heavier 30-grain bullet, compared to the much more powerful .405 Winchester. The latter was preferred by most purchasers of the Model 1895. Black-powder cartridges of the 1890s suffered from competition with the newly introduced smokeless powder cartridges of that era. Most black-powder cartridges introduced at that time had no chance to establish any degree of popularity. Although longer, this case has the same basic body as the .30-40 Krag. Because headspacing is on the rim, it may not be possible to safely use that case to make the .40-72, except for very low-pressure loads.

.40-72 Winchester Loading Data and Factory Ballistics

Bullet (grains/type)	Powder	Grains	Velocity	Energy	Source/Comments
330 Lead	IMR 3031	40.0	1,435	1,510	Lyman No. 406150
300 Lead	FL		1,425	1,350	Winchester factory load

Bullet (grains/type)	Powder	Grains	Velocity	Energy	Source/Comments
330 Lead	FL		1,407	1,451	Winchester factory load

.401 Winchester Self-Loading (.401 WSL)

Historical Notes: The .401 was introduced by Winchester, in 1910, for its new Model 10 Autoloading rifle, which was a minor modification of the Model 1907. Both the cartridge and the rifle were discontinued in 1936, but the ammunition was loaded by most ammunition companies until after World War II. It is another obsolete "self-loading" cartridge.

General Comments: The .401 is the most powerful of the Winchester Autoloading line and the only one suitable for deer. The .401 found favor with many hunters as a quick, short-range number for hunting deer and black bear. Velocity is too low and the trajectory too high for this to be a useful cartridge beyond about 150 yards. It can be reloaded but, like all cartridges used in semi-auto guns, it is necessary to stick to the factory ballistics or the rifle action may not function properly. Proper bullet diameter is .406-inch, but .410-inch revolver bullets can sometimes be used safely—verify chamber clearance. With a bit of lathe work, .35 Remington cases can be converted to work perfectly in .401 WSL chambered rifles.

.401 Winchester Loading Data and Factory Ballistics

Bullet (grains/type)	Powder	Grains	Velocity	Energy	Source/Comments
200 SP	2400	24.7	1,915	1,625	Lyman
212 Lead	IMR 4227	29.0	2,074	2,025	Lyman
240 Lead	IMR 4227	27.5	1,968	2,150	Lyman
200 SP	FL		2,135	2,020	Winchester factory load
250 SP	FL		1,870	1,940	Winchester factory load

.40-82 Winchester (WCF)

Historical Notes: Introduced in 1885 for the Winchester single-shot and also available for the Model 1886 lever-action repeater, this cartridge was popular enough to make the transition into the smokeless powder era. It was loaded up to 1935.

General Comments: The .40-82 WCF gained a favorable reputation on elk and heavy game. It developed a higher muzzle velocity than many other black-powder cartridges, which made it easier to make contact with over unknown distances. Despite the relative popularity, rifles in this chambering are seldom encountered. Most of the original single-shots and Model 1886s have been rebarreled to some more modern chambering. It should be possible to convert the .45-70 case to work in these rifles, but the neck would be very short. The .45 Basic will make perfect cases. Although groove diameter was typically .408-inch, bullets used in original loads were only .406-inch diameter.

.40-82 Winchester Loading Data and Factory Ballistics

Bullet (grains/type)	Powder	Grains	Velocity	Energy	Source/Comments
260 Lead	IMR 4198	28.0	1,425	1,180	Lyman No. 403169
260 Lead	FL		1,490	1,285	Winchester factory load

.40-70 Peabody "What Cheer"

Historical Notes: Made for the Peabody-Martini rifles by the Providence Tool Co., this is one of a series of cartridges named for the What Cheer rifle range outside Providence, R.I., which opened in 1875. The first of the Peabody sporting and target rifles was said to have been exhibited at the opening celebration, but the .40-70 cartridge actually was not introduced until 1877 or 1878. The Union Metallic Cartridge Co. loaded the round, and so did Winchester.

General Comments: This is an odd-shaped cartridge, with a long, tapered shoulder and short body. Most samples have Berdan priming. Bullet diameter is .408-inch, but most nominal .406-inch bullets will cast sufficiently oversized to meet this diameter. This is not a common cartridge in collections, and rifles in this chambering are rare. For these low-pressure loads, .348 Winchester cases could be converted to work in this chamber.

.40-70 Peabody "What Cheer" Loading Data and Factory Ballistics

Bullet (grains/type)	Powder	Grains	Velocity	Energy	Source/Comments
330 Lead	IMR 4198	22.0	1,350	1,340	Lyman No. 406150
380 Lead	FL		1,420	1,710	Factory load

.40-90 Peabody "What Cheer"

Historical Notes: This unusually shaped cartridge was for the Peabody-Martini Rifle No. 3, introduced in 1877-'78. This rifle was a fancy model similar to the No. 2 Creedmoor, but was designated the "What Cheer." This was in line with the Peabody policy of naming its rifles after famous target ranges of the day, in this case the What Cheer Range of Greenwood, R.I., which was originally opened in 1875.

General Comments: The .40-90 Peabody "What Cheer" is a bottlenecked case similar to other "What Cheer" cartridges. This was a popular match cartridge, until the early 1900s. Proper bullet diameter is .408-inch. Cast bullets intended for the .405 Winchester can be sized down and used in this round. No one lists a mould for a 500-grain bullet for this cartridge. For these low-pressure loads, .348 Winchester cases could be converted to work in this chamber.

.40-90 Peabody "What Cheer" Loading Data and Factory Ballistics

Bullet (grains/type)	Powder	Grains	Velocity	Energy	Source/Comments
330 Lead	IMR 4198	27.0	1,450	1,550	Lyman No. 406150
500 Lead	FL		1,250	1,735	Factory load

.405 Winchester

Historical Notes: The .405 is another of the rimmed cartridges developed for the Winchester Model 1895 lever-action rifle. Introduced in 1904, the rifle became obsolete in 1936, but has been reproduced recently in limited runs; most were chambered for cartridges that are somewhat more modern, but one run was promised in .405. The Winchester single-shot also chambered the .405, and a number of double rifles were turned out in this chambering in England and Europe. The Remington-Lee bolt-action rifle was available in .405-caliber, between 1904 and 1906. The old Eley-Kynoch catalog lists the .405 Winchester with a 300-grain soft-point bullet at the standard factory load velocity.

General Comments: The .405 Winchester is the most powerful rimmed cartridge ever developed for the lever-action rifle. It is adequate for any North American big game at short to medium ranges and has been used successfully in Africa on all species. In the old Model 1895 Winchester, with its curved buttplate and poorly designed stock, it had a reputation for punishing recoil. Theodore Roosevelt used the .405 in Africa and thought very highly of it as a lion cartridge. However, John Taylor, in his excellent book, *African Rifles and Cartridges*, rates it as a poor choice compared to other available chamberings for African use. The short, fat, 300-grain round-nosed bullet loses velocity rapidly and lacks the sectional density necessary for deep penetration of heavy game. Nevertheless, it is quite adequate for any North American animals at ranges of 100 to 150 yards. Although longer, this case has the same basic body as the .30-40 Krag. However, because headspacing is on the rim, it is not possible to safely use that case to make .405s, except for very low-pressure loads (which the original author of this book did). With modern jacketed pistol bullets, one can thus make perfectly adequate short-range deer loads. A-Square (www.a-square.com) has recently reintroduced .405 ammunition. Buffalo Arms ((208) 263-6953; www.buffaloarms.com) offers modified .30-40 cases that are the correct length and have a modified rim to give the correct headspace.

.405 Winchester Loading Data and Factory Ballistics

Bullet (grains/type)	Powder	Grains	Velocity	Energy	Source/Comments
290 Cast	IMR 3031	40.0	1,500	1,449	Lyman No. 412263
300 SP	IMR 4895	56.0	2,230	3,321	NA
300 SP	IMR 3031	57.0	2,250	3,380	NA
300 SP	FL		2,200	3,220	Winchester factory load

.40-90 Bullard

Historical Notes: This rather odd bottlenecked cartridge was developed for the Bullard single-shot and repeating rifles, introduced in 1886-'87. Both Winchester and Remington manufactured this round for a number of years.

General Comments: This is a rather large, fat cartridge with ballistics similar to other .40-caliber cartridges of the period, such as the .40-82 Winchester. There was not a lot to choose from, regarding performance between any of these. Cartridges designed by the big manufacturers for their rifles were more widely advertised and distributed and, consequently, won the popularity race. Cartridges like the Bullard line gradually faded into the background. The .40-90 Bullard was undoubtedly an effective big-game cartridge, particularly if the now-rare 400-grain loading was used. Considering the low-pressure loads used, it should be possible to convert .50-90 Sharps cases for safe use in rifles so chambered.

.40-90 Bullard Loading Data and Factory Ballistics

Bullet (grains/type)	Powder	Grains	Velocity	Energy	Source/Comments
300 Lead	black powder (Fg)	90.0	1,569	1,648	Lyman No. 415175
300 Lead	IMR 4198	29.0	1,450	1,405	Lyman No. 415175
300 Lead	FL		1,569	1,648	Factory load

.40-75 Bullard

Historical Notes: Introduced, in 1887, for the Bullard lever-action repeating rifle and available for the single-shot, the .40-75 was the same case with a different bullet weight and powder charge as the .40-60 Bullard.

General Comments: This is a big-game cartridge similar in performance to the .40-60 Marlin or the .40-65 Winchester. Winchester's cartridge achieved the greatest popularity of these three. Proper diameter for a cast bullet is

.413 inch, which is significantly larger than many of the other .40-caliber cartridges, which used a bullet of .403-inch diameter. The old Bullard catalog states that the .40-60 Marlin can be fired in guns of the above chambering. If so, then the .40-65 WCF could also be used, as it is the same case as the Marlin round. It should be possible to convert .45-70 cases to work in these rifles.

.40-75 Bullard Loading Data and Factory Ballistics

Bullet (grains/type)	Powder	Grains	Velocity	Energy	Source/Comments
260 Lead	black powder (Fg)	75.0	1,513	1,315	Lyman No. 412174
260 Lead	IMR 4198	20.0	1,500	1,302	Lyman No. 412174
258 Lead	FL		1,513	1,315	Factory load

.40-40 Maynard (1882)

Historical Notes: A cartridge for the Maynard 1882 rifle, Improved Hunting or Target No. 9, and the Mid Range Target or Hunting No. 10, it was advertised as a combination hunting and target cartridge.

General Comments: In performance, the .40-40 is similar to the .44-40 WCF. Maynard made only two bullet weights in .40-caliber; the 330-grain was intended for the longer .40-60, but was sometimes used in the .40-40. Bullet diameter of these cartridges is not the same as the .403-inch of most Sharps and Winchester cartridges. The Maynard Co. sold moulds or factory-made bullets for its rifles. The .40-caliber Maynard bore is usually .415- to .417-inch diameter. It should be possible to convert .303 British cases to work in these rifles.

.40-40 Maynard 1882 Loading Data and Factory Ballistics

Bullet (grains/type)	Powder	Grains	Velocity	Energy	Source/Comments
260 Lead	IMR 4198	24.0	1,400	1,140	Lyman No. 413174
270 Lead	FL		1,425	1,222	Factory load
330 Lead	FL		1,260	1,168	Factory load

.40-60 Maynard (1882)

Historical Notes: This is an intermediate-range match cartridge for the 1882 Maynard Models 10, 12, and 13 Hunting and the Models 15-16 Target rifles. It does not use the same case as the longer .40-70 Maynard.

General Comments: The .40-60 Maynard is an elongated version of the .40-40 and differs mainly in the longer case length. Unfortunately, it duplicated the performance of similar Marlin, Sharps, and Winchester cartridges and, for that reason, it did not become popular or widely used. It should be possible to convert .303 British cases to work in these rifles.

.40-60 Maynard 1882 Loading Data and Factory Ballistics

Bullet (grains/type)	Powder	Grains	Velocity	Energy	Source/Comments
300 Lead	IMR 4198	26.0	1,370	1,248	Lyman No. 413175
330 Lead	FL		1,370	1,380	Factory load

.40-70 Maynard (1882)

Historical Notes: This has the longest case of the three .40-caliber cartridges chambered in the 1882-type Maynard single-shot rifle, which was available in both Target and Hunting models.

General Comments: Some publications show the .40-70 Maynard to be the same as the .40-60, but with a different load. Others indicate that it is identical except for length. Actually, it has a little longer case (.21-inch), with a slightly larger rim and base diameter. The .40-60 can be fired in a .40-70 chamber, but the reverse is not true. In overall length, this is the shorter of the two cartridges, because of the lighter bullet seated farther down in the case. This is more of a hunting cartridge, although it was also available in the target rifle models. It should be possible to convert .303 British cases to work in these rifles.

.40-70 Maynard (1882) Loading Data and Factory Ballistics

Bullet (grains/type)	Powder	Grains	Velocity	Energy	Source/Comments
260 Lead	IMR 4198	27.0	1,450	1,211	Lyman No. 413174
270 Lead	FL		1,645	1,620	Factory load

.44 Evans Long
.44-40 Straight
.44-40-300

Historical Notes: The .44 Evans Long was developed for the 1877 New Model Evans sporting rifle. It is sometimes referred to as the .44-40 Straight or the .44-40-300, because of its different loadings.

General Comments: The New Model Evans rifle was similar to the Old Model, except for the change to a longer, more powerful cartridge. The magazine capacity was only (!) 26 rounds, compared to 34 for the Old Model. Again, this is not a strong action, so it is advisable to use only black-powder loads. The cartridge was loaded with 275- to 300-grain bullets and 40 to 43 grains of black powder. Although this case is somewhat larger in diameter, usable cases might be made by cutting off .303 Savage cases, as with the Henry Center Fire Flat. As with all similar numbers, it is best to load only with black powder or Pyrodex. Also, either the case mouth must be thinned or an undersized bullet must be used, to provide adequate case-neck to chamber-wall clearance.

.44 Evans Long Factory Ballistics

Bullet (grains/type)	Powder	Grains	Velocity	Energy	Source/Comments
280 Lead	FL		200	903	Factory load

.44 Evans Short

Historical Notes: This is the cartridge for the various Old Model Evans rifles, introduced in 1875. Winchester loaded the ammunition until the early 1920s.

General Comments: The Evans rifle was designed for military use, but, when it was turned down by the U.S. Ordnance Department, it was manufactured as a sporting number. The Evans had a magazine capacity of 34 cartridges held in the four-column tubular magazine located in the butt. This was an odd-looking lever-action rifle. Evans rifles were once somewhat common items, and box lots of ammunition could be purchased until 1940-'41. This is not a particularly strong action, so only use black-powder loads. A load of 28 grains of Fg or FFg was used in the original round. Cases can be made by cutting off .303 Savage cases and perhaps thinning the rim, as required. (As in similar rim-thinning situations, pistol primers may have to be used, but those work well in most black-powder or black-powder pressure loads anyway.) Also, either the case mouth must be thinned or an undersized bullet must be used to provide adequate case-neck to chamber-wall clearance.

.44 Evans Short Factory Ballistics

Bullet (grains/type)	Powder	Grains	Velocity	Energy	Source/Comments
215 Lead	FL		850	350	Winchester factory load

.44 Henry Center Fire Flat

Historical Notes:	This is a centerfire version of the rimfire .44 Henry Flat. In 1891, 1,020 M1866 Winchester rifles were chambered for this cartridge and shipped to Brazil.
General Comments:	Rifles for this cartridge are extremely rare. The 1866 Henry rifle was not very strong. Those who want to shoot one should stick to black powder. The proper charge is 26 or 28 grains of FFg or FFFg. Cast bullets for the .44-40 WCF can be used. Cases can be made by cutting off .303 Savage cases and perhaps thinning the rim, as required. (In rim-thinning situations, pistol primers may have to be used, but these are preferable in almost every black-powder or black-powder pressure load anyway.)

.44 Henry Center Fire Flat Factory Ballistics

Bullet (grains/type)	Powder	Grains	Velocity	Energy	Source/Comments
200 Lead	FL		1,150	594	Factory load
227 Lead	FL		1,200	725	Factory load

.44 Game Getter
.44-40 Marlin
.44 Colt Lightning

Historical Notes:	In 1908, Marble Arms Corp. introduced its Game Getter, a double-barrel, over/under pistol with a removable skeleton buttstock. The upper barrel was rifled and chambered for the .22 rimfire cartridge; the lower barrel was smoothbore and chambered for the .44 shot cartridge. The introduction of this pistol bolstered the popularity of the several varieties of .44 shot cartridges.
	The Stevens Model 101 Featherweight rifle (1914-'16) was chambered for this cartridge, as well as the .44 XL and .44 WCF shot cartridges. The .44 WCF shot cartridge was a crimped case with cardboard wadding; others were loaded with a wood or paper "bullet" that enclosed the shot. The Marble catalog of 1914 stated, "Shot cartridges with paper or wooden ends are especially adapted to rifled barrels. However, they can be used in the Game Getter, but give uncertain results." UMC loaded a .44 round ball cartridge before the introduction of the Game Getter, using 34 grains of black powder and a 115-grain round lead ball. This combination of gun and cartridge became very popular and Winchester and U.S. Ammunition Co. began to offer it, calling it the .44 Game Getter.
General Comments:	The .44-40 is, of course, still loaded today, but, during its life span as a black-powder cartridge (and the early smokeless powder days), it was available in a variety of loads that are now obsolete.
	The standard load of 40 grains of black powder and a 200-grain bullet of the .44 WCF was altered slightly (a 217-grain bullet was used), and the resulting cartridge was called the .44-40 Marlin or the .44 Colt Lightning Magazine Rifle. All are nothing more than load variations on the standard .44-40 Winchester—some rifles may require shorter overall cartridge lengths. Also obsolete today are the high-velocity smokeless powder loads that were offered for rifles with stronger actions.

.44-40 Extra Long

General Comments: The .44-40 Extra Long is listed in various publications, and sample rounds are common. It has a longer body and neck than the standard .44-40 WCF. The original author of this book was unable to find any record indicating the gun for which this cartridge was designed. It is listed so the reader will not confuse it with the straight Ballard or Wesson Extra Long .44 cartridges. Some believe this is the .44-40 shot case with a conical bullet. According to William R. Small, of Ojo Caliente, N.M., the Stevens Model 101 Featherweight rifle (1914-'16) chambered this round, as well as the .44 XL and .44 WCF shot cartridges. Cases can be made by shortening and necking .444 Marlin cases.

.44 Long Center Fire (Ballard)

Historical Notes: The .44 Long Center Fire (Ballard) was introduced, in 1875-'76, as one of the chamberings for the J.M. Marlin Ballard Sporting Rifle No. 2. It was also used in a number of other single-shot rifles, including those of Frank Wesson. It was replaced by the .44 Extra Long CF, and then both were phased out by the more popular .44-40 WCF. It is the centerfire equivalent of the .44 Long rimfire.

General Comments: This is a more-or-less transitional cartridge from the rimfire to the better centerfires. Most early breech-loading rifles were developed for rimfire cartridges, and it was a simple matter to bring out a similar centerfire for the same basic rifle. This allowed the shooter to reload. However, most of these cartridges were no more effective than the rimfire they replaced and, so, did not last long. The original load used 35 grains of black powder and a 227-grain bullet. Muzzle velocity was low—only about 1100 to 1200 fps. As with the .44 Evans Long, Short, or Henry Flat Center Fire, cases can be made by cutting off .303 Savage cases, but stick to black-powder and cast bullets.

.44 Extra Long/
.44 Extra Long Center Fire (Ballard)

Historical Notes: This cartridge is sometimes listed simply as the .44 Extra Long. It is a straight case and is the centerfire version of the .44 Rimfire Extra Long. As near as can be determined, it was introduced, in 1876, for the J.M. Marlin Ballard Sporting Rifle No. 2. It was only available for a few years, before being replaced in the Ballard rifles by the .44-40 WCF. Rifles in this chambering are rare today.

General Comments: The .44 Extra Long was not a loved Ballard number, as there were too many better .44-caliber cartridges available. The .44-40 WCF was already popular by the time the Ballard round hit the market, and the .44 Extra Long was available only in the single-shot. It did, however, provide a reloadable case for those used to the .44 EL rimfire, and quite a few of the old rimfire rifles were probably converted to use the centerfire. Remington loaded this with 50 grains of black powder and a 265-grain bullet. Cases can be made by cutting .303 Savage cases as mentioned in the discussion about the .44 Henry Flat Center Fire.

.44 Extra Long (Ballard) Factory Ballistics

Bullet (grains/type)	Powder	Grains	Velocity	Energy	Source/Comments
265 Lead	FL		1,320	1,030	Remington factory load

.44 Wesson Extra Long

Historical Notes:	Made for the Frank Wesson tip-up rifles, this cartridge appears to be identical to the .44 Extra Long Ballard except for the shape of the bullet. The Wesson bullet shows two grease grooves when loaded in the case, while the Ballard shows only one.				
General Comments:	Many of the Wesson tip-up rifles were furnished with a patented adjustable hammer, permitting the use of both rim- and centerfire cartridges. Lyman No. 419182 (240-grain) or 424100 (170-grain) bullets can be adapted to this cartridge. Original loads used 48 to 50 grains of black powder. Wesson rifles in this chambering are very rare. As discussed with the .44 Henry Flat Center Fire, cases can be made by cutting off .303 Savage cases.				

.44 Wesson Extra Long Factory Ballistics

Bullet (grains/type)	Powder	Grains	Velocity	Energy	Source/Comments
250-257 Lead	FL		1,340	1,010	Factory load

.44-100 Remington "Creedmoor"/.44-90 Remington Straight

Historical Notes:	The .44-100 cartridge was for the Remington-Hepburn or No. 3 Long-Range Creedmoor rifle. It was introduced in 1880. This special 2 6/10-inch shell had various loadings and bullets, plus the usual variety of designations for the same round. As if to add more confusion, a 24/10-inch version was also made. This may have been designed to furnish a straight case as an alternative to some of the necked Sharps .44 cartridges.				
General Comments:	Also known as the .44-26/10-inch and .44-90 Remington Straight, this was designed as a match cartridge for long-range shooting out to 1,000 and even 1,400 yards. It was moderately popular, but rifles in this chambering are scarce. The cartridge is a collector's item. Remington manufactured a number of match rifles designated "Creedmoor," and this is the correct spelling of the Creedmoor, Long Island, rifle range. However, the company also made various cartridges under the Creedmore label (note the different spelling). Ammunition so designated had a target-type bullet and very often was intended for rifles that the manufacturer had never called Creedmoor. This has caused much confusion, although Remington changed the spelling to try to prevent it. Both Remington and Winchester furnished empty cases and bullets for handloading. Cases can be converted from the .45 Basic.				

.44-100 Remington "Creedmoor" Loading Data and Factory Ballistics

Bullet (grains/type)	Powder	Grains	Velocity	Energy	Source/Comments
470 Lead	IMR 4198	27.0	1,410	2,080	Lyman No. 446187
520 Lead	FL		1,435	2,380	Remington factory load
550 Lead	FL		1,380	2,338	Remington factory load

.44-90 Remington Special (Necked)

Historical Notes: The .44-90 Remington Special looks like the .44-90 Sharps but, on closer inspection, it has a shorter case with a slightly larger body diameter—these are not interchangeable. The .40-90 was introduced as a match cartridge for the Remington rolling block Creedmoor series, in 1873. Remington catalogs listed empty cases and bullets for this cartridge as late as 1910.

General Comments: The .44-77 Sharps had a 2¼-inch case, the .44-90 Sharps a 2 -inch case. The .44-90 Remington Special case was 27/16-inch, or 2.44 inches long. The Remington cartridge was regularly loaded with a 550-grain patched or lubricated lead bullet, which is heavier than the normal bullet used in Sharps cartridges. Remington probably designed its .44-90 so that a heavy bullet and 90 grains of powder could be used without increasing the overall length of the cartridge. The loaded length is actually less than the similar Sharps cartridges. This is primarily a match cartridge, but would also be effective on almost any big game. Lighter bullets and more powder could be used to increase black-powder ballistics for hunting. The only safe source of cases (those that have been extensively modified from .348 Winchester size) is Buffalo Arms (208-263-6953; www.buffaloarms.com).

.44-90 Remington Special Loading Data and Factory Ballistics

Bullet (grains/type)	Powder	Grains	Velocity	Energy	Source/Comments
470 Lead	IMR 4198	30.0	1,270	1,688	Lyman No. 446187
470 Lead PP	black powder (Fg)	90.0			Factory load, early paper patch
550 Lead	black powder (Fg)	90.0	1,250	1,812	Remington factory load

.44-95 Peabody "What Cheer"
.44-100 Peabody "What Cheer"

Historical Notes: The .44-95 Peabody also had a 100-grain loading and was occasionally referred to as the .44-100 Peabody. It is the largest of the Peabody "What Cheer" cartridges. It was the original chambering for the Peabody-Martini Long-Range Creedmoor Rifle. The straight stock version was the No. 3 "What Cheer," and, eventually, the cartridge was given this name. Some authorities say it was introduced in 1877, but it may have made its debut as early as 1875. It was popular primarily as a target round.

General Comments: Peabody and Peabody-Martini rifles were manufactured by the Providence Tool Co. of Providence, R.I. The action was patented by H.L. Peabody, of Boston, Mass., in 1862. Peabody-Martini military rifles were manufactured for the Turkish government, during 1873, and something like 600,000 were delivered. The original Peabody pivoting block action had a side-hammer, but the Swiss Martini modification did away with this, instead employing an internal lock. The British Martini-Henry rifle is based on this modified American design. This is one of the strongest of the old single-shot actions.

Adding the phrase "What Cheer" was in line with the Peabody policy of naming its rifles after famous target ranges of the day, in this case the What Cheer Range, of Greenwood, R.I., which was originally opened in 1875.

.44-95 Peabody "What Cheer" Loading Data and Factory Ballistics

Bullet (grains/type)	Powder	Grains	Velocity	Energy	Source/Comments
470 Lead	black powder (Fg)	100.0	1,380	1,990	Lyman No. 446187
470 Lead	IMR 4759	21.0	1,380	1,990	Lyman No. 446187
550 Lead	FL		1,310	2,100	Factory load

.44-70 Maynard (1882)

Historical Notes: Introduced for the 1882-type Maynard single-shot rifle, the .44-70 was also available for the Hunters Model No. 11 and the Creedmoor No. 14 match rifle.

General Comments: The .44-70 Maynard is a .44-caliber version of the popular .45-70 Government military round. Many riflemen of the late 1880s preferred the .44-caliber over the larger .45 bore, although there is little difference in bore dimensions. The Maynard company furnished a 430-grain bullet for hunting and general shooting and a 520-grain for target work. Although somewhat too short, .45-70 cases will work in these rifles.

.44-70 Maynard (1882) Loading Data and Factory Ballistics

Bullet (grains/type)	Powder	Grains	Velocity	Energy	Source/Comments
470 Lead	IMR 4198	26.0	1,300	1,768	Lyman No. 446187
430 Lead	FL		1,310	1,640	Factory load

.44-100 Ballard

Historical Notes: The .44-100 Ballard Everlasting was one of the chamberings introduced with the various J.M. Marlin Ballard rifles. It is first listed for the 1876 Model Pacific No. 5 and Long Range No. 7A. It was discontinued about 1880 and does not appear as a standard chambering in later Marlin Fire Arms Co. catalogs. However, the 1888 Marlin & Ballard catalog again lists brass shells under obsolete sizes at 12 cents each. The .45-100 Ballard, which came out later, is based on this same case with the neck reamed out to accept the larger-diameter bullet.

General Comments: This is another rare Ballard cartridge. It was an accurate target number and had considerable knockdown power for big game. Ballard rifles were manufactured by several companies. The best known of these were made by the Marlin Fire Arms Co., after it was incorporated, in 1881. Most of its models and cartridges are not particularly scarce. John M. Marlin organized the Marlin Fire Arms Co. but, prior to that, he turned out Ballard rifles under the name of J.M. Marlin (1875-1881). The first Ballard arms were for rimfire cartridges, and these were introduced by Ball & Williams, in 1861, and continued until 1866 under its brand. From 1866 to 1869, these were made by Merrimack Arms & Manufacturing Co. and, from 1869 to 1873, by Brown Manufacturing Co. Some of these early models and cartridges are rare and valuable. Although the .44-100 Ballard is larger and somewhat longer in diameter, it might be possible to form .45-70 cases to work in these rifles. Basic .45s could be cut to the proper length. In either case, one might have to turn down the rim to fit the chamber.

.44-100 Ballard Loading Data and Factory Ballistics

Bullet (grains/type)	Powder	Grains	Velocity	Energy	Source/Comments
365 Lead	black powder (Fg)	110.0	1,500	1,830	Lyman No. 446109
365 Lead	IMR 4198	26.0	1,350	1,480	Lyman No. 446109
535 Lead	FL		1,400	2,328	Factory load

.44-75 Ballard Everlasting

Historical Notes: The .44-75 is one of the rarer Ballard cases. Seldom found in collections and not mentioned in most cartridge books, L.D. Satterlee* lists it as available for the J.M. Marlin Ballard Perfection No. 4, Pacific No. 5 and Schuetzen No. 6, all introduced in 1876. He gives case length as 2¼-inch.† This chambering is not listed in the Marlin Fire Arms Co. after Marlin began making Ballard rifles, in 1881. James J. Grant ** says this was one of the special Marlin Everlasting cases using the shallow Berdan-type No. 2 primer similar to the .40-65. He also has specimens using Large Rifle primers.

General Comments: The 44-75-2½-inch can be made by trimming and sizing Sharps .45-2⁹/₁₀-inch cases. This must have been intended as both a target and hunting cartridge, since it was available in rifles of both types. Marlin and Ballard catalogs listed a patched 405-grain, .44-caliber bullet, which was probably one of the weights used in the .44-75. Bullets for .44-caliber Sharps cartridges of .446-inch diameter can be adapted to the .44-75 Ballard. No factory ballistics are available, so it is probable that only empty cases and bullets were furnished.

The so-called Everlasting, or reloadable case, was popular with hunters and target shooters during the 1880-'90 period. These heavy cases could be reused repeatedly. In fact, they were made so heavy that powder capacity was often reduced by five or 10 grains. To get around this, the Everlasting case was often made longer than the standard.

* *op. cit.*

** *More Single Shot Rifles (New York, 1959).*

† *John T. Amber, the first editor of this book, owned a fine No. 7 Ballard in .44-75 chambering, complete in case with hunting and target sights, etc., and including a score or more of cases. All were 2½ inches long, not 2¼ inches, and were Berdan-primed Everlasting type.*

.44-100 Wesson

Historical Notes: As with the .44-85 Wesson, this one was found on a U.S. Cartridge Co. advertising sheet printed in 1881-'82. This is also a straight case, with the length listed as 33/8 inches. The bullet is seated deeply so the total length of the loaded cartridge is 39/10 inches. The load is given as 100 or 120 grains of black powder with a 550-grain, paper-patched bullet.

General Comments: What date and what rifle? There is no information given on this. As previously stated, all .44-caliber Sharps cartridges are necked and, perhaps, this is intended as the straight case counter to the necked .44-100 or 105 (25/8-inch) Sharps. This is speculation, but many shooters of this period did prefer the straight case. The .44-100 Wesson is not listed in any previous cartridge book, and now that its existence has been brought to the attention of collectors, additional information may be forthcoming. Muzzle velocity of this combination would be approximately 1350 to 1400 fps, depending on charge, barrel length, etc.

.44-85 Wesson

Historical Notes: The .44-85 Wesson is another of the mysterious and little-known Wesson cartridges. The little information available was gathered from a United States Cartridge Co. (U.S.C.C.) advertising sheet printed in 1881-'82. The .44-85 is a straight case with a length of 27/8 inches. All .44-caliber Sharps cartridges were necked, so it is not similar to any of those. There is nothing to indicate which Wesson rifle it was for, but, with that length, it was probably meant for the Creedmoor models.

General Comments: It is well to point out that, during the late 1800s, many riflemen did not like bottlenecked cases. It may be that Frank Wesson introduced this cartridge because all the Sharps .44 cases were necked and some individuals wanted the same performance in a straight case. The U.S.C.C. load had a 390-grain patched bullet backed by 85 grains of Fg black powder. This would have developed a muzzle velocity of approximately 1450 fps in the average rifle.

Bullet (grains/type)	Powder	Grains	Velocity	Energy	Source/Comments
390 Lead	black powder (Fg)	85.0	1,450	1,821	Factory load

.44-77 Sharps & Remington

Historical Notes: This is the 2¼-inch Sharps bottlenecked case introduced in 1869 for the Model 1869 Sharps breech-loading sporting rifle. It was also one of the chamberings available for the Remington-Hepburn or No. 3. It was a popular target round, used more for this purpose than hunting. The design of the .44-77 is said to have been based on a combination of the .42 Russian and the .43 Spanish military cartridges.

General Comments: A variety of factory loadings were turned out for the .44-77, with bullet weights from 300 grains to 470 grains. It is sometimes listed as the .44-70 or .44-75, depending on the powder charge used. Remington made an unusual two-piece reloadable case with a steel head and brass body.

.44-77 Sharps & Remington Loading Data and Factory Ballistics

Bullet (grains/type)	Powder	Grains	Velocity	Energy	Source/Comments
365 Lead	IMR 4198	28.0	1,480	1,782	Lyman No. 446109
470 Lead PP	black powder (Fg)	77.0	UNK	UNK	Factory load, early paper patch
365 Lead	FL		1,460	1,730	Factory load

.44-90 Sharps Necked (.44-100 Sharps 2⅝-inch/ .44-105 Sharp Necked)

Historical Notes: This is the .44-90 Sharps 2⅝-inch case of larger capacity than the .44-77 Sharps. It was the chambering for the Sharps 1873 Creedmoor rifle made by the old Sharps Rifle Manufacturing Co. before its reorganization, in 1875-'76, and was chambered in later side-hammer models. Advertisements list it as early as June of 1873. Sharps rifles of .44-caliber were discontinued, during 1878, in favor of the more popular .45-caliber.

General Comments: These are just different loadings and bullet weights. Ammunition was available with bullets weighing 277, 450, 470, 500, and 520 grains. It was not as popular for hunting as some of the other Sharps chamberings, but was used for 1,000-yard match shooting. A version with a .19-inch shorter case also existed. Both are listed in the 1910 Winchester catalog. The only safe source of cases is Buffalo Arms; it extensively modifies .348 Winchester cases to properly fit these chambers. (208) 263-6953; www.buffaloarms.com).

.44-90 Sharps (Necked) Loading Data and Factory Ballistics

Bullet (grains/type)	Powder	Grains	Velocity	Energy	Source/Comments
470 Lead	IMR 4198	28.0	1,300	1,630	Lyman No. 446187
520 Lead	FL		1,270	1,860	Factory load

.44-60 Sharps & Remington (Necked)

Historical Notes: This 1-inch .44 case was loaded by Remington and Winchester. It was introduced, in 1869, for the 1869 Sporting Rifle and used in Sharps, Winchester, and Remington single-shot rifles.

General Comments: This was a general purpose cartridge for hunting or target shooting. It was listed by Remington and labeled as one of its "Creedmore" types (note the spelling), which has caused some confusion identifying the round. Sharps match rifles for long-range shooting were named after the famous range at Creedmoor, Long Island. Other rifle makers also used this name. Remington applied the name to cartridges not originally chambered in the Sharps Creedmoor line. It is interesting to compare this cartridge with the .42 Russian Berdan Carbine round. Except for bullet diameter, the two are practically identical. This suggests the possibility that the .44-60 was developed by expanding the neck of the Russian Carbine cartridge, much as some modern wildcats are made. The .44-60 necked Peabody, Winchester, Remington, etc., appear to be the same as the .44-60 (1-inch) Sharps cartridge.

.44-60 Sharps (Necked) Loading Data and Factory Ballistics

Bullet (grains/type)	Powder	Grains	Velocity	Energy	Source/Comments
315 Lead	IMR 4198	24.0	1,300	1,188	Lyman No. 446110
396 Lead	FL		1,250	1,375	Factory load

.45-50 Peabody (Sporting)

Historical Notes: A sporting cartridge for the Peabody-Martini single-shot rifle, the .45-50 was introduced in 1873-'74, shortly after the Martini modification of the Peabody action was adopted.

General Comments: The .45-50 bears a close resemblance to the Peabody .45-55 Turkish carbine cartridge. It is probable that it is a modification of the Turkish military round, adapted to sporting use. Physical measurements of the two are not identical, but very close. This is a rare cartridge, and rifles in this chambering are seldom encountered. Almost any .45-caliber rifle bullet can be sized down to .454-inch diameter and used; the Lyman No. 456191 (300-grain) will work fine. Powder charge can be varied from 50 to 55 grains of Fg black powder, depending on bullet weight and seating depth. For smokeless powder loads, use 22 to 23 grains of Du Pont (IMR) 4198. This will more or less duplicate original black-powder ballistics. It could be possible to cut and form .45-70 cases to work in these rifles. This is one of the few Peabody designs close enough to common current chamberings to offer hope of conveniently shooting the rifle chambered for it.

.45-50 Peabody (Sporting) Loading Data and Factory Ballistics

Bullet (grains/type)	Powder	Grains	Velocity	Energy	Source/Comments
255 Lead	IMR 4198	25.0	1,350	1,080	Lyman No. 454190
300 Lead	black powder (Fg)	50.0	1,285	1,080	Lyman No. 456191
290 Lead	FL		1,295	1,085	Factory load

.44-60 Winchester
.44-60 Peabody "Creedmoor"

Historical Notes:	This cartridge is for the Peabody-Martini Creedmoor rifle, introduced in 1877-'78. It is not a well-known cartridge and apparently was of limited popularity. Winchester loaded this round under its own name, which it introduced in 1874-'75. This is the same as the Sharps .44-60-1 -inch necked cartridge.
General Comments:	Examination of these cartridges in comparison with the .42 Russian Carbine indicates they are identical except for neck and bullet diameter. The .44-60 was likely developed by expanding the neck of the Russian cartridge, very much as some of our modern wildcats are made. The Russian Carbine cartridge is a shortened version of the .42 Berdan.

.44-60 Peabody "Creedmoor" Loading Data and Factory Ballistics

Bullet (grains/type)	Powder	Grains	Velocity	Energy	Source/Comments
365 Lead	black powder (Fg)	65.0	1,280	1,410	Lyman No. 446109
395 Lead	FL		1,250	1,375	Winchester factory load

.45-75 Winchester (Centennial)

Historical Notes:	The .45-75 Winchester was the original chambering for the Model 1876 Centennial rifle. Other chamberings were added later. The Kennedy repeating rifle also used this round. Winchester continued to produce this cartridge until 1935. The Canadian Northwest Mounted Police adopted the Model 76 Winchester in the .45-75 chambering and used it for 27 years.
General Comments:	To compete with the big Sharps and other single-shot cartridges, Winchester needed a longer repeating action. The Model 76 was designed to fill that need. However, as produced, it wasn't long enough to handle cartridges with an overall length exceeding 2¼ inches. The .45-75 gives performance equal to, or slightly better than, the .45-70 Government by use of a shorter, fatter, bottlenecked case. The Model 76 action is not noted for great strength, and heavy smokeless powder charges should be avoided. The .45-75 would be a good short-range deer or black bear cartridge, by modern standards. It was favored by Theodore Roosevelt for grizzly bear. Usable cases can be made from .348 Winchester cases.

.45-75 Winchester Loading Data and Factory Ballistics

Bullet (grains/type)	Powder	Grains	Velocity	Energy	Source/Comments
350 Lead	IMR 4198	24.0	1,380	1,480	Lyman No. 456192
350 Lead	FL		1,383	1,485	Factory load

.45-60 Winchester

Historical Notes:	The .45-60 is one of several cartridges designed for the Winchester 1876 Centennial Model rifle. The .45-60 cartridge was introduced in 1879. Winchester continued production of this cartridge until 1935, although the rifle was discontinued in 1897. The Kennedy lever-action repeating rifle used this cartridge, as did the Colt Lightning pump-action repeater.

General Comments: The .45-60 was brought out, with others of the Model 1876 cartridge line, to provide greater power than the .44-40 and other short cartridges used in the Model 1873 Winchester. The .45-60 design was probably influenced by the. 45-70 Government round. The Model 1876 rifle had a medium-length action that would not handle the long cartridges used in the single-shots of the period. The .45-60 would be a better deer cartridge than the .44 WCF, but would not be suitable for larger game. Rifles for this cartridge are not strong, so one should not attempt to exceed original ballistics. It should be easy to form .45-70 cases to work in these rifles.

.45-60 Winchester Loading Data and Factory Ballistics

Bullet (grains/type)	Powder	Grains	Velocity	Energy	Source/Comments
300 Lead	IMR 4198	25.0	1,450	1,410	Lyman No. 456191
300 Lead	FL		1,315	1,152	Winchester factory load

.45-100 Ballard

Historical Notes: Satterlee* indicates that this cartridge was introduced, in 1878, with the Ballard Sporting No. 4½ rifle. However, Grant first shows it with the 1882 (Marlin Fire Arms Co.) Pacific No. 5. Manufacture of Ballard single-shot rifles was discontinued between 1888 and 1890. The .45-100 cartridge was still listed as a standard chambering in the 1888 Marlin & Ballard catalog. This was the last catalog that advertised the Ballard, according to some authorities.

General Comments: The .45-100 is not a common cartridge, although it was available up to the time Ballard rifles were discontinued. It is the same case as the .44-100 Ballard, but the inside of the neck was reamed, to accommodate the larger .45-caliber bullet. Almost any .45-caliber lead rifle bullet can be sized to fit this case. The company offered .45-caliber bullets in 285, 405, 420, and 550 grains for loading this and other cartridges. Lighter bullets left room for up to 120 grains of black powder. This was used as both a target and hunting round and was equal in power to some of the big Sharps and Winchester cartridges of similar capacity. The old Ballard action is not particularly strong, and caution is advised when using smokeless powder. Although the base is a bit smaller than the .45-70, one suspects usable cases could be made from .45-70 cases. If so, Basic .45 cases could be cut to the proper length to duplicate this cartridge, which is very similar to the .45-90 Winchester, only longer.

*op. cit.

.45-100 Ballard Loading Data and Factory Ballistics

Bullet (grains/type)	Powder	Grains	Velocity	Energy	Source/Comments
500 Lead	black powder (Fg)	100.0	1,400	2,180	Lyman No. 457125
500 Lead	IMR 4198	22.0	1,250	1,740	Lyman No. 457125
550 Lead	FL		1,370	2,300	Factory load

.45-125 Winchester (.45 Express)

Historical Notes: Introduced in 1886 as a special-order chambering for the Winchester single-shot rifle, the .45-125 was not widely used and was discontinued after a few years. Winchester continued to load this ammunition until 1916.

General Comments: The .45-125 has a long bottlenecked case and was furnished with the 300-grain copper-tubed, Express bullet. Lyman No. 456191 is the proper bullet for reloading. In appearance, this cartridge resembles the British .500/465 Nitro, but they are not the same and can be distinguished by head markings, bullet diameter, etc.

This is a powerful black-powder number and would do for most big game in North America. One reason it became obsolete is that the .45-90 WCF will do the same thing with a smaller case and less powder.

.45-125 Winchester Loading Data and Factory Ballistics

Bullet (grains/type)	Powder	Grains	Velocity	Energy	Source/Comments
300 Lead	IMR 4198	35.0	1,475	1,456	Lyman No. 456191
300 SP	FL		1,690	1,903	Winchester factory load

.45-70 Van Choate

Historical Notes: This cartridge was originally designed for the experimental Van Choate military bolt-action rifle made by the Brown Manufacturing Co., in 1872. It is similar to the .45-70 Government, but has a case length of 2¼ inches instead of 21/10 inches. It was used in other rifles as well, because it was listed in Remington and Winchester catalogs as late as 1910-'12. The paper patched bullet weighed 420 grains.

General Comments: There are a number of variations of the basic .45-70 Government cartridge. Most of these vary by bullet weight, but a few use a different case length. One of these was the .45-78-475 Wolcott with a 2.31-inch case. There was also a .45-80 Sharpshooter cartridge that was used in special target rifles. This had a 24/10-inch case that was very similar, if not identical, to the Sharps 24/10-inch case. Although these cartridges are identical in all dimensions except length, a rifle would have to be chambered to accept the extra-long case, so these would not be interchangeable. Just what the originators hoped to gain from these variations is hard to imagine. It was probably done to allow a full or increased powder charge with a heavier or longer-than-standard bullet. Most of these variations have an odd-shaped bullet. For any of these, one can use the same bullets and loading data given with the .45-70. Standard .45-70 cases chamber in these rifles. To duplicate the original case, trim Basic .45s to the proper length.

.45-75 Sharps (Straight)
.45-70 Sharps 2¹/₁₀-inch

Historical Notes: This cartridge is identical to the .45-70 Government. It represents another instance of a manufacturer adding his name to a cartridge when chambered for his rifles. Also known as the .45-70 Sharps, it was added to the company product line early to mid-1875. It was one of the loadings designated as the Sharps .45-2-1/10-inch case.

General Comments: Use the same loading data as that given for the .45-70 Government. Most original Sharps rifles have black-powder steel barrels, so it is advisable to stick to lead bullets to reduce wear on the bore. Any load safe for the 1873 "Trapdoor" Springfield will be okay in Sharps rifles of any vintage.

.45-75 Sharps (Straight) Factory Ballistics

Bullet (grains/type)	Powder	Grains	Velocity	Energy	Source/Comments
400 Lead	FL		1,330	1,580	Factory load

.45-82 Winchester
.45-85 Winchester
.45-90 Winchester
.45-90 Winchester High Velocity

Historical Notes: These designations are often listed separately, giving different case dimensions. However, these are nothing more than different loads and bullet weights in the same basic .45-90 case. All loads were for the Winchester Model 1886 repeater or the 1885 single-shot. The .45-90 was introduced in 1886. The other loads followed. The Marlin Model 1895 was also chambered for the group. The smokeless powder .45-90 came out in 1895 and was discontinued about 1936.

General Comments: For many decades after its introduction, the .45-90 was a popular sporting cartridge. Once offered in a high-velocity loading with its standard 300-grain bullet at nearly 2000 fps and generating over 2,900 ft-lbs of energy, it was no doubt a good killer. With a 200 fps advantage over the high-velocity .45-70-300 load, it would shoot a bit flatter and give, perhaps, 50 yards more usable range.

The .45-90 case is practically identical to the .45-70, only longer. It is common practice to fire the .45-70 in these rifles, when the proper ammunition is not available. The .45-90 is adequate for any North American big game at moderate ranges. Use standard .458-inch diameter bullets for loading. For handloading, use only lead bullets to avoid excessive barrel wear.

.45-82, .45-85, .45-90 Winchester Loading Data and Factory Ballistics

Bullet (grains/type)	Powder	Grains	Velocity	Energy	Source/Comments
300 Lead	IMR 4198	38.0	1,530	1,565	NA
405 Lead	IMR 4198	32.0	1,410	1,790	Lyman No. 457483 gas checked
405 Cast	IMR 3031	40.0	1,500	2,023	Lyman No. 457124
300 Lead	FL		1,554	1,609	Factory load
350 Lead	FL		1,510	1,775	Factory load
405 Lead	FL		1,468	1,938	Factory load

.45-90 Sharps (Straight)
.45-100 Sharps (Straight)
.45-110 Sharps (Straight)
.45 Sharps Special

Historical Notes: When the Sharps company adopted the .45-caliber, it developed a variety of loads and case lengths. The first of these was introduced in mid-1876 (2 inches), and different case lengths were added late in 1876 (26/10 inches), and mid-1877 (24/10 inches). The principal difference in these cartridges was in bullet weight, powder charge, and case length. Other dimensions are the same. Some are heavy reloadable cases that had to be lengthened slightly to hold the same charge as the originals.

General Comments: The .45-100 (24/10 inches), .45-100 (26/10 inches), .45-90 (2¾ inches), .45-100 (2 inches) and the .45-110 (2 inches), all appear to be identical except for loading and/or case length. The .45-2¾-inch case, listed in the 1876 catalog, is otherwise unknown. There is no point listing all of these separately because of slight differences. However, the reader should know that each exists, as these are encountered in literature referring to Sharps rifles or loading data for them. The .45-90 Winchester case can be fired in any of the above chambered rifles by seating the bullet well out of the case. With cast bullets, .45-70 cartridges can be fired in these rifles. These cases can be made from Basic .45 cases, and many custom bullet moulds are currently available.

.45-90 Sharps (Straight), .45-100 Sharps (Straight), .45-110 Sharps (Straight)

Bullet (grains/type)	Powder	Grains	Velocity	Energy	Source/Comments
485 Lead	IMR 4198	24.0	1,300	1,822	Lyman No. 451112
550 Lead	FL		1,360	2,240	Factory load

.45-120 (3¼-inch) Sharps (Straight)
.45-125 (3¼-inch) Sharps (Straight)

Historical Notes: The .45-caliber 3¼-inch case is the largest Sharps cartridge of this caliber. Because of differences in case thickness, it usually came in two versions, the .45-120 and the .45-125. It was introduced, in 1878-'79 for the Sharps-Borchardt rifles, although there is no documentary evidence that the Sharps factory produced rifles in this chambering or any of the 3¼-inch cases, either .40, .45, or. 50. Original rifles in this chambering and original ammunition are collector's items. The Sharps Rifle Co. failed in 1881, so the big 3¼-inch case did not have a particularly long life, although other single-shot rifles could be (and were) chambered for it. In 1991-'92, Eldorado Cartridge made a run of cases and loaded this ammunition.

General Comments: The .45-120 Sharps is a very powerful black-powder cartridge adequate for any North American big game. It is usually considered one of the big buffalo cartridges, but it could not have participated in the slaughter of these animals to any great extent, because it arrived on the scene very late. Western buffalo hunting reached its peak in 1875-'76 and, by 1880, was on the wane. The last of the great herds was destroyed in 1884, and the need for the big, powerful buffalo rifles and cartridges passed with the last of these animals. The repeating rifle and the small-bore, high-velocity cartridge would, within a decade, give them the final shove into obsolescence. Most of the Sharps-Borchardt single-shot rifles in this and other chamberings have been rebarreled and made into modern small-bore varmint rifles.

.45-120 (3¼-inch) Sharps (Straight), .45-125 (3¼-inch) Sharps (Straight)

Bullet (grains/type)	Powder	Grains	Velocity	Energy	Source/Comments
485 Lead	IMR 4198	26.0	1,360	2,000	Lyman No. 451112
500 Cast	Black powder (FFg)	85.0	1,299	1,873	Lyman No. 457125
500 Lead	FL		1,520	2,561	Factory load

.45-100 Remington (Necked)

Historical Notes: The .45-100 Remington necked cartridge is listed in the 1880-'81 United States Cartridge Co. advertising sheet. It must have been a special-order chambering for Remington single-shot rifles, because there are no references to it concerning a specific rifle. It was also available as a special order item for some of the late Sharps rifles, for it is listed in the 1875 Sharps catalog as the .45-2¼-inch case.

General Comments: The .45-100 Remington uses a 2 -inch necked case, which appears to be identical to the .44-90 Remington except for the larger diameter and longer neck. As we have mentioned before, some shooters liked the straight case, while others preferred the necked case. All Sharps .45-caliber cases are straight. Perhaps Remington offered a choice to the man who wanted a necked .45-caliber cartridge. Since the U.S. Cartridge Co. shows this as loaded ammunition, at least a moderate demand must have existed. Shorter, .348 Winchester cases can be modified for use in these rifles.

.50-90 Sharps
.50-100 Sharps
.50-110 Sharps

Historical Notes: The 2½-inch .50-caliber Sharps was introduced in the 1872 Sharps catalog, which also listed the .50-70, among others. This was the heyday of buffalo hunting, and there was a strong demand for more potent game loads. The .50-90 offered more power. When western writers refer to the "Big 50" Sharps buffalo rifle and cartridge, this is the cartridge they mean, whether they know it or not. The longer Sharps (3¼-inch) .50-caliber cartridge did not arrive until after the buffalo were finished.

General Comments: Soon after its introduction, it was the "Big 50" or "Poison Slinger." The .50-90 is also called the .50-100 or .50-110, depending on what bullet weight and powder charge was used. Sharps discontinued its .40- and .50-caliber cartridges, except on special order, when it adopted the .45-caliber. Correct bullet diameter is .509-inch; several Lyman moulds in this size are available. One should not confuse various loadings of this cartridge with the .50-110 Winchester. Cases are readily available from several sources.

.50-90 Sharps, .50-100 Sharps, .50-110 Sharps Loading Data and Factory Ballistics

Bullet (grains/type)	Powder	Grains	Velocity	Energy	Source/Comments
365 Lead	AA 5744	37.0	1,652	2,210	Accurate Arms
422 Cast	IMR 4198	25.5	1,129	1,194	Lyman No. 515141
440 Lead	AA 5744	33.0	1,418	1,965	Accurate Arms
465 Lead	IMR 4198	30.0	1,320	1,804	Lyman No. 509133
550 Lead	AA 5744	30.0	1,275	1,985	Accurate Arms
335 Lead	FL		1,475	1,630	Factory load
473 Lead	FL		1,350	1,920	Factory load

.50-140 (3¼-inch) Sharps
.50-140 Winchester Express

Historical Notes: This is another special-order Sharps cartridge. It was introduced in 1880, but specific reference is lacking. Dimensions, except for length, are the same as the .50-90 Sharps. Some authorities believe rifles were made by rechambering .50-90s. None of the Sharps catalogs lists this cartridge or chambering.

General Comments: Winchester loaded the .50-140 with a 473-grain bullet, but many handloaders used the 700-grain paper-patched type, which could be purchased on a commercial basis. UMC also offered empty cases. Rifles chambered for this round are rare, and cartridges are collector's items. This was the most powerful of the Sharps "buffalo" cartridges, but it was introduced after most of the great herds were long gone. By 1880, buffalo hunting had almost ended, though it continued sporadically until 1884, when the last remaining herd was destroyed. Buffalo hunting for scattered individuals or small groups was not economically feasible. Sharps rifles used .509-inch diameter bullets, while Winchester used .512-inch diameter. The Basic .50 duplicates this case.

.50-140 Sharps, .50-140 Winchester Express Loading Data and Factory Ballistics

Bullet (grains/type)	Powder	Grains	Velocity	Energy	Source/Comments
422 Cast	IMR 4198	39.0	1,386	1,780	Lyman No. 515141
440 Lead	AA 5744	55.0	1,978	3,820	Accurate Arms
550 Lead	AA 5744	50.0	1,736	3,680	Accurate Arms
465 Lead	IMR 4198	33.0	1,450	2,190	Lyman No. 509133
700 Lead	AA 5744	48.0	1,529	3,635	Accurate Arms
473 Lead	FL		1,580	2,520	Winchester factory load
700 Lead	FL		1,355	2,850	Factory load

.50-100 Winchester
.50-105 Winchester
.50-110 Winchester
.50-110 Winchester High Velocity

Historical Notes: Here we have another example of different loadings in the same case causing confusion, as if they had been used in differently chambered guns. These are all variations of the original .50-110 Winchester, introduced in or before 1916 for the Model 1886 repeating rifle. The original .50-110 was cataloged in November 1887, the .50-100-450 version was offered in August 1895, and the High Velocity version came along sometime after 1910, but is shown in the 1916 catalog. This chambering was also available for the single-shot. Winchester listed cartridges until 1935.

General Comments: Originally a black-powder number, both a standard- and high-velocity smokeless powder version also were developed. The high-velocity load pushed the 300-grain bullet at 2225 fps and developed 3298 ft-lbs of energy at the muzzle. This was quite a potent number, being comparable to some of the British-designed African cartridges. For loading, use the Lyman No. 512139 (290-grain) hollow-point, No. 512138 (450-grain), or one of those bullets listed with the loading data. In spite of being a bit shorter, straightened .348 Winchester cases should work in most rifles.

.50-100, .50-105, .50-110 Winchester Loading Data and Factory Ballistics

Bullet (grains/type)	Powder	Grains	Velocity	Energy	Source/Comments
285 Lead	black powder (Fg)	110.0	1,600	1,710	Lyman No. 518144
285 Lead	IMR 4198	39.0	1,750	2,045	Lyman No. 518144
450 Lead	black powder (Fg)	100.0	1,475	2,190	Lyman No. 515141
300 Lead	FL		1,605	1,720	Winchester factory load, standard
300 Lead	FL		2,225	3,298	Winchester factory load, high velocity

.50-115 Bullard

Historical Notes: This, the largest of the Bullard cartridges, was introduced in 1886. It is unique in being both the first semi-rimmed and solid-head cartridge produced in the United States. It was chambered in the repeating Bullard rifles and possibly the single-shot. No other rifle makers used it.

General Comments: The .50-115 Bullard has a slight shoulder. With its larger body diameter, it is shorter than similar .50-caliber cartridges. It delivers the same performance as the longer .50-110 Winchester. It is another rare cartridge and would be difficult to duplicate out of some other case because of the semi-rim construction, although one could turn down the rim on the .470 Nitro Express to make usable cases.

.50-115 Bullard Loading Data and Factory Ballistics

Bullet (grains/type)	Powder	Grains	Velocity	Energy	Source/Comments
290 Lead	black powder (Fg)	115.0	1,539	1,580	Lyman No. 512139
290 Lead	IMR 4198	32.0	1,570	1,647	Lyman No. 512139
300 Lead	FL		1,539	1,583	Factory load

.50-95 Winchester
.50-95 Winchester Express

Historical Notes: The .50-95 is another of the short-necked cartridges developed for the Winchester 1876 Centennial Model repeater. This is the big bore of the group and was introduced in 1879. It was not as popular as some of the others and had a relatively short production life. The Colt New Lightning pump-action rifle was also available in this chambering.

General Comments: The .50-70 Government cartridge gained a certain following among buffalo hunters of the period, and the .50-95 is essentially an improved, repeating rifle version of that cartridge. Lyman hollow-point bullets No. 512137 (350 grains) or 512139 (290 grains) can be used for loading. It is advisable to stick to black-powder or low-pressure smokeless powder loads for the Model 76 Winchester; it is not a strong action, although entirely adequate for any black-powder load. Shortened .348 Winchester cases should work in most rifles, with very light loads. Cases from the .50-90 Sharps can be converted into perfectly fitting .50-95 WCF cases.

.50-95 Winchester Loading Data and Factory Ballistics

Bullet (grains/type)	Powder	Grains	Velocity	Energy	Source/Comments
285 Lead	IMR 4198	26.0	1,420	1,302	Lyman No. 518144
350 Lead	IMR 4198	23.0	1,350	1,420	Lyman No. 518145
300 Lead	FL		1,557	1,615	Winchester factory load

.50-50 Maynard (1882)

Historical Notes: This is the Maynard version of the .50 U.S. Carbine cartridge. It was used in the 1882 Model Maynard single-shot rifle.

General Comments: Some of the .50-50 Maynard cartridges have a smaller base diameter than that listed, but this is more a matter of manufacturing tolerance than design difference. Ammunition for old rifles of this chambering can be made by trimming .50-70 cases to the correct length. Powder charge is 50 to 60 grains of black powder, depending on bullet weight and type. Lyman No. 518144 (285-grain) or 518145 (350-grain) make good cast bullets for these old rifles. By shortening and possibly thinning the rim, .348 Winchester cases can be used in these rifles.

.50-50 Maynard Factory Ballistics

Bullet (grains/type)	Powder	Grains	Velocity	Energy	Source/Comments
350 Lead	FL		1,270	1,260	Factory load
400 Lead	FL		1,210	1,305	Factory load

.50 U.S. Carbine (.50 Carbine)

Historical Notes: Introduced as a carbine loading for the 1870 Trapdoor Springfield single-shot rifle or carbine, this is a centerfire modification of similar rimfire types developed during and immediately after the Civil War.

General Comments: The .50 Carbine round is a short-case variation of the standard .50-70 military cartridge. It can be fired in the rifle, but the standard .50-70 case is too long to fit in carbines. The carbine load consisted of a 400-grain bullet and 45 to 50 grains of Fg black powder. Lyman No. 518144 (285 grains) is a good bullet for loading these old shells. If your gun will not take the regular .50-70, just trim the case to the proper length. The 1870 Springfield has a weak action, so do not try any hot smokeless powder loads. Cases can be converted from .50-90 Sharps cases.

.50 U.S. Carbine Loading Data and Factory Ballistics

Bullet (grains/type)	Powder	Grains	Velocity	Energy	Source/Comments
400 Lead	IMR 4198	22.0	1,200	1,285	NA
400 Lead	FL		1,200	1,285	Factory load

.55-100 Maynard

Historical Notes: This cartridge is for the Maynard Improved Hunters Rifle No. 11, 1882-type. The .55-100 listed here was introduced the same year as the rifle. This is a little known and seldom encountered round. There was also a shotshell version.

General Comments: Some Maynard rifles were available as combination guns with interchangeable shot or rifled barrels. The .55-100 was one of the cartridges for this arrangement. Shells for both shot and bullet loading were advertised in its catalog. This is an odd bullet diameter (.551-inch), and no one makes a suitable mould. However, some of the .54-caliber musket balls or Minié bullets could probably be resized to work. Although significantly undersized at the base, for the low pressures of black-powder loading in this cartridge, the .470 Nitro Express case could probably be converted for safe use in one of these rifles.

.55-100 Maynard Factory Ballistics

Bullet (grains/type)	Powder	Grains	Velocity	Energy	Source/Comments
530 Lead	FL		1,410	2,340	Factory load

.58 Carbine (Berdan)

Historical Notes: This is the carbine version of the .58 Berdan Musket cartridge, introduced in 1869. The two differ only in case length and powder charge. The carbine case is 1½ inches long, whereas the musket case is 1¾ inches long. There is no other difference except the powder charge.

General Comments: Rifles for .58 Berdan cartridges are scarce items. Proper load for the carbine version is 40 to 45 grains of Fg black powder. Use Lyman No. 585213 (476-grain) bullet. For a good smokeless powder load, try 22 grains of Du Pont (IMR) 4198.

.58 Berdan Carbine Factory Ballistics

Bullet (grains/type)	Powder	Grains	Velocity	Energy	Source/Comments
530 Lead	FL		925	1,012	Factory load

.58 U.S. Musket (Berdan)

Historical Notes: Introduced in 1869 for use in the Berdan breech-loading conversion of the Springfield rifled musket, this cartridge was produced in both a rifle version (listed here) and a carbine version (listed above). Bullet weight is the same in both cartridges. This cartridge was never officially adopted by the United States armed forces, but was used experimentally. The centerfire cartridge evolved from earlier rimfire and inside-primed types. The Springfield muzzle-loading musket used a 500-grain bullet and 60 grains of powder for 950 to 1000 fps, before conversion to breech loading.

General Comments: Colonel Hiram Berdan, noted chiefly for his part in organizing and leading Berdan's Sharpshooters during the Civil War, was also a firearms designer of considerable importance in the post-war period. The breech-loading conversion system he designed was not used by the United States, but was adopted by Spain, Russia, and other European powers. His Berdan I (hinged cam-lock) and Berdan II (bolt-action) single-shot rifles were both officially adopted and used by Russia for a number of years. In 1895, his widow was awarded a judgment for patent infringement in a suit filed against the U.S. Government; the 1866 Springfield rifle used a breech system that copied essential features of the Berdan design.

In 1870, Col. Berdan developed the priming form that bears his name, the Berdan system that is used almost universally outside the United States. Evidently, Berdan was truly unappreciated by his homeland. The Boxer primer used here was invented by an Englishman who seems to have been equally unappreciated by his homeland. The .58 Musket cartridge is common, but arms in this chambering are scarce.

.58 U.S. Musket (Berdan) Loading Data and Factory Ballistics

Bullet (grains/type)	Powder	Grains	Velocity	Energy	Source/Comments
476 Lead	black powder (Fg)	80-85	1,230	1,608	Lyman No. 585213
476 Lead	IMR 4198	25.0	1,230	1,608	Lyman No. 585213
530 Lead	black powder (Fg)	80-85	1,100	1,420	Factory load

.70-150 Winchester

Historical Notes: The .70-150 cartridge appeared on the 1888 Winchester cartridge boards. Some say it was an advertising novelty for display only. According to Paul Foster (*Gun Digest*, 1952, 6th Edition, p. 173), the only gun chambered for it was a specially made Model 1887 shotgun with rifled barrel. It was never produced on a commercial basis.

General Comments: The .70-150 is based on the brass 12-gauge shotshell shortened and necked slightly. It is mentioned only to complete the record. No guns were produced for it; therefore, no loading or ballistics data is available. However, the case would hold about 150 grains of powder, and bullets of this caliber could weigh anywhere from 600 to 900 grains. The muzzle velocity this combination could develop would be approximately 1,300 to 1,500 fps, depending on bullet weight. This would suggest a muzzle energy of about 4,000 ft-lbs!

.70-150 Winchester Ballistics

Bullet (grains/type)	Powder	Grains	Velocity	Energy	Source/Comments
600 Lead			1,500	3,000	Theoretical ballistics
900 Lead			1,300	3,380	Theoretical ballistics

Dimensional Data

Cartridge	Case	Bullet Dia.	Neck Dia.	Shoulder Dia.	Base Dia.	Rim Dia.	Rim Thick.	Case Length	Ctge. Length	Primer	Page
.219 Zipper	A	.224	.252	.364	.421	.497	.058	1.94	2.26	L	165
.222 Remington Magnum	C	.224	.253	.355	.375	.375	.041	1.85	2.21	S	166
.22 Accelerator	A	.224	.30?	Various	Various	Various	UNK/NA	Various	Various	UNK/NA	166
.228 Weatherby Magnum	E	.224	.395	UNK/NA	.455	.522	UNK/NA	1.76	2.24	S	167
.22-15-60 Stevens	B	.226	.243	UNK/NA	.265	.342	UNK/NA	2.01	2.26	S	168
.22 Winchester Center Fire (WCF)	A	.228	.241	.278	.295	.342	.058	1.39	1.61	S	168
.22 Extra Long (Maynard)**	B	.228	.252	UNK/NA	.252	.310	UNK/NA	1.17	1.41	S-0***	169
.22 Savage High Power	A	.228	.252	.360	.416	.500	.056	2.05	2.51	L	169
6mm Bench Rest Remington	C	.243	.263	.457	.466	.468	.045	1.52	2.19	S	170
.244 Remington (.236 Navy)	C	.243	.276	.429	.470	.472	.045	2.23	2.90	L	171
6mm Lee Navy	C	.244	.278	.402	.445	.448	UNK/NA	2.35	3.11	L	171
.25-20 Marlin	A	.257	.274	.329	.349	.405	UNK/NA	1.33	UNK/NA	S	172
.25-20 Single Shot	A	.257	.275	.296	.315	.378	UNK/NA	1.63	1.90	S	172
.25-21 Stevens	B	.257	.280	UNK/NA	.300	.376	UNK/NA	2.05	2.30	S	173
.25 Remington	C	.257	.280	.355	.420	.421	.045	2.04	2.54	L	173
.25-36 Marlin	A	.257	.281	.358	.416	.499	.056	2.12	2.50	S	174
.25-25 Stevens	B	.257	.282	UNK/NA	.323	.376	UNK/NA	2.37	2.63	S	174
.256 Winchester Magnum	A	.257	.283	.370	.378	.440	.055	1.30	1.53	S	175
.256 Newton	C	.264	.290	.430	.469	.473	.045	2.44	3.40	L	175
6.5mm Remington Magnum	E	.264	.300	.490	.512	.532	.047	2.17	2.80	L	176
7x61mm Sharpe & Hart Super	E	.284	.320	.478	.515	.532	.048	2.40	3.27	L	177
.275 H&H Magnum	E	.284	.375	.375	.513	.532	.048	2.50	3.30	L	177
.28-30-120 Stevens	B	.285	.309	UNK/NA	.357	.412	UNK/NA	2.51	2.82	L	178
.30 Remington	C	.307	.328	.402	.420	.421	.045	2.03	2.525	L	178
.30-30 Wesson	A	.308	.329	.330	.380	.440	UNK/NA	1.66	2.50	L	179
.30 USA/.30-40 Rimless	C	.308	.333	.417	.454	.456	.054	2.31	3.10	L	179
.30-03 Springfield/Gov't.	C	.308	.340	.441	.470	.473	.045	2.54	3.34	L	180
.30 Newton/.30 Adolph Express	C	.308	.340	.491	.523	.525	UNK/NA	2.52	3.35	L	180
.32-40 Remington	A	.309	.330	.358	.453	.535	UNK/NA	2.13	3.25	S	181
.303 Savage/.301 Savage	A	.308/.311	.334 (.3322)	.408 (.4135)	.439	.501	.058	2.00 (2.015)	2.52	L	181
.32-20 Marlin	A	.312	.326	.338	.353	.405	UNK/NA	1.32	UNK/NA	S	182
.32-30 Remington	A	.312	.332	.357	.378	.437	UNK/NA	1.64	2.01	S	182
.32-35 Stevens & Maynard	B	.312	.339	UNK/NA	.402	.503	UNK/NA	1.88	2.29	S	183
.32-40 Bullard	A	.315	.332	.413	.453	.510	UNK/NA	1.85	2.26	S	183
.32 Long, CF*	B	.317	.318	UNK/NA	.321	.369	UNK/NA	0.82	1.35	S	184
.32 Ballard Extra Long*	B	.317	.318	UNK/NA	.321	.369	UNK/NA	1.24	1.80	S	184
.32-40 Ballard & Winchester	B	.320	.338	UNK/NA	.424	.506	.058	2.13	2.59	L	184
.32 Winchester SL (WSL)	H	.320	.343	UNK/NA	.346	.388	UNK/NA	1.28	1.88	S	185
.32 Remington	C	.320	.344	.396	.420	.421	.045	2.04	2.57	L	186
.32 Ideal	B	.323	.344	UNK/NA	.348	.411	UNK/NA	1.77	2.25	S	186
.33 Winchester	A	.333	.365	.443	.508	.610	.065	2.11	2.80	L	187
.35 Winchester SL (WSL)	H	.351	.374	UNK/NA	.378	.405	.045	1.14	1.64	S	187
.351 Winchester SL (WSL)	H	.351	.374	.378	.407	1.38	.045	1.91	UNK/NA	S	188
.350 Griffin & Howe Mag.	E	.357	.382	.446	.511	.528	.048	2.848	3.64	L	188
.35 Winchester	A	.358	.378	.412	.457	.539	UNK/NA	2.41	3.16	L	189
.35 Newton	C	.358	.383	.498	.523	.525	2.52	3.35	12		189
.38-45 Stevens	B	.363	.395	UNK/NA	.455	.522	UNK/NA	1.76	2.24	S	190
.35-30 Maynard (1882)	B	.359	.395	UNK/NA	.400	.494	UNK/NA	1.63	2.03	S	190
.35-40 Maynard (1882)	B	.360	.390	UNK/NA	.400	.492	UNK/NA	2.06	2.53	S	191
.35-30 Maynard (1865)	B	.370	.397	UNK/NA	.408	.771/ 1.076	.037	1.53	1.98	ext. primed	191
.38-40 Remington-Hepburn	B	.372	.395	UNK/NA	.454	.537	UNK/NA	1.77	2.32	S	191
.38-45 Bullard	A	.373	.397	.448	.454	.526	UNK/NA	1.80	2.26	S	192
.38 Long, CF*	B	.375	.378	UNK/NA	.379	.441	UNK/NA	1.03	1.45	S	192
.38 Ballard Extra Long*	B	.375	.378	UNK/NA	.379	.441	UNK/NA	1.63	2.06	S	193

Dimensional Data

Cartridge	Case	Bullet Dia.	Neck Dia.	Shoulder Dia.	Base Dia.	Rim Dia.	Rim Thick.	Case Length	Ctge. Length	Primer	Page
.38-35 Stevens	B	.375	.402	UNK/NA	.403	.492	UNK/NA	1.62	2.43	S	193
.38-50 Maynard (1882)	B	.375	.415	UNK/NA	.421	.500	.069	1.97	2.38	S	193
.38-50 Remington-Hepburn	B	.376	.392	UNK/NA	.454	.535	UNK/NA	2.23	3.07	S	194
.38-50 Ballard Everlasting	B	.376	.395	UNK/NA	.425	.502	UNK/NA	2.00	2.72	S	194
.38-90 Winchester Express	A	.376	.395	.470	.477	.558	UNK/NA	3.25	3.70	L	195
.38-56 Winchester	A	.376	.403	.447	.506	.606	.065	2.10	2.50	L	195
.38-72 Winchester	A	.378	.397	.427	.461	.519	UNK/NA	2.58	3.16	L	196
.40-70 Sharps (Straight)	B	.403	.420	UNK/NA	.453	.533	.078	2.50	3.18	L	196
.38-70 Winchester	A	.378	.403	.421	.506	.600	UNK/NA	2.31	2.73	L	196
.40-50 Sharps (Straight)	B	.403	.421	UNK/NA	.454	.554	.078	1.88	2.63	B-1	197
.40-50 Sharps (Necked)	A	.403	.424	.489	.501	.580	UNK/NA	1.72	2.37	B-1	197
.40-85/.40-90 Ballard Everlasting	B	.403	.425	UNK/NA	.477	.545	UNK/NA	2.94	3.81	S	198
.40-60 Marlin	B	.403	.425	UNK/NA	.504	.604	UNK/NA	2.11	2.55	S	198
.40-60 Colt	A	.403	.425	.445	.504	.600		2.31	2.73	L	199
.40-90 Sharps (Straight)	B	.403	.425	UNK/NA	.477	.546	UNK/NA	3.25	4.06	B-1	199
.40-65 Ballard Everlasting	B	.403	.435	UNK/NA	.508	.600	UNK/NA	2.38	2.55	B-1	200
.40-90/.40-100 Sharps (Necked)	A	.403	.435	.500	.506	.602	UNK/NA	2.63	3.44	B-1	200
.40-70 Sharps (Necked)	A	.403	.426	.500	.503	.595	UNK/NA	2.25	3.02	L	200
.40-110 Winchester Express	A	.403	.428	.485	.565	.651	UNK/NA	3.25	3.63	L	201
.40-63/.40-70 Ballard Everlasting	B	.403	.430	UNK/NA	.471	.555	UNK/NA	2.38	2.55	S	201
.40-60 Winchester	A	.404	.425	.445	.506	.630	UNK/NA	1.87	2.10	S	202
.40-70 Winchester	A	.405	.430	.496	.504	.604	UNK/NA	2.40	2.85	L	202
.40-70 Remington	A	.405	.434	.500	.503	.595	UNK/NA	2.25	3.00	L	202
.40-65 Winchester	B	.406	.423	UNK/NA	.504	.604	UNK/NA	2.10	2.48	L	203
.40-72 Winchester	B	.406	.431	UNK/NA	.460	.518	UNK/NA	2.60	3.15	L	203
.401 Winchester (WSL)	H	.406	.428	UNK/NA	.429	.457	.055	1.50	2.00	L	204
.40-82 Winchester (WCF)	A	.406	.428	.448	.502	.604	.060	2.40	2.77	L	204
.40-70 Peabody	A	.408	.428	.551	.581	.662		1.76	2.85	L	204
.40-90 Peabody "What Cheer"	A	.408	.433	.546	.586	.659	UNK/NA	2.00	3.37	B-1	205
.405 Winchester	B	.412	.436	UNK/NA	.461	.543	.075	2.58	3.18	L	205
.40-90 Bullard	A	.413	.430	.551	.569	.622	UNK/NA	2.04	2.55	L	206
.40-75 Bullard	B	.413	.432	UNK/NA	.505	.606	UNK/NA	2.09	2.54	S	206
.40-40 Maynard (1882)	B	.415	.450	UNK/NA	.456	.532	UNK/NA	1.78	2.32	S	207
.40-60 Maynard (1882)	B	.417	.448	UNK/NA	.454	.533	UNK/NA	2.20	2.75	S	207
.40-70 Maynard (1882)	B	.417	.450	UNK/NA	.451	.535	UNK/NA	2.42	2.88	B-1	208
.44 Evans Long/.440-40 Straight	B	.419	.434	UNK/NA	.449	.509	UNK/NA	1.54	2.00	L	208
.44 Evans Short	B	.419	.439	UNK/NA	.440	.513	UNK/NA	0.99	1.44	S	208
.44 Henry Center Fire Flat	B	.423	.443	UNK/NA	.445	.523	UNK/NA	0.88	1.36	S	209
.44 Game Getter/.44-40 Marlin/ .44 Colt Lightning	A	.427	.443	.458	.471	.520	.065	1.31	Varies	L	209
.44-40 Extra Long	A	.428	.442	.463	.468	.515	UNK/NA	1.58	1.96	S	210
.44 Long Center Fire (Ballard)*	B	.439	.440	UNK/NA	.441	.506	UNK/NA	1.09	1.65	S	210
.44 Extra Long Center Fire (Ballard)*	B	.439	.441	UNK/NA	.441	.506	UNK/NA	1.63	2.10	S	210
.44 Wesson Extra Long*	B	.440	.441	UNK/NA	.441	.510	UNK/NA	1.63	2.19	S	211
.44-100/.44-90/.44-110 Creedmoor	B	.442	.465	UNK/NA	.503	.568	UNK/NA	2.60	3.97	L	211
.44-90 Rem. Special (Necked)	A	.442	.466	.504	.520	.628	.075	2.44	3.08	L	212
.44-95/.44-100 Peabody "What Cheer"	A	.443	.465	.550	.580	.670	UNK/NA	2.31	3.32	B-1	212
.44-70 Maynard (1882)	B	.445	.466	UNK/NA	.499	.601	UNK/NA	2.21	2.87	B-1	213
.44-100 Ballard	B	.445	.485	UNK/NA	.498	.605	.080	2.81	3.25	L	213
.44-75 Ballard Everlasting	B	.445	.487	UNK/NA	.497	.603	UNK/NA	2.50	3.00	B-2	214
.44-100 Wesson	B	.445	UNK/NA	UNK/NA	.515-.520	.605-.610	UNK/NA	3.38	3.85	L	214
.44-85 Wesson	B	.446	UNK/NA	UNK/NA	.515-520	.605-.610	UNK/NA	2.88	3.31	L	214
.44-77 Sharps & Remington	A	.446	.467	.502	.516	.625	UNK/NA	2.25	3.05	L-B1	215
.44-90 Sharps (Necked)	A	.446	.468	.504	.517	.625	.065	2.63	3.30	B-1	215
.44-60 Sharps & Remington (Necked)	A	.447	.464	.502	.515	.630	UNK/NA	1.88	2.55	L-B1	215

Dimensional Data

Cartridge	Case	Bullet Dia.	Neck Dia.	Shoulder Dia.	Base Dia.	Rim Dia.	Rim Thick.	Case Length	Ctge. Length	Primer	Page
.45-50 Peabody (Sporting)	A	.454	.478	.508	.516	.634	2.08	2.08	2.08	UNK/NA	216
.44-60 Winchester/ Peabody "Creedmoor"	A	.447	.464	.502	.518	.628	UNK/NA	1.89	2.56	B-1	217
.45-75 Winchester (Centennial)	A	.454	.478	.547	.559	.616	UNK/NA	1.89	2.25	L	217
.45-60 Winchester	B	.454	.479	UNK/NA	.508	.629	UNK/NA	1.89	2.15(?)	L	217
.45-100 Ballard	B	.454	.487	UNK/NA	.498	.597	UNK/NA	2.81	3.25	L	218
.45-125 Winchester/.45 (Express)	A	.456	.470	.521	.533	.601		3.25	3.63	L	218
.45-70 Van Choate	B	.457	UNK/NA	Same as 45-70, see Chapter 1	UNK/NA	UNK/NA	UNK/NA	2.25	2.91	L	219
.45-75/.45-70 Sharps 2 1/10-inch (Straight)	B	.457	UNK/NA	Same as 45-70, see Chapter 1	UNK/NA	UNK/NA	UNK/NA	2.10	2.90	L	219
.45-82/.45-85/.45-90 Winchester & .45-90 Winchester High Velocity	B	.457	.477	UNK/NA	.501	.597	.065	2.40	2.88	L	220
.45-90/.45-100/.45-110 Sharps (24/10, 26/10, 2¾, 27/8-inch) Straight	B	.458	.489	.500	.597	.065	2.40, 2.60, 2.75, 2.87	2.85, 3.00	18-20	B-1	220
.45-120/.45-125 (31/4-inch) Sharps	B	.458	.490	UNK/NA	.506	.597	.065	3.25	4.16	L	221
.45-100 Remington (Necked)	A	.458	.490	.550	.558	.645	UNK/NA	2.63	3.26	L	221
.50-90/.50-100/.50-110 Sharps	B	.509	.528	UNK/NA	.565	.663	.060	2.50	3.20	L	221
.50-140 (31/4") Sharps & Winchester	B	.509/ .512	.528	UNK/NA	.565	.665	.060	3.25	3.94	L	222
.50-100/50-105/.50-110 Winchester/.50-110 Winchester High Velocity	B	.512	.534	UNK/NA	.551	.607	.063	2.40	2.75	L	223
.50-115 Bullard	G	.512	.547	.577	.585	.619	UNK/NA	2.19	2.56	L	223
.50-95 Winchester/Win. Express	A	.513	.533	.553	.562	.627	UNK/NA	1.94	2.26	L	223
.50-50 Maynard (1882)	B	.513	.535	UNK/NA	.563	.661	UNK/NA	1.37	1.91	L	224
.50 U.S. Carbine	B	.515	.535	UNK/NA	.560	.660	UNK/NA	UNK/NA	UNK/NA	B-1	224
.55-100 Maynard 1882	B	.551	.582		.590	.718	UNK/NA	1.94	2.56	L	225
.58 Carbine (Berdan)	B	.589	.625	UNK/NA	.640	.740	UNK/NA	UNK/NA	UNK/NA	B-2	225
.58 U.S. Musket (Berdan)	B	.589	.625	UNK/NA	.646	.740	.062	1.75	2.15	B-1	226
.70-150 Winchester	A	.705	.725	.790	.805	.870	UNK/NA	2.18	2.63	L	226

Case Type: A = Rimmed, bottleneck. B = Rimmed, straight. C = Rimless, bottleneck. D = Rimless, straight. E = Belted, bottleneck. F = Belted, straight. G = Semi-rimmed, bottleneck. H = Semi-rimmed, straight. I = Rebated, bottleneck. J = Rebated, straight. K = Rebated, belted bottleneck. L = Rebated, belted straight. Primer Type: S = Small rifle (.175"). SP = Small pistol (.175"). L = Large rifle (.210"). LP = Large pistol (.210"). 50 BMG = CCI-35/VihtaVuori-110/RWS-8212. B-1 = Berdan #1. B-2 = Berdan #2. Other Codes: V = OAL depends upon bullet used. V = Rifling twist varies, depending upon bullet and application. Belt/Rim Diameter. Unless otherwise noted, all dimensions in inches. UNK/NA = Unknown/Not Applicable

* Cartridges so marked used an outside lubricated bullet when originally introduced, and this was of a diameter about the same as the neck or shell mouth. Later, inside lubricated loadings used a much smaller diameter bullet than listed, usually with a long, hollow base. Before the recent advent of effective wax-type lubricants, outside lubricated bullets were never very popular or effective. The inside lubricated hollow-base bullets were cleaner to handle and use and the hollow base was intended to expand the bullet to fit the larger barrel. This never worked very well and accuracy suffered.

** Original 22-10-45 Maynard case length was 1.25".

*** This is a black-powder primer smaller than the small rifle or pistol size. It has not been made for many years.

Note on black-powder primers: Not all companies used the same primer type or size in the same cartridge or length case. For example, the 45-70 or its equivalent was usually loaded with the large rifle size primer. However, the Marlin version had the small rifle size and Sharps Co. ammunition had Berdan primers. Primer type and size listed is what appears to have been the most general size and type used. Unless otherwise noted, all dimensions are in inches. So-called 44-caliber black-powder rifles had groove diameters varying from about .446-inch to about .460-inch. Most use bullets of about .448-inch to .452-inch diameter.

Wildcat Cartridges
(Rifle & Handgun)

Wildcat cartridges have been around for a long time; at least 100 years. Originally, wildcats were developed by some gunsmith or individual experimenter attempting to improve on the ballistics of a commercial cartridge to fulfill a personal or special requirement, and possibly to increase the effective range for varmint shooting or the knockdown power on big game. I do not know who coined the term "wildcat" to describe these efforts, but, for our purposes, we will define wildcat cartridges as cartridge designs and loads not available from major manufacturers as over-the-counter ammunition, or cartridges not generally available even in custom loadings. To shoot wildcat cartridges, you have to load them yourself or contract that loading with a custom handloader or ammunition producer.

A great proliferation of wildcat cartridge designs has occurred in the past 30 years or so, some of those quite good and some not. In some instances, the wildcat filled, or was perceived to fill, some niche not accommodated by commercially available ammunition. Good examples include the .35 Whelen and the .45 Alaskan. The former lingered in wildcat limbo for a generation before being commercially adopted. The latter, though certainly useful, will likely never achieve commercialization, chiefly because the only rifle appropriate for it was long ago discontinued. (As an aside, Ruger offered its short-barreled Super Redhawk Alaskan in .45 Alaskan for a while, but the 2012 website no longer shows this revolver offered in this cartridge.) In other instances, the only basis for a wildcat was to offer ballistics previously unavailable in a certain type of firearm, such as the entire genre of current Thompson/Center custom chamberings. Benchresters have long experimented with wildcats, creating designs in which the only criterion was potential inherent accuracy. These wildcats are built to precisely fit a single firearm and, though these are nominally of the same specifications, cannot be interchanged in other so-chambered firearms with impunity.

Several new entries describe recent developments, while others describe Australian wildcats from the post-World War II era that are almost unknown in the United States. Still others describe wildcats of historical importance that have not previously appeared here. Some older wildcats of historical or developmental interest are retained because many younger or new shooters do not know that these exist. Such ignorance is probably one reason for the development of wildcats that are just a variation on a theme and do not offer anything new.

It is quite impossible to include every known wildcat cartridge, because so many exist. Previous editions claimed the number to be in excess of 300. Your current editor suspects the number is now well into the thousands, which seems to be substantiated by Dave Kiff of Pacific Precision reamer manufacturing company, who holds drawings for more than 6,000 distinctly named wildcats!

Wildcat cartridges tend to be regional in nature—what is popular in one area may be completely unknown in the rest of the country—so some viable numbers will never find representation in these pages. Even those wildcats that have been written up and published in gun magazines may have only a limited following. Probably the best indicator of the popularity of a cartridge is the number of loading die sets sold in that particular type. RCBS in Oroville, Calif., is the world's largest manufacturer of wildcat loading and case-forming dies. They make up special-order die sets to customer specifications at relatively modest prices. Quite a few wildcat cartridges have retained sufficient popularity over the years to warrant RCBS carrying those as standard stocked items. Less popular numbers are available on special order, subject to minor delays in delivery.

For many years, the trend in wildcat cartridge development has been toward increased case capacity and higher velocity. Currently, wildcat cartridge design and chambering simply for the sake of improved performance has declined from enthusiastic to almost nonexistent. One explanation for this is a maturity among shooters. We have grown into the realization that there really are no magic cartridges. Within safe pressure parameters, no wildcat chambering in any standard case chambered in any standard gun is going to deliver ballistics significantly different from what is already available in commercial form. Of course, some will disagree, and one must admit that exceptions always exist. However, it is safe to say that the vast majority of recent wildcatting has been directed toward filling target-shooting and gun-type chambering niches, e.g., the aforementioned Thompson/Center chamberings.

Wildcat cartridges are made in a number of ways, from the simple to the more complex. Wildcats can be grouped into basic categories: those with increased case capacity, created by modifying an existing cartridge; those with unusual case capacity for bore diameter, made by necking up or down a case that is larger or smaller than any common commercial example; those with unusual bullet sizes, created by necking an existing case to accept a different size bullet; and those with unusually close cartridge-to-chamber tolerances, building the rifle and loading dies to match the custom handloaded ammunition. Most recently, we have seen entire new lines of unusually short cases, based upon an unusually large diameter case, which, for any given capacity, provides a shorter cartridge and powder column, and possibly superior accuracy.

Let us look at some examples. A very early wildcat became the .22 Hornet. In this instance, no change in the case was required, since the cartridge was based on the .22 WCF black-powder cartridge and simply loaded with smokeless powder and jacketed 45-grain bullets designed for the 5.5mm Velo Dog revolver cartridge. Early wildcats were rather simple and are good examples of simply necking a standard commercial cartridge case either up or down. The .35 Whelen is an example of the former, the .25-06 the latter, both being based on the standard .30-06 case. Improved cartridges are examples of increasing performance in the original case in an uncomplicated manner. Here, the standard cartridge is fired in the Improved chamber, from which it emerges with less body taper and a sharper shoulder. This increases powder capacity and general reloading of the Improved case provides improved performance over the standard-case load. The Ackley Improved .250 Savage and .257 Roberts chamberings, along with the various improved versions of the .300 H&H Magnum, are good examples of improved wildcats that result in a noticeable, but still modest, ballistic enhancement over the original cartridge. The same cannot be said of some of the others.

One advantage of Improved chambers is that these will also chamber and fire factory cartridges designed for the original chambering. This is very handy if you happen to run out of Improved reloads in some place far from home. This practice will, of course, result in a slight velocity reduction. Another potentially significant advantage, such as in the .35 Whelen, is improved headspace control.

Some readers might think that someone who develops a popular wildcat eventually adopted by one of the big commercial ammunition companies will make a lot of money. Not true. He will be lucky if he even gets credit as the originator. No major company is going to adopt a wildcat cartridge until it has a long-term, proven record. By that time, it will have been around so long it will fall into the category of general public knowledge, and no one will have any claim to it. It is also futile to patent a cartridge design, because any slight variation becomes a new cartridge. I mention this because occasionally we hear from someone who thinks developing a "new" cartridge is the road to fame and fortune.

A good number of commercial cartridges originated as wildcats. Some prime examples are: .17 Remington, .22 Hornet, .22-250 Remington, .243 Winchester, .244 Remington, .257 Roberts, .25-06 Remington, .280 Remington, 7mm-08 Remington, 7-30 Waters, and the .35 Whelen. Moreover, a large number of commercial cartridges are simply variations of what were originally wildcats themselves. These include practically all of the American 7mm and .30-caliber factory magnum cartridges. Remington has been the leader in adopting wildcat designs, and this has been very beneficial to the shooting sports. The .300 Whisper / AAC Blackout is a perfect example.

Working with wildcat cartridges is very instructive. Those of us who have done so have learned a great deal about the relationship between case size and configuration, bore diameter, and powder combustion. One of the areas that has provided some real surprises is in working with short rifle cartridges (case lengths of around 1½ inches). This is a trend begun by the Germans during World War II, with the 7.92x33mm assault rifle cartridge, which uses a 1.3-inch long case. The Russians recognized a good idea when they saw one and so developed the 7.62x39mm (M43) cartridge, with a case 1.52 inches long.

As a group, wildcatters tend to be advanced handloaders and true devotees of the shooting sports. Wildcat rifles and cartridges are also a good topic of conversation around the hunting campfire, and, if you happen to have a rifle so chambered, it sort of sets you apart as someone who is at least a little above average in gun knowledge. However, one should never enter lightly into the wildcat arena, because this usually entails a custom-built rifle, plus the investment in forming and loading dies. Rifles chambered for wildcat cartridges are much more difficult to trade or sell in the event you decide that what you have is not exactly what you want. Nevertheless, individuals who have developed wildcat cartridges have spurred major advances to our knowledge of internal ballistics and have spawned a number of very fine cartridges that eventually entered the commercial line. Large companies such as Federal, Remington, and Winchester are, by nature, rather conservative and disinclined to market something that will not sell. It is in the area of innovation that the wildcatters make their major contributions, and we have not seen the end yet. No telling what great ideas will come to fruition over the next decade or so.

— F.C.B., with additional text by Stan Skinner

Pocket Manual for Shooters and Reloaders by Parker O. Ackley. Salt Lake City, 1964.

Practical Dope on the .22 by F.C. Ness. New York and Harrisburg, PA, 1947.

Small Game and Varmint Rifles by Henry F. Stebbins. New York city, 1950.

Twenty-Two Caliber Varmint Rifles by Charles S. Landis. Plantersville, SC, 1947.

Why Not Load Your Own? by Col. Townsend Whelen. Washington, DC, 1949 and later eds.

Wildcat Cartridges by Richard F. Simmons. New York city, 1947.

Woodchucks and Woodchuck Rifles by C.S. Landis. New York city, 1951. 10 Eichelberger Long Rifle

15th Edition Update

There is always plenty of development in the Wildcat chapter, and it's always interesting to see if a one-off round can find a home with a certain maker, prove itself as a Proprietary round, then move into the broader Current American Sporting Cartridges chapter.

This time around, we've added thirteen new offerings that shooters and collectors may find of interest: .17 Javelina, 6.5 SAUM, .257 Condor, 7mm-300 Weatherby Magnum, 300 Raptor, .30 ARX, and .300 ICL Grizzly, .458 Hubel Express, .458 B&M EX, .475 B&M, .499 Hubel Express No. 2, .585 Hubel Express, .700 Hubel Express.

The .17 Javelina finds acceptance among a merry band of pipsqueak shooters who love to tinker at the lower edge of bullet-weight ranges. It has the enviable advantage of having a great name and the pedigree of highly accurate rifles built to shoot it. At the top end of the spectrum, the Hubels are big for bigness's sake — how much powder can be crammed into various containers and still fit in a shoulderable firearm? Ed Hubel continues to tinker with 50 BMG and 20mm cannon cases to find out. — W.T.W.

.10 Eichelberger Long Rifle

Historical Notes:	The .10 Eichelberger Long Rifle is the smallest wildcat cartridge known to exist at this time. Pioneering sub-caliber experimenter Bill Eichelberger created this wildcat in 1999 by necking down .22 Long Rifle cases to accept a bullet measuring .103 inch. Over the years, Eichelberger crafted more than 10,000 cartridge cases for the .10 Eichelberger Long Rifle and its bigger siblings in .12-, .14-, and .17-caliber. As a rimfire cartridge, each .10 Eichelberger Long Rifle case, after forming, loading, and bullet seating, can be fired only one time.
General Comments:	The .10 Eichelberger Long Rifle cartridge uses Winchester .22 Long Rifle brass as the parent case. Since this cartridge is a rimfire, careful and safe reloading practices are needed to remove the bullet from the internally primed .22 Long Rifle case. Using a series of case forming dies, the live (primed) brass is necked down to .10-caliber and given a 25-degree shoulder—resulting in a diminutive bottleneck shape. After many repetitions of necking down and annealing, the case is trimmed to the final overall length dimension. To avoid excess pressure, extreme care is appropriate in measuring the tiny powder charge. The cartridge works well with 21-inch barrels having a rifling twist of 1:7. Suitable actions to rebarrel and chamber for the .10 Eichelberger Long Rifle include modern .22 LR bolt-actions and single-shots, such as the Thompson/Center Contender and G2. SSK Industries (www.sskindustries.com) can supply Contender barrels and .10-caliber bullets for this cartridge on a special-order basis.

.10 Eichelberger LR Loading Data

Bullet (grains)	Powder	Grains	Velocity	Energy	Source/Comments
7.2	AA9	1.8	2,160	74	Bill Eichelberger

.10 Eichelberger Pup

Historical Notes: In the diminutive world of experimenter Bill Eichelberger, no cartridge case seems too small to transform into a sub-caliber wildcat. The .10 Eichelberger Pup, built on the less common Cooper CCM brass around 1999, can drive .10-caliber bullets weighing 7.2 grains at velocities over 3600 fps. The .10 Eichelberger Pup is intended for small game at ranges approaching 75 to 100 yards. With quality barrels, bullets, and shooting techniques, it is capable of MOA or better performance.

General Comments: The .10 Eichelberger Pup uses .22 Cooper CCM brass as its parent case. The brass is necked down in a series of dies to accept .103-inch diameter bullets and given a 30-degree shoulder. After many repetitions of necking down and annealing, the case is trimmed to the final overall length dimension. The cartridge uses Federal No. 205 primers. To avoid excess pressure, extreme care is required in measuring the tiny powder charge. The cartridge works well with 21-inch barrels having a rifling twist of 1:7. Suitable actions for the .10 Eichelberger Pup include the Thompson/Center Contender and G2. SSK Industries (www.sskindustries.com) can supply Contender barrels and .10-caliber bullets for this cartridge on a special-order basis.

.10 Eichelberger Pup Loading Data

Bullet (grains)	Powder	Grains	Velocity	Energy	Source/Comments
7.2	AA9	3.5	3,230	160	Bill Eichelberger
7.2	2400	3.9	3,615	208	Bill Eichelberger
10	AA1680	3.9	3,134	218	Bill Eichelberger

.10 Eichelberger Squirrel

Historical Notes: In a decades-long quest to explore sub-calibers in small cases, Bill Eichelberger found ways to transform brass cases most folks would consider small into tiny powerhouses. His pre-1999 era .10 Squirrel comes very close to breaking the 4000 fps threshold with 7.2-grain, .103-inch diameter bullets. The .10 Squirrel is the fastest .10-caliber cartridge created by Eichelberger. It is suitable for small game at ranges up to 100 yards. Eichelberger also designed .12-caliber and .14-caliber versions of this cartridge.

General Comments: The .10 Squirrel uses rimmed Remington .22 Hornet brass as its parent case. The brass is necked down in a series of steps to accept .103-inch diameter bullets and given a 30-degree shoulder. After many repetitions of necking down and annealing, the case is trimmed to the final overall length dimension. The cartridge uses Federal No. 205 primers. To avoid excess pressure, extreme care is required in measuring the tiny powder charge. The cartridge works well with 21-inch barrels having a rifling twist of 1:7. Suitable actions for the .10 Squirrel include the Thompson/Center Contender and G2. SSK Industries (www.sskindustries.com) can supply Contender barrels and 10-caliber bullets for this cartridge on a special-order basis.

.10 Squirrel Loading Data

Bullet (grains)	Powder	Grains	Velocity	Energy	Source/Comments
7.2	Win 748	6.5	3,924	246	Bill Eichelberger
10	H380	6.4	3,290	240	Bill Eichelberger

.12 Eichelberger LR

Historical Notes: In a 21-inch barrel, the .12 Eichelberger Long Rifle can zip a 10-grain .12-caliber bullet to faster than 2800 fps—blistering performance, compared to an ordinary .22 Long Rifle cartridge. Another of Bill Eichelberger's sub-caliber wildcat cartridges dating back to 1982, the .12 Eichelberger Long Rifle was designed for short- to mid-range small game and target shooting. Eichelberger also designed .10-caliber and .14-caliber versions of this cartridge.

General Comments: The .12 Eichelberger Long Rifle cartridge uses Winchester .22 Long Rifle brass as the parent case. Since this cartridge is a rimfire, careful and safe reloading practices are needed to remove the bullet from the internally primed .22 Long Rifle case. Using a series of case forming dies, the live (primed) brass is necked down to accept .123-inch diameter bullets and given a 25-degree shoulder, resulting in a diminutive bottleneck shape. After multiple cycles of necking down and annealing, the case is trimmed to the final overall length dimension. To avoid excess pressure, extreme care is appropriate in measuring the tiny powder charge. The cartridge works well with 22-inch barrels having a rifling twist of 1:5½. Suitable actions to rebarrel and chamber for the .12 Eichelberger Long Rifle include modern .22 LR bolt actions, and single shots such as the Thompson/Center Contender and G2. SSK Industries (www.sskindustries.com) can supply Contender barrels and .12-caliber bullets for this cartridge on a special-order basis.

.12 Eichelberger LR Loading Data

Bullet (grains)	Powder	Grains	Velocity	Energy	Source/Comments
10	Accurate Arms 9	2.6	2,810	175	Bill Eichelberger

.12 Eichelberger Winchester Rimfire Magnum

Historical Notes: Strictly a one-shot proposition, the .12 Eichelberger WRM wildcat cartridge rockets an 11.5-grain, .123-inch diameter bullet to almost 3500 fps—stellar performance from a rimfire case. During testing, in 1982, of his family of wildcats based on rimfire cartridge cases, designer Bill Eichelberger necked down more than 10,000 rimfire cases (both Long Rifle and WRM), without one of the internally primed cases discharging. This cartridge is tailored for short- to mid-range varmint and informal target shooting. Eichelberger also designed a .14-caliber version of this cartridge.

General Comments: The .12 Eichelberger WRM cartridge uses Winchester .22 WRM brass as the parent case. Since this cartridge is a rimfire, careful and safe reloading practices are needed to remove the bullet from the internally primed case. Using a series of case forming dies, the live (primed) brass is necked down to accept .123-inch diameter bullets and given a 25-degree shoulder, resulting in a diminutive bottleneck shape. After multiple repetitions of necking down and annealing, the case is trimmed to the final overall length dimension. To avoid excess pressure, extreme care is appropriate in measuring the tiny powder charge. The cartridge works well with 21-inch barrels having a rifling twist of 1:5½. Suitable actions to rebarrel and chamber for the .12 Eichelberger WRM include modern .22 WRM bolt actions, and single-shots such as the Thompson/Center Contender and G2. SSK Industries (www.sskindustries.com) can supply Contender barrels and .12-caliber bullets for this cartridge on a special-order basis.

.12 Eichelberger Winchester Rimfire Magnum Loading Data

Bullet (grains)	Powder	Grains	Velocity	Energy	Source/Comments
7.2	Win 748	6.5	3,924	246	Bill Eichelberger
10	H380	6.4	3,290	240	Bill Eichelberger

.12 Cooper (CCM)

Historical Notes: The .12 Cooper, as designed by Bill Eichelberger in 1996, is a rimmed, sub-caliber wildcat cartridge capable of driving 10-grain .12-caliber bullets to velocities of almost 3800 fps. It is suitable for small-game hunting and target shooting.

General Comments: The .12 Cooper uses rimmed Cooper CCM brass as its parent case. The brass is necked down in a series of dies to accept .123-inch diameter bullets and given a 32-degree shoulder. After multiple repetitions of necking down and annealing, the case is trimmed to the final overall length dimension. The cartridge uses Federal No. 205 primers. To avoid excess pressure, extreme care is required in measuring the tiny powder charge. The cartridge works well with 15-inch barrels having a rifling twist of 1:5½. Suitable actions for the .12 Cooper include the Thompson/Center Contender and G2. SSK Industries (www.sskindustries.com) can supply Contender barrels and .12-caliber bullets for this cartridge on a special-order basis.

.12 Cooper (CCM) Loading Data

Bullet (grains)	Powder	Grains	Velocity	Energy	Source/Comments
10	Win 680	6.6	3,770	315	Bill Eichelberger
11.5	Win 680	6.1	3,500	312	Bill Eichelberger

.12 Eichelberger Carbine

Historical Notes: The original designers of the .30 Carbine cartridge would be amazed to learn sub-caliber experimenter Bill Eichelberger used their military brass to drive knitting needle-sized bullets to .220 Swift and higher velocities. Conceived in 1997, the .12 Eichelberger Carbine is the fastest wildcat .12-caliber cartridge known to exist. For small-game hunting and shooting, it can drive 10-grain bullets to almost 4400 fps. Eichelberger also designed a .14-caliber version of this cartridge.

General Comments: The .12 Eichelberger Carbine uses Winchester .30 Carbine brass as its parent case. The brass is necked down in a series of dies to accept .123-inch diameter bullets and given a 25-degree shoulder. After multiple repetitions of necking down and annealing, the case is trimmed to the final overall length dimension. The cartridge uses Federal No. 205 primers. To avoid excess pressure, extreme care is required in measuring the tiny powder charge. The cartridge works well with 15-inch barrels having a rifling twist of 1:5½. Suitable actions for the .12 Eichelberger Carbine include the Thompson/Center Contender and G2. SSK Industries (www.sskindustries.com) can supply Contender barrels and .12-caliber bullets for this cartridge on a special-order basis.

.12 Eichelberger Carbine Loading Data

Bullet (grains)	Powder	Grains	Velocity	Energy	Source/Comments
10	H335	13.8	4,390	427	Bill Eichelberger
11.5	H335	13.5	4,145	438	Bill Eichelberger

.14 Eichelberger Bee

Historical Notes: The .218 Bee cartridge, introduced by Winchester, in 1938, never achieved great popularity, even though it offered greater case capacity than the contemporary .22 Hornet round. In 1980, Bill Eichelberger exploited the case capacity of the .218 Bee, when he modified the brass to accept .144-inch diameter bullets in a cartridge named the .13 Eichelberger Bee. It is capable of driving 15-grain bullets about 150 fps faster than Eichelberger's Hornet-based wildcat, and can speed the heavier 18-grain bullets to more than 3600 fps. The .14 Eichelberger Bee fits into the small-game and target-shooting niches and falls within the 100-yard limitation of the sub-caliber wildcats.

General Comments: The .14 Eichelberger Bee uses .218 Bee brass as the parent case. The brass is necked down in a series of bushings to accept .144-inch diameter bullets and given a 30-degree shoulder. After several cycles of necking down and annealing, the case is trimmed to the final overall length dimension. The cartridge uses Remington No, 7½ primers. To avoid excess pressure, extreme care is required in measuring the tiny powder charge. The cartridge works well with 21-inch barrels having a rifling twist of 1:10. Suitable actions for the .14 Eichelberger Bee include the Thompson/Center Contender and G2. SSK Industries (www.sskindustries.com) can supply Contender barrels and .14-caliber bullets for this cartridge on a special-order basis.

.14 Eichelberger Bee Loading Data

Bullet (grains)	Powder	Grains	Velocity	Energy	Source/Comments
13	H335	14.6	4,124	490	Bill Eichelberger
15	Accurate Arms 2460	14.6	3,910	509	Bill Eichelberger
18	Accurate Arms 2495	14.2	3,634	527	Bill Eichelberger

.14 Eichelberger Dart

Historical Notes: Essentially similar to its smaller .10- and 12-caliber siblings, the .14 Eichelberger Dart turns the .25 ACP pistol case, holding a precisely measured powder charge, into a velocity powerhouse for 10-grain and 13-grain bullets measuring .144 inch in diameter. About 1983, wildcatter Bill Eichelberger designed the .14 Eichelberger Dart to push these micro-sized bullets in the 2330 to 2960 fps range, creating a sub-caliber cartridge for small game and paper punching.

General Comments: The .14 Eichelberger Dart uses Winchester .25 ACP brass as its parent case. The brass is necked down in a series of dies to accept .144-inch diameter bullets and given a 30-degree shoulder. After several repetitions of necking down and annealing, the case is trimmed to the final overall length dimension. The cartridge uses Federal No. 205 primers. To avoid excess pressure, extreme care is required in measuring the tiny powder charge. The cartridge works well with 15-inch barrels having a rifling twist of 1:9. Suitable actions for the .14 Eichelberger Dart include the Thompson/Center Contender and G2. SSK Industries (www. sskindustries.com) can supply Contender barrels and .14-caliber bullets for this cartridge on a special-order basis.

.14 Eichelberger Dart

Bullet (grains)	Powder	Grains	Velocity	Energy	Source/Comments
10	Accurate Arms 9	3.5	2,967	195	Bill Eichelberger
12.7	H110	3.2	2,614	192	Bill Eichelberger
13	H110	3.3	2,692	209	Bill Eichelberger

.14-222

Historical Notes: In the decade following World War II, there was considerable interest and experimentation with sub-caliber cartridges of .14- and even .12-caliber. Although interest subsided, it never completely died out, and a small but persistent group continued to work with the .14-caliber. The .14-222 is among these cartridges. It was originated by Helmut W. Sakschek about 1985. It is based on the .222 Remington case necked down to .14-caliber. Information covering the cartridge was published in the 1988 issue (20th Edition) of *Guns Illustrated* (DBI Books, Inc., edited by Harold A. Murtz). Mild report and practically zero recoil are characteristics of these small-caliber rifles. With initial velocities of faster than 4000 fps, these are quite deadly on smaller species of vermin.

General Comments: An 11-grain bullet starting out at 4465 fps develops 505 ft-lbs of energy, which doesn't sound very impressive. However, anything moving at such velocity imparts a sizable portion of that velocity to the molecular structure of whatever it impacts, with devastating results. On the other hand, once remaining velocity drops below about 3500 fps, the effectiveness of these small, lightweight bullets diminishes rapidly, so these are not really all that good for long-range shooting. There are also many problems in working with such small projectiles. For example, metal fouling can be a serious problem, and such cartridges generally exhibit extreme sensitivity to charge variations. Wind drift with such light projectiles is also a frequent complaint. Some older .14-caliber cartridges used bullets of 20 to 25 grains, which are easier to handle and load but cannot be pushed at quite the velocity of the lighter projectiles. In any event, the sub-calibers are extremely interesting and represent an area that may see additional development. Bullet-making equipment is available through Corbin Inc. (www.corbins.com). The advent of cleaner powders, such as those now available from Ramshot, and moly-plated bullets (NECO process) can significantly mitigate bore fouling.

.14-222 Loading Data

Bullet (grains/type)	Powder	Grains	Velocity	Energy	Source/Comments
11.4 HP	IMR 4198	20.0	4,200	445	NA
11.4 HP	IMR 3031	21.0	4,465	505	NA

.14 Cooper (CCM)

Historical Notes: The .14 Cooper, as designed by Bill Eichelberger, in 1993, is a rimmed, sub-caliber wildcat cartridge capable of driving 10-grain .14-caliber bullets to velocities of almost 3900 fps. It is suitable for small-game hunting and target shooting.

General Comments: The .14 Cooper uses rimmed Cooper CCM brass as its parent case. The brass is necked-down in a series of dies to accept .144-inch diameter bullets, and given a 32-degree shoulder. After several repetitions of necking-down and annealing, the case is trimmed to the final overall length dimension. To avoid excess pressure, extreme care is required in measuring the tiny powder charge. The cartridge works well with 21-inch barrels having a rifling twist of 1:8¾. Suitable actions for the .14 Cooper include the Thompson/Center Contender and G2. SSK Industries (www.sskindustries.com) can supply Contender barrels and .14-caliber bullets for this cartridge on a special-order basis.

.14 Cooper (CCM) Loading Data

Bullet (grains)	Powder	Grains	Velocity	Energy	Source/Comments
10	H110	7.4	3,895	336	Bill Eichelberger
12	H110	7.1	3,491	343	Bill Eichelberger
13	H110	7.0	3,443	342	Bill Eichelberger
15	H110	7.5	3,487	404	Bill Eichelberger

.14 Walker Hornet

Historical Notes: As designed by David Walker, the .14 Walker Hornet combines a straight body, sharp shoulder angle, and long neck to drive 10-grain bullets to almost 4200 fps. It was one of the first .14-caliber wildcats and served as the basis for the .14 Eichelberger Hornet, which achieves greater case volume and resulting higher velocities. Like all the .14-caliber wildcats, the .14 Walker Hornet is a short-range, small-game cartridge.

General Comments: The .14 Walker Hornet uses Remington .22 Hornet brass as its parent case. The brass is necked down in a series of dies to accept .144-inch diameter bullets and given a 30-degree shoulder. After several cycles of necking down and annealing, the case is trimmed to the final overall length dimension. The cartridge uses Remington No. 7½ primers. To avoid excess pressure, extreme care is required in measuring the tiny powder charge. The cartridge works well with 21-inch barrels having a rifling twist of 1:8¾. Suitable actions for the .14 Walker Hornet include the Thompson/Center Contender and G2. SSK Industries (www.sskindustries.com) can supply Contender barrels and .14-caliber bullets for this cartridge on a special-order basis.

Bullet (grains)	Powder	Grains	Velocity	Energy	Source/Comments
10	Accurate Arms	10.3	4,198	391	Bill Eichelberger
13	Accurate Arms	9.9	3,757	407	Bill Eichelberger
15	Win 748	11.2	3,737	469	Bill Eichelberger

.14/222
Eichelberger Magnum

Left to right: a factory .222 Rem. case, three stages of progressively swagged necks, resized case with neck turned to correct thickness, fireformed case trimmed to length, and finished .14-222 with bullet seated.

Historical Notes: The .14/222 Eichelberger Magnum is the big brother to the .14/221 Eichelberger. As conceived in 1978, Bill Eichelberger adapted the .222 Remington Magnum case, an unsuccessful contender for the small-bore U.S. M16 rifle, as the dynamo for this sub-caliber wildcat. The 47mm-long case allows for greater powder capacity, enabling heavier bullets to be driven over 3900 fps, and lighter ones to over 4300 fps. The .14/222 Eichelberger Magnum is the ultimate .14-caliber wildcat now available to the serious, curious, and dedicated shooter with considerable time and money to invest.

General Comments: The .14/222 Eichelberger uses .222 Remington Magnum brass as the parent case. The brass is necked down in a series of bushings to accept .144-inch diameter bullets and given a 23-degree shoulder with a short neck. After several repetitions of necking down and annealing, the case is trimmed to the final overall length dimension. The cartridge uses Remington No. 7½ primers. To avoid excess pressure, extreme care is required in measuring the tiny powder charge. The cartridge works well with 21-inch barrels having a rifling twist of 1:8¾. Suitable actions for the .14/222 Eichelberger Magnum include the Thompson/Center Contender and G2. SSK Industries (www.sskindustries.com) can supply Contender barrels and .14-caliber bullets for this cartridge on a special-order basis.

.14/222 Eichelberger Magnum Loading Data

Bullet (grains)	Powder	Grains	Velocity	Energy	Source/Comments
13	H380	24.5	4,368	550	Bill Eichelberger
15	Win 780	24.3	4,155	574	Bill Eichelberger
18	Accurate Arms 3100	24.4	3,959	626	Bill Eichelberger

.14 Jet Junior

Historical Notes: The almost forgotten, 1961-vintage .22 Remington Jet cartridge inspired the .14 Jet Junior. Originally intended as a small-game hunting cartridge, the .22 Remington Jet had a long shoulder tapering gently from case body to the neck. It originally pushed a 40-grain bullet to about 2460 fps and was a solid, but not spectacular, cartridge. Sometime before 1998, the late Bud Pylinski transformed it into the .14 Jet Junior, which sends 10-grain bullets screaming downrange at almost twice the velocity of the .22 Remington Jet—4570 fps! In addition, the .14 Jet Junior can handle relatively heavy (for a .14-caliber) bullets weighing 18 grains. Across the full range of bullets, though, the .14 Jet Junior is best suited for target shooting and small game at ranges up to 100 yards.

General Comments: The .14 Jet Junior uses .22 Remington Jet brass as the parent case. The brass is necked down in a series of bushings to accept .144-inch diameter bullets, and given a 10-degree shoulder. After several repetitions of necking down and annealing, the case is trimmed to the final overall length dimension. The cartridge uses Remington No. 7½ primers. To avoid excess pressure, extreme care is required in measuring the tiny powder charge. The cartridge works well with 21-inch barrels having a rifling twist of 1:8¾. Suitable actions for the .14 Jet Junior include the Thompson/Center Contender and G2. SSK Industries (www.sskindustries.com) can supply Contender barrels and .14-caliber bullets for this cartridge on a special-order basis.

.14 Jet Junior Loading Data

Bullet (grains)	Powder	Grains	Velocity	Energy	Source/Comments
10	Win 748	14.8	4,570	463	Bill Eichelberger
13	Win 748	13.8	4,087	482	Bill Eichelberger
15	Win 748	14.3	3,925	513	Bill Eichelberger
18	H380	13.3	3,479	483	Bill Eichelberger

.17 Ackley Hornet

Historical Notes: The .17 Ackley Hornet is simply the .22 Hornet Improved necked down to .17-caliber. It was originated by P.O. Ackley in the early 1950s, and he describes this cartridge as one of the most balanced of the .17-caliber cartridges. Although small, it delivers ballistics equal to some of the larger .17-caliber cartridges. It is an effective 200-yard varmint cartridge and is quite accurate. It is normally used in single-shot rifles, although the small Sako bolt-action was favored by many, because it was made to handle rimmed cartridges such as the .22 Hornet or .218 Bee.

General Comments: The .17 Hornet is a good cartridge for use in settled areas where mild report and minimum ricochet are desirable characteristics. It is one of the most accurate of the .17-calibers. Its use should be confined to varmint shooting. The standard twist is 1:10, the same as most other .17-caliber rifles. Reportedly, IMR 4198 gives the most uniform results, although Ball BL-C2, as well as several of the newer powders, should work well. Berger Bullets (www.bergerbullets.com) has recently offered .17-caliber bullets of various styles and weights. This significantly improves the versatility of all .17-caliber cartridges.

.17 Ackley Hornet Loading Data

Bullet (grains/type)	Powder	Grains	Velocity	Energy	Source/Comments
25 HP	BL-C2	15.0	3,040	510	N/A
25 HP	IMR 4198	11.0	3,300	600	Ackley
25 HP	IMR 4198	12.0	3,585	710	Ackley
25 HP	H4227	11.5	3,570	705	Ackley

.17-32 Magnum

Historical Notes: The .17-32 Magnum was developed by Carroll Pilant, a long time employee of Sierra Bullets. Carroll was trying to figure out what to do with the more than 1,000 .32 H&R Magnum cases he had on hand, in 1994. Carroll says he woke up in the middle of the night with the idea to neck the case down to .17-caliber. The first rifle was built on a Ruger single shot No. 3 action and, according to Carroll, was very accurate.

General Comments: The .17-32 Magnum offers ballistics that fall between the rimfire .17 HMR and the newer Hornady .17 Hornet. From a practicality standpoint, it offers no advantage over either cartridge, unless you have a large store of .32 H&R Magnum brass on hand. For those looking for more performance, a wildcat similar to this cartridge but built on the newer .327 Federal Magnum case would offer more capacity and a much higher velocity. Either would be a good option in a rifle set up for use with a rimmed cartridge.

.17 - 32 Magnum Loading Data

Bullet (grains/type)	Powder	Grains	Velocity	Energy	Source/Comments
25 Hornady HP	AA 1680	7.4	3,250	418	Carroll Pilant
20 V-Max	N 130	7.4	3,320	489	Carroll Pilant

.17 VHA
(Varmint Hunter Association)

Historical Notes: The .17 VHA was developed by the John Anderson who is the editor of the Varmint Hunter Association's magazine. Anderson used the 4.6x40 HK submachine gun round as the parent case for this wildcat and simply necked it down to .17 caliber. By working with M.L. McPherson, a previous editor of *Cartridges of the World* (Editions 8 and 9), Anderson developed the load data for the .17 VHA. Ballistically, the .17 VHA offers similar velocities to the .17 Hornet, which is a rimmed cartridge. It is capable of pushing a 20-grain bullet to 3700 fps. According to John Anderson, because of the diminutive size of this case, it is necessary to use Small Pistol primers, as opposed to Small Rifle primers. Rifle primers are a bit potent for this small-sized case, and accuracy will be better with the pistol primers.

General Comments: Anderson's intent with the .17 VHA was to provide a low-recoil, small-caliber cartridge suitable for ground squirrels and prairie dogs. This cartridge offers some advantages over the rimfire .17 HMR and the .17 Hornet. For starters it is reloadable and the .17 HMR is not. It is also rimless, which means feeding is not an issue. The case walls on the .17 VHA are also thicker than those of the Hornet, which should extend case life. Reamers are available from Pacific Tool & Gauge (www.pacifictoolandgauge.com), and dies are available on a custom basis from Redding (www.redding-reloading.com).

Bullet (grains/type)	Powder	Grains	Velocity	Energy	Source/Comments
20 V-Max	AA 1690	10.9	3,562	563	John Anderson
20 V-Max	Lil' Gun	8.7	3,577	568	John Anderson
25 V-Max	AA 1680	10.0	3,263	590	John Anderson

.17 Mach IV
.17 Mach III

Historical Notes: The .17/221 was created by P.O. Ackley, who gave permission to Vern O'Brien, owner of O'Brien Rifle Company, of Las Vegas, Nev., to rename it .17 Mach IV when building custom rifles for it on the small Sako action. O'Brien also offered it in custom single-shot pistols built on the XP-100 action, in which case he called it the .17 Mach III, due to lower velocities in a short barrel. It succeeded on both counts, but could not compete against a factory chambering, i.e., the .17 Remington.

General Comments: This short cartridge can be used in short rifle actions. Efficiency is much better than in the various full-power .17s available. This diminutive chambering can produce more than 3850 fps with 25-grain bullets and is fully capable of delivering good varmint accuracy to about 250 yards, perhaps a bit further on a calm day. Muzzle blast is in a different league from larger .17s and the various high-performance .22s. While by no means "quiet," the .17 Mach IV generates so much less report, the difference is significant. Use of the faster powders listed, while necessitating a slight velocity sacrifice, results in much quieter loads. Since it uses significantly less powder than the .17 Remington, the 17 Mach IV generally produces much less barrel fouling, an important consideration in this diminutive bore size. Berger Bullets has recently offered .17-caliber bullets of various styles and weights. This significantly improves the versatility of all .17-caliber cartridges.

.17 Mach IV, .17 Mach III Loading Data

Bullet (grains/type)	Powder	Grains	Velocity	Energy	Source/Comments
25	2400	13.1	3,600	720	Hornady
25	H4227	14.6	3,700	760	Hornady
25	H4198	15.6	3,700	760	Hornady
25	2015	18.5	3,850	820	Accurate
25	2230	20.3	3,861	825	Accurate
25	2460	20.5	3,883	835	Accurate (Compressed)
25	2520	20.5	3,768	785	Accurate (Compressed)

.17/222

Historical Notes: The .17/222 is simply the .222 Remington case necked-down to .17-caliber. There are several versions of this cartridge, but the one listed here is the most popular. The .17/222 dates back to about 1957, possibly earlier. Many shooters considered the .17/222 more accurate and less sensitive to load variations than the wildcat .17/223, which was the forerunner of the later .17 Remington. P.O. Ackley considered the .222 Remington case about maximum capacity for the .17-caliber and states in his book *Handbook for Shooters and Reloaders* that larger cases tend to be inflexible. Those who have experimented with larger cases have usually found him to be right.

General Comments: The .17/222 did not achieve great popularity, but was well liked by those who worked with it. Performance is practically the same as the .17 Remington, which has a larger case. Best accuracy is usually with IMR 4198 powder and the 25-grain bullet. Recommended twist is 1:10. Cases are simple and easy to form by necking-down .222 Remington cases with no other modification. There has been some renewed interest in this cartridge during the past couple of years.

.17 Javelina — *NEW*

Historical Notes: Designed by Paul Marquart of A&M Gunshop in Prescott, Arizona, about 1956, the .17 Javelina has never been as popular as other wildcats in this caliber because forming its cases is expensive and difficult. It is based on the .222 Rem. case, which Marquart shortened and blew out, pushing the shoulder back about 0.150 inch. The .17-.222, in contrast, has a little more case capacity and is easily formed from .222 brass by simply necking down the case and not moving the shoulder. Of course, the .17 Rem. is a factory-loaded option in this size range.

General Comments: Circa 1961, A&M often used the highly regarded Sako L461 short-action, usually with custom McMillan or Shilen barrels with 1:9 or 1:10 twist, depending on the bullet weight, and gorgeous wood. Unquestionably, the quality of the rifles gave a boost to the .17 Javelina's prospects, but the case-manufacturing effort doomed it. The cases are necked down to .17 caliber, and then trimmed and formed. Forming the Javelina cases usually requires a forming die set, made by RCBS and Redding.

.17 Javelina Loading Data

Bullet (grains/type)	Powder	Grains	Velocity	Energy	Source/Comments
25 Sisk	H322	18.7	3,680	752	A&M Gunshop
25 Sisk	IMR 3031	18.6	3,850	823	A&M Gunshop

.17 Ackley Improved Bee

Historical Notes: The .17 Ackley Bee is a step up from the .17 Hornet, as it is based on the .218 Improved Bee case, which has significantly larger powder capacity. This cartridge was developed by P.O. Ackley, back in the 1950s, and he considered it the ideal small case for a .17-caliber cartridge. There is relatively little— gain in ballistic performance by using cartridge cases larger than the .17 Bee. In fact, cases of very much larger capacity often produce erratic results and poor accuracy.

General Comments: The .17 Bee, like the .17 Hornet, is chambered mostly in single-shot rifles, usually of the under-lever type. Bolt-actions are sometimes used, but will not always handle the rimmed case well when feeding from the magazine. The small Sako bolt-action was favored, when available. Like most of the smaller .17-caliber cartridges, the .17 Bee is noted for its mild report and low recoil. This is a good 200- to 225-yard varmint cartridge for use in settled areas. P.O. Ackley recommended IMR 4198 or H4198 as the propellants that produce the most uniform results, and several new choices now available should work, as well. Bullets are available from Hornady (www.hornady.com). Berger Bullets (www.bergerbullets.com) has recently offered .17-caliber bullets of various styles and weights. This significantly improves the versatility of all .17-caliber cartridges.

.17 Ackley Bee Loading Data

Bullet (grains/type)	Powder	Grains	Velocity	Energy	Source/Comments
20	H4227	11.0	3,845	655	Ackley
25 HP	BL-C2	16.5	3,190	565	NA
25 HP	H335	17.0	3,285	595	NA
25 HP	IMR 4198	13.0	3,180	555	NA

.17-357 RG (.17-357 Real Guns)

Historical Notes: The .17-357 RG is a .172-caliber wildcat cartridge based on the 357 SIG commercial cartridge. The 17-357 RG was developed to function in both rifle- and handgun-length barrels. The cartridge was designed by Joseph D'Alessandro and was documented in a series that first appeared on the RealGuns.com website. The first article was posted in June 2004 and the series concluded in November 2004.

According to the RealGuns.com website, the original 357 SIG shoulder is bumped back, extended and formed to a 40-degree angle to ensure an adequate 0.200 neck length. The 17-357 RG is subjected to a number of cold-forming steps and sees significant dimensional change, which results in work-hardened brass. Annealing increased case longevity. The rimless case head at 0.424 is between a .223 Remington and .308 Winchester in diameter, so lots of rifles can be chambered for the cartridge.

General Comments The author claimed a 50 percent performance improvement over the 17 HMR. Parent brass is inexpensive and readily available, powder consumption is small, and wear and tear on firearms is negligible. Overall length can run from 1.140 for pistols to 1.300 or so for heavy, long 17-caliber bullets, so case capacity can be preserved.—*W.T.W.*

.17-357 RG Loading Data and Factory Ballistics

Bullet (grains/type)	Powder	Grains	Velocity	Energy	Source/Comments
20 Hornady	Power Pistol	6.1	2,560	291	Realguns.com
20 Hornady	Blue Dot	7.5	3,048	413	Realguns.com

.19 Badger

Historical Notes: In one shooting day, in 2001, Jim Harrison, and Jim Leahy of James Calhoon Mfg. shot seven Montana badgers with a .19-caliber cartridge based on the .30 Carbine case. The results from this small-caliber (4.85mm) cartridge effectively ended the search for a reliable, 300-yard, flat-shooting varmint cartridge with low recoil, noise, fouling, and barrel heating characteristics, and its makers gave the cartridge its name, the .19 Badger. Harrison, the cartridge designer, previously tested many .19-caliber and parent case combinations, but found most exceeded the "too large and too fast" threshold.

General Comments: The .30 Carbine parent case, when necked to .19-caliber with a 30-degree shoulder, creates a short powder column with thick case walls at the case neck. Both features contribute to varmint-grade accuracy. Suitable for any firearm capable of accommodating the Hornet case, the .19 Badger works well in 24-inch barrels using a 1:13 twist. Incidentally, the .19 Badger holds about 25 percent more powder than the .19 Calhoon cartridge (which uses the .22 Hornet as its parent case). James Calhoon (www.jamescalhoon.com) offers rifles, barrel kits, loaded ammunition, reloading supplies, and components for the .19 Badger cartridge. Cooper Firearms (www.cooperfirearms.com) also chambers single-shot rifles for this cartridge on special order.

.19 Badger Loading Data and Factory Ballistics

Bullet (grains/type)	Powder	Grains	Velocity	Energy	Source/Comments
27 Calhoon DBL HP	Accurate Arms 1680	16.3	3,775	854	James Calhoon
32 Calhoon DBL HP	FL	N/A	3,550	895	James Calhoon

.19 Calhoon

Historical Notes:	Around 1997, Jim Leahy (James Calhoon Mfg.) decided to adapt a military cartridge development, the 4.85mm (.19-caliber), to varmint cartridges. His decision reflected two consideration: (1) ballistic superiority over the .22-calibers, and (2) consistency and ease of loading over .17-calibers. One of his resulting .19-caliber cartridge offerings, the .19 Calhoon, is the most powerful proprietary cartridge based on the .22 Hornet case.
General Comments:	Occasionally described as a Hornet on steroids, the .19 Calhoon adds an additional 100-yards range over the factory .22 Hornet and easily drives a 32-grain bullet as fast as the wildcat .17 Hornet cartridge can drive a 25-grain bullet. This performance translates into a significant range—best at 250 yards and effective to 350 yards—and killing power advantage. Using the parent Hornet case blown out and given a 30-degree shoulder, it can be chambered in any firearm suitable for the Hornet case, such as the CZ 527 and Ruger 77. The chambering works well with 24 inch barrels using a 1:13 twist. The .19 Calhoon delivers performance similar to the .17 Mach IV (.17-221) in a compact and reliable cartridge. James Calhoon (www.jamescalhoon.com) offers rifles, barrel kits, loaded ammunition, reloading supplies, and components. Cooper Firearms (www.cooperfirearms.com) also chambers single-shot rifles for this cartridge.

.19 Calhoon Loading Data and Factory Ballistics

Bullet (grains/type)	Powder	Grains	Velocity	Energy	Source/Comments
27 Calhoon DBL HP	Accurate Arms 1680	14.7	3,610	781	James Calhoon
32 Calhoon DBL HP	FL		3,400	821	James Calhoon
36 Calhoon DBL HP	Accurate Arms 2200	15.0	3,165	800	James Calhoon
40 Calhoon DBL HP	Accurate Arms 2200	14.5	3,060	831	James Calhoon

.19-223 Calhoon

Historical Notes:	During 1970 NATO trials intended to identify a superior infantry cartridge, the 4.85mm Experimental provided exceptional performance to 500-plus meters, outperforming other competitors. Essentially a .222 Magnum case adapted to a .19-caliber bullet, the 4.85mm Experimental led to the creation of the .19-223 Calhoon by James Leahy, in 1997. Leahy's cartridge, however, used the readily available .223 Remington for its parent case. It offers less recoil and a flatter trajectory than the .223 Remington, and is a superb long-range, flat-shooting varmint cartridge with abundant terminal energy.
General Comments:	This cartridge offers significant bullet weight versatility, ranging from 32 grains for pelt hunting to 44 grains for improved long-range shooting. The .19-223 Calhoon drives heavier (better ballistic coefficient) bullets than the .17 Remington at similar velocities. The .223 parent case is necked down to .19-caliber in one pass through a forming die, and the case shape is subsequently formed by fire-forming. With a 30-degree shoulder, the fire-formed case attains the powder capacity of the .222 Remington Magnum and delivers velocities normally associated with the .220 Swift. The .19-223 Calhoon can be accommodated in firearms suitable for the .223 Remington-length cases. It works well with 26-inch barrels using a 1:13 twist. James Calhoon Mfg. offers rifles, barrel kits, loaded ammunition, reloading supplies, and components. Cooper Firearms also chambers single-shot rifles for this cartridge.

.19-223 Calhoon Loading Data and Factory Ballistics

Bullet (grains/type)	Powder	Grains	Velocity	Energy	Source/Comments
32 Calhoon DBL HP	BLC-2	27.0	4,025	1,151	James Calhoon
36 Calhoon DBL HP	Accurate Arms 2015 BR	24.5	3,840	1,178	James Calhoon
40 Calhoon DBL HP	FL		3,750	1,248	James Calhoon
44 Calhoon DBL HP	VV N550	27.0	3,670	1,315	James Calhoon

.20 Vartarg

Historical Notes: The .20 Vartarg (varmint/target) is a very efficient .20-caliber cartridge based on the .221 Fireball case. Like the PPC cartridges, it has a very good bore-to-powder capacity ratio and is popular with varmint hunters, because it uses very little power compared to other .20-caliber cartridges. It was developed by Todd Kindler, who is also responsible for the .20 Tactical wildcat cartridge. However, the .20 Vartarg is a bit easier to work with; just run a .221 Fireball case through a .20 Vartarg sizing die, load, and shoot.

General Comments: Of all the .20-caliber factory and wildcat cartridges, the .20 Vartarg probably has the best reputation for accuracy. It is a great cartridge for high-volume varmint shooting out to around 300 yards, due to its high velocity, accuracy, and minimal recoil, this last of which will allow the shooter to observe bullet impact through the rifle scope.

.22 Vartarg Loading Data and Ballistics

Bullet (grains/type)	Powder	Grains	Velocity	Energy	Source/Comments
32 Sierra	X-Terminator	20.4	3,556	898	Ramshot
40 V-Max	X-Terminator	18.8	3,356	1,000	Ramshot

.20 Tactical

Historical Notes: This cartridge might be considered the forerunner to the .204 Ruger. It is a wildcat cartridge developed by Todd Kindler well before the .204 Ruger became a factory loaded cartridge. The .20 Tactical is based on the .223 Remington case, but is, of course, necked down to .20-caliber. It also has a steeper, 30-degree shoulder. Brass for the .20 Tactical is made by pushing a full-length and sized .223 Remington case into a .20 Tactical forming die and then into a .20 Tactical sizing die. For all practical ballistic purposes, the .20 Tactical is identical to the .204 Ruger.

General Comments: The .20 Tactical does use a slightly shorter case than the .204 Ruger. This can be beneficial when working with certain long or heavy-for-caliber bullets, where maximum overall cartridge length might require they be seated into the case mouth past the ogive. This, of course, will depend on the configuration of the rifles chamber and magazine box, as well. Cooper and Dakota both offer .20 Tactical rifles, something that can also be built by any good custom gunsmith. Lapua is now offering .20 Tactical brass, which eliminates the need for forming cases with dies followed by fire forming in chambers. This cartridge has a reputation for fine accuracy, and it is surprising that it has not caught on faster with AR-15 shooters.

Bullet (grains/type)	Powder	Grains	Velocity	Energy	Source/Comments
33 V-Max	H 335	26.7	3,917	1,124	Hodgdon
36 Berger HP	H 4895	26.5C	3,746	1,121	Hodgdon

.20 PDK

Historical Notes: This cartridge was designed to shoot varmints and targets with 40-, 45-, and 50-grain .20-caliber bullets. It was conceptualized by Illinois wildcatter Roy Winnett, in collaboration with Dave Kiff at Pacific Tool & Gauge and benchrest shooter John Hutchins. The parent case for the .20 PDK (Prairie Dog Killer) is the 6.8 Remington SPC. The .20 PDK will work well in either a bolt rifle or AR-15.

General Comments: Both Roy Winnett and John Hutchins are avid long-range shooters and have conducted extensive testing with the .20 PDK on both paper and prairie dogs. They have found a 1:9 twist best for stabilization of 40- to 50-grain bullets. A re-barreled Savage rifle chambered for the .20 PDK was tested by this editor and was found to deliver both excellent accuracy and velocities on par with those shown below. Cartridge cases and handloading dies are available directly from Roy Winnett, (309) 367-4867; www.pdk20.com.

.20 PDK Loading Data

Bullet (grains/type)	Powder	Grains	Velocity	Energy	Source
40 V-Max	10 X	27.5	4,077	1,476	Roy Winnett
50 Berger	Benchmark	25.5	3,603	1,441	Roy Winnett

.22 Reed Express

Historical Notes: In 2004, Fred Zeglin and Ron Reed began working on a high-velocity .22-caliber pistol for varminting and self-defense. As the foundation for their idea, they selected the inexpensive CZ-52 pistol, a quality military pistol currently available from surplus firearm dealers and chambered in the 1930s-vintage 7.62x25 Tokarev cartridge. This cartridge was widely used by the former Soviet Union and its allies, before Soviet Bloc countries switched to the 9x18 Makarov cartridge, after WWII. Zeglin and Reed necked the 7.62x25 round to .22-caliber and loaded it with bullets ranging from 30 to 50 grains to create a high-velocity round. Interestingly, the .22 Reed Express achieves velocities with 50-grain bullets that rival those of the FN 5.7x28 cartridge with 26-grain bullets.

General Comments: The .22 Reed uses 7.62x25 brass as the parent case. The brass is necked-down to accept .224-inch bullets and the shoulder angle changed. With heavier bullets, the powder charge must be reduced to allow the longer bullets to fit into the CZ-52 pistol magazine. Barrels in .22 Reed Express chambering are also available for the Thompson/Center Contender. Reed's Ammunition & Research (www.reedsammo.com) offers barrels, reloading components, and ammunition.

Bullet (grains/type)	Powder	Grains	Velocity	Energy	Source/Comments
30 Berger	H110	12.7	2,782	515	Fred Zeglin
35 V-Max	H110	12.6	2,721	575	Fred Zeglin
50	Accurate Arms 9	10.0	2,401	639	Fred Zeglin

.22 Taranah Hornet

Historical Notes: The Taranah Hornet was developed by Andy Montgomery, assistant technical editor of Guns and Game magazine, in Australia. An article on that cartridge appeared in issue No. 27, July-September 2000, of that magazine. The .22 Taranah Hornet is essentially a .22 K-Hornet shortened by .15-inch. The reason for the shorter length is to allow the long-for-weight 40-grain Nosler Ballistic Tip projectile to be used, without running into overall-length problems. The cartridge was specifically designed to operate through the ZKW 465 and CZ 527 Hornet detachable magazines. Montgomery reports velocities in excess of the standard Hornet, and only marginally behind the conventional K-Hornet. The original rifle was chambered by Sprinter Arms of South Australia, using one of its 1:10 twist barrel.

General Comments: The Taranah Hornet is an ideal small-game cartridge that utilizes ballistically efficient bullets to gain better down-range performance. It not only produces higher velocities than the original Hornet, but, when 40-grain Nosler Ballistic Tip bullets are used, it also shoots flatter. It is a very efficient cartridge, has a mild report, and is economical to shoot. Montgomery has found good case life and excellent accuracy from the cartridge. It would be suitable for most small game and varmints, and it extends the effective range of the standard Hornet a little. The cartridge can be fed through the magazine of popular bolt-action rifles.

.22 Taranah Hornet Loading Data

Bullet (grains/type)	Powder	Grains	Velocity	Energy	Source/Comments
40 Nosler BT	Win 680	11.5	2,831	712	Andy Montgomery
40 Nosler BT	2400	10.5	2,827	710	Andy Montgomery
50 Speer SP	2400	10.0	2,489	688	Andy Montgomery
50 Sierra SP	Win 680	11.5	2,571	734	Andy Montgomery

.224 Texas Trophy Hunter

Historical Notes: Every year, Texas hunters take an incredible number of whitetail deer, and more than a few take whitetails with hot .22s. The .224 Texas Trophy Hunter, conceived by gun writer Ralph Lermayer in 1998, uses the greater capacity of the 6mm Remington case to deliver more power than the .22-250 and .220 Swift.

General Comments: Following extensive experiments with the .220 Swift, .22-250, and .240 Weatherby cases, Lermayer settled on the 6mm Remington case as the best balance of case taper, shoulder angle, length, and capacity. Necking the 6mm Remington case down to .224 (with the factory's 26-degree shoulder angle), the designer created a cartridge that would deliver heavier, well-constructed, 70- to 80-grain .224 bullets accurately at relatively high velocities. The 6mm case provides optimum capacity for the .224 bore, brass is readily available, and standard actions and magazines require no modification other than a new barrel. Proper rifling twist for the .224 Texas Trophy Hunter is 1:8 or 1:9. Bullet construction is the key to success; it takes a stout, thick jacket solid or bonded core bullet to hold up to the velocity potential. Stoutly constructed bullets can be driven in excess of 3500 fps. Dies are available from Redding (www.redding-reloading.com). Nosler recently endorsed its .22-caliber 60-grain Partition bullet for whitetail deer hunting.

.224 Texas Trophy Hunter Loading Data

Bullet (grains/type)	Powder	Grains	Velocity	Energy	Source/Comments
55 Trophy Bonded	H4831	46.5	3,840	1,800	Ralph Lermayer
60 Nosler Partition	H4831	46.0	3,780	1,903	Ralph Lermayer
75 Hornady A-Max	Win Mag Rifle	47.0	3,780	2,379	Ralph Lermayer
79 Lost River	VV N165	45.0	3,520	2,173	Ralph Lermayer

.218 Mashburn Bee

Historical Notes: The .218 Mashburn Bee is an Improved version of the factory .218 Bee. Cases are made by firing factory ammunition in the Mashburn chamber, so no special case-forming dies are required. The cartridge was the work of A.E. Mashburn, of the Mashburn Arms Co., in Oklahoma City, Oklahoma. As near as can be determined, the cartridge originated in or about 1940. The Improved case produced better ballistics than the original Bee and offered longer case life. There are other Improved versions of the .218 Bee, but all are rather similar. The Mashburn Bee will deliver about the same velocity with the 55-grain bullet as the factory Bee does with the 45-grain bullet.

General Comments: The Mashburn Bee was popular until the advent of the .222 Remington. It was, and still is, a very accurate varmint cartridge. The recommended powders for loading these small cartridges are similar to IMR 4198 and IMR 4227.

.218 Mashburn Bee Loading Data

Bullet (grains/type)	Powder	Grains	Velocity	Energy	Source/Comments
40 HP	IMR 4227	16.5	3,300	960	NA
45 SP	IMR 4227	16.3	3,319	1,100	Ackley
50 SP	IMR 4198	17.3	3,300	1,210	Ackley

.22 K-Hornet

Historical Notes: Originated by Lysle Kilbourn, in 1940, this was one of the first of the so-called "Improved" cartridges. It is based on the fire-formed and blown-out .22 Hornet case, with a straight body, sharp shoulder, and short neck. There are other versions, but this is the most popular and is representative of the lot. It has been used for a good many years and is still popular in varmint-shooting circles. Extensive experience with this cartridge in the Thompson Contender shows substantial improvements over the .22 Hornet.

General Comments: The popularity of the .22 K-Hornet was based on increased performance, plus the fact that any regular factory-loaded ammunition could also be fired in the same chamber. In addition, the conversion is quite cheap, and any Hornet rifle can be re-chambered. Ammunition is no problem, because the round is based on easily obtainable factory ammunition. It brings the .22 Hornet into the same class as the .218 Bee, with the added advantage that the .22 Hornet was chambered in several good bolt-action rifles. It is suitable for the same range of varmints and small game as the .218 Bee. Those lucky enough to find an original Kimber rifle chambered for the .22 K-Hornet can pride themselves in owning a superb rifle. The very similar Harvey Kay-Chuck was developed by Jim Harvey, about 1956. In that round, loading length was kept short enough so that the ammunition would chamber in modified S&W K-22 revolvers.

.22 K-Hornet Loading Data

Bullet (grains/type)	Powder	Grains	Velocity	Energy	Source/Comments
45 SP	IMR 4227	12.5	2,875	825	Ackley
45 SP	2400	11.5	2,900	840	Ackley
45	IMR 4198	14.5	2,800	780	Ackley
50 SP	2400	11.0	2,700	810	Ackley

.22 Waldog

Historical Notes:	The .22 Waldog was originated by Dan Dowling of Accuracy Gunsmithing, in Arvada, Colo., in 1980. He named it after a friend, Waldo G. Woodside, thus the Waldog, or Waldo-G. The cartridge is made by running .220 Russian cases through a shortened .22-250 die and trimming the case to a length of 1.375 inches. It is, in effect, a shortened .22 PPC. The idea was to create a more efficient case than the .22 PPC by reducing volumetric capacity to approximately that of the .222 Remington. This cartridge was originally used exclusively in heavy benchrest rifles. Several 100-yard benchrest world records have been broken by the .22 Waldog.
General Comments:	The .22 Waldog is another effort to develop a super-accurate benchrest cartridge. The current trend is toward smaller, more efficient cases, and the Waldog has proven to be a very accurate cartridge. Best accuracy has been obtained with 52-grain match bullets and 24 grains of H322 powder, but any powder that works well in the .222 Remington should give comparable results in the Waldog. Although not as widely used as the .22 PPC, the Waldog has found a significant following among benchrest shooters. It is reminiscent of the 308x1.5-inch necked down to .22 caliber, also known as the .22 Remington BR, as the two have similar case capacities. However, the .22 Remington BR case is larger in diameter and length is about .12-inch longer.

.22 BR Remington

Historical Notes:	The .22 BR Remington is based on the .308x1.5-inch Barnes case necked down to .22-caliber and lengthened by .02-inch, with the shoulder angle increased to 30 degrees. It is difficult to determine who originated the .22 version of the necked-down 308x1½, because there are a number of versions dating back to about 1963. J. Stekl is credited with having developed the Remington rendition. In any event, Remington standardized the dimensions, in 1978, as its .22 BR. It is one of a series of BR cartridges, including the 6mm and 7mm, all based on the same case. The .22 BR is a factory wildcat, because loaded ammunition is not available. Cases must be made from special Remington or necked BR cases, which have a Small Rifle primer pocket, or from full-size Remington 6mm or 7mm BR cases. The .22 BR has won many honors in benchrest competition and has great accuracy potential.
General Comments:	The .22 BR is similar to the .22 PPC, but has a case of larger base diameter and slightly greater powder capacity with the same case length. Anything one can do, the other can duplicate. Both can push a 55-grain bullet at over 3000 fps and duplicate the performance of the .223 Remington. Both are extremely accurate and make excellent varmint cartridges, as well as competitive benchrest numbers.

.22 BR Remington Loading Data

Bullet (grains/type)	Powder	Grains	Velocity	Energy	Source/Comments
53 HP Hornady	2460	32.8	3,653	1,570	Accurate, 26-inch barrel

.22 BR Remington Loading Data

Bullet (grains/type)	Powder	Grains	Velocity	Energy	Source/Comments
55 BT Nosler	2460	32.5	3,605	1,585	Accurate, 26-inch barrel
60 HP Hornady	2460	31.7	3,455	1,590	Accurate, 26-inch barrel

R-2 Lovell

Historical Notes: The development of the R-2 Lovell is unusual, because it is an example of a wildcat cartridge developed from what was originally a wildcat. It is believed to have been developed in 1937 by Harvey Donaldson, of New York. It derived its name from the fact that the second chambering reamer (made by M.S. Risley, Earlville, N.Y.) appeared to be correct in providing what the designer was striving to produce. It is actually an Improved, or blown-out version, of the original .22 Lovell or .22-3000 developed by Hervey Lovell, about 1934. Both are based on the long obsolete .25-20 Single-Shot case necked down, itself a wildcat, when it first appeared in 1882.

General Comments: The R-2 Lovell is probably the most popular wildcat .22-caliber cartridge ever designed. It was so popular that the late J. Bushnell Smith, of Middlebury, Vermont, and Griffin & Howe, of New York City, custom loaded ammunition in large quantities; when the supply of .25-20 Single-shot cases was exhausted, Griffin & Howe arranged for the manufacture of R-2 cases. This is a fine varmint cartridge and was often chambered in bolt-action and single-shot rifles, where it delivered excellent accuracy. Performance is pretty close to the .222 Remington, but the R-2 Lovell has long since been displaced by this more recent factory chambering, and the R-2 is no longer a viable choice, since suitable cases are no longer available. It is included here only for historical significance.

R-2 Lovell Loading Data

Bullet (grains/type)	Powder	Grains	Velocity	Energy	Source/Comments
45 SP	IMR 4227	8.0	1,880	350	Ackley
45 SP	IMR 4227	16.0	3,280	1,070	Ackley
50 SP	IMR 4198	17.0	3,050	1,030	Ackley
55 SP	IMR 4198	17.0	3,050	1,135	Ackley

.22 Eargesplitten Loudenboomer

Historical Notes: P.O. Ackley created this concept cartridge in the 1960s in an attempt to break the 5,000 fps barrier. Based on the .378 Weatherby Magnum cartridge case necked down to accept a .224-diameter bullet, it did achieve 4,600 fps with a 50-grain bullet.

General Comments: There is only so much powder that can burn in a rifle barrel, and the smaller the bore, the less powder you can burn. Machinist Zac Weighman makes an inert novelty cartridge called the .22 Earspliting-loudenboomer that's based on a .50 BMG cartridge as the parent, employing the same steps he uses to manufacture the .17 Incinerator. —*W.T.W.*

.22 Eargesplitten Loudenboomer Loading Data

Bullet (grains/type)	Powder	Grains	Velocity	Energy	Source/Comments
50	H570	105	4,600	2,349	Handload

.22 CHeetah

Historical Notes: The .22 CHeetah was developed by Jim Carmichael, shooting editor of *Outdoor Life* magazine, and Fred Huntington, of RCBS fame, thus the capital "C" and "H" for each of their surname initials. It appears to have originated in the late 1970s. The cartridge is essentially a full-length Remington .308 BR case—with the Small Rifle primer pocket—necked down to .22-caliber, but with the shoulder moved forward. What you end up with is a variation of the .308 Winchester necked down to .22, but using a special match case. This is not exactly new, because there are in existence several slightly different versions made by necking the .243 Winchester case down (such as the .243 Middlestead, which used a 30-degree shoulder angle), and these date back to the early 1960s. However, the .22 CHeetah is an original, with regard to the .308 BR case and its Small Rifle primer pocket.

General Comments: The major differences between the .22 CHeetah and its predecessors are the use of the lighter, more uniform BR case, blown-out 40-degree shoulder angle, and short neck. In other words, the case has been designed to benchrest specifications. It also has greater powder capacity than any of the older versions. There are actually two case types, the MKI, with the 40-degree shoulder angle, and the MKII, with the original 28-degree shoulder. The .22 CHeetah is somewhat more powerful than the .220 Swift, but ballistics were measured from a 27-inch barrel. The cartridge has proven to be superbly accurate and a very effective 300-yard varmint cartridge.

.22 CHeetah Loading Data (MKI)

Bullet (grains/type)	Powder	Grains	Velocity	Energy	Source/Comments
50 SP	IMR 4064	46.0	4,285	2040	NA
52 HP	IMR 4064	44.0	4,135	1970	NA
55 SP	IMR 4350	49.0	4,090	1990	NA

.219 Donaldson Wasp

Historical Notes: This cartridge originated in 1937, shortly after Winchester introduced the .219 Zipper. It is made by shortening, re-necking, and blowing-out .219 Zipper cases. The Donaldson Wasp became the most popular version of such adaptations, and more or less the standard. Many benchrest matches have been won with the .219 Wasp, and it has a well-deserved reputation for excellent accuracy. It has been used mostly in custom-made single-shot rifles, because of the rimmed case.

General Comments: The .219 Wasp is another .22 wildcat that achieved notable, continued popularity. This is one of the better wildcat numbers, but like most of the other offbeat .22s, it was overshadowed by the .222 Remington. The .219 Improved Zipper, developed by P.O. Ackley, in 1938, is a more practical cartridge, because it is made by simply fire-forming standard .219 Zipper cases in the Improved chamber. The Improved version offers velocities similar to the standard Wasp, but with significantly lower pressures. Cases for these wildcats can also be made from .25-35 and .30-30 cases. It was claimed, by some authorities, that breech pressures developed by popular loads in the Wasp ran as high as 55,000 to 60,000 psi, which, in a strong action, is of no consequence.

.219 Donaldson Wasp Loading Data

Bullet (grains/type)	Powder	Grains	Velocity	Energy	Source/Comments
45 SP	IMR 3031	30.0	3,780	1425	Ackley
45 SP	H380	33.0	3,510	1215	NA
50 SP	IMR 4064	32.0	3,605	1440	Ackley
50 SP	H380	32.0	3,370	1255	NA

.22 Spitfire (.22-30 Carbine, 5.7x33mm, MMJ 5.7mm Johnson)

Historical Notes: The 5.7x33mm Johnson Spitfire was designed by Melvin Johnson, Jr., a Boston lawyer and captain in the Marine Corps Reserve. In 1963, he built and tested both a pistol and selective-fire M2 Carbine chambered for the round. Johnson promoted it as a survival rifle caliber. Loaded with a .224 bullet, it had a case length of 1.29 and an overall loaded length of 1.65.

General Comments: The .22 Spitfire/5.7mm Johnson is a .30 Carbine case necked down to take a .224 bullet. Metrically, it would be a 5.7x33mm. Ballistically, it would split the difference between the 5.56x45mm and 5.7x28mm. If it were chambered in an M1 Carbine, it would make a heck of a PDW (personal defense weapon). Midway sells an RCBS neck reamer and dies for the 5.7mm Johnson. Sample cartridges are available from Ammo-One.com. —*W.T.W.*

.22 Spitfire (5.7mm Johnson) Loading Data

Bullet (grains/type)	Powder	Grains	Velocity	Energy	Source/Comments
40 FMJ			2,850	720	Johnson Guns, Inc.
40 FMJ			3,000	795	Johnson Guns, Inc.
50 FMJ			2,700	810	Johnson Guns, Inc.

.224 Montgomery

Historical Notes: This wildcat centerfire cartridge was designed by IHMSA shooter and instructor Tim Montgomery. The round is made by necking down a .25 ACP case to accept a .224 bullet. He said, "I have been shooting this cartridge since 1990, and it is not too hard to get a few sub-MOA groups out of each range session."

General Comments: A typical load for the Montgomery is 1.8 grains of Bullseye, or two grains of Unique with a 40-grain Hornady V-Max or a Nosler 40-grain boattail. These loads will produce around 1,300 fps. One load Montgomery likes uses 40-grain BlitzKing bullets and 2.8 grains of AA#5. Another load for a 12-inch T/C Contender 1:12 twist is 2.8 grains of Vihtavuori 3n3 under a 45-grain Sierra Hornet soft-point. A Federal 100M primer fires the charge, and it averages a little over 1,400 fps. This would make a super pest-getter: little noise, no recoil, and deadly accurate.

Bullberry Barrel Works of Hurricane, Utah, chambers for this round. RCBS has dies (No. 55000 Shell holder No. 29, .25 ACP). —*W.T.W.*

.224 Montgomery Loading Data

Bullet (grains/type)	Powder	Grains	Velocity	Energy	Source
30 Berger	AA#7	4.0	2,000	266	Tim Montgomery
45 Sierra Hornet SP	Vihtavuori 3n37	2.8	1,400	196	Tim Montgomery

.224 Clark

Historical Notes: Every few years, someone will neck down the 6mm Remington case to .22-caliber, fire-form it to the Improved configuration, and proclaim it to be the greatest invention since the round wheel. Occasionally, one of those cartridge development "pioneers" will manage to sell his story to a young and innocent magazine editor, who is unaware that the idea is far from new. No one knows for certain who was first to try it, but the one who received the most attention was varmint shooter and gunsmith Kenneth Clark, of Madera, Calif. Back in 1962, he necked down the .257 Roberts case to .22-caliber, blew it out to less body taper and a 30-degree shoulder angle, and called it the .224 Clark. And, since the 6mm Remington case is nothing more than the .257 Roberts case necked down with a minor change made to its shoulder angle, the .22-6mm Remington Improved and the .224 Clark are performance peas of the same pod. An avid shooter of California ground squirrels at extreme ranges, Clark wanted something capable of bucking wind better than the .22-250 and .220 Swift did, so he talked friend Joyce Hornady into making .224-inch 80-grain bullets for his cartridge. That may be the only time in history a major company has made bullets specifically for a wildcat cartridge on a production basis. Kenneth Clark was also a deer hunter, so he designed an 85-grain bullet for his cartridge and made it in his shop. Like the Hornady 80-grain varmint bullet, it was a hollow-point, but his early design was of double-jacket construction for expansion control.

General Comments: When building rifles for his cartridge, Clark used barrels with a rifling twist rate of 1:9 to stabilize the extremely long 80- and 85-grain bullets in flight. Since those bullets weren't as long as match bullets of the same weight now being made (Sierra 80-grain MatchKing being an example), anyone building a rifle in .224 Clark today would be wise to go with a twist rate of 1:8. Even after 6mm Remington cases became available, Clark stayed with Winchester .257 Roberts brass for forming his cartridge because, in his opinion, it handled higher pressures. Whether or not this is true today is debatable and, in reality, a moot argument, since .257 Roberts cases are as easy to come by as 6mm Remington cases.

.224 Clark Loading Data and Factory Ballistics

Bullet (grains/type)	Powder	Grains	Velocity	Energy	Source
80 Clark HP	H4831	50.0	3,500	2174	Ken Clark
85 Clark HP	H870	59.0	3,518	2333	Ken Clark

WARNING: These powder charges are maximum and must be reduced by 10 percent for starting loads.

.22 Fawn

Historical Notes: Carroll Pilant is an employee of Sierra Bullets and has been the face of the company for many years. Carroll is an avid shooter and reloader. When Carroll's son Hunter was young, he wanted to design his own wildcat cartridge and was continually putting drawings in front of his father, who would repeatedly tell him, "It's already been done. " That changed, in October 1992, when Hunter showed Carroll a .41 Magnum case necked down to .22-caliber. Hunter had named it after his sister, Fawn. Carroll then worked with Clymer Reamers and Bullberry Barrel Works and had a Thompson/Center single-shot rifle built for his son for Christmas. The only change Carroll made to his son's drawing and design was to open the primer pocket to accept Large Rifle primers. Carroll later found out that, in 1969, Dennis Hrusosky had developed a similar cartridge with a 30-degree shoulder that he called the .224 Rimmed Critter Gitter.

General Comments: The .22 Fawn is capable of driving a 50-grain bullet faster than 3200 fps. This cartridge offers similar ballistics to the .222 Remington Magnum, the .22 PPC, and the .223 Remington, but in a much shorter configuration. The .22 Fawn is a rimmed cartridge that is well-suited to single-shot rifles and pistols like the Thompson/Center Contender. Aside from the rimmed case, the .22 Fawn offers little advantage over these other cartridges, unless you have a large stash of .41 Magnum cases lying around and nothing else to use them for. It is mostly unique in that it was conceived by a young man as opposed to a seasoned wildcatter.

.22 Fawn Loading Data

Bullet (grains/type)	Powder	Grains	Velocity	Energy	Source/Comments
50 Sierra SPT	AA 2015	22.0	3,250	1,172	Carroll Pilant

.22 PDK

Historical Notes: The intent of the .22 PDK was to offer a high-velocity .22-caliber cartridge that consumed less powder than a .22-250 or .220 Swift. It was conceptualized by Illinois wildcatter Roy Winnett, in collaboration with benchrest shooter John Hutchins. The parent case was the .20 PDK (Prairie Dog Killer), which is based on the 6.8 Remington SPC case. The .22 PDK will work well in either a bolt rifle or AR-15. It has a 30-degree shoulder and a case capacity of 36 grains of water.

General Comments: The .22 PDK may be especially appealing to AR-15 shooters looking for a higher velocity option to the .223 Remington for shooting targets or varmints at long range. This cartridge is also capable of driving premium, heavy-for-caliber bullets suitable for medium-sized game like deer to much higher velocities than the .223 Remington. While the cartridge does not offer a substantial advantage over the .22-250 in a bolt-action rifle, it is indeed a lightning rod in an AR-15. A twist rate of 1:9 or 1:10 is ideal for this cartridge. Cartridge cases are available from Silver State Armory, and handloading dies and cases are available directly from Roy Winnett: (309) 367-4867; www.pdk20.com.

.22 PDK Loading Data

Bullet (grains/type)	Powder	Grains	Velocity	Energy	Source/Comments
50 Nosler BT	H 4895	31.0	3,880	1,672	Roy Winnett
55 V-Max	W 748	31.5	3,770	1,735	Roy Winnett
60 Berger	AA 2230	31.0	3,580	1,707	Roy Winnett
65 JLK	H4895	31.0	3,520	1,788	Roy Winnett
80 JLK VLD	VV 540	29.5	3,230	1,852	Roy Winnett

.220 Weatherby Rocket

Historical Notes: The .220 Weatherby Rocket is the only Weatherby development for which loaded ammunition or empty cases are not available. For this reason, it must be placed in the wildcat category. Developed, in 1943, by the late Roy Weatherby, it was the first in the long line of his excellent and successful cartridges. However, it was never very popular. It is important primarily as it notes the beginning of the Weatherby ammunition line and the initial stimulant to a career of rifle and cartridge manufacture that has had a considerable impact on American thinking.

General Comments: The .220 Weatherby Rocket is actually one of a number of improved wildcat cartridges based on the .220 Swift case. The Ackley and Kilbourn versions are similar, and none have any particular advantage over any other. In addition, none of these is sufficiently superior to the original .220 Swift or offer anything of outstanding value, insofar as performance is concerned. As is typical of improved cartridges in which the original design features significant body taper, the Improved Swift extracts somewhat more easily and, with proper headspacing, gives longer case life.

.220 Weatherby Rocket Loading Data

Bullet (grains/type)	Powder	Grains	Velocity	Energy	Source/Comments
50 SP	IMR 3031	40.0	4,005	1,775	Ackley

.220 Weatherby Rocket Loading Data

Bullet (grains/type)	Powder	Grains	Velocity	Energy	Source/Comments
55 SP	IMR 3031	39.0	3,767	1,730	Ackley
55 SP	IMR 4064	42.0	3,860	1,820	Ackley

Warning: Start all loads 10 percent below these figures and work up gradually.

.22-243 Middlestead

Historical Notes: The .243 Winchester cartridge, released in 1955, was an ideal candidate for wildcat experimentation, such as necking down the .243 case to .224 to produce the .22-243 Winchester wildcat. In the 1960s, Californian Paul Middlestead made his version with a 30-degree shoulder, a modification that provided a longer neck for more flexible bullet-seating depth. A flat-shooting varmint cartridge, it predates the .22 CHeetah by 10 years.

General Comments: Recoil is slightly less than the parent .243. No factory ammunition is produced for it. The Middlestead performs similarly to the .223 WSSM, and, because of its neck length, it can accept 50-grain bullets (4150 fps), 55-grain bullets (3900 fps), 60- to 65-grain bullets (3700 fps), and even 80-grainers such as the Hornady A-Max (3300 fps). Of course, when shooters are building a rifle for this wildcat, they must consider barrel twist rates for the bullet weights they intend to use most often. —*W.T.W.*

.22-243 Middlestead Loading Data

Bullet (grains/type)	Powder	Grains	Velocity	Energy	Source/Comments
30 Berger HP MEF	Alliant Reloader 15	48.0	5,029	1,681	ReloadersNest.com
52 Sierra HP	Norma 204	52.0	3,942	1,790	ReloadersNest.com
77 Sierra MatchKing	Alliant Reloader 22	45.8	3,700	2,236	ReloadersNest.com

.220 Wotkyns-Wilson Arrow

Historical Notes: The .220 Wotkyns-Wilson Arrow was the work of Grosvenor Wotkyns and L.E. Wilson and is the .220 Swift with the shoulder angle increased from 21 degrees to 30 degrees. It dates back to the 1940s. Cases are made by reforming unfired .220 Swift cases in full-length sizing dies. Because of the longer neck, standard Swift ammunition will not fully enter the Arrow chamber and cases cannot be made by fire-forming.

General Comments: The .220 Wotkyns-Wilson Arrow represented an effort to remedy a problem by making a minor change in cartridge configuration. Factory Swift cases had the reputation of lengthening after only a few firings, thus requiring frequent trimming. Changing to a steeper shoulder angle improved headspacing and made for longer case life. The Arrow was a popular benchrest cartridge and a true long-range varmint number. It delivers ballistics comparable to the .220 Swift.

.220 Wotkyns-Wilson Arrow Loading Data

Bullet (grains/type)	Powder	Grains	Velocity	Energy	Source/Comments
45 SP	H450	47.0	3,985	1,580	NA
50 SP	H450	46.0	3,850	1,640	NA
50 SP	IMR 4064	40.0	3,915	1,695	NA
55 SP	H380	39.0	3,510	1,500	NA

.228 Ackley Magnum

Historical Notes: The .228 Ackley Magnum dates back to about 1938, and although it has been around for a number of years, it developed only a limited popularity. Like the .22 Newton, it was designed as a combination varmint and big-game cartridge. Ammunition is made by necking-down and shortening .30-06 or .308 Winchester cases. There are several versions of this cartridge, but Ackley's design is the most popular.

General Comments: Rifles for .228-inch diameter, heavy-jacketed bullets designed for big game have been used very successfully all over the world. Bullets of this type were made in weights from 70 to more than 100 grains by Fred Barnes, but are now difficult to obtain. Rifles in this class have proven rather conclusively that the difficulties encountered with the .220 Swift and other high-velocity .22s have been mostly a result of improper bullet design. Factory .22-caliber centerfire loads are all made for varmint shooting and do not hold together or penetrate deeply enough on big game—most of the time. Sometimes these do and the results are spectacular, but mostly these blow up on contact and inflict a massive, but not immediately fatal, wound. Consequently, hunting deer with any .22-caliber centerfire rifle is illegal in most states. Bear this matter of bullet construction in mind next time you get in an argument over the effectiveness of small-caliber rifles on big game.

.228 Ackley Magnum Loading Data

Bullet (grains/type)	Powder	Grains	Velocity	Energy	Source/Comments
70 SP	IMR 4350	46.0	3,650	2,070	Ackley
90 SP	IMR 4350	43.0	3,480	2,420	Ackley

6x45mm (6mm-223 Remington)

Historical Notes: The 6mm-223 Remington, also known as the 6x45mm, came into being in late 1965, shortly after Remington introduced the .223 Remington as a sporting round. Various experimenters built rifles for the cartridge (in order to take advantage of the reduced wind drift offered by the 6mm, as opposed to the original .22-caliber bullet), for benchrest or varmint shooting. Jim Stekl, then-manager of Remington's custom shop, set an IBS 200-yard Sporter aggregate record of .3069 MOA in 1973 using the 6x45mm. For a time, some owners of AR-15 rifles rebarreled their rifles to this chambering for use in NRA National Match Course competition. However, the 6x45mm cannot compete successfully with the 7.62x51mm NATO (.308 Winchester) round at ranges beyond 300 yards. After its brief flurry as a benchrest and match cartridge, the 6x45mm has now been relegated to designation primarily as a varmint cartridge used by those who want more power than the .223 with the added advantage of being able to utilize inexpensive military cases. Reloading dies are available from RCBS, and chambering reamers from Clymer (www.clymertool.com).

General Comments: The 6x45mm is one of a series of 6mm benchrest cartridges based on necking up .223 Remington and .222 Remington Magnum cases. None have any great advantage over the other and all are capable of extremely fine accuracy. Probably the only advantage of the 6x45mm is that it is based on the 5.56mm (.223 Remington) military case, which assures a good supply of cases. On the other hand, its shorter case permits the use of bullets of up to 100 grains to be seated to an overall length that will feed through magazine rifles such as the Colt AR-15, Ruger Mini-14, or Remington 788. In power, the 6x45mm is between the old .25-35 and the .250 Savage, which would make it rather marginal as a deer cartridge, except under ideal conditions. It is, however, close to ideal as a varmint and small-game cartridge out to 300 yards. This cartridge has become very popular in the Thompson/Center Contender and Remington XP-100 handguns. Bob Milek, the late field editor of *Guns & Ammo* and *Petersen's Hunting* magazines, shot a custom XP-100 in 6x45mm for a number of years. Rifles chambered for cartridges in this group are pleasant to shoot, have a relatively low report, and are noted for long barrel life.

6x45mm (6mm-223 Remington) Loading Data

Bullet (grains/type)	Powder	Grains	Velocity	Energy	Source/Comments
70 HP	W748	27.5	2,890	1,295	NA
75 HP	H335	27.0	2,900	1,400	NA
80 HP	W748	27.0	2,780	1,370	NA

6mm Dasher

Historical Notes: Early in 1998, this cartridge, based upon the .22 Dasher, was announced in a Precision Shooting magazine article that was co-authored by Al Ashton and Dan Dowling. The .22 Dasher was developed as a means of approximating .22-250 ballistics in a shorter case, but using cases with the same base diameter. Thinner case walls and the modern Ackley case shape make it possible for the significantly shorter BR case to achieve that goal. This 6mm version is simply the .22-caliber Dasher necked up to accept 6mm bullets with no other changes.

General Comments: Lighter 6mm varminting bullets can come very close to matching the trajectory of best .22 Dasher loads; heavier 6mm varmint bullets can exhibit significantly less wind drift. This cartridge will push Nosler's excellent 55-grain BT 150 fps faster than the .22 Dasher will push the same weight bullet. Perhaps a more important advantage is that, since the 6mm version is much easier on the barrel, one can expect double the barrel life. Moreover, it is much harder to overheat the barrel during an extended shooting string. The latter fact is a significant consideration to all serious varmint hunters. Concerns over undue barrel heating prompt many varminters to carry several rifles, so they can switch between guns during any extended period of shooting. For this reason alone, the 6mm Dasher is a superior high-performance varminting choice. This cartridge, like the 6mm Norma BR, is finding application in 1,000-yard benchrest events, where it can excel on calm days.

6mm-250 (6mm International) Loading Data

Bullet (grains/type)	Powder	Grains	Velocity	Energy	Source/Comments
55 Nosler BT	H335	39.0	4,000	1,955	Al Aston (2.175-inch OAL)
70 Nosler BT	H335	36.8	3,650	2,070	Al Aston (2.175-inch OAL)

.25-222 Copperhead

Historical Notes: The .25-222 Copperhead was created during the early 1970s by firearms writer John Wootters in his search for a varmint cartridge with more punch than the .222 Remington and yet small enough to work in a lightweight rifle built on the Sako L-461 action. The custom rifle he ended up with had a barrel measuring 183/8 inches long with a rifling twist rate of 1:14. The rifle wore a Mannlicher-style stock, and a clamp on its scope allowed easy attachment of a spotlight for calling coyotes and bobcats at night. Wootters also developed several reduced-velocity loads with the Lyman 257463 cast bullet for use on Rio Grande turkeys, which are abundant in his home state of Texas. The case is formed by necking up the .222 Remington case to .25-caliber with no other change.

General Comments: The .25-222 Copperhead is in the same performance class as the 6x45mm and 6x47mm wildcats, and choosing between them boils down to a preference in .24- or .25-caliber.

.25-222 Copperhead Loading Data and Factory Ballistics

Bullet (grains/type)	Powder	Grains	Velocity	Energy	Source
60 Hornady FP	H4227	19.5	2,955	1,162	John Wootters

.25-222 Copperhead Loading Data and Factory Ballistics

Bullet (grains/type)	Powder	Grains	Velocity	Energy	Source
72 Lyman 257463	IMR-4198	16.0	2,070	684	John Wootters
75 Hornady HP	IMR-4198	21.0	2,765	1,272	John Wootters
87 Sierra SP	IMR-4198	20.5	2,590	1,294	John Wootters

.22 Tuba II Rimmed
.22 Tuba II Unrimmed

Historical Notes: The .22 Tuba II has been a working cartridge—but is now mainly a collectible—made by machinist Zachary Weighman. Weighman said, "I started making these up for friends of mine, after seeing a drawing of 'Dingbat cartridges'—drawings of mythical cartridges. In one of them, the shoulder started at the rim. Being a machinist, I decided to turn up a few of these from solid brass. I gave them a primer pocket and drilled out the neck, too. I seated snapped primers and bullets in them. Being as how I'm a cartridge collector, I have lots of friends who think this kind of stuff is pretty cool, so I made them up to give away to my friends."

"One day a friend said, 'Wouldn't it be cool if you could make up an actual cartridge like this?' So, after giving it some thought, I decided to make up a die for necking down a .45 Long Colt case, to see what it would look like. The die has inserts that progressively get smaller. It took five sizing steps to neck the .45 LC cases down to .22. I had moderate success with this, but I did not have a lot of .45 LC cases on hand. However, I did have lots of .44 Magnum cases, so I changed to them. After refining the process a bit, I was having much better success with these. I later decided to try using .45 ACP cases to make a rimless version of the .22 Tuba. I decided to call my cartridges the .22 Tuba II.

"At this point, they were still just dummies for giving away. Once again, the same friend said, 'It would be really cool if you had a gun that would shoot these cartridges.' I had an old Marlin single-shot .410 bolt-action shotgun. Because the head of a .410 shell and a .44 Magnum cartridge are very close to the same diameter, I thought the action would work. It was just a matter of changing the barrel and cutting a chamber. So I removed the .410 barrel and installed a .22 rimfire barrel onto the action."

Weighman continued, "I had already cut the chamber into the barrel, using drills and lather tools on my lathe. The whole deal worked really well. The extractor even worked with no other modifications. Then I turned to the rimless version. With this, I decided to use a single-shot .410 shotgun again, but this time it was a break-action New England Firearms gun. I cut the barrel off at about seven inches, creating a sort of mono-block. Then I drilled it, reamed it, and threaded the inside of this mono-block. I then took another .22 rimfire barrel and threaded the outside area to match the threads in the mono-block. The barrel was threaded into the mono-block and, after some extractor work and adding a scope mount and scope, it was ready to go."

General Comments: Weighman said he's done very little chronograph work with the Tuba rounds, except for 40-grain lead bullets, which he pulls out of .22 LR cases and reforms in a swaging die. With this bullet over 8.0 grains of IMR 4227 (which is about all it will hold), he gets just under 2,300 fps velocity. The inert Tubas he sells nowadays are dummies loaded with 55-grain FMJ bullets. He told us, "I do this because they just plain look and sell better than ones with lead bullets. They're popular and they sell well."

For more information, e-mail Weighman at cartguy@torchlake.com.— *W.T.W*

.22 Tuba II Loading Data

Bullet (grains/type)	Powder	Grains	Velocity	Energy	Source
40 swaged lead .22 LR	IMR-4227	8.0	2,300	470	Zac Weighman

.22 Newton

Historical Notes: One of a series of cartridges developed by Charles Newton, this one did not appear in full commercial version. It was designed about 1912, following the introduction of the .22 Savage Hi-Power for the Model 99 lever-action rifle. Newton concluded during his development work on the .22 Savage that it was not entirely adequate for deer. He believed the 70-grain bullet at 2800 fps could be improved by using a larger case. Newton may have used the 7x57mm Mauser case for some of his early experiments. However, the final version of the .22 Newton appears to have been based on the .30-06 case shortened about ¼-inch and necked-down to take 0.228-inch-diameter bullets. The .22 Newton did not appear as a Newton rifle chambering until about 1914 or later and did not have a very long life. The original loading had a 90-grain bullet driven at 3100 fps. The .22 Newton was soon displaced by the .256 Newton, which had superior potential as a big-game cartridge.

General Comments: This is another cartridge somewhat ahead of its time. The new 5.6x57, developed by RWS, is very similar in performance and case capacity. It pushes a 74-grain bullet at 3400 fps (.224-inch diameter), and is a necked-down 7x57 case. With a 90-grain bullet, this 5.6mm round would probably just about duplicate .22 Newton performance. Because of the relatively heavy .22-caliber bullet, the .22 Newton would be a satisfactory deer, antelope or similar game cartridge, provided proper bullet construction was used. The .220/257 Gipson is a very similar cartridge based on the .257 Roberts case necked-down to .22-caliber. This latter cartridge was designed by Vernon Gipson, a gunsmith and wildcatter from Worth, Illinois. (The .22 Gebby was a similar round on the .257 case.) Rifles for the .22 Newton require a very fast twist (1:8 inches) to stabilize this long, small-caliber bullet.

.22 Newton Loading Data

Bullet (grains/type)	Powder	Grains	Velocity	Energy	Source/Comments
70 SP	IMR 4350	40.0	3,250	1,640	NA
90 SP	IMR 4350	38.0	3,100	1,920	NA

6mm CHeetah

Historical Notes: The 6mm CHeetah, designed by *Outdoor Life's* shooting editor Jim Carmichael, is a highly accurate, long-range varmint cartridge. It is best described as a variation of Jim's earlier (and racy) .22 CHeetah cartridge necked up to accommodate 6mm bullets. Based on a modified .243 Winchester parent case, the cartridge employs both fire-forming and neck-turning techniques and requires knowledge of advanced reloading practices.

General Comments: The principle advantage of the 6mm CHeetah is accuracy. This performance results from a combination of precise cartridge case preparation steps (especially neck turning to a diameter of .267-inch to achieve precision bullet alignment), and chambering in high-quality rifles with target-grade barrels and expert gunsmithing. The case design is not a true Improved cartridge, and factory .243 Winchester ammunition can not safely be fired in the 6mm CHeetah. Loading data for the .243 AI cartridge can be used for the 6mm CHeetah. The fire-forming load uses 46.5-grains of Reloader 19 and a Sierra 85-grain bullet seated for an overall loaded cartridge length of 2.747 inches. Rifles using the Remington 40X or modern benchrest-type actions provide the best platform for the 6mm CHeetah. Reamers are available from JGS Precision Tool Mfg (www.jgstools.com); rifles for the 6mm CHeetah can be supplied by gunsmiths specializing in high precision firearms.

6mm CHeetah Loading Data

Bullet (grains/type)	Powder	Grains	Velocity	Energy	Source/Comments
55 Nosler Ballistic Tip	H4350	51.0	3,627	1,606	Jim Carmichael
70 Speer TNT	H4350	47.5	3,525	1,931	Jim Carmichael

6mm CHeetah Loading Data

Bullet (grains/type)	Powder	Grains	Velocity	Energy	Source/Comments
100 Sierra Boat-tail	H4350	45.0	3,074	2,098	Jim Carmichael

6x47mm

Historical Notes: Simply the .222 Remington Magnum case necked up for .243-inch bullets, the 6x47mm is thought to be a brainchild of Mike Walker who, in addition to working for Remington at the time, was an avid benchrest competitor. Introduced to the sport during the early 1960s, it and the .222 Remington absolutely dominated benchrest shooting, until the 6mm PPC came along. The popularity of the 6x47mm prompted Federal to start making nickel-plated cases during the 1970s, but they are long out of production.

General Comments: While most often thought of as a competition cartridge, the 6x47mm is a fine varmint cartridge when loaded with relatively light bullets for its caliber. As for bigger game, there are better deer cartridges, but a good marksman who desires a lightweight rifle with very little recoil could get by with it by handloading the Nosler 85-grain Partition to a velocity of 2800 fps and restricting shots to no farther than 200 yards. Benchrest shooters customarily stick with relatively light bullets in various 6mm cartridges, and the 1:14 twist rate in barrels they choose are too slow to stabilize bullets much heavier than 75 grains. When the 6x47mm is used for applications where heavier bullets are needed, the twist should be quicker with 1:10 or even 1:9, recommended for hunting bullets up to 100 grains. A good bolt-action rifle chambered for any member of the .222 Remington family of cartridges can be converted to 6x47mm by simply rebarreling it. True to its benchrest competition heritage, the 6x47mm can be incredibly accurate in a good barrel, although some competitors consider it to be more finicky than the 6mm PPC that replaced it.

6x47mm Loading Data and Factory Ballistics

(Note: *Excellent 200-yard deer and pronghorn load)

Bullet (grains/type)	Powder	Grains	Velocity	Energy	Source
58 Hornady V-Max	A-2230	28.8	3,500	1,576	Hornady
65 Hornady V-Max	IMR-3031	27.8	3,300	1,570	Hornady
70 Hornady SP	BL-C(2)	30.7	3,200	1,590	Hornady
75 Hornady HP	H322	25.9	3,000	1,497	Hornady
85 Nosler Partition*	H335	27.5	2,810	1,489	Layne Simpson

WARNING: All powder charges are maximum and must be reduced by 10 percent for starting loads.

6mm-250 (6mm International) Walker Version

Historical Notes: Prior to World War II, the 6mm (.243-caliber) was nearly an exclusive British and European development, with some cartridges dating back to the early 1900s. Immediately after World War II, American wildcatters began to work with this caliber. The simple process of necking the .250 Savage case down to take .243 bullets probably occurred to several individuals, but was obscured by other 6mm developments. Several versions exist, and two of these have become popular with benchrest and match shooters. The Donaldson 6mm International was developed by Harvey Donaldson, of Fultonville, New York, the man known as the father of modern benchrest shooting. The Remington 6mm International originated with Mike Walker, of the Remington Arms Co.

General Comments: Cartridges of 6mm based on the .250 Savage case are all similar, but vary slightly in length and shoulder angle. Original design was the .250 case necked down with no other change. Donaldson's version used a ¼-inch shortened case with the shoulder pushed back; on that version, shoulder angle is 30 degrees. The Walker 6mm retains the standard length, but pushes the shoulder back, creating a long neck. Body taper and shoulder angle are the same as the .250. The Remington 40X match rifle has been chambered on special order for the Walker cartridge. Robert Hutton, long-time experimenter and gun writer, has worked with these cartridges, and his results were presented in the 1962 (16th edition) of *Gun Digest*. The late John T. Amber reported 5/8-inch averages for five-shot, 100-yard groups with the Walker cartridge in the Remington 40X target rifle, impressive performance for that era.

6mm-250 (6mm International) Loading Data

Bullet (grains/type)	Powder	Grains	Velocity	Energy	Source/Comments
60 HP	IMR 3031	32.0	3,450	1,630	NA
75 HP	IMR 3031	32.0	3,390	1,910	NA
90 SP	IMR 3031	30.0	3,160	2,000	NA
100 SP	IMR 3031	28.0	2,900	1,870	NA

6mm/30-30 Ackley Improved

Historical Notes: There are actually two common versions of the 6mm/30-30, one based on the .30-30 Winchester case necked down without any other change, and the other using the Improved configuration. The Improved version was the most popular and the one recommended. The 6mm/30-30 has the same dimensions as the .22/30-30, except for a larger .243-inch neck diameter. The cartridge dates back to the 1940s or earlier, and the version referred to here is the Ackley Improved, although there may be others. One of the original purposes of the 6mm/30-30 was for use in re-bored and re-chambered .22 Hi-Power Model 99 Savage lever-actions. This chambering has also been used in single-shot actions. Cases can be formed from .30-30 or .32 Special cases, which might require a set of forming dies plus a final fire-forming. More recent versions use a shortened case for application to single-shot pistols.

General Comments: The 6mm/30-30, when used in a strong action, can be loaded to almost equal the .243 Winchester. It is a good varmint-through-deer cartridge, but its current usefulness is primarily as a chambering for single-shot actions.

6mm/30-30 Improved Loading Data

Bullet (grains/type)	Powder	Grains	Velocity	Energy	Source/Comments
75 HP	IMR 3031	37.0	3,450	1,980	Ackley
75 HP	IMR 4895	36.0	3,265	1,770	Ackley
*85 HP	IMR 4895	37.0	3,300	2,060	Ackley
90 SP	IMR 4320	38.0	3,065	1,880	Ackley

*Ackley, op cit.

Spitzer 6mm-06

Historical Notes: The earliest 6mm cartridge of American design was the 6mm Lee Navy, with its 112-grain bullet at around 2600 fps. No one knows for certain when wildcatters begin to take a serous look at bullets measuring .243-inch in diameter, but it probably didn't happen in great numbers until the 1940s. The Canadians had their 6mm-303 Epps on the .303 British case, while Americans necked down about everything they could get their hands on. Three of the more popular were the .240 Cobra (on the .220 Swift case); Fred Huntington's. 243 Rockchucker, which eventually became known as the .244 Remington; and Warren Page's .240 Page Pooper, which was eventually produced commercially as the .243 Winchester. Wildcats on the .30-06 case went by various names, but the most popular were probably the plain-vanilla 6mm-06 and the .240 Super Varminter, the latter created by Jerry Gebby, who also popularized the .22-250. With its minimum body taper, stubby neck length, and extremely sharp shoulder angle, another wildcat called the

.240 Gibbs was basically an Improved version of the Super Varminter. Others of similar powder capacities that came along later are the 6mm-284, on the .284 Winchester case, and the 6mm-350, on the .350 Remington Magnum case.

General Comments: The 6mm-06 case is easily formed by necking down the .30-06 case in two steps, first with a 6.5-06 or .25-06 full-length resizing die, and then with a 6mm-06 die, all available from RCBS (www.rcbs.com) and Redding (www.redding-reloading.com). An intermediate sizing die is not required when necking down .270 Winchester or .25-06 cases. Regardless of the case used, neck diameter with a bullet seated must be held to .290-inch or smaller, and should a batch of formed cases exceed that dimension, their neck walls will need to be thinned by the necessary amount by reaming or outside turning. Maximum case length of 2.494 inches is the same as for the .30-06, so cases formed from .270 Winchester brass will require trimming back by a slight amount. While pressure-tested load data are not available for the 6mm-06, its powder capacity is quite close to those of the .240 Weatherby Magnum and the 6mm-284, so starting loads published for them in various reloading manuals can be used. The chamber of the Weatherby Mark V in .240 Magnum is not freebored, as is the case for that same rifle chambered for other Weatherby cartridges, but its throat is a bit longer than is commonly seen in rifles chambered for other 6mm cartridges, so, to be on the safe side, starting loads published for the .240 Magnum should be reduced by 5 percent when used in the 6mm-06. Continuing on with a note of caution, starting loads found in the Hornady manual for the 6mm-284 should also be reduced by the same amount when used in the 6mm-06.

A gross-capacity comparison of 6mm-06 cases formed from Remington .25-06 cases, .240 Magnum cases, and 6mm-284 cases formed from Winchester .284 brass reveals that the 6mm-06 averages a half grain greater capacity than the .240 Magnum, and 2.3 grains less than the 6mm-284. This gives the 6mm-284 a slight edge over the other two, but only when it is used in a rifle with an action long enough to allow seating the heavier bullets out of its powder space. More often, that cartridge is used in a short-action rifle in which deep seating of bullets is required, and this reduces its net powder capacity to about the same as for the .240 Magnum and the 6mm-06.

Like the .240 Weatherby Magnum, the 6mm-06 has an extremely flat trajectory, making it an excellent choice for hunting deer and pronghorn antelope in open country. When the Swift 90-grain Scirocco exits a 26-inch barrel at 3425 fps and is zeroed three inches high at 100 yards, it strikes about four inches high at 200 yards, dead on at 300, and low by about half the body depth of a whitetail deer at 400 yards, where it is still packing close to 1200 ft-lbs of punch.

Spitzer 6mm-06 Loading Data and Factory Ballistics

Bullet (grains/type)	Powder	Grains	Velocity	Energy	Source
55 Nosler Ballistic Tip	H414	52.0	3,817	1,777	Layne Simpson
75 Sierra HP	V-N160	53.0	3,644	2,209	Layne Simpson
80 Sierra HP	Magnum	55.0	3,382	2,030	Layne Simpson
85 Barnes XBT	IMR-4350	49.0	3,479	2,282	Layne Simpson
90 Swift Scirocco	H4831	53.0	3,428	2,346	Layne Simpson
100 Nosler Partition	IMR-7828	52.0	3,272	2,375	Layne Simpson
105 Speer SP	RL-22	51.0	3,210	2,400	Layne Simpson

WARNING: All powder charges are maximum and should be reduced by 15 percent for starting loads. Cases were formed by necking down Remington .25-06 brass.

.240 Hawk

Historical Notes: Unlike other members of the Hawk cartridge family, the Fred Zeglin-designed .240 Hawk is an overbored, velocity-addicted varmint cartridge. It is capable of shooting groups as small as .300-inch at 100 yards and offers one of the flattest trajectories available in 6mm varmint cartridges. Performance comes at a price, however, and .240 Hawk barrel life may be shorter than other 6mm varmint cartridges using lighter powder charges. Devout long-range varmint shooters may decide the trade-off is okay.

General Comments: All Hawk cartridges fit into standard .30-06 length actions and use a .473-inch bolt-face. The .240 Hawk uses .280 Remington brass as its parent case. The brass is necked down in a sizing die and fire-formed in a .240 Hawk chamber. The .240 Hawk is designed for lighter weight 6mm varmint bullets. Reloading data for the .240 Weatherby can be used as a starting point, as the .240 Hawk enjoys a four-percent greater case capacity advantage. However, barrel life will be less than other 6mm varmint cartridges that use lighter powder charges. It is best suited for bolt-action rifles with 28-inch barrels with a 1:14 twist. Z-Hat Custom (www.z-hat.com) offers rifles, dies, and reloading information. Use caution with the listed loads, as Z-Hat has not conducted pressure tests on them.

.240 Hawk Loading Data

Bullet (grains/type)	Powder	Grains	Velocity	Energy	Source/Comments
60 Sierra HP	VV N150	53.0	3,968	2,097	Z-Hat Custom
75 Speer HP	H4064	49.0	3,652	2,220	Z-Hat Custom
80 Remington HP	RL-15	53.0	4,055	2,920	Z-Hat Custom
87 Hornady SPT	Win 748	51.0	3,954	3,019	Z-Hat Custom

6mm-284

Historical Notes: It is anybody's guess who might have been first to size Winchester's rebated-rim .284 down to 6mm. The conversion is good for those interested in achieving maximum velocity with this bullet size. This cartridge can be chambered in medium-length actions.

General Comments: The 6mm-284 has practically the same capacity as the .240 Weatherby Magnum and the 6mm-06. If loaded to similar chamber pressures, it will produce similar velocity. Therefore, ballistics are indistinguishable. However, it has advantages over the Weatherby offering; cases are easier to come by and non-belted. The 6mm-284 can also be chambered in medium-length actions.

Just like the 6mm-06 and .240 Weatherby, when loaded with 100-grain bullets, the 6mm-284 produces only about 100 fps more velocity than the 6mm Remington, when loaded to the same peak pressures and fired from equal-length barrels. Likely, with heavier-than-standard bullets, this difference could reach 150 fps. As to whether such an advantage might justify conversion of a .243 Winchester or 6mm Remington rifle to 6mm-284, consider that this performance difference exceeds the performance difference between the .280 Remington and 7mm Remington Magnum!

6mm-284 Loading Data (26-inch barrel)

Bullet (grains)	Powder	Grains	Velocity	Energy	Source/Comments
70	IMR 4320	45.0	3,600	2,015	Hornady
70	IMR 4350	49.5	3,600	2,015	Hornady
70	H4831	52.5	3,600	2,015	Hornady
75	H4831	54.1	3,600	2,155	Hornady
87	H4831	51.7	3,400	2,230	Hornady
100	IMR 4350	49.0	3,200	2,275	Hornady
100	H4831	51.4	3,200	2,275	Hornady

.25 Gibbs

Historical Notes: The .25 Gibbs was designed in the 1950s by firearms experimenter R.E. "Rocky" Gibbs. It was a natural follow-up to Gibbs' original .270 Gibbs, which he developed while seeking the optimum case capacity for the .270 bore size in combination with a 150-grain bullet.

General Comments: The .25 Gibbs is a blown-out .30-06 (or .270 Winchester) case with a steep shoulder and short neck. The shoulder is pushed forward about .196-inch, compared to the standard .270 case, and the case holds about six grains more IMR4350 powder than a standard .270 Winchester. Although Gibbs used this and his other wildcats as front ignition cartridges, the following is a "standard" loading, without the front ignition tube.

.25 Gibbs Loading Data

Bullet (grain/type)	Powder	Grains	Velocity	Energy	Source/Comments
87 Sierra SP	IMR4350	62.0	3,617	2,527	R.E. Gibbs

.25-303
(.303-25)

Historical Notes: The .25-303, also known in reverse as the .303-25, was a wildcat centerfire rifle cartridge based on necking down a .303 British case to fire a .257 projectile. Originating in Australia in the 1930s, it was popular to take a cheap and plentiful Lee Enfield action (No. 1, No. 4, No. 5, and P14), and rebarrel it for the .25-caliber round. For the do-it-yourselfer of today, sometimes the magazine feed lips also need adjusting.

The smaller round was better suited to small-game hunting than the .303 British itself, and civilian ownership of rifles chambered for military rounds was severely restricted. The 87-grain bullet produced about 2,650 fps and was the most popular load, partly because it didn't damage the skins of kangaroos. The .25-303 sits between the .250-3000 and .257 Roberts, in terms of velocity and power and resembles the once-popular .25 Krag. Nearly all rifles converted to .25-303 featured 1:12 barrel twists.

General Comments: Loaded ammunition and brass was produced by Sportco, Super Cartridge Company in Melbourne, ICI, and Riverbrand, using military Berdan-primed cases and new Boxer primed cases. Up until the mid-1980s, .25-303 was available as factory-loaded ammo in Australia. Brass for the .303 British is available from Remington, Federal, Winchester, Sellier & Bellot, and others. Reloading dies are made by RCBS, Lyman, and others. To find loads to work up, the .25-303 is a near twin of the .257 Roberts. The Roberts case holds 56 grains of water and a .303 case 57 grains, so any manufacturer's published load for the .257 Roberts should be safe in a .25-303.—*W.T.W.*

.25-303 (.303-25) Loading Data

Bullet (grain/type)	Powder	Grains	Velocity	Energy	Source/Comments
87 Speer spitzer	H4350	36.9	3,010	1,750	GunBoards.com
100 Speer spitzer	IMR4831	44.5	3,024	2,030	GunBoards.com
117 Sierra BTSP	IMR4831	44.0	2,850	2,110	GunBoards.com

.250 Humdinger

General Comments: The .250 Humdinger is a .243 case expanded to .25-caliber and fire-formed in the Humdinger chamber. The case has absolute minimum body taper and a 45-degree shoulder angle. This produces about as much capacity as can be squeezed from an Improved .243 case. The .25-caliber is ideally suited to hunting wild pigs, feral goats, and most deer species, as well as varmint shooting with lighter bullets. Most short-action rifles designed for the .243 or .308 could quite successfully be chambered for this cartridge. Ballistics from a 23-inch barrel exceed factory .25-06 loads, and it could be considered quite an efficient cartridge.

.250 Humdinger Loading Data

Bullet (grains/type)	Powder	Grains	Velocity	Energy	Source/Comments
75 Sierra HP	H4350	50.0	3,577	2,131	Breil Jackson
87 Sierra SP	H4350	48.5	3,437	2,282	Breil Jackson

.250 Humdinger Loading Data

Bullet (grains/type)	Powder	Grains	Velocity	Energy	Source/Comments
100 Nosler BT	H4350	46.0	3,194	2,266	Breil Jackson
100 Nosler BT	RL 19	48.5	3,175	2,239	Breil Jackson
117 Hornady SPBT	IMR4831	46.0	3,085	2,473	Breil Jackson
120 Nosler Partition	IMR4831	45.0	3,040	2,462	Breil Jackson

.257 Kimber

Historical Notes: When Jack Warne and his son, Greg, founded the original Kimber of Oregon, the rifle they introduced to American hunters and shooters was the Model 82 in .22 Long Rifle. Rifles in .22 Hornet, .218 Bee, and .25-20 Winchester were also built on that same action, but, when the time came to add the .223 Remington to the lineup, a new Model 84 with front locking lugs on its bolt was developed. In addition to eventually being chambered for a number of other factory cartridges, such as the .17 Remington, .221 Remington Fire Ball, and .222 Remington Magnum, a limited number of Model 82 rifles were built in various wildcat chamberings, one being the .257 Kimber, introduced in 1987. It was also offered in the Kimber Predator, a single-shot handgun built on the Model 84 action. Developed by Mike Hill, the .257 Kimber case is formed by necking up the .222 Remington Magnum case and fire-forming it to the Improved configuration with minimum body tape and a 40-degree shoulder angle. Hill received the first rifle built in this caliber.

General Comments: As combination varmint/deer cartridges go, the .257 Roberts is a better choice for rifles with actions large enough to handle it, but it is too long for the Kimber Model 84 action, thereby explaining the reasoning behind the .257 Kimber. Since the little cartridge pretty much duplicates the performance of the .250 Savage, it has to be considered the best deer cartridge to be offered by Kimber in its Model 84 rifle. Reloading dies are available from Redding. When fire-forming the .257 Kimber case, the shoulder of the .222 Magnum case is moved forward for a considerable increase in the headspace dimension. This requires seating of bullets out of the case for hard contact with the rifling in preparation for fire-forming. Doing so holds the head of the case firmly in contact with the face of the bolt, thus preventing case stretching and separation in the web area. Failure to follow this procedure can result in case separation, with possible damage to rifle and shooter.

.257 Kimber Loading Data and Factory Ballistics

Bullet (grains/type)	Powder	Grains	Velocity	Energy	Source
75 Sierra HP	H335	31.5	3,195	1,698	Hodgdon
87 Sierra SP	H4895	31.0	3,056	1,802	Hodgdon
87 Sierra SP	IMR-3031	30.0	3,040	1,783	Hodgdon
100 Sierra SP	H4895	28.0	2,760	1,690	Hodgdon
117 Sierra SP	H4895	24.0	2,223	1,282	Hodgdon

.250/3000 Ackley Improved

Historical Notes: The .250/3000 Improved was originated by P.O. Ackley in the late 1940s and, although one of the best of the Ackley Improved line of cartridges, has never achieved great popularity. This statement about it being the best is based upon the observation that it offers the greatest percentage velocity increase of any of the Improved line of wildcats. Increased shoulder angle affects performance chiefly because it increases case capacity. However, it also improves headspacing and decreases case stretching. There are no significant internal ballistic effects related to any particular shoulder design. There are several versions of the .250 Improved, but the Ackley configuration is the best known. The Savage Model 99 lever-action has recently been offered chambered for the .250/3000, and tens of thousands of these fine rifles are in the hands of hunters. Handloading owners of these rifles should be interested in this excellent conversion, which improves extraction, extends case life, and increases performance markedly.

General Comments: The .250/3000 Improved offers performance equal to or better than the .257 Roberts. It will, for example, push the 100-grain bullet at a muzzle velocity of 3200 fps, compared to the factory .257 loading of the same bullet that is listed at 2900 fps. The commercial .250/3000 loading of the 100-grain bullet, incidentally, is rated at 2820 fps.

.250/3000 Ackley Improved Loading Data

Bullet (grains/type)	Powder	Grains	Velocity	Energy	Source/Comments
87 SP	IMR 4350	42.0	3,310	2,110	Ackley
100 SP	IMR 4350	41.0	3,045	2,060	Ackley
100 SP	IMR 4350	42.0	3,200	2,275	Ackley
120 SP	IMR 4350	40.0	2,650	1,870	Ackley
120 SP	IMR 4350	41.0	2,750	2,020	Ackley

.25-284

Historical Notes: It is anybody's guess who might have been the first to size the .284 Winchester down to the quarter-bore. This conversion is a good one, offering usable capacity practically identical to the .25-06 in a cartridge that can be chambered in medium-length actions.

General Comments: The .25-284 is ballistically indistinguishable from the .25-06, but offers several advantages. First, the sharper case shoulder of the shorter case reduces case stretching and extends case life, compared to the .25-06. Second, the shorter powder column promises superior accuracy potential. Finally, this more compact cartridge is easier to handle. Nevertheless, the .25-06 was easier to make, because .30-06 cases have long been plentiful. Further, the .25-06 enjoyed decades of wildcat history. For these reasons, it is not surprising that the .25-06 was the round chosen to achieve factory chambering. This is too bad, because the .25-06 offers no ballistic advantages over the .25-284, and the aforementioned facts would tend to suggest the .25-284 as a better all-around choice.

Capacity and chamber pressure are essentially identical to the .25-06, and that data can be used, providing a prudent reduction in starting loads and adherence to standard loading practices to ensure against inadvertent use of too-hot loads.

.257 STW (Shooting Times Westerner)

Historical Notes: The .257 STW is the third member of the *Shooting Times* Westerner family of wildcats developed by firearms writer Layne Simpson (the 7mm STW and .358 STA were the first and second). It was introduced in the June 1998 issue of *Shooting Times* magazine. Custom rifle builder Lex Webernick built the first rifle in .257 STW for Simpson, and the first game taken by the writer with it was a Coues deer, in Mexico. The .257 STW case is formed by necking down the 7mm STW case to .25-caliber with no other change. Reloading dies are available from Redding (www.redding-reloading.com) and RCBS (www.rcbs.com).

General Comments: The .257 STW is capable of accelerating a 100-grain bullet to a muzzle velocity of 3700 fps, making it one of the flattest-shooting big-game cartridges in existence. When a 100-grain bullet of high-ballistic coefficient is zeroed three inches high at 100 yards, it strikes about an inch high at 300 yards and six inches low at 400 yards, where it is still moving along at close to 2600 fps. Due to the extremely high velocities of this cartridge, lightly constructed bullets may blow up before penetrating to the vitals of big game and, for this reason, only those of extreme controlled-expansion design should be used.

A cartridge capable of burning such a heavy powder charge in a relatively small bore can be finicky to work with, making the .257 STW a cartridge for experienced handloaders only. Those of less experience should stick with the time-proven .257 Weatherby Magnum, which is not a bad deal, since it is only about 200 fps slower with bullets of various weights, not to mention that factory ammunition is available.

Bullet (grains/type)	Powder	Grains	Velocity	Energy	Source
75 Sierra HP	RL-22	85.0	4,036	2,710	Shooting Times
85 Nosler Ballistic Tip	RL-22	83.0	3,914	2,888	Shooting Times
100 Nosler Partition	H1000	86.0	3,709	3,051	Shooting Times
100 Swift A-Frame	RL-25	82.0	3,712	3,056	Shooting Times
120 Nosler Partition	H1000	82.0	3,466	3,197	Shooting Times
120 Swift A-Frame	RL-25	78.0	3,419	3,111	Shooting Times
120 Swift A-Frame	H50BMG	88.0	3,410	3,095	Shooting Times

WARNING: All powder charges are maximum and must be reduced by 10 percent for starting loads.

.257 Allen Xpress

Historical Notes:
In 2007, a new family of wildcats came out of Kirby Allen's Allen Precision Shooting shop. The goal of these wildcats was to offer a high level of performance in the .257, 6.5mm, .270, .300, .338, and .375 calibers, but do so in a package that offered measurably longer barrel life than the company's Allen Magnum siblings in the same calibers (.257 Allen Magnum, 6.5mm Allen Magnum, .270 Allen Magnum, 7mm Allen Magnum, .338 Allen Magnum, and .375 Allen Magnum).

The Allen Xpress line of wildcats was designed to offer a high-performance option to those who do not need or want the extreme performance level of the Allen Magnums. (Allen Magnums are found in Chapter 4, Proprietary Cartridges, because, while APS will chamber other actions for its Xpress line of cartridges, the company actually manufactures actions for these Magnum cartridges. The line between wildcat and proprietary is a small one in this case, but we feel that, as of the 14th Edition, this is the proper way to categorize these two subtly different lines of cartridges from the same maker.) Even though the Allen Xpress wildcats are slightly less potent then their Allen Magnum siblings, they are still at the very top of the performance ladder, compared to other commercial, proprietary, and wildcat chamberings.

General Comments:
The .257 Allen Xpress is best used on pronghorn and deer, and other big game where live weight is limited to around 300 pounds or less. Because of the lack of high-BC bullets in the .25-caliber family, it is not recommended to use the .257 Allen Xpress at ranges past 700 yards, simply due to the fact that retained velocity and bullet energy have fallen to the point where consistent bullet expansion is not guaranteed. The .257 Allen Xpress can be chambered in standard-length magnum actions, if desired, with a short throat. The parent case, the .300 Dakota Magnum, is more costly than some of the other brass on the market, and case forming is a bit more involved than with other .25-caliber magnum wildcats. The .257 Allen Xpress will match the much longer .257 STW and do so in a chambering that can be fitted into a standard-length receiver. For more information, check the website APSRifles.com or e-mail Kirby Allen at allenmagnum@gmail.com.—*W.T.W.*

.257 Allen Xpress Loading Data

Bullet (grains/type)	Powder	Grains	Velocity	Energy	Source/Comments
100 Nosler Ballistic Tip	N/A	N/A	3,850	3,290	Allen Precision Shooting
100 Nosler Accubond	N/A	N/A	3,750	3,435	Allen Precision Shooting
115 Nosler Ballistic Tip	N/A	N/A	3,700	3,495	Allen Precision Shooting
120 Nosler Ballistic Tip	N/A	N/A	3,700	3,495	Allen Precision Shooting

.257 Ackley Improved

Historical Notes: A number of "Improved" versions of the .257 Roberts exist. Most were developed in the late 1940s and early 1950s. The .257 Ackley Improved is one of the best and certainly the most popular of the crop. This cartridge has rather straight, blown-out case walls with very little taper and a 40-degree shoulder angle. As with the other Ackley Improved cartridges, cases are made by firing factory ammunition in the Improved chamber. The .257 Improved has about the ideal case capacity for the .25-caliber and is quite efficient in the velocity it produces with a given charge of powder. The gains achieved by Improved cartridges are a matter of increasing case capacity by changing shoulder angle and sometimes moving the shoulder forward to lengthen the body and, at the same time, reducing body taper. Shoulder angle affects performance chiefly because it increases case capacity. It also improves headspacing and decreases case stretching. However, there are no significant internal ballistic effects related to any particular shoulder design. The .257 Improved will develop from 100 to 300 fps more velocity than the standard .257 Roberts, depending on bullet weight. In fact, velocities are only slightly below those developed by the .25-06 with the same weight bullets (capacities of these two are quite similar).

General Comments: The .257 Improved has proven to be an excellent cartridge for long-range varmint shooting and for big game such as deer, antelope, black bear, big horn sheep, etc. This is one of the best of the Improved cartridge line, in terms of useful velocity and energy gain.

.257 Improved (Ackley) Loading Data

Bullet (grains/type)	Powder	Grains	Velocity	Energy	Source/Comments
75 HP	IMR 4895	44.0	3,570	2,365	Ackley
87 SP	IMR 4895	43.0	3,352	2,160	Ackley
100 SP	IMR 4831	51.0	3,200	2,280	Ackley
100 SP	IMR 4350	49.0	3,160	2,220	Ackley
117 SP	IMR 4831	47.0	2,850	2,112	Ackley
120 SP	IMR 4831	46.0	2,875	2,210	Ackley

.257 Condor — *NEW*

Historical Notes: The .257 Condor was a wildcat the development of which is credited to Dr. Ramon Somavia, circa 1946, who wished to build a cartridge with long projectiles with high sectional density and heavy for their diameter for long-range hunting in southern California.

The Condor used some interesting ideas. The cartridge used extremely long, heavy .25-caliber bullets weighing at least 160 grains. .257 Condor cases are made by simply necking down 7x61 Sharpe & Hart brass (which see). .257 Condor barrels were made with 1:7 twist for the 160-grain bullets. Case length was 2.400 inches, with a loaded length of 3.30 inches. The case measured .532 at the belt, with the head diameter above belt measuring .413. It had a neck length of .300. The name was copyrighted and could be used only under license, which might explain its disappearance from the scene.

General Comments: The experiment proved that a flat trajectory was possible using this case formula. When the rifle was sighted in at 200 yards, the point of impact was 2 inches above the point of aim at 100 yards. Sighted in for 300 yards, point of impact was still just 2 inches high at 100 yards.

Norma built cases for it (see nearby headstamped case). Many folks don't know the company has always produced limited runs of cases for specialist manufacturers and dedicated wildcatters. As a modern example, the 6mm PPC was first run as a commercial and correctly headstamped case by Norma.

Bullet (grains/type)	Powder	Grains	Velocity	Energy	Source/Comments
120 Norma	IMR #4350	60	3,436	3,145	P.O. Ackley
160 Norma	IMR #4350	54.5	2,918	3,024	P.O. Ackley
160 Norma	IMR #4831	57	2,919	3,026	P.O. Ackley

.25 Hunter

Historical Notes: In 1994, Elgin Gates designed the .414 Super Mag. cartridge and was having it chambered in Dan Wesson and Thomson/Center handguns. Gates passed away before he could see his project come to fruition, but a few years later, Starline made brass for the .414 Super Mag. and Carroll Pliant worked with the cartridge to develop data for the Sierra loading manual. Carroll necked this case down to .25-caliber, reamed the primer pocket deeper to accept Large Rifle primers, and named the wildcat the .25 Hunter after his son, who is now Media Relation/Tech at Starline Brass (www.starlinebrass.com). This is a good hunting cartridge with mild recoil that offers performance just shy of the .250-3000 Savage. It works well in single-shot break-open rifles like the Thomson/Center, and single-shot bolt-action rifles, as well.

General Comments: For all practical purposes the .25 Hunter duplicates .250 Savage performance, but in a rimmed case that is more suited to single-shot rifles and pistols. Current brass availability is questionable, so, while this cartridge does have a practical application, it is unlikely it will receive much attention. It is the third in a line of wildcat cartridges developed by Carroll Pilant from pistol cartridges that were primarily designed for use in a rifle, and the project does illustrate the usefulness of this type of conversion.

.25 Ackley Krag
.25 Ackley Krag Short

Historical Notes: Ackley offered at least two versions of this cartridge. The .25 Ackley Krag Short holds about 50 grains of IMR-type powder, compared to the full-length .25 Ackley Krag, which holds about 55 grains. The shorter version seems to have been Ackley's favorite, and he preferred it for chambering in P14 Enfields and various single-shot actions. In the heyday of Ackley's developments, the slowest powders available limited performance gains with case capacity increases much beyond this level in the quarter-bore. This fact explains the similar performance he reported for the two versions.

General Comments: The Short version of the .25 Ackley Krag offers very impressive performance, when properly loaded in a strong modern action, but it is now overshadowed by the full-length version of the .25 Ackley Krag and other larger-capacity cases, such as the .25-06. Nevertheless, either of these cartridges are fully capable as big-game cartridges for smaller North American species. These can be highly recommended for single-shot rifle conversions. Very similarly performing .25-caliber versions of the .303 British were championed in Canada and other former British-ruled lands for use in the British SMLE (Enfield) or the much stronger P14 Enfield or Martini single-shot action.

.25 Ackley Krag Short Loading Data

Bullet (grains/type)	Powder	Grains	Velocity	Energy	Source/Comments
87	H380	49.0	3,460	2,310	Ackley
100	IMR 4064	43.0	3,265	2,365	Ackley
100	H380	49.0	3,412	2,585	Ackley
100	IMR 4350	50.0	3,300	2,415	Ackley
117	H4831	50.0	3,285	2,855	Ackley

.25 Ackley Krag (full-length .30-40 conversion) Loading Data

Bullet (grains/type)	Powder	Grains	Velocity	Energy	Source/Comments
87	IMR 4064	48.0	3,360	2,180	Ackley
100	IMR 4350	50.0	3,090	2,120	Ackley
100	IMR 4895	49.0	3,414	2,585	Ackley
125	IMR 4350	50.0	3,000	2,495	Ackley

6.5 STW
(Shooting Times Westerner)

Historical Notes: The 6.5 STW is the fourth member of the *Shooting Times* Westerner family of wildcats developed by firearms writer Layne Simpson (the 7mm STW, .358 STA, and .257 STW came first, in that order). He introduced it in the September 1999 issue of *Shooting Times* magazine, soon after taking a huge Vancouver Island black bear with the new cartridge. Simpson's first rifle in this caliber was built by the Canadian firm of Prairie Gun Works (www.pgwdti.com). The 6.5 STW case is formed by necking down the 7mm STW case for bullets of .264-inch diameter with no other change. Reloading dies are available from Redding (www.redding-reloading.com) and RCBS (www.rcbs.com).

General Comments: The 6.5 STW is capable of accelerating a 140-grain bullet to a muzzle velocity of 3300 fps, making it an extremely flat-shooting big-game cartridge capable of handling anything up to the size of elk and moose. When a 140-grain bullet of high-ballistic coefficient is zeroed three inches high at 100 yards, it strikes about an inch high at 300 yards and only seven inches low at 400 yards, where it is still packing close to 2000 ft-lbs of energy. Due to the extremely high velocities of this cartridge, lightly constructed bullets may blow up before penetrating to the vitals of big game and, for this reason, only those of extreme controlled expansion design should be used. A good 140-grain bullet is hard to beat for elk and such, but the Swift 120-grain A-Frame, Nosler 125-grain Partition, or Swift 130-grain Scirocco are tough to beat on deer and pronghorn antelope at long range. A cartridge capable of burning such a heavy powder charge in a relatively small bore can be finicky to work with, making the 6.5 STW a cartridge for experienced handloaders only.

6.5 STW (Shooting Times Westerner) Loading Data and Factory Ballistics

Bullet (grains/type)	Powder	Grains	Velocity	Energy	Source
85 Sierra HP	IMR-7828	85.0	4,016	3,041	Shooting Times
100 Nosler Partition	H1000	88.0	3,863	3,310	Shooting Times
120 Swift A-Frame	H1000	83.0	3,511	3,281	Shooting Times
125 Nosler Partition	H1000	83.0	3,460	3,319	Shooting Times
130 Swift Scirocco	H50BMG	88.0	3,461	3,454	Shooting Times
140 Nosler Partition	A-8700	90.0	3,316	3,414	Shooting Times
140 Swift A-Frame	H870	88.0	3,312	3,406	Shooting Times

WARNING: All powder charges are maximum and must be reduced by 10 percent for starting loads.

6.5x52mm American

Historical Notes: The 6.5x52mm American was created by firearms writer Layne Simpson, in response to requests from his readers for a cartridge short enough to work in a short-action rifle and capable of duplicating the performance of the 6.5x55mm Swedish. It was introduced in the August 1994 issue of *Shooting Times*, about three years before the .260 Remington was introduced commercially. The case was originally formed by necking down the 7mm-08 Remington case and fire-forming it to the Improved shape with minimum body taper and a 40-degree shoulder angle. It can also be formed from the .260 Remington and .308 Winchester cases. With the exception of its neck diameter, the case is identical to Simpson's earlier 7mm SGLC. The first rifle chambered for the cartridge was a custom job on the Remington Model Seven action with a Lilja 21-inch barrel and a McMillan fiberglass stock.

General Comments: When the three cartridges are loaded to the same chamber pressure and fired in barrels of the same length, the 6.5x62mm American is a bit faster than the 6.5x55mm Swedish and .260 Remington. The velocities published for it were from a 21-inch barrel, and about 100 fps can be added for a 24-inch barrel. Like the other two cartridges, it is an excellent choice for hunting deer-sized game and, when loaded with the Sierra 85-grain bullet, it is not a bad choice for varminting. Best bullets for open-country hunting of deer are those weighing from 120 to 130 grains, with the Swift 130-grain Scirocco a great choice for use on everything from whitetail deer and pronghorn antelope to caribou and black bear. Clymer (www.clymertool.com) offers the chamber reamer, and reloading dies are available from Redding (www.redding-reloading.com).

6.5x52mm American Loading Data and Factory Ballistics (21-inch barrel)

Bullet (grains/type)	Powder	Grains	Velocity	Energy	Source
85 Sierra HP	H414	51.0	3,381	2,155	Layne Simpson
100 Nosler Partition	W760	49.0	3,054	2,345	Layne Simpson
120 Swift A-Frame	H4350	48.0	2,968	2,354	Layne Simpson
125 Nosler Partition	N-204	47.0	2,914	2,448	Layne Simpson
130 Swift Scirocco	A-4350	46.0	2,829	2,398	Layne Simpson
140 Swift A-Frame	H414	45.0	2,731	2,316	Layne Simpson
140 Sierra MatchKing	W760	45.0	2,712	2,284	Layne Simpson

WARNING: All powder charges are maximum and must be reduced by 15 percent for starting loads.

6.5 Gibbs

Historical Notes: The 6.5 Gibbs was designed in the 1950s by firearms experimenter R.E. "Rocky" Gibbs. It was a natural follow-on to Gibbs' original .270 Gibbs, which he developed while seeking the optimum case capacity for the .270 bore size in combination with a 150-grain bullet.

General Comments: The 6.5 Gibbs is a blown-out .30-06 (or .270) case with a steep shoulder and short neck. The shoulder is pushed forward about .196-inch compared to the standard .270 case, and the case holds about six grains more IMR4350 powder than a standard .270 Winchester. Although Gibbs used this and his other wildcats as front-ignition cartridges, the following is a "standard" loading without a front ignition tube.

6.5 Gibbs Loading Data

Bullet (grains/type)	Powder	Grains	Velocity	Energy	Source/Comments
120 SP	IMR4350	60.0	3,325	2,995	R.E. Gibbs
140 Speer	H4831	62.0	2,967	2,736	R.E. Gibbs

EABCO 6.5mm Bench Rest Magnum (EABCO 6.5 BRM)

Historical Notes: In 1996, Eben Brown lengthened the .219 Donaldson Wasp benchrest cartridge by a ¼-inch and opened the neck to 6.5mm to create the 6.5 Bench Rest Magnum cartridge. This cartridge was developed to give big-game hunting performance from small-frame single-shot rifles and pistols, such as the Thompson/Center Contenders and Encores, BF pistols, Ruger No. 1 rifles, and EABCO model 97D rifles.

General Comments: Brass is mechanically formed from virgin .30-30 Winchester cases and given a longer body with a slight taper, sharp 30-degree shoulder, and 6.5mm neck. A long, skinny cartridge body keeps bolt thrust manageable for small-frame firearms. In suitable single-shot firearms, the 6.5mm BRM works well with barrel lengths of 24 inches and 1:8 rifling. The sectional density of 140-grain 6.5mm bullets is similar to 190-grain bullets in .30-caliber cartridges. For large game, such as moose or elk, suitable bonded core or partition bullets should be loaded. EABCO (www.eabco.com) provides rifles, barrels, loaded ammunition, and reloading supplies for the 6.5 BRM cartridge. In addition, it offers a family of cartridges in .224, 6mm, 7mm, and .300 BRM chamberings. All loads listed use EABCO custom-formed brass and CCI BR Large Rifle primers.

EABCO 6.5mm Bench Rest Magnum (6.5 BRM) Loading Data and Factory Ballistics

Bullet (grains/type)	Powder	Grains	Velocity	Energy	Source/Comments
100 Sierra	VV N150	38.0	2,877	1,837	EABCO
140 Sierra GameKing	FL	N/A	2,400	1,790	EABCO
140 Sierra GameKing	VV N160	38.0	2496	1936	EABCO
140 Hornady A-Max	H4831SC	39.5	2401	1791	EABCO

.264 LBC-AR

Historical Notes: The .264 LBC-AR cartridge is, for all practical purposes, a 6.5 Grendel. Alexander Arms has held the trademark on the name 6.5 Grendel since that cartridge was introduced. Les Baer started offering rifles for the 6.5 Grendel, but, apparently, there was some contention between the two companies. Les Baer Custom subsequently introduced a new cartridge called the ".264 LBC-AR." As best as can be determined, the cartridge is identical to the 6.5 Grendel, but the chambers in rifles are cut slightly different. However, .264 LBC-AR and 6.5 Grendel ammunition and rifles are interchangeable.

General Comments: This is an example of what can happen when a wildcatter holds his creation as proprietary. Another company can produce a very similar and even compatible cartridge, call it by another name, put marketing dollars behind it, and a cartridge war begins. Currently, and according to Les Baer Custom, Black Hills is offering .264 LBC-AR factory ammunition. Hornady and Wolf both offer 6.5 Grendel ammo. However, just recently, Alexander Arms released its trademark on the 6.5 Grendel cartridge. This led to SAAMI standardization in November 2011, which, in turn, will most probably lead to the availability of 6.5 Grendel firearms from other manufacturers, as well as an assortment of factory ammunition. Ultimately, one can speculate that now the 6.5 Grendel will regain its title as the most prolific 6.5mm AR-15 cartridge extant.

Bullet (grains/type)	Powder	Grains	Velocity	Energy	Source
123 Sierra Matchking	FL		2,650	1,917	Les Baer Custom

6.5mm Allen Xpress

Historical Notes: Built by gunsmith Kirby Allen, owner of Allen Precision Shooting, the 6.5mm Allen Xpress was designed as a big-game hunting round useful out to 700 yards in portable rifles. It is best used on pronghorn and smaller deer, where the live weight of animals is limited to no more than 300 pounds. The 6.5mm Allen Xpress will easily match the 6.5mm S.T.W., but do so in a significantly shorter case design. The 6.5mm Allen Xpress is the baby brother to the 6.5mm Allen Magnum

General Comments: Parent case is the .300 Dakota Magnum, so the 6.5 Allen Xpress can be chambered in standard-length magnum actions, if desired. It is better suited to lighter bullet weights then the 6.5mm Allen Magnum, and is slightly easier on throat life than the 6.5mm Allen Magnum. Allen Magnums are found in Chapter 4, Proprietary Cartridges, because, while APS will chamber other actions for its Xpress line of cartridges, the company actually manufactures actions for these Magnum cartridges. The line between wildcat and proprietary is a small one in this case, but we feel that, as of the 14th Edition, this is the proper way to categorize these two subtly different lines of cartridges from the same maker.) Even so, Allen recommends this only for big-game hunting and not high-volume varmint shooting. The parent case is more costly than some of the other brass on the market, and case forming is more involved than some other 6.5mm-caliber magnum wildcats. For more information, check the website APSRifles.com or e-mail Kirby Allen at allenmagnum@gmail.com.—*W.T.W.*

6.5mm Allen Xpress Loading Data

Bullet (grains/type)	Powder	Grains	Velocity	Energy	Source/Comments
120 Nosler Ballistic Tip	*	N/A	3,550	3,357	Allen Precision Shooting
130 Nosler Accubond	*	N/A	3,450	3,435	Allen Precision Shooting
140 Nosler Accubond	*	N/A	3,350	3,488	Allen Precision Shooting
142 Sierra MatchKing	*	N/A	3,350	3537	Allen Precision Shooting

6.5mm Leopard

Historical Notes: In 2001, *Outdoor Life's* shooting editor Jim Carmichael designed a 6.5mm long-range hunting and target cartridge, based on newly available Winchester Short Magnum brass. The resulting cartridge, the 6.5 Leopard, proved successful in long-range competitive shooting and offers a highly competitive alternative to the 6.5x284 cartridges used by some shooters. At top-end loadings, the 6.5 Leopard is capable of pushing a Sierra 142-grain Match King bullet to velocities exceeding 3200 fps.

General Comments: Following initial experimentation with .300 WSM cases, the 6.5 Leopard case construction became a simple, one-step necking down operation, once .270 WSM cases became available. No other case changes are needed, because the .270 WSM case length, shoulder diameter, and shoulder angle are optimal. The 6.5 Leopard works well in 26-inch barrels with a 1:9 twist. The cartridge is suitable for short-action rifles, such as the Remington 700. Reamers are available from JGS Precision Tool (www.jgstools.com), and Redding (www.redding-reloading.com) offers reloading dies. Rifles for the 6.5 Leopard can be supplied by Borden Rifles (www.bordenrifles.com) and other gunsmiths specializing in high precision firearms. Listed loads are starting loads.

6.5 Leopard Loading Data

Bullet (grains/type)	Powder	Grains	Velocity	Energy	Source/Comments
107	IMR 4831	62.0	3,404	2,752	Jim Carmichael
120	RETUMBO	65.0	3,203	2,733	Jim Carmichael
140	RETUMBO	60.0	3,036	2,865	Jim Carmichael

.264 Hawk

Historical Notes:	Designed by Wyoming gunmaker Fred Zeglin, in 1998, the .264 Hawk, one of the proprietary Hawk cartridge family, is a flat-shooting, open-country hunting cartridge. For antelope, mule deer, and similarly sized game, the .264 Hawk can speed 6.5mm bullets to impressive velocities.
General Comments:	All Hawk cartridges fit into standard .30-06 length actions and use a .473-inch bolt face. The .264 Hawk uses .280 Remington brass as its parent case. The brass is necked down in a sizing die and fireformed in a .264 Hawk chamber. The .264 Hawk can accommodate bullet weights ranging from light 6.5mm varmint bullets up to 140-grain big-game hunting bullets. It is best suited for bolt-action rifles with 26-inch barrels having a 1:14 rifling twist. Z-Hat Custom (www.z-hat.com) offers rifles, dies, and reloading information.

.264 Hawk Loading Data

Bullet (grains/type)	Powder	Grains	Velocity	Energy	Source/Comments
85 Sierra HP	H4895	51.0	3,575	2,411	Z-Hat Custom
120 Nosler BP	VV N160	57.0	3,440	3,152	Z-Hat Custom
129 Hornady SP	H4831	56.0	2,970	2,526	Z-Hat Custom
140 Nosler	IMR 7828	54.0	2,955	2,714	Z-Hat Custom

6.5mm-06 Ackley Improved

Historical Notes:	This cartridge was a natural outgrowth from the 6.5-06. After World War II, many military rifles of 6.5mm were surplused by various countries. Most found their way to the shores of the United States, as a means of bringing much needed cash to countries that would have otherwise simply scrapped these guns. Since ammunition for these chamberings was difficult or impossible to obtain, it was natural for gunsmiths to consider re-chambering them to 6.5-06, since abundant, inexpensive .30-06 cases are easily necked-down to 6.5 and the conversion offered the promise of more power than the original chambering. Similarly, bullet manufacturers responded to the availability of 6.5mm guns by offering component bullets for handloading. This later served only to increase demand for wildcat conversions. It was only reasonable for customers to want to chamber for the Improved version of the 6.5mm-06, because this added nothing to the cost of the conversion and promised a ballistic benefit and increased case life. With the powders then available, the latter was delivered; the former was not.
General Comments:	Ackley's experiences with this chambering are most interesting. He first chambered a 6.5mm barrel to 6.5mm-06 and worked up load data. Then, he re-chambered the same barrel to the Improved version and again worked up data. We can only assume that he used the same pressure criteria and the same components for both studies, but, perhaps, this is an erroneous assumption. The reason for doubt stems from the fact that Ackley reported higher velocities with the standard 6.5-06 than with the Improved version. It must be noted that he was limited to powders no slower burning than H4831. Using the slower powders now available, he might have found the Improved version to have the ballistic edge. In any case, the difference in ballistics is marginal. It should be noted that the .25-06 and the 6.5mm-06 Improved have almost exactly the same relative case capacity. Therefore, considering bullet availability, including light

varmint-style bullets and hunting bullets that are much heavier than anything available in .257-inch, the 6.5mm-06 Improved is everything the .25-06 will ever be, and more.

6.5mm-06 Ackley Improved Loading Data

Bullet (grains/type)	Powder	Grains	Velocity	Energy	Source/Comments
120	IMR 4350	53.0	3,100	2,560	Ackley
140	IMR 4350	51.0	2,920	2,650	Ackley
140	H4831	53.0	2,950	2,705	Ackley
150	IMR 4350	49.0	2,780	2,575	Ackley
150	H4831	51.0	2,760	2,535	Ackley
165	IMR 4350	46.0	2,550	2,090	Ackley
165	H4831	48.0	2,550	2,090	Ackley

6.5 SAUM — *NEW*

Historical Notes: The 6.5mm SAUM (or RSAUM) is a necked-down case made from a 7mm Remington Short Action Ultra Magnum (7mm SAUM) or a 300 SAUM case. The SAUM cases are short, fat and unbelted, and are designed to work in short-action rifles. They were introduced in 2001. The 6.5mm SAUM's niche might be to displace the need for magnums for long-range hunting and competition. Loaded with long, high-BC bullets, the 6.5 RSAUM's case capacity allows great downrange performance with lower pressure and lower recoil. Also, many magnums run 65,000 psi in the chamber, which erodes the barrel throat faster than many shooters would like. This round solves that problem by running at .308 Win. pressures.

General Comments: Compared to the 6.5mm Grendel, which fires a 123-grain A-Max bullet at 2,580 fps, and the 6.5mm Creedmoor, which fires a 140-grain A-Max at 2,710 fps, the 6.5mm SAUM can push a 140-grain A-Max to 3,180 fps. In fact, the 6.5 SAUM even compares favorably with the 7mm Remington Magnum shooting a Hornady 139-grain InterLock SP.

G.A. Precision (GAPrecision.net), a custom rifle builder in North Kansas City, Missouri, has made something of a speciality in chambering rifles for the round, to the point that a variant, the 6.5 SAUM GAP 4S, exists. GAP founder George Gardner said that after August 2013, any rifle chambered in GAP's 6.5 4S SAUM will have a .028 shorter throat to provide more room to use 140-grain VLD bullets.

Copper Creek Cartridge Co. sells commercially loaded 6.5 SAUM GAP 4S rounds for about $65 a box. Bullets include a 143-grain Hornady ELD-X (3,065 fps in a 24-inch barrel), a 130-grain Berger VLD Hunting (3,150 fps) and a 140-grain Berger Hybrid (3,050 fps), all loaded in new Hornady brass. Copper Creek Cartridge also loads the 130-grain Berger VLD in Norma brass, one of which has the Norma 300 RSAUM necked to 6.5mm, trimmed square and the neck turned to .015-inch neck-wall thickness.

6.5 SAUM Loading Data

Bullet (grains/type)	Powder	Grains	Velocity	Energy	Source/Comments
130 Berger VLD	H1000	61.5	3,161	2,883	G.A. Precision

.270 Gibbs

Historical Notes: The .270 Gibbs was designed in the 1950s by firearms experimenter R.E. "Rocky" Gibbs. It was developed while seeking the optimum case capacity for the .270 bore size in combination with a 150-grain bullet. Gibbs wanted a case with more capacity than a .270 Ackley, but believed the capacity of "short magnum" .270 cases to be excessive. He wanted to seat a heavy (150-grain) bullet to "normal depth" and leave very little air space to produce high loading-density maximum loads.

General Comments: The .270 Gibbs is a blown-out .30-06 (or .270) case with a steep shoulder and short neck. The shoulder is pushed forward about .196-inch, compared to the standard .270 case, and the case holds about six grains more of IMR4350 powder than a standard .270 Winchester. Although Gibbs used this and his other wildcats as front-ignition cartridges, the following is a "standard" loading without a front ignition tube.

.270 Gibbs Loading Data

Bullet (grains/type)	Powder	Grains	Velocity	Energy	Source/Comments
150 SPBT	H4831	63.0	3,175	3,357	R.E. Gibbs

.270 REN

Historical Notes: Designed in 1985 by Charles Rensing and Jim Rock, this cartridge was developed in response to NRA Hunter Pistol Silhouette competition rules. This category only allows use of straight-walled cartridges. This diminutive number fulfills that requirement while producing minimal recoil, as intended by the inventors.

General Comments: The .270 REN is based on the .22 Hornet simply necked straight to accept .270 bullets. Recoil is very mild in typical guns, and this little chambering can propel the excellent 90-, 100-, and 110-grain bullets available to considerable velocity with modest powder charges. Guns chambered for the .270 REN are currently available from several manufacturers, including RPM, Thompson/Center, and Merrill.

.270 REN Loading Data (10-inch barrel)

Bullet (grains/type)	Powder	Grains	Velocity	Energy	Source/Comments
90	AA No. 7	8.2	1,650	540	Accurate
90	AA No. 9	11.1	1,888	710	Accurate
90	A1680	14.5	1,811	655	Accurate
100 Hornady	H110	10.2	1,600	565	Hornady
100 Hornady	AA 5744	10.4	1,600	565	Hornady
100 Hornady	W296	11.0	1,600	565	Hornady
100 Hornady	AA No. 7	8.2	1,566	540	Accurate
100 Hornady	AA No. 9	10.8	1,799	715	Accurate
100 Hornady	A1680	14.5	1,815	730	Accurate
110 Sierra	AA No. 7	8.0	1,474	530	Accurate
110 Sierra	AA No. 9	10.2	1,666	675	Accurate
110 Sierra	A1680	14.0	1,,675	685	Accurate

.270 IHMSA

Historical Notes: Just one of an entire series of cartridges designed by Elgin Gates, the .270 IHMSA (International Handgun Metallic Silhouette Association) is among the more popular of the group, which ranges from .25- through .35-caliber. All are similar and are designed specifically for chambering in single-shot handguns. The intention was to offer competitors a choice of easy-to-make chamberings that could deliver the desired momentum to distant targets. In this endeavor, Gates appears to have been notably successful. Other IHMSA numbers include 7mm and .30-caliber versions.

General Comments: The .270 IHMSA is based on the .300 Savage case. Cases are formed by simply necking the case down to accept .270 bullets. The sizing die also drives the inside of the shoulder back to achieve a 38-degree shoulder angle, providing superior headspace control and a longer case neck. The same treatment is utilized for all cases in the IHMSA line.

Bullet (grains)	Powder	Grains	Velocity	Energy	Source/Comments
90	H414	45.0	2,691	1,445	Hodgdon
90	BL-C(2)	40.0	2,719	1,475	Hodgdon
100	H414	45.0	2,654	1,560	Hodgdon
100	H4895	38.0	2,654	1,560	Hodgdon
110	H414	44.0	2,626	1,680	Hodgdon
110	H4895	37.0	2,590	1,635	Hodgdon
130	H414	41.0	2,442	1,720	Hodgdon
130	H450	44.0	2,423	1,695	Hodgdon
140	H4831	43.0	2,449	1,860	Hodgdon
140	H4350	41.0	2,394	1,780	Hodgdon
150	H4350	40.0	2,291	1,745	Hodgdon
150	H4895	33.0	2,274	1,720	Hodgdon

.270 Hawk

Historical Notes:	Like the .270 Ackley Improved, the .270 Hawk delivers about 50 fps more velocity than the factory .270 Winchester cartridge with identical bullets. Fred Zeglin designed the .270 Hawk as a member of his proprietary Hawk cartridge family, about 1998. The .270 Hawk is an excellent deer and antelope cartridge.
General Comments:	All Hawk cartridges fit into standard .30-06 length actions and use a .473-inch bolt face. The .270 Hawk uses .280 Remington brass as its parent case. The brass is necked up to .30-caliber, full length sized, and fire-formed in a .270 Hawk chamber. The .270 Hawk works well in bolt-action rifles with 24- to 26-inch barrels and a 1:10 rifling twist. Quality Cartridge (www.qual-cart.com) supplies ammunition and correctly headstamped brass. Z-Hat Custom (www.z-hat.com) offers rifles, dies, and reloading information.

.270 Hawk Loading Data

Bullet (grains/type)	Powder	Grains	Velocity	Energy	Source/Comments
130 gr.	H4350	61.0	3,295	3,133	Z-Hat Custom
140 gr.	H4350	58.0	3,161	3,105	Z-Hat Custom
150 gr.	H4350	57.0	3,051	3,100	Z-Hat Custom

.270 Savage (270 Titus)
.270 Ackley Improved Savage

Historical Notes:	The .270 Savage was, in its day, a very good cartridge for the Model 99 Savage, and it remains so today. With the standard 130-grain bullet, it delivers performance reasonably close to factory .270 Winchester loads. Heavier bullets intrude much of the available powder space and, therefore, do not perform as well. The Ackley Improved version comes very close to .270 Winchester ballistics and is a much better Model 99 chambering option in all respects (see discussion at .250-300 Ackley Improved).
General Comments:	While the .250 Savage is a fine deer cartridge, the .270 version offers the potential to use heavier bullets at about the same velocity. Therefore, this chambering (particularly the Ackley version), is a much better big-game hunting option. With properly constructed bullets, this is also a much better elk cartridge.

Barrel twist rates were commonly 1:10, though some were 1:12. Charles A. Evans also developed a version of this cartridge, which he called the .270 Evans. Still later, Bliss Titus started working with it, so it is also known as the .270 Titus.

.270 Savage Loading Data

Bullet (grains/type)	Powder	Grains	Velocity	Energy	Source/Comments
100 SP	IMR 4064	42.0	3,107	2,140	Ackley
100 SP	IMR 3031	39.0	2,950	1,930	Ackley
130 SP	IMR 4064	39.0	2,763	2,200	Ackley
150 SP	IMR 4350	43.0	2,574	2,205	Ackley

.270 Allen Xpress

Historical Notes: The .270 Allen Xpress, like the .257 Allen Xpress and the 6.5 Allen Xpress, is based on the .300 Dakota Magnum case and is suited for hunting medium big-game animals out to a half-mile, depending on the rifle design employed. Riflesmith Kirby Allen, of Allen Precision Shooting, says it is best suited for big game up to 500 pounds in live body weight, but, in good conditions, it can be used effectively on heavier game, such as elk.

General Comments: Allen said, "The .270 Allen Xpress competes head to head against the 7mm STW, 7mm Remington Magnum, and .270 Winchester. It easily outperforms the 7mm Magnum and .270, and it will match the 7mm STW with the same bullet weights. It has very impressive performance for its case length, equal to the highest performing .270 and 7mm magnum wildcats on the market today." (Allen Magnums are found in Chapter 4, Proprietary Cartridges, because, while APS will chamber other actions for its Xpress line of cartridges, the company actually manufactures actions for these Magnum cartridges. The line between wildcat and proprietary is a small one in this case, but we feel that, as of the 14th Edition, this is the proper way to categorize these two subtly different lines of cartridges from the same maker.) For more information, check the website APSRifles.com or e-mail Kirby Allen at allenmagnum@gmail.com.— *W.T.W.*

.270 Allen Express Loading Data (28-inch barrel) (Note: * Ramshot Magnum, Reloader 25)

Bullet (grains)	Powder	Grains	Velocity	Energy	Source/Comments
130 Nosler Accubond	*	N/A	3,500	3,535	Allen Precision Shooting
140 Nosler Accubond	*	N/A	3,400	3,592	Allen Precision Shooting

7mm TCU (7mmx223)

Historical Notes: The 7mm TCU is another of the series of cartridges developed by Wes Ugalde for Thompson/Center and offered as a standard chambering in the single-shot Contender pistol. All are based on the .223 Remington case necked up, this one to 7mm (.284-inch). The 7mm TCU dates back to about 1980 and has become quite popular for metallic silhouette pistol shooting. It is also known as the 7mmx223. Other TCU numbers include 6mm, .25-caliber, and 6.5mm versions of this same basic case.

General Comments: The 7mm TCU has a reputation for exceptional accuracy and makes a good varmint cartridge in the T/C Contender pistol, particularly with the 14-inch barrel, which provides an extra couple hundred feet per second over the 10-inch barrel. It is on the marginal side for deer or other medium game. The originators recommend that only commercial .223 Remington cases be used for forming cases. Do not use military cases. Cases are easy to make and can be formed in one operation once the dies are properly adjusted. Proper case length is 1.740 inches.

7mm TCU (7mmx223) Loading Data

Bullet (grains/type)	Powder	Grains	Velocity	Energy	Source/Comments
100 SP	BL-C2	28.0	2,100	980	14-inch barrel
115 SP	IMR 4198	23.0	2,185	1,220	14-inch barrel
130 SP	IMR 4198	22.0	2,050	1,215	14-inch barrel
140 SP	H4895	24.0	1,880	1,100	14-inch barrel
150 SP	BL-C2	25.0	1,910	1,220	14-inch barrel

7mm Gibbs

Historical Notes: The 7mm Gibbs was designed in the 1950s by firearms experimenter R.E. "Rocky" Gibbs. It was a natural follow-up to Gibbs' original .270 Gibbs, which he developed while seeking the optimum case capacity for the .270 bore size in combination with a 150-grain bullet.

General Comments: The 7mm Gibbs is a blown-out .30-06 (or .270) case with a steep shoulder and short neck. The shoulder is pushed forward about .196-inch, compared to the standard .270 case, and the case holds about six grains more of IMR4350 powder than a standard .270 Winchester. Although Gibbs used this and his other wildcats as front ignition cartridges, the following is a "standard" loading without a front ignition tube.

7mm Gibbs Loading Data

Bullet (grains/type)	Powder	Grains	Velocity	Energy	Source/Comments
140 Sierra	H4831	67.0	3,293	3,370	R.E. Gibbs
160 Speer	H4831	67.0	3,173	3,574	R.E. Gibbs

.30 Gibbs

Historical Notes: The .30 Gibbs was designed in the 1950s by firearms experimenter R.E. "Rocky" Gibbs. He called it "The world's most powerful .30-06." It was a natural follow-up to Gibbs' original .270 Gibbs, which he developed while seeking the optimum case capacity for the .270 bore size in combination with a 150-grain bullet.

General Comments: The .30 Gibbs is a blown-out .30-06 case with a steep shoulder and short neck. The shoulder is pushed forward about .196-inch, compared to the standard .30-06 case, and the case holds about seven grains more of IMR4350 powder than a standard .30-06 Winchester. Although Gibbs used this and his other wildcats as front ignition cartridges, the following is a "standard" loading without a front ignition tube.

.30 Gibbs Loading Data

Bullet (grains/type)	Powder	Grains	Velocity	Energy	Source/Comments
150 Hornady	IMR4064	60.0	3,285	3,593	R.E. Gibbs
180 Barnes	IMR4350	65.0	3,139	3,937	R.E. Gibbs

7mm JRS

Historical Notes: The 7mm JRS was designed by Jon R. Sundra. It is based on the .280/7mm Express Remington case, but is more than an Improved .280 in that it cannot be made by fire-forming .280 Remington ammo in a 7mm JRS chamber. Attempting to do so is dangerous, because the 7mm JRS pushes a 35-degree shoulder more than .05-inch forward of where it would be on the .280 Improved. Therefore, headspace is increased commensurately.

To give some idea of relative case capacities, the .280 Remington/7mm Express holds about 63 grains of water to the base of the neck; the .280 RCBS holds about 66 grains; the 7mm JRS about 70.5 grains (Norma cases). The 7mm Remington Magnum holds about 82 grains.

General Comments: Chamber reamers for the 7mm JRS are made by Clymer Mfg. (www.clymertool.com), while reloading dies are made by Hornady. Sundra found that very little load development work was necessary with this cartridge. Norma MRP and Reloader 22 are the best powders, with H4831, IMR 4831, and IMR 7828 coming in as close seconds. Other slow burners like IMR 4831 and H450 also do well. Depending on the individual rifle and case (Remington, Norma, or Winchester), maximum loads range between 60.5 to 63.5 grains of Rl-22 with a 150-grain Nosler. Velocity has ranged from 3060 to 3120 fps in various barrels of 23½ to 24 inches.

The 7mm JRS is chambered by E.R. Shaw (www.ershawbarrels.com). Standard length actions like the Ruger 77 and Mauser (commercial or military) can be used. To take full advantage of case capacity, these loads assume bullet bases seated no deeper than the shoulder (overall length of 3 7/10-inch with a 154-grain Hornady, 33/8-inch with a 150-grain Nosler). Sundra recommends that chambers be throated so a dummy round with either of the above bullets will have a 1/16-inch leade. To accommodate cartridges of this length, you will need a Model 70, Remington 700, or long Sako action. Grayback Wildcats (541-882-3492), offers fire-formed (once-fired) cases for the 7mm JRS. Similar "pushed shoulder '06-based" Improved cartridges exist in .30-, .338-, .35-, and .375-caliber. All are very good, but those in otherwise factory chamberings (.280, .30-06, and, now, the .35 Whelen) create serious safety concerns. Any rifle thus chambered will chamber the factory cartridge of the proper bore diameter, which will then have enough headspace to separate and destroy the gun, and perhaps even the shooter and bystanders.

7mm JRS Loading Data

Bullet (grains/type)	Powder	Grains	Velocity	Energy	Source/Comments
145 SP	Rl-22	63.0	3,130	3,155	Jon Sundra
154 SP	Rl-22	61.5	3,020	3,120	Jon Sundra

.285 OKH
7mm-06 Mashburn
7mm-06

Historical Notes: These cartridges are lumped together, because all are practically identical and, except for headspace specification, are very similar to the .280 Remington. The .285 OKH is another O'Neil-Keith-Hopkins development that originally used a duplex loading consisting of different powders with different burning rates loaded one on top of the other. It also employed a long flash tube that ignited the powder at the front of the case instead of the rear. This was supposed to improve ballistics and apparently did so, but was a lot of trouble, proving rather impractical for the average handloader. All of these cartridges originated in the late 1940s and early 1950s.

General Comments: Because these cartridges hold about two grains of powder less than the .280 Remington, maximum .280 Remington loads are not recommended. The various 7mms based on the .30-06 case are worthy of mention, because these were the wildcat forerunners of the commercial .280.

Bullet (grains/type)	Powder	Grains	Velocity	Energy	Source/Comments
100 SP	IMR 3031	45.0	3,110	2,150	N/A
125 SP	IMR 4350	57.0	3,195	2,840	N/A
150 SP	IMR 4895	48.0	2,890	2,780	N/A
165 SP	IMR 4350	52.0	2,820	2,920	N/A
175 SP	IMR 4350	55.0	2,720	2,880	N/A

.280 Hawk

Historical Notes: In 1997, Wyoming gunmaker Fred Zeglin designed the Hawk family of proprietary hunting cartridges suitable for varminting through dangerous game. Fred's .280 Hawk offers a modest ballistic advantage over factory .280 Remington ammunition. Using the same bullets and barrel length, the .280 Hawk produces about 50 fps more velocity. The cartridge is well suited for most North American big game, except for the Alaskan and Canadian grizzly and brown bears.

General Comments: All Hawk cartridges use standard length actions with a .473-inch bolt face. The .280 Hawk uses .280 Remington brass as the parent case. The brass is necked up to .30-caliber, sized in a .280 Hawk die to set the headspace, and fire-formed in a .280 Hawk chamber. The cartridge is well suited for bolt-action and modern single-shot rifles. Barrel lengths of 24 to 26 inches with a 1:10 twist are recommended. Loaded ammunition and correctly headstamped brass are available from Quality Cartridge (www.qual-cart.com). Z-Hat Custom (www.z-hat.com) offers rifles, dies, and reloading information.

.280 Hawk Loading Data

Bullet (grains)	Powder	Grains	Velocity	Energy	Source/Comments
140	H4831	60.0	3,015	2,825	Z-Hat Custom
154	RL-22	59.0	2,827	2,732	Z-Hat Custom
160	RL-22	60.0	2,845	2,875	Z-Hat Custom

7mm SGLC
(Simpson's Good Little Cartridge)

Historical Notes: Back in the 1970s, determined to have a rifle that hung light on the shoulder at an affordable price, firearms writer Layne Simpson decided to convert a 6½-pound Weatherby Varmintmaster from .22-250 to a flat-shooting cartridge powerful enough for handling most mountain game. The wildcat cartridge he came up with is the .308 Winchester case necked down to 7mm and blown out to the Improved shape with minimum body taper and a 40-degree shoulder angle. Gunsmith Wally Strutz, of Eagle River, Wisconsin, re-barreled the Weatherby rifle and modified its magazine to handle the cartridge. The first animal taken by Simpson with the outfit was a Shiras moose, and shortly thereafter, on a hunt in Rhodesia (now Zimbabwe), he used the rifle to take 12 animals ranging from impala to greater kudu with a total of 14 cartridges. The story of that hunt was published in the March-April 1979 issue of *Rifle* magazine.

Simpson eventually made a switch-barrel rifle of his Varmintmaster with a barrel in 250 Savage Improved added to his collection. Years later, Roy Weatherby's son, Ed, who was running the company by that time, found a copy of the *Rifle* magazine article in his father's files. Ed liked the idea and decided to offer the Varmintmaster in a .250 Savage version called the Whitetail Deluxe. A page in the 1993 Weatherby catalog was devoted to the new rifle, and a couple of those rifles were on display at the SHOT show that year. Unfortunately, not many people buy rifles in .250 Savage any more, so Ed Weatherby wisely took Simpson's idea a step further by increasing the length of the Varmintmaster action by about an inch, introducing it in 1997 as the standard Mark V. This made the action long enough to handle not only short cartridges, such as the .22-250, .243 Winchester, and .308 Winchester, but longer best-sellers such as the .30-06 and .270 Winchester, as well. And it was all started by a wildcat cartridge and a firearms writer who had a hankering for a light big-game rifle.

General Comments: Simpson is quick to admit today that, if the 7mm-08 Remington had been available during the mid-1970s, he probably would have chosen it for his Varmintmaster conversion, since factory ammo is available. A bit older now, he also says that, if he were developing the cartridge today, he wouldn't give it such a "silly, tongue-twisting name." The 7mm SGLC case can be formed the original way by necking down and fire-forming the .308 Winchester case, or by firing 7mm-08 Remington factory ammunition in a rifle properly chambered for the 7mm SGLC. Simpson's favorite bullet, and the one he's used to take most of the game bagged with this cartridge, is the Nosler 140-grain Partition, but he also likes the performance of the Speer 130-grain spitzer on whitetail deer and pronghorn antelope. Excellent choices of powders for handloads with all bullet weights are H414, W760, and Reloader 19.

7mm SGLC Loading Data and Factory Ballistics (24-inch barrel)

Bullet (grains/type)	Powder	Grains	Velocity	Energy	Source
120 Hornady HP	W760	53.0	3,210	2,743	Layne Simpson
130 Speer SP	H414	52.0	3,177	2,910	Layne Simpson
140 Nosler Partition	H414	49.0	3,010	2,813	Layne Simpson
150 Nosler Partition	RL19	52.0	2,968	2,931	Layne Simpson
160 Nosler Partition	RL19	51.0	2,902	2,989	Layne Simpson
175 Nosler Partition	RL19	49.0	2,738	2,910	Layne Simpson

WARNING: All powder charges are maximum and must be reduced by 10 percent for starting loads.

7mm *Shooting Times* Easterner (7mm STE)

Historical Notes: The 7mm *Shooting Times* Easterner (7mm STE) was designed in 1987 by gun writer Layne Simpson for Marlin 336 and Winchester Model 94 lever-action rifles. This cartridge is the .307 Winchester case necked down and fire-formed to the Improved configuration with minimum body taper and a 40-degree shoulder. The .307 Winchester is actually a rimmed version of the .308 Winchester, thus providing the 7mm STE with more powder capacity than either the .30-30 Winchester or the 7-30 Waters. Load data for the 7mm STE was developed with the Nosler 120-grain and Hornady 139-grain flat-nosed bullet, as these are compatible with the tubular magazines of the lever guns. Maximum velocities for these bullets in a 22-inch barrel are 2,900 fps and 2,700 fps, respectively.

General Comments: This cartridge has enjoyed fair success on whitetails, mule deer, pronghorns, black bear, caribou, and wild hogs. Performance of the Nosler bullet on all of these has been nothing less than outstanding. A favorite open-country "single-shot" recipe for loading directly into the chamber (i.e., not for use in a tubular magazine), is the Nosler 140-grain Ballistic Tip loaded to 2700 fps. Chamber pressures generated by the 7mm STE are comparable to those developed by the .307 Winchester. Consequently, only Model 336 and 94 rifles of recent manufacture and in excellent condition should be considered for this conversion. Those rifles in .30-30 Winchester, .307 Winchester, .356 Winchester, and .444 Marlin are easily converted to the 7mm STE by rebarreling with no other modifications necessary.

7mm Shooting Times Easterner (STE) Loading Data

Bullet (grains/type)	Powder	Grains	Velocity	Energy	Source/Comments
120 SP	H414	47.0	2,915	2,265	Layne Simpson
120 SP	H4895	41.0	2,910	2,250	Layne Simpson
139 SP	W760	45.0	2,710	2,265	Layne Simpson
139 SP	Rl-22	50.0	2,710	2,265	Layne Simpson

7mm-300 Weatherby — *NEW*

Historical Notes: The 7mm-300 Weatherby is the full-length 300 Weatherby case necked down to .284. It has about the same case capacity as the 7mm STW. The separate 7mm Weatherby Magnum is based on a shortened .300 Weatherby case.

Custom gunsmith and target shooter Howard Wolfe of Mifflinburg, Pennsylvania, is credited with doing early load development of the round and building several long-range rifles chambered for this wildcat. It was reportedly first tested by Robert Hutton of Guns & Ammo in 1961 and 1962. In October 1970, Mary Louise DeVito of Williamsport, Pennsylvania, used this cartridge with a Sierra 168-grain MatchKing bullet to break a 1,000-yard benchrest record, firing a record group of 7-11/16 inches (see load specs below).

General Comments: Longer barrels (26 inches-plus) are required to give this round room to perform. Devito's benchrest barrel was 30 inches long, according to historical records. Midway sells 7mm-300 brass as well as Redding 2-Die Sets ($104 in 2016), a Redding Neck Sizer Die for the 7mm-300 Weatherby Magnum, RCBS Case Forming Dies and other reloading equipment.

This cartridge has appeared in previous editions of COTW and is restored for this edition because factory-made 6.5mm-300 Weatherby is now available. What's interesting vis-a-vis the 6.5-300 Weatherby is the factory's recent adoption of the necked-down wildcat concept using the big .300 Weatherby Magnum case was pioneered more than 50 years ago.

7mm-300 Weatherby Loading Data

Bullet (grains/type)	Powder	Grains	Velocity	Energy	Source/Comments
168 Sierra Matchking	H570	87	3,254	3,949	Sierra; Federal 215 Primer

.30 American

Historical Notes: The .30 American is not actually a cartridge. It is, in fact, a specially annealed .30-30 Winchester case with a small primer pocket and small flash hole made to match-grade tolerances by Federal Cartridge Co. The idea for this originated with David Brennan (editor of *Precision Shooting* magazine), Bill Diefenderfers, David Tooley, et al. The purpose of the special case is to provide the basis for forming a series of wildcat cartridges that are variations of the original .22 Donaldson Wasp. Various versions in calibers from .22 to .35 have been made. All this came about in 1986 and was written up in the 1988 4*2nd Edition of Gun Digest*.

General Comments: The idea behind the .30 American was to field a benchrest cartridge that will beat the .22 and 6mm PPC cartridges developed by Dr. Lou Palmisano and Ferris Pindell. Along the way, it could also provide match-grade cases for making up some of the other wildcats based on the .30-30 case, such as the .30 and .357 Herrett, plus a host of others. Cases are no longer available.

.30-30 Ackley Improved

Historical Notes: The .30-30 Winchester is one of the most popular sporting cartridges ever produced. It is the standard American deer cartridge, but its popularity is due more to the light, handy carbines that chamber it than to its ballistics. Many hunters have wished that the .30-30 had a little more oomph. The .30-30 Improved does just that by providing an additional 200 to 300 fps within the working pressure limits of the standard Model 94 Winchester action. There are various versions of the .30-30 Improved, but the Ackley version is the most popular. The exact date of introduction is not known, but was probably sometime in the early 1950s or, perhaps, even earlier.

General Comments: Basically, the .30-30 Improved requires only a simple re-chambering job. Cases are made by firing standard .30-30 Winchester ammunition in the Improved chamber, then reloading the fire-formed cases. However, anyone who favors the Model 94 Winchester or Marlin 336 and wants more power than the standard .30-30 can simply buy one in .307 Winchester. This would seem to make the Improved .30-30 obsolete for new rifles, but it is still a good modification for older Model 94s and Marlins.

Editor's note: Since the .307 Winchester appears on its way to obsolescence, perhaps one should not be so hasty in condemning Ackley's solution.

.30-30 Ackley Improved Loading Data

Bullet (grains/type)	Powder	Grains	Velocity	Energy	Source/Comments
100 SP	RI-7	36.0	2,750	1,680	N/A
110 HP	RI-7	35.0	2,610	1,660	N/A
130 SP	W748	36.0	2,385	1,645	N/A
150 SP	RI-7	30.0	2,270	1,720	N/A
150 SP	IMR 3031	37.0	2,617	2,280	Ackley
170 SP	IMR 3031	35.0	2,310	2,020	N/A

.30 ARX — NEW

Historical Notes: The .30 ARX is an AR-15-compatible wildcat cartridge made from a necked-up 6.5 Grendel case in 2011. The originator is Robert Whitley of AR-X Enterprises LLC, a small ordnance and accessories manufacturer in Doylestown, Pennsylvania.

General Comments: By changing the case from a .223 base to a 6.5 Grendel base, the shooter gains 14 grains of case capacity over the 300 BLK, providing near-.30-30 Win. performance with common 6.5 Grendel bolts. It's possible this higher-taper cartridge will make feeding and extraction more reliable than the BLK, and the .30 ARX has 57 percent more case capacity than the 300 AAC Blackout.

It uses commercial 6.5 Grendel brass necked up to 30 caliber. The .30 ARX works well with many .30-caliber bullets loaded at magazine length while taking advantage of its case capacity for maximum power and velocity. Suitable powders for the .30 ARX include Hodgdon H4198, Reloder 7 & Norma 200 and AA1680.

AR-X Enterprises has .30 ARX uppers in stock, and die sets are available. For more information, log on to 6mmAR.com, or call (215) 348-8789.

Cartridge Name Loading Data and Factory Ballistics

Bullet (grains/type)	Powder	Grains	Velocity	Energy	Source/Comments
125 Nosler BallisticTip	H4198	28	2,419	1,624	AR-X Enterprises
150 Sierra BT	H4198	28	2,363	1,859	AR-X Enterprises

.30 Herrett

Historical Notes: The .30 Herrett was developed as a handgun hunting cartridge by grip-maker Steve Herrett and the late noted gun writer Bob Milek. It was intended for use in the Thompson/Center single-shot pistol, and the first barrels were made up in 1972, although Thompson/Center did not offer it as a standard chambering until 1973. The cartridge is based on a shortened and reformed .30-30 Winchester case reduced to 1.6 inches, as compared to the original length of 2.04 inches. The case is longer and has greater powder capacity than the .30 Carbine and, when fired in the 10-inch barrel of the Thompson/Center pistol, delivers a rather impressive performance. Muzzle velocities of more than 2000 fps are possible with the 125- or 130-grain bullet.

General Comments: Conceived as a superior handgun hunting cartridge, the .30 Herrett has been used successfully on everything from varmints to deer. However, as loaded and used in the Thompson/Center pistol, it develops less velocity and energy than the standard .30-30 rifle and must be considered on the marginal side as a medium-game cartridge in the hands of the average hunter. Much of its success has been due in no small part to the skill of the people who have used it. On the other hand, it offers greater power than the .357 Magnum cartridge, which some consider adequate for big game in the hands of a skilled hunter. As with all big-game hunting with a handgun, it boils down to the question of who is doing the hunting. What Bob Milek or someone in that class can do and what the average person can do are two different things. In any event, the .30 Herrett is an outstanding long-range handgun varmint cartridge, particularly with 110-, 125-, or 130-grain bullets. It has also been used with success for silhouette shooting, although most shooters prefer the .357 Herrett for that sport. The .30 Herrett is a good example of a wildcat cartridge designed for a specific purpose not really covered by anything in commercial lines, and one that fulfills its design purpose extremely well.

.30 Herrett Loading Data

Bullet (grains/type)	Powder	Grains	Velocity	Energy	Source/Comments
100 SP	2400	19.0	2,210	1,090	NA
110 HP	2400	20.0	2,270	1,260	NA
125 SP	IMR 4227	23.0	2,205	1,350	NA
130 SP	2400	19.0	2,000	1,160	NA
150 SP	Norma 200	27.0	2,100	1,470	NA

.30 Kurz

Historical Notes: The .30 Kurz is made by shortening the .30-06 or .308 Winchester to 1.290 inches. This produces a short cartridge very similar to the German 7.92 Kurz assault rifle cartridge of World War II. The idea originated in the 1960s, and there are other versions of this cartridge. It is intended for use in modified M1 carbines and is the same length as the .30 Carbine case.

General Comments: The .30 Carbine cartridge is not very flexible and is not a particularly good choice for hunting. Because of this, many efforts have been made to improve the performance of the handy little M1 Carbine through wildcat cartridge designs. The .30 Kurz is one of these. The problem is that the cartridge has capabilities beyond the ability of the M1 Carbine. When loaded within the pressure limits of the gun, it does not provide much of an improvement. It is, however, an interesting development as one of the shortest of the short .30-calibers. It is usually loaded with a 110-grain bullet.

.308x1.5-inch Barnes

Historical Notes: The .308x1.5-inch was developed by the original author of this book, Frank C. Barnes, in March 1961. It is based on the .308 Winchester case shortened from the original 2.01 inches to a length of 1.50 inches. The only other difference is in shoulder diameter, which is .003-inch larger than the original cartridge. Two rifles were made up for the developmental work, one on a Swedish Model 96 short military bolt-action (1:12 twist) by Les Corbett, the other on a Remington rolling block single-shot action (1:10-inch twist) by P.O. Ackley. Both rifles proved to be extremely accurate, although the 1:12 twist appears to be the one that has become more or less standard for this cartridge. The .308x1.5 inch is similar to the Russian 7.62x39mm (M43) military round, but is larger in base diameter and has a greater powder capacity. Consequently, it can be loaded to produce higher velocity with any given bullet weight. At the time this cartridge was introduced, several gun designers, working on assault rifle designs they hoped to sell to the government, chambered guns to handle the .308x1.5 inch. However, nothing came of these efforts, and the cartridge has never been seriously considered as a military round.

A number of individual experimenters have worked with variations of the original .308x1.5-inch case configuration by lengthening it to 1.6 inches, 1.7 inches, etc., and it has been necked down to .22, 6mm, and 7mm, and necked up to .375-inch. Case capacity of the .308x1.5 inch is close to that of the .223 Remington and, if necked down to .22-caliber, it delivers approximately the same ballistics. The original case-forming and loading dies were made up by RCBS (www.rcbs.com), and these can still be ordered as a regular stock item.

General Comments: As originally conceived, the .308x1.5-inch was envisioned as a varmint-through-deer sporting cartridge that could be chambered in very lightweight, short-action rifles for hunting under conditions in which reduced bulk and heft would be important. As a secondary possibility, it could provide a very efficient .30-caliber match or even a benchrest cartridge. However, it has emerged as more of a special-purpose handgun cartridge for use in custom single-shot pistols for silhouette shooting. Many custom barrels have been made for the popular Thompson/Center Contender single-shot pistol in .308x1.5-inch chambering and, in addition, the Wichita Silhouette Pistol, made by Wichita Arms (www.wichitaarms.com), offers it as a standard chambering. In addition, a number of custom pistolsmiths who make up single-shot pistols based on the Remington XP-100 bolt-action offer it as a chambering choice.

As a rifle cartridge, the .308x1.5-inch delivers initial velocities in excess of the factory-loaded .30-30 Winchester (a true 2530 to 2540 fps with the 150-grain bullet, as opposed to the advertised 2410 fps of the commercial .30-30). Actually, as demonstrated through chronograph tests, the factory 150-grain loading of the .30-30 develops only about 2250 fps from a 22-inch barrel, and most of the .30-30s sold have 20-inch barrels. Since the .308x1.5-inch is used exclusively in bolt- or single-shot actions, this allows the use of spitzer bullets, which means that the retained velocity at the longer ranges will also be greater than the flat-pointed .30-30 bullet. Frank Barnes had great success with this little cartridge in hunting deer, feral pigs, and feral goats. Properly loaded, it has good killing power on animals up to deer-size at ranges out to about 150 yards or so.

Small cartridges such as the .308x1.5-inch are very efficient and deliver performance out of all proportion to their size. However this is only achieved at relatively high pressure levels. When loading the .308x1.5-inch or any similar cartridges to maximum performance levels, adding only a few tenths of a grain of powder can run the pressure up to unsafe levels. Also, if military cases are used, all maximum charges must be reduced, because those cases are generally heavier, which reduces capacity and increases loading density, again thereby increasing pressure. A number of shooters have been using the .308x1.5-inch for shooting cast bullets. Lou Delgado of Thousand Oaks, Calif., experimented with cast bullets and various twists from 1:12 through 1:16.

Editor's note: This cartridge would be a good choice for the "Hunter Benchrest" game, but is not allowed, owing to insufficient case capacity to satisfy the rule requiring that the case must have at least as much capacity as the .30-30 case. Since .308x1.5-inch performance far outclasses any factory .30-30 loading, some might question the common sense of such a rule.

.308x1.5-inch Barnes Loading Data

Bullet (grains)	Powder	Grains	Velocity	Energy	Source/Comments
80	IMR 4198	28.0	2,875	1,468	N/A
80	IMR 4198	29.0	2,938	1,533	N/A
93	IMR 4198	28.5	2,835	1,659	N/A
100	IMR 4198	28.5	2,810	1,755	N/A
125	H380	30.0	2,015	1,125	N/A
125	H380	30.0	2,015	1,126	N/A
125	IMR 3031	29.0	2,352	1,548	N/A
125	IMR 4198	27.0	2,557	1,814	N/A
125	IMR 3031	29.0	2,350	1,535	N/A
125	IMR 4198	28.0	2,640	1,935	N/A
150	IMR 4198	27.0	2,530	2,130	N/A
150	H380	23.0	1,589	850	N/A
150	IMR 4064	27.0	2,032	1,375	N/A
150	IMR 4198	21.0	2,027	1,368	N/A
150	IMR 4198	26.0	2,456	2,008	N/A

Bullet (grains)	Powder	Grains	Velocity	Energy	Source/Comments
150	IMR 3031	28.0	2,370	1,870	N/A
170	IMR 3031	27.5	2,112	1,653	N/A
170	IMR 4198	24.5	2,233	1,882	N/A
180	IMR 4198	24.0	2,180	1,900	N/A
180	IMR 3031	26.0	2,035	1,655	N/A

.30-06 Ackley Improved

Historical Notes: The .30-06 Ackley Improved is made by firing the standard .30-06 in the Improved chamber. Headspace is the same, but the Improved case has a more abrupt shoulder, less body taper, and a larger shoulder diameter. The most popular version was developed by P.O. Ackley, in 1944, but there are other versions as experiments going back to 1940 and earlier. This has always been a controversial cartridge, with its detractors claiming it was not as good as the standard '06, and its defenders claiming it was better than the .300 H&H Magnum. Actual chronograph tests have proven it definitely superior to the standard .30-06 cartridge with slow-burning powders. However, it could never match the various magnums, since usable case capacity is significantly less.

General Comments: The advantage of owning a wildcat-chambered rifle that will also shoot standard factory ammunition is obvious. The various Improved cartridges from .22- through .35-caliber are all designed to do exactly that. The idea is to provide superior performance by handloading the Improved case, without preventing use of the standard factory round when an ammunition shortage or other occasion demands.

The .30-06 Ackley Improved is one of the most popular and widely used of the Improved breed. With the proper powder, it will add a little over 100 fps muzzle velocity to any bullet weight, as compared to the standard factory-loaded cartridge. This does make it equal to the original factory-loaded .300 H&H Magnum with 150-, 180-, and 220-grain bullets, but, of course, the .300 Magnum can also be handloaded to exceed anything possible in the Improved '06. Best results are obtained with slow-burning powders such as IMR 4350 or Hodgdon 4831. The .30-06 Improved would be adequate for any North American game. As is typical of Ackley's improved series of cartridges, this design exhibits reduced case stretching and easier extraction, compared to the more tapered standard version.

.30-06 Ackley Improved Loading Data

Bullet (grains/type)	Powder	Grains	Velocity	Energy	Source/Comments
130 SP	IMR 4895	54.0	3,150	2,860	Ackley
150 SP	IMR 4350	59.0	3,070	3,150	Ackley
165 SP	IMR 4350	58.0	2,940	3,180	Ackley
180 SP	IMR 4350	56.0	2,825	3,200	Ackley
200 SP	H4831	59.0	2,760	3,180	Ackley
200 SP	IMR 4350	54.0	2,675	3,190	Ackley
220 SP	IMR 4350	54.0	2,620	3,365	Ackley

.30-338 Winchester Magnum

Historical Notes: This cartridge was developed specifically for use in 1,000-yard benchrest competition and is now popular in NRA High Power competition for the long-range events. It was created by simply necking the .338

Winchester Magnum to .30-caliber and almost exactly duplicates the .308 Norma Magnum. (Norma's commercial offering has slightly less case taper and is slightly longer.)

General Comments: The .30-338 Winchester Magnum fills a void in Winchester's Magnum line, created when Winchester introduced the .300 Magnum. The .264, .338, and .458 Magnum all share a 2½-inch case length. Evidently to avoid direct competition with the existing .308 Norma Magnum and to better compete with the well-established and substantially longer .300 Weatherby Magnum, Winchester opted to increase case length and push the shoulder forward on its new .30-caliber magnum (actual usable capacity increase was marginal). The Wildcat .30-338 is likely exactly what Winchester would have offered had Norma not offered it first. Ballistics are very similar to the .300 Winchester Magnum, despite the slight reduction in powder capacity. Compared to that commercial chambering, a slightly longer case neck provides superior purchase for longer bullets. Remington and other mainstream manufacturers have offered rifles chambered for this round as a cataloged item.

.30-338 Winchester Magnum Loading Data (26-inch barrel)

Bullet (grains/type)	Powder	Grains	Velocity	Energy	Source/Comments
150 PSP-CL (Rem)	A4350	71.5	3,203	3,415	Accurate
150 PSP-CL (Rem)	A3100	76.0	3,145	3,295	Accurate
168 Sierra MK	A3100	68.5	3,047	3,460	Accurate
168 Sierra MK	A4350	73.5	3,076	3,530	Accurate
180 Sierra MK	A3100	72.5	2,964	3,510	Accurate
180 Sierra MK	A4350	66.0	2,929	3,430	Accurate
190 Sierra MK	A3100	72.3	3,006	3,810	Accurate
190 Sierra MK	A4350	65.0	2,888	3,520	Accurate
200 Sierra MK	A3100	71.0	2,921	3,790	Accurate
200 Sierra MK	A4350	64.0	2,811	3,510	Accurate
220 Sierra MK	A3100	70.0	2,735	3,655	Accurate
220 Sierra MK	A4350	63.0	2,646	3,420	Accurate
220 Sierra MK	AA 8700	80.0	2,528	3,120	Accurate

.300 ICL Grizzly — *NEW*

Historical Notes: The .300 ICL Grizzly stands as an exemplar of a class of hunting wildcat cartridges built in the 1960s by Arnold and Vern Juenke, gunsmiths who owned Saturn Gun Works in Reno, Nevada. Members of the Increased Case Load line feature 45-degree shoulders and straight case-body lines. They are "improved" in the sense that they have more powder space than the parent cartridge, and we include one in the wildcat entries as a marker for other cartridge designers to note.

Cartridges in the line include the .22 ICL Gopher, .218 ICL Bobcat, .224 ICL Benchrester, .219 ICL Wolverine, .224 ICL Marmot, .25 ICL Magnum, .25-35 ICL Coyote, .257 ICL Whitetail, .25-270 ICL Ram, 6.5 ICL Boar, 6.5mm ICL Magnum, .277 ICL Flying Saucer, .270 ICL Magnum, 7mm ICL Magnum, 7mm ICL Tortilla, 7mm ICL Wapiti, .300 ICL Tornado, .30/06 ICL Caribou, .30 ICL Grizzly Cub, .30 ICL Magnum, .300 ICL Magnum, .303 ICL Improved, .375 ICL Kodiak and .375 ICL Magnum.

General Comments: The .300 ICL Grizzly was based on a .300 H&H Mag. case and could run a 150-grain bullet to nearly 3,600 fps, according to Ackley data. Quality Cartridge is the only manufacturer making new brass cases correctly headstamped for many ICL cartridges.

.300 ICL Grizzly Loading Data

Bullet (grains/type)	Powder	Grains	Velocity	Energy	Source/Comments
150 SP	IMR 4350	80	3,590	4,292	Saturn Gun Works

.300 ICL Grizzly Loading Data

Bullet (grains/type)	Powder	Grains	Velocity	Energy	Source/Comments
180 Nosler Partition	IMR 7828	78	3,460	4,784	Saturn Gun Works
200 Accubond	H4831	78	3,200	5,002	Saturn Gun Works

.300 Raptor — *NEW*

Historical Notes: Around 2010, this cartridge and the similar .338 Raptor became developmental wildcats made by riflesmith Kirby Allen, the creator of the Allen Magnum and Allen Xpress lines (which see). Allen's customers were interested in the performance level of the .338 Allen Magnum but wanted a more portable rifle design and better barrel life. The Raptors are based on the .338 Excalibur parent case, with the shoulder moved forward and sharpened, and more case-body taper put in to improve extraction performance with top-pressure loads. Also, Allen increased the Excalibur's case-body length to 3.050 inches, the same as the 338 Allen Magnum. Allen believes it is the largest-capacity and highest-performance .30-caliber magnum on the market that can be used in a conventionally sized receiver suitable for the .338 Lapua-diameter chamberings.

General Comments: The .300 Raptor will chamber in a repeating version of the Raptor LRSS or Stalker receiver. The .338 Raptor with the 300-grain SMK or the 300-grain Nosler Accubond should work in the Seekins Precision 3.990-inch detachable bottom-metal systems. Headstamped .300 Raptor and .338 Raptor brass is available from Bertram Brass. For more information, check the website APSRifles.com, or e-mail Kirby Allen at allenmagnum@gmail.com.

.300 Raptor Loading Data (* Hodgdon US869, WC860, WC872)

Bullet (grains/type)	Powder	Grains	Velocity	Energy	Source/Comments
180 Accubond	*		3,650	5,323	Kirby Allen
200 Accubond	*		3,565	5,642	Kirby Allen
230 Berger Hybrid	*		3,340	5,695	Kirby Allen
240 Sierra Matchking	*		3,280	5,731	Kirby Allen

.300 Allen Xpress

Historical Notes: The .300 Allen Xpress is the first of Kirby Allen's APS Xpress family of wildcats that can be considered a heavy magnum wildcat chambering. It is also the first APS wildcat that works as well at conventional big-game hunting ranges as it does at long and extreme ranges. Based on the extremely strong and high-quality .338 Lapua Magnum case, the .300 Allen Xpress is specifically designed for use on heavy game at long to extreme range. It offers dramatically longer throat life than any of the smaller Allen Xpress wildcats, such as the .257 Allen Xpress, the 6.5 Allen Xpress, and the .270 Allen Xpress, all based on the .300 Dakota Magnum case.

General Comments: The .300 Allen Xpress is on the top of the performance ladder, easily matching the performance of the much larger .30-378 Weatherby, yet doing so with roughly 12 grains less powder capacity and also a much shorter COAL. This makes it easier to chamber in repeating receivers.

The .300 Allen Xpress brass is easy to form, and brass is available from APS fully formed. There's a range of suitable bullets and powders, and it's comfortable to shoot, when you consider the power it develops. For more information, check the website APSRifles.com or e-mail Kirby Allen at allenmagnum@gmail.com.—*W.T.W.*

.300 Allen Xpress Loading Data (Note: * Hodgdon Retumbo, Reloader 25, Reloader 33, Ramshot Magnum)

Bullet (grains/type)	Powder	Grains	Velocity	Energy	Source/Comments
200 Nosler Accubond	*	N/A	3,500	5,438	Allen Precision Shooting
210 Sierra MatchKing	*	N/A/	3,450	5,548	Allen Precision Shooting
210 Sierra MatchKing	*	N/A	3,250	5,548	Allen Precision Shooting

.327 Martin Meteor

Historical Notes: The .327 Martin Meteor was developed in December of 2008 to provide terminal performance that far exceeded that of the new .327 Federal in a revolver. It was engineered by Lee Martin, of Arlington, Virginia, and is based off the .357 Maximum cartridge case. Cases are formed by running virgin .357 Maximum brass through a full-length .327 Martin Meteor sizing die, and they are then are lathe-turned to a length of 1.52. Final length adjustment is completed on a case trimmer so that cases measure 1.50 inches. This is a bottleneck pistol cartridge developed to work in converted Ruger Blackhawk revolvers.

General Comments: Eight-inch barrels are preferred for this cartridge to extract maximum performance. Custom cylinders made from 416 stainless provide the necessary strength. With an extremely flat trajectory and incredibly high velocities, this cartridge should work well on smallish big game like hogs and deer. Be careful with bullet selection; few .312-caliber bullets are engineered to withstand the high velocity impacts this cartridge can deliver. Speer's 110- and 115-grain Gold Dots and Hornady's 100-grain XTP bullets should be excellent choices. Do not try to duplicate these loads in a .327 Federal Magnum; you will ruin your revolver and possible some of your body parts.

327 Martin Meteor Loading Data and Ballistics

Bullet (grains/type)	Powder	Grains	Velocity	Energy	Source/Comments
85 Hornady XTP	H 110	26.0	2,203	915	Lee Martin
100 Hornady XTP	Lil' Gun	24	2,108	986	Lee Martin

8mm-06

Historical Notes: Immediately after World War II, many shooters found themselves in possession of 8mm Mauser military rifles for which they could not obtain suitable ammunition. What could have been more natural than to re-chamber those rifles for the .30-06 case, with the neck expanded to take .323-inch bullets? Presto! The 8mm-06 was born. It is impossible to state positively who first accomplished this, as it probably happened at several places about the same time.

General Comments: The 8mm-06 in standard or Improved form is one of the better wildcat developments. It is similar to the German 8x64mm(S) Brenneke in both dimensions and performance. Using European nomenclature, this would be the 8x63mm(S). With the 125-grain bullet, it makes a very good varmint cartridge, while the 200- to 250-grain bullets are adequate for any North American big game. For those who do not like the performance of the standard 8mm cartridge, the 8mm-06 provides an inexpensive means of altering Mauser military rifles to a more powerful cartridge. However, the conversion eliminates the use of cheap, surplus military ammunition and requires use of handloads. Ballistics of the standard version well exceed .30-06 performance, while the Improved version adds another 100 fps and suggests serious big-game hunting performance potential.

8mm-06 Loading Data

Bullet (grains/type)	Powder	Grains	Velocity	Energy	Source/Comments
150	IMR 4895	59.0	3,026	3,050	Ackley
170 SP	IMR 4064	57.0	2,930	3,240	Ackley
200 SP	IMR 4350	61.0	2,700	3,260	
225 SP	IMR 4350	58.0	2,515	3,165	
250 SP	IMR 4831	62.0	2,380	3,145	Ackley

.333 OKH

Historical Notes: The .333 OKH was developed by Charles O'Neil, Elmer Keith, and Don Hopkins (thus, the OKH represents the first initial in each man's surname), in 1945. It is the .30-06 case necked up to accept .333-inch diameter bullets. At the time the cartridge was developed, .338-inch diameter bullets were not generally available, but .333-inch bullets were. When the .338 Winchester Magnum was introduced in 1958 a variety of .338-inch bullets became available, which led to rifles made for the .338-06 cartridge. The difference between the .333 OKH and the .338-06 is miniscule, and one can use loading data interchangeably. However, the two bullet diameters are *not* interchangeable. The .333 OKH was a very good cartridge but is now obsolete.

.333 OKH Loading Data

Bullet (grains)	Powder	Grains	Velocity	Energy	Source/Comments
250	IMR 4350	62.0	2,400	3,200	Ackley
275	IMR 4895	45.0	2,202	2,960	Ackley
275	IMR 4831	57.0	2,314	3,270	Ackley

.334 OKH

Historical Notes: The .334 OKH is another development by O'Neil, Keith, and Hopkins, this one dating back to the late 1940s. It is based on the .300 H&H Magnum necked up to use .333-inch bullets. Bullets of this size were made by Fred Barnes in weights from 200 to 300 grains. The .334 OKH is the forerunner of a number of developments leading up to the .338 Winchester Magnum. After the Winchester Magnum was introduced, everyone switched to .338-inch diameter bullets.

General Comments: The .334 OKH is an excellent big-game cartridge for North American hunting and is adequate for most soft-skinned African big game. Like all other .33-caliber cartridges, it was made obsolete by the .338 Winchester Magnum, which used standard .338-inch diameter bullets. Bullets of .333-inch diameter are no longer available.

.338-223 Straight

Historical Notes: The .338-223 Straight originated, in 1972, with Max Atchisson of Atlanta, Georgia. It was intended as the cartridge for a blow-back semi-auto rifle he'd designed. It also had a secondary purpose as a possible cartridge for use in re-barreled Model 1907 Winchester self-loading rifles chambered for the .351 Winchester SL. At that time, .351 WSL ammunition was no longer manufactured and difficult to obtain in quantity. Winchester eventually reintroduced .351 WSL ammunition and eliminated that problem.

Although strictly an experimental development, the .338-223 is interesting, because it is the ultimate possibility in necking up the .223 Remington or similar cases. There are two versions of the cartridge, one made by necking up the full-length .223 case, the other based on cutting off the .223 case at the shoulder and trimming it to 1.412 inches. The full-length version presented two problems. First it was difficult to make without splitting the case neck. Second, with an overall length of 2.54 inches, it was too long to function through the action of re-barreled Model 1907 Winchester rifles. The short case, on the other hand, is almost the same length as the .351 Winchester SL and can be made to work in the Model 1907 rifle.

General Comments: The .351 Winchester SL is loaded with a 180-grain bullet at a muzzle velocity of 1850 fps. The .338-223 has a 200-grain bullet at 1820 fps, so the two are ballistically almost identical. Both cartridges are considered marginal for deer, but do very well on coyotes, bobcats, mountain lions, or similar predators at close range. The .338-223 project was eventually dropped, because the reappearance of .351 Winchester ammunition made such a cartridge non-viable. One problem with the .338-223 is that it is a rimless case, which must headspace on the case mouth. This works well with short pistol cartridges, but not as well with high-powered rifle cartridges. Finally, there seems to be no real need for such a cartridge.

.338-223 Loading Data

Bullet (grains/type)	Powder	Grains	Velocity	Energy	Source/Comments
200 SP	2400	18.3	1,820	1,880	NA
200 SP	IMR 4227	19.0	1,750	1,370	NA
Loading data for the short case only.					

.338 Allen Xpress

Historical Notes: The .338 Allen Xpress is one of only two wildcats in the entire APS family of wildcats that can fire a commercially available round, the .338 Lapua Magnum, with perfect safety and generally fine accuracy. The other is the .510 Allen Magnum. The .338 Allen Xpress will easily match the .338-378 Weatherby and .338-416 Rigby chamberings, but do so with powder charges nearly 10 grains smaller and in a significantly shorter overall length. The .338 Allen Xpress is best used for long to extreme-range big-game hunting, and it performs exceptionally well on heavier game such as elk. It is also the first of the APS wildcats that offers enough barrel life so that it can be used for very-long-range varmint hunting and competition.

General Comments: Rifles chambered for the .338 Allen Xpress can fire .338 Lapua ammunition for fireforming or field use, if needed. The brass is easy to form, and brass is available from APS fully formed. There are many suitable bullets and powders for the wildcat. It does supply increased recoil over the smaller Allen Xpress choices—the .257 Allen Xpress, the 6.5 Allen Xpress, the .270 Allen Xpress, and the .300 Allen Xpress. Shooting this round is much more comfortable with the APS Painkiller muzzle brake installed. (Allen Magnums are found in Chapter 4, Proprietary Cartridges, because, while APS will chamber other actions for its Xpress line of cartridges, the company actually manufactures actions for these Magnum cartridges. The line between wildcat and proprietary is a small one in this case, but we feel that, as of the 14th Edition, this is the proper way to categorize these two subtly different lines of cartridges from the same maker.)

Fully formed brass is available for the .338 Allen Xpress for those who want to take their rifles overseas and where the airlines require the headstamp on ammunition to match that of the rifle's chambering engraving. This custom brass is made by Jamison International, and while it is not as strong as Lapua brass, it is plenty strong to handle the top loads developed for this round. For more information, check the website APSRifles.com or e-mail Kirby Allen at allenmagnum@gmail.com.—*W.T.W.*

.338 Allen Xpress Loading Data

(Note: *Hodgdon Retumbo)

Bullet (grains/type)	Powder	Grains	Velocity	Energy	Source/Comments
225 Nosler Accubond	*	N/A	3,400	5,774	Allen Precision Shooting
250 Nosler Accubond	*	N/A	3,300	6,043	Allen Precision Shooting
265 Barnes TTSX	*	N/A	3,200	6,024	Allen Precision Shooting
300 Berger Gen 2 Hybrid	*	N/A	3,000	5,993	Allen Precision Shooting

.338/50 Talbot

Historical Notes:	The .338/50 is the work of Skip Talbot, of Talbot's Custom Equipment, in Fallon, Nevada. Skip began development of the cartridge, in 1984, as an outgrowth of working with the .50-caliber Browning Machine Gun cartridge. The .338/50 is the .50 BMG necked-down to .33-caliber and with the shoulder angle increased to 35 degrees. The primary purpose of the .338/50 is long-range target shooting at ranges out to 3,000 yards. Forming dies are made by RCBS (www.rcbs.com).
General Comments:	The .338/50 is a highly specialized cartridge and not intended for hunting. It is, of course, adequate for any big game. Owing to the unusually large capacity, severe throat erosion occurred within 250 rounds. Talbot also tried a shortened version of the cartridge, about one inch shorter than the full-length case, in order to increase loading density. In the full-length version, a maximum load of 170 grains of Accurate Arms 8700 powder occupied only about 77 percent of the volumetric capacity. However, the short version was unsuccessful, because muzzle velocity was reduced about 500 fps. The full-length case developed a muzzle velocity of 3700 fps with the 250-grain bullet when fired from a 44-inch barrel. By comparison, the .340 Weatherby Magnum pushes the 250-grain bullet at an initial velocity of 2850 fps from a 26-inch barrel, so the .338/50 develops an additional 850 fps with the same bullet. The internal ballistic predictor program, QuickLOAD, shows that 581 fps of this difference results solely from the longer barrel. Equally, given a 44-inch barrel and loaded to similar pressures, the .340 Weatherby would produce 3350 fps. Therefore, these ballistics are not so impressive. However, with a much slower powder and bullets of 300 grains or heavier, the results might be spectacular. It is an interesting cartridge, but not very practical for most purposes until ceramic barrel liners come into vogue.

.338/50 Talbot Loading Data

Bullet (grains/type)	Powder	Grains	Velocity	Energy	Source/Comments
250 SP	AA 8700	170.0	3,700	7,625	N/A

9x25mm Dillon

Historical Notes:	Final design of the 9x25mm was completed in 1988, but the cartridge languished until top IPSC competitor Rob Leatham began testing, in 1991. This cartridge was developed by a group of people at Dillon, but was chiefly Randy Shelly's concept, and he is primarily responsible for the design. Randy's intention was to create a 9mm cartridge that would function through standard pistols and still produce IPSC Major Power Factor without requiring excessive pressures. In an effort to achieve Major Power Factor ratings with light bullets, which reduce recoil, many IPSC competitors have routinely used .38

Super loads generating rifle-type peak pressures! The 9x25mm is based on the 10mm Automatic case necked to 9mm. Its increased capacity allows loads to achieve the Major level with more reasonable pressure.

General Comments: The 9x25 Dillon is formed by necking the 10mm Automatic case to 9mm with a sharp shoulder and a short neck. This creates a relatively high-capacity pistol cartridge, which is based on a high-pressure case. With the proper bullet and powder, the 9x25mm Dillon can generate significant muzzle energy and easily achieves IPSC Major-Power levels. VihtaVuori has recently designed a powder (called Vit N105) specifically for this and similar cartridges. Appropriate 9mm bullets are readily available. The future is bright for this cartridge, and McNett's Double Tap Ammunition (www.doubletapammo.com) is currently offering 10 loads for this round. Springfield Armory offers guns in this chambering, and several custom barrel makers chamber tubes for this round. Representing an increasingly unique example of the breed, the 9x25mm Dillon meets a recognized need. For more information on the 9x25mm and Randy's more recent development, the 9x30mm, contact him at Dillon Precision (www.dillonprecision.com).

9x25mm Dillon Loading Data (8-inch barrel)

Bullet (grains/type)	Powder	Grains	Velocity	Energy	Source/Comments
100 FMJ RN	AA No. 9	15.3	1,751	680	Lyman
100 FMJ RN	W296	17.2	1,769	690	Lyman
115 JHP	Her-2400	13.0	1,587	640	Lyman
115 JHP	W296	15.0	1,566	625	Lyman
124 FMJ FP	W296	14.4	1,529	640	Lyman
130 Cast	W296	13.5	1,479	630	Lyman (No. 356634)

9mm Action Express

Historical Notes: This is a 1988 innovation by Evan Whildin, who was vice president of Action Arms, Ltd. at that time. The 9mm Action Express (9mm AE) is the .41 Action Express case necked-down to 9mm. It retains the .41 AE rebated rim, which is the same diameter as the standard 9mm Luger. The advantage of this in the 9mm AE is that the cartridge offers a larger case that can be used in firearms originally designed for the 9mm Luger without the necessity of changing the bolt or breech face. This will allow a number of .41 AE semi-auto pistols and carbines to be changed to the 9mm version through the installation of kits made available for specific guns.

General Comments: The 9mm AE has been tested in the Uzi semi-auto pistol and in specially altered 1911 Colt pistols. As a commercial round, it appeared chambered in the Action Arms TZ-75S88. It is a sort of super 9mm and, as such, is more powerful than the .38 Colt Super Auto. It has an advantage over the 9mm Winchester Magnum, since it is shorter and most 9mm pistols can be adapted to it. Tests in a 10-inch pressure barrel gave muzzle velocities with a 95-grain bullet of 1880 fps at 31,760 CUP, and 1903 fps with a 100-grain bullet at 34,880 CUP. These pressures are a bit on the high side for some semi-auto pistols. On the other hand, these are top loads and can be reduced and still maintain impressive velocities. A 124-grain bullet was measured at 1590 fps and 28,550 CUP, a load that could be digested by most 9mm autos. The 9mm AE is a potentially good self-defense and field cartridge. Of course, converted auto pistols are not likely to have 10-inch barrels, five inches being more normal. However, safe loads of around 1500 fps with the 124-grain bullet have been tested in converted Colt 1911 autos with five-inch barrels. This beats the .38 Colt Super Automatic and its 130-grain bullet at 1275 fps. Currently, this cartridge is not being commercially manufactured.

9mm Action Express Loading Data

Bullet (grains/type)	Powder	Grains	Velocity	Energy	Source/Comments
115 JHP	AA No. 9	16.1	1,825	850	Action Arms
124 JHP	IMR 4227	13.3	1,225	415	Action Arms
124 JHP	H110	16.5	1,530	645	Action Arms

.357 Auto Mag

Historical Notes: The .357 Auto Mag is an outgrowth of the .44 Auto Mag and is based on the .44 Auto Mag case necked-down to .35-caliber. The .44 Auto Mag, in turn, is made by cutting off .30-06 or .308 Winchester case to a length of 1.298 inches and inside reaming to accept a .429-inch diameter bullet. The first Auto Mag pistols were announced in 1970 and delivered in late 1971. These were, of course, in .44-caliber. The .357 Auto Mag did not appear until 1973. One could purchase both the .357 and .44 barrel and slide assembly units to convert the pistol to handle either cartridge with a relatively easy parts change. Auto Mag ammunition was made in Mexico for a time, and by Norma in Sweden. Conversion of .44 Auto Mag cases to a smaller caliber is routine. Auto Mag semi-auto pistols are no longer in production.

General Comments: The .357 and .44 Auto Mag pistols were made of stainless steel, had a 6½-inch barrel, an overall length of 11½ inches and weighed 3.4 pounds. In other words, these were quite large and heavy, much like the Desert Eagle pistols currently available from Magnum Research. The .357 Auto Mag pushed the 158-grain jacketed bullet at a muzzle velocity of 1600 fps, and the 110-grain bullet at over 1900 fps, when loaded to maximum performance levels. This is certainly well in excess of anything feasible from a .357 Magnum revolver. Auto Mag pistols in .357 have been used with success on everything from varmints to deer. Like many of the more powerful handgun cartridges, ballistics of the .357 Auto Mag are marginal for big game, but, like the others, it can do the job in the hands of a good shot and accomplished hunter. As a self-defense gun, the Auto Mag pistols are a bit unwieldy and overpowered. These are strictly for sporting use.

.357 Auto Mag Loading Data

Bullet (grains/type)	Powder	Grains	Velocity	Energy	Source/Comments
110 JHP	BlueDot	19.0	1,935	920	NA
125 JHP	BlueDot	18.0	1,810	915	NA
140 JHP	BlueDot	17.0	1,725	930	NA
158 JSP	BlueDot	16.0	1,500	795	NA
158 JSP	H110	22.0	1,635	940	NA

.357 Herrett

Historical Notes: Although the .30 Herrett proved a good handgun hunting cartridge when used in the 10- or 14-inch barrel of the Thompson/Center Contender single-shot pistol, it needed to be improved for hunting heavy game. One solution was to neck it up to .35-caliber, to take advantage of larger diameter, heavier bullets. This was done in the initial development. However, it appeared desirable to increase the powder capacity of the original .30 Herrett case, and, so, the final design used a case length of 1.75 inches, which is .15-inch longer than the .30 Herrett case. The development of the .357 Herrett was the work of Steve Herrett and gun writer Bob Milek. It was introduced as a standard chambering for the Thompson/Center pistol, in 1974. Cases are made by reforming, shortening, and necking up .30-30 or .32 Winchester Special cases. The case has a 30-degree shoulder angle. After forming, the cases are fire-formed to the final configuration.

General Comments: The .357 Herrett is another example of a wildcat cartridge developed for a specific firearm and purpose, filling a gap in the commercial line of ammunition. It was intended primarily as a hunting cartridge for the heavier varieties of medium game, although it also has become quite popular among silhouette shooters. It serves both purposes well, but one must bear in mind that, as a hunting cartridge, it delivers ballistics inferior to the .35 Remington fired from a rifle. While it is perfectly capable of handling large animals under average conditions, much depends on the skill of the user, something that is true of all handguns and handgun cartridges when used for hunting. The .357 Herrett is, nevertheless, one of the best of the handgun cartridges for field use on medium or small game and varmints.

.357 Herrett Loading Data

(Note: These loads are for the Thompson/Center Pistol with 14-inch barrel.)

Bullet (grains/type)	Powder	Grains	Velocity	Energy	Source/Comments
110 JHP	2400	28.0	2,600	1,650	N/A
110 JHP	IMR 4227	33.0	2,685	1,710	N/A
125 JHP	IMR 4227	31.0	2,565	1,820	N/A
150 JHP	IMR 4227	30.0	2,380	1,910	N/A
158 JSP	IMR 4227	29.0	2,310	1,870	N/A
180 JSP	IMR 4227	27.0	2,130	1,820	N/A
180 JSP	Norma 200	32.0	2,125	1,810	N/A

.35-30/30
(.35-30)

Historical Notes: Although not widely known, the .35-30/30 is one of our oldest wildcats, having originated around the turn of the century. Its original purpose was to salvage worn-out .32-40 and .32 Winchester Special barrels by reboring these to .35-caliber. The idea was also applied to improve the performance of Winchester Model 1894 rifles and carbines, while staying within the cartridge length and pressure limitations of that action. While the .35-30/30 cartridge is based on necking up .30-30 or .32 Winchester Special cases without any other change, a few rifles have been made up to accept the somewhat superior Ackley Improved version. Recently, there has been a rebirth of interest in this cartridge by silhouette shooters who like to use cast bullets. In 1976, Arizona gunsmith Paul Marquart built several .35-30/30 silhouette rifles based on the Remington 788 action, and these quickly established a reputation as being both accurate and effective for the intended sport. Information on these rifles was published in *The Fouling Shot*, published by the Cast Bullet Association (www.castbulletassoc.org), and other shooters found it promising as a target and hunting cartridge. The .35-30/30 can be loaded to about equal the ballistics of the .35 Remington, and, in fact, if Remington had not introduced its rimless .35, in 1908, it is highly possible that the necked-up .30-30 would have become much more popular than it did. In any event, it has gained a new but modest following.

General Comments: With jacketed bullets there is little, if any, difference between the ballistics and killing power of the .35-30/30 and the .35 Remington. On paper, the .35 Remington appears to have an edge over the .35-30/30, because it has about a 14 percent greater powder capacity, but the factory 200-grain bullet loading rarely attains 2000 fps, except in a 24-inch test barrel, chiefly because of rather anemic loading pressures. As a cast bullet cartridge, the .35-30/30, with its longer neck, permits use of cast bullets as heavy as 270 grains seated to a depth that will feed through magazine rifles designed for the .30-30. This is not possible with the .35 Remington and its short neck. In a strong action, the .35-30/30 can be loaded to deliver performance approaching the .375 Winchester. However, in a strong action, the .35 Remington can be stepped up quite a bit, too. It is possible to attain 1800 fps with a 300-grain bullet in a strong action chambered for the .35-30/30, which would make it suitable for elk or moose at short range. It is a good cartridge for upping the performance of .30-30 rifles or for salvaging worn-out .32 Special barrels. For a wildcat, it is rather a special-purpose cartridge, but one that may fill the needs of a number of shooters. Dies are available from RCBS (www.rcbs.com) and chambering reamers from Clymer (www.clymertool.com).

.35/30-30 Loading Data

Bullet (grains/type)	Powder	Grains	Velocity	Energy	Source/Comments
200 JSP	IMR 4198	25.0	1,925	1,650	N/A
208 Lead	IMR 4198	25.0	1,895	1,660	N/A
210 Lead	W630	15.0	1,520	1,080	Lyman 35875
245 Lead	H335	30.0	1,770	1,710	Lyman 358318
282 Lead	H335	28.0	1,700	1,810	Lyman 3589

Bullet (grains/type)	Powder	Grains	Velocity	Energy	Source/Comments
292 Lead	W748	33.5	1,620	1,580	N/A

.358 BFG (1.625-Inch)

Historical Notes: In 2007, the Indiana Natural Resources Commission made a significant change to the State's deer hunting regulations, making it legal to hunt deer with a rifle as long as the cartridge case used measured no longer than 1.625 inches in length and fired a bullet that was no less than .35-caliber (.358-inch in diameter). Immediately, wildcat rifle cartridges that met these restrictions started appearing. The .358 BFG (1.625 inches) cartridge was designed by Bryan Farrington, from Clinton, Ind., and utilizes the .25 WSSM cartridge case necked up to .358-caliber. It should be noted that, as with many wildcats based on new cartridge cases, this particular .35/.25 WSSM is not the only version of this conversion being used. However, the .358 BFG (1.625 Inch) cartridge does fall within the guidelines of a legal Indiana rifle cartridge for deer hunting.

On September 20, 2011, the Indiana Natural Resources Commission made a significant change to the State's deer hunting regulations. The allowable centerfire rifle case length was increased from 1.625 inches—made legal in 2007—to 1.80 inches. The previous restriction limited hunters to using rifles chambered for pistol-caliber cartridges, and the increase in case length was, it is thought, to allow the use of the .460 Smith & Wesson. The regulation also specifies a minimum cartridge caliber of .358.

General Comments: This cartridge closely duplicates the ballistics of the .358 Winchester, which has long been considered a sublime deer cartridge. I discovered this in 2005 when I worked with Charlie Sisk of Sisk Rifles and Dave Kiff of Pacific Tool & Gauge to produce an almost identical version of this wildcat. Bryan Farrington indicates that necks will need to be trim turned for his cartridge, and I had the same experiences when I worked with my version of the .35/.25 WSSM. It is also necessary to neck up from .25 to .35 in at least a two-stage process, going from .25- to .30-caliber and then to .35 using a tapered expander ball. As noted, various versions of this cartridge exist, and neck diameter and free-bore vary a great deal from one chamber to another, so approach with caution. It is strongly suggested that you utilize one source for a rifle and dies to eliminate this issue.

.358 BFG (1.625 Inch) Loading Data and Ballistics

Bullet (grains/type)	Powder	Grains	Velocity	Energy	Source
180 Hornady SP/SSP	Reloader 10X	48.0	2,700	2,913	Bryan Farrington
200 Hornady SP	Reloader 10X	46.0	2,550	2,887	Bryan Farrington

.358 Gremlin

Historical Notes: The .358 Gremlin is a wildcat based on the 6.5 Grendel cartridge, which uses the 7.62X39 cartridge case as a base. It was developed, in 2008 by Bryan Farrington, from Clinton, Ind., to meet the requirements established in 2007 by the Indiana Natural Resources Commission (INRC). In that year, the INRC made it legal to hunt deer with a rifle with any cartridge using a case that measured no longer than 1.625 inches and fired a bullet that no less than .35-caliber (.358-inch in diameter.) Immediately, wildcat rifle cartridges that met these restrictions started appearing. The .358 lure of the .358 Gremlin is that it was designed to utilize the AR-15 platform. Conversion to the .358 Gremlin is easy with any AR-15 that is set up for the 7.62X39 or 6.5 Grendel cartridge.

On Sept. 20, 2011, the Indiana Natural Resources Commission made a significant change to the State's deer hunting regulations. The allowable length of a centerfire rifle case was increased from 1.625 inches—made legal in 2007—to 1.80 inches. The previous restriction had been in place to limit hunters to using rifles chambered for pistol caliber cartridges, and the increase in case length was, it is thought, to allow the use of the .460 Smith & Wesson. The regulation also specifies a minimum cartridge caliber of .358.

General Comments: This cartridge closely duplicates the ballistics of the .35 Remington, a cartridge with a stellar track record in the deer woods. Although conceived for the AR-15 platform, in Indiana, it has become a popular conversion for bolt-action rifles like the Ruger 77 and CZ 527 that started life out as 7.62X39mm. Hunters are also chambering this cartridge in Thompson G2/Encore rifles. Though conceived as a one-state answer to newly passed hunting laws, the cartridge has great merit in a rifle specifically designed for young hunters or those who maybe intolerant of excessive recoil. Additionally, anyone looking for a cartridge for an AR-15 that offers more punch than a .223 Remington for hunting wild hogs might want to consider the .358 Gremlin.

.358 Gremlin Loading Data and Ballistics

Bullet (grains/type)	Powder	Grains	Velocity	Energy	Source
140 Hornady XTP	Lil Gun	25.5	2,460	1,880	Bryan Farrington
180 Hornady SS/SP	Lil Gun	25.5	2,350	2,206	Bryan Farrington
200 Hornady SP	H 4227	25.0	2,025	1,820	Bryan Farrington

.35 Indiana

Historical Notes: While working on the *13th Edition of Cartridges of the World*, I used my "Empty Cases" blog (www.gunwriter.wordpress.com), to gain feedback for the book and to uncover new wildcat cartridges. A reader from Indiana by the name of Scott Jones contacted me about wildcats that would meet the .35-caliber/1.8-

inch case length requirements for deer hunting in Indiana with a rifle. (On Sept. 20, 2011, the Indiana Natural Resources Commission made a significant change to the State's deer hunting regulations. The allowable length of a centerfire rifle case was increased from 1.625 inches—made legal in 2007—to 1.80 inches. The previous restriction had been to limit hunters to using rifles chambered for pistol-caliber cartridges, and the increase in case length was, it is thought, to allow the use of the .460 Smith & Wesson. The regulation also specifies a minimum cartridge caliber of .358.) Scott and I decided that the simplest solution was to just shorten a .35 Remington case from 1.92 to 1.8 inches. Factory .35 Remington dies can still be used. Additionally, since Jones intended to chamber this new wildcat in a bolt-action rifle, the cartridge could be loaded to pressures well in excess of factory .35 Remington ammunition.

General Comments: Another factoid not realized by many is that even though the .35 Remington has a rim diameter that is 0.013 smaller than cartridges based on the common .308 rim diameter of 0.473, it will still function perfectly in Remington 700 rifles originally set up for a cartridge with a 0.473 rim. No alterations to the Remington 700 magazine box are required, either. The .35 Indiana can drive a 180-grain bullet to 2450 fps from a 22-inch barrel. This is more than sufficient for deer hunting out to 250 yards or so.

.35 Indiana Loading Data & Ballistics

Bullet (grains/type)	Powder	Grains	Velocity	Energy	Source
180 Barnes Tipped TSX	AA 2015	25.5	2,455	2,408	Richard Mann
200 Core-Lokt PSP	AA 2015	43.5	2,400	2,557	Richard Mann

.35 SuperMann

Historical Notes: Developed by the editor of this book's 13th Edition, Richard A. Mann, the .35 SuperMann is nothing more than an Improved version of the classic .35 Remington cartridge intended for use in bolt-action rifles only. The cartridge was developed by Mann and custom rifle builder Charlie Sisk (www.siskguns.com) by blowing out or increasing the shoulder diameter of the .35 Remington case to from .419 to .437. Mann is a fan of the .358 Winchester cartridge, but factory ammunition is sometimes hard to come by, and necking up .308 Winchester cases can be time consuming. He wanted a .35-caliber cartridge that offered .358 Winchester power, but liked the idea of being able to use the less expensive factory .35 Remington ammunition for practice or as low-recoil hunting loads. The difference in the two cartridges is twofold; diameter of the shoulder, and pressure. This very slightly increases powder capacity, but, more importantly, it prevents the hotter loaded cartridge from being chambered in weak actions intended for .35 Remington operating pressures. Dies and reamers are available on a custom basis from Pacific Tool & Gauge (www.pacifictoolandgauge.com).

General Comments: A rifle in .35 SuperMann is easy to assemble. All that is needed is a short-action Remington 700 with a .473 bolt face—one in .308 Winchester is perfect—and a new barrel. Even though the .35 Remington has a slightly smaller rim diameter of .460, it will still function fine with a Remington 700 bolt sized for a .308 case. Loaded to a maximum average pressure of 58,000 psi, the .35 SuperMann delivers some impressive ballistics from a 16¼-inch barrel; a 200-grain bullet can be pushed to 2,400 fps. A bolt-action rifle in .35 SuperMann will function perfectly with and accurately shoot factory .35 Remington ammunition. For the handloader, this makes for a versatile Eastern woods rifle for deer, bear, or hogs that can also be used with factory ammunition for practice or recoil-sensitive hunters.

.35 SuperMann Loading Data

Bullet (grains/type)	Powder	Grains	Velocity	Energy	Source
158 Hornady XTP (.357 Pistol)	AA 2015	43.5	2,480	2,157	Richard Mann / Sisk Rifles
150 LeHigh Brass HP	AA 2015	44.5	2,520	2,114	Richard Mann / Sisk Rifles
180 Hornady SP	AA 2015	44.0	2,456	2,410	Richard Mann / Sisk Rifles
200 Remington Whelen PSP	AA 2015	43.5	2,410	2,578	Richard Mann / Sisk Rifles
200 Barnes TSX	AA 2015	44.0	2,420	2,600	Richard Mann / Sisk Rifles
200 Remington PSP	AA 1680	36.5	2,359	2,470	Richard Mann / Sisk Rifles
225 Nosler Partition	AA 2015	41.5	2,261	2,553	Richard Mann / Sisk Rifles

.358 Hoosier

Historical Notes: On September 20, 2011, the Indiana Natural Resources Commission made a significant change to the State's deer hunting regulations. The allowable length of a centerfire rifle case was increased from 1.625 inches—made legal in 2007—to 1.80 inches. The previous restriction had been in place to limit hunters to using rifles chambered for pistol caliber cartridges, and the increase in case length was, it is thought, to allow the use of the .460 Smith & Wesson. The regulation also specifies a minimum cartridge caliber of .358. For several years, wildcatters have been building rifles chambered for .35-caliber bullets on a short 1.625-inch case. The recent allowance of the longer case increases the allowable powder capacity and potential performance. Indiana rifleman, hunter, and wildcatter Bill Herring saw the potential for shortening the .358 Winchester case for use as a legal deer cartridge in his state. The first incarnation of this cartridge had a 1.625-inch case. More recently, Herring lengthened the case to 1.80 inches, and the result is what he calls the .358 Hoosier.

General Comments: The .358 Hoosier case is formed by cutting off the .358 Winchester case to 1.8 inches and then running it through a .358 Hoosier die one time. After this single pass through the die, the case will need to be trimmed back to 1.8 inches, but no other modifications are necessary. Pacific Tool and Gauge (www.pacifictoolandgauge.com) can supply chamber reamers, and dies are available from Hornady on a custom basis. The resulting cartridge performs best with 180- and 200-grain bullets and will deliver muzzle velocities of 2600 and 2500 fps, respectively, from a 22-inch barrel. The .358 Hoosier comes close to matching standard .358 Winchester velocities and greatly enhances the power that an Indiana deer hunter can apply to a whitetail deer. At the same time, when compared to the pistol caliber cartridges this regulation was intended to encompass, an Indiana deer hunter now has a firearm with a much longer effective range. It is questionable if any major manufacturer will adopt this cartridge, since the potential for sales is mostly limited to one state. However, that does not take anything away from the .358 Hoosier, which would be just as effective for deer or larger game anywhere else on earth.

.358 Hoosier Loading Data and Ballistics

Bullet (grains/type)	Powder	Grains	Velocity	Energy	Source
180 Hornady SP/SSP	Reloader 7	42.6	2,690	N/A	Bill Herring
180 Barnes TTSX	Reloader 10X	43.0	2,640	N/A	Bill Herring
200 Hornady PSP	Reloader 10X	43.0	2,550	N/A	Bill Herring

.35 Sambar

Historical Notes: Breil Jackson, Editor of Australia's *Guns and Game* magazine, developed the .35 Sambar. David Stendell built the first rifle on a Model 70 Classic .300 WSM action. The .35 Whelen is a popular sambar deer cartridge in southeast Australia, and Jackson was trying to improve upon its performance, while allowing for the use of a short-action compact rifle for hunting in thick brush. The project was launched in 2001, and development of the .35 Sambar was featured in a series of articles in *Guns and Game* magazine throughout 2002.

General Comments: The .35 Sambar is the .300 WSM case necked up to .35-caliber with no other changes. Using 250-grain bullets of good construction, it is a very powerful cartridge in a short-action rifle, suitable for most big game. Velocities of 2700 fps can be achieved with 250-grain bullets from a 23-inch barrel. Lighter bullets can also be used for smaller game and longer range, especially the Nosler Ballistic Tip bullets.

.35 Sambar Loading Data

Bullet (grain/type)	Powder	Grains	Velocity	Energy	Source/Comments
200 Hornady SP	Varget	65.0	2,771	3,410	Breil Jackson
200 Hornady SP	Varget	68.0	2,920	3,787	Breil Jackson
225 Nosler BT	Varget	65.0	2,755	3,793	Breil Jackson
225 Nosler BT	H4350	75.0	2,843	4,039	Breil Jackson
250 Speer GS	H4350	72.0	2,700	4,048	Breil Jackson

.358 UMT (Ultra Mag Towsley)

Historical Notes: A 1999 idea of gun writer Bryce Towsley, the .358 Ultra Mag Towsley puts zip back into the family of .35-caliber cartridges. The 358 UMT shoots flatter than the 7mm Remington Magnum or the .300 Winchester Magnum. The cartridge is intended for elk, big bears, moose, and larger African plains game. Towsley tested the cartridge in Africa, taking kudu, zebra, nyala, gemsbok, and waterbuck at ranges from 10 to 450 yards. If Remington ever decided to extend the Ultra Mag series to .35-caliber, odds are the new cartridge would be a spitting image of the .358 UMT.

General Comments: Based on necking up the available and affordable .300 Remington Ultra Mag parent case, the .358 UMT maintains the same body taper, 30-degree shoulder, and headspacing datum line. Only the larger neck and resulting shorter shoulder distinguish the .358 UMT from its non-belted parent case and, naturally, Remington 700 actions are well-suited for this cartridge. The high velocities possible with this wildcat demand premium bullets, such as the Barnes X-bullet, Nosler Partition, or Swift A-Frame. Many .35-caliber bullets are designed for lower velocity cartridges and may not perform well in the .358 UMT. Loads listed below were tested in the Barnes Ballistic Lab.

.358 Ultra Mag Towsley Loading Data

Bullet (grains/type)	Powder	Grains	Velocity	Energy	Source/Comments
180 X-Bullet	MRP	101.5	3,408	4,641	Barnes/59,000 psi
225 XLC	IMR7828	95.0	3,039	4,613	Barnes/59,100 psi
250 X-Bullet	RL-25	90.0	2,965	4,879	Barnes/58,000 psi

.358 Ultra Mag Towsley Loading Data

Bullet (grains/type)	Powder	Grains	Velocity	Energy	Source/Comments
250 Nosler Partition	H-1000	102.0	3,029	5,092	Barnes/61,400 psi
250 Nosler BT	H-1000	104.0	3,011	5,032	Barnes/57,300 psi

.358/300 WSM

Historical Notes: As soon as wildcatters heard about Winchester's new .300 WSM cartridge, their brains started turning. This short fat case with a large powder capacity and a rebated rim has been necked up and down. Winchester did the same necking it down to both .277- and .284-caliber for its .270 and 7mm WSM cartridges. Necking the case up to .358-caliber was an obvious choice. Almost every factory .30-caliber cartridge has had the same treatment; consider the .358 Winchester, which is based on the .308 Winchester case, and the .35 Whelen, which is based on the .30-06 case. The .358-300 WSM caries on this tradition, and though a number of wildcatters have made this conversion, not all of them followed the same design criteria. You can find several versions of this wildcat chambering where the dimensions differ slightly. Anyone looking to work with this cartridge should take care in assuring that their handloading dies match the chamber dimensions of their rifle.

General Comments: Gun writer Bryce Towsley took the most logical approach, as have several others. He simply necked the .300 WSM case up to .358-caliber, but did not alter the shoulder diameter, datum line, base-to-shoulder, or base-to-neck dimensions. This method of wildcatting is the common-sense approach, when necking up to a larger caliber. However, when necking down, especially by one caliber, care should be taken to slightly alter these dimensions so that the larger caliber cartridge cannot chamber in the smaller caliber cartridge firearm.

The .358-300 WSM is a powerful medium-bore cartridge suitable for any game in North America, and all but the most dangerous game anywhere else. It will push a 225-grain Nosler Accubond in excess of 2800 fps. This is a clear 150 fps advantage over the .35 Whelen, which requires a longer action, and at least a 300 fps velocity advantage when compared to the .358 Winchester.

.358 / 300 WSM Loading Data and Ballistics

Bullet (grains/type)	Powder	Grains	Velocity	Energy	Source
220 Speer FP	Reloader 17	76.0	2,929	4,190	Bryce Towsley
225 Nosler Accubond		75.0	2,816	3,961	Bryce Towsley

.366 DGW

Historical Notes: A high performance, medium-bore wildcat cartridge crafted by Maine gunsmith Judson Stewart Bailey, the .366 DGW is identified with the initials of its creator, David G. Walker. Walker's idea was to achieve optimum performance from the .416 Rigby parent case, directly necking it down to accept .366 (9.3mm) bullets. With a 24-inch barrel propelling high sectional density and ballistic coefficient bullets at relatively low pressures, Bailey believes the .366 DGW will shoot flatter and out-penetrate the Remington Ultra Magnums, the .338 Lapua, and the .338/378 Weatherby. In 2001, Bailey successfully hunted with the cartridge in South Africa, taking zebra, kudu, warthog, wildebeest, nyala, blesbok, and gemsbok.

General Comments: Strictly a custom rifle proposition, the .366 DBW cartridge has been chambered in Ruger No. 1 single-shot and converted Enfield P14 bolt-action rifles. The Beretta/SAKO TRG-s and longer BRNO ZKK 602 and CZ actions would also be suitable for this .416 Rigby-based cartridge. Reloading dies are available from RCBS (www.rcbs.com). Suitably dimensioned bullets are available from various manufacturers, including Nosler, Woodleigh, Swift, Barnes, and Speer.

.366 DGW Loading Data

Bullet (grains/type)	Powder	Grains	Velocity	Energy	Source/Comments
250 Nosler BT	IMR4350	98.0	3,253	5,875	Judson Bailey
286 Nosler Partition	IMR7828	103.0	3,020	5,775	Judson Bailey
300 Swift A-Frame	H4831	97.0	2,911	5,607	Judson Bailey

9.3 Sisk

Historical Notes: Charlie Sisk of Sisk Rifles (www.siskguns.com) in Dayton, Texas, has an affinity for cartridges that shoot a .366 (9.3mm) bullet and so has developed several wildcats in this caliber. The one he has used and sold the most is the 9.3 Sisk, which is an 8mm Remington Magnum case necked up to .366. This is indeed a powerful cartridge that will drive a 286-grain Nosler Partition in excess of 2800 fps, besting the time-honored 9.3x62mm cartridge by at least 300 fps.

General Comments: Initially, Sisk has used his 9.3 Sisk cartridge on a variety of large game in America and Africa, with very fine results. An awakened interest in the 9.3x62mm in the states has brought about an interest in 9.3-caliber rifle cartridges in general, and the 9.3 Sisk is one of the most powerful of the lot. Matched with a 250-grain Barnes Triple Shock or 286-grain Nosler Partition, it is capable of cleanly taking any game animal on the planet.

9.3 Sisk Loading Data and Ballistics

Bullet (grains/type)	Powder	Grains	Velocity	Energy	Source/Comments
250 Barnes Triple Shock	H 4350	88.0	2,920	4,732	Sisk Rifles
286 Nosler Partition	H 4350	84.0	2,820	5,049	Sisk Rifles

9.3 BS

Historical Notes: Developed partially as a joke—hence the "BS"—that pokes fun at the notion the world needs another wildcat cartridge, but also to take advantage of some modern 9.3-caliber big-game bullets and a shorter-actioned rifle than will work with the famous 9.3x62 mm, the 9.3 BS is the brainchild of gun writer John Barsness (B) and custom rifle builder Charlie Sisk (S). The 9.3 BS is based off the .350 Remington Magnum case, which is simply necked up to 9.3-caliber.

General Comments: Initially, Sisk (www.siskguns.com) made two rifles chambered for this cartridge, one for Barsness and the other for himself. After an article in *Handloader* magazine and some savvy Internet promotion, several other custom rifles were built by those who recognized the virtues of the cartridge or by those who were readers and fans of Barsness' writings. Even though the cartridge was initially conceived as sort of a joke, it is a viable big-game cartridge suitable for use anywhere in the world. Both Barsness and Sisk have taken several animals to include Asian water buffalo and grizzly. Brass with the 9.3 BS head stamp is available from Sisk Rifles, reamers are available from Pacific Tool & Gauge (www.pacifictoolandgauge.com), and custom dies can be obtained from Redding (www.redding-reloading.com). The 9.3 BS will do anything the much older 9.3x62 mm will do.

9.3 BS Loading Data

Bullet (grains/type)	Powder	Grains	Velocity	Energy	Source/Comments
250 Barnes Triple Shock	TAC	58.0	2,610	3,780	Sisk Rifles
286 Nosler Partition	H 4895	54.0	2,460	3,842	Sisk Rifles

.375 Whelen (.375-06)
.375 Ackley Improved

Historical Notes: The .375 Whelen, also known as the .375-06, was not developed by the late Col. Townsend Whelen, but was named in his honor. The cartridge was actually the work of the late gunsmith and writer L.R. "Bob" Wallack, in 1951, and is based on the .30-06 case necked up. There are two versions, one based on the standard case and retaining the original 17-degree, 30-minute shoulder angle, the other the Improved case with a 40-degree shoulder angle. The Improved case holds slightly more powder and provides vastly superior headspace control, so it is the more popular version. An increment of .375-inch is about as far as one can go in expanding the .30-06 case without running into headspace problems, due to lack of a distinct shoulder. Experiments with larger diameter bullets have invariably led to headspacing problems. An example of this was the .400 Whelen, which never became popular and is no longer chambered.

General Comments: The .375 Whelen is not as powerful as the .375 H&H Magnum, but is, nevertheless, a good medium bore for application against most dangerous game. It is certainly adequate for any North American big game. It uses bullets from 200 to 300 grains and, because it is strictly a handloading proposition, can be quite flexible. It can be loaded down with 200- or 250-grain bullets for deer hunting, as well as loaded to full power for larger animals. This is one advantage of wildcat cartridges; these must be handloaded and, so, can be tailored to fit different game and hunting situations. As with the .338 and .35 versions of the '06, Ackley's Improved design is superior. In this instance, it is mandatory to ensure adequate headspace control.

Bullet (grains/type)	Powder	Grains	Velocity	Energy	Source/Comments
200 SP	IMR 4895	58.0	2,450	2,265	N/A
235 SP	IMR 4064	60.0	2,475	3,205	N/A
270 SP	IMR 4064	57.0	2,380	3,400	N/A
300 SP	IMR 4064	52.0	2,110	2,975	N/A

.375 Allen Xpress

Historical Notes: The .375 Allen Xpress will easily match the .378 Weatherby Magnum in downrange ballistics and do so with 10 grains less powder and in a much shorter overall length. The .375 Allen Xpress was developed as a dual-role wildcat design. In one, it can be used as a dangerous-game chambering when loaded with conventional 300-grain big-game bullets. Loaded with the 350-grain Sierra MatchKing, it will perform well as a long- to extreme-range chambering in a medium- to heavy-rifle platform. Ballistic performance is slightly less than the .338 Allen Xpress (which see), but the larger frontal area of the 375-caliber bullet would be more authoritative on big game.

General Comments: Based on a blown-out 338 Lapua Magnum case, this wildcat offers extreme performance out of an extremely strong and high-quality parent case. The brass is easy to form, and formed brass is also available. A range of suitable powders and bullets gives the shooter a lot of flexibility in building exactly what he needs. In particular, Allen says, "There's a selection of bullets from 260 through 350 grains which has proven to be very impressive in the 375 AX rifles: The new 260-grain Accubond, a load of good 300-grain bullets, and the new 350-grain Barnes TSX bullet." Naturally, the .375 Allen Xpress produces more recoil over smaller caliber choices, so shooting this round is much more comfortable with the APS Painkiller muzzle brake installed. (Allen Magnums are found in Chapter 4, "Proprietary Cartridges," because, while APS will chamber other actions for its Xpress line of cartridges, the company actually manufactures actions for these Magnum cartridges. The line between wildcat and proprietary is a small one in this case, but we feel that, as of the 14th Edition, this is the proper way to categorize these two subtly different lines of cartridges from the same maker.) For more information, check the website APSRifles.com or e-mail Kirby Allen at allenmagnum@gmail.com.—*W.T.W.*

.375 Allen Xpress Loading Data (Note: * Hodgdon H-4831, H-1000, Reloader 22)

Bullet (grains/type)	Powder	Grains	Velocity	Energy	Source/Comments
260 Nosler Accubond	*	N/A	3,350	6,477	Allen Precision Shooting
300 Nosler Accubond	*	N/A	3,050	6,195	Allen Precision Shooting
350 Nosler Accubond	*	N/A	2.900	6.545	Allen Precision Shooting

.400 Whelen

Historical Notes: Of the various cartridges named after the late Col. Townsend Whelen, recent research indicates that he actually developed both the .35 and the .400 rounds that bear his name. According to Phil Sharpe,* Col. Whelen developed this cartridge while he was commanding officer at Frankford Arsenal, during the early 1920s. The .400 Whelen is based on the .30-06 case necked up with no other changes.

General Comments: The .400 Whelen was not a successful development, because expansion of the .30-06 case neck to this size leaves only a very slight shoulder. This can give rise to serious headspace problems—particularly with incautious handloading and sloppy chambering practices. Nonetheless, properly built custom rifles in this chambering were used successfully in the United States, Canada, and Africa on big game. The .37-caliber bore size is the maximum for the .30-06 case without creating a potential for headspace problems. The combination of careful chambering and ammunition production can evidently mitigate this potential, because G&H rifles in .400 Whelen were used extensively, with no known complaints. J.D. Jones, at SSK Industries (www.sskindustries.com), now offers a .416-06 Improved using a 60-degree shoulder and a body taper similar to Ackley's design. The .400 Whelen works perfectly with no headspace complaints to date. Had Whelen utilized an Improved design, perhaps his .400 would have fared better. Good evidence also suggests that one reason for its short popularity was that most shooters considered it both unnecessarily powerful for North American hunting and only marginally powerful for the most serious of African applications.

Sharpe, Phillip B., Complete Guide to Handloading, Funk & Wagnalls Co., 1941, p. 398.

.400 Whelen Loading Data

Bullet (grains/type)	Powder	Grains	Velocity	Energy	Source/Comments
300 JSP	IMR 3031	60.0	2,265	3,415	
350 JSP	IMR 3031	57.0	2,100	3,430	

.41 Special

Historical Notes:	It would be impossible to guess who might have been the first to think of this cartridge as a wildcat chambering. Almost certainly, the first gun was completed within a few years of introduction of the .41 Magnum (1964). Basically, the .41 Special is nothing more than the .41 Magnum case shortened to 1.16 inch, which matches case length for both .38 and .44 Special, hence the "Special" moniker. Typically, gunsmiths fit and re-chamber a .38 or .357 cylinder to a .41 Magnum gun or install a converted cylinder and new barrel into some other large-frame revolver. Ruger's Flattop and Old Model (three-screw frame) and Smith & Wesson's 586 and 686 are some of the better revolvers for this conversion.
General Comments:	In 1932, Colt's pursued development of a .41 Special cartridge for police use. At least three versions were tested. These differed only in case length (and ballistics). That .41 Special used a .385-inch bullet and, except for the name, had no relationship whatsoever to this wildcat. Commercial production was not pursued.

Compared to the longer-cased .41 Magnum, this cartridge gives better ballistic uniformity with so-called mid-range loads—200- to 220-grain bullets launched at about 1000 fps—which is a fine self-defense combination. Top loads can approach the ballistics of .41 Magnum factory levels, but that defeats the intended purpose of providing sufficient energy and velocity for serious self-defense use, or for hunting of smaller big-game species up to deer. This is a very good cartridge and deserves more attention than it has heretofore received. Note that bullets as light as 135 grains are offered for .40-caliber pistols. This would suggest that 140-grain, .41-caliber JHP bullets should be workable. Supposing revolvers of essentially the same weight with loads generating about 500 ft-lbs of energy, the lighter bullet would generate 15 percent less recoil energy. This is a significant difference and would reduce recovery time and make the gun easier for shooters to manage and master.

.41 Special Ballistic Data

Bullet (grains/type)	Powder	Grains	Velocity	Energy	Source/Comments
200 Speer JHP	H4227	14.5	1,035	475	John Taffin
200 Speer JHP	Unique	7.0	1,043	480	John Taffin
200 Speer JHP	2400	12.5	1,082	520	John Taffin
215 Cast SWC	Unique	7.0	1,027	500	John Taffin
215 Cast SWC	2400	12.5	1,063	385	John Taffin
215 Cast SWC	H4227	14.5	1,037	500	John Taffin

.416 Barnes

Historical Notes: The .416 Barnes was the last cartridge design of the late Frank Barnes, the original author of this book. In the late 1980s, Barnes began to think about various .40-caliber rifle cartridges. He realized that, though there were many available, most were designed for use in Africa. Barnes felt there would be strong interest in a .416 designed for American game and hunting conditions, rather than the dangerous African species. Additionally, he felt it would be advantageous if it could be adapted to several different rifle actions, rather than being limited to a single type. After studying the old .40-caliber cartridges, which are too long for today's actions, Barnes settled on the final version, which uses the .45-70 Government cartridge as its base. By using the .45-70, a number of current actions become available, which make for easy conversions to the .416 Barnes. Readily available and very reasonably priced in particular is Marlin's M-1895 lever-action. Unfortunately, few commercial bullets in .416 are available in the weight range intended and appropriate for use in tubular-magazine rifles.

General Comments: The .416 Barnes would be an excellent cartridge for North American big game. Loading data for this cartridge is limited. Barnes recommended using 37 grains of Rl-7 to push a 400-grain bullet at 1625 fps. IMR 3031 is another good, general-purpose powder for the .416 Barnes in a lever-action rifle. Barnes found an accurate load of 50 grains of IMR 3031 behind a 330-grain bullet. It gave him a velocity of 2045 fps. This cartridge really comes into its own when used with 270- and 330-grain bullets. Though it provides no real advantage for the deer hunter, it would prove to be an excellent elk, moose, or brown bear cartridge.

.416 Barnes Loading Data

Bullet (grains/type)	Powder	Grains	Velocity	Energy	Source/Comments
300 SP	IMR 4198	52.0	2,355	3,695	NA
300 SP	Rl-7	54.0	2,270	3,435	NA
330 Lead	IMR 3031	50.0	2,045	3,065	NA
400 SP	IMR 4198	44.0	1,920	3,275	NA
400 SP	IMR 4064	58.0	2,140	4,070	NA
400 SP	H335	59.0	2,155	4,125	NA
400 Lead	IMR 4198	39.0	1,830	2,975	NA

.416 UMT
(Ultra Mag Towsley)

Historical Notes: The .416 UMT, (the "UMT" stands for Ultra Mag Towsley) was the second of a pair of cartridges gun writer Bryce M. Towsley designed and based on the Remington Ultra Mag case. Towsley worked with custom gunmaker Mark Basner (www.basnersrifles.com) to build the rifles. Like the .358 UMT, the .416 UMT is not a complicated wildcat. It is simply a .375 Remington Ultra Mag case necked up to take a .416 bullet. The shoulder angle, base-to-shoulder length, and datum line are all the same as the .375 RUM. The case holds 120.2 grains of water. By comparison, the .416 Remington holds 103.4 grains of water, and the .416 Rigby 129.6 grains. The Ultra Mag class of cartridges were all designed to operate at a maximum average pressure of 65,000 psi, which is the same as the .416 Remington, but much higher than the Rigby. The .416 UMT generates more muzzle energy than either the .458 Winchester or the mighty .470 Nitro

Express. It's actually in the same class as the .500 Nitro Express and very close to the .458 Lott, which is enough power to handle anything on earth, in any circumstance.

General Comments: Towsley first tested his .416 UMT rifle in Tanzania, on Cape buffalo and several smaller species. It was also used by his son, Nathan, a few months later to take a moose in their home state of Vermont. While it's designed for African dangerous game up to and including elephant, the .416 UMT is also an excellent choice in North America for big animals like moose or brown bear. It shoots much flatter than the .458 or .500 cartridges, which are in the same power range, and is a better choice for moderate long-range work.

.416 UMT Loading Data and Ballistics

Bullet (grains/type)	Powder	Grains	Velocity	Energy	Source
400 Swift A Frame	Reloader 15	85.4	2,525	5,662	Bryce Towsley
400 Barnes Solid	IMR 4350	94.0	2,486	5,488	Bryce Towsley

.416 Aagaard

Historical Notes: Named as a tribute to the late African professional hunter and writer Finn Aagaard, the .416 Aagaard delivers .404 Jeffery ballistics in a compact cartridge suitable for a medium-length action. Fred Zeglin designed this cartridge in 2002 for Frank Selman, a friend and hunting partner of Aagaard's.

General Comments: The .416 Aagaard uses Hornady's .376 Steyr brass as the parent case. The modern Hornady brass is necked up to .416 and sized to create a new shoulder before fire-forming in a .416 Aagaard chamber. The cartridge is well suited for bolt-action rifles using a 24-inch barrel and a 1:14 rifling twist. Note that the .376 Steyr case requires a special bolt face diameter. Z-Hat Custom (www.z-hat.com) offers rifles, dies, and reloading information. Hornady sells .376 Steyr brass. Ballistics data cited below was measured in a 21-inch barrel.

.416 Aagaard Loading Data

Bullet (grains/type)	Powder	Grains	Velocity	Energy	Source/Comments
350 Speer	VV N133	62.0	2,239	3,895	Z-Hat Custom
350 Speer	H4895	65.0	2,316	4,168	Z-Hat Custom
400 Hawk	RL-15	64.0	2,160	4,143	Z-Hat Custom

.416 SM²
(.416/300 WSM)

Historical Notes: Designed by Charlie Sisk of Sisk Rifles and gun writer Richard Mann, the .416 SM2 was intended as a dangerous-game cartridge that would work in a standard length short-action rifle. The SM2 designation stands for Sisk/Mann and Short/Magnum. Essentially, this cartridge slightly betters the performance of the great .404 Jeffery and another wildcat cartridge, the .416 Aagaard designed by Fred Zeglin of Z-hat Custom. This wildcat has been conceptualized by several other wildcatters, but no standardized SAAMI measurements exist. It is nothing more than a .300 WSM necked up to .416-caliber.

General Comments: This cartridge was developed by Sisk and Mann for an African buffalo hunt that never materialized. It is indeed a very powerful cartridge for a short-action rifle and, when loaded with proper bullets, is suitable for use on any dangerous game animal. Interest in short magnum cartridges has somewhat waned in recent years, and rifles with a proper bolt face are not as readily available as one may have thought just a few years back. Still, there are quite a few .300 WSM rifles around, and all one needs to do to convert to a .416 SM2 or .416/300 WSM is chamber and install a new barrel. Handloading dies are available from Redding (www.redding-reloading.com)on a custom basis, and chamber reamers can be supplied by Pacific Tool & Gauge (www.pacifictoolandgauge.com).

.416 SM2 Loading Data

Bullet (grains/type)	Powder	Grains	Velocity	Energy	Source
350 Barnes TSX	Ramshot TAC	67.5.0	2,450	4,664	Sisk Rifles
400 Barnes TSX	AA 2495	60.0	2,300	4,697	Sisk Rifles

.45 Wildey Magnum

Historical Notes: In 1997, the .45 Wildey Magnum became the first big-bore bottleneck magnum cartridge chambered for a production autoloading pistol. Wildey Moore designed the cartridge for a gas-operated, autoloading pistol featuring a three-lug rotary bolt and interchangeable barrel assemblies. Revising the armament planned for the movie *Death Wish III*, actor Charles Bronson replaced the original .45 Wildey Magnum pistol with its bigger brother, the .475 Wildey Magnum, to maximize the power effect of Wildey's big-bore magnums on the audience.

General Comments: Wildey recommends this cartridge for hunting and target shooting, but not for self-defense purposes, due to the potential for damage or injury to bystanders. The cartridge is suited for barrel lengths of eight to 18 inches and a 1:16 rifling twist. A 10-inch barrel offers the best blend of performance and carrying convenience. The .45 Wildey Magnum uses readily available .451-inch diameter pistol bullets. Wildey Guns (www.wildeyguns.com) offers pistols, carbines, barrel assemblies, reloading data, and dies for the .45 Wildey Magnum.

.45 Wildey Magnum Loading Data and Factory Ballistics

Bullet (grains/type)	Powder	Grains	Velocity	Energy	Source/Comments
230	Blue Dot	22.0	Not Given	UNK	Wildey/FA
250	FL		1,829	1,856	Wildey/FA
260	Blue Dot	19.5	Not Given	UNK	Wildey/FA

.450 KNR

Historical Notes: Developed, in 1992, by Kase Reeder for an African safari, the proprietary .450 KNR readily fits into the classic family of big, cigar-sized dangerous-game cartridges. Kase, the son of Arizona gunmaker Gary Reeder, successfully dropped all of Africa's Big Five game animals with the .450 KNR. A few hardy souls purchased Thompson/Center Encore pistols in this chambering, but the general consensus suggests the cartridge is too much of a bone-crusher to be shot from a handgun.

General Comments: The .450 KNR, essentially a .470 Nitro Express necked down to accept industry-standard .458-caliber bullets, works very well in heavy-barreled Ruger No. 1 rifles. Gary Reeder Custom Guns (www. reedercustomguns.com) offers dies, barrels, firearms, reloading components, and information. When using Reeder's reloading information for lighter loads, a kapok or facial tissue filler is advisable, in order to hold the powder closer to the primer to prevent misfires.

Bullet (grains/type)	Powder	Grains	Velocity	Energy	Source/Comments
500 Hornady	H414	105.0	2,300	5,872	Gary Reeder
510 Hornady	IMR 4350	100.0	2,300	5,990	Gary Reeder

.45 Silhouette

Historical Notes: The .45 Silhouette is an approach to a big-bore silhouette cartridge using the full-length .45-70 Government case, which is inefficient when used in 10- or 12-inch barrels. Initial development was carried out by Frank Barnes (not the original author of this book) and Dick Smith of the Washoe County Crime Laboratory during 1984. The idea resulted from earlier experience with the 458x1.5-inch cartridge, which is based on the .458 Winchester Magnum shortened to 1½ inches. The .45 Silhouette is made by cutting back the .45-70 case from 2.1 inches to 1½ inches. Performance of these two is similar, although the .45 Silhouette is a rimmed case, while the 458x1½-inch is a belted case. The rimmed case is better suited to break-open type actions, such as the Thompson/Center Contender, and might even be used in a revolver. Original testing was in a Siamese Mauser bolt-action rifle with a 20-inch barrel. The idea is neither brilliant nor highly original. The result is very similar to the old .45-50 Peabody sporting cartridge or the 11.75Rmm Montenegrin revolver cartridge, both of black-powder vintage. In any event, those wanting to work with the .45 Silhouette can obtain a set of trim and loading dies from RCBS.

General Comments: The .45 Silhouette is intended primarily to shoot a 300-grain bullet of .457- or .458-inch diameter. Lighter or heavier bullets can be used, but this detracts somewhat from the original purpose, which is to provide a .45-caliber handgun cartridge that shoots a 300-grain bullet. We think the late Elmer Keith would have approved of this. Although developed as a silhouette cartridge, this would obviously also make a pretty good hunting number for anything from small game on up through deer and black bear, at least when fired from a 20-inch or longer rifle barrel. After all, a 300-grain bullet with a muzzle velocity of over 1800 fps and 2100 ft-lbs of energy outperforms a number of popular deer-class cartridges. Loading data listed below was developed in a Siamese Mauser bolt-action rifle with 20-inch barrel, and a custom-barreled and modified Thompson/Center Contender pistol with a 10-inch barrel. A twist of 1:16 or 1:18 is recommended with a ¼-inch of freebore. (Note: One could argue that this was the intellectual forerunner of the .475 Linebaugh.)

.45 Silhouette Loading Data (Note: *Compressed charge)

Bullet (grains/type)	Powder	Grains	Velocity	Energy	Source/Comments
200 Lead	Unique	12.0	1,325	785	10-inch barrel
300 Lead	SR 4759	23.0	1,420	1,350	10-inch barrel
300 JHP	IMR 4198	34.0	1,240	1,030	10-inch barrel
300 Lead	IMR 4198	36.0	1,610	1,732	Lyman 456191/20-inch barrel
300 Lead	Black powder	44.0 (FFg)	1,170	930	Lyman 456191/20-inch barrel
300 JHP	IMR 4198	35.0	1,485	1,470	20-inch barrel
300 JHP	IMR 4198	38.0	1,670	1,860	20-inch barrel
300 JHP	IMR 4198	40.0*	1,810	2,180	20-inch barrel

.458 Hubel Express — NEW

Historical Notes: The .458 Hubel Express was the first of many wildcat cartridges made by Ed Hubel, who has developed the 12 Gauge From Hell cartridge (which see). The .458 Hubel Express was a .450 Nitro Express case with the rim removed and an extractor groove cut and a belt swaged onto the case head. Developed in the early 1990s, it was chambered in a Ruger Model 77 action and an Enfield action.

General Comments: In many ways, this short-run wildcat resembles the .458 Win. Mag., except longer. With Hubel's modifications, both are belted straight-case designs, but the Hubel's .450 Nitro parent case is three-quarters of an inch longer than the Win. Mag., so it was capable of a lot more downrange effect. Hubel claimed his Express load pushed a 450-grain bullet up to 2,900 fps, substantially better than the Win. Mag.

The irony of using the Nitro case for this custom load is amusing because the .458 Win. Mag. was introduced as a bolt-rifle round to compete against the .450 Nitro Express and .470 Nitro Express cartridges in British double rifles. All said, an affordable wildcat in this power range would have been nice to have because commercial .450 Nitro Express ammo runs about $5.80 a shot (Hornady #8255).

.458 Hubel Express Loading Data

Bullet (grains/type)	Powder	Grains	Velocity	Energy	Source/Comments
450 Roundnose	NA	NA	2,900	8,401	Ed Hubel

.458x1.5-inch Barnes

Historical Notes: The .458x1.5-inch, which was never intended to be anything except an abstract experiment, has surfaced in a number of roles, including a military one (see Chapter 6). It all goes back to 1962, when the original author of this book was playing around with the .458 Winchester Magnum and cutting it off to various lengths. That work culminated in the .458x2-inch. All this was reported in the June 1963 issue of *Guns & Ammo* magazine. Nothing noteworthy developed with this very short version as a sporting round until the metallic silhouette game came into bloom, at which point several individuals built up special silhouette pistols based on the Remington XP-100 action and chambered for the .458x1.5-inch. One of these was Larry Stevens of Carson City, Nevada, who won a number of matches in the Unlimited class with this combination. He reports that recoil with bullets over 300 grains is rather heavy.

General Comments: The 458x1.5-inch will certainly knock down the metallic pigs and rams, when fired from either a pistol or a rifle. Also, a 300-grain bullet exiting the muzzle at 1500 to 1800 fps is a potent field load and could be effective for anything from small game and varmints on up to deer-size animals. Cases are easy to make by cutting off a standard magnum case to 1.50 inches. No one makes loading dies for the cartridge, but one can improvise by using .45 Colt or other .45 pistol dies.

.458x1.5-inch Barnes Loading Data

Bullet (grains/type)	Powder	Grains	Velocity	Energy	Source/Comments
300 JSP	IMR 4198	40.0	1,805	2,180	24-inch barrel
300 JSP	IMR 4198	40.0	1,680	1,885	15-inch barrel
*350 JSP	2400	23.0	1,376	1,470	12-inch barrel
*350 JSP	2400	24.0	1,435	1,602	12-inch barrel
*430 Lead	IMR 4227	26.0	1,348	1,740	12-inch barrel

*Loading data furnished by Larry Stevens

.458x2-inch American

Historical Notes: This belted cartridge was designed by the original author of this book, Frank C. Barnes, in mid-1962. It uses the .458 Winchester Magnum case, shortened from 2½ inches to two inches. It is designed as a medium-power, big-bore cartridge for North American hunting conditions and game. It is short enough to work through either standard- or medium-length rifle actions. The original rifle was made up on the short

Remington Model 722 action, as a lightweight carbine with 21-inch barrel. This provides an extremely powerful rifle for its size and weight of 7¼ pounds. The cartridge also works very well in re-barreled Winchester Model 94 Big Bore rifles.

General Comments: The standard .458 Winchester Magnum and the .460 Weatherby Magnum are overpowered for North American big game. Both have very heavy recoil and require heavy, expensive rifles. Efforts have been made by various designers to provide a medium-power, big-bore cartridge more suited to American needs. The .450-348 and .450 Alaskan are examples of this, but these are rimmed cases suitable only for lever-action or single-shot rifles. The .458x2-inch fills the need for a bolt-action round of modern design tailored to game found on the North American continent. The .458x2-inch American is intended for 300- to 405-grain bullets. It gives good performance with these and is adequate for the heaviest North American game at short to medium ranges. It would also be quite handy for use against any but the more dangerous varieties of African game in close cover. Case dimensions and capacity are similar to the .45-70, but modern rifles permit heavier loads. This cartridge is, in effect, a belted .45-70, rather than just a shortened .458 Magnum. Ammunition can easily be made from .458 Magnum or most other belted Magnum cases. Dies are available from RCBS (www.rcbs.com). Early in 2000, Marlin began shipping Model 1895 rifles chambered for its version of this cartridge, the .450 Marlin. That case features a different belt and is slightly longer; the 458x2-inch is definitely not safe for use in .450 Marlin-chambered rifles.

Note: The loads shown here are economical, accurate, and pleasant to shoot. The heavier bullet loads are adequate for deer out to 150 yards. Jacketed bullet loads are intended for big game.

.458x2-inch Cast Bullet Loading Data

Bullet (grains/type)	Powder	Grains	Velocity	Energy	Source/Comments
210	IMR 4198	23.0	1,285	778	Lyman No. 457127 Light plinking load
250	IMR 4198	28.0	1,828	1,860	Lyman No. 454485 gas checked sized .457-inch
300	IMR 4198	25.0	1,370	1,257	Lyman No. 457191
405	IMR 3031	45.0	1,535	2,120	Lyman No. 457483 gas checked
300 H SJ	IMR 4198	36.0	1,650	1,820	
300 H JHP	IMR 4198	40.0	1,825	2,223	Very accurate deer load
300 Barnes SP	IMR 4198	55.0	2,412	3,900	N/A
405 Win SP	IMR 4198	51.0	2,110	4,005	N/A

Note: All loads fired from 24-inch barrel, average temperature 78 degrees F. Winchester .458 Magnum cases and Federal No. 215 primers used for all loads. Velocity measured with Avtron Model T333 electronic chronograph.

.460 Alliance

Historical Notes: The .460 Alliance was developed by Michael A. Wayne of Alliance Armament LLC in 2010, specifically for use in the AK-47 platform. It was intended as a short-range hunting/tactical cartridge. It is based on the Remington Short Action Ultra Mag case.

General Comments: This cartridge substantially changes the bark of the AK-47 by allowing it to fire a .458-caliber bullet to velocities of that of the .44 Magnum and duplicate those of most factory .45-70 loads. It should be a great cartridge for short-range wild hog and deer hunting, and it has tactical applications, as well. Factory loaded ammunition is available from Alliance Armament (www.alliancearmament.com).

Bullet (grains/type)	Powder	Grains	Velocity	Energy	Source
300 JHP	FL		2,000	2,665	Alliance Factory Load
405 JSP	FL		1,650	2,448	Alliance Factory Load
405 JFP	Lil' Gun	29.0	1,650	2,448	Alliance Armament

.450 Bonecrusher

Historical Notes: The .450 Bonecrusher was developed by Lee Martin, of Arlington, Va., in 2002, as a lower pressure alternative to another .45-caliber wildcat he had been working with. Cases are made by full-length sizing a .500 Linebaugh case in a .450 Bonecrusher die. Subsequent fire-forming extends the shoulder to 30 degrees with minimal body taper. The operating pressure of the .450 Bonecrusher is set at 40,000 psi. The .450 Bonecrusher is capable of pushing a 405-grain bullet to over 1400 fps from an 8.5-inch-barreled revolver.

General Comments: The .450 Bonecrusher is indeed a specialty round and is not intended for everyone. While it might have some nostalgic and entertainment appeal due to its sheer power, the real draw of this cartridge is its ability to turn an 8.5-inch barreled Ruger Super Blackhawk Revolver into a .45-70. This would make a great short-range revolver hunting cartridge for large game—for anyone who can withstand the recoil.

.450 Bonecrusher Loading Data and Ballistics

Bullet (grains/type)	Powder	Grains	Velocity	Energy	Source/Comments
300 Hornady	H 110	42.0	1,783	2,117	Lee Martin
350 Hornady	H 110	38.0	1,705	2,259	Lee Martin

.450 Howell

Historical Notes: The .450 Howell is one of three cartridges designed by Ken Howell. Howell's idea was to design a series of cartridges capable of taking African game and that would fit in a standard-length bolt-action. Ken began his design sometime in the mid 1970s, when magnum-length Mauser actions were prohibitively expensive and relatively rare. The cartridge cases of the .375 H&H Magnum and .416 Rigby were much longer than needed for efficient use with modern smokeless powders. The original version, the .375 Howell, was designed for approximately the optimum smokeless powder capacity for its bore size. All cartridges are based on the .404 Jeffery case, which measures .540-inch in diameter at the base, versus the .532-inch diameter of the H&H base, thus offering substantial powder capacity in a short case. The .450 Howell is actually based on Ken's .416 Howell, which was the first of the three he designed; the .450 was just a necked-up version. The design of these non-belted magnums is exceptional,but, unfortunately, was never picked up by any of the commercial cartridge companies, although similar numbers are now offered by Dakota Arms and others.

General Comments: With about a 10 percent increase in capacity over the .458 Winchester Magnum, this cartridge can generate fully 100 fps more velocity at the same pressure and with the same cartridge length. It has the further significant advantage of superior accuracy potential, because it headspaces on the shoulder, rather than a belt and, therefore, can be aligned better in the chamber.

.450 Alaskan
(.45-348 Winchester Improved)

Historical Notes: The .450 Alaskan was designed by Harold Johnson, a resident of Cooper's Landing, Alaska. This cartridge was designed to meet the demands of hunters who wanted a lever-action rifle that could deliver substantial energy and bullet mass for use against the largest and most dangerous of Alaskan game. Winchester Model 71s converted to this chambering are among the most prized rifles in Alaska. Belted Magnum bolt-action rifles are legion on used gun racks in Alaska at certain times of the year, but Alaskan-chambered Model 71s are never seen for sale at any price! This is ample testimony to the power, dependability, accuracy, and ruggedness this combination delivers.

General Comments: Ackley might have been the first to open the hole through the barrel and improve the chamber of a Model 71 Winchester. However, by Ackley's own testimony, Johnson's version of the .45-caliber .348 Improved is a better choice. The .450 Alaskan will function through the Model 71's action with little or no alteration to the feeding mechanism, while Ackley's version will not. Ackley's version has slightly less body taper and holds slightly more powder, but ballistics are very similar. The .450 Fuller is essentially identical to the .450 Alaskan, except for a different shoulder angle. Conversion to any of these cartridges produces a Model 71 lever-action rifle capable of delivering ballistics practically duplicating the .458 Winchester Magnum. Any such conversion necessitates special attachment measures to prevent the magazine and fore-end from being separated from the receiver under the stresses of the substantial recoil these cartridges generate. The data shown below is based on Ackley's recommendation of reducing .450-348 Ackley Improved data 5 percent for use in the .450 Alaskan chambering (velocities are estimates only).

.450 Alaskan Loading Data (26-inch barrel)

Bullet (grains/type)	Powder	Grains	Velocity	Energy	Source/Comments
350	IMR 3031	67.0	2,415	4,535	Adapted .450-348 Ackley data, see text
400	IMR 4064	67.0	2,095	3,900	Adapted .450-348 Ackley data, see text
400	IMR 3031	67.0	2,215	4,360	Adapted .450-348 Ackley data, see text
500	IMR 4064	66.0	2,005	4,465	Adapted .450-348 Ackley data, see text

.460 G&A Special

Historical Notes: On a 1971 Uganda safari, then *Guns and Ammo* magazine publisher and wildcatter Tom Siatos designed the .460 G&A Special to provide the optimum velocity—2350 fps with 500-grain soft-point or solid bullets—for hunting dangerous game. Considered more efficient and effective than the .458 Winchester Magnum, the .460 G&A compiled a most successful track record on African Cape buffalo and rhino, and on water buffalo in Brazil and Australia. Professional hunters have used the .460 G&A extensively in elephant culling operations. Firearms authority Jeff Cooper considers it suitable medicine for crumpling irritated Cape buffalo at ping-pong table distances, should a hunter step into an unwise circumstance.

General Comments: Testing 500-grain solids against hard pine boards, the .460 G&A cartridge reliably penetrates to a depth of 48 inches before stopping. The .460 G&A uses the beltless .404 Jeffery parent case with the shoulder moved forward, neck expanded to accept .458 bullets, and fire-formed in a .460 G&A chamber. Barrels of 23 to 24 inches with a 1:14 twist work well with the .460 G&A cartridge. The cartridge adapts readily to magnum Mauser bolt-action rifles and accepts .458-inch diameter bullets. For tough, nasty, and otherwise dangerous game, premium hunting bullets should be the responsible hunter's first consideration.

458 B&M EX — *NEW*

Historical Notes: This wildcat is a project by William V. Bruton and Michael McCourry, whose main lines of B&M cartridges are covered in the Proprietary chapter. The EX in the name can be thought to mean "Extra" or "Express," because it has more case capacity than the 458 B&M proprietary cartridge (which see). It is formed from 500 MDM brass with a 2.5-inch-long case.

General Comments: The 458 B&M EX been chambered in a couple of dangerous-game rifles made by the company. In a rifle with a 20-inch barrel, the 458 B&M EX will deliver 458 Lott velocities or slightly better with 450-grain bullets.

458 B&M EX Loading Data

Bullet (grains/type)	Powder	Grains	Velocity	Energy	Source/Comments
450 CEB BBW#13 Solid	IMR 8208	98	2,440	5,947	B&M Load Data Sheet

.460 G&A Special Loading Data

Bullet (grains/type)	Powder	Grains	Velocity	Energy	Source/Comments
500 Hornady SP	IMR 4064	88.0	2,370	6,235	J. P. Lott & Bob Forker
500 Hornady FMJ	IMR 4064	88.0	2,375	6,261	J. P. Lott & Bob Forker

.450 Watts Magnum

Historical Notes: The .450 Watts Magnum is made by necking up .375 H&H Magnum cases to accept .458-inch diameter bullets. According to P.O. Ackley*, it was originated by Watts and Anderson of Yakima, Wash. It dates back to the 1950s or earlier. The case is .35-inch longer than the .458 Winchester Magnum. Because it holds more powder, it can be loaded to slightly higher velocities than the .458 Winchester Magnum.

General Comments: The .450 Watts is a powerful cartridge that can push a 500-grain bullet a couple of hundred feet per second faster than the .458 Winchester. This makes the .450 Watts a fine choice for the handloader. Arizona Ammunition (www.arizonaammunition.net), now offers factory-loaded custom ammunition for this and practically any other chambering. Guns so chambered safely shoot .458 Winchester Magnum loads.

op cit, P.O. Ackley, p. 501

.450 Watts Magnum Loading Data*

Bullet (grains/type)	Powder	Grains	Velocity	Energy	Source/Comments
400 SP	IMR 4198	85.0	2,670	6,320	Ackley
500 SP	IMR 4320	98.0	2,500	6,920	Ackley

.475 Ackley Magnum
.475 OKH Magnum

Historical Notes: These two cartridges are listed together, because they are virtually identical. Both are formed by necking up .375 H&H cases without any other change. The Ackley .475 Magnum originated in the middle 1950s. The bullet used is the Barnes 600-grain soft-point or solid at a muzzle velocity of 2250 fps. The cartridge is normally chambered in bolt-action rifles.

General Comments: A 600-grain bullet at 2250 fps develops 6752 ft-lbs of energy, making for a very powerful cartridge, adequate for any dangerous African game. However, for those who like lots of energy and power, the .475 Ackley/OKH is not as powerful as either the .460 Weatherby or the .475 A&M Magnum. In actual practice, this probably wouldn't make much difference, because any of these cartridges is capable of dispatching an elephant or Cape buffalo with one shot. Of course, this has also been done with smaller numbers developing less energy. Therefore, in the final analysis, a great deal depends on the hunter and his skill. This cartridge is overpowered for North American big game.

.475 Ackley Magnum Loading Data

Bullet (grains/type)	Powder	Grains	Velocity	Energy	Source/Comments
600*	IMR 4320	90.0	2,250	6,750	Ackley

*Ackley, op. cit.

.475 Wildey Magnum

Historical Notes: The .475 Wildey is the brainchild of Wildey J. Moore. This cartridge was designed to be used in a big-bore, gas-operated, semi-automatic handgun, which was also designed by Wildey. The original pistol was chambered for the .45 Winchester Magnum. In order to build the gun, Moore decided to sell stock in his company to raise capital for production. In time, some of the investors wanted to take active roles in production and marketing of this particular handgun. Unfortunately, many of these were not shooters or people knowledgeable about firearms. Moore's share in the Wildey company was diluted to 25 percent and, without his knowledge, other shareholders in the company formed a separate investment company to gain control of Wildey, Inc. In January 1983, Moore was fired from his own company, but the new management ended up in bankruptcy less than a year later.

It took a few years for Moore to get back on his feet. Using this time to his advantage, he designed an entirely new pistol with improved ballistics and a new cartridge, the .475 Wildey Magnum. The .475 Wildey is based on the .284 Winchester cartridge shortened to 1.395 inches, and then neck reamed to handle .475-inch bullets. The cartridge is the same length as the .45 Winchester Magnum, but of greater diameter. Case forming dies for this cartridge are available from RCBS (www.rcbs.com). Bullets for the 475 Wildey are available from Barnes Bullets (www.barnesbullets.com). Several designs are available, in both soft-points and solids.

General Comments: The Wildey is a very heavy handgun, designed to handle breech pressures exceeding 48,000 psi. Due to its size and weight, usefulness will most likely be limited to hunting and some sport shooting. Accuracy has proven to be outstanding. Five-shot, 25-yard groups consistently average less than one inch. Ballistics are also impressive, with 100-yard remaining energies exceeding .44 Magnum muzzle energy. Load data from Wildey indicates that 18 grains of BlueDot powder should be used with a 300-grain jacketed bullet. With that load, a 300-grain Barnes JSP gives an impressive muzzle velocity of 1610 fps with a muzzle energy of 1727 ft-lbs.

.475 Wildey Magnum Loading Data

Bullet (grains/type)	Powder	Grains	Velocity	Energy	Source/Comments
250 SP	BlueDot	21.0	1,850	1,900	Wildey, Inc.
300 SP	BlueDot	18.0	1,610	1,727	Wildey, Inc.

.475 A&M Magnum

Historical Notes: This monster round was developed by the Atkinson & Marquart Rifle Co., of Prescott, Arizona, in 1958-'59. It is based on the .378 Weatherby case necked-up to .47-caliber. Bullets of this diameter are made by Barnes (www.barnesbullets.com). Only a few custom-made rifles have been produced in this chambering.

General Comments: The .475 A&M Magnum can develop nearly 10,000 ft-lbs of muzzle energy, which makes it one of the most powerful sporting cartridges ever developed. It is not available on a commercial basis and is neither widely used nor known. However, no serious need exists for a cartridge of this power to hunt anything on this planet. Rifles in this class have little practical value for North American hunting conditions. Recoil of a properly built rifle is around 90 ft-lbs, so six or eight shots should provide a workout equal to going a couple of rounds with the world's heavyweight boxing champ.

Editor's note: Around 1960, Fred Barnes (of Barnes bullet fame and no relation to Frank Barnes, the originator of this book) built himself a .475 A&M-chambered rifle, based upon a sporterized Enfield action. With its open sights, that rifle weighed no more than eight pounds. Being Fred Barnes, his initial handloading effort combined stiff charges of IMR 3031 behind his 600-grain bullets. He, some friends, and a small group of well-wishers went to an informal shooting range near Grand Junction, Colorado. Fred sat down on the pea gravel of the parking area and crossed his legs to fire from the sitting position. He took dead aim at the base of a small juniper tree, which was tenuously hanging on at the top edge of a roadway cutbank. When Fred pulled the trigger, everyone was watching for the impact. The shot went low. The tree was summarily uprooted! All watchers cheered as the tree fell, then, as a group, they looked around to find what Barnes' reaction might be. There he was, located several feet behind his original position, lying on his back, arms outstretched, holding the rifle above his head. Dust from the muzzle blast and his ignoble recoil-induced slide (he had absorbed well over 110 ft-lbs of energy) was still stirring, when Fred asked, matter-of-factly, "Anybody want to buy a rifle?" He found no takers.

475 B&M — NEW

Historical Notes: In 2011, Bruton & McCourry designed the acronymic 475 B&M as part of a series of rounds designed for the Winchester M70 Winchester Short Magnum control-feed bolt action. Like others in the B&M series, it is fashioned from a 2.240-inch Remington Ultra Mag case, which is then necked-up to take .474-caliber bullets. At the time of this writing, all 475 B&Ms have been built with 18-inch barrels and fire bullets from Cutting Edge and North Fork that have been designed specifically for the 475 B&M.

It is a coin flip to put this in the Proprietary chapter alongside other B&M cartridges or with the Wildcats. But because only a handful of rifles have been reamed for this round, we place it here.

General Comments: The 475 B&M, like its 416 B&M stablemate, is a versatile rifle and cartridge combination, and it handles a range of bullets that's slightly heavier than the 416. For lighter game — moose, bears and elk, — the 475 B&M runs a 320-grain hollowpoint up to 2,628 fps while keeping a reasonable 56K psi pressure reading. For hardier game, the next step up is a 350-grain solid, which makes 2,524 fps at 56,050 psi, according to B&M data. B&M supplies load recipes up to 450-grain solids for the biggest and most dangerous game.

475 B&M Loading Data

Bullet (grains/type)	Powder	Grains	Velocity	Energy	Source/Comments
425 North Fork CPS	H-322	73	2,268	4,853	B&M Load Data Sheet
450 CEB Solid	H-322	72	2,204	4,852	B&M Load Data Sheet

.475 A&M Magnum Loading Data

Bullet (grains/type)	Powder	Grains	Velocity	Energy	Source/Comments
400 SP	IMR 3031	120.0	3,227	9,250	Ackley

Bullet (grains/type)	Powder	Grains	Velocity	Energy	Source/Comments
500 SP	IMR 3031	110.0	2,980	9,860	Ackley
600 SP	IMR 3031	105.0	2,502	8,340	Ackley

.475 Lehigh

Historical Notes: This wildcat handgun cartridge was developed in September 2011, by Michael Cyrus of Cross Outdoors for Lehigh Defense. It is based on the .480 Ruger case, but the rim is turned down to match that of the .45 Auto, and an extractor groove is cut into the base of the cartridge case. The result is a rebated rimmed cartridge that is basically the same length as a .45 Auto cartridge, but for .475-caliber bullets. The intent was to offer a larger caliber option to .45 Auto handguns for hunting and personal protection and that would only require a barrel swap to complete the conversion.

General Comments: The .475 Lehigh offers performance very close to that of the 10mm Auto, but with a larger caliber bullet. Converting about any double-stacked magazine .45 Auto generally only requires a barrel swap, and barrels and brass are available form Lehigh Defense. Most currently available .475-caliber pistol bullets were developed for the higher velocities achievable from a .480 Ruger and, therefore, will not expand reliably at .475 Lehigh velocities. However, Lehigh Defense (www.lehighdefense.com) is offering its penetrator and controlled-fracturing hollow-point bullet in .47-caliber, and both perform admirably from this cartridge.

.475 Lehigh Loading Data

Bullet (grains/type)	Powder	Grains	Velocity	Energy	Source
200 Lehigh CFHP/penetrator	AA No. 7	14.3	1,250	693	Lehigh Defense
275 Speer Deep Curl	True Blue	8.0	800	390	Lehigh Defense

.499 Hubel Express (.499 HE) — *NEW*

Historical Notes: Development of this round began in the late 1990s, when wildcatter Ed Hubel initially began work on a .510 Hubel Express. To chamber it in an NEF Handi-Rifle break-action already set up for the .500 S&W Mag., he switched to a .500-diameter bullet and renamed it the .499 Hubel Express. That switch in bullet diameter meant he only had to lengthen the existing .500 S&W Mag. chamber to accommodate the .499 Hubel Express's finished case length of 3.55 inches.

General Comments: This .499 HE creates a handy .50-caliber rifle with much more power than the .500 S&W Mag., and at lower pressures than the .500 S&W generates. To improve shooter comfort, Hubel adds weight and a thicker buttpad to the NEF rifle. The latest incarnation (No. 2) of the .499 HE came along in 2010, when Hubel switched parent cases from the .475 No. 2 Nitro Express to .450 No. 2 Nitro Express cases to save money.

Bullet (grains/type)	Powder	Grains	Velocity	Energy	Source/Comments
500 Roundnose	NA	NA	3,000	9,989	Ed Hubel

.500 Cyrus

Historical Notes: This true .500-caliber rifle cartridge was developed by wildcatter Michael Cyrus, of Cross Outdoors, Prichard, W. Va. The idea was to provide big-bore enthusiasts with a short-action—3.00 inches or less—rifle capable of matching .470 Nitro performances. Cyrus also wanted to take advantage of the new wave of .500-caliber handgun bullets that were becoming available. The parent case for the .500 Cyrus is a straight-wall .416 Rigby case that has had the rim turned down from 0.586 to 0.531. Then the case is shortened and necked to .500-caliber.

General Comments: The .500 Cyrus may represent the most power that can be harnessed in a short, three-inch action. It will drive a 500-grain bullet at almost 2300 fps. The problem with the concept is a lack of .500-caliber bullets capable of handling impact velocities this high. To solve this, Cyrus turned to Lehigh Defense and had special .500-caliber all-copper or -brass bullets machined. These bullets expand and then the petals break off, creating additional wound channels inside game animals. I used the .500 Cyrus to take two eland and a wildebeest in Africa with as many shots using somewhat reduced loads. Cross Outdoors currently offers custom .500 Cyrus rifles, ammunition, bullets, and dies. A neat aspect of this cartridge is that it can be downloaded to fire .500-caliber pistol bullets and even saboted muzzleloading bullets, making it a very versatile choice for hunting any big-game animals anywhere.

.500 Cyrus Loading Data

Bullet (grains/type)	Powder	Grains	Velocity	Energy	Source
325 Barnes XPB	Benchmark	92.0C	2,720	5,338	Hodgdon
400 Lead w/ Gas Check	Trail Boss	30.0C	1,388	1,710	Hodgdon
500 Hornady	H 4895	87.0C	2,291	5,826	Hodgdon

.510 Nitro Express

Historical Notes: The .510 Nitro Express is the brainchild of Bob Schneidmiller and custom gun maker D'Arcy Echols. Schneidmiller grew up in the West and, from early childhood, developed a passion for buffalo hunting. He read virtually everything he could get his hands on and dreamed of owning a .50 Sharps. As he grew up, his interests broadened to include the Dark Continent. On his first trip to Africa, Schneidmiller carried a .50-90 Sharps, with which he took a Cape buffalo, but the performance of the .50-90 left much to be desired. After his return, he met D'arcy Echols, and thoughts of building a bigger, more powerful rifle were discussed. Schneidmiller had hoped to build a .500 Nitro, but case supplies for that particular cartridge was drying up fast. He had a good supply of Sharps .50-140 3¼-inch cases, but D'arcy was not keen about building a custom rifle for an obsolete cartridge. So, instead, they used the same basic case design as the .50-140-3¼ Sharps with modern bullets and powders to achieve or better .500 Nitro Express ballistics. Schneidmiller suggested they call the new cartridge the .510 Echols Express, but Echols didn't favor the idea. They finally settled on the .510 Nitro Express. The rifle was built on a Martin Hagn falling-block action and proved superbly accurate. Originally, the rifle was built without a muzzle brake. However, recoil was so heavy that the forearm was torn off with the first shot. The barrel was then so equipped, and Schneidmiller claims it is now a pussycat. Some might disagree.

General Comments: The .510 Nitro Express is a superb cartridge for anyone desiring a single-shot rifle for dangerous game. This cartridge and rifle combination can offer plenty of power, without the expense of a double rifle. Though many hunters shy away from the thought of a single-shot rifle for dangerous game, there is still a strong following for the single-shot. For those not wishing to spend the time and money for a custom rifle, the Ruger No. 1 action would probably be an excellent choice for this cartridge.

.510 Nitro Express Loading Data

Bullet (grains/type)	Powder	Grains	Velocity	Energy	Source/Comments
500 SP/FMJ	IMR 4895	90.0	2,337	6,062	Bob Schneidmiller
550 SP	IMR 4895	88.0	2,172	5,762	Bob Schneidmiller
600 SP	IMR 4831	102.0	2,053	5,614	Bob Schneidmiller
700 SP	IMR 4350	85.0	1,942	5,860	Bob Schneidmiller

.50 TAC

Historical Notes: Developed from the .500 Cyrus cartridge, in 2008, the .50 TAC is a .510-caliber version of the .500 Cyrus. It was developed to provide a tactical rifle that would work off a long-action, but that would be capable of firing .510-caliber (.50 BMG bullets). The parent case for the .50 TAC is the .500 Cyrus or a straight-wall .416 Rigby case that has had the rim turned down from 0.586 to 0.531. Then the case is shortened and necked to .510-caliber.

General Comments: The .50 TAC is a good alternative to the .50 BMG for tactical teams that need the penetration power of the big Browning round, but who do not want to deal with the heavy rifles and intense recoil of that cartridge. The .50 TAC offers about 70 percent of the .50 BMG's capabilities, but in a much more portable rifle. This cartridge is also conducive to subsonic loading and is one of the few .50-caliber cartridges that can be said about. Cross Outdoors in Prichard, W. Va., currently offers custom .50 TAC rifles, ammunition, bullets, and dies.

.50 TAC Loading Data

Bullet (grains/type)	Powder	Grains	Velocity	Energy	Source
645 Lehigh	H 4895	70.0	2,050	6,018	Cross Outdoors
606 Lehigh	H 5744	30.0	1,050	1,438	Cross Outdoors

.500 Belted Magnum

Historical Notes: Gunsmiths Frederick Teal and James C. Tucker designed this medium-length cartridge, in mid-1998. It uses the .460 Weatherby belted case, opened and trimmed to 2½ inches with a maximum cartridge length of 3¼ inches. It was designed to provide a cartridge for dangerous game hunting that does not require the use of a magnum-length action. The original rifle was made up on a P14 Enfield with a 26-inch barrel. This provided an extremely powerful rifle weighing in at 11 pounds. Reloading dies are available from RCBS (www.rcbs.com), chamber reamers from JGS (www.jgstools.com), and jacketed bullets from Barnes and Woodleigh.

General Comments: The .500-bore cartridges and the rifles chambered for them are very expensive and generate excessive recoil. Also, quality loaded ammunition and cases can be problematic. The .500 Belted Magnum offers a practical alternative. This cartridge is, in effect, a .500 Nitro-Express in a .30-06-length case, designed for use in common, low cost, Mauser 98-pattern bolt-action rifles. Classic Nitro Express performance is achieved using Weatherby cases and updated, improved magnum powders. A 535-grain bullet with a charge of up to 80 grains generates the required velocity and muzzle energy to stop dangerous game. Recoil is acceptable with all heavy loads. Working chamber pressures are kept to moderate levels, so as to ensure positive extraction in the tropics. For more information on this interesting development, contact James C. Tucker, custom stockmaker, at P. O. Box 366, Medford, OR 97501.

.500 Belted Magnum Load Data

Bullet (grains/type.)	Powder	Grains	Velocity	Energy	Source/Comments
440 SP	RL -7	67	2,135	4,452	Woodleigh BPE SP
500 Cast	SR4759	36	1,515	2,545	Cast Lee 515-500-F
450 FN	IMR4198	66	2,163	4,675	Barnes
535 SP	IMR3031	78	2,150	5,489	Woodleigh
535 FMJ	H.335	78	2,174	5,612	Woodleigh
535 BS	H.4895	80	2,178	5,633	Barnes Jeffrey
570 BS	Varget	80	2,131	5,745	N/A

.50 McMillan FatMac

Historical Notes: The late Gale McMillan and his son, Rock, developed this cartridge in 1996. Their primary goal was to create a modern (short, fat) case like those now used in benchrest competitive events, but designed to launch .50-caliber match bullets for use in 1,000-yard (or longer-range) Fifty Caliber Shooters Association (FCSA) matches. This case was derived by significantly shortening the bottlenecked 20mm cannon case. The primer pocket has been modified to accept a steel insert. This bushing insert sizes the primer pocket to accept a .50 BMG primer and doubles as a flash tube. The latter carries the primer blast to near the front of the powder charge, which provides significant internal ballistic benefits, including improved shot-to-shot uniformity and increased muzzle velocity.

General Comments: Case capacity exceeds 415 grains of water, which is probably more than is necessary for the intended application (this is comparatively similar to a .30-caliber case of 150-grain capacity). Barrel length in .50-caliber match rifles is commonly quite long, up to about 42 inches. Chronographing showed that this cartridge easily launches 750-grain match bullets in excess of 3400 fps (using 330 grains of powder), without placing any undue stress on the case. The .50 BMG manages only about 2700 fps (using about 225 grains of powder).

It seems likely that anyone seriously interested in pushing the envelope of .50-caliber performance might do well to consider an even shorter version of this case (perhaps about 350 grains of water capacity). The forward ignition feature is probably a worthwhile addition; this system is routinely used in artillery, where it is more feasible than in small arms. Generally, forward ignition adds measurably to ballistic efficiency (performance) and ballistic uniformity (accuracy). Since McMillan conceived this number strictly as a benchrest cartridge, he used a very short case neck. This could allow one to partially seat a bullet into a case that has been sized to provide very modest neck tension. Then, during chambering, the ogive would come to rest against the rifling before the bolt was fully closed. As the bolt was locked, the short, loose case neck would allow the bullet to seat more deeply. As that occurred, the bullet could center and align to the chamber and bore—all are good features for such a cartridge. Shoulder angle is 30 degrees. The rifle uses a custom receiver built by Rock McMillan's McMillan Machine Company and a stock built by Kelly McMillan's McMillan Fiberglass Stocks (both at www.mcmfamily.com).

.50 McMillan FatMac Ballistic Data

Bullet (grains/type)	Powder	Grains	Velocity	Energy	Source/Comments
750 Hornady A-Max	N/A	N/A	3,425	19,545	McMillan (4.666-inch OAL)

.50 McMurdo

Historical Notes: Developed by Fifty Caliber Shooter Association member, and later president, Lynn McMurdo, in 1995, the .50 McMurdo (12.7x92mm) is a long-range sporting cartridge successfully used for 1,000-yard shooting competition. It proved to be a worthy contender in the art of extreme long-range accuracy shooting with .50-caliber rifles. The .50 McMurdo enjoyed wide use by five-time world champion .50-caliber shooter Scott Nye, the late Skip Talbot, and other long-range competitive shooters in Fifty Caliber Shooter Association matches.

General Comments: The .50 McMurdo is an accurate competition cartridge. The .50 McMurdo is strictly a handloading proposition for custom rifles—the .50 BMG parent case is shortened by seven millimeters and given a 30-degree shoulder. The resulting case was designed to provide optimum loading densities for the 800-grain bullets. The .50 McMurdo uses the McMurdo "Ironhand" solid brass projectile.

.50 McMurdo Loading Data

Bullet (grains/type)	Powder	Grains	Velocity	Energy	Source/Comments
800 McMurdo Ironhand	VV N29	238.0	2,650	12,473	Lynn McMurdo

.505/530 Woodleigh

Historical Notes: The .505/530 Woodleigh was developed by Geoff McDonald, of Woodleigh Bullets, for an African elephant hunter. Several of these rifles have been built on Enfield P14 actions, which handle the large case head of the .505. BRNO 602 or CZ550 Magnum actions would also be suitable. The rifles are fitted with Ashley ghost ring peep sights and custom-built mercury recoil reducers and weigh 13½ pounds. The .505/530 Woodleigh was preceded by the .530 Woodleigh Magnum created, in 1982, by necking up the .460 Weatherby case to fit .530-inch, 750-grain bullets. Its maximum muzzle velocity, with acceptable pressures, is 2,150 fps.

General Comments: The .505/530 Woodleigh is the .505 Gibbs case necked up to take .530-inch bullets. With a muzzle velocity of up to 2350 fps (9200 ft-lbs), it is quite a handful. Having a groove and bullet diameter of .530-inch and firing 750-grain FMJ and soft-nose bullets, it is suitable, and more than adequate, for all dangerous game. Field-testing in Zimbabwe in 2001 delivered excellent results on elephant, hippo, and buffalo. Woodleigh Bullets of Australia (www.wooodleighbullets.com.au/), makes .530-inch bullets.

505/530 Woodleigh Factory Ballistics and Loading Data   (Note: Use only Federal No. 215 Magnum Primer.)

Bullet (grains/type)	Powder	Grains	Velocity	Energy	Source/Comments
750 Soft Nose or FMJ	H4350	130.0	2,100	7,346	Geoff McDonald
750 Soft Nose or FMJ	H4350	136.0	2,200	8,062	Working load
750 Soft Nose or FMJ	H4350	146.0	2,352	9,215	Geoff McDonald

.585 Nyati

Historical Notes: With available muzzle energy exceeding 10,000 ft-lbs, the .585 Nyati deserves mention as very likely the world's most powerful shoulder-gun cartridge. The .50 Browning Machine Gun cartridge is used for sporting purposes, generating vastly more power than the .585 as it launches bullets of the same weight 300 to 400 fps faster. However, the .50 BMG is not, by any stretch of the imagination, a shoulder firearm cartridge. The .585 is.

This cartridge was created by Ross Seyfried, who modified .577 Nitro cases. Besides case forming, the rim has to be turned down to fit the bolt face. Either standard belted magnum or .416 Rigby rim size is used, as the bolt requires. Length allows chambering in "magnum-length" Mauser actions with minimal modifications. Modified magazine capacity is three cartridges. Seyfried reports very satisfactory accuracy, no doubt a result of careful chambering and quality workmanship throughout the rifle and load. Nyati (en-YAH-tee) means "Cape buffalo" in several African languages, and this is certainly a good name for a cartridge delivering so much bullet and energy.

General Comments: The .585 gives those who really want power a much more affordable option than the big British double rifles, which can often cost tens of thousands of dollars. However, one must mention recoil. It is an open question as to how many among us can tolerate the kind of recoil this cartridge will generate with full-power loads. In a 10-pound rifle with a good muzzle brake, top loads will generate more than 150 ft-lbs of recoil energy. Compare this to a .30-06 generating a mere 20 ft-lbs. Perhaps a better understanding of what this means is this: Imagine having this 10-pound rifle dropped off a 32-foot cliff and catching it with your shoulder. The originator suggests maximum loads defeat the design purpose. He recommends loads in the 2,200 fps range. Sound advice. A quality muzzle brake can significantly mitigate recoil and is almost certainly necessary on such a rifle. Bullets for the .585 are available from Barnes, Woodleigh, and numerous custom manufacturers. This cartridge also performs superbly with pure-lead cast bullets.

.585 Nyati Loading Data

(Note: All recoil data for vented barrel. *10-pound rifle,14-pound rifle,***18-pound rifle)**

Bullet (grains/type)	Powder	Grains	Velocity	Energy	Recoil Energy*	**	***
650 Barnes TC Solid	IMR 4350	160.0	2,402	8,325	130	80	65
750 Barnes	IMR 4350	130.0	1,925	6,175	105	65	58
750 Barnes	IMR 4350	140.0	2,040	6,935	130	80	65
750 Woodleigh	IMR 4350	140.0	2,196	8,035	140	90	70
750 Barnes Solid	IMR 4350	140.0	2,210	8,135	145	92	68
750 Barnes	IMR 4350	150.0	2,287	8,715	150	95	75
750 Barnes	IMR 4350	160.0	2,487	10,300	180	115	90
750 Barnes	RI-15	120.0	2,070	7,140	115	70	58
750 Barnes	RI-15	130.0	2,235	8,320	135	85	68
750 Barnes	RI-15	140.0	2,420	9,755	155	100	78
750 Barnes	RI-15	Max (147.0)	2,525	10,620	175	110	88
545 Lead Patched	IMR 4198	72.0	1,641	3,255	35	25	18
650 Lead Patched	IMR 4198	73.0	1,660	3,975	55	35	28

.585 Hubel Express
(.585 HE) — NEW

Historical Notes: In 2004, wildcat cartridge designer Ed Hubel created the .585 Hubel Express, made from the parent .585 Nyati case with a belt swaged onto the head area. Chambered in NEF break-action Handi-Rifles, it competes with cartridges such as the .577 Nitro Express, .585 Nyati, .577 Tyrannosaur and .585 GMA Express at a lower cost of rifle and cartridge production.

Because the .585 HE has a proper side taper, fired cases can be extracted from the chamber using only fingers or sometimes just gravity. To fire this stout round, Hubel uses a modified mono-block NEF single-shot weighted to 15 pounds, with a 32-inch barrel and a thick recoil pad.

General Comments: The .585 HE is one of several cartridges Hubel has worked on in this caliber.

The .585 Short Hubel Express (.585 SHE), developed in 2009, uses a .505 Gibbs case shortened to 2.7 inches. This cartridge is short enough to fit in standard-length bolt-action rifles, such as a Ruger Model 77, and Hubel claims it can drive a 650-grain bullet up to 2,300 fps.

Another is the .585 Hubel Indiana (.585 HI), which is a .505 Gibbs case shortened to 1.785 inches. It's so named because it's made to comply with Indiana hunting regulations, which now allow the use of centerfire rifles with case lengths up to 1.80 inches. The .585 Hubel Indiana works best with 440- to 540-grain Minie bullets made for muzzleloaders. It pushes a 440-grain bullet up to 2,200 fps in .58-caliber muzzleloader barrels with slow rifling twists.

In 2010, Hubel developed the .585 Rimmed Hubel Magnum (.585 RHM), the parent case of which is the British .55 Boys Anti-Tank Rifle case. This monster's case length is 4.0 inches long, and the COAL is 4.60 inches.

.585 Hubel Express Loading Data

Bullet (grains/type)	Powder	Grains	Velocity	Energy	Source/Comments
650 Woodleigh	RL 25	167	2,900	12,134	Ed Hubel

.700 Hubel Express
(.700 HE) — NEW

Historical Notes: Wildcatter Ed Hubel uses a .50 Browning Machine Gun case as the parent for the .700 Hubel Express. However, Hubel straightens the case neck and swages a belt onto the head of the BMG case. Though development on this round began in the late 1990s, the first rifle chambered for the .700 Hubel Express appeared in 2008; a Vulcan single-shot bolt action.

General Comments: Like with the .585-series Hubel Expresses, the .700 Hubel Express is part of a family of cartridges. The little brother is the .700 Short Hubel Express, a very simple cartridge design created in 2010. To fashion the .700 SHE, Hubel starts with the .50 BMG case, trims it to 2.7 inches long and expands the mouth to accept the .700-caliber bullet. Filled with a proper powder, the rimless straight case will drive an 825-grain bullet up to 2,100 fps. COAL is 3.15 inches.

The bigger brother is the .700 Hubel Express Long, the case of which alone (4.27 inches) is nearly the length of the .700 HE. It, too, is made from .50 BMG cases, these with extended necks. COAL is 4.75 inches.

The even bigger step-brother from a different parent is the .700 Hubel Super Magnum, which was made from a 20mm case (20×110mm Hispano) and necked down to .70 caliber. Hubel says it holds 650 grains of ball powder under the bullet, and that it pushes a 1,000-grain bullet. This one is unusual for a Hubel cartridge because it has a shoulder, .940 inch, to go along with a case length of 4.33 inches and a COAL of 5.04 inches.

.729 Jongmans

Historical Notes: About 1990, Clive Downie, of Ripplebrook, in Victoria, Australia, began experimenting with parallel-sided Browning .50-caliber machine gun cases, with the idea of producing a huge-caliber rifle. He gave the project to John Jongmans, a riflemaker with experience with .50-caliber arms, and Jongmans perfected the design by putting a slight shoulder on the case and using a .727-inch bullet. John Jongmans gave it the .729 designation. The rifle was built on a Jongmans action with a 30½-inch barrel and a huge, homemade muzzle brake produced by Downie. The gun weighs 21 pounds, bare.

General Comments: The .729 Jongmans is needlessly over-powerful for any game on earth and is, perhaps, as large a bullet as one could reliably get to work in a Browning .50 case. Loads were worked up with an 896-grain solid-copper turned bullet and then, later, with a 1,048-grain turned copper bullet. Up to 340 grains of powder is used, and recoil is brutal. Downie suggests that 15 shots maximum in any session is all a seasoned shooter could handle. He estimated the Taylor Knock-Out scale figure is about 250.

.729 Jongmans Loading Data

Bullet (grain/type)	Powder	Grains	Velocity	Energy	Source/Comments
895 solid copper	H50BMG	270	1,847	6,781	Clive Downie
895 solid copper	H50BMG	300	2,210	9,700	Clive Downie
895 solid copper	H50BMG	340	2,367	11,137	Clive Downie
1,048 solid copper	H50BMG	280	1,955	8,890	Clive Downie
1,048 solid copper	H50BMG	310	2,205	11,317	Clive Downie
1,048 solid copper	H50BMG	330	2,265	11,941	Clive Downie

12 Gauge From Hell (GFH)
— *NEW*

Historical Notes: Cartridge researcher and collector Zachary Weighman has documented several shotshell-based cartridges designed by Ed Hubel of Lake, Michigan, one of which is the 12 Gauge From Hell, also known as 12 GFH. Hubel has been building wildcat rounds since the early 1990s, and they range in caliber from .458 to .700 with various Hubel designations and a full line of shotgun cartridges, namely the 28 GFH, 20 GFH, 16 GFH, 12 GFH, 10 GFH and 8 GFH, along with the 4 Bore. Reportedly, he's also working on a 2 Bore.

General Comments: Hubel said Rod Garnick and John McMorrow are co-designers of the 12 GFH, dating back to 2004, and, in fact, the original concept was Garnick's idea. The 12 GFH was made from a necked-up .50 BMG case, 3.85 inches overall, made to fire in a falling-block Borchardt action. Hubel later used a Savage 210 bolt-action slug shotgun with a rifled barrel and a New England Firearms break-action with a lengthened chamber.

Hubel said he has fired 12 GFH cases three dozen times with no visual signs of case thinning, and he estimates a case should last for a couple of hundred firings.

On later versions, Hubel made 12 GFH cases using high-base cups from new unfired plastic hulls, and he fits the base/rim area of a BMG case (turned down about .008 inch) into the base cup using an arbor press, along with other processes. Top loads tested have been 600-grain bullets at 3,400 fps, but more shootable current loads run out at 1,650 to 1,700 fps. Brass cases are available from Rocky Mountain Cartridge in Worland, Wyoming.(www.rockymountaincartridge.com).

Hubel also manufactures a 12 GFH Belted from from .55-caliber Boys anti-tank rifle cases.

12 Gauge From Hell Loading Data

Bullet (grains/type)	Powder	Grains	Velocity	Energy	Source/Comments
600 Dixie Slug	RE-17	NA	3,400	15,396	Ed Hubel

Dimensional Data

Cartridge	Case	Bullet Dia.	Neck Dia.	Shoulder Dia.	Base Dia.	Rim Dia.	Rim Thick.	Case Length	Ctge. Length	Primer	Page
.10 Eichelberger LR	A	.103	.122	.223	.225	.275	.043	.568	UNK	RF	231
.10 Eichelberger Pup	A	.103	.122	.247	249	.308	.050	.767	UNK	S	232
.10 Eichelberger Squirrel	A	.103	.122	.291	.294	.350	.065	.613	UNK	S	232
.12 Eichelberger LR	A	.123	.140	.224	.225	.275	.043	.568	UNK	RF	233
.12 Eichelberger WRM	A	.123	.140	.238	.241	.293	.050	1.064	UNK	RF	233
.12 Cooper	A	.123	.145	.247	.249	.308	.050	1.106	UNK	S	234
.12 Eichelberger Carbine	C	.123	.147	.356	.356	.360	.050	1.240	UNK	S	234
.14 Eichelberger Bee	A	.144	.162	.329	.349.	.408	.065	1.310	UNK	S	234
.14 Eichelberger Dart	A	.144	.164	.274	.278	.301	.043	.640	UNK	S	235
.14-222	C	.144	.165	.356	.375	.375	.041	1.70	1.92	S	235
.14 Cooper	A	.144	.166	.247	.249	.3085	.051	1.104	UNK	S	236
.14 Walker Hornet	A	.144	.170	.285	.294	.350	.065	1.350	UNK	S	236
.14/222 Eichelberger Magnum	C	.144	.170	.356	.376	.378	.045	1.850	UNK	UNK	237
.14 Jet Junior	A	.144	.177	.366	.378	.440	.059	1.260	UNK	SP	237
.17 Ackley Hornet	A	.172	.195	.290	.295	.345	.060	1.39	1.47	S	238
.17-32 Magnum	A	.172	.196	.335	.335	.375	.055	.900	1.450	S	239
.17 VHA (Varmint Hunters Assn.)	C	.172	.196	.305	.316	.315	.043	1.201	1.60	S	239
.17 Mach IV/Mach III	C	.172	.199	.361	.375	.378	.041	1.40	UNK	S	240
.17/222	C	.172	.199	.355	.375	.375	.041	1.69	1.82	S	240
.17 Javelina	C	0.172	0.201	0.353	0.374	0.378	0.045	1.53	1.85	S	241
.17 Ackley Improved Bee	A	.172	.201	.341	.350	.408	.060	1.35	1.78	S	241
.17-357 RG	C	.172	.203	.424	.425	.424	.055	.865	1.31	SP	242
.19 Badger	C	.198	UNK	UNK	UNK	UNK	UNK	UNK	1.3	S	242
.19 Calhoon	A	.198	.215	.286	.294	.350	.063	1.39	1.47	S	243
.19-223 Calhoon	C	.198	.224	.364	.373	.373	.041	1.76	2.0	S	243
.20 Vartarg	C	.204	.232	.360	.374	.375	.048	1.40	1.90	S	244
.20 Tactical	C	.204	.233	.360	.373	.375	.041	1.755	2.1	S	244
.20 PDK	C	.204	.247	.400	.421	.417	.049	1.683	2.236	S	245
.22 Reed Express	C	.224	UNK	UNK	UNK	UNK	UNK	UNK	UNK	UNK	245
.22 Taranah Hornet	A	.224	UNK	UNK	.294	.350	.063	UNK	UNK	UNK	246
.224 Texas Trophy Hunter	C	.224	UNK	UNK	.470	.472	.045	UNK	UNK	UNK	246
.218 Mashburn Bee	A	.224	.241	.340	.349	.408	.060	1.34	1.75	S	247
.22 K-Hornet	A	.224	.242	.286	.294	.345	.060	1.39	1.70	S	247
.22 Waldog	C	.224	.245	.431	.440	.441	.053	1.375	1.820	S	248
.22 BR Remington	C	.224	.245	.450	.466	.468	.045	1.502	2.00	S	248
R-2 Lovell	A	.224	.246	.295	.315	.382	UNK	1.63	1.80	S	249
.22 Eargensplitten Loudenboomer	E	.224	.246	.560	.582	.579	.063	2.913	3.35	L	249
.22 CHeetah	C	.224	.250	.451	.466	.470	.048	2.00	2.36	S	250
.219 Donaldson Wasp	A	.224	.251	.402	.418	.497	.058	1.71	2.10	L	250
.22 Spitfire	D	.224	.253	.332	.353	.356	.050	1.2902	1.65	SR	251
.224 Montgomery	G	.224	.254	.277	.277	.298	.064	.62	1.13	SP	251
.224 Clark	C	.224	.255	.455	.471	.473	.049	2.235	3.075	L	251
.22 Fawn	A	.224	.255	.430	.435	.492	.060	1.30	1.90	S	252
.22 PDK	C	.224	.256	.400	.421	.417	.049	1.750	2.25	S	253
.220 Weatherby Rocket	G	.224	.260	.430	.443	.472	.045	2.21	2.68	L	253
.22-243 Middlestead	C	.224	.260	.454	.470	.470	.049	2.05	2.71	L	254
.220 Wotkyns-Wilson Arrow	G	.224	.261	.402	.443	.472	.045	2.205	2.70	L	254
.228 Ackley Magnum	C	.228	.265	.445	.470	.473	.045	2.25	2.55	L	255
6x45mm (6-223 Rem)	C	.243	.266	.354	.376	.378	.041	1.76	2.26	S	255
6mm Dasher	C	.224	.271	.462	.470	.470	.050	1.54	V	S	256
.25-222 Copperhead	C	.224	.285	.357	.375	.378	.045	1.695	2.130	S	256
.22 Tuba II Rimmed/unrim	A	.224	.300	.457	.457	.514	.055	1.29	1.62	LP	257
.22 Newton	C	.228	.256	.420	.471	.474	.045	2.23	2.85	L	258
6mm CHeetah	C	.243	.260	.456	.470	.473	.049	2.00	UNK	L	258

Dimensional Data

Cartridge	Case	Bullet Dia.	Neck Dia.	Shoulder Dia.	Base Dia.	Rim Dia.	Rim Thick.	Case Length	Ctge. Length	Primer	Page
6x47mm	C	.243	.266	.357	.375	.378	.045	1.85	2.485	S	259
6mm-250 Walker	C	.243	.274	.420	.468	.470	.045	1.91	2.21	L	259
6mm/30-30 Ackley Improved	A	.243	.275	.392	.422	.502	.058	2.03	2.55	L	260
Spitzer 6mm-06	C	.243	.276	.441	.470	.473	.049	2.494	3.350	L	260
.240 Hawk	C	.243	.276	.454	.471	.473	.049	2.485	UNK	L	261
6mm-284	I	.243	.276	.475	.500	.473	.049	2.165	2.80	L	262
.25 Gibbs	C	.257	UNK	UNK	.440	.468	.045	UNK	UNK	UNK	262
.25-303	A	.257	.257	.412	.460	.540	.064	2.185	2.85	L	263
.250 Humdinger	A	.257	UNK	UNK	.471	.473	UNK	UNK	UNK	UNK	263
.257 Kimber	C	.257	.279	.365	.376	.373	.041	1.82	2.985	UNK	264
.250/3000 Ackley Improved	C	.257	.284	.445	.467	.473	.045	1.91	2.52	L	264
.25-284	I	.257	.285	.495	.500	.473	.049	2.17	2.80	L	265
.257 STW	E	.257	.285	.487	.511	.532	.050	2.850	3.600	L	265
.257 Allen Xpress	C	.257	.287	.532	.544	.544	.046	2.535	3.35	Fed 215 L	266
.257 Ackley Improved	C	.257	.288	.457	.471	.474	.045	2.23	2.78	L	267
.257 Condor	E	0.257	0.288	0.451	0.532	0.532	0.050	2.400	3.300	LRM	267
.25 Hunter	A	.257	.293	.430	.435	.492	.046	1.625	2.30	L	268
.25 Ackley Krag	A	.257	.293	.415	.457	.540	.059	2.24-2.31	V	L	268
.25 Ackley Krag Short	A	.257	.293	.442	.457	.540	.059	2.31	UNK	L	268
6.5 STW	E	.264	.298	.487	.511	.532	.050	2.850	3.600	L	269
6.5x52mm American	C	.264	.297	.465	.470	.473	.054	2.024	2.735	L	270
6.5 Gibbs	C	.264	UNK	UNK	.440	.468	.045	UNK	UNK	UNK	270
EABCO 6.5mm BRM	A	.264	UNK	UNK	.422	.502	.058	UNK	UNK	UNK	271
.264 LBC-AR	C	.264	.293	.428	.439	.441	.059	1.526	2.20	S	271
6.5 Allen Xpress	C	.264	.295	.532	.544	.544	.046	2.54	3.375	Fed 215 L	272
6.5mm Leopard	C	.264	.295	.539	.551	.533	.049	2.093	UNK	L	272
.264 Hawk	C	.264	.296	.454	.471	.473	.049	2.485	UNK	L	273
6.5mm-06 Ackley Improved	C	.264	.300	.455	.471	.473	.045	2.50	3.30	L	273
6.5 SAUM	I	0.264	0.295	0.534	0.550	0.534	0.050	2.015	2.226	L	274
.270 Gibbs	C	.277	UNK	UNK	.440	.468	.045	UNK	UNK	UNK	274
.270 REN	B	.277	.295	UNK	.298	.350	.060	1.29	UNK	S	275
.270 IHMSA	C	.277	.305	.448	.471	.473	.045	1.866	2.60	L	275
.270 Hawk	C	.277	.308	.453	.471	.473	.049	2.485	UNK	L	276
.270 Savage	C	.277	.308	.413	.470	.470	.045	1.88	2.62	L	276
.270 Ackley Improved Savage	C	.277	.308	.450	.470	.470	.045	1.88	2.62	L	276
.270 Allen Xpress	C	.277	.308	.535	.544	.544	.046	2.545	3.40	Fed 215 L	277
7mm TCU (7mmx223)	C	.284	.302	.350	.373	.375	.041	1.74	2.28	S	277
7mm Gibbs	C	.284	UNK	UNK	.440	.468	.045	UNK	UNK	UNK	278
.30 Gibbs	C	.308	UNK	UNK	.440	.468	.045	UNK	UNK	UNK	278
7mm JRS	C	.284	.312	.454	.470	.467	.045	2.525	3.455	L	279
.285 OKH/7mm-06	C	.284	.315	.442	.470	.472	.045	2.55	3.35	L	279
.280 Hawk	C	.284	.315	.454	.471	.473	.049	2.485	UNK	L	280
7mm SGLC	C	.284	.315	.465	.470	.473	.054	2.024	2.735	L	280
7mm STE	A	.284	.315	.454	.467	.502	.059	2.1	2.54	L	281
7mm-300 Weatherby Magnum	E	0.284	0.310	0.492	0.513	0.530	0.048	2.825	3.560	L	282
.30 American	A	.308	.328	.402	.422	.502	.058	2.03	2.53	S	282
.30-30 Ackley Improved	A	.308	.328	.405	.422	.502	.058	2.04	2.54	L	282
.30 ARX	C	0.308	0.330	0.428	0.439	0.441	0.059	1.526	2.26	CCI BR-4	283
.30 Herrett	A	.308	.329	.405	.421	.505	.058	1.61	2.01	L	283
.30 Kurz	C	.308	.334	.443	.470	.473	.045	1.29	1.65	L	284
.308x1.5-Inch Barnes	C	.308	.338	.450	.466	.470	.048	1.50	2.05	L	284
.30-06 Ackley Improved	C	.308	.340	.454	.470	.473	.045	2.49	3.35	L	286
.30-338 Winchester Magnum	E	.308	.340	.491	.513	.532	.048	2.50	UNK	L	286
.300 ICL Grizzly	E	0.308	0.340	0.460	0.532	0.532	0.050	2.610	3.540	LRM	287
.300 Raptor	C	0.308	0.338	0.566	0.590	0.580	0.058	3.050	4.285	Fed 215	288

Dimensional Data

Cartridge	Case	Bullet Dia.	Neck Dia.	Shoulder Dia.	Base Dia.	Rim Dia.	Rim Thick.	Case Length	Ctge. Length	Primer	Page
.300 Allen Xpress	C	.308	.340	.560	.590	.590	.060	2.70	3.70	Fed 215 L	288
.327 Martin Meteor	A	.312	.336	.379	.379	.440	.060	1.50	1.77	S	289
8mm-06	C	.323	.351	.441	.470	.473	.045	2.47	3.25	L	289
.333 OKH	C	.333	.365	.443	.470	.473	.045	2.49	3.37	L	290
.334 OKH	E	.333	.367	.480	.513	.530	.048	2.86	3.65	L	290
.338-223 Straight	D	.338	.362	UNK	.376	.378	.041	1.41	2.25	S	291
.338 Allen Xpress	C	.338	.366	.561	.590	.590	.060	2.70	3.6-3.96	Fed 215 L	291
.338/50 Talbot	C	.338	.380	.748	.774	.782	.080	3.76	4.25	.50 BMG	292
9x25 Dillon	C	.355	.382	.423	.423	.424	.050	0.99	1.26	SP	292
9mm Action Express	I	.355	.390	.433	.435	.394	.045	.866	1.152	S	293
.357 Auto Magnum	C	.357	.382	.461	.470	.473	.048	1.298	1.60	LP	294
.357 Herrett	A	.358	.375	.405	.420	.505	.058	1.75	2.10	L	294
.35-30/30	A	.358	.378	.401	.422	.506	.058	2.04	2.55	L	295
.358 BFG	I	.358	.382	.539	.555	.535	.054	1.625	2.370	L	296
.358 Gremlin	C	.358	.384	.427	.438	.440	.059	1.495	2.250	S	297
.35 Indiana	C	.358	.384	.437	.458	.460	.046	1.80	2.780	L	297
.35 SuperMann	C	.358	.384	.437	.458	.460	.046	1.91	2.780	L	298
.358 Hoosier	C	.358	.388	.454	.470	.473	.048	1.80	2.70	L	299
.35 Sambar	I	.358	UNK	.538	.555	.535	.054	2.10	2.86	UNK	300
.358 UMT (Ultra Mag Towsley)	E	.358	.390	.525	.550	.534	.054	2.85	3.5	UNK	300
.358/300 WSM	I	.358	.390	.538	.555	.535	.054	2.10	2.560	L	301
.366 DGW	C	.366	UNK	UNK	.589	.586	.058	UNK	UNK	UNK	302
9.3 Sisk	C	.366	.388	.486	.512	.532	.047	2.85	3.57	L	302
9.3 BS	E	.366	.390	.495	.5126	.532	.046	2.165	2.80	L	303
.375 Whelen & Ackley Imp. Whelen	C	.375	.403	.442/.455	.470	.473	.045	2.50	3.42	L	303
.375 Allen Xpress	C	.375	.403	.560	.590	.590	.060	2.70	3.6-3.95	Fed 215 L	304
.400 Whelen	C	.405	.436	.462	.470	.473	.048	2.49	3.10	L	304
.41 Special	B	.410	.432	UNK	.433	.488	.056	1.16	1.60	LP	305
.416 Barnes	A	.416	.432	.484	.505	.608	.065	2.112	2.95	L	306
.416 UMT	C	.416	.440	.525	.550	.534	.050	2.850	3.540	L	306
.416 Aagaard	C	.416	.441	.492	.506	.496	.049	2.35	UNK	L	307
.416 SM2	B	.416	.447	.538	.555	.535	.054	2.072	3.75	L	307
.445 Super Mag	B	.432	.456	UNK	.457	.514	.055	1.60	1.985	LP	308
.45 Wildey Magnum	C	.451	UNK	UNK	.500	.473	.048	1.295	1.580	L	308
.450 KNR	A	.458	UNK	UNK	UNK	UNK	UNK	UNK	UNK	UNK	308
.45 Silhouette	B	.458	.477	UNK	.501	.600	.065	1.51	1.97	L	309
.458 Hubel Express	F	0.458	0.481		0.527	0.532	0.050	3.400	3.950	L	309
.458x1.5-inch Barnes	F	.458	.481	UNK	.513	.532	.048	V	UNK	L	310
.458x2-inch American	F	.458	.478	UNK	.508	.532	.048	2.00	2.60	L	310
.460 Alliance	I	.458	.485	.530	.550	.534	.045	1.575	2.015	L	311
.450 Bonecrusher	A	.458	.488	.530	.535	.610	.060	1.40	1.77	L	312
.450 Howell	C	.458	.480	.515	.545	.534	.045	2.50	3.25	L	312
.450 Alaskan	A	.458	.480	.515	.547	.605	.062	2.25	2.79	L	313
.460 G&A Special	C	.458	.480	.530	.545	.545	.049	2.86	UNK	L	313
.458 B&M EX	I	0.458	0.485	0.531	0.550	0.538	0.048	2.510	3.586	Fed 215	314
.450 Watts Magnum	F	.458	.481	UNK	.513	.530	.048	2.85	3.65	L	314
.475 Ackley/OKH Magnum	F	.474	.496	UNK	.508	.528	.048	2.739	3.518	L	315
.475 Wildey Magnum	I	.475	.497	UNK	.500	.473	.048	1.295	1.58	L	315
.475 A&M Magnum	E	.475	.502	.560	.589	.603/.580	.060	2.90	3.75	L	316
.475 B&M	I	0.474	0.506	0.533	0.553	0.526	0.056	2.244	3.040	Fed 215	316
.475 Lehigh	J	.475	.504	UNK	.504	.480	.044	.950	1.17	LP	317
.499 Hubel Express No. 2	F	0.500	0.523		0.565	0.630	0.050	3.550	3.920	L	317
.500 Cyrus	L	.500	.528	.580	.582	.531	.058	2.333	2.90	L	318
.510 Nitro Express	B	.510	.535	UNK	.565	.665	UNK	3.245	4.185	L	318
.50 TAC	I	.510	.538	.580	.582	.531	.058	2.333	3.75	L	319

Dimensional Data

Cartridge	Case	Bullet Dia.	Neck Dia.	Shoulder Dia.	Base Dia.	Rim Dia.	Rim Thick.	Case Length	Ctge. Length	Primer	Page
.500 Belted Magnum	L	.510	.540	N/A	.584	.603/.580	.062	2.50	3.25	L	320
.50 McMillan FatMac	C	.510	.550	1.111	1.152	1.158	.090	2.645	V	.50 BMG	320
.50 McMurdo	C	.510	.554	.725	.800	.802	.078	3.700	5.722	.50 BMG	321
.505/530 Woodleigh	C	.530	UNK	UNK	UNK	UNK	UNK	UNK	UNK	UNK	321
.585 Nyati	I	.585	.605	.650	.660	.532/.586	UNK	2.79	3.525	L	322
.585 Hubel Express	F	0.585	0.607		0.634	0.637	0.050	3.250	3.900	L	323
.700 Hubel Express	F	0.700	0.735		0.775	0.775	0.050	3.850	4.300	50 BMG	323
.729 Jongmans	C	.727	UNK	UNK	.804	.804	.080	UNK	UNK	UNK	324
12 Gauge From Hell (12 GFH)	B	0.729	0.770		0.803	0.880	0.072	3.850	4.300	Rem 209	324

Case Type: A = Rimmed, bottleneck. B = Rimmed, straight. C = Rimless, bottleneck. D = Rimless, straight. E = Belted, bottleneck. F = Belted, straight. G = Semi-rimmed, bottleneck. H = Semi-rimmed, straight. I = Rebated, bottleneck. J = Rebated, straight. K = Rebated, belted bottleneck. L = Rebated, belted straight.

Primer Type: S = Small rifle (.175"). SP = Small pistol (.175"). L = Large rifle (.210"). LP = Large pistol (.210"). 50 BMG = CCI-35/VihtaVuori-110/RWS-8212. B-1 = Berdan #1. B-2 = Berdan #2.

Other codes: V = OAL depends upon bullet used. V = Rifling twist varies, depending upon bullet and application. Belt/Rim Diameter. Unless otherwise noted, all dimensions in inches.

Proprietary Cartridges
(Rifle & Handgun)

These proprietary cartridges and guns so chambered are special. These developments represent the culmination of efforts of serious gunsmiths to provide guns and ammunition that are a cut above the ordinary. All represent a level of hand fitting and precision that is simply not feasible in run-of-the-mill offerings. For those shooters willing and able to pay a premium price, these rifles offer the option of a factory gun that is, in many instances, equal to the best of the fully custom numbers in both fit and function. The cartridges used in these guns represent an effort toward ballistic perfection. Some are more successful than others.

The concept of the proprietary cartridge was well developed in Great Britain beginning in the late 1800s. That tradition continued until quite recently, when unfortunate and thoroughly nonsensical political developments probably destroyed the practice forever. Under our current definition, many of the reasonably well-known cartridges associated with such firms as Holland & Holland were originally strictly proprietary. Those cartridges were designed to fulfill some specific need in the best possible way. For a fuller understanding of this relationship, one should review the introductory text and cartridge write-ups in Chapter 7, British Sporting Rifle Cartridges.

A good example is the belted .375 H&H Magnum. That case was designed to provide solid headspace control while facilitating reliable functioning under extreme and adverse conditions in a bolt-action rifle. Considerations included functionality under extremely hot conditions, and when either the ammunition or the rifle chamber might not be perfectly clean. The belt provided for solid headspacing, despite a comparatively loose fit of the case body in the chamber of the rifle. Caliber, capacity, bullet design, and loading pressure (case capacity) were also chosen with consideration of the intended applications—in this instance, chiefly short- to medium-range shots on smaller species of dangerous African game.

Similarly, Sharps and many other stateside manufacturers followed the same route during the era of Buffalo exploitation and development of long-range target shooting competitive events. Most of those cartridge developments are long obsolete, but others moved into the mainstream and are still with us. An example of the former is the .44-50 Peabody, while the .38-55 Ballard (now known as the .38-55 Winchester), exemplifies the latter group.

In many instances, cartridges we now think of as standard items were once essentially proprietary. A good example is the .348 Winchester. Here was a cartridge designed by Winchester, which was commercially chambered only by Winchester (in its Model 71 rifle). For many years, Winchester was the only source of .348 ammunition. Similarly, the .444 Marlin was designed for use in only one rifle (Marlin's .444) and, until the advent of Buffalo Bore ammunition's new offerings, was never commercially loaded by anyone other than Remington. While these are SAAMI standard chamberings, both are, in some manner, proprietary. Other examples abound. In some sense, practically every factory chambering that did not originate as a military cartridge was once proprietary. Nevertheless, we will maintain an arbitrary and perhaps unfair distinction between offerings from mainstream manufacturers and those from smaller producers.

Regarding the wildcat connection, consider the .35 Whelen. While this fine cartridge might seem to fit the proprietary bill, really it does not. For many decades it was a widely chambered wildcat cartridge, but was not commercially loaded. Now it is commercially loaded and chambered as a mainstream offering. Even before that, it was too widely known and chambered for inclusion in this chapter.

While many cartridges discussed in this chapter had antecedents in the wildcat arena (or among European developments), they have not yet achieved standard commercial status. The distinction seems significant. It would be convenient if all proprietary cartridges were unique developments and if no wildcat cartridges fit into this category. However, that is not the situation. Gray areas of overlap are noteworthy and somewhat abundant.

Most proprietary offerings detailed in this chapter followed a developmental path similar to the aforementioned historical British proprietary cartridges. Some custom gun manufacturer noted a void in the offerings from major arms manufacturers. That manufacturer then designed a cartridge to fill that void in the best way possible —according to his likes and based upon what basic case types were available for improvement. Here, we might consider the history of the major commercial cartridge offerings with which, in many instances, these proprietary chamberings compete.

Big-bore (.50-caliber and up) rifles convey almost romantic images and historic links to the great dangerous game hunters of years past. However, the years between then and now have seen the introduction of legal restrictions on the ownership of these firearms. When proprietary cartridges contain a projectile larger than a half-inch in diameter, they may be considered as destructive devices, according to the United States' Code of Federal Regulations, Title 27, Volume 1. The statutory authority granted to the BATFE allows the director to determine that the device, among other things, is a rifle that the owner intends to use solely for sporting purposes. Certain combinations of firearms actions, barrel lengths, and bore diameter may not meet the criteria of "being a rifle that the owner intends to use solely for sporting purposes" and would otherwise constitute a destructive device. Possession of an unauthorized destructive device may subject the possessor to criminal or civil penalties. For shooters interested in purchasing or possessing one of the ,50-caliber or larger cartridges documented in this chapter, it is important to confirm that the manufacturer of the rifle and cartridge combination has an exemption from the BATFE for its manufacture.

15th Edition Update

Proprietary Cartridges are the efforts of restless minds that believe a little more accuracy, a little more power, and a little more distance is always possible, if the developer is willing to invest the time and money necessary to explore the options available out there. Proprietary rounds are different from Wildcats because someone wants to sell them to folks who have specialized wants and desires, so that usually means firearms support as well as cartridge development.

This time around, we've collected a range of 15 new Proprietary listings for folks to peruse. The bulk of the chapter is provided by various B&M listings: 9.3 B&M, .375 B&M, .416 B&M, .458 B&M, .458 B&M Super Short, .475 B&M Super Short, 50 B&M, 500 MDM, 500 B&M, 50 B&M Alaskan, and 50 B&M Super Short. They originate from the minds of hunters William V. Bruton and Michael McCourry, who built their line of cartridges so they could offer SSK Industries-built short, handy safari rifles that stop big and dangerous game at extremely close ranges. Many of the standard B&M Cartridges are based on a 2.240-inch-long (trimmed) Remington Ultra Magnum case, but some have other provenance that is interesting to examine.

The .45 Raptor is yet another attempt to put more power in an AR platform, this time by necking up a .308 Win. case; whereas the .502 Thunder Sabre approaches the problem from a different direction, by necking down a .50 AE case to fit into an AR-profile hog gun.

The .400 A-Square DPM is a big concept: making a round flexible enough to load with lighter bullets for plains game then heavier bullets for bigger or dangerous game. What catches the reader's eye, of course, is the "A-Square" name, which despite some troubles, still exists under another owner's care. —W.T.W.

2.34mm SwissMiniGun (Rimfire)

Historical Notes: This diminutive cartridge fits a diminutive handgun—the SwissMiniGun. Together, they are the smallest revolver and rimfire ammunition in the world. According to Guinness World Records, the MiniGun itself is 5.5cm long (2.2 inches), 3.5cm tall (1.4 inches), 1cm wide (0.4-inch) and weighs 19.8 grams (0.7 ounces). It fires the 2.34mm-caliber rimfire ammunition, which likewise is the smallest rimfire ammunition in the world.

This miniature handgun is a double-action revolver and has the same features as a real-size gun. SwissMiniGun is a fully authorized and licensed gunsmith company in Switzerland. The .092-caliber round develops 399.6 fps velocity and 0.7154 ft-lbs. of energy, or about a tenth of what some BB guns create.

General Comments: The miniature revolver is legally classified as a "non-firearm" in Canada, due to the low velocity of the 2.34mm cartridge it discharges. However, the MiniGun remains a firearm for certain sections of the Criminal Code and Firearms Act, but is exempt from licensing and registration. The revolver is not classified as a firearm in France, because its ammunition power is less than 2 joules. In Switzerland, the miniature revolver is classified as a real firearm, so customers must ask their police department for a permit. The U.S. does not allow import of the miniature revolver, because it does not meet the minimum size prerequisites on ATF Form 4590.

2.43 SwissMiniGun (Rimfire) Loading Data and Factory Ballistics

Bullet (grains/type)	Powder	Grains	Velocity	Energy	Source
1.9753 RN	N/A	.772	399.6	0.7154	Factory Load

.17 Incinerator (inert)

Historical Notes: The .17 Incinerator is a collector cartridge made by machinist Zachary Weighman, who stuffs a .17-caliber bullet into a heavily worked and necked-down .50 BMG case. Weighman says the cartridge is inert; it contains no powder and the primer is a spent .50 BMG unit.

Weighman said, "I started making these up for friends of mine, after seeing a drawing of 'Dingbat cartridges'—drawings of mythical cartridges. I thought they were really cool, so I started trying to figure out how to make them. As you can see, I did get it figured out." Weighman also makes other novelty cartridges, including the .30 Hottie (.30/50 BMG), the 7.18mm Pookster (a 7mm/50 BMG, nicknamed for his daughter and her July birthday), and the .24 Wolverine (.24/50 BMG).

General Comments: Weighman says the process takes many sizing and annealing steps and some lathe work to machine. Weighman, a machinist, has a small mill and lathe at home. He made a die that holds inserts for necking down the .50 BMG cases. Each insert has a progressively smaller-diameter hole in it. It takes 13 sizing steps to neck the cases down to the proper size. He also anneals the cases at least three times at different points in the process. Then he uses a small lathe to clean up neck and shoulder imperfections, and then reams the inside diameter of the necks and trims them to length. He "sanitizes" the headstamp area by turning them in a lathe, and then he etches the headstamp onto them. Last, he seats the bullets into the cases and polishes.

.222 Remington Rimmed

Historical Notes: During the 1950s and 1960s, thousands of rifles built on the small Martini action and chambered for a rimmed cartridge called the .310 Cadet (also known as the .310 Greener) were sold on the military surplus market. Manufactured from 1910 to 1940 by Birmingham Small Arms (BSA), Greener, Webley & Scott, and other English firms, they were used as training rifles by military cadets in Great Britain and Australia. Once those rifles became available on the surplus market, many custom rifles were built on the action and, since its extractor was designed for a rimmed cartridge, some of the more common cartridges chosen were the .22 Hornet, .218 Bee, .22 Jet, .256 Winchester, and Improved versions of same. The action became popular enough in Australia to prompt the Super Cartridge Company of that country to manufacture a rimmed version of the .222 Remington specifically for it. Since the action was also quite popular among custom rifle builders in America, the Williams Gun Sight Company (www.williamsgunsight.com) imported the cases. Think of the .222 Remington case with the rim diameter of the .38 Special pistol cartridge, and you have the .222 Remington Rimmed.

General Comments: Not much can be said about the .222 Rimmed that has not already been said many times about the .222 Remington, except that, for a time, it was a way to give a wonderful little military surplus rifle a second useful life. In the United States, the cartridge became unnecessary, after Michigan gunsmith Robert Snapp started making rimless extractors that allowed the standard .222 Remington cartridge compatible with the Martini Cadet action. Reloading data for the two cartridges are interchangeable.

.222 Remington Rimmed Loading Data and Factory Ballistics

Bullet (grains/type)	Powder	Grains	Velocity	Energy	Source
40 Sierra BlitzKing	RL-7	22.0	3,358	1,000	Layne Simpson
50 Nosler Ballistic Tip	RL-7	21.0	3,316	1,219	Layne Simpson
52 Sierra MatchKing	RL-7	21.0	3,334	1,282	Layne Simpson
55 Sierra BlitzKing	RL-7	20.5	3,118	1,186	Layne Simpson

.224-32 FA
(.224-32 Freedom Arms)

Historical Notes: The .224-32 FA is a proprietary cartridge of Freedom Arms, Inc. (FreedomArms.com) that utilizes the .327 Federal case. The goal in designing this cartridge was to get a high-performance .22 centerfire cartridge that would work in a revolver. As of this writing, the .224-32 FA is available only for hand forming and loading. Loading dies designed specifically for the .224-32 FA are available from Freedom Arms.

General Comments: The .224-32 FA case is very simple to make. Lube the .327 Federal case and run it into the properly adjusted sizing/forming die, then trim the case to 1.115/1.120 overall length. The sizing/forming die should be adjusted to set the headspace at .005 to .010. This cartridge headspaces off the shoulder, not the rim. This is easily checked by inserting a formed and trimmed case into a chamber, rotate it around so the case head shows at the top of the loading gate cutout in the receiver, and then use a .005 shim as a go gage and a .010 shim as a no-go gage between the case head and firewall.

If forming primed cases, care must be taken to not get lube inside the case. An/nealing is not required or even suggested, as annealing will cause premature case sticking when fired. After fire-forming the case, it can still take two to four additional firings (depending on the load used) before the case is fully formed.

Therefore, be careful using the top loads before the cases are fully formed, as case capacity will be slightly less, and this will cause higher pressure. It is important to keep the cases in batches according to how many times the cases have been fired.

You may lose an occasional case when forming, but the majority of cases will last through at least 10 firings. Usually, when using the upper-end loads, the primer pockets will stretch enough by the time 10 to 15 shots have been fired that the cases should be discarded. Before loading the cases, check for neck cracks. Also, if you don't feel sufficient resistance when seating a new primer, discard the case. If you experience case separation close to the head, it is usually due to too much headspace. —*W.T.W.*

.224-32 FA (Freedom Arms) Loading Data and Factory Ballistics

Bullet (grains/type)	Powder	Grains	Velocity	Energy	Source
40 Sierra BlitzKing or V-Max	IMR 4227	9.5	1,830	297	Freedom Arms Starting Load
40 Sierra BlitzKing or V-Max	IMR 4227	10	1,940	334	Freedom Arms Max Load
40 Sierra BlitzKing or V-Max	AA 1680	12	1,900	321	Freedom Arms Starting Load
40 Sierra BlitzKing or V-Max	AA 1680	12.5	2,020	362	Freedom Arms Max Load
40 Sierra BlitzKing or V-Max	IMR 4227	10	1,900	321	Freedom Arms Starting Load
40 Sierra BlitzKing or V-Max	IMR 4227	12	2,270	458	Freedom Arms Max Load
40 Sierra BlitzKing or V-Max	AA 1680	12.5	1,965	343	Freedom Arms Starting Load
40 Sierra BlitzKing or V-Max	AA 1680	14.5	2,295	468	Freedom Arms Max Load

.22 TCM
(.22 Tuason Craig Micromagnum)

Historical Notes:	Armscor President Martin Tuason and master gunsmith Fred Craig developed the .22 TCM (Tuason Craig Micromagnum) using the .223 Remington case shortened so that the shoulder is at approximately the same length as the case mouth of a 9x19mm cartridge. The result: Fired from a 1911, the TCM delivers 2,100 fps with a 40-grain bullet. The bottlenecked cartridge is similar in case capacity, general shape, and performance to the 5.7x28 FN.
General Comments:	Currently, only Rock Island Armory catalogs firearms chambered in .22 TCM. These include a 1911-style semi-auto pistol and a bolt-action rifle that can use the same magazines as the pistol. The base pistol is a wide-body, high-capacity 1911 based on a Para-Ordnance frame. Only Armscor, the parent company of Rock Island Armory, manufactures ammunition. The maximum overall loaded length is the same as a .45 ACP. The cartridge is designed to feed from a Para-Ordnance-style double-column .38 Super or 9x19mm magazine. The flush magazines hold 17+1 rounds of .22 TCM. Armscor Precision's ammunition line is made in Marikina City, Philippines.

.22 TCM Factory Ballistics (24-inch barrel)

Bullet (grains)	Powder	Grains	Velocity	Energy	Source/Comments
40 JHP	FL	FL	1,875	312	Armscor USA

.226 JDJ

Historical Notes:	Designed by J.D. Jones, in 1979, this cartridge is the .225 Winchester, Improved. It provides a reduction in chamber pressure, which improves Contender functioning; factory .225 Winchester ammunition sometimes gave extraction difficulties in Contender barrels. This design solved that problem. Factory .225 Winchester ammunition can be used.

General Comments: As is typical of the JDJ line, this chambering offers ½ MOA accuracy potential with proper handloads. New barrels feature a 1:9 twist for use with heavier bullets, which are gaining popularity in the .22-caliber bore. Typical loads with the 40-grain bullet easily exceed 3600 fps from a 16-inch barrel. The Barnes 45-grain XBT is an effective choice for peccary-size game species. However, use of this bullet requires special handloading techniques (deeper bullet seating and a reduction in powder charge). Further, those bullets work best when a minimum-friction coating (such as moly-plating) is used. For this reason, SSK does not support the use of X-style bullets in its guns. While no bullet substitution is benign, never substitute any X-style bullet in any load—begin with data specifically created for that bullet. For information on components, loading data, barrels, and guns designed for this cartridge, contact SSK Industries at (720) 264-0176 or www.sskindustries.com.

.226 JDJ Loading Data (Note: These loads for use only in SSK barrels.)

Bullet (grains/type)	Powder	Grains	Velocity	Energy	Source/Comments
50 Hornady	IMR 3031	32.0	2,864	905	SSK/maximum load, SSK barrel only
55	IMR 4064	33.0	2,808	960	SSK/maximum load, SSK barrel only
55 Hornady SX	BL-C (2)	32.0	2,637	849	SSK/maximum load, SSK barrel only
60 Hornady SP	H414	35.0	2,732	995	SSK/maximum load, SSK barrel only
63 Sierra	H4831	38.5	2,831	1,115	SSK/maximum load, SSK barrel only

6 Whisper

Historical Notes: Created by J.D. Jones, the 6 Whisper uses a modified .221 Fireball case necked up to 6mm to propel heavy bullets at subsonic velocities and lighter bullets at higher velocities. In a 10-inch-barreled Contender pistol, the 6 Whisper can propel 115-grain bullets to 1,054 fps, and lighter 55-grain bullets to over 3,000 fps.

General Comments: This cartridge is well-suited for Thompson/Center Contenders, bolt-action rifles, and AR15-type rifles. At subsonic velocities, it functions quietly and accurately in suppressed firearms. For information on components, loading data, barrels, and guns designed for this cartridge, contact SSK Industries: (720) 264-0176; www.sskindustries.com.

6mm JDJ

Historical Notes: This cartridge was designed and developed by noted gun writer and experimenter J.D. Jones, hence the "JDJ" designation. Jones began development of his series of cartridges around 1978, and they are generally fired in barrels furnished by his company, SSK Industries. The purpose of this cartridge is to give added range and power to the Thompson/Center Contender pistol for the primary purpose of hunting varmints and small game. Some of his cartridges have proven to be excellent metallic silhouette numbers, as well. The JDJ series of cases is easy to make. All JDJ cartridges are proprietary, and SSK neither sells reamers nor permits the reamer maker to duplicate any of SSK's reamers.

General Comments: Based on the .225 Winchester case, itself a modified .30-30 case, this improved chambering provides ample capacity to deliver maximum 6mm velocity from handgun-length barrels (14 to 16 inches). Best applications are in handgun varminting and hunting of the smallest big-game species. With the proper 70- to 75-grain bullet, this chambering can deliver 300-yard varmint accuracy and trajectory. Heavier, well-constructed bullets can deliver adequate performance for smaller big-game out to perhaps 100 yards. The Barnes 75-grain and 85-grain X bullets offer serious hunting performance. However, use of these bullets requires special handloading techniques (deeper bullet seating and a reduction in powder charge). Further, those bullets work best when a minimum-friction coating (such as moly-plating) is used. For this reason, SSK does not support the use of X-style bullets in its guns. While no bullet substitution is benign, never substitute any X-style bullet in any load—begin with data specifically created for that bullet. For information on components, loading data, barrels, and guns designed for this cartridge, contact SSK Industries: (720) 264-0176; www.sskindustries.com.

6 JDJ No. 2 Loading Data (Note: These loads for use only in SSK barrels.)

Bullet (grains/type)	Powder	Grains	Velocity	Energy	Source/Comments
70 HP	RI-7	29.0	2,845	1,260	SSK/maximum load/SSK barrel only
*70 HP	AA 2700	35.0	2,540	1,000	SSK/maximum load/SSK barrel only
80 HP	RI-19	37.0	2,370	1,000	SSK/maximum load/SSK barrel only

6.17 Spitfire

Historical Notes: Lazzeroni Arms designed this cartridge in 1997. While somewhat related to an older case, for all practical purposes, this is a new case design. This cartridge was created in response to requests for a high-performance cartridge that would work in a 2.8-inch action and yet deliver the ballistics of a full-length belted magnum. Case diameter is similar to conventional belted case rim diameter, so adaptation to a standard action is quite simple.

General Comments: Bullet diameter is .243-inch (Lazzeroni bases its designations on bullet diameter, instead of bore diameter, which is the common practice). Ballistics are quite impressive for such a short cartridge. The Spitfire comes very close to top .240 Weatherby ballistics. Case design is typical of the Lazzeroni line: moderate body taper, 30-degree shoulder, sufficiently long neck, and thick rim of approximate case-body diameter. In other words, this is a well-designed case. For more information on Lazzeroni custom guns, ammunition, and reloading data, contact (888) 492--7247 or www.lazzeroni.com.

6.17 Spitfire Factory Ballistics (24-inch barrel)

Bullet (grains)	Powder	Grains	Velocity	Energy	Source/Comments
70	N/A	N/A	3,750	2,186	Lazzeroni factory load
85	N/A	N/A	3,550	2,379	Lazzeroni factory load
100	N/A	N/A	3,350	2,493	Lazzeroni factory load

6.17 Flash

Historical Notes: Lazzeroni Arms designed this cartridge in 1996. While somewhat related to an older case, for all practical purposes, this is a new case design. John Lazzeroni believes that those hunters who will take the time to become competent marksmen can legitimately take game at ranges out to about 500 yards, given a gun with the requisite accuracy and a bullet that will perform properly. This cartridge was created to provide sufficient velocity that would enable medium-weight hunting bullets with dependable expansion at maximum ranges. Adaptation to standard actions is quite simple. Lazzeroni has recently discontinued this as a standard chambering, but still offers it on a special-order basis.

General Comments: Bullet diameter is .243-inch (Lazzeroni bases its designations on bullet diameter instead of bore diameter, which is the common practice). Flash ballistics surpass any other current 6mm cartridge. Case design is typical of the Lazzeroni line: moderate body taper, 30-degree shoulder, sufficiently long neck, and thick rim of approximate case-body diameter. In other words, this is a well-designed case. Designed specifically for hunting, with limited barrel life (no more than 500 rounds), this cartridge is not recommended for any other use. While 27-inch barrels are standard, all the smaller-caliber, full-length Lazzeroni numbers would benefit significantly from even longer barrels. Most of Lazzeroni's full-length cartridge loadings use specially lubricated (proprietary process) premium bullets from Nosler, Barnes, or Swift. This is a superior performer for those who only hunt the smaller species of big game and who will not abuse the barrel via incautious shooting. The 85-grain Nosler Partition works extremely well. For more information on Lazzeroni custom guns, ammunition, and reloading data, contact (888) 492--7247 or www.lazzeroni.com.

6.17 Flash Factory Ballistics (27-inch barrel)

Bullet (grains/type)	Powder	Grains	Velocity	Energy	Source/Comments
70	N/A	N/A	4,150	2,678	Lazzeroni factory load
85	N/A	N/A	3,900	2,871	Lazzeroni factory load
100	N/A	N/A	3,700	3,041	Lazzeroni factory load

.255 Banshee

Historical Notes: Gary Reeder's Banshee series of cartridges is based on the .22 K Hornet case. Gary wanted a pistol cartridge that was capable of pushing a 65- to 75-grain bullet to 2000 fps from a 12-inch barrel. The Banshee will even work in a revolver.

General Comments: According to Gary Reeder, the .255 Banshee will work well with bullets as heavy as 87 grains and performs admirably on smaller-bodied deer. He takes the .22 K Hornet cases, which are necked up and then fire formed with loads reduced by 10 percent. This is a fun cartridge to shoot from a revolver and should be great fun for snooping around grown-up pastures holding groundhogs, badgers, and such. Information on custom guns, ammunition, and reloading data can be obtained by contacting Gary Reeder Custom Guns, (928) 527-4100 or www.reedercustomguns.com.

.255 Banshee Loading Data and Ballistics

Bullet (grains/type)	Powder	Grains	Velocity	Energy	Source/Comments
60 Hornady FP	H 110	12.0	2,178	631	Gary Reeder
75 Hornady HP	AA # 9	10.0	1,960	639	Gary Reeder
85 Nosler Ballistic Tip	H 110	10.0	1,810	618	Gary Reeder

.257 Raptor

Historical Notes: Becoming less enthralled with powerful, hard-kicking cartridges, Gary Reeder decided to put together a couple very practical wildcat cartridges based on the .204 Ruger case. The 257 Raptor was one of three Raptor cartridges he developed. Reeder's first .257 Raptor was put together on a Thompson/Center Encore with the help of Dave Manson, who supplied the reamers.

General Comments: Ballistically, the .257 Raptor is in the same class as the old .25-35 Winchester. However, the .257 Raptor comes in a much smaller package and, since it's a rimless cartridge, can work in a wider range of rifles including AR-15s. Reeder has used the .257 Raptor to take a bunch of whitetail deer, as well as several wild hogs and assorted exotic game animals. For more information on custom guns, ammunition, and reloading data, contact Reeder Custom Guns, (928) 527-4100 or www.reedercustomguns.com.

.257 Raptor Loading Data and Ballistics

Bullet (grains/type)	Powder	Grains	Velocity	Energy	Source/Comments
75 HP	H 335	29.0	2,608	1,132	Gary Reeder
85 Nosler Ballistic Tip	IMR 3031	27.0	2,539	1,216	Gary Reeder

.257 JDJ

Historical Notes: This is another cartridge designed and developed by J.D. Jones. Jones began development of his cartridges around 1978, and they are generally fired in barrels furnished by his company, SSK Industries. The purpose of these cartridges is to give added range and power to the Thompson/Center Contender pistol. Some of Jones' cartridges have also proven to be excellent metallic silhouette numbers. JDJ cartridges are relatively easy to make. All JDJ cartridges are proprietary, and SSK neither sells reamers nor has permitted the reamer maker to duplicate any of the reamers for the series.

General Comments: Based on the .225 Winchester case, itself a modified .30-30 case, this Improved chambering provides ample capacity to deliver near-maximum quarter-bore velocity from handgun-length barrels (14 to 16 inches). Best applications are in handgun varminting and hunting of smaller big-game species. A preferred bullet for the latter application is Nosler's 85-grain Ballistic Tip. This cartridge can launch this bullet to about 2,900 fps with top loads from a 14-inch barrel. This combination is said to provide good terminal performance to 300 yards. One can use heavier bullets to deliver more energy. However, reduced velocity limits expansion; trajectory errors increase. Therefore, hunters should limit use of such bullets to shorter ranges. For information on components, loading data, barrels, and guns designed for this cartridge, contact SSK Industries, (720) 264-0176 or www.sskindustries.com.

.257 JDJ Loading Data (Note: These loads for use only in SSK barrels.)

Bullet (grains/type)	Powder	Grains	Velocity	Energy	Source/Comments
75 HP	H322	30.0	2,310	890	SSK/maximum load/SSK barrels only
75 HP	W748	37.0	2,645	1,165	SSK/maximum load/SSK barrels only
100 SP	W748	34.0	1,405	1,285	SSK/maximum load/SSK barrels only
117 SP	IMR 4350	35.0	2,195	1,250	SSK/maximum load/SSK barrels only

.25/06 JDJ

Historical Notes: Virtually identical to the 6.5/270 JDJ, the .25/06 JDJ uses a modified .270 Winchester case, necked down to handle .25-caliber bullets. Other changes include shortening the neck, reducing case taper to maximize powder capacity, and forming a 60-degree shoulder to achieve ballistics normally associated with belted magnum cartridges in similar length (15-inch) Encore barrels.

General Comments: The .25/06 JDJ is well-suited for Thompson/Center Encore firearms, Ruger No. 1 rifles, or appropriate bolt-action rifles. This cartridge provides long case life, consumes less powder than belted magnum cartridges, and uses relatively inexpensive cases. For information on components, loading data, barrels, and guns designed for this cartridge, contact SSK Industries, (720) 264-0176 or www.sskindustries.com.

6.53 Scramjet

Historical Notes: Lazzeroni Arms designed this cartridge in 1996. While somewhat related to an older case, for all practical purposes this is a new case design. John Lazzeroni believes that those hunters who will take the time to become competent marksmen can legitimately take game at ranges out to about 500 yards, given a gun with the requisite accuracy and a bullet that will perform properly. This cartridge was created to launch lightweight hunting bullets with sufficient velocity to provide dependable expansion at maximum ranges. Adaptation to standard actions is quite simple. While this case does not sell well, Lazzeroni will continue to handle it, owing to the founder's love for this bore size.

General Comments: Bullet diameter is .257-inch (Lazzeroni bases its designations on bullet diameter, instead of bore diameter, which is the common practice.). Scramjet ballistics exceed any other current .25-caliber cartridge. Case design is typical of the Lazzeroni line: moderate body taper, 30-degree shoulder, sufficiently long neck, and thick rim of approximate case-body diameter. In other words, this is a well-designed case. Designed specifically for hunting, and with limited barrel life, this cartridge is not recommended for any other use. While 27-inch barrels are standard, all the smaller-caliber, full-length Lazzeroni numbers would benefit significantly from even longer barrels. Most of Lazzeroni's full-length cartridge loadings use specially lubricated (proprietary process) premium bullets from Nosler, Barnes, or Swift. For hunting, John prefers the 100-grain Nosler Partition and the 90-grain Barnes XBT, while the 85-grain Nosler BT is especially accurate and makes a superb long-range varminting choice. A significant portion of the accuracy and ballistic potential of these cartridges results from the unusually effective reduced-friction coating used. For more information on Lazzeroni custom guns, ammunition, and reloading data, contact (888) 492--7247 or www.lazzeroni.com.

6.53 Scramjet Factory Ballistics (27-inch barrel)

Bullet (grains/type)	Powder	Grains	Velocity	Energy	Source/Comments
85	FL	N/A	4,000	3,021	Lazzeroni factory load
100	FL		3750	3123	Lazzeroni factory load
120	FL		3,550	3,219	Lazzeroni factory load

.257 Mini Dreadnaught

Historical Notes: This cartridge was designed by J.D. Jones, at SSK Industries. Application is to Thompson/Center Encore or Contender single-shot pistols fitted with a custom SSK barrel. Typical barrel length is 15 inches. Cases are fire formed from empty .220 Swift cases. Neck length is minimal, which is acceptable for a cartridge used in a single-shot gun. Shoulder angle is 60 degrees, which seems to work just fine. Body taper is minimal. Therefore, this is a maximized .25-caliber version of the .220 Swift case. Capacity is similar to the .257 Roberts (about 57 grains) and working pressure is higher (about 60,000 psi), so ballistics are quite similar, despite the significant deficit in barrel length.

General Comments: Since the Swift case has a rim, it is possible to fire-form necked-up Swift cases to fit this chamber. For this purpose, use loads that are near the maximum level. Jones recommends 100- to 120-grain bullets for big-game hunting applications on smaller species. Nosler's Ballistic Tip and Partition bullets have demonstrated superior performance. However, it would appear this cartridge is capable of driving 120-grain bullets fast enough to give dependable expansion. While one could use the lightest Barnes X bullets, which can offer impressive terminal performance, the handloader must use X-bullet-specific loading data and special handloading techniques (e.g., the bullet ogive must be seated a minimum of .050-inch from the rifling). Further, those bullets work best when a minimum-friction coating (such as moly-plating) is used. For this reason, SSK does not support the use of X-style bullets in its guns. While no bullet substitution is benign, never substitute any X-style bullet in any load—begin with data specifically created for that bullet. For information on components, loading data, barrels, and guns designed for this cartridge, contact SSK Industries, (720) 264-0176 or www.sskindustries.com.

.257 Mini Dreadnaught Loading Data (Note: These loads for use only in SSK barrels.)

Bullet (grains/type)	Powder	Grains	Velocity	Energy	Source/Comments
100 Nosler BT	AA 4350	48.7	3,008	2,005	SSK/maximum load/SSK barrels only

.257 Allen Magnum

Historical Notes: In 2005, gunsmith Kirby Allen marked the start of the Allen Magnum family of proprietary rounds based on the .338 Remington Ultra Magnum parent case, forming the .257 Allen Magnum, 6.5mm Allen Magnum and .270 Allen Magnum. The .257 Allen Magnum, with the same bullet weights, produces 500 fps more muzzle velocity than the .257 Weatherby and 200-plus fps more velocity than the .257 STW. Looked at another way, the .257 Allen Magnum will drive a 156-grain bullet to the same velocity as a .257 Weatherby with a 120-grain bullet.

Allen says this round is not intended for high-volume shooting. It is designed for light to medium big game such as pronghorns. This round easily fits into most commercial long-action magnum receivers.

General Comments: With the proper bullets, this round shoots flat, with a muzzle velocity north of 4,000 fps, but barrel life is limited. Also, forming cases is an involved process, and handloads must use ultra slow-burning ball powders. Preferred bullets are Nosler's 100- and 115-grain Ballistic Tips, 110-grain Accubonds, and 100- and 115-grain Barnes TSXs. Allen Precision supplies wildcat brass and loading dies. Custom handloading dies include Redding or Hornady Custom FL sizing dies and converted Forster Ultra BR seating dies. Allen Precision also supplies fully formed APS brass for the .257 Allen Magnum and correctly headstamped, fully formed brass. For more information, check the website APSRifles.com or e-mail Kirby Allen at allenmagnum@gmail.com.—*W.T.W.*

.257 Allen Magnum Loading Data (Note: * Powders include Ramshot Magnum, Hodgdon AA8700, Hodgdon US869, WC-860, and WC872, but grain loadings are information proprietary to Allen Precision Shooting.)

Bullet (grains/type)	Powder	Grains	Velocity	Energy	Source/Comments
110 Nosler BT	*	N/A	4,050	3,641	Allen Precision Shooting
110 Accubond	*	N/A	3,900	3,714	Allen Precision Shooting
115 Barnes TSX	*	N/A	3,800	3,686	Allen Precision Shooting
120 Barnes TSX	*	N/A	3,750	3,746	Allen Precision Shooting
130 Custom	*	N/A	3,650	3,752	Allen Precision Shooting
142 Custom	*	N/A	3,450	3,844	Allen Precision Shooting
156 Custom	*	N/A	3,350	3,886	Allen Precision Shooting

6.5mm JDJX30

Historical Notes: This J.D. Jones cartridge is the 7-30 Waters necked down to 6.5mm and Improved. Its purpose is to meet customer demand for improved performance with readily obtained cases. Since the 7-30 is based on the .30-30 Winchester, one can easily use those abundant cases to form this round. Other than rim diameter and a slight increase in case length, this is essentially identical to the 6.5mm JDJ.

General Comments: Excellent bullets are available and, with proper loads and in the hands of a good shot, this chambering is capable of 300-yard shots on the smaller species. Jones considers this one of the premier small-bore hunting choices. For information on components, loading data, barrels, and guns designed for this cartridge, contact SSK Industries, (720) 264-0176 or www.sskindustries.com.

6.5mm JDJ x30 Loading Data (Note: These loads for use only in SSK barrels.)

Bullet (grains/type)	Powder	Grains	Velocity	Energy	Source/Comments
85 Sierra	W760	42.0	2,710	1,385	SSK/maximum load/SSK barrel only (14")
120 Speer	W760	40.0	2,477	1,635	SSK/maximum load/SSK barrel only (14")
120 Nosler BT	IMR 4064	37.5	2,580	1,770	SSK/maximum load/SSK barrel only (14")
129 Hornady	IMR 4350	40.7	2,481	1,760	SSK/maximum load/SSK barrel only (14")
140 Sierra	IMR 4350	40.7	2,376	1,755	SSK/maximum load/SSK barrel only (14")

6.5mm Whisper

Historical Notes:	Designed by J.D. Jones, in the early 1990s, this cartridge was intended for use in sound-suppressed M-15s, bolt-action rifles, and T/C Contenders. As with most of Jones' line, this cartridge was designed at SSK Industries. This cartridge is based upon the .221 Remington case.
General Comments:	When combined with a very quick rifling twist, this chambering will deliver 155-grain very low drag (VLD) bullets from SSK Contender barrels with ½ MOA accuracy at subsonic velocities (1040 fps). Lighter bullets can achieve a more typical muzzle velocity, but such applications sacrifice the design purpose of this chambering. The 6.5mm Whisper performs well as a short-range deer cartridge. For information on components, loading data, barrels, and guns designed for this cartridge, contact SSK Industries, (720) 264-0176 or www.sskindustries.com.

6.5mm Whisper Loading Data (Note: These loads for use only in SSK barrels.)

Bullet (grains/type)	Powder	Grains	Velocity	Energy	Source/Comments
100 Hornady	H110	19.0	2,300	1,170	Maximum load/SSK barrel only (10")
120 Nosler BT	A-1680	19.0	2,150	1,230	Maximum load/SSK barrel only (10")
155	H110	8.3	970	320	SSK/M-16 (gas port open)
155	H110	8.3	1,051	375	SSK/M-16 (gas port blocked)
155	AA No. 9	8.4	1,050	375	SSK/M-16 (gas port open)
155	AA No. 9	8.4	1,074	395	SSK/M-16 (gas port blocked)

6.5x25 CBJ

Historical Notes:	The 6.5x25 CBJ was developed by CBJ Tech AB in Sweden, which was founded in 1997 by C. Bertil Johansson, who is also the inventor of the cartridge. The purpose of the cartridge is to increase the performance of pistols and shoulder weapons chambered for 9x19 Parabellum cartridge, in terms of range, penetration, and wounding effect.
General Comments:	The geometry of this case—up to the shoulder, as well as overall cartridge length—is identical to the 9x19 Luger (Parabellum) cartridge and it generates the same level of impulse (pressure). This means

that most weapons currently chambered for the 9mm Luger can be converted to the 6.5x25 CBJ by only changing the barrel. The cartridge has several different proprietary projectiles, all of which can be used interchangeably to meet different requirements. The main variant is the 6.5x25 CBJ Ball, which has a sub-caliber projectile consisting of a 4mm tungsten core encased in a discarding plastic sabot. When shot from an eight-inch barrel—when zeroed at 100 meters—it will have a maximum trajectory height of ¾-inch. It is also capable of defeating an 8mm hardened armor plate at 100 yards. CBJ Tech AB is currently working with several countries and major military units worldwide who are interested in this cartridge. The 6.5x25 CBJ is a high-velocity pistol/sub-machine pistol cartridge with subsonic capability. Both subsonic and supersonic cartridges function with the same reliability. At this time, CBJ Tech AB has no plans for commercial sales.

6.5x25 CBJ Factory Ballistics

Bullet (grains/type)	Powder	Grains	Velocity	Energy	Source/Comments
30.9 Sub-caliber AP	FL	N/A	2,788	533	CBJ Tech AB
38.6 Frangible	FL	N/A	2,788	666	CBJ Tech AB
123.5 MC (Subsonic)	Fl	N/A	1,049	302	CBJ Tech AB t

6.5mm JDJ No. 2

Historical Notes: This J.D. Jones cartridge is the .307 Winchester necked down to 6.5mm and Improved. It provides a 6.5mm chambering based upon the .307 Winchester case.

General Comments: Excellent bullets are available and, with proper loads and in the hands of a good shot, this chambering is fine for 300-yard shots on smaller species. In handgun-length barrels, ballistics are not significantly superior to the smaller 6.5mm JDJ cartridges and so do not justify the existence of this chambering. For information on components, loading data, barrels, and guns designed for this cartridge, contact SSK Industries, (720) 264-0176 or www.sskindustries.com.

6.5mm JDJ No. 2 Loading Data (Note: These loads for use only in SSK barrels.)

Bullet (grains)	Powder	Grains	Velocity	Energy	Source/Comments
120	IMR 4350	43.0	NA	NA	SSK/maximum load/SSK barrel only
129	IMR 4350	42.0	NA	NA	SSK/maximum load/SSK barrel only
140	IMR 4350	41.0	NA	NA	SSK/maximum load/SSK barrel only

6.5mm JDJ

Historical Notes: Designed by J.D. Jones, at SSK Industries, this is the .225 Winchester case Improved and necked up to 6mm. The purpose was to provide a Contender hunting cartridge for smaller big-game species.

General Comments: Excellent bullets are available and, with proper loads and in the hands of a good shot, this chambering is capable of 300-yard shots on smaller big-game species. Jones considers this cartridge one of the premier small-bore hunting choices. For information on components, loading data, barrels, and guns designed for this cartridge, contact SSK Industries, (720) 264-0176 or www.sskindustries.com.

6.5mm JDJ Loading Data (Note: These loads for use only in SSK barrels.)

Bullet (grains/type)	Powder	Grains	Velocity	Energy	Source/Comments
85 Sierra	IMR 4320	35.0	2,644	1,315	SSK/maximum load/SSK barrel only (14")
100 Sierra HP	H322	35.0	2,714	1,635	SSK/maximum load/SSK barrel only (14")

6.5mm JDJ Loading Data (Note: These loads for use only in SSK barrels.)

Bullet (grains/type)	Powder	Grains	Velocity	Energy	Source/Comments
120 Speer	IMR 4350	38.5	2,467	1,620	SSK/maximum load/SSK barrel only (14")
125 Nosler Part	IMR 4320	33.0	2,410	1,610	SSK/maximum load/SSK barrel only (14")
129 Hornady	IMR 4320	32.0	2,342	1,570	SSK/maximum load/SSK barrel only (14")
140 Speer	IMR 4350	34.0	2,097	1,365	SSK/maximum load/SSK barrel only (14")

6.5/270 JDJ

Historical Notes: If anyone produced more successful cartridge designs than J.D. Jones of SSK Industries, they're not widely recognized. In creating the 6.5/270 JDJ, Jones used a modified .270 Winchester case, necking it down to handle 6.5mm bullets, shortening the neck, reducing case taper, and forming a 60-degree shoulder to achieve ballistics normally associated with belted magnum cartridges in similar length (15-inch) Encore barrels.

General Comments: The 6.5/270 JDJ is well suited for Thompson/Center Encore firearms, Ruger No. 1 rifles, or appropriate bolt-action rifles. This cartridge provides long case life, consumes less powder than belted magnum cartridges, and uses relatively inexpensive cases. For information on components, loading data, barrels, and guns designed for this cartridge, contact SSK Industries, (720) 264-0176 or www.sskindustries.com.

6.5 MPC (Multi Purpose Cartridge) — *NEW*

Historical Notes: The 6.5 MPC (Multi Purpose Cartridge) is an SSK Industries development that seems to have gone fallow, despite its promise. According to the company's webpage for this round (sskindustries.com/6-5-mpc/), it is based on the 5.56 cartridge shortened and opened to 6.5mm, with the same COAL as the 5.56. Also, the case must be shortened by 3 millimeters and the shoulder pushed back to increase the size of the case neck so it will accept a 6.5mm bullet.

General Comments: Like the similar 6.8 SPC, the 6.5 MPC is superior to the 5.56 NATO downrange, but the 6.5 MPC offers some benefits over the 6.8 SPC. The 6.8 round requires conversion of barrels, bolts and caliber-specific magazines. In M16/AR-15 rifles, the 6.5 MPC uses the 5.56 bolt and magazines as well as all other parts, except for the barrel. Factory ammunition is not available for the 6.5 MPC. Contact SSK for brass and dies.

6.5 MPC Loading Data

Bullet (grains/type)	Powder	Grains	Velocity	Energy	Source/Comments
95 SSK Solid	NA	NA	2,600*	1,426	SSK Industries
95 SSK Solid	NA	NA	2,800**	1,653	SSK Industries
110 Sierra HP	NA	NA	2,480*	1,502	SSK Industries
110 Sierra HP	NA	NA	2,731**	1,821	SSK Industries
120 SMK	NA	NA	2,220*	1,313	SSK Industries
120 SMK	NA	NA	2,400**	1,534	SSK Industries

*12-inch barrel; **20-inch barrel

6.5 Mini Dreadnaught

Historical Notes: This cartridge was designed by J.D. Jones, at SSK Industries. Application is to Thompson/Center Encore or Contender single-shot pistols fitted with a custom SSK barrel. Typical barrel length is 15 inches. Cases are formed from empty .220 Swift cases. Neck length is minimal, which is acceptable for a cartridge used in a single-shot gun. Shoulder angle is 60 degrees, which seems to work just fine. Body taper is minimal, similar to the Ackley Improved designs. Therefore, this is a maximized, 6.5mm version of the .220 Swift case. Capacity is similar to the .257 Roberts (about 56 grains) and with a larger bore and higher working pressure (about 60,000 psi), ballistics easily duplicate the Roberts, despite the significant deficit in barrel length.

General Comments: Since the Swift case has a rim, it is possible to fire-form necked-up Swift cases to fit this chamber. For this purpose, use loads that are near the maximum level. Jones recommends 120- to 140-grain bullets for big-game hunting applications on smaller species. Nosler's Ballistic Tip and Partition bullets have demonstrated superior performance. However, it would appear that this cartridge is capable of driving 155-grain bullets fast enough to give dependable expansion. While one could use 100-grain Barnes X bullets, which can offer impressive terminal performance, the handloader must use X bullet-specific loading data and special handloading techniques (e.g., the bullet ogive must be seated a minimum of .050-inch from the rifling). Further, those bullets work best when a reduced-friction coating (such as moly-plating) is used. For this reason, SSK does not support use of X-style bullets in its guns. While no bullet substitution is benign, never substitute any X-style bullet in any load—begin with data specifically created for that bullet. This cartridge has a significantly shorter case body than the .257 Mini Dreadnaught, so it fails to exceed the ballistic potential of its smaller-bored sibling. For information on components, loading data, barrels, and guns designed for this cartridge, contact SSK Industries, (720) 264-0176 or www. sskindustries.com.

6.5 Mini Dreadnaught Load Data (Note: These loads for use only in SSK barrels.)

Bullet (grains/type)	Powder	Grains	Velocity	Energy	Source/Comments
120 Sierra	Vit N560	52.0	2,852	2,165	SSK/maximum load/SSK barrels only
120 Sierra	AA 2700	49.5	2,775	2,050	SSK/maximum load/SSK barrels only
140 Remington	Vit N560	52.0	2,736	2,325	SSK/maximum load/SSK barrels only
140 Hornady	AA 2700	48.2	2,618	2,130	SSK/maximum load/SSK barrels only

6.71 Phantom

Historical Notes: Lazzeroni Arms designed this cartridge, in 1997. While somewhat related to an older case, for all practical purposes, this is a new case design. This cartridge was created in response to requests for a high-performance cartridge that would work in a 2.8-inch action and yet deliver the ballistics of a full-length belted magnum. Case diameter is similar to rim diameter of the conventional belted case, so adaptation to a standard action is quite simple.

General Comments: Bullet diameter is .264-inch (Lazzeroni bases its designations on bullet diameter, instead of bore diameter, which is the common practice). Ballistics are quite impressive for such a short cartridge. The Phantom essentially duplicates 24-inch barrel .264 Winchester Magnum ballistics. Case design is typical of the Lazzeroni line: moderate body taper, 30-degree shoulder, sufficiently long neck, and thick rim of approximate case-body diameter. In other words, this is a well-designed case. For more information on Lazzeroni custom guns, ammunition, and reloading data, contact (888) 492-7247 or www.lazzeroni.com.

Bullet (grains)	Powder	Grains	Velocity	Energy	Source/Comments
100	FL		3,450	2,643	Lazzeroni factory load
120	FL		3,250	2,815	Lazzeroni factory load
140	FL		3,050	2,892	Lazzeroni factory load

6.71 Blackbird

Historical Notes: Lazzeroni Arms designed this cartridge, in 1996. Lazzeroni no longer routinely chambers this number, but will still do so on a special-order basis. While somewhat related to an older case, for all practical purposes, this is an original case design. John Lazzeroni believes that those hunters who will take the time to become competent marksmen can legitimately take game at ranges out to about 500 yards, given a gun with the requisite accuracy and a bullet that will perform properly. This cartridge was created to provide sufficient velocity to medium-weight hunting bullets so as to enable dependable expansion at maximum ranges. Adaptation to standard actions is quite simple.

General Comments: Bullet diameter is .264-inch (Lazzeroni bases its designations on bullet diameter, instead of bore diameter, which is the common practice). Ballistics exceed any other current 6.5mm cartridge. Case design is typical of the Lazzeroni line: moderate body taper, 30-degree shoulder, sufficiently long neck, and thick rim of approximate case-body diameter. In other words, this is a well-designed case. Intended specifically for hunting, and with limited barrel life (typically between 700 and 1,000 rounds, when the rifle is not overheated and is properly cleaned), this cartridge is not recommended for any other use. While 27-inch barrels are standard, all the smaller-caliber, full-length Lazzeroni numbers would benefit significantly from even longer barrels. This is a superior performer for those who only hunt smaller species of big game and who will not abuse the barrel via incautious shooting. The 125-grain Nosler Partitions and 100-grain Barnes Xs work extremely well. For more information on Lazzeroni custom guns, ammunition, and reloading data, contact (888) 492-7247 or www.lazzeroni.com.

6.71 Blackbird Factory Ballistics (27-inch barrel)

Bullet (grains)	Powder	Grains	Velocity	Energy	Source/Comments
100	FL		4,000	3,021	Lazzeroni factory load
120	FL		3,750	3,123	Lazzeroni factory load
140	FL		3,550	3,219	Lazzeroni factory load

6.5mm Allen Magnum

Historical Notes: The 6.5mm Allen Magnum is one of seven such cartridges in a line of proprietary products manufactured by riflesmith Kirby Allen, operating out of Fort Shaw, Montana, as Allen Precision Shooting. It is based on the .338 Remington Ultra Magnum case. Allen says the 6.5mm Allen Magnum is a dedicated hunting round for use on light to medium big game at moderate to long range. With 100- to 130-grain bullet weights, the 6.5mm Allen Magnum is extremely flat shooting, but 140- and 142-grain bullets perform better at long range. The 6.5mm Allen Magnum is not intended as a high-volume varmint round, because barrel life is relatively short.

General Comments: According to ballistics posted on the APSRifles.com website, the 6.5mm Allen Magnum in a 30-inch barrel will generate 3,800 fps with a 120-grain Accubond bullet. There seems to be a good selection of commercial bullets for the load. However, case forming is an involved process and suitable reloading powders are limited.

Allen says he uses only surplus ball powders for these very low expansion ratio wildcat designs. Stick powders cause powder bridging problems, with excessive pressure spikes. The ultra slow-burning ball powders do not have these problems. Because these powders can vary significantly in burn rate from lot to lot, he recommends the shooter use one of his supplied recipes, but reduced by 10 percent, as a starting load. Then the shooter can work up loads over a chronograph, watching for any pressure signs. Best powders are H-US869, WC860, AA8700, and WC-872.

Full-length sizing dies for the 6.5mm Allen Magnum chamberings are made by Redding. Seating dies are made from reaming Forster Ultra BR seating dies with the same chambering reamer used in each rifle. For more information, check the website APSRifles.com or e-mail Kirby Allen at allenmagnum@gmail.com.—*W.T.W.*

6.5 Allen Magnum Factory Ballistics (27-inch barrel) (Note: * Hodgdon US869, AA8700, WC-860, WC-872)

Bullet (grains)	Powder	Grains	Velocity	Energy	Source/Comments
100 Nosler BT	*	N/A	4,100	3,731	Allen Precision Shooting
120 Accubond	*	N/A	3,800	3,846	Allen Precision Shooting
130 Accubond	*	N/A	3,700	3,950	Allen Precision Shooting
140 Accubond	*	N/A	3,550	3,916	Allen Precision Shooting
142 Sierra MatchKing	*	N/A	3,550	3,972	Allen Precision Shooting

.270 JDJ

Historical Notes: This is another cartridge designed and developed by J.D. Jones, around 1978. It is generally fired in barrels furnished by his company, SSK Industries. The purpose of these cartridges is to give added range and power to the Thompson/Center Contender pistol for hunting medium game. All of the JDJ cartridges are proprietary, and SSK neither sells reamers nor has permitted the reamer maker to duplicate any of the reamers for this series.

General Comments: Based on the .225 Winchester case (itself a modified .30-30 case) this Improved chambering provides ample capacity to deliver impressive velocity from handgun-length barrels, now commonly 14 to 16 inches. Best applications are in handgun varminting and hunting of smaller big-game species through mule deer-size. For varminting, best performance is probably achieved with bullets of 100 grains. Either Hornady's or Sierra's 110-grain bullets would be good choices for pronghorn hunting. For hunting deer and similar-sized game, the best bullet weight is 130 grains. Heavier bullets can deliver more energy, but expansion is unreliable. This chambering has seen considerable use in various types of handgun competition. This is ample testimony to the potential accuracy of this chambering and the quality of gunsmithing involved in such alterations. For information on components, loading data, barrels, and guns designed for this cartridge, contact SSK Industries, (720) 264-0176 or www.sskindustries.com.

.270 JDJ Loading Data (Note: These loads for use only in SSK barrels.)

Bullet (grains/type)	Powder	Grains	Velocity	Energy	Source/Comments
100 SP	RI-7	34.0	2,795	1,735	SSK/maximum load/(SSK barrels only)
110 SP	IMR 4320	36.0	2,520	1,555	SSK/maximum load/(SSK barrels only)
130 SP	RI-7	30.7	2,370	1,625	SSK/maximum load/(SSK barrels only)
130 SP	IMR 3031	35.0	2,470	1,765	SSK/maximum load/(SSK barrels only)

.270 JDJ No. 2

Historical Notes: Another creation of J. D. Jones, the .270 JDJ No. 2 uses a modified .30-06 family of cases with a shortened neck, reduced case taper, and 60-degree shoulder to achieve ballistics normally associated with belted magnum cartridges in similar length barrels. In a short-barreled Encore pistol, the .270 JDJ No. 2 can propel 130-grain bullets to 2487 fps. The cartridge can accommodate a range of .270 bullet weights ranging from 90 grains to 150 grains, including some fine hunting bullets. For information on components, loading data, barrels, and guns designed for this cartridge, contact SSK Industries, (720) 264-0176 or www.sskindustries.com.

General Comments: The .270 JDJ No. 2 is well suited for Thompson/Center Encore firearms or appropriate bolt-action rifles. Capable of sub-MOA accuracy, this cartridge provides long case life, consumes less powder than belted magnum cartridges, and uses relatively inexpensive cases. For information on components, loading data, barrels, and guns designed for this cartridge, contact SSK Industries, (720) 264-0176 or www.sskindustries.com.

.270 Allen Magnum

Historical Notes: Kirby Allen, of Allen Precision Shooting (APS), designed the .270 Allen Magnum for hunting medium-sized big game in the 200- to 600-pound class. Based on a 7mm Remington Ultra Magnum or .300 Remington Ultra Magnum parent case, the .270 Allen Magnum was the first APS wildcat to offer more than one ton of energy at 1,000 yards. It also retains up to 2,300 fps at this range, which ensures full bullet expansion.

General Comments: Preferred bullets are 130- and 140-grain Accubonds, 130-, 140-, and 150-grain Ballistic Tips, and, when available, the 169.5-grain ULD RBBT from Wildcat bullets. With commercial bullets, the .270 Allen Magnum is best used at ranges up to 800 yards on medium-size game. For elk hunting with conventional commercial bullets, range should be limited to 600 yards.

Allen said, "Berger is currently working on a new 170-grain VLD bullet design, and Matrix Bullets is working on a heavy-jacketed version of its 175-grain .277 bullets that will replace the old 169.5-grain ULD RBBT and will bring the .270 Allen Magnum back to its original extreme performance level."

This round is easy to form brass for, and formed brass is available through APS with rifle orders. It offers decent barrel life for its performance level and fits easily in Remington 700 receivers. Full-length sizing dies for the .270 Allen Magnum are made by Redding. Seating dies are made from reaming Forster Ultra BR seating dies with the same chambering reamer used in each rifle. For more information, check the website APSRifles.com or e-mail Kirby Allen at allenmagnum@gmail.com.—*W.T.W.*

.270 Allen Magnum Loading Data

Bullet (grains/type)	Powder	Grains	Velocity	Energy	Source/Comments
130 Accubond	*	N/A	3,750	4,058	Accubond
140 Accubond	*	N/A	3,650	4,140	Accubond
150 Nosler BT	*	N/A	3,550	3,972	Accubond
170 Custom	*	N/A	3,450	4,492	Accubond

7mm Whisper

Historical Notes: Designed by J.D. Jones in the early 1990s, this cartridge was designed for use in sound-suppressed M-15s, bolt-action rifles, and T/C Contenders. As with most of the JDJ line, this cartridge was designed at SSK Industries. The 7mm Whisper is based upon the .221 Remington case.

General Comments: When combined with a very quick rifling twist, this chambering will deliver heavy 7mm bullets from SSK Contender barrels, with ½ MOA accuracy at subsonic velocities (1040 fps). Lighter bullets can achieve velocities that are more typical, but they sacrifice the design purpose of this chambering. For information on components, loading data, barrels, and guns designed for this cartridge, contact SSK Industries, (720) 264-0176 or www.sskindustries.com.

7mm Whisper Loading Data

Bullet (grains/type)	Powder	Grains	Velocity	Energy	Source/Comments
120	AA 1680	20.0	2,250	1,345	SSK/maximum load/16½" barrel
140 Nosler BT	AA 1680	18.5	2,060	1,315	SSK/maximum load/6½" barrel
168	AA 1680	9.5	1,056	415	SSK/subsonic
168	Vit N540	12.6	1,064	420	SSK/subsonic

7mm-30 JDJ

Historical Notes: This JDJ cartridge is the 7-30 Waters, Improved. The purpose is to meet customer demand for improved performance with readily obtained cases. Since the 7-30 is based on the .30-30 Winchester, one can easily use those abundant cases to form this round. Other than rim diameter and a slight increase in length, this chambering is essentially similar to the 7mm JDJ.

General Comments: Excellent bullets are available. With proper loads and in the hands of a marksman, this chambering is capable of 300-yard shots on smaller game species. Significantly, it delivers substantially more energy than the 6.5mm JDJ offerings. Despite a shorter barrel, this Improved cartridge will drive a 140-grain bullet at about the same velocity as the 7-30 Waters will drive the 120-grain bullet. For information on components, loading data, barrels, and guns designed for this cartridge, contact SSK Industries, (720) 264-0176 or www.sskindustries.com.

7mm GNR

Historical Notes: One of the most experienced cartridge wildcatters of all time, Gary Reeder is, as you would expect, an avid shooter and hunter. The 7mm GNR was developed as a handgun hunting round for a single-shot pistol like the Thompson/Center Contender. The 7mm GNR is a very close ballistic performer to the 7-30 Waters, but a serious ballistic comparison will show it is capable of velocities about 300 to 350 fps faster. The 7mm GNR, when fired from a 14-inch barrel, will duplicate the external ballistics of a 7-30 Waters out of a 24-inch barrel. Originally based on the .30-30 Winchester case, due to the compatibility of its rim with single-shot actions, Reeder later switched to the .375 Winchester case, but found pressures were too high. Reeder switched back to .30-30 brass, but with the availability of factory new 7-30 Waters brass, that became the go-to choice for making brass for the 7mm GNR.

General Comments: Though it must be handloaded, and even though cases must be fire-formed from .30-30 Winchester or 7-30 Waters brass, the 7mm GNR is a great cartridge for deer- or antelope-sized game, particularly if you are a lover of single-shot, break-action pistols like the Contender. Gary Reeder has no qualms about designing a niche cartridge that has a specific, if narrow, use, and the 7mm GNR is a perfect example of his skill at wildcatting. Like with all the cartridges developed by Reeder, Gary figures out the ballistics he wants from a specific platform and for a specific purpose and then builds a cartridge accordingly. Information on custom guns, ammunition, and reloading data can be obtained by contacting Gary Reeder Custom Guns, (928) 527-4100 or www.reedercustomguns.com.

7mm GNR Loading Data and Ballistics (14-inch barrel T/C Contender)

Bullet (grains/type)	Powder	Grains	Velocity	Energy	Source/Comments
120	H-322	32	2,300	1,409	Gary Reeder (Fire-form load)
120	H-4895	38	2,650	1,871	Gary Reeder
130	AA 2520	38	2,625	1,988	Gary Reeder
139 Hornady BTSP	H 4350	36	2,475	1,890	Gary Reeder

7mm JDJ

Historical Notes: This is another cartridge designed and developed by J.D. Jones. Its purpose is to give added range and power to the Thompson/Center Contender pistol for the primary purpose of hunting medium game. This cartridge has also proved to be an excellent choice for metallic silhouette competition. All JDJ cartridges are relatively easy to make. These are proprietary, and SSK neither sells reamers nor has permitted the reamer maker to duplicate any of the reamers for the series.

General Comments: Based on the .225 Winchester case (itself a modified .30-30 case), this Improved chambering provides ample capacity to deliver impressive velocity, especially with longer handgun-length barrels (14 to 16 inches). Best applications are in handgun hunting of smaller big-game species through mule deer-size. Best hunting performance is probably achieved with bullets of 120 to 140 grains. Experts have tallied many kills at ranges exceeding 200 yards. Heavier bullets can deliver more energy, but expansion is not reliable. Heavier bullets have proven effective in the handgun silhouette game; bullets of about 150 grains are noted for their effectiveness in toppling the ram target. This is ample testimony to the potential accuracy of this chambering and the quality of gunsmithing involved in such alterations. For information on components, loading data, barrels, and guns designed for this cartridge, contact SSK Industries, (720) 264-0176 or www.sskindustries.com.

7mm JDJ Loading Data (Note: These loads for use only in SSK barrels.)

Bullet (grains/type)	Powder	Grains	Velocity	Energy	Source/Comments
120 SP	H4895	34.0	2,480	1,640	SSK/maximum load/SSK barrels only
139-140 SP	IMR 4320	34.0	2,145	1,420	SSK/maximum load/SSK barrels only
150-154 SP	IMR 4320	34.0	2,110	1,520	SSK/maximum load/SSK barrels only

.280 JDJ

Historical Notes: This cartridge was designed by J.D. Jones, at SSK Industries. Application is to Thompson/Center Encore single-shot pistols fitted with a custom SSK barrel. Typical barrel length is 15 inches. Cases are formed from empty .280 Remington cases by special means and cannot be fire-formed from any other case. Neck length is minimal, which is acceptable for a cartridge used in a single-shot gun. Shoulder angle is

60 degrees, which seems to work just fine. Body taper is minimal, similar to Ackley's Improved designs. Therefore, this is a maximized, .28-caliber version of the .280 case. Case capacity is a whopping 76 grains of water, which is only 10 grains less than the 7mm Remington Magnum. Working pressure is about 60,000 psi, so ballistics are quite impressive. Best handloads in SSK barrels come close to duplicating .280 (rifle) ballistics.

General Comments: Since this case has no rim, it is not generally safe to directly fire-form it in the conventional manner. However, owing to the captive extractor system used in the Encore, it is possible to use a special technique in those guns, to wit: In a standard .280 case (sized), seat a jacketed bullet hard against the rifling so that the gun will just close. The correct powder charge is about 5 percent below the maximum SSK-recommended load. Jones recommends 140-grain bullets for big-game hunting applications on smaller species and bullets up to 175 grains on larger species. With the velocity potential of this chambering, premium bullets are probably a superior choice for hunting applications. While one could use 120-grain Barnes X bullets, which can offer impressive terminal performance, the handloader must use X bullet-specific loading data and special handloading techniques (e.g., the bullet ogive must be seated a minimum of .050-inch from the rifling). Further, those bullets work best when a friction-reducing application (such as moly-plating) is used. For this reason, SSK does not support use of X-style bullets in its guns. While no bullet substitution is benign, never substitute any X-style bullet in any load—begin with data specifically created for that bullet. Speer's 110-grain TNT should provide impressive varminting performance. For information on components, loading data, barrels, and guns designed for this cartridge, contact SSK Industries, (720) 264-0176 or www.sskindustries.com.

.280 JDJ Loading Data (Note: These loads for use only in SSK barrels.)

Bullet (grains/type)	Powder	Grains	Velocity	Energy	Source/Comments
120 Nosler BT	IMR 4831	70.0	3,119	2,590	SSK/maximum load/SSK barrels only
140 Nosler BT	IMR 4831	67.5	2,975	2,750	SSK/maximum load/SSK barrels only
150 Nosler Part	RI-22	68.4	2,775	2,565	SSK/maximum load/SSK barrels only
175 Remington	IMR 4831	64.3	2,670	2,770	SSK/maximum load/SSK barrels only

7mm JDJ No. 2

Historical Notes: This JDJ cartridge is the .307 Winchester necked down to 7mm and Improved. The purpose was to provide a 7mm chambering based upon the .307 Winchester case.

General Comments: Excellent bullets are available for this cartridge. With proper loads and in the hands of a good shot, this chambering is capable of 300-yard shots on smaller big-game species. In handgun-length barrels, ballistics are not significantly superior to the smaller 7mm JDJ offerings to justify the existence of this chambering. For information on components, loading data, barrels, and guns designed for this cartridge, contact SSK Industries, (720) 264-0176 or www.sskindustries.com.

7mm JDJ No. 2 Loading Data (Note: These loads for use only in SSK barrels.)

Bullet (grains/type)	Powder	Grains	Velocity	Energy	Source/Comments
100 Hornady	W760	47.0	2,532	1,420	SSK/maximum load/14" barrel
115 Speer	W760	46.0	2,453	1,535	SSK/maximum load/14" barrel
139 Hornady	H4350	45.0	2,369	1,730	SSK/maximum load/14" barrel
140 Nosler SB	H414	43.0	2,257	1,580	SSK/maximum load/14" barrel
140 Nosler SB	W760	44.0	2,303	1,645	SSK/maximum load/14" barrel

7mm Dakota

Historical Notes: The 7mm Dakota is based on the .404 Jeffery case. This case is long enough to create standard- or magnum-length cartridges. In any given cartridge length, use of the non-belted .404 Jeffery case offers about 15-percent more case capacity, compared to the standard belted magnum case. Because maximum case diameter is slightly larger than the standard belted magnum, re-chambering to 7mm Dakota often reduces magazine capacity by one cartridge, unless a slight deepening of the magazine well is accomplished.

General Comments: This cartridge functions properly through standard-length (3.35-inch) actions. Guns chambered for the 7mm Remington Magnum are easily converted to 7mm Dakota with only re-chambering and slight bolt-face alterations. This chambering offers capacity similar to the much longer 7mm STW (3.65 inches). If loaded to similar pressures with appropriate powders, the 7mm Dakota offers a useful velocity advantage over the 7mm Remington Magnum; with the heaviest bullets, this advantage might be significant. For those interested in getting all the performance possible from the 7mm bore, the 7mm Dakota is worth considering. The 7mm STW has a slight capacity advantage, but the ballistic difference is marginal and the STW requires a longer action. Finally, because this cartridge headspaces between the case shoulder and bolt face, it's easier to get it to line up properly in the rifle's chamber. This can lead to superior accuracy. It is worth noting that there are no disadvantages to the rimless bottleneck design for most applications. Contact Dakota Arms for more information: (605) 347-4686 or www.dakotaarms.com.

7mm Dakota Loading Data

Bullet (grains)	Powder	Grains	Velocity	Energy	Source/Comments
140	IMR 4831	73.0	3,355	3,495	Dakota/maximum load
140	H4831	76.0	3,295	3,375	Dakota/maximum load
140	RI-22	77.0	3,365	3,515	Dakota/maximum load
140	IMR 7828	80.0	3,421	3,645	Dakota/maximum load
160	IMR 4831	68.0	3,064	3,335	Dakota/maximum load
160	H4831	74.0	3,156	3,535	Dakota/maximum load
160	RI-22	74.5	3,212	3,660	Dakota/maximum load
160	IMR 7828	75.0	3,171	3,570	Dakota/maximum load
140	FL	N/A	3,400	3,593	Dakota factory load
160	FL	N/A	3,200	3,637	Dakota factory load

.280 GNR

Historical Notes: Gary Reeder is one of the most experienced cartridge wildcatters of all time. He makes not just any wildcat cartridges. Rather, he typically designs a group of wildcats based on a particular case. The .280 GNR is a perfect example. After developing the .310 and 8mm GNR rounds, Reeder decided he wanted to make a 7mm (.284). He put the entire project together in the six weeks leading up to an African safari. This is a spin-off on the .405 Winchester case, which is simply necked down to 7mm with a 40-degree shoulder. One reason Reeder chose the .450 case is because it has about 18-percent more capacity than the .30-06 case, which is the parent case for the .280 Remington. Without the time available to get dies in hand, Reeder necked the .405 case down to .308-caliber using his .310 GNR dies. Then he took the cases to 7mm with a set of 7mm-08 Improved dies, and, with nothing but load workup left, he was ready for Africa.

General Comments: The .280 GNR was specifically developed for medium to large deer-sized game at long range. It will drive a 140-grain bullet in excess of 2,950 fps out of a single-shot pistol with a 15-inch barrel. This is very similar to 7mm Remington Magnum performance, but from a rimmed cartridge that works great in single-shot rifles or handguns. Information on custom guns, ammunition, and reloading data can be obtained through Gary Reeder Custom Guns, (928) 527-4100 or www.reedercustomguns.com.

.280 GNR Loading Data

Bullet (grains/type)	Powder	Grains	Velocity	Energy	Source/Comments
139 Hornady BTSP	H 4350	56	2,965	2,713	Gary Reeder

7mm Allen Magnum

Historical Notes: The 7mm Allen Magnum was the first Allen Precision Shooting (APSRifles.com) wildcat to step away from the Remington Ultra Magnum parent case in favor of a slightly shorter and fatter design based on the .338 Lapua Magnum parent case. The .338 Lapua Magnum offers a slightly larger case capacity and increased strength, allowing it to handle pressures exceeding anything the RUM case can survive and doing so with long brass life. However, the large-diameter Lapua parent case requires receivers designed for its size.

General Comments: Should the shooter have the skills, the 140- and 160-grain Accubonds are capable of cleanly taking big game up to 800 yards. Likewise, the 175-grain Sierra MatchKing and 180-grain Berger VLD deliver more than a ton of energy on target well past 1,000 yards. When it was available, the Ultra Low Drag RBBT 200-grain from Wildcat Bullets put just under 2,200 ft-lbs of energy on target at 1,200 yards.

Fully formed brass is available from APS with rifle orders. This round can be loaded with powders that are very stable over wide temperature changes. The relatively short overall length works in standard-length receivers and magazine boxes. For more information, check the website APSRifles.com or e-mail Kirby Allen at allenmagnum@gmail.com.—*W.T.W.*

7mm Allen Magnum Loading Data (Note: *Hodgdon Retumbo, Reloader 33, Hodgdon US869, AA 8700, WC-860, WC-872)

Bullet (grains)	Powder	Grains	Velocity	Energy	Source/Comments
140 Accubond	*	N/A	3,700	4,254	Allen Precision Shooting
160 Accubond	*	N/A	3,550	4,476	Allen Precision Shooting
175 Sierra MatchKing	*	N/A	3,450	4,624	Allen Precision Shooting
180 Berger VLD	*	N/A	3,400	4,619	Allen Precision Shooting
200 Custom	*	N/A	3,300	4,835	Allen Precision Shooting

7.21 Tomahawk

Historical Notes: Lazzeroni Arms designed this cartridge in 1997. While somewhat related to an older case, for all practical purposes, this is a new case design. This cartridge was created in response to requests for a high-performance cartridge that would work in a 2.8-inch action and yet deliver the ballistics of a full-length belted magnum. Adaptation to a standard action is feasible, but is not recommended.

General Comments: Bullet diameter is .284-inch (Lazzeroni bases its designations on bullet diameter, instead of bore diameter, which is the common practice). Ballistics are impressive for such a short cartridge. Given equal-length barrels, the Tomahawk essentially duplicates top 7mm Weatherby Magnum ballistics, coming very close to the 7mm STW. Case design is typical of the Lazzeroni line: moderate body taper, 30-degree shoulder, sufficiently long neck, and thick rim of approximate case-body diameter. In other words, this is a well-designed case. For more information on Lazzeroni custom guns, ammunition, and reloading data, contact (888) 492-7247 or www.lazzeroni.com.

7.21 Tomahawk Factory Ballistics (24-inch barrel)

Bullet (grains)	Powder	Grains	Velocity	Energy	Source/Comments
120	FL	N/A	3,525	3,310	Lazzeroni factory load
140	FL	N/A	3,300	3,386	Lazzeroni factory load
150	FL	N/A	3,200	3,412	Lazzeroni factory load
160	FL	N/A	3,100	3,415	Lazzeroni factory load

7.21 Firehawk

Historical Notes: Lazzeroni Arms designed this cartridge in 1996. It was discontinued from standard chambering in 1999, but is still available as a special order. It was replaced by the 7.21 Firebird. While somewhat related to an older case, for all practical purposes, this is a new case design. John Lazzeroni believes that those hunters who will take the time to become competent marksmen can legitimately take game at ranges out to about 500 yards, given a gun with the requisite accuracy and a bullet that will perform properly. This cartridge was created to provide velocity to medium-weight hunting bullets sufficient to enable dependable expansion at maximum ranges. Adaptation to standard actions is quite simple.

General Comments: Bullet diameter is .284-inch (Lazzeroni bases its designations on bullet diameter instead of bore diameter, which is the common practice). Until the introduction of the 7.21 Firebird (also from Lazzeroni), ballistics exceeded any other current 7mm cartridge. Case design is typical of the Lazzeroni line: moderate body taper, 30-degree shoulder, sufficiently long neck, and thick rim of approximate case-body diameter. In other words, this is a well-designed case. Designed specifically for hunting and with limited barrel life, this cartridge is not recommended for any other use. While 27-inch barrels are standard, all smaller-caliber, full-length Lazzeroni numbers would benefit significantly from even longer barrels. Most of Lazzeroni's full-length cartridge loadings use specially lubricated (proprietary process) premium bullets from Nosler, Barnes, or Swift. These are the only bullets providing the necessary accuracy and terminal performance to meet Lazzeroni's strict requirements. A significant portion of the accuracy and ballistic potential of these cartridges results from the unusually effective, reduced-friction coating used. For more information on Lazzeroni custom guns, ammunition, and reloading data, contact (888) 492-7247 or www.lazzeroni.com.

7.21 Firehawk Factory Ballistics (27-inch barrel)

Bullet (grains)	Powder	Grains	Velocity	Energy	Source/Comments
120	FL	N/A	3,800	3,848	Lazzeroni factory load
140	FL	N/A	3,600	4,030	Lazzeroni factory load
150	FL	N/A	3,500	4,081	Lazzeroni factory load
160	FL	N/A	3,400	4,108	Lazzeroni factory load

7.21 Firebird

Historical Notes: Lazzeroni Arms designed this cartridge in 1998 by necking down the 7.82 Warbird. John Lazzeroni believes that hunters who will take the time to become competent marksmen can legitimately take game at ranges out to about 500 yards, given a gun with the requisite accuracy and a bullet that will perform properly. This cartridge was created to eliminate the intermediate Lazzeroni case size and stay one step ahead of the competition. Lazzeroni believes that 7mm is the ideal bore size for North American hunting needs and that there is no such thing as too much velocity. This cartridge can provide sufficient velocity to medium-weight hunting bullets for dependable expansion at maximum ranges. Adaptation to standard actions is not recommended.

General Comments: Bullet diameter is .284-inch (Lazzeroni bases its designations on bullet diameter, instead of bore diameter, which is the common practice). Ballistics exceed any other current 7mm cartridge. Case design is typical of the Lazzeroni line: moderate body taper, 30-degree shoulder, sufficiently long neck, and thick rim of approximate case-body diameter, making this a well-designed case. Designed specifically for hunting and with limited barrel life, this cartridge is not recommended for any other use. While a 27-inch barrel is standard, this number would benefit significantly from use of a longer barrel. Only the best premium bullets provide the necessary accuracy and terminal performance. Factory loads use specially lubricated (proprietary process) premium bullets from Nosler, Barnes, or Swift. A 27- or 28-inch barrel with specially prepared Lazzeroni/Barnes 120-grain XBT bullets produces the flattest shooting (shortest time of flight to 1,000 yards) combination of any commercially available hunting or target rifle. One would be hard-pressed to do better with any wildcat. For more information on Lazzeroni custom guns, ammunition, and reloading data, contact (888) 492-7247 or www.lazzeroni.com.

7.21 Firebird Factory Ballistics (27-inch barrel)

Bullet (grains)	Powder	Grains	Velocity	Energy	Source/Comments
120	FL	N/A	3,950	4,155	Lazzeroni factory load
140	FL	N/A	3,750	4,370	Lazzeroni factory load
150	FL	N/A	3,650	4,435	Lazzeroni factory load
160	FL	N/A	3,550	4,475	Lazzeroni factory load
175	FL	N/A	3,400	4,490	Lazzeroni factory load

7mm Canadian Magnum

Historical Notes: This cartridge was developed about 1989 by North American Shooting Systems (NASS) and is similar to the 7mm Imperial Magnum. This design features a slightly rebated, rimless bottleneck case. Design intent was to provide maximum powder capacity available in a standard action with minimal gunsmithing. (Without deepening the magazine well slightly, magazine capacity is usually reduced by one round.) Bolt face alteration is not necessary. Cartridge feeding and headspacing characteristics are improved.

General Comments: The Canadian Magnum series is similar to the Dakota cartridge family in both design and purpose. However, Canadian Magnums all take advantage of the entire 3.65-inch magazine length of the long-action Remington M700 and similar rifles. On these cartridges, body diameter is significantly larger than the standard belted magnum (.544-inch versus .513-inch at the base). Re-chambering of nominal belted magnums with the same bore diameter is generally quite simple, requiring no other rifle alterations. For any given case length, capacity is fully 15-percent greater than can be achieved with the belted version. Body taper is minimal, and the shoulder is comparatively sharp. However, neck length is sufficiently generous to provide good bullet purchase for hunting ammunition. Performance is commensurate with the generous capacity and pressures used in these loadings. We must note that one should expect this chambering to be rather hard on barrels.

7mm Canadian Magnum Loading Data and Factory Ballistics

Bullet (grains)	Powder	Grains	Velocity	Energy	Source/Comments
140	H4831	82.0	3,426	3,645	NASS/maximum load
140	RI-22	85.0	3,523	3,855	NASS/maximum load
140	IMR 7828	86.5	3,480	3,760	NASS/maximum load
160	RI-22	82.0	3,264	3,780	NASS/maximum load

7mm Canadian Magnum Loading Data and Factory Ballistics

Bullet (grains)	Powder	Grains	Velocity	Energy	Source/Comments
160	IMR 7828	83.5	3,257	3,765	NASS/maximum load
160	H1000	87.0	3,288	3,835	NASS/maximum load
175	IMR 7828	79.0	3,018	3,540	NASS/maximum load
175	H1000	83.0	3,098	3,725	NASS/maximum load
175	H870	93.0	3,109	3,750	NASS/maximum load
140	FL	N/A	3,525	3,860	NASS factory load

7.62 Micro-Whisper

Historical Notes: Designed by J.D. Jones at SSK Industries in the early 1990s, this is simply the .30 Luger case adapted to use .30-caliber rifle bullets. Case dimensions are identical, but chambering specifications are different. The design intent was for an extremely quiet, sound-suppressed load that would shoot 180-grain bullets to about 1,040 fps.

General Comments: This cartridge provides much better subsonic performance than the .308 Winchester. Civilian applications are limited. Nevertheless, performance is startling. For those looking for minimal recoil and noise for short-range use, this is an interesting choice. For information on components, loading data, barrels, and guns designed for this cartridge, contact SSK Industries, (720) 264-0176 or www.sskindustries.com.

7.62 Micro-Whisper Loading Data

Bullet (grains/type)	Powder	Grains	Velocity	Energy	Source/Comments
93 Norma SP	AA No. 9	11.5	1,762	640	SSK/maximum load/8¾" barrel
150 Hornady FMJ	H110	7.0	1,018	345	SSK/subsonic/8¾" barrel
150 Hornady FMJ	AA No. 9	8.0	1,259	525	SSK/subsonic/8¾" barrel
168 Hornady Match	AA No. 9	7.1	1,056	445	SSK/subsonic/8¾" barrel
180 Speer	H110	7.0	1,025	420	SSK/subsonic/8¾" barrel
180 Speer	H110	8.0	1,161	535	SSK/subsonic/8¾" barrel

7.63 Mini-Whisper

Historical Notes: Designed by J.D. Jones at SSK Industries in the early 1990s, this is simply the .30 Mauser case adapted to use .30-caliber rifle bullets. Case dimensions are identical, but chambering specifications are different. The design intent was for an extremely quiet, sound-suppressed load that would shoot 200-grain bullets to about 1,040 fps.

General Comments: This cartridge provides much better subsonic performance than the .308 Winchester. Civilian applications are limited. Nevertheless, performance is startling. For those looking for minimal recoil and noise for short-range use, this is an interesting choice. For information on components, loading data, barrels, and guns designed for this cartridge, contact SSK Industries, (720) 264-0176 or www.sskindustries.com.

7.63 Mini-Whisper Loading Data

Bullet (grains/type)	Powder	Grains	Velocity	Energy	Source/Comments
93 Norma	Clays	7.5	1,727	615	SSK/maximum load/7" barrel
110 Speer Carb	Clays	7.5	1,588	615	SSK/maximum load/7" barrel (1.415" OAL)

7.63 Mini-Whisper Loading Data

Bullet (grains/type)	Powder	Grains	Velocity	Energy	Source/Comments
110 Speer Carb	AA No. 7	11.4	1,742	740	SSK/maximum load/7" barrel (1.415" OAL)
150 Hornady FMJ	AA No. 2	4.5	1,025	350	SSK/subsonic/7" barrel
150 Hornady FMJ	AA No. 9	10.5	1,445	695	SSK/maximum load/7" barrel
168 Hornady Match	AA No. 2	5.2	1,031	395	SSK/subsonic/7" barrel
168 Hornady Match	HP-38	5.7	1,035	395	SSK/subsonic/ 7" barrel

.300 Whisper
(See also .300 AAC Blackout)

Historical Notes: The .300 Whisper is a new concept in the development of small case-capacity, highly efficient cartridges combined with bullets of extreme ballistic efficiency. This is a special-purpose design, by J.D. Jones of SSK Industries, based on a .221 Remington case necked up to .308-caliber. It is intended to fire extremely heavy, accurate, ballistically efficient bullets at subsonic velocities in suppressed guns. It delivers more energy more accurately than any other subsonic round at 200 yards. In addition, it has interesting supersonic capabilities above 1160 fps, thus offering greater versatility than any other cartridge capable of performing in these vastly differing arenas. Because powder charges are very small, suppressor size is proportionately smaller.

General Comments: Bullet weights from 100 to 240 grains can be used. Best accuracy is obtained with heavier bullets. For silhouette shooting, 220- to 240-grain bullets are best. With 125- or 150-grain projectiles, this cartridge is outstanding for deer and other medium game, with better performance than the .30-30 Winchester in the T/C Contender pistol and less than half the felt recoil. In suppressed guns, noise can be reduced to less than that of a .177-caliber spring-air rifle. For information on components, loading data, barrels, and guns for this cartridge, contact SSK Industries, (720) 264-0176 or www.sskindustries.com.

.300 Whisper Loading Data

Bullet (grains/type)	Powder	Grains	Velocity	Energy	Source/Comments
125 Nosler BT	H110	20.6	2,283	1,445	SSK/maximum rifle load/AR-15
150 Nosler BT	H110	18.0	2,073	1,430	SSK/maximum rifle load
165	AA 1680	10.3	1,013	375	SSK/subsonic/AR-15
125 Nosler BT	H110	20.6	2,283	1,445	SSK/maximum load/AR-15
125 Nosler BT	H110	18.0	2,014	1,350	SSK/maximum load/AR-15
165	AA 2015	12.6	1,046	400	SSK/subsonic/AR-15
168	AA 1680	20.2	1,906	1355	SSK/maximum load/rifle
200	AA 2015	12.0	1,007	450	N/A
220	AA No. 9	8.5	1,013	500	SSK/subsonic/AR-15
250	H110	8.6	980	530	SSK/subsonic/AR-15

.308 CorBon

Historical Notes: This cartridge was designed by CorBon and announced at the 1999 Shooting, Hunting, Outdoor Trade (SHOT) Show. The purpose was to achieve the greatest feasible performance from an action designed to handle 2.8-inch cartridges, but without the necessity of any significant magazine or action modifications. In a crowded market, Peter Pi (CEO at CorBon) seems to have found a combination that fills a useful niche. Ballistics approximate those of the conventional .30-caliber belted magnum, which is designed to work in a 3.3-inch (or longer) action.

General Comments: A significant trend in the wildcat and proprietary arena is toward shorter cartridges. This design promises advantages in both rifle and ballistics. This shorter case chambers in a shorter, lighter, more rigid action that is faster and easier to manipulate. This cartridge might also have intrinsic accuracy advantages; the big push in accuracy competition is toward shorter and fatter cases. Evidently, such a design might promote earlier and more consistent ignition of individual powder granules. Contact CorBon for more information: (800) 626-7266 or www.shopcorbon.com.

.308 CorBon Factory Ballistics

Bullet (grains/type)	Powder	Grains	Velocity	Energy	Source/Comments
165 SPBT	FL	N/A	3,100	3,520	CorBon factory load
180 SPBT	FL	N/A	3,000	3,600	CorBon factory load

.307 GNR

Historical Notes: Custom gun builder and cartridge designer Gary Reeder will tell you that, while he has taken most of the game he has hunted with T/C Contenders and Encores, he is really a revolver man at heart. Reeder wanted a cartridge that would duplicate .300 GNR and .30 Herret ballistics from a revolver, and the .307 GNR was his answer. The case is formed by necking a .357 Maximum case down to .308-caliber with one pass through a sizing die.

General Comments: This cartridge requires a revolver with a longer than normal frame; one sized for the .357 Maximum like Ruger's .357 Maximum Blackhawk is what is needed. Recoil is tolerable, considering this cartridge generates a good bit of power from a revolver. With proper bullets, the .307 GNR should be sufficient for hunting all medium-sized, non-dangerous game. Information on custom guns, ammunition, and reloading data can be obtained by contacting Gary Reeder Custom Guns, (928) 527-4100 or www.reedercustomguns.com.

.307 GNR Loading Data & Ballistics

Bullet (grains/type)	Powder	Grains	Velocity	Energy	Source
110 FP	H 110	21.0	2,303	1,295	Gary Reeder
125 FP	IMR 4227	20.0	2,084	1,205	Gary Reeder

.309 JDJ

Historical Notes: This cartridge was designed and developed by J.D. Jones about 1978. It is generally fired in barrels furnished by SSK Industries. Its purpose is to give added power and range to the T/C Contender pistol for hunting medium game. The JDJ series of cartridges are easy to make. All JDJ designs are proprietary rounds, and SSK neither sells reamers nor allows the reamer maker to duplicate the reamers for sale. Should you desire to chamber a JDJ cartridge, contact SSK Industries (www.sskindustries.com).

General Comments: The .309 JDJ is based on a .444 Marlin case necked down to .30-caliber in a .308 full-length sizing die, and then fire-formed to obtain the sharp shoulder. This cartridge offers about 2600 fps with a 125-grain bullet, 2450 fps with a 150-grain bullet, and 160-grainers can be driven at 2400 fps. For general use, 165-grain bullets are an excellent choice. Jones has taken large plains game in Africa with this round. In a pinch, it would do for elk with 180-grain bullets. The .309 is easy to shoot and can be extremely versatile. With the proper load and bullet sighted to shoot about three inches high at 100 yards, it will be dead on at about 225 to 250 yards. It can be very effective on moderate-sized game to that range, with the right bullet and a shooter possessing adequate skills. For information on components, loading data, barrels, and guns designed for this cartridge, contact SSK Industries, (720) 264-0176 or www.sskindustries.com.

.309 JDJ Loading Data (Note: These loads for use only in SSK barrels.)

Bullet (grains/type)	Powder	Grains	Velocity	Energy	Source/Comments
150 SP	IMR 4320	41.0	2,010	1,360	SSK/maximum load/SSK barrels only
150 SP	IMR 4350	43.0	2,370	1,875	SSK/maximum load/SSK barrels only
165 SP	IMR 4350	52.0	2,430	1,775	SSK/maximum load/SSK barrels only
180 SP	IMR 4350	49.0	2,135	1,825	SSK/maximum load/SSK barrels only

.30-06 JDJ

Historical Notes: This cartridge was designed by J.D. Jones at SSK Industries. Application is to Thompson/Center Encore single-shot pistols fitted with a custom SSK barrel. Typical barrel length is 15 inches. Cases are formed from empty Remington .30-06 cases by special means and cannot be fire-formed from any other case. Neck length is minimal, which is acceptable for a cartridge used in a single-shot gun. Shoulder angle is 60 degrees, which works fine. Body taper is minimal, similar to Ackley's Improved designs. Therefore, this is a maximized version of the .30-06 case. Capacity is a whopping 75 grains of water, which is significantly greater than the .30-06 (about 70). Working pressure is about 60,000 psi, so ballistics are quite impressive. Best handloads in SSK barrels come very close to duplicating .30-06 (rifle) ballistics.

General Comments: Since this case has no rim, it is not generally safe to directly fire-form it in the conventional manner. However, owing to the captive extractor system used in the Encore, it is possible to use a special technique in those guns. To fire-form, use a standard .30-06 case (sized), seat a jacketed bullet hard against the rifling so that the gun will just close. Correct powder charge is about 5 percent below the maximum SSK-recommended load. Jones recommends 150-grain bullets for big-game hunting applications on smaller species, and bullets up to 200 grains on larger species. With the velocity potential of this chambering, premium bullets are probably a superior choice for hunting applications. While one could use 140-grain Barnes X bullets, which can offer impressive terminal performance, the handloader must use X bullet-specific loading data and special handloading techniques (i.e., the bullet ogive must be seated a minimum of .05-inch from the rifling). For this reason, SSK does not support use of the X-stle bullets in its guns. Further those bullets work best when a reduced-friction coating (such as moly-plating) is used. While no bullet substitution is benign, never substitute any X-style bullet in any load, rather begin with data specifically created for that bullet. For information on components, loading data, barrels, and guns designed for this cartridge, contact SSK Industries, (720) 264-0176 or www.sskindustries.com.

30-06 JDJ Loading Data (Note: These loads for use only in SSK barrels.)

Bullet (grains/type)	Powder	Grains	Velocity	Energy	Source/Comments
125	IMR 4064	62.0	3,167	2,785	SSK/maximum load/SSK barrels only
150	IMR 4064	60.0	2,930	2,860	SSK/maximum load/SSK barrels only
165 Hornady	RI-15	58.3	2,790	2,850	SSK/maximum load/SSK barrels only
180 Speer	RI-19	66.2	2,666	2,840	SSK/maximum load/SSK barrels only
200 Speer	Vit N560	63.4	2,504	2,785	SSK/maximum load/SSK barrels only

.300 Dakota

Historical Notes: The .300 Dakota is based upon the .404 Jeffery case. In this application, the case is shortened to create a cartridge of .30-06 length (3.34 inches). The rim of the .300 Dakota is slightly larger than the rim on a standard belted-magnum case, so, besides re-chambering, the gunsmith must also perform a minor bolt-face alteration. In any given-length cartridge, use of the non-belted .404 Jeffery case provides about a 15-percent increase in usable case capacity, compared to the standard belted case. Because maximum case diameter is slightly larger (.544-inch versus .532-inch), magazine capacity is usually reduced by one round. However, minor gunsmithing alterations will usually remedy that situation.

General Comments: The .300 Dakota functions properly through standard-length actions (3.35 inches). This cartridge provides a significant capacity advantage over the .300 Winchester Magnum and comes close to duplicating capacity and performance of the much longer .300 Weatherby Magnum. Re-chambering to .300 Dakota is possible in most rifles originally chambered for any standard belted .300 Magnum. One thereby gains the improved feeding and accuracy advantages offered by this non-belted case. If loaded to similar pressures using appropriate powders, the .300 Dakota offers a worthwhile velocity advantage over the .300 Winchester Magnum. For those interested in an all-around .30-caliber hunting cartridge, the .300 Dakota is worth considering. The .300 Weatherby does have a slight capacity advantage, but the ballistic difference is marginal, and Weatherby's cartridge requires a longer action. Contact Dakota Arms for more information: (605) 347-4686 or www.dakotaarms.com.

.300 Dakota Loading Data and Factory Ballistics

Bullet (grains)	Powder	Grains	Velocity	Energy	Source/Comments
165	IMR 4350	77.0	3,247	3,860	Dakota/maximum load
165	H4831	82.0	3,283	3,945	Dakota/maximum load
165	RI-22	83.0	3,307	4,000	Dakota/maximum load
165	IMR 7828	85.0	3,277	3,930	Dakota/maximum load
180	H4831	77.5	3,114	3,875	Dakota/maximum load
180	RI-22	81.0	3,249	4,215	Dakota/maximum load
180	IMR 7828	82.0	3,221	4,140	Dakota/maximum load
200	H4831	77.5	2,965	3,900	Dakota/maximum load
200	RI-22	78.0	3,052	4,130	Dakota/maximum load
200	IMR 7828	80.5	3,026	4,060	Dakota/maximum load
200	H1000	82.5	2,986	3,955	Dakota/maximum load
150	FL	N/A	3,300	3,626	Dakota factory load
180	FL	N/A	3,100	3,840	Dakota factory load

.300 Pegasus

Historical Notes: This 1994 chambering is based upon an entirely original case that features a .580-inch head size. The rim is essentially identical to the .378 Weatherby case, but the design has no belt. Therefore, case capacity is substantially greater for any given cartridge length. This standard rimless bottleneck design also facilitates proper chambering with tight tolerances. Design intent was the acceleration of 180-grain hunting bullets to a velocity in excess of 3500 fps from a 26-inch barrel, without exceeding about 62,000 psi (piezo transducer pressure units)—a typical modern cartridge pressure limit. The .300 Pegasus easily achieves this goal.

General Comments: This cartridge seems a good choice for those who feel they need a flat-shooting round that can deliver substantial energy to targets at long range. Rifles originally chambered for the .378 and .460 Weatherby numbers can be rebarreled to accept this cartridge. The slowest handloader powders now available offer the best velocity potential. In a typical rifle, recoil would have to be classed as a bit heavy, and barrel life is quite limited.

.300 Pegasus Loading Data and Factory Ballistics

Bullet (grains/type)	Powder	Grains	Velocity	Energy	Source/Comments
150 Nosler BT	IMR 7828	N/A	3,642	4,420	A-Square/maximum load
150 Nosler BT	RI-22	N/A	3,675	4,495	A-Square/maximum load
150 Nosler BT	AA 8700	N/A	3,703	4,565	A-Square/maximum load
180 Nosler BT	RI-22	N/A	3,371	4,540	A-Square/maximum load
180 Nosler BT	IMR 7828	N/A	3,413	4,655	A-Square/maximum load
180 Nosler BT	AA 8700	N/A	3,456	4,775	A-Square/maximum load
180 Nosler BT	H870	N/A	3,505	4,910	A-Square/maximum load
150 Nosler BT	FL	N/A	3,780	4,760	A-Square Factory load
180 Nosler BT	FL	N/A	3,523	4,960	A-Square Factory load

7.82 Patriot

Historical Notes:	Lazzeroni Arms designed this cartridge in 1997. While somewhat related to an older case, for all practical purposes, this is a new case design. This cartridge was created in response to requests for a high-performance cartridge that would work in a 2.8-inch action yet deliver the ballistics of a full-length belted magnum. While feasible, adaptation to a standard action (3.35-inch) is not recommended.
General Comments:	Bullet diameter is .308-inch (Lazzeroni bases its designations on bullet diameter instead of bore diameter, which is the common practice). Ballistics are quite impressive for such a short cartridge. Given equal-length barrels, the Patriot essentially duplicates .300 Winchester Magnum ballistics. Case design is typical of the Lazzeroni line: moderate body taper, 30-degree shoulder, sufficiently long neck, and thick rim of approximate case-body diameter. In other words, this is a well-designed case. This cartridge has already become quite popular and successful in the various 1,000-yard target-shooting games. Dick Davis, of Lazzeroni Arms, is doing quite well with it. This case is the basis for several wildcat and target chamberings (6mm Thermos Bottle, 6mm LBFM, 6.5 LBFM, 7mm LBFM, and .30-LBFM.) For more information on Lazzeroni custom guns, ammunition, and reloading data, contact (888) 492-7247 or www.lazzeroni.com.

7.82 Patriot Factory Ballistics (24-inch barrel)

Bullet (grains)	Powder	Grains	Velocity	Energy	Source/Comments
130	FL		3,550	3635	Lazzeroni factory load
150	FL		3,300	3628	Lazzeroni factory load
180	FL		3,100	3842	Lazzeroni factory load
200	FL		2,950	3866	Lazzeroni factory load

7.82 Warbird

Historical Notes: Lazzeroni Arms designed this cartridge in 1995. While somewhat related to an older case, for all practical purposes this is a new case design. John Lazzeroni believes that those hunters who will take the time to become competent marksmen can legitimately take game at ranges out to about 500 yards, given a gun with the requisite accuracy and a bullet that will perform properly. This cartridge was created to provide sufficient velocity for medium-weight hunting bullets to provide dependable expansion at maximum ranges and to have sufficient energy for taking larger species at longer ranges. Adaptation to standard actions is feasible, but is not recommended.

General Comments: Bullet diameter is .308-inch. (Lazzeroni bases its designations on bullet diameter instead of bore diameter, which is the common practice.) Ballistics equal or exceed any other factory .30-caliber cartridge. Case design is typical of the Lazzeroni line: moderate body taper, 30-degree shoulder, sufficiently long neck, and thick rim of approximate case-body diameter. In other words, this is a well-designed case. Designed specifically for hunting, and with limited barrel life, this cartridge is not recommended for any other use. While 27-inch barrels are standard, all the smaller-caliber, full-length Lazzeroni numbers would benefit significantly from even longer barrels. Most of Lazzeroni's full-length cartridge loadings use specially lubricated (proprietary process) premium bullets from Nosler, Barnes, or Swift. These are the only bullets providing the necessary accuracy and terminal performance to meet Lazzeroni's strict requirements. One could argue that this is a superior all-around choice for lighter species. The premium 130-grain bullet will handle most species in North America, while a 200-grain bullet is adequate for most critters anywhere in the world. For more information on Lazzeroni custom guns, ammunition, and reloading data, contact (888) 492-7247 or www.lazzeroni.com.

7.82 Warbird Factory Ballistics (27-inch barrel)

Bullet (grains)	Powder	Grains	Velocity	Energy	Source/Comments
130	FL	N/A	4,000	4,620	Lazzeroni factory load
150	FL	N/A	3,800	4,810	Lazzeroni factory load
165	FL	N/A	3,600	4,750	Lazzeroni factory load
180	FL	N/A	3,550	5,040	Lazzeroni factory load
200	FL	N/A	3,350	4,985	Lazzeroni factory load

.300 Canadian Magnum

Historical Notes: This cartridge was developed about 1989 by North American Shooting Systems (NASS) and is somewhat similar to the .300 Imperial Magnum. This design features a slightly rebated, rimless bottleneck case. Design intent was to provide maximum powder capacity available in a standard action with minimal gunsmithing. (Without deepening the magazine well slightly, magazine capacity is usually reduced by one round.) Bolt face alteration is unnecessary. Cartridge feeding and headspacing characteristics are improved.

General Comments: The Canadian Magnum series are similar to those in the Dakota cartridge family in both design and purpose. However, this cartridge takes advantage of the entire 3.65-inch magazine length of the long-action Remington M700 and similar rifles. On the Canadian Magnums, body diameter is significantly larger than the standard belted magnum (.544-inch versus .513-inch at the base). Re-chambering of nominal belted magnums with the same bore diameter is generally quite simple, requiring no other rifle alterations. For any given case length, capacity is about 15 percent greater than can be achieved with the standard belted magnum case. Body taper is minimal and the shoulder is comparatively sharp. However, neck length is sufficiently generous to provide good bullet purchase for hunting ammunition. Performance is commensurate with the generous capacity and pressures used in these loadings. Barrel life is a consideration—there are no free lunches. Note: This cartridge is similar to Remington's Ultra round.

Bullet (grains)	Powder	Grains	Velocity	Energy	Source/Comments
165	H4831	86.0	3,231	3,820	NASS/maximum load
165	RI-22	87.0	3,434	4,315	NASS/maximum load
165	IMR 7828	89.5	3,466	4,395	NASS/maximum load
180	RI-22	83.0	3,354	4,490	NASS/maximum load
180	IMR 7828	87.5	3,367	4,525	NASS/maximum load
180	H1000	92.0	3,163	3,995	NASS/maximum load
200	RI-22	79.0	3,053	4,135	NASS/maximum load
200	IMR 7828	82.0	3,093	4,245	NASS/maximum load
200	H870	95.0	3,070	4,180	NASS/maximum load
180	FL	N/A	3,425	4,685	NASS factory load

8mm JDJ

Historical Notes: Designed by J.D. Jones of SSK Industries about 1980, this cartridge uses the .444 Marlin case necked down to 8mm with a sharp shoulder. Design intent was a Thompson/Center chambering that would surpass .35 Remington rifle ballistics.

General Comments: With a 200-grain Nosler Partition loaded to top handgun velocity (2100 fps), this chambering can deliver substantial energy within the useful range. The Barnes 180-grain X bullets can deliver superior terminal performance, but its use requires special handloading techniques (deeper bullet seating and a reduction in powder charge). Effectiveness on the lightest of species is improved with Hornady's 150-grain bullet at 2400 fps muzzle velocity. For information on components, loading data, barrels, and guns designed for this cartridge, contact SSK Industries, (720) 264-0176 or www.sskindustries.com.

8mm JDJ Loading Data (Note: These loads for use only in SSK barrels.)

Bullet (grains/type)	Powder	Grains	Velocity	Energy	Source/Comments
150 Hornady	IMR 4320	47.5	2,286	1,740	SSK/maximum load/SSK barrel only (14")
150 Hornady	H322	47.5	2,420	1,950	SSK/maximum load/SSK barrel only (14")
170 Hornady	IMR 4320	47.5	2,254	1,915	SSK/maximum load/SSK barrel only (14")
170 Hornady	AA 2520	49.5	2,373	2,125	SSK/maximum load/SSK barrel only (14")
200 Speer	H4350	52.0	2,192	2,130	SSK/maximum load/SSK barrel only (14")
225	H4350	51.5	2,131	2,265	SSK/maximum load/SSK barrel only (14")

.338 Woodswalker

Historical Notes: Created during the late 1990s by J.D. Jones of SSK Industries, the .338 Woodswalker was designed specifically for use in the T/C Contender pistol with a 10-inch barrel. The case is formed by necking up and fire-forming the European-designed 8.15x46R case for .338-inch bullets. At the time of this cartridge's development, those cases were being imported by RWS.

General Comments: One of very few to write about the .338 Woodswalker was Layne Simpson, who used it to take several whitetail deer and wild boar. When fired in a 10-inch barrel, it is not far behind the velocity of the old .33 Winchester and, for this reason, the 200-grain flat-nose bullet made by Hornady for that cartridge is the best choice for deer. Unfortunately, it has been discontinued, and other bullets of its caliber are constructed for much higher velocities. The Nosler 180-grain AccuBond and 200-grain Ballistic Tip work satisfactorily on deer out to about 150 yards, but expansion decreases rapidly as the range is increased beyond that. For information on components, loading data, barrels, and guns designed for this cartridge, contact SSK Industries, (720) 264-0176 or www.sskindustries.com.

.338 Woodswalker Loading Data and Factory Ballistics

Bullet (grains/type)	Powder	Grains	Velocity	Energy	Source
180 Nosler AccuBond	H335	41.0	2,044	1,668	Layne Simpson
200 Nosler Ballistic Tip	H335	39.5	1,927	1,647	Layne Simpson
200 Nosler Ballistic Tip	H4198	33.0	2,009	1,790	Layne Simpson
200 Hornady FP	H335	39.5	1,910	1,618	Layne Simpson
200 Hornady FP	RL-7	32.0	1,852	1,522	Layne Simpson
200 Hornady FP	H4198	33.0	1,979	1,737	Layne Simpson
200 Hornady FP	BL-C(2)	40.0	1,908	1,615	Layne Simpson
200 Hornady FP	W748	39.0	1,867	1,546	Layne Simpson
210 Nosler Partition	BL-C(2)	37.0	1,909	1,697	Layne Simpson

WARNING: All powder charges are maximum and must be reduced by 10 percent for starting loads.

.338 Whisper

Historical Notes: Designed by J.D. Jones of SSK Industries in the early 1990s, this chambering is the 7mm BR opened up to accept .338-inch bullets with no other changes. JDJ's intention was the delivery of significant long-range energy from a low-noise rifle. This combination certainly succeeded in attaining that goal.

General Comments: Usually this cartridge is chambered in rebarreled .308 Winchester rifles. With a quick rifling twist, 300-grain Sierra MatchKings will deliver superb accuracy past 600 yards. Long-range penetration and energy are surprising. For information on components, loading data, barrels, and guns designed for this cartridge, contact SSK Industries, (720) 264-0176 or www.sskindustries.com.

.338 Whisper Loading Data

Bullet (grains/type)	Powder	Grains	Velocity	Energy	Source/Comments
200 Nosler BT	H4227	11.5	1,075	510	SSK/subsonic/12" barrel
200 Nosler BT	HP-38	8.8	1,077	515	SSK/subsonic/12" barrel
250 Nosler BT	HP-38	9.6	1,029	585	SSK/subsonic/12" barrel
250 Nosler BT	Vit N350	10.8	1,040	600	SSK/subsonic/12" barrel
300 Nosler BT	Vit N350	12.3	1,040	720	SSK/subsonic/12" barrel
300 Nosler BT	HP-38	10.8	1,050	735	SSK/subsonic/12" barrel

.338 Spectre

Historical Notes: The .338 Spectre was developed by Marty ter Weeme, founder of Teppo Jutsu LLC. He was also the developer of the .458 SOCOM. The Spectre is the result of improvements to the earlier .358 CQB cartridge, which came about during the design of the .458 SOCOM. The concept behind the .338 Spectre was to offer a cartridge with broad-spectrum application, but one that was primarily designed to deliver a heavy, subsonic bullet with a very high ballistic coefficient at extended distances. The designer boasts that the .338 Spectre is capable of MOA accuracy out to 500 yards. Like the .300 AAC Blackout, the .338 Spectre was developed to also provide supersonic and subsonic loads from the same weapon system. The cartridge is based on a shortened 6.8 SPC case that has been necked up to .338-caliber. All of the dimensions in the accompanying drawing—with the exception of the shoulder angle and case length from the base to the shoulder—were provided by Marty ter Weeme, who told me he hopes to "... avoid having non-licensed folks copying the reamer ... ." These unknown dimensions were estimated by measuring.

General Comments: The ballistics of the .338 Spectre cartridge are similar to that of a .357 Magnum. However, it should be noted that commercial .338-caliber bullets are not designed to expand at such low velocities. Still, the cartridge is quite versatile and does have some tactical applications. Subsonic loads will work through and can be suppressed by a 9mm-caliber suppressor. And, with an overall cartridge length similar to that of the .223 Remington, 7.62x39, and 6.8 SPC, it will work from the AR-15 platform. Handloading dies can be obtained from CH Tool & Die or the Hornady Custom Shop. Loaded ammunition is available from Southern Ballistics Research: (912) 264-5822 or www.sbr-usa.com.

.338 Spectre Loading Data and Factory Ballistics

Bullet (grains/type)	Powder	Grains	Velocity	Energy	Source/Comments
	H 4350	57	2,710	2,935	Gary Reeder
250 Hornady	AA 1680	17.0	1,300	938	SBR
300 Sierra BTHP	IMR 4227	9.5	985	646	SBR
250 Hornady	FL	N/A	1,450	1,166	SBR Factory Load
300 Sierra HPBT	FL	N/A	990	652	SBR Factory Load

.338 Allen Magnum

Historical Notes: Based on the .375 Cheyenne Tactical (.375 CheyTac) case, Kirby Allen, of Allen Precision Shooting, designed the .338 Allen Magnum specifically for hunting medium to heavy big game at long distances. Terminal performance of the .338 Allen Magnum with most bullets actually improves once targeting range extends past 1,000 yards. This is because the retained velocity has dropped to a level more suitable for most bullet designs. It's an ideal long-range elk round. The .338 Allen Magnum, when loaded with a 300-grain Sierra MatchKing, offers a 500- to 600-fps muzzle velocity advantage over the .338 Lapua Magnum.

General Comments: This is pretty much the top of the performance ladder, even when taking into consideration .50-caliber rounds. The round's very large chambering requires a complete custom receiver designed specifically for the CheyTac parent case. Rifles are long and heavy, starting at 15 pounds minimum for single-shots and up to 19 pounds for standard Xtreme Heavy Sporter Rifles. The primary bullets used in the .338 Allen

Magnum are the 300-grain Sierra MatchKing and the 300-grain Berger Hybrid Gen 2 bullets. At 1,800 yards, velocity is 1,781 fps and energy is 2,114 ft-lbs with a 300-grain Berger HG2. Fully formed brass is available from APS with rifle orders, along with loading dies and load data. For more information, check the website APSRifles.com or e-mail Kirby Allen at allenmagnum@gmail.com.—*W.T.W.*

.338 Allen Magnum Loading Data (Note: *Hodgdon H-50BMG, Vhitavuori 20N29)

Bullet (grains/type)	Powder	Grains	Velocity	Energy	Source/Comments
265 Barnes TTSX	*	N/A	3,550	7,413	Allen Precision Shooting
300 Berger HG2	*	N/A	3,350	7,473	Allen Precision Shooting

.338 JDJ

Historical Notes: Like several other chamberings based upon the same basic case (.444 Marlin), this cartridge was designed and developed by J.D. Jones about 1978. Barrels in this chambering are furnished by SSK Industries. The purpose is to provide increased power and range for T/C Contender and other single-shot hunting handguns. Like most of the JDJ line, these cases are easily formed from the parent case.

General Comments: Based on the .444 Marlin necked down, this chambering provides ample capacity and bullet area to produce impressive muzzle energy, especially with longer handgun-length barrels (14 to 16 inches). With bullets of only slightly lighter weight, the .338 JDJ offers muzzle velocities similar to the .375 Winchester, when fired from a rifle. Since this cartridge uses spitzer bullets, performance at normal hunting ranges is significantly superior to the parent .444 Marlin. Conventional bullets of 180 to 220 grains are good choices. However, the Barnes 160-grain X bullet can deliver superior terminal performance, reduced recoil, and a flatter trajectory, but requires special handloading techniques (e.g., deeper bullet seating and a reduction in powder charge). With proper hunting bullets loaded to maximum velocity (necessary to ensure proper terminal performance), recoil can be rather stiff. For information on components, loading data, barrels, and guns designed for this cartridge, contact SSK Industries, (720) 264-0176 or www.sskindustries.com.

.338 JDJ Loading Data and Ballistics

Bullet (grains)	Powder	Grains	Velocity	Energy	Source/Comments
225	Win 760	42.5	1,561	1,217	SSK 12" barrel
250	Win 760	42.5	1,488	1,228	SSK 12" barrel
275	IMR 4831	945.5	1,609	1,580	SSK 12" barrel

.338 A-Square

Historical Notes: This 1978 design is a modified .378 Weatherby Magnum necked down to accept .338-inch bullets. The intention was to provide a flat-shooting cartridge capable of delivering substantial energy to medium-sized game animals at normal hunting ranges. It can deliver massive energy to long-range targets. With minor modifications, most 3.65-inch bolt-action magazines will handle this cartridge.

General Comments: Ballistics are close to A-Square's .338 Excaliber, but this cartridge will not feed from a magazine as smoothly as that beltless design. The basic design incorporates a sharp shoulder for good headspace control but features a comparatively generous body taper. Ballistics are impressive. For more information on, contact (605) 234-0500 (South Dakota), (307) 436-5677 (Wyoming) or www.a-squareco.com.

Bullet (grains/type)	Powder	Grains	Velocity	Energy	Source/Comments
200 Nosler BT	H4831	104.0	3,259	4,715	A-Square/maximum load
200 Nosler BT	IMR 7828	106.0	3,353	4,990	A-Square/maximum load
200 Nosler BT	RI-22	104.0	3,355	4,995	A-Square/maximum load
250 Sierra SBT	IMR 7828	95.0	2,879	4,600	A-Square/maximum load
250 Sierra SBT	RI-22	95.0	2,965	4,880	A-Square/maximum load
250 Sierra SBT	H870	118.0	3,094	5,310	A-Square/maximum load
250 Sierra SBT	AA 8700	120.0	3,100	5,330	A-Square/maximum load
200 Nosler BT	FL	N/A	3,500	5,435	A-Square factory load
250 Sierra SBT	FL	N/A	3,120	5,400	A-Square factory load
250 Triad	FL	N/A	3,120	5,400	A-Square factory load

8.59 Galaxy

Historical Notes: Lazzeroni Arms designed this cartridge in 1997. While somewhat related to an older case, for all practical purposes, this is a new case design. This cartridge was created in response to requests for a high-performance cartridge that would work in a 2.8-inch action, yet deliver the ballistics of a full-length belted magnum. Adaptation to a standard action is feasible, but is not recommended.

General Comments: Bullet diameter is .338-inch (Lazzeroni bases its designations on bullet diameter instead of bore diameter, which is the common practice.) Ballistics are quite impressive for such a short cartridge. Given equal-length barrels, the Galaxy easily exceeds the .338 Winchester Magnum. Case design is typical of the Lazzeroni line: moderate body taper, 30-degree shoulder, sufficiently long neck, and thick rim of approximate case-body diameter. It is a well-designed case. For more information on Lazzeroni custom guns, ammunition, and reloading data, contact (888) 492-7247 or www.lazzeroni.com.

8.59 Galaxy Factory Ballistics (24-inch barrel)

Bullet (grains)	Powder	Grains	Velocity	Energy	Source/Comments
200	FL	N/A	3,100	4,269	Lazzeroni factory load
225	FL	N/A	2,950	4,349	Lazzeroni factory load
250	FL	N/A	2,750	4,199	Lazzeroni factory load

.338 Lehigh

Historical Notes: Developed to offer a larger caliber, harder hitting option for hunters and tactical operatives using the AR-15 platform, the .338 Lehigh is based on the 6.5 Grendel cartridge from Alexander Arms. Both the .338 Lehigh and the 6.5 Grendel are based on the old Russian 7.62x39mm cartridge. The development of the

.338 Lehigh comes on the heels of the introduction of the .300 AAC Blackout cartridge and fills the same niche, that being a larger caliber AR-15 cartridge capable of both subsonic and supersonic performance. From a subsonic standpoint, the .338 Lehigh is similar to the .338 Spectre, but due to the Lehigh's larger case capacity, it well outperforms the Spectre when loaded to supersonic velocities.

General Comments: Conversions for .338 Lehigh AR-15s are simple with rifles that have a 0.441 bolt face, like the .65 Grendel and the 7.62X39mm, i.e., a new barrel is all that is needed. Bolt guns chambered for the 7.62x39mm can be converted to the .338 Lehigh just as easily. The .338 Lehigh offers superior supersonic ballistics, when compared to both the .300 AAC Blackout and the .338 Spectre. It can drive a 145-grain bullet in excess of 2400 fps. This would make a great multi-purpose tactical cartridge and would be great for hunting big game at close to moderate ranges. Ammunition, dies, brass, and bullets for both subsonic and supersonic applications are available from Lehigh Defense at (267) 217-3539 or www.lehighdefense.com.

.338 Lehigh Loading Data

Bullet (grains/type)	Powder	Grains	Velocity	Energy	Source
145 Lehigh CFHP	AA 1680	24	2,410	1,869	Lehigh Defense Factory Load
240 Lehigh Subsonic	AA No. 2	9.0	1,050	489	Lehigh Defense Factory Load

.338 Federal (.33-08)

Historical Notes: There was a time when, immediately after the introduction of a new cartridge, wildcatters would scream out with glee and neck its case up and down to various calibers. They had a field day in 1952 when the .308 Winchester arrived on the scene. Winchester quickly covered two bases with its .243 Winchester and .358 Winchester cartridges, and, many years later, Remington took a couple of wildcats under its wing and called them the .260 Remington and 7mm-08 Remington. One that got away for an even longer period of time was the .33-08 which, as its name implies, is the .308 case necked up for bullets of .338 caliber. One of the first reports on this one was filed by Roy Smith in *Rifle* magazine. A fan of the Winchester Model 88 lever-action rifle, Smith had one of those rifles rebarreled to .33-08. Federal adopted the cartridge in 2006 and renamed it the .338 Federal.

General Comments: When it comes to performance on game, the .33-08 and the .358 Winchester are in the same league, but the .33-caliber cartridge has the advantage of a better selection of bullets for handloading. Same goes for factory ammunition. Only one loading of the .358 is available from Winchester, while Federal offers seven .338 Federal loadings as this volume goes to print. Like the .338 Federal, this cartridge is seen at its best on big game when loaded with bullets weighing from 200 to 225 grains, with the Nosler 210-grain Partition an old favorite. Starting loads published by various reloading component manufacturers for the .338 Federal can be used in this cartridge as well.

.338 Canadian Magnum

Historical Notes: This cartridge was developed about 1989 by North American Shooting Systems (NASS) and is somewhat similar to the .338 Imperial Magnum. This design features a slightly rebated rimless bottleneck case. Design intent was to provide maximum powder capacity available in a standard action with minimal gunsmithing. (Without deepening the magazine well slightly, magazine capacity is usually reduced by one round.) Bolt face alteration is not necessary. Cartridge feeding and headspacing characteristics are improved.

General Comments: The Canadian Magnum series is similar to the Dakota cartridge family in both design and purpose. However, this cartridge takes advantage of the entire 3.65-inch magazine length of the long-action Remington M700 and similar rifles. On the Canadian Magnums, body diameter is significantly larger than the standard belted magnum (.544-inch versus .513-inch at the base). Re-chambering of nominal belted magnums with the same bore diameter is generally quite simple, requiring no other rifle alterations. For any given case length, capacity is about 15 percent greater than can be achieved with the standard belted-magnum case. Body taper is minimal, and the case shoulder is comparatively sharp. However, neck length is sufficiently generous to provide good bullet purchase for hunting ammunition. Performance is commensurate with the capacity and pressures used in these loadings. As with the .300 Canadian Magnum, one is impressed with the similarity to Remington's Ultra cartridge in the same bore size.

.338 Canadian Magnum Loading Data and Factory Ballistics

Bullet (grains)	Powder	Grains	Velocity	Energy	Source/Comments
225	IMR 4831	88.0	3,083	4,745	NASS/maximum load
225	H4831	91.0	3,047	4,635	NASS/maximum load
250	IMR 4831	88.0	2,924	4,740	NASS/maximum load
250	RI-19	89.0	2,977	4,915	NASS/maximum load
250	H4831	91.0	2,951	4,830	NASS/maximum load
225	FL	N/A	3,110	4,830	NASS factory load

8.59 Titan

Historical Notes: Lazzeroni Arms designed this cartridge in 1994 based upon an earlier 1992 design. This was the first Lazzeroni cartridge. While somewhat related to an older case, for practical purposes, this is a new case design. John Lazzeroni believes that those hunters who will take the time to become competent marksmen can legitimately take game at longer ranges. This cartridge was created to launch medium- to heavy-weight hunting bullets with sufficient velocity to provide dependable expansion at longer ranges and to have sufficient energy for taking the largest species. Adaptation to standard actions is feasible, but is not recommended.

General Comments: Bullet diameter is .338-inch (Lazzeroni bases its designations on bullet diameter instead of bore diameter, which is the common practice). Ballistics equal or exceed any factory .33-caliber cartridge. Case design is typical of the Lazzeroni line: moderate body taper, 30-degree shoulder, sufficiently long neck, and thick rim of approximate case-body diameter. In other words, this is a well-designed case. While designed specifically for hunting, this cartridge does have application to long-range target shooting. Standard barrel length is 27 inches, which provides a good measure of the ballistic potential of this cartridge. Most of Lazzeroni's full-length cartridge loadings use specially lubricated (proprietary process) premium bullets from Nosler, Barnes, or Swift. These are the only bullets providing the necessary accuracy and terminal performance to meet Lazzeroni's strict requirements. He designed this as the ultimate North American hunting cartridge for the hunter who is interested primarily in elk. His experience with a .33-caliber magnum that would not deliver the accuracy necessary to take an elk cleanly at somewhat beyond 350 yards prompted this development and the entire subsequent Lazzeroni line. For more information on Lazzeroni custom guns, ammunition, and reloading data, contact (888) 492-7247 or www.lazzeroni.com.

8.59 Titan Factory Ballistics (27-inch barrel)

Bullet (grains)	Powder	Grains	Velocity	Energy	Source/Comments
200	FL	N/A	3,450	5,287	Lazzeroni factory load *
225	FL	N/A	3,300	5,442	Lazzeroni factory load *
250	FL	N/A	3,150	5,510	Lazzeroni factory load *

*RI-25 will produce superior velocity, but accuracy has so far been dismal. RI-19 is the preferred powder for this cartridge.

.338 GNR

Historical Notes: Developed in early 1985 by Gary Reeder, the .338 GNR was specifically designed for an African safari. Reeder wanted an extra-long-range cartridge for a Thompson/Center Contender, one that still had plenty of power for 650- to 750-pound animals. The .338 GNR is based on the .405 Winchester case.

General Comments: Reeder has used the .338 GNR on a number of big-game hunts with great success. It does best with bullets in the 180- to 225-grain weight range. Due to the large amounts of powder this cartridge consumes, Contender barrels in the 15- to 16-inch range work best. Gary Reeder also recommends a muzzle brake to prolong scope life, as the recoil is quite intense. Information on custom guns, ammunition, and reloading data can be obtained by contacting Gary Reeder Custom Guns, (928) 527-4100 or www.reedercustomguns.com.

.338 GNR Loading Data and Ballistics

Bullet (grains/type)	Powder	Grains	Velocity	Energy	Source
180 SP	H 4350	57	2,710	2,935	Gary Reeder
225 SP	Reloader 15	50	2,510	3,147	Gary Reeder

.338-06 JDJ

Historical Notes: This cartridge was designed by J.D. Jones of SSK Industries. Application is to Thompson/Center Encore single-shot pistols fitted with a custom SSK barrel. Typical barrel length is 15 inches. Cases are formed from .30-06 or .35 Whelen cases by special means and cannot be fire-formed from any other case. Neck length is minimal, which is acceptable for a cartridge used in a single-shot gun. Shoulder angle is 60 degrees, which seems to work just fine. Body taper is minimal, similar to Ackley's Improved designs. Therefore, this is a maximized .338-06 case. Capacity is a whopping 76 grains of water, which is significantly greater than the .338-06 (about 71). Working pressure is about 60,000 psi, so ballistics are quite impressive. Best handloads in SSK barrels can approach .338-08 A-Square (rifle) ballistics.

General Comments: Since this case has no rim, it is not generally safe to directly fire-form it in the conventional manner. However, owing to the captive extractor system used in the Encore, it is possible to use a special technique in those guns, to wit: Resize and neck-expand a .30-06 case, then seat a .338-inch jacketed bullet hard against the rifling so that the gun will just close. Correct powder charge is about 5 percent below the maximum SSK-recommended load. Jones recommends 180-grain bullets for big-game hunting applications on smaller species, and bullets up to 250 grains on larger species. This cartridge generates sufficient energy for hunting on any continent. Not all shooters have equal abilities and tolerances—while Jones' 9-year old grandson proved capable of handling this combination, recoil may exceed what some adult shooters can handle. For information on components, loading data, barrels, and guns designed for this cartridge, contact SSK Industries, (720) 264-0176 or www.sskindustries.com.

.338-06 JDJ Loading Data

Bullet (grains/type)	Powder	Grains	Velocity	Energy	Source/Comments
175 Barnes X	IMR 4064	62.5	2,863	3,185	SSK/max. load, SSK barrels only

Bullet (grains/type)	Powder	Grains	Velocity	Energy	Source/Comments
180 Nosler BT	IMR 4064	62.5	2,850	3,245	SSK/max. load, SSK barrels only
200 Hornady	IMR 4064	61.5	2,693	3,220	SSK/max. load, SSK barrels only
225 Speer BT	IMR 4064	60.5	2,643	3,490	SSK/max. load, SSK barrels only
250 Speer GS	IMR 4064	58.0	2,481	3,415	SSK/max. load, SSK barrels only

.330 Dakota

Historical Notes: The .330 Dakota is based upon a shortened version of the rimless bottleneck .404 Jeffery case. The .330 Dakota is dimensioned to function through a standard-length action (3.35 inches). Design intent was to offer a factory alternative to the .338 Winchester Magnum with .340 Weatherby performance. This also offers .338 Winchester Magnum rifle owners a simple conversion to improve ballistics and cartridge-feeding characteristics.

General Comments: Like the 7mm and .300 Dakota cartridges, the .330 Dakota functions properly through .30-06 length (3.35-inch) actions. This cartridge provides a significant case capacity advantage over the .338 Winchester Magnum (about 15 percent) and comes very close to duplicating capacity and performance of the much longer .340 Weatherby Magnum. Most rifles chambered for the .338 Winchester Magnum are easily converted to .330 Dakota. This conversion offers advantages in function, accuracy, and ballistics, because of the non-belted case. If loaded to similar pressures with appropriate powders, the .330 Dakota should produce 5 percent more velocity (10 percent more energy) than Winchester's .338 Magnum. With the heaviest bullets, the advantage is more significant. For those interested in a hunting cartridge geared to larger big game, the .330 Dakota is a serious contender. Combined with the right bullets, this flat-shooting cartridge can deliver more energy to targets a quarter-mile away than factory .270 ammunition produces at the muzzle! The .340 Weatherby does have a slight capacity advantage, but the ballistic difference is marginal, and Weatherby's cartridge requires the use of a longer action. For hunters who want maximum performance from the .338-inch bore, the Canadian Magnum, A-Square, and Lazzeroni offerings are better choices. Contact Dakota Arms for more information: (605) 347-4686 or www.dakotaarms.com.

.330 Dakota Loading Data and Factory Ballistics

Bullet (grains)	Powder	Grains	Velocity	Energy	Source/Comments
200	IMR 4350	80.0	3,082	4,215	Dakota/maximum load
200	RI-22	86.5	3,146	4,390	Dakota/maximum load
200	H4831	88.0	3,200	4,545	Dakota/maximum load
200	IMR 7828	88.0	3,100	4,265	Dakota/maximum load
250	IMR 4350	76.0	2,853	4,515	Dakota/maximum load
250	RI-22	80.5	2,849	4,500	Dakota/maximum load
250	H4831	81.5	2,878	4,595	Dakota/maximum load
250	IMR 7828	82.0	2,829	4,440	Dakota/maximum load
210	FL	N/A	3,200	4,480	Dakota factory load
250	FL	N/A	2,900	4,668	Dakota factory load

.338 Excaliber

Historical Notes: This 1994 chambering is based upon an entirely new case that features a .580-inch head size. The rim is essentially identical to the .378 Weatherby case, but there is no useless belt. Therefore, case capacity is substantially greater for any given cartridge length. This standard rimless bottleneck design also facilitates proper chambering with tight tolerances. Design intent was acceleration of a 200-grain hunting bullet in excess of 3500 fps without exceeding about 62,000 psi (piezo transducer pressure units)—a typical pressure for modern cartridges. The .338 Excaliber accomplishes this goal.

General Comments: This cartridge is a superior choice for those who feel they need a flat-shooting cartridge that can deliver substantial energy to medium-sized game targets at long-range. Rifles originally chambered for the .378 and .460 can be re-barreled to accept this cartridge. The slowest handloader powders now available offer the best velocity potential. In a typical rifle, recoil would have to be classed as heavy, especially when shooting heavier bullets. As is normal with .338-inch chamberings, trajectories are essentially indistinguishable from the similar .30-caliber counterpart, but with the delivery of a heavier bullet carrying more energy.

.338 Excaliber Loading Data

Bullet (grains/type)	Powder	Grains	Velocity	Energy	Source/Comments
200 Nosler BT	RI-22	113.0	3,434	5,240	A-Square/maximum load
200 Nosler BT	H870	138.0	3,480	5,380	A-Square/maximum load
200 Nosler BT	AA 8700	140.0	3,493	5,415	A-Square/maximum load
200 Nosler BT	IMR 7828	116.0	3,497	5,430	A-Square/maximum load
250 Sierra SBT	IMR 7827	105.0	2,966	4,885	A-Square/maximum load
250 Sierra SBT	H5010	128.0	3,109	5,365	A-Square/maximum load
250 Sierra SBT	RI-22	110.0	3,192	5,655	A-Square/maximum load
250 Sierra SBT	H870	128.0	3,200	5,685	A-Square/maximum load
250 Sierra SBT	AA 8700	130.0	3,202	5,690	A-Square/maximum load

.38 Casull

Historical Notes: Repeatedly proven for nearly a century, the story of the endurance and reliability of John Browning's 1911 pistol approaches the status of legend. Not well known, however, is the adaptability of the 1911 design to different cartridges. Casull Arms used improved steels and technologies to update its 1911-design pistol to accommodate a new short cartridge, the .38 Casull. Created by Dick Casull in 1998, its case capacity equals or exceeds the .357 Magnum, while fitting in a .45 ACP magazine.

General Comments: The cartridge is for long-range target and hunting uses, or for when self-defense needs call for a more powerful cartridge than its parent case, the .45 ACP. (It is also said to be similar to the wildcat .38-45 Clerke, developed around 1963 by Bo Clerke, a New Mexico gunsmith, but the .38 Casull has thicker case walls.) The .38 Casull uses a longer case neck and rebated rim for more reliable feeding. For handgun hunters, the .38 Casull demonstrates high accuracy and flat trajectories at 100 yards. The barrel is five inches long with 1:18 rifling. Shooters are advised that only Casull Arms pistols are designed and constructed for this cartridge; chambering in other firearms is strongly discouraged. Loaded ammunition was available from Casull Arms, and initial chronograph testing indicates the factory ammo does attain the specified velocities.

This round was previously categorized in the "Handgun Cartridges" chapter, but would, in fact, have been a proprietary loading of Casull Arms. That company was formed by Dick Casull after he parted ways with Wayne Baker and Freedom Arms, the company they'd founded together, but Casull Arms doesn't seem to be in existence at this point. There's little to no information on the availability of brass or bullets for this round, let alone more than just a handful of guns chambered for it out there, so for all intents and purposes, this round seems to be obsolete. For these reasons, it seems we had a toss-up between slotting it in the proprietary or wildcat cartridges, but, given its history, we have opted for the proprietary designation as being most appropriate at this time.

.38 Casull Loading Data and Factory Ballistics

Bullet (grains/type)	Powder	Grains	Velocity	Energy	Source/Comments
124 Hornady	FL	N/A	1,800	N/A	Casull Arms
147 Hornady	FL	N/A	1,600	N/A	Casull Arms

.356 GNR

Historical Notes: One of Gary Reeder's favorite Thompson/Center Contender cartridges has been the .357/44 B&D. Gary wanted to chamber that cartridge in a revolver, but had problems making the combination work; the case constantly set back and pulled crimp, locking up the cylinder. In the mid-1990s, Reeder decided to give it another go, but this time he took a .41 Magnum case and necked it down to .357. He made the case walls straight and put in a sharp shoulder with a short neck—and it worked perfectly. The .356 GNR was originally developed for bullets ranging in weight from 125 to 140 grains, and it has worked very well as a deer cartridge.

General Comments: Additional experimentation has also shown the .356 GNR to work very well with 180-grain cast LBT bullets. This discovery proved that the .356 GNR was suitable not just for deer, but would work for big game, as well. Reeder has chambered the .356 GNR in many T/C Contender barrels, but he feels it is best at home in a six-shot revolver like the Ruger Blackhawk and Redhawk and the S&W Models 27 and 28. Those looking for a .357-caliber alternative to a .357 Magnum that has more punch and will still work in revolvers with cylinders shorter than those used for the .357 Maximum should find the .356 GNR to their liking. Information on custom guns, ammunition, and reloading data can be obtained by contacting Gary Reeder Custom Guns, (928) 527-4100 or www.reedercustomguns.com.

.356 GNR Loading Data and Ballistics

Bullet (grains/type)	Powder	Grains	Velocity	Energy	Source
125 JHP	H 110	24.0	2,000	1,110	Gary Reeder
140 JHP	W 296	24.0	1,870	1,086	Gary Reeder
180 Cast LBT	H 110	24	1,700	1,154	Gary Reeder

.358 JDJ

Historical Notes: Another cartridge designed and developed by J.D. Jones. Jones began development of his cartridges, around 1978, to give added range and power to the Thompson/Center Contender pistol. Some of his cartridges have also proven to be excellent metallic silhouette numbers. JDJ cartridges are relatively easy to make. All JDJ cartridges are proprietary and SSK does not sell reamers, nor has it permitted the reamer maker to sell them. For information, contact SSK Industries (www.sskindustries.com).

General Comments: The first version of this cartridge used the .303 British case, but was later changed to the .444 Marlin necked down. This chambering provides ample capacity and bullet area to produce impressive muzzle energy, especially with longer handgun-length barrels (14 to 16 inches). Any .357 Magnum, .35 Remington, or .35 Herrett Thompson/Center Contender barrel is easily re-chambered to use this cartridge. The .358 JDJ offers muzzle velocities similar to the .375 Winchester (rifle loads) with bullets of equal weight. Since this chambering uses spitzer bullets, delivered energy at normal hunting range is significantly higher than with the parent .444 Marlin, even when the latter is fired from a rifle. Bullets of 180 to 225 grains are good choices. Top loads in this chambering generate significant recoil. An effective muzzle brake (which increases the already significant muzzle blast effect) is essential. Recoil of top loads compares to top .44 Magnum revolver loads, a recoil level many shooters cannot learn to tolerate. When bullets of proper hunting weight are driven at full velocity (necessary to assure proper terminal performance), even the seasoned handgunner would describe the recoil generated as rather brisk. For information on components, loading data, barrels, and guns designed for this cartridge, contact SSK Industries, (720) 264-0176 or www.sskindustries.com.

.358 JDJ Loading Data (Note: These loads for use only in SSK barrels.)

Bullet (grains/type)	Powder	Grains	Velocity	Energy	Source/Comments
180 JSP	RI-7	49.0	2,295	2,105	SSK/maximum load/SSK barrels only
200 SP	RI-7	48.0	2,275	2,295	SSK/maximum load/SSK barrels only
225 SP	RI-15	52.5	2,145	2,300	SSK/maximum load/SSK barrels only
250 SP	AA 2520	50.0	2,100	2,205	SSK/maximum load/SSK barrels only

.35-06 JDJ

Historical Notes: This cartridge was designed by J.D. Jones of SSK Industries. Application is to Thompson/Center Encore single-shot pistols fitted with a custom SSK barrel. Typical barrel length is 15 inches. Cases are formed from empty .30-06 or .35 Whelen cases by special means and cannot be fire-formed from any other case. Neck length is minimal, acceptable for a cartridge used in a single-shot. Shoulder angle is 60 degrees, which seems to work fine. Body taper is minimal, similar to Ackley's Improved designs, therefore, this is equivalent to a maximized .35 Whelen. Capacity is a whopping 76 grains of water, which is significantly greater than the .35 Whelen (about 72). Working pressure is about 60,000 psi, so ballistics are quite impressive. Best handloads in SSK barrels can approach .35 Whelen (rifle) ballistics.

General Comments: Since this case has no rim, it is not generally safe to directly fire-form it in the conventional manner. However, owing to the captive extractor system used in the Encore, it is possible to use a special technique in those gun. To wit, resize a .35 Whelen case, and then seat a .358-inch jacketed bullet hard against the rifling so that the gun will just close. Correct powder charge is about 5 percent below the maximum SSK-recommended load. Jones recommends 200-grain bullets for big-game hunting of smaller species, and bullets up to 250 grains on larger species. This cartridge generates sufficient energy for hunting on any continent. SSK has not yet fully developed optimal loading data for this number. Recoil may exceed what some shooters can learn to handle. For information on components, loading data, barrels, and guns, contact SSK Industries, (720) 264-0176 or www.sskindustries.com.

.35-06 JDJ Loading Data (Note: These loads for use only in SSK barrels.)

Bullet (grains)	Powder	Grains	Velocity	Energy	Source/Comments
180	H335	67.0	2,742	3,005	SSK/maximum load/SSK barrels only
220	IMR 4064	62.8	2,584	3,260	SSK/maximum load/SSK barrels only
225	IMR 4064	62.8	2,614	3,415	SSK/maximum load/SSK barrels only
250	RI-15	61.8	2,415	3,235	SSK/maximum load/SSK barrels only

.358 Shooting Times Alaskan (.358 STA)

Historical Notes: The .358 STA was the second cartridge developed by firearms writer Layne Simpson on the 8mm Remington Magnum case, and it is second in popularity to the 7mm STW, which came first. It has been reported that the first version of the .358 STA was formed by necking up the 8mm Remington Magnum with no other change, but this is not true. It is true for the 7mm STW, because the 8mm Magnum case holds all the powder that can be burned in a bore of that size at an acceptable level of efficiency. But, more powder can be burned in a .35-caliber bore and, right from the start, Simpson chose to reform the case to the Improved configuration with minimum body taper and a 35-degree shoulder angle. The case is formed by necking up the 8mm Remington Magnum case and loading it with a reduced powder charge with 80 grains of H4350 behind a 250-grain bullet for a popular fireforming load. The first rifle chambered for this cartridge was built by gunsmith Kenny Jarrett, and the first commercial rifles chambered for it were built by A-Square. That company was also first to offer loaded ammunition. Layne Simpson introduced the cartridge in the September 1992 issue of Shooting Times, soon after using it to bag an Alaskan brown bear.

General Comments: Powerful enough to handle any big-game animal in North America, the .358 STA shoots as flat as a .300 Magnum and delivers more energy to the target than the .375 H&H Magnum. When loaded with a 250-grain bullet, it is about 200 fps faster than the .358 Norma Magnum and duplicates the performance of a cartridge of the 1920s called the .350 Griffin & Howe Magnum. For more information on A-square custom rifles and ammunition, contact (605) 234-0500 (South Dakota), (307) 436-5677 (Wyoming) or www.a-squareco.com.

.358 STA Loading Data and Factory Ballistics

Bullet (grains/type)	Powder	Grains	Velocity	Energy	Source
180 Barnes XFB	RL-19	95.0	3,357	4,501	Barnes
200 Barnes XFB	IMR-4831	90.0	3,217	4,591	Barnes
225 Nosler Partition	H4350	87.0	3,182	5,053	Hodgdon
225 Barnes XFB	IMR-4831	87.0	3,183	4,883	Barnes
250 Barnes XFB	IMR-4831	86.0	2,995	4,974	Barnes
250 Nosler Partition	H4350	89.0	2,981	4,928	Layne Simpson
275 A-Square LL	H4831	90.0	2,857	4,979	A-Square
300 Barnes SN	RL-19	84.0	2,714	4,901	Layne Simpson
300 Barnes SN	H4831	86.0	2,719	4,919	Layne Simpson
275 A-Square Lion Load	FL	N/A	2,850	4,954	A-Square
275 A-Square Dead Tough	FL	N/A	2,850	4,954	A-Square

WARNING: All powder charges are maximum and must be reduced by 10 percent for starting loads.

9.09 Eagle

Historical Notes: Lazzeroni Arms designed this cartridge in 1998. While somewhat related to an older case, for all practical purposes, this is a new case design. This cartridge was created in response to requests for a high-performance cartridge that would work in a 2.8-inch action and yet deliver the ballistics of a full-length belted magnum. Adaptation to a standard action is feasible but is not recommended. Although standardized, this is essentially a wildcat chambering using Lazzeroni's Patriot case. Lazzeroni does offer dies and reamer specifications, but does not normally chamber for this cartridge or provide properly headstamped cases.

General Comments:	Bullet diameter is .358-inch (Lazzeroni bases its designations on bullet diameter instead of bore diameter, which is the common practice). Ballistics are quite impressive for such a short cartridge. Given equal-length barrels, the Eagle essentially duplicates .358 Norma Magnum ballistics. Case design is typical of the Lazzeroni line: moderate body taper, 30-degree shoulder, sufficiently long neck, and thick rim of approximate case-body diameter. In other words, this is a well-designed case. For more information on Lazzeroni custom guns, ammunition, and reloading data, contact (888) 492-7247 or www.lazzeroni.com.

9.09 Eagle Factory Ballistics (24-inch barrel)

Bullet (grains)	Powder	Grains	Velocity	Energy	Source/Comments
250	FL	N/A	2,850	4,510	Lazzeroni factory load

9.3mm JDJ

Historical Notes:	Designed by J.D. Jones of SSK Industries, this chambering is the .444 Marlin case necked down to 9.3mm with no other changes. Design intent was a Thompson/Center chambering that would surpass .35 Remington rifle ballistics and use the newly available U.S.-manufactured 9.3mm bullets.

General Comments:	Any ballistic difference between this chambering and the .358 JDJ would be very hard to demonstrate. This chambering is reported to deliver impressive performance against deer and black bear-sized game when heavy bullets are used. The primary market is European, where the 9.3mm bore is quite popular. This chambering generates significant recoil. An effective muzzle brake (which increases the already significant muzzle-blast effect) is essential. Recoil of top loads compares to top .44 Magnum revolver loads, a recoil level many shooters cannot learn to tolerate. When bullets of proper hunting weight are driven at full velocity (necessary to assure proper terminal performance), even the seasoned handgunner would describe the recoil as very brisk. For information on components, loading data, barrels, and guns, contact SSK Industries, (720) 264-0176 or www.sskindustries.com.

9.3mm JDJ Loading Data (Note: These loads for use only in SSK barrels.)

Bullet (grains/type)	Powder	Grains	Velocity	Energy	Source/Comments
270 Speer	H322	44.0	1,906	2,175	SSK/maximum load/SSK barrel only (14")
270 Speer	H414	57.3	1,924	2,240	SSK/maximum load/SSK barrel only (14")
270 Speer	IMR 4064	52.0	1,974	2,335	SSK/maximum load/SSK barrel only (14")
270 Norma	RI-15	53.0	2,027	2,465	SSK/maximum load/SSK barrel only (14")
270 Speer	RI-15	54.0	2,077	2,585	SSK/maximum load/SSK barrel only (14")

9.3 B&M — *NEW*

Historical Notes:	This line of proprietary dangerous-game cartridges includes the 9.3 B&M, covered here, plus the 416 B&M, 458 B&M, 475 B&M, and 50 B&M (which see). B&M is an acronymic shortening of two gentlemen's last names; Bruton and McCourry, respectively William V. Bruton and Michael McCourry. In 2005, they wanted a .500-caliber cartridge on par with the 500 S&W, only in a short, handy rifle for safari, where some shots might be — unintentionally — at extremely close range.

General Comments:	The standard B&M Cartridges are based on a 2.240-inch-long (trimmed) Remington Ultra Magnum case. B&M's favorite bullet for the 9.3 cartridge is the 210-grain ESP (Enhanced System Projectile) Raptor. The 9.3 B&M runs this bullet faster than 2,900 fps in a 20-inch barrel, according to the maker. Properly head-stamped brass is available, or you can make your own brass, the process for which is detailed on the B&M website.

The B&M line is chambered in Winchester M70 WSM bolt-actions with barrels of 18 or 20 inches. The rifles weigh 6.5 to 7.5 pounds rather than the 10-plus pounds of more traditional African big-game rifles.

All of the B&M series rifles are built by SSK Industries; (740) 264-0176 (SSKindustries.com). For those who do not handload, custom-loaded ammo is also available from Superior Ammunition; (843) 830-3139 (SuperiorAmmo.com).

9.3 B&M Loading Data

Bullet (grains/type)	Powder	Grains	Velocity	Energy	Source/Comments
210 ESP Raptor HP	IMR 4320	73	2,910	3,947	B&M Load Data Sheet
255 CEB BBW#13	RL 15	69	2,713	4,166	B&M Load Data Sheet
286 Hornady	AA 2520	64	2,511	4,003	B&M Load Data Sheet
320 Wood FMJ	IMR 4320	66	2,466	4,250	B&M Load Data Sheet

.375 Whisper

Historical Notes: Created by J.D. Jones, the .375 Whisper, like all other Whisper cartridges, must be capable of subsonic extreme accuracy with very heavy bullets, while maintaining excellent accuracy with light bullets at moderate to high velocity.

General Comments: Using a 7mm Bench Rest Remington case necked up to .375-caliber, the .375 Whisper launches a 300-grain Hornady projectile at just under sub-sonic speeds (1050 fps). It can propel 250-grain bullets to 2,250 fps. The .375 Whisper can be chambered in suitably barreled Thompson/Center Contender firearms, as well as other single-shot and many bolt-action firearms. For information on components, loading data, barrels, and guns, contact SSK Industries, (720) 264-0176 or www.sskindustries.com.

.375/454 JDJ Woodswalker

Historical Notes: Another big-bore, short-range hunting round from SSK Industries, the .375/454 JDJ Woodswalker is based on necking the powerful .454 Casull cartridge to .375-caliber. Barrels, dies, and cases for the 375/454 JDJ are available from SSK Industries (www.sskindustries.com).

General Comments: Using a .375-caliber, 200-grain Sierra projectile in modified .454 Casull cases and 15-inch SSK barrels, the .375/454 JDJ achieves about 2,375 fps. With 270-grain Hornady Spire Points, it can achieve velocities exceeding 1900 fps. It is suitable for the Thompson/Center Encore.

.375 JDJ

Historical Notes: This is another cartridge designed and developed by J.D. Jones, hence the JDJ designation. Development of his cartridges began around 1978, and these are generally fired in barrels furnished by his company, SSK Industries. The purpose of these cartridges is to give added range and power to the Thompson/Center Contender pistol for hunting. Some of Jones' cartridges have also proven to be excellent metallic silhouette numbers. JDJ cartridges are relatively easy to make. All JDJ cartridges are proprietary, and SSK neither sells reamers nor allows the reamer maker to sell them.

General Comments: Based on the .444 Marlin necked down, this chambering provides ample capacity and bullet area to produce muzzle energy similar to what .30-06-chambered rifles deliver, especially with longer handgun-length barrels (14 to 16 inches). The .375 JDJ loaded to top velocity with 250-grain bullets is fully capable of taking elk-sized game with proper shot placement. However, the Barnes 210-grain X bullet can deliver superior terminal performance, reduced recoil, and a flatter trajectory, but does require special handloading techniques (deeper bullet seating and a reduction in powder charge). With heavier bullets of proper construction, this chambering is adequate for species to the one-ton class. Jones himself has repeatedly proven this fact. An excellent selection of good bullets that work well when loaded to top .375 JDJ velocities is available.

This chambering generates significant recoil. An effective muzzle brake (which increases the already significant muzzle-blast effect) is essential. Top loads generally produce more recoil than top .44 Magnum revolver loads, a recoil level many shooters cannot learn to tolerate. When bullets of proper hunting weight are driven at full velocity (necessary to assure proper terminal performance), even the seasoned handgunner would describe the recoil as very brisk. For information on components, loading data, barrels, and guns, contact SSK Industries, (720) 264-0176 or www.sskindustries.com.

.375 JDJ Loading Data (Note: These loads for use only in SSK barrels.)

Bullet (grains/type)	Powder	Grains	Velocity	Energy	Source/Comments
220 SP	H4895	51.0	2,350	2,365	SSK/maximum load/12-14" SSK barrels only
270 SP	IMR 4064	48.0	2,100	2,165	SSK/maximum load/12-14" SSK barrels only
270 SP	IMR 4064	49.2	2,100	2,400	SSK/maximum load/12-14" SSK barrels only
300 SP	W748	50.8	1,950	2,405	SSK/maximum load/12-14" SSK barrels only

9.53 Hellcat

Historical Notes: Lazzeroni Arms designed this cartridge in 1997. While somewhat related to an older case, for all practical purposes, this is a new case design. The Hellcat was created in response to requests for a high-performance cartridge that would work in a 2.8-inch action and yet deliver the ballistics of a full-length belted magnum. Adaptation to a standard action is feasible, but is not recommended.

General Comments: Bullet diameter is .375-inch (Lazzeroni bases its designations on bullet diameter, instead of bore diameter, which is the common practice.) Ballistics are quite impressive for such a short cartridge. Given equal-length barrels, the Hellcat essentially duplicates the ballistics of the legendary .375 H&H Magnum. This well-designed case is typical of the Lazzeroni line: moderate body taper, 30-degree shoulder, sufficiently long neck, and thick rim of approximate case-body diameter.

Bill George owns the first Hellcat rifle ever built. With very modest assistance from a former editor of this book, George assembled some extremely accurate handloads (well under 1 MOA accuracy) using the 300-grain Nosler Partition. He took those to Africa and proceeded to kill everything he shot at, using exactly one round for each animal in almost every instance. This Hellcat load dropped George's Cape buffalo in its tracks, a feat that left his guide practically in shock. The quote was, "Never seen that happen before in my life!" Shot placement and bullet performance count. For more information on Lazzeroni custom guns, ammunition, and reloading data, contact (888) 492-7247 or www.lazzeroni.com.

9.53 Hellcat Factory Ballistics (24-inch barrel)

Bullet (grains)	Powder	Grains	Velocity	Energy	Source/Comments
300	FL	N/A	2,600	4,500	Lazzeroni factory load

.375-06 JDJ

Historical Notes: This cartridge was designed by J.D. Jones of SSK Industries. Application is to Thompson/Center Encore single-shot pistols fitted with a custom SSK barrel. Typical barrel length is 15 inches. Cases are best formed from empty .30-06 or .35 Whelen cases by special means. Neck length is minimal, which is acceptable for a cartridge used in a single-shot gun. Shoulder angle is 60 degrees, which seems to work just fine and is probably necessary to maintain headspace against the firing pin blow and primer blast. Body taper is minimal, similar to Ackley's Improved designs. Therefore, this is equivalent to a maximized .375 Whelen. Capacity is a whopping 77 grains of water, which is significantly greater than the .375 Whelen (about 73). Working pressure is about 60,000 psi, so ballistics are quite impressive. Best handloads in SSK barrels easily exceed the energy of top factory .35 Whelen (rifle) loads.

General Comments: Since this case has no rim, it is not generally safe to directly fire-form it in the conventional manner. However, owing to the captive extractor system used in the Encore, it is possible to use a special technique in those guns, to wit: Resize and neck expand a .35 Whelen case, and then seat a .375-inch jacketed bullet hard against the rifling so that the gun will just close. Correct powder charge is about 5 percent below the maximum SSK-recommended load. Jones recommends 220-grain bullets at reduced velocity for big-game hunting applications on smaller species and bullets up to 300 grains for the largest species. While one could use 210- and 235-grain Barnes X bullets, which can offer impressive terminal performance, handloaders must use X bullet-specific loading data and special handloading techniques (e.g., bullet ogive must be seated a minimum of .050-inch from rifling). Further, those bullets work best when a reduced-friction coating (such as moly-plating) is used. For this reason, SSK does not support use of X-style bullets in its guns. While no bullet substitution is benign, never substitute any X-style bullet in any load—begin with data specifically created for that bullet. This cartridge generates sufficient energy for hunting on any continent. SSK has not fully developed optimal loading data for this number at this time. With heavy bullets and top loads, recoil may exceed what even seasoned shooters want to experience. For information on components, loading data, barrels, and guns designed for this cartridge, contact SSK Industries, (720) 264-0176 or www.sskindustries.com.

.375-06 JDJ Loading Data (Note: These loads for use only in SSK barrels.)

Bullet (grains)	Powder	Grains	Velocity	Energy	Source/Comments
220	AA 4350	55.6	1,825	1,625	SSK/maximum load/SSK barrels only
220	VarGet	67.3	2,601	3,305	SSK/maximum load/SSK barrels only
270	Vit N140	65.2	2,421	3,515	SSK/maximum load/SSK barrels only
300	IMR 4320	63.4	2,330	3,615	SSK/maximum load/SSK barrels only

.375 Allen Magnum

Historical Notes: Kirby Allen, of Allen Precision Shooting, made the .375 Allen Magnum for big-game hunting, but the round's larger bore diameter also makes it suitable for extreme-range target shooting. Like its smaller-caliber brother the .338 Allen Magnum, the .375 Allen Magnum is extremely effective for big-game hunting at long range. With the larger frontal area and heavier bullet weight, this round is suitable for the heaviest animals, especially elk, moose, and other big game at long ranges.

General Comments: With its primary bullet (350-grain Sierra MatchKing), the .375 Allen Magnum will sustain supersonic velocity to a range of roughly 2,800 yards, depending on elevation. With the weight and diameter of this bullet, the .375 Allen Magnum will easily take big game at any supersonic range, assuming the hunter has the ability to put the bullet through the vital area. Even if bullet expansion is minimal, the .375-caliber projectile is effective at cleanly killing big game because of its large frontal area and subsequent large amount of tissue displacement.

Fully formed custom brass is available from APS with rifle orders. Longer barrel life will be had with this round than with the .338 Allen Magnum. The round does have a trajectory similar to the .338 Allen Magnum, but with more terminal authority on heavier big game. Rifles are long and relatively heavy, starting around 16 pounds. For more information, check the website APSRifles.com or e-mail Kirby Allen at allenmagnum@gmail.com.—*W.T.W.*

.375 Allen Magnum Loading Data (Note: *Hodgdon Retumbo, Reloader 33)

Bullet (grains/type)	Powder	Grains	Velocity	Energy	Source/Comments
300 Sierra MatchKing	*	N/A	3,450	7,926	Allen Precision Shooting
350 Sierra MatchKing	*	N/A	3,300	8,461	Allen Precision Shooting

.375 Dakota

Historical Notes: The .375 Dakota is a shortened and necked-down version of the basic, rebated rimless .404 Jeffery case, but the rim is enlarged slightly to eliminate the rebated feature. Design purpose was to create a cartridge that would duplicate .375 H&H performance from a .30-06-length action (3.35 inches). The case features a rim that is slightly larger than the standard belted-magnum cases; using this cartridge in a rifle with a standard belted-magnum bolt face will require a slight bolt alteration. Despite its similar capacity, maximum case diameter of this much shorter case is only slightly larger than the .375 H&H Magnum. Typically, magazine capacity is reduced by one cartridge. This is perhaps a significant consideration for a dangerous-game rifle, but a minor magazine alteration will remedy the problem.

General Comments: The .375 Dakota, just like the 7mm, .300, and .330 Dakota cartridges, functions properly through standard-length (3.35-inch) actions. Usable case capacity is nearly identical to the .375 H&H Magnum and, if loaded to equal pressures, ballistics are the same. This cartridge provides superior feeding and a potential accuracy advantage over the .375 H&H. This should be a good choice for those who feel lesser calibers are inadequate for larger species. Combined with some superior bullets, this cartridge can rival the long-range trajectory of the best .270 Winchester loads. When loaded with proper dangerous-game bullets and in the hands of an expert, this cartridge would suffice for any game worldwide. Contact Dakota Arms for more information: (605) 347-4686 or www.dakotaarms.com.

.375 Dakota Loading Data and Factory Ballistics

Bullet (grains)	Powder	Grains	Velocity	Energy	Source/Comments
270	RI-15	75.0	2,829	4,795	Dakota/maximum load
270	IMR 4350	85.0	2,895	5,020	Dakota/maximum load
270	H4350	85.0	2,883	4,980	Dakota/maximum load
300	IMR 4350	78.0	2,660	4,710	Dakota/maximum load
300	H4350	78.0	2,648	4,670	Dakota/maximum load
300	IMR 4831	79.0	2,641	4,640	Dakota/maximum load
300	RI-19	83.5	2,662	4,720	Dakota/maximum load
270	FL	N/A	2,800	4,680	Dakota factory load
300	FL	N/A	2,600	4,502	Dakota factory load

.375 Canadian Magnum

Historical Notes: This cartridge was developed about 1994 by North American Shooting Systems (NASS), and is simply a .375-caliber version of the .338 Canadian Magnum. This design features a slightly rebated, rimless bottleneck case. Design intent was to provide the maximum feasible powder capacity in a standard action with minimal gunsmithing (without deepening the magazine well slightly, magazine capacity is usually reduced by one round). Bolt face alteration is unnecessary. Cartridge feeding and headspacing characteristics are improved.

General Comments: The Canadian Magnum series is similar to Dakota's cartridge family in both design and purpose. However, this cartridge (like the entire Canadian line) takes advantage of the full 3.65-inch magazine length of the long-action Remington M700 and similar rifles. On the Canadian Magnums, body diameter is significantly larger than the standard belted magnum (.544-inch versus .513-inch at the base). Re-chambering of nominal belted magnums with the same bore diameter is generally quite simple, requiring no other alterations to the gun. For any given case length, case capacity is about 15-percent greater than can be achieved with the belted version. Body taper is minimal and the shoulder is comparatively sharp. However, neck length is sufficiently generous to provide good bullet purchase for hunting ammunition. Performance is commensurate with the capacity and pressures used in these loadings. Actual performance of this number is very close to the vaunted .378 Weatherby Magnum.

.375 Canadian Magnum Loading Data and Factory Ballistics

Bullet (grains)	Powder	Grains	Velocity	Energy	Source/Comments
270	H4831	103.0	3,010	5,430	NASS/maximum load
270	FL	N/A	3,000	5,395	NASS factory load

.375 A-Square

Historical Notes: This is a somewhat modified .378 Weatherby Magnum designed in 1975 and intended to allow duplication of .378 Weatherby Magnum performance in a .375 H&H magazine length (3.65 inches).

General Comments: Ballistics duplicate the parent .378 Weatherby Magnum, and chambering is easily achieved in any of the many .375 H&H-chambered magazine rifles. Cases are easily converted from .378 Weatherby Magnum cases. This chambering is a viable choice for a light rifle in Africa. The heavier solids offered are certainly capable of use against the heaviest of game, with proper shot placement. Recoil is distinctly less than recoil with any of the .40-caliber and larger dangerous-game chamberings. For more information on A-square custom rifles and ammunition, contact (605) 234-0500 (South Dakota), (307) 436-5677 (Wyoming) or www.a-squareco.com.

.375 A-Square Loading Data and Factory Ballistics

Bullet (grains/type)	Powder	Grains	Velocity	Energy	Source/Comments
250 Sierra SBT	IMR 4831	106.0	3,184	5,625	A-Square/maximum load
250 Sierra SBT	H4831	114.5	3,186	5,630	A-Square/maximum load
250 Sierra SBT	RI-22	113.0	3,217	5,740	A-Square/maximum load
300 Monolithic Solid	RI-22	105.0	2,839	5,370	A-Square/maximum load
300 Monolithic Solid	IMR 4831	101.0	2,911	5,640	A-Square/maximum load
300 Monolithic Solid	H4831	110.0	2,974	5,890	A-Square/maximum load
300 Sierra & TRIAD	FL	N/A	2,920	5,675	A-Square factory load (3 A-Square bullet types)

9.53 Saturn

Historical Notes: Lazzeroni Arms designed this cartridge in 1996. While somewhat related to an older case, for all practical purposes, this is a new case design. John Lazzeroni believes that those hunters who will take the time to become competent marksmen can legitimately take game at longer ranges. This cartridge was created to provide sufficient velocity for medium-weight or heavyweight hunting bullets to enable dependable expansion at longer ranges, and to have sufficient energy for taking the largest species. Adaptation to standard actions is feasible, but is not recommended.

General Comments: Bullet diameter is .375-inch (Lazzeroni bases its designations on bullet diameter, instead of bore diameter, which is the common practice). Ballistics equal or exceed any factory .37-caliber cartridge. Case design is typical of the Lazzeroni line: moderate body taper, 30-degree shoulder, sufficiently long neck, and thick rim of approximate case-body diameter. In other words, this is a well-designed case. Although designed specifically for hunting, this cartridge does have application to long-range target shooting. While a 27-inch barrel was originally standard, Lazzeroni has recently changed to a 24-inch barrel for this number, and there is no significant sacrifice in performance. Lazzeroni's cartridge loadings use premium bullets from Nosler, Barnes, or Swift. These are the only bullets providing the necessary accuracy and terminal performance to meet Lazzeroni's strict requirements. For more information on Lazzeroni custom guns, ammunition, and reloading data, contact (888) 492-7247 or www.lazzeroni.com.

9.53 Saturn Factory Ballistics (24-inch barrel)

Bullet (grains/type)	Powder	Grains	Velocity	Energy	Source/Comments
300	FL	N/A	3,010	6,035	Lazzeroni factory load *

* Lazzeroni has used loads exceeding 3,100 fps, but that is pressing the issue rather hard. RI-19 is a preferred powder for this number.

.375 JRS Magnum

General Comments: The .375 JRS was designed by noted gun writer Jon R. Sundra. It is based on the 8mm Remington Magnum case necked up to .375 with no other changes. It can be made by fire-forming .375 H&H factory ammunition; by necking up the 8mm Rem. Mag. using tapered expanders of .358-inch, and then .375-inch; or by fire-forming, using blank loads in 8mm Rem. Mag. cases. Of these, Sundra recommends the latter, because only the neck is worked. The procedure for making the blanks requires a load of 35 grains of IMR SR 4756, a small over-powder wad of tissue, and then filling the remainder of the case to the base of the neck with Cream of Wheat cereal (uncooked, of course). Seal off the case mouth with a plug of soap by pushing the case neck into a soap bar. The resultant blank will expand the neck perfectly in a .375 JRS chamber.

As of 1990, A-Square Co. began offering .375 JRS unprimed cases, as well as loaded ammunition with its headstamp. In 1992, U.S. Repeating Arms began chambering the Winchester Model 70 Super Grade (the pre-'64 action with controlled round feeding) for the .375 JRS. E.R. Shaw and the H-S Precision also chamber for the .375 JRS. It ballistically duplicates the .375 Weatherby Magnum and other older wildcats of the same general design. Hornady and RCBS make reloading dies.

General Comments: Case capacity of the .375 JRS is about 8 percent greater than that of the .375 H&H. The best powder for 270- to 330-grain bullets is IMR 4350. Velocity in 24-inch barrels for a 300-grain bullet will average between 2,700 and 2,750 fps. Any max load listed for the .375 H&H can be used for a starting load in the .375 JRS.

.375 JRS Loading Data

Bullet (grains/type)	Powder	Grains	Velocity	Energy	Source/Comments
270 SP	IMR 4350	85.0	2,750	4,535	Jon Sundra
300 SP	IMR 4350	83.0	2,700	4,855	Jon Sundra

375 B&M — *NEW*

Historical Notes: The 375 B&M is one of a line of proprietary cartridges based on 2.240-inch-long (trimmed) Remington Ultra Magnum cases. The makers, William V. Bruton and Michael McCourry, wanted rounds that would fit in lighter, short Winchester M70 WSM bolt-actions with barrels of 18 or 20 inches. This B&M variation fits in a 7-pound rifle, where lighter weight and shorter OAL make it a top-notch choice for elk hunting.

General Comments: When the RUM brass is cut to 2.240 inches, it's run through an appropriate B&M-size die to make this and other chamberings; 475 B&M, 458 B&M, 416 B&M and 9.3 B&M (which see). A new and unfired case should just go into the rifle with slight resistance, meaning the shoulder is bumping the chamber, which keeps the brass from flowing too far forward when it is fired. This prevents head separation. After the case is fire-formed, the shooter can full-length size the cases so they chamber with ease.

All B&M-series rifles are built by SSK Industries. Custom-loaded ammo is also available from Superior Ammunition. Properly head-stamped brass is available, or you can make your own brass, the process for which is detailed on the B&M website.

Bullet (grains/type)	Powder	Grains	Velocity	Energy	Source/Comments
235 Barnes TSX	RL 15	75	2,807	4,110	B&M Load Data Sheet
300 Hornady	RL 15	70	2,498	4,155	B&M Load Data Sheet

.400 A-Square Dual Purpose Magnum (400 Pondoro) — *NEW*

Historical Notes: The .400 A-Square Dual Purpose Magnum was introduced in 2006 by the A-Square Co., though it is essentially the same as the 400 Pondoro developed in 1992, also by A-Square. The case for the .400 ASDPM is a blown-out full-length .375 H&H Mag. The 400 Pondoro was a necked-down .416 Rigby.

Col. Arthur B. Alphin called the .400 "dual purpose" to signify that factory loads extended down to varmint weights as well as having dangerous-game applications. The A-Square .400 Dual Purpose round has a place as an African cartridge and is also suitable for bears, elk, moose and other big game.

A-Square was sold to Sharps Rifle Co. in 2011, which then sold out to the Wyoming-based Broadsword Group, LLC. A-Square branded ammunition and rifles are still listed on Broadsword's company website, Broadsword.com. Thus this round's inclusion in the Proprietary chapter and not the Obsolete chapter.

General Comments: In designing this 40-caliber belted magnum, Alphin did not use classic .416-diameter bullets, such as those found in the .416 Rigby, .416 Taylor and .416 Rem. He designed the new cartridge around a .410-inch-diameter bullet like that found in the .41 Mag. handgun cartridge. As a result, lighter .41-caliber pistol bullets were already available, and A-Square made its own 400-grain big-game bullets.

.400 A-Square Dual Purpose Magnum Factory Ballistics

Bullet (grains/type)	Powder	Grains	Velocity	Energy	Source/Comments
400 A-Square DPM			2,400	5116	A-Square Ammunition

.400 CorBon

Historical Notes: Peter Pi, CEO of CorBon, designed this cartridge in 1995 by simply necking down the .45 Automatic to .40-caliber with a 25-degree shoulder. Unlike some earlier necked-down .45 Automatic designs, this case has a reasonably long neck. With the advent of plentiful .40-caliber pistol bullets, this was an obvious high-performance cartridge choice.

This design offers several advantages. First, in most pistols, conversion is completed by a simple barrel replacement. Second, the feed ramp in the chamber can easily be shortened or eliminated, thus allowing safe use of loads generating significantly higher pressure. Third, owing to the bottleneck design, this case can function better with a wider variety of bullet shapes and is generally more forgiving toward machining, fit, and finish tolerances. Finally, for any given energy level, the .400 CorBon produces significantly less recoil than the .45 Automatic (lighter bullets, launched faster).

General Comments: This is a very fine cartridge for those who do not like excessive recoil. Factory loads offer significant self-defense ballistics in a package that most shooters can easily learn to handle. Those who are satisfied with the .45 Automatic will probably find little appeal with the .400 CorBon. On the other hand, those who are dissatisfied with 9mm and .40 S&W ballistics might find this a viable option. Cases are easily converted from the ubiquitous .45 Automatic, but Starline (www.starlinebrass.com) offers these as a component. Owing to increased case capacity, ballistics of the .400 CorBon approach those of the 10mm Automatic, but with significantly less pressure. For more information on CorBon ammunition, contact (800) 626-7266 or www.shopcorbon.com.

Bullet (grains/type)	Powder	Grains	Velocity	Energy	Source/Comments
135 JHP	Vit N340	9.7	1,400	585	Cor-Bon
155 JHP	WAP	10.5	1,310	590	Cor-Bon
165 JHP	Vit N105	10.5	1,250	570	Cor-Bon
180 Cast	Unique	7.0	1,100	480	Cor-Bon
135 JHP	FL	N/A	1,450	625	CorBon factory load
155 JHP	FL	N/A	1,350	625	CorBon factory load
165 JHP	FL	N/A	1300	615	Cor-Bon factory load

.40-44 Woodswalker

Historical Notes: This cartridge was designed by J.D. Jones of SSK Industries. Application is to Thompson/Center Encore or Contender single-shot pistols fitted with a custom SSK barrel. Typical barrel length is 10 inches. Cases are formed from empty .44 Magnum cases, running the case into a full-length sizing die. Neck length is rather short, acceptable for use in a single-shot gun. Shoulder angle is 30 degrees.

General Comments: This is reminiscent of the .357 Bain & Davis. The only advantage of such a conversion is the ability to launch lighter bullets at higher velocities (compared to the parent cartridge). Working pressure is about 60,000 psi. Energy of top loads approaches that for .454 Casull revolver loads. It is an open question as to whether any readily available JHP bullet will function properly when used at twice the designed velocity. However, broadside lung shots on smaller game (and some not so small) have resulted in spectacular kills, when using 180-grain and heavier bullets For information on components, loading data, barrels, and guns, contact SSK Industries, (720) 264-0176 or www.sskindustries.com.

.40-44 Woodswalker Loading Data (Note: These loads for use only in SSK barrels.)

Bullet (grains/type)	Powder	Grains	Velocity	Energy	Source/Comments
150 Sierra	AA No. 9	30.7	2,404	1,925	SSK/maximum load/SSK barrels only
165 Speer	Vit N110	25.2	2,122	1,650	SSK/maximum load/SSK barrels only
170 Sierra	H110	31.4	2,213	1,845	SSK/maximum load/SSK barrels only
190 Speer	AA No. 9	27.5	2,116	1,885	SSK/maximum load/SSK barrels only

.40-454 JDJ

Historical Notes: This cartridge was designed by J.D. Jones, of SSK Industries. Application is to Thompson/Center Encore and Contender single-shot pistols fitted with a custom SSK barrel. Typical barrel length is 12 inches. Cases are formed from empty .454 Casull cases by simply running the case into the full-length sizing die. Neck length is rather short, which is acceptable for a cartridge used in a single-shot gun. Shoulder angle is 30 degrees.

General Comments: This is very reminiscent of the .357 Bain & Davis (the .44 Magnum necked to .35-caliber). The only advantage of such a conversion is the ability to launch lighter bullets at higher velocity (compared to the parent cartridge). Working pressure is about 60,000 psi. Muzzle energy of top loads can exceed any feasible .454 Casull revolver load. It is an open question as to whether any readily available JHP bullet will function properly, when used at almost three times the designed velocity. Use on smaller game species with broadside lung shots has resulted in spectacular kills, when using 180-grain and heavier bullets. For information on components, loading data, barrels, and guns designed for this cartridge, contact SSK Industries, (720) 264-0176 or www.sskindustries.com.

.40-454 JDJ Loading Data (Note: These loads for use only in SSK barrels.)

Bullet (grains/type)	Powder	Grains	Velocity	Energy	Source/Comments
165 Speer	AA No. 9	36.6	2,825	2,925	SSK/maximum load
190 Speer	AA No. 9	34.5	2,525	2,690	SSK/maximum load

.408 CheyTac

Historical Notes: The .408 CheyTac may just be the ultimate long-range sniper and anti-material cartridge. Designed in 2001 by Dr. John Taylor and his technical team to fill a gap between the .50 BMG and .338 Lapua, the .408 CheyTac can drive a 419-grain bullet to a supersonic range exceeding 2,200 yards. After 400 yards, the retained energy of the .408 CheyTac exceeds that of .50 BMG ball ammunition. With high kinetic energy retention, the .408 can defeat any material the .50 BMG can defeat, unless an explosive projectile is required. In testing, the cartridge delivered sub-MOA accuracy at ranges beyond 2,500 yards. Doppler radar testing at the U.S. Army Proving Ground, in Yuma, Arizona, confirmed the .408's ballistics. The .408 CheyTac advantages over the .50 BMG include less weight, a more compact cartridge, improved velocity and accuracy, and lower recoil, and shorter flight time to the target. Special Ops soldiers tested .408 CheyTac rifles and cartridges in Iraq and Afghanistan (2004). Informal reports of a first-shot hit exceeding 2,300 yards have circulated within the military community.

General Comments: Using new, high-quality brass, the .408 CheyTac is based on a redesigned and strengthened .505 Gibbs case with a modified web area. The cartridge works well with 25- to 29-inch barrels using a 1:13 twist. The 305-grain and 419-grain bullets for the .408 are CNC-turned bullets of copper-nickel alloy and encompass a patented "balanced flight" design. A tungsten carbide penetrator (armor-piercing) bullet is also available. CheyTac LLC (www.cheytac.com) offers bolt-action and self-loading rifles, ballistic computers, ammunition, and cases.

.408 CheyTac Factory Ballistics

Bullet (grains/type)	Powder	Grains	Velocity	Energy	Source/Comments
305 Solid	FL	N/A	3,500	N/A	CheyTac
419 Solid	FL	N/A	3,000	N/A	CheyTac

.41 GNR

Historical Notes: Gary Reeder has been a long-time fan of the .41 Auto Mag cartridge, which is simply a .44 Auto Mag necked down to .41-caliber. Gary desired to run this cartridge in a revolver, but its rimless design made that difficult. Gary found a simple solution by necking a .44 Remington Magnum case down to .41-caliber.

General Comments: The .41 GNR was an early success and continues to be one of the most popular cartridges Gary Reeder offers. It is frequently chambered in Thompson/Center Contender barrels, custom revolvers, and even Marlin lever-action rifles. It will drive a 170-grain bullet to 1980 fps from a 10-inch Contender barrel, and, from a 20-inch lever gun, velocities are well in excess of 2000 fps. Using the 170-grain Sierra jacketed hollow point bullet, this cartridge has taken everything from coyotes to caribou with one shot. Information on custom guns, ammunition, and reloading data can be obtained by contacting Gary Reeder Custom Guns, (928) 527-4100 or www.reedercustomguns.com.

.41 GNR Loading Data and Ballistics

Bullet (grains/type)	Powder	Grains	Velocity	Energy	Source
170 JHP	W 296	29.5	1,980	1,479	Gary Reeder
210 JHP	W 296	28.0	1,900	1,683	Gary Reeder
250 Cast LBT	W 296	28	1,810	1,818	Gary Reeder

.410 GNR

Historical Notes: The .410 GNR was an effort by Gary Reeder to develop another .41-caliber revolver cartridge. It was developed in 2001. Out of a six-inch revolver, the .410 GNR will almost match .41 GNR performance when fired from a 10-inch Contender. It is based on the .454 Casull case, which is necked down to .41-caliber. Due to the high pressures generated by this cartridge, Reeder only offers it in Contender barrels and in revolvers with a five-shot cylinder.

General Comments: This is a powerful revolver cartridge suitable for taking any game animal on earth. Within two months of its release, it was used to take seven buffalo (some African, some Asian), some American bison, and one Australian water buffalo. All but two were taken with one shot each. A 250-grain bullet moving at 1,645 fps out of a six-inch revolver is not something to be taken lightly, regardless of which end of the gun you are on. Information on custom guns, ammunition, and reloading data can be obtained by contacting Gary Reeder Custom Guns, (928) 527-4100 or www.reedercustomguns.com.

.410 GNR Loading Data and Ballistics

Bullet (grains/type)	Powder	Grains	Velocity	Energy	Source
170 Sierra JHP	W 296	33.0	1,900	1,362	Gary Reeder
210 Hornady JHP	Accurate # 9	32.0	1,795	1,502	Gary Reeder
250 Cast LBT	W 296	30.0	1,645	1,502	Gary Reeder

.411 Express

Historical Notes: Created by Z-Hat Custom owner Fred Zeglin in 2002, the .411 Express is the longest version of the .30-06 case that will function in a standard-length action. The .411 Express uses the largest diameter bullet that will fit into the .30-06 case. With good shooting and good bullets, the cartridge is capable of and succeeded in taking North American elk at ranges exceeding 300 yards. The .411 Express is a powerful, large-bore cartridge with stout, but manageable, recoil.

General Comments: This cartridge fits into standard-length actions with a .473-inch bolt face. The .411 Express uses .30-06 cylindrical brass as the parent case. Since the case manufacturer does not neck down cylindrical brass, only experienced handloaders should attempt to form the .411 Express case. The parent brass is necked to .411-inch and then fire-formed in a .411 Express chamber. This Z-Hat offering is best suited for bolt-action rifles using 24-inch barrels with a 1:18 or 1:20 rifling twist. Loaded ammunition and correctly headstamped brass are available from Quality Cartridge (www.qual-cart.com). Z-Hat Custom (www.z-hat.com) offers rifles, dies and reloading information.

.411 Express Loading Data

Bullet (grains)	Powder	Grains	Velocity	Energy	Source/Comments
300	H4895	66.0	2,561	4,368	Z-Hat Custom
360	Accurate Arms 2230	60.0	2,296	4,212	Z-Hat Custom
400	RL-15	59.0	2,160	4,361	Z-Hat Custom

.411 Hawk

Historical Notes: The .411 Hawk is the most popular member in the Hawk family of hunting cartridges. Building on an idea of Bob Fulton's in 1997, Fred Zeglin created the .411 Hawk to accept the largest diameter bullets that can be loaded into the .30-06 case. With the right bullets, the .411 Hawk can produce more than 4,000 ft-lbs of energy from a .30-06 case! This is a premier big-game cartridge, suitable for anything on the North American continent and most game in Africa.

General Comments: All Hawk cartridges fit into standard-length actions with a .473-inch bolt face. The .411 Hawk uses .30-06 cylindrical brass or .35 Whelen brass as the parent case. Since the case manufacturer does not neck down cylindrical brass, only experienced handloaders should attempt to form the .411 Express case from .30-06 cylindrical brass. The cylindrical brass is necked down in a cold forming step and then fire-formed in a .411 Hawk chamber. As an alternative, .35 Whelen brass can be expanded using a .430 tapered expander, and then sized in a full length die and fire-formed in a .411 Hawk chamber. While the .411 Hawk shoulder appears minimal, extensive testing confirmed the shoulder area was ample to safely headspace this powerful cartridge. This Hawk cartridge is suited for bolt-action, single-shot, and lever-action rifles (such as the Browning/Winchester 1895 and BLR) using 24- to 26-inch barrels with a 1:20 rifling twist. Hunters who plan to shoot only 400-grain bullets can use 1:24 twist rifling. Loaded ammunition and correctly headstamped brass are available from Quality Cartridge (www.qual-cart.com). Z-Hat Custom (www.z-hat.com) offers rifles, dies, and reloading information.

.411 Hawk Loading Data

Bullet (grains/type)	Powder	Grains	Velocity	Energy	Source/Comments
300 Hawk	H4895	64.0	2,553	4,341	Z-Hat Custom
325 North Fork	H4895	64.0	2,479	4,434	Z-Hat Custom
350 A-Frame	IMR 4064	61.0	2,366	4,350	Z-Hat Custom
360 North Fork	Accurate Arms 2230	57.0	2,281	4,158	Z-Hat Custom
400 Hawk	RL-15	57.0	2,159	4,139	Z-Hat Custom

.411 JDJ

Historical Notes: Based upon the .444 Marlin case, this cartridge is designed to take advantage of the plentiful .41-caliber pistol and revolver bullets now on the market. With cast rifle bullets sized properly, it provides more versatility than the .416-inch bore. J.D. Jones designed this at SSK Industries.

General Comments: Various pistol and revolver bullets can be loaded to achieve as high as 2400 fps from a 14-inch Contender barrel. Special cast bullets in the 400-grain range are easily loaded to achieve 1,800 fps in the same guns. This approaches top .45-70 modern rifle ballistics. Even with the best Pachmayr Decelerator grips and the most effective muzzle brake possible, this combination will generate massive recoil. Many otherwise competent shooters simply cannot learn to master such a chambering in a handgun. The Barnes 300-grain X bullet offers reduced recoil with potentially superior terminal performance and a flatter trajectory, but requires special handloading techniques (deeper bullet seating and a reduction in powder charge). With the proper bullets, those who can handle the recoil will find this a serious handgun chambering for use against any species in the world. For information on components, loading data, barrels, and guns designed for this cartridge, contact SSK Industries, (720) 264-0176 or www.sskindustries.com.

.411 JDJ Loading Data (Note: These loads for use only in SSK barrels.)

Bullet (grains/type)	Powder	Grains	Velocity	Energy	Source/Comments
210 Sierra	H4198	45.0	1,878	1,640	SSK/maximum load
275 Harrison	H4227	38.0	1,990	2,415	SSK/maximum load
295 Cast	H322	45.0	1,683	1,855	SSK/maximum load
330 Harrison	Rl-7	46.0	2,000	2,930	SSK/maximum load
385 Cast	Rl-7	46.0	1,711	2,500	SSK/maximum load

.416 JDJ

Historical Notes: Based upon the .444 Marlin case, this cartridge is designed to take advantage of the plentiful .416-caliber rifle bullets now on the market. With cast rifle bullets sized properly, it provides some versatility, but is only intended for big-game hunting. J.D. Jones designed this at SSK Industries, after the advent of .416 handloader bullets.

General Comments: Rifle bullets in the 400-grain range are easily loaded to achieve 1800 fps from a 14-inch Contender barrel. This approaches top .45-70 ballistics from a modern rifle. Even with the best Pachmayr Decelerator grips and the most effective muzzle brake possible, this combination will generate massive recoil. Many otherwise competent shooters simply cannot learn to master such a chambering in a handgun. The Barnes 300-grain X bullet offers reduced recoil with potentially superior terminal performance and a flatter trajectory, but requires special handloading techniques (deeper bullet seating and a reduction in powder charge). With the proper bullets, those who can handle the recoil will find this a serious handgun chambering for use against any species in the world. For information on components, loading data, barrels, and guns designed for this cartridge, contact SSK Industries, (720) 264-0176 or www.sskindustries.com.

.416 JDJ Loading Data (Note: These loads for use only in SSK barrels.)

Bullet (grains/type)	Powder	Grains	Velocity	Energy	Source/Comments
300 Hawk	Rl-7	51.0	2,016	2,705	SSK/maximum load
350 CB	AA 2230	56.0	1,908	2,830	SSK/maximum load
400 Hornady	Rl-15	53.5	1,727	2,650	SSK/maximum load
400 Hawk	Rl-15	56.5	1,810	2,910	SSK/maximum load

.416-06 JDJ

Historical Notes: This cartridge was designed by J.D. Jones of SSK Industries. Application is to Thompson/Center Encore single-shot pistols fitted with a custom SSK barrel. Typical barrel length is 15 inches. Cases are formed from empty .35 Whelen cases by special means. Neck length is minimal, which is acceptable for a cartridge used in a single-shot gun. Shoulder angle is 60 degrees, which seems to work just fine. An unusually sharp case shoulder is certainly necessary to maintain headspace against firing pin impact and primer blast. Body taper is minimal, similar to Ackley's Improved designs. Therefore, this is equivalent to a maximized, .41-caliber .30-06 case. Capacity is a whopping 78 grains of water, compared to about 100 grains for the .416 Rem. Mag. Working pressure is about 60,000 psi, so ballistics are, nevertheless, quite impressive. Best handloads in SSK barrels far surpass any normal .35 Whelen loads.

General Comments: Since this case has no rim, it is not generally safe to directly fire-form it in the conventional manner. However, owing to the captive extractor system used in the Encore, it is possible to use a special technique in those guns, to wit: Resize and neck-expand a .35 Whelen case, and then seat a jacketed .416-inch bullet hard against the rifling so that the gun will just close. Correct powder charge is about 5 percent below the maximum SSK-recommended load. Jones recommends 300-grain bullets for big-game hunting applications on medium species, and bullets up to 400 grains for the largest species. Never substitute any bullet without beginning with specific loading data developed for that bullet. Achieving sufficient velocity to assure bullet expansion is an issue. Lightly constructed bullets would seem to be in order here. On the other hand, velocity is adequate with the 400-grain solid to make this a thoroughly acceptable cartridge for hunting any species on this planet. SSK has not fully developed optimal loading data for this number at this time. With heavy bullets and top loads, recoil probably exceeds what most shooters want to experience or could ever learn to handle. Whether this cartridge has sufficient headspace control seems to be an open question. Do not anneal the case, as doing so will almost certainly allow excessive case stretching. For information on components, loading data, barrels, and guns designed for this cartridge, contact SSK Industries, (720) 264-0176 or www.sskindustries.com.

.416-06 JDJ Loading Data (Note: These loads for use only in SSK barrels.)

Bullet (grains)	Powder	Grains	Velocity	Energy	Source/Comments
300	AA 2015	62.3	2,229	3,310	SSK/maximum load/SSK barrels only
400	AA 2015	60.0	2,065	3,785	SSK/maximum load/SSK barrels only

.416 BGA

Historical Notes: A large-bore, high performance cartridge, the .416 BGA was designed in 2003 by Raymond Oelrich, publisher of *Big Game Adventures* magazine, as one of a family of proprietary BGA cartridges. The .416 BGA uses standard-length actions, bolt faces, and magazines. It is a competent peer to other .416 magnum cartridges. The cartridge should do well on elk, moose, bear, and large North American and African game, where reach and good retained energy are needed.

General Comments: The .416 BGA parent case is the European 9.3x64 manufactured to BGA proprietary specifications. The BGA cartridges are not offered for handloaders. Proprietary ammunition is available from A-Square (www.a-squareco.com) and Superior Ammo (www.superiorammo.com).

.416 BGA Factory Ballistics

Bullet (grains)	Powder	Grains	Velocity	Energy	Source/Comments
350	FL	N/A	2,350	4,291	Raymond Oelrich
400	FL	N/A	2,200	4,298	Raymond Oelrich

.416 Dakota

Historical Notes: The .416 Dakota uses a modified full-length .404 Jeffery case, which features a rim that is only slightly larger than the standard belted-magnum rim. In any given-length cartridge, use of the non-belted .404 Jeffery case offers about 15 percent more case capacity than the standard belted magnum. Because maximum case diameter is only slightly larger, one can retain full magazine capacity through minor magazine well modifications. Dakota designed its .416 to offer maximum .416-bore ballistics in a standard-size action.

General Comments: With about 15 percent more usable capacity, the .416 Dakota offers ballistic performance substantially superior to the .416 Remington Magnum. Lacking the belt, this cartridge also feeds better from the magazine and offers potentially superior accuracy. This cartridge requires use of a so-called magnum-length action (3.65 inches). Gunsmiths can easily rechamber most .416 Remington Magnum rifles to .416 Dakota. Restrictive laws often prohibit taking of dangerous game with cartridges of lesser caliber (although often there is no restriction on bullet weight, type, or velocity!), so the various .416s present themselves as a minimum-caliber alternative in some African countries. Many find the reduction in recoil, compared to larger bores shooting heavier bullets, a worthwhile advantage. When loaded with proper spitzer bullets, the .416 Dakota offers a trajectory similar to the .270 Winchester and can deliver energy levels at extended ranges that rival the muzzle energies of many magnum cartridges. However, even with an effective muzzle brake, recoil becomes a bit stiff in typical rifles. Contact Dakota Arms for more information: (605) 347-4686 or www.dakotaarms.com.

.416 Dakota Loading Data and Factory Ballistics

Bullet (grains)	Powder	Grains	Velocity	Energy	Source/Comments
400	IMR 4350	90.0	2,489	5,500	Dakota/maximum load
400	IMR 4831	95.0	2,527	5,670	Dakota/maximum load
400	RI-19	100.0	2,558	5,810	Dakota/maximum load
400	H4831	100.0	2,556	5,800	Dakota/maximum load
400	FL	N/A	2,450	5,330	Dakota factory load

10.57 Maverick

Historical Notes: Lazzeroni Arms designed this cartridge in 1998. While somewhat related to an older case, for all practical purposes, this is a new case design. This cartridge was created in response to requests for a high-performance cartridge that would work in a 2.8-inch action and yet deliver the ballistics of a full-length belted magnum. Adaptation to a standard action is feasible, but is not recommended.

General Comments: Bullet diameter is .416-inch (Lazzeroni bases its designations on bullet diameter, instead of bore diameter, which is the common practice.) Ballistics are quite impressive for such a short cartridge. Given equal-length barrels, the Maverick easily duplicates .416 Remington Magnum ballistics, although in a short-action rifle. Case design is typical of the Lazzeroni line: moderate body taper, 30-degree shoulder, sufficiently long neck, and thick rim of approximate case-body diameter. In other words, this is a well-designed case. For those who feel .37-caliber rifles are a bit on the light side for dangerous-game hunting, this is a fine choice. For more information on Lazzeroni custom guns, ammunition, and reloading data, contact (888) 492-7247 or www.lazzeroni.com.

10.57 Maverick Factory Ballistics (24-inch barrel)

Bullet (grains)	Powder	Grains	Velocity	Energy	Source/Comments
400	FL	N/A	2,400	5,117	Lazzeroni factory load

10.57 Meteor

Historical Notes: Lazzeroni Arms designed this cartridge in 1997. While somewhat related to an older case, for all practical purposes, this is a new case design. This cartridge was created to provide sufficient velocity for heavyweight hunting bullets to provide dependable expansion at intermediate ranges and to have sufficient energy for taking the largest species. Adaptation to standard actions is feasible, but is not recommended.

General Comments: Bullet diameter is .416-inch (Lazzeroni bases its designations on bullet diameter, instead of bore diameter, which is the common practice.) Ballistics equal or exceed any factory .41-caliber cartridge. Case design is typical of the Lazzeroni line: moderate body taper, 30-degree shoulder, sufficiently long neck, and thick rim of approximate case-body diameter. In other words, this is a well-designed case. Designed specifically for dangerous-game hunting, this cartridge is not recommended for any other use. A 24-inch barrel is standard. A longer barrel will not significantly improve ballistics. Muzzle energy approaches 7000 ft-lbs. Lazzeroni's full-length cartridge loadings use premium bullets from Nosler, Barnes, or Swift. These are the only bullets providing the necessary accuracy and terminal performance to meet Lazzeroni's strict requirements. For more information on Lazzeroni custom guns, ammunition, and reloading data, contact (888) 492-7247 or www.lazzeroni.com.

10.57 Meteor Factory Ballistics (24-inch barrel)

Bullet (grains/type)	Powder	Grains	Velocity	Energy	Source/Comments
300 Barnes X	FL	N/A	3,100	6,400	Lazzeroni factory load
400	FL	N/A	2,750	6,719	Lazzeroni factory load

.416 Rimmed

Historical Notes: This cartridge was designed by A-Square about 1991, at the behest of several Continental rifle makers. This is essentially a lengthened and rimmed .416 Rigby. Cartridge length (capacity) was chosen to allow 400-grain bullets to reach 2400 fps, with pressures that are acceptable in double rifles (about 40,000 psi). The basic design is quite good. For the first time, the hunter who prefers a double rifle in .41-caliber can achieve the vaunted ballistics of typical .41-caliber bolt-action rifle/cartridge combinations. Older .41-caliber double-rifle numbers fall short of this mark by several hundred feet per second.

General Comments: A-Square (www.a-squareco.com) specializes in cartridges and bullets intended for dangerous game applications. This new number is an interesting mix of old and new. Professional dangerous game hunters have long recognized that a muzzle velocity of about 2400 fps seems to be about ideal for these applications. Equally, the .41-caliber bore size launching 400-grain bullets has long been recognized as a fine combination. In guns of reasonable weight, recoil is manageable, while both delivered energy and penetration potential are significant. For more information on A-square custom rifles and ammunition, contact (605) 234-0500 (South Dakota), (307) 436-5677 (Wyoming) or www.a-squareco.com.

.416 Rimmed Loading Data and Factory Ballistics

Bullet (grains/type)	Powder	Grains	Velocity	Energy	Source/Comments
400 Lion	IMR 7828	112	2,437	5,275	A-Square
400 Lion	RI-22	108	2,402	5,125	A-Square
400	FL	N/A	2,400	5,115	A-Square factory load

.416 Taylor

Historical Notes: The .416 Taylor was developed by Robert Chatfield-Taylor in 1972. It is based on the .458 Winchester Magnum case necked-down to .416-caliber. However, it can also be made by necking up .338 Winchester Magnum cases. The late Chatfield-Taylor was a writer and hunter of note, and he used the cartridge in Africa and reported very favorably on it. It was also checked out on Cape buffalo, elephant, and lion by several others with success, including John Wootters. At one time, there were rumors that the cartridge would be commercialized by Remington or Winchester, but it remained for A-Square to do that. The .416 Taylor is ballistically similar to the .416 Rigby and is adequate for the same range of game, including the tough, dangerous, African varieties. It is overpowered for most North American big game, but would be good backup against brown bears.

General Comments: The .416 Taylor came about partly because .416 Rigby cartridges and cases were difficult to obtain, and partly because the .416-caliber represents a gap in the lineup of American commercial cartridges. The .416 Taylor can also be used in a standard-length action. This gap has now been filled by Remington with its .416 Remington Magnum based on the 8mm Remington Magnum case, and by Weatherby with its new .416. In 1988, Federal introduced .416 Rigby ammunition, thus ending the shortage of .416 Rigby ammunition.

The .416 Taylor can be considered something of a forerunner to the Remington .416, because it proved the feasibility and effectiveness of a new .416-caliber to replace the venerable .416 Rigby. The cases are easy to make, and RCBS (www.rcbs.com) can furnish loading dies. Originally, the problem was the availability of good .416-inch bullets. However, that deficiency has been eliminated by Barnes and Hornady. A-Square (www.a-squareco.com) currently furnishes rifles, cases, bullets, and loaded ammunition in .416 Taylor, so it has become a proprietary cartridge.

.416 Taylor Loading Data and Factory Ballistics

Bullet (grains/type)	Powder	Grains	Velocity	Energy	Source/Comments
400 SP	IMR 4320	70.0	2,270	4,595	N/A
400 SP	IMR 4320	71.0	2,305	4,700	N/A
400	FL	N/A	2,350	4,905	A-Square factory load

.416 Hoffman

Historical Notes: The .416 Hoffman is another wildcat cartridge adopted by A-Square Co., with bullets and loaded ammunition currently available there. It originated with George L. Hoffman, of Sonora, Texas, in the late 1970s, and is based on the necked-up and Improved .375 H&H Magnum case. Ballistically, it duplicates the .416 Rigby and the .416 Taylor, except that the case is about 3/10-inch longer than the Taylor and holds more powder. The case is of smaller base diameter than the Rigby, which allows an extra round to be carried in a magazine of equal size. A-Square can also furnish rifles of this caliber.

General Comments: The .416 Hoffman is the most practical of the .416 wildcats, because it does not require reworking .375 H&H cases. With its 400-grain bullet at 2,400 fps, it is relatively flat shooting to 200 yards and extremely accurate. It would be a good candidate for a one-gun cartridge to use on whatever Africa has to offer. Although overpowered for most North American big game, it would nevertheless do very well on moose or grizzly bear and could be loaded down for use on some of the smaller species. It is a very good cartridge for those who need or favor the .416-bore. Being very similar, Remington's .416 seems a superior option. For more information on A-square custom rifles and ammunition, contact (605) 234-0500 (South Dakota), (307) 436-5677 (Wyoming) or www.a-squareco.com.

.416 Hoffman Loading Data and Factory Ballistics

Bullet (grains/type)	Powder	Grains	Velocity	Energy	Source/Comments
400 SP	IMR 4064	77.0	2,400	5,125	N/A
400 SP	IMR 4895	74.0	2,350	4,910	N/A
400 SP	IMR 4895	77.0	2,425	5,230	N/A
400 SP	IMR 4320	77.0	2,400	5,125	N/A
400 SP	IMR 4350	88.0	2,375	5,040	N/A
400	FL	N/A	2,400	5,125	A-Square factory load

.416 Barrett

Historical Notes: The .416 Barrett was developed by Pete Forrest, of Barrett Firearms, a well-known Tennessee manufacturer of bolt-action and semiautomatic rifles chambered for the .50 Browning Machine Gun cartridge. A number of rifles built by Barrett have been used successfully by American troops deployed in Iraq and Afghanistan. The .416 Barrett is the .50 BMG case shortened to a length of 3.273 inches and necked down to accept bullets of .416-inch diameter, the same diameter as bullets loaded in the .416 Remington Magnum and .416 Rigby. Shoulder angle of the case is 25 degrees. It was initially loaded with a solid bronze bullet of Very Low Drag (VLD) form weighing 395 grains. As of early 2009, Barrett, McMillan, and EDM Arms offer rifles chambered to .416 Barrett.

General Comments: How the performance of the .416 Barrett stacks up against the .50 BMG in performance depends on which loading of the .50 the .416 Barrett is compared. The Barrett cartridge is more accurate than standard military loadings of the Big Fifty, but, since that cartridge has proven to be capable of sub-minute-of-angle accuracy out to 1,000 yards when loaded with a match bullet such as the Hornady 750-grain V-Max, the accuracy potential of the two cartridges is probably about the same. Ballistic coefficient of the Barrett bullet is .730, lower than the 1.050 of the Hornady bullet. That, along with the additional weight of the latter, gives the larger caliber a considerable edge in downrange energy delivery. When the 395-grain VLD bullet of the .416 Barrett exits the muzzle at 3,290 fps, its residual energy at 1,000 yards is 3710 ft-lbs. When the Hornady .50-caliber, 750-grain V-Max starts out at 2,850 fps, it is packing 6,900 ft-lbs at 1,000 yards. Bullet drop and wind deflection are also less for the .50 BMG. In the favor of the .416 Barrett is a lower level of recoil and less ammo weight, both important characteristics in a combat cartridge designed to be used in shoulder-fired weapons. Contact Barrett at (615) 896-2938 or www.barrett.net.

.416 Barrett Loading Data and Factory Ballistics

Bullet (grains/type)	Powder	Grains	Velocity	Energy	Source
395 Solid VLD	FL	N/A	3,290	9,517	Barrett

416 B&M — *NEW*

Historical Notes: The 416 B&M (Bruton & McCourry) is designed for the Winchester M70 Winchester Short Magnum control-feed action with 18- and 20-inch barrels, but 20-inch barrels are optimum because some loads lose velocity in 18-inch tubes. However, the shooter might be willing to sacrifice velocity for handling and ease of use in the field in certain situations.

General Comments: The 416 B&M is a versatile rifle and cartridge combination that is at its best with 350-grain bullets. In 20 inches of barrel, it runs most 350-grain bullets faster than 2,450 fps, and in 18 inches of barrel, 2,400 fps and more. It makes an awfully good Alaskan rifle, as it's only 38 inches long and weighs 6.5 pounds. The 325-grain Cutting Edge Bullets' BBW#13 NonCon hollowpoint is more than enough for anything you might encounter in Alaska.

For plains game, moose and elk, the 416 B&M fires a Cutting Edge 225-grain hollowpoint, seated deeply to accommodate a Talon Tip nose safely, at 2,926 fps in 18-inch barrels and 2,992 fps in 20-inch barrels. It's also suitable for dangerous game such as lions, bears and leopards. Heavier bullets, such as the the 325 and 350 solid Safari bullets from Cutting edge, are better for buffalo and other dangerous game.

To make 416 B&M brass, cut the .300 RUM case close to 2.240 inches, and then trim, lube and run through the 416 sizing die. The formed case should bump against the shoulder just a bit when chambering. The maker says the 416 B&M can suffer from case-head separation with ball powders. If you use an extruded tubular powder such as RL-15, IMR 4320, and IMR 8208 with the heavier bullets, you can full-length resize the case, and it will be easy to chamber and will last more than 10 firings.

Bullet (grains/type)	Powder	Grains	Velocity	Energy	Source/Comments
300 ESP Raptor	AA 2520	75	2,627	4,596	B&M Load Data Sheet

.425 Express

Historical Notes: The .425 Express was developed as a joint effort between Cameron Hopkins and Whit Collins, with John French building the prototype rifle. The entire story was published in the May 1988 issue of Guns magazine. The cartridge is based on the .300 Winchester Magnum case shortened from 2.620 inches to 2.550 inches, then fire-formed in the .425 chamber. Loading dies are available from Redding Reloading Equipment (www.redding-reloading.com). The prototype rifle was built on a Ruger Model 77 action.

General Comments: The .425 Express fills a gap in the medium-bore cartridge lineup between the 3.75 Holland & Holland Magnum and the .458 Winchester Magnum. This cartridge fits standard-length bolt actions, such as the Winchester Model 70, 1917 Enfield, Mauser 98, or other similar-length actions. This cartridge uses either a 350-grain or a 400-grain bullet and has proven very effective on heavy African game. It is overpowered for most North American hunting, but would provide a margin of safety if going after brown bears in the far North. Colonel Charles Askins used the .425 Express very successfully on buffalo in Australia. A-Square (www.a-squareco.com) now loads .425 Express ammunition.

.425 Express Loading Data

Bullet (grains/type)	Powder	Grains	Velocity	Energy	Source/Comments
350 SP	IMR 4064	79.0	2,535	5,000	Cameron Hopkins
350 SP	H4895	77.0	2,490	4,825	Cameron Hopkins
350 SP	W760	77.0	2,210	3,795	Cameron Hopkins
400 SP	H4895	73.0	2,420	5,210	Cameron Hopkins
400 SP	IMR 4064	76.0	2,370	4,995	Cameron Hopkins
400 SP	W760	76.0	2,155	4,120	Cameron Hopkins

.44/454 JDJ Woodswalker

Historical Notes: A big-bore, short-range hunting round from SSK Industries, the .44/454 JDJ Woodswalker is based on necking the powerful 454 Casull cartridge to 44-caliber. Barrels, dies, and cases for the 44/454 JDJ are available from SSK Industries (www.sskindustries.com).

General Comments: Using a .44-caliber, 300-grain Nosler projectile in modified .454 Casull cases and 15-inch SSK barrels, the .44/454 JDJ achieves about 2100 fps. With the Hornady 240-grain XTP bullet, it can reach 2300 fps. It is suitable for the Thompson/Center Encore.

.440 CorBon

Historical Notes: CorBon designed this cartridge in 1997 by the simple expedient of necking down the .50 Action Express to .44-caliber (actually, a .429-inch bullet). This case has a reasonably long neck. With the advent of the

.50 AE and the existence of plentiful .44-caliber pistol bullets, this was an obvious choice for a high-performance hunting chambering geared toward those who prefer a semi-automatic handgun.

Compared to the parent case, this design offers several advantages. First, conversion of the gun is completed by a simple barrel replacement. Second, owing to the bottleneck, this cartridge can give better functioning with a wider variety of bullet shapes and is generally more forgiving toward machining, fit, and finish tolerances. Finally, for any given energy level, the .440 CorBon produces significantly less recoil than the .50 AE and shoots flatter (lighter bullets, launched faster). However, with top loads, the .440 cannot match the energy of the .50 AE.

General Comments: This is a very fine cartridge for those who do not like excessive recoil. Factory loads offer significant hunting handgun ballistics in a package that most shooters can easily learn to handle (providing only that they have large enough hands to properly hold the gun). Except for a flatter trajectory with the .440 CorBon, those who are satisfied with the .50 AE will probably find little appeal to this conversion. On the other hand, those who are dissatisfied with the .44 Magnum and who can handle the big AE pistol might find this a viable option. Cases are easily converted from .50 AE cases. This chambering offers the handloader a wide selection of bullets, which is not the case with the .50 AE. Ballistics of the .440 CorBon are essentially those of the .454 Casull. For more information on CorBon ammunition, contact (800) 626-7266 or www.shopcorbon.com.

.440 CorBon Loading Data and Factory Ballistics

Bullet (grains)	Powder	Grains	Velocity	Energy	Source/Comments
240	H110 | W296	30.0	1,800	1,725	CorBon
260	IMR 4227	27.5	1,700	1,665	CorBon
240	FL	N/A	1,900	1,920	CorBon factory load
260	FL	N/A	1,700	1,665	CorBon factory load
305	FL	N/A	1,600	1,730	CorBon factory load

45 Raptor — *NEW*

Historical Notes: The 45 Raptor is a new round for the AR-10 rifle platform developed by Arne Brennan. The case is a necked-up .308 Win. case with a case length and body dimensions of a .460 S&W. In effect, the 45 Raptor turns the .460 S&W revolver cartridge into a rifle cartridge by modifying the existing rimmed cartridge case and changing it into a rimless profile, matching the rim and extractor specifications of the .308 Win. It fits the AR-10 rifle platform to take advantage of the case strength and operating pressures of the .308 Win.

The 45 Raptor was developed as a big-bore hunting cartridge for deer, hogs, elk, moose and bears within 200 yards, supplying one-third more energy at 100 yards than the .50 Beowulf, .450 Bushmaster or .458 SOCOM. The designer limited the case length to 1.800 inches, which would make the cartridge legal for rifle hunting in Indiana.

Contact Brennan at arne@northamericansportsman.com or RaptorShootingSystems.com.

General Comments: Differentiated from the .460 S&W Mag, the 45 Raptor's rimless design head-spaces off the case mouth and has additional clearances in the chamber for use in a semi-automatic rifle. In addition, the throat design has increased freebore and a shallower lead angle than the .460 S&W Mag.'s SAAMI-specified chamber dimensions.

Brass, magazines and muzzle brakes are available for order at Raptor Shooting Systems. Barrels are available for order from Satern Custom Machine. 460 S&W Mag. reloading dies are available from multiple manufacturers and multiple large reloading tool and component dealers, including MidwayUSA.com and Brownells.com. Bullets and published load data designed for the .460 S&W Mag. and .454 Casull are suitable for the 45 Raptor. The 45 Raptor maintains the same magazine capacity as a similarly-sized .308 Win. magazine; that is, a 20-round .308 Win. magazine also holds 20 45 Raptor cartridges. Currently, five- and 20-round magazines are available by special order from Medesha Firearms.

Initially, the 45 Raptor is being offered with a 16-inch barrel, with the muzzle threaded ¾-24 for brakes and suppressors.

Starline produces 45 Raptor brass to the same pressure capacity specifications as the .460 S&W Mag. The manufacturer advises that handloaders don't full-length-resize new brass, which can make it brittle and can lead to splitting cases, especially if the round is overcrimped. Also, only minimally flare the case mouth to seat bullets in the case. When using a taper-crimp die, do not overcrimp the case. Only taper-crimp the loaded round to return the flared portion of the case to the remainder of the case. Recommended powders include Accurate 5744, Accurate 1680, Accurate LT-30, IMR 4227, Hodgdon H4198 and Alliant 300MP, following established load-development practices.

45 Raptor Loading Data

Bullet (grains/type)	Powder	Grains	Velocity	Energy	Source/Comments
225 Barnes X	H110	42.0	2,500	3,122	Hodgdon
240 Hdy XTP	H4227	45.0	2,500	3,330	Hodgdon
250 Barnes X	Li'l Gun	42.0	2,400	3,916	Hodgdon

.458 SOCOM

Historical Notes: After a bloody 1993 battle in Mogadishu, Somalia, several individuals addressed the opportunity to increase single-hit stopping power from the U.S. military's M-16 and M-4 family of rifles and carbines. Maarten ter Weeme (Teppo Jutsu LLC) developed the .458 SOCOM cartridge to provide the equivalent of .45-70 firepower from M-16 rifles. The .458 SOCOM hurls big chunks of metal at substantial velocity from unaltered lower receivers and magazines—in full auto and suppressed, if desired. During testing, the cartridge defeated Level IIIa protective vests.

General Comments: The .458 SOCOM uses the .50 AE as the parent case, lengthened to 1.575 inches (40mm) and necked to accept .458-inch bullets. It features a rebated .473-inch rim. It accepts readily available .458-caliber bullets ranging from 250 grains to 600 grains and in a wide variety of bullet styles and construction. Using standard M-16 lower receivers and unmodified magazines, 10 .458 SOCOM rounds will fit into a military 30-round M-16 magazine; the 20-round magazine will hold seven rounds. In 16-inch barreled rifles, the 600-grain subsonic load works well with a 1:14 rifling twist. The 300-grain bullets do better with a 1:18 twist. CorBon supplies loaded .458 SOCOM ammunition (www.shopcorbon.com); Starline offers new brass cases (ww.starlinebrass.com), CH4D lists reloading dies (www.ch4d.com); and Teppo Jutsu LLC provides reloading data (www.teppojutsu.com).

.458 SOCOM Factory Ballistics

Bullet (grains)	Powder	Grains	Velocity	Energy	Source/Comments
300	FL	N/A	2,000	N/A	Teppo Jutsu LLC
500	FL	N/A	1,300	N/A	Teppo Jutsu LLC

.458 Whisper

Historical Notes: Designed by J.D. Jones of SSK Industries in 1993, this chambering uses a shortened .458 Winchester Magnum case. With custom 600-grain very low drag (VLD) bullets, this cartridge will function through standard-length magazines. The design intent was to create a hard-hitting subsonic round with superior penetration potential.

General Comments: This is a rather esoteric chambering. For proper use, it requires very expensive custom bullets. Nevertheless, ballistic consistency and accuracy are impressive. When launched at subsonic velocities (1040 fps is typical for the .458 Whisper), the long and heavy VLD bullet loses velocity so slowly that crosswinds have little effect. It also retains much of its muzzle energy beyond one mile! For information on components, loading data, barrels, and guns designed for this cartridge, contact SSK Industries, (720) 264-0176 or www.sskindustries.com.

.458 Whisper Loading Data

Bullet (grains/type)	Powder	Grains	Velocity	Energy	Source/Comments
500 H.T.	W231	15.6	1,021	1,155	SSK/subsonic
560 H.T.	BlueDot	18.0	1,101	1,505	SSK/subsonic
600 H.T.	AA 2015	27.0	1,044	1,450	SSK/subsonic

458 B&M — *NEW*

Historical Notes: The 458 B&M is another proprietary cartridge in a series made by William V. Bruton and Michael McCourry. They based the B&Ms on 2.240-inch-long (trimmed) Remington Ultra Magnum cases to fit in lighter, short Winchester M70 WSM bolt-actions with barrels of 18 or 20 inches.

The 458 B&M is derived from the 50 B&M (which see). The original specs for the 458 B&M called for a case length of 2.295 inches, but McCourry said available .458-caliber bullets would not seat to a proper overall length at 2.295. So he shortened the case to 2.240 inches.

General Comments: The 458 B&M has the same case capacity as the 458 Win. Mag. But the 458 Win. takes a 24-inch barrel to reach its potential, where the 458 B&M produces similar speeds in an 18-inch barrel on a 7- to 8-pound rifle.

When the RUM brass is cut to 2.240 inches, it's run through an appropriate B&M-size die to make this and other B&M chamberings (which see). All B&M-series rifles are built by SSK Industries. Custom-loaded ammo is also available from Superior Ammunition. Properly head-stamped brass is available, or you can make your own brass, the process for which is detailed on the B&M website.

458 B&M Loading Data

Bullet (grains/type)	Powder	Grains	Velocity	Energy	Source/Comments
450 Swift A	2520	78	2,251	5,061	B&M Load Data Sheet

458 B&M Super Short — *NEW*

Historical Notes: Premiering in 2011, the 458 B&M Super Short is the smallest in this line made by William V. Bruton and Michael McCourry. Like its larger stablemates (50 B&M Super Short and 475 B&M Super Short), the 458 B&M Super Short is a Winchester Short Magnum case cut and trimmed to 1.65 inches and then formed in a sizing die. Some trimming might be required after forming.

General Comments: The B&M Super Shorts are made to fit in a Winchester M70 WSSM control-feed action and chambered in a 16.25-inch barrel with a 1:14 twist rate. The rifle weighs only 6.25 pounds and measures 36 inches in overall length and can handle a range of bullet weights. A Cutting Edge 250-grain BBW#13 NonCon HP hits 2,700 fps muzzle velocity out of a 16.25-inch barrel. A North Fork 300-grain Soft Point hits 2,505 fps. The case accepts a 325-grain BBW #13 solid and runs it at 2,314 fps.

458 B&M Super Short Loading Data

Bullet (grains/type)	Powder	Grains	Velocity	Energy	Source/Comments
250 CEB BBW#13 Talon Tip	LilGun	52	2,618	3,804	B&M Load Data Sheet
300 Remington HP	WW 297	45	2,185	3,179	B&M Load Data Sheet

.460 A-Square Short

Historical Notes: The A-Square series of cartridges was designed, in 1974, by Col. Arthur Alphin, in response to a hunting incident involving a Cape buffalo and a hunter equipped with a .458 Winchester Magnum. (Alphin first designed the .500 A-Square, with the purpose of providing maximum stopping power.) In order to gain more powder capacity and more power, all original A-Square cartridges were based upon the .460 Weatherby case.

General Comments: The .460 A-Square Short provides better ballistics than the .458 Winchester, but with the same length cartridge. It would be an excellent choice for re-chambering a .458 Winchester. Aside from re-chambering, this would require work on the magazine well and feed ramp, as well as opening up the bolt face. This cartridge can easily push a 500-grain bullet at velocities of 2400 fps or more. The .460 Short is an efficient cartridge, as well as a very accurate one. Groups tighter than one inch at 100 yards have been reported on numerous occasions. For more information on A-square custom rifles and ammunition, contact (605) 234-0500 (South Dakota), (307) 436-5677 (Wyoming) or www.a-squareco.com.

.460 A-Square Short Loading Data

Bullet (grains/type)	Powder	Grains	Velocity	Energy	Source/Comments
500 SP	IMR 4064	88.0	2,385	6,315	A-Square
500 SP	IMR 4895	91.0	2,450	6,670	A-Square
500 SP	IMR 4320	91.0	2,435	6,580	A-Square
500 SP	IMR 4320	91.0	2,435	6,580	A-Square

.458 Canadian Magnum

Historical Notes: North American Shooting Systems (NASS) developed this cartridge about 1994. This cartridge features a slightly rebated, rimless bottleneck case. Design intent was provision of maximum powder capacity in a standard action with minimal gunsmithing. (Without deepening the magazine well slightly, use of this cartridge usually reduces magazine capacity by one round.) Bolt face alteration is unnecessary. Cartridge feeding and headspacing characteristics are improved. This particular cartridge is factory loaded to modest pressures to provide proper functioning in the hottest climes—a worthwhile consideration.

General Comments: This cartridge takes advantage of the entire 3.65-inch magazine length of the long-action Remington M700 and similar rifles. This represents the maximum feasible bullet size for use in this beltless case—headspace control, while adequate, is marginal with such a narrow case shoulder (one would be well advised to avoid magnum-strength striker springs). Body diameter is significantly larger than the standard belted magnum (.544-inch versus .513-inch at the base). Re-chambering of nominal belted magnums with the same bore diameter is generally quite simple, requiring no other rifle alterations. For any given case length, capacity is about 15 percent greater than can be achieved with the belted version. Body taper is minimal and the case shoulder is comparatively sharp. However, neck length is sufficiently generous to provide good bullet purchase for hunting ammunition.

.458 Canadian Magnum Loading Data and Factory Ballistics

Bullet (grains)	Powder	Grains	Velocity	Energy	Source/Comments
500	IMR 4064	89.0	2,360	6,180	NASS/maximum
350	FL	N/A	2,575	5,150	NASS factory load

.450 Dakota

Historical Notes: Formerly, Dakota had based its entire cartridge line on the .404 Jeffery case. With the introduction of the .450 Dakota, that changed. Dakota's latest addition, the .450 Dakota, uses an Improved .416 Rigby case. Design purpose was to provide a cartridge capable of driving a 500-grain bullet at about 2,400 fps with moderate chamber pressures.

General Comments: Since the .450 Dakota uses an Improved full-length .416 Rigby case, capacity is substantially identical to the .460 Weatherby Magnum. Obviously, if loaded to similar pressures, these two will produce similar ballistics. However, Dakota does not advocate loading this cartridge to full Weatherby pressures. The logic: By slightly reducing peak pressure, one can ease the effort of extracting a fired case. This approach also helps to minimize pressure excursions related to use under extreme tropical heat. Since that is what this cartridge was designed for, such an approach seems reasonable. When loaded to similar peak pressures, the .450 Dakota can propel a 500-grain bullet about 350 fps faster than the .458 Winchester Magnum. The nominal .450 Dakota loading gives up only about 150 fps to full-power .460 Weatherby loads. If one follows Dakota's advice, one ends up with a load propelling a 500-grain bullet at about 2450 fps. Most dangerous-game experts agree that 2,450 fps is nearly the perfect muzzle velocity for maximizing terminal performance with solids. Because of its non-belted design, this cartridge offers superior functioning from a box magazine and can deliver superior accuracy. However, most would agree that recoil is a bit heavy for a day of shooting holes in paper targets. Contact Dakota Arms for more information: (605) 347-4686 or www.dakotaarms.com.

.450 Dakota Loading Data and Factory Ballistics

Bullet (grains)	Powder	Grains	Velocity	Energy	Source/Comments
400	RI-15	105.0	2,732	6,625	Dakota/maximum load
400	IMR 4064	105.0	2,763	6,775	Dakota/maximum load
400	IMR 4350	115.0	2,650	6,235	Dakota/maximum load
500	H4350	110.0	2,460	6,715	Dakota/maximum load
500	IMR 4350	110.0	2,470	6,770	Dakota/maximum load
500	IMR 4831	112.0	2,444	6,630	Dakota/maximum load
500	FL	N/A	2,450	6,663	Dakota factory load

.450 Ackley Magnum

Historical Notes: The late, great gunsmith and master experimenter Parker Ackley designed this cartridge about 1960. Ackley describes the genesis of the .458 Ackley as an effort to achieve maximum feasible case capacity using the full-length (2.85-inch) H&H belted magnum case necked to .45-caliber. Obviously, this required elimination of most of the case body taper and incorporation of a sharp case shoulder with a comparatively short neck. Ackley recognized that several others had designed very similar cartridges with the same goals and essentially identical results. A-Square (www.a-squareco.com), which now offers factory ammunition, adopted this chambering about 1995.

General Comments: Compared to the tapered-case .458 Watts, this Ackley-designed number does achieve the same velocity with somewhat less pressure. Conversely, this cartridge does provide for slightly more muzzle velocity when loaded to any given peak chamber pressure. Ackley noted that any difference is essentially academic. All similar numbers can deliver similarly large doses of energy and recoil in guns of reasonable weight. According to Ackley, an advantage the .458 Watts has over this chambering is that one can safely fire .458 Winchester Magnum ammunition in the Watts chamber. Field testing has confirmed this. Further, Ackley reported that some users complained of limited case life with this number. Evidently, the modest case shoulder can allow excessive brass working during the firing and resizing cycle.

.450 Ackley Magnum Loading Data and Factory Ballistics

Bullet (grains/type)	Powder	Grains	Velocity	Energy	Source/Comments
465 Solid	H4895	86.0	2,422	6,055	A-Square
465 Solid	IMR 4064	86.0	2,376	5,830	A-Square
465 Solid	RI-12	88.0	2,395	5,925	A-Square
465 Solid	FL	N/A	2,400	5,950	A-Square factory load

.450 Assegai

Historical Notes: This cartridge was designed by A-Square at the behest of several professional African hunters. The .450 Assegai case is similar to a lengthened, rimmed .416 Rigby case. This makes it suitable for application to double rifles. Cartridge length (capacity) was chosen to allow 500-grain bullets to reach 2,400 fps with acceptable double rifle pressures (about 40,000 psi). The basic design is quite good. The hunter who prefers a double rifle in .45-caliber can achieve the vaunted ballistics of the best .45-caliber bolt-action rifle/cartridge combinations, with a case of reasonable capacity. Older .45-caliber double rifle numbers cannot achieve this velocity with acceptable pressures. The Assegai (pronounced, approximately, as AS-sa-guy) is the ancient stabbing spear of the Zulu, which makes this an interesting moniker for this thoroughly modern cartridge.

General Comments: This new number is an interesting mix of old and new. Professional dangerous-game hunters have long recognized that a muzzle velocity of about 2400 fps seems to be about ideal for these applications. Some prefer more bullet weight than smaller calibers can manage. Compared to the .41-caliber with a 400-grain bullet, the .45-caliber launching a 500-grain bullet has long been recognized as a fine combination for those who can handle the heavier rifle and increased recoil. A-Square (www.a-squareco.com) can supply brass. For more information on A-square custom rifles and ammunition, contact (605) 234-0500 (South Dakota), (307) 436-5677 (Wyoming) or www.a-squareco.com.

.450 Assegai Loading Data and Factory Ballistics

Bullet (grains/type)	Powder	Grains	Velocity	Energy	Source/Comments
500 Lion	H4831	125	2,480	6,830	A-Square
500 Lion	IMR 4831	117	2,379	6,285	A-Square
500 Lion	RI-22	120	2,378	6,280	A-Square
500	FL	N/A	2,400	6,400	A-Square factory load

.475 Linebaugh

Historical Notes: The .475 Linebaugh is the creation of John Linebaugh, of Maryville, Missouri. It is a current favorite in the contest to develop the world's most powerful revolver cartridge, a role it fills rather well. The cartridge is based on the .45-70 government case cut off at 1½ inches and loaded with .475-inch diameter bullets weighing from 320 to 440 grains. The gun used is a modified, large-frame Ruger Bisley revolver fitted with a five-shot cylinder and 5½-inch barrel. Longer barrels are available if so desired. Freedom Arms (www.freedomarms.com) now chambers this round.

Cutting .45-70 cases to a length of 1½ inches is not a new idea—the original author of this book did this in 1984 to make the .45 Silhouette. However, adapting the 1½-inch rimmed case to handle .47-caliber bullets is definitely an innovative move.

The .475 Linebaugh was first announced in an article written by Ross Seyfried, in the May 1988 issue of

Guns & Ammo magazine. Loading dies are available from RCBS (www.rcbs.com) and Redding (www.redding-reloading.com).

General Comments: The .475 Linebaugh, like all other super-magnum handgun cartridges, is intended primarily for hunting big game or as a backup when confronting dangerous animals. A 370-grain bullet starting out at 1,495 fps develops 1,840 ft-lbs of energy, and a 440-grain bullet at 1,360 fps develops 1800 ft-lbs. This is 108 ft-lbs greater than top .454 Casull loadings, so we can accept the claim that the .475 Linebaugh is one of the world's most powerful revolver cartridge. However, other factors would probably make it even more effective, because the top energy load for the .454 Casull is a 260-grain bullet at 1,723 fps muzzle velocity. If we compare the 300-grain .454 bullet at 1,353 fps and 1,220 ft-lbs, with the 370-grain .475 bullet at 1,495 fps and 1,840 ft-lbs, the difference is even more pronounced in favor of the .475. In fact, this works out to be 620 ft-lbs more energy on the side of the .475 Linebaugh. On the other hand, if we are talking about handgun cartridges in general, a number of silhouette cartridges fired in single-shot pistols produce more energy than the .475. In any event, the .475 Linebaugh should make a very fine big-game revolver cartridge for those who insist on the biggest or the most. Buffalo Bore (www.buffalobore.com) now offers factory loaded ammunition.

.475 Linebaugh Loading Data and Factory Ballistics

Bullet (grains/type)	Powder	Grains	Velocity	Energy	Source/Comments
370 SP	W296	25.0	1,000	825	John Linebaugh
370 SP	H110	29.0	1,285	1,360	John Linebaugh
370 SP	H110	33.0	1,495	1,840	John Linebaugh
440 SP	W296	27.0	1,280	1,605	John Linebaugh
440 SP	W296	29.0	1,360	1,800	John Linebaugh
420 LFN	FL	N/A	950	840	Buffalo Bore factory load
420 LFN	FL	N/A	1,350	1,695	Buffalo Bore factory load
420 WFN	FL	N/A	1,350	1,695	Buffalo Bore factory load
440 ExWN	FL	N/A	1,300	1,650	Buffalo Bore factory load
350 JHP	FL	N/A	1,500	1,745	Buffalo Bore factory load
400 JFN	FL	N/A	1,400	1,740	Buffalo Bore factory load

.475 JDJ

Historical Notes: This cartridge was designed and developed by J.D. Jones, hence the JDJ designation. Jones began development of his series of cartridges in 1978. They are generally fired in barrels furnished by his company, SSK Industries. The purpose of these cartridges is to give added range and power to the Thompson/Center Contender pistol for the primary purpose of hunting. Some of Jones' cartridges have proven to be excellent metallic silhouette cartridges. The JDJ series is relatively simple and easy to make. All of the JDJ cartridges are proprietary, and SSK neither sells reamers nor permits the reamer maker to sell them. If you desire a JDJ cartridge, contact SSK Industries (www.sskindustries.com).

General Comments: The .475 JDJ is the first .475-caliber handgun cartridge. It is made by straightening out the tapered .45-70 Government case to a straight-wall configuration. This is easily done by expanding the neck and firing a .475-inch bullet. Cast bullets work very well in this cartridge, and many good designs are available. Standard .475-inch rifle bullets will not expand reliably. However, a .475-inch diameter 500-grain bullet pushed at 1650 fps does expand—big animals fall down quickly. Jones has taken several buffalo with the .475. When properly loaded, it is very impressive on animals in the 2,000-pound category. It is noticeably more effective than the .45-70 Government, when loaded correctly. Recoil exceeds what most shooters can tolerate. On deer, 400-grain Hornady pistol bullets deliver excellent results. For information on components, loading data, barrels, and guns designed for this cartridge, contact SSK Industries, (720) 264-0176 or www.sskindustries.com.

.475 JDJ Loading Data

Bullet (grains/type)	Powder	Grains	Velocity	Energy	Source/Comments
298 Cast	H322	54.0	Fire-forming	N/A	SSK Industries, Inc.
400 Hornady	2015BR	53.0	Not Specified	N/A	SSK Industries, Inc.
440	H322	54.0	1,727	N/A	SSK Industries, Inc.
500 Cast	IMR 3031	48.5	1,338	N/A	SSK Industries, Inc.
500 Woodleigh	IMR 3031	48.5	1,140	N/A	SSK Industries, Inc.

.470 Capstick

Historical Notes: This cartridge was designed by Col. Arthur B. Alphin and is named after the famous author and African big-game hunter Peter Capstick. It delivers the maximum possible power from the .375 H&H Magnum case size while retaining the greater magazine capacity of the H&H over the Weatherby or Rigby cartridges. The .475-inch diameter bullets deliver much more shock than the .458-caliber cartridges. The .470 Capstick is designed for heavy game out to 200 yards, and dangerous game at close ranges. Trajectory is flat enough to allow taking medium-size game at ranges up to 250 yards.

General Comments: The .470 Capstick was designed to deliver 500-grain bullets at a muzzle velocity of approximately 2400 fps. It offers a muzzle energy of 6394 ft-lbs and retains well over 5200 ft-lbs of energy at 100 yards. The .470 Capstick is nearly identical in dimensions to the .475 Ackley Magnum, designed quite a few years prior. Probably the most notable difference is the use of a 500-grain bullet in the .470 Capstick (as opposed to a 600-grain bullet), in order to obtain a flatter trajectory. Capstick was a legend in his own time and did much to promote African hunting. He certainly deserves to have a cartridge with his name on it.

.470 Capstick Loading Data and Factory Ballistics

Bullet (grains/type)	Powder	Grains	Velocity	Energy	Source/Comments
500 Solid	H4895	85.0	2,387	6,325	A-Square/maximum load
500 Solid	RI-12	89.5	2,410	6,450	A-Square/maximum load
500 Solid	IMR 4064	88.0	2,404	6,420	A-Square/maximum load
500 Solid	RI-15	91.0	2,385	6,315	A-Square/maximum load
500	FL	N/A	2,400	6,400	A-Square factory load

12.04 Bibamufu

Historical Notes: Lazzeroni Arms designed this cartridge in 1999 at the request of world hunter and famed gun writer Col. Craig Boddington. While somewhat related to an older case, for all practical purposes, this is a new case design. This cartridge was created to provide sufficient velocity for heavyweight hunting bullets to deliver significant doses of energy to the world's biggest and most dangerous game. Adaptation to standard actions is feasible, but is not recommended.

General Comments: Bullet diameter is .475-inch (Lazzeroni bases its designation on bullet diameter, instead of bore diameter, which is the common practice). Ballistics are impressive. Case design is typical of the Lazzeroni line: moderate body taper, 30-degree shoulder, sufficiently long neck, and thick rim of approximate case-body diameter. As produced, the case shoulder is sufficiently hard and thick to provide adequate headspace control. However, the margin of strength is small enough to suggest that one should not anneal these cases. Designed specifically for dangerous-game hunting, this cartridge makes no sense for any other purpose. Recoil is significant by any measure. A 24-inch barrel is standard, and adding a few inches of barrel length will not significantly improve ballistics. Muzzle energy exceeds 7505 ft-lbs. Ammunition is offered only as a special-order item and can be equipped with any bullet the customer desires. For more information on Lazzeroni custom guns, ammunition, and reloading data, contact (888) 492-7247 or www.lazzeroni.com.

Bullet (grains)	Powder	Grains	Velocity	Energy	Source/Comments
500	FL	N/A	2,600	7,505	Lazzeroni factory load

.470 Turnbull

Historical Notes: Firearms restoration guru Doug Turnbull made the similar .475 Turnbull cartridge for the Model 1886 Winchester. "So to ensure shooters using Marlin rifles were not left out," he said, "we developed a slightly shorter version of the .475 Turnbull—the .470 Turnbull." The .470 Turnbull rifle cartridge is designed specifically for use in the Marlin Model 1895 lever-action, including original rifles, new production Model 1895 Marlin rifles, and Guide Guns. Older rifles will require rebarreling.

General Comments: Like the .475 Turnbull, the parent case is the .348 Winchester. The major case differences between the .470 Turnbull and the .475 Turnbull are overall length (2.55 for the .470, 2.78 for the .475) and shoulder angle (10 degrees for the .470, 17 degrees 15 minutes for the .475). The .470's ballistics resemble those of the .450 Marlin.—*W.T.W.*

.470 Turnbull Loading Data

Bullet (grains/type)	Powder	Grains	Velocity	Energy	Source/Comments
350 Barnes TSX	IMR 4198	57.0	2,010	3,139	Turnbull Mfg.

475 B&M Super Short — *NEW*

Historical Notes: Premiering in late 2011, the 475 B&M Super Short is the middle of this line made by William V. Bruton and Michael McCourry. Like its stablemates (50 B&M Super Short and 458 B&M Super Short, which see), the 475 B&M Super Short is a Winchester Short Magnum case cut and trimmed to 1.65 inches and then formed in a sizing die. Some trimming might be required after forming.

General Comments: The B&M Super Shorts are made to fit in a Winchester M70 WSSM control-feed action and chambered in a 16.25-inch-long barrel with a 1:10 twist. The resulting rifle comes in less than 36 inches in overall length. The 475 B&M Super Short can handle bullets weights from 320 to 400 grains with pressures less than 64,297 psi. Maximum pressure listed on the B&M load data is 65,103 psi for a 350-grain bullet on top of 48 grains of WW296.

475 B&M Super Short Loading Data

Bullet (grains/type)	Powder	Grains	Velocity	Energy	Source/Comments
325 Speer Flat Nose	WW 296	46	2,167	3,388	B&M Load Data Sheet
350 CEB #13	WW 296	48	2,214	3,808	B&M Load Data Sheet*
*65,103 psi, maximum load					

.475 Turnbull — *NEW*

Historical Notes: Doug Turnbull has been restoring high-quality firearms for more than 20 years, and in 2007, he began working on a modern cartridge for vintage lever-action rifles, specifically the Model 1886 Winchester. The eponymous result was this round, built from a blown-out necked-up .348 Winchester case. Turnbull has said that vintage Winchester 1886 actions are strong enough to handle the 40,000-plus psi pressures the .475 Turnbull generates, but they must be rebarreled with modern steel alloys.

General Comments: The .475 Turnbull shoots widely available .475-caliber bullets seated in a .502 neck. The shoulder diameter is .5371 with a 17-degree, 15-minute shoulder angle, its SAAMI drawing shows. The rim diameter measures .610 and is .070 thick. The base diameter is .5517. The case is 2.20 inches long and the COAL is 2.78. Turnbull Mfg. supplies headstamped brass and bullets manufactured by Barnes, Nosler, and Hawk. Others are available. Reloading data is available on the Turnbull Mfg. website (Turnbullmfg. com), and reloading dies (either RCBS or Hornady brand with shellholder) are also available. Cor-Bon sells .475 Turnbull factory-loaded ammunition. Caution is advised shooting full-power .475s in a traditional Winchester stock with a steel crescent buttplate.—*W.T.W.*

.475 Turnbull Loading Data

Bullet (grains/type)	Powder	Grains	Velocity	Energy	Source/Comments
350 Barnes TSX	H322	66	2,300	4,110	Turnbull Mfg.

.500 Wyoming Express

Historical Notes: This large-capacity revolver cartridge was introduced in 2005 by Freedom Arms to be chambered in the FA Model 83 single-action revolver. The 1.370-inch case is belted to provide reliable headspacing in the Model 83 revolver. Freedom Arms designed the case to minimize forcing cone erosion by matching powder column length, volume, and bullet diameter with bullet weights, pressure levels, and velocity ranges.

General Comments: Case shortening and slight belt expansion is normal with maximum loads. Tests show as much as .002-inch expansion on the first firing, with much less expansion on subsequent firings, for a total expansion of about .003-inch after 10 firings with the case still usable. More than .004-inch expansion may render the case unusable, because of interference between the belt and chamber headspace area. This cartridge was designed to use bullets weighing from 350 to 450 grains. Freedom Arms does not recommend using bullets outside this weight range. Maximum loads should not be exceeded, because small increases in the powder charge can cause a dramatic increase in chamber pressure. Powder charges in reduced loads should not be below 90 percent of case capacity. The .500 WE uses a Large Rifle primer for reliable and consistent ignition. Contact (307) 883-2468 or www.freedomarms.com.

.500 Wyoming Express Loading Data

Bullet (grains/type)	Powder	Grains	Velocity	Energy	Source/Comments
350 XTP	TrailBoss	10.0	831	537	Freedom Arms
370WFNGC	Li'lGun	31.0	1,528	1,918	Freedom Arms
370WFNGC	H4227	34.0	1,535	1,936	Freedom Arms
370WFNGC	H110	36.0	1,607	2,122	Freedom Arms
400WFNGC	Li'lGun	31.0	1,565	2,175	Freedom Arms
400WFNGC	H4227	33.0	1,509	2,022	Freedom Arms

.500 Wyoming Express Loading Data

Bullet (grains/type)	Powder	Grains	Velocity	Energy	Source/Comments
400FWNGC	H110	34.5	1,589	2,242	Freedom Arms
440WFNGC	Li'lGun	28.0	1,450	2,054	Freedom Arms
440WFNGC	H4227	30.0	1,413	1,951	Freedom Arms
440FWNGC	H110	29.5	1,415	1,956	Freedom Arms

.510 GNR

Historical Notes: The 510 GNR is the largest caliber proprietary handgun cartridge designed by Gary Reeder, who chambers it in specially prepared Ruger Blackhawk and Super Blackhawk revolvers. In 2002, Reeder designed this cartridge to accommodate a loading range varying from the .50 Special to the .500 Linebaugh. At the top end loading, recoil is somewhat less than the .500 Linebaugh. Hunters have used the .510 GNR to take large Alaskan bear and African dangerous game.

General Comments: The .510 GNR uses .500 Linebaugh brass as the parent case shortened by .100 inch – about the same length as a 44 Magnum case. The 510 GNR works well in heavy-duty single-action revolvers with five-shot cylinders and five-inch barrels. Custom loaded ammunition (varying from mild to hot) is available from Cartridge Performance Engineering. Correctly headstamped brass, dies, firearms, reloading components and information are available from Reeder Custom Guns. Ballistic data was recorded in a five-inch custom revolver barrel. Note: H4227 loads are based on crimping the LBT bullet at the first lube groove to increase internal powder capacity.

510 GNR Loading Data

Bullet (grains/type)	Powder	Grains	Velocity	Energy	Source/Comments
350-gr LBT	Win 296	30.0	1,250	N/A	Gary Reeder
350-gr LBT	H4227	34.0	1,320	N/A	Gary Reeder
435-gr LBT	H4227	32.0	1,200	N/A	Gary Reeder

.50 Beowulf

Historical Notes: In 1999, Bill Alexander (Alexander Arms) designed the .50 Beowulf to be the biggest possible cartridge that could be chambered in the AR-15 family of rifles and carbines. No contemporary cartridges existed at the time, so Bill re-worked the .50 AE parent cartridge case, extended it slightly and rebating the rim to fit an AR-15 bolt face. For close range and brush hunting, the .50 Beowulf is superbly suited for wild hogs and even larger game.

General Comments: The .50 Beowulf delivers exceptional stopping power at short to medium ranges using ½-inch diameter bullets ranging in weight from 325 grains to 400 grains at velocities from 1900 to 2050 fps. The .50 Beowulf shares the .445-inch case rim dimension with the military 7.63x39 cartridge case. Seven cartridges will fit into an Alexander Arms-supplied magazine dimensioned to fit into the magazine well of an AR15's lower. The cartridge performs well in a 16-inch barrel using a 1:19 twist. Factory loads do not exceed 33,000 psi. Alexander Arms (www.alexanderarms.com) supplies rifles, magazines, ammunition, reloading dies, and brass.

.50 Beowulf Factory Ballistics

Bullet (grains/type)	Powder	Grains	Velocity	Energy	Source/Comments
300r Gold Dot	FL	N/A	1,900	2,404	Alexander Arms
325 Unicor	FL	N/A	1,950	2,743	Alexander Arms
334 HP	FL	N/A	1,900	2,677	Alexander Arms
334 FMJ	FL	N/A	1,900	2,677	Alexander Arms
400 SP	FL	N/A	1,800	2,877	Alexander Arms

.50 GI

Historical Notes: Frustrated by laws that banned .50-caliber handguns in his native Denmark, Alex Zimmerman created the proprietary .50 GI cartridge, in 2002, Zimmerman having moved to the United States a decade earlier. First seen publicly at the 2004 SHOT Show, the .50 GI cartridge is not a magnum cartridge. Zimmerman engineered a 1911-style pistol and .50 GI cartridge combination to achieve highly controllable knock-down power for self-defense and IPSC shooting.

General Comments: One .50 GI factory load drives a 300-grain bullet at 700 to 725 fps (translating into a 210 power factor), with felt recoil comparable to a 230-grain .45 ACP hardball round. For serious stopping power, a second factory load drives a 275-grain bullet at 875 fps, with felt recoil similar to a 10mm. With hotter loads, the .50 GI is suitable for feral hog and deer hunting at moderate ranges. To fit 1911 frames and slides, the .50 GI cartridge features a .45 ACP base and rim on a proprietary cartridge case manufactured by Starline (www.starlinebrass.com). This feature allows the use of a standard .45 breech face, extractor, and ejector on 1911-style pistols. Changing a Guncrafters Industries (www.guncraftersindustries.com) .50 GI-chambered pistol to .45 ACP requires only a different barrel and magazine. A firm taper crimp must be applied when reloading the .50 GI, and finished cartridges should measure .5235/.5240-inch at the case mouth. Guncrafter Industries offers 1911-type pistols, ammo, empty cases, reloading dies and magazines for the .50 GI cartridge. Hornady (www.hornady.com) and Lee Precision (www.leeprecision.com) sell reloading dies.

.50 GI Loading Data

Bullet (grains/type)	Powder	Grains	Velocity	Energy	Source/Comments
275 GI HP (copper clad)	Herco	8.0	875	467	Factory Load
300 GI FP (copper clad)	Titegroup	5.1	700	326	Factory Load
300 IMI JHP	Titegroup	5.9	800	426	OAL 1.220 "
240 Lead SWC	VV N310	4.4	750	299	OAL 1.230 "
300 Speer TMJ	Herco	8.0	875	509	OAL 1.220 "

.500 Phantom

Historical Notes: In 2005, Maarten ter Weeme (Teppo Jetsu, LLC) and Garber Supply Co. jointly created the .500 Phantom, specifically for AR-10 firearms. The .500 Phantom is the largest cartridge case that will function through the AR-10 action. The case design accommodates a wide range of .50-caliber bullet weights, including match-grade projectiles and smaller calibers in sabots. It produces velocity levels varying from 2000 fps to subsonic. The .500 Phantom is intended for law enforcement and special operations applications.

General Comments: The .500 Phantom cartridge uses a special .50-caliber non-belted short magnum brass case manufactured by Garber Supply Company, with a rebated head and strengthened web for the higher operating pressures. Factory bolt faces for WSM or RSAUM cases readily accept the .500 Phantom cartridge case. Remarkably, unmodified .308 Winchester magazines can accept eight .500 Phantom rounds, and AR-10 lower receivers require no modification. Suitable firearms for the .500 Phantom include the AR-10 and DPMS LR-308 rifles. Teppo Jutsu LLC (www.teppojutsu.com) offers AR-10 upper receivers and information on the .500 Phantom. Both Quality Cartridge (www.qual-cart.com) and Reed's Ammunition & Research (www.reedsammo.com) sell loaded ammunition. New brass and loading data are available from Garber Supply Co (gsc.feistyrooster.com).

.500 Phantom Factory Ballistics

Bullet (grains/type)	Powder	Grains	Velocity	Energy	Source/Comments
525 Barnes RN	FL	N/A	2,000	4,664	Teppo Jutsu LLC
750 Hornady A-Max	FL	N/A	1,040	1,802	Teppo Jutsu LLC

.502 Thunder Sabre — *NEW*

Historical Notes: The .502 Thunder Sabre is a .50 Action Express case with the rim trimmed down (rebated) to .440 inch. The round was designed by Robyn Church of Cloud Mountain Armory in 2004. The rebated rim enables use of a modified AR bolt in an AR-style rifle, and the feed ramp and ejection port are also widened. Its niche is that even though the .502 TS is less powerful than other .50-caliber AR-style rounds, it costs less to shoot.

General Comments: R&J Firearms (RJFirearms.com), a small firearms manufacturer in McMinnville, Oregon, offers a complete .502 TS rifle, as well as uppers and proprietary ammo, which runs $30 to $50 per box of 30 without shipping. Other R&J production loads include 325-grain JHP rounds ($47/30), 300-grain FTX rounds ($47/30) and 330-grain hard-cast slugs for $45/30. Production loads use 30 to 32.6 grains of Winchester 296 powder, developed for the .357 Mag. and .44 Rem. Mag. cartridges.

The .502 Thunder Sabre would be adequate to hunt wild pigs out to 100 yards, pushing a 335-grain jacketed hollowpoint to about 1,700 fps. Recoil is about the same as a rifle chambered in 44 Mag. The brass for the .502 TS is built and stamped by Starline.

Cartridge Name Loading Data and Factory Ballistics

Bullet (grains/type)	Powder	Grains	Velocity	Energy	Source/Comments
335 JHP	Win 296	30	1,700	2,149	R&J Firearms Production Load

.510 Whisper

Historical Notes: Created by J. D. Jones, the .510 Whisper, like all other Whisper cartridges, must be capable of subsonic extreme accuracy with very heavy bullets, while maintaining excellent accuracy with light bullets at moderate to high velocities. Barrels, dies, and cases for the .510 Whisper are available from SSK Industries (www.sskindustries.com).

General Comments: Using a .338 Lapua case shortened to 1.875 inches and necked up to .50-caliber, the .510 Whisper launches a 750-grain Hornady A-Max projectile at just under 1050 fps. The case neck is turned for accuracy and to create a shoulder for headspacing. SSK testing in suppressed, re-barreled, SAKO TRG-S rifles achieved MOA accuracy at 600 yards, with occasional groups of ½ MOA. For information on components, loading data, barrels, and guns designed for this cartridge, contact SSK Industries, (720) 264-0176 or www.sskindustries.com.

.500 A-Square

Historical Notes: The A-Square series of cartridges was designed in 1974 by Col. Arthur Alphin, after a hunting incident with Cape buffalo using the .458 Winchester Magnum. Alphin first designed the .500 A-Square to provide maximum stopping power. In order to gain more powder capacity and more power, all original A-Square cartridges were based on the .460 Weatherby case. A-Square Co. (www.a-squareco.com) offers cases and loaded ammunition for each of the A-Square cartridges.

General Comments: The .500 A-Square requires a long magazine (3.77 inches, same as a .416 Rigby and .460 Weatherby). This cartridge delivers high energy and stopping power from a bolt-action rifle. This was Alphin's first design and is based on the .460 Weatherby cartridge necked up and blown out. Alphin reports that this cartridge is the backbone and main reason for the formation of the A-Square Co. in 1979. In addition to custom rifles made for this caliber, A-Square makes its own rifles so chambered. The .500 A-Square is an excellent choice for a backup rifle and has stopping power about equal to the .577 Nitro Express. Naturally, recoil from this dangerous-game cartridge can be extremely heavy. For more information on A-square custom rifles and ammunition, contact (605) 234-0500 (South Dakota), (307) 436-5677 (Wyoming) or www.a-squareco.com.

.500 A-Square Loading Data

Bullet (grains/type)	Powder	Grains	Velocity	Energy	Source/Comments
600 SP	IMR 4320	116.5	2,475	8,155	A-Square

.50 Peacekeeper

Historical Notes: This cartridge was designed by J.D. Jones, of SSK Industries in 1999. This is simply the .460 Weatherby Magnum necked up to .50-caliber with no other changes. Therefore, this is nothing new—this case is essentially identical to the .500 A-Square. What is unique about the .50 Peacekeeper are the loads used and the intended purpose. This combination is specifically designed to launch heavy, long-range match bullets from highly accurate rifles of moderate weight. It is intended to compete directly with the various 30-pound class of .50 BMG-chambered rifles. Fired from a rifle of about half that weight, recoil energy is similar—bullets are launched at somewhat less velocity, but using much less powder.

General Comments: Muzzle ballistics are sufficient to suggest that this number is worth considering for those who believe they need a .50 BMG-class rifle. Several rifles will easily handle this cartridge in single-shot mode: Ruger M-77 Magnum, Sako large action, Weatherby large action, Ed Brown action, and Prairie Gun Works' new action (which will also feed this round from the magazine). The .50 Peacekeeper can be chambered in the large Sako action. For information on components, loading data, barrels, and guns designed for this cartridge, contact SSK Industries, (720) 264-0176 or www.sskindustries.com.

.50 Peacekeeper Loading Data (23-inch barrel)

Bullet (grains/type)	Powder	Grains	Velocity	Energy	Source/Comments
650 Ball	H335	108	2,350	7,975	SSK/maximum load
700 AP	AA 2700	117	2,200	7,525	SSK/maximum load
750 A-Max	AA 2520	105	2,205	8,100	SSK/maximum load

.500 Linebaugh

Historical Notes: The .500 Linebaugh is the design creation of John Linebaugh, of Maryville, Mo. Linebaugh started out by converting a .45 Colt revolver from six-shot to five-shot, thus offering more strength in the cylinder. It was a successful venture, but he continued to search for a more powerful handgun. The result is the .500 Linebaugh. The .500 Linebaugh is based on the .348 Winchester cartridge, which is cut down to 1½ inches and reamed to .50-caliber. He uses a large-frame Ruger Bisley revolver, as he has found the Ruger frame is the only one that can withstand the severe recoil of this cartridge. He replaces the Ruger barrel with one of .50-caliber, usually 5½ inches long. However, he will cut a barrel of any length the customer desires.

The .500 proved to be a very successful round, pushing 500-grain bullets at more than 1200 fps. Accuracy is outstanding, but recoil can only be described as severe. Not long after Linebaugh designed this cartridge, the supply of .348 Winchester cases began to dry up, which is why he designed the .475 Linebaugh based on the readily available .45-70 Government case. Not long after the .475 was designed, Browning reintroduced its Model 1871 rifle in .348 Winchester, and so those cases are again readily available.

General Comments: There are more powerful pistol cartridges, but primarily for single-shot handguns, such as the T/C Contender. When it comes to the revolver, this is close to the ultimate in power. Generally, in these revolvers, the .475 Linebaugh can safely be loaded to higher pressure and, therefore, can deliver more energy. Due to its accuracy and easy handling, this cartridge could prove to be an excellent heavy-game handgun cartridge and possibly a revolver cartridge suitable for taking African game. Specialized bullets are made by Bear Ammunition (www.dkgtrading.com). The jackets for these bullets are turned on a screw machine, and a lead core is swaged in. These bullets have been found to be excellent performers in terms of both accuracy and penetration. The .500 Linebaugh should find a strong following in the wilds of Alaska or the plains of Africa, where it could be used as a primary hunting gun or a backup. Buffalo Bore (www.buffalobore.com) offers factory-loaded ammunition.

.500 Linebaugh Loading Data and Factory Ballistics

Bullet (grains/type)	Powder	Grains	Velocity	Energy	Source/Comments
400 Cast	H110	27.0	1,200	1,280	John Linebaugh
410 SP	H110	29.0	1,250	1,425	John Linebaugh
410 SP	H110	31.0	1,320	1,590	John Linebaugh
500 SP	FL	N/A	1,200	1,599	John Linebaugh
435 LFN	FL	N/A	950	870	Buffalo Bore factory load
435 LFN	FL	N/A	1,300	1,630	Buffalo Bore factory load
440 WFN	FL	N/A	1,300	1,650	Buffalo Bore factory load
400 JHP	FL	N/A	1,400	1,740	Buffalo Bore factory load

500 B&M — *NEW*

Historical Notes: The 500 B&M is another proprietary cartridge in a series made by William V. Bruton and Michael McCourry, this one in 2013. This in-between cartridge occupies space between the 500 MDM (which see, 2.8-inch-long case) and the 50 B&M (which see, 2.240-inch-long case), but it is based on the same .375 RUM case, trimmed to a length of 2.5 inches. It resembles a shortened 500 MDM.

General Comments: The 500 B&M cartridge, like its bigger brother the 500 MDM, favors many of the same powders, such as IMR 8208, H-4895, V-N530, H-322, X-Terminator and the current version of RL 10X. With V-N530 and H-4895, it can safely run 450-grain #13 Solids faster than 2,400 fps. McCourry says adding a Talon Tip to a 410-grain Raptor bullet makes capable of taking on buffalo with ease. The penetration of the 450-grain #13 Solid can handle elephants, hippos and buffalo from any angle.

When the RUM brass is cut to 2.240 inches, it's run through an appropriate B&M-size die to make this and other B&M chamberings (which see). All B&M-series rifles are built by SSK Industries. Custom-loaded ammo is also available from Superior Ammunition. Properly head-stamped brass is available, or you can make your own brass, the process for which is detailed on the B&M website.

500 B&M Loading Data

Bullet (grains/type)	Powder	Grains	Velocity	Energy	Source/Comments
410 Raptor HP	V-N530	95	2,517	5,766	B&M Load Data Sheet

500 MDM — *NEW*

Historical Notes: The 500 MDM is currently the largest cartridge that can be put into a Winchester M70 action without major modifications, according to B&M Rifles and Cartridges of Conway, South Carolina. It is a true .500-caliber load designed to exceed the ballistics of the .500 Nitro express, firing custom-designed 550-grain bullets at 2,250 fps out of a 20-inch barrel. The parent case is a .375 Remington Ultra Magnum necked up to .50-caliber. The case length is trimmed to 2.80 inches.

General Comments: All B&M-series rifles are built by SSK Industries. Properly head-stamped brass is available, or you can make your own brass, the process for which is detailed on the B&M website. Case forming can be done by using a die or fire-forming it with low-powered charges.

Among the best handloads B&M recommends is a 300-grain nonconventional #13 hollowpoint. B&M Rifles and Cartridges stocks dies from RCBS and Hornady, as well as brass and custom bullets, along with all the necessary load data. Custom-loaded ammo is also available from Superior Ammunition.

500 MDM Loading Data

Bullet (grains/type)	Powder	Grains	Velocity	Energy	Source/Comments
300 BBW#13 NonCon HP	H-4198	96	2,898	5,593	B&M Load Data Sheet

Short Nose DGBR-HP W25

.495 A-Square

Historical Notes: The A-Square series of cartridges was designed in 1974 by Col. Arthur Alphin, as a result of a hunting incident with Cape buffalo using the .458 Winchester Magnum. Alphin first designed the .500 A-Square to provide maximum stopping power. In order to gain more powder capacity and more power, all original A-Square cartridges were based on the .460 Weatherby case. A-Square (www.a-squareco.com) offers cases and loaded ammunition for each of the A-Square cartridges.

General Comments: The .495 A-Square was designed to push 600-grain, .510-inch bullets from a cartridge that could be used in .375 Magnum-length actions. Though the .495 A-Square may not have as much energy as the .460 Weatherby, it does have the advantage of a larger diameter bullet. For a .50-caliber cartridge, recoil is reported as relatively low. It has also been reported that this cartridge does well with cast bullets. For more information on A-square custom rifles and ammunition, contact (605) 234-0500 (South Dakota), (307) 436-5677 (Wyoming) or www.a-squareco.com.

.495 A-Square Loading Data

Bullet (grains/type)	Powder	Grains	Velocity	Energy	Source/Comments
600 SP	IMR 4895	100.0	2,275	6,890	A-Square
600 SP	IMR 4320	103.0	2,280	6,925	A-Square

50 B&M Alaskan — *NEW*

Historical Notes: The 50 B&M Alaskan is made for Marlin 1895 or Winchester/Browning M71 lever-guns, but the first gun chambered for this round was a Marlin Guide Gun in early 2007. The 50 B&M Alaskan is yet another Bruton and McCourry .500-caliber cartridge, this one based on a 50 Alaskan case, the bullet of which is .510 in diameter. The .50 Alaskan was a wildcat cartridge based on the .348 Win. It was developed by Harold Johnson and Harold Fuller in the 1950s as a bear-capable cartridge that would function in lever-action rifles. A less-necked-up variation was the .450 Alaskan (which see), also called a .45-348 Winchester Improved.

The 50 B&M Alaskan is merely the older Alaskan necked down from .510 to .500, easily done in a sizing die. Although the .50 Alaskan is a fine cartridge for lever-guns, only a handful of .510-caliber bullets will function properly in those rifles. But there are many .500-caliber bullets to chose from, in many weights and configurations, that will function well.

General Comments: Typical rifles have 18-inch barrels and 1:12 twists. This cartridge also can be used in a Ruger No. 1 or Winchester M1885, as well as Encores and Contenders. SSK Industries has reamers to chamber rifles in 50 B&M Alaskan.

The 50 B&M Alaskan can run a 500-grain Hornady right at 1,850 fps, making it a good choice for thin-skinned dangerous game. Many lighter .500-caliber bullets — such as the 325 Swift, 400 Sierra, North Fork 450 Premium Bonded, and Cutting Edge Bullets' Solids and Non-Conventional bullets — make the lever-action extremely versatile and suitable for most hunting in its namesake state.

Cartridge Name Loading Data and Factory Ballistics

Bullet (grains/type)	Powder	Grains	Velocity	Energy	Source/Comments
500 Hornady	H-4198	57	1,873	3,894	B&M Load Data Sheet

50 B&M — *NEW*

Historical Notes: The 50 B&M is a true .500-caliber cartridge made in 2012 by designers William V. Bruton and Michael McCourry (B&M) for use in Winchester M70 WSM control-feed bolt-action safari rifles. The parent cartridge is the .300 Remington Ultra Magnum case cut and trimmed to 2.25 inches. The 50 B&M is capable of pushing 500-grain bullets at 2,150 fps or better.

General Comments: B&M rifles chambered in this round have 1:12-twist 18-inch barrels and weigh 6.5 pounds with the Winchester Ultimate Stock and 7.5 to 8 pounds with Accurate Innovations Wood Stocks, which B&M recommends. With an overall length of 38 inches, this is a handy and powerful package.

Although the 50 B&M is capable of shooting all available commercial .500-caliber bullets, these bullets do not qualify as dangerous-game bullets in most circumstances. B&M argues on its website that a class of bullets the makers prefer, which they tag as "non-conventional," or "Non-Cons," work in a different manner than conventional expanding bullets. Non-Cons can come in several configurations, but they cite the North Fork Expanding Cup Point as a example of the type. To boil down a long blog post, B&M says Non-Con bullets are capable of expansion and out-of-the-animal penetration. It's worth reading at www.b-mriflesandcartridges.com/Non-Conventional-Bullets.html.

Cartridge Name Loading Data and Factory Ballistics

Bullet (grains/type)	Powder	Grains	Velocity	Energy	Source/Comments
300 CEB #13 NonCon HP	H-4198	76	2,502	4,169	B&M Load Data Sheet

.500 Whisper

Historical Notes: Designed by J.D. Jones in 1993 at SSK Industries, this chambering is based upon a shortened .460 Weatherby Magnum case. Custom very low drag (VLD) bullets up to 900 grains have been tested. Design intent was to create a very hard-hitting subsonic round with superior penetration potential for use against lightly armored vehicles.

General Comments: This is a very esoteric chambering. Proper use requires expensive custom bullets. Nevertheless, ballistic consistency and accuracy are impressive when launched at subsonic velocities (1,040 fps is typical). Typical heavy VLD bullets lose velocity so slowly that crosswinds have little effect, and retained energy exceeds one-half of muzzle energy well beyond one mile. Yes, such bullets will travel that far with exceedingly good accuracy! For information on components, loading data, barrels, and guns designed for this cartridge, contact SSK Industries, (720) 264-0176 or www.sskindustries.com.

.500 Whisper Loading Data

Bullet (grains)	Powder	Grains	Velocity	Energy	Source/Comments
650 to 750	Vit N110	36.6	1,050	1,590/1,835	SSK/Load must be tuned to individual gun

.510 Allen Magnum

Historical Notes: Kirby Allen of Allen Precision Shooting designed the .510 Allen Magnum off the .50 BMG case, primarily as an extreme-range target and competition wildcat. The goal was to increase the ballistic performance of the .50 BMG by adding velocity to what the parent case can produce. The .510 Allen Magnum does this very well. Using the same bullet weights, velocity gains in the 150- to 200-fps range are not uncommon

The effective range of the .510 Allen Magnum, much like the .338 Allen Magnum and .375 Allen Magnum, is more limited by the shooter's ability to handle a .50-caliber-class weapon and read environmental conditions than the performance of the chambering itself. For consistent target shooting, the .510 Allen Magnum will offer sustained supersonic velocity beyond 3,000 yards in most elevations and shooting conditions.

General Comments: The 750-grain A-Max is the recommended bullet because it has a good BC, is easy to purchase, and is generally very user friendly and accurate. The .510 Allen Magnum can also be used for big-game hunting at pretty much any range you can effectively place your bullets. For this purpose, the 750-grain A-max is a good choice, because it is considered an expanding-bullet design, which is required by many Western states. Of course, the .510 Allen Magnum is excessively powerful for any big-game hunting, but, with proper shot placement, it is fully capable of cleanly taking any big-game animal on this planet and, perhaps, other planets, as well. The more mundane restriction on the .510 Allen Magnum as a sporting cartridge is carrying around the 30-pound rifle that shoots it. If you like to shoot and you like to load, this is a good round for those pursuits, since the .510 Allen Magnum requires fireformed brass and special handloading equipment. For more information, check the website APSRifles.com or email Kirby Allen at allenmagnum@gmail.com.— *W.T.W.*

.510 Allen Magnum Loading Data (Note: *US869, AA 8700, H-50BMG, Vhitavuori 20N29, WC860, WC872)

Bullet (grains/type)	Powder	Grains	Velocity	Energy	Source/Comments
750 Hornady A-Max	*	N/A	3,000	14,983	Allen Precision Shooting

50 B&M Super Short — *NEW*

Historical Notes: Premiering in 2010, the 50 B&M Super Short is the smallest in this line made by William V. Bruton and Michael McCourry. Like its smaller stablemates (458 B&M Super Short and 475 B&M Super Short, which see), the 50 B&M Super Short is a Winchester Short Magnum case cut and trimmed to 1.65 inches and then formed in a sizing die. Some trimming might be required after forming.

The 50 B&M Super Short is a unique rifle and cartridge combination. The cartridge is designed to work in the Winchester M70 WSSM bolt action with 16-inch barrels — making such a rifle the same overall length as a Marlin Guide Gun. With the Ultimate stock from Winchester, these B&M rifles come in as low as 6.25 pounds.

General Comments: Initially, McCourry said he did not consider the 50 B&M Super Short to be suitable for heavy game — elephant, hippo and buffalo. But after he witnessed the 50 B&M Super Short take big Australian buffalo, he revised his thinking. Bullet choices for dangerous game are critical, but the B&M site features several loads that have proven to deliver deep penetration in thick-skinned game.

50 B&M Super Short Loading Data

Bullet (grains/type)	Powder	Grains	Velocity	Energy	Source/Comments
300 Hornady	WW 296	56	2,425	3,916	B&M Load Data Sheet

.50 American Eagle

Historical Notes: SSK Industries designed the .50 American Eagle for a single shot M 16 rifle in suppressed applications. Barrels, dies, and cases are available from SSK Industries (www.sskindustries.com).

General Comments: Using a .50-caliber 650-grain projectile in Speer .50 AE cases opened to accept .510-inch bullets, the .50 American Eagle achieves about 1000 fps. Case heads are reduced in diameter to fit 7.62x39-sized bolt faces in the M-16. It is suitable for the Thompson/Center Encore, AR-15, bolt-action firearms, and Ruger No. 1 rifles.

14.5 JDJ

Historical Notes: The 14.5 JDJ, the latest in an amazing series of big-bore boomers from J.D. Jones, uses the .50 BMG case with the neck expanded and case fire-formed to launch .585-inch diameter bullets at high velocities. Using a quality McMillan bolt-action built into an SSK rifle, the 14.5 JDJ is capable of achieving sub-MOA groups at 1,000 yards using SSK Industries CNC-machined bronze bullets. A 2005 offering from SSK Industries (www.sskindustries.com), the 14.5 JDJ cartridge should be considered as the very top end of proprietary cartridges based on the .50 BMG parent case. It can accommodate bullet weights ranging from 750 grains to 1,200 grains and works well with powders suitable for .50 BMG.

General Comments: Rifles for the 14.5 JDJ are strictly custom creations and can use only those actions suitable for the .50 BMG cartridge. The 14.5 JDJ can be quite expensive to own and shoot. A typical 14.5 JDJ rifle will weigh about 42 pounds with the recommended 36-inch barrel and muzzle brake. SSK possesses a BATFE destructive device exemption for the 14.5 JDJ cartridge, which enables the company to manufacture this cartridge and rifles chambered for it. Interestingly, the Barnes 750-grain bullet can be driven faster than 3000 fps. Listed reloading data are the fireforming loads. SSK Industries (www.sskindustries.com) offers rifles, reloading dies, bullets, and loading data.

Bullet (grains/type)	Powder	Grains	Velocity	Energy	Source/Comments
750 Barnes	FL	N/A	3,000	14,986	SSK Industries
750 Barnes	5010	250.0	2,900	14,004	SSK Industries
1,173 SSK Bronze	5010	235.0	2,600	17,605	SSK Industries

.577 Tyrannosaur

Historical Notes: This entirely new cartridge was designed in 1993 in response to the demands of two professional African hunting guides who'd had bad experiences with lesser chamberings as backup guns when clients were hunting dangerous species. There is no secret to the design: This is the longest, largest-diameter case that will properly function through a standard-size, bolt-action rifle. Bullet diameter is limited by the necessity of a sufficient case shoulder to control headspace. Design pressure assures proper functioning in even the hottest climes and will not overstress the action.

General Comments: Case capacity is on par with the .600 Nitro Express. When loaded to .30-30 Winchester pressure levels, this cartridge can develop 10,000 ft-lbs of muzzle energy. When chambered in a 13-pound rifle with a properly designed stock containing three mercury recoil suppressors, recoil of the .577 Tyrannosaur is claimed to be less punishing than Weatherby's Mark V chambered for the much less powerful .460 WM. Nevertheless, by no means should one call this a "mildly recoiling" combination. For those looking for the ultimate in affordable, repeating rifle firepower, the .577 is the factory option of choice. Compared to purchasing a typical top-quality, big-bore British double rifle, one could buy several .577 Tyrannosaurs, a lifetime supply of .577 ammunition, and a new 4x4 pickup to haul the lot around in—with considerable leftover change!

.577 Tyrannosaur Loading Data and Factory Ballistics

Bullet (grains/type)	Powder	Grains	Velocity	Energy	Source/Comments
750 Monolithic Solid	RI-19	177.5	2,473	10,180	A-Square/max. load
750 Monolithic Solid	FL	N/A	2,400	9,590	A-Square factory load

.600/577 JDJ

Historical Notes: Long considered the epitome of big-bore elephant cartridges, the .577 Nitro Express was chambered by premier English gun-makers in top-end double rifles. The .600/577 JDJ, as crafted by SSK Industries, expands the .577 Nitro case to a straight taper to accept .620-inch diameter bullets.

General Comments: The .600/577 JDJ fires a 900-grain bullet at approximately 1800 fps. Muzzle brakes and hydraulic counter-coil recoil-reducing devices are highly recommended in this caliber. It can be chambered in suitably converted Ruger No. 1 rifles. The BATFE does not classify this cartridge as a destructive device. For information on components, loading data, barrels, and guns designed for this cartridge, contact SSK Industries, (720) 264-0176 or www.sskindustries.com.

.700 JDJ

Historical Notes: Prolific cartridge designer J.D. Jones created the .700 JDJ, in 1995. Using a .50-caliber BMG case necked up to .70-caliber, the .700 JDJ launches an 1100-grain projectile at about 2,200 fps.

General Comments: The .700 JDJ is still in production and can be chambered in any action suitable for the .50 BMG cartridge. SSK Industries uses special-order Krieger barrels for the .700 JDJ. The BATFE does not classify this cartridge as a destructive device. For information on components, loading data, barrels, and guns designed for this cartridge, contact SSK Industries, (720) 264-0176 or www.sskindustries.com.

.950 JDJ

Historical Notes: At .95-caliber, this cartridge defines the upper limit of rifle cartridges. As its creator, J.D. Jones described that the .950 JDJ it is not for the faint of heart, nor the financially-challenged shooter. The cartridge is based on the 20mm Vulcan case fired in rotary barrel cannon on U.S. Air Force fighter aircraft. Using a shortened, bottlenecked 20mm case, the .950 JDJ launches a 3,600-grain projectile at approximately 2,200 fps.

General Comments: Developed in 1996, the .950 JDJ is no longer in production. SSK Industries developed a few custom rifles in the chambering, using super-sized McMillan single-shot rifles and Krieger special-order barrels. When completed, these bolt-action rifles looked like .50-caliber rifles on steroids, weighing between 100 and 110 pounds. The muzzle brake alone weighed about 18 pounds, but, even so, recoil was brisk. The BATFE does not classify this cartridge as a destructive device. For information on components, loading data, barrels, and guns designed for this cartridge, contact SSK Industries, (720) 264-0176 or www. sskindustries.com.

Dimensional Data

Cartridge	Case	Bullet Dia.	Neck Dia.	Shoulder Dia.	Base Dia.	Rim Dia.	Rim Thick.	Case Length	Ctge. Length	Primer	Page
2.34 SwissMiniGun (rimfire)	B	.092	.092126	UNK/NA	.092126	.110236	UNK/NA	.240157	.359449	UNK/NA	330
.17 Incinerator (.17/50)	C	.172	.220	.720	.804	.804	.080	3.99	4.40	.50 BMG (spent)	330
.222 Remington Rimmed	A	.224	.253	.357	.375	.440	.049	1.700	2.130	S	331
.224-32 FA	A	.224	.255	.337	.337	.371	.050	1.2	1.60	SP	331
.22 TCM	C	.224	.255	.362	.372	.370	.049	1.025	1.265	SP	332
.226 JDJ	A	.224	.256	.410	.419	.467	.045	1.93	V	L	322
6 Whisper	C	.243	UNK	UNK	.370	.375	.040	UNK	UNK	UNK	333
6mm JDJ	A	.243	.272	.415	.421	.470	.045	1.905	2.65	L	333
6.17 Spitfire	C	.243	.275	.510	.530	.530	.050	2.05	2.8	L	334
6.17 Flash	C	.243	.275	.510	.530	.530	.050	2.80	3.55	L	334
.255 Banshee	A	.257	.278	.297	.298	.345	.050	1.335	1.80	S	335
.257 Raptor	C	.257	.283	.370	.376	.378	.045	1.860	2.135	S	335
.257 JDJ	A	.257	.288	.415	.421	.473	.045	1.905	2.81	L	336
.25-06 JDJ	C	.257	UNK	UNK	.440	.468	.045	UNK	UNK	UNK	336
6.53 Scramjet	C	.257	.289	.510	.530	.530	.055	2.80	3.575	L	337
.257 Mini Dreadnaught	G	.257	.290	.425	.445	.467	.045	2.145	V	L	337
.257 Allen Magnum	I	.257	.290	.538	.550	.532	.050	2.75	3.655	Fed 215 L	338
6.5mm JDJx30	A	.264	.285	.409	.419	.497	.058	2.03	V	L	338
6.5mm Whisper	C	.264	.286	.357	.372	.375	.041	1.36	V	S	339
6.5x25 CBJ	C	.264	.287	.379	.390	.393	.049	.984	1.169	S	339
6.5mm JDJ No. 2	A	.264	.292	.450	.466	.502	.059	2.00	V	L	340
6.5mm JDJ	A	.264	.293	.410	.419	.467	.045	1.93	V	L	340
6.5/270 JDJ	C	.264	UNK	UNK	.440	.468	.045	UNK	UNK	UNK	341
6.5 MPC	C	0.264	0.297	0.349	0.373	0.375	0.041	1.760	2.26	Bx	341
6.5 Mini Dreadnaught	G	.263	.296	.425	.445	.467	.045	2.150	V	L	342
6.71 Phantom	C	.264	.297	.510	.530	.530	.055	2.05	2.8	L	342
6.71 Blackbird	C	.264	.297	.524	.544	.544	.055	2.80	3.575	L	343
6.5mm Allen Magnum	I	.264	.297	.538	.550	.532	.050	2.75	3.655	Fed 215 L	343
.270 JDJ	A	.277	.305	.415	.419	.467	.045	1.905	2.875	L	344
.270 JDJ No. 2	C	.277	UNK	UNK	.440	.468	.045	UNK	UNK	UNK	345
.270 Allen Magnum	I	.277	.310	.534	.550	.532	.050	2.835	3.78	Fed 215 L	345
7mm Whisper	C	.284	.306	.357	.372	.375	.041	1.36	V	S	346
7mm-30 JDJ	A	.284	.306	.409	.419	.497	.058	2.03	V	L	346
7mm GNR	A	.284	.312	.400	.420	.502	.058	2.055	2.65	L	346
7mm JDJ	A	.284	.312	.415	.421	.473	.045	1.905	V	L	347
.280 JDJ	C	.284	.312	.455	.470	.467	.045	2.505	V	L	347
7mm JDJ No. 2	A	.284	.313	.450	.466	.502	.059	2.00	V	L	348
7mm Dakota	C	.284	.314	.531	.544	.544	.042	2.50	3.33	L	349
.280 GNR	A	.284	.316	.448	.463	.543	.075	2.525	3.0	L	349
7mm Allen Magnum	C	.284	.316	.536	.590	.590	.060	2.71	3.65	Fed 215 L	350
7.21 Tomahawk	C	.284	.318	.557	.577	.577	.060	2.05	2.80	L	350
7.21 Firehawk	C	.284	.318	.524	.544	.544	.055	2.80	3.55	L	351
7.21 Firebird	C	.284	.318	.557	.577	.577	.060	2.80	3.6	L	351
7mm Canadian Magnum	I	.284	.322	.530	.544	.532	.046	2.83	3.60	L	352
7.62 Micro-Whisper	C	.308	.328	.382	.389	.392	.045	.846	V	SP/S	353
7.63 Mini-Whisper	C	.308	.329	.375	.381	.385	.045	.985	V	SP/S	353
.300 Whisper	C	.308	.330	.369	.375	.375	.041	1.50	2.575	S	354
.308 CorBon	C	.308	.333	.532	.545	.532	.050	2.08	2.80	L	354
.307 GNR	A	.308	.336	.379	.380	.433	.055	1.55	2.00	S	355
.309 JDJ	A	.308	.335	.453	.470	.514	.058	2.20	3.16	L	355
.30-06 JDJ	C	.308	.335	.455	.470	.467	.045	2.455	V	L	356
.300 Dakota	C	.308	.338	.531	.544	.544	.046	2.55	3.33	L	357
.300 Pegasus	C	.308	.339	.566	.580	.580	.058	2.99	3.75	L	357
7.82 Patriot	C	.308	.340	.557	.577	.577	.060	2.05	2.8	L	358
7.82 Warbird	C	.308	.340	.557	.577	.577	.060	2.80	3.60	L	359

Dimensional Data

Cartridge	Case	Bullet Dia.	Neck Dia.	Shoulder Dia.	Base Dia.	Rim Dia.	Rim Thick.	Case Length	Ctge. Length	Primer	Page
.300 Canadian Magnum	I	.308	.342	.530	.544	.532	.046	2.83	3.60	L	359
8mm JDJ	A	.323	.356	.455	.470	.514	.058	2.22	V	L	360
.338 Woodswalker	A	.338	.360	.410	.420	.482	.060	1.860	2.510	L	360
.338 Whisper	C	.338	.360	.457	.463	.466	.048	1.47	V	S	361
.338 Spectre	C	.338	.361	.415	.425	.420	.049	1.25	2.10	L	362
.338 Allen Magnum	C	.338	.363	.610	.637	.640	.065	3.025	4.20	Fed 215 L	362
.338 JDJ	A	.338	.365	.453	.470	.514	.058	2.20	V	L	363
.338 A-Square	K	.338	.367	.553	.582	.603/.580∂	.060	2.85	3.67	L	363
8.59 Galaxy	C	.338	.368	.557	.577	.577	.060	2.05	2.80	L	364
.338 Lehigh	C	.338	.369	.4268	.439	.441	.053	1.40	2.26	S	364
.338 Federal (.33-08)	C	.338	.369	.454	.470	.470	.049	2.015	2.820	L	365
.338 Canadian Magnum	I	.338	.369	.530	.544	.532	.046	2.83	3.60	L	365
8.59 Titan	C	.338	.369	.557	.577	.577	.060	2.80	3.60	L	366
.338 GNR	A	.338	.370	.435	.463	.543	.075	2.545	3.20	L	367
.338-06 JDJ	C	.338	.370	.455	.470	.467	.045	2.465	V	L	367
.330 Dakota	C	.338	.371	.530	.544	.544	.045	2.57	3.32	L	368
.338 Excaliber	C	.338	.371	.566	.580	.580	.058	2.99	3.75	L	369
.38 Casull	C	.357	UNK	UNK	.476	.476	.044	UNK	1.170	UNK	369
.356 GNR	A	.358	.360	.433	.434	.498	.054	1.250	UNK	UNK	370
.358 JDJ	A	.358	.362	.453	.470	.514	.058	.220	3.065	L	370
.35-06 JDJ	C	.358	.385	.455	.470	.467	.045	2.445	V	L	371
.358 Shooting Times Alaskan (STA)	E	.358	.386	.502	.513	.532	.048	2.85	3.65	L	372
9.09 Eagle	C	.358	.387	.557	.577	.577	.060	2.05	2.80	L	372
9.3mm JDJ	A	.366	.389	.455	.465	.506	.058	2.22	V	L	373
9.3 B&M	I	0.366	0.403	0.530	0.552	0.532	0.048	2.256	2.950	L	373
.375 Whisper	C	.375	UNK	UNK	.466	.468	.045	UNK	UNK	UNK	374
.375/454 JDJ Woodswalker	B	.375	UNK	UNK	.480	.515	.055	UNK	UNK	UNK	374
.375 JDJ	A	.375	.396	.453	.470	.514	.058	2.20	3.13	L	374
9.53 Hellcat	C	.375	.404	.557	.577	.577	.060	2.05	2.80	L	375
.375-06 JDJ	C	.375	.405	.457	.470	.467	.045	2.435	V	L	375
.375 Allen Magnum	C	.375	.401	.605	.637	.640	.065	3.025	4.20	Fed 215 L	376
.375 Dakota	C	.375	.402	.529	.544	.544	.046	2.57	3.32	L	377
.375 Canadian Magnum	I	.375	.402	.530	.544	.532	.046	2.83	3.60	L	377
.375 A-Square	K	.375	.405	.551	.582	.603/.580∂	.060	2.85	3.65	L	378
9.53 Saturn	C	.375	.404	.557	.577	.577	.060	2.80	3.60	L	378
.375 JRS Magnum	E	.375	.498	.485	.535	UNK/NA	.048	2.84	3.69	L	379
.375 B&M	I	0.375	0.410	0.530	0.550	0.532	0.048	2.251	2.950	Fed 215	379
.400 A-Square DPM	E	0.410	0.450	0.520	0.521	0.530	0.046	2.85	3.600	L	380
.400 CorBon	C	.401	.423	.469	.470	.471	.050	.898	1.20	LP	380
.40-44 Woodswalker	A	.401	.428	.455	.455	.510	.055	1.295	V	LP	381
.40-454 JDJ	A	.401	.428	.470	.470	.510	.055	1.395	V	LP	381
.408 CheyTac	C	.408	.438	.601	.637	.640	.065	3.04	4.307	L	382
.41 GNR	A	.410	.436	.458	.461	.514	.055	1.240	1.60	L	382
.410 GNR	A	.410	.439	.477	.480	.512	.055	1.349	1.69	L	383
.411 Express	C	.411	UNK	UNK	.440	.468	.045	UNK	UNK	UNK	383
.411 Hawk	C	.411	UNK	UNK	.440	.468	.045	UNK	UNK	UNK	384
.411 JDJ	A	.411	.425	.455	.465	.506	.058	2.235	V	L	384
.416 JDJ	A	.416	.430	.455	.465	.506	.058	2.22	V	L	385
.416-06 JDJ	C	.416	.443	.455	.470	.467	.045	2.415	V	L	385
.416 BGA	C	.416	UNK	UNK	.504	.492	UNK	UNK	UNK	UNK	386
.416 Dakota	C	.416	.441	.527	.544	.544	.042	2.85	3.645	L	386
10.57 Maverick	C	.416	.445	.557	.577	.577	.060	2.05	2.80	L	387
10.57 Meteor	C	.416	.445	.557	.577	.577	.060	2.80	3.62	L	387
.416 Rimmed	A	.416	.446	.549	.573	.665	.060	3.300	4.100	L	388
.416 Taylor	E	.416	.447	.491	.513	.532	.048	2.50	3.34	L	388

Dimensional Data

Cartridge	Case	Bullet Dia.	Neck Dia.	Shoulder Dia.	Base Dia.	Rim Dia.	Rim Thick.	Case Length	Ctge. Length	Primer	Page
.416 Hoffman	E	.416	.447	.491	.513	.532	.048	2.85	3.60	L	389
.416 Barrett	C	.416	.460	.730	.803	.804	.083	3.273	4.563	Bx	390
.416 B&M	I	0.416	0.450	0.534	0.552	0.526	0.056	2.253	3.000	Fed 215	390
.425 Express	E	.423	.429	.490	.513	.532	.048	2.552	3.34	L	391
.44/454 JDJ Woodswalker	B	.429	UNK	UNK	.480	.515	.055	UNK	UNK	UNK	391
.440 CorBon	I	.429	.461	.529	.538	.510	.055	1.280	1.59	LP	391
.45 Raptor	D	0.452	0.478		0.478	0.473	0.055	1.800	2.300	L	392
.458 SOCOM	I	.458	.452	.530	.538	.473	.048	1.575	2.015	UNK	393
.458 Whisper	F	.458	.485	UNK/NA	.506	.525	.048	1.75	V	L	393
.458 B&M	I	0.458	0.487	0.529	0.554	0.525	0.048	2.250	2.950	Fed 215	394
.458 B&M Super Short	I	0.458	0.490	0.534	0.554	0.534	0.052	1.648	2.245	Fed 210	394
.460 A-Square Short	K	.458	.484	.560	.582	.603/.580∂	.060	2.50	3.50	L	395
.458 Canadian Magnum	I	.458	.485	.530	.544	.532	.046	2.83	3.60	L	395
.450 Dakota	C	.458	.485	.560	.582	.580	.058	2.90	3.74	L	396
.450 Ackley Magnum	E	.458	.487	.503	.512	.532	.048	2.85	3.65	L	396
.450 Assegai	A	.458	.487	.549	.573	.665	.060	3.300	4.100	L	397
.475 Linebaugh	B	.475	.495	UNK/NA	.501	.600	.065	1.50	1.77	L	397
.475 JDJ	B	.475	.497	UNK/NA	.502	.604	.065	2.10	V	L	398
.470 Capstick	F	.475	.499	UNK/NA	.513	.532	.048	2.85	3.65	L	399
12.04 Bibamufu	C	.475	.500	.557	.577	.577	.060	2.80	3.62	L	399
.470 Turnbull	A	.4755	.502	.5371	.5517	.610	.070	2.205	2.56	L	400
.475 B&M Super Short	I	0.474	0.506	0.538	0.557	0.535	0.052	1.650	2.318	Fed 210	400
.475 Turnbull	A	.4755	.504	.5371	.5517	.610	.070	2.205	2.78	L	401
.500 Wyoming Express	F	.500	UNK/NA	UNK/NA	UNK/NA	UNK/NA	UNK/NA	1.370	1.765	LR	401
.510 GNR	B	.500	.514	.548	.550	.614	.070	1.190	UNK	UNK	402
.50 Beowulf	J	.500	.525	UNK/NA	.535	.445	.055	1.650	2.125	UNK	402
.50 GI	J	.500	.526	UNK/NA	.526	.480	.048	.899	1.221	UNK	403
.500 Phantom	I	.500	.535	UNK/NA	.620	.532	UNK/NA	1.525	2.280	UNK	403
.502 Thunder Sabre	J	0.500	0.540		0.538	0.440	0.055	1.286	1.690	LP	404
.510 Whisper	C	.510	UNK	UNK	.590	.590	.060	1.875	UNK	UNK	404
.500 A-Square	K	.510	.536	.568	.582	.603/.580∂	.060	2.90	3.74	L	405
.50 Peacekeeper	K	.510	.538	.565	.586	.603/.580∂	.058	2.882	V	L	405
.500 Linebaugh	B	.510	.540	UNK/NA	.553	.610	.062	1.405	1.755	L	406
500 B&M	I	0.500	0.525	0.540	0.550	0.538	0.048	2.506	3.224	Fed 215	406
500 MDM	I	0.500	0.525	0.543	0.550	0.538	0.048	2.800	3.463	Fed 215	407
.495 A-Square	L	.510	.542	UNK/NA	.582	.603/.580∂	.060	2.80	3.60	L	407
50 B&M Alaskan	B	0.500	0.529	0.539	0.548	0.592	0.070	2.104	2.580	Fed 215	408
50 B&M	J	0.500	0.532		0.552	0.534	0.050	2.258	2.940	Fed 215	408
.500 Whisper	K	.510	.549	.563	.580	.603/.580∂	.060	2.90	V	L	409
.510 Allen Magnum	C	.510	.552	.77	.800	.800	.080	3.90	5.750	CCI-35	409
50 B&M Super Short	I	0.500	0.535		0.555	0.536	0.055	1.645	2.258	Fed 210	410
.50 American Eagle	I	.510	.560	.714	.804	.440	.053	UNK	UNK	UNK	410
14.5 JDJ	C	.585	UNK	UNK	.804	.804	.080	UNK	UNK	UNK	410
.577 Tyrannosaur	C	.585	.614	.673	.688	.688	.060	2.99	3.71	L	411
.600/577 JDJ	B	.620	UNK	UNK	.660	.748	.052	UNK	UNK	UNK	411
.700 JDJ	C	.727	UNK	UNK	.804	.804	.080	UNK	UNK	UNK	412
.950 JDJ	C	.950	UNK	UNK	UNK	UNK	UNK	4.00	UNK	UNK	412

Case Type: A = Rimmed, bottleneck. B = Rimmed, straight. C = Rimless, bottleneck. D = Rimless, straight. E = Belted, bottleneck. F = Belted, straight. G = Semi-rimmed, bottleneck. H = Semi-rimmed, straight. I = Rebated, bottleneck. J = Rebated, straight. K = Rebated, belted bottleneck L = Rebated, belted straight.

Primer Type: S = Small rifle (.175"). SP = Small pistol (.175"). L = Large rifle (.210"). LP = Large pistol (.210"). B-1 = Berdan #1. B-2 = Berdan #2.

Other codes: V = OAL depends upon bullet used. V = Rifling twist varies, depending upon bullet and application. ∂ = Belt/Rim Diameter. Unless otherwise noted, all dimensions in inches.

Handgun Cartridges of the World

(Current & Obsolete—Black-Powder and Smokeless)

It can be stated unequivocally that the United States is the only country where the handgun has developed fully as a sporting arm, used for hunting, as well as various kinds of match and silhouette shooting. This has had a profound effect on the development of handguns and handgun cartridges in America. Shortly after World War II, for instance, there was renewed interest in the single-action revolver. This resulted in the introduction of new single-action models by Sturm, Ruger & Co. In turn, it became profitable for Colt to reintroduce its single-action revolver, which had been considered obsolete. Now, Ruger and several other manufacturers and importers continue the single-action tradition.

Handgun hunting was responsible for new cartridges designed primarily for field use, such as the .22 Remington Jet, .221 Remington Fireball, .44 Magnum, .454 Casull, .475 Linebaugh, and .500 Linebaugh. The increasing popularity of silhouette pistol competition has given rise to specialized types of handguns designed particularly for this sport, such as the Thompson/Center Contender, Wichita Silhouette Pistol, Merrill Sportsman (now the RPM XL), and a number of custom handguns based on the Remington XP-100 action and the 7mm BR Remington cartridge. Some of these silhouette pistols chamber cartridges that are suitable for varmint and big-game hunting.

The sporting handgun is a uniquely American innovation. Using a handgun for hunting reduces the effective range to about 100 yards, depending on the skill of the shooter. However, handguns offer the advantages of lightness and easy portability, decided advantages in rough terrain or heavy brush.

Handguns are divided into several types, depending on intended use. Military and police handguns are designed for defensive use at short range. Typical bore sizes vary from 9mm to .45-caliber. The semi-automatic pistol is preferred by the world's military establishments, although the revolver is still used by some military police agencies. In recent years, police organizations in the United States have switched to the 9mm or .40 Auto and, in some instances, the .45 Automatic. Military and police handguns are usually of medium weight and have three- to five-inch barrels. Caliber is represented by the 9mm Luger, .40 S&W, and .45 Automatic (ACP). Off-duty or special assignment police arms are usually lighter and have shorter barrels than standard arms.

Pocket-type self-defense handguns have generally been small, lightweight, and of relatively small caliber, varying from .22 to .38. Today, the trend is toward pocket-type handguns chambered for cartridges that are more substantial. These high-end models are often of superior quality and capable of surprising accuracy and dependability.

Well-made pocket or self-defense handguns can be good small-game and plinking guns. Target pistols are characterized by adjustable target sights and usually a barrel of six inches or so in length. Match pistols often are so specialized as to be of little practical use for anything else.

Hunting handguns also tend to be specialized, due to their long barrels and heavy frames. Because most also have adjustable sights, these can be used for target shooting, too. Any handgun can be used for hunting small game at short ranges, provided its user can hit with it. Serious hunting handguns vary in caliber from .22 to .50, depending on the game to be hunted. Magnum cartridges are preferred for big game. Some single-shot pistols, such as the Thompson/Center Contender, are chambered for rifle cartridges like the .30-30 and the .223 Remington.

Because handgun cartridges are limited in velocity, an important consideration is the type of bullet used. The semi-wadcutter, as designed by the late Elmer Keith, is probably the best type of cast-lead bullet. Some modern jacketed handgun bullets with a large area of exposed lead at the nose have also proven highly effective on lighter species. In competent and practiced hands, the .357 Magnum has given a good account of itself on deer-size animals and, in some cases, even larger quarry. One must realize that handgun cartridges used for big game deliver marginal ballistics for that purpose, compared to high-powered rifle cartridges. Thus, shooter skill is critical.

Some handgun cartridges have also become popular as rifle cartridges. This includes the .357 and .44 Magnums, as well as the venerable .44-40 Winchester and .45 Colt. These make a good combination for owners of handguns in these chamberings, because standard factory ammunition can then be used interchangeably in rifles and pistols. However, some rifles can withstand much higher pressures than most handguns, and handloads that are safe in a rifle may wreck a handgun. Use caution and common sense when handloading.

Handgun cartridges are divided into three major types, those intended for semi-automatic pistols, those to be used in revolvers, and those for single-shot pistols. Those designed for semi-automatic pistols are either rimless or semi-rimmed to facilitate feeding from the magazine. Revolver cartridges are, in general, of rimmed construction, although some revolvers have been made to handle semi-rimmed or rimless cartridges, such as the .32 Automatic, .30 Carbine, 9mm Luger, .380 Automatic, and the .45 Automatic. Single-shot pistol cartridges are often bottlenecked and rimmed or rimless. At one time, bullets intended for revolver cartridges were of lead, while those for auto-pistol cartridges were jacketed to facilitate feeding. At present, it is common practice to use jacketed bullets in revolvers, particularly for hunting, although match shooters prefer light loads and lead bullets. Lead bullets are also used for target loads in pistols. Jacketed bullets have been used in some military revolvers since before World War I because of international agreements.

Owing to limitations in the design strength of typical revolvers and pistols, smokeless powder did not improve the performance of handgun cartridges to the extent it did rifle cartridges. Consequently, black-powder cartridges of medium to large caliber are almost as effective as modern non-magnum handgun cartridges. In fact, many modern handgun cartridges originated as black-powder numbers, and their performances with smokeless powder is about the same as it was with their original black-powder loadings.

When selecting a handgun or handgun cartridge, give careful consideration to the gun's intended use. Most individuals have a tendency to overdo it regarding power, following the idea that bigger is better. While a few experts can achieve long-range hits, most handgun hunting is for small game or varmints at ranges of 50 yards or less. It takes a great deal of practice before one can hit a target with any consistency at 100 yards and beyond. Power will not compensate for poor marksmanship, so it is best to start with something you can handle and move up to a larger chambering after proficiency has improved. Remember, the average person must expend hundreds of rounds to develop proficiency with a .22 rimfire pistol, and it takes even more practice with larger chamberings.

The .22 Long Rifle rimfire is probably the most popular handgun cartridge, followed by the .38 Special and 9mm Luger among the centerfires. The .22 rimfire is adequate for small game at close ranges and can serve as a house gun for home protection. The .38 Special has the advantage of reloadability, and it is possible to regulate the power to cover shooting situations from very light target loads to full-power self-defense or field loads. For serious self-defense, the .38 Special and the .380 Automatic are considered minimum. The .38 Special and the .357 Magnum are probably the most widely used revolver cartridges, while the 9mm, .40 S&W, and .45 Automatic are the most popular pistol cartridges. For match competition, the .22 rimfire, .38 Special, and 45 Automatic may still lead the pack, although other centerfire numbers have recently made gains. —F.C.B.

15th Edition Update

This chapter also has a substantial number of new entries, 11 to be exact. Three have the same goal in mind: improve the venerable .45 ACP without requiring a change in the 1911 pistol's form factor.

Thus, while the .45 Super is externally and dimensionally identical to the 45 ACP, it is designed to be used in semi-auto pistols with stronger recoil springs and a shock buffer. We have previously covered the .451 Detonics Magnum, but we reinsert it in this edition because the company that initially made it has restarted under a different owner, which is worth noting. The .450 SMC, or .450 Short Magnum Cartridge, is basically a

.45 Super with a small primer pocket. External dimensions of the .450 SMC are the same as the .45 Super and .45 ACP.

Elsewhere, we update and expand our coverage of three powerful handgun-silhouette rounds: .375 Super Magnum, .414 Super Magnum, and the .445 Super Magnum. "Super" in this case means "Longer," which means more powerful, both for hunting and competition shooting. All three require heavily modified revolvers to work, but if you're going to go big in terms of power, then strengthening a wheelgun to do that isn't any big deal.

There are also two "Atomic" rounds, which, curiously, have nothing to do with each other. The 9.4mm Dutch and and 10.6 German Ordnance are both obsolete handgun rounds that paid forward ideas that shaped thinking about what a sidearm can, and should do. The .401 Bobcat is yet another example of a rifle round being converted into a pistol round — something the aspiring designer should consider. — W.T.W.

2.7mm Kolibri Auto

Historical Notes:	The 2.7mm Kolibri Auto is the smallest commercially manufactured centerfire pistol cartridge. It was used in the equally small Kolibri semi-auto pistol introduced about 1914. There was also a single-shot parlor-type pistol chambered for the round. The Kolibri automatic is of conventional blowback design. The cartridge has been obsolete for many years and is a collector's item.
General Comments:	Small pistols and miniature cartridges may have some value for indoor target practice, but have no other practical use. The tiny 2.7mm Kolibri jacketed bullet is of .105-inch to .108-inch diameter and weighs about three grains. Actual ballistics are unknown, but muzzle velocity is estimated to be 650 to 700 fps. This would develop an energy of only three ft-lbs. When you consider that the .25 Automatic develops 73 ft-lbs at the muzzle, you can see what a pipsqueak this cartridge is. However, it is by no means a toy. It is claimed that the bullet will penetrate 1½ inches of pine, which is sufficient to inflict a serious wound at close range. It should be treated with the same respect accorded any firearm. The 2.7mm Kolibri could not be considered a humane cartridge for hunting anything. However, it might do to dispatch a trapped mouse or eliminate an overly aggressive cockroach. It is not practical to reload these small cartridges.

2.7mm Kolibri Auto Factory Ballistics (Note: *Estimated velocity)

Bullet (grains/type)	Powder	Grains	Velocity	Energy	Source/Comments
3 FMJ	FL	N/A	650-700	2.8-3.25	Factory load *

4.5x39Rmm SPS

| Historical Notes: | The 4.5mm SPP-1M Underwater Pistol was developed in the late 1960s as a combat arm for divers. According to *The New World of Russian Small Arms & Ammo,* by Charlie Cutshaw, the team of Pytor Sazonov and Oleg Kravcheno designed the 4.5x39mm (SSP-1M) cartridge. Vladimir Simonov is credited as the designer of the SPP-1 underwater pistol, which consists of four smoothbore barrels grouped in a square formation. Alongside the pistol, an Avtomat Podvodnyi Spetsialnyi (Special Underwater Assault Rifle) was also developed, but chambered for the 5.66x39mm MPS Underwater Rifle Cartridge round. The |

Russian company TsNIITochMash built them and began offering them to the public in 1993. The pistol is still in use by Russian Navy Special Forces.

General Comments: Initially, the designers found that standard bullets fired underwater had very limited range, so they patterned their projectiles after the long darts used for spear fishing. In "Russian Underwater Guns," an August 2011 article in the *Small Arms Defense Journal*, author Robert G. Segel described the specifications for cartridges fired in the Soviet 4.5mm SPP-1M Underwater Pistol. The proprietary cartridge is a rimmed bottleneck case 1.575 inches long and sealed against water. The complete cartridge is 5.71 inches long and weighs .617 ounce. It uses a dart with a flattened point. The 4.53-inch dart weighs .452 ounce. This projectile is stabilized by its flattened point. Lethal range in water is assessed by the dart being able to penetrate a padded underwater diving suit or a 5mm-thick organic glass face mask. Depending on the depth at which it's fired, the dart can be lethal from six to 17 meters. 4.5mm cartridges for the SPP-1M pistol are packed in boxes of 24 rounds.—*W.T.W.*

3mm Kolibri

General Comments: There is some confusion surrounding the 3mm Kolibri. Some say it is the same as the 2.7mm Kolibri, but physical measurements disprove this. The bullet and case are larger in diameter, compared to the 2.7mm round. In addition, 3mm rounds have lead bullets, while 2.7mm cartridges use a jacketed projectile. Power and general characteristics would be about the same as the 2.7, which is covered above.

4.25mm Liliput Auto
(4.25mm Erika Auto)

Historical Notes: Another of the miniature European auto-pistol cartridges, this 4.25mm (.17-caliber) cartridge was used in the German Liliput pistol, introduced in 1920, and this name stuck to it. However, this cartridge actually originated in Austria, about 1913-'14, for the Erika auto pistol. Thus, it is sometimes referred to as the 4.25mm Erika. Both gun and cartridge have been obsolete for many years.

General Comments: The 4.25mm round is of greater power than the 2.7 or 3mm Kolibri, but that still doesn't mean it's much of a cartridge. With a 12- to 15-grain bullet and a muzzle velocity around 800 fps, it develops only 17 ft-lbs of muzzle energy—still far below the 73 ft-lbs of the .25 Automatic. It could not be considered effective for serious self-defense or any kind of hunting. However, it would kill rats or mice at short range. As with all these miniature cartridges, it is potentially dangerous and could inflict a serious wound at short range. Its principal use would be for indoor target practice. Ammunition is scarce and too expensive to shoot in quantity, regardless. This case is not reloadable.

4.25mm Liliput Auto Factory Ballistics (Note: *Estimated velocity)

Bullet (grains/type)	Powder	Grains	Velocity	Energy	Source/Comments
12-15	FL		800	17-21.3	Factory load *

5mm Clement Auto

Historical Notes: The 5mm Clement cartridge originated in Spain, in 1897, for the obscure Charola-Anitua auto pistol. In 1903, the Belgian-made Clement auto pistol was adapted to the round, and this resulted in the change of name. The cartridge is listed in the 1904 and 1934 DWM catalog (No. 484) and was loaded in Germany, until about 1938. It was replaced by the more effective .25 Automatic.

General Comments: The Clement auto pistol was well made and popular in Europe. The 5mm cartridge is of bottleneck type, and the 36-grain bullet has a muzzle velocity of 1030 fps. Because of the high velocity, it develops slightly greater energy than the .25 Automatic. However, it is no more effective. Like the .25 Automatic, it is not entirely satisfactory for self-defense, and is unsuitable for hunting anything but rats, mice, sparrows, or similar pests. It is now a collector's item, and ammunition is far too expensive to shoot.

5mm Clement Auto Factory Ballistics

Bullet (grains/type)	Powder	Grains	Velocity	Energy	Source/Comments
36 FMJ	FL		1,030	78	Factory load, DWM

5mm Bergmann

Historical Notes: This was a cartridge for the obsolete Bergmann No. 2 auto pistol, introduced in 1894 and produced commercially from 1896 until about 1900. This cartridge is listed in the 1904 DWM catalog (No. 416A), but not in the 1934 issue. It has been obsolete since around 1930, being replaced by the 6.35mm Browning (.25 Automatic).

General Comments: The 5mm Bergmann has a straight, tapered, rimless case. The bullet is of .20- to .21-inch diameter and was available in a 37-grain lead or 34-grain full metal jacket or soft-point. According to White and Munhall, muzzle velocity is just a little under 600 fps. Muzzle energy would be about 30 ft-lbs, less than half that of the .25 Automatic. The cartridge has little practical value, except for indoor target practice. As originally manufactured, the cartridge had no rim or extractor groove, but, after a short time, the extractor groove was added. This is another collector's cartridge, much too expensive to shoot.

5mm Bergmann Factory Ballistics

Bullet (grains/type)	Powder	Grains	Velocity	Energy	Source/Comments
34 FMJ	FL		600	27	Factory load
37 Lead	FL		600	30	Factory load

5.45x18mm Soviet

Historical Notes: This modern pistol cartridge was developed in the Soviet Union in the 1970s for the PSM compact semi-automatic pistol. Its design follows Soviet tradition, in that the case is bottlenecked and bullet caliber is the same as for the service rifle (the 5.45mm AK-74). Case length and overall loaded length are similar to the 9mm Makarov cartridge, although the base and rim diameter of the 5.45x18mm Soviet is smaller. Thus far, Russia is the only country to have adopted this cartridge and the PSM pistol for it.

General Comments: The concept behind this cartridge is unknown. By Western standards, this cartridge is a very poor choice for self-defense. Muzzle energy is about the same as the .22 Long Rifle. However, a key to its purpose may be bullet construction, which consists of a gilding metal jacket around a two-piece core consisting of a steel front and lead rear halves. If penetration is the purpose, then this bullet should prove effective against body armor. Beyond this, it seems to have little value. It is one of the few new cartridges to enter production in Russia for many years. Manufactured only in the Commonwealth of Independent States, cases are normally lacquered steel with a Berdan primer. Bullet diameter is about .210-inch.

5.45x18mm Soviet Factory Ballistics

Bullet (grains/type)	Powder	Grains	Velocity	Energy	Source/Comments
40 FMJ	FL		1,034	95	Factory load

.22 Remington Jet Magnum
.22 Center Fire Magnum

Historical Notes: The .22 Remington Jet, also known as the .22 Center Fire Magnum, was introduced jointly by Remington and Smith & Wesson. The former developed the cartridge, the latter the revolver. The first news of this cartridge leaked out in 1959, but production revolvers and ammunition were not available until 1961. The

S&W Model 53 revolver is the only revolver ever to chamber this cartridge, and it was discontinued in 1971. The .22 Jet grew out of popular wildcat handgun cartridges, such as the Harvey .22 Kay-Chuk and others based on the altered .22 Hornet case. However, the .22 Jet is actually based on a necked-down .357 Magnum case. Marlin once offered the Model 62 lever-action rifle for the .22 Jet, H&R offered it in the Topper, and Thompson/Center offered it in the Contender, for a time.

General Comments: The .22 Jet is strictly a hunting number, intended to provide high velocity and flat trajectory in the field. The M53 revolver will also fire regular .22 Long Rifle ammunition by use of supplemental steel chamber inserts and an adjustable firing pin. This cartridge has ample performance for small game at ranges out to 100 yards, for those who can shoot a revolver that well.

When this round was first announced, most gun writers praised its fantastic performance. A muzzle velocity of 2460 fps was supposed to be developed in an 8½-inch barrel. Chronograph tests by various individuals, including the book's original author, indicated an actual velocity of only around 2000 fps in this barrel length. Quite a letdown, but it is still a good cartridge. The S&W Model 53 in .22 Jet was discontinued because of problems with the cylinder locking up when firing full-powered loads. This ammunition is no longer manufactured commercially.

.22 Remington Jet Magnum Loading Data and Factory Ballistics

Bullet (grains/type)	Powder	Grains	Velocity	Energy	Source/Comments
40 HP	2400	10.5	1,800	288	Hornady, Sierra
45 SP	2400	12.8	1,700	288	Hornady, Sierra
40 HP	FL		2,460	535	Factory load

Cartridges and cylinder must be free of grease or oil to prevent setback of cases when fired.

.221 Remington Fireball

Historical Notes: This cartridge was introduced early in 1963 for the Remington XP-100 bolt-action, a single-shot pistol based on a shortened, lightened 700 series rifle action. The pistol had a streamlined nylon-plastic stock, ventilated barrel rib, and adjustable sights. This was the first handgun made by Remington since its pocket automatics were discontinued back in 1935. The Thompson/Center Contender was also available in .221 Remington for a time, but no longer. Remington was the only source for .221 Fireball ammunition. It is still available.

General Comments: The .221 Fireball follows the modern design in .22-caliber high-velocity pistol cartridges for small-game and varmint hunting at long range. The rimless case is a shortened version of the .222 Remington. The cartridge is well adapted to rifles, as well as pistols. The bullet is designed for quick expansion on small animals and is very deadly at all practical ranges. The XP-100 pistol has a 10-inch barrel and is intended for use with a scope. It is capable of sub-MOA 100-yard groups, when fitted with a scope and fired from a rest. It is much more powerful than the older .22 Remington Jet used in the S&W .22 WMR revolver. Muzzle energy of the .221 Fireball is greater than the .357 Magnum. Despite the caliber designation, .224-inch is the proper bullet diameter. The .221 Fireball was chambered in the Remington Model 700 Classic rifle on a limited-run basis in the late 2000s.

.221 Remington Fireball Loading Data and Factory Ballistics

Bullet (grains/type)	Powder	Grains	Velocity	Energy	Source/Comments
50 SP	IMR 4198	17.0	2,610	755	Speer, Hornady, Sierra, Nosler
50 SP	IMR 4227	15.5	2,600	750	Speer, Hornady, Sierra, Nosler
55 SP	IMR 4198	16.0	2,400	704	Speer, Hornady, Nosler
50 SP	FL		2,650	780	Remington factory load

5.5mm Velo Dog Revolver

Historical Notes: This round was introduced in 1894 for the Velo Dog revolver, manufactured by Galand, of Paris. It derives its name from the French word velocycle, meaning, roughly, "bicycle." Later, a number of Belgian and German revolvers also chambered this round. The cartridge was loaded in the United States by Peters, Remington, and Winchester, up until about 1940. However, no American company made a gun for it. Fiocchi of Italy still loads this cartridge.

General Comments: The 5.5mm Velo Dog is a centerfire .22 of slightly less power than the .22 Long Rifle rimfire. It bears some resemblance to the obsolete .22 Extra Long Maynard centerfire rifle cartridge. However, it is easy to distinguish between these by the head markings, and because the 5.5mm has a metal-cased bullet. The Velo Dog revolver was designed for cyclists to shoot pursuing dogs. This was a unique period in history—can you imagine what would happen today if some cyclist shot a dog! The cartridge became obsolete because it is ballistically inferior to the popular .22 Long Rifle.

Editor's note: Others might argue that the present period is historically unique. Try to fathom the logic that suggests it's OK for an unrestricted dog to attack a harmless cyclist or pedestrian, but that it is not OK for that person to effectively defend himself!

There is some uncertainty as to the proper designation for this cartridge. There is also a loading called the 5.75 Velo Dog, which could be the correct name for this cartridge—it would seem that we should have been able to resolve this, but that is not yet the case. Maybe we will solve the mystery next edition.

5.5mm Velo Dog Revolver Factory Ballistics

Bullet (grains/type)	Powder	Grains	Velocity	Energy	Source/Comments
45 FMJ	FL		750	55	Fiocchi factory load

5.8x21mm DAP 92

Historical Notes: This cartridge was introduced in the United States in 1908 with the Browning-designed Colt-manufactured .25 Vest Pocket Automatic pistol. It had been introduced in Europe a few years earlier in the FN Baby Browning, which is practically identical to the Colt. The design of these two pistols has been copied by manufacturers all over the world. Dozens of different pistols have used this cartridge. The original Browning is still made (for European consumption), but Colt did not resume manufacture of its Vest Pocket model after World War II. American Arms, Beretta, Iver Johnson, Jennings, Lorcin, Phoenix Arms, Sundance, Taurus, Astra, Star, Kel-Tech, Rohrbaugh, and Walther have all made pistols in this chambering.

General Comments: The 5.8×21mm is slightly less powerful than the 5.7×28mm and 4.6×30mm, but serves the same function as those smallbore PDW cartridges. The pistol can hold up to 20 cartridges per magazine. According to the PLA, the 45-grain FMJ-BT-AP will penetrate a 1.3mm-thick plate of 232 helmet steel and two inches of wood planking at 50 meters. Yawing in soap media is significant. It offers light recoil and reasonable accuracy around 2.1 inches at 25 meters.—*W.T.W.*

5.8x21mm DAP 92 Loading Data and Factory Ballistics

Bullet (grains/type)	Powder	Grains	Velocity	Energy	Source/Comments
45 FMJ-BT-AP, Steel Penetrator	Dual-based, noncorrosive	FL	1,574	247	Government load

.25 (6.35mm) Automatic (.25 ACP)

Historical Notes: This cartridge was introduced in the United States in 1908 with the Browning-designed Colt-manufactured .25 Vest Pocket Automatic pistol. It had been introduced in Europe a few years earlier in the FN Baby Browning, which is practically identical to the Colt. The design of these two pistols has been copied by manufacturers all over the world. Dozens of different pistols have used this cartridge. The original Browning is still made (for European consumption), but Colt did not resume manufacture of its Vest Pocket model after World War II. American Arms, Beretta, Iver Johnson, Jennings, Lorcin, Phoenix Arms, Sundance, Taurus, Ortgies, Astra, Star, Kelt-Tech, Rohrbaugh,and Walther have all made pistols in this chambering.

General Comments: The .25 Automatic offers surprising velocity for such a small cartridge. However, delivered energy is quite modest. This, combined with the full metal jacketed bullet of the conventional load, adds up to very poor stopping or killing power on anything. Lighter, expanding bullets lack adequate penetration or delivered energy to suggest any significant improvement. The .25 Auto is not powerful enough for hunting anything but pests, nor is it adequate for serious self-defense. However, .25 Automatic pistols are popular because of their small size and low cost. Their principal usefulness might be as a threat, because no sane person wants to be shot if that can be avoided, not even with the little .25. Winchester and Hornady recently have offered hollow-point loads in an effort to improve terminal ballistics.

Editor's note: Three important facts are often overlooked when discussing the value of this cartridge. First, compared to any rimfire chambering, the .25 Automatic provides superior functioning in typical concealable pistols. Despite being very underpowered, well-placed shots from a .25 Auto do beat throwing rocks and will certainly disable or kill. Second, owing to a properly designed case and bullet, this cartridge is dramatically more dependable in a pocket pistol than any rimfire round. Finally, any functional gun that a person can and will carry and use correctly has significant defensive value.

.25 (6.35mm) Automatic (.25 ACP) Loading Data and Factory Ballistics

Bullet (grains/type)	Powder	Grains	Velocity	Energy	Source/Comments
50 FMJ	Bullseye	1.2	810	73	Hornady, Sierra
45 JHP	FL	UNK/NA	815	66	Factory load, Winchester new
50 FMJ	UNK/NA	UNK/NA	760	64	NA

.25 North American Arms (NAA)

Historical Notes: First developed in 1999 by Kentucky firearms writer J.B. Wood, the .25 NAA cartridge is a .32 ACP case necked to .25-caliber. Wood's goal was to increase reliable expansion of .25-caliber bullets when fired from a short-barreled handgun. The concept of bottleneck cases to drive smaller-diameter bullets to greater speeds is more than a century old.

General Comments: Fired in a re-barreled Savage model 1908 self-loading pistol with Hornady test ammo, bullet expansion ranged from .360- to .412-inch. With perceived recoil in the .22 Long Rifle range, the improved feeding of a bottleneck cartridge and consistent hollow-point bullet expansion, the North American Arms corporation decided to offer this chambering in its Guardian mini-pistol product line in 2002 or 2003. CorBon produces the ammo, which bears a CorBon .25 NAA headstamp and claims a muzzle velocity of 1200 fps with a 35-grain JHP bullet for 121 ft-lbs from a two-inch barrel.

.25 North American Arms Loading Data

Bullet (grains/type)	Powder	Grains	Velocity	Energy	Source/Comments
35 Hornady XTP	Herco	2.6	1,050	85	Test Load by Hornady

.256 Winchester Magnum

Historical Notes: The .256 Winchester Magnum handgun cartridge was announced in 1960. However, no arms were available until late in 1962, and most of these were not on the market in quantity before 1963. The Marlin Model 62 lever-action rifle was the first rifle officially announced for this cartridge. This was followed by a new Ruger single-shot pistol named the Hawkeye, which made the scene ahead of the Marlin. The

Ruger Hawkeye was discontinued in 1966, and the Marlin 62 was dropped a few years later. The .256 Magnum is based on the .357 Magnum case necked-down to accept .257-inch diameter bullets. Some difficulty developed trying to design a revolver for this cartridge due to the cylinder gap and high pressure. The Ruger Hawkeye has a completely enclosed breech. Thompson/Center single-shot pistols were also available in this chambering.

General Comments: Fired in the Ruger Hawkeye, with its enclosed breech and 8½-inch barrel, the .256 Magnum develops an average muzzle velocity of about 2360 fps. From a 24-inch rifle barrel, muzzle velocity is over 2800 fps—this with the 60-grain SP bullet originally loaded by Winchester. When first announced, the velocity was listed as 2200 fps, as the factory used a test barrel shorter than 8½ inches. Although similar to the old .25-20 cartridge, the .256 has greater powder capacity, is loaded to higher pressures and, therefore, gives superior performance. When used in a rifle, many shooters prefer 75- or 85-grain bullets. The .256 Magnum should be an excellent varmint and small-game round at close ranges. In a rifle, it would be effective out to 200 or 225 yards. See the *18th Edition of Gun Digest* for an excellent report by Yard and Helbig on shooting the .256. Winchester was the only source of this ammunition. Though Winchester ceased production of this cartridge in the early 1990s, cases are easily formed from .357 Magnums, so the handloader has no problem.

.256 Winchester Magnum Handgun Loading Data and Factory Ballistics

Bullet (grains/type)	Powder	Grains	Velocity	Energy	Source/Comments
60 SP	2400	14.6	2,300	705	Hornady
60 SP	H4227	16.0	2,300	705	Hornady
75 SP	2400	13.0	2,000	668	Hornady
60 SP	FL	FL	2,200	650	Winchester factory load

6.5mm Bergmann

Historical Notes: Another in the series of cartridges developed by Bergmann in the 1894-'96 period, the 6.5mm round is listed in the 1904 DWM catalog (No. 413A), but by 1934 had been dropped. Theodor Bergmann designed a number of special cartridges for his auto pistols. These ranged from 5mm to 11mm in diameter, and practically all of these were obsolete by about 1930. The original version of the 6.5mm was both rimless and grooveless, but, because of the problem of extracting an unfired or dud cartridge, this was soon altered to standard rimless design. The more popular Bergmann cartridges were loaded in England, as well as on the continent.

General Comments: The 6.5mm Bergmann cartridge is a necked, rimless-type that looks very powerful, but really isn't. It is actually less powerful than the .32 Automatic. While not an entirely adequate self-defense round, it could be used for shooting small pests or birds. It is more powerful than the .25 Automatic. However, ammunition is scarce and expensive, so no one is likely to do much shooting with it anyway. The 6.5mm Bergmann is one of the few 6.5mm pistol cartridges.

6.5mm Bergmann Factory Ballistics

Bullet (grains/type)	Powder	Grains	Velocity	Energy	Source/Comments
65 to 88 FMJ	FL	FL	780	94	Factory load

7mm Nambu

Historical Notes: This unusual pistol cartridge was manufactured only in Japan for the Japanese "Baby" Nambu semi-auto pistol, which was introduced about 1920. It was not an official Japanese military cartridge, but was specially made for high-ranking officers who were required to purchase their own sidearms. The 7mm Nambu pistol is a scaled-down version of the original model Nambu, which was developed about 1904. The 7mm Nambu pistol was something of a mystery until after World War II, when quantities were brought back by returning GIs. The 7mm Nambu cartridge is a collector's item, and the pistols are scarce.

General Comments: By Western standards, the 7mm Nambu would not be considered an adequate self-defense cartridge. For sporting use, it would be effective only on small game or birds. The pistol has a seven-shot magazine, 3¼-inch barrel, weighs only 16 ounces, and is extremely well made and of good material and finish. The 1963 *17th Edition of Gun Digest* includes an article by Roy D. Strengholt, which covers the 7mm Nambu pistol and cartridge in considerable detail. The 7mm Nambu is unusual in that it is one of the very few pistol cartridges to use a 7mm (.283-inch)-diameter bullet.

7mm Nambu Factory Ballistics

Bullet (grains/type)	Powder	Grains	Velocity	Energy	Source/Comments
56 FMJ	FL	FL	1,250	196	Factory load *

*Approximate

7mm Bench Rest Remington

Historical Notes: Originally not a commercial cartridge, but a chambering only for the Remington Model XP-100 Silhouette target pistol, the 7mm BR has graduated to a full-fledged commercial cartridge. It has also become a rifle as well as a pistol round. It is based on the .308x1½-inch Barnes case necked-down to 7mm. Originally the cartridge was made by shortening and necking-down the Remington BR case, a special .308 Winchester case with a Small Rifle primer pocket made especially for this purpose. Remington's Mike Walker was instrumental in developing the 7mm BR.

This idea isn't new, because the British had developed a similar, although slightly longer, cartridge as an experimental military round, as early as 1945. In addition, more than one person has necked the .308x1½-inch case down to 7mm. Elgin Gates worked with a similar cartridge in 1952. The Remington BR line of cartridges originated, according to company literature in 1978. There is also a .22 BR and a 6mm BR covered elsewhere in this book. This cartridge was designed to provide an out-of-the-box silhouette cartridge, with ballistics calculated to strike the best balance for accuracy, velocity, and bullet weight to hit and knock down the metal targets.

General Comments: External dimensions of the Remington .308 BR case are identical to the .308 Winchester. However, the walls are thinner and are annealed to facilitate reforming, and the primer pocket is sized for the Small Rifle primer. Ballistics of the factory cartridge showed a 140-grain bullet at a muzzle velocity of 2215 fps and 1525 ft-lbs of energy, as registered from a 15-inch barrel. It would do better in a slightly longer barrel. These short 1½-inch cartridges often develop maximum velocity in a relatively short barrel, usually about 16 to 18 inches.

The 7mm BR would be a good medium-range varmint and short-range deer cartridge. It cannot be improved to any extent by handloading, since the standard factory load is about tops for the 140-grain bullet. Remington no longer catalogs this cartridge.

7mm Bench Rest Loading Data and Factory Ballistics

Bullet (grains)	Powder	Grains	Velocity	Energy	Source/Comments
100	W748	34.0	2,400	1,279	Sierra, Hornady
120	748	32.0	2,300	1,410	Sierra, Hornady
130	H322	27.0	2,100	1,277	Sierra, Speer, Nosler
140	748	30.0	2,150	1,450	Sierra, Hornady, Speer
150	H335	28.0	2,000	1,333	Sierra, Speer, Nosler
160	748	28.0	2,000	1,421	Sierra, Hornady, Speer
140	FL		2,215	1,525	Remington factory load

7.62mm Russian Nagant Revolver

Historical Notes: This military revolver cartridge was adopted by Russia in 1895 and used in the Nagant and Pieper revolvers, which were both seven-shot designs, as opposed to the usual six. The Nagant design is unique in that when the hammer is cocked, the cylinder moves forward over the barrel shank to form a gas seal. The velocity gain from this arrangement is significant. No other revolver has ever used this ingenious, though complicated, system.

General Comments: Russian Nagant revolvers have been sold in moderate quantities in the United States, but are more of a collector's item than a practical gun. Ammunition in shooting quantities is difficult to find, but can be made from .32-20 Winchester cases, which are very similar. Power and effectiveness are about the same as the .32 S&W Long. Most versions of the cartridge have the bullet seated completely inside the case. Velocity of the 108-grain FMJ flat-nose bullet in the Nagant revolver is about 1100 fps, but the conventional Pieper revolver delivers only 725 fps. Bullet diameter is .295-inch. Both guns and ammunition were recently in production in Russia. Fiocchi manufactured this cartridge quite recently.

7.62 Russian Nagant Revolver Loading Data and Factory Ballistics

Bullet (grains/type)	Powder	Grains	Velocity	Energy	Source/Comments
115 Cast	Bullseye	3.0	800	165	Lyman No. 311008
98 FMJ	FL		750	122	Fiocchi factory load
108 FMJ	FL		725	125	Factory load – Pieper revolver
108 FMJ	FL		1,100	290	Factory load – Nagant revolver

.32 Protector

Historical Notes: This cartridge was chambered in the Protector palm pistol that was manufactured by the Minneapolis Fire Arms Co. Winchester offered this cartridge late in 1898 and continued to catalog it until at least 1916. Evidently, despite what must have been very modest power, this combination had some appeal.

General Comments: Performance must have been quite anemic. However, just as with similar pocket pistols carried today, there is a certain deterrence value to any gun—very few persons really want to be shot at or hit with anything. When the chips are down, having almost any gun available can far surpass the value of throwing rocks.

.32 Protector (Estimated ballistics.)

Bullet (grains)	Powder	Grains	Velocity	Energy	Source/Comments
40	Black powder	4.0	550	26	QuickLOAD

7.65mm Roth-Sauer

Historical Notes: The 7.65mm Roth-Sauer originated in 1901 as one chambering for the Frommer pocket-type auto pistol. About 1905, the Roth-Sauer pistol was adapted to a reduced loading of the Frommer cartridge. Due to the popularity of the Roth-Sauer pistol, the name became attached to the cartridge. Winchester loaded the round during the 1920s, but it has been obsolete since 1930.

General Comments: The eight-shot Roth-Sauer pistol was a compact pocket or self-defense, type. Despite the low power of the cartridge, the pistol had a complicated, long-recoil locked breech. The 7.65mm Roth-Sauer cartridge looks like the .32 Automatic, but has a shorter case and a bullet of slightly smaller diameter (.301 inch). The 70- to 74-grain bullet has a muzzle velocity of 1070 fps, which means it develops a bit more energy than the

.32 Automatic. Regardless, both are in the same class, and there is not much difference between them. It is possible to make 7.65mm R-S ammo from .32 Automatic cases by turning down the rim, shortening, and reforming.

7.65mm Roth-Sauer Factory Ballistics

Bullet (grains/type)	Powder	Grains	Velocity	Energy	Source/Comments
70 to 74 FMJ	FL		1,070	184	Factory load

7.7mm Bittner

Historical Notes: Gustav Bittner created this cartridge for the Bittner Lever Action Pistol (Bittner'sche Repetir Pistole), circa 1893, in Weipert, a town that's in what is now the Czech Republic. Fewer than 500 of these rare pistols were made. The clip-fed pistol had the housing in front of action. In the action, the bolt stays retracted until the ring trigger is pulled, which moves bolt forward, stripping a round into the chamber. Because it appeared about the same time as more functional semi-automatics, the Lever Action Pistol was a short-lived design.

General Comments: The straight-rimmed case with Berdan priming is typical of designs of the time.—*W.T.W.*

7.62x25mm Russian Tokarev

Historical Notes: The 7.62x25mm Tokarev was the official Soviet pistol cartridge, adopted in 1930 for the Tokarev Model TT-30 and modified Model TT-33 automatic pistols. The pistols are a basic Browning-type design similar to the Colt .45 Auto pistol. However, these incorporate many original features to simplify manufacturing processes, and must be considered an advance over Browning's original patented design. These pistols often have a crude finish, but are well made and of excellent design. These have a 4½-inch barrel and a magazine capacity of eight rounds. Large quantities have been sold as military surplus. Some were made in communist China and Hungary, as well as Russia. The Hungarian-made Tokarev, in a modified form called the "Tokagypt," is chambered for the 9mm Parabellum cartridge. The Chinese began exporting both pistols and ammunition to the United States in 1987, at very reasonable prices.

General Comments: The cartridge is very similar in dimension to the 7.63mm (.30) Mauser, and most brands of Mauser ammunition can be fired in the Tokarev pistol. The 7.62mm Tokarev is a fair field cartridge for small game, with good velocity and flat trajectory, but needs soft-point bullets for maximum effectiveness. The handloader can use loading data for the 7.63 Mauser. The Speer .30-caliber plinker bullet of 100 grains makes a good hunting bullet, but, because it is slightly heavier than the standard weight, it must be loaded to lower velocity.

Chinese and Russian ammunition are steel-cased and Berdan-primed with corrosive primers. Such ammunition is not reloadable. Hansen Cartridge has imported quantities of 7.62x25mm ammunition with reloadable cases and non-corrosive Boxer primers.

7.62x25 Russian Tokarev Loading Data and Factory Ballistics

Bullet (grains/type)	Powder	Grains	Velocity	Energy	Source/Comments
86	Bullseye	5.0	1,390	365	Duplicate factory ball
87 FMJ	FL	FL	1,390	365	Factory load

.30 (7.65mm) Borchardt

Historical Notes: Also known as the 7.65mm Borchardt, this is the cartridge for the Model 1893 Borchardt auto pistol. Cartridge and pistol were designed by American Hugo Borchardt, but were manufactured by Loewe, in Berlin. The .30 Borchardt is listed in the 1905 and 1918-'19 Remington catalogs and was loaded in this country for a number of years.

General Comments: The .30 Borchardt is the predecessor of the 7.63 (30) Mauser, 7.65mm Mannlicher, and 7.62x25mm Russian Tokarev. These all have similar physical measurements, but the modern rounds are loaded to higher pressures and velocity than the original Borchardt cartridge. The .30 Borchardt fired an 85-grain bullet at 1280 fps, whereas the .30 Mauser fires an 86-grain bullet at 1410 to 1450 fps. Modern ammunition should *not* he used in the Borchardt or Mannlicher pistols. Borchardt cartridges are now scarce collector's items and should *not* be fired.

.30 (7.65mm) Borchardt Factory Ballistics

Bullet (grains/type)	Powder	Grains	Velocity	Energy	Source/Comments
85 FMJ	FL		1,280	312	Factory load

7.63mm (7.65) Mannlicher

Historical Notes: This straight-walled rimless cartridge was used in the Models 1900, 1901, and 1905 Mannlicher military automatic pistols. These were manufactured in Austria (Steyr) and in Spain. Austrian guns are well-made and finished, but the Spanish types are sometimes of doubtful quality. These pistols were common military surplus items in the 1950s. Some dealers also had ammunition.

General Comments: The 1900 and slightly-modified 1901 and 1905 Mannlicher pistols operate on the delayed blowback system. The non-detachable magazine is in the grip and holds eight rounds, the 1905 with 10. These guns are loaded from the top by means of a special charger, after retracting the slide. The 7.63 cartridge is only slightly more powerful than the .32 Automatic, and its use in the field would have to be confined to small game. There is also a locked-breech Model 1903 Mannlicher auto pistol that fires a lower-powered cartridge that is otherwise similar to the bottlenecked 7.63 Mauser. The standard Mauser cartridge must not be fired in these Model 1903 pistols, as that will quickly damage the action.

7.63 (7.65) Mannlicher Loading Data and Factory Ballistics

Bullet (grains/type)	Powder	Grains	Velocity	Energy	Source/Comments
86	Unique	3.2	1,000	193	Mauser bullet
85 FMJ	FL	FL	1,025	201	Factory load

.30 (7.65x21mm) Luger

Historical Notes: Introduced in 1900 by Deutsche Waffen u. Munitions Fabriken in Germany, the 7.65mm was designed by Georg Luger for the Luger automatic pistol. The cartridge is still used chiefly in the Luger pistol, although some SIG, Beretta M951, Browning Hi-Power, Ruger P89, and Walther P-38 pistols are chambered for this round. It was adopted as standard issue by the Swiss, Brazilian, Bulgarian, and Portuguese armies, but none of them currently issue it for front-line service.

General Comments: This is another bottlenecked rimless cartridge similar to the .30 Mauser, but shorter and not quite as powerful. It is not noted for great stopping power because of the small-diameter, lightweight, full jacketed bullet. It is used occasionally for small-game hunting and will do a fair job on rabbits and the like, provided the bullets are properly placed. The only manufacturer still offering this cartridge is Winchester. Bullet diameter is .308-inch.

Bullet (grains/type)	Powder	Grains	Velocity	Energy	Source/Comments
93	Unique	5.0	1,115	257	Lyman duplication of
100	Unique	4.8	1,210	325	Speer plinker
93 FMJ	FL	FL	1,220	305	Factory load

.30 (7.63x25mm) Mauser

Historical Notes: The .30 Mauser cartridge was developed by American gun designer Hugo Borchardt for the first successful commercial, automatic pistol of the same name. The Borchardt pistol was made by Ludwig Loewe & Co. (later DWM) of Berlin, Germany. Both the pistol and cartridge were introduced in 1893. The Borchardt automatic pistol was later redesigned, emerging as the well-known Luger pistol. This cartridge was adopted by Paul Mauser for his famous Model 1896 pistol, though with increased power for his more rugged design. It has been used mainly in the Mauser M1896 military automatic pistol and various imitations or copies manufactured in Spain and China.

General Comments: Until the .357 Magnum cartridge came along, the .30 Mauser was the high-velocity champion of the pistol world. It has a flat trajectory that makes long-range hits possible, but lacks stopping power because of the light, full jacketed bullet. However, it has been used successfully for hunting small game and varmints at moderate ranges. Handloading with soft-point or hollow-point hunting bullets improves performance considerably. At one time, both Remington and Winchester loaded this cartridge, but it has been dropped.

.30 (7.63x25mm) Mauser Loading Data and Factory Ballistics

Bullet (grains/type)	Powder	Grains	Velocity	Energy	Source/Comments
86 FMJ	Bullseye	4.5	1,160	257	Lyman
86 FMJ	Unique	6.0	1,230	289	Lyman
86 FMJ	FL		1,410	375	Factory load

7.62x38mm SP-3
7.62x42mm SP-4
7.62x63mm PZAM

Historical Notes: These "silent cartridges" were made for Soviet assassination weapons and special forces use. Designer Igor Ya. Stechkin developed a special type of ammunition that required no external silencer to be fired silently. Stechkin silenced the cartridges internally by encapsulating the blast of the propellant within the cartridge case. The 7.62x63mm PZAM cartridge was fired from the derringer-style S4M pistol in the mid-1960s. The 7.62x38mm SP-3 cartridge was used in the two-barrel Soviet MSP Groza pistol, circa 1972. The 7.62x42mm SP-4 was employed in the special forces PSS semi-auto sidearm circa 1983.

General Comments: Charlie Cutshaw, in *The New World of Russian Small Arms & Ammo,* says these three cartridges are closely related. The 7.62x63mm PZAM and 7.62x38mm SP-3 used a small propelling charge that drove two internal pistons forward to expel a standard M1943 bullet out of the case. The first piston hits against the cartridge case's internal shoulder, while the smaller, second piston continues forward to expel the bullet and then hits against the internal shoulder of the first piston. That retains all of the propelling gases and the resulting sound.

The 7.62x63mm SP-3 cartridge had thicker walls than the SP-2 earlier version and had its own built-in firing pin. According to Cutshaw, the hammer of the S4M pistol struck the cartridge firing pin, which, in turn, struck the primer. The firing mechanism of the SP-3 cartridge was actually screwed into the base of the cartridge.

The 7.62x42mm SP-4 cartridge was used in the PSS silent semi-automatic pistol, a sidearm probably intended for special operations use rather than assassinations. The cartridge had a single-stage piston that did not project from the case when fired. It used a cylindrical bullet made of mild steel and was fitted with a brass driving band at the front. Feeding from a six-shot magazine in the blowback-operated PSS pistol, it apparently could also be fired from the single-shot NRS-1 scout shooting knife.—*W.T.W.*

7.62x38mm, 7.62x42mm, 7.62x63mm Loading Data and Factory Ballistics

Bullet (grains/type)	Powder	Grains	Velocity	Energy	Source/Comments
123 PZAM 7.62	ML	ML	570	90	Military Loading
123 SP-3 7.62	ML	ML	490	66	Military Loading
143 SP-4 7.62	ML	ML	655	136	Military Loading

.32 H&R Magnum

Historical Notes: The .32 H&R Magnum was the result of a joint project between Harrington & Richardson and Federal Cartridge Co. It was introduced in 1984 for the five-shot H&R Model 504, 532, and 586 revolvers. This was followed later in the same year by Charter Arms and its six-shot .32 H&R Magnum Police Undercover revolver, and, in 1985, by the Ruger New Model .32 Magnum Single-Six and SP101 revolvers.

The .32 H&R Magnum is simply the older .32 Smith & Wesson Long case lengthened by .155-inch. Therefore, any .32 Magnum revolver will also accept and fire both the .32 S&W and the .32 S&W Long. This makes for a convenient situation, because the shooter has a choice of three different cartridges that will work in one handgun. Two loadings of the cartridge were offered, a lead semi-wadcutter bullet of 95 grains, or an 85-grain jacketed hollow-point.

General Comments: According to factory ballistics, the .32 Magnum delivers double the energy of the .32 S&W Long and 13 percent more energy than the standard .38 Special load. However, chronograph tests demonstrated that actual velocity at the muzzle ranges 60 to 100 fps below factory-advertised figures. Nevertheless, the cartridge performance level is well above that of any other .32-caliber handgun cartridge currently available. The .32-20 can be handloaded to equal the .32 Magnum in a revolver, but new .32-20 revolvers have not been available since before World War II.

What kept H&R from chambering its revolvers for the .32-20? To do so would have required extensive design changes in its revolvers, because the .32-20 is too long. In fact, .32-20 case length is nearly the same as .32 Magnum overall cartridge length. By the late 1980s, both H&R and Charter Arms had gone out of business (both are again producing firearms), leaving Ruger and Dan Wesson as the sole supplier of revolvers in this chambering. Federal was the only ammunition maker to undertake production. H&R no longer manufacturers handguns and was acquired by The Freedom Group through Marlin Firearms. Charter Arms is back in business and offers four revolvers for the .32 H&R. Dan Wesson has been acquired by CZ-USA, but offers no .32-caliber revolvers. Smith & Wesson and Ruger do manufacturer revolvers for the .32 H&R, and any revolver chambered for the newer .327 Federal Magnum can also safely fire .32 H&R Magnum cartridges. Currently a modest but serviceable selection of .32 H&R Magnum loads are available from Federal, Black Hills, Buffalo Bore, and DoubleTap ammunition.

.32 H&R Magnum Loading Data and Factory Ballistics

Bullet (grains/type)	Powder	Grains	Velocity	Energy	Source/Comments
85 JHP	Unique	4.0	900	153	Hornady
90 Lead	Unique	3.4	815	145	Hornady
98 Lead	Unique	3.0	815	145	Speer
85 JHP	FL	FL	1,100	230	Factory load
85 JHP	FL	FL	1,300	318	Buffalo Bore Factory Load
90 Sierra JHC	True Blue	6.5	1,150	264	Sierra
130 Keith Style Hard Cast	FL	FL	1,125	365	Buffalo Bore Factory Load

.32 Smith & Wesson

Historical Notes: Designed for the Smith & Wesson Model 1½, hinged-frame, single-action revolver introduced in 1878, the .32 S&W is an old and very popular cartridge, widely used in the United States and Europe for low-priced, pocket-type revolvers. Originally a black-powder cartridge, it has been loaded with smokeless powder exclusively since 1940. In the United States, Colt, Harrington & Richardson, Hopkins & Allen, Iver Johnson, Smith & Wesson, and others have made revolvers for this cartridge. In England, Webley & Scott made revolvers for it. Elsewhere in Europe, the Bayard and Pickert revolvers chambered it. The original loading used nine grains of black powder.

General Comments: The .32 Smith & Wesson formerly ranked with the .32 Automatic in general popularity, and for the same reasons. It is low-powered and adaptable to small, light, inexpensive, pocket-type handguns. Ballistically, it is not quite as good as the .32 Automatic. It is very similar to the .32 Short Colt, but the two are not interchangeable, because of a difference in bullet and case diameter. Like the .32 Automatic, the .32 S&W is about the minimum cartridge for self-defense. It is considered inadequate for police work. It is used occasionally for hunting small game at very short ranges, but is too underpowered for consideration as a sporting cartridge. This ammunition is still available.

.32 Smith & Wesson Loading Data and Factory Ballistics

Bullet (grains/type)	Powder	Grains	Velocity	Energy	Source/Comments
85 Lead	Bullseye	1.1	705	93	NA
85 Lead	Black powder (Fg)	9.0	680	90	Factory load
98 Lead	Smokeless powder		705	115	Factory load

.32 Smith & Wesson Long
.32 Colt New Police

Historical Notes: This cartridge was developed for the Smith & Wesson First Model, solid-frame, hand-ejector revolver, introduced in 1903. The same cartridge, loaded with a flat-nose bullet, is called the .32 Colt New Police. Colt, Harrington & Richardson, Iver Johnson, and Smith & Wesson were the principal companies making revolvers in this chambering in the United States. Many Spanish and other European revolvers, such as the Bayard and Pickert, chambered the round. In Europe, it had not been as widely used as the shorter .32 S&W until some ISU centerfire target shooters discovered the .32 S&W Long, and now there are several high-class European target autoloaders for the wadcutter loading of this cartridge.

General Comments: The .32 S&W Long is the smallest revolver cartridge deemed adequate for police use in the United States, and it has been fairly popular with detectives or plainclothes officers. It has always been available in a variety of short, light, small-frame revolvers, some of which are very well made. It has a reputation for excellent accuracy and has been used for target and match shooting in the past, as well as in ISU shooting. It is as accurate as the .38 S&W Special, but not as versatile. It is the minimum size for sporting use and with handloaded, hunting-type bullets it is quite effective on small game. It is not as popular or widely used for self-defense as it once was, because of the development of compact .38-caliber revolvers. Its range and effectiveness can be increased by handloading. The original load was 13 grains of black powder and a 98-grain bullet.

Previous editions of this book incorrectly listed the .32-44 Target as being interchangeable with the .32 Smith & Wesson Long. Not so. The .32-44 was a chambering for the S&W No. 3 Target revolver and will not chamber in .32 S&W Long revolvers. The .32-44 designation translates as "a .32 on a .44 frame." Like its larger sibling, the original .38-44 S&W Target, the .32-44 S&W Target featured an elongated case with a bullet that was loaded flush with the case mouth, somewhat in the spirit of the 7.62mm Russian Nagant Revolver cartridge.

Bullet (grains/type)	Powder	Grains	Velocity	Energy	Source/Comments
90 Lead	700X	1.8	700	98	Hornady
98 Lead	Unique	1.8	665	96	Speer
98 Lead	Black powder (Fg)	13.0	780	132	Factory load
98 Wadcutter	Smokeless powder	FL	705	115	Factory load

.32 North American Arms (NAA)

Historical Notes: Culminating from a joint development effort between North American Arms and writer Ed Sanow, the .32 NAA uses an ordinary .380 ACP case necked-down to house a .32-caliber bullet. In 2002, North American Arms decided to offer this chambering in its Guardian mini-pistol product line.

General Comments: Behind the neck, all case dimensions and configurations, including the extractor groove, rimless case, cartridge diameter, and bolt face engagement are identical to the .380 ACP. CorBon produces the ammo, which will bear a CorBon .32 NAA headstamp. The cartridge uses a proprietary bullet designed by Hornady.

.32 North American Arms Factory Ballistics

Bullet (grains/type)	Powder	Grains	Velocity	Energy	Source/Comments
60 JHP	FL	FL	1,222	199	CorBon factory load (2.5"bbl)

7.92x24mm

Historical Notes: In 2006, the 7.92×24mm pistol cartridge was designed by firearms company VBR-Belgium (Van Bruaene Rik–Belgium) for use in PDWs, pistols, submachine guns, and carbines. In a PDW, it performs more like the 9×19mm NATO pistol round than a 4.6×30mm or 5.7×28mm. The 7.92×24mm is shorter than those other chamberings, to allow its use in compact and sub-compact weapons. To be compatible with 9×19mm and .45 Auto grip frames, the 7.92×24mm case accepts different bullet lengths, "S" for 9mm and "N" for the .45.

General Comments: The 7.92×24mm round exceeds the minimum FBI penetration requirements—12-inch penetration when fired into ballistic gelatin—and is available on the civilian, law enforcement, and military markets. Several variants are made, including the 3P (contains three projectiles roughly the size of 12-gauge buckshot); the BAP (Brass Armor Piercing); AP-HPF (Armor Piercing-Hollow Point Fragmenting, with a 5.7mm hardened steel penetrator and a brass fragmenting hollow-point sabot); and FRA (Frangible) bullets, suitable for indoor shooting.—*W.T.W.*

7.92x24mm Factory Ballistics

Bullet (grains/type)	Powder	Grains	Velocity	Energy	Source/Comments
71 FMJ RN	FL	FL	1,650	429	Factory Load
110 FMJ BT	FL	FL	1,000	269	Factory Load

.327 Federal Magnum

0.375" 0.337" 0.337"

1.200"

Historical Notes: Introduced in 2008 by the Federal Cartridge Company, the .327 Federal Magnum is an attempt to improve the performance of the .32 H&R Magnum. Factory .32 H&R Magnum ammunition, as per SAAMI specifications, is not loaded to the cartridge's full potential. This is due to the weaker H&R revolvers chambered for this cartridge. Cartridge performance for the .32 H&R Magnum can be substantially improved with handloads, when fired in Ruger or S&W revolvers. The .327 Federal Magnum takes this performance to a new level. This was accomplished by increasing the case capacity and loading the cartridge to a substantially higher pressure (45,000 psi) than the .32 H&R Magnum has at 21,000 CUP. In fact, the .327 Federal Magnum is loaded to a higher pressure than any other commercially loaded defensive handgun cartridge. Since .327 Federal Magnum cartridges cannot be chambered in any other .32-caliber revolver, there is no concern of over-pressure issues. Ruger worked with Federal during the development of this cartridge and initially offered a three-inch version of its SP 101 six-shot revolver in this chambering. With factory loads, a 100-grain bullet will leave the barrel of the SP 101 at about 1,400 fps.

General Comments: Many who had never fired this cartridge initially considered it similar to its predecessor—the .32 H&R Magnum—as suitable for ladies or other recoil-conscious shooters. That's not the case. The .327 Federal Magnum is a handful in a 28-ounce SP 101 with full power loads. Federal does offer an 85-grain, low-recoil load that is much more controllable, but it is still markedly more powerful than any factory .32 H&R Magnum load. The terminal performance of this cartridge with both the 100- and 115-grain Speer Gold Dot loads approaches that of the .357 Magnum with similar bullets. Penetration in 10 percent gelatin is in excess of 14 inches, and bullets exhibit wide expansion. The design of these two Gold Dot bullets is very important to this cartridge, because prior to them, there were no .312-diameter bullets that could withstand the velocity this cartridge is capable of producing.

Over the last three years, I have spent a great deal of time shooting, testing, and handloading this cartridge for three revolvers and a Marlin 1894 re-chambered from .32 H&R Magnum. I was always a fan of the .32 H&R Magnum, and the .327 Federal has become my favorite revolver cartridge. If you can manage the recoil from a handgun, it is a viable self-defense option, and, from a rifle, it is capable of taking deer-sized game out to 100 yards. From the 16-inch barreled Marlin, the 110-grain bullet speeds along at over 2000 fps. One thing that sets the .327 Federal Magnum apart from all other revolver cartridges is the fact that any revolver so chambered will also fire .32 Short, .32 Long, and .32 H&R Magnum ammunition. This cartridge's versatility is unmatched.

327 Federal Magnum Loading Data and Factory Ballistics

Bullet (grains/type)	Powder	Grains	Velocity	Energy	Source/Comments
85 JHP	True Blue	8.7	1,644	510	Ramshot
90 Lead SWC	True Blue	7.9	1,536	471	Ramshot
100 JHP	True Blue	7.7	1,441	461	Ramshot
85 JHP	FL	FL	1,400	370	Federal Factory load
100 Gold Dot HP	FL	FL	1,500	500	Speer Factory load
100 JSP	FL	FL	1,500	500	Federal Factory load
100 Keith Hard Cast	FL	FL	1,300	375	Buffalo Bore Factory load
100 JHP	FL	FL	1,450	466	Buffalo Bore Factory load
115 Gold Dot HP	FL	FL	1,300	375	Speer Factory load

.32 Automatic Colt Pistol (.32 ACP)/7.65mm Browning

Historical Notes: Designed by John Browning for his first successful automatic pistol, this cartridge was first manufactured by FN, in Belgium, and introduced in 1899. It was marketed in the United States when Colt turned out a pocket automatic on another Browning patent in 1903. The .32 Automatic Colt Pistol (ACP) is one of the more popular pistol cartridges ever developed. In the United States, Colt, Remington, Harrington & Richardson, Smith & Wesson, and Savage chambered pistols for this cartridge. In Europe, every company that made automatic pistols chambered the .32 ACP. It was also used in the German Pickert revolver. In Europe, it is known as the 7.65mm Browning.

General Comments: This cartridge uses a semi-rimmed cartridge case and a .308-inch diameter bullet. The .32 Automatic is the minimum cartridge that should really be seriously considered for self-defense. In the United States, it is used exclusively for small pocket-type guns and is not considered adequate for police or military use. However, in Europe it is often used in police pistols and as an alternative, but unofficial, chambering for military sidearms. As a hunting cartridge, it is not powerful enough for anything larger than small game.

Loading tables generally give bullet diameter of the .32 Automatic as .312-inch or .314-inch. It is actually closer to .308-inch, and this is important if you handload. Effective small-game loads can be made by using 100-grain .30-caliber rifle bullets intended for light loads and plinking, such as the Speer .30-caliber Plinker. All major ammunition makers offer this cartridge. Winchester recently introduced a load with a jacketed hollow-point bullet. Other makers have followed suit.

.32 (7.65mm) Automatic/.32 ACP Loading Data and Factory Ballistics

Bullet (grains/type)	Powder	Grains	Velocity	Energy	Source/Comments
71 FMJ	Bullseye	2.2	800	100	Sierra, Hornady
71 FMJ	700X	2.0	850	114	Sierra, Hornady
60 JHP	FL	FL	970	125	Winchester factory load
71 FMJ	FL	FL	905	129	Factory load
74 FMJ/JSP	FL				Factory load, early

.32 Short Colt
.32 Long Colt
.32 S&W Gallery

Historical Notes: Introduced by Colt in 1875 along with the New Line model revolvers, this was originally a black-powder cartridge using a 90-grain outside-lubricated bullet. There is also a .32 Short Colt, which is identical, except for a shorter case length. In England and Europe, this is known as the .320 caliber revolver. The .32 Short and Long Colt cartridges are actually obsolete, having been displaced by the .32 S&W and .32 S&W Long. Colt is the only company that used this cartridge in the United States. It was more popular in Europe, where a number of black-powder .320 revolvers were made.

General Comments: The .32 Colt cartridge was originally of the outside-lubricated type, which used a bullet of .313-inch diameter. Later, this was changed to an inside-lubricated type, which necessitated a bullet of .299-inch diameter, so that the lubricating grooves would fit inside the case. Bullet weight was reduced from 90 to 80 or 82 grains in the inside-lubricated type, and this shortened overall length a little. In power and usefulness, the Colt cartridges are nearly the same as the .32 S&W Short and Long, but not nearly as accurate. Winchester only recently discontinued this loading.

.32 Short Colt/.32 Long Colt Loading Data and Factory Ballistics

Bullet (grains/type)	Powder	Grains	Velocity	Energy	Source/Comments
55 Lead	Black powder	4.5	N/A	N/A	Wadcutter lead in 32 Short Colt
80 Lead	Bullseye	1.8	732	94	Approximate Factory Equivalent 32 Short Colt
80 Lead	FL	FL	745	100	Factory Load - Short Colt
82 Lead	FL	FL	755	104	Factory Load - Long Colt

.32 Colt

Historical Notes: This cartridge was Colt's attempt at solving the problems associated with outside-lubricated cartridges. The .32 Colt utilized a longer case to fully cover the lubricated portion of the bullet and carried a hollow-based bullet to help obturation in the bore. This was necessary, because the bullets had to be undersized to fit in the case. Reports were that the effort was not very successful. Loading was an 82-grain lead bullet with 12 grains of black powder.

.320 Revolver

Historical Notes: The .320 Revolver cartridge originated in England about 1870. It was the first used in the Webley revolver, but later, a number of other British and European pocket-type guns chambered it. The .320 served as the inspiration for the .32 Short Colt. It is no longer loaded by European ammunition manufacturers. At one time, it was also manufactured in the United States, but was discontinued in the late 1920s.

General Comments: The .320 Revolver is nearly identical to the .32 Short Colt in ballistic performance. The 320 is a short-range small-game number only. Use the same loading data as given for the .32 Short Colt. Recently, .320 Revolver ammunition was offered by Fiocchi.

.320 Revolver Factory Ballistics

Bullet (grains/type)	Powder	Grains	Velocity	Energy	Source/Comments
80 Lead	FL	FL	550	54	Factory load

7.5mm Swiss Army Revolver

Historical Notes: This cartridge was adopted by the Swiss Army in 1882 and officially used until 1903. The Swiss Army revolver is based on a modified Nagant system. In the early 1960s, quantities of these revolvers were sold on the American market by surplus dealers. These are quite well made and finished. Both black-powder and smokeless powder ammunition is encountered.

General Comments: The 7.5mm Swiss revolver cartridge is identical to and fully interchangeable with the 7.5mm Swedish and Norwegian rounds. Modern smokeless powder ammunition was loaded by Norma for the Swedish Nagant, and this can be used in the Swiss revolver. The two cartridges differ only in bullet type. Most Swedish cartridges use an outside-lubricated bullet, whereas the Swiss also used an inside-lubricated type. Ballistics are about the same as the .32 S&W Long. For additional information, see the 7.5mm Swedish Nagant Revolver. Fiocchi now produces this ammunition.

7.5mm Swiss Army Factory Ballistics

Bullet (grains/type)	Powder	Grains	Velocity	Energy	Source/Comments
102 to 110 Lead	ML	ML	700	115	Military load

.35 Smith & Wesson Auto/.35 Automatic

Historical Notes: Smith & Wesson introduced this cartridge and a new auto pistol in 1913. The S&W pistol is the only one that ever chambered this cartridge. It was discontinued (in .35 S&W chambering), in 1921. The pistol was based on designs of the Belgian C.P. Clement. Commercial ammunition was loaded until about 1940.

General Comments: The .35 S&W Auto is actually a .32-caliber cartridge and is similar to the .32 Automatic. In fact, it is possible to fire .32 Automatic ammo in some .35 semi-auto pistols. The cartridge designation was probably to prevent confusion with the .32 Automatic. However, it has created more confusion than it prevented. The .32 Automatic is a better cartridge, and Smith & Wesson eventually chambered its pistol for that more popular round.

.35 Smith & Wesson Auto Loading Data and Factory Ballistics

Bullet (grains/type)	Powder	Grains	Velocity	Energy	Source/Comments
76 FMJ	Bullseye	1.6	809	110	Duplicate factory load
76 FMJ	FL	FL	809	110	Factory load

8mm Rast-Gasser

Historical Notes: The 8mm Rast-Gasser military cartridge was introduced in 1898 for the solid-frame Rast-Gasser military revolver patented in 1873. A number of different revolvers manufactured in Belgium and Germany chambered the round. Although popular in Europe, the 8mm Rast-Gasser was never manufactured in the United States. The round is obsolete and ammunition difficult to obtain.

General Comments: The Gasser solid-frame revolver design is noted for its simplicity of disassembly. It also has a rebounding hammer and a spring-mounted, separate firing pin. These are usually well made and rather sturdy. Quantities have been sold at various times in surplus stores.

The cartridge resembles the 8mm French Lebel Revolver round quite closely. Bullet diameter is .320-inch. Rim and body diameter are nearly identical to the .32 S&W Long. The .32 S&W case is shorter, but both cartridges are of approximately the same power. Lyman cast bullet No. 313445 (95 grains) can be adapted for handloading. Loading data for the .32 S&W can be used as a guide in working up loads. This ammunition is now offered by Fiocchi.

8mm Rast-Gasser Factory Ballistics

Bullet (grains/type)	Powder	Grains	Velocity	Energy	Source/Comments
115 to 126 Lead	FL	FL	750 - 785	140 - 170	Factory load
125	FL	FL	787	170	1914-1918 factory load
126 Lead	FL	FL	770	166	Fiocchi factory load

8mm Nambu

Historical Notes: This was the official Japanese military pistol cartridge introduced in 1904 for the Nambu auto pistol. It was also used in the modified 1925 model and the odd-looking 1934 model. This was the official Japanese pistol cartridge in World War II, although other pistols and cartridges were used. It was used only by Japan.

General Comments: Quite a few 8mm Nambu pistols were brought back from the Pacific battle areas by returning GIs at war's end. Ammunition has been a problem, because most captured stores were destroyed. Externally, the cartridge resembles the 7.65mm Luger, but uses a larger diameter bullet and a semi-rimmed case. In power, it is slightly superior to the .32 Automatic. Most Nambu cartridges are collector's items.

Bullet diameter is .320-inch. Cast .32-caliber revolver bullets sized as close to this as possible would undoubtedly work in weights of 83 to 100 grains. Use only light charges of powder. In the 1980s, Brass Extrusion Laboratories, Ltd. of Bensenville, Illinois (now MAST Technology, Inc.; www.masttechnology. com), manufactured 8mm Nambu cases for Midway (www.midwayusa.com), though Midway no longer sells this ammunition. Today this cartridge is commercially loaded by the Old Western Scrounger (www. ows-ammo.com) and the Buffalo Arms Co (www.buffaloarms.com).

8mm Nambu Loading Data and Factory Ballistics

Bullet (grains/type)	Powder	Grains	Velocity	Energy	Source/Comments
83 Lead	Unique	3.0	950	165	Estimated velocity
102 FMJ	ML		960	202	Military load

8mm Lebel Revolver

Historical Notes: This cartridge is for the French 1892 Ordnance Revolver, commonly called the Lebel. This is a six-shot, solid-frame, double-action gun. Bayard and Pieper also made revolvers in this chambering. Small lots have shown up in surplus stores, but these are of interest mostly to military collectors.

General Comments: The 8mm Lebel revolver cartridge closely resembles the .32-20 WCF, and ammunition can be made by sizing .32-20 cases. This is not a common item, but surplus stores have occasionally offered this ammunition. The .32 Smith & Wesson Long can be fired in these revolvers, but the cases bulge badly and accuracy is poor. When cooking up your own loads, stick to moderate charges and velocity, as the Lebel revolver is not designed for high pressures. For field use, this is another .32 S&W Long-class cartridge suitable only for small game. Bullet diameter is .330-inch, and one can use the Lyman No. 32359 cast bullet. Fiocchi currently offers this ammunition.

8mm Lebel Revolver Loading Data and Factory Ballistics

Bullet (grains/type)	Powder	Grains	Velocity	Energy	Source/Comments
115 Lead	Bullseye	2.8	700	126	Lyman No. 32359
102 Lead	ML	ML	625	104	Military load

7.5mm Swedish Nagant Revolver

Historical Notes: The cartridge listed here is the 7.5mm Swedish, designed for the 1887 Swedish Nagant military revolver manufactured by Husqvarna. Since the end of World War II, large quantities of these revolvers have been sold as surplus in the United States. This has a short, rimmed case with an outside-lubricated bullet and is usually loaded with black powder. The revolver is long obsolete, but Norma of Sweden loaded this cartridge with Berdan-primed cases and smokeless propellants.

General Comments: The 7.5mm Swedish Nagant Revolver cartridge was practically unknown in the United States prior to 1948. It is listed here, because of the large number of these revolvers imported. Many Nagant revolvers were altered to use the .22 Long Rifle, by lining the barrel and bushing the cylinder. The .32 Short or Long Colt can be fired in these revolvers, but they fit loosely and accuracy is terrible. Cartridge cases can be made from empty .32-20 cases trimmed back to .895 inch in length. The Australian .310 Martini cartridge will also work, if cut to the proper length. The Swedish Nagant revolver was intended for black powder, and only low-pressure smokeless powder loads are safe. Ballistically, the 7.5mm cartridge is in the same class as the .32 S&W Long. Fiocchi loads the 7.5mm Swiss, which is essentially the same case with a different loading and which can be used in these guns.

7.5mm Swedish Nagant Revolver Loading Data and Factory Ballistics

Bullet (grains/type)	Powder	Grains	Velocity	Energy	Source/Comments
105 Lead	Bullseye	2.0	720	120	Duplicates factory load
105 Lead	Black powder (FFFg)	11.5	725	121	Duplicates factory load
104 Lead	FL	FL	725	121	Factory load
107 Lead	FL	FL	710	108	Fiocchi factory load

8.5mm Mars

Historical Notes: The obsolete 8.5mm Mars was an experimental centerfire pistol cartridge developed in the late nineteenth century. It was based on necking down the .45 Mars Long case. Though the .45 Mars Long itself produced an impressive muzzle velocity of 1,250 fps, the 8.5mm version hit 1,750 fps, far outperforming the 9mm Parabellum of the time (approximately 1,100 fps). The similar .360 Mars cartridge fired a 156-grain lead round-nose bullet at 1,400 fps.

General Comments: The bullet used in the 8.5mm Mars had two cannelures, with the case crimped into both to withstand the feeding action of the Mars Automatic Pistol. The cartridge headspaces on the shoulder behind the neck. The case has a thin rim and deep extractor groove, in comparison to most rimless pistol cartridges. This was among the most powerful handgun cartridges made in the early twentieth century, but fewer than 100 of the complicated pistols were made.—*W.T.W.*

8mm Mars Loading Data and Factory Ballistics

Bullet (grains/type)	Powder	Grains	Velocity	Energy	Source/Comments
139 FMJ	Fl	FL	1,550	740	Factory Load

9mm Ultra

Historical Notes: This cartridge was designed for the Walther PP Super semi-auto pistol introduced in 1972-'73. This seven-shot autoloader was designed particularly for the West German police. It was not available to the civilian market until 1975, and then only in small numbers. Quite a few guns in this chambering have shown up in the United States, as the West German police discontinued using this chambering. In recent years, the SIG Sauer P230 and the Benelli B76 auto pistols have also been chambered for the 9mm Ultra. The cartridge was actually developed, in 1936, for the German Air Force, but was never officially adopted.

The 9mm Ultra is one millimeter longer than the .380 Auto and one millimeter shorter than the 9mm Luger, with the same general case dimensions. In terms of inches, the .380 case length is .680-inch, the 9mm Ultra is .720-inch, and the 9mm Luger is .760-inch.

Original loading of the 9mm Ultra (by Hirtenberger, of Austria) used a 100-grain full-jacketed bullet at a muzzle velocity of 1060 fps. GECO (Dynamit-Nobel) loads a 94-grain full-jacketed bullet at an initial velocity of 1054 fps. Both bullets are of truncated cone shape. Ammunition is hard to find in the United States, and American companies do not load it. The case has a slightly rebated rim .02-inch smaller than the base.

General Comments: European police have traditionally carried small .32 Automatic and .380 Automatic pistols. However, with the increase in crime and attacks by terrorist groups, they found themselves outgunned by those on the other side of the law. There was some reluctance to adopt the full-powered 9mm military auto-pistol, which is heavier and bulkier than the more convenient .32 and .380 autos. The 9mm Ultra was an effort to provide greater stopping power, while retaining the small, handy pistols police were used to carrying. This was not successful, and most German police now carry 9mm Luger-chambered pistols.

The best that can be said about the 9mm Ultra is that it is as good as and probably more effective than the .380 Automatic. Handloaded with 9mm jacketed hollow-point bullets, it would certainly be satisfactory for small-game hunting. Hirtenberger, Fiocchi, and Dynamit Nobel still offer this cartridge. It is sometimes called the 9mm Police.

9mm Ultra Loading Data and Factory Ballistics

Bullet (grains/type)	Powder	Grains	Velocity	Energy	Source/Comments
100	W231	3.6	1,010	225	NA
123 FMJ	FL		1,070	350	Fiocchi factory load
124 FMJ	ML		1,050	308	Military load

9mm Bayard Long
(9mm Bergmann-Bayard Long)

Historical Notes: This cartridge is for the 1910 Model Bergmann-Bayard automatic pistol, which was the official Danish military sidearm for many years. The Spanish also used both pistol and cartridge and, consequently, many Spanish-made pistols were made for this round. The Astra and various Colt-Browning copies or modifications are found in the 9mm Bayard chambering.

General Comments: The 9mm Bayard has never been manufactured in the United States. Pistols in this chambering are mostly military surplus, which were imported and sold after World War II. The cartridge is quite similar to the .38 Automatic but longer. The Astra Model 400 is designed for the 9mm Bayard and will handle the .38 Automatic without any adjustment, but most other pistols will not. It is a potent round and makes a good field cartridge if loaded with hunting-type bullets. Bullet diameter is .355 inch, and any 9mm Luger bullet can be used, cast or jacketed. Standard loads for the 9mm Luger or the .38 Colt Automatic will work fine in these pistols.

9mm Bergmann-Bayard Long Loading Data and Factory Ballistics

Bullet (grains/type)	Powder	Grains	Velocity	Energy	Source/Comments
116 JSP	Unique	7.0	1,280	420	N/A
125 FMJ	FL	FL	1,120	352	Factory load

9mm Browning Long

Historical Notes: This Browning-designed pistol cartridge was popular in Europe but never adopted by American manufacturers. It was introduced with the FN Browning 1903 Model pistol. Sweden used the pistol and cartridge as an official military sidearm starting in 1907 and sold most of these pistols as surplus after World War II. Most were altered to use the standard .380 Automatic for the American market. In addition to the Browning, Le Francais and Webley & Scott pistols used this cartridge.

General Comments: The 9mm Browning Long has been used only to a very limited extent in the United States. In size, it is a shortened .38 Automatic, and, in power, is between the .380 and .38 Colt Automatic. For field use, it would be strictly a small-game number. Bullet diameter is the same as the 9mm Luger. Bullets for reloading are easy to obtain. Like all auto pistol cartridges, killing power can be improved with soft-point or half-jacketed hunting bullets. Even in Europe, this cartridge is essentially obsolete.

9mm Browning Long Loading Data and Factory Ballistics

Bullet (grains/type)	Powder	Grains	Velocity	Energy	Source/Comments
75 Lead	Unique	5.0	1,078	192	Lyman No. 358101
95 FMJ	Unique	5.0	1,050	230	Estimated Velocity
116 FMJ	Unique	4.8	1,000	255	Estimated Velocity
110 FMJ	FL	FL	1,100	300	Factory load

9mm Mauser

Historical Notes: Introduced in 1908, this cartridge was developed for the Export Model Mauser auto pistol. Both cartridge and pistol had a relatively short life and were discontinued in 1914 with the outbreak of World War I. Production was not resumed after the war. The 9mm Mauser was designed as a more powerful round than the 7.63mm Mauser, in an effort to capture sales in Africa and South America. It failed in this effort and never became popular, although it is potentially a good field cartridge. The 9mm Mauser was revived, in 1933-'34, when the Swiss-designed Neuhausen submachine gun and, later, the Austrian Steyr-Solothurn were chambered for this round. Manufacture of this cartridge then resumed in several European countries. Today, the 9mm Mauser (DWM No. 487) is a collector's item.

General Comments: The 9mm Mauser is more powerful than the 9mm Luger and has an edge on the .38 Colt Super Automatic. It develops 534 ft-lbs of energy at the muzzle, compared to 465 and 430 for top factory loadings of the 9mm Luger and .38 Colt Super, respectively. According to the DWM catalog, the 9mm Mauser is loaded with a 123- or 128-grain full-jacketed bullet at an initial velocity of 1362 fps. With modern bullets, this would make a good small- to medium-game hunting cartridge. The case is approximately .23 inch longer than the 9mm Luger and is rimless and Berdan-primed. Empty cases are easily reloaded with any standard 9mm (.355-inch) 100- to 130-grain bullet.

9mm Mauser Loading Data and Factory Ballistics

Bullet (grains/type)	Powder	Grains	Velocity	Energy	Source/Comments
125	BlueDot	10.6	1,300	467	Estimated Velocity
128 FMJ	FL	FL	1,362	534	Factory load

9mm Winchester Magnum

Historical Notes: Reports on the 9mm Winchester Magnum were circulating as early as 1977, but 11 years later in late 1988, it was still not exactly an over-the-counter item, although a few individuals were using it in Thompson/Center pistols. This cartridge was listed in the 1988 Winchester-Western Sporting Arms and Ammunition Catalog. In any event, the 9mm Magnum is one of two cartridges developed by Winchester for the stainless steel Wildey gas-operated semi-automatic pistol. This is a rather large handgun (weighing more than three pounds unloaded), and holding 14 of these 9mm Magnum rounds. That gun was advertised as available in five-, six-, seven-, eight-, or 10-inch barrel lengths. It had a ventilated, raised rib over the barrel and an adjustable, target-type rear sight. This pistol and cartridge are intended primarily for silhouette competition, but have an obvious field application for hunting small to medium game or even big game in the hands of an expert.

General Comments: The 9mm Winchester Magnum bears some resemblance to the older 9mm Mauser cartridge and develops roughly comparable ballistics. The Mauser 9mm fires a 128-grain bullet at 1362 fps, whereas the Winchester version has a 115-grain bullet that starts out at 1475 fps. The energies developed are 534 and 556 ft-lbs, respectively, so these are not very far apart. A 115-grain bullet with a muzzle velocity of 1475 fps (five-inch barrel) is impressive, but less than top handloads in the .357 Magnum, which can develop over 1550 fps with 125-grain bullets. The 9mm Magnum is certainly more powerful than either the 9mm Luger or the .38 Colt Super and, if loaded with hunting-type bullets, should prove to be very effective for a broad range of hunting situations.

9mm Winchester Magnum Factory Ballistics

Bullet (grains/type)	Powder	Grains	Velocity	Energy	Source/Comments
115 FMJ	FL		1,475	556	Factory load

.356 TSW (Team Smith & Wesson)

Historical Notes: The centerfire pistol cartridge was designed by Smith & Wesson in 1994 as an IPSC round. The .356 TSW fit in a 9mm magazine, and S&W convinced Federal to load it and submit it for SAAMI-spec approval, where it saw promise as a Limited-class competition round. However, because of a rules change, USPSA didn't approve it for that class, and there were other rounds that were better choices for Open guns. S&W scrapped the project, effectively killing the .356 TSW. Federal case heads and the box were marked "356 TSW." The load was a 147-grain FMJ Match product number GM356SW.

General Comments: The TSW is simply a slightly longer 9mm case (9x21.5mm), and it uses ordinary 9mm bullets for reloading purposes. To meet IPSC's major power factor back then, the TSW had to send a 124-grain 9mm bullet at about 1,450 fps. A .356 TSW performs on par with hot 9x21 IPSC loads or full-house .357 SIG loads, but it has an advantage over the .357 SIG. The SIG cartridge is a bottleneck round, a .40 S&W casing necked down to 9mm. The .356 TSW is a straight-walled 9mm casing, thus, more .356 rounds can fit into a magazine. The .356 TSW was mainly chambered in 150 Smith & Wesson Model 3566 Performance Center .356 TSW pistols.

.356 TSW (Team Smith & Wesson) Factory Ballistics

Bullet (grains/type)	Powder	Grains	Velocity	Energy	Source/Comments
147 Federal Match FMJ	FL	FL	1,220	486	Federal GM356SW
124 Winchester FMJ	VV-3N37	9.1	1,446	576	IPSC Loads List 2001

9mm Glisenti

Historical Notes: Adopted for the Italian military Model 1910 Glisenti auto pistol, the 9mm Glisenti was also used in other pistols and submachine guns. It was the official Italian pistol cartridge, during World War I and II. It is similar in physical measurement to the 9mm Luger (Parabellum), but is not loaded as heavily. Regular 9mm Luger ammunition should not be fired in pistols intended for the Glisenti cartridge or loading.

General Comments: The 9mm Glisenti is in about the same class as the .38 Automatic and is not quite as powerful as the standard 9mm Luger. Quite a few Glisenti pistols have been sold on the American market through military surplus dealers. Ammunition can be made by loading 9mm Luger cases down to the proper velocity and pressure levels. Bullet diameter is .355-inch, so standard 9mm Luger bullets can be used. This cartridge is now obsolete, but Fiocchi has recently manufactured it.

9mm Glisenti Loading Data and Factory Ballistics

Bullet (grains/type)	Powder	Grains	Velocity	Energy	Source/Comments
116 FMJ	Bullseye	4.0	1,070	294	
123 FMJ	FL		1,070	350	Fiocchi factory load
124 FMJ	ML		1,050	308	Military load

9mm ABC Mi-Bullet

Historical Notes: Advanced Ballistics Concepts, LLC (ABC) has invented two handgun cartridges, the 9mm ABC Mi-Bullet and the 45 ABC Mi-Bullet, whose multi-part bullet chunks joined by Kevlar tethers immediately unlock and expand to a predetermined diameter and pattern of spread. The round is designed to improve hit probability in self-defense situations. The Multiple Impact Bullet (Mi-Bullet) is similar to buckshot, in that both deliver multiple strike points.

The Mi-Stopper second-generation bullet is formed of high-density materials (e.g., lead, copper, tungsten, and the company's Zuerillium zinc alloy, aka Green Lead). The 9mm Mi-Bullet has an unusual construction. The tip of the round is the spool for the tethers. The spool sits atop three fitted fragments, which effectively form the bottom of the "bullet" next to the powder charge. The Mi-Bullets connect three separate segments with ballistic-grade tethers that allow the fragments to expand like a web to a predetermined diameter.

General Comments: A good application for this round might be a two-shot Derringer or other minimal-capacity handgun. The projectile is designed to expand to its maximum width at 12 feet, then "lock out" to maximum width for three feet, and then begin contracting, thus, the sweet spot for self-defense use is between about 12 feet and 21 feet, where most encounters occur. ABC offers Mi-Bullet cartridges in three categories: Less-lethal (Mi-Stinger), semi-lethal (Mi-Stunner), and fully-lethal (Mi-Stopper). Mi-Bullets fit existing firearms.—W.T.W.

9mm ABC Mi-4 Bullet (Lethal) Loading Data and Factory Ballistics

Bullet (grains/type)	Powder	Grains	Velocity	Energy	Source/Comments
85 Lead RN	Win 231	5.0	1,100	228	Stopper Factory Load

9mm ABC Mi-4 Bullet (Semi-Lethal, aka Green Load) Loading Data and Factory Ballistics

Bullet (grains/type)	Powder	Grains	Velocity	Energy	Source/Comments
70 Zuerillium Alloy	Win 231	5.2	950	140	Stopper Factory Load

9mm Luger (9x19mm Parabellum) 9mm Luger +P

Historical Notes: The 9mm Luger, or 9mm Parabellum, was introduced in 1902 with the Luger automatic pistol. It was adopted first by the German Navy in 1904 and then by the German Army in 1908. Since that time, it has been adopted by the military of practically every non-Communist power. It has become the world's most popular and widely used military handgun and submachine gun cartridge. In the United States, Colt, Smith & Wesson, Ruger, and many others chamber the 9mm, as do many foreign-made pistols. In 1985, the 9mm Luger was adopted as the official military cartridge by U.S. Armed Forces, along with the Beretta Model 92-F (M-9) 15-shot semi-auto pistol.

General Comments: Although the 9mm Luger delivers good performance for police, military, or sporting use, it was not popular in the United States until fairly recently. The principal reason was that no American-made arms were chambered for it initially. In 1954, Smith & Wesson brought out its Model 39 semi-automatic in this chambering, and Colt chambered its lightweight Commander for the 9mm Luger, in 1951. This plus the influx of military pistols chambered for the 9mm greatly increased both popularity and acceptance in this country. Currently the 9mm Luger is the most widely used cartridge in the United States, though a principal complaint has always been that the 9mm Luger lacks stopping power as a defensive cartridge.

However, the only automatic pistol cartridge with proven stopping power is the .45 Automatic. For hunting use, the 9mm Luger is adequate for most small game, if hollow-point bullets are used. Modern, premium jacketed hollow-point loads can dramatically improve performance. A variety of 9mm loadings are offered by every major U.S. ammunition maker.

The term "stopping power" as referred to in the above text is really nothing more than words used to describe something that gun writers have never been able to quantify like they do with velocity and group size. Since the 1980s, when the 9mm became a very popular cartridge for use by law enforcement officers, those who have conducted research into the ability of a handgun cartridge to actually "stop" a bad guy have learned a great deal. Additionally, modern bullet engineering, combined with the moderately high velocities obtainable with a 9mm Luger, 9mm Luger +P, and 9mm Luger +P+ loads has changed not only the outlook on but the performance of the 9mm Luger. Extensive tests in 10 percent ordnance gelatin have shown that many defensive loads for the 9mm expand to a wider diameter and penetrate as deeply as many .45 Auto loads—and they do this with a higher impact velocity, which translates to more tissue destruction. Anyone armed with a 9mm and good defensive ammo should feel just as safe as if they were carrying a .45 Auto.

9mm Luger (9x19mm Parabellum, 9mm Luger +P) Loading Data and Factory Ballistics

Bullet (grains/type)	Powder	Grains	Velocity	Energy	Source/Comments
100	Unique	5.1	1,150	294	Hornady
115	Herco	6.0	1,200	368	Speer
115	Bullseye	4.8	1,250	399	Speer, Hornady, Sierra
115	231	5.2	1,150	338	Speer, Hornady, Sierra
124/125	Unique	5.5	1,150	364	Speer, Sierra
124/125	700X	4.3	1,150	364	Speer, Sierra
80 TAC-XP JHP	FL	FL	1,560	433	DoubleTap Factory Load
115 FMJ	FL	FL	1,160	345	Factory load
124 JHP	FL	FL	1,300	465	Buffalo Bore Factory Load
124 FMJ	ML	ML	1,299	465	Military load, U.S.
124 FMJ	FL	FL	1,120	345	Factory load
147 JHP	FL	FL	975	310	Factory load

9x21mm

Historical Notes: In many countries, such as Italy, Mexico, and France, it is illegal for private citizens to own semi-automatic pistols in military chamberings, such as 9x19mm Parabellum (9mm Luger). Faced with a strong demand for a powerful, semi-automatic pistol in a non-military chambering, the 9x21mm cartridge was developed, in the mid-1980s. It is a 9x19mm Parabellum case lengthened two millimeters. However, a blunt, truncated-cone bullet seated deeply in the case mouth is used. Overall loaded length is, therefore, the same as the 9mm Luger cartridge. Thus, magazines, breech faces, and feed ramps that are suitable for one cartridge work fine with the other with little or no modification.

General Comments: Ballistically, the 9x21mm offers the same performance as the 9mm Luger, so those barrels and recoil springs can be used. Firearms manufacturers find it easy to transition from 9mm to 9x21 to produce this chambering as needed for specialized markets.

For self-defense, the 9x21mm is fully the ballistic equal of the 9mm Luger. It is suitable for small-game hunting with expanding bullets. For handloading, 9mm Luger data can be used. Despite its similarity, these two cartridges are not interchangeable.

With the Western European Union consolidating firearms laws, the prohibition against private ownership of pistols in military chamberings will be ended. The purpose for which the 9x21mm was developed will no longer exist. Therefore, the 9x21mm will probably become history. Fiocchi recently offered this ammunition.

Bullet (grains/type)	Powder	Grains	Velocity	Energy	Source/Comments
90 JHTP	Blue Dot	10.2	1,482	437	Lyman
124 FMJ	AA No. 7	9.8	1,335	490	Lyman
147 Lead	AA No. 7	8.0	1,089	385	Lyman No. 356637
123 FMJ	FL	FL	1,181	380	Patronen factory load (Hungarian)
124 FMJ	FL	FL	1,110	340	Fiocchi factory load

9mm Steyr

Historical Notes: The standard Austrian military pistol cartridge for the Steyr Model 1912 auto pistol, the case is approximately 23 millimeters long, as compared to the 9mm Luger, which is 19 millimeters. Apparently, the only other countries besides Austria to use this as a military round were Romania and Chile, which adopted both the Steyr pistol and cartridge in 1912. This cartridge is very similar to the 9mm Bergmann-Bayard, and these two are often confused. However, 9mm Steyr ammunition is usually found with a nickel-jacketed bullet. The 9mm Bayard case is slightly longer. Quantities of 9mm Steyr pistols have appeared on the United States surplus military market and, for awhile, ammunition was readily available.

General Comments: The 9mm Steyr is quite similar to the 9mm Bayard. The Astra Model 400 will sometimes handle both, but other pistols will not. The 9mm Steyr is a good field cartridge, similar to the .38 Colt Automatic in performance. Bullet diameter is the same as the 9mm Luger, and one can use Luger bullets for reloading. Any standard load for the 9mm Luger or .38 Automatic will work in the Steyr pistol. Fiocchi of Italy still loads this round.

9mm Steyr Loading Data and Factory Ballistics

Bullet (grains/type)	Powder	Grains	Velocity	Energy	Source/Comments
119 Lead	Unique	6.5	1,200	379	Lyman No. 356402
115 FMJ	FL	FL	1,200	360	Factory load
116 FMJ	ML	ML	1,200	370	Military load

9x23 Winchester

Historical Notes: Winchester introduced this cartridge early in 1996, announcing it at the annual NRA convention. This chambering was designed to meet a specific requirement of the International Practical Shooting Confederation (IPSC) competition, and is not well known outside that discipline.

IPSC competitors have struggled for years to concoct the lowest recoiling load that will qualify for Major Power Factor designation. IPSC Power Factor (PF) is bullet weight in grains, times muzzle velocity in feet per second, divided by 1,000. To qualify as a "Major Cartridge," a load must generate at least 175 PF units. To qualify as a "Minor," it must produce 125 PF units (new rules are now under consideration). Scoring includes a bonus for competitors using a Major power factor cartridge. Owing to magazine capacity and grip size considerations, the 9mm-bore size is highly preferred. Because of the muzzle braking devices used, combining a heavy charge of powder with a light bullet to achieve a given PF results in a load that generates less disruption to the shooter's hold, compared to a heavier bullet loaded at lower velocity but generating the same PF. This allows the shooter to get back on target faster. Therefore, the standard approach has been to load unusually light bullets at unusually high velocities. The trouble is that, for any given PF, the lighter the bullet, the greater the muzzle energy. Since we have found no free lunches in the world of kinetics, it follows that to achieve more muzzle energy, the load must also generate more chamber pressure. Therefore, IPSC loads tend to generate unusually high chamber pressures—many loads commonly used by top competitors have approached the pressure levels of magnum rifle proof loads!

When firing such loads in a conventional pistol, one thing is certain Eventually, something will give. Winchester's solution to this significant problem was to design a new case.

General Comments: While the 9x23 looks like a stretched 9mm Luger, there are significant internal differences. The 9x23 has an unusually thick web section. This prevents the dangerous case wall blowout that can occur with any conventional pistol cartridge when an unusually high-pressure loading is fired in a gun with a feed ramp in the bottom of the chamber that extends further forward than the "solid" portion of the case (the web). The 9x23mm case has sufficient capacity to allow IPSC shooters to achieve Major Power Factor using relatively light bullets and without generating gun-wrecking pressures. Nevertheless, IPSC shooters who insist upon using ever-lighter bullets will eventually run into trouble. Ballistics are quite impressive. Given proper loads, this cartridge would seem to qualify as a serious self-defense number.

9x23mm Winchester Factory Ballistics

Bullet (grains/type)	Powder	Grains	Velocity	Energy	Source/Comments
124	FL	FL	1,450	577	Winchester factory load
124	FL	FL	1,460	585	Winchester factory load

9mm Federal

Historical Notes: The 9mm Federal was developed by Federal Cartridge Co. and first appeared in its 1989 ammunition catalog. It is a rimmed version of the 9mm Luger, intended for use in revolvers. The first handgun specifically chambered for it was the Charter Arms Pit Bull revolver, also introduced in 1989. This was a five-shot double-action revolver with a 2½-inch barrel similar to the older Police Bulldog model. The use of any rimless cartridge in double-action revolvers has never been entirely satisfactory, because of extraction difficulties. The 9mm Federal was designed to eliminate this problem in the same way that the .45 Auto Rim removed the need for the half-moon clips in .45 Automatic revolvers. However, the 9mm Federal lacks the very thick rim characteristic of the .45 Auto Rim. Shortly after this round's introduction, Charter Arms went out of business, though that company has since been resurrected. No other manufacturer chambered this cartridge.

General Comments: Initial loading of the 9mm Federal was a 115-grain jacketed hollow-point bullet at 1280 fps muzzle velocity from a four-inch test barrel. Ballistically, this equals or exceeds most +P .38 Special loads and is pushing close to .357 Magnum performance. The principal advantage of the 9mm Federal was the short case length, which would allow shortening the length of the cylinder and frame of revolvers designed for it, thus reducing weight and bulk. However, no gun manufacturer ever did this; Charter Arms merely chambered it in a .38 Special-sized cylinder. As a self-defense or field cartridge, this would be equal to the 9mm Luger.

Unfortunately, the 9mm Federal will chamber in most .38 S&W revolvers. Firing such a combination, particularly in the old top-break type, would almost certainly result in destruction of the revolver and injury or death to the shooter and bystanders. Also, some lots or makes of .38 S&W ammunition will fit the 9mm Federal chamber, but it might not be safe to fire these in 9mm Federal guns, because of the grossly oversize bullet. Last, but not least, 9mm Luger cartridges will chamber and fire in 9mm Federal revolvers, but this can create extraction and other mechanical problems. In all cases, stick to the ammunition for which the gun is chambered. Reloading data for the 9mm Luger can be used as a guide in working up reloads. In 1992, Federal ceased manufacture of this exceedingly ill-conceived cartridge.

9mm Federal Loading Data and Factory Ballistics

Bullet (grains/type)	Powder	Grains	Velocity	Energy	Source/Comments
115	HS 6	7.7	1,270	410	NA
115 JHP	FL	FL	1,280	420	Factory load

.380 Automatic Colt Pistol (9mm Kurz/9x17mm/.380 ACP)

Historical Notes: This cartridge was designed by John Browning and introduced in Europe by FN of Belgium in 1912, as the 9mm Browning Short. It had previously been added to the Colt Pocket Automatic line, in 1908. Several governments have adopted it as the official military pistol cartridge. These include Czechoslovakia, Italy, and Sweden. It is also much used by European police. Colt, High Standard, Remington, and Savage have made pistols in this chambering, in the United States. In Europe, Browning, Beretta, Bayard, CZ, Frommer, Astra, Star, Llama, Walther and others made or make .380 Automatic-chambered pistols. This cartridge is also called 9x17mm.

General Comments: This is another cartridge that has been very popular, because of the light, handy pistols that are chambered for it. The .380 Auto has more stopping power and is a far better cartridge for almost any purpose than the .32 Auto. It is about the minimum pistol cartridge considered adequate for police or military use. For self-defense, it is not as powerful as the 9mm Luger, .38 Auto, and a few others, but this is offset, to a certain extent, by the reduced size and weight of the arms it is used in. For hunting or field use, it will do a good job on rabbits, birds, or other small game. It offers high velocity, which is an advantage for field use. With cast or swaged half-jacketed bullets of hunting type, it will do a good job on small game, but not many shooters want to bother handloading it.

Shortly after the 2008 presidential election, there was a renewed nationwide interest in super-compact concealed carry handguns. All of a sudden, .380 Autos became the most popular handguns of all time. Sales sky-rocketed for itty-bitty pistols like the Ruger LCP, and it was almost impossible to find .380 Auto ammunition on retailers' shelves. The renewed interest in this cartridge has driven ammo manufacturers to engineer some very effective .380 ammunition for defensive handguns. Those from Buffalo Bore, DoubleTap, and Winchester are perfect examples and take the .380 Auto into .38 Special performance range. The Buffalo Bore load is indeed a +P load, but it should be noted that +P .380 Auto ammunition is not recognized by SAAMI and should only be fired in handguns designed for it or in those specified to be safe for its use by the ammunition manufacturer.

.380 Automatic Colt Pistol (9mm Kurz/9x17mm/.380 ACP) Loading Data and Factory Ballistics

Bullet (grains/type)	Powder	Grains	Velocity	Energy	Source/Comments
90 JHP	Bullseye	3.0	900	162	Sierra, Hornady, Speer
95 FMJ	Bullseye	3.2	900	171	Speer, Sierra
95 FMJ	Unique	3.7	900	171	Speer, Sierra
80 Barnes TAC-XP	FL		1,050	196	DoubleTap Factory Load
85 JHP	FL		1,000	189	Factory load
88 JHP	FL		990	191	Factory load
90 JHP +P	FL		1,200	288	Buffalo Bore Factory Load
90 JHP	FL		1,000	200	Factory load
95 FMJ	FL		955	192	Factory load
95 Bonded PDX1	FL		1,000	211	Winchester Factory Load
100 Hard Cast Lead FN	FL		1,150	294	Buffalo Bore Factory Load

.38 Dardick Tround

Historical Notes: The tround was a triangular-shaped cartridge used in inventor David Dardick's Model 1100 and 1500 open-chamber revolvers. The Model 1500 had interchangeable barrels in .38 Dardick, .30 Dardick, and .22

Dardick, and a carbine adaptor kit was available. The Dardick was a magazine-fed double-action revolver. The August 1957 issue of *Mechanix Illustrated* said, "The revolutionary new Dardick open chamber revolver is as versatile as a six-armed monkey." And about as useful. Dardick's patent No. 2,847,784, issued in August 1958, is for a "pre-stressed open chamber gun with rotatable cylinder."

General Comments: Patent No. 2,865,126, issued in late 1958, covered Dardick's design of the tround. Named for its convex triangular shape, the tround allowed the firearm's chamber to be open on one side. That supposedly made it able to eject and load faster than with a standard cartridge. One of the downfalls of the Dardick was the magazine was not detachable and needed stripper clips to be loaded rapidly. There were several versions. The Dardick 1100 had a 10-tround magazine that fired .38 Dardick. A simple adapter allowed the user to shoot with any standard ammunition.—*W.T.W.*

.38 AMU
(.38 Army Marksmanship Unit)

Historical Notes: The .38 AMU is a specially headstamped round developed in the early 1960s for the Army Marksmanship Unit. It was designed to feed in specially chambered 1911s and a few S&W Model 52s that were also chambered for it. Herman Gano, an AMU gunsmith, is attributed as the round's creator.

The .38 AMU fired a flush-seated, hollow-base wadcutter much like a standard .38 Special HBWC target load. On the Winchester load, "SR" in its headstamp stands for "semi-rimmed." The rim was modified to solve feeding problems the rimmed .38 Special caused in a box magazine. A Colt .38 AMU conversion kit consisted of a slide with a breechface and extractor designed for the .38 AMU, and, of course, a barrel chambered for the cartridge. The barrel had only one forward locking lug, so the gun wouldn't lock up too tightly and hinder proper cycling with midrange ammo. The Army contracted Federal, Winchester-Western, and Remington to produce the .38 AMU cartridge, but once military teams started using .45s in centerfire matches, the .38 AMU project passed into history.

General Comments: The .38 AMU is basically a .38 Special with a semi-rimmed head, like the .38 Super. It's made by cutting the rim to .406 and cutting a extractor groove 0.03-inch deep with a 67-degree back chamfer. The rest of the cartridge remains the same as the .38 Special; load data for the .38 AMU can be derived from .38 Special wadcutter numbers.—*W.T.W.*

.38 AMU Factory Ballistics

Bullet (grains/type)	Powder	Grains	Velocity	Energy	Source/Comments
148 Speer HBWC	Bullseye	3.1	799	210	Speer #13 Manual

.38 Short & Long Colt

Historical Notes: The .38 Long Colt was once the official United States Army revolver cartridge (1892 to 1911). The short version was used mainly in the Colt Army & Navy Model revolver with swing-out cylinder, developed in 1887. The .38 Long Colt was introduced in 1875 as one of several chamberings for Colt New Line, New Police and New House revolvers.

General Comments: Since this was once a military cartridge, a number of Colt and S&W revolvers in this chambering are still around. The .38 Long Colt cartridge can be fired in a .38 Special revolver, but not vice versa. During the Spanish-American War and the Philippine insurrection, the Army found that the .38 Long Colt had insufficient stopping power for combat use. The cartridge was therefore dropped in 1911, in favor of the .45 Automatic. This was the experience that made the U.S. Army reluctant to adopt the 9mm Luger. It was forced to do so, in 1985, largely as a NATO-inspired political decision. Advocates of a smaller caliber admit the superior stopping power of the .45, but point out that extra weight and reduced magazine capacity are detrimental factors that should also be considered. The .38 Long Colt is in about the same class as the standard .38 Special loading, but it is not nearly as accurate or as versatile. Some of the old .38 Long Colt revolvers will accept .38 Special or .357 Magnum ammunition, but never fire these in the old .38s. Firing the .357 Magnum would be particularly dangerous, probably wrecking the gun and possibly injuring the shooter or bystanders. Remington has recently manufactured .38 Short Colt ammunition. Black Hills Ammunition has recently reintroduced .38 Long Colt ammunition in response to demands from the cowboy action shooting fraternity.

.38 Short & Long Colt Factory Ballistics

Bullet (grains/type)	Powder	Grains	Velocity	Energy	Source/Comments
150 Lead	FL	FL	770	195	Factory load

.357 Remington Maximum

Historical Notes: The .357 Maximum was announced as a joint venture between Remington Arms Co. and Sturm, Ruger and Co. This cartridge is a .310-inch elongation of the .357 Magnum case. The first handgun to chamber the round was the Ruger Blackhawk .357 Maximum single-action revolver, introduced in 1983. This was followed, in 1984, by the Dan Wesson double-action, stainless-steel revolver, the Seville single-action stainless-steel revolver, and the Thompson/Center Contender single-shot pistol. During the same year, Harrington & Richardson chambered its Model 258 single-shot rifle for the round, as did Savage in its Model 24V and Model 24VS Camper over/under rifle shotgun combination guns. Although Remington developed the commercial .357 Maximum, a similar wildcat cartridge was actually developed by Elgin Gates at an earlier time.

Unfortunately, the .357 Maximum revolvers all developed excessive gas-cutting on the top strap, just forward of the cylinder, within 1,000 rounds or so, when fired with full factory loads. Ruger withdrew its Blackhawk .357 Maximum revolver from production, pending additional research and possible engineering changes. Dan Wesson, when its revolvers were still in production, prior to that company's purchase by CZ, eliminated the problem by establishing a .002-inch barrel/cylinder gap for its .357 Maximum revolvers. (The Dan Wesson revolvers have interchangeable barrels that are easily replaced and fine-tuned by the customer, using a furnished gap tool.) Top strap erosion, of course, is not a problem with the single-shot Thompson/Center Contender or the rifles chambering the .357 Maximum.

General Comments: Efforts to develop ultra high-velocity revolvers have not been crowned with unbridled success. The .22 Remington Jet in the Model 53 Smith & Wesson revolver is another example of a combination that was discontinued because of mechanical troubles. In the case of the .357 Maximum, the cartridge differs from the standard .357 Magnum only in case length, so one can drop back to shooting the .357 Magnum in any Maximum revolver, or simply handload to lower velocity levels using the Maximum case. Factory ballistics were taken in a 10½-inch vented test barrel, and actual muzzle velocity from a revolver with the same-length barrel is about 200 fps lower than the advertised figure.

The .357 Maximum was conceived primarily as an ultra-velocity, flat-trajectory silhouette cartridge. That it would also make a good field cartridge for hunting small and medium game is obvious. Many would consider it a good deer cartridge, but, when used in a handgun, it would be rather marginal for that purpose. Of course, a good deal depends on the skill of the person using it and, as noted elsewhere, the older, less powerful .357 Magnum has killed its share of big game. Certainly, the .357 Maximum has been used as a big-game handgun cartridge, but the measure of success has reflected more upon the person behind the gun than the cartridge.

.357 Remington Maximum Loading Data and Factory Ballistics

Bullet (grains/type)	Powder	Grains	Velocity	Energy	Source/Comments
125 JHP	W296	25.0	1,800	900	Hornady, Speer
140 JHP	W296	23.5	1,700	899	Hornady, Speer
158 JHP	W296	21.0	1,550	843	Hornady, Speer
180 FMJ	H4227	18.4	1,300	676	Sierra, Nosler, Speer, Hornady
158 JHP	FL	FL	1,825	1,168	Factory load
180 JHP	FL	FL	1,550	960	Factory load

.38 Special (.38 Special +P/.38-44 High Velocity/.38 Smith & Wesson Special)

Historical Notes: Also known as the .38 Colt Special and, more generally, as simply the .38 Special, this cartridge was developed by S&W and introduced with its Military & Police Model revolver, in 1902. This was originally a military cartridge meant to replace the unsatisfactory .38 Long Colt then in use by the Army. Colt brought out its version in 1909, which differs from the original only in bullet shape, the Colt being a flat-point style. Colt, Smith & Wesson, and others make revolvers specifically for this cartridge. Several Belgian, Brazilian, German, and Spanish firms also make .38 Special revolvers. The S&W 52 Target Auto, available until 1993, was made for the mid-range wadcutter load. A number of good quality, lever-action Winchester clones (1866, 1873, 1892) are chambered for the .38 Special.

General Comments: The .38 Special is considered one of the best-balanced, all-round handgun cartridges ever designed. It is also one of the most accurate and is very widely used for match shooting. Any .357 Magnum revolver will also shoot the .38 Special. At one time, it was the standard police cartridge here and largely in Mexico and Canada. It is also usable in lightweight pocket revolvers. Several companies make over/under, two-shot, derringer-type pistols in this chambering that are compact and relatively powerful for close-in self-defense. The .38 Special is also a very popular sporting cartridge for hunting small to medium game and varmint-type animals. With modern hunting bullets, it is effective for this purpose. Because of its moderate recoil, the average person can learn to shoot well with it in a short time, something not true of the .357 or .44 Magnums. The .38 Special is loaded by all major commercial ammunition manufacturers. Bullet weights from 95 to 200 grains have been available.

Note: Previous editions of this book incorrectly listed the .38-44 Target as being interchangeable with the .38 Special. Not so. The .38-44 was a chambering for the top-break S&W No. 3 Target revolver and is not to be confused with the later .38-44 High Velocity chambered in the N-frame Hand Ejector Outdoorsman. (In both cases, the .38-44 designation translates as "a .38 on a .44 frame.") The .38-44 for the No. 3 revolver featured a bullet loaded flush with the case mouth, which will not chamber in revolvers intended for the .38 Special.

.38 Smith & Wesson Special Loading Data and Factory Ballistics

Bullet (grains/type)	Powder	Grains	Velocity	Energy	Source/Comments
110 JHP	Bullseye	4.7	1,000	244	Hornady, Speer, Sierra
125 JHP	231	5.5	1,000	278	Sierra, Speer, Nosler
140 JHP	2400	10.4	950	281	Speer, Sierra
158 JHP	Herco	5.0	900	284	Speer, Nosler, Sierra
148 WC	Bullseye	3.1	800	210	Speer, Hornady
95 JHP	FL	FL	1,175	291	Factory load
110 JHP	FL	FL	995	242	Factory load
125 JHP	FL	FL	945	248	Factory load
130 FMS	ML	ML	950	260	Military load
148 WC	FL	FL	710	132	Factory load
150 LRN	FL	FL	890	270	Factory load
158 Hard Core Cast +P	FL	FL	1,250	548	Buffalo Bore Factory Load
200 LRN	FL	FL	730	236	Factory load

.357 Atomic — *NEW*

Historical Notes: The .357 Atomic, in essence, was a trade-named cartridge that was a .357 Mag. +P. For a brief time in 1954 to 1955, Great Western Arms Co. offered this load for a specialized series of Frontier revolvers with heat-treated cylinders. It was claimed to be the most powerful handgun in the world for pushing a 158-grain .357 slug at 1,600 fps and better. There doesn't seem to be any case differences between it and regular .357 Mag. ammo.

General Comments: When Smith & Wesson introduced the .44 Mag. in the mid-1950s, the .357 Atomic was no longer the world's most powerful handgun cartridge. Great Western went to a conventional .357 Mag. rollmark in 1958. Herters and Hawes reportedly chambered some SAA clones in .357 Atomic.

.357 Atomic Loading Data

Bullet (grains/type)	Powder	Grains	Velocity	Energy	Source/Comments
158 LSWC	Alliant 2400	16	1,600	898	Great Western Arms Co. Collectors

.357 Magnum (.357 S&W Magnum)

Historical Notes: This chambering was introduced in 1935 by Smith & Wesson for its heavy-frame revolver. Ammunition was developed by Winchester, in cooperation with Smith & Wesson. Major Douglas B. Wesson (of S&W) and Philip B. Sharpe are credited with much of the final development work. The .357 Magnum is based on the .38 Special case lengthened about 1/10-inch, so it will not chamber in standard .38 Special revolvers. This was the most powerful handgun cartridge in the world, until the .44 Magnum was introduced, in 1955. Colt, Ruger, Smith & Wesson, and many others manufacture revolvers for this cartridge. There has also been a proliferation of imported single- and double-action revolvers, and several single-shot pistols chamber it. There is even a semi-auto pistol in this chambering. American .357 Magnum revolvers have been used in Canada, Mexico, and other countries.

General Comments: This is probably the most popular high-velocity handgun cartridge in the United States for police, hunting, and target work. The .357 Magnum provides nearly double the velocity and more than three times the energy of standard .38 Special loads. It is noted for its flat trajectory, deep penetration, and great knockdown power. It has been used successfully on deer, black bear, elk, and even grizzly bear. However, it is not fully adequate for these larger animals, unless used by an excellent marksman. It is also used in repeating and single-shot rifles as matched arms to go along with a revolver. In a 20- to 24-inch rifle barrel, standard factory 158-grain loads develop about 1650 fps muzzle velocity, and special (rifle only) handloads will develop over 2000 fps. It is considered the best all-round handgun-hunting cartridge for small and medium game and, under proper conditions, for deer at short range. During the Korean conflict, it was very effective against the body armor used by the Communist forces. Nearly every major commercial ammunition manufacturer offers .357 Magnum ammunition.

.357 Magnum Loading Data and Factory Ballistics

Bullet (grains/type)	Powder	Grains	Velocity	Energy	Source/Comments
110 JHP	2400	19.0	1,500	550	Sierra, Speer
125 JHP	2400	16.0	1,200	400	Nosler, Speer, Hornady
140 JHP	W296	16.0	1,200	448	Speer, Hornady, Sierra
158 JHP	2400	13.5	1,200	505	Hornady, Speer, Sierra, Nosler
110 JHP	FL	FL	1,295	410	Factory load
125 JHP	FL	FL	1,450	583	Factory load
140 JHP	FL	FL	1,360	575	Factory load
158 JHP, Lead	FL	FL	1,235	535	Factory load
180 JHP	FL	FL	1,090	475	Factory load
140 FTX	FL	FL	1,440	644	Hornady Factory Load

.357 SIG

Historical Notes: This cartridge is based upon the .40 S&W case, simply necked down with a short neck and a sharp shoulder. The design purpose was to achieve .357 Magnum revolver ballistics from typical semi-automatic pistols. This cartridge design offers several potential advantages. First, its compact nature allows use of a smaller (shorter) grip frame in pistols so chambered. For shooters with smaller hands, this is significant; many find guns chambered for the .45 Automatic and 10mm cartridges entirely too big for proper handling and accurate shooting. Second, compared to the parent cartridge, the .357 SIG can effectively launch lighter bullets at greater velocity to achieve similar muzzle energy with less recoil. All of these considerations figured in the development of this cartridge.

General Comments: The .357 SIG is loaded to a comparatively high pressure level—the same as top factory .357 Magnum loads and 14 percent higher than the .40 S&W or the 9mm Luger. The combination of high pressure, reasonable case capacity, and no barrel venting (as seen in .357 Magnum revolvers) allows this petite cartridge to generate significant ballistics—fully the equal of the .40 S&W in terms of muzzle energy. However, in the typical short pistol barrels used, there is a price to pay for this level of performance— muzzle blast is significant. Compared to the .40 S&W, the .357 SIG has only one advantage, that being a slight reduction in recoil. Time will tell if that will prove sufficient cause to popularize this cartridge.

.357 SIG Loading Data and Factory Ballistics

Bullet (grains/type)	Powder	Grains	Velocity	Energy	Source/Comments
88 JHP	AA No. 5	11.1	1,616	510	Accurate/1.13" OAL
95 FMJ	AA No. 5	11.0	1,572	520	Accurate/1.135" OAL
115 XTP	AA No. 9	13.5	1,434	525	Accurate/1.14" OAL
124 XTP	AA No. 9	13.0	1,387	530	Accurate/1.14" OAL
147 XTP	Vit N350	6.9	1,170	445	VihtaVuori/1.135" OAL
95 FMJ	AA No. 5	11.0	1,572	520	Accurate/1.135" OAL
125 JHP	FL	FL	1,350	505	Speer & Federal factory load

.38 Automatic (.38 ACP)

Historical Notes: This is another cartridge designed by John Browning and introduced by Colt in 1900 for its .38 Automatic. In its original form, this pistol was designed as a military gun. From this evolved the seven-shot sporting and eight-shot military models of 1902. This cartridge was stepped up in power in 1929 and the improved round called the .38 Super Auto. In the United States, only Colt chambered it. In England, Webley & Scott chambered it in one version of its military automatic. In Spain, a number of automatics have been made for the .38 ACP.

General Comments: Although developed for military and self-defense uses, the .38 Colt Auto achieved a degree of popularity for sporting use through its relatively high velocity. The military turned it down, because of previous poor results with the .38 Long Colt. No guns designed for this cartridge have been made since 1928, but plenty of the older model Colt pistols are still used. In power, it is about the same as the 9mm Luger, but it has a longer semi-rimmed case. This cartridge is now obsolete and is no longer loaded by any major ammunition maker.

.38 Automatic/.38 Automatic Colt Pistol (ACP) Loading Data and Factory Ballistics

Bullet (grains/type)	Powder	Grains	Velocity	Energy	Source/Comments
115 FMJ	Bullseye	5.0	1,150	338	Hornady
125 JHP	Bullseye	4.7	1,100	336	Hornady

Bullet (grains/type)	Powder	Grains	Velocity	Energy	Source/Comments
130 FMJ	FL	FL	1,040	312	Factory load

.38 Super Automatic
.38 Super Automatic +P

Historical Notes: Introduced by Colt in 1929 as an improved version of the older .38 Auto, the Super Auto is identical to the original cartridge, except that it uses a more powerful loading. This is a fine high-speed sporting cartridge for the improved Government Model automatic pistol, but it should not be used in the older Colt pocket models. The Thompson submachine gun was once available in a .38 Super chambering. In Spain, Llama has made pistols for it. It is not popular in Europe, but is very popular in Canada, Mexico, and South America, where pistols in military chamberings have been prohibited.

General Comments: This was, for many years, the most powerful automatic pistol cartridge made in the United States, from the standpoint of both velocity and energy. It makes a good sporting cartridge for hunting small to medium game, because the flat trajectory permits accurate long-range shots. However, the original metal-cased bullet did not bring out the full potential. With good expanding-type bullets, it is one of our better hunting cartridges for a pistol. It is more powerful than the 9mm Luger, but both are adequate for about the same range of game. It can give greater penetration than the .45 Automatic, but is inferior in stopping power for defensive use. For handloading, any 9mm bullet can be used. However, unless proper round-nosed or conical shapes are used, it will be necessary to single load most rounds. This chambering has been extremely popular among IPSC competitors. Both Remington and Winchester offer this cartridge.

.38 Super Automatic +P Loading Data and Factory Ballistics

Bullet (grains/type)	Powder	Grains	Velocity	Energy	Source/Comments
115 FMJ	Bullseye	5.0	1,200	368	Hornady, Sierra, Speer
125 JHP	231	5.4	1,150	500	Sierra, Hornady, Speer
115 JHP	FL	FL	1,300	431	Factory load
125 JHP	FL	FL	1,240	427	Factory load
130 FMJ	FL	FL	1,215	426	Factory load

.360 Mars

Historical Notes: The Mars Automatic Pistol was a semi-automatic pistol developed in 1900 and chambered in this loading, as well as the 8.5mm Mars, and the .45 Mars Short and Long. The handgun was manufactured by Webley & Scott and other gun makers in Birmingham and London, until 1907. The Gabbet-Fairfax "Mars" Self-Loading Pistol measured about 11¼ inches overall and had a blued barrel with raised sighting rib. It had a round rotating bolt with twin cocking lugs, a blued frame with two long cylinders housing the recoil springs extending under the barrel, bright hammer, grooved trigger, a magazine with lanyard-ring, smooth walnut grips, and some original blued finish.

The handgun had a complex and long recoil mechanism, which made it expensive to produce. Also, apparently, fired cases were ejected directly into the shooter's face. Gabbet-Fairfax declared bankruptcy in 1903 and production was resumed by the Mars Pistol Syndicate, which in turn went bankrupt in 1907.

General Comments: The .360 Mars was made by necking down the .45 Mars Long case. In comparison to other rimless pistol cartridges, the case had a thin rim and deep extractor groove. To withstand the pistol's vigorous feeding action, the chamfered case mouth fits flush into the forward cannelure. The cartridge headspaces on the shoulder adjacent to the neck.—*W.T.W.*

Bullet (grains/type)	Powder	Grains	Velocity	Energy	Source/Comments
156 LRN	FL	FL	1,400	679	Kynoch

.38 Smith & Wesson/.38 Colt New Police/ .38 Super Police/.380/200 (British)

Historical Notes: Designed by Smith & Wesson for its hinged-frame revolvers introduced about 1877, the .38 S&W is one of the more widely adopted American revolver cartridges; it has been used all over the world. England began using it as an official service cartridge prior to World War II, and it is well-distributed through the British Commonwealth. Large numbers of Spanish-made revolvers in this chambering are used in Mexico and South America, but it has never been very popular in Europe outside the UK. It is also known as the .38 Colt New Police and, with a 200-grain bullet, as the .38 Super Police. Colt, H&R, Hopkins & Allen, Iver Johnson, Ruger, and S&W have made revolvers in this chambering, in the United States. Webley & Scott made many of the British service arms. The British service load is called the .380/200.

General Comments: The .38 S&W is another cartridge that owes most of its popularity to the fact that it is well-suited to lightweight pocket guns. It is also a good short-range cartridge for defense use and has better stopping power than any of the .32s and even some of the larger automatic pistol cartridges. The British military figured out that the shocking power of this cartridge with a 200-grain bullet was about the same as its older .455 military cartridge. In actual combat, this proved correct, thus permitting the use of lighter guns. The .38 S&W is not a particularly satisfactory hunting cartridge, because the curved trajectory limits its use to short ranges. However, it can be improved for hunting through judicious handloading. Remington still offers .38 S&W ammunition.

.38 Smith & Wesson Loading Data and Factory Ballistics

Bullet (grains/type)	Powder	Grains	Velocity	Energy	Source/Comments
148 Lead	Bullseye	2.5	700	161	Speer
158 Lead	Unique	3.0	700	172	Speer
145 Lead	FL	FL	685	150	Factory load
200 Lead	ML	ML	630	176	Military load, British

9mm Russian Makarov

Historical Notes: This is the current Russian military cartridge used in the Makarov and Stechkin auto-pistols. It was adopted shortly after the end of World War II, and its design may have been inspired by an experimental German cartridge called the 9mm Ultra. Other countries from the former Warsaw Pact also use the round. Chinese-made Makarov pistols have recently appeared on surplus shelves, along with 9mm Makarov ammunition.

General Comments: The Soviet 9mm pistol cartridge is intermediate in size and power between the .380 Automatic and the 9mm Luger. Technically, it can be described as a 9x18mm, although it differs dimensionally from the 9x18 Ultra and is not interchangeable with that cartridge. It is a well-designed cartridge for its purpose, although a little underpowered by Western standards. It is satisfactory for small game, when loaded with hunting-type bullets, which are now available. Loading data and components are available from various manufacturers. The Makarov pistol is of medium size and is similar to the German Walther. The Stechkin is a selective-fire type that can be used with the holster stock as a submachine gun. Both pistols are well made. Cases are easily formed by passing 9mm Luger cases over an expander ball and then trimming to length.

9mm Russian Makarov Loading Data and Factory Ballistics

Bullet (grains/type)	Powder	Grains	Velocity	Energy	Source/Comments
90 JHP	Unique	4.3	966	185	Lyman
95 FMJ	AA No. 5	5.0	909	173	Lyman
95 Lead	Unique	4.0	1,016	215	Lyman No. 364653
100 JHP	Unique	4.1	887	173	Lyman
95 FMJ	ML	ML	1,060	237	Military load

.380 Short & Long Revolver

Historical Notes: The .380 Revolver cartridge is a British innovation for the Webley revolver and originated somewhere between 1868 and '70. It was loaded in the United States until shortly after World War I. The .38 Short Colt was copied from it, and most .380 revolvers will accept the Colt version. It has been largely replaced by the inside-lubricated .38 S&W.

General Comments: The .380 is in the same class as the .38 Short Colt or .38 S&W. Use the same loading data. This ammunition recently has been available from Fiocchi.

.380 Revolver Factory Ballistics

Bullet (grains/type)	Powder	Grains	Velocity	Energy	Source/Comments
124 Lead	FL	FL	625	110	Factory load

9.4mm Dutch — *NEW*

Historical Notes: Innumerable obsolete cartridges have great stories, but few are as long-lived as the 9.4x21mm Dutch, which was initially chambered in Dutch Model 1873 New Model revolvers as a black-powder round and then converted to modern powders in later versions of the handgun. In the Dutch Model 91 double-action revolver, it entered service in 1895 and stayed in military and law-enforcement use into World War II, particularly for the KNIL (Koninklijk Nederlandsch-Indisch Leger, also known as the Royal Dutch East Indies Army). As a result, this cartridge became synonymous with the Netherlands, thus its nickname.

General Comments: The 9.4mm round was altered many times to increase power, and the final case took up almost the full length of the M91 cylinder and used a flat-nosed bullet. Handloaders can fashion suitable brass most easily by cutting down and resizing .41 Rem. Mag. cases. No commercial bullets are available, so swaging bullets is required as well, so be sure to slug the barrel to ensure you have the right bullet diameter before attempting loads. CH Tool & Die of Mt. Vernon, Ohio, has a full set of dies for the round.

Pistol photo courtesy of Bob Adams.

9.4mm Dutch Loading Data

Bullet (grains/type)	Powder	Grains	Velocity	Energy	Source/Comments
135 Copper-Plated Flatnose	Unique	4.5	720	155	Collector's Forum

.375 SuperMag — *NEW*

Historical Notes: The SuperMag family of handgun cartridges was produced by Elgin Gates, a founder of the International Handgun Metallic Silhouette Association, in the 1970s. The siblings were the .375 SuperMag, along with .357-, .44-, .45-, .50-, and .60-caliber SuperMag iterations. All were 1.610 inches long, or about 0.3 inch longer than standard magnums such as the .357 Mag., .41 Mag. and .44 Mag. All of Gates' Super Mags required special long-frame, long-cylinder revolvers. Dan Wesson chambered several models for these specialty cartridges.

General Comments: The SuperMags used the same bullets as the original magnum cartridges on top of extra powder capacity that gained 30 percent more muzzle velocity over the original magnum rounds. The .375 SuperMag was based on the .375 Win. rifle cartridge. It could also be made from .30-30 Win. brass, cut to length and filed in a trim die. SuperMag .375 brass can be made from .375 Win. brass using a trim die.

Quality Cartridge (qual-cart.com) offers properly headstamped brass for $35/20. To ensure a round case mouth, cases must be sized, or have the expander ball of the sizing die run through case neck and deburred or chamfered before loading. Also, the handloader might see a light staining on the case neck of new brass because of annealing. Annealing makes cases the proper hardness to hold a bullet securely, and it imparts flexibility so the case can expand and contract upon firing and repeated forming. This stain can be removed by tumbling before loading.

Reed's Ammunition & Research of Oklahoma City (ReedsAmmo.com) offers production loads for this round.

.375 SuperMag Loading Data

Bullet (grains/type)	Powder	Grains	Velocity	Energy	Source/Comments
220 Hornady	H110	22.9			Hornady Manual
220 Hornady	H110	26.5			Elgin Gates
200 Speer FP Power Jacket			1,390	858	Reed's Ammunition 375SM200PJ
220 Hornady SP			1,340	877	Reed's Ammunition 375SM220HDY

.375 Atomic — *NEW*

Historical Notes: Lee Martin is credited with developing the round in 1997. .375 Atomics are .375 Win. rifle cases cut to 1.40 inches in length and used in custom Ruger Blackhawks. But .375 Win. brass isn't always available and costs more, so .30-30 Winchester brass can also be the parent case. Brass prep involves cutting a .30-30 slightly oversized, and then expanding the necks and full-length sizing them. Fire-forming thereafter is minimal.

General Comments: Velocities with the .375 Atomic resemble the .375 Supermag. For more, visit www.singleactions.com.

.375 Atomic Loading Data

Bullet (grains/type)	Powder	Grains	Velocity	Energy	Source/Comments
200 Sierra Pro Hunter FN	H110	21.0	1,555	1,073	Lee Martin
220 Hornady Flat Point	H110	20.0	1,505	1,106	Lee Martin

9.8mm Automatic Colt
(9.65 Browning Automatic Colt)

Historical Notes: This cartridge is also known as the 9.8 Colt Auto Pistol and was developed by Colt about 1912, probably for the Model 1911 pistol. Its development was said to be part of an effort to secure a contract with the Romanian government, whose military didn't like the .45 Automatic. In any event, the Romanians opted for the 9mm Steyr Model 1912 automatic pistol produced in Austria. Only a very few Colt pistols chambered in 9.8mm were ever made, and the cartridge was not introduced in this country. However, an identical cartridge appears to have been produced in Belgium, listed as the 9.65mm Browning Automatic Pistol. American cartridges are headstamped "WRA" and were manufactured by Winchester, while the Belgian cases are marked "FN."

General Comments: The 9.8mm Colt is a true .38-caliber, with a bullet diameter that varies from .378- to .381-inch and weighs 130 grains. Actual ballistics are not available, but the muzzle velocity must have been in excess of 1000 fps, which would put it into the same class as the .38 Automatic. It would have made a good military or self-defense cartridge. With all the new handgun cartridges that have appeared in the last few years, it's a wonder that someone hasn't latched onto this basic design. Increase the bullet weight to 140 grains and start it out at 1250 fps, and you would have a great self-defense and field cartridge. This chambering is long obsolete, and 9.8mm cartridges are collector's items.

9.8mm Automatic Colt (9.65 Browning Automatic Colt) Factory Ballistics (Note: *Estimated ballistics)

Bullet (grains/type)	Powder	Grains	Velocity	Energy	Source/Comments
130 FMJ	FL		1,000	289	Factory load *

.41 Long Colt

Historical Notes: Introduced by Colt, with its double-action or Lightning Model revolver in 1877, it was later used in the New Army, New Navy, Army Special, Single Action Army, and the Bisley. No revolvers have chambered this cartridge since about the early 1930s. The .41 Short Colt is identical to this cartridge, except for case length (.65-inch) and the 160-grain bullet used. Both rounds were originally black-powder cartridges using outside-lubricated bullets with a diameter of .401-inch. Smokeless powder, inside-lubricated cartridges have hollow-base bullets of .387-inch diameter intended to expand into the bore upon exiting the case.

General Comments: Although obsolete for a long time, the .41 Long Colt was, for some years, quite popular. It is largely a short-range number, with its slow, heavy bullet, but it has good stopping power. Its performance can be duplicated by using the 200-grain bullet in the .38 Special. It actually is no more powerful than the .38 Special and, in addition, is neither as accurate nor as versatile. It was never popular for hunting, although it would certainly be adequate for small to medium game. These cartridges are now collector's items, as there has been no commercial manufacture for many years until recently; Midway USA (www.midwayusa.com) is currently carrying the round, manufactured by Ultramax, intended for cowboy action shooters. Brass is available from Starline (www.starlinebrass.com).

.41 Long Colt Loading Data and Factory Ballistics

Bullet (grains/type)	Powder	Grains	Velocity	Energy	Source/Comments
200 Lead	Bullseye	3.4	730	235	Duplicate factory load
200 Lead	FL	FL	730	235	Factory load

.40 Smith & Wesson

Historical Notes: This cartridge was developed as an in-house joint venture between Winchester and Smith & Wesson within six months from the time it was first discussed in June 1989. Mr. Bersett at Winchester, and Mr. Melvin at S&W, were primarily responsible for this cartridge's development and standardization.

At that time, the FBI had been working with the 10mm Automatic, developing a load that met its criteria for bullet diameter, weight, and velocity. The folks at Winchester and Smith & Wesson realized that the power level the FBI had settled on could easily be achieved using a much shorter cartridge. This would facilitate accuracy and allow use of a smaller, more comfortable grip frame.

General Comments: Until quite recently, none of the factory loads available actually took full advantage of this cartridge's potential. Several now offered actually generate about 500 ft-lbs of energy in typical guns. This is serious power for such a small package and rivals the best the .45 Automatic can offer. However, such a powerful and compact package requires comparatively high pressures. High peak pressure and a short barrel equate to high noise and muzzle blast. Nevertheless, for its purpose, this has to be considered a superior cartridge design. It has already completely eclipsed the similar .41 Action Express.

.40 S&W Auto Loading Data and Factory Ballistics

Bullet (grains/type)	Powder	Grains	Velocity	Energy	Source/Comments
135 JHP	Universal	7.5	1,324	524	Hodgdon
155 JHP	Universal	6.6	1,186	482	Hodgdon
180 JHP	Universal	5.8	1,046	435	Hodgdon
200 JHP	HS 7	7.4	907	363	Hodgdon
155 JHP	FL	FL	1,140	447	Factory load
155 JHP	FL	FL	1,205	500	Factory load
155 FMJ-SWC	FL	FL	1,125	436	Factory load
180 JHP	FL	FL	990	392	Factory load
180 JHP	FL	FL	1,015	412	Factory load

10mm Automatic

Historical Notes: The 10mm Auto was introduced in 1983 as the cartridge for the Bren Ten semi-auto pistol, made by the now-defunct Dornaus & Dixon Enterprises, Inc., of Huntington Beach, Calif. Ammunition was loaded by Norma, with a 200-grain full-jacketed truncated cone bullet, similar to some 9mm Luger and .45 Automatic loads of some years back. According to data furnished by Norma, the ammunition is loaded to a mean working pressure of 37,000 psi, with a maximum pressure of 44,400 psi. This is getting up in the area of some rifle loads and makes this a rather hot handgun cartridge. Muzzle velocity is listed as 1200 fps, and energy at the muzzle as 635 ft-lbs. This makes this cartridge more powerful than the .357 Magnum or the obsolete lead bullet .41 Magnum police load. Muzzle energy is about double that of the .45 Automatic. Gun and cartridge are the creation of Jeff Cooper and associates, who were trying to develop the ideal combat weapon. Colt and several others have offered the 10mm chambering.

General Comments: The Bren Ten semi-auto pistol was based on a modification of the much-praised Czech CZ-75 pistol design. It had a five-inch barrel, 11-shot magazine, and weighed 39 ounces. It was a full-size combat-type pistol intended primarily for law enforcement/self-defense use, but it had many design problems.

The 10mm cartridge is an ideal combat round with good stopping power, particularly with an expanding-type bullet. However, recoil is quite heavy. It would also be a good field cartridge for small to medium game or larger animals, in the hands of a good shot and skilled hunter. In the late 1980s, the FBI adopted this cartridge in a slightly reduced loading, along with a matching S&W pistol, as standard issue. Problems with the guns delayed general issue. Ammunition was initially quite expensive. This discouraged non-handloaders from doing much shooting with the round. Overall, the Bren Ten pistol and cartridge represent an excellent concept for a combat handgun, and it reflects the extensive background and experience of Cooper.

Hornady, Speer, Sierra, and Nosler offer suitable bullets. The 10mm Auto cartridge has been loaded by Federal, Winchester, Remington, CCI, and other U.S. ammunition manufacturers. Actual ballistics are generally about 100 fps slower than early factory claims, so actual 10mm Automatic factory loads do not significantly exceed .45 Automatic +P ballistics.

10mm Automatic Loading Data and Factory Ballistics

Bullet (grains/type)	Powder	Grains	Velocity	Energy	Source/Comments
155 JHP	BlueDot	12.0	1,250	538	Hornady, Sierra
180 JHP	BlueDot	10.0	1,150	529	Hornady, Sierra
200 FMJ	BlueDot	8.5	1,100	537	Hornady
170 JHP	FL	FL	1,340	680	Norma factory load
180 JHP	FL	FL	1,030	425	Factory load
180 JHP	FL	FL	950	361	FBI factory loading
200 FMC	FL	FL	1,200	635	Factory load

.41 Short Colt

Historical Notes: The .41 (Short) Colt uses a heel-base bullet of about .401-inch maximum diameter. One of an entire line of cartridges designed for application in various revolvers with cylindrical (i.e., non-shouldered) chambers, this was never a very successful cartridge. The chief complaints involved limited case support for the bullet, as well as the problems associated with the necessary external grease grooves, which tended to attract dirt. In fact, it was said that this type of cartridge was among the deadliest on the frontier, not because of its ballistic effect, but because the dirt and grime it carried into even a minor wound was almost certain to lead to a fatal infection.

The historical reason for the invention of heel-based cartridges stemmed from the era of the conversion cap-and-ball revolver. It was a simple matter to bore a hole of cylinder-mouth diameter full-length through the cylinder. The heel-base bulleted cartridge was invented for use in guns so converted. The original loading used a 160-grain lead bullet and 14 grains of black powder.

General Comments: The .41 Short Colt was never a popular chambering and offered limited ballistics. It was also very difficult to handload properly. Lyman once offered moulds that cast hollow-base bullets of inside case diameter. These were easier to load and removed the problem of the external-lube groove but were not sufficiently accurate to engender any following.

.401 Bobcat — NEW

Historical Notes: Designed in April 1994, this is another wildcat devised by Lee Martin of Arlington, Virginia, as a .40-caliber round suited for a revolver that offered better bullet selection than the .41 Rem. Mag. It is based on the .220 Swift case trimmed to a 1.40-inch overall length and inside-case-reamed for heavy 10mm bullets. Because of cylinder-length availability in Ruger Blackhawks, a shorter 1.29-inch-long configuration was also made.

General Comments: Handguns for this round were heavily modified, including having customer cylinders machined for them, as well as custom barrels — in particular, tubes from Pac-Nor (Pac-Nor.com). The longer Bobcat holds about 5 more grains more of H110/W296 than the 1.29-inch-long case. This increase in volume provides a bump of 150 fps to 200 fps for the 1.4-inch-long case. As with most magnum revolver rounds, H110 and W296 seem to be the optimal propellants.

.401 Bobcat Loading Data (1.4-inch case)

Bullet (grains/type)	Powder	Grains	Velocity	Energy	Source/Comments
180 Hornady XTP	H110/W296	27.0	1,730	1,196	Lee Martin
200 Hornady XTP	H110/W296	26.0	1,660	1,123	Lee Martin
265 Cast	H110/W296	20.0	1,410	1,169	Lee Martin

.401 Herter Powermag

Historical Notes:	This is a proprietary cartridge developed by Herter's, Inc., of Waseca, Minnesota, in 1961. Herter's was a mail-order gun, ammunition, and loading supply house that once offered a series of excellent products to the gun trade. The .401 Powermag was chambered in the Herter Powermag single-action revolver. The cartridge is very similar to the .41 Remington Magnum, but the two are *not* interchangeable. The case of the .41 Remington Magnum is .005-inch larger in diameter and .009-inch longer than the .401 Powermag. Since the .401 Powermag preceded the .41 Magnum by three years, it is difficult to escape the possibility that it served as the inspiration for Remington round. On the other hand, the wildcat .400 Eimer existed in 1924. It is also similar to the .401 and the .41 Magnums, so it is difficult to decide who influenced whom. Ammunition and loading components for the .401 Powermag are no longer available.
General Comments:	The .401 Powermag is an excellent self-defense or field cartridge. It is capable of doing anything the .41 Magnum can do. It has been used successfully on everything from small game and varmints on up to deer and black bear. With the availability of the commercial .41 Magnum and the many fine guns chambered for it, there is no need for the .401 Powermag, although it was, and still is, a fine cartridge.

.401 Herter Powermag Loading Data

Bullet (grains/type)	Powder	Grains	Velocity	Energy	Source/Comments
160 JSP	Unique	11.0	1,325	625	NA
180 JSP	Unique	10.0	1,270	650	NA
200 JSP	Unique	8.5	1,140	580	NA
200 JSP	BlueDot	13.0	1,280	735	NA

.41 Remington Magnum

Historical Notes:	The .41 Remington Magnum revolver cartridge was introduced in June 1964 along with the S&W Model 57 revolver. This is a heavy-frame gun, essentially the same as the older .44 Magnum, but of smaller caliber. The .41 Magnum is very similar to an old, but little-known wildcat cartridge called the .400 Eimer. Bore diameter of the .41 Magnum is a true .410-inch, rather than the .401-inch of the .41 Long Colt. Both a police load and a more powerful soft-point hunting round were originally introduced.
	Like most new cartridges, a number of individuals claim to have originated or influenced the design of the .41 Magnum. It might be well to mention that the .400 Eimer appeared around 1924. Possibly, a number of persons working over a span of time convinced Remington that it would be a good idea to bring out such a round. Probably Elmer Keith deserves the major credit.
General Comments:	There has been much argument, as to the need for a police cartridge with greater stopping power than the .357 Magnum. Few understand why a blunt, 200-grain bullet for the .357 would not have served this purpose. In addition, a lighter 210-grain police load could have been worked up for the .44 Magnum. However, someone wanted a new cartridge, and the .41 Magnum was the result.
	Actually, the new round was a more practical all-round hunting cartridge for the average individual than was the .44 Magnum. The .357 is not entirely adequate for big game, except in the hands of a good shot and experienced handgun hunter. The .44 Magnum is overpowered for anything but big game, and most people do not shoot very well with it. The .41 Magnum covers the small-game, medium-game, and

varmint-through-deer classes quite adequately. Its effectiveness on anything heavier than deer would depend upon who was using it and under what conditions.

Recoil and muzzle blast of the .41 Magnum are slightly less than the .44 Magnum, but still heavy. For the average shooter, mastering either will require about the same amount of training and practice. The 210-grain lead police load, with its 1150 fps velocity, is relatively pleasant to shoot and quite adequate for small game or varmints at average handgun ranges. Factory-claimed velocities are for an 8-3/8 inch barrel. Velocities developed from the six-inch barrel is about 1000 fps for the police load, and 1360 to 1400 fps for the soft-point hunting load. In summation, the .41 Magnum is not quite as powerful as the .44 Magnum, but it is all the gun the average handgun hunter needs. A number of police departments have adopted the .41 Magnum, but most have since dropped it in favor of 9mm Luger or .40 S&W semi-automatic pistols. All major domestic commercial ammunition makers have offered this cartridge, but, as of this writing, it has yet to find truly widespread popularity.

.41 Remington Magnum Loading Data and Factory Ballistics

Bullet (grains/type)	Powder	Grains	Velocity	Energy	Source/Comments
170 JHP	2400	21.0	1,400	740	Sierra
210 JHP	W296	20.0	1,200	672	Speer, Nosler, Sierra, Hornady
210 JHP	H110	20.0	1,200	672	Speer, Nosler, Sierra, Hornady
170 JHP	FL	FL	1,420	761	Factory load
175 JHP	FL	FL	1,250	607	Factory load
210 Lead	FL	FL	965	434	Factory load
210 JHP	FL	FL	1,300	788	Factory load

.41 Action Express

Historical Notes: The .41 Action Express (.41 AE) was designed in 1986 by Evan Whildin, vice president of Action Arms. The cartridge is unique among modern handgun cartridges, in that it has a rebated rim that will fit 9mm bolt faces and can be used in guns originally designed for the 9mm without the need for extensive changes. The .41 AE is chambered in the Action Arms AT-88, which is a beefed-up copy of the Czech CZ-75 auto pistol. The cartridge was originally developed with a 170-grain JHP bullet at 1130 fps initial velocity. However, the first commercial ammunition, loaded by Samson, in Israel, and imported into the United States, has a 200-grain flat-nose bullet with a muzzle velocity of 1000 fps, and a 180-grain JHP bullet, also at 1,000 fps.

General Comments: The .41 AE cannot be readily formed from any other case, although it is possible to make cases from .41 Magnum cases by trimming to .866-inch and turning down the rim on a lathe. This is, in fact, how the first experimental cartridges were made by Whildin. According to Bob Olsen, of Action Arms, the cross-sectional area of the bullet is 33 percent greater than the 9mm, and the bullets are one-third heavier. He also says that the Samson cases have been strengthened to prevent any bulging in blowback guns. Bullet diameter is the same as the .41 Magnum: .410-inch.

The .41 AE delivers practically the same ballistics as the .41 Magnum police load, which should make it an effective police or self-defense cartridge. The AT-88 pistol is based on a well-proven design and is accurate and pleasant to shoot. Recoil of the .41 AE is quite noticeably less than the .45 Automatic. The 180-grain load should be a good field load. However, one can handload cases with lighter jacketed or cast bullets. Israel Military Industries (Samson) is the only commercial manufacturer of this round. This concept is so good and performance so nearly ideal for this type of gun that it is quite surprising that this innovative round did not catch on.

.41 Action Express Loading Data and Factory Ballistics

Bullet (grains/type)	Powder	Grains	Velocity	Energy	Source/Comments
170 JHP	Unique	6.9	1,100	457	Sierra
170 JHP	Herco	7.1	1,100	457	Sierra

Bullet (grains/type)	Powder	Grains	Velocity	Energy	Source/Comments
210 JHP	Unique	5.5	900	378	Sierra, Hornady
180 JHP	FL	FL	1,000	400	Factory load
200 FMJ	FL	FL	1,000	448	Factory load

.414 Super Mag — *NEW*

Historical Notes:	Designed for silhouette shooting, this cartridge is basically a heavy-duty, lengthened version of the .41 Mag., the concept for which was begun in the 1970s by the late Elgin Gates. He originally made up SuperMag cartridges in .357, .375, .44, .45, .50 and .60 caliber, and then later added the .414 caliber. All the SuperMags by Gates had cases measuring 1.610 inches, or about 3/10 inch longer than standard magnum cartridges, requiring the production of a new revolver with a longer frame and cylinder.
General Comments:	The old Dan Wesson company manufactured .414 SuperMag revolvers ‚Äî about 25 of them, in fact ‚Äî before the company went bankrupt and suddenly closed its doors, leaving the .414 in limbo. When a new Dan Wesson company emerged, it chambered the .414 SuperMag in the New Generation Standard Silhouette Series. The blued model was # 414 V8S, and the stainless version was #7414 V8S and listed for $1,169 in 2002. Dan Wesson also offered them in the Super Ram Silhouette Series revolvers, 414 V8S SRS-1 and 7414 V8S SRS-1, blued and stainless respectively, for $1399 in 2002.
	The 414's case holds just more than 15 percent more powder than the 44 Mag. Reloading for the 414 requires a heavy crimp on the bullets to ensure they don't move forward during recoil. Firearms for this caliber have also been produced by Thompson/Center. Starline Brass offers properly headstamped cases.

.414 Super Mag Loading Data

Bullet (grains/type)	Powder	Grains	Velocity	Energy	Source/Comments
210 Sierra JHP	H 110	27.4	1,500	1,049	Sierra
210 Sierra JHP	AA 1680	30.6	1,450	980	Sierra

.44 Merwin & Hulbert

Historical Notes:	Winchester offered this cartridge beginning in 1882 and continued to catalog it until at least 1916. The Merwin & Hulbert revolver was quite popular and well liked on the frontier. Reproduction guns have even shown up in a few Hollywood productions.
General Comments:	While this cartridge and gun never received widespread lasting fame, review of the cartridge suggests that it was quite well designed, superior in several ways to many contemporary numbers. Without looking at the headstamp, it would be hard for most shooters to tell that this is not a thoroughly modern cartridge. Ballistics were comparable to the various .44-caliber revolver cartridges of the day.

10.4mm Italian Revolver

Historical Notes:	This cartridge was developed for the Italian Model 1874 service revolver, but was also used in the Glisenti Model 1889 revolver. It is sometimes listed as the 10.35 Italian Revolver or 10.35 Glisenti. Black-powder and smokeless powder ammunition is encountered. Both of the above revolvers have been sold from time to time in surplus stores.

General Comments: The 10.4 Italian cartridge is similar to the .44 S&W Russian. It would be an effective short-range self-defense or small-game hunting number. This ammunition is still commercially available from Fiocchi.

10.4mm Italian Revolver Factory Ballistics

Bullet (grains/type)	Powder	Grains	Velocity	Energy	Source/Comments
177 Lead	Black powder	ML	735	212	Military load
177 Lead	Smokeless powder	FL	800	240	Factory load

.44 Smith & Wesson Russian

Historical Notes: This cartridge was designed by S&W for its Russian Model military revolver in 1870, the first models of which were made for the Imperial Russian Army. A civilian or commercial model was also manufactured, beginning in 1878. Colt's Bisley Target Model and its regular single-action were available in this chambering. The German firm of Ludwig Loewe made copies of the S&W Russian Model revolver in the same chambering.

General Comments: Originally loaded with black powder, the .44 S&W Russian was one of the most accurate and popular cartridges of its day. It was the favorite of Buffalo Bill Cody and many other western characters. Good accuracy to 200 yards was reported, and some of the first precision handgun shooting was accomplished with this cartridge. It was made obsolete by the .44 S&W Special, which was better suited to early smokeless powders. Any gun chambered for the .44 Special or the .44 Magnum will also shoot the .44 Russian. This makes a good field cartridge, but it is not as good as the .44 Special, due to the old black-powder revolvers it was used in and the fact that it cannot be handloaded to the same level. Cases can be made by trimming .44 Special cases to a length of .97-inch. Fiocchi and Black Hills offer .44 Russian ammunition, and others may soon offer it for use in cowboy action shooting.

.44 Smith & Wesson Russian Factory Ballistics

Bullet (grains/type)	Powder	Grains	Velocity	Energy	Source/Comments
246 Lead	Bullseye	3.6	700	265	N/A
246 Lead	Black powder (FFFg)	20.0(?)	770	324	Factory load

.44 Smith & Wesson Special

Historical Notes: With the coming of bulkier smokeless powders, the .44 Russian cartridge case proved too small to permit efficient use of full charges of the new propellants. Though originally a black-powder cartridge, the .44 Special—which is about .2-inch longer than the Russian—eliminated this problem and provided more power, while using the same bullets as the older .44 Russian. This cartridge was introduced about 1907. Both Colt and S&W made revolvers in this chambering, and a few Spanish and other European revolvers were also made to handle it. There has been a rebirth of interest in the .44 Special in the past few decades.

General Comments: The .44 S&W Special is one of the most accurate and powerful big-bore revolver cartridges. However, it was never factory loaded to its full potential. It was left to the handloader to develop truly effective hunting loads. Experiments to maximize .44 Special's big game hunting potential, by men like Elmer Keith, culminated in the .44 Magnum. The .44 S&W Special is still popular for target or field use. Revolvers for the .44 Special are not strong enough to handle loads as heavy as those used in Magnum guns. Winchester, Remington, Federal, Black Hills, CorBon, and others load this ammunition.

.44 Smith & Wesson Special Loading Data and Factory Ballistics

Bullet (grains/type)	Powder	Grains	Velocity	Energy	Source/Comments
180 JHP	231	6.8	900	324	Sierra, Hornady

Bullet (grains/type)	Powder	Grains	Velocity	Energy	Source/Comments
200 JHP	231	6.0	800	284	Speer, Nosler, Hornady
240 JHP	HS-6	7.5	750	300	Hornady, Speer
200 JHP	FL	FL	900	360	Factory load
200 L-SWC	FL	FL	1,035	476	Factory load (very optimistic data)
246 Lead	Smokeless powder	FL	755	310	Factory load

.44 Remington Magnum

Historical Notes: This cartridge was developed by Smith & Wesson and Remington and introduced in 1955 for a new, heavy-frame .44 Magnum revolver. Ruger, Colt, Smith & Wesson, and others make revolvers for this cartridge. Its development was inspired and much preliminary work done by Elmer Keith and that era's group of hand-cannon fanatics, who insisted on the ultimate in handgun accuracy, range, and power. Ruger introduced a semi-auto carbine in .44 Magnum chambering, in 1961, and Marlin introduced its Model 94 lever-action, in 1967.

General Comments: In addition to having been the world's most powerful commercial handgun cartridge for many years, the .44 Magnum also has a well-deserved reputation for superb accuracy. It is used more as a field or hunting round than anything else, but a few police officers favored it because of its ability to penetrate an automobile body. It takes a seasoned handgunner to shoot it well, as both recoil and muzzle blast are considerable. This is one of the few commercial handgun cartridges that can be considered fully adequate for big-game hunting. It has been used to take deer, black bear, elk, moose, and big Alaskan brown bears. It has often been chambered in rifles, with the Model 1894 Winchester or the Remington rolling-block action generally used. In a 20- or 24-inch rifle barrel, the standard factory load will develop about 1720 fps at the muzzle and 1580 ft-lbs of energy. This equals the energy of the .30-30 rifle cartridge. It is a very flexible cartridge when handloaded and can be made to cover any situation within the scope of the modern revolver. Very few, if any, police departments use it, because it is simply too much for the average police officer to handle. Its use in police work is largely a personal thing. All major manufacturers of commercial ammunition offer this cartridge in a variety of bullet weights.

.44 Remington Magnum Loading Data and Factory Ballistics

Bullet (grains/type)	Powder	Grains	Velocity	Energy	Source/Comments
180 JHP	Unique	14.0	1,500	900	Hornady, Sierra
200 JHP	W296	26.0	1,450	934	Hornady, Speer
240 JHP	H110	23.0	1,350	971	Speer, Hornady, Sierra, Nosler
250 FMJ	2400	21.0	1,250	868	Sierra
180 JHP	FL	FL	1,610	1,035	Factory load
210 JHP	FL	FL	1,495	1,042	Factory load
210 JHP	FL	FL	1,250	729	Factory load
240 Lead	FL	FL	1,350	971	Factory load
240 JHP	FL	FL	1,180	741	Factory load
240 Lead	FL	FL	1,000	533	Factory load
240 Lead	FL	FL	1,350	971	Factory load
250 FMJ	FL	FL	1,180	775	Factory load
255 FTX	FL	FL	1,410	993	Hornady Factory Load

.44 Auto Mag

Historical Notes: Introduced late in 1971, this cartridge was developed for the Auto Mag pistol designed by the late Harry Sanford of Pasadena, Calif. The gun was also made and marketed for a few years by High Standard. The cartridge is made by cutting off .30-06 or .308 Winchester cases to a length of 1.30 inches, inside reaming the case neck to accept .429-inch bullets, and trimming to a length of 1.298 inches. The newly formed case is then loaded with .429-inch jacketed bullets of 200 to 240 grains. For a time, .44 Auto Mag cases were made in Mexico, by Cartuchos Deportivos Mexico and headstamped CDM. Loaded ammunition was later offered by Norma of Sweden. A few custom loaders furnished loaded rounds. Dies are made by RCBS (www.rcbs.com). The .44 Auto Mag cartridge was used only in the Auto Mag semi-auto pistol, which is no longer in production.

General Comments: The Auto Mag semi-auto pistol operates on the short recoil principle, with a six-lug, front-locking rotary bolt. Made almost entirely of stainless steel, it has a 6½-inch barrel, an overall length of 11½ inches, and weighs about 3½ pounds. This was the most powerful commercial semi-auto pistol manufactured at that time. When loaded to maximum, a 200-grain bullet can be pushed at over 1500 fps, and the 240-grain to 1400 fps. Unfortunately, the Auto Mag pistol had a rather short and stormy career marked by more than its share of manufacturing, marketing, and mechanical troubles. The .44 Auto Mag pistol was developed primarily as a sporting gun. It has been used to take all kinds of big game, including deer, elk, moose, and Kodiak bear. It is in the same class as the .44 Magnum.

.44 Auto Mag Loading Data

Bullet (grains/type)	Powder	Grains	Velocity	Energy	Source/Comments
180 JHP	2400	25.0	1,600	1,024	Sierra
200 JHP	W296	26.5	1,500	999	Hornady
240 JHP	W296	24.0	1,350	972	Sierra, Hornady
240 JHP	H110	23.0	1,400	1,045	Hornady

.44 Smith & Wesson American

Historical Notes: The .44 S&W American was one of the earliest American centerfire revolver cartridges. It was used in the Smith & Wesson single-action Model 3 revolver, known more generally as the .44 S&W American model. It is known to have been in use late in 1870 and was probably introduced as early as 1869. The U.S. Army used this cartridge and revolver for a short time, between 1871 and 1873. The Merwin Hulbert & Co. Army revolver also was made for this round. Commercial ammunition in black-powder and smokeless powder types was manufactured until about 1940.

General Comments: The .44 S&W American is another obsolete black-powder number that survived an amazing number of years. It used an outside-lubricated bullet of the same diameter as the .44 S&W Russian inside the case, and a slightly larger diameter outside the case. Ammunition with both Boxer- and Berdan-type primers was loaded. Reloadable cases can probably be made by reforming .44 Magnum cases, and dies to do this are available from RCBS (www.rcbs.com). Revolvers for this cartridge are of the older black-powder type and loads should be kept mild. The .44 American could be used for hunting at short range, but there are better and more modern cartridges available. In power, it is comparable to the .41 Long Colt. Cartridges are now collector's items.

.44 Smith & Wesson American Loading Data and Factory Ballistics

Bullet (grains/type)	Powder	Grains	Velocity	Energy	Source/Comments
200 Lead	Unique	5.5	765	259	Lyman No. 419180

Bullet (grains/type)	Powder	Grains	Velocity	Energy	Source/Comments
205 Lead	FL		682	212	Factory load
218 Lead	Black powder (FFg)	25.0	660	196	Factory load

.44 Webley/.442 RIC/ .442 Revolver Center Fire/ .442 Kurz/10.5x17Rmm

Historical Notes: The 44 Webley originated in 1868 for the Webley Royal Irish Constabulary (RIC) model revolver. In England, it is listed as the .442 Revolver Center Fire. In the United States, it was loaded as the .44 Webley, up to about 1940. At least one H&R revolver model chambered it. It was also loaded in Europe, where it is called the 10.5x17Rmm or 442 Kurz (DWM No. 221).

General Comments: The .44 Webley was popular for use in pocket-type or self-defense pistols. In power, it is in about the same class as the .41 Long Colt or .44 S&W American. It has much better stopping power than some of the smaller calibers, but is strictly a short-range proposition. Original loading was 15 to 19 grains of black powder and a 200- or 220-grain bullet. Late-manufactured ammunition used smokeless powder. It is long obsolete, and these cartridges are now collector's items.

.44 Webley/442 RIC Factory Ballistics

Bullet (grains/type)	Powder	Grains	Velocity	Energy	Source/Comments
200 Lead	FL	FL	715	230	Remington factory load
220 Lead	FL	Fl	700	239	Kynoch factory load

.44 Bull Dog

Historical Notes: The .44 Bull Dog appears to have originated about 1880, perhaps a year or two prior to that. The first reference the original author of this book could locate was in the 1880 Homer Fisher gun catalog, reproduced in L.D. Satterlee's *Ten Old Gun Catalogs*; British Webley Bull Dog revolvers were advertised therein. American companies loaded the round up to about 1938-'39. The 1933 Winchester catalog lists it as for "Webley, British Bull Dog and H&R revolvers."

General Comments: The Bull Dog-type pocket revolver was quite popular through the late 1800s. The .44 Bull Dog cartridge was much superior to some of the rimfire cartridges of that period. It provided reasonably good short-range stopping power in a compact gun. However, it is solely a short-range, self-defense round and of little value for anything else. It is in the same general class as the .41 Short Colt. The cartridge has been obsolete for a good many years. Both black-powder and smokeless powder loadings are encountered.

.44 Bull Dog Factory Ballistics

Bullet (grains/type)	Powder	Grains	Velocity	Energy	Source/Comments
168 to 170 Lead	FL	FL	460	80	Factory load

10.6mm German — *NEW*

Historical Notes: The cartridge aficionado will take note of the 10.6mm German Ordnance's appearance — and fairly rapid disappearance — because it reflected thinking at the time that handgun cartridges had to be wide in diameter to be effective, because they couldn't be pushed to high velocities with the powders of the day.

If you're into collecting turn-of-the century military sidearms, you'll likely come across the Models 1879 and 1883 Reichsrevolver, which fired the 10.6mm German Ordnance round and are often called the 10.6 Reichsrevolver. The cartridge is also referred to as the 10.6mm Reichsrevolver, 10.6mm Service Ordnance and 10.55mm German. Usually described as a 10.6x25mm cartridge, it was actually a 10.43x24.64mm straight case with a rim.

General Comments: The service revolvers were used by the German Army from 1879 to 1908, and they have the distinction of being superseded by the Luger. Last major commercial production of the 10.6mm round was in 1939.

Heinrich E. Harder authored the definitive work to date on these weapons, Der Reichsrevolver und seine Varianten, which is written in German, but the illustration captions and chapter notes are translated into English.

.44 Colt

Historical Notes: The .44 Colt is yet another black-powder cartridge of importance, primarily because it was once used by the U.S. Army. It was introduced about 1871 and used by the Army from then until 1873. It was used in the metallic cartridge conversion of the Colt 1860 percussion revolver, and it could also be fired in the Remington Model 1875 .44 Army revolver. Commercial ammunition was loaded in both black-powder and smokeless powder types, up to about 1940.

General Comments: The .44 Colt uses an outside-lubricated bullet. It is similar to the .44 S&W American, but has a longer case of slightly larger diameter. Early ammunition used the inside Benet cup and Martin folded-type primers. Ammunition has become a collector's item, and revolvers for this cartridge are very seldom encountered. Ballistically it is about the same as the .44 S&W American.

.44 Colt Factory Ballistics

Bullet (grains/type)	Powder	Grains	Velocity	Energy	Source/Comments
210	Bullseye	4.0	700	226	Lyman No. 429185
210 Lead	Black powder (FFg)	23.0	660	206	Factory load
225 Lead	Black powder FFg)	23.0	640	207	Military load
210 Lead	FL		660	206	Factory load
225 Lead	FL		640	207	Factory load

11.75mm Montenegrin Revolver/ 11mm Austrian Gasser/ 11.25x36mm Montenegrin

Historical Notes: This cartridge was for the long-obsolete Montenegrin and Austro-Hungarian revolvers based on the Gasser system. The round was introduced about 1870 and is known as the 11mm Austrian Gasser and 11.25x36mm Montenegrin. The revolver for the cartridge is a large, massive hinged-frame type, weighing around 4½ pounds. G. Roth manufactured ammunition (No. 287), and, apparently, so did a number of other companies, including a few lots made by Winchester. Both the 11.75mm cartridge and revolver are now in the realm of the collector.

General Comments: The 11.75mm is quite a large revolver cartridge, being longer and larger in diameter than the .44 Magnum. The 282- to 313-grain, .445-inch bullet is also unusually heavy for a handgun cartridge. As a black-powder number, it should have knockdown and stopping power on a par with the .44 S&W Special or the .45 Colt, possibly better, with the heavier bullet. There is no loading data, but some information says that ammunition can be made by shortening and extensively reworking empty .45-70 cases.

.445 Super Magnum — *NEW*

Historical Notes: Designed by Elgin T. Gates for silhouette shooting, the .445 Super Magnum is a heavy-duty, lengthened version of the .44 Mag. .445 SuperMag revolvers were available only from Dan Wesson in blued and stainless-steel versions and in competition and hunting models, such as the Model 7445 Alaskan Guide Special, available from the factory as late as 2006.

General Comments: Headstamped ".445 Gates" brass is available, and factory-loaded rounds are available from Reed's Ammunition & Research of Oklahoma City.

If you handload for this round, a good, heavy crimp is required to keep bullets from moving forward in recoil. The same bullets that work in the .44 Mag. also work well in the .44 SuperMag. With a 240 Speer silhouette bullet, 33.0 grains of H110 or 38.0 grains of WW680 will do 1,350 to 1,450 fps in 6- and 8-inch Dan Wesson barrels. For hunting, the 300-grain Sierra Jacketed Flat Point on top of 31.0 grains of H110 will get the shooter 1,300 fps.

.445 Super Mag Factory Ballistics

Bullet (grains/type)	Powder	Grains	Velocity	Energy	Source/Comments
200 Barnes X			1,700	1,283	Reed's Ammunition & Research #45SM200BX
300 Nosler HP			1,400	1,305	Reed's Ammunition & Research #445SM300NOS
320 Hard Cast GC			1,400	1,392	Reed's Ammunition & Research #445SM320GLH

11.75mm Montenegrin Revolver Factory Ballistics

Bullet (grains/type)	Powder	Grains	Velocity	Energy	Source/Comments
282 to 313 Lead	FL		700	328	Factory load

.45 Mars Short
.45 Mars Long

Historical Notes: The Mars Automatic Pistol, aka the Webley-Mars, was a semi-automatic pistol developed in 1900 and chambered in these loadings as well as two other bottlenecked cartridges with large powder charges, the 8.5mm Mars and 9mm Mars. The British War Office rejected the Mars Automatic Pistol as a replacement for the Webley & Scott revolver, because of the former's large recoil and considerable muzzle flash. Some say the pistol inspired the design of the present day Desert Eagle, but that seems apocryphal. The handgun was manufactured by Webley & Scott and other gun makers in Birmingham and London, until 1907.

General Comments: Hugh Gabbet-Fairfax, a Birmingham inventor, developed the Mars pistol in 1900 with the idea of producing the most powerful military pistol possible, and the .45 Mars Long was the most powerful handgun in the world for a time. The .45 Long produced a muzzle velocity of 1,250 fps, very impressive compared to others of the time, such as the .45 Colt Auto (855 fps), .455 Webley Auto (700 fps) and the 9mm Parabellum (1,100 fps). The Short was likely developed because of the Long's unpleasantness. An observer of the time called the Long a "young cannon."—*W.T.W.*

Bullet (grains/type)	Powder	Grains	Velocity	Energy	Source/Comments
220 FMJ	FL	FL	1,200	700	Kynoch

11mm German Service Revolver

Historical Notes: This cartridge was for the German Model 1879 and 1883 service revolvers. It has been obsolete since 1904, but a few of these revolvers were used in World War I and even the last stages of World War II. The cartridge is also listed as the 10.6 or 10.8mm German service or ordnance revolver load (DWM No. 200 & 200A). Moderate numbers of these revolvers have been sold by surplus dealers in the United States. This cartridge used a heel-based bullet of about .451-inch maximum diameter.

General Comments: The 11mm German ordnance cartridge bears a close resemblance to the .44 S&W Russian. The two are of the same power. The old German revolvers were designed for black powder, and only low-pressure smokeless powder loads should be fired in these. Ammunition can be made by shortening and reforming .44 S&W Special cases. This cartridge is obsolete. Ammunition has become a collector's item.

11mm German Service Revolver Factory Ballistics

Bullet (grains/type)	Powder	Grains	Velocity	Energy	Source/Comments
262 Lead	Black powder	ML	700	288	Military load

11mm French Ordnance Revolver

Historical Notes: This was an early French military cartridge for the Model 1873 Ordnance Revolver. It became obsolete in 1892 on adoption of the smaller 8mm Lebel revolver and cartridge. A few of the old M73 revolvers have been sold in surplus stores, although ammunition is very scarce. Evidently, 11mm refers to bore diameter, as barrels measure close to .451-inch across the grooves.

General Comments: Most military establishments of the period around 1870 used similar handgun cartridges, usually of .43-, .44-, or .45-caliber. The 11mm French round is another one not very much different from the .44 S&W Russian. Satisfactory ammunition can probably be made by shortening and reforming .44 S&W Special cases. Lyman No. 42798 (205-grain) cast bullets can be used, although they will be undersized. Bullet No. 452460 (200-grain) can also be used, if swaged down to about .447- to .450-inch. There really is not an entirely satisfactory bullet for this particular cartridge. Power is a little less than the .44 S&W Russian, but the 11mm French cartridge would make an effective short-range self-defense or small-game field round. This ammunition has been obsolete for many years. Cartridges are scarce collector's items.

11mm French Ordnance Revolver Factory Ballistics

Bullet (grains/type)	Powder	Grains	Velocity	Energy	Source/Comments
180 Lead	Black powder	ML	695	195	Military load

.45 Winchester Magnum

Historical Notes: The .45 Magnum was first listed in the 1979 Winchester gun and ammunition catalog, although reports of its impending release had circulated some two years earlier. The cartridge was chambered in the on-again, off-again Wildey gas-operated semi-automatic pistol and has been adopted as a standard chambering for the Thompson/Center Contender single-shot pistol. The cartridge is, essentially, an elongated version of the .45 Automatic. Both gun and cartridge were developed, initially, for silhouette competition, but with the ballistics developed (a 230-grain bullet at a muzzle velocity of 1,400 fps), the cartridge should prove an effective hunting round.

General Comments: The .45 Winchester Magnum develops 72 percent higher velocity and 200-percent greater muzzle energy than the standard .45 Automatic, and it's in the same class as the .44 Magnum revolver cartridge. With its rimless case, it is a natural for use in a semi-automatic rifle, if one were ever developed. The Wildey .45 Magnum, along with the. 44 Auto Mag, the Desert Eagle, and the LAR Grizzly, are the only automatic pistols that truly qualify as big-game handguns. The potential is there for a fine combination silhouette and hunting pistol. The price is high, and for strictly silhouette shooting, the much lower-priced Thompson/Center Contender in the same chambering might appeal to many potential buyers. The availability of commercial ammunition with hunting-type bullets would also be a factor, although there is a good variety of such bullets available to the handloader.

.45 Winchester Magnum Loading Data and Factory Ballistics

Bullet (grains/type)	Powder	Grains	Velocity	Energy	Source/Comments
185 JHP	BlueDot	20.0	1,850	1,406	Hornady
200 JHP	2400	22.5	1,500	999	Speer
225 JHP	H110	26.0	1,500	1,124	Speer
230 FMJ	BlueDot	17.0	1,550	1,227	Hornady
260 JHP	W296	25.0	1,500	1,300	Speer
230 FMJ	FL	FL	1,400	1,001	Factory load, Winchester

All of the above loads were developed in a Thompson/Center Contender pistol with a 10-inch barrel. These loads are not recommended for any other handgun.

.451 Detonics Magnum — *NEW*

Historical Notes: An entry about the .451 Detonics Magnum has previously appeared in these pages, and we reinsert it in this edition because the company that initially made it has restarted. The .451 Detonics was basically a .45 Win. Mag. case shortened to fit in a 1911 magazine, yet long enough that it would not chamber in a .45 ACP barrel.

Detonics is historically recognized as the innovator of the compact 1911 as a new design and not a cut-down version of a full-size handgun. In November 2007, ownership of Detonics USA and all of its predecessors was purchased by Bruce Siddle and Dr. Steve Stahle, and corporate operations were relocated to Millstadt, Illinois. It now operates as Detonics Defense Technologies, LLC. More information about the company can be found at DetonicsDefense.com.

However, the Detonics Defense Technologies website is explicit about its not supporting parts for .451 Detonics-chambered rounds and suggests rebarreling older handguns in the .451 Detonics chambering with the more-common .45 ACP.

Headstamped .451 Detonics brass is available from Quality Cartridge, $59/50. Midway also stocks the QC brass for $64/50.

General Comments: The cartridge was introduced in 1983, and Detonics furnished empty cases headstamped ".451 Det/Mag." Cases can also be made from cut-down .308 Win. brass.

In its search for a more potent .45-caliber round for its .45-caliber pistols, the Detonics Mfg. Co. decided to take advantage of this by trimming the .45 Win. Mag. from its normal length of 1.198 inches to that of .942 inch. This is still sufficiently longer than the .45 ACP, so the .451 Detonics cartridge will not chamber in handguns intended for .45 ACP. The newly created case will handle much higher pressures than the original .45 ACP and still function through actions of the same length.

Various mechanical features of the Colt M1911 A1 auto pistol have prevented any significant ballistic advantage in the cartridges it chambers. One of these weaknesses is that a portion of the cartridge head is unsupported, so operating pressures are dictated by the strength of that portion of the case. The .45 Win. Mag. has a substantially stronger case head and dimensions identical to the .45 ACP except for greater length. Detonics not only chambered its Scoremaster and Combat Master semi-auto pistols for the .451 Detonics, it also offered a conversion kit for the Colt Government, Gold Cup and Commander pistols.

.451 Detonics Magnum Loading Data

Bullet (grains/type)	Powder	Grains	Velocity	Energy	Source/Comments
200 JHP			1,200	639	Cor-Bon Load

.460 Rowland

0.476"	0.476"		0.476"

0.955"

Historical Notes:	This cartridge was developed by northwest Louisiana native Johnny Rowland, who grew up on a farm shooting guns and enjoying the outdoors. Rowland has developed a number of gun-related products, including the .460 Rowland. The idea with this round was to develop a handgun hunting cartridge for the 1911 pistol that would offer .44 Magnum levels of power. To do this, Rowland increased the .45 Auto case by 1/16-inch, to ensure .460 Rowland cartridges could not be loaded in .45 Auto handguns. The other main difference between the .460 Rowland and the .45 Auto is that the Rowland round is loaded to a much higher pressures, 40,000 psi as compared to 19,000 psi. Despite the .460 designation, the .460 Rowland uses .451-diameter bullets just like a .45 Auto.
General Comments:	The .460 Rowland is indeed a powerhouse cartridge, something you will realize the first time you fire one. Most 1911s in .460 Rowland are built with a compensator to combat the intense recoil. Currently, Buffalo Bore, CorBon, and Wilson Combat all offer factory loaded ammunition for the .460 Rowland in various bullets weights from 185- to 255-grain. External ballistics are very similar to that of the .44 Magnum, as is terminal performance, when similar bullets are compared. As of now, a .460 Rowland handgun is a custom option, and Wilson Combat offers its Hunter 1911 in this cartridge.

.460 Rowland Loading Data and Factory Ballistics

Bullet (grains/type)	Powder	Grains	Velocity	Energy	Source/Comments
185 JSWC	Longshot	13.5	1,503	927	Hodgdon
200 JHP	Longshot	13.8	1,456	941	Hodgdon
230 XTP	Longshot	12.0	1,336	911	Hodgdon
185 JHP	FL	FL	1,425	834	CorBon Factory load
230 JHP	FL	FL	1,250	798	CorBon Factory load
230 XTP	FL	FL	1,200	735	Wilson Combat Factory load
255 HC FN (Lead)	FL	FL	1,300	957	Buffalo Bore Factory load

.45 Webley

Historical Notes:	The earliest reference that could be located regarding the .45 Webley was in the 1876 James Brown & Son gun catalog.* However, it may have originated a year or two earlier than that. American companies manufactured it up to about 1939. The 1933 Winchester catalog says it is for "Webley and Bull Dog double-action revolvers." It is obsolete.

General Comments: The .45 Webley is similar to the .450 Revolver cartridge, but has a slightly longer case. The two will interchange in most revolvers. Originally a black-powder cartridge, the .45 Webley was loaded with 20 grains of powder and a 230-grain bullet. Smokeless powder was also used in late loadings. In power, it is in the same class as the .41 Short Colt, but probably has superior stopping power, because of the larger, heavier bullet. Ammunition could probably be made by cutting off .455 Webley cases.

L.D. Satterlee op. cit.

.45 Webley Factory Ballistics

Bullet (grains/type)	Powder	Grains	Velocity	Energy	Source/Comments
230 Lead	FL		550	150	Factory load, U.S.

.45 Automatic Rimmed (.45 Auto Rim)

Historical Notes: During World War I, both Colt and Smith & Wesson manufactured revolvers for the .45 Automatic cartridge. This required use of a half-moon clip to support and then eject the rimless .45 Automatic. Thousands of these revolvers were sold on the civilian market after the war ended. In 1920, the Peters Cartridge Co. introduced a rimmed version of the .45 Automatic, which eliminated the need for half-moon clips in the revolver. The round was also loaded with a lead bullet, to reduce rifling wear inherent with use of the jacketed .45 Automatic bullets in the unusually soft barrels used.

General Comments: Cylinder throats in these revolvers were considerably oversized. Bill Falin, chief ballistician at Accurate Arms, has suggested that this might have been done by design as a simple means of mitigating chamber pressure when standard .45 Automatic military rounds were used. Bill's testing demonstrated that heavily jacketed full metal jacket bullets do not obturate until the rifling is contacted and, so, a significant amount of gas escapes before peak chamber pressure occurs. Considering the significant pressure of original .45 Automatic loads, which launched 230-grain bullets from the 1911 at an honest 930 fps with powders such as Unique, this might well have been necessary to keep these somewhat fragile revolvers in one piece. In any case, this is certainly an interesting conjecture.

The .45 Auto-Rim (.45 Automatic Rimmed), while similar in performance to the .45 Automatic, is probably a better field or hunting cartridge, because it can be handloaded with semi-wadcutter, hollow-point, and other lead hunting bullets. When using such bullets at slightly increased velocities, it is every bit as good as the .45 Colt revolver cartridge for small through medium game. Many war-surplus .455 Webley revolvers have been altered to shoot the .45 Auto-Rim, and many of these are used in the field. The cartridge is probably more widely used than at anytime since it was introduced. This cartridge is no longer offered by commercial ammunition makers.

.45 Automatic Rimmed Loading Data and Factory Ballistics

Bullet (grains/type)	Powder	Grains	Velocity	Energy	Source/Comments
185 JHP	Bullseye	5.5	850	297	Hornady
200	Bullseye	4.90	750	250	Hornady, Sierra
230	Unique	6.6	800	327	Speer, Sierra
230 Lead	FL		805	331	Factory load

.45 Glock Auto Pistol (.45 GAP)

Historical Notes: In 2003, Winchester announced ammunition for a new Glock auto pistol. The .45 GAP (Glock Auto Pistol) cartridge is 1/8-inch shorter than the timeless .45 ACP cartridge, but delivers similar performance. The shorter cartridge case allows a trimmer, more-ergonomic shape in the Glock Model 37 pistol.

General Comments: Many knowledgeable pistol shooters consider the 230-grain bullet to be about the best available for

.45-caliber autoloading pistols. For law enforcement use, the frontal area of a .45-caliber bullet offers a stopping power advantage, given correct bullet design. During load development, Winchester engineers achieved .45 ACP velocities in the shorter .45 GAP case using 230-grain bullets. Winchester also developed Law Enforcement-Only loads for this cartridge for duty use, with its proprietary T-Series bullets, and for training with frangible bullets. Speer offers ammunition in a variety of loads.

.45 Glock Auto Pistol (.45 GAP) Loading Data and Factory Ballistics

Bullet (grains/type)	Powder	Grains	Velocity	Energy	Source/Comments
175 Frangible	FL	FL	1,000	N/A	Winchester
185 TMJ FN	FL	FL	1,020	N/A	Speer
185 SilverTip	FL	FL	1,000	N/A	Winchester
200 GDHP	FL	FL	950	N/A	Speer
230 FMJ	FL	FL	850	N/A	Winchester
230 JHP	FL	FL	880	N/A	Winchester
185 Hdy XTP	Longshot	7.5	1,075	N/A	Hodgdon
200 Speer GDHP	Longshot	6.8	1,000	N/A	Hodgdon

.45 Automatic Short/.45 HP

Historical Notes:	In many countries, such as Italy, France, and Mexico, it has been illegal for private citizens to own semi-automatic pistols in military chamberings such as .45 Automatic. Gun owners in these countries created a strong demand for a powerful, semi-auto pistol in a non-military chambering. The .45 Automatic Short was developed in response to that demand. It is sometimes called the .45 HP.
	This cartridge uses a .45 Automatic case shortened by one millimeter. All other case dimensions remain the same. A standard 230-grain FMJ bullet is used, but is seated out so that cartridge overall length and muzzle velocity are identical to the .45 Automatic using the same loads. Pistols originally designed for the .45 Automatic can quickly be converted to the Short by installing a new barrel. All other parts remain the same.
General Comments:	Because the chamber of the .45 Automatic Short is shorter than the .45 Automatic, the latter round will not chamber in a .45 Short barrel. The letter of the law in the appropriate countries is, therefore, preserved, while shooters can still obtain .45 Automatic performance. The .45 Automatic is famous for its stopping power, and the Short offers identical ballistics. Loading data for the two is interchangeable. With the Western European Union consolidating firearm laws, the prohibition against private ownership of pistols in military chamberings will soon end. Therefore, the purpose for which the .45 Automatic Short exists will end, and this cartridge will become obsolete. Only Hirtenberger AG, of Austria, has commercially loaded this ammunition.

.45 Automatic Short Factory Ballistics

Bullet (grains/type)	Powder	Grains	Velocity	Energy	Source/Comments
230 FMJ	FL	FL	835	356	Hirtenberger factory load

.45 Automatic Match

Historical Notes:	This can be seen as a variation of the .45 ACP or as a separate match round. To the latter point, it has its own SAAMI drawing, with the name as listed. The chambering dimensions for the two rounds are the same, but the cartridge dimensions vary. The .45 Automatic Match has an overall length (OAL) of approximately 1.140, which is substantially shorter than a 1.275 OAL .45 ACP full metal jacket. The .45

Automatic Match also has a reduced powder load. At one time, Winchester (.45 Automatic Super Match X45AWCP), Remington (Remington High Velocity R45AP1), and Federal (Gold Match 185-grain SWC GM45B) all loaded this match round. It's been dropped from the Winchester and Remington lines, but Federal continues to produce it.

General Comments: The .45 Automatic Match's length, bullet shape, and power rating make it suitable for a bull's-eye gun and likely to malfunction in most other 1911s with full-power recoil springs.—*W.T.W.*

.45 Automatic Match Factory Ballistics

Bullet (grains/type)	Powder	Grains	Velocity	Energy	Source/Comments
185 FMJ-SWC Match	FL	FL	794	259	Federal Gold Match, GM45B Factory Load
185 Wadcutter	FL	FL	784	252	Remington High Velocity, R45AP1 Factory Load

.45 ABC Mi-Bullet

Historical Notes: Advanced Ballistics Concepts, LLC (ABC) has invented two handgun cartridges, the 45 ABC Mi-Bullet and the 9mm ABC Mi-Bullet, with multi-part bullets that immediately unlock and expand to a predetermined diameter and pattern of spread upon leaving the tip of a rifled barrel. They're designed to improve hit probability in self-defense situations.

The new Multiple Impact Bullet (Mi-Bullet) is similar to multi-pellet buckshot, in that both deliver multiple strike points. The Mi-Bullets connect three separate segments with ballistic-grade tethers that allow the fragment to expand like a web to a predetermined diameter. ABC offers Mi-Bullet cartridges in three categories: Less-lethal (Mi-Stinger), semi-lethal (Mi-Stunner), and fully-lethal (Mi-Stopper). Mi-Bullets fit existing firearms.

General Comments: The Mi-Stopper second-generation bullet is formed of high-density materials (e.g., lead, copper, tungsten, and Zuerillium zinc alloy, or Green Lead). The .45 Mi-Bullet has an unusual construction. The tip of the round is the spool for the tethers. The spool sits atop three fitted fragments, which effectively form the bottom of the "bullet" next to the powder charge.

A good application for this round might be a two-shot Derringer or other minimal-capacity handgun, where the shooter can't afford to miss. The projectile is designed to expand to its maximum width at 12 feet, and then "lock out" to maximum width for three feet, then begin contracting, so the sweet spot for self-defense use is between about 12 feet and 21 feet, where many encounters occur.—*W.T.W.*

.45 ABC Mi-3 Stopper Bullet (Lethal) Factory Ballistics

Bullet (grains/type)	Powder	Grains	Velocity	Energy	Source/Comments
200 Lead RN	Win 231	6.2	950	400	Stopper Factory Load

.45 ABC Mi-3 Stunner Bullet (Semi-Lethal) Factory Ballistics

Bullet (grains/type)	Powder	Grains	Velocity	Energy	Source/Comments
120 Zuerillium Alloy	Win 231	4.4	700	130	Stunner Factory Load (aka Green Load)

.45 Automatic Colt Pistol
(.45 Automatic +P/.45 ACP)

Historical Notes: This cartridge was developed by John Browning in 1905 and adopted by the United States Ordnance Department, with the Colt-Browning automatic pistol in 1911. It has also been made the official military handgun chambering by several other governments, notably Argentina, Mexico, and Norway. The .45 Automatic is the most powerful military handgun cartridge in use today. It is also one of the most difficult to master. The Colt Government Model auto-pistol and its copies, as well as the Colt and Smith & Wesson Army Model 1917 revolvers, are the principal arms chambered for the .45 Automatic in the United States. Ruger, S&W, Springfield Armory, Glock, Numrich, and many other companies now also offer guns in this chambering. Several submachine guns have used it. About 1943, a number of Reising semi-automatic rifles were marketed in this chambering. Imitations of the Colt auto pistol have been made in Argentina, China, Korea, Norway, Spain, and the United States. It was replaced in 1985 as the official U.S. military handgun cartridge by the 9mm Parabellum. However, it remains in U.S. Marine Corps service and has proven increasingly popular with police agencies in the United States.

General Comments: The .45 Automatic has been proven in combat all over the world as having excellent stopping power. It has also developed into a first-class match cartridge, with accuracy equal to the best. It requires practice for the average person to develop skill with this cartridge, particularly when fired in some untuned semi-automatics. It is used far more for target shooting than hunting, its curved trajectory limiting its effective range. Despite this, it is quite adequate for any small or medium game. Like all the other semi-auto pistol cartridges, it is a better hunting round with soft-point and hollow-point bullets. At one time, a number of police departments switched from the .38 Special to the .45 Automatic. All major and minor commercial ammunition manufacturers offer this cartridge. After several years of declining sales, it is enjoying a resurgence of popularity, especially after its centennial celebration in 2011.

.45 Automatic (.45 ACP/.45 Auto) Loading Data and Factory Ballistics

Bullet (grains/type)	Powder	Grains	Velocity	Energy	Source/Comments
185 JHP	Bullseye	5.0	900	333	Hornady, Sierra, Nosler
200 JHP	BlueDot	10.0	900	360	Speer, Sierra
230 FMJ	Bullseye	5.0	800	327	Nosler, Speer, Sierra
230 FMJ	Unique	6.0	800	327	Speer, Nosler, Hornady, Sierra
185 FMJ SWC	FL	FL	770	244	Factory load
185 JHP	FL	FL	1,000	411	Factory load
185 JHP	FL	FL	1,140	534	Factory load (+P)
230 FMJ	FL	FL	835	356	Factory load
230 JHP	FL	FL	875	391	Factory load
230 FMJ	ML	FL	855	405	Military load

45 Super — NEW

Historical Notes: The 45 Super was developed in 1988 by Dean Grennell, Tom Fergerson and Ace Hindman, owner of Ace Custom 45s (Cleveland, Texas [281] 659-1017), by shortening a .451 Detonics case (which see). The .451 Detonics has a thicker case wall than the ACP and is loaded to higher pressures. The 45 Super offers about 300 fps more muzzle velocity than even hot .45 ACP +P loads. Garey Hindman, Ace's son, trademarked the .45 Super name in 1994.

Externally and dimensionally identical to the .45 ACP, the 45 Super is designed to be used in semi-auto pistols with stronger recoil springs and a shock buffer. Although you can "occasionally" shoot 45 Super out of some stock +P-rated pistols such as the Glock 21, HK USPs or full-sized steel 1911s, they will likely break unless they're modified to handle the extra pressure and slide velocity of the 45 Super.

General Comments: Recoil and noise are noticeably higher than what 230-grain JHP +Ps produce. In a gun the size of an H&K Mark 23 or other large-frame sidearms, recoil is more tolerable.

Factory ammo for the 45 Super is available from Underwood Ammunition Co. (UnderwoodAmmo.com) and Buffalo Bore. Starline Brass offers headstamped 45 Super brass (large pistol primer) that's 0.892 to 0.897 in COAL, and the company's website says, "45 Super is the same externally as the .45 Auto, but has a thicker web, denser grain structure in the metal, and [has a] special heat-treat process that enhances the durability of the case. Similar internal capacity as the .45 Auto."

45 Super Factory Ballistics

Bullet (grains/type)	Powder	Grains	Velocity	Energy	Source/Comments
120 Lehigh Xtreme Defense			1,600	682	Underwood Ammunition #845-20
170 Lehigh Defense CF			1,250	590	Underwood Ammunition #825-20
185 JHP			1,300	694	Buffalo Bore #45S185
200 JHP			1,200	639	Buffalo Bore #45S200
230 FMJ Flatnose			1,100	618	Buffalo Bore #45S230
255-gr. HARD CAST-FLAT NOSE			1,075	654	Buffalo Bore #45S255

.450 SMC — *NEW*

Historical Notes: In late 2000, Triton Ammunition Corp. announced a new cartridge based on the .45 ACP case head — the .450 SMC, or .450 Short Magnum Cartridge or .450 Small Magnum Cartridge. It is basically a .45 Super with a small primer pocket. External dimensions of the .450 SMC are the same as the .45 Super and .45 ACP. The smaller primer pocket means more brass in the web area, and it differentiates the .450 SMC from the .45 Super. The .450 SMC uses a small magnum rifle primer rather than the standard large pistol primer of the .45 ACP. It was initially offered in Triton's Quik-Shok and Hi-Vel lines.

However, Triton went under, and Mike McNett, founder of Doubletap Ammunition, picked up the rights and tooling for the .450 SMC cartridge. Doubletap is currently the sole producer of .450 SMC.

General Comments: This round is meant to be fired through any firearm that is rated for .45 ACP +P pressure. It pushes a 185-grain JHP to 1,350 fps, a 230-grain JHP to 1200 fps, and a 255-grain hardcast to 1,100 fps. At one point, STI chambered 1911 and 2011 frames in the .450 SMC. This ammunition should only be fired in pistols that have been modified to handle the increased pressure of this round. Several gunsmiths specialize in converting pistols to .450 SMC. The case length is the same as standard .45 ACP, so the same magazines and reloading dies can be used.

.450 SMC Factory Ballistics

Bullet (grains/type)	Powder	Grains	Velocity	Energy	Source/Comments
160 Barnes TAC-XP Lead Free			1,350	648	Doubletap Ammunition
255 SWC Hardcast			1,030	601	Doubletap Ammunition

.454 Casull

Historical Notes: The .454 Casull, originally called the .454 Magnum Revolver, was developed by Dick Casull and Jack Fulmer in 1957. The first public announcement was made by P.O. Ackley in the November 1959 issue of *Guns & Ammo* magazine. Solid-head .45 Colt cases and specially altered Colt's and Ruger single-action revolvers were used for initial development. The .454 Casull employs a special case, originally offered only by Federal, that is .1-inch longer than the .45 Colt case, to prevent this round from chambering in .45 Colt revolvers. A five-shot single-action revolver, designed by Dick Casull and manufactured by Freedom Arms Co., is chambered for this cartridge. The revolver is made of stainless steel throughout, has a 7½-

inch barrel and weighs 50 ounces in standard configuration. Ammunition is now loaded and marketed by Winchester, Hornady, Buffalo Bore, CorBon, and Black Hills Ammunition.

General Comments: The .454 Casull is primarily a hunting cartridge, although it will probably find acceptance among metallic silhouette shooters. The .454 Casull is one of the most powerful revolver cartridges available. Anyone who contemplates hunting dangerous game with a handgun should seriously consider the .454 Casull and the Freedom Arms revolver. For those wishing a reduced load, standard .45 Colt ammunition can be fired in the .454 revolver. There has been a persistent call for a magnum .45 revolver ever since the .44 Magnum was introduced, and the .454 certainly provides all that could be desired in .45-caliber. Firing lead-bullet .45 Colt loads in a .454 can leave a lead ring deposit in the front of the chamber. If this deposit is not removed before chambering and firing full-power .454 loads with the unusually hard bullets used in such rounds, the cylinder can be damaged beyond repair. This is not conjecture—it has happened.

.454 Casull Loading Data and Factory Ballistics

Bullet (grains/type)	Powder	Grains	Velocity	Energy	Source/Comments
240 FA JHP	AA No. 9	31.0	1,916	1,955	Accurate
260 FA JFP	AA No. 9	30.0	1,835	1,945	Accurate
300 H XTP	AA No. 9	26.0	1,623	1,755	Accurate
260 JHP	FL	FL	1,723	1,730	Factory load
300 JHP	FL	FL	1,353	1,220	Factory load
300 Spr UniCore	FL	FL	1,500	1,500	Buffalo Bore factory load
325 LBT LFN	FL	FL	1,525	1,675	Buffalo Bore factory load
360 LBT LWN	FL	FL	1,425	1,630	Buffalo Bore factory load

.460 Smith & Wesson

Historical Notes: Announced in 2005 as a joint Hornady-Smith & Wesson development, the .460 Smith and Wesson (S&W) is the fastest revolver cartridge ever produced, reaching velocities of about 2200 fps with 200-grain bullets. It is chambered in the S&W M460 Extreme Velocity Revolver for long-range handgun hunting. Used by a skilled pistol shooter, the .460 S&W cartridge can achieve MOA accuracy at 100 yards.

General Comments: The .460 S&W uses the .454 Casull case lengthened to 1.8 inches as its parent case. It is the first commercial revolver cartridge to use tipped bullets. Hornady and CorBon offer loaded ammunition for the .460 S&W. Hornady and Starline supply reloading components and data for this cartridge. It is well suited for whitetail deer hunting at 150 yard-plus ranges.

.460 Smith & Wesson Loading Data and Factory Ballistics

Bullet (grains/type)	Powder	Grains	Velocity	Energy	Source/Comments
220 Hornady SST	FL		2,200	2,149	Hornady
225 Barnes X	H110	42.0	2,243	2,513	Hodgdon
240 Hdy XTP	H4227	45.0	2,198	2,574	Hodgdon
250 Barnes X	Li'l Gun	42.0	2,044	2,319	Hodgdon

.45 Colt

Historical Notes: This was introduced in 1873 by Colt as one of the cartridges for its famous Peacemaker single-action revolver. Both the cartridge and the revolver were adopted by the U.S. Army in 1875. This served as the official handgun cartridge of the Army until 1892 (some 17 years), when it was replaced by the .38

Long Colt. The .45 Colt is one of the cartridges that helped civilize and settle the American West. It was originally a black-powder number, loaded with 40 grains of FFg powder and a 255-grain lead bullet. Testing has demonstrated that muzzle velocity of the original loading almost certainly exceeded 900 fps in the original revolvers. Various importers offer excellent Italian-made replicas of the original Colt model, and Ruger and several other makes of more modern single-action revolvers are currently chambered in .45 Colt.

General Comments: This is one of the most famous American handgun cartridges and still a favorite with big-bore advocates. It is extremely accurate and has more knockdown and stopping power than nearly any common handgun cartridge except the .44 Magnum. It is a popular field cartridge and can be safely handloaded to velocities in excess of 1000 fps with 250-grain cast bullets. Black-powder revolvers should not be used with any load developing more than about 800 fps muzzle velocity. Although the .45 Colt has a larger case than the .45 Automatic or the .45 Auto-Rim, it is not quite as efficient with factory-duplicating loads using smokeless powder. Using special revolvers, some very heavy loads have been established for the .45 Colt case. These put it in almost the same class as the .44 Magnum. Such loads should not be attempted except by an experienced person who fully understands what he is doing and who will ensure that those loads are only used in a revolver that will withstand the pressures generated. This is another cartridge that has developed a rebirth of interest. Federal, Remington, Winchester, Black Hills Ammunition, CorBon, and others all offer .45 Colt loads.

.45 Colt Loading Data and Factory Ballistics

Bullet (grains/type)	Powder	Grains	Velocity	Energy	Source/Comments
185 JHP	700X	9.0	1,100	497	Sierra
225 JHP	Unique	9.0	950	451	Speer
240 JHP	Unique	8.7	850	385	Sierra
250 JHP	IMR 4227	17.0	800	355	Hornady, Nosler
250 JHP	Unique	7.5	800	355	Hornady
260 JHP	IMR 4227	16.0	850	417	Speer
255 Lead	Black powder (FFg)	40.0	930	490	Factory load
225 JHP	Smokeless powder	FL	920	423	Factory load
255 Lead	Smokeless powder	FL	860	420	Factory load

.455 Revolver MkII
.455 Webley Revolver MkII

Historical Notes: This is a British military revolver cartridge adopted in 1897 and designated the .455 Revolver MkII. It is a modification of an earlier round originally designed for blackpowder, the .455 Revolver MkI. Modern revolvers will chamber and fire either the old or the new cartridge. The .455 Webley was used officially in both World War I and II, although it was partly replaced by the .380/200 (.38 S&W), which was adopted in the mid-1930s. In addition to the Webley revolver, both Colt and Smith & Wesson chambered arms for this cartridge. Ammunition was loaded by American companies up to about 1940.

General Comments: The .455 Webley Revolver cartridge was never very popular or widely used in the United States, because standard American sporting and military arms in .45 Automatic were more easily obtainable. However, after World War II, many obsolete .455 revolvers were sold at low prices in the United States, and this changed the situation somewhat. It is better known and more widely used than previously, but most .455 revolvers have been altered to shoot the .45 Automatic through the use of half-moon clips or the rimmed .45 Auto-Rim cartridge. The .455 Revolver is not a very satisfactory field cartridge because of the low velocity and curved trajectory. On the other hand, it has excellent short-range stopping power. It can be improved by handloading and with the use of semi-wadcutter, hunting-type bullets. It is now essentially obsolete. However, Fiocchi of Italy still produces commercial ammunition labeled .455 Webley (MKI).

Bullet (grains/type)	Powder	Grains	Velocity	Energy	Source/Comments
260 Lead	Unique	5.0	610	213	NA
262 FMJ	FL	FL	700	285	Fiocchi factory load
265 FMJ	ML	ML	600	220	Military load

.45 Colt Government

Historical Notes: This was something of a bastardized cartridge, combining the length of the S&W Schofield revolver round with the rim of the Colt SAA round. Army ordnance described at least one version of this cartridge officially as Revolver Ball Cartridge, Caliber .45. The Remington-UMC version was labeled (on the box and case heads) as .45 Colt. The evident military incentive for such a loading seems obvious: With both S&W and Colt .45-caliber revolvers (similar, but differently chambered) in use, supplying the correct ammunition to far-flung outposts must have been something of a logistical nightmare. One has to wonder how often troopers found themselves in possession of ammunition that would not work in the gun they had been issued. The .45 Colt ammunition is longer than the Schofield cylinder; chambering Schofield ammunition in the Colt leaves precious little room for rim clearance. It seems likely that some early .45 Colt SAAs would not have chambered some Schofield ammunition, even when the gun was clean. Conversely, the .45 Colt Government, combining the shorter case and smaller rim, worked (after a fashion) in either gun. Ballistically, it differed little from the standard .45 Colt ordnance loading, which was significantly lighter than the original commercial loading. Available information suggests that this cartridge was available between the late 1870s and the 1930s.

General Comments: When the chips are down, having any ammunition that will fit and work in the gun at hand is much better than throwing rocks. However, the Schofield does not function as dependably using the smaller-rimmed .45 Colt Government cases; incautious manipulation or a somewhat worn gun can result in the extractor slipping past the rim of one or more partially extracted cases. The gun cannot, then, be closed. Worse, if the cylinder is the slightest bit dirty (black powder, remember), removing the offending case can require a dowel, a hammer, and at least three hands!

.45 Colt Government Factory Ballistics

Bullet (grains/type)	Powder	Grains	Velocity	Energy	Source/Comments
255 LRNFP	Black powder (FFFg)	28.0	800	360	Factory load, 1.10-inch case *

*QuickLOAD estimated data. Semi-balloon head sample, headstamped "REM-UMC" over ".45 COLT;" slightly rounded primer stamped "U;" 255-grain RNFP bullet appears to match bullets used in original .45 (Long) Colt loads.

.45 Smith & Wesson (.45 S&W Schofield)

Historical Notes: This cartridge was introduced in 1875 for the Smith & Wesson Schofield revolver. This revolver was adopted by the U.S. Army in that year and used until 1892, when it and the .45 Colt Army revolver were replaced by the Colt Army & Navy Model in .38-caliber. Commercial .45 S&W ammunition was loaded continuously until about 1940 and was reintroduced about 1997 by Black Hills Ammunition, in response to demands from cowboy action shooters for a superior, reduced-power .45-caliber cartridge. Some authorities believe Gen. George A. Custer used a Schofield revolver at the Battle of the Little Big Horn.

General Comments: The Smith & Wesson Schofield revolver was a single-action, hinged-frame type. It employed a special heavy barrel latch designed by Gen. Schofield, hence the name. The cylinder of this revolver was not long enough to accept the .45 Colt cartridge, so a shorter round was designed. In addition, to improve extraction, rim diameter was enlarged slightly. Later, to simplify supply contingencies, a .45-caliber cartridge designed with a rim to fit both .45 Colt-chambered revolvers and .45 S&W-chambered revolvers was loaded by government arsenals. A similar commercial loading, eventually called the .45 Colt Government, followed. This cartridge was used in both the Schofield Model and the Colt Army Model. Ammunition for the .45 S&W can be used in most .45 Colt revolvers, but the reverse is not true. Although the Colt Single Action Army revolver is the one always depicted as the universal sidearm of the Old West, the S&W was also quite popular. These old guns were made for black powder, so heavy smokeless powder charges should never be used. This cartridge and handgun are again in production, with Black Hills Ammunition supplying loads that duplicate the original, and Navy Arms and others marketing the replica revolver.

.45 Smith & Wesson (.45 S&W Schofield) Loading Data and Factory Ballistics

Bullet (grains/type)	Powder	Grains	Velocity	Energy	Source/Comments
230 Lead	Bullseye	4.6	740	277	NA
230 Lead	Black powder (FFFg)	28.0	730	276	NA
250 Lead	Black powder (FFFg)	28.0	710	283	Factory load
230 Lead	Smokeless powder	FI	730	276	Factory load
250 Lead	Smokeless powder	FL	710	283	Factory load

.455 Webley Automatic

Historical Notes: The .455 Webley semi-rimmed pistol cartridge was adopted by the British Navy in 1912 for use in the 455 Webley self-loading pistol. The pistol was not entirely satisfactory and was replaced by the end of World War I. The cartridge resembles the .45 Automatic, but uses a very blunt pointed bullet.

General Comments: This cartridge has seen very little use in the United States, although a number of Webley pistols in this chambering were sold in military surplus stores after World War II. In performance, it is inferior to the .45 Automatic. Because of the relatively low velocity, it is not as good a field cartridge as the .45 Automatic.

.455 Webley Automatic Loading Data and Factory Ballistics

Bullet (grains/type)	Powder	Grains	Velocity	Energy	Source/Comments
200 Lead	Unique	6.2	775	265	Lyman No. 452460
224 FMJ	Smokeless powder	ML	700	247	Military load

.455 Revolver MkI
.455 Colt/.455 Enfield

Historical Notes: The .455 Revolver MkI was adopted by the British Army in 1892 to replace the .476 MkIII and the .455 Enfield MkI ammunition. Despite the different designations, these two cartridges actually have the same case dimensions; they differ only in bullet diameter, type, and construction. The .476 was a black-powder cartridge, and so was the 455 MkI at its inception. However, in 1894, the propellant was changed to the new cordite, and, after a few years, it was found that the smokeless powder burned more efficiently in a shorter case. Consequently, a shorter case was adopted in 1897 and this altered round was designated the .455 Revolver MkII. This is the .455 Webley familiar to American shooters. It has a case .11-inch to .14-inch shorter than the original round.

The .455 Colt is nothing more than Colt's commercial designation of the .455 Revolver MkI, in a somewhat improved loading. It is listed in various publications and was loaded by American companies under this name, but was discontinued in the late 1930s. This is not a Colt-designed cartridge, but it does have different ballistics than the British MkI. Later, new cartridge dimensions were adopted, and this round was called the .455 Colt MkII.

General Comments: The .455 MkI, .455 MkII, .455 Colt, and the original .476 Revolver rounds are all interchangeable and can be fired in early British service arms. The .450 Revolver cartridge can also be fired in .455 revolvers. However, the .455 Webley is the only one still commercially loaded. Use the same bullet and .455 Webley loading data for any of the .455 cartridges listed here. Power and performance are the same. Fiocchi has recently offered this ammunition.

Editor's note: Those not at least slightly confused by the profusion of large-caliber British cartridge designations are a rare breed.

.455 Revolver MkI, .455 Colt Factory Ballistics

Bullet (grains/type)	Powder	Grains	Velocity	Energy	Source/Comments
265 Lead	Black powder	FL	700	289	Kynoch factory load
265 Lead	Cordite powder	FL	600	212	Kynoch factory load
265 Lead	Smokeless powder	FL	757	337	Factory load, U.S.
262 Lead	FL	FL	850	420	Fiocchi factory load

.450 Revolver/.450 Adams/ .450 Short/.450 Colt

Historical Notes: This was the first centerfire revolver cartridge adopted by the British Army. It was adopted for the Adams revolver in November 1868, and saw service until replaced by the .476 Enfield (Mks I & II) in 1880. It was not a satisfactory military round, but became a popular commercial cartridge. American companies loaded it to about 1940, and both Colt and Smith & Wesson chambered revolvers for it. Also loaded in Europe, it is now obsolete. It is often listed as the .450 Short, .450 Adams, or .450 Colt. A .450 MkIII was used in World War I as a reserve arm cartridge in Britain.

General Comments: The .450 Revolver cartridge was originally a black-powder round, loaded with 13 grains of black powder and a 225-grain bullet. Smokeless powder loads were also manufactured. The .450 can be fired in any .455 Webley revolver, and it was often used as a light target-load option. It is in about the same class as the old .44 S&W Russian and makes a good short-range self-defense cartridge. Ammunition can be made from shortened .455 Webley cases. It has been essentially obsolete for decades, though Fiocchi still occasionally offers this loading.

.450 Revolver/.450 Adams Factory Ballistics

Bullet (grains/type)	Powder	Grains	Velocity	Energy	Source/Comments
225 Lead	Black powder	FL	650	211	Kynoch factory load
225 Lead	Smokeless powder	FL	700	245	Kynoch factory load
226 Lead	FL	FL	700	245	Fiocchi factory load

.476 Eley/.476 Enfield MkIII/ .476 Revolver (.455/476)

Historical Notes: This was a British military cartridge used from late 1881 to mid-1891, when the .455 Webley Revolver MkI cartridge was introduced. Sometimes called the .455/476, this round has the same case and bullet dimensions as the .455 MkI, except that the latter has a .05 mm shorter case. Unlike the .476 MkII, the MkIII has a clay plug in the hollow base. The charge was 18 grains of black powder. Also known as the .476 Eley and .476 Revolver, the MkIII can be used in any British service .455, but the bullet may be a bit oversized for use in .455 Colts or S&Ws of late manufacture.

General Comments: The .476 has caused much confusion among collectors. Here are the facts we believe. In November 1868, the British Army adopted the .450 Adams revolver cartridge. Generally unsatisfactory, nevertheless the .450 was used in World War I as a reserve weapon, with a MkIII .450 cartridge introduced at the same time. The .450 was officially replaced in 1880 by the .476 Enfield MkI, shortly followed by the .476 MkIII as outlined in the preceding text. In July 1891, the .455 MkI Webley appeared. Next was a black-powder load, then a .455 MkI Cordite round (6.5 grains) in September 1894. About the same time, the .442 cartridge for the R.I.C. was adopted (June 4, 1892), made in only one Mark as a service round. There were also blank cartridges in use—as there were with about all these British handgun cartridges. The .455 MkII cordite load was adopted July 1897, this being the first "short" case load, case length being reduced to 19 millimeters from the original 22 millimeters. Two cordite loads—a MkIII round approved February 1898, and a MkIV approved May 1912—were dropped because of bullet form (both were considered of "dumdum" or "explosive" quality). The last of the .455 ball cartridges was the Mk VI, adopted September 1939, carrying a jacketed bullet and loaded with Cordite (5.5 t7.5 grains) or nitrocellulose (5.5 grains). A Mk V had briefly appeared, which was similar to the MkIV, but with antimony in the bullet as a hardening agent.

.480 Ruger

Historical Notes: After a half-century of production, millions of shooters use Bill Ruger's firearms—but only one very special pistol cartridge bears the man's name. The .480 Ruger was never intended to be the biggest and heaviest-recoiling handgun cartridge on the block. It splits the difference between the .44 Remington Magnum and .454 Casull cartridges.

General Comments: Using a Hornady 325-grain XTP Magnum bullet (diameter .475-inch) and Hornady brass, the .480 Ruger offers a significant velocity and energy increase over the .44 Remington Magnum cartridge, but without the recoil disadvantage of other super-powered handgun cartridges. The key to delivering the two-thirds of a ton of muzzle energy is a well-reasoned balance between bullet weight, velocity, and operating pressure, in a cartridge derived from the venerable .45-70 case. The cartridge is chambered in Ruger's rugged double-action six-shooter, the Super Redhawk, which wears an integral scope mounting system on the top strap. It should serve big-game handgun hunters and metallic silhouette target shooters with distinction.

.480 Ruger Factory Ballistics

Bullet (grains/type)	Powder	Grains	Velocity	Energy	Source/Comments
325 Hornady XTP	FL	FL	1,350	1,315	Hornady

.500 JRH

Historical Notes: The .500 JRH is the brainchild of Jack Huntington, a gunsmith out of Northern California. Jack wanted a full-power, no-compromise, .50-caliber cartridge that would fit in a standard-frame revolver, like the Freedom Arms Model 83, with a maximum case length of 1.4 inches. Huntington turned a dummy case in his lathe in 1993, and the .500 JRH became an honest to goodness commercially loaded reality, when Starline began producing brass and Buffalo Bore began offering loaded ammunition.

General Comments: The very first .500 JRH revolver was a Model 83 from Freedom Arms and, today, Magnum Research is offering its BFR chambered for the .500 JRH. Brass for the round, which is manufactured by Starline, is available from JRH Advanced Gunsmithing, though .500 Smith & Wesson brass can be easily cut down to form .500 JRH brass. The specifications call for turning down the rim, but Magnum Research BFR revolvers will accept the larger rim of the .500 Smith & Wesson case. The .500 JRH has a reputation for fine accuracy, and is should be very effective for hunting large and even dangerous game.

.500 JRH Loading Data and Factory Ballistics

Bullet (grains/type)	Powder	Grains	Velocity	Energy	Source/Comments
350 JFP	FL	FL	1,350	1,416	Grizzly Cartridge Factory Load
400 WFN - Cast	FL	FL	1,300	1,501	Grizzly Cartridge Factory Load

Bullet (grains/type)	Powder	Grains	Velocity	Energy	Source/Comments
425 TCFN - Cast	FL	FL	1,380	1,797	Buffalo Bore Factory Load
440 LFN - Cast	FL	FL	950	882	Buffalo Bore Factory Load
440 LFN - Cast	W 231	10	950	882	Jack Huntington
440 TC	W 296	29.5	1,350	1,780	Jack Huntington

.500 Smith & Wesson

Historical Notes: Introduced by Smith and Wesson in 2003 for big-game hunting in the first commercial .50-caliber revolver, the .500 S&W became the most powerful factory production cartridge in history. The M500 revolver and .500 S&W cartridge constitute an effective combination for big-game hunting at reasonable ranges.

General Comments: The .500 S&W uses a rimmed case 1.625 inches long, with a rim diameter of .560 inch. To fit in the M500 revolver's cylinder, the overall length for a loaded cartridge cannot exceed 2¼ inches. The .500 S&W cartridge is best suited to heavy-duty hunting revolvers or modern single-shot pistols and rifles. Factory ammunition is available from Hornady, CorBon, and Winchester. Hornady and Starline offer reloading components.

.500 Smith & Wesson Loading Data and Factory Ballistics

Bullet (grains/type)	Powder	Grains	Velocity	Energy	Source/Comments
350 Hornady XTP	FL	FL	1,900	2,805	Hornady
500 Hornady SP	FL	FL	1,425	2,254	Hornady
275 Barnes XPB	Li'lGun	44.0	2,137	2,788	Hodgdon
350 Hdy XTP	H110	43.0	1,877	2,737	Hodgdon
400 Sierra JSP	Li'l Gun	37.0	1,725	2,642	Hodgdon
500 Hdy SP	H110	32.2	1,436	2,286	Hodgdon

.50 Action Express

Historical Notes: The .50 Action Express (.50 AE) was developed in 1988 for the IMI Desert Eagle semi-auto pistol, imported by Magnum Research, Inc. It is another development by Evan Whildin, then of Action Arms. It was part of a program to upgrade performance of the semi-auto pistol through new cartridge design. The .50 AE has the same rim diameter, case length, and overall length as the .44 Magnum. However, base diameter is .547-inch, so, like the .41 AE, the .50 AE has a rebated rim. This allows simple adaptation to the Desert Eagle pistol, which was designed for use with the .44 Magnum. Since the rim is the same, it is possible to change chamberings by the simple process of installing a new barrel, a very practical design.

General Comments: The .50 AE uses a .500-inch bullet * weighing 325 grains at a muzzle velocity of 1400 fps. This load develops 1414 ft-lbs of muzzle energy, which makes the .50 AE one of the world's most powerful pistol cartridges. This is an excellent field cartridge for deer-size animals or as a backup when hunting dangerous game. Speer now offers factory ammunition.

* The original design featured a standard .50-caliber .510-inch bullet, but when a polygonally-rifled bore was adopted, the gauge plug defining the limit of "Sporting Devices" fell through the barrel. This rendered the .50 AE a "destructive device," so bore size was reduced and the case was tapered to accommodate the smaller bullet.

.50 Action Express Loading Data and Factory Ballistics

Bullet (grains/type)	Powder	Grains	Velocity	Energy	Source/Comments
300 JHP	AA No. 7	27.5	1,579	1,568	Accurate Arms
325 Speer Uni-Core	AA 1680	37.8	1,305	1,227	Accurate
325 JHP	FL	FL	1,400	1,414	Factory load

.50 Remington (M71 Army)

Historical Notes: This cartridge was introduced, in its original version, as the .50 Remington Pistol, Navy Model 1867. The cartridge listed here is the 1871 Army modification. Both were used in slightly different models of the Remington single-shot rolling block pistol. The older Navy cartridge had a straight, tapered case, while the Army round had a slight but distinct bottleneck. The Army cartridge also had a larger-diameter rim that prevented it being fired in the Navy pistol. However, the Navy cartridge would chamber and fire okay in the Army pistol. Commercial ammunition was available until about 1920 and used the Navy dimensions. Ammunition was loaded by both Remington and Winchester.

General Comments: This is an obsolete black-powder cartridge of the early centerfire-type originally made with an inside primer. The old Remington rolling-block pistols are much esteemed for conversion to modern cartridges and for target shooting. The standard load was 25 grains of FFg black powder. The large, heavy bullet should have been a good man-stopper and would certainly have been adequate for the usual run of small to medium game at short range. Ammunition for the Army-type pistol can be made from .50-70 cases. Cases with the early inside primers are *not* reloadable. Some commercial cartridges made with Boxer primers could be reloaded. Both cartridge types are now collector's items.

.50 Remington (M71 Army) Loading Data and Factory Ballistics

Bullet (grains/type)	Powder	Grains	Velocity	Energy	Source/Comments
265 Lead	Unique	7.0	750	330	Lyman No. 518144
300 Lead	ML	ML	600	240	Military load

Dimensional Data

Cartridge	Case	Bullet Dia.	Neck Dia.	Shoulder Dia.	Base Dia.	Rim Dia.	Rim Thick.	Case Length	Ctge. Length	Primer	Page
2.7mm Kolibri	D	.107	.139	UNK/NA	.140	.140	UNK/NA	.37	.43	UNK/NA	417
4.5x39Rmm SPS	A	.177	UNK/NA	UNK/NA	UNK/NA	UNK/NA	UNK/NA	1.575	5.71	UNK/NA	417
3mm Kolibri	D	.120	.150	–	.150	.150		.32	.43	UNK/NA	418
4.25mm Liliput	D	.167	.198	–	.198	.198		.41	.56	UNK/NA	418
5mm Clement Auto	C	.202	.223	.277	.281	.281	.025	.71	1.01	UNK/NA	418
5mm Bergmann	D	.203	.230	–	.273	.274	.020	.59	.96	UNK/NA	419
5.45X18mm Soviet	C	.210	.220	UNK/NA	.300	.300	UNK	.7	.98	SB	419
.22 Remington Jet (.22 CF Magnum)	A	.223	.247	.350	.376	.440	.055	1.28	1.58	SP	419
.221 Remington Fireball	C	.224	.251	.355	.375	.375	.040	1.40	1.82	SP	420
5.5mm Velo Dog Revolver	B	.225	.248	UNK/NA	.253	.308	UNK	1.12	1.35	SP-B	421
5.8x21mm DAP 92	C	.236	.259	.306	.313	.314	.044	.827	1.28	SP	421
.25 Automatic Colt Pistol (.25 ACP)	D	.251	.276	UNK/NA	.277	.298	.038	.62	.91	SP	421
.25 North American Arms (NAA)	C	.251	.276	.330	.337	.337	.046	.745	.960	UNK/NA	422
.256 Winchester Magnum	A	.257	.277	.378	.378	.440	.055	1.30	1.53	SP	422
6.5mm Bergmann	C	.264	.289	.325	.367	.370	.025	.87	1.23	UNK/NA	423
7mm Nambu	C	.280	.296	.337	.351	.359	UNK	.78	1.06	B	423
7mm Bench Rest Remington	Based on Rem. 308 BR case shortened to 1.50									SP	424
7.62mm Russian Nagant Revolver	B	.295	.286	UNK/NA	.335	.388	UNK/NA	1.53	1.53	B	425
.32 Protector	B	.300	.310	UNK/NA	.310	.352	.040	.350	.555	UNK/NA	425
7.65mm Roth-Sauer	D	.301	.332	UNK/NA	.335	.335	UNK/NA	.51	.84	14.2	425
7.7mm Bittner	B	.302	.319	UNK/NA	.337	.390	UNK/NA	.665	1.00	B	426
7.62X25mm Russian Tokarev	C	.307	.330	.370	.380	.390	UNK	.97	1.35	B	426
.30 Borchardt	C	.307	.331	.370	.385	.390	UNK/NA	.99	1.34	UNK/NA	427
7.63mm (7.65) Mannlicher	D	.308	.331	UNK/NA	.332	.334	.030	.84	1.12	B	427
.30 (7.65x21mm) Luger	C	.308	.322	.374	.388	.391	.045	.75	1.15	SP-B	427
.30 (7.63x25mm) Mauser	C	.308	.332	.370	.381	.390	.045	.99	1.36	SP-B	428
7.62x38mm Silent Cartridge	C	.311	.434	.438	.438	.440	.053	1.496	1.654	S	428
7.62x42mm Silent Cartridge	C	.311	.434	.438	.438	.440	.053	1.654	2.05	S	428
7.62x63mm Silent Cartridge	C	.311	.434	.438	.438	.440	.053	2.48	3.031	S	428
.32 H&R Magnum	B	.312	.333	UNK/NA	.333	.371	.050	1.08	1.35	SP	429
.32 S&W	B	.312	.334	UNK/NA	.335	.375	.045	.61	.92	SP	430
.32 S&W Long/.32 Colt New Police	B	.312	.335	UNK/NA	.335	.375	.048	.93	1.27	SP	430
.32 North American Arms (NAA)	C	.312	.337	.373	.374	.374	.045	.68	.984	UNK/NA	431
7.92x24mm	D	.312	.360	.360	.360	.339	.050	.94	1.276	SP	431
.327 Federal Magnum	B	.312	.337	UNK/NA	.337	.371	.050	1.20	1.46	S	432
.32 Automatic Colt Pistol (ACP)	H	.3125	.3365	UNK/NA	.337	.358	.045	.68	.984	SP	433
.32 Short Colt	B	.313	.313	UNK/NA	.318	.374	.045	.63	1.00	SP	433
.32 Long Colt	B	.313	.313	UNK/NA	.318	.374	.045	.92	1.26	SP	433
.32 Colt	B	?	.313	UNK/NA	.318	.374	.052	.755	1.26	SP	434
.320 Revolver	B	.317	.320	UNK/NA	.322	.350	UNK/NA	.62	.90	B	434
7.5mm Swiss Army	B	.317	.335	UNK/NA	.345	.407	UNK/NA	.89	1.29	B	434
.35 S&W Auto/.35 Automatic	D	.320	UNK	UNK/NA	UNK	UNK/NA	UNK/NA	UNK/NA	UNK/NA	UNK/NA	435
8mm Rast-Gasser	B	.320	.332	UNK/NA	.334	.376	UNK/NA	1.037	1.391	UNK/NA	435
8mm Nambu	G	.320	.338	.388	.408	.413	UNK/NA	.86	1.25	B	435
8mm Lebel Revolver	B	.323	.350	UNK/NA	.384	.400	UNK/NA	1.07	1.44	B	436
7.5mm Swedish Nagant Revolver	B	.325	.328	UNK/NA	.350	.406	UNK/NA	.89	1.35	B	436
8.5 Mars	C	.335	.336	.415	.505	.491	.04	1.128	1.583	B	437
9mm Ultra	D	.355	.374	UNK/NA	.386	.366	UNK	.72	1.03	SP-B	437
9mm Bayard Long	D	.355	.375	UNK/NA	.390	.392	UNK	.91	1.32	B	438
9mm Browning Long	D	.355	.376	UNK/NA	.384	.404	UNK	.80	1.10	B	438
9mm Mauser	D	.355	.376	UNK/NA	.389	.390	.050	.981	1.38	B	439
9mm Winchester Magnum	D	.355	.379	UNK/NA	.392	.394	.046	1.16	1.545	SP	439
.356 TSW (Team Smith & Wesson)	D	.355	.380	.3904	.3907	.394	.066	.85	1.16	SP	440
9mm Glisenti	D	.355	.380	UNK/NA	.392	.393	UNK	.75	1.15	B	440
9mm ABC Mi Bullet	D	.355	.380	UNK/NA	.392	.393	.042	.754	1.16	SP	441

Dimensional Data

Cartridge	Case	Bullet Dia.	Neck Dia.	Shoulder Dia.	Base Dia.	Rim Dia.	Rim Thick.	Case Length	Ctge. Length	Primer	Page
9mm Luger (9x19mm Parabellum)	D	.355	.380	UNK/NA	.392	.393	.042	.754	1.16	SP-B	441
9x21mm	D	.355	.380	UNK/NA	.392	.393	UNK	.830	1.16	SP	442
9mm Steyr	D	.355	.380	UNK/NA	.380	.381	UNK	.90	1.30	B	443
9x23mm Winchester	D	.355	.380	UNK/NA	.390	.392	.042	.900	1.245	LP	443
9mm Federal	B	.355	.382	UNK/NA	.386	.435	UNK	.754	1.163	SP	444
.380 Automatic Colt Pistol (ACP)/ 9mm Browning Short/9mm Kurz	D	.356	.373	UNK/NA	.373	.374	.040	.68	.98	SP	445
.38 Dardick Tround	N/A	UNK/NA	UNK/NA	UNK/NA	UNK/NA	UNK/NA	UNK/NA	UNK/NA	UNK/NA	UNK/NA	445
.38 AMU	H	.357	.259	.373	.376	.404	.047	1.153	1.153	SP	446
.38 Short and Long Colt	D	.357	.357	UNK/NA	.378	.433	.055	.76	1.10	SP	446
.357 Remington Maximum	B	.357	.375	UNK/NA	.375	.433	.055	1.59	1.97	SP	447
.38 Special (.38 S&W Special)	B	.357	.379	UNK/NA	.379	.440	.054	1.16	1.55	SP	448
.357 Atomic GWA	B	0.357	0.379		0.379	0.440	0.055	1.29	1.51	SP	448
.357 Magnum S&W	B	.357	.379	UNK/NA	.379	.440	.055	1.29	1.51	SP	449
.357 SIG	C	.357	.381	.424	.425	.424	.055	.865	1.140	SP	450
.38 Automatic/.38 Super Automatic	H	.358	.382	UNK/NA	.383	.405	.045	.90	1.28	SP	451
.360 Mars	C	.359	.370	.455	.505	.491	.040	1.045	1.414	B	451
.38 S&W/.38 Colt New Police	B	.359	.386	UNK/NA	.386	.433	.055	.78	1.20	SP	452
9mm Russian Makarov	D	.363	.384	UNK/NA	.389	.396	UNK/NA	.71	.97	B	452
.380 Short & Long Revolver	B	.375	.377	UNK/NA	.380	.426	.046	.70	1.10	SP-B	453
9.4mm Dutch	B	0.380	0.430		0.433	0.480	0.054	1.070	1.310	B	453
.375 Super Magnum	B	0.375	0.415		0.416	0.506	0.063	1.610	1.965	LP	453
.375 Atomic	B	0.375	0.400		0.415	0.502	0.063	1.4	1.62	L	454
9.8mm Auto Colt	D	.378	.404	UNK/NA	.404	.405	UNK/NA	.912	1.267	UNK/NA	455
.41 Long Colt	B	.386	.404	UNK/NA	.405	.430	.052	1.138	1.39	SP	455
.40 S&W Auto	D	.400	.423	UNK/NA	.423	.424	.050	.850	1.135	SP	455
10mm Automatic	D	.400	.423	UNK/NA	.423	.424	.050	.99	1.26	LP	456
.41 Short Colt	D	.401	.404	UNK/NA	.405	.430	.052	UNK/NA	UNK/NA	SP	457
.401 Bobcat	B	0.401	0.425		0.442	0.472	0.045	1.400	1.550	L	457
.401 Herter Powermag	B	.401	?	UNK/NA	.428	UNK/NA	UNK/NA	1.271	UNK/NA	UNK/NA	458
.41 Remington Magnum	B	.410	.432	UNK/NA	.433	.488	.054	1.28	1.58	LP	458
.41 Action Express	J	.410	.434	UNK/NA	.435	.394	.045	.866	1.17	SP	459
.414 Super Mag	B	.410	.434	UNK/NA	.435	.492	.059	1.610	1.965	L	460
.44 Merwin & Hulbert	B	.424	.442	UNK/NA	.442	.502	.060	1.15	1.53	UNK/NA	460
10.4mm Italian Revolver	B	.422	.444	UNK/NA	.451	.505	UNK/NA	.89	1.25	B	460
.44 S&W Russian	B	.429	.457	UNK/NA	.457	.515	.050	.97	1.43	LP	461
.44 S&W Special	B	.429	.457	UNK/NA	.457	.514	.055	1.16	1.62	LP	461
.44 Remington Magnum	B	.429	.457	UNK/NA	.457	.514	.055	1.29	1.61	LP	462
.44 Auto Mag	D	.429	.457	UNK/NA	.470	.473	.048	1.298	1.620	LP	463
.44 S&W American	B	.434	.438	UNK/NA	.440	.506	.050	.91	1.44	20	463
.44 Webley	B	.436	.470	UNK/NA	.472	.503	UNK/NA	.69	1.10	20	464
.44 Bull Dog	B	.440	.470	UNK/NA	.473	.503	UNK/NA	.57	.95	SP-B	464
10.6 German Ordnance	B	0.417	0.430	0.453	0.454	0.509	0.060	0.981	1.45	B	464
.44 Colt	B	.443	.450	UNK/NA	.456	.483	UNK/NA	1.10	1.50	16	464
11.75mm Montenegrin	B	.445	.472	UNK/NA	.490	.555	UNK/NA	1.40	1.73	UNK/NA	465
.445 Super Magnum	B	0.429	0.456		0.457	0.514	0.055	1.610	1.965	LP	466
.45 Mars Short	D	.450	.470	.480	.505	.491	.040	0.841	1.162	B	466
.45 Mars Long	D	.450	.470	.480	.505	.491	.040	1.152	1.485	B	466
11mm German Service	B	.451	.449	UNK/NA	.453	.509	UNK/NA	.96	1.21	23	467
11mm French Ordnance	B	.451	.449	UNK/NA	.460	.491	.035	.71	1.18	16	467
.45 Winchester Magnum	D	.451	.475	UNK/NA	.477	.481	.045	1.198	1.55	LP	467
.451 Detonics Magnum	D	0.451	0.475		0.477	0.481	0.045	0.944	1.294	LP	468
.460 Rowland	D	.451	.476	UNK/NA	.476	.476	.044	.955	1.27	LP	469
.45 Webley	B	.452	.471	UNK/NA	.471	.504	UNK/NA	.82	1.15	LP-B	469
.45 Auto-Rim	B	.452	.472	UNK/NA	.476	.516	.085	.898	1.28	LP	470

Dimensional Data

Cartridge	Case	Bullet Dia.	Neck Dia.	Shoulder Dia.	Base Dia.	Rim Dia.	Rim Thick.	Case Length	Ctge. Length	Primer	Page
.45 Glock Auto Pistol (GAP)	D	.452	.473	UNK/NA	.476	.470	.049	.760	1.137	LP	470
.45 Automatic Short/.45 HP	D	.452	.476	UNK/NA	.476	.476	.044	.860	1.17	LP	471
.45 Automatic Match	D	.452	.476	UNK/NA	.476	.476	.044	.898	1.14	LP	471
.45 ABC Mi Bullet	D	.452	.476	UNK/NA	.476	.476	.044	.898	1.17	LP	472
.45 Automatic Colt Pistol (ACP)	D	.452	.476	UNK/NA	.476	.476	.044	.898	1.17	LP	473
.45 Super	D	0.452	0.476		0.476	0.476	0.044	0.898	1.17	LP	473
.450 SMC	D	0.452	0.476		0.476	0.476	0.044	0.898	1.17	SR	474
.454 Casull	B	.452	.476	UNK/NA	.480	.512	.055	1.39	1.70	S*	474
.460 Smith & Wesson	B	.452	.478	UNK/NA	.478	.520	.059	.1.80	2.290	LP	475
.45 Colt	B	.454	.476	UNK/NA	.480	.512	.055	1.29	1.60	LP	475
.455 Webley Revolver Mk-II	B	.454	.476	UNK/NA	.480	.535	UNK/NA	.77	1.23	LP-B	476
.45 Colt Government	B	.454	.478	UNK/NA	.478	.506	.055	1.10	1.44	LP	477
.45 S&W Schofield	B	.454	.478	UNK/NA	.478	.522	.055	1.10	1.43	LP	477
.455 Webley Automatic	H	.455	.473	UNK/NA	.474	.500	UNK/NA	.93	1.23	B	478
.455 Enfield (.455 Colt)	B	.455	.473	UNK/NA	.478	.530	.035	.87	1.35	LP-B	478
.450 Revolver	B	.455	.475	UNK/NA	.477	.510	UNK/NA	.69	1.10	16	479
.476 Enfield	B	.472	.474	UNK/NA	.478	.530	UNK/NA	.87	1.33	UNK/NA	479
.480 Ruger	B	.475	.504	UNK/NA	.540	.540	.065	1.285	1.650	UNK	480
.500 JRH	B	.500	.527	UNK/NA	.527	.545	.055	1.40	1.80	L	480
.500 Smith & Wesson	B	.500	.530	UNK/NA	.530	.560	.059	2.250	UNK/NA	LP	481
.50 Action Express	J	.500	.540	UNK/NA	.547	.514	.055	1.285	1.610	LP	481
.50 Remington Army	A	.508	.532	.564	.565	.665	UNK/NA	.875	1.24	UNK/NA	482

Notes on handgun primers: Magnum pistol cartridges are usually loaded with Magnum pistol primers and the ..22 Remington Jet and 2.56 Winchester are sometimes loaded with Small Rifle primers. During WWI, Frankford Arsenal made .45 Automatic cases with special No. 70 primers of .204" diameter instead of the standard .210."

Case Type: A = Rimmed, bottleneck. B = Rimmed, straight. C = Rimless, bottleneck. D = Rimless, straight. E = Belted, bottleneck. F = Belted, straight. G = Semi-rimmed, bottleneck. H = Semi-rimmed, straight. I = Rebated, bottleneck. J = Rebated, straight. K = Rebated, belted bottleneck. L = Rebated, belted straight.

Primer Type: S = Small rifle (.175"). SP = Small pistol (.175"). L = Large rifle (.210"). LP = Large pistol (.210"). B = Berdan type. B-1 = Berdan #1. B-2 = Berdan #2.

Other Codes: V = OAL depends upon bullet used V – Rifling twist varies, depending upon bullet and application. ∂ = Belt/Rim Diameter. Unless otherwise noted, all dimensions in inches. Twist (factory) is given as inches of barrel length per complete revolution, e.g., 12 = 1 turn in 12", etc.

For full-power loads always use Small Rifle primers.

Military Rifle Cartridges of the World

(Current & Obsolete—Black-Powder and Smokeless)

The sale and use of surplus military firearms in the United States goes back to at least the Civil War, and probably earlier. During World War I, American companies manufactured rifles for the British, French, and Russian governments. At war's end, when military orders were canceled, they found themselves stuck with undelivered quantities. As a result, a lot of new Enfields, Lebels, and Mosin-Nagant rifles showed up in the civilian market and, for a time, 7.62mm Russian and 8mm Lebel sporting ammunition was loaded by American companies. However, nothing in previous history matched the variety and quantity of military arms marketed in the United States after World War II. The first influx occurred about 1947-'48 and were mostly captured enemy guns. However, in the 1950s, practically all the world powers were in the process of adopting new and more modern military small arms. They sold their older models to surplus dealers, who immediately offered those guns in the United States. This period offered unprecedented opportunities to shoot, experiment with, and remodel military rifles. Dealers sold many fine and brand new military rifles and handguns at very low prices. Few of these arms sold at prices over $35 to $40, and many sold at $10 to $25. Some of these same guns will bring upward of $300 on today's market. Not a single issue or model ever went down in value.

The Gun Control Act of 1968 ended the importation of surplus guns on such a scale. It is doubtful we will ever again see anything comparable to the war surplus phenomenon during the period between 1948 and 1968, although recently the surplus market did loosen up again. Consequently, a variety of military rifles are used for target practice, plinking, and small- and big-game hunting in America. Tinkers and gunsmiths can convert most military rifles into first-class sporting arms, and tens of thousands were so altered. Naturally, the cartridges used by these various rifles are of interest to those shooting the guns because, after all, the gun is of no use without the ammunition. That era exposed the American sportsman to chamberings all but unknown prior to World War II, which influenced subsequent cartridge development in this country.

Military ammunition represents one of the most highly developed categories of the metallic cartridge. Military ballisticians have spent untold millions of dollars in research to determine the best and most efficient combination of primer, case, powder, and bullet. The resulting degree of perfection explains why military cartridges are so popular for sporting use and why any cartridge adopted as a nation's official military chambering is so likely to become popular in civilian applications. American military cartridges have been highly esteemed in sporting circles, and all but the old 6mm Lee and .50-70 are still loaded and used. (Manufacturers have recently reintroduced .50-70 components, and sportsmen are again using this cartridge for sports like cowboy action shooting, for example). Foreign military chamberings do not offer the American sportsman anything new or different, although most are quite good in basic design and performance. These cartridges largely parallel what we already have available. The exceptions are the various 6.5mm and 7mm chamberings, which represent an area that was formerly neglected here.

Middle European, Mediterranean, Scandinavian, and Asian countries have favored 6.5mm cartridges for their military rifles. These cartridges are all quite similar in performance and power and offer little to choose from for sporting use. From the American viewpoint, the 6.5mm Mannlicher-Schoenauer and the 6.5x55mm Swedish are the best choices. However, any of these are good deer and antelope cartridges, superior to anything in the .30-30 class for this purpose. Most are appropriate for use against larger game, when loaded with heavier bullets. The 7x57mm

Mauser is another cartridge well known in sporting circles and is well adapted to North American game and hunting conditions. It is listed along with the 8x57mm Mauser and the .303 British under American sporting cartridges, because all three are loaded in this country and have been for many years. An interesting recent development has been the widespread availability of the 7.62x53R Russian and 7.62x39mm Soviet cartridges and guns to shoot them.

A surprising number of obsolete single-shot and repeating black-powder military rifles have shown up since 1948. Many of these rifles are brand new or in first-class condition. This has spurred shooting interest. The centerfire black-powder cartridges listed include those that an average neophyte might encounter, along with a few comparatively rare, albeit interesting, examples. Calibers vary from .32 to .60, with bullet weights from 250 to over 500 grains. The original powder used was coarse granulation black powder similar to what we know as Fg. The charge ranged from 40 grains to more than 80 grains. There was also variation of the powder charge within the same cartridge, owing to use of different bullets and lot-to-lot variations in powder density and performance. Most countries also had a carbine loading, which was lighter than standard. In power, all these old cartridges are similar to our own .45-70 and are adequate for most North American big game at short to moderate range. Standard loadings from these rounds all have a very curved trajectory, which makes it difficult to hit anything beyond 200 yards, although these will kill much further away. At known ranges, these are typically quite accurate and will turn in good scores out to 500 or even 1,000 yards.

Continued use of black-powder military rifles will eventually require reloading of fired cases. All but the American cartridges use Berdan primers, usually of 6.37mm (.251-inch), 6.46mm (.254-inch) or 6.5mm (.256-inch) size. These sizes are available from RWS. Lyman, Hornady, RCBS, and others make loading dies for the more popular black-powder cartridges. It is often possible to make reloadable cases from similar modern cases by trimming and reforming. To produce good ballistics and proper burning, black-powder charges should fill the case to the base of the bullet; while seating the bullet, it should slightly compress the charge. When using smokeless powder to load black-powder cartridges, *never* exceed original velocities or pressures, as few rifles are strong enough to safely withstand such treatment. Accurate Arms offers simple instructions for loading AA 5744, so as to duplicate the pressure and velocity of the original black-powder load in any typical rifle cartridge. In brief, begin with a charge that fills 45 percent of the available powder space in the case (room left over with bullet seated normally). Increase the charge as needed, until the load duplicates the velocity of the original black-powder loading. After firing with black powder, cases must be soaked and scrubbed in soap or detergent to remove the fouling, then dried before reloading. A bullet alloy of one part tin to 16 or 20 parts lead is about right for black powder, but a mixture of one-to-10 is more satisfactory with smokeless charges. Use of hard, jacketed bullets in black-powder rifles is not good practice, as these will often rapidly wear the bore, sometimes destroying accuracy within only 100 rounds or so. If you use common sense and exercise reasonable caution, shooting obsolete military rifles is a lot of fun and is perfectly safe, if the gun is in good condition.

The subject of military rifles is too broad and involved to be covered adequately in a book devoted primarily to cartridges. However, we have included tables listing the more common smokeless and black-powder military rifles and their characteristics. In passing, it might be well to at least mention two badly abused phases of the military rifle subject—safety and value. Some authors who should know better have bluntly stated, and without qualification, that all surplus military arms are unsafe, worthless pieces of junk. This simply is not true. The idea that any military power would arm its troops with guns inherently dangerous to fire is too silly to merit serious discussion. Toward the end of World War II, Germany and Japan turned out some shoddy, makeshift arms for drill, guard, or civilian use, and some used castings that were definitely not safe to fire. Others looked like hell, but were actually quite stout. In any event, these were not standard military issue, and the surplus gun market handled very few of these. For marketers to have sold dangerous and unsafe guns would have ended the big surplus military boom long before the Gun Control Act of 1968. That is just a matter of common sense.

I believe it is entirely correct to state that no standard military rifle is any more dangerous than any other if it is in good condition and fired with the cartridge and load for which it was designed. Use the correct ammunition and exercise common sense in handloading, and you will not get in trouble. Alteration of military rifles to other than the original chambering is alright, too, if you know what you're doing. On the other hand, this can be dangerous if mishandled, for it requires knowledge of the relative strength, mechanics, and metallurgy of military rifle actions.

Value? Only you can determine the value a certain gun has for you. "Value," as such, has really been beaten to death. Such terms as "good," "bad," "worthless," or a "good buy" are all relative, for their meaning will vary with the buyer and his individual ideas. As late as 1940, one could buy U.S. 1873 .45-70 Springfield rifles for $6.50 used and $11 brand new. I owned several and wish I'd had both the money and the foresight to have purchased a whole garage full, because these rifles are currently worth quite a bit in good condition. One must understand, though, that alteration of a military rifle destroys its value as a collector's item.

American-made sporting ammunition included the more popular foreign military chamberings up until about the mid-1930s. The 6.5mm Mannlicher-Schoenauer, 7x57mm Mauser, 7.65mm Mauser, 7.62mm Russian, 8mm Mauser, and 8mm Lebel were all made in the United States, along with the .303 British. At present, few American sporting rifles chamber foreign military cartridges, and only the 6.5x55mm Swedish, 7mm and 8mm Mauser, and .303 British are loaded here. However, Norma and RWS have recently loaded some of these cartridges in sporting versions. Most of these are imported through U.S. dealers.

Hunters should not use military ammunition loaded with full metal jacket bullets. These bullets are designed to wound, not necessarily kill.

Also, bear in mind that full jacketed bullets will not break up on contact; more often than not, these will ricochet badly. This is also true of the big, low-velocity bullets fired by black-powder rifles.

Handloading will improve the performance of most military cartridges to varying degrees. Most European ammunition is loaded with corrosive Berdan-type primers which (without special tools) are not as quick or easy to decap and re-prime as the Boxer-primed cases used by American manufacturers. Many others use steel cases that are not routinely reloadable. Norma continues to import ammunition and cases made for American primers in a number of military chamberings. Availability of reloadable cases is an important consideration, because the supply of surplus ammunition is not inexhaustible. The ultimate use of your rifle may depend on just such a small item as this.

Some military cartridges have never been loaded as sporting ammunition, but the handloader can correct this deficiency. Some of the old black-powder military rifles have been relegated as wall hangers, because of lack of ammunition, but this situation is changing, as small manufacturers now offer these cases to the handloader. Buffalo Arms (www.buffaloarms.com) offers many such cases. Many cartridges listed in Chapter 6 are obsolete, from the military viewpoint. The United States, the United Kingdom, and all NATO countries have adopted the 7.62x51mm NATO round, as have Japan, Australia, and many Asian countries. In addition, practically all these countries now use the 5.56x45mm (.223 Remington) for their military rifles. The U.S. used this smaller round almost exclusively in Vietnam. Russia and most former satellite countries have adopted the Russian M43 or 7.62x39mm cartridge. In 1974, the Soviet Union adopted a new .22-caliber round designated the 5.45x39mm.

Recent development in military cartridges has been in the realm of caseless cartridges, something that hasn't been fully successful to date. The word from ordnance circles is, "Happiness is still a cartridge case." — F.C.B.

15th Edition Update

Chapter 6 has two new entries, the 5.2x68mm Mondragon and the 5x58 Sturtevant. The former is interesting to the cartridge aficionado because this 100-year-old plus design is similar to short, bottleneck high-velocity cartridges currently chambered in 22 caliber — and it had a piston inside the case. The latter was developed in Germany and built by a British firm, showing that the notion of producing military rounds in smaller calibers has been going on since the beginning. They are both right at home alongside a 5.56 NATO.

4.85mm British

Historical Notes:	This was an experimental British military cartridge of less than .22-caliber that more or less parallels similar developments by Germany. Although entered in the NATO trials of 1977, none of these small-caliber cartridges were ever adopted, even though some of these cartridges developed initial velocities in excess of 4000 fps. The problem with these small, lightweight, high-velocity bullets is that all lose velocity and energy rapidly and, from a military viewpoint, are not very effective beyond moderate range. A gilding, metal-clad, steel jacketed bullet of .192-inch diameter with lead alloy core and flat base was used. Both Ball and tracer types were made. Further development ended after the 1977 NATO trials.
General Comments:	The dimensions of the 4.85mm British are practically identical to the wildcat 5mm/223 except that the case is about a 1/5-inch longer, due to a longer neck. Muzzle velocity would be similar.

4.85mm British Factory Ballistics

Bullet (grains/type)	Powder	Grains	Velocity	Energy	Source/Comments
56	ML	ML	3,117	1,210	Military load (L1E1 Ball)

5x58 Sturtevant — *NEW*

Historical Notes: This cartridge was developed in Germany and built by a British firm, Sturtevant Engineering Co. What‚Äôs interesting to the current observer about this obsolete round is that the notion of producing military rounds in smaller calibers has been going on since the beginning. The round had a cupronickel bullet more than an inch long. The case and charge were based on the 7.92x57 Mauser.

General Comments: This unique high-velocity experimental cartridge was an early German-British effort. The case type (DWM 469A) was manufactured in Germany by DWM. The cartridges were loaded by the British firm Sturtevant Engineering, which produced them under contract for the German Rifle Examination Commission (Deutsche Gewehr Prufungs Kommission), which examined new rifles for possible use by the German military.

If you are attempting to build a Deutsche Waffen & Munitionsfabrik cartridge collection, the Sturtevant is one to watch for. It‚Äôs an exceptionally rare 20-caliber round from the turn of the 19th century.

5.2x68mm Mondragon (with piston) — *NEW*

Historical Notes: This early small-caliber round was designed in 1894 by the Swiss Col. Rubin to fit a semi-automatic rifle design by Mexican Manuel Mondragon. According to the Rubin patent, a piston ring around the base of the bullet was used to drive the projectile. The piston ring stopped at the shoulder while the projectile continued out the barrel. A smooth cannelure on the case identifies where the piston ring sits. The piston was eventually dropped as better powders made the piston unnecessary.

General Comments: The rifle that shot this round is an exceptionally rare early Model 1894 Swiss/SIG experimental Type IIA Mondragon. SIG, in Neuhausen, built this development of the original 1893 Mondragon rifles. The cartridge is similar to short, bottleneck, high-velocity cartridges currently chambered in .22-caliber, only this cartridge has a piston inside the case. The piston inside the case had the powder charge located below the piston. The top of the piston rod was positioned below the actual bullet, and when the primer and powder were ignited, the piston would drive the bullet at a high muzzle velocity, with most velocities around the 1,500 to 1,800 fps.

5.2x68mm Mondragon Loading Data

Bullet (grains/type)	Powder	Grains	Velocity	Energy	Source/Comments
90 Roundnose		48	2,650	1,403	Factory Load

5.7x28mm FN P90 (Belgium)

Historical Notes: Developed in the late 1980s by FN for its then new P90 personal-defense gun, this cartridge is intended to replace the 9x19mm Parabellum pistol cartridge. Claimed ballistic performance is much superior to the 9mm cartridge. As yet, no major country has adopted this new chambering.

General Comments: The 5.7x28mm cartridge is somewhat similar in shape to the commercial .221 Fireball cartridge. However, the two are not interchangeable. A sharply pointed ball bullet weighing only 23 grains is used, as intended range is limited. Despite this, the bullet has been designed to penetrate helmets and body armor at 50 meters without breaking up.

FNH USA now produces the Five-seveN series of pistols and PS90 carbines that chamber this round. Numerous law enforcement agencies and military personnel around the world, including, it is reported, the U.S. Secret Service, are regularly employing this round and numerous firearms chambered for it, such as the AR-57.

Bullet (grains/type)	Powder	Grains	Velocity	Energy	Source/Comments
23 FMJ-BT Ball	ML	ML	2,790	400	Military Load

5.45x39mm Soviet

Historical Notes: This is a Russian cartridge introduced about 1974 for use in the new AK-74 assault rifle. There are both fixed-stock and folding-stock versions, and the 5.45mm rifle has a redesigned flash reducer/muzzle brake that distinguishes it from the earlier AK-47. This cartridge has a more slender case and a thicker rim than the 7.62x39mm (M43) cartridge. The bullet is .221- to .222-inch in diameter and weighs 53 to 54 grains. This bullet is almost one-inch long and has a very sharp spitzer point, a boat-tail base, a mild steel core, a short lead filler on top, and an air space in the nose. The bullet is designed to be unstable in tissue, thus producing a more severe wound. The British used somewhat the same idea in the design of their MKVII .303 bullet, used in World War II. Casualty reports from Afghanistan, where the new 5.45mm cartridge and rifle first appeared, tend to confirm the lethality of the bullet. Muzzle velocity is approximately 2,950 fps.

The first 5.45mm Soviet cartridges publicly available to western military intelligence were brought out of Afghanistan by writer Galen Greer, while on assignment for Soldier of Fortune magazine, in 1980, and the first information made public was in the October 1980 issue of that magazine. Until that time, the existence of a new Russian military cartridge had mostly been rumor. Later, the round was withdrawn from service in Afghanistan. Cases are lacquered steel with Berdan primers.

General Comments: The Russians apparently designed this cartridge as a result of experience on the receiving end of the U.S. M-16 rifle and 5.56mm round, in Vietnam. The 5.45mm Russian is a well-designed cartridge, for its intended purpose. The long, thin, boat-tail bullet reduces aerodynamic drag to the minimum and results in a higher retained velocity at long range. The bullet is designed to be stable in flight and provide good accuracy at all ranges out to maximum, but unstable on contact, so as to tumble easily, which enhances lethality. It is a better designed military bullet than the original used in the United States M193 5.56mm cartridge. However, the new 5.56mm SS109 (M855) NATO standard round, with its heavier bullet and improved shape, probably has an edge over the Soviet bullet.

5.45x39mm Russian Factory Ballistics

Bullet (grains)	Powder	Grains	Velocity	Energy	Source/Comments
54	ML	ML	2,950	1,045	Military load (SBT Ball)

5.66x39mm MPS

Historical Notes: The Special Underwater Assault Rifle (Avtomat Podvodnyi Spetsialnyi) was built by the Russian company TsNIITochMash and chambered for a 5.66mm dart. The MPS underwater cartridge was developed in conjunction with the 4.5x39Rmm SPS Underwater Pistol Cartridge. The rifle cartridge is slightly larger in diameter and overall length than the pistol cartridge.

General Comments: The MPS cartridge uses a standard 5.45x39mm Soviet rimless case that's sealed against water intrusion and functions in the automatic APS underwater assault rifle. The projectile is a 120mm-long 5.66mm-diameter dart. Given the larger case volume, the velocity of the 5.9-inch MPS bullet is greater than that of the SPS pistol bullet. The rifle dart weighs about 284 grains and has a maximum range underwater of 30 meters, 100 meters in air.—W.T.W.

5.56x45mm NATO

Historical Notes: The 5.56x45mm cartridge was originally developed for the Armalite AR-15 rifle. It was first tested by the U.S. Air Force as a possible replacement for the M-1 Carbine in 1960-'61. The AR-15 later evolved into the selective-fire M-16 adopted by the U.S. military in 1964 after several years of testing by the U.S. Continental Army Command at Fort Monroe, Virginia. The rifle and cartridge were first combat tested in Vietnam in the early 1960s.

General Comments: As initially loaded, the 5.56x45mm Ball cartridge had a 55-grain spitzer boat-tail bullet at a muzzle velocity of 3250 fps. It was the standard U.S. military loading until 1984. In 1980, the 5.56mm, FN-designed, 62-grain SS109 bullet was adopted by NATO. Designated the M855 in the United States, the new load uses a spitzer boat-tail bullet with a mild steel penetrator in front of the lead base. Muzzle velocity is 3100 fps. Adoption also involved changes in 5.56mm rifles to a quicker rifling twist of 1:7, to stabilize the longer, heavier bullet. This much improved bullet resulted in higher retained velocity and greater accuracy at long range. It also has much improved penetration characteristics over the old M193 55-grain projectile at all ranges.

The 5.56mm case is similar in configuration to and interchangeable with the commercial .223 Remington, although SAAMI warns that dimensional differences between military chambers and commercial chambers may make it unsafe to fire military ammunition in sporting rifles. Additional information and loading data can be found under that listing in Chapter 1.

5.56x45mm NATO Factory Ballistics

Bullet (grains/type)	Powder	Grains	Velocity	Energy	Source/Comments
55 FMJ-BT M193 Ball	ML	ML	3,250	1,325	U.S. Military load, old
62 FMJ-BT M855 Ball	ML	ML	3,100	1,325	NATO load, new

5.8x42mm Chinese

Historical Notes: Surprisingly, in the mid-1990s, the Chinese military introduced a new, indigenous, 5.8x42mm Small-Caliber High-Velocity (SCHV) assault rifle round and a new family of small arms to use it. This was the result of research spanning more than two decades. Like the Russians, the advantages of SCHV assault rifle ammo observed in Vietnam War battle reports did not go unnoticed by the Chinese military. So in March 1971, the Chinese military logistic department commenced a small arms research project, in Beijing, known as the "713 Conference," in order to develop the design criteria for an indigenous SCHV assault rifle cartridge.

The design criteria called for a cartridge of approximately 6mm-caliber at 1,000 meters per second muzzle velocity, with the goals of reducing recoil and ammo weight, while improving accuracy and terminal ballistics over the Type 56/M43 7.62x39mm full-caliber intermediate round. The following "744 Conference" narrowed down the calibers under consideration to 5.8mm and 6mm. The project completed its development in 1987, and the new SCHV assault rifle cartridge was officially designated as the DBP87.

The Chinese military has since developed a variety of small arms chambered for the new 5.8mm cartridge. The first was the QBZ87 assault rifle primarily used as the test bed for further 5.8mm ammo development. The QBZ87 was an undated 7.62mm Type 81 assault rifle chambered for the new 5.8mm round. The QBZ87 has now been largely withdrawn from frontline services and handed over to paramilitary, military academies, and reservists.

Next came the QBZ95 assault rifle family, comprised of the QBZ95 assault rifle, QBB95 squad automatic rifle/light machine gun, and the QBZ95B carbine. The QBZ95 (Qing, Bu-Qiang, Zi-Dong, 1995 Si, or Infantry Rifle Automatic, Model 1995), is a modern looking 7.1-pound (3.25-kilogram) assault rifle in a bullpup configuration. Like other bullpup rifles, such as French FAMAS, Austrian AUG, and the British SA80, the QBZ has its magazine and action located behind its trigger and pistol grip.

General Comments: The 5.8mm ammo is much more conventional than the weapons chambered for it. The 5.8mm standard rifle load has a 64-grain (4.15g) bullet, with a full metal jacket made of steel and wearing a copper-washed coating. The 24.3mm long projectile has a very streamlined external shape, with a sharp bullet ogive and a sizeable boat-tail. The 5.8mm bullet has a composite core that consists of a pin-shaped hardened steel penetrator located near the base of the bullet, with lead as the filling material between the penetrator and the jacket, as well as in the tip cavity.

The 5.8mm cartridge has a 42mm long case, with a one-degree taper in the body from its 10.5mm-diameter base. The bottleneck shoulder and the neck are both 4 millimeters long. The shorter but wider 5.8mm case is more space efficient than the long and slim case of the 5.56mm. The tapered case design also helps with both ammo feeding and extraction. However, the straight-wall case design of the 5.56mm has better accuracy.

5.8x42mm Chinese Factory Ballistics

Bullet (grains/type)	Powder	Grains	Velocity	Energy	Source/Comments
64 FMJ BT	Corrosive	approx. 28.0	3,050	1,325	Timothy G. Yan

6mm SAW (U.S.)

Historical Notes: In the early 1970s, the U.S. Army began studies to develop a new infantry squad machine gun called the Squad Automatic Weapon (SAW). Frankford Arsenal began computerized parametric design analyses in July 1971 to design a cartridge to meet user requirements. After several experimental designs based on the 5.56x45mm case proved unsuccessful, a new case having a larger .410-inch diameter head and a length of 1.779 inches was adopted. A 6mm diameter (.243-inch) 105-grain full metal jacket boat-tail bullet was used.

General Comments: Cartridge cases for the 6mm SAW will be found in both steel (with a phenolic varnish finish) and in aluminum (with an anodized finish). The aluminum case is longer than the steel case. The 6mm SAW was never adopted, although considerable quantities of ammunition were loaded experimentally by Frankford Arsenal. This cartridge is frequently encountered in collections. It is historically significant as the first cartridge designed using computerized parametric design analysis. Interestingly, ballistics are quite similar to the circa-1895 Lee Navy cartridge.

6mm SAW Factory Ballistics

Bullet (grains/type)	Powder	Grains	Velocity	Energy	Source/Comments
105 FMJ-BT	ML	ML	2,520	1,480	Military load, XM732 Ball

6x49mm "Unified"

Historical Notes: The 6mm "Unified" machine gun was developed by the Central Research Institute for Precision Machine Building (aka TsNIITochMash) during the late 1980s and early 1990s in the U.S.S.R. and, later, in Russia, to replace the Kalashnikov PKM general-purpose machine gun. Reportedly, the 6mm Unified MG had an effective range of up to 1,500 meters and was almost twice as accurate as the PKM.

Some military thinkers in the last half-century have suggested that a 6mm caliber would be the ideal military cartridge, offering more rounds per unit weight than the 7.62mm and better ballistic and terminal performance than 5.45/5.56mm rounds. However, 6mm-caliber rounds are not making inroads in any major military arsenals. In this case, part of the issue has to be cost. Russia already has several standard military cartridges, and adding another would complicate ammunition logistics and add massive production costs. Other than basic dimensions and a few references in periodicals, data regarding the 6mm experimental cartridges is hard to come by.

General Comments: The 6x49 "Unified" cartridge had a rimless bottlenecked steel case with a distinctive case groove just above the base. An 80-grain pointed bullet would deliver muzzle velocities around 3,700 fps. As a full-power cartridge, the 6x49mm is not very impressive when compared to a 6.5mm general-purpose cartridge in retained energy, barrier penetration ability, and armor penetration ability at 1,000 meters. It likely developed high chamber pressures and caused too much barrel wear to be an effective long-use military round.—*W.T.W.*

Bullet (grains/type)	Powder	Grains	Velocity	Energy	Source/Comments
77	ML	ML	3,772	2,432	Military load

6.5x54mm Mannlicher-Schoenauer (Greek)

Historical Notes: This original Greek military cartridge was designed in 1900 and used in the 1903 Mannlicher bolt-action rifle. It is also a popular sporting number in Europe and the United States. All major American ammunition companies loaded the 6.5mm Mannlicher, until about 1940. The Austrian-made Mannlicher-Schoenauer sporting rifle was the only rifle routinely available in this chambering. Sporting ammunition is loaded in Europe, and RWS has imported Boxer-primed, reloadable cases and a good variety of sporting loads. European ammunition uses the Berdan primer, usually the 5.5mm or .217-inch size.

General Comments: The 6.5mm M-S has always had a certain following in the United States, even though American rifle makers do not chamber it as a standard option. It is a very fine cartridge for North American hunting, with far better killing power than the .30-30 or anything in that class. In fact, every species of big game on earth has been taken with this cartridge. A great many elephants were killed by ivory hunters using this little 6.5mm and heavy, solid bullets. It did not make enough noise to bother a herd and gave deep penetration for well-placed brain shots. In the hands of an experienced hunter, it will do for any North American big game. However, by today's standards, it is considered primarily a deer, sheep, antelope, and black bear cartridge. In power, it is often compared to the .257 Roberts, and there is some validity for this. On the other hand, the 6.5mm M-S is loaded with bullets of around 160 grains in weight, compared to the 120-grain top weight of the .257. It is the long, heavy bullet that makes this a good killer on the tougher varieties of game.

6.5x54mm Mannlicher-Schoenauer (Greek) Loading Data and Factory Ballistics

Bullet (grains/type)	Powder	Grains	Velocity	Energy	Source/Comments
139-140 SP	IMR 3031	35	2,510	1,950	Antelope, deer
139-140 SP	IMR 4895	36	2,400	1,790	N/A
156 SP	IMR 4350	38	2,510	2,182	N/A
156 SP	IMR 3031	34	2,460	2,100	Duplicates original military load
160 SP	IMR 4064	38	2,450	2,140	Heavy game
140 SP	FL	FI	2,250	1,575	Hirtenberger factory load
159 SP	FL	FL	2,330	1,740	RWS factory load
159 Ball	ML	ML	2,223	1,740	Military load

6.5x50mm Japanese Arisaka

Historical Notes: This cartridge, best known for its use in the modified Mauser-type Model 38 Japanese bolt-action rifle of 1905, was actually introduced in 1897, intended for a discontinued rifle found to be unsafe in service. It was introduced in the United States after World War II, as the result of captured rifles brought back by returning GIs and, later, by the surplus arms dealers who sold large numbers of the Model 38 rifles and carbines. Sporting ammunition in 6.5x50mm has recently been loaded by Norma, using the American-type Boxer primer. Military ammunition has a Berdan-type primer, usually of .199-inch or .217-inch size. Military ball ammunition of recent production, with steel cases and Berdan primers, has recently been imported from China.

General Comments: The 6.5x50mm has a semi-rimmed case, but is otherwise not radically different from other 6.5mm military cartridges. It has the shortest case and shortest powder capacity of any of the military 6.5mms, but is, nonetheless, an efficient design with smokeless powder. The Japanese Model 38 rifle has an unusually strong action, which allows the cartridge to be loaded to its full potential. Because commercial sporting ammunition and reloadable cases are available, this is one of the more useful military cartridges. In power, it is on a par with any of the other 6.5 military rounds and is fine for antelope, deer, sheep, and black bear. It makes a far more effective deer cartridge than the .30-30. To solve the ammunition availability problem, some 6.5mm Arisaka rifles have been re-chambered to the wildcat 6.5-257 Roberts, which makes a fine conversion.

6.5x50mm Japanese Arisaka Loading Data and Factory Ballistics

Bullet (grains/type)	Powder	Grains	Velocity	Energy	Source/Comments
120 SP	IMR 4350	43	3,000	2,400	Maximum load
120 SP	H380	36	2,680	1,918	N/A
120 SP	IMR 4895	34	2,650	1,870	N/A
140 SP	IMR 4350	40	2,680	2,240	N/A
140 SP	H380	34	2,360	1,735	N/A
156 SP	IMR 4064	28	2,060	1,460	Duplicates factory loading
160 SP	IMR 4320	34	2,500	2,408	N/A
139 Ball	ML	ML	2,500	1,930	Military load
139 SP	FL	FL	2,430	1,815	Norma factory load
156 SP	FL	FL	2,070	1,475	Norma factory load

6.5x53Rmm Mannlicher (Dutch & Romanian)

Historical Notes: This is an earlier rimmed version of the 6.5x54mm Greek cartridge. It was designed by Mannlicher and used in the bolt-action Dutch Models 1892 and 1895 and Romanian Models 1892 and 1893. The cartridge was dropped by both countries after World War II.

General Comments: This cartridge delivers ballistics practically identical to the regular 6.5x54mm Mannlicher-Schoenauer known for many years in the United States and, at one time, loaded by most cartridge companies. The rimmed version is used in a few single-shot and combination European sporting rifles. Commercial hunting ammunition for rifles so chambered was once loaded in both England and Europe.

This cartridge was introduced in the United States after World War II, when quantities of the Dutch and Romanian military rifles and carbines were sold in surplus stores. Only imported sporting ammunition is available, but some dealers have furnished hunting loads based on the military round with the bullet replaced. Rifles in this chambering are suitable for deer, antelope, black bear, and the like. The British listed this cartridge as the .256 Mannlicher, and many bolt-action rifles were turned out for it by Jeffery and others. It has been popular in parts of Africa. No commercial manufacturer currently offers this ammunition. Brass can be made from .303 British cases.

6.5x53Rmm Mannlicher Loading Data and Factory Ballistics

Bullet (grains/type)	Powder	Grains	Velocity	Energy	Source/Comments
120 SP	IMR 4895	33	2,440	1,590	N/A
120 SP	IMR 4064	35	2,650	1,875	N/A
140 SP	IMR 3031	35	2,550	2,360	N/A
156 SP	IMR 3031	34	2,445	2,095	Duplicates military ball load
156 SP	IMR 4350	38	2,510	2,192	N/A
160 SP	IMR 3031	34	2,250	1,810	N/A
156 – 159 Ball	ML	ML	2,433	2,085	Military load
160 SP	FL	FL	2,350	1,960	Factory load

6.5x53.5mm Daudeteau

Historical Notes:　A collector's item today, this semi-rimmed 1895 design was introduced originally as a military cartridge for the French Navy. It was used in the Daudeteau bolt-action rifle and, evidently, commercial ammunition was also produced.

General Comments:　Rifles and ammunition are quite rare, and you are not likely to have one with which to hunt. If you do, it would probably be satisfactory for anything up to deer. According to Aivaro Casal, this cartridge was adopted by Uruguay in 1895 and used until 1898.

6.5x53.5mm Daudeteau Factory Ballistics

Bullet (grains/type)	Powder	Grains	Velocity	Energy	Source/Comments
150 RN Ball	ML	40	2,395	1,922	Military load

6.5x55mm Swedish Mauser

Historical Notes:　A Mauser- and Swedish-designed military cartridge adopted in 1894, the 6.5x55mm was used in the Swedish Models 94, 96, and 38 rifles and carbines. These are based on a modification of the Spanish Mauser 1893 bolt-action. Norway also adopted this cartridge for its 1894 and 1912 Krag-Jorgensen rifles. Ammunition for sporting use is loaded by Norma and others. Military ammunition uses the Berdan primer, usually of .199-inch or .216-inch diameter. Sporting rifles are currently available on the American market in this chambering. Federal and PMC produce 6.5x55mm ammunition. Remington apparently produced a few rifles in 6.5x55mm some years ago, and one version of the Model 70 Winchester was also so chambered. The military ball is a spitzer boat-tail of very advanced design. Both copper and clad-steel jacket types exist.

General Comments:　The 6.5x55 Swedish cartridge is another surplus, post-war immigrant that has become quite popular in the United States. For North American hunting, it is one of the best of the foreign military cartridges. It has been highly developed as a match and hunting round in the Scandinavian countries and has a reputation for superb accuracy. With lighter bullets (77- to 100-grain), it will do very well for varmint shooting of all kinds. The 120-grain bullet is fine for antelope or deer, and heavier (140- to 160-grain) bullets make it suitable for most types of big game. The Swedish Mauser and the Norwegian Krag are intended for working pressures of only about 45,000 psi, and this must be considered when handloading. With a stronger action, maximum loads and performance could be notably increased. Except for a slightly larger rim and base diameter and a shorter neck, this cartridge is very similar to the 6.5x57mm Mauser cartridge. It is not known exactly who designed it, but, undoubtedly, its design was influenced by Mauser developments. Chapter 1 contains more information on this round.

6.5x55mm Swedish Mauser Loading Data and Factory Ballistics

Bullet (grains/type)	Powder	Grains	Velocity	Energy	Source/Comments
100 HP	IMR 3031	44	3,100	2,140	Varmint load
120 SP	IMR 4350	50	2,780	2,062	Deer, antelope
129 SP	IMR 4895	41	2,625	1,990	N/A
140 SP	IMR 4350	45	2,520	1,980	N/A
140 SP	IMR 4831	50	2,590	2,090	N/A
156 SP	IMR 4350	43	2,500	2,168	N/A
160 SP	IMR 4350	42	2,430	2,100	Heavy game
77 FMJ	FL	FL	3,120	1,660	Norma bird factory load
139 SP	FL	FL	2,790	2,395	Norma factory load

Bullet (grains/type)	Powder	Grains	Velocity	Energy	Source/Comments
156 SP	FL	FL	2,490	2,150	Norma factory load
139 Ball	ML	ML	2,625	2,126	Military load

6.5x52mm Italian (Mannlicher-Carcano)

Historical Notes: This was the official Italian military cartridge adopted in 1891 for the bolt-action Mannlicher-Carcano rifle. This rifle was a Mannlicher-inspired design in every respect except the bolt, which is a Mauser-type with double locking lugs at the front. It is also the only military rifle of smokeless powder design to use gain-twist rifling. This Italian 6.5mm cartridge is very similar to the 6.5mm Mannlicher-Schoenauer in size, shape, and performance. Both unprimed cases and loaded ammunition have been made by Norma.

General Comments: The Italian 6.5mm military cartridge was unfamiliar to American shooters, until after World War II. Large quantities of Italian Model 91 rifles and carbines have been sold at very low prices, and because we are a great nation of bargain hunters, this is now a fairly widely used cartridge. Many surplus arms dealers furnished hunting ammunition that consisted of the military round with the full-jacketed bullet replaced by a soft-point. Reloadable cases can be made very easily from 6.5x54mm Mannlicher cases. This is a good deer, antelope, or black bear cartridge, but the low working pressure limit of the Carcano rifle prevents loading it as heavily as similar military 6.5mms.

6.5x52mm Italian Mannlicher-Carcano Loading Data and Factory Ballistics

Bullet (grains/type)	Powder	Grains	Velocity	Energy	Source/Comments
140 SP	IMR 4895	33	2,250	1,570	Maximum for Carcano rifle
140 SP	IMR 3031	34	2,320	1,730	N/A
156 SP	IMR 4064	37	2,280	1,806	N/A
156 SP	IMR 4350	35	2,340	1,898	N/A
160 SP	IMR 4350	35	2,320	1,919	N/A
139 SP	FL	FL	2,580	2,045	Norma factory load
156 SP	FL	FL	2,430	2,045	Norma factory load
162 Ball	ML	ML	2,296	1,902	Military load

6.8x57mm Chinese

Historical Notes: While we have no sample cartridge and very little data on this number—we are uncertain even as to the correct name—we feel compelled to include a brief mention of it here. Why? Because other than the .270 Winchester, Roy Weatherby's subsequent .270 Magnum, and the new short magnums, this is the only other commercial or military cartridge of which we are aware that used a bullet of .277-inch diameter. One must speculate that this number might have had something to do with Winchester's decision to use an unusual bullet size in what became one of the most successful, commercially inspired hunting cartridges of all time. If so, the 6.8x57mm Chinese most assuredly deserves honorable mention.

.280 British

Historical Notes: This was an experimental cartridge developed by the British Army concurrently with a semi-automatic/full-auto assault-type rifle, the EM-2. Work began in 1945, immediately after the end of the war and by 1947 the rifle/cartridge combination was ready for field trials. It was tested by both the British and the

U.S. Its ultimate rejection was mostly a political decision to satisfy U.S. military higher-ups, who were wedded to the .30-caliber. By 1954, the British had adopted and were manufacturing the 7.62mm NATO round. The EM-2 rifle was a short, bullpup design, weighing seven pounds and using a 20-round clip. The British continued field-testing both rifle and cartridge until as late as 1951. The cyclic rate of the EM-2 was 600 to 650 rounds per minute.

General Comments: In 1948, the rim of the .280 British case was slightly enlarged to match the .30-06 and the name was changed to .280/30. Ballistics remained the same. The .280/30 case was developed by shortening and necking down the standard .30-06 case so that the rim and case diameter of the two cases are the same. The .280/30 case has a slightly tapered body, probably an aid to feeding and extraction. Various bullet weights were used, ranging from 130 to 140 grains; muzzle velocity of the various loads ranged from 2400 to 2530 fps. When tested in the United States and loaded with American powders, velocity was increased to 2600 fps.

The .280/30 would have made a good sporting round, but we don't know of anyone who has used it for that purpose. In a good, strong, bolt- or single-shot action and loaded to maximum performance with American powders, the .280/30 could probably push the 139-grain bullet at something like 2700 to 2800 fps muzzle velocity. For some reason, very little, if any, work has ever been done with this cartridge in the sporting field. It is worth mentioning here, because some experimenters as early as 1962 necked the .308x1.5-inch down to 7mm, creating a very similar round. However, the .280/30 British case is .20 inch longer than the .308x1.5-inch, and case capacity is probably about 10 percent greater. Remington picked up this idea in its 7mm BR handgun cartridge used in the XP-100 Silhouette pistol. No commercial sporting ammunition has ever been made.

In an interesting aside, Lewis Potter, proprietor of Potter & Walker (Eversham, Worcestershire, UK), reported that he had shot 90 deer, ranging in size from a 25-pound muntjac to a 350-pound red deer, with the .280 British cartridge in rifles built on Winchester and Sako actions (using chamber reamers by Clymer, www.clymertools.com, and reforming and reloading dies by RCBS, www.rcbs.com). He reported good results with 120-grain bullets at an average muzzle velocity of 2750 fps from a 20-inch barrel. Potter also noted, "These short, dumpy cases usually make good combustion chambers, and you get a fair bit out for what you put in. Originally designed for a 130-grain bullet, the military changed to a 140-grain to get better retained energy at the longer ranges. It was reported that they were disappointed it would only pierce one side of a steel helmet at 1,600 yards. Originally, the cartridge had been designed as a .270, was also called the .276, and changed to .280 on 7 November, 1947."

.280 British Military Ballistics

Bullet (grains/type)	Powder	Grains	Velocity	Energy	Source/Comments
139 Ball	ML	ML	2,530	1,980	Military load, typical

7x57mm Mauser

Historical Notes: The 7x57mm Mauser is another cartridge that, although designed as a military round, was widely adapted for sporting purposes. Contrary to what most cartridge books say, it was not introduced in 1893. It was actually developed in 1892 and used in a limited number of Model 1892 Mauser rifles, a modification of the Belgian-Mauser pattern of 1889. In 1893, Mauser introduced an improved bolt-action rifle in 7x57mm that was officially adopted by the Spanish military. Subsequently, with minor modifications, the 7mm-chambered rifle was adopted by other European and many Latin-American governments. The Remington Model 1902 rolling block rifle was also manufactured in 7x57mm Mauser, as was the Model 70 Winchester. More recently, several U.S. gun makers have chambered it in their finest guns.

The original 7mm military round employed a 173-grain bullet with a muzzle velocity of 2296 fps and an energy of 2025 ft-lbs. Other loadings were used by various countries, with bullets ranging in weight from 139 grains up to the original 173 grains. Those loads on which data is available are listed below.

Model 93 Mauser rifles in 7mm were used by Spanish troops in Cuba, during the Spanish-American War. The effectiveness of this combination against American forces was responsible for the eventual adoption of the Mauser-system 1903 Springfield rifle. San Juan Hill was defended by only about 700 Spaniards armed with the new Mauser 7mm rifles, but they inflicted some 1,400 casualties on the 15,000 Americans who attacked their position.

General Comments: The United States saw a large influx of surplus 7mm military rifles after World War II. Many who purchased those fine rifles immediately wanted the gun altered to use a more familiar American sporting cartridge. This was foolish, because the 7x57mm is one of the best all-round cartridges available for North American big-game hunting. With the proper bullet for the job at hand, the 7mm will handle any big game here. It might not be the choice for grizzly bear in heavy brush, but, in the hands of an experienced hunter, it will be far superior to the .30-30 for any purpose. If the barrel is in good shape, it is best to leave a 7mm military rifle in its original chambering. Loading data is in Chapter 1. All major manufacturers offer 7x57mm sporting ammunition.

7x57mm Mauser Factory Ballistics

Bullet (grains/type)	Powder	Grains	Velocity	Energy	Source/Comments
139 Ball	ML	ML	2,950	2,580	Military load, Brazil & Colombia
142 Ball	ML	ML	2,740	2,365	Military load, Uruguay
155 Ball	ML	ML	2,300	1,820	Military load, Mexico
162 Ball	ML	ML	2,295	1,890	Military load, Mexico
173 Ball	ML	ML	2,296	2,025	Original military loading used by Spain & others

.276 Enfield

Historical Notes: The .276 Enfield was an experimental military cartridge developed by the British beginning in 1909 for what later became the proposed Pattern 13 bolt-action rifle. It is very similar to the Canadian .280 Ross cartridge. Although the rifle and cartridge were issued for troop trials, these were not adopted due to the onset of World War I. However, the rifle was produced in a slightly modified form as the Pattern 14 Enfield and chambered for the .303 British cartridge. Many of these were manufactured in the United States, for the British government. Most .276 Enfield ammunition was manufactured by Royal Laboratories, Woolwich, England, and headstamped R-L. Bullet diameter is .282-inch. Bullet weights vary from 144 to 190 grains.

General Comments: The .276 Enfield is primarily a collector's item, because it was never officially adopted or used as a military cartridge. Also, it was not used as a sporting cartridge and is therefore interesting mostly as a development that might have replaced the .303 British, had World War I had not intervened. After the war, between 1923 and 1932, the United States experimented with a smaller, similar cartridge, the .276 Pedersen. Sporting ammunition has never been made for this chambering.

.276 Enfield Loading Data

Bullet (grains/type)	Powder	Grains	Velocity	Energy	Source/Comments
165 Ball	ML	ML	2,800	2,881	Military load, experimental

.276 Pedersen

Historical Notes: The .276 Pedersen was a U.S. Army experimental cartridge developed between 1923 and 1932 for the experimental Pedersen semi-automatic rifle. There were actually several variations of this cartridge (perhaps as many as 10), with differences in case length, diameter, and other dimensions. It appears that the most common version of this cartridge was developed by necking the 6.5 Carcano up to 7mm. One version, the T2, had the same rim and head dimensions as the .30-06, while another, the T2-E1, was modified specifically for testing in an early version of the Garand rifle.

The .276 was tested with bullets weighing from 120 grains at 2550 fps to 150 grains at 2360 fps. Performance was not spectacular, but was acceptable for a military cartridge at the time. However, in 1932, General Douglas MacArthur, then Army Chief of Staff, disapproved any caliber reduction, and that ended the development program for the .276.

J.D. Pedersen, the originator of the .276 program, was a famous arms designer, whose successful creations included the Remington Model 10 shotgun, the Model 12 line of .22 pump-action rifles, the Model 14 and Model 25 centerfire pump-action rifles, and the World War I Pedersen device. The Pedersen semi-auto military rifle design employed a toggle breech block system similar to the Luger pistol and Maxim machine gun. However, the Pedersen system differed in that the barrel did not recoil with the breech block, but rather remained stationary. The Garand system was adopted over the Pedersen rifle prior to World War II.

General Comments: The .276 Pedersen was never manufactured as a commercial cartridge, and no commercial sporting rifles were chambered for it. It would have made a good deer cartridge, but there were plenty of other cartridges in the same class that served just as well, and there was no reason to bring out a sporting version. The .276 ammunition was quite common for a few years after World War II and it is found in many collections.

.276 Pedersen Factory Ballistics

Bullet (grains/type)	Powder	Grains	Velocity	Energy	Source/Comments
120 Ball	ML	ML	2,550	1,732	Military load, experimental
150 Ball	ML	ML	2,360	1,858	Military load, experimental

7.35mm Italian Carcano

Historical Notes: The 7.35mm cartridge was adopted by Italy in 1938 to replace the 6.5x52mm round that had been used since 1891. Experience in Ethiopia and other places had demonstrated the desirability for a larger caliber in combat use. The Model 91 Carcano rifle was modified slightly for the new cartridge, but retained the same basic action. That happened about the time Italy became involved in various military actions, and the new cartridge created a critical supply problem, causing it to be withdrawn from service. Quantities of 7.35mm rifles were used against the Russians by Finnish troops and reportedly gave good service. No sporting ammunition is currently loaded for this chambering, although Norma offered it for many years.

General Comments: Many thousands of the Italian Model 38 service rifles and carbines were sold here as surplus. These rifles were sold at extremely low prices and are now in rather widespread use all over the country. In power, the 7.35mm is between the .30-30 and the .300 Savage, making it a good deer and black bear cartridge, if the proper hunting bullet is used. It is actually a better cartridge than the .30-30 in many respects. Reloadable cases can be made from empty 6.5x54mm Mannlicher cases as imported by RWS. This is done by expanding the neck, running the shell through a full length sizing die, and then trimming back to proper length. The Carcano action is designed for working pressures of only about 38,000 psi, and the loads given below should not be exceeded. In a strong, modern action, it would be possible to equal the .300 Savage in performance, but this cannot be done safely in the military Carcano.

7.35mm Italian Carcano Loading Data and Factory Ballistics

Bullet (grains/type)	Powder	Grains	Velocity	Energy	Source/Comments
128 SP	IMR 3031	38	2,495	1,776	Approximates military load ballistics
128 SP	IMR 4895	40	2,500	1,782	N/A
150 SP	IMR 4320	40	2,550	2,175	N/A
150 SP	IMR 4895	38	2,450	2,005	N/A
150 SP	H380	41	2,490	2,070	N/A
128 Ball	ML		2,483	1,749	Military load

7.62x45mm Czech M52

Historical Notes: This cartridge was independently developed in Czechoslovakia in the late 1940s. It was adopted for official Czech military use in 1952 along with the M52 semi-auto carbine and the M52 machine gun. In the interest of standardization in the Warsaw Pact, the 7.62x45mm cartridge was dropped in the 1960s in favor of the 7.62x39mm Soviet round. The Czech cartridge is of interest historically, as it is one of the very few successful, independently developed assault rifle rounds outside the 7.62x39mm or 5.56x45mm cartridges. It is now obsolete.

General Comments: The 7.62x45mm cartridge offers ballistic performance very similar to the Soviet 7.62x39. A .309-inch diameter spitzer boat-tail bullet weighing 130 grains was used at a muzzle velocity of 2440 fps. Cases were either brass or lacquered steel with Berdan primers. Both ball and tracer types were made. The semi-automatic Czech M52 rifle was almost unknown in the United States until recently, and substantial quantities of the model have been imported.

7.5x55mm Swiss Schmidt-Rubin

Historical Notes: The first Swiss 7.5mm cartridge was adopted in 1889 for the Schmidt-Rubin straight-pull rifle of the same year. The original loading used a .299-inch diameter, 213-grain paper-patched lead bullet and a charge of 29 grains of semi-smokeless powder. Muzzle velocity was 1970 fps. Later, a steel-capped hollow-base lead bullet was used, followed by a 190-grain copper or iron-jacketed round-nose bullet with a smokeless powder loading (Model 90/03). In 1911, the 174-grain spitzer boat-tail bullet was adopted and the diameter increased to .308-inch. Golden State Arms Corp. once imported Japanese-made cases with Boxer primer pockets for loading sporting ammunition. Both unprimed cases and loaded rounds are available from Norma.

General Comments: The 7.5mm Swiss military cartridge is another of the surplus items that has become well known to American shooters only since the end of the war. The Swiss army made a number of improvements in the straight-pull Schmidt-Rubin rifle, and the older, less desirable models were sold off as obsolete surplus. The original Model 89, with rear locking lugs, a very long receiver, and a protruding box magazine, was one of those. The improved Model 1911, with its shorter receiver, forward-located locking lugs, and a less conspicuous magazine, is another.

The 190-grain load develops about 37,000 psi breech pressure, and the 174-grain load about 45,500 psi, (the latter also uses a slightly larger diameter bullet. The 1911 cartridge, considerably more powerful than the older loading, should not be used in the Model 89 rifle. In a suitable action, the 7.5mm Swiss cartridge can be loaded to deliver performance equal to the .308 Winchester and is suitable for the same range of applications. Reloadable cases can be readily made by necking up .284 Winchester brass. The .284's rebated rim works just fine in the Schmidt-Rubin rifle.

7.5x55mm Swiss Schmidt-Rubin Loading Data and Factory Ballistics
(Model-1911 rifle, or later models, using .308-inch diameter bullets)

Bullet (grains/type)	Powder	Grains	Velocity	Energy	Source/Comments
130 SP	IMR 3031	46	3,000	2,608	Varmint load
150 SP	IMR 3031	45	2,820	2,658	N/A
165 SP	IMR 4895	42	2,570	2,430	N/A
180 SP	IMR 4064	45	2,570	2,642	N/A
200 SP	IMR 4350	49	2,460	2,700	N/A
174 Ball	ML	ML	2,560	2,540	Military load
180	FL	FL	2,650	2,805	Factory load

.30 Carbine (.30 M-1 Carbine)

Historical Notes: In 1940, the U.S. Ordnance Department concluded that a light carbine might have certain advantages over the .45-caliber semi-auto pistol in many combat situations. Various designs were submitted by a number of private manufacturers and, in the end, Winchester's offering was selected. The semi-auto .30 M-1 Carbine was officially adopted in 1941. This cartridge, a modification of the .32 Winchester self-loading round of 1906, was hardly a revolutionary new design, but it served the purpose. About the same time, the Germans developed their assault rifle and the 7.92mm Kurz (short) cartridge. The M-1 Carbine is not an assault rifle, and the military insists it was designed to fulfill a different purpose. A few sporting rifles and handguns have chambered the .30 Carbine (See Chapter 1).

General Comments: In mid-1963, the government released .30 M-1 Carbines for sale to civilians through the National Rifle Association at the very moderate price of around $20. Thousands of these rifles, as a result, have been used for sporting purposes. Federal, Winchester, and Remington load soft-point sporting ammunition and, so, the M-l Carbine must be considered from other than a strictly military viewpoint. The .30 Carbine cartridge is in the same class as the .32-20 WCF, but slightly more powerful. It is wholly a small-game and varmint number, despite contrary claims by those who love the short, light, and handy M-1 Carbine. The modest accuracy of the Carbine, combined with the ballistics of this cartridge, limit the effective sporting accuracy range to about 150 yards. The original author of this book used an M-1 Carbine to hunt small game and deer as early as 1943, before most people could get their hands on one of these guns, so he had a pretty good idea of the capability of this cartridge. Remember that the .32 Winchester self-loading round became obsolete in 1920, because it was ineffective and more or less useless for sporting purposes. The .30 Carbine was derived from that round and shares the same shortcomings. However, the .30 Carbine can shoot relatively cheaper military ammunition, and this allows use of the gun in many situations not economically feasible with the .32 SL. However, don't kid yourself about the so-called "terrific power" of the .30 Carbine cartridge, because it's just not there. Despite this, it can be a very useful cartridge within its limitations, and its use and popularity have increased considerably over the years.

One final note: Had the military adopted a normal, modern rifle pressure standard, instead of the inexplicably modest 40,000 psi specified, we might have a somewhat different opinion of this cartridge. Loading to normal .30-06 pressures provides about 400 fps more velocity, which seems significant.

.30 Carbine Loading Data and Factory Ballistics

Bullet (grains/type)	Powder	Grains	Velocity	Energy	Source/Comments
100 Plinker	2400	15.5	2,170	1,045	Speer
110 SP	IMR 4227	15.0	2,010	985	N/A
125 Lead RN	AA 1680	15.0	1,756	855	Accurate Arms
110 Ball	ML	ML	1,975	955	Military load, M-1
110 SP	FL	FL	1,990	965	Factory load

.30 Army (.30-40 Krag)

Historical Notes: The .30 U.S. Army, or .30-40 Krag, was the first small-bore military cartridge adopted by the U.S. Army. It was adopted in 1892 for the Norwegian-invented, American-modified Krag-Jorgensen bolt-action rifle. Original loads used 40 grains of smokeless powder with a 220-grain full metal jacket round-nose bullet. The .30-40 Krag cartridge remained in service only a few years, before being replaced, in 1903, by the rimless .30-03 cartridge, predecessor to the .30-06.

General Comments: In 1893, Winchester began offering its High Wall single-shot rifle chambered for the .30-40 Krag, thus becoming the first commercial producer in the United States to offer a small-bore, smokeless-powder sporting cartridge. This was nearly two years before the smokeless powder .30-30 loading was offered.

A glance at the following ballistics might suggest, to the astute reader, that original loads used pressures that would today seem excessive for the Krag rifle. Indeed, this seems to have been the case, as the rated velocity was routinely achieved in production rifles and, considering the limited case capacity and characteristics of contemporary domestic smokeless powders, pressures had to have been rather brisk, perhaps exceeding 55,000 psi. It seems at least possible that use of such unusually high-pressure loads contributed to the subsequent problems that earned the single locking lug Krag action a reputation, perhaps undeserved, for weakness.

.30-40 Krag Factory Ballistics

Bullet (grains/type)	Powder	Grains	Velocity	Energy	Source/Comments
220 FMJ-RN Ball	ML	ML	2,200	2,365	Military load, special

7.62x51mm NATO
(.308 Winchester)

Historical Notes: For the NATO small arms trials in the early 1950s, the U.S. submitted its new T-65 cartridge. This was basically a shortened .30-06 case using the same caliber bullet and similar case head dimensions. Case length was reduced from 63 millimeters in the .30-06 to 51 millimeters for the 7.62mm T-65. This allowed a lighter, more compact cartridge and rifle. Some of the other NATO Allies submitted entries that were far more advanced than the T-65 cartridge. However, the U.S. used its considerable influence to override all Allied objections, in order to have the 7.62x51mm NATO cartridge adopted; it remains a NATO standard to this day. In 1957, the U.S. Army adopted the M-14 rifle in 7.62x51mm. The M60 machine gun is also chambered for this cartridge, as are various sniper rifles.

General Comments: During the Vietnam War, the U.S. military adopted the 5.56x45mm cartridge for the new M-16 rifle, which greatly upset the other NATO Allies. A new series of NATO tests was begun in the late 1970s, which resulted in the 5.56x45mm cartridge being standardized, in 1980. Both 7.62x51mm and 5.56x45mm remain NATO standard rounds. Recent tendencies have been to chamber infantry assault rifles for the 5.56x45mm, leaving the 7.62x51mm cartridge for machine guns. Nearly all NATO Allies manufacture the 7.62x51mm cartridge. Many non-NATO countries, such as Japan, Australia, Brazil, Taiwan, South Africa, and others also use this cartridge. Ball, tracer, match, armor piercing, and frangible types exist.

7.62x51mm NATO Factory Ballistics

Bullet (grains/type)	Powder	Grains	Velocity	Energy	Source/Comments
150 FMJ-BT Ball	ML	ML	2,750	2,520	Military load, M80
168 HP-BT Match	ML	ML	2,680	2,680	Military load, M852

.30-06 Springfield
(7.62x63mm U.S./.30-06
Government/.30-06 U.S.)

Historical Notes: The .30-06 Springfield is a United States military cartridge adopted in 1906 for the Model 1903 Springfield service rifle, which was based on the Mauser bolt-action system. The .30-06 is actually a slightly modified version of the original 1903 cartridge, which was loaded with a 220-grain round-nose bullet at a muzzle velocity of 2300 fps. Because of cartridge developments in Europe, it was considered advisable to change to a lighter weight, pointed 150-grain bullet at an increased velocity (2,700 fps). At the same time, the case neck was shortened by .07-inch. This improved round was designated the "Ball Cartridge, caliber .30, Model of 1906," but, in practice, this cumbersome nomenclature was shortened to .30-06. The .30-06 version can be chambered and fired in any rifle made for the original 1903 round, but the reverse is not true, because of the difference in case neck length. For many years, both the 1903 and 1906 configurations were loaded by sporting ammunition manufacturers. Shooting the '06 in the '03 chamber reportedly gave poor accuracy. Old catalogs list both rounds. Occasionally, the 1903 version is called the .30-45, because the original loading used 45 grains of smokeless powder. For additional discussion, see the .30-03 listing in Chapter 2.

Again, because of military developments in Europe, the Army switched to a 172-grain bullet with a nine-degree boat-tail, in 1926. This new round was designated the "Ball, caliber .30, M1." Muzzle velocity, originally the same as the 150-grain load of 2700 fps, was later reduced to 2640 fps, because of difficulty maintaining pressure specifications at the higher velocity. In 1940, the 150-grain flat-base bullet was re-adopted as the "Cartridge, Ball, caliber .30, M2," and that was the load used in World War II. The return to the lighter bullet came about, at least in part, because of difficulties adapting the new Garand semi-automatic rifle to handle the 172-grain load. The heavier boat-tail bullet was superior for machine gun use, because of its greater maximum range of nearly 6,000 yards, compared to about 3,500 yards for the 150-grain loading.

The rimless .30-03 and .30-06 replaced the older rimmed .30-40 Krag as the official U.S. military round. The .30-06 has, in turn, been superseded by the 7.62x51mm, also known as the 7.62mm NATO or, in its commercial version, the .308 Winchester. In Europe, the .30-06 is known as the 7.62x63mm and is widely used.

General Comments: During World War II, the U.S. government supplied .30-06 arms and ammunition to many Allied nations, including Great Britain, Netherlands, France, China, Australia, New Zealand, and Brazil. To keep their inventory of guns ready, many countries undertook manufacture of .30-06 ammunition after the war.

In the 1950s and 1960s, vast quantities of surplus .30-06 ammunition were sold on the U.S. market; shooters will often encounter ball, armor-piercing, and tracer types. Ammunition loaded before and during World War II is corrosively primed. Practically all U.S. military ammunition loaded after 1952 has non-corrosive primers. The principal exception is Frankford Arsenal Match ammunition marked FA 53, 54 or 56, which used the old-style corrosive priming, because it provided superior accuracy.

.30-06 Springfield Factory Ballistics

Bullet (grains/type)	Powder	Grains	Velocity	Energy	Source/Comments
150 FMJ Ball	ML	ML	2,740	2,500	Military load, M2
172 FMJ-BT Ball	ML	ML	2,640	2,660	Military load, M1
220 FMJ-RN Ball	ML	ML	2,300	2,585	Military load, M-1903

Note: Myriad other M-1906 military loadings were adopted for various applications, with differing bullet weights and muzzle velocities.

7.5x54mm French MAS

Historical Notes: In 1924, the French army adopted a new cartridge, the 7.5x58mm MLE 1924C, for a new automatic rifle. In 1929, to avoid ammunition mix-ups with the 7.92x57mm, the French changed to a 4mm shorter cartridge of slightly larger diameter, creating the 7.5x54mm MLF 1929C. This cartridge was originally used in light machine guns and other automatic arms, but in 1934, the Berthier Model-07/15 bolt-action rifle was also modified for this round. In 1936, a newly designed bolt-action rifle (MAS 36) in the new 7.5mm was adopted. This rimless cartridge replaced the rimmed 8mm Lebel, which the French army had used since 1886.

General Comments: Fair quantities of French military rifles in this chambering have appeared on the surplus market from time to time, as the French are noted for hanging on to their obsolete military hardware long after it's of any real value. Sporting ammunition for this chambering has never been manufactured. However, A.L.M. Arsenal, in France, recently produced this cartridge with a Boxer primer. Some of the surplus dealers made up hunting ammunition by replacing the military bullet with a similar soft-point type. The 7.5mm MAS is in the same class as the .30-40 Krag or the .303 British and can be used for the same range of game. Performance can be improved a little in handloading, but only Berdan-primed military cases have formerly been available. The military load develops about 40,000 psi breech pressure. The initials "MAS" represent the French arsenal that developed this cartridge and rifle, Manufacture d'Armes de Saint Etienne.

7.5x54mm French MAS Loading Data and Factory Ballistics

Bullet (grains/type)	Powder	Grains	Velocity	Energy	Source/Comments
150 SP	IMR 4831	54	2,680	2,400	Duplicates military ball
150 SP	IMR 4895	48	2,800	2,620	N/A
180 SP	IMR 4895	44	2,590	2,692	N/A
140 Ball	ML	ML	2,600	2,100	Military load, MLE 1929C

7.62x53Rmm Russian

Historical Notes: Sometimes called the 7.62x54Rmm Russian, this cartridge was adopted in 1891 with the Model 1891 Mosin-Nagant bolt-action rifle. Its 150-grain spitzer bullet was adopted in 1909. This cartridge was standard issue in the Russian army, during World War II. It is still standard issue for medium machine guns and the SVD sniper rifle. It was also adopted by Finland, China, and most ex-satellite nations. It remains one of the few rimmed military cartridges still in standard issue. Early in World War I, Winchester made M95 lever-action muskets, and Remington made rolling block rifles for Imperial Russia. Later, Russian Nagant rifles were manufactured in the United States by New England Westinghouse Co., Remington, and Winchester. After the war, a large number of surplus rifles were sold commercially, and Remington loaded a 150-grain bronze-point hunting round. Additional Russian Nagant rifles and carbines have been sold in surplus stores, since the end of World War II. Many of these rifles were captured during the Korean conflict. Surplus Mosin rifles are being imported from China, Finland, Hungary, Poland, Romania, and Russia.

General Comments: The 7.62x54Rmm Russian cartridge has been kicked around since about 1919 and is fairly well known to American shooters. Remington discontinued loading this round about 1950. It was recently offered by Norma and Lapua. Various surplus military ammunition (corrosive Berdan primed and steel cased) has recently been imported into the United States. Russian military cartridges use Berdan primers, usually of 6.45 mm (.254-inch) diameter.

With the 150-grain bullet, the 7.62mm Russian is in the same class as the .30-06. However, since the rifle has a shorter magazine, it will not do as well as the .30-06 when loaded with heavier bullets. Although military bullets measure .309- to .311-inch in diameter, rifles with tighter bores will shoot .308-inch bullets just fine. However, many rifles have grossly oversized bores. In such rifles, .308-inch jacketed bullets are hopelessly inaccurate, though .311-inch bullets will shoot with a modicum of accuracy. Properly sized cast bullets will shoot with impressive accuracy (minute-of-angle groups are no problem). Unfortunately, there is no ready source of appropriate commercial jacketed or cast bullets sized large enough for specimens with bores running larger than about .313-inch. Standard working pressure is about 45,000 psi.

7.62x53Rmm Russian Loading Data and Factory Ballistics

Bullet (grains/type)	Powder	Grains	Velocity	Energy	Source/Comments
150 SP	IMR 3031	49	2,800	2,620	Approximates military ball load
180 SP	IMR 4320	48	2,630	2,772	N/A
220 SP	IMR 4350	45	2,350	2,705	N/A
147 Ball	ML	ML	2,886	2,727	Military load, Type LPS bullet
150 SP	FL	FL	2,950	2,820	Norma factory load
180 SP	FL	FL	2,580	2,650	Norma factory load
185 Ball	ML	ML	2,660	2,910	Military load, Type O bullet

.303 British

Historical Notes: As a military cartridge, the .303 British must be considered one of the most successful of its type. Developed during 1887 and adopted in 1888, it was the official military cartridge of the British Commonwealth in World War I and II. In 1957, the 7.62x51mm NATO cartridge replaced it.

Originally, the .303 cartridge was loaded with a 215-grain round-nose bullet encased in a cupro-nickel jacket. This bullet, backed by 70 grains of compressed black powder, developed a muzzle velocity of 1850 fps. Muzzle energy was 1630 ft-lbs. In the 1890s, in response to reports from the frontier that the jacketed round-nose solid bullet was ineffective against tribesmen, Capt. Bertie Clay, at the arsenal at Dum Dum, India, perfected an expanding bullet, with the jacket open at the nose to expose the lead core. This bullet mushroomed on impact. Such projectiles became known as Dum Dum bullets, which has led to much confusion and nonsense through the common parlance and lay misunderstanding of what expanding bullets are, how they work, and why they are beneficial.

In 1892, propellant charging was changed to use the new Cordite smokeless powder. Muzzle velocity of the new loading was 1970 fps, which produced 1850 ft-lbs of energy. Owing to the efficiency of the new powder, this worthwhile ballistic improvement was accompanied by a significant reduction in peak chamber pressure. In 1910, a load using a 174-grain pointed flat-base bullet was adopted; velocity for that loading was 2440 fps, which produces 2310 ft-lbs of energy. This was the MkVII round, still in use when the .303 was discontinued.

Bullets for the MkVII cartridge had an aluminum- or fiber-filled tip, with a base of conventional lead alloy. This made the bullet longer than normal for its weight. It also produced a stable projectile in flight that would tumble easily on contact, thus increasing wounding potential.

The .303 cartridge was designed for the Lee-Metford MkI magazine rifle, a turn-bolt type invented by James Paris Lee, an American. (In studying these things, it is surprising how often significant firearms and cartridge inventors were forced to travel beyond their own shores to find acceptance.) In 1895, the segmental and shallow Metford-type rifling was discontinued in favor of the deeper Enfield-type. (Interestingly, Metford had also patented the so-called Enfield rifling, prior to his segmental form.) From this point on, the rifle was known as the Lee-Enfield. Many variations and types exist.

General Comments: The .303 British cartridge has been used extensively in Africa, Canada, and India by settlers and government workers. It gained a bad reputation, because the full jacketed military bullets tended to tumble on impact. However, with proper sporting bullets, it does quite well on the lighter, non-dangerous game varieties. Norma offers one loading, a 150-grain soft-nose. U.S. companies now load it with a 180-grain soft-point.

Although usually classed with the .30-40 Krag, the .303 actually has a worthwhile edge over the Krag. For one thing, it has a nominal operating pressure of 45,000 to 48,000 psi, compared to 40,000 to 42,000 psi for the .30-40. In addition, late model Enfield rifles are much stronger than the Krag. Enfield No. 4 MkI rifles have been successfully converted to use the 7.62mm NATO, which has a nominal maximum pressure of 62,000 psi. Finally, the modest increase in bore area gives the edge to the .303.

Ammunition for the .303 loaded in Britain had the Berdan primer and, in older lots, usually Cordite powder. Military ammunition loaded by American companies has the Boxer primer and American-type nitrocellulose powder. Proper jacketed bullet diameter for the .303 is .311-inch. Cast bullets may run to .312-inch or even .313-inch. Loading data will be found in Chapter 1.

.303 British Factory Ballistics

Bullet (grains/type)	Powder	Grains	Velocity	Energy	Source/Comments
215 Ball	FFg	70.0	1,850	1,630	Original black powder load
215 Ball	Cordite	N/A	1,970	1,850	Original Cordite load
175 Ball	ML	ML	2,440	2,310	Military load, MkVII Ball
215 Ball	ML	ML	2,050	2,010	Military load, MkVI Ball

7.7x58mm Japanese Arisaka

Historical Notes: The 7.7mm cartridge was adopted by the Japanese in 1939 to replace the older 6.5mm, but they ended up using both cartridges during World War II. They also adopted a new rifle, the Model 99 Arisaka, which was a modification of the earlier 1905 gun. Norma has offered empty cases and sporting ammunition for this chambering with American Boxer-type primer pockets. No sporting rifles have ever been manufactured in this chambering.

General Comments: The 7.7mm, or .31 Jap, as it is sometimes called, is ballistically very similar to the .303 British cartridge and uses the same .311-inch diameter bullets. However, it is a rimless type, whereas the British case is rimmed. There is also a semi-rimmed Japanese version for machine gun use. The 7.7mm Japanese can be used for the same kinds and sizes of game as the .303 British. With good Norma sporting ammunition available, this has become one of the more useful military cartridges for North American hunting. Military loads develop about 42,000 psi, which, as with the 6.5mm Arisaka, seems unusually mild for a modern military chambering, particularly when one considers the unusual strength of these rifles.

7.7x58mm Japanese Arisaka Loading Data and Factory Ballistics

Bullet (grains/type)	Powder	Grains	Velocity	Energy	Source/Comments
130 SP	IMR 3031	46	2,950	2,510	Duplicates factory loading
150 SP	IMR 3031	41	2,680	2,400	N/A
180 SP	IMR 4064	45	2,490	2,470	Duplicates factory loading
215 SP	IMR 4064	42	2,240	2,405	N/A

7.7x58mm Japanese Arisaka Loading Data and Factory Ballistics

Bullet (grains/type)	Powder	Grains	Velocity	Energy	Source/Comments
130 SP	FL	FL	2,950	2,510	Norma factory load
175 Ball	ML	ML	2,400	2,237	Military load
180 SP	FL	FL	2,490	2,470	Norma factory load

7.62x39mm (7.62x39mm Soviet M43)

Historical Notes: This "assault rifle" cartridge was adopted by Russia in 1943. It did not come into general use until after World War II, but the Russians now use it as their principal infantry small-arms cartridge. Original use was in the SKS semi-automatic carbine, later replaced by the AK-47 selective-fire assault rifle. The RPD light machine gun also uses the M43 cartridge. Finland, and those ex-satellite countries in the Soviet bloc, use the M43 cartridge in arms furnished by Russia or of their own design. This cartridge was adopted as the result of Russian military experience against German assault rifles chambered for the 7.92mm Kurz. Ruger introduced its Mini-30 semi-automatic rifle chambered for the 7.62x39mm in 1987 and the bolt-action M77 Mark II rifle, in 1991. Most military ammunition has a steel case and corrosive Berdan primer, but reloadable cases are now readily available.

General Comments: The M43 is a ¼-inch longer than the German 7.92mm Kurz and will give substantially better performance with newer powders. This cartridge has been loaded commercially by Federal, Winchester, Remington, and Black Hills with Boxer-primed reloadable cases. Better handloads and factory ammunition using soft-point bullets up to about 150 grains place this cartridge far ahead of any reasonable .30-30 load, in terms of delivered energy beyond 100 yards.

7.62x39mm Loading Data and Factory Ballistics

Bullet (grains/type)	Powder	Grains	Velocity	Energy	Source/Comments
110 Sierra HP	AA 1680	27.5	2,547	1,580	Accurate Arms, Maximum load (.308")
125 Sierra SP	AA 1680	25.5	2,368	1,555	Accurate Arms, Maximum load (.311")
150 Sierra SP	AA 2015	26.0	2,072	1,430	Accurate Arms, Maximum load (.311")
122 Ball	ML	ML	2,329	1,470	Military load
123 SP	FL	FL	2,300	1,440	Black Hills factory load
150 SP	FL	FL	2,200	1,610	Black Hills factory load

7.65x53mm Mauser (Argentine)

Historical Notes: Mauser-designed for the 1889 Belgian pattern rifle, the 7.65mm was also adopted by Argentina, Bolivia, Columbia, Ecuador, Peru, and Turkey. In the United States, Remington and Winchester loaded sporting ammunition and furnished rifles in this chambering, until about 1936. It has been obsolete in the United States since that time, but sporting ammunition has always been loaded in Europe. The Remington Model 30 and Winchester Model 54 bolt-action rifles were chambered for the 7.65mm, and it enjoyed a limited popularity for a few years. With the influx of 1891 Argentine Mauser military rifles, it is having another go-around on the American market. Evidently, a very similar but unique Belgian Mauser cartridge also exists. The catalog drawing suggests that it has slightly smaller case head, probably less body taper and, perhaps, a slightly shorter case neck (the sketch is insufficiently dimensionally denoted to establish facts).

General Comments: The 7.65mm is among the best designed of all Mauser cartridges. This number gives excellent performance for North American hunting. In power, its slightly larger usable case capacity and slight bore-size increase place it ahead of the .308 Winchester and quite close to factory .30-06 loads, particularly with bullets up to about 165 grains, which makes it adequate for all medium game.

Arsenal primers are Berdan 5.5mm or .217-inch, a size available in several European makes. Occasionally one encounters discontinued American-made cases or ammunition, and these use conventional Boxer Large Rifle primers. Cases can be made from empty .30-06 cases through the use of case-forming dies available from several American manufacturers. Bullet size is .313-inch, but .311-inch or .312-inch diameter bullets will give satisfactory accuracy. Norma-made cases and loaded ammunition use Boxer primers.

7.65x53mm Mauser Loading Data and Factory Ballistics

Bullet (grains/type)	Powder	Grains	Velocity	Energy	Source/Comments
150 SP	IMR 4895	47	2,810	2,638	N/A
150 SP	IMR 4895	42	2,550	2,172	N/A
174 SP	IMR 4895	45	2,590	2,600	N/A
175 SP	IMR 4350	49	2,560	2,550	N/A
175 SP	IMR 4831	53	2,456	2,346	N/A
180 SP	FL	FL	2,590	2,685	Norma factory load
150 SP	FL	FL	2,920	2,841	Norma factory load
155 FMJ-BT Ball	ML	ML	2,710	2,530	Military load, Type S
174 FMJ-BT Ball	ML	ML	2,460	2,340	Military load, Type SS
211 FMJ Ball	ML	ML	2,130	2,150	Military load, Original

8x53Rmm Japanese Murata

Historical Notes: This Japanese service cartridge was adopted in 1887 for the tube-magazine Murata turn-bolt rifle, a modification of the earlier single-shot and repeating 11mm Murata rifles. It is similar to the French Chassepot in design. The 8mm Murata was the principal rifle used by the Japanese, in the Sino-Japanese War of 1894. It was known officially as the Meiji 20 8mm rifle and cartridge. "Meiji" refers to the period of the Emperor Meiji's reign (1868-1912). This cartridge was replaced in 1897 by the 6.5mm round.

General Comments: Both 8mm Murata rifles and cartridges are collector's items, and rare ones at that. This cartridge was loaded with smokeless powder and a jacketed flat-nose bullet (safe for use in the tubular magazine) that measured .320 inch in diameter and weighed 238 grains. No reader is likely to have one of these rifles available for hunting or anything else. However, if you do, the cartridge would be adequate for anything to elk-sized animals at moderate range. The 8x53Rmm is unusual among military cartridges, because it has a protected primer that appears as a primer within a primer.

8x53Rmm Japanese Murata Factory Ballistics

Bullet (grains/type)	Powder	Grains	Velocity	Energy	Source/Comments
238 Ball	ML	ML	1,850	1,810	Military load

8x50Rmm Siamese Mauser (Type 45)

Historical Notes: Originally adopted in 1902, this cartridge actually derives its name from the Thai year of adoption—1945. It was a standard Siamese military cartridge from 1902 until World War II. It is historically significant for two reasons. First, the 8x50Rmm Siamese is the first rimmed military cartridge adapted to a unique variation of the popular Mauser rifle. Second, it was the first cartridge to be manufactured in quantity in Thailand (National Arsenal, Bangkok). During World War II, the production machinery was moved to the hills to escape Japanese seizure. The machinery served to supply the guerrilla movement. When the war ended, it was moved back to Bangkok.

General Comments: The 8x50Rmm cartridge was loaded with a .321-inch-diameter, round-nose bullet with a copper-nickel jacket, in a brass cartridge case with Berdan priming. Some manufacture of this cartridge was also contracted out to Japan and Germany. In 1923, a new cartridge was adopted, the 8x52Rmm, and existing rifles for the older round were re-chambered and rear sights modified. During the late 1970s, thousands of these surplus rifles were sold in the United States. It is hard to avoid noticing the similarity between this circa-1895 cartridge and the circa-1955 7.62x51mm NATO round.

8x50Rmm Siamese Mauser Factory Ballistics

Bullet (grains/type)	Powder	Grains	Velocity	Energy	Source/Comments
237 Ball	FL	FL	2,050 (est.)	2,210	N/A

8x52Rmm Siamese (Type 66)

Historical Notes: In 1923, the Siamese army adopted a new cartridge with a pointed bullet. Case length was two millimeters longer than the older 8x50Rmm Siamese cartridge, so the two are not interchangeable. The new round was adapted to a new Mannlicher infantry rifle and carbine, as well as to Madsen, Browning, and Vickers machine guns. Older rifles for the 8x50Rmm cartridge were re-chambered. The 8x52Rmm cartridge remained in production in Thailand until 1953 after which ball ammunition was contracted out (chiefly to Kynoch, in England), until finally discontinued, in the late 1960s.

General Comments: The pointed, flat-base ball bullet of the 8x52Rmm cartridge will be found with both cupro-nickel-clad steel and gilding metal jackets. Cases are of brass with Berdan primers. Boxer-primed cases will also be encountered. In addition to ball loadings, there were tracer, armor-piercing, and armor-piercing incendiary types. This cartridge was also made by Kynoch (U.K.), in Japan and Denmark, and by Sako of Finland. Surplus rifles in this chambering are often encountered in the United States.

8x52Rmm Siamese Factory Ballistics (Note: *Estimated ballistics)

Bullet (grains/type)	Powder	Grains	Velocity	Energy	Source/Comments
181 Ball	ML	ML	2,250	2,615	Military load *

8x58Rmm Danish Krag

Historical Notes: This Danish-designed military cartridge was adopted in 1889 for the M89 Krag-Jorgensen bolt-action rifle. The cartridge was adopted by Norway in 1888 for a Remington carbine, and then by both Denmark and Sweden in 1889. The original loading was the 237-grain round-nose bullet, but, in 1908, this was changed to a 196-grain spitzer bullet at a muzzle velocity of 2460 fps. This was, at one time, a popular sporting and target cartridge in Scandinavian countries, where rifles based on the Remington rolling block action and chambered for this round were used. A few of those were imported into the United States.

General Comments: The Danish 8mm military cartridge has a good reputation for accuracy in the Danish Krag rifle. It is also noted for very satisfactory killing power on European big game. It was practically unknown in the United States, until after World War II, when a number of surplus Danish Krags were sold. As a military cartridge, it is in the same class as our own .30-40 Krag or the .303 British. However, the sporting ammunition once offered by Norma was far more powerful than any commercial loads for the .30-40 or .303. In fact, the 198-grain bullet at 2740 fps develops far more energy than any commercial .30-06 load. This is one of the better military cartridges, from the point of view of the North American hunter. European sporting cartridges are loaded to pressures of 42,000 to 45,000 psi. This cartridge is no longer commercially loaded, and ammunition has become scarce.

8x58Rmm Danish Krag Loading Data and Factory Ballistics

Bullet (grains/type)	Powder	Grains	Velocity	Energy	Source/Comments
159 SP	IMR 3031	52.4	2,870	2,920	Duplicates factory loading
196 SP	IMR 4895	54	2,630	3,020	Duplicates factory loading
198 SP	IMR 4895	54.5	2,740	3,310	Duplicates factory loading
159 SP	FL	FL	2,870	2,920	Norma factory load
196 SP	FL	FL	2,630	3,020	Norma factory load
198 SP	FL	FL	2,740	3,310	Norma factory load
237 Ball	ML	ML	1,968	2,041	Military load

8x50Rmm Lebel

Historical Notes: The 8mm Lebel was the first smallbore, smokeless powder military cartridge developed by any world power. The cartridge and the Lebel bolt-action rifle were both adopted in 1886. The original loading used a 232-grain, jacketed flat-nose flat-base bullet called the Balle M. In 1898, a solid bronze, spitzer boat-tail, 198-grain bullet was adopted, the famous Balle D. The cartridge was further updated in 1932 with the adoption of the Balle 32M, which had a cupro-nickel-clad steel jacket over a lead core. This spitzer boat-tail bullet weighed 190 grains. Its rimmed case was not well adapted to automatic arms, so it was replaced by the rimless 7.5x54mm MAS round in 1929. Remington manufactured rolling blocks and Mannlicher-Berthier chambered in 8x50Rmm Lebel for the French government during World War I. When the war ended, all the surplus was sold commercially, and Remington turned out sporting ammunition with a 170-grain, bronze-pointed bullet. Few rifles have been made in this chambering. Military production of this cartridge in France continued, even under German occupation.

General Comments: Probably more 8mm Lebel rifles were sold during the 1920s and '30s than after World War II. The Remington factory products were all brand new and in perfect condition, which is more than can be said for the more recent war surplus models that have shown up. The 8mm Lebel cartridge is in the .308 Winchester-class and makes a fine cartridge for deer or elk hunting. Modern 8mm Lebel sporting ammunition is difficult to find. Plenty of good .323-inch bullets are available, and American cases can easily be reloaded. Military cases have Berdan primers of .199-inch or .216-inch size and are less practical to reload.

8x50Rmm Lebel Loading Data and Factory Ballistics

Bullet (grains/type)	Powder	Grains	Velocity	Energy	Source/Comments
170 SP	IMR 4895	49	2,570	2,500	N/A
198 SP	IMR 3031	46	2,380	2,481	Duplicates military ball
198 SP	IMR 4895	45	2,450	2,645	N/A
170	FL	FL	2,640	2,630	Remington factory load
198	ML	ML	2,380	2,481	Military load, Balle D, Balle 32M

8x50Rmm Austrian Mannlicher

Historical Notes: This was an Austrian military cartridge adopted in 1888 for the Mannlicher Model 88 straight-pull rifle, and also used in the later improved Model 95. This cartridge was also used by Bulgaria, Greece, and Hungary. It remains fairly popular as a sporting cartridge in Europe, and many Mannlicher rifles have been chambered for it. Sporting ammunition is still loaded in Europe by Hirtenberger, and this cartridge was recently imported to the United States. This was originally a black-powder design. A smokeless powder loading was adopted about 1890.

General Comments: During the 1920s and '30s, a few European sporting rifles chambered for the 8x50Rmm cartridge were imported into the United States and used, to a limited extent, for big-game hunting. This is another cartridge in the .30-40 Krag class, which is adequate for most North American big game. It uses .323-inch bullets, of which there is a good variety available for handloading. Berdan-primed cases appear to use the 5.1mm or .199-inch primer, although this is variable. Hirtenberger ammunition is Boxer primed and loaded at 40,000 to 42,000 psi.

The Model 88 Mannlicher straight-pull rifle uses a hinged block on the underside of the bolt to lock the action. This design is not noted for great strength, and pressures must be kept quite low for safety. The Model 95 has a revolving bolt head and forward locking lugs, which provide greater strength. Many 95s were altered to shoot the standard German 8mm Mauser service cartridge.

8x50Rmm Austrian Mannlicher Loading Data and Factory Ballistics (Loads are for Model 88 action in good condition.)

Bullet (grains/type)	Powder	Grains	Velocity	Energy	Source/Comments
159 SP	IMR 3031	48	2,460	2,142	N/A
227 SP	IMR 3031	45	2,040	2,102	N/A
244 SP	IMR 3031	45	2,010	2,200	Approximates military load
196 SP	FL	FL	2,310	2,320	Hirtenberger factory load
244 Ball	ML	ML	2,030	2,240	Military load, smokeless powder

7.92x33mm Kurz

Historical Notes: This cartridge was developed during 1940-'41 for use in the newly conceived German MKB42 assault rifle. It first was tested in combat against the Russian army at Cholm, Russia, in late 1942. Several changes and modifications culminated in the Sturmgewehr rifle, or Stg-44. This was the first successful assault rifle cartridge and, as such, marks an important milestone in military history that has had a profound effect on small arms development.

The 7.92mm Kurz is a short version of the standard 7.92mm (8mm) Mauser cartridge. No commercial sporting rifle has ever been made for this round. Ammunition was manufactured in East Germany for some years for export customers.

General Comments: This is a medium-range cartridge designed to increase infantry firepower by permitting more accurate and controlled full-automatic fire. That is not possible with lightweight shoulder guns using full-powered cartridges, such as the .30-06 or the German 8x57mm Mauser. This combination must have been quite effective, because it was used against the Russians, who almost immediately copied it and brought out a similar assault rifle and cartridge. It has been demonstrated that, in close combat in cities, jungles, or similar areas, these reduced-power cartridges have all the range and penetration necessary.

The German Sturmgewehr, or assault rifle, had a 16-inch barrel, weighed 10 to 11 pounds loaded and used a 30-shot magazine. As a sporting cartridge, the 7.92mm Kurz would be less powerful than the .30-30 and not very well suited for anything but small to medium game. Because guns for this cartridge are capable of full-automatic fire, none have been sold in fireable condition, because these come under the National Firearms Act and require a special license to own. This ammunition has never been commercially manufactured. Military ammunition is not reloadable, as it is steel cased and Berdan primed.

7.92x33mm Kurz Loading Data and Factory Ballistics

Bullet (grains/type)	Powder	Grains	Velocity	Energy	Source/Comments
125	4198	20	2,070	1,193	N/A
125	4198	23	2,310	1,485	Maximum load
125 Ball	ML	ML	2,247	1,408	Military load

7.9x57mmJ and 7.9x57mm JS (8mm German Mauser)

Historical Notes: The 8mm Mauser is one of the world's truly great military cartridges. It was the official German military cartridge in both World Wars and was also adopted by Czechoslovakia, Poland, China, and other countries. It is also a popular sporting round in many parts of the world.

Although designated the 8mm "Mauser," the original military round was designed for the German Model 88 commission rifle, which was a modified Mannlicher-type, not a Mauser design. This rifle was known officially as the Gewehr 88, or German Infantry Model 1888. It was designed by the German Infantry Board or Commission at Spandau Arsenal. It was replaced in 1898 by the superior Mauser model of that year.

The original J Patrone cartridge used a round-nose 226-grain bullet of .318-inch diameter. Muzzle velocity was 2093 fps. In 1905, the Germans adopted an improved cartridge that retained the original 8x57mm case, but employed a larger-diameter bullet (.323-inch). The new S Patrone bullet was lighter (154 grains) and was pointed or spitzer-type. Muzzle velocity was upped to 2880 fps. Although the rifle had a significantly longer barrel than the '03 Springfield, the 17 percent muzzle energy advantage that the 7.9x57mmJS load had over the .30-06 ball loading is quite surprising. There is evidence that German smokeless powder of that era was vastly superior to anything available in this country and, perhaps, anywhere else. This no doubt accommodated the above noted ballistic potential of the 7.9x57mmJS loading. External ballistic calculations prove that the German military loading was a significantly superior battlefield cartridge compared to the U.S. military loading. All German military rifles manufactured since 1905 originated with the .323-inch bore. All earlier military and many civilian arms were re-rifled to accommodate .323-inch bullets.

The original German 8mm military cartridge was designated by a "J" for "Infanterie." (The story is that U.S. military intelligence officers who were tasked to discover the secret of the superior performance of the German cartridge captured classified German documents toward the end of World War I and then mistook the ornate German script "I" for a "J." If true, it is indeed ironic that, worldwide, including Germany, the designation has been bastardized to "J.") The later bullet, for the .323-inch diameter groove, is indicated by an "S," for spitzer-type. Sporting ammunition in 8mm is labeled by the same system. The 8x57mmJ or 1888 cartridge can be fired safely in the 1905 or "S"-bore rifles, though accuracy is poor. However, it is not safe to fire the larger "S" (.323-inch) bullet in the smaller "J" (.318-inch) bore.

General Comments: Thousands of 8mm military rifles have been sold through surplus dealers since the end of World War II. Most were bought to obtain the 98 Mauser action, which served as the basis for building a sporting rifle for some U.S. cartridges. In many instances, the cost of making up a custom rifle on a military action wasn't justified. However, if the original chambering was retained and modifications held to the minimum, many of these rifles were a good buy.

The 8x57mmJS Mauser is an outstanding sporting cartridge in its own right, being in the same class as our .30-06. U.S. ammunition companies load only the "S" version of the 8mm, but hold it to a very mild pressure level, so the round could safely be fired in a "J"-bored rifle. This has a 170-grain bullet at 2360 fps, which about duplicates the .30-40 Krag in power. Norma makes both 165- and 196-grain sporting loads that bring out the full potential of this cartridge. Sporting loads and handloading data will be found in Chapter 1.

7.9x57mmJ and 7.9mmJS Factory Ballistics

Bullet (grains/type)	Powder	Grains	Velocity	Energy	Source/Comments
154 Ball	ML	ML	2,880	2,835	Military load, S Patrone
226 Ball	ML	ML	2,095	2,200	Military load, J Patrone

WARNING! Many "J"-bore (.318-inch) rifles still exist and will fire "S"-bore (.323-inch) cartridges, potentially creating dangerous pressures. When in doubt, check the bore diameter CAREFULLY!

8x63mm Swedish

Historical Notes:	This is a Swedish round introduced in 1932 for use in various Browning air- or water-cooled machine guns and for the m/40 rifle. (Note that the lower-case "m" and the slash between it and the numeral "40" is the frequently encountered representation of the designation for this particular Swedish rifle. It is, of course, not the same as the U.S. M40 rifle.) Swedish military rifles and light machine guns are chambered for the standard 6.5x55mm cartridge. Its use is confined to Sweden, and it is practically unknown outside there. It was never actually loaded as a sporting cartridge.				
General Comments:	The 8x63mm nearly duplicates the wildcat 8mm-06 cartridge, which is the .30-06 necked up to accept .323-inch bullets. However, the 8x63mm has a larger-diameter case and should be capable of delivering about 15 percent more energy if loaded to the same pressure. The 8x63mm Swedish is significantly more powerful than the .30-06 Springfield.				

8x63mm Swedish Loading Data and Factory Ballistics

Bullet (grains/type)	Powder	Grains	Velocity	Energy	Source/Comments
150 SP	4895	60	3,050	3,100	N/A
170 SP	4320	57	2,820	3,020	N/A
225 SP	4350	57	2,450	2,960	N/A
218 Ball	ML	ML	2,493	3,025	Military load

8x60Rmm Guedes M85 Portuguese

Historical Notes:	Portugal adopted the 8mm Guedes rifle and cartridge, in 1885. The gun was a single-shot, under-lever type based on the Martini-Henry design. These rifles were manufactured by Steyr in Austria and were well made and finished. One of the last of the military single-shots, it had a very short life. A very similar cartridge called the 8x60mm Kropatschek was adapted in 1896 by Portugal. These two may have been generally interchangeable.
General Comments:	The 8mm Guedes cartridge represented a ballistic advance similar to the 9.5mm Turkish Mauser. However, the Guedes rifle was a step in the wrong direction, because all the powers of the time were rapidly developing repeating rifles. Both rifle and cartridge are rare.
	The 8mm Guedes was replaced in 1896 by an apparently interchangeable cartridge, the 8x60Rmm Kropatschek (later shortened to a 56mm case length). This cartridge was used in the Austrian-made Kropatschek rifle, a tube-magazine repeater. No sporting rifles were made for either of these rounds.

8x60Rmm Guedes M85 Portuguese Loading Data and Factory Ballistics

Bullet (grains/type)	Powder	Grains	Velocity	Energy	Source/Comments
175 Lead	Black powder (Fg)	75	1,740	1,182	Lyman #321232
175 Lead	IMR 4198	28	1,670	1,090	Lyman #321232
247 Ball	Black powder (Fg)	70	1,706	1,605	Military load

8x59mm Breda

Historical Notes: This cartridge was for the Italian Breda Model 1937 and 1938 machine guns. Insofar as can be established, it has never been used as a sporting cartridge.

General Comments: Different bullet weights and muzzle velocities are listed for the 8mm Breda, and this may reflect the various military loadings. Bullet diameter varies from .322-inch to .326-inch. The cartridge case is fatter and 1/10-inch longer than the 8mm Mauser. The original purpose of the 8mm Breda was to replace the 6.5mm Italian cartridge as a more effective machine gun round. Since case capacity and published ballistics both suggest that this cartridge came close to matching modern .300 Magnum energy levels, it would seem that it was indeed a significant step up from the 6.5mm Italian Carcano.

8x59mm Breda Loading Data

Bullet (grains/type)	Powder	Grains	Velocity	Energy	Source/Comments
210 Ball	ML	ML	2,600	3,160	Military load

8x56Rmm Austrian-Hungarian Mannlicher (8mm Hungarian M31)

Historical Notes: This cartridge was developed in 1930 for the Solothurn machine gun. It was subsequently adopted by Hungary about 1931. Design goes back to the mid-1920s, when it was developed to replace the 8x50Rmm Austrian round. It was designated the M30 in Austria, and the M31 in Hungary. It differs from the older Austrian 8x50Rmm, having a longer tapered shoulder, plus a bullet of slightly larger diameter. It was used in the Hungarian Model 35 Mannlicher bolt-action rifle, and also the modified Model 95 straight-pull Mannlicher. In 1940, Hungary adopted the standard German 8mm military round, and many of its rifles were then altered to that chambering. As far as we know, no sporting rifles were turned out in the 8mm Hungarian chambering.

General Comments: This cartridge is often confused with the 8x56mm Mannlicher-Schoenauer, which is a rimless sporting cartridge, whereas the Hungarian military round is rimmed. The two are not interchangeable, as there is considerable difference in case dimensions, as well as bullet diameter.

Rifles in this chambering are common on the American market, and ammunition is also readily available. The .329-inch diameter bullet makes handloading a problem, because bullets of this size are not normally available. It is possible to use .323-inch bullets, but accuracy is poor. Military rifles in this chambering should be considered primarily collector's items, because of the ammunition supply problem. In power, the 8x56Rmm Hungarian and the 8x50Rmm Austrian cartridge are in the .30-40 Krag class.

8x56Rmm Hungarian Mannlicher Loading Data and Factory Ballistics

Bullet (grains/type)	Powder	Grains	Velocity	Energy	Source/Comments
198 SP	IMR 3031	46	2,310	2,358	.323-inch bullet
206 Ball	IMR 3031	45	2,300	2,420	Military load

9x21mm Russian (9x21mm Gyurza)

Historical Notes: The 9x21 Russian resembles the 9x21mm cartridge in the West, but it is based on the 9x18mm Makarov, not the 9x19mm. Case head dimensions of 9x21mm Russian cartridges are identical to 9x18mm cases. WARNING: 9x21mm Russian should never be fired in a western 9x21mm pistol, though it will likely chamber. Originally built by the Russian firm of TsNIITochMash in 1993, the 9x21 Russian was built specifically for the Gurza pistol, which so far is the only known firearm chambered for this cartridge. In performance, the 9x21mm's ballistics are in the lower end of .357 Magnum class.

General Comments: The 9x21 Russian comes in two variations, the RG-052 and RG-054. The RG-054 cartridges have a steel penetrator. The RG-052 has a gilding metal case, and the RG-054 has lacquered steel cases. The 9x21mm Russian will probably never be widely distributed outside Russia because it was designed to be an armor-piercing round. The 9x21 P (7N28) bullet consists of a lead core in a bi-metallic shell. The 9x21 PS (7N29) has an armor-piercing tracer bullet that is used jointly with the 9x21 P. The 9x21mm with tracer (7BT3) is a frangible type used where ricochets are a concern.—*W.T.W.*

9x21 Russian Loading Data and Factory Ballistics

Bullet (grains/type)	Powder	Grains	Velocity	Energy	Source/Comments
103 7N28	ML	ML	1,410	455	Military Load
111 7BT3	ML	ML	1,300	415	Military load
122 7N29	ML	ML	1,300	458	Military load

9x39mm SP-5 & SP-6

Historical Notes: In the 1980s, the 9x39mm subsonic cartridge was developed by TsNIITochMash for use in its AS and VSS suppressed rifles. The cartridge was designed by N. Zabelin, L. Dvoryaninova, and Y. Frolov of TsNIITochMash. The case appears to be no more than a 7.62x39mm case necked-up to accept the 9mm bullet, so the 9x39mm has essentially the same head diameter and case length. The 250-grain bullets for the 9x39mm are about twice the weight of the 7.62×39mm.

General Comments: The SP-5 ball round is primarily used in the VSS sniper rifle, and the SP-6 armor piercing round in the AS assault rifle. They are not intended to be used beyond 400 to 500 meters. The 250-grain SP-5 ball round is a boat-tail configuration with a hollow base and steel-lead core. —*W.T.W.*

9x39mm SP-5 & SP-6 Loading Data and Factory Ballistics

Bullet (grains/type)	Powder	Grains	Velocity	Energy	Source/Comments
250 SP-5 (ball)	ML	ML	950	501	Military Load
246.2 SP-6 (AP)	ML	ML	950	493	Military load

9.5x60Rmm Turkish Mauser

Historical Notes: This cartridge was adopted by Turkey in 1887 with the M87 Mauser bolt-action repeating rifle, which was a modification of the German Model 71/84. This last Mauser-designed black-powder cartridge is one of the most efficient ever developed. Mauser concluded, after extensive testing and experimenting, that the 9.5mm bullet gave the maximum performance possible with this propellant. The cartridge was used for three years, before it was made obsolete by smokeless powder. In 1890, Turkey adopted the 7.65mm Mauser cartridge. The 9.5mm is often referred to as the Turkish Peabody, because it was also used extensively in the Peabody-Martini single-shot rifle.

General Comments: The Turkish Mauser Model 87 rifle is largely a collector's item, because the Turks scrapped most of the original guns when they adopted the 7.65mm, in 1890. However, a good number of the single-shot Peabody-Martini rifles in this chambering survived. This cartridge has been obsolete in Europe since the turn of the century. As a hunting number, the 9.5mm Turkish would be adequate for North American big game at moderate ranges.

9.5x60Rmm Turkish Mauser Loading Data and Factory Ballistics

Bullet (grains/type)	Powder	Grains	Velocity	Energy	Source/Comments
290 Lead	IMR 4198	34	1,500	1,445	Lyman #403173
285 Lead	Black powder (Fg)	70	1,758	1,955	Military load, paper-patched bullet
284 Lead	ML	ML	1,758	1,950	Military load

10.15x61Rmm Jarmann

Historical Notes: This cartridge was adopted by Norway and Sweden in 1881 for use in the Jarmann repeating rifle, which featured a turn bolt and tube magazine. It was officially adopted in 1884, with a modified version adopted in 1887. It was used for only seven years, before being replaced by the 6.5x55mm cartridge and the Krag rifle.

General Comments: The 10.15mm Jarmann is nearly unknown in the United States, and the Jarmann rifle is a collector's item. The cartridge was not used long enough to build much of a following, even in the Scandinavian countries, although it was used to a limited extent in Norway and Sweden for sporting purposes. It is one of the more efficient black-powder cartridges and is comparable to the 9.5mm Turkish Mauser.

10.15x61Rmm Jarmann Loading Data and Factory Ballistics

Bullet (grains/type)	Powder	Grains	Velocity	Energy	Source/Comments
290 Lead	IMR 4198	32	1,430	1,315	Lyman #403173
337 Lead	Black powder (Fg)	80	1,625	1,975	Military load, paper-patched bullet
337 Lead	ML	ML	1,625	1,975	Military load

10.15x63Rmm Serbian Mauser

Historical Notes: This cartridge was adopted in 1878 by Serbia, for use in the Mauser Model 78/80 single-shot rifle, which was nothing more than a slight modification of the Mauser Model 71 rifle. In the Serbian model, the left receiver wall enclosed the bolt more fully than did the original M71. This modification was later incorporated into the design of the Mauser 71/84 repeating rifle. Quantities of the German 71/84 were also chambered for the Serbian cartridge and sold to that country. It is reported that various 10.15 Serbian Mauser rifles were observed in the Balkans as late as World War II.

General Comments: This is another rare military cartridge not likely to be used for sporting purposes. We do not know of any of these Serbian Mauser rifles being sold in the United States. If any of these rifles do show up, the handloader can make ammunition by sizing 11mm Mauser cases full length in a 10.15mm die.

10.15x63Rmm Serbian Mauser Factory Ballistics

Bullet (grains/type)	Powder	Grains	Velocity	Energy	Source/Comments
290 Lead	IMR 4198	34.0	N/A	N/A	Lyman #412263, sized to .411-inch
340 Lead	Black powder	ML	1,460	1,612	Military load

10.4x38Rmm Swiss Vetterli M69/81

Historical Notes: This Swiss cartridge was adopted in 1869 for use in the Vetterli turn-bolt rifle. The official military round is a rimfire, but a centerfire version was also loaded in Europe. The cartridge and rifle were discontinued in 1889.

General Comments: The 10.4mm, or .41 Swiss, cartridge is quite well known in the United States, and most American companies loaded it, until about 1942. Thousands of surplus Swiss Vetterli rifles have been sold in this country, and a surprising number have been used for hunting deer. For a time, there was a good supply of both rifles and cartridges on dealers' shelves. American ammunition was loaded with smokeless powder. The .41 Swiss would be a barely adequate short-range cartridge for deer-class animals. The rimfire military version cannot be reloaded. This cartridge is unusual, in that it is one of the few rimfire military rounds. One note: Some sources list muzzle velocity as 1,427 fps, and this, perhaps, refers to a later smokeless loading.

10.4x38Rmm Swiss Vetterli M69/81 Factory Ballistics

Bullet (grains/type)	Powder	Grains	Velocity	Energy	Source/Comments
334 Lead	ML	ML	1345 *	1,330	Military load

10.4x47Rmm Italian Vetterli M70

Historical Notes: This Italian cartridge was adopted in 1870, used in the Vetterli single-shot turn-bolt rifle and, later, a modified box-magazine repeater (Vitali system). Many were loaded with a brass-coated bullet.

General Comments: The 10.4 Italian service cartridge has not been produced for many years, but occasional lots of surplus ammunition have appeared in stores. In performance, it is practically identical to the 10.4mm Swiss Vetterli. Italian Vetterli rifles are fairly common in the United States.

10.4x47Rmm Italian Vetterli M70 Loading Data and Factory Ballistics

Bullet (grains/type)	Powder	Grains	Velocity	Energy	Source/Comments
250 Lead	IMR 4198	27	1300	935	Lyman #429251
313	Black powder (Fg)	62	1,345	1,255	Military load

10.75x58Rmm Russian Berdan (.43 Russian Berdan)

Historical Notes: The 10.75x58Rmm was adopted by Russia in 1868 and used in the Berdan I and the Krnka M69 rifles. After 1871, it was used in the Berdan II rifle. These were all single-shot arms. This was the first military cartridge with the outside centerfire Berdan primer and a bottleneck case. Large quantities of these cartridges were manufactured in the United States by Remington and Winchester, for the Russian government. Most of the Berdan rifles were made by Colt's, but the Russians also manufactured these guns at their Tula arsenal.

General Comments: This was primarily a military cartridge and was not used to any great extent for sporting purposes. During the 1950s and '60s, a fair number of the old Colt's-made Berdan I and II rifles showed up in various surplus stores, along with suitable black-powder ammunition. In the United States, this was known as the .43 Russian Berdan cartridge.

The Berdan I rifle is a forward-hinged, lift-block type (striker-fired), and the Berdan II is a turn-bolt single-shot, somewhat similar to the Model 71 Mauser. The Krnka is a breech-loading conversion of the Russian muzzleloading rifle. In 1867, the Berdan I-type action was tested by an American military board as a possible means of converting the muzzleloading Springfield to breech-loading.

10.75x58Rmm Russian Berdan Loading Data and Factory Ballistics

Bullet (grains/type)	Powder	Grains	Velocity	Energy	Source/Comments
250 Lead	IMR 4198	33	1,400	1,085	Lyman #429251
370 Lead	IMR 4198	31	1,410	1,630	N/A
370 Lead	Black powder (Fg)	77	1,450	1,725	Military load, paper-patched bullet

11x60Rmm Japanese Murata

Historical Notes: This is the original Japanese military cartridge designed by Maj. Murata for his single-shot turn-bolt rifle. Different authorities give varying dates for the introduction of the rifle and cartridge. The rifle is called the Meiji 13 11mm by the Japanese, which would make the date of introduction 1880. It was later replaced by an 8mm round. The Japanese purchased obsolete European military rifles until they developed their own. They used quantities of the French Chassepot, and the Murata rifle is based on this French design. The 11mm Murata cartridge is also quite similar to the 11mm Gras, which was used in the modified Chassepot.

General Comments: The 11mm Murata is another collector's item, too rare and valuable to shoot, even if you had several of these cartridges. Less valuable ammunition can be made by reforming .348 Winchester cases. Bullet diameter is .432-inch, but Lyman's No. 439186 (370-grain) bullet could probably be sized down and made to work. Use loading data for the 11mm Gras or the 11mm Mauser.

11x60Rmm Japanese Murata Factory Ballistics

Bullet (grains/type)	Powder	Grains	Velocity	Energy	Source/Comments
420 Lead	ML	ML	1,487	2,060	Military load

11x50Rmm Belgian Albini M67/72

Historical Notes: This Belgian military cartridge was adopted in 1867 and used in the Albini-Braendlin single-shot, lift-block rifle. It is often confused with the 11mm Comblain, which it resembles. It was originally loaded with black powder and a paper-patched bullet. Most original Albini rifles were sold off, and many were remodeled into sporter-types or re-chambered for sporting cartridges of the late 1800s.

General Comments: Moderate numbers of the old Albini Braendlin rifles have been sold in the U.S. as collector's items. Most were in good condition and sold for low prices. Ammunition is scarce and much too valuable to shoot. Usable cases for black-powder loads might be converted from modern .470 Nitro Express cases.

11x50Rmm Belgian Albini M67/72 Loading Data and Factory Ballistics

Bullet (grains/type)	Powder	Grains	Velocity	Energy	Source/Comments
370 Lead	IMR 4198	29	1,350	1,495	Lyman #439186
386 Lead	Black powder (Fg)	75	1,368	1,605	Military load, paper-patched bullet

11x53Rmm Belgian Comblain M71

Historical Notes: The 11mm Belgian Comblain was never an official military round, but was used by the Belgian civil guard. It was introduced in 1871 as the cartridge for the falling-block type Comblain single-shot rifle. Rifles in this chambering were used, to a limited extent, by some of the South American countries. The 11mm Albini was the official Belgian military cartridge.

General Comments: The 11mm Belgian Comblain is similar to the Brazilian Comblain, but these cartridges are *not* interchangeable. Cases for black-powder loads could probably be made from .470 Nitro Express cases.

11x53Rmm Belgian Comblain M71 Loading Data and Factory Ballistics

Bullet (grains/type)	Powder	Grains	Velocity	Energy	Source/Comments
370 Lead	IMR 4198	32	1,460	1,750	Lyman #439186
386 Lead	Black powder (Fg)	76	1,445	1,787	Military load, paper-patched bullet

11.15x58Rmm (.43) Spanish Remington (11x53mm Spanish)

General Comments: The 11mm (.43) Spanish Remington was not seen in the United States until after WWII, when large numbers of Remington rolling-block rifles were sold as surplus. Black-powder ammunition was available for a short time, but is now a collector's item. Many of these rifles have been re-barreled to some other chambering. It is possible to have these rifles re-chambered to accept the full-length .348 Winchester case, which can easily be neck-expanded to take .439-inch diameter bullets.

General Comments: Three distinct black-powder Spanish military 11.15mm cartridges exist. The one here, a carbine version with a case length of 17/8 inches, was loaded with 60 grains of black powder and a 400-grain bullet. The original centerfire cartridge, with its straight case and .454-inch-diameter bullet, is covered later in this chapter as the "Spanish Reformado." The carbine round had the same case configuration as the standard cartridge and although shorter, could undoubtedly be fired in the standard rifle chamber, but the reverse would not be true. The carbine round is now a rare and valuable collector's item. Like most of the old black-powder military cartridges, the .43 Spanish would make a good big-game hunting cartridge for anything from deer through elk at close range.

11.15x58Rmm (43) Spanish Remington Loading Data and Factory Ballistics

Bullet (grains/type)	Powder	Grains	Velocity	Energy	Source/Comments
387 Lead	IMR 4198	32	1,360	1,590	Lyman #439186
387 Lead	IMR 3031	40	1,310	1,475	Lyman #439186
375 Lead	Black powder (Fg)	78	1,380	1,585	Military load

11.15x58Rmm Austrian Werndl M77

Historical Notes: This is an improved bottlenecked cartridge adopted by Austria, in 1877, to replace the earlier straight case of the 11.4 mm. It originally was used in the Werndl rotating block single-shot rifle, but from 1886 to 1888, it was also used in the Mannlicher straight-pull rifle.

General Comments: Rifles for the 11.15mm Werndl cartridge are scarce, as is the ammunition. At one time, Winchester and other American companies loaded this round, but it has been used very little in the United States. It is in the same class as the 11mm Mauser for sporting use.

11.15x58Rmm Austrian Werndl M77 Loading Data and Factory Ballistics

Bullet (grains/type)	Powder	Grains	Velocity	Energy	Source/Comments
370 Lead	IMR 4198	32	1,360	1,520	Lyman #439186
370 Lead	Black powder (Fg)	75	1,437	1,695	Military load; paper-patched bullet

11x59Rmm French Gras
11x59mm Vickers

Historical Notes: This French cartridge was adopted in 1874 for the Gras single-shot rifle, a metallic cartridge breech-loaded conversion of the Chassepot needle gun. This was the first modern French military cartridge. It was replaced in 1886 by the then-revolutionary 8mm Lebel. Many Remington rolling block rifles were chambered for the 11mm Gras, and these, along with the Gras rifle, were used extensively in the Balkans and French colonial areas. Remington loaded this cartridge at one time. The Japanese purchased and used many of the Gras-modified rifles and the 11mm Gras cartridge.

The 11mm Vickers was used by the British and French during World War I in the Vickers aircraft machine gun, to shoot down German artillery observation balloons; the cartridge is also referred to as the 11mm Vickers Balloon Gun cartridge. It uses the same case as the 1874 French Gras rifle cartridge and was actually developed by the French for their Hotchkiss anti-balloon gun. The more reliable Vickers machine gun was later modified to shoot the same cartridge. By 1917, the standard rifle cartridge was not as satisfactory for shooting down observation balloons as a larger caliber carrying a heavier tracer/incendiary bullet. This was the reason for the development of a special-purpose cartridge. Rather than waste time, the French simply used what was immediately available and adopted the Gras rifle case. Some of these cartridges are headstamped "WESTERN 2-17," indicating that these cartridges were manufactured in the U.S. by Western Cartridge Co., in February 1917.

General Comments: Neither this rifle nor this cartridge have ever been used to any degree in the United States. It would be suitable for North American big-game hunting at short range, like most of the other black-powder military cartridges. It is similar in performance to the 11mm Mauser. The 11mm Vickers appears to have a longer, heavier bullet than the original Gras cartridge. It is also of the full jacketed type, and some are brass covered. One should be cautious of rounds bearing tracer/incendiary bullets.

11x59Rmm French Gras Loading Data and Factory Ballistics

Bullet (grains/type)	Powder	Grains	Velocity	Energy	Source/Comments
365 Lead	IMR 4198	36	1,420	1,635	Lyman #446109
385 Lead	IMR 4198	33	1,400	1,675	N/A
385 Lead	Black powder (Fg)	78	1,493	1,903	Military load

11.15x60Rmm (.43) Mauser (11x60Rmm Mauser)

Historical Notes: The first of a long line of military cartridges designed by Paul Mauser. It was adopted by the German military in 1871 with the M71 bolt-action single-shot Mauser rifle. Later, this rifle was converted to a tubular magazine repeater in the Model 71/84. This cartridge became a popular sporting cartridge in Europe and East Africa, but it is no longer loaded in Europe. Canadian Industries Limited (Dominion Brand) once offered a smokeless powder version that was imported into the United States.

General Comments: A popular military and sporting round through the 1870s and '80s, the 11mm Mauser was loaded in the United States by Remington and Winchester. It enjoyed only limited popularity here because our own .45-70 military load was easier to obtain. A modernized version using smokeless powder was produced for H. Krieghoff, of Suhl, Germany, and chambered in Mauser bolt-action rifles, in the 1920s. A few were imported into the United States. The 11mm Mauser is still a potent short-range cartridge for North American big game. Most military ammunition uses the Berdan primer, usually of 6.5mm (.254-inch) size. Correct bullet diameter is .446-inch.

11.15x60Rmm (43) Mauser Loading Data and Factory Ballistics

Bullet (grains/type)	Powder	Grains	Velocity	Energy	Source/Comments
370 Lead	Black powder (Fg)	77	1,430	1,680	Duplicates military load, paper-patched bullet
387 Lead	IMR 4198	32	1,335	1,530	N/A
387 Lead	IMR 4198	35	1,510	1,955	Maximum load
385	FL	FL	1,360	1,580	CIL factory load
386 Lead	ML	ML	1,425	1,740	Military load

.45 Remington Thompson

Historical Notes: This cartridge was developed for use in the Thompson M-1923 "Military Model" submachine gun. While it has been described as a stretched .45 Automatic, case and bullet diameter are smaller (.472 versus .476 inch, and .447 versus .451 inch, respectively). The sample cartridge is headstamped "REM-UMC" over ".45 ACP." Development was in 1923, as a joint venture of Remington Arms and Auto Ordnance Corp. Intended application was a long-barreled version of the Thompson that could provide significantly improved ballistics over the standard .45 Automatic-chambered versions.

General Comments: When one considers that this number generated ballistics exceeding any standard .44 Magnum factory loading fired from a pistol, this was, indeed, a significant ballistic improvement, compared to the .45 Automatic. However, it seems likely that the Thompson, despite its significant weight and good design, must have been something of a handful when firing such loads fully automatic.

.45 Remington Thompson

Bullet (grains/type)	Powder	Grains	Velocity	Energy	Source/Comments
250	FL	FL	1,450	1,165	Factory load

11.43x55Rmm Turkish/
.45 Peabody-Martini/
.450 Turkish Peabody-Martini

Historical Notes: This cartridge was used by Turkey from 1874 until 1887. It was replaced by the 9.5mm Mauser. This round was used primarily in the Peabody-Martini single-shot rifle, many of which were made in the United States. This cartridge was loaded in England and called the .450 Turkish Peabody-Martini and the .45 Peabody-Martini in the United States. It was popular in the Balkans and on occasion is still used there.

General Comments: This is another cartridge that was not distributed very extensively in the United States. A few of the old, single-shot under-lever Peabody-Martini rifles have been sold at various times, but 11.43mm ammunition is hard to come by. A Lyman #446187 cast lead bullet weighing 465 grains can be used for handloading.

11.43x55Rmm Turkish Loading Data and Factory Ballistics

Bullet (grains/type)	Powder	Grains	Velocity	Energy	Source/Comments
465 Lead	Black powder (Fg)	80	1,280	1,690	Approximates military load
465 Lead	IMR 4198	36	1,410	2,050	Lyman #446187
486 Lead	ML	ML	1,263	1,720	Military load

11.43x50Rmm
.43 Egyptian Remington

Historical Notes: This cartridge was adopted by Egypt in 1870 for use in the single-shot Remington rolling block rifle. The Egyptian government ordered 60,000 of these rifles, between 1870 and 1876. Remington rifles in this chambering were also used by France in 1870-'71 during the Franco-Prussian War. In fact, those rifles were part of a shipment intended for Egypt, but the Egyptians defaulted, so the French bought them. The Egyptians accepted a later order. Remington loaded huge quantities of this ammunition.

General Comments: In appearance, the .43 Egyptian looks similar to the .43 Spanish Remington cartridge. Performance is almost identical, but the two are *not* interchangeable. The 11mm Egyptian also resembles and is very close to the 11x52Rmm Beaumont in physical measurements. Early Remington catalogs list the 11mm Egyptian as also suitable for the Beaumont rifle, so this cartridge can be fired in both guns.

Obsolete Egyptian rolling block rifles were sold off in widely scattered places all over the world. Many turned up on the American market. The 11mm Egyptian is adequate for most American game and is comparable in power to the 11mm Mauser.

11.43x50Rmm (43) Egyptian Remington Loading Data and Factory Ballistics

Bullet (grains/type)	Powder	Grains	Velocity	Energy	Source/Comments
465 Lead	Black powder (Fg)	70	1,280	1,690	Lyman #446187
465 Lead	IMR 4198	34	1,440	2,140	Lyman #446187
400 Lead	Black powder (Fg)	75	1,330	1,570	Military load; paper-patched bullet

11.4x50Rmm Austrian Werndl M73

Historical Notes: This was the official Austrian military cartridge from 1873 to 1877. It was used in the Werndl single-shot rifle, which featured a breech block that rotated after the hammer was cocked. The block was turned via a protruding thumb-piece, so as to expose the loading groove cut on the bottom. Both rifle and cartridge are relatively rare in the United States.

General Comments: From time to time, a few Model 73 Werndl rifles are sold as collector's items. The cartridge is a scarce collector's item in the United States. In power, it is on a par with similar black-powder cartridges. It might be possible to convert .45-70 cases to work in these rifles.

11.4x50Rmm Austrian Werndl M73 Loading Data and Factory Ballistics

Bullet (grains/type)	Powder	Grains	Velocity	Energy	Source/Comments
465 Lead	IMR 4198	29	1,300	1,745	Lyman #446187
340 Lead	Black powder (Fg)	62	1,270	1,215	Military load

11.4x50Rmm Brazilian Comblain M74

General Comments: The Brazilian Comblain cartridge is quite similar in appearance to the Belgian cartridge of the same name. However, the two are *not* interchangeable. It has seen very little use in the United States. In performance, it is about the same as the .45-70.

11.4x50Rmm Brazilian Comblain M74 Loading Data and Factory Ballistics

Bullet (grains/type)	Powder	Grains	Velocity	Energy	Source/Comments
485 Lead	IMR 4198	27	1,280	1,765	Lyman #451112
486 Lead	Black powder (Fg)	72	1,310	1,850	Military load

11.5x57Rmm (.43) Spanish Reformado

Historical Notes: This was the original centerfire, Berdan-primed Spanish military cartridge. It was adopted about 1867 and used in early Remington rolling block rifles for the Spanish government. It was also used in some Berdan and Snider conversions of the Spanish muzzleloader. Over a million rounds of this ammunition and many rolling block rifles were captured by American troops in Cuba, during the Spanish-American War. It was replaced by the 11.15mm Spanish Remington cartridge in 1871.

General Comments: Although this cartridge is listed as .43-caliber, the bullet has a base band that is actually .454-inch. The bullet is brass covered and has a 10-degree beveled base. In the tropical climate of Cuba, the brass-covered bullets often turned green with verdigris and were thought to be "poisoned" bullets by American troops. In terms of bacterial count and infectious wounds, these probably were poisonous. Rim, base diameter, and case length are almost identical to the 11.15mm Spanish Remington, and cases could be made by expanding and trimming 11.15mm cases.

Bullet (grains/type)	Powder	Grains	Velocity	Energy	Source/Comments
250 Lead	IMR 4198	32	1,220	825	Lyman #454485
395 Ball	Black powder (Fg)	74	1,280	1,435	Military load

.577/450 Martini-Henry

Historical Notes: This cartridge was adopted by Great Britain in 1871 for use in the Martini-Henry falling-block, single-shot rifle. Originally a rolled-type cartridge case, it was later changed to a drawn case. To some extent, it still is a popular sporting cartridge in England, the British Commonwealth, and Africa. It was loaded, in England, with both black and smokeless powders having nearly identical ballistics.

The .577/450 cartridge entered history with the B Company, 24th Regiment of the British Army, on January 22-23, 1879. On that day, Lieutenants John Chard and Gonville Bromhead, with some 140 men, defended Rork's Drift, in Natal, South Africa, from more than 4,000 Zulu warriors. When the battle was over, more than 20,000 rounds of .577/450 ammunition had been fired by the defenders.

General Comments: Many Martini-Henry rifles were imported into the United States, which created mild interest in this cartridge. With its large diameter and heavy lead bullet, it is a good killer on most game at close range. It has been used in Africa and India on all kinds of animals, including the dangerous varieties.

.577/450 Martini-Henry Loading Data and Factory Ballistics

Bullet (grains/type)	Powder	Grains	Velocity	Energy	Source/Comments
400 Lead	IMR 4198	38	1,450	1,865	Lyman #457124
500 Lead	Black powder (Fg)	80	1,320	1,935	Lyman #457125
325 Lead	FL	FL	1,600	1,845	Kynoch factory load
370 Lead	FL	FL	1,450	1,725	Kynoch factory load
480 Lead	ML	ML	1,350	1,940	Military load

11x52Rmm Netherlands Beaumont M71/78

Historical Notes: The cartridge listed here is the modified version of the Dutch Beaumont military round introduced in 1878. It was used in the turn-bolt single-shot Beaumont rifle, which is very similar to the French Gras. In 1888, the Beaumont single-shot was altered to a box magazine repeater based on the Italian Vitali system. This employed a single vertical column of cartridges, inserted in the bottom of the action. It is similar to the Lee magazine. For additional information, see the 11.3x50Rmm Beaumont entry.

General Comments: This modification of the original Beaumont cartridge has caused considerable confusion in collecting circles. The longer 11x52Rmm will chamber in any rifle made for the original 11.3x50Rmm cartridge, but the reverse is *not* true, because of the larger diameter of the case and bullet. The 11mm Egyptian Remington will chamber in Beaumont rifles, and early catalogs list it as being for those, but the 11.3mm and 11mm Beaumont are not identical to the 11mm Egyptian. The cartridge listed here is the most common and the one usually found in collections. Beaumont rifles and cartridges were not widely used in the United States, and only a few rifles were occasionally sold in surplus stores.

Bullet (grains/type)	Powder	Grains	Velocity	Energy	Source/Comments
400 Lead	Black powder (Fg)	55	1,360	1,640	Lyman #457124
400 Lead	IMR 4198	31	1,430	1,815	Lyman #457124, maximum load
345 Lead	Black powder (Fg)	60	1,476	1,670	Military load

11.63x33mm Belted (.458x1½-inch Barnes)

Historical Notes: To paraphrase the late Robert Ripley, believe it or not, the .458x1½-inch Barnes cartridge was actually an experimental military cartridge by U.S. Armed Forces during the Vietnamese war. The cartridge was developed by the original author of this book in mid-1962 as part of the work on the .458x2-inch cartridge, which involved cutting the .458 Winchester Magnum case back to various lengths. All of this was duly reported in the June 1963 issue of *Guns & Ammo* magazine. Someone in the military establishment read the article and decided that the short .45-caliber cartridge just might have a certain specialized military application.

It appears there was a problem using the 5.56mm cartridge and the M-16 rifle in jungle ambush situations. The light, high-velocity bullet didn't always arrive on target, when fired through intervening jungle growth. It was concluded that, because the range of such shooting was fairly short, a proper loading of the .458x1½-inch might solve these problems. The military shortened the Barnes original 1½-inch version to 1.312 inches and developed a load using a 500-grain full metal jacket bullet at a muzzle velocity of about 1,100 fps (below the speed of sound; 1,150 fps). The load was accurate and worked well with a silencer.

At least five bolt-action, match-type rifles equipped with heavy barrels, scopes, and silencers were built and sent to Vietnam for experimental use. This was probably one of the best-kept secrets of the war, as very few people know about it, even today. The experiment was not an unqualified success, because the troops didn't like the heavy, cumbersome rifles. A lighter 20- or 22-inch barrel carbine might have been better accepted in that particular combat environment. In any event, the .458x1½-inch cartridge must be listed as an unofficial experimental military cartridge. After all, it actually *did* achieve combat status, which is more than can be said for other experimental cartridges, such as the .276 Pedersen, a cartridge on which the military spent considerable time and money but then abandoned.

The last of the .458x1½-inch round-nose military ammunition was destroyed, in Herlong, Calif., about 1984 or 1985. This is destined to become one of the rarer collector's cartridges, because very few got into general circulation. It just goes to show that, when you start something, you never know exactly how it's going to end.

11.63x33mm Belted Factory Ballistics   (Note: *Estimated velocity)

Bullet (grains/type)	Powder	Grains	Velocity	Energy	Source/Comments
500 FMC	ML	ML	1,050-1,100 *	1,225-1,340	Military load, experimental

11.7x51Rmm Danish Remington/ .45 Danish Remington

Historical Notes: This cartridge was adopted by Denmark in 1896. It was used in the Remington rolling block rifle. This cartridge and guns chambered for it were available as early as 1878. Some were made by Remington, and some by the Danes. Remington also loaded this cartridge for many years.

General Comments: The 11.7mm, or .45 Danish Remington, has seen considerable use as a target and hunting loading in Scandinavian countries. It is less known in the United States, only because of the few Danish rolling block rifles that have trickled in. It is similar to the .45-70, but the case is a little (.09-inch) shorter. Performance is practically identical. Any load used in the .45-70 will give almost the same results in the 11.7mm.

However, such loads should be reduced by at least one grain, to compensate for the slightly smaller case of the Danish cartridge. It would be adequate for any North American game at short range.

11.7x51Rmm Danish Remington Loading Data and Factory Ballistics

Bullet (grains/type)	Powder	Grains	Velocity	Energy	Source/Comments
300 Lead	IMR 4198	34	1,480	1,460	Lyman #457191
405 Lead	IMR 4198	29	1,340	1,615	Lyman #457124
380 Lead	Black powder (Fg)	50	1,350	1,535	Remington factory load
387 Lead	ML	ML	1,345	1,550	Military load

11.3x50Rmm Beaumont M71

Historical Notes: This was the original Dutch Beaumont cartridge adopted in 1871 for use in the Beaumont single-shot rifle, a turn-bolt type similar to the French Gras. A few years after it was adopted, the rifle was altered to a box magazine repeater. In 1878, the Beaumont cartridge was slightly redesigned to use a shorter case and a bullet of .457-inch diameter.

General Comments: Among cartridge collectors, there is considerable argument regarding the Dutch Beaumont cartridge. Some claim it is identical to the 11mm Egyptian Remington, while others say it is not. The difficulty is caused partly by the fact that both versions of the Beaumont cartridge are similar to the Egyptian Remington. The cartridge listed here is the original version. The slightly modified cartridge is the 11x52Rmm M71/78, which has a longer case and a heavier bullet of .457-inch diameter. Old Remington catalogs list the .43 Egyptian as "adapted to Remington, Egyptian model military and Beaumont rifles." Undoubtedly, the 11mm Egyptian can be fired in Beaumont rifles. However, these three cartridges are not identical in physical measurements.

11.3x50Rmm Beaumont M71 Loading Data and Factory Ballistics

Bullet (grains/type)	Powder	Grains	Velocity	Energy	Source/Comments
360 Lead	Black powder (Fg)	55	1,300	1,350	Lyman #509134
360 Lead	IMR 4198	35	1,420	1,610	Lyman #509134, maximum load
336 Lead	Black powder (Fg)	58	1,378	1,415	Military load

.50 Browning 12.7x99mm

Historical Notes: The German 13mm TUF anti-tank rifle of World War I made quite an impression on U.S. Army higher-ups, who began developing a similar cartridge before the end of the war. Design genius John M. Browning undertook the project, completing his work in 1921. Both gun and cartridge were adopted by the U.S. Army in 1923. It has remained the standard ever since. The cartridge has been adopted and made by at least 30 countries, including the United States, Britain, Canada, France, Belgium, Israel, Netherlands, Japan, Singapore, and Taiwan. Many bullet types will be encountered, including ball, armor-piercing, tracer, incendiary, sabot hyper-velocity, and others.

General Comments: This cartridge is normally found with a Boxer-primed brass case, although steel cases will occasionally be encountered. There are two FMJ-BT ball bullet types, both with mild steel cores. The M2 ball weighs 720 grains and has a muzzle velocity of 2810 fps, while the M33 Ball weighs 668 grains and has a muzzle velocity of 2910 fps. Recently, long-range target rifles from McMillan, Barrett, and others have chambered this round. It has, thus, moved down from exclusive use in heavy machine guns. The Fifty

Caliber Shooters Association (FCSA) holds 1,000-yard (and longer) competitive events. In modern rifles, five-shot groups at 1,000 yards often fall within a six-inch circle, and many groups under three inches have been recorded. With known wind conditions, it is routine to hit a 55-gallon drum at ranges of about a mile.

.50 Browning Factory Ballistics

Bullet (grains/type)	Powder	Grains	Velocity	Energy	Source/Comments
668 FMJ-BT Ball	ML	ML	2,910	12,550	Military load, M33
720 FMJ-BT Ball	ML	ML	2,810	12,600	Military load, M2

12.7x107mm

Historical Notes:	The U.S.S.R. began developing large-caliber cartridges as early as 1927, and in 1930, the military 12.7x108mm cartridge appeared with armor-piercing bullets. Subsequently, the 12.7x108mm took on a host of bullet types for different jobs, just as the .50 BMG did in this country. Among those bullet types were AP incendiary, AP incendiary tracers, incendiary, ranging, and other types. Their development was conducted originally at Tula and then Ulyanovsk Cartridge Works and TsNIITochMash. All 12.7mm cartridges are made with brass cases. The 12.7x107mm's case capacity is 350.6 grains of H2O, and its maximum pressure is 52,000 psi.
General Comments:	The 12.7x107mm could penetrate 16 millimeters of armor plate at a range of 500 meters, making it an effective anti-materiel round, as well as anti-personnel. In 1971, the round was used in a then-new machine gun, the NSV-12.7 (Nikitin-Sokolov-Volkov), a gas-operated model with a rate of fire of 700 to 800 rounds a minute. The cartridge found its way into many other Soviet machine guns, including the Kord-12.7 (1998) and YAkB-12.7 (Yakushev-Borzov, a remotely controlled four-barrel Gatling gun for the Mil Mi-24 attack gunship), as well as large-caliber sniper rifles, such as the gas-operated OSV 96.—*W.T.W.*

12.7x107mm Loading Data and Factory Ballistics

Bullet (grains/type)	Powder	Grains	Velocity	Energy	Source/Comments
745 API B32	ML	ML	2,700	11,980	Military load
855 API BS	ML	ML	2,700	13,737	Military load

.50-70 Musket (.50 Gov't.)

Historical Notes:	The .50-70 was the United States' military rifle cartridge from 1866 to 1873. It was the first centerfire cartridge in general use by the U.S. military. The design was derived from the .50-60-400 Joslyn rimfire. It was used in various models and modifications of the single-shot Springfield rifle, until replaced by the .45-70 in 1873. It was also chambered in the Remington single-shot military rifle and in a variety of sporting rifles, both single-shot and repeating. The original cartridge had the inside, Benet-type primer. It has been obsolete since the turn of the century.
General Comments:	The .50-70, or .50 Government, was a popular cartridge through the 1870s and '80s. It was said to be very effective on buffalo and other heavy game. It was the popularity of this cartridge that induced Winchester to bring out the .50-110, which was, in effect, an improved and more powerful version of the .50-70. Very few rifles in this chambering remain in use, and ammunition is almost non-existent. However, it would be adequate for any North American big game at short range. Cases with the later Boxer-type priming can be reloaded. Most .50-70 rifles were intended for black powder; only very light charges of smokeless powder

can be considered safe. In 1934, Francis Bannerman & Sons, of New York City, advertised both .50-70 Springfield rifles and ammunition. Rifles were still available as late as 1940. Until recently, no sporting rifles chambered this round since the early 1900s. The rise of cowboy action shooting and black-powder metallic cartridge silhouette competition has renewed interest in this round. Cases and guns have recently been produced. There was also a carbine version with a shorter case (1.35 inches instead of 1.94 inches).

.50-70 Musket (.50 Gov't.) Loading Data and Factory Ballistics

Bullet (grains/type)	Powder	Grains	Velocity	Energy	Source/Comments
350 Lead	IMR 3031	38.0	1,310	1,333	Lyman No. 518145
422 Cast	IMR 4198	25.5	1,129	1,194	Lyman No. 515141
425 Lead	AA 5744	30.0	1,419	1,900	Accurate Arms
550 Lead	AA 5744	25.0	1,208	1,780	Accurate Arms
450 Lead	IMR 3031	36.0	1,270	1,611	Lyman No. 515141
450 Lead	IMR 4198	26.0	1,410	1,987	N/A
425 Lead	FL	FL	1,275	1,535	Factory load
450 Lead	FL	FL	1,260	1,488	Factory load

.50-70 Government (.50 Gov't.)

Historical Notes: The .50-70 was the United States' military rifle cartridge from 1866 to 1873. It was the first centerfire cartridge in general use by the U.S. military. The design was derived from the .50-60-400 Joslyn rimfire. It was used in various models and modifications of the single-shot Springfield rifle, until replaced by the .45-70 in 1873. It was also chambered in the Remington single-shot military rifle and in a wide variety of sporting rifles, both single-shot and repeating. The original cartridge had the inside, Benet-type primer. It has been obsolete since the turn of the century.

General Comments: The .50-70, or .50 Government, was a popular cartridge through the 1870s and '80s. It was said to be very effective on buffalo and other heavy game. It was the popularity of this cartridge that induced Winchester to bring out the .50-110, which was, in some sense, an improved and more powerful version of the .50-70. Until recently, very few rifles in this chambering were in use. The recent rise of popularity of the cowboy action game has changed that, and now both cartridge and gun are once again available. The .50-70 is adequate for any North American big game at short range. Cases with the later Boxer-type priming can be reloaded. Most .50-70 rifles were intended for black powder; only very light charges of smokeless powder can be considered safe in these firearms. In 1934, Francis Bannerman & Sons, of New York City, advertised both .50-70 Springfield rifles and the ammunition. Rifles were still available as late as 1940. No sporting rifles have chambered this round, since the early 1900s. There was also a carbine version with a shorter case (1.35 inches instead of 1.94 inches).

Black-powder metallic cartridge silhouette rifle competition continues to be a popular, if niche sport, and this round is often encountered on the firing line. Cowboy action shooting participants also use this round. Shiloh Sharps (ww.shilohrifle.com) continues to make very fine guns of the applicable era in this round for competition, hunting, and other sporting use.

.50-70 Government Loading Data (Note: *Estimated ballistics)

Bullet (grains/type)	Powder	Grains	Velocity	Energy	Source/Comments
300 Lead	Black powder (Fg)	N/A	1,323	1,165	QuickLOAD *
450 Lead	Black powder (Fg)	N/A	1,113	1,235	QuickLOAD *

.577 Snider (14.7mm)

Historical Notes: This British cartridge was adopted in 1867 and used in the Snider breech-loading conversion of the Enfield Musket. The Snider system was invented by Joseph Snider, an American who first offered it to his home country, but was turned down. The converted rifle was usually referred to as the "Snider Enfield." The original cartridge had a cardboard body with a metal base—essentially identical to more recent "paper" shotgun shells. Later, this was improved by using a coiled-brass case designed by Col. Boxer, inventor of the Boxer-type primer. Modern .577 ammunition has a drawn-brass case. Some Martini-Henry single-shot rifles were also chambered for this cartridge. This cartridge was replaced in British military service by the .577/450 in 1871.

General Comments: A large number of Snider Enfield rifles were sold in the United States by Francis Bannerman & Sons, of New York City. Small numbers were also imported during the 1950s by various surplus military arms dealers. The .577 cartridge was loaded in England, with either a solid lead or a lead-base, copper-tube bullet. The case appears to be straight, at first glance, but it has a slight taper and shoulder similar to some American black-powder cartridges of the same period. The dimensions of the .577 case are very similar to those of the 24-gauge shotgun shell, and brass 24-gauge shells can be used to make ammunition by trimming about a half-inch from the length. Neither the Snider rifle nor the .577 cartridge are very practical for American hunting, but these guns are a lot of fun to shoot.

.577 Snider Loading Data and Factory Ballistics

Bullet (grains/type)	Powder	Grains	Velocity	Energy	Source/Comments
350 Lead	Black powder (Fg)	73	1,310	1,330	NA
350 Lead	IMR 4198	31	1,380	1,480	NA
450 Lead	Black powder (Fg)	73	1,270	1,610	NA
450 Lead	IMR 4198	30	1,300	1,690	NA
476 Lead	IMR 4198	30	1,250	1,650	Lyman #575213
480 Lead	Black powder (Fg)	70-73	1,250	1,665	Military load

14.5x114mm

Historical Notes: In December 1942, the U.S.S.R. developed the 14.5x114mm cartridge as an anti-tank machine gun. The round also saw use in anti-aircraft machine guns. Several designers, including S.V. Vladimirov, based the new round on the 20mm V-20 aircraft cannon. The 14.5mm appeared in the KPV-44 Vladimirov heavy machine gun and anti-aircraft prototypes in May 1945, making them the world's most powerful mass-produced heavy machine guns of the time. The cartridge was reportedly designed in 1939.

General Comments: The 14.5 cartridge with armor-piercing incendiary bullets (B-32) was intended to defeat lightly armored targets and low-flying aircraft. It had a case capacity of 656.3 grains of water and was rated up to 52,000 psi chamber pressure. A common rifling twist was 1:17.91. Versions of the round included the B-32 and the BS-41 (armor piercing incendiary), the BZT-44 (armor piercing incendiary tracer), the PZ (adjustment incendiary), and the MDZ (instant incendiary). A 14.5mm with an armor piercing, incendiary, hard alloy-cored bullet to defeat armor was tested as early as 1989. A common barrel length for the gun was 1,350mm, and the KPV-44 produced a rate of fire of 600 to 650 rounds a minute. The modified KPVT tank machine gun was mounted on heavy tanks, combat reconnaissance vehicles, and armored personnel carriers. —*W.T.W.*

Bullet (grains/type)	Powder	Grains	Velocity	Energy	Source/Comments
921 MDZ HEI	ML	ML	3,300	22,020	Military load

Dimensional Data

Cartridge	Case	Bullet Dia.	Neck Dia.	Shoulder Dia.	Base Dia.	Rim Dia.	Rim Thick.	Case Length	Ctge. Length	Primer	Page
4.85mm British	C	.197	.220	.353	.375	.376	.041	1.925	2.455	B	487
5x58 Sturtevant	I	0.204	0.236	0.424	0.466	0.466	0.0453	2.277	3.374		488
5.2x68 Mondragon	J	0.208	0.243	0.450	0.489	0.491	0.067	2.650	3.060		488
5.7x28mm FN P90 (Belgium)	C	.220	.249	.309	.310	.310	UNK	1.13	1.71	B	488
5.45x39mm Soviet	C	.221	.246	.387	.395	.394	.053	1.56	2.22	B	489
5.66x39mm MPS	C	.223	.246	.364	.395	.394	.053	1.568	5.90	SR	489
5.56x45mm NATO	C	.224	.249	.349	.373	.375	.041	1.76	2.26	Bx	490
5.8x42mm Chinese	C	.224	UNK	UNK	UNK	UNK	UNK	1.660	2.30	UNK	490
6mm SAW (U.S.)	C	.243	.273	.382	.410	.410		1.779	2.58	Bx	491
6x49mm Unified	C	.248	UNK/NA	UNK/NA	.444	UNK/NA	UNK/NA	1.92	2.736	UNK/NA	491
6.5x54mm Mannlicher-Schoenauer (Greek)	C	.263	.287	.424	.447	.450	UNK/NA	2.09	3.02	B	492
6.5mm Japanese Arisaka	G	.263	.293	.425	.455	.471	.045	2.00	2.98	B	492
6.5x53Rmm Mannlicher (Dutch & Romanian)	A	.263	.297	.423	.450	.526	.066	2.10	3.03	B	493
6.5x53.5 Daudeteau	G	.263	.298	.466	.480	.524	.065	2.09	3.02	UNK/NA	494
6.5x55mm Swedish Mauser	C	.264	.297	.435	.480	.480	UNK/NA	2.16	3.15	B	494
6.5x52mm Italian (Mannlicher-Carcano)	C	.265	.295	.430	.445	.448	.045	2.05	3.02	B	495
6.8x57mm Chinese	C	.277	UNK/NA	UNK/NA	UNK/NA	UNK/NA	UNK/NA	UNK/NA	2.25	UNK/NA	495
.280 British	C	.283	.313	.448	.470	.473	UNK/NA	1.71	2.54	B	495
7x57mm Mauser	C	.284	.320	.420	.470	.474	.055	2.23	3.06	B	496
.276 Enfield	C	.284	.321	.460	.528	.521	UNK/NA	2.35	3.25	B	497
.276 Pederson	C	.285	.314	.389	.449	.451	UNK/NA	2.02	2.85	Bx	497
7.35mm Italian Carcano	C	.298	.323	.420	.445	.449	UNK/NA	2.01	2.98	B	498
7.62x45mm Czech M52	C	.309	.334	.412	.441	.440	UNK/NA	1.77	2.36	B	498
7.5x55mm Swiss Schmidt-Rubin	C	.308	.334	.452	.494	.496	.058	2.18	3.05	B	499
.30 Carbine (.30 M-1 Carbine)	D	.308	.335	.335	.3567	.3598	.050	1.29	1.679	Bx	499
.30 Army (.30-40 Krag)	A	.308	.338	.415 (.419)	.457	.540	UNK/NA	2.31	3.10	Bx	500
7.62x51mm NATO (.308 Win.)	C	.308	.338	.447	.466	.470	UNK/NA	2.01	2.75	Bx	501
7.62x63mm U.S. (.30-06 Springfield))	C	.308	.340	.441	.470	.473	UNK/NA	2.49	3.34	Bx	501
7.5x54mm French MAS	C	.308	.340	.441	.480	.482	.054	2.11	2.99	B	502
7.62x53Rmm Russian	C	.310	.340	.394	.443	.445	UNK/NA	1.52	2.20	B	502
.303 British	A	.311	.337	.402	.458	.530	UNK	2.21	3.05	B	503
7.7x58mm Japanese Arisaka	C	.311	.338	.431	.472	.474	.042	2.28	3.13	B	504
7.62x39mm Soviet (M43)	C	.311	.340 (.337)	.344 (.396)	.438 (.433)	.440	.053	1.52 (1.528)	2.20	S	505
7.65x53mm Mauser (Argentine)	C	.313	.338	.429	.468	.470	.040	2.09	2.95	B	505
8x53Rmm Japanese Murata	?	.320	UNK/NA	UNK/NA	UNK/NA	UNK/NA	UNK/NA	UNK/NA	UNK/NA	UNK/NA	506
8x50Rmm Siamese Mauser (Type 45)	A	.321	.347	.450	.480	.550	UNK/NA	1.98	2.97	B	506
8x52Rmm Siamese (Type 66)	A	.321	.347	.460	.500	.550	UNK/NA	2.04	2.96	B, Bx	507
8x58Rmm Danish Krag	A	.322	.355	.460	.500	.575	.060	2.28	3.20	B	507
8x50Rmm Lebel	A	.323	.347	.483	.536	.621	.068	1.98	2.75	B	508
8x50Rmm Austrian Mannlicher	A	.323	.351	.462	.501	.553	.040	1.98	3.00	B	508
7.92x33mm Kurz	C	.323	.352	.440	.470	.470	UNK/NA	1.3	1.88	B	509
7.9x57mm J&JS (8mm Mauser JS)	C	.323	.353	.443	.469	.473	UNK/NA	2.24	3.17	B	510
8x63mm Swedish	C	.323	.356	.456	.488	.479	UNK/NA	2.48	3.36	B	511
8x60Rmm Guedes M/85 Portuguese	A	.326	.354	.490	.543	.620	.080	2.34	3.25	B	511
8x59mm Breda	C	.326	.357	.433	.491	.469	UNK/NA	2.33	3.17	B	512

Dimensional Data

Cartridge	Case	Bullet Dia.	Neck Dia.	Shoulder Dia.	Base Dia.	Rim Dia.	Rim Thick.	Case Length	Ctge. Length	Primer	Page
8x56Rmm Austrian-Hungarian Mannlicher (M31)	A	.329	UNK/NA	UNK/NA	UNK/NA	UNK/NA	UNK/NA	UNK/NA	UNK/NA	UNK/NA	512
9x21mm Russian (9x21mm Gyurza)	D	.356	UNK/NA	.380	.390	.390	.047	0.82	1.38	UNK/NA	513
9x39mm SP-5 & SP-6	C	.356	.380	.408	.447	.447	.059	1.528	2.20	S	513
9.5x60Rmm Turkish Mauser	A	.389	.411	.487	.511	.612	.082	2.37	2.97	B	513
10.15x61Rmm Jarmann	A	.403	.430	.540	.548	.615	.078	2.40	3.06	B	514
10.15x63Rmm Serbian Mauser	A	.411	.433	.515	.520	.592	.082	2.46	3.13	B	514
10.4x38Rmm Swiss Vetterli	A	.415	.437	.518	.540	.630	.055	1.60	2.20	B-RF	515
10.4x47Rmm Italian Vetterli M/70	A	.430	.437	.517	.540	.634	.058	1.87	2.46	B	515
10.75x58Rmm Russian Berdan (.43 Russian Berdan)	A	.430	.449	.506	.567	.637	.080	2.24	2.95	B	515
11x60Rmm Japanese Murata	A	.432	.465	.526	.542	.632		2.36	3.13	B	516
11x50Rmm Belgian Albini	A	.435	.472	.535	.580	.678		2.00	2.6	B	516
11x53Rmm Belgian Comblain	A	.436	.460	.532	.575	.673	.082	2.10	2.76	B	517
11.15x58Rmm (.43) Spanish Rem.	A	.439	.458	.512	.516	.635	.082	2.25	2.82	B	517
11.15x58Rmm Austrian Werndl M/77	A	.441	.466	.536	.545	.617	.100	2.27	3.02	B	518
11x59Rmm French Gras/ 11x59mm Vickers	A	.445	.468	.531	.544	.667	.075	2.34	3.00	B	518
11.15x60Rmm (43) Mauser/ 11x60Rmm Mauser	A	.446	.465	.510	.516	.586	.075	2.37	3.00	B	518
.45 Remington Thompson	D	.447	.470	UNK	.472	.471	.044	1.12	1.45	LP	519
11.43x55Rmm Turkish/ .45 Peabody-Martini	A	.447	.474	.560	.582	.668	UNK/NA	2.30	3.12	B	520
11.43x50Rmm/.43 Remington Egyptian	A	.448	.479	.542	.581	.668	.065	1.94	2.73	B	520
11.4x50mm Austrian Werndl M/73	B	.449	.472	UNK/NA	.493	.571	UNK/NA	1.97	2.55	B	521
11.4x50Rmm Brazilian Comblain	A	.452	.494	.530	.588	.682	UNK/NA	2.02	2.62	B	521
11.5x57Rmm Spanish Reformado	B	.454	.466	UNK/NA	.525	.631	UNK/NA	2.26	3.06	B	521
.577/450 Martini Henry	A	.455	.487	.628	.668	.746	.050	2.34	3.12	B	522
11x52mm Netherlands Beaumont M/71	A	.457	.484	.528	.576	.665	.065	2.04	2.54	B	522
11.63x33mm Belted (.458x1½-inch Barnes)	F	.458	.493	UNK/NA	.509	.530	UNK/NA	1.50	2.19	Bx	523
11.7x51Rmm Danish Remington/ .45 Danish Remington	B	.462	.486	UNK/NA	.514	.579	UNK/NA	2.01	2.45	B	523
11.3x50mm Beaumont M71	A	.464	.486	.530	.581	.666	.060	1.97	2.49	B	524
.50 Browning/12.7x99mm	C	.510- (.511)	.555- (.560)	.708- (.714)	.800- (.804)	.800- (.804)	.080	3.90 (3.91)	5.43- (5.545)	Bx	524
12.7x107mm	C	.511	.549	.744	.856	.854	.075	4.30	5.807	UNK/NA	525
.50-70 Gov't. Musket	B	.515	.535	UNK/NA	.565	.660	.060	1.75	2.25	L	525
.50-70 Gov't.	B	.515	.535	UNK/NA	.565	.660	.060	1.75	2.25	Bx	526
.577 Snider (14.7mm)	B	.570	.602	UNK/NA	.660	.747	.052	2.00	2.45	B	527
14.5x114mm	C	.586	.650	1.004	1.061	1.061	.098	4.50	6.134	UNK/NA	527

Case Type: A = Rimmed, bottleneck. B = Rimmed, straight. C = Rimless, bottleneck. D = Rimless, straight. E = Belted, bottleneck. F = Belted, straight. G = Semi-rimmed, bottleneck. H = Semi-rimmed, straight. I = Rebated, bottleneck. J = Rebated, straight. K = Rebated, belted bottleneck. L = Rebated, belted straight. **Primer Type:** B = Berdan. Bx = Boxer. RF = Rimfire. **Other Codes:** Unless otherwise noted, all dimensions in inches. Twist (factory) is given as inches of barrel length per complete revolution, e.g., 12 = 1 turn in 12", etc. * = Gain twist. Dimensions shown in some instances do not exactly coincide with dimensions found in *The Book of Rifles* (W.H.B. Smith, Harrisburg, Pa., 1960). Differences amount to only a few thousandths of an inch, doubtless attributable to specimen variations. Parentheses indicate maximum cartridge specifications.

British Sporting Rifle Cartridges

(Current & Obsolete – Black-Powder and Smokeless)

By Ray Ordorica

It has been 20 years since I compiled the first-ever update of the British section of this book pursuant to the volume's inception. Now, thanks to two friends, I have been given the opportunity to again update it, and I have tried to set it right once again.

Sadly, there are still lots of folks who have no familiarity with British rifles or cartridges, but that has not stopped them from writing about them. The editor of a major publication recently put his ignorance on public display by claiming that good double rifles print their two barrels together at some distance from the firing point, and after that point, the bullets cross. That is not so. Good rifles put their bullets a small distance apart on parallel paths and the bullets never cross. I had hoped everyone would know that by now.

My interest in British cartridges and rifles dates to about 1950, when I first read John "Pondoro" Taylor's *African Rifles and Cartridges*. Along the way, I've owned 15 double rifles, all but two of them English, those rifles ranging in caliber from .360 Express (2¼-inch) to 12-bore. I well remember buying my Churchill .470 back in 1974. With the rifle in front of me, my first thought was, *"Where do I get ammunition?"* If you had told me Federal and Hornady would be loading it within my lifetime, I would have told you that you were crazy. For only three of my double rifles has it been relatively easy to organize ammo, and one of those was a muzzleloader! Getting ammo was by no means easy when the guns were first acquired. The easy part came decades after I had bought them.

Many years ago, Ross Seyfried and I wrapped paper patches around smaller bullets to make them work in bigger bores (*The American Rifleman*, June 1978). Today's reloader can simply buy whatever bullet size and weight he might need to get his odd old English rifle shooting. The Internet also makes it relatively easy to find what's needed. Not only can the big boomers again sing their old songs, but many of the odd and generally ignored British cartridges can be brought back to life with today's myriad reloading supplies. Even better, brand-new guns for the old cartridges are being made. Who would have believed, 20 years ago, that Ruger would build its No. 1 Tropical Rifle in .400 Jeffery, and that Hornady would make ammo for it? Certainly not I. That's a happy celebration of the fact that many of these old cartridges are no longer obsolete and instead have new life, thanks to modern brass, bullet, cartridge, and rifle makers.

Back when Ross and I were struggling to make our big doubles shoot, there was no easy way to get bullets of the correct size and weight, so we did what we had to. We begged and borrowed brass, cobbled up bullets, and made guesses at powder charges. However, today's easy component availability and the convenience of loaded ammunition would most likely not exist but for the work of early experimenters who wrote up their successes, and, thus, helped reestablish a demand for British cartridge cases and bullets, as well as for the rifles that shoot them. Just several decades ago, very few new firearms were being made that were chambered for most of the British cartridges. Back then, I wanted a .416 Rigby; I ended up having to build one for myself. Today, Rigby, CZ, Kimber, Dakota, and quite a few others will happily make you a .416 Rigby rifle. I'm pleased to see that Holland & Holland, Purdey, Westley Richards, John Rigby & Co., Cogswell & Harrison, and several other famous names are still going strong, but be prepared for massive sticker shock if you want one of those rifles.

Believe it or not, some new British cartridges have appeared. My friend Paul Roberts introduced the .450 Rigby in 1995, when he owned Rigby's. Then, in 2003, Holland & Holland brought out the .400 H&H Magnum and the .465 H&H Magnum, both belted cartridges designed for use in magazine rifles intended for time in Africa. The former is based on the .375 H&H case, the latter roughly on the .460 Weatherby case. The .400 H&H with 400-grain bullets of 0.411-inch diameter at 2,375 fps competes with the .416 Rigby and .416 Remington. The .465 H&H cartridge competes with the .450 Rigby and similar cartridges designed for magazine rifles. We finally have illustrations of these two H&H cartridges and some up-to-date information on both of them. H&H has produced rifles in both these calibers and has plenty of good ammo for both.

More good news is that John Rigby & Co. (Gunmakers) Ltd. has moved back to London, and is now in partnership with Mauser (and Blaser). The company is resurrecting the finest of its fine old rifles, beginning with single- and double-square bridge German magnum Mauser actions made up by British hands into new rifles that closely match the configuration of the original .416 Rigby bolt rifles. Around the end of the nineteenth century, John Rigby contacted Paul Mauser and asked for a longer version of the Mauser action. The result was the Magnum Mauser action, which was first used for the popular rimmed .400/.350, but was also suitable for other calibers. It's the action on which Rigby built his famous .416 rifle. Those rare, unadorned, original .416 Rigbys today bring astonishing prices. The new versions look to be close copies of the early guns and will be in .375, .416, and .450 calibers, with smaller chamberings to come. The makers also plan to resurrect the original rising-bite third lockup of early Rigby double rifles. My old Rigby in .450 Nitro had that rising bite, and it closed like a bank vault. I wish the new enterprise the best of luck.

These days, the resurrection of the manufacture of top-quality brass, bullets and, now, ammunition for the great rifles of old Africa has helped close the knowledge gap and generate more enthusiasm for the old English bundooks. Although they are far more rare than Rugers, Winchesters, and Remingtons, these grand old British firearms—some bearing names centuries old—are out there in profusion for those who know where to look. For decades, many of them lay hidden away in the vaults of collectors who cherished them and their strange and wonderful (but entirely unavailable) British cartridges. Now, with new ammunition production on several important fronts and with excellent bullets and brass being made, these old guns can once again be fired. Thanks to great manufacturers such as Federal, Hornady, Kynoch and others producing excellent ammunition, collectors can shoot the old guns without having to reload.

***

Beginning in the late nineteenth century, the British went hunting in Africa, at a time when no rifles or cartridges suitable for the task at hand existed anywhere in the world. Their need for proper dangerous-game rifles and cartridges was unique, because the British were just about the only ones hunting in Africa. The British development of the double rifle as the best of the best for hunting dangerous game also came out of that need.

The first elephant guns were muzzleloaders, commonly smoothbores. The first cartridge-firing elephant guns also used black powder and lead bullets. These cartridges and guns were so big as to be nearly unbelievable by today's standards. These were the "gauge rifles." They were ponderous 4-, 6-, or 8-bore guns that weighed up to 25 pounds. A 4-bore rifle has a bore diameter of about an inch. Some of these early guns were smoothbores, but most were rifled. Early hunters considered the 10- and 12-bores too small for safe use against the biggest game. When they went up against the big stuff, they usually used 8-bores and larger. The big lead bullets slung by those huge old cannons were not all that effective against elephants, as is well recorded by early African hunters like Selous. To improve performance the bullets were often made with a hollow, which was then filled with an explosive compound. While that helped, it still didn't answer every question.

The .450 Express, .500 Express, and even the .577 Express of the latter days of the nineteenth century were essentially deer and medium-game rifles, not the elephant stompers they became when loaded with cordite and full-patch ("solid") bullets. The medium-game Express cartridges were loaded with lead bullets that either had grease-filled grooves or were made without grooves and then paper patched. Paper patching is simply wrapping the bullet with, usually, two layers of paper, which was put on wet and allowed to dry. The paper-patched bullet was then trimmed, lubricated, and loaded. This provided a non-fouling bullet of soft lead that was one of the most deadly projectiles ever devised. These paper-patched bullets performed very well in the hunting fields 130 years ago and still do today.

The so-called Paradoxes (Holland & Holland's name), Exploras (Westley Richards), and the like were light smoothbores, usually 8-, 10-, or 12-bores, with a few inches of rifling near the muzzle. These fired shotshells quite well and also gave enough spin to round balls or conical bullets to provide adequate accuracy and performance on medium-size game at reasonable ranges.

The coming of cordite (smokeless) powder gave ammunition makers headaches, as they tried to develop new bullets that would work well at the higher velocities the new propellant provided. The ammo makers aimed most of their research at Africa and India. Along the development road, it was discovered that full-patch or solid bullets (the bullet nose fully covered or protected with gilding metal or, with Rigby's bullets, mild steel) would reach the brain of a tusker, rhino, or Cape buff quite easily; therefore, elephant rifles could be built lighter than ever before and of smaller bore size.

Because there were no precedents, the British made many mistakes in their early rifle- and smokeless-cartridge production. Common among those were building rifles too heavy for the new cartridges and retaining brass case designs that had worked well with black powder, but were not so good with cordite. One example is the .450/.400 3¼-inch NE, which was originally a successful black-powder design. With cordite, it gave problems. Some of the first rifles made for the cordite version weighed over 11 pounds. A quarter-century later, with plenty of practical experience behind them, English gun makers commonly built them to weigh 9½ pounds. Another problem with the .450/.400 3¼-inch NE, as claimed by those who were there, was that early brass cases for the cartridge weren't stout enough. The case design has a long neck and a thin rim. If the rifle were neglected and became pitted or fouled, the fired case would sometimes stick in the chamber. When this happened and the rifle was opened, the rim would be ripped off by the extractor, leaving the hunter unarmed. Eventually, that problem was eliminated through better cartridge designs, better brass, and thicker rims. Those who kept their rifles clean apparently did not have any trouble with that cartridge.

Another problem was determining how small the bore should be for any given game size, a problem that's still with us. Many hunters today believe the biggest gun is the best, while others try to make the smallest work for everything. Clearly, the biggest guns will be adequate for the smallest game, but the converse has never been true. This may be one reason behind the myriad early British cartridges, of which there are a great many more than have ever appeared in these pages. The British were hunting worldwide and were among the very few hunting dangerous game and large plains game at a time when nothing was known about the new cordite loads and their jacketed bullets. Eventually things settled out, but it took a while.

***

Many British cartridges were decades ahead of their time, good ideas that needed better powders and better steels to let them bloom. The .275 H&H Belted Rimless Magnum came out around 1912, 50 years before the nearly identical 7mm Remington Magnum. Too often, the British gun developers are overlooked by U.S. shooters. Westley Richards was the first to draw brass into cartridges, a fact seldom mentioned in Ameri-

can gun journals. One must remember the British were hunting game of all sizes worldwide, while the U.S. hunters were shooting deer and elk. The bison were gone. In America, there was no need to develop rifles or cartridges capable of killing an elephant, let alone lion, tiger, gaur, Cape and water buffalo, eland, giraffe, and the like. One would therefore expect cartridge development during the late nineteenth and early twentieth centuries to have been quite furious in England. In the U.S., the first serious step toward Africa didn't come until 1956, when Winchester brought out its .458 Winchester Magnum to compete with a cartridge nearly 60 years old.

From its inception in 1898, with its cordite charge and steel-covered bullets, Rigby's rimmed .450 3¼-inch Nitro Express cartridge quickly became the king of the cordite elephant slayers. It threw a 480-grain jacketed bullet of 0.458-inch diameter at just over 2,100 fps. Every maker offered rifles in that caliber, and most of the world's hunters of dangerous game were happy. Then, for political reasons, the British government prohibited the importation of .450-bore rifles into India and the Sudan. In response, British gun makers brought out new elephant cartridges and rifles in the form of Holland's .465, Lang's .470, Westley's .476, and several others. All of them worked just about like the old .450 Nitro had, and you paid your money and took your choice. During the period from about 1900 to 1940, if you wanted more power than was offered by these .450- to .470-class elephant cartridges, there were three choices. The .500 Nitro Express was somewhat more powerful than all of the .470 class, but the .577 NE and the .600 NE were tops. They were the ultimate life insurance policies for those who were frequently involved in close encounters with elephant.

Today's gun collector or shooter is not as unfamiliar with British cartridges as perhaps he was a half-century ago. As noted, it used to be difficult to get cases or bullets for the British cartridges. Today, we have Bruce Bertram of Australia to thank for producing his array of fine brass for the British calibers. Another Aussie outfit, Woodleigh Bullets, makes some of the finest projectiles ever seen. They have a huge selection of bullets that are as close as you can get to original sizes, shapes, and weights of the early English projectiles. Barnes and Hornady have many types of superb quality bullets made for the big English rifles. So does Hawk Precision, Ballard Built, and many other companies. Don't overlook the bullet casting companies, including the old standby Lyman, for another viable bullet options.

Some of our component makers have disappeared over the past two decades, but there are many new outfits. The clever reloader with a truly odd-caliber rifle might be able to use brass from a company that makes, say, metric calibers. With careful comparisons and measurements, you might find just the right size of brass that, suitably reworked, can let your odd British rifle shoot once again. Besides Bertram in Australia, a few other brass-making companies are Bell, Horneber (brass for .505 Gibbs and .476 Westley, among others), Graf, Jamison (.30 Newton and big Brits), Magtech (12-bore brass cases), Norma, RWS, Federal, and Hornady. There are many others. Don't overlook all the easily found U.S.-based makers. Huntington Die Specialties on the Internet is a good place to start your search.

As to reference books, John "Pondoro" Taylor's classic *African Rifles and Cartridges* has been reprinted many times and is still the best book ever written on the hunting of African game with most of the British cartridges. There are many other reference books on British rifles and cartridges, and the collector or shooter has a much easier time finding information on these than ever before. The Internet is simply the biggest library on the face of the earth. Use it.

If you want to take your British rifle hunting or target shooting today, please make sure it is safe to shoot. Getting ammo made up for it may not be much of a problem, but that's only half the battle. Check the dimensions of your barrel by slugging it. Verify the chambering is correct, the ammo is a proper fit, and the gun is in acceptable condition, before you attempt to shoot it. Not all the old guns are in a condition that will permit shooting. Best-quality Damascus barrels on older rifles are, in most cases, perfectly acceptable, if the barrels are in excellent condition both inside and out. Damascus steel was rightly considered superior to common steel barrels long after plain steel barrels came along, because Damascus barrels could withstand proof charges that plain steel ones could not.

Age in and of itself may not be a problem. I have a fine old Erskine 12-bore double rifle that is lots of fun to shoot. It's in perfect condition and it's 150 years old. My .470 Churchill, formerly pictured on these pages, was made around 1925. It went to Tanzania with me, in 1995, and killed a Cape buff. It has now been converted into my Citabria, so you won't see it here again. I suggest you shoot loads that are very conservative and thoroughly safe in your old English firearms. There's no point in pushing the limits. If you must push, buy a Ruger, Winchester, or other modern rifle. Because we cannot personally inspect your firearms and advise you on the wisdom of shooting them, we give very limited loading data here.

Another old caution is still in order. It is the opinion of David Winks, the now-retired chief barrel maker for Holland & Holland, that no one should ever fire homogeneous bullets of any type through fine rifle barrels, specifically those on British double rifles. Because of the bullet's non-flexing, extremely tough construction, these bullets are too hard on the bore, in his expert opinion. Twenty years ago, Winks told this writer his people used *Cartridges of the World* nearly every day at the H&H shop, a philosophy echoed back then by the folks at John Rigby & Co. We sincerely hope this updated chapter will be of equal value to them and to the many lovers of British rifles and their cartridges worldwide. We wish all of you good shooting with your British firearms.

.297/230 Morris Short, Long, Extra Long & Lancaster Sporting

Historical Notes: These cartridges are listed together because all are very similar. The Morris Long has a long neck, the Extra Long has a really long neck (11/8-inch case length), and the Lancaster Sporting resembles the Short, but its shoulder is farther forward. These first appeared in an Eley ad in 1882. These cartridges are target or practice rounds to be fired from a barrel insert for the British .577/.450 Martini-Henry service rifle. The idea originated with Richard Morris and was adopted by the British army. Some models of the .303 Enfield rifle used an insert for the Morris cartridges. In addition, barrel and chamber inserts were available for the Webley & Scott .450 and .455 revolvers. European-made single-shot pistols and rifles are occasionally found chambered for the Morris cartridges. These cartridges were listed in Eley-Kynoch catalogs as late as 1962. B.S.A. made Martini-actioned rifles for these cartridges.

General Comments: The .297/.230 cartridges were used for target practice and small-game shooting. Power is about the same as the standard .22 rimfire. The Morrises lost adherents—even though the centerfire Morris cartridges can be reloaded—because .22 rimfire ammunition is cheaper. They were originally black-powder loadings, but late-issue ammunition used smokeless powder. Bullets were of lead in solid or hollow-point types.

.297/230 Morris Short, Long, and Extra Long Loading Data and Factory Ballistics

Bullet (grains/type)	Powder	Grains	Velocity	Energy	Source/Comments
43 lead	Unique	3.0	900	75	Lyman #225438
43 lead	2400	4.0	1,200	137	Lyman #225438
37 lead	Black powder	3.25	875	62	Eley factory load
37 lead	Black powder	5.5	1,200	118	Eley factory load

.240 Magnum Flanged
.240 Magnum Rimless
.240 Apex
.240 Super Express

Historical Notes: This pair of 6mm cartridges was introduced by Holland & Holland in the early 1920s. The rimmed cartridge was, of course, designed for double rifles, and the belted rimless version for magazine rifles. H&H also called it the .240 Super Express, but original ammunition boxes from the maker carry the names in the header here.

General Comments: Performance of these two .240s is similar to that of the .243 Winchester. Holland data gives a velocity of 2,900 fps with a 100-grain bullet for the belted version. In a strong, modern single-shot or bolt-action rifle using modern powders, performance could be increased significantly. However, this usually doesn't work for double rifles, because they are sighted and regulated for a specific loading. If you change things, the rifle may not shoot your loads to the same point of impact as the original load. That is why most rimmed British cartridges have a limited selection of bullet weights and velocities.

The British were well ahead of the U.S. in the development of good 6mm cartridges. Either of these cartridges would do anything that could be done by the .243 or 6mm Remington.

.240 Magnum Flanged and Rimless H&H (.240 Apex) Factory Ballistics

Bullet (grains/type)	Powder	Grains	Velocity	Energy	Source/Comments
100 SP	FL		2,900	1,865	Factory load

.244 H&H Magnum

Historical Notes: This, the last belted magnum developed by Holland & Holland (until 2003), was introduced in 1955 for its Mauser-type bolt-action sporting rifles. Custom-made rifles in this chambering are seen occasionally. American loading handbooks have listed it in the past.

General Comments: The high-velocity .244 Holland & Holland Magnum is based on the .375 H&H Magnum case necked down to 6mm. This is a very large capacity case for the caliber. Only very slow-burning powders will develop maximum velocity in a case this big, so the British were forced to use something other than cordite for this cartridge. American powders such as IMR-4350, IMR-4831, and the like give good results with bullets of 100 grains. Holland & Holland advertises a muzzle velocity of 3,500 fps with the 100-grain bullet.

The .244 H&H Magnum is a long-range, light-game cartridge. It would also be an excellent varmint and small-game number under any conditions.

.244 H&H Magnum Factory Ballistics

Bullet (grains/type)	Powder	Grains	Velocity	Energy	Source/Comments
Bullet (grains/type)	Powder	Grains	Velocity	Energy	Source/Comments
100 SP	FL		3,500	2,720	Factory load
100 SP	FL		2,900	1,865	Factory load

.246 Purdey

General Comments: A rimmed, necked cartridge designed in 1921 for use in Purdey double rifles, the .246 Purdey was not popular nor widely used. With a 100-grain bullet at 2950 fps, it is only slightly less powerful than the .243 Winchester or 6mm Remington. It's long obsolete. As with most cartridges designed for double rifles, only one loading was available. Bullet diameter ranges from 0.251- to 0.253-inch.

.246 Purdey

Bullet (grains/type)	Powder	Grains	Velocity	Energy	Source/Comments
Bullet (grains/type)	Powder	Grains	Velocity	Energy	Source/Comments
100 SP	FL		2,950	1,930	Factory load

.297/.250 Rook

Historical Notes: Introduced by Holland & Holland for its semi-smoothbore rifles, this load dates back prior to 1880. It is a target and small-game cartridge usually used in single-shot rifles based on the small Martini action, though it's occasionally seen in very fine break-action single-shot and double-barreled rifles. Incidentally, the English rook is a bird similar to the American crow.

General Comments: In performance, the .297/.250 is similar to the old .25 Stevens rimfire. However, it is a centerfire bottlenecked cartridge and can be reloaded. There were a half-dozen or more of these so-called "rook" cartridges. None were very widely used outside Britain. Like the others, this is entirely a small-game cartridge. Bullet diameter is 0.250 inch.

.255 Jeffery Rook

Historical Notes: This small, rimmed, necked cartridge was introduced by Jeffery and used in rook rifles. It is long obsolete in Britain, and quite rare in the United States.

General Comments: This is a small-game and target number. Several loadings were provided, with three or nine grains of black powder, and several with 3½ to 4¼ grains of smokeless powder. The usual bullet was a 65-grain lead solid or hollowpoint bullet at a standard muzzle velocity of 1,200 fps. The round may have been used in single-shot pistols, as well as in rifles.

.255 Jeffery Rook

Bullet (grains/type)	Powder	Grains	Velocity	Energy	Source/Comments
Bullet (grains/type)	Powder	Grains	Velocity	Energy	Source/Comments
65 Lead	FL		1,200	208	Factory load

.242 Rimless Nitro Express

Historical Notes: Developed in 1923 by Kynoch, for J. Manton & Co. (Calcutta), this cartridge was first called the .242 Manton. It was listed in late, post-war Kynoch catalogs.

General Comments: The .242 Rimless is very similar to the .243 Winchester and 6mm Remington in power and capacity. The case is a little longer than the American 6mms, but not quite as large in diameter. When loaded with American powders and used in a strong, modern bolt-action, it will deliver performance very similar to the .243 Winchester. This would be an effective cartridge for the same general range of game and shooting conditions as the .243 Winchester. Bullets are .249- to .253-inch diameter, so .243-inch bullets would not give satisfactory accuracy. One might be able to swage down .25-caliber bullets to fit, but be sure to slug your bore before attempting to handload for this cartridge.

.256 Mannlicher

Historical Notes: Much of the rest of the world called this round the 6.5x53R Mannlicher, particularly the Dutch and Romanians, both of which used it as a military round in the late 1800s, but the British used this moniker. (See the chapter on the world's military cartridges for more information.) This rimmed round was essentially identical in performance to that of the 6.5x54 M-S. The Brits developed four target loads from this rimmed (flanged) case and from the rimless 6.5x54 Mannlicher-Schönauer. These were the .256 Fraser Flanged and Rimless, and the .256 Swift Flanged and Rimless.

.256 Fraser Flanged/.256 Fraser Rimless/.256 Swift Flanged/ .256 Swift Rimless

Historical Notes: There were four target loads developed from the basic shape of the 6.5x54mm Mannlicher-Schoenauer case (.256 Mannlicher). These were the .256 Fraser Flanged and Rimless and the .256 Swift Flanged and Rimless. None achieved any great popularity.

.256 Gibbs Magnum

Historical Notes: This cartridge is a rimless, necked 6.5mm, introduced by George Gibbs in 1913 for Mauser-type magazine rifles of his design. It is a 6.5x57 Mauser round with the neck shortened by 2mm, and differs from the 6.5x55mm Swedish round, its base diameter being .470 inches.

General Comments: Brass can be made from 6mm Remington, .257 Roberts, 7x57 Mauser, or most of the other 57mm-long cases. Powder capacity and ballistics are about the same as the 6.5x57 or 6.5x55, so loading data from those rounds are great places to start with handloading. The case length is 2.17 inches.

.256 Gibbs Magnum Factory Ballistics

Bullet (grains/type)	Powder	Grains	Velocity	Energy	Source/Comments
145 SP	FL		2,600	2,178	Factory load

.26 BSA
(.26 Rimless Belted Nitro Express)

Historical Notes: The .26 Rimless Belted Nitro Express originated in 1921. It was introduced by Birmingham Small Arms (BSA) for its sporting rifles based on the bolt-action 1914 Enfield. It is actually a belted rimless case of advanced design.

General Comments: The .26 BSA was intended to appeal to those interested in high velocity, and it does this well with the light 110-grain bullet. It is also an example of what happens when every other feature is sacrificed for the last few feet-per-second of velocity. It looks good on paper, but it isn't very effective. On the other hand, some other .26-caliber cartridges with heavier bullets at lower velocities have a fine reputation on all kinds of game.

As factory loaded, the .26 BSA was not a suitable cartridge for North American hunting conditions. If handloaded with bullets of heavier weight, it can be made as effective as any other .26-caliber cartridge of similar case capacity. Head diameter is close to that of the .300 H&H Magnum, and cases can be made by reforming .300 H&H brass. Bullet diameter of existing cartridge specimens ranges from 0.266- to 0.269-inch, so be sure to slug your bore.

.26 BSA Factory Ballistics

Bullet (grains/type)	Powder	Grains	Velocity	Energy	Source/Comments
110 SP	FL		3,100	2,345	Factory load

.275 Rigby (7x57mm)

Historical Notes: This round, identical to the 7x57mm Mauser, was adopted by John Rigby & Co. in 1907 for Rigby bolt-action magazine rifles. Rigby was, at that time, the British outlet for Mauser. Rigby's original rifle featured the 175-grain bullet. In its 1924 catalog, Rigby listed three versions of the Mauser, the No. 1 rifle for the 175-grain bullet, and the No. 2 and No. 3 rifles for the 140-grain bullet. All were designed for deer stalking. The No. 1 and 2 rifles weighed 7½ pounds, and the No. 3 was built to weigh 6¾ pounds.

General Comments: This cartridge was made famous by Walter D.M. Bell, the British hunter who slew nearly a thousand elephants with it in the early years of the twentieth century. He killed them all with solid bullets of 175-grain weight, usually with one shot apiece. Bell was one of the finest marksmen the world has seen. You can read about his successes in his The Wanderings of an Elephant Hunter, Bell of Africa, and Karamojo Safari. Unfortunately, many men who read Bell's books and tried to emulate his success with this little cartridge without Bell's skill or luck have gotten themselves killed.

The .275 Rigby is a fine deer cartridge. A light No. 3 Rigby, stoked with the 140-grain Nosler Partition, is one of the finest rifles available for thin-skinned game in the 200-pound-and-under class. Don't use it on elephant.

.275 Rigby (7x57) Factory Ballistics

Bullet (grains/type)	Powder	Grains	Velocity	Energy	Source/Comments
140 Solid or LT Capped SN-SP	FL		3,000	2,800	Factory load
175 Solid or SN	FL		2,300	2,066	Factory load

.275 Belted Magnum (H&H)
.275 Flanged Magnum (H&H)

Historical Notes: Introduced in England in 1911-'12, the belted version for bolt-actions and the flanged for single-shot and double-barrel rifles, these are the first 7mm Magnums. These cartridges came out shortly after the .280 Ross created quite a stir in the smallbore high-velocity field. A fair number of American custom rifles have been made for this round, but no factory rifles. The belted version, known in the United States as the .275 H&H Magnum, was loaded by the Western Cartridge Co. until 1939. The rimmed load was slightly reduced from the belted. It was developed by F.W. Jones, as an improvement of the .280 Ross. Eley and Kynoch loaded bullets of 105, 140, 143, 150, 160, and 180 grains.

General Comments: The .275 H&H Magnum is similar to the 7mm Remington Magnum. With modern powders in a good rifle, this ancient British number will do anything that can be done by the 7mm Magnum. Both the flanged and belted versions are still on Holland's list of current cartridges. Be sure to slug your rifle to get the correct bore size and fit your bullets accordingly. These two cartridges are good long-range calibers for mountain or plains hunting of light game.

.275 Belted Magnum & Flanged Magnum (H&H) Factory Ballistics

Bullet (grains/type)	Powder	Grains	Velocity	Energy	Source/Comments
140 SP	FL		2,650	2,184	Factory load, British
160 SP	FL		2,700	2,600	Factory load, British
175 SP	FL		2,680	2,800	Western factory load

.275 No. 2 Magnum
(7mm Rigby Magnum Flanged)

Historical Notes: This is a rimmed necked cartridge designed for Rigby double rifles. It was introduced in 1927 and was still available in the early 1960s. It is advertised for "deer-stalking and all classes of non-dangerous game." It is another cartridge in roughly the same class as the 7x57mm Mauser.

.275 No. 2 Magnum Factory Ballistics

Bullet (grains/type)	Powder	Grains	Velocity	Energy	Source/Comments
140 SP	FL		2,675	2,230	Factory load

.280 Flanged (.280 Lancaster)

Historical Notes: Developed by Lancaster, this rimmed .280 cartridge is similar to the rimless .280 Ross and was used in single-shot and double rifles. It was introduced shortly after the Ross cartridge appeared in 1906. It is said to have been a favorite with King George V.

General Comments: The rimmed .280 is loaded to slightly lower velocities than the .280 Ross. When the rimless Ross cartridge was introduced, it created considerable interest all over the world. It was only natural to bring out a rimmed version, for the man who preferred the double rifle. Both cartridges have practically the same power and effectiveness. These high-speed .280 cartridges lost popularity after a few big-game hunters were killed while using them on heavy or dangerous game under adverse conditions. One of the most famous of these was Sir George Grey, killed by a lion in Africa.

.280 Flanged (.280 Lancaster) Factory Ballistics

Bullet (grains/type)	Powder	Grains	Velocity	Energy	Source/Comments
140 SP	FL		2,800	2,440	Factory load
160 SP	FL		2,600	2,400	Factory load
180 SP	FL		2,400	2,300	Factory load

.280 Ross (.280 Rimless)

Historical Notes: This timeless cartridge was designed by F.W. Jones, a consultant to Eley and Sir Charles Ross, and introduced in 1906 for the Canadian straight-pull Ross rifle. This was one of the first modern, high-velocity, smallbore cartridges. It was originally a military design, but quickly caught the fancy of sportsmen, because of its high velocity, flat trajectory, and excellent killing power. The German .280 Halger Magnum is based on the Ross case. At one time, Remington and Winchester loaded .280 Ross ammunition. American companies discontinued it in 1935. It is actually a semi-rimmed case.

General Comments: The .280 Ross is an example of what happens when hunters get overly enthusiastic about something new. It proved to have fantastic killing power on thin-skinned game. Even dangerous species were dispatched occasionally as if struck by lightning. However, there is a big difference between killing dangerous game under ideal conditions and stopping them cold when conditions get rough. Some men gave their lives to find this out, and the .280 Ross hit the skids. The original Ross bullet was made to expand quickly on medium-size game. However, no one bullet weight or type will do all things. This and many other cartridges have been maligned, because someone used them on game or under conditions for which they were not designed. The .280 Ross can be adequate for most North American game and non-dangerous African plains varieties, if you select the proper bullets.

.280 Ross Factory Ballistics

Bullet (grains/type)	Powder	Grains	Velocity	Energy	Source/Comments
140 SP	FL		2,900	2,620	Factory load
150 SP	FL		2,800	2,610	Factory load
160 SP	FL		2,700	2,600	Factory load
180 SP	FL		2,550	2,600	Factory load

.280 Jeffery (.33/.280 Jeffery)

Historical Notes: The .280 Jeffery is another of the series of .28-caliber cartridges designed as answers to the .280 Ross. The exact date of introduction of this one has not been established, but would have been around 1915. The firm of Jeffery built Mauser-type magazine rifles for this cartridge.

General Comments: This cartridge is based on the .333 Jeffery case necked down to accept bullets of 0.288-inch diameter. It has a larger case than the .280 Ross and holds more powder, but is not loaded to a much higher velocity. With modern powders, it could be handloaded to deliver a good deal higher velocity within safe pressure limits, but, today, there are better and more modern 7mm cartridges available. The .280 Jeffery would be a good cartridge for non-dangerous game at moderate to long ranges, with good bullets.

.300 (.295) Rook

Historical Notes: Another of the small British Rook cartridges, this one is of rather obscure origin and use. It dates prior to 1874, and was originally a black-powder cartridge. It was used in single-shot rifles and, possibly, pistols or revolvers. It was listed in the 1962 Eley-Kynoch catalog.

General Comments: Aside from bullet diameter, the .300 Rook closely resembles the obsolete American .32 Extra Long centerfire. The .300 Rook case is shorter than the .32 Extra Long, making it possible to fire .300 Rook cartridges in old rifles chambered for the American cartridge (though cartridge collectors would frown on this). This possibility might interest owners of old Ballard or Stevens rifles. The .300 Rook is strictly a small-game or target number.

.300 (.295) Rook Factory Ballistics

Bullet (grains/type)	Powder	Grains	Velocity	Energy	Source/Comments
80 lead	Black powder	10.0	1,100	215	Factory load

.300 Sherwood

Historical Notes: This was introduced by Westley Richards in 1901 as its answer to the .310 Greener cartridge. It was intended for use in Martini-action and Sherwood target rifles. Both solid lead and the amazing LT-capped bullets (designed by Leslie Taylor, then the director of Westley Richards), were available. About eight years later, Westley Richards came out with a similar cartridge called the .298 Minex—with a slightly shorter and slightly bottlenecked case—and a bolt-action rifle to shoot it.

General Comments: This is another British cartridge seldom encountered today. It is of interest primarily to cartridge collectors. In terms of power, it is on a par with .357 Magnum revolver ballistics, but has a smaller-diameter bullet. It would be useful for small-game or pest shooting, at short to moderate ranges.

.300 Sherwood Factory Ballistics

Bullet (grains/type)	Powder	Grains	Velocity	Energy	Source/Comments
140 JHP	FL		1,400	610	Factory load

.300 Belted Rimless Magnum (H&H)/.30 Flanged Magnum (H&H Super .30)

Historical Notes: The belted version here is the .300 Holland & Holland Magnum familiar to most of the world. The flanged version is for double rifles and is loaded a bit lighter. These cartridges originated in 1925. Additional data on the belted version is located in Chapter 1.

General Comments: The performance of this pair, with original factory loads, is on a par with or just a bit better than that of the .30-06. The flanged version must be loaded to give proper regulation in the double rifle, but the belted version in a good bolt-action rifle can easily beat the performance of the .30-06.

.300 Belted Rimless Magnum (H&H Super .30) Factory Ballistics

Bullet (grains/type)	Powder	Grains	Velocity	Energy	Source/Comments
150 SP	FL		3,000	3,000	Factory load, British

.300 Belted Rimless Magnum (H&H Super .30) Factory Ballistics

Bullet (grains/type)	Powder	Grains	Velocity	Energy	Source/Comments
180 SP	FL		2,750	3,020	Factory load, British
220 SP	FL		2,300	2,115	Factory load, British

.30 Flanged Magnum Factory Ballistics

Bullet (grains/type)	Powder	Grains	Velocity	Energy	Source/Comments
150 SP	FL		2,875	2,755	Factory load
180 SP	FL		2,575	2,653	Factory load
220 SP	FL		2,250	2,475	Factory load

.375/.303 Westley Richards
.375/.303 Axite

Historical Notes: This cartridge was introduced in 1905, and was listed in Westley Richards' catalogs for several years thereafter. It was also listed in the 1909 Charles Lancaster & Co. catalog. It was used in high-velocity double rifles by Westley with Lancaster oval-bore rifling, in single-shot falling-block rifles, and in Lee-action magazine rifles.

General Comments: Power is about the same as the .300 H&H Magnum. It was loaded with Axite, a new Kynoch powder said by the makers to be "comparatively free from erosive and corrosive effects."

.375/303 Westley Richards Factory Ballistics

Bullet (grains/type)	Powder	Grains	Velocity	Energy	Source/Comments
215 SP	FL		2,500	2,981	Factory load
200 SP	FL		2,726	2,980	Factory load

.303 British

General Comments: The .303 British military cartridge is a popular sporting round throughout the British Commonwealth and much of the world. It is covered in detail under military cartridges (Chapter 6), and also listed with American sporting cartridges (Chapter 1). English and Canadian loads offer greater variety and performance than those loaded in the United States.

.303 British Factory Ballistics

Bullet (grains/type)	Powder	Grains	Velocity	Energy	Source/Comments
150 SP	FL		2,700	2,440	Factory load, British
174 SP	FL		2,450	2,315	Factory load, British
180 SP	FL		2,540	2,580	Factory load, Canadian
192 SP	FL		2,200	2,070	Factory load, British
210 SP	FL		2,050	1,960	Factory load, British
215 SP	FL		2,050	2,010	Factory load, British

.303 Magnum

Historical Notes: This cartridge was introduced by Jeffery in 1919 and subsequently adopted by the British Match Rifle Committee. It had a short life, being listed by Kynoch only until 1930. Case configuration is the same as the experimental .276 military round and case capacity is the same as the .30-06.

General Comments: This cartridge was designed for long-range target shooting at long ranges. Performance is identical to that of the .30-06.

.303 Magnum Factory Ballistics

Bullet (grains/type)	Powder	Grains	Velocity	Energy	Source/Comments
174 FMJ	FL		2,850	3,050	Factory load

.310 Cadet (.310 Greener)

Historical Notes: This cartridge was introduced by Greener in 1900 as a target round for the small Martini sporting and training rifles. Many of those rifles were made for the Australian government as cadet trainers. The .310 Cadet also became a popular sporting cartridge for small-game shooting. Thousands of the Australian Martini cadet rifles were imported into the U.S. after World War II, and the .310 cartridge is rather well known in the U.S., as a result.

General Comments: The .310 Cadet cartridge is similar in size and performance to the .32-20. In fact, .310 ammunition can be made from .32-20 cases. Back in the 1950s, Winfield Arms Co. and Klein's Sporting Goods of Chicago sold several hundred .310 Martini rifles and actions. According to a 1955 data circular, those Martini actions were tested with proof loads of up to 60,000 psi, in order to determine what pressure the actions could safely handle. Some were rechambered for the .32 Winchester Special. Others were rebored to .357 Magnum. Quite a few have been rebarreled to .22 Hornet or .218 Bee. Former Gun Digest editor Ken Warner had one for the .44 Magnum. The .310 Cadet cartridge is a good small-game and pest number at moderate ranges, and it also is a good target round.

.310 Cadet Factory Ballistics

Bullet (grains/type)	Powder	Grains	Velocity	Energy	Source/Comments
84 lead	FL		UNK	UNK	Factory load
120 lead	Black powder	6.0	1,200	385	Factory load
125 lead	FL		UNK	UNK	Factory load

.318 Rimless Nitro Express
.318 Westley Richards
.318 Accelerated Express

Historical Notes: This cartridge was developed by Westley Richards in 1910 for its bolt-action, Mauser-type magazine rifles. It was intended for use in Africa, and it made a fine name for itself there. It was one of the most popular medium-bore cartridges in Africa, even after the advent of the .375 H&H Magnum. Many gun makers have chambered bolt-action rifles for this round. It is very similar to Elmer Keith's .333 OKH and the popular wildcat, the .338-06 (.338 OKH). There was a square-shouldered version of this cartridge, as well, designed to improve headspace control. Because this was not a major problem, the square-shouldered version did not last. It was fired in the standard chamber.

General Comments: The .318 can be used in standard-length bolt-actions of fairly light weight. This cartridge threw bullets of good weight at respectable velocities that proved very deadly on all sorts of game and, as a result, it became very popular. It worked so well on all medium-sized African game that it got some hunters in trouble, when they tried to extend its usefulness to dangerous game, sometimes at the cost of their lives. The .318 Westley Richards has been used with great success on all North American big game, though it is not recommended for use against the biggest bears or any kind of dangerous game in a tight spot.

The .318 case is very similar to the .30-06 in size, shape, and capacity. The 180-grain bullet was used on the lighter animals, while the 250-grain was preferred for all medium to heavy game. Bullet types were solid, soft-point, and the Westley Richards copper-capped. Fraser had a "ratchet" bullet load for this cartridge. Bullets of the necessary .330-inch diameter for the .318 Westley Richards can be obtained by swaging existing .33-caliber bullets. In addition, Woodleigh makes best-quality bullets in soft-nose or solid persuasion of the exact size. Cases can be made from .30-06 brass.

.318 Rimless Nitro Express Factory Ballistics

Bullet (grains/type)	Powder	Grains	Velocity	Energy	Source/Comments
180 SP	FL		2,700	2,920	Factory load
250 SP	FL		2,400	3,200	Factory load

.333 Jeffery Flanged & Rimless

Historical Notes: These are the two versions of the .333 Jeffery, introduced in 1908. The rimmed cartridge was intended for double rifles. The rimless type, intended for magazine rifles, became more popular. The rimmed .333 was discontinued after World War II. Both versions have about the same power. German-made Mauser rifles were also chambered for the rimless version.

General Comments: The .333 Jeffery earned a fine reputation on all varieties of African big game, including picked shots at elephants. Of course, most professional ivory hunters knew it was on the light side for such animals and, so, used their heavy rifles when in close cover or when they needed to drop dangerous game quickly. On soft-skinned game, it gave excellent penetration, particularly with the 300-grain bullet. This cartridge was the inspiration for the domestic wildcat .333 OKH, designed by Elmer Keith, Charlie O'Neil, and Don Hopkins.

.333 Jeffery Flanged and Rimless Factory Ballistics

Bullet (grains/type)	Powder	Grains	Velocity	Energy	Source/Comments
250 SP	FL		2,500	3,480	Factory load, Rimless
300 SP	FL		2,200	3,230	Factory load, Rimless
250 SP	Cordite	67.0	2,400	3,200	Factory load, Flanged
300 SP	Cordite	63.0	2,150	3,090	Factory load, Flanged

.33 BSA
(.33 Belted Rimless/.330 BSA)

Historical Notes: This belted cartridge was introduced by Birmingham Small Arms in 1921 for its bolt-action sporting rifles based on the military Enfield. It was never very popular and was discontinued many years ago.

General Comments: Like the rimless .26 BSA, the .33 was an effort to furnish a high-velocity cartridge in a popular caliber. Neither was a commercial success. The 165-grain bullet starts out at 3,000 fps, but its poor sectional density causes it to slow down quite rapidly; after only 100 yards, its velocity was down to about 2,650. The .33 BSA offered good killing power on light game, but failed to penetrate properly on heavy game.

For this reason, it was not a successful general-purpose cartridge for African game. Why the manufacturer did not offer a choice of bullets with weights up to, say, 250 grains, is a mystery.

This is a good case design for modern rifles, and the handloader can improve this one and put it in the same class as the .338-06 or the .318 Westley Richards. Properly handloaded, the .33 BSA would do well on most North American big game. This cartridge uses .338-inch diameter bullets. In fact, if you lengthen the case an eighth of an inch and move the shoulder forward a bit, you have the .338 Winchester Magnum. When handloading this cartridge, remember that the British Enfield action will not stand the same high working pressure as will the Mauser 98.

.33 BSA Factory Ballistics (Note: *Estimated ballistics)

Bullet (grains/type)	Powder	Grains	Velocity	Energy	Source/Comments
165 SP	FL		3,000	3,290	Factory load
175 SP	FL		2,900	3,265	Factory load *

.400/.350 Rigby

Historical Notes: The first of John Rigby & Co.'s .350s, this cartridge was introduced in November 1899. This is the old .400 Purdey case necked down to .35-caliber. Rigby provided single-shot, double, and bolt-action rifles in this chambering. The cartridge utilized outstanding soft-points and solids of 310 grains at about 2,100 fps. The .400/.350 was, at one time, the most popular and widely used medium-bore cartridge for African hunting. It was succeeded by the .350 No. 2, which is identical in case dimensions, but has a bullet of only 225 grains at somewhat higher velocity. That cartridge was also loaded in a rimless version, but this one—the original and, some say, the best of the .350 Rigbys—was available only as a rimmed case. The magazine boxes of Rigby's bolt rifles were slanted to accommodate the rim.

General Comments: The .400/.350 is a rimmed case that resembles the old .35 Winchester in general appearance. However, it is longer and uses heavier .358-inch-diameter bullets. The popularity of the .400/.350 was due, in a large part, to the excellent bullet design, which gave uniform and dependable results. The incomparable John "Pondoro" Taylor had a single-loader in this chambering, and that rifle was a great favorite of his. He used it on lion and other big game and reported that penetration and overall performance were excellent. The .400/.350 would be a good cartridge for most North American big game, particularly where ranges are short.

.400/.350 Rigby Factory Ballistics

Bullet (grains/type)	Powder	Grains	Velocity	Energy	Source/Comments
310 SP	FL		2,100	3,035	Factory load

.350 Rigby Magnum & .350 No. 2 Rigby

Historical Notes: The rimmed version of this cartridge, the .350 No. 2, was the successor to the .400/.350 Rigby. The cases of the two are identical. The difference from the .400/.350 is in the use of a lighter bullet at higher velocity. The rimless .350 Rigby Magnum was designed for bolt-action magazine rifles. Both cartridges came out in 1908, and both used a bullet of only 225 grains to increase the velocity of what was already a fully successful cartridge. This, it was felt, was necessary to compete with speedier cartridges that were all the rage at the time.

General Comments: The .350 Rigby Magnum and the No. 2 were popular with many African and Asian hunters. The performances of these rounds are similar to that of the .35 Whelen. Many hunters preferred the .350 Rigby Magnum over the .375 H&H Magnum, because the Rigby had less recoil. Either of these Rigby rounds would be a fine cartridge for any North American big game short of large bears, although some hunters who can put up with the poorer trajectory prefer the heavier bullet of the original .400/350. Bullet diameter is 0.358-inch, so bullets are easy to find for the reloader.

Bullet (grains/type)	Powder	Grains	Velocity	Energy	Source/Comments
225 SP	FL		2,625	3,440	Factory load, Rimless
225 SP	FL		2,575	3,312	Factory load, No. 2

.360 No. 5 Rook

Historical Notes: Introduced between 1875 and 1880, this cartridge was loaded until World War II. It was used in handguns and rifles. The 1909 Charles Lancaster & Co. catalog illustrates it for its underlever single-shot rifle and the Webley New "Express" revolver. Many other arms chambered the .360 No. 5.

General Comments: In addition to the versions listed below, shot and blank cartridges were also offered. Although ammunition catalogs separate rifle and revolver loadings, in actual practice, any version could be used in rifles or in late-model revolvers. The .360 No. 5 cartridge is very similar to the .380 Long and the .38 Long Colt. This is a small-game and target load.

.360 No. 5 Rook Factory Ballistics

Bullet (grains/type)	Powder	Grains	Velocity	Energy	Source/Comments
82 lead	Black powder		UNK	UNK	Factory load
125 lead	Black powder		1,050	310	Factory load
134 lead	Black powder		1,025	312	Factory load
134 lead	Smokeless powder		1,025	312	Factory load
145 lead	Smokeless powder		1,075	373	Factory load
134 lead	Black powder		1,025	312	Factory load

.360 Express (2¼-inch)
.360 Nitro-For-Black .360 Nitro Express

Historical Notes: The .360 (2¼-inch) is a black-powder cartridge that first appeared before 1873. In that guise, it was loaded with a great variety of bullet weights, from 71 to 215 grains. Cartridge case length also varied considerably. The 2¼-inch version was the most common, but a length of 2 7/16 inches was also common and a favorite length of Alexander Henry, who was, arguably, the best craftsman of the nineteenth century. Some cases were as long as 2¾ inches. Nitro loadings were with bullet weights of 190, 200, 250, and 300 grains (at least). Nitro versions date from around 1900 to 1902. Some black-powder loads were paper patched, others were of bare lead.

General Comments: This cartridge would be useful for small, thin-skinned game. In power, it is about the same as the .38-55 and would not be a bad short-range woods cartridge for deer-size animals. It was used mostly in single-shot and double rifles. If you have a rifle in this bore size, be sure to make a chamber cast to find out the true dimensions before you attempt to handload for it. Bertram of Australia makes cases for the .360 that are long enough to produce suitable loads for any version.

.360 Express (2¼-inch)/.360 Nitro-For-Black Factory Ballistics

Bullet (grains/type)	Powder	Grains	Velocity	Energy	Source/Comments
134 lead	Smokeless powder		1,025	312	Factory load
190 (360 NBP)	Smokeless powder		1,700	1,222	Factory load
300 (360 NE)	Smokeless powder		1,650	1,820	Factory load

.400/.360 Nitro Express (2¾-inch) Westley Richards/ Fraser/Evans/Purdey

Historical Notes: Although these cartridges have similar names, these are not interchangeable. The Purdey version uses a bigger bullet than the others—.367-inch diameter. The other versions have bullets from .358- to .360-inch diameter. The Purdey is usually marked .400/.360P or .400/.360B. There are significant variations in bullet weight, as well as in rim thickness. In addition, Westley Richards had a rimless version of the .400/.360 loaded with a 314-grain bullet. They all appeared about 1900.

General Comments: These cartridges all generate about the same power. All are fine for use against medium-sized game, particularly for close-range hunting. The Purdey and Evans versions use a 300-grain bullet at 1,950 fps, and the Westley Richards version threw a 314-grain bullet at 1,900 fps. The Fraser used a 289-grain bullet. Often, the correct load is engraved on the rifle in question, other times, information leading to the correct loading is given in the proofmarks on British firearms. These rifles are quite common today, and the true chambering is often difficult to determine. Some may have been rechambered. To determine what you have, make a chamber cast and measure it precisely. Be sure to slug your bore.

.400/.360 Nitro Express (2¾-inch) Factory Ballistics

Bullet (grains/type)	Powder	Grains	Velocity	Energy	Source/Comments
289 SP	FL		UNK	UNK	Fraser factory load
300 SP	FL		1,950	2,537	Purdey factory load
300 SP	FL		1,950	2,537	Evans factory load
314 SP	FL		1,900	2,520	Westley Richards factory load

.360 No. 2 Nitro Express

Historical Notes: The fine .360 No. 2 was introduced by Eley Brothers in 1905 for single-shot rifles and doubles. The .360 No. 2 was quite popular during its first years of existence, but could not compete with the .375 H&H Magnum that appeared on the market only a few years later. The ballistics of this cartridge are similar to those of Holland's .375 with its 300-grain bullets. The .360 No. 2's case is basically a necked-down .400 Jeffery with a rounded shoulder. Cases can be made from modern .400 Jeffery cases or bought from Bertram.

General Comments: This is a large, rimmed, bottlenecked case noted for the low pressure it develops, the lowest of any cartridge in its class. It was a good all-around cartridge for thin-skinned African or Indian game. It would be adequate for any North American big game at moderate ranges and would be an excellent cartridge for elk in heavy timber. Kynoch loads it today. Bullet diameter is 0.366-inch, but be sure to check your rifle's bore, as there were some barrel variations, particularly early in the twentieth century.

.360 No. 2 Nitro Express Factory Ballistics

Bullet (grains/type)	Powder	Grains	Velocity	Energy	Source/Comments
320 SP	FL		2,200	3,442	Factory load

.375 Flanged Nitro Express (2½-inch) (.370 Flanged)

Historical Notes: Introduced in 1899, this is a straight, rimmed case not to be confused with the .375 Flanged Magnum, which has a larger necked case. This one was used in single-shots and double rifles, and BSA made a bolt-action Lee magazine rifle in this chambering.

General Comments: The straight .375 rimmed cartridge is suitable for much hunting use and would be adequate for almost any North American big game, particularly for hunting in woods or brush. Bullets are no problem. This one is very similar in concept to the .375 Winchester, but the two are not interchangeable. This cartridge lends itself to some improvement by handloading, an acceptable practice for use in a single-shot or magazine rifle. One can make cases from .405 Winchester cases. Bertram also makes brass for it. Elmer Keith had a Lancaster oval-bore double rifle in this chambering, which he used for elk on occasion. The grand old master liked the rifle and chambering very much, once he got it regulated properly, something he said was quite a chore.

.375 Flanged Nitro Express (2½-inch) Factory Ballistics (Note: *Estimated ballistics)

Bullet (grains/type)	Powder	Grains	Velocity	Energy	Source/Comments
270 SP	FL		2,000	2,400	Factory load
300 SP	FL		1,900	2,405	Factory load *

.400/.375 Belted Nitro Express (H&H)

Historical Notes: This was the world's first belted case. It was introduced by Holland & Holland in 1905 to compete with the rising popularity of the 9.5mm Mannlicher-Schönauer. The .400/.375 was used mainly in bolt-action rifles, but some double and single-shot rifles also chambered it. It was listed in British ammunition catalogs until 1936-'38. Many of Holland & Holland's rifles in this chambering were apparently takedowns on Mannlicher actions and, later, on Mauser 98 actions.

General Comments: The power of the .400/.375 is nearly identical to that of the 9.5mm Mannlicher and in the same class as the .358 Winchester. It would be adequate for most North American big game at moderate ranges. Cases can be made from .240 Weatherby brass. Bullets designed for .375 Magnum velocities will perform poorly at these low velocities, but one might have good luck with cast bullets or those designed for the .375 Winchester rifle.

.400/.375 Belted Nitro Express (H&H) Factory Ballistics (Note: *Estimated ballistics)

Bullet (grains/type)	Powder	Grains	Velocity	Energy	Source/Comments
270 SP/FMJ	FL		2,175	2,840	Factory load
320	Cordite	43.0	2,000	2,840	Factory load *

.375 Rimless Nitro Express (2¼-inch) (9.5x57mm Mannlicher-Schönauer)

General Comments: This is the British designation for the 9.5mm Mannlicher-Schönauer, and it may be listed either or both ways. There is a very slight difference in loading between the two listings, but they are interchangeable. This cartridge takes bullets of 0.375-inch diameter. Performance is similar to that of the .400/.375. The 9.5mm Mannlicher-Schönauer is not carried in late European catalogs. Additional data for this one is in the chapter on European cartridges.

.375 Rimless Nitro Express (2¼-inch) (9.5x57mm MS) Factory Ballistics

Bullet (grains/type)	Powder	Grains	Velocity	Energy	Source/Comments
270 SP	FL		2,150	2,771	Factory load, European
270 SP	FL		2,100	2,643	Factory load, British

.369 Nitro Express (Purdey)

Historical Notes: This cartridge was brought out in 1922 by Purdey, for double-barrel rifles of its manufacture.

General Comments: The .369 Purdey was loaded with only one bullet weight (270 grains) and offers ballistics practically identical to the .375 H&H Flanged Magnum with the same bullet. The .369 uses bullets of .375-inch diameter. It is a good cartridge suitable for any of the heavier varieties of North American big game. It could be improved by handloading, but, because it was only used in double-barrel rifles, it is not normally practical to change performance of the load.

.369 Nitro Express (Purdey) Factory Ballistics

Bullet (grains/type)	Powder	Grains	Velocity	Energy	Source/Comments
270 SP	FL		2,500	3,760	Factory load

.375 Flanged Magnum
.375 Belted Rimless Magnum
.375 H&H Magnum

Historical Notes: In 1912, Holland & Holland brought out perhaps the most famous pair of cartridges ever devised, the .375 Magnum in belted and flanged versions. The belted version was for magazine rifles and the rimmed or flanged for doubles and single-loaders. When these cartridges were introduced, nothing similar was available. Their only competitors were the .450/.400 3-inch and 3¼-inch for doubles, the somewhat more powerful .404 Jeffery and .416 Rigby for magazine rifles, and the smaller .350 Rigby Magnum and No. 2. Holland's new .375 Magnum offered three bullet weights that regulated well in double rifles, something unheard of before—or since. The round gave a flat trajectory, three bullet weights, and outstanding performance in handy rifles of top quality. The belted version has always been with us, and Kynoch and others again load the rimmed version today.

General Comments: This cartridge has been very successful and, hence, very popular in Africa, India, and, in fact, throughout the hunting world. Nearly every manufacturer in the world makes or has made rifles in the belted version of this cartridge, and double rifles are still being made for the flanged version.

The .375 rimmed is loaded to slightly less velocity than the belted case, but not enough to make any real difference. One can use the same loading data as the .375 belted magnum. However, you can't change the ballistics without causing the barrels of a double rifle to shoot to different points of impact. You must adjust your load to the individual rifle by trial and error. A rifle in either version of this cartridge makes a fine all-around hunting tool for anything on the face of the earth short of dangerous game at close quarters.

.375 H&H Flanged Magnum Loading Data and Factory Ballistics

Bullet (grains/type)	Powder	Grains	Velocity	Energy	Source/Comments
270 SP	IMR 4350	83.0	2,620	4,115	N/A
300 SP	IMR 4350	80.0	2,500	4,160	N/A
235 SP	FL		2,750	3,945	Factory load
270 SP	FL		2,600	4,050	Factory load
300 SP	FL		2,400	3,835	Factory load

.375 Belted Magnum Factory Ballistics

Bullet (grains/type)	Powder	Grains	Velocity	Energy	Source/Comments
235 SP	FL		2,800	4,090	Factory load
270 SP	FL		2,650	4,200	Factory load
300 SP	FL		2,500	4,160	Factory load

.380 Short and Long (Rifle)

Historical Notes: These are old black-powder cartridges dating back to the early 1870s. These cartridges were used in single-shot rifles, pistols, and revolvers. Ammunition was loaded by DWM in Germany, and chambered in inexpensive, European-made handguns.

General Comments: The .380 Long is similar to the old .38 Long Colt. It is suitable for short-range target and small-game use. If you have a gun chambered for one of these, it is possible to make ammunition from .38 Special brass. The .380 has an outside-lubricated bullet of up to 0.376-inch diameter. Use similar loading data as for the .38 Long Colt.

.380 Short and Long (Rifle) Factory Ballistics

Bullet (grains/type)	Powder	Grains	Velocity	Energy	Source/Comments
124 lead	Black powder		1,050	304	Factory load

.400 Purdey (3-inch) Light Express/.400 Straight 3-inch

Historical Notes: Numerous .40-caliber straight cases were chambered in British rifles from the dawn of the breechloading era. Some were made of paper, some of coiled brass. Some were as short as two inches, others as long as 3¼. Around 1905, Purdey used this three-inch case loaded with "light cordite" for its double rifles. Kynoch offered a shot cartridge slightly longer than three inches, perhaps for use in oval-bored rifles of .40-caliber. Oval boring was a speciality of Lancaster's.

General Comments: According to a Purdey catalog, "The light .400 is an excellent firearm for deer, wild boar, etc., and has gained great popularity for tiger shooting in India, having the advantage of being a really powerful firearm and no heavier than a heavy 12-bore gun. The bullet is lead with a nickel base (a gas check), and at 100 yards has a striking energy of 1,443 foot-pounds." We hope not too many tiger hunters had to defend themselves with this one. A .40-caliber bullet weighing only 230 grains would work fine on deer, as it has about the sectional density of a typical (240-grain) .44 Magnum bullet, though at significantly greater velocity. Penetration would depend on bullet construction. These rifles generally require 0.405-inch bullets, but be sure to slug your bore.

.400 Purdey (3-inch) Factory Ballistics

Bullet (grains/type)	Powder	Grains	Velocity	Energy	Source/Comments
230 lead	Cordite	47.0	2,050	2,150	Factory load

.400 H&H Magnum

Historical Notes: When Holland & Holland began receiving inquiries asking them to develop a cartridge that would increase in power over its legendary .375 H&H Magnum, Technical Director Russell Wilkin began working on the problem. The requests were for a cartridge that could produce 6,000 ft-lbs of energy at the muzzle, which is an enormous leap over the .375's 4,160 ft-lbs, so Wilkin decided to create two cartridges, a .465 and a more manageable .411-caliber cartridge that could be called the ".400 Holland & Holland Magnum." This bore diameter fit neatly between the .375 and the .465 calibers and would be legal in those African countries that require a minimum .40-caliber rifle to hunt dangerous game.

General Comments: Holland retained the belted case head of the .375 H&H, mostly for aesthetic reasons. The shoulder has been moved back to lengthen the neck, providing plenty of grip on the bullet to withstand inertia under recoil in the magazine of a bolt-action rifle. A shallow shoulder angle ensures a smooth feed from magazine to chamber. Field testing shows the .400 has a very similar trajectory to the .375 at normal hunting ranges.

.400 H&H Magnum Factory Ballistics

Bullet (grains/type)	Powder	Grains	Velocity	Energy	Source/Comments
400 Woodleigh	FL		2,400	5,115	Holland & Holland

.450/.400 2 3/8-inch BPE
.450/.400 2 3/8-inch Nitro-For-Black
.450/.400 2 3/8-inch Nitro Express

Historical Notes: These are different loadings of the same cartridge, which was a black-powder load that originated circa 1880. The Nitro-For-black and Nitro Express versions originated circa 1899. These are based on the old .450-bore base-diameter case shortened and necked down to .40-caliber, and then loaded with 80 grains of black powder and a 210- to 270-grain lead bullet. The Nitro-For-Black version, made for use in black-powder rifles, was loaded with 270-grain bullets and developed very low pressure. The full Nitro version featured 300- to 400-grain bullets over 40 to 43 grains of cordite. There was a similar BP Express cartridge of 2 7/8-inch length and some other rather rare variations on this theme.

General Comments: The British worked up smokeless loads for many of their old black-powder cartridges. For single-shot rifles, this wasn't difficult, but, with a double rifle, the load had to be balanced to shoot to the same point of impact as the original black-powder load. With these doubles, simply working up the same velocity for the same bullet didn't always work. Various bullets and velocities had to be tried to arrive at the right combination.

With the correct load for the individual rifle, this cartridge gave fine deer-hunting performance at short ranges. The Nitro Express version with 43 grains of cordite and the 400-grain bullet would be quite a bit more powerful and generally more useful.

.450/400 2 3/8-inch BPE, Nitro-For-Black, and Nitro Express Factory Ballistics

Bullet (grains/type)	Powder	Grains	Velocity	Energy	Source/Comments
210 - 270 lead	Black powder (FFg)	79.0 - 84.0	N/A	N/A	N/A
270 RN copper-tubed lead	Cordite	38.0	1,650	1,630	Factory load, Nitro for black powder
300 RN HP	Cordite	40.0	N/A	N/A	Factory load, Nitro Express
400 RN HP	Cordite	42.0-43.0	N/A	N/A	Factory load, Nitro Express

.400 Jeffery Nitro Express
.450/.400 3-inch

Historical Notes: This cartridge was introduced by Jeffery in 1902. According to John "Pondoro" Taylor, this shorter cartridge was brought out because the longer, formerly black-powder, .450/.400 3¼-inch cartridge had a tendency to stick in the chamber after firing, when it was fired in its cordite version. The Jeffery case is shorter, but its shoulder is moved forward, providing more volume. The .400 Jeffery was designed exclusively for cordite and was never a black-powder cartridge. As with the 3-¼-inch version, this round was very popular before the .375 H&H Magnum appeared. It is still one of the most effective all-around cartridges for Africa. Today, Hornady and quite a few others load this round.

General Comments: The .400 Jeffery throws a 400-grain bullet at adequate velocity and, hence, is more effective on the largest game than is the 300-grain .375 H&H Magnum loading. However, it is less versatile when it comes to available guns and loads, and that is where the .375 shines. Taylor wrote that he considered either of the .450/.400s (3- or 3-¼-inch), adequate for any African game under almost any conditions, if used by an experienced hunter. Taylor killed about 1,500 elephants. He used about every suitable English and German cartridge in the process, so his opinion is something to consider. Elmer Keith wrote that a double rifle for this cartridge would be his first choice for crawling through an Alaskan alder thicket after big bear. Note that loads using 55 or 57 grains of cordite were offered for use in extremely hot climates. A 300-grain loading was also offered, but it was not particularly popular.

Bullets of proper diameter (0.411-inch) may be obtained from Hornady, Barnes, Woodleigh, Hawk, and others. Hornady and Bertram and a few others make cases. The availability of new and excellent bullets in this size, along with some new rifles, has given this cartridge a new lease on life. Ruger chambered its No. 1 rifle for it in 2014. Good double rifles for the .400 Jeffery are being made in 2014 by Sabatti, Searcy, and a few English companies. We expect this cartridge to be around for many years to come.

.400 Jeffery (.450/400 Nitro Express 3-inch) Factory Ballistics

Bullet (grains/type)	Powder	Grains	Velocity	Energy	Source/Comments
400 SP	Cordite	60.0	2,100	3,920	Factory load, standard

.450/.400 3¼-inch BPE

.450/.400 3¼-inch Nitro-For- Black

.450/.400 3¼-inch Nitro Express

Historical Notes: The .450/.400 3¼ is basically a necked-down .450 3¼ case. In black-powder form, it was loaded with 110 to 120 grains of powder. Bullet weight varied from 230 to 300 grains. The Nitro-For-Black version was stoked with 45 to 48 grains of cordite and with bullets weighing from 270 to 316 grains. The Nitro Express version was loaded with 400-grain soft-points or solids over 56 to 60 grains of cordite. In black-powder versions, it extracted easily, but, with the increased pressure of the Nitro version, corrosion or fouling in the chamber could cause the case to stick, and the rim could be torn off.

General Comments: The black-powder version of this cartridge was generally used for deer or similar-size game. The Nitro version is the smallest of the British cartridges that can be considered appropriate for use on dangerous game and is a fine all-around cartridge for African and Indian game or for big Alaskan bear. Before the introduction of the .375 H&H Magnum, it was one of the most popular cartridges worldwide. If one is a cool and good shot, they can take this cartridge against the biggest elephant, which is just what John "Pondoro" Taylor did many times. He speaks quite highly of it in African Rifles and Cartridges.

Many double rifles are encountered today for both black-powder and Nitro versions of this cartridge. Note that Jeffery's later .40-caliber three-inch round, the .400 Jeffery, is not interchangeable with this one. The early Nitro rifles tend to be too heavy for the chambering. A double rifle for this round in Nitro version needs to weigh only about 9½ pounds.

.450/400 3¼-inch BPE, Nitro-For-Black, and Nitro Express Factory Ballistics

Bullet (grains/type)	Powder	Grains	Velocity	Energy	Source/Comments
230 to 300 lead	Black powder (FFg)	110.0	N/A	N/A	Factory load
270 to 316 SP	Cordite	45.0 – 48.0	N/A	N/A	Factory load, Nitro For Black
400 SP	Cordite	56.0 – 60.0	2,150	4,110	Factory load, Nitro Express

.400 H&H Magnum
Belted Rimless

Historical Notes: Over the years, Holland & Holland has received many requests to develop a cartridge more powerful than its legendary .375 H&H Magnum. Technical Director Russell Wilkin came up with two new H&H cartridges, the .400 and the .465 H&H Magnums. The .400 H&H Mag uses bullets of 0.411-inch of 400-grain weight. This bore diameter would be legal in those African countries that require a minimum .40-caliber rifle to hunt dangerous game. One wonders why H&H didn't make it a .416-caliber, with the hosts of fine bullets out there. Perhaps such a consideration would have made it too close to the .416 Remington for legal comfort.

General Comments: Holland & Holland retained the belted case head of the .375 H&H and also the tapered case found on all its cartridges. The shoulder has been moved back to lengthen the neck, which helps the case grip the bullet and better withstand recoil. The new .465 H&H Belted Mag has a similar design. The shallow shoulder angle should provide very smooth feeding. Field testing has shown the trajectory of the new .400 to be similar to that of the .375.

.400 H&H Magnum Belted Rimless Factory Ballistics

Bullet (grains/type)	Powder	Grains	Velocity	Energy	Source/Comments
400 Woodleigh	FL		2,400	5,115	Holland & Holland

.404 Jeffery/
.404 Rimless Nitro Express
10.75x73mm

Historical Notes: Introduced by W.J. Jeffery in 1909, the .404 Jeffery was vastly popular for many years, and then died slowly over many decades. It now has a new lease on life. In 1993, Dynamit Nobel announced it would restart production of .404 Jeffery ammunition and Ruger announced that the M77 rifle would be chambered for that cartridge. A Canadian company, NASS, recently announced a line of proprietary cartridges ranging from 7mm to .458 based on the .404 case. In the United States, Dakota Arms, of Sturgis, S.D., (and now part of the Freedom Group, which includes Remington and Marlin, among others) has introduced its own line of proprietary cartridges based on the .404 case, these ranging from 7mm to .416. Bullets of .423-inch diameter are now available for the .404. Norma, RWS, and Bertram make cases. The .404 was designed to be a bolt-action cartridge that would duplicate the ballistics of the rimmed .400 Jeffery and the .450/.400 3¼-inch. The .404 is also popular on the Continent, where it is metrically named the 10.75x73mm. Today, it is loaded a bit hotter than originally.

General Comments: The .404 made a great name for itself in Africa, where inexpensive bolt rifles let its performance be experienced by those who could not afford a double-barrel rifle for one of the .400 Nitro Express rounds. At one time, a higher-velocity 300-grain load was available for the .404. It gave good results on thin-skinned game, but proved rather unreliable on the heavier species. With the standard 400-grain bullet, the .404 was a very popular, general-purpose cartridge in Africa and India. Properly used, it is adequate for any game found there. It is somewhat overpowered for North American game and lacks the flat trajectory and long-range potential necessary for much of our hunting stateside. The .404 is a good cartridge for hunting bear or other big game at close quarters. The .404 uses .423-inch diameter bullets, which are available from Barnes, Woodleigh, and RWS.

.404 Jeffery Factory Ballistics

Bullet (grains/type)	Powder	Grains	Velocity	Energy	Source/Comments
300 SP	FL		2,600	4,500	Factory load
400 SP	FL		2,125	4,020	Factory load

Bullet (grains/type)	Powder	Grains	Velocity	Energy	Source/Comments
400 SP	FL		2300	4700	Factory load, modern

.416 Rigby

Historical Notes:	The .416 Rigby began life as a proprietary cartridge, introduced by John Rigby in 1911, for magnum Mauser-actioned rifles. The cartridge and rifle quickly established a solid record of reliability on dangerous game that endures to this day. Over the years, many makers have built rifles around this cartridge. Today, John Rigby & Co., in conjunction with Mauser, is again producing .416 rifles on German magnum Mauser actions that are close copies of the originals. Also, CZ, Kimber, Dakota, and probably a few more outfits will make you a .416 Rigby rifle. Federal Cartridge Co. makes .416 Rigby ammunition, as do Hornady, Norma, Kynoch, Nosler, and others.
General Comments:	The .416 Rigby is one of the best magazine-rifle cartridges for big game ever offered. At its inception, it was almost unique, with only the .404 Jeffery having similar power. Today, we also have the .400 H&H Magnum, the .416 Remington Magnum, and the .416 Weatherby Magnum. All of these use a belted case, which may not give quite as smooth feeding as does the big beltless Rigby case. The .416 Rigby delivers greater striking energy than the .404 Jeffery. For those who preferred the bolt-action rifle (or couldn't afford a good double), the .416 Rigby was a great favorite for use against dangerous game in almost any situation.
	Because the .416 Remington and Weatherby are now standard items, many great bullets are available in this caliber. This cartridge is a handloader's dream. Numerous moulds are available for those who want to shoot cast bullets.

.416 Rigby Factory Ballistics

Bullet (grains/type)	Powder	Grains	Velocity	Energy	Source/Comments
410 SP	FL	N/A	2,370	5,100	Factory load
400 SP	FL	N/A	2,430	5,245	Federal factory load

.425 Westley Richards Magnum

Historical Notes:	Westley Richards introduced this cartridge in 1909. It was a good cartridge and quite successful. It had a rebated rim that fits the standard-diameter Mauser bolt face. Westley made double rifles as well as bolt-action rifles for the .425. The round was loaded with only one bullet weight, 410 grains, but with about a half-dozen varieties of soft-noses and solids.
General Comments:	The .425 Westley is a sort of poor-man's magnum. Designed for use against dangerous game, it was intended to take the place of the .450-bore in India, though Westley Richards also offered its .476 for use in both Africa and India. The .425 proved to be a fine cartridge and was offered not only with solids, but also with the Leslie Taylor-designed capped soft-nose bullets. Taylor was the director of Westley Richards at the beginning of the twentieth century and was personally involved in bullet design, among many other things. The so-called "LT-capped bullets" worked very well and were incorporated into most other Westley Richards cartridges, including the .318 and .476.
	The .425's rebated rim is .30-06 size, so any .30-06 or 8mm Mauser action can be made to accept it with minimal gunsmithing. The result can be a good and powerful big-game rifle at a reasonable cost. Bullet diameters ranged from 0.428 to 0.435 inch, so be sure to check your rifle's bore carefully before shooting it or handloading for it.

Bullet (grains/type)	Powder	Grains	Velocity	Energy	Source/Comments
410 SP	FL		2,350	5,010	Factory load

.500/.450 No. 1 Carbine
.500/.450 No. 1 Express
.500/.450 No. 1 Musket
.500/.450 No. 2 Musket

Historical Notes:	Perhaps no cartridges in the world are more abundant or more confusing than those of British origin labeled .500/.450 and followed by one or another length designation. There are no fewer than 19 listings of individually identified cartridges in Bill Fleming's British Sporting Rifle Cartridges. Many of them were loaded with a great variety of bullet weights. All of them were bottleneck cartridges, and all began life loaded with black powder. The No. 1 Carbine was Westley Richards' first drawn-brass case. It appeared just before 1880. Westley Richards was also responsible for the Musket and the 2¾-inch No. 1 Express, and possibly others of this lot. The oldest of the .500/.450s had a coiled-brass case of 2½-inch length that dates to 1871. Some of these cartridges were loaded well into the twentieth century.
General Comments:	All the .500/.450s are in the same class as the .45-70 and would be fairly effective short-range cartridges for North American game. Because of the great variation in designs, the handloader should be careful to determine exactly which of the many variants they have before attempting to build cartridges for it.

.500/.450 No. 1 Express Factory Ballistics

Bullet (grains/type)	Powder	Grains	Velocity	Energy	Source/Comments
270 lead	Black powder	N/A	1,900	2,160	Factory load

.500/.450 No. 2 Musket Factory Ballistics

Bullet (grains/type)	Powder	Grains	Velocity	Energy	Source/Comments
480 lead	Black powder	N/A	1,300	1,805	Factory load
480 lead	Smokeless powder	N/A	1,300	1,805	Factory load
500 lead	Smokeless powder	N/A	1,350	2,025	Factory load

.450 3¼-inch BPE

Historical Notes:	There were a great many "straight" British cartridges of nominal .450 designation, ranging from the .450 No. 1—barely longer than the .45 Colt—up to the .450 3¼-inch. In Bill Fleming's British Sporting Rifle Cartridges, there is a progression of no fewer than nine different lengths illustrated, in coiled paper, coiled brass, and drawn brass. The 3¼-inch drawn-brass version originated prior to 1877, and coiled-brass versions were in existence before 1871.
	This cartridge was the first attempt to replace the .577 Snider, when Britain was looking for a new military cartridge. It was first loaded with 480-grain bullets, but didn't work well in the Martini-Henry rifle. Loaded with lighter bullets and more powder, it became a favorite of Victorian-age sportsmen. As

an Express, bullet weights ran from about 260 grains up to 365 in the Nitro-For-Black versions. Powder charges were from 105 to 120 grains of black (Greener indicates 150 grains). Nitro loadings for black-powder rifles used up to 55 grains of cordite. The .450 3¼ Express was loaded in France, Germany, Austria, Canada, and, most likely, elsewhere. It was one of the best black-powder cartridges in the world and was loaded well into the twentieth century in Nitro-For-Black versions.

General Comments: The 3¼-inch Express became one of the most popular cartridges ever devised. It was a deer cartridge or one intended for medium-sized game at best. Selous and Taylor both used this cartridge to take elephant, but they both knew this was something of a stunt. The .450 3¼-inch Express became known as the .450 3¼-inch BPE in the nitro age. The .450 3¼-inch Express lasted well into the twentieth century, and many rifles that chamber it are still in use. The author of this chapter once owned a fine Watson Bros. hammer double that regulated well with bullets from 300 to 400 grains.

.450 3¼-inch Nitro Express

Historical Notes: When cordite and suitable full-patch bullets were loaded into what had been one of the world's most popular deer cartridges, the result was the new standard-of-the-world in elephant cartridges. This replaced the ponderous 8-, 6-, and 4-bore black-powder rifles. John Rigby and Co. introduced this cartridge, in 1898. For many years, it was considered the standard elephant or dangerous-game cartridge and enjoyed great popularity. It utilizes 480-grain bullets of .458-inch diameter.

General Comments: The .450 Nitro is considered adequate for dangerous African game—or any other game, for that matter—under almost any conditions. It would most likely have been the only British cartridge used for big-game hunting, except for a British law that prohibited importation of .45-caliber rifles or cartridges into India. British rifle makers had to come up with something new, so the .425, .470, .476, and others came into being. Nevertheless, the .450 NE was, and still is, a winner, and a great many double-barrel rifles for this cartridge are still in service.

In the 13th Edition, we noted that A-Square Ammunition was offering this cartridge for a time, but its website at the time of the 13th Edition update stated:

"The .450 N.E. (3¼-inch) has been discontinued and can no longer be supported. This cartridge started out as a black-powder cartridge in the 1870s. It has gone from there to Black Powder Express, to Nitro for Black Powder, and thence to Nitro Express. Cartridge, chamber and throat dimensions have gone all over the map in the ensuing 130 years. Further, we have seen barrels with grooves as tight as .450 inch and bores as tight as .438 inch to grooves as loose as .461 inch. Though these dimensional variations may work with black powder and cast lead bullets, they are totally unsafe with smokeless powder and jacketed bullets. For smokeless powder and modern .458-inch bullets to safely work, the groove diameter must be .458 inch with a bore diameter of .450 inch. There are too many rifles in .450 N.E. (3¼-inch) that do not have barrels of such dimensions and therefore we cannot safely support this cartridge."

Indeed, A-Square, which was sold to Sharps Rifle Company in 2011, which then sold out to the Wyoming-based Broadsword Group, LLC (A-Square branded ammunition and rifles can still be had, as of this writing, at Broadsword's company website, www.broadsword.com), does not list the .450 NE at all. Nonetheless, the editors of this book feel it is worth continuing to include the issues A-Square noted about the the cartridge and which we first included in the 13th Edition. One can never be too careful.

.450 3¼-inch Nitro Express Factory Ballistics

Bullet (grains/type)	Powder	Grains	Velocity	Energy	Source/Comments
465 (various)	N/A		2,150	4,770	A-Square
480 lead	Smokeless powder		2,150	4,930	Factory load

.500/450 3¼-inch Magnum Express (BPE)

Historical Notes: This cartridge originated with a coiled-brass case in the 1870s. Loaded with about 140 grains of black powder in the drawn-brass version, it was once very popular in Africa. Typical express bullet weight was 325 grains.

General Comments: This was popular enough that it was loaded in both black and smokeless (Nitro-for-Black) versions, until the start of World War II. As was the case with many of the early black-powder cartridges, this one was later loaded with cordite, thereby becoming vastly more powerful. If you made a mistake ordering replacement cartridges while you were a long distance from supply centers, you might end up with light and useless loads for your nitro rifle, or elephant-grade loads for your deer rifle. Sadly, this was a common occurrence for early British sportsmen.

.500/450 3¼-inch Magnum BPE Factory Ballistics

Bullet (grains/type)	Powder	Grains	Velocity	Energy	Source/Comments
325 SP	Black powder	N/A	1,950	2,745	Factory load
325 SP	Smokeless powder	N/A	1,950	2,745	Factory load
365 SP	Smokeless powder	N/A	1,875	2,850	Factory load

.500/.450 3¼-inch Nitro Express

Historical Notes: This is a rimmed, necked case introduced (probably by Holland & Holland) around the end of the nineteenth century. It is the cordite version of the black-powder .500/.450 Magnum Express. In Nitro guise, it was used in single-shot and double rifles and made a great name for itself in Africa. It was usually loaded with 480-grain soft-point or solid bullets, but there were other, slightly lighter loadings. It was a fine performer. Theodore Roosevelt had a double rifle in this chambering. H&H opened this one up to become the .500/.465, after the ban on .450-bore rifles in India and the Sudan.

General Comments: This was a prime competitor of Rigby's .450 3¼-inch Nitro Express, but performance of the two was practically identical. The British developed several .45-caliber large bores, all of which produced about 5,000 ft-lbs of muzzle energy. These cartridges all had about the same killing power, so the hunter chose whichever one he preferred. All these large rimmed cartridges develop low pressures, making them well suited to the hot climates where dangerous game abounds. Younger African guides have, in many instances, switched to bolt-action rifles in contemporary chamberings, because magazine rifles are less costly than the classic English doubles, if not as quick for the second shot. The bullet used in British .45-caliber cartridges varies from 0.454- to 0.458-inch in diameter, so there are plenty of jacketed or cast bullets available to fit almost any of them.

.500/.450 Magnum Nitro-Express (3¼-inch) Factory Ballistics

Bullet (grains/type)	Powder	Grains	Velocity	Energy	Source/Comments
480 SP	FL		2,175	5,080	Factory load

.450 No. 2 Nitro Express (3½-inch)

Historical Notes: This case is a quarter-inch longer than the .500/.450 Magnum, but the cartridge uses the same bullet weight loaded to the same velocity. It was introduced about 1900 to 1902 by Eley. It was designed to give very low pressure in single-shot and double rifles and has a thick rim to aid extraction. It was loaded with 480-grain bullets, 70 to 80 grains of cordite, and with a great variety of bullet types. It later was opened up to become the .475 No. 2, for importation into India.

General Comments: The only logical reason for designing a larger-capacity case to deliver the identical ballistics of a smaller cartridge is to reduce breech pressure. It appears that some British cartridges gave extraction difficulties during the era of transition from black to smokeless powder. At first, this was believed to be the result of the higher pressure developed by smokeless powder. Later, the manufacturers discovered most of the trouble could be eliminated by making the case walls thicker. Some rifles in this chambering are still around, and Bertram has brass for them, Woodleigh has bullets, and Kynoch has loaded ammo for this and for the .475 No. 2.

.450 No. 2 Nitro-Express (3½-inch) Factory Ballistics

Bullet (grains/type)	Powder	Grains	Velocity	Energy	Source/Comments
480 SP	FL	N/A	2,175	5,050	Factory load

.450 Rigby

Historical Notes: Introduced in 1995, Rigby's newest cartridge was the idea of Rigby's former director Paul Roberts. John "Pondoro" Taylor said that Rigby's always had Africa in mind, when it brought out a new cartridge. This round is one more feather in the hat of this very old (1775) but still progressive and innovative company. That tradition continues today with the company under new management and back in London. Now in partnership with Mauser, the company has introduced new but very close copies of the old Rigby Mauser rifles, first in .416 and .450 Rigby calibers, with smaller calibers to come. The .450 Rigby cartridge has made a good name for itself in Africa, and has already become another of the all-time great classics.

General Comments: Rigby offers the .450 Rigby in bolt-action rifles only as of 2014. In the standard factory loading, this cartridge throws a 480-grain Woodleigh soft-nose or solid bullet at 2,350 fps. This gives it a trajectory and terminal performance edge on the .450 to .470 group, and it far surpasses the somewhat overstrained .458 Winchester Magnum.

The case is basically the same one that the .416 Rigby uses. It retains the sharp-shoulder design of the .416 for good and consistent resistance to the striker blow. It throws a 0.458-inch bullet. Similar in size to the .460 Weatherby, this improved design is unhampered by a belt and, thus, gives smooth, quiet, and sure feeding from the magazine. This will be a good choice for the person wanting to take only one rifle to Africa. It will also be right at home with anyone who appreciates a good, powerful rifle. Nosler, Kynoch, and others offer loaded ammo for this one.

.465 H&H Belted Magnum

Historical Notes: Holland & Holland Technical Director Russell Wilkin developed this cartridge and also the .400 H&H Magnum in 2003 in response to requests for more power in a magazine rifle than is provided by the company's .375 H&H Magnum. Guy Davies of Holland & Holland's New York offices assured me in 2014 that Holland & Holland has built rifles for this cartridge and has good stocks of ammunition, originally made by Wolfgang Romey.

General Comments: The case has a belted base similar in size to the .460 Weatherby. It also has a long, tapered shoulder, which gives good feeding, and a long neck to better grip the bullet. The body taper is increased in typical H&H fashion, to ensure easy extraction in the heat of Africa.

The .465 H&H Magnum has a head diameter of .580-inch, measured just in front of the belt. The case is 2.89 inches long and has the sloping profile characteristic of Holland's cartridge offerings. The bullets are 0.467-inch in diameter of 480-grain weight, and the bullet leaves the rifle at 2,375 fps. This cartridge should quickly make a significant name for itself in Africa, for which use it was designed. The .465 H&H Magnum has as much energy at 200 yards as the .375 H&H does at the muzzle.

.465 H&H Belted Magnum Factory Ballistics

Bullet (grains/type)	Powder	Grains	Velocity	Energy	Source/Comments
480 Woodleigh	FL		2,375	6,012	Holland & Holland

.500/.465 Nitro Express

Historical Notes: This rimmed, necked cartridge was introduced by Holland & Holland in 1907 to replace .450-caliber rifles when the .450s were outlawed by the British-controlled governments of India and the Sudan. This was an act of military expediency intended to prevent rebel forces from obtaining components that could be used in old, .45-caliber military weapons against regular British troops. H&H was, of course, well known for producing top-quality firearms that performed well. When the .500/.465 (or just .465, as it is known), became H&H's new elephant cartridge, replacing the .500/.450 Nitro, it quickly became very popular in Africa. Holland & Holland has made double rifles in .465-caliber ever since.

General Comments: The .500/.465 Nitro Express launches 480-grain solids or soft-point bullets of 0.467- to 0.468-inch diameter at roughly 2,150 fps with 4,930 ft-lbs of energy at the muzzle. Kynoch currently produces this round. MidwayUSA provides Bertram brass and also retails loaded ammunition, as do several other outlets. Woodleigh makes bullets.

.500/.465 Nitro Express Factory Ballistics

Bullet (grains/type)	Powder	Grains	Velocity	Energy	Source/Comments
480 SP	Cordite	73	2,150	4,930	Factory load
480 (various)	FL	N/A	2,150	4,930	A-Square factory load

.470 Nitro Express

Historical Notes: The .470 was introduced in 1900, and, according to John Taylor, was designed by Joseph Lang. Today, it is the most popular of the British elephant cartridges. It was adopted by most rifle makers along the way and was a specialty of Rigby's for many years, when that company had to change from the .450 Nitro. It was used mostly in double rifles and was (and still is) a favorite of elephant hunters. Like most cartridges in this general category, it originated as a replacement for the .450 Nitro Express, which was banned in India and the Sudan. Holland & Holland, Purdey, Searcy, Sabatti, and many others make rifles in this chambering.

General Comments: The .470 Nitro is probably the most popular and widely used of the various .460- to .475-caliber English elephant cartridges. It is certainly the most enduring. It has plenty of killing power for any of the heavy or dangerous varieties of game, and it is potent lion or tiger medicine in a tight spot. It can, like any powerful cartridge, be used for smaller game than that for which it was designed, and that is exactly how a great many of the big double rifles are used today.

Federal Cartridge Co. began making loaded ammunition in 1989, using best-quality 500-grain solids and soft-points at 2,150 fps. Handloading components are widely available, and many makers offer double rifles in this chambering. Indeed, until just recently, it was one of the best choices in a new double rifle, because of ammunition and component availability, though today's market gives the shooter a few other viable options. Still, the .470 is universally known and accepted all over the world, which might sway one's choice toward it. Brass and best-quality bullets are available from Barnes, Trophy Bonded Bullets, Woodleigh, Hornady, Norma, and many smaller custom shops. Ammunition may be found from many sources, including Federal, Hornady, Nosler, and Kynoch.

.470 Nitro-Express Factory Ballistics

Bullet (grains/type)	Powder	Grains	Velocity	Energy	Source/Comments
500 SP/FMJ	FL	N/A	2,150	5.130	Factory load, British
500 SP/FMJ	FL	N/A	2,150	5,130	Federal factory load

.475 3¼-inch Nitro Express

Historical Notes:	This cartridge, like the .470, was designed to replace .45-caliber British cartridges used in India and the Sudan. Most were introduced between 1905 and 1910. This one came out about 1900. It is a straight, rimmed shell intended for single-shot or double rifles and took a 480-grain bullet of apparently varying diameters. Cartridges with bullets as small as 0.474-inch and as large as 0.483-inch have been encountered. Be sure to check your rifle barrel's dimensions, before attempting to shoot it with modern components.
General Comments:	The .475 Nitro has about the same performance as the .470, .465, etc., and was considered a good, general-purpose round for heavy and dangerous game of all types. Barnes, Woodleigh, and others offer bullets for loading this cartridge.

.475 3¼-inch Nitro Express Factory Ballistics

Bullet (grains/type)	Powder	Grains	Velocity	Energy	Source/Comments
480 SP	FL	N/A	2,175	5,040	Factory load, British

.475 No. 2 Nitro Express
.475 No. 2 Jeffery

Historical Notes:	This round was developed to replace the .450 No. 2, when the British government prohibited .45-caliber cartridges in India and the Sudan. The .475 No. 2 Nitro Express was used, of course, in double rifles. The standard version used a 480-grain bullet with 80 or 85 grains of cordite. Jeffrey's load used a 500-grain bullet and three different powder charges: 75, 80, and 85 grains of cordite. The various cartridges would interchange, but, unless the load matched the rifle, it would not regulate properly. There were some bullet variations, but the most common was of 0.489-inch diameter.
General Comments:	The .475 is a very large, impressive-looking cartridge with an overall length of almost 4½ inches. It undoubtedly gave its user some added bravado or confidence that might have been well needed in a tight spot, in spite of the fact that performance was about the same as that of shorter cartridges. It has ample power for any African or Indian game and would also take care of anything in North America. The .475 case is made unusually heavy, to reduce expansion and facilitate extraction. Pressure is quite low.

.475 No. 2 Nitro Express Factory Ballistics

Bullet (grains/type)	Powder	Grains	Velocity	Energy	Source/Comments
480 SP	FL	N/A	2,200	5,170	Factory load, standard

Bullet (grains/type)	Powder	Grains	Velocity	Energy	Source/Comments
480 (various)	FL	N/A	2,200	5,170	A-Square factory load
500 SP	FL	N/A	2,150	5,140	Jeffery factory load

.476 Nitro Express
.476 Westley Richards

Historical Notes: This cartridge was a Westley Richards development introduced in 1907. It was used in single-shot and double rifles, but was not as popular as others of the same class. The 520-grain bullets were of 0.476-inch diameter and the impressive LT-capped bullets (Leslie Taylor's design) were available as soft-points.

General Comments: Nothing much can be said about the .476 Nitro Express that has not already been mentioned about other cartridges in the same class. All are nearly identical in power. The .476 is considered adequate for any and all African or Indian big game, and the round was a favorite of Elmer Keith's. Barnes and others offer bullets of this size and Kynoch and others offer loaded cartridges.

.476 Nitro Express Factory Ballistics

Bullet (grains/type)	Powder	Grains	Velocity	Energy	Source/Comments
520 SP	FL	N/A	2,100	5,085	Factory load

.577/.500 No. 2 Express
Westley Richards No. 2 Express

Historical Notes: The .577/500 No. 2 Express was a black-powder cartridge with a 2 13/16-inch case, introduced sometime before 1879. There were several longer cartridges bearing the .577/.500 designation, such as the .577/.500 NA&A, and two versions of the 3 1/8-inch case, black and Nitro. The shoulder of the latter is farther forward. This 2 13/16-inch case load was favored, if not originated, by Westley Richards. Bullet weight varied from 300 grains up to 380 grains in front of 130 grains of black powder. With Nitro-For-Black loads, bullet weight was from 340 to 440 grains. This never was a full nitro cartridge.

General Comments: The .577/.500 No. 2 Express was popular in India, for shooting thin-skinned game such as tiger. The black-powder and Nitro-For-Black versions were used for plains game in Africa, in the later years of the nineteenth century and was an excellent light to medium game load, but was not powerful enough for heavier game or for general use.

.577/500 No. 2 BP Express Factory Ballistics

Bullet (grains/type)	Powder	Grains	Velocity	Energy	Source/Comments
300 lead	FL	N/A	1,870	2,340	Factory load
340 lead	Black powder	N/A	1,925	2,800	Factory load

.577/.500 31/8 -inch Nitro Express

Historical Notes: This was a black-powder cartridge based on the .577 case and necked to .50-caliber. Its case is 5/16-inch longer than the .577/.500 No. 2 Express. It evolved into a full Nitro cartridge and enjoyed moderate popularity, that load being 60 grains of cordite with jacketed bullets of 440, 480, and 570 grains.

General Comments: This cartridge in black-powder form would be adequate for deer, bear, elk, or moose at moderate ranges and would be fine for woods hunting. In full Nitro guise, it was a grand powerhouse.

.577/.500 31/8-inch Nitro Express Factory Ballistics

Bullet (grains/type)	Powder	Grains	Velocity	Energy	Source/Comments
440 lead	Axite	58.0	UNK	UNK	Factory load, Nitro-For-Black powder
570 FMJ	Cordite	UNK	UNK	UNK	Factory load, Nitro Express

.500 Express (BPE) Nitro-For-Black

Historical Notes: The straight .500 was offered in a great variety of lengths, including 1½, 2, 2¼, 2½, 2 , 3, and 3¼ inches. All were black-powder cartridges. Some were quite successful and lasted, while others faded long before the end of the nineteenth century. This cartridge size originated about the mid- to late 1860s, and, over time, a great many lengths were tried. The most successful of these was the three-inch version. Bullet weights for that case length ran from 340 to 440 grains and the charge was from 123 to 142 grains of black powder. In the early 1900s, Fraser had a load with 120 grains of black and a 570-grain bullet, which is the bullet weight of the full Nitro cartridge.

Around the beginning of the smokeless era, Westley Richards came out with two versions of this cartridge, one three-inch, the other in a shorter case. Both were called the Long Range cartridge. These cartridges utilized heavier bullets and either light charges of cordite or heavy black-powder loads.

General Comments: The black-powder .500 was popular in India, as a good general-purpose firearm, but was not highly regarded in Africa. This cartridge is similar to the .50-140 Sharps and, of course, would be adequate for any North American big game. There are many bullet molds available that will make just about any of the .500 BP cartridges work. The author of this chapter had a fine Alexander Henry sidelock hammer double rifle with Damascus barrels for the three-inch version of this cartridge. The rifle was cased with a mold for two types of paper-patched bullets, a case crimping tool, and other loading accessories. The rifle was extremely accurate and lots of fun to shoot with proper black-powder loads.

.500 Express (BPE) Nitro-For-Black-Powder Factory Ballistics

Bullet (grains/type)	Powder	Grains	Velocity	Energy	Source/Comments
400 SP	FL	N/A	1,900	3,530	Factory load

.500 Nitro Express (3-inch and 3¼-inch)

Historical Notes: The .500 Nitro Expresses were derived from what were originally black-powder cartridges. The Nitro versions were introduced in the early 1900s. A 570-grain bullet is used in both case lengths and ballistics are about identical, though the longer case works at lower pressure. There were also loadings utilizing a 480-grain bullet and slightly reduced charges of cordite.

General Comments: The .500 Nitro Express was considered a real killer on practically anything. John A. Hunter, who did game control work for the Kenya Game Department for 26 years, considered it his favorite. His book Hunter is recommended reading, because it provides the stories of firsthand experiences that show what real-life hunting in Africa is all about. This cartridge has somewhat more power than all the .470-class cartridges, but not nearly as much as the .577 and .600 Nitros.

.500 Nitro Express (3-inch, 3¼-inch) Factory Ballistics

Bullet (grains/type)	Powder	Grains	Velocity	Energy	Source/Comments
570 SP	Smokeless powder	N/A	2,150	5,850	Factory load
570 (various)	Smokeless powder	N/A	2,150	5,850	A-Square

.505 Gibbs (.505 Rimless)

Historical Notes: The .505 Gibbs was introduced, somewhere around 1911 to 1913, as a proprietary cartridge by Gibbs for use in Mauser magazine rifles. Rifles in this caliber were imported by a few American dealers and used in the U.S. to a limited extent. Hoffman Arms in the U.S. built rifles chambered for this cartridge in the 1920s and '30s. Formerly hard to find, ammo for this cartridge is again being loaded by Nosler, Kynoch, and a few others. Bullets and cases are again available from several sources.

General Comments: When the first of the .505 rifles showed up in the United States, there were all kinds of stories floating around about the horrendous recoil. Several claims were made that shooters had suffered broken shoulders or collarbones as a result of firing this cartridge. This sort of nonsense made "heroes" out of those who fired these guns, but hardly contributed to the popularity of the cartridge. Elmer Keith fired several of the Hoffman-made rifles and said the recoil was about as bad as he'd care to experience. A rifle in this caliber ought to weigh 10 to 11 pounds, not less.

The .505 is slightly less powerful than the .500 Jeffery, but both have an edge over the .458 Winchester. The .505 Gibbs is considered adequate for anything in Africa and has a good reputation against elephant, buffalo, and lion. Barnes and Nosler and possibly others make bullets specifically designed for this cartridge. Nosler and others provide loaded ammunition in 2014.

.505 Gibbs (.505 Rimless) Factory Ballistics

Bullet (grains/type)	Powder	Grains	Velocity	Energy	Source/Comments
525 SP	FL	N/A	2,300	6,190	Factory load
525 (various)	FL	N/A	2,300	6,190	A-Square factory load

.500 Jeffery
12.7x70 Schuler

Historical Notes: The .500 Jeffery is not an English cartridge. Germany introduced it in the early 1900s, and was used by that country's sportsmen in German holdings in Africa. It was known as the 12.7x70 Schuler.

Jeffery chambered very few magazine rifles for it, calling it the .500 Jeffery. Its design is relatively poor for use in dangerous-game rifles, the cartridge having a short neck (0.375-inch) that might not hold the bullet securely, a rebated rim that, in some cases, might not provide sufficient extraction, and pressure that might be too high for use in an elephant rifle. Despite those shortcomings, it has been recently resurrected. You can buy .500 Jeffery ammo, in 2014, loaded by Kynoch, CorBon, Norma, and Nosler. There are also several new rifles for it from CZ, Heym, and Searcy.

General Comments: The .500 Jeffery is similar to the .505 Gibbs, but has a shorter case and is loaded to higher pressure and velocity. The .500 Jeffery was the most powerful cartridge used in any of the British magazine rifles. Bullet diameter is 0.510 inch. Variations over the years in ammunition manufacture and chamberings by different makers abound; while new rifles and new ammo should work well together, if you have an older rifle, be sure to verify its barrel and chamber dimensions before shooting.

.500 Jeffery Factory Ballistics

Bullet (grains/type)	Powder	Grains	Velocity	Energy	Source/Comments
535 SP	FL	N/A	2,400	6,800	Factory load, British
570 (various)	FL	N/A	2,300	6,695	A-Square factory load

.577 BP Express
2½-, 2¾-, 3-, and 3¼-inch

Historical Notes: The .577 Express series began about 1870 with the 2½-inch version. Its predecessors were the .577 Snider variants, which date from 1866. Numerous shorter coiled-brass and drawn-brass .577-bore cartridges were developed, but the best were the Expresses, specifically those that lasted long enough to become nitro cartridges. The shortest of these is the 2¾-inch version. Bore size evolved into 0.585-inch diameter, and the best Express bullets weighed about 520 to 650 grains. The charge was 135 to 190 grains of black.

General Comments: All of these were for use on the heavier non-dangerous game, though, as happens, some hunters used these cartridges against tigers and lions, with varying success. There was a great variety of bullets available, and success was directly tied to utilizing the proper bullet. To prevent rapid damage to the bore, only cast or swaged-lead bullets should be used in just about all older rifles. Paper-patched bullets are probably best.

.577 Nitro Express
2¾-, 3-, and 3¼-inch

Historical Notes: These were all originally black-powder cartridges, but, when loaded with cordite and proper bullets, they became some of the best stoppers for dangerous game. All three originated around the end of the nineteenth century. The shorter- and longer-cased cartridges were overshadowed by the 3-inch loading, which earned a wonderful name for itself in Africa.

General Comments: The .577 enjoyed a great reputation as an elephant killer and was a standard chambering found in any battery of African rifles. It was popular with professional ivory hunters for close cover work. Many claimed it was superior to the .600 Nitro, because it gave greater penetration. Rifles for the .577 could also be made a few pounds lighter than those for the .600 Nitro, which contributed to the .577's popularity.

Cartridges of this size were usually for emergency use under difficult conditions. Most hunters used lighter rifles of smaller caliber for ordinary shooting, but had the big .577 as a backup. Rifles for the .577 weighed 13 pounds or more, and that's a lot of weight, if you have to carry it very far at the ready. Gun bearers usually carried the heavy guns until needed, but not because the British were lazy. An exhausted man just can't handle a rifle of such heft and weight in a pinch.

.577 Nitro Express Factory Ballistics

Bullet (grains/type)	Powder	Grains	Velocity	Energy	Source/Comments
750 SP/FMJ	FL	N/A	2,050	7,010	Factory load
750 (various)	FL	N/A	2,050	7,010	A-Square factory load

.600 Nitro Express
(2.8-inch & 3-inch)

Historical Notes: The .600 in either case length was the largest and most powerful of the English cordite elephant cartridges until the advent of the .700 Nitro, in 1988. The 2.8-inch version was loaded with an 800-grain bullet and 110 grains of cordite. The 3-inch loading had bullets of 900 grains in a variety of types in front of loads of 100 or 110 grains of cordite. The 3-inch .600 was introduced by Jeffery, just before 1901. The 2.8-inch version came out in 1899, and may have been a developmental stage of the cartridge.

The .600 was chambered in single-shot and double rifles. It was not based on any earlier black-powder cartridge. Despite its reputation, only a small number of rifles have been made for the .600. In the early 1990s, Germany's Heym introduced the Magnum Express bolt-action rifle chambering this cartridge.

General Comments: At one time, the .600 Nitro Express was the most powerful commercial rifle cartridge in the world. The .700 Nitro Express now overshadows it. The .600 was designed to deliver the maximum possible stopping power against elephants, under the most difficult and dangerous conditions. Even professional ivory hunters considered it overpowered for anything but emergency use. It is said that a head shot that missed the brain of an elephant would still knock it down for a considerable length of time. John Taylor said the tusker would stay down for up to 30 minutes. Rifles for the .600 usually weighed 16 pounds or more.

There were at least three loadings for the cartridge, giving 2,050, 1,950, and 1,850 fps. It is necessary to use the load for which the rifle is regulated to get the two barrels to shoot to the same point of impact. Components for handloading are available from Barnes, Huntington, Bertram, and Woodleigh.

.600 Nitro Express Factory Ballistics

Bullet (grains/type)	Powder	Grains	Velocity	Energy	Source/Comments
900 SP/FMJ	Cordite	120.0	2,050	8,400	Factory load
900 SP/FMJ	Cordite	110.0	1,950	7,600	Factory load
900 SP/FMJ	Cordite	100.0	1,850	6,840	Factory load

.700 Nitro Express

Historical Notes: The .700 Nitro Express is an original design not based on altering the caliber or configuration of any existing cartridge. It was developed in 1988 by two Americans, Jim Bell and William Feldstein. It is chambered in double rifles made by Holland & Holland. The round came about, because Feldstein wanted H&H to build him a .600 Nitro Express. The company refused, because it had already completed its official last .600 Nitro Express some years before and was uninterested in reviving the chambering. Bell and Feldstein then decided to approach H&H on the possibility of building a series of rifles in a new chambering, something completely different from anything previously made. Since H&H was actually looking for a new big-bore cartridge, the .700 Nitro Express was born.

According to Bell, the .700 is based on scaling up the old .600 Nitro, using a totally new case that's a full half-inch longer. This bullet is a true 0.700-inch diameter and weighs 1,000 grains. Although these rifles are expensive, H&H has a backorder amounting to millions of dollars worth of .700 Nitro Expresses—one must therefore conclude the concept is a raging success.

Several years after the first .700 NE was built, H&H was faced with an unending din of protest from potential customers. Accordingly, they came to terms with the owner of the "official last" .600 Nitro H&H and went back into the business of building new .600 Nitro double rifles.

General Comments: A .70-caliber bullet weighing 1,000 grains with a muzzle velocity of 2,000 fps generates a muzzle energy of 8,900 ft.-lbs. of energy. This is the most powerful production sporting cartridge in the world. The Taylor Knockout Value is 200. It will, of course, be more than adequate for any game animal found anywhere on this planet. For those who insist on the biggest, this is it. The .700 H&H double rifles for this cartridge are very lively and handy, not at all cumbersome. These are fully usable, if costly, tools. However, keeping the weight of such a rifle down to a level that will allow the average hunter to use it properly guarantees that recoil will be heavy.

700 Nitro Express Factory Ballistics

Bullet (grains/type)	Powder	Grains	Velocity	Energy	Source/Comments
1,000 SP/FMJ	FL	N/A	2,000	8,900	A-Square factory load

Dimensional Data

Cartridge	Case	Bullet Dia.	Neck Dia.	Shoulder Dia.	Base Dia.	Rim Dia.	Rim Thick	Case Length	Ctge. Length	Berdan Primer Size/Kynoch #	Page
.297/.230 Morris Short	A	.225	.240	.274	.294	.347	UNK/NA	.58	.89	.177/69	532
.297/.230 Morris Long	A	.225	.240	.274	.295	.345	UNK/NA	.80	1.1	.177/69	532
.297/.230 Morris Extra Long	A	.223	.240	.274	.296	.248	UNK/NA	1.125	1.45	UNK/NA	532
.240 Magnum Flanged	A	.245	.274	.402	.448	.513	UNK/NA	2.50	3.25	.217/81	532
.240 Magnum Rimless H&H (.240 Apex)	E	.245	.274	.403	.450	467	.035	2.49	3.21	.217/81	532
.244 H&H Magnum	E	.244	.263	.445	.508	.532	UNK/NA	2.78	3.58	.217/60	533
.246 Purdey Flanged	A	.253	.283	.401	.474	.544	UNK/NA	2.24	2.98	UNK/NA	533
.297/.250 Rook	A	.250	.267	.294	.295	.343	UNK/NA	.82	1.1	.177/69	533
255 Rook	A	.255	1.150	.274	.344	.401		1.150	1.430		534
.242 Rimless Nitro Express	C	.253	.281	.405	.465	.465	UNK/NA	2.38	3.20	.217/59	534
.256 Gibbs Magnum	A	0.264	0.292	0.430	.470/.471	0.474	NA	2.17	3.09	0.217	534
.26 BSA	C	0.266+	0.292	0.405	0.465	0.465	NA	2.38	3.20	.217/59	535
.275 Rigby (7x57mm)	C	.284	.324	.428	.474	.475	UNK/NA	2.24	3.07	.217	535
.275 Belted Magnum	E	.284	.325	.454	.513	.532	UNK/NA	2.50	3.42	.217/81	536
.275 No. 2 Magnum	A	.284	.318	.450	.510	.582	UNK/NA	2.50	3.26	217	536
.280 Flanged (.280 Lancaster)	A	.287	.316	.423	.535	.607	UNK/NA	2.60	3.62	.217/60	536
.280 Ross (.280 Rimless)	G	.287	.317	.404	.534	.556	UNK/NA	2.59	3.50	.217/59	537
.280 Jeffery (.33/280 Jeffery)	C	.288	.317	.504	.542	.538	UNK/NA	2.50	3.45	.217/59	537
.300 Rook	B	.300	.317		.319	.369		1.170	1.380		538
.300 Sherwood	B	.300	.318		.320	.370		1.540	2.020		538
.300 Belted Rimless Magnum	E	.308	.338	.447	.513	.530	UNK/NA	2.85	3.60	.217/60	538
.375/303 Westley Richards (Axite)	A	.311	.343	.390	.457	.505	UNK/NA	2.50	3.36	UNK/NA	539
.303 British	A	.312	.340	.401	.460	.540	UNK/NA	2.21	3.05	UNK/NA	539
.303 Magnum	C	.312	.345	.462	.530	.557	UNK/NA	2.35	3.25	UNK/NA	540
.310 Cadet (.310 Greener)	B	.324	.320	UNK/NA	.353	.405	.035	1.12	1.72	.177/69	540
.318 Rimless Nitro Express	C	.330	.358	.445	.465	.465	UNK/NA	2.39	3.40	.217/81	540
.333 Jeffery Rimless	C	.333	.359	.496	.540	.538	UNK/NA	2.48	3.48	.217/59	541
.33 BSA	E	.338	.369	.453	.534	.534	UNK/NA	2.40	3.10	.217/59	541
.400/.350 Rigby	A	.358	.380	.415	.470	.520	UNK/NA	2.75	3.60	.241/34	542
.350 Rigby Magnum	C	.358	.380	.443	.519	.525	UNK/NA	2.75	3.60	.241/34	542
.360 No. 5 Rook	B	.362	.375	UNK/NA	.380	.432	UNK/NA	1.05	1.45	UNK/NA	543
.360 Express (2¼-inch)	B	.365	.384	UNK/NA	.430	.480	.040	2.25	3.00	.241/34	543
.400/.360 Nitro Express (2¾-inch)	A	.358	.375	.437	.470	.590	UNK/NA	2.75	3.59	.241	544
.360 No. 2 Nitro Express	A	.367	.393	.517	.539	.631	.045	3.00	3.85	.254/40	544
.375 Flanged Nitro Express (2½-inch)	B	.375	.397	UNK/NA	.456	.523	UNK/NA	2.50	3.10	.217/34	544
.400/.375 Belted Nitro Express (H&H)	E	.375	.397	.435	.470	.466	UNK/NA	2.50	3.00	.217	545
.375 Rimless Nitro Express 2¼ (9.5x57mm)	C	.375	.400	.460	.471	.473	.40	2.25	2.94	.217	545
.369 Nitro Express (Purdey)		.375	.398	.475	.543	.616	UNK/NA	2.69	3.60	.254/40	546
.375 Flanged Magnum	A	.375	.404	.450	.515	.572	UNK/NA	2.94	3.80	.217/40	546
.380 Short	B	.375	.379		.380	.430		.600	1.110		547
.400 Purdey	B	.405	.427		.469	.516		3.000	3.600		547
.400 H&H Magnum	C/E	.411	.441	.492	.513	.532	.050	2.846	3.55	L	547
.450/.400 (23/8-inch)	A	.407	.427	.456	.545	.616	.035	2.38	2.95	UNK/NA	548

Dimensional Data

Cartridge	Case	Bullet Dia.	Neck Dia.	Shoulder Dia.	Base Dia.	Rim Dia.	Rim Thick	Case Length	Ctge. Length	Berdan Primer Size/Kynoch #	Page
.400 Jeffery Nitro Express (.450/400 3-inch)	A	.410	.434	.518	.545	.613	UNK/NA	3.00	3.75	.254/40	548
.450/400 Nitro Express (3¼-inch) & BPE	A	.405	.432	.502	.544	.615	.040	3.25	3.85	.254/40	549
.400 H&H Magnum Belted Rimless	E	.371	.397	.435	.465	.466		2.470	3.000		550
.404 Jeffery (.404 Rimless Nitro Express)	C	.422	.450	.520	.544	.537	.045	2.87	3.53	.217/81	550
.416 Rigby	C	.416	.445	.539	.589	.589	.062	2.90	3.72	Bx	551
.425 Westley Richards Magnum	I	.435	.456	.540	.543	.467	UNK/NA	2.64	3.30	UNK/NA	551
.500/450 No. 1 Express	A	.458	.485	.530	.577	.660	UNK/NA	2.75	3.38	.241/31A	552
.450 3¼-inch BPE	A	.405	.432	UNK/NA	UNK/NA	UNK/NA	UNK/NA	UNK/NA	UNK/NA	.254/40	552
.450 Nitro Express (3¼-inch)	B	.458	.479	UNK/NA	.545	.624	.040	3.25	4.11	.254/40	553
.500/450 Magnum Express BPE (3¼-inch)	A	.458	.479	.500	.570	.644	UNK/NA	3.25	3.91	.254/40	554
.500/450 Nitro Express (3¼-inch)	A	.458	.479	.500	.570	.644	UNK/NA	3.25	3.91	.254/40	554
.450 No. 2 Nitro Express (3½-inch)	A	.458	.477	.518	.564	.650	UNK/NA	3.50	4.42	.254/40	555
.450 Rigby	B	.458	.475	.539	.589	.589	UNK/NA	2.90	3.80	Bx	555
.465 H&H Magnum	F	.468	.494	.531	.582	.579	UNK/NA	UNK/NA	UNK/NA	UNK/NA	555
.500/.465 Nitro Express	A	.466	.488	.524	.573	.650	UNK/NA	3.25	3.89	.254/40	556
.470 Nitro Express	A	.475	.500	.528	.572	.646	.035	3.25	4.00	.254/40	556
.475 Nitro Express (3¼-inch)	B	.483	.502	UNK/NA	.545	.621	UNK/NA	3.25	4.00	.254/40	557
.475 No. 2 Nitro Express/Jeffery	A	.489	.510	.547	.576	.666	UNK/NA	3.50	4.33	.254/40	557
.476 Nitro Express/Westley Richards	A	.476	.508	.530	.570	.643	UNK/NA	3.00	3.77	.254/40	558
.577/.500 No. 2 BPE	A	.507	.538	.560	.641	.726	.055	2.83	3.40	.251/31A	558
.577/.500 Nitro Express (31/8-inch)	A	.508	.526	.585	.645	.717	.055	3.13	3.74	.251/31A	559
.500 Express Nitro-For-Black (3-inch)	B	.510	.535	UNK/NA	.580	.660	.055	3.01	3.39	.251/31A	559
.500 Nitro Express (3- & 3¼-inch)	B	.510	.535	UNK/NA	.580	.660	.040	3.25	3.63	.251/31A	559
.505 Gibbs	C	.505	.530	.588	.635	.635	UNK/NA	3.15	3.85	.254/40	560
.500 Jeffery	I	.510	.535	.615	.620	.575	UNK/NA	2.75	3.47	.254/40	560
.577 BP Express (2¼, 2¾, 3-, & 3¼-inch)	B	.584	.608	UNK/NA	.660	.748	.052	3.25	UNK/NA	.254/40	561
.577 Nitro Express (2¾, 3-, & 3¼-inch)	B	.584	.608	UNK/NA	.660	.748	.052	3.00	3.70	.254/40	561
.600 Nitro Express	B	.620	.648	UNK/NA	.697	.805	UNK/NA	3.00	3.68	.254/40	562
.700 Nitro Express	B	.700	.728	UNK/NA	.780	.890	UNK/NA	3.50	4.20	Bx	562

Case Type: A = Rimmed, bottleneck. B = Rimmed, straight. C = Rimless, bottleneck. D = Rimless, straight. E = Belted, bottleneck. F = Belted, straight. G = Semi-rimmed, bottleneck. H = Semi-rimmed, straight. I = Rebated, bottleneck. J = Rebated, straight. K = Rebated, belted bottleneck. L = Rebated, belted straight.

Primer Type: B = Berdan. Bx = Boxer. RF = Rimfire.

Other codes: Unless otherwise noted, all dimensions in inches. Dimensions shown in some instances do not exactly coincide with dimensions found in *The Book of Rifles* (W.H.B. Smith, Harrisburg, Pa., 1960). Differences amount to only a few thousandths of an inch, doubtless attributable to specimen variations. Parentheses indicate maximum cartridge specifications. UNK/NA = Unknown/Not Available

European Sporting Rifle Cartridges

(Current & Obsolete – Black-Powder and Smokeless)

European sporting cartridges are, at least nowadays, better known than those of British origin. European arms makers are well represented by a world-wide distributing system and they advertise what they make. They also manufacture products for a mass market at prices that place them within economic reach for those who could not possibly afford a fine British double-barrel gun.

The Mauser and Mannlicher turn-bolt systems have been the backbone of European sporting rifle manufacture since the 1890s, long before American companies adopted the type. Because the designers intended these cartridges for the same type of rifle, there is great similarity between many modern European and American cartridge designs. We have borrowed freely from each other, and it is often difficult to tell who originated what. Continental gunmakers have also produced very fine, handcrafted double-barrel rifles and combination guns as good as anything turned out by the British. Unfortunately, there has always been a certain prejudice against double-barrel rifles not made in Britain. This resulted because some cheap rifles of this type were turned out on the continent and simply didn't measure up to the required high standards. The Austrians and Germans, on the other hand, developed the drilling or combination gun—the over/under rifle-shotgun—to a greater extent than anyone else did. These multi-purpose firearms feature various combinations of rifled tubes and shot barrels. When it comes to an all-around gun, nothing is superior to a good combination gun.

Gun makers have produced sporting arms all over Europe, including Russia. Today, guns from that latter country are seeing more use outside the Soviet bloc. For decades, the Japanese have made superb firearms. Many of these are now being sold by their own marketing branches here in the United States. Of course, some of our old-line companies with a tradition as American as Yankee Doodle have been, for years, selling guns under their own names that are actually made in Europe or Japan.

European sporting ammunition originates mostly in Italy, Austria, Germany, Finland, Sweden, and Britain. The French chemist Vieille developed the first commercially successful smokeless powder, in 1885. The French adapted this to the 8mm Lebel military cartridge. Commercial manufacture of ammunition started in Germany, during 1856, when Heinrich Utendoerffer founded a plant to make percussion caps and, later, primers. By 1871, he was turning out Berdan-primed centerfire cases for the Bavarian Werder rifle. This enterprise later grew into the great Rheinisch-Westfäflishe-Sprengstoff-AG, or RWS, as we know it today. Early cartridges or cases made by the firm have "H. Utendoerffer" stamped into the head, sometimes with raised letters.

RWS developed the non-mercuric, non-corrosive primer, in the 1920s, and began to market this significantly improved product under the trade name Sinoxid. Deutsche Waffen und Munitionsfabriken (DWM) is another important German firm that is, unfortunately, no longer in the commercial ammunition business. Hirtenberger-Patronenfabrik, located near Vienna, Austria, was one of the world's largest munitions makers, until destroyed during World War II; organized, in 1860, by the Mandl brothers, both industrial fires and acts of war have razed it several times. The company has started production again and has once more become an important source of sporting ammunition. Norma Precision (formerly Norma Projektilfabrik), manufactures sporting ammunition and components in Sweden. Norma has exported products to the United States since shortly after the end of World War II. It makes the Weatherby line of cases and ammunition and also offers cases for many of the more popular American and European cartridges. The firm of G. Roth manufactured a large variety of sporting ammunition, but did not survive World War II. Lapua of Finland exports to the United States, as does Fiocchi of Italy, and Eley of Britain.

European cartridges, with few exceptions, have metric designations, usually expressed in millimeters. By international agreement, one millimeter equals .03937-inch, or one inch equals 2.54 centimeters (which equals 25.4 millimeters). Metric cartridge designation is quite simple, once you understand it. The first figure represents bore diameter, the second figure represents case length. An "R" indicates a rimmed case, and its absence a rimless one. The designer or manufacturer can tack a name on the end of the numeric designation. Europeans used single-shot and combination guns that extract better with a rimmed case, so they have an "R," or rimmed, version of almost all popular rimless cartridges. Ballistics and case dimensions are usually, though not always, identical.

Some confusion surrounds two different 8mm cartridges. The original 8mm German military cartridge, adopted in 1888, used a .318-inch diameter bullet designed to work in a 7.92mm bore. So did 8mm sporting rounds of the same period. However, in 1905, the German army altered the cartridge and bore design to use a .323-inch diameter bullet—bore diameter was unchanged, but the grooves were deepened to improve accurate barrel life. Shortly thereafter, 8mm sporting cartridges also reflected this change. The old diameter is indicated by a "J" (actually the old German letter form for "I," standing for "Infanterie"), and the new one by an "S." For example, the 8x57mmJ has a .318-inch bullet, and the 8x57mmS (or 8x57mmJS) the .323-inch bullet. It will not hurt anything but accuracy to use the .318-inch bullet in a .323-inch bore—but it might blow up the gun to do the opposite! The proper designation is always on the box, and it is usually stamped on the cartridge head. Read the label! Modern rifles are practically all chambered for the "S" (.323-inch) bullet. European arms and ammunition firms seized upon many American and British cartridges over the years, but they never took to the British belted-type case as we here in the U.S. did. The .22 WCF (5.6x35Rmm), .22 Savage HP (5.6x52Rmm), .25-35 (6.5x52Rmm), and .30-06 (7.62x63) are popular in Europe and listed in late catalogs. The .30-30 WCF is also popular, but Europeans firms don't currently load it. Cartridges of 6mm and 7mm were highly developed in Europe, long before these cartridges became popular here. The 8mm is to Europeans what the .30-caliber is to Americans and, consequently, they have a large variety of cartridges in this caliber, some of advanced design. The 8x68mmS, for example, is a magnum round more powerful than the .300 Weatherby or the .300 Winchester Magnum.

German Mauser-system bolt-action rifles once competed with the more expensive British rifles for use in African hunting. The Germans developed some unusually potent cartridges for dangerous game, but currently use American or British magnum cartridges. They have revived few of their African cartridges since the war.

European centerfire ammunition of modern production by RWS, Norma, Hirtenberger, IMI, Fiocchi, Lapua, and Sako use Boxer primers. RWS still offers nine different types of Berdan primers, as well as Boxer types to satisfy the needs of handloaders. Ammunition for obsolete cartridge rifles is a problem, but, in some instances, handloaders can easily re-form available metric or American cases to work satisfactorily. (Buffalo Arms—www.buffaloarms.com—offers commercially reformed cases that accommodate loading of practically any cartridge you might encounter. These cases, along with a set of custom dies from RCBS, will get you shooting in no time.)

European hunting is quite different from that found in the United States. Differences include both game and methods of taking. Europeans have no large, predatory dangerous game, although the wild boar can be a rough customer, under certain conditions. Conservation is highly developed, and the shooting of game very selective; weeding out old or undesirable animals is as important as collecting a trophy. In most countries, one must pass a rigid course in gun handling and hunting knowledge before being eligible for a permit or license. The German test is especially difficult. Also, in Europe, there is no wide-open hunting. One must get permission or make advance arrangements, and a guide of some sort is usually required. Hunters stalk several varieties of deer, ranging in size from the 40-pound class roebuck to the hirsch or red stag, which is almost as large as an American elk. The chamois, a prime trophy, is present in the higher mountainous areas. Hunters also pursue small game, mostly hare, and they have good bird shooting opportunities. They do not indulge in formal varmint hunting, although I understand pest shooting has developed some following. Along open fields, long shots are not unusual, but great velocity and flat trajectory are not as important as in some areas of North America. Great knockdown and killing power is not required for European hunting, and their cartridges reflect this. The more popular hunting cartridges develop from around 2000 ft-lbs of energy to not much over 2500 ft-lbs of energy, while the trend in the United States is toward energy in excess of 3000 ft-lbs.

The Germans once did a great deal of social target shooting, and many older cartridges originated for this. The Schuetzen, or free rifle, arrived here with German immigrants and was highly popular, off and on, from about 1850 to 1920—its heyday the 1890-1910 period. Many of our cartridges and bolt-action rifles reflect European ideas and design.

Although more information is available on European cartridges than British, the same problem exists in attempting to establish the exact dates of introduction. I sent letters to the principal European manufacturers requesting such information, but, in many instances, records no longer existed. Old catalogs and books were of considerable assistance. If nothing else, these provided sufficient information to establish the period of introduction within a few years. We know that most black-powder cartridges originated in the 1870s and 1880s, and early smokeless numbers after 1885. Sometimes a cartridge was designed for a specific rifle. The rifle's introduction date then provides a good estimate of cartridge origination date. Individual gunmakers or small companies operated during fixed dates, and their designs can often be approximately dated on that basis. Again, if the reader has specific information of this nature and finds what he believes to be an error in dating, let us know. This way, corrections or new data can be included at a future time.—*F.C.B.*

5.6x35Rmm Vierling
.22 Winchester Centerfire

Historical Notes:	This is the European, or metric designation, for the .22 Winchester Centerfire, which was introduced in 1885 and picked up by European gunmakers a year or so later. It was loaded to much higher velocity there than in the United States, thus providing the inspiration for the .22 Hornet, which is based on the same case. Single-shot, combination, and repeating rifles of European manufacture have been chambered for the 5.6x35Rmm Vierling.
General Comments:	The 5.6x35Rmm (.22 WCF) is a popular small-game and target round in Europe. Although originally a black-powder number, the Germans adapted it to smokeless powder and stepped up the velocity long before wildcatters created the .22 Hornet in the United States. As loaded in Europe, it is a good 100- to 150-yard small-game or target cartridge. The 5.6x35Rmm Vierling can easily be formed from .22 Hornet cases.

5.6x35Rmm Vierling (22 Winchester Centerfire) Loading Data and Factory Ballistics

Bullet (grains/type)	Powder	Grains	Velocity	Energy	Source/Comments
48 SP	2400	8.0	2,120	480	Lyman #225414
39 SP	FL	FL	1,940	325	RWS factory load
39 SP	FL	FL	2,630	600	RWS factory load
46 SP	FL	FL	2,030	418	RWS factory load

5.6x33mm Rook & Tesching
5.6x33Rmm Rook & Tesching

Historical Notes:	Except for rim design (rimmed and rimless), these two cartridges are identical. They date back to around 1900 or earlier and were originally loaded with black powder. Both have been obsolete since about 1936. Like the British, the Germans had a series of rook (a rook is a bird akin to our crow), or parlor cartridges, for short-range target practice or small-game shooting. These were listed in catalogs as for *tesching gewehre*, i.e., small-game or rook rifles. Although popular in Europe, these cartridges were not used to any extent elsewhere.
General Comments:	When Winchester introduced the .22 WCF, in 1885, it not only replaced most other .22 centerfires in the United States, but also in Europe. The 5.6x33mm is of similar performance and was probably made

obsolete by the .22 WCF. Both are strictly small-game or target cartridges. The Winchester round is still loaded in Europe, where it is known as the 5.6x35Rmm Vierling. The 5.6x33mm was also listed as the 5.7x33mm. These are said to be for single-shot rifles, but must have also been used in repeating rifles. The rimless 5.6x33mm bears some resemblance to certain wildcat .22 rounds, based on necking-down the .30 U.S. carbine.

5.6x33mm Rook, 5.6x33Rmm Rook Loading Data and Factory Ballistics (Note: *Approximate ballistics only.

Bullet (grains/type)	Powder	Grains	Velocity	Energy	Source/Comments
60 Lead	2400	5.0	1,600	343 *	Lyman #225462GC
65 Lead	FL	FL	1,500	327 *	Factory load

5.6x50mm Magnum
5.6x50Rmm Magnum

Historical Notes: Most authorities agree that the 5.6x50mm Magnum was developed by DWM in cooperation with Friedrick W. Heym, a noted German gunmaker, and was introduced in 1968 or 1969. It is an offshoot of the 5.6x47Rmm (basically a rimmed version of the .222 Remington Magnum), dating back to about 1967. However, the 5.6x50mm case is .118-inch longer than the .222 Remington Magnum and has greater powder capacity, resulting in a higher muzzle velocity. The rimmed version was intended for use in single-shots, combination guns, and drillings, with the rimless cartridge for bolt-action rifles. Neither is very well known or used to any extent in the United States.

General Comments: In Germany, the 5.6x50mm was used for deer hunting and was loaded with a bullet designed for that purpose. In the United States, it would be primarily a varmint cartridge. Where more power than the .222 or .223 Remington is desired, most Americans would opt for the .22-250 Remington or the .220 Swift, because both rifles and ammunition are available here on an over-the-counter basis. Loading dies for the 5.6x50mm are available from RCBS, Forster/Bonanza, and Lyman. RWS and Hirtenberger have recently offered 5.6x50mm Magnum ammunition.

Hirtenberger as its own entity is no longer in business, having been taken over by Swedish conglomerate RUAG Ammotec (www.ruag.com/en/Ammotec/Ammotec_Home). Original Hirtenberger ammo is occasionally found in the surplus marketplace. RUAG is also the parent company of the European brands RWS, Rottweil, GECO, and Norma, and markets ammo for both civilian and law enforcement use under those original names, as well as the Hitenberger brand. Also, Forster/Bonanza is now simly Forster Products, www.forsterproducts.com.

5.6x50mm Magnum, 5.6x50Rmm Magnum Loading Data and Factory Ballistics

Bullet (grains/type)	Powder	Grains	Velocity	Energy	Source/Comments
50 SP	IMR 3031	28.5	3,400	1,284	Hornady
50 SP	W748	29.5	3,500	1,360	Hornady
55 SP	IMR 4064	27.5	3,300	1,330	Hornady
55 SP	W748	28.5	3,300	1,330	Hornady
60 SP	IMR 4064	27.0	3,200	1,360	Hornady
50 SP	FL	FL	3,590	1,430	Factory load – 5.6x50mm
50 SP	FL	FL	3,510	1,365	Factory load – 5.6x50mm
55 SP	FL	FL	3,280	1,310	Factory load – 5.6x50Rmm

5.6x57mm RWS
5.6x57Rmm RWS

Historical Notes: The 5.6x57mm was introduced by RWS about 1964 as a cartridge for hunting deer and chamois. Germany has a law that requires a minimum remaining energy level at 200 meters in order for a cartridge to be legal for taking these animals. The 5.6x57mm was designed with this in mind. It is also loaded with a properly designed bullet for these larger animals, and there is a rimmed version.

General Comments: The 5.6x57mm is in about the same class as the .220 Swift and, as loaded in Europe, would probably do very well for American deer or antelope. However, it would be classed as a varmint cartridge here in the U.S. It is a good cartridge, but the difficulty of finding ammunition would rule out any great popularity in this country. Twist used in rifles of this chambering is 1:10, as opposed to what used to be conventional for .22-caliber centerfires in the U.S., 1:12 to 1:14 inches (newer .22-centerfires often have 1:10 twists; rifles designed for long-range target shooting often have 1:8 twist). The cartridge also has an unusually thick neck, which allows the use of .22 rimfire adapter units, but it presents problems to the handloader. It is manufactured by RWS and by Hirtenberger. Factory ballistics of both versions are identical.

Hirtenberger, as a stand-alone entity, is no longer in business, having been taken over by Swedish conglomerate RUAG Ammotec (www.ruag.com/en/Ammotec/Ammotec_Home). Original Hirtenberger ammo is occasionally found in the surplus marketplace. RUAG is also the parent company of the European brands RWS, Rottweil, GECO, and Norma, and RUAG markets ammo for both civilian and law enforcement use under those original names, as well as the Hitenberger brand.

5.6x57mm, 5.6x57Rmm RWS Loading Data and Factory Ballistics

Bullet (grains/type)	Powder	Grains	Velocity	Energy	Source/Comments
50 SP	IMR 4320	40.0	3,900	1,689	Hornady
55 SP	W760	42.5	3,800	1,764	Hornady
55 SP	IMR 4350	41.0	3,700	1,672	Hornady
55 SP	IMR 4320	39.0	3,790	1,758	Hornady
60 SP	IMR 4320	38.5	3,700	1,824	Hornady
74 SP	RI-22	43.0	3,400	1,890	NA
55 SP	FL	FL	3,510	1,505	Hirtenberger factory load
74 SP	FL	FL	3,410	1,910	RWS factory load

5.6x61mm & 5.6x61Rmm
Vom Hofe Super Express

Historical Notes: These two cartridges were introduced in 1937 by E.A. Vom Hofe for his line of German-made Mauser-action express rifles. Some were exported to the United States between the wars. These chamberings were reintroduced by Stoeger Arms Corp. in 1962. The new rifles were based on the Swedish Husqvarna-Mauser action. Both the rimless and rimmed versions were listed in late DWM catalogs. Dimensions and ballistics are identical; these cartridges differ only in the rim.

General Comments: The 5.6x61mm Vom Hofe came out two years after the Winchester .220 Swift. It is one of the very few ultra-velocity .22 cartridges developed in Europe. Bullet diameter is identical to the .22 Savage Hi-Power, but the standard bullet is 10-percent heavier. The .22 Savage has remained popular in Europe, and is still loaded there. Velocity is close to the .220 Swift and, with its 77-grain bullet, the 5.6 is much more effective on deer-size animals. By American standards, it would be considered a long-range varmint cartridge. In Europe, it is looked on as a proper cartridge for deer or boar. If the bullet is designed for the job, there is no reason why it would not be entirely effective for use in open country. The heavier bullet should also have superior wind-bucking ability at long range. The 5.6 bears some resemblance to the .228 Ackley Magnum, which is made from the necked-down and shortened .30-06 case. Although neither cartridge is now loaded in Europe, new empty cases are available from Old Western Scrounger (www.ows-ammo.com)/Gibbs Rifle Co. (www.gibbsrifle.com) and from Huntington's Sportsman's Store (www.huntingtonsports.com). Bullets are available from both sources and from Hornady (www.hornady.com).

5.6x61mm & 5.6x61Rmm Vom Hofe Super Express Loading Data and Factory Ballistics

Bullet (grains/type)	Powder	Grains	Velocity	Energy	Source/Comments
70 SP	IMR 4895	37.0	2,800	1,215	RWS
77 SP	H870	61.0	3,460	2,050	RWS
87 SP	IMR 4350	52.0	3,310	2,110	RWS
77 SP	FL	FL	3,708	2,350	RWS factory load (obsolete, very optimistic)
77 SP	FL	FL	3,480	2,070	RWS factory load (obsolete)

6x29.5Rmm Stahl

Historical Notes: This is a small, 6mm rimmed cartridge for single-shot and combination guns that dates back prior to 1900. It was originally a black-powder number for guns made by B. Stahl, of Suhl, Germany. It has been obsolete for a long time and is largely a collector's item.

General Comments: This cartridge resembles the .25-20 WCF, but has a smaller-diameter lead bullet. It is entirely a small-game, plinking or target round. Ammunition could probably be made using .25-20 cases, although the rim would have to be turned down to proper diameter. Factory ballistics are unknown, but should be similar to the .25-20-86 black-powder load.

6x29.5Rmm Stahl Loading Data

Bullet (grains/type)	Powder	Grains	Velocity	Energy	Source/Comments
85 Lead	2400	7.0	1,460	405	Lyman #245496

6x62mm Freres
6x62Rmm Freres

Historical Notes: This is a recent German development by Metallwerk Elisenhutte GmBH (MEN). While it appears to be based on the .30-06, case-head diameter is greater, and the 6x62mm should not be made from .30-06 cases. Instead, use 9.3x62mm cases, which was undoubtedly what was used as a basis for this new number and which should be available from Norma and others. The 6x62mm is the first new 6mm cartridge developed in Europe in many years. This number is almost unknown in the United States.

General Comments: What we have here is a super, or magnum, 6mm suitable for all types of small and medium game at long range. The 6x62mm offers more performance than the .243 Winchester or 6mm Remington and requires a long action to accommodate its length. For U.S. hunting conditions, the 100-grain SP bullet load should be selected.

6x62mm Freres Factory Ballistics

Bullet (grains/type)	Powder	Grains	Velocity	Energy	Source/Comments
85 SP	FL	FL	3,460	2,260	MEN factory load
100 SP	FL	FL	3,313	2,442	MEN factory load

6x57mm Mauser
6.2x57mm RWS

Historical Notes: This is a little-known German cartridge that dates back to around 1895. Physical measurements indicate it is the 6.5x57mm Mauser necked down to 6mm. The 6.5mm, in turn, was based on the 1893 7x57mm Mauser necked down. This is a very interesting situation, because it means the 6x57mm is practically identical to the modern .244/6mm Remington. The two differ only by a minor variation in the shoulder angle. The .244 Remington is the .257 Roberts necked down to 6mm (.244) with the shoulder angle increased from 20 degrees/45 minutes to 26 degrees. The commercial .257 Roberts was originated by necking down the original 7x57mm Mauser without other notable changes.

By a long and devious process, different individuals and companies arrived at practically the same point, but at different times. It just goes to prove that there is very little new under the sun. For all practical purposes, the .244 Remington originated, or at least existed, before the turn of the century—it's just that it took 60 years before Remington finally got around to offering the ammunition!

General Comments: Records of ballistics or the specific rifle that the 6x57mm was used in are lacking. However, two bullet weights were available, a 120-grain soft-point and a 123-grain hollow-point. Considering the time and powders available, muzzle velocity was probably near 2600 fps. This would be a fine deer, antelope, or black bear cartridge. Standard ballistics are not known, and no loading data duplicating the original loads has been developed.

6x58mm Forster
6x58Rmm Forster

Historical Notes: These two cartridges are identical except that one is rimless and the other rimmed. These cartridges were introduced about 1904 and have been obsolete for a good many years. Physical measurement indicates this round is based on the 6.5x58mm Mauser necked-down. It is listed for the Forster (forester) stalking rifle. It apparently was used in bolt-action, single-shot, or combination guns.

General Comments: The rimless version of the 6x58mm closely resembles the .244 Remington, although these cartridges differ in shoulder angle and length of the neck. Available ballistics list a 127-grain bullet, but, at one time, a 119-grain and a 123-grain were also available. Performance is a little below the .243 Winchester, but with modern powders and a strong bolt-action, one could undoubtedly equal the .243 or the .244 in any given bullet weight. This would be a good deer and, possibly, elk cartridge. Ammunition could be made by necking-down 6.5x58mm cases for the rimless version, but the rimmed type would be a problem.

6x58mm Forster 6x58Rmm Forster Loading Data and Factory Ballistics

Bullet (grains/type)	Powder	Grains	Velocity	Energy	Source/Comments
105 SP	IMR 4320	35.0	2,750	1,762	NA
108 Lead	IMR 3031	24.0	2,200	1,165	Lyman #245499GC
127 SP	FL	FL	2,788	2,176	Factory load

.244 Halger Magnum

Historical Notes: Although this cartridge has an English cartridge designation, it is a 6mm magnum that originated in Germany. It was introduced, in the 1920s, by Halger Arms Co., of Hamburg.* The originators were named Halbe and Gerlich, and the Halger was formed by combining the first three letters of each name. The case is rimless (actually no more than the 6.5x57mm case), intended for use in Mauser bolt rifles, but there were some rimmed cases also made.

General Comments: The velocity of the .244 Halger is impressive, at least on paper. However, the Halger line of cartridges turned out to be somewhat overrated, when tested here. Regardless, this would still be a highly effective cartridge, even if velocity was a couple of hundred feet per second below claims. An 87-grain bullet would be mostly for varmint shooting, but heavier bullets could be handloaded for deer or larger animals. In size and general performance, it is very similar to the 6mm Remington. Bullet diameter is .243-inch, so any 6mm bullet would be suitable for handloading with proper data.

* See "Halger and His Rifles" by Phil Sharpe (*Gun Digest, 7th Edition.*).

.244 Halger Magnum Loading Data and Factory Ballistics

Bullet (grains/type)	Powder	Grains	Velocity	Energy	Source/Comments
90 SP	IMR 4350	47.0	3,270	2,142	N/A
105 SP	IMR 4350	44.0	3,020	2,130	N/A
87 SP	FL	FL	3,770	2,745	DWM factory load (optimistic)

6.5x40Rmm

General Comments: An obsolete cartridge for single-shot and combination guns, the 6.5x40Rmm case has considerable body taper. The Germans used a number of similarly shaped cartridges in varying calibers and lengths, with a case of similar design. All were black-powder cartridges, and while one or two made the transition to smokeless powder, most were discontinued after World War I or before 1930. Factory ballistic data is unavailable.

6.5x40Rmm Loading Data

Bullet (grains/type)	Powder	Grains	Velocity	Energy	Source/Comments
100 SP	2400	5.0	1,200	324	Lyman #245498GC

6.5x52Rmm
(.25-35 Winchester)

General Comments: This is the metric version of the .25-35 WCF. This load was used in European single-shot and combination guns. It is not listed in the latest RWS catalogs, although it has been popular in Germany for many years. European loading was practically identical to that used by U.S. ammunition companies.

6.5x52Rmm (.25-35 Winchester) Factory Ballistics

Bullet (grains/type)	Powder	Grains	Velocity	Energy	Source/Comments
117 SP	FL	FL	2,230	1,285	RWS factory load

6.5x27Rmm
6.5Rmm Ronezewski

General Comments: A short, rimmed, bottlenecked cartridge that resembles the .25-20 WCF, the 6.5x27Rmm is fatter and shorter. Performance is practically the same as with the 86-grain loading of the .25-20. The 6.5x27Rmm was listed as the kal. 6.5mm Einzelladerbüchse, which literally means "caliber 6.5mm single-loading gun." (Actually, what is meant is a cartridge that is "single-loaded" by the shooter, using powder charges contained in paper envelopes or closed tubes. RWS, for one, offered these for the 8.15x46Rmm cartridge (in the 1934 period), loaded with a variety of powders and in a choice of charge weights.) It was used mostly in low-priced, single-shot guns, but, apparently, also in some combination guns. It dates back to the 1890s or earlier and has been obsolete for a long time.

6.5x27Rmm Loading Data and Factory Ballistics

Bullet (grains/type)	Powder	Grains	Velocity	Energy	Source/Comments
86 SP	2400	7.0	1,425	394	25-20 bullet
86 SP	IMR 4227	9.0	1,500	434	25-20 bullet
82 SP	FL	FL	1,570	465	Factory load

6.5x48Rmm Sauer

General Comments: An obsolete black-powder cartridge developed for use in Sauer-made single-shot and combination guns. Because some samples have jacketed soft-point bullets, it must have also been furnished with smokeless powder. This is entirely a target or small-game number.

6.5x48Rmm Sauer Loading Data and Factory Ballistics

Bullet (grains/type)	Powder	Grains	Velocity	Energy	Source/Comments
120 lead	IMR 4198	12.0	1,260	428	Lyman #266455GC
126 lead	Black powder	FL	1,155	378	Factory load

6.5x53.5mm Daudeteau

General Comments: A collector's item today, this semi-rimmed type was introduced, originally, as a military cartridge for the French Navy, in 1895. It was used in the Daudeteau military bolt-action rifle, but commercial ammunition was also produced. Rifles and ammunition are quite rare, and you are not likely to have one to hunt with. If you do, it would probably be satisfactory for anything up to deer. According to Aivaro Casal, this cartridge was adopted by Uruguay in 1895 and used until 1898.

6.5x53.5mm Daudeteau Factory Ballistics

Bullet (grains/type)	Powder	Grains	Velocity	Energy	Source/Comments
150 SP	FL	40.0	2,395	1,922	Factory load

6.5x54mm Mauser

Historical Notes: This is one of the shortest of the Mauser rimless necked cases and was introduced around 1900. It was chambered mostly in the K Model (Kurz) or short-action carbine. The deluxe type M sporter was also available in 6.5x54. This Mauser cartridge was gradually displaced by the more universally popular 6.5x54mm Mannlicher-Schoenauer. It was once listed in DWM catalogs.

General Comments: In both appearance and performance, the 6.5x54mm Mauser is similar to the Mannlicher round. These cartridges are suitable for the same general size and type of big game. Mauser rifles in this chambering were imported into the United States until World War II. The case has a shorter body of slightly larger diameter than the 6.5 Mannlicher. Ammunition can be made by reforming and trimming .308 Winchester or .300 Savage cases. One can use the same loading data as for 6.5 Mannlicher with very similar results. However, when using home-swaged cases, reduce maximum loads by three or four grains to account for the reduced capacity, compared to original cases.

6.5x54mm Mauser Loading Data and Factory Ballistics

Bullet (grains/type)	Powder	Grains	Velocity	Energy	Source/Comments
120 SP	IMR 4895	36.0	2,500	1,665	N/A
119 SP	FL	FL	2,362	1,468	DWM factory load

6.5x58Rmm Sauer

General Comments: This is the longest of the rimmed, tapered, 6.5mm cartridges developed for the Sauer-made single-shot and combination guns, as well as some Mauser repeating rifles. The others were the 6.5x40Rmm and the 6.5x48Rmm. All have the same type of tapered case. The 6.5x58Rmm, the most popular, is not listed in recent RWS catalogs. It is less powerful than the .25-35 WCF and, by American standards, would be underpowered for deer-sized animals.

6.5x58Rmm Sauer Loading Data and Factory Ballistics

Bullet (grains/type)	Powder	Grains	Velocity	Energy	Source/Comments
120 Lead	4198	15.0	1,480	588	Lyman #266455GC
120 Lead	4895	21.0	1,650	730	Lyman #266455GC
127 SP	3031	24.0	2,100	1,288	RWS bullet
127 SP	FL	FL	2,020	1,140	Factory load

6.5x57mm Mauser & RWS
6.5x57Rmm Mauser & RWS

Historical Notes: The 6.5x57mm Mauser was developed about 1893-'94 as a necked-down version of the 7x57mm Mauser. Listed as a hunting cartridge, it was never adopted as an official military cartridge by any power. However, it undoubtedly influenced the design of many of the 6.5mm military cartridges, such as the 6.5x55mm Swedish and 6.5x68mm Portuguese. The three have similar dimensions and performance, but are not the same and can not be interchanged. The rimmed version is used mostly in combination guns. Both are listed in late RWS and Hirtenberger catalogs.

General Comments: As a commercial cartridge, the 6.5x57mm has not been widely used in the United States, although German-made rifles in this chambering have been imported. On the other hand, several virtually identical wildcat numbers have enjoyed limited popularity. These are based on either necking down the 7x57mm case or necking up the .257 Roberts case. The two cases are similar, except for shoulder angle and length. The funny thing is that several individuals claim to have "invented" the wildcat version, not knowing that Paul Mauser beat them to it by 100 years. There are a number of chamber configurations used in making up wildcat versions of the 6.5x57, and few, if any, will interchange. Immediately after World War II, a number of Japanese 6.5mm Arisaka military rifles were re-chambered to handle various 6.5/.257 or 6.5/7mm wildcat cartridges. However, this is a tricky thing that should be checked out by a gunsmith before actually doing any shooting—better safe than sorry. It should be noted that reforming 6mm Remington, .257 Roberts or 7x57mm cases into 6.5x57mm cases by simply neck sizing the case will not necessarily accommodate proper headspace control. To solve this problem, neck the case up to at least .30-caliber before forming it in the 6.5x57mm full-length sizing die.

Bullet (grains/type)	Powder	Grains	Velocity	Energy	Source/Comments
129 SP	IMR 4350	44.5	2,800	2,246	Hornady
140 SP	IMR 4350	43.5	2,700	2,267	Hornady
160 SP	IMR 4350	41.5	2,500	2,221	Hornady
93 FMJ	FL	FL	3,320	2,255	RWS factory load
96 FMJ	FL	FL	3,290	2,290	Factory load
119 SP	FL	FL	2,821	2,097	Factory load
123 SP	FL	FL	2,683	1,967	Factory load
127 SP	FL	FL	2,850	2,290	RWS factory load
154 SP	FL	FL	2,670	2,435	RWS factory load
157 SP	FL	FL	2,450	2,080	DWM factory load

6.5x58mm Portuguese

General Comments: The 6.5x58mm Portuguese (used in the Portuguese Mauser-Vergueiro rifle) is often confused with the 6.5x57mm Mauser. Performance is about the same, but these cartridges are not interchangeable. The 6.5x57mm was never adopted as a military round. There is also a 6.5x58Rmm Sauer and a 6.5x58Rmm Krag-Jorgensen, which are distinct cartridges. See also Chapter 6 for more information.

6.5x65mm RWS
6.5x65Rmm RWS

Historical Notes: Developed by RWS about 1988, this is the first new European 6.5mm cartridge in many years. Case-head diameter matches the 9.3x62mm (which is about .004-inch larger than the .30-06), but this case is, as indicated, three millimeters longer than the 9.3x62mm. A rimmed version is offered for single-shot and combination guns. RWS is the only manufacturer.

General Comments: Ballistic performance of this modern 6.5mm is superior to most European 6.5mm cartridges. It is in the same class as the 6.5mm Remington Magnum. This would be a good choice for small and medium game at long range. While the lighter-weight bullets are popular for European hunting, American shooters should select the heavier bullet.

6.5x65mm, 6.5x65Rmm RWS Factory Ballistics

Bullet (grains/type)	Powder	Grains	Velocity	Energy	Source/Comments
108 SP	FL	FL	3,460	2,260	RWS factory load
127 SP	FL	FL	3,313	2,442	RWS factory load

6.5x61mm Mauser
6.5x61Rmm Mauser

Historical Notes: Developed by DWM for various German-made Mauser action rifles, the 6.5x61mm was introduced in the 1930s. There is also a rimmed version for single-shot and combination guns. This cartridge was only moderately popular and has not been revived.

General Comments: The 6.5x61mm is very similar to the .256 Newton. According to the late Phil Sharpe,* it was developed after RWS had imported and tested a .256 Newton rifle. Performance is similar, and .256 loading data could be used as a starting point for working up handloads. The 6.5x61mm would be adequate for most North American game, under proper conditions.

Op cit.

6.5x61mm, 6.5x51Rmm Mauser

Bullet (grains/type)	Powder	Grains	Velocity	Energy	Source/Comments
120 SP	4831	55.0	2,860	2,180	N/A
140 SP	4350	50.0	2,640	2,170	N/A
119 SP	FL	FL	3,090	2,510	N/A
139 SP	FL	FL	2,906	2,596	N/A
157 SP	FL	FL	2,749	2,617	N/A

6.5x58Rmm Krag-Jorgensen

Historical Notes: This Danish target cartridge was developed in 1933 by necking-down the 8mm Model 89 military round. It is used in single-shot match rifles based on the Krag-Jorgensen action. Its use is confined almost entirely to Denmark.

General Comments: The 6.5mm is popular in the Scandinavian countries for target and hunting use. This particular round was designed to adapt the local military rifle to that caliber without altering the action in any way. By retaining the same rimmed case, only a new barrel is required. Rifles for this cartridge are quite rare in the United States. However, if you can find the now-obsolete Norma 8x58Rmm Danish Krag cases with Boxer primers, you can neck these down to make ammunition. This would make a good deer cartridge.

6.5x58Rmm Krag-Jorgensen Loading Data and Factory Ballistics (Note: *Approximate ballistics only.)

Bullet (grains/type)	Powder	Grains	Velocity	Energy	Source/Comments
140 SP	IMR 4350	46.0	2,500	1,935 *	N/A
139 SP	FL	FL	2,500	1,930 *	Factory load

6.5x68mm RWS
6.5x68Rmm RWS

Historical Notes: This cartridge was developed by RWS about 1938-'39 and marketed in the spring of 1940. While this has been called the 6.5x68mm Schuler, such a name is erroneous, because that particular gunmaker had nothing to do with its development. It was originally chambered in German-made, Mauser-action rifles. However, the Mannlicher-Schoenauer bolt-action was imported by Stoeger in 6.5x68mm, and Charles Leavell, of Sumpter, S.C., also brought in 6.5x68mm and 8x68mm rifles. At one time, the German-made Vom Hofe rifles were available for this round, and it is occasionally referred to as the 6.5mm Vom Hofe Express. It is listed in late RWS and Hirtenberger catalogs, and a few American-made custom rifles have been made for it.

General Comments: The 6.5x68mm is the most powerful of the many European 6.5mm cartridges. In dimensions and performance, it is similar to the .264 Winchester Magnum, except that the .264 has a belted case. On paper, the 6.5x68mm boasts a higher velocity with the 93-grain bullet than the .264 does with the 100-grain. It has an extremely flat trajectory. With the light bullet, this would be important mostly for long-range varmint shooting. Arguments as to which of the two is more powerful are rather academic because, with the same bullet weight, chamber pressure, and barrel length, there really isn't much difference. It is largely a matter of personal choice and which rifle you prefer. Regardless, the 6.5x68mm is a terrific ultra-velocity small-bore cartridge and would be a good all-round cartridge for North American hunting. It is capable of cleanly killing anything from varmint to grizzly bear, if the hunter does his part and uses the proper bullet.

Bullet (grains/type)	Powder	Grains	Velocity	Energy	Source/Comments
87 SP	H4831	73.0	3,700	2,710	Hodgdon
120 SP	H4831	68.0	3,300	2,980	Hodgdon
140 SP	H4831	63.0	3,000	2,800	Hodgdon
93 SP	FL	FL	3,950	3,180	RWS factory load (optimistic)
123 SP	FL	FL	3,450	3,255	RWS factory load (optimistic)
140 SP	FL	FL	2,920	2,651	Hirtenberger factory load

7x33mm Sako
7x33mm Finnish

Historical Notes: This cartridge originated in 1942 when Sako was producing 9mm Parabellum cartridges in large quantities. The base of the 7x33mm is the same size as the 9mm, but the case was lengthened to the maximum possible for the available case-making equipment. It was then necked down to 7mm. The original bullet weight was 92.6 grains, but was soon changed to 78 grains, which has been standard ever since. Both soft-point and full metal jacket bullets are available.

This caliber was originally developed for capercaillie and black grouse hunting. These birds were widely hunted and were the most important hunting species in Finland, following World War II. For bird hunting, full metal jacket bullets were standard.

General Comments: The ballistics of the 7x33mm are similar to the .30 Carbine, and velocity at 200 yards is only 1500 fps. Post-WWII hunting in Finland was mostly for food, and the slow, round-nose bullet is a good killer that does not destroy much meat. The 7x33mm is considered effective for bird hunting to about 150 yards. The first rifles chambered for the 7x33mm were the Sako L42 and later L46 models, and about 6,000 guns were produced, before this caliber was dropped from production in the 1960s. The popularity of the .222 Remington was the principal reason for the demise of the 7x33mm.

7x33mm Sako (7x33mm Finnish) Loading Data and Factory Ballistics

Bullet (grains/type)	Powder	Grains	Velocity	Energy	Source/Comments
78 SP	N110 (Vihta Vuori)	16.5	2,430	1,030	Sako
78 SP or FMJ	FL	FL,	2,400	998	Sako factory load

.270 Schuster — *NEW*

Historical Notes: The .270 Schuster deserves note here because it was an attempt by its designer, Reinhard Schuster, to patent a cartridge design. United States Patent Application 20110048269, filed March 3, 2011, was for a "rifle cartridge formed to have an overall length of about 2.800 inches, or 71.12 millimeters. The shell case has a case length between 1.900 inches and 1.950 inches and a neck forming a mouth for a standard .270 caliber bullet." In short, the "novel" cartridge named in the application was for a .308 Winchester to be necked down to a 6.8mm caliber.

General Comments: Or, looked at another way, the resulting .270 Schuster would be a .270-08 — a notion that began in the 1950s when the 7.62 NATO case was necked to .270. The .270 Redding and the .270 SABI also plow this same ground. Then there's the .260 Rem. and the 7mm-08 bracketing this caliber in factory-loaded ammo for the same, or almost the same, ballistics, and it's easy to see why this round was obsoleted practically at conception.

Bullet (grains/type)	Powder	Grains	Velocity	Energy	Source/Comments
150 Nosler			2,657	2,351	Patent Application US20110048269

7x64mm Brenneke
7x65Rmm Brenneke

Historical Notes: This cartridge was developed by Wilhelm Brenneke in 1917 and used in various Mauser-action sporting rifles. Ammunition is listed in the current RWS, Norma, Federal, and Remington catalogs. Brenneke never fabricated ammunition, because he was a designer and gunmaker, and this task was left to the companies equipped to turn out commercial ammunition. There is a near-identical rimmed version, listed as the 7x65Rmm, used in single-shot or combination firearms.

General Comments: Those who think everything new and worthwhile always originates as the result of good old Yankee ingenuity better take a close look at this cartridge. The 7x64mm Brenneke is virtually identical to the .280 Remington and the wildcat 7mm-06, and has been around for more than 75 years. The base diameter of the 7x64mm is a little smaller than the .280, so these cartridges will not actually interchange, but differences are slight. Visibly, the only way an expert can tell these cartridges apart without reading the head markings is by the brass texture or the German-type bullet.

The 7x64mm Brenneke is adequate for any North American big game with the proper bullet. In its original form, it was loaded with a special bullet designed by Brenneke, called the Brenneke Torpedo. Quite a large variety of bullet types are offered in each weight to adapt the cartridge to practically any game or shooting situation.

7x64mm Brenneke, 7x65Rmm Brenneke Loading Data and Factory Ballistics

Bullet (grains/type)	Powder	Grains	Velocity	Energy	Source/Comments
139 SP	IMR 4350	54.5	3,000	2,810	Hornady (7x65Rmm)
154 SP	IMR 4350	52.5	2,900	2,877	Hornady (7x65Rmm)
175 SP	IMR 4350	50.5	2,700	2,833	Hornady (7x65Rmm)
139 SP	FL	FL	2,955	2,690	Factory load
139	FL	FL	2,806	2,430	Patronen (Hungarian)
154 SP	FL	FL	2,822	2,772	Norma factory load
162 SP	FL	FL	2,890	3,000	RWS factory load
170	FL	FL	2,625	2,600	Patronen (Hungarian)
173 SP	FL	FL	2,790	2,990	Factory load

7mm Blaser Magnum

Historical Notes: The idea for four new Blaser cartridges originated in a Las Vegas hotel. Bernhard Knöbel, who was relatively new at Blaser, wanted something fresh to add to the brand. Working with Christer Larsson of Norma, a man who is a very savvy ballistics engineer, they decided on a new line of cartridges based on the .404 Jeffery case, but without a magnum belt. The plan was to develop four cartridges—a 7mm, .30, .338, and .375—that would have a ballistic advantage over the 7mm Remington Magnum, .300 Winchester Magnum, .338 Winchester Magnum, and the famed .375 H&H. An additional requirement was that all four of these cartridges would operate at a maximum average pressure of 58,000 psi. Norma engineers, after extensive testing and evaluation, decided on barrels with four grooves, a case with more taper than the Winchester Short Magnums, a neck length that was 1.1-caliber in length, and a shoulder angle of 30 degrees.

General Comments: The 7mm Blaser Magnum cartridge is currently available only in rifles from Blaser currently sold in Europe. Therefore, it is listed as a European Sporting Rifle cartridge. In the near future, Blaser expects to offer its rifles chambered for all four of its new magnum cartridges in the United States. Norma currently catalogs one 7mm Blaser load; a 156-grain Norma Oryx bullet at 3035 fps, but ballistic reports from Norma show load development work with a 140-grain Nosler Accubond being driven to 3,150 fps. These ballistics almost exactly mirror the performance of the 7mm Remington Magnum. But remember, the 7mm Blaser is a beltless magnum. Whether this cartridge will gain a following in the States remains to be seen, but that prospect seems doubtful, unless American sporting arms manufacturers start chambering it in more affordable rifles.

7mm Blaser Magnum Factory Ballistics

Bullet (grains/type)	Powder	Grains	Velocity	Energy	Source
140 Nosler Accubond	FL	FL	3,150	3,085	Norma
156 Norma Oryx	FL	FL	3,035	3,192	Norma

7x72Rmm

Historical Notes: A popular, straight, tapered case for single-shot and combination guns, this load was last listed in the 1960 RWS catalog, but it is not currently available. Date of origin is not determined, but it is also shown in RWS manuals of circa 1934. This is seldom used in the United States, except for an occasional combination gun brought back from Europe. In terms of energy or power, it is in the .30-30 class and would not be satisfactory for anything larger than deer at short to moderate range. Bullet diameter is standard, and one can use any American-made .284-inch bullets for handloading. This round has occasionally been loaded, as demand dictates.

7x72Rmm Loading Data and Factory Ballistics

Bullet (grains/type)	Powder	Grains	Velocity	Energy	Source/Comments
139 SP	IMR 4198	23.0	1,850	N/A	N/A

Bullet (grains/type)	Powder	Grains	Velocity	Energy	Source/Comments
139 SP	IMR 4198	28.0	2,300	1,640	N/A
160 SP	IMR 4895	27.0	1,810	1,168	N/A
139 SP	FL	FL	2,440	1,835	Factory load

7x73mm Vom Hofe (Belted)

Historical Notes: Developed by E.A. Vom Hofe and his partner Schnienmann in 1931, this cartridge is unusual in that it has a belted case, something German designers normally avoided. Original rifles were based on the Mauser 98 action and made by the firm of Hoffmann, in Berlin. After 1936, Vom Hofe made rifles in his own name. The 7x73mm was not as popular as other Vom Hofe cartridges and manufacture of it was not resumed after World War II.

General Comments: The 7x73mm belted delivered the same ballistics as the smaller and shorter 7mm Super Express rimless introduced later. Dimensions of the 7x73mm case are close to the .300 H&H Magnum, but the Vom Hofe has a larger base and belt diameter (about .013-inch greater). It is at least possible that the 7x73mm was originally developed by necking down the full-length .300 H&H case. Some American wildcats, such as the 7mm Mashburn (Long) were made much the same way. Velocity must have been taken in a 30-inch barrel, because similar United States cartridges (usually chronographed in 24- to 26-inch barrels) do not achieve such velocities with the same weight bullet.

The 7x73mm is scarce and practically unknown in the United States. It would be entirely adequate for North American big game. In power, it has a slight edge over the 7mm Weatherby Magnum.

7x73mm Vom Hofe (Belted) Factory Ballistics

Bullet (grains/type)	Powder	Grains	Velocity	Energy	Source/Comments
170 SP	FL	FL	3,290	4,120	Factory load (very optimistic)

7x66mm Vom Hofe Super Express

Historical Notes: This is a rimless 7mm magnum, developed for the post-World War II Vom Hofe rifles built on the Swedish Husqvarna-Mauser action. These rifles were first advertised in the United States by Stoeger in 1962, but the 7mm Super Express cartridge was introduced in Germany about 1956. What is apparently the same cartridge has also been listed as the 7x66mm Vom Hofe, and also as the 7.6x66mm Vom Hofe. It was once loaded by DWM. E.A. Vom Hofe has been dead for some years, and the operation was reactivated by Walter Gehmann, once a world-champion rifle shot, although the Vom Hofe name was retained. Gehmann operates a large gun and sport shop in Karlsruhe, with a branch in Stuttgart (www.gehmann.com). The cartridge he offered differed ballistically and in form from the pre-war type. The case is 66 millimeters long, the rim measures .507 inch, the head is .544 inch, and the shoulder measures .504 inch. Thus, it will be seen that the rim diameter is of the type smaller than the head, a lá the .284 Winchester. The shoulder form is unusual, being of modified venturi style.

General Comments: Ballistics claimed for the 7mm Super Express are quite impressive. With the 170-grain bullet, it beats out the 175-grain load of the 7mm Remington Magnum by almost 300 fps, and the 7mm Weatherby Magnum by 164. Not even some of the oversized wildcat 7mm magnum cartridges claim such performance. This makes one wonder what barrel length was used for the velocity tests. American cartridges are usually chronographed from 24- or 26-inch barrels, but Europe ballisticians often use a 30-inch barrel. Regardless, the 7mm Vom Hofe Super Express is as good as any of the other 7mm magnums. It would be an excellent all-round cartridge for North American hunting. It would also do for most non-dangerous African game. It would be at its best for plains or mountain hunting, or anytime long shots entered the picture. Case capacity significantly exceeds the 7mm Remington and Weatherby Magnums.

Bullet (grains/type)	Powder	Grains	Velocity	Energy	Source/Comments
130 SP	IMR 4350	68.0	3,350	3,250	N/A
175 SP	IMR 4350	60.0	2,900	3,280	N/A
120 SP	FL	FL	3,520	3,340	Gehmann factory load
123 SP	FL	FL	3,640	3,630	Factory load
140 SP	FL	FL	3,356	3,540	Gehmann factory load
169 SP	FL	FL	3,300	4,090	Factory load (very optimistic)
170 SP	FL	FL	3,052	3,540	Gehmann factory load

7x75Rmm Vom Hofe Super Express

Historical Notes: This big cartridge was introduced by Vom Hofe about 1939 and is currently loaded by the Walter Gehmann Co. in Germany (www.gehmann.com). The 7x75Rmm is quite potent, in the same general class as the 7mm Remington Magnum. It is more than adequate for North American game. Cases are imported by Old Western Scrounger. (www.ows-ammo.com). Loading data and factory ballistics are not available.

7x57mm Mauser
7x57Rmm Mauser

General Comments: An extremely popular sporting round over much of the world. European loads are much more diverse and useful than those generally provided by American companies. RWS ammunition is available in the larger cities of the United States and many parts of the world. See Chapter 1 for United States and other load data; see Chapter 6 for military load information; and consult the RWS/DWM ballistic tables for data.

7x57mm, 7x57Rmm Mauser Factory Ballistics

Bullet (grains/type)	Powder	Grains	Velocity	Energy	Source/Comments
123 SP	FL	FL	2,955	2,390	RWS factory load
139 SP	FL	FL	2,625	2,125	RWS factory load
154 SP	FL	FL	2,690	2,473	RWS factory load
177 SP	FL	FL	2,460	2,385	RWS factory load

.300 Blaser Magnum

Historical Notes: The idea for four new Blaser cartridges originated in a Las Vegas hotel. Bernhard Knöbel, who was relatively new at Blaser, wanted something fresh for the brand. Working with Christer Larsson of Norma, a man who is a very savvy ballistics engineer, they decided on a new line of cartridges based on the .404 Jeffery case, but without a magnum belt. The plan was to develop four cartridges—a 7mm, .30, .338, and .375—that would have a ballistic advantage over the 7mm Remington Magnum, .300 Winchester Magnum, .338 Winchester Magnum, and the famed .375 H&H. An additional requirement was that all four of these cartridges would operate at a maximum average pressure of 58,000 psi. Norma engineers, after extensive testing and evaluation, decided on barrels with four grooves, a case with more taper than the Winchester Short Magnums, a neck length that was 1.1-caliber in length, and a shoulder angle of 30 degrees.

General Comments: The .300 Blaser Magnum cartridge is currently available only in rifles from Blaser currently sold in Europe. Therefore, it is listed as a European sporting rifle cartridge. In the near future, Blaser expects to offer its rifles chambered for all four of its new magnum cartridges in the United States. Norma currently catalogs one .300 Blaser load; a 200-grain Norma Oryx bullet at 2822 fps, but ballistic reports from Norma show load development work with a 180-grain Barnes Tipped Triple Shock being driven to 3050 fps. This level of performance exceeds that of the .300 Winchester Magnum by about 100 fps. Whether this cartridge will gain a following in the States remains to be seen, but that seems doubtful, unless American sporting arms manufacturers start chambering it in more affordable rifles.

.300 Blaser Magnum Factory Ballistics

Bullet (grains/type)	Powder	Grains	Velocity	Energy	Source
180 Barnes Tipped TSX	FL	FL	3,050	3,719	Norma
200 Norma Oryx	FL	FL	2,822	3,538	Norma

.308 Norma Magnum

Historical Notes: The .308 Norma Magnum was introduced in 1960 by Å.B. Norma Projektilfabrik, of Åmotfors, Sweden. In its original form, this cartridge was something of a semi-wildcat, because only unprimed brass cases were available and no commercial rifles were chambered for it. However, about 18 months after it was introduced, Norma began producing factory ammunition. Several European manufacturers chamber the round as standard or on order.

General Comments: The .308 Norma Magnum is practically identical to the wildcat .30-338, which is the .338 Winchester Magnum necked-down to .30-caliber. However, the two cases are not interchangeable because of a difference in body length. Almost any standard-length .30-06 rifle can be rechambered to take the .308 Norma cartridge. This cartridge is also similar to a number of .30-caliber wildcat magnums, based on the blown-out and shortened .300 H&H case, and known collectively as the .300 "short magnum" group; the .30 Luft, .300 Apex, and Ackley Short .30 Magnum are representative of this class. The .308 Norma Magnum is adequate for any North American big game and should do well on African plains game. Powder capacity is only a hair greater than the .300 H&H, but the shape of the case is radically different.

This is a proprietary cartridge of European origin designed specifically for the American market. It has previously been placed with the American cartridges because most U.S. readers will look for it here. Technically, it belongs in the chapter covering European cartridges.

.308 Norma Magnum Loading Data and Factory Ballistics

Bullet (grains/type)	Powder	Grains	Velocity	Energy	Source/Comments
100 SP	H380	70.0	3,500	2,721	Speer
110 SP	IMR 4350	75.5	3,400	2,824	Sierra, Hornady
125 SP	IMR 4350	76.0	3,400	3,209	Sierra, Hornady
150 SP	IMR 4350	72.0	3,200	3,420	Hornady, Nosler, Sierra, Speer
150 SP	IMR 4831	73.0	3,150	3,306	Nosler, Speer
165 SP	IMR 4350	71.0	3,100	3,522	Sierra, Speer, Nosler
180 SP	IMR 4831	73.0	3,000	3,598	Sierra
220 SP	IMR 4350	68.0	2,800	3,831	Hornady
180 SP	FL		3,100	3,842	Norma factory load

.300 Norma Magnum

Case dimensions: 2.500", 20.5°, 0.587", 0.585", 0.562", 0.341", 1.892", 2.185"

Historical Notes: In early 2007, a ballistician by the name of Jimmie Sloan began looking into long-range shooting and what it took to achieve success at 1,000 and 1,500 yards with a portable individual weapon system. Sloan was unsatisfied with the cartridges available at the time. He wanted a rifle cartridge capable of shooting a bullet with a very high ballistic coefficient, one that weighed 300 grains and traveled at velocities around 2800 fps. A wildcat cartridge known as the .338R was the result. In 2009, Norma AB Precision legitimized the cartridge as the .338 Norma Magnum. The .300 Norma Magnum is nothing more than the .338 Norma Magnum necked down to .308-caliber. Aside from that, the case dimensions are almost identical.

General Comments: The .300 Norma Magnum generates .30-378 Weatherby ballistics from a non-belted case with a standard, radius-free shoulder. Though yet to be offered as a factory loading by any American ammunition manufacturers, wildcatters have already gone to work by Ackley Improving the case so that it has a 40-degree shoulder. Brass for the .300 Norma Magnum is available from MidwayUSA (www.midwayusa.com). Though similar in name and caliber to the .308 Norma Magnum, these cartridges are not the same; the .300 Norma Magnum will push a 200-grain bullet to the same velocities the .308 Norma Magnum will push a 180-grain bullet. It's too early to predict with any certainty the future of this cartridge, but long-range shooters are showing a real interest—R.A.M.

.300 Norma Magnum Loading Data and Ballistics

Bullet (grains/type)	Powder	Grains	Velocity	Energy	Source/Comments
208 Hornady A-Max	H-1000	89.3	3,089	4,406	Jimmie Sloan
220 Sierra Matchking	H-1000	86.3	3,003	4,404	Jimmie Sloan
240 Sierra Matchking	Ramshot Magnum	85.0	2,943	4,615	Jimmie Sloan

.30R Blaser

Historical Notes: Blaser (www.blaser-usa.com) and RWS (www.rws-munition.de/en.html) cooperated in developing this round in 1990. Being rimmed, it is intended for use in single-shot and combination guns. RWS is the only manufacturer. Note the nomenclature is a combination of European and United States practices.

General Comments: Ballistically, this newer cartridge fills the slot between the .30-06 and the .300 H&H Magnum. It is suitable for all types of large North American game. Bullet diameter is .308-inch. Bullets of 150 to 180 grains work best for most applications.

.30R Blaser Loading Data and Factory Ballistics

Bullet (grains/type)	Powder	Grains	Velocity	Energy	Source/Comments
150 SP	RI-22	68.0	3,069	3,110	RWS
180 SP	RI-22	64.0	2,870	3,290	RWS
220 SP	RI-22	58.0	2,481	3,008	RWS
250 SP	RI-22	57.0	2,335	3,026	RWS
150 SP	FL	FL	3,085	3,165	RWS factory load
180 SP	FL	FL	2,820	3,190	RWS factory load

8x48Rmm Sauer

General Comments: This obsolete black-powder cartridge was used in single-shot and combination guns. It is shown in post-World War II RWS catalogs as a discontinued number. It was popular in its day, and rifles in this chambering are common. In power, it is similar to the .32-40 WCF and would qualify as a deer cartridge for short-range shooting. Quality Cartridge (www.qual-cart.com) currently lists brass for this round.

8x48Rmm Sauer Factory Ballistics

Bullet (grains/type)	Powder	Grains	Velocity	Energy	Source/Comments
155 Lead	IMR 4198	18.0	1,500	780	Lyman #316475GC
196 SP	FL	FL	1,665	1,215	DWM factory load

8x51mm Mauser
8x51Rmm Mauser

Historical Notes: An 8mm round designed for the K-Model, or short-action, Mauser rifles. The rimmed version is identical, but made for single-shot or combination guns. Both were introduced in 1888. The rimless cartridge is a shortened version of the German 8x57mm military round developed the same year. It was fairly popular, but has been replaced by the 8x56mm Mannlicher-Schoenauer.

General Comments: The 8x51mm Mauser reached its peak popularity before World War I. It was a favorite, in Germany, for short-action rifles and carbines. Mauser Type A, K, and M sporters were imported into the U.S. in this chambering to a limited extent. Ammunition in shooting quantities is almost impossible to find. In power, the 8x51mm is a .30-30-class cartridge and would be good for anything up to deer-size animals. For handloading, .318-inch bullets should be used.

Bullet (grains/type)	Powder	Grains	Velocity	Energy	Source/Comments
125 SP	IMR 4198	30.0	2,370	1,560	N/A
150 SP	IMR 4064	41.0	2,350	1,840	N/A
157 SP	FL	FL	2,155	1,627	Factory load
158 SP	FL	FL	2,380	1,990	Factory load
196 SP	FL	FL	2,099	1,887	Factory load

8.15x46Rmm

Historical Notes: This is an old, popular target cartridge that was sometimes used for hunting. The exact date of introduction has not established, but it dates back to the period between 1890 and 1900. Single-shots, combination guns, and repeating rifles were chambered for the round. It is listed in current RWS catalogs. Modern loads have jacketed bullets, usually flat-nose soft-points, but, at one time, lead bullets were commonly used. A variety of diameters were factory offered, designed to fit different rifles. According to Fred Datig, this cartridge was developed by Frohn, of Suhl, Germany. For many years, it was the cartridge for 200-meter off-hand target shooting, in Germany and Austria.

General Comments: The 8.15x46Rmm was practically unknown in the United States, until after World War II, when returning GIs brought back various rifles in this chambering (mostly single-shots). Older rifles are intended for low pressure, so one should be careful when handloading and stick to moderate loads, if there is any doubt. Ammunition can be made from resized or fire-formed .32-40 cases. In power, the 8.15x46Rmm is comparable to the .32-40. Thus, it is a little underpowered for deer-sized animals, but would be fine for any small to medium game. Cases are available from RWS (http://rws-munition/de/en.html) and are imported by Old Western Scrounger (www.ows-ammo.com). Quality Cartridge (www.qual-cart.com) also lists brass for this round.

8.15x46Rmm Loading Data and Factory Ballistics

Bullet (grains/type)	Powder	Grains	Velocity	Energy	Source/Comments
151 SP	IMR 4895	30.0	1,900	1,240	N/A
190 Lead	IMR 3031	23.0	1,500	956	Lyman #338237
151 SP	FL	FL	1,805	1,090	RWS factory load

8x75mm
8x75Rmm

Historical Notes: These two cartridges are listed together, because one is a rimmed version of the other. These cartridges were introduced around 1910 and are based on the older 9.3x74Rmm case necked down. These cartridges were intended to provide a powerful 8mm for African use. The rimless version was for bolt-action express rifles, the rimmed for combination guns or single-shots.

General Comments: At the turn of the century and until start of World War I, there was considerable competition between German and British gunmakers for the African gun trade. The Germans made good repeating rifles at moderate prices and gained sales by underselling the British. However, the British seemed to always keep one jump ahead, in the matter of popular cartridge design. The Germans were constantly trying to come up with something that would compete with the British offerings. The 8x75mm is one of a number of

German efforts to produce an express 8mm cartridge. Two bullet diameters were used, the earlier .318-inch, and the later .323-inch, or "S," size. The large-diameter bullet should not be used in the smaller bore. Many 8mm cartridges come in two different bullet diameters. One must be very careful about this, because the large-diameter "S" round is often loaded to higher velocity and pressure. The 8x75mm is in about the same class as the .300 H&H Magnum and is powerful enough for any North American big game.

8x75mm, 8x75Rmm Factory Ballistics

Bullet (grains/type)	Powder	Grains	Velocity	Energy	Source/Comments
180 SP	RI-22	71.0	2,791	3,115	RWS
200 SP	RI-22	68.0	2,713	3,270	RWS
196 SP	FL	FL	2,715	3,230	Factory loading for .318-inch bore rifles
198 SP	FL	FL	3,050	4,120	Factory loading for S-bore rifles

WARNING! Many J-bore (.318-inch) rifles still exist and, depending upon throat and cartridge neck dimension, it can be possible to chamber "S" bore (.323-inch) cartridges. Firing such a combination can create dangerous pressures. When in doubt, check bore diameter CAREFULLY!

8x57Rmm 360

Historical Notes: Based on the 9.3x72Rmm case, this old German cartridge is a copy of the British .360 Nitro Express No. 2. Loaded first with black powder and, later, with smokeless, a fair number of combination guns will be found chambered for this round. Bore diameter is .318-inch.

General Comments: Due to low breech pressure, ballistic performance of the 8x57Rmm is only moderate. It is suitable for all types of small and medium game at close range, but falls off badly at longer ranges. This cartridge is now obsolete. For handloading, use only .318 diameter bullets. Quality Cartridge (www.qual-cart.com) currently lists brass for this round.

8x57Rmm 360 Loading Data and Factory Ballistics (Note: *Estimated ballistics.)

Bullet (grains/type)	Powder	Grains	Velocity	Energy	Source/Comments
196 SP	RI-19	37.5	1,893	1,561	RWS
196 SP	IMR 3031	26.0	1,560	1,059	RWS
196 SP	IMR 4350	37.0	1,820	1,441	RWS
196 SP	FL	FL	1,800	1,410 *	N/A

8x58Rmm Sauer

General Comments: This black-powder cartridge was once used in single-shot and combination guns. A popular schüetzen cartridge in its day, it is long obsolete. It differs from the 8x48Rmm only in length. This cartridge is based on the 9.3x72Rmm case and offers similar performance to the 8x57Rmm 360. Power is about the same as the .32-40 WCF, and it could be used for deer at short range. For handloading, use only .318-inch diameter bullets. Quality Cartridge (www.qual-cart.com) currently lists brass for this round.

8x58Rmm Sauer Loading Data and Factory Ballistics

Bullet (grains/type)	Powder	Grains	Velocity	Energy	Source/Comments
196 SP	IMR 4064	34.0	1,942	1,642	N/A
196 SP	RI-19	39.0	1,877	1,533	RWS

Bullet (grains/type)	Powder	Grains	Velocity	Energy	Source/Comments
196 SP	FL	FL	1,690	1,248	Factory load

8x42Rmm – M-88

Historical Notes: Introduced in 1888, this is a shortened version of the 8x51Rmm Mauser round. It is listed as a hunting cartridge, and was used primarily in single-shot or combination guns. It has been obsolete for many years.

General Comments: The need for a less powerful version of the 8x51Rmm must have been rather limited, because the 8x42Rmm was not nearly as popular as the longer cartridge. In power, the 8x42Rmm is in the same class as the .32-40 WCF and would just about qualify as a deer cartridge. It would be best for small to medium game at moderate ranges.

8x42Rmm – M-88 Loading Data and Factory Ballistics

Bullet (grains/type)	Powder	Grains	Velocity	Energy	Source/Comments
175 lead	IMR 4227	22.0	1,580	975	Lyman #319295GC
157 SP	FL	FL	1,780	1,110	Factory load

8x71mm Peterlongo

General Comments: Johann Peterlongo was an Austrian gunmaker and designer in Innsbruck. While his products are virtually unknown in the United States, he had a certain following in Europe. He turned out combination guns and other sporting arms of high quality. He designed 8mm and 9mm cartridges based on a long rimless case of necked type. These cartridges are of interest mostly to collectors today. The Peterlongo cartridges were loaded by G. Roth and Hirtenberger-Patronenfabrik.

8x71mm Peterlongo Factory Ballistics (Note: *Estimated ballistics.)

Bullet (grains/type)	Powder	Grains	Velocity	Energy	Source/Comments
200 SP	FL	FL	2,650	3,132 *	Factory load
154	N/A	N/A	2,854	2,785	1932 Catalog (German)

8x57mmJ Mauser

Historical Notes: This original 8x57mm cartridge was adopted in 1888 along with the Model-88 Commission rifle, by the German Army. Many sporting rifles were subsequently chambered for this cartridge. Ammunition is still being manufactured by RWS in Germany. Bullet diameter is .318-inch.

General Comments: The later 8x57mmJS uses a .323-inch diameter bullet and is loaded to higher pressures. Never fire 8x57mmJS ammunition in rifles chambered for 8x57mmJ ammunition. American manufacturers offer only the 8x57mmJS load, but it is deliberately loaded down to be safe to fire in 8x57mmJ chambers. The 8x57mmJ would be adequate for any large North American game at medium ranges. Use only .318-inch diameter bullets.

This cartridge is now universally called the 8x57mmJ Mauser or, simply, the 8mm Mauser, and has caused considerable historical confusion. The story goes that the fancy German script capital "I" in the German word "Infanterie" (Infantry) was mistaken by interpreters as a capital "J." If true, this represents an interesting bit of irony, since even the Germans now routinely refer to this cartridge using the bastardized "J" designation. Quality Cartridge (www.qual-cart.com) currently lists brass for this round.

8x57mmJ Mauser Loading Data and Factory Ballistics

Bullet (grains/type)	Powder	Grains	Velocity	Energy	Source/Comments
150 SP	IMR 3031	47.0	2,800	2,611	RWS
170 SP	IMR 3031	45.0	2,600	2,552	RWS
196 SP	RI-1550	46.0	2,225	2,145	RWS
196 SP	FL	FL	2,391	2,488	Factory load
198 SP	FL	FL	2,647	3,075	Factory load

8x56mm Mannlicher-Schoenauer

Historical Notes:	Introduced about 1908 for various Mannlicher-Schoenauer rifles and carbines, the 8x56mm became quite popular and was picked up by other European gunmakers. It was also manufactured for a short time by American ammunition companies, but no U.S. commercial sporting rifles were chambered for it.
General Comments:	The 8x56mm Mannlicher has seen only limited use in the United States, although it is popular in Europe. Ballistically, it is a little more powerful than the .35 Remington. Both shoot approximately the same weight bullet at similar velocity. By American standards, this would be a good short-range cartridge for deer or black bear. While it is a good cartridge, performance is no better than what is available in American chamberings. Western Cartridge Co. discontinued it about 1938. Bullets of .323-inch diameter are used for handloading. This cartridge should not be confused with the 8x56mm Hungarian. Quality Cartridge (www.qual-cart.com) currently lists brass for this round.

8x56mm Mannlicher-Schoenauer Loading Data and Factory Ballistics

Bullet (grains/type)	Powder	Grains	Velocity	Energy	Source/Comments
170 SP	IMR 4895	44.0	2,260	1,935	N/A
200 SP	IMR 3031	40.0	2,050	1,875	N/A
200 SP	FL	FL	2,165	1,920	Western factory load
200 SP	FL	FL	2,200	2,150	Eley-Kynoch factory load
202 SP	FL	FL	2,170	2,105	RWS factory load

8x64mmJ Brenneke
8x64mmS Brenneke
8x65RmmJ Brenneke
8x65RmmS Brenneke

Historical Notes:	These two cartridges were developed by Wilhelm Brenneke about 1912 for Mauser rifles and combination guns. Originally, loaded ammunition was furnished only by DWM, but RWS made empty cases for Brenneke. Mauser-system Brenneke rifles are again available for the 8x64mmS cartridge, made in Berlin by the original W. Brenneke firm. The 8x64mm cartridge is based on the 9.3x62mm case, while the 8x65Rmm is based on the 9.3x74Rmm case.
General Comments:	Like most other 8mm cartridges, the 8x64mm and 8x65Rmm are loaded with both .318-inch "J" and .323-inch "S" bullets. Modern rifles are always chambered for the "S"-type bullet. This is a constant source of confusion to Americans who own or are interested in 8mm rifles. It is also the principal reason 8mm

cartridges are not popular here, because even the sporting goods dealers do not want to bother with two bullet diameters and the difficulty they can cause typical customers. The 8x64mmS is very similar to the wildcat 8mm-06 and has plenty of punch for North American big game.

8x64mmJ, 8x65RmmJ, 8x64mmS & 8x65RmmS Brenneke Loading Data and Factory Ballistics

Bullet (grains/type)	Powder	Grains	Velocity	Energy	Source/Comments
150 SP	IMR 4350	60.0	2,770	2,560	N/A
170 SP	IMR 4064	52.0	2,710	2,760	N/A
225 SP	IMR 4831	61.0	2,400	2,900	N/A
225 SP	IMR 4350	57.0	2,450	2,955	N/A
154 SP	FL	FL	2,952	2,986	Factory load
185 SP	FL	FL	2,890	3,420	Factory load
227 SP	FL	FL	2,578	3,347	Factory load

8x57mmJS Mauser

Historical Notes: Information on the 8x57mm is given in Chapters 1 and 6. As a military round, the 8mm Mauser is another casualty of World War II, replaced by the .30-06 and the 7.62x51mm NATO round in the West and by the Russian M-43 or 7.62x39mm in the East. As a sporting round, the 8mm Mauser is still popular, and many rifles in this chambering are in use. European sporting loads put it in the same class as the .30-06, fully capable of handling any game or situation the .30-06 can. American manufacturers load this cartridge to lower velocity and pressure than European makers. The "S" bullet diameter is .323-inch.

8x57mmJS Mauser Loading Data and Factory Ballistics

Bullet (grains/type)	Powder	Grains	Velocity	Energy	Source/Comments
150 SP	IMR 4064	50.0	2,800	2,612	Sierra, Hornady
170 SP	H380	49.0	2,500	2,360	Hodgdon, Hornady
200 SP	H205	55.0	2,500	2,776	Speer
220 SP	IMR 4064	39.0	2,200	2,365	Sierra, Barnes
250 SP	RI-15	42.0	2,250	2,811	Barnes
165 SP	FL	FL	2,854	2,985	Norma factory load
170 SP	FL	FL	2,657	2,666	Hirtenberger factory load
198 SP	FL	FL	2,732	3,282	RWS factory load

8x57RmmJS Mauser

Historical Notes: This is the rimmed version of the 8x57mmJS German military round, for use in single-shot and combination guns. Introduced in 1888 with the .318-inch "J" bullet, it was adapted in 1905 to the larger "S"-type, or .323-inch diameter bullet, corresponding to a similar change in the military round. Popular in Europe and listed in the latest RWS and Hirtenberger catalog, it is seldom seen in the United States.

General Comments: The 8x57RmmJS gives the same performance as the Rimless 8x57mmJS Mauser familiar to American shooters. It is in the same class as the .30-06 and would do for any North American big game. RWS and Hirtenberger cases and ammunition with American Boxer primers are available, but other European brand cases are made for the Berdan primer. Be sure you use the proper bullet diameter for your particular gun. RWS cartridges for the .323-inch, or "S," bore size have a blackened primer and a cannelured bullet.

Bullet diameters are clearly marked on the box. The "S" is available in heavier loadings and higher velocities than the "J" (.318-inch) loading.

Hirtenberger, as its own entity, is no longer in business, having been taken over by Swedish conglomerate RUAG Ammotec (www.ruag.com/en/Ammotec/Ammotec_Home). Original Hirtenberger ammo is occasionally found in the surplus marketplace. RUAG is also the parent company of the European brands RWS, Rottweil, GECO, and Norma and markets ammo for both civilian and law enforcement use under those original names, as well as the Hitenberger brand.

8x57RmmJS Mauser Loading Data and Factory Ballistics

Bullet (grains/type)	Powder	Grains	Velocity	Energy	Source/Comments
170 SP	IMR 4895	49.0	2,650	2,660	8x57mmJR (.318-inch bullet)
196 SP	IMR 4064	45.0	2,440	2,600	N/A
225 SP	IMR 4350	50.0	2,230	2,498	N/A
170 SP	FL	FL	2,591	2,535	Hirtenberger factory load, 8x57RmmJS (.323-inch bullet)
178 SP	FL	FL	2,380	2,230	Factory load, 8x57RmmJ (.318-inch bullet)
196 SP	FL	FL	2,312	2,327	Hirtenberger factory load, 8x57RmmJS (.323-inch bullet)
227 SP	FL	FL	2,130	2,290	Factory load, 8x57RmmJ (.318-inch bullet)

8x54mm Krag-Jorgensen

Historical Notes: This cartridge is based on the necked-up 6.5x55mm Swedish-Norwegian military round. The purpose of this chambering was to provide an 8mm cartridge that would operate in the 6.5mm Krag-Jorgensen bolt-action rifle used by Norway. By retaining the original case, this could be done by re-barreling alone with no alteration of the action or magazine. The 8x54mm was used for target shooting and hunting and is seldom encountered outside the Scandinavian countries. It is of practically the same power as the 8x58Rmm Danish Krag military round. It could be used for almost any North American big game. It is no longer in production, and this ammunition has become a collector's item. For handloading, use bullets of .323-inch diameter.

8x54mm Krag-Jorgensen Loading Data and Factory Ballistics

Bullet (grains/type)	Powder	Grains	Velocity	Energy	Source/Comments
150 SP	IMR 3031	52.0	2,850	2,718	N/A
196 SP	IMR 4895	47.0	2,370	2,560	N/A
196 SP	FL	FL	2,295	2,300	Factory load

8x68mmS RWS

Historical Notes: First loaded by RWS in 1938-'39 for marketing in the spring of 1939, this cartridge is still listed in its latest catalogs, as well as in Hirtenberger catalogs. This is one of the most modern and powerful of the 8mm cartridges. After the 1:9½ twist of the standard 8mm barrel was found to be unnecessarily fast, a 1:11 twist was adopted.

General Comments: The 8x68mmS is in the same class as the .338 Winchester Magnum, although it has a slightly smaller-diameter bullet of less weight. It is powerful enough for the largest and toughest North American big game and would be superior to the .300 H&H Magnum for African hunting. Some authorities compare it to the .300 Weatherby or the .300 Winchester Magnum, but the 8x68mmS has an edge over both.

This is one 8mm furnished only in a single bullet size, .323-inch. Case dimensions are similar to the belted .300 Magnums, but the 8x68mmS is a rimless cartridge with no belt. It has not been used in the United States very widely to date, but would be popular if more hunters were familiar with it. It is one of the best European cartridges for all-round use in North America. Performance is almost identical to the 8mm Remington Magnum.

Hirtenberger, as its own entity, is no longer in business, having been taken over by Swedish conglomerate RUAG Ammotec (www.ruag.com/en/Ammotec/Ammotec_Home). Original Hirtenberger ammo is occasionally found in the surplus marketplace. RUAG is also the parent company of the European brands RWS, Rottweil, GECO, and Norma, and markets ammo for both civilian and law enforcement use under those original names, as well as the Hitenberger brand.

8x68mmS RWS Loading Data and Factory Ballistics

Bullet (grains/type)	Powder	Grains	Velocity	Energy	Source/Comments
125 SP	W760	81.0	3,500	3,401	Hornady
150 SP	W760	76.0	3,300	3,628	Hornady
150 SP	IMR 4350	73.5	3,200	3,412	Hornady
170 SP	IMR 4831	75.5	3,100	3,629	Hornady
170 SP	IMR 4350	72.0	3,100	3,629	Hornady
200 SP	RI-22	78.0	2,971	3,920	RWS (optimistic)
220 SP	IMR 4831	67.0	2,700	3,562	Hornady
187 SP	FL	FL	3,180	4,195	Factory load (optimistic)
196 SP	FL	FL	2,985	3,879	Hirtenberger factory load (optimistic)
200 SP	FL	FL	2,985	3,958	Hirtenberger factory load (optimistic)

8x60mmJ Mauser & RWS
8x60mmS Mauser & RWS
8x60RmmJ Mauser & RWS
8x60RmmS Mauser & RWS

Historical Notes: The 8x60mmS and 8x60RmmS were introduced, soon after World War I, to replace the 8x57mmJS in sporting rifles. After the war, German civilians were forbidden to own rifles in the military chambering, yet many did! Converting these to 8x60mmS was a simple chamber lengthening job, not costly, and many were so altered to be legally licensed. A few years later, the 8x60mm was offered in the old bullet diameter (.318-inch) as well, probably to add performance to older 8x57mmJ sporting rifles, via the same easy conversion.

General Comments: The 8x60mm comes in a confusing variety of types and loads. Both rimless and rimmed case are available for the .318-inch and "S" (.323-inch) diameter bullets. There is a standard and a magnum loading, as well as one called the Magnum-Bombe. Case dimensions are the same, but there is a difference in bullet weight and velocity. In the standard load, the 8x60mm is almost identical to the .30-06 in power, but the magnum loading brings it up to the .300 H&H Magnum performance level. It has sufficient power for North American big game and could be used for anything the .30-06 can handle. On heavy game, such as moose, elk, or grizzly bear, it would have an edge over the .30-06, if one used maximum loads. It is a popular round in Europe and has been used to some extent in Africa, although most African hunters do not consider it any better than the .300 H&H. It is still loaded by RWS (http://rws-munition/de/en.html). Quality Cartridge (www.qual-cart.com) currently lists brass for the 8x60mmS Mauser round.

Bullet (grains/type)	Powder	Grains	Velocity	Energy	Source/Comments
159 SP	IMR 3031	48.0	2,820	2,805	N/A
196 SP	IMR 4895	49.0	2,570	2,875	N/A
159 SP	FL	FL	2,820	2,805	Norma factory load ("S" bore)
187 SP	FL	FL	2,810	3,275	RWS factory load ("S" bore)
196 SP	FL	FL	2,580	2,890	RWS factory load

8x72Rmm Sauer/8x72Rmm Jugdewehr/8x72R .360-inch

Historical Notes: This straight, rimmed case was developed by Sauer & Sohn for use in combination guns. The 8x72Rmm is sometimes listed as the 8x72Rmm S&S. Date of introduction has not been established, but the old DWM case No. 574 would indicate sometime around 1910. It is obsolete.

General Comments: The 8x72Rmm was derived from the older 9.3x72Rmm. The principal difference between the two is caliber. Instead of having a conventional bottleneck, the 8x72Rmm case is full-length tapered to accommodate an 8mm bullet. Late RWS catalogs list this as a discontinued number. In power, it compares more or less with the .35 Remington. The 8x72Rmm would be useful mostly for woods hunting of deer-size animals. For handloading, bullets of .323-inch diameter should be used.

8x72Rmm Sauer Loading Data and Factory Ballistics

Bullet (grains/type)	Powder	Grains	Velocity	Energy	Source/Comments
150 SP	Rl-15	45.0	2,334	1,815	RWS
170 SP	Rl-15	43.0	2,240	1,810	RWS
210 Lead	IMR 4198	28.0	1,850	1,602	Lyman #323471GC
225 SP	IMR 3031	38.0	1,910	1,830	N/A
227 SP	FL	FL	1,900	1,825	Factory load

.338 Blaser Magnum

Historical Notes: The idea for four new Blaser cartridges originated in a Las Vegas hotel. Bernhard Knöbel, who was relatively new at Blaser, wanted something fresh for the brand. Working with Christer Larsson of Norma, a man who is a very savvy ballistics engineer, they decided on a new line of cartridges based on the .404 Jeffery case without a magnum belt. The plan was to develop four cartridges—a 7mm, .30, .338, and .375—that would have a ballistic advantage over the 7mm Remington Magnum, .300 Winchester Magnum, .338 Winchester Magnum, and the famed .375 H&H. An additional requirement was that all four of these cartridges would operate at a maximum average pressure of 58,000 psi. Norma engineers, after extensive testing and evaluation, decided on barrels with four grooves, a case with more taper than the Winchester Short Magnums, a neck length that was 1.1-caliber, and a shoulder angle of 30 degrees.

General Comments: The .338 Blaser Magnum cartridge is currently available only in rifles from Blaser currently sold in Europe. Therefore, it is listed as a European Sporting Rifle cartridge. In the near future, Blaser expects to offer its rifles chambered for all four of its new magnum cartridges in the United States. Norma currently catalogs one .338 Blaser load, a 230-grain Norma Oryx bullet at 2822 fps, but ballistic reports from Norma show load development work with a 210-grain Barnes Tipped Triple Shock being driven to 2950 fps, demonstrating about a 100 fps advantage over the .338 Winchester Magnum, but from a beltless case. Whether this cartridge will gain a following in the States remains to be seen, but that seems doubtful, unless American sporting arms manufacturers start chambering it in more affordable rifles.

.338 Blaser Magnum Factory Ballistics

Bullet (grains/type)	Powder	Grains	Velocity	Energy	Source
210 Barnes Tipped TSX	FL	FL	2,950	4,059	Norma
230 Norma Oryx	FL	FL	2,822	4,068	Norma

.338 Norma Magnum

Historical Notes: In early 2007, a ballistician by the name of Jimmie Sloan began looking into long-range shooting and what it took to achieve success at 1,000 and 1,500 yards with a portable individual weapon system. Sloan was unsatisfied with the cartridges available at the time. He wanted a rifle cartridge capable of shooting a bullet with a very high ballistic coefficient, one that also weighed 300 grains and traveled at velocities around 2800 fps. A wildcat cartridge known as the .338R was the result, and the first reamers for the cartridge were manufactured by Dave Kiff at Pacific Tool & Gauge. Norma AB Precision showed interest in the cartridge, and the .338 Norma Magnum was born. The U.S. Military has also shown interest in this cartridge, since its legitimization by Norma. The cartridge case for the .338 Norma Magnum is very similar to the .338 Lapua Magnum, however, the .338 Norma Magnum has a slightly larger diameter shoulder and is about a quarter-inch shorter.

General Comments: Many that are in the know, when it comes to long-range shooting, consider the .338 Norma Magnum superior to the .338 Lapua Magnum. Balistically, the .338 Norma Magnum is very similar to the .338 Lapua Magnum. However, with the .338 Norma Magnum, a 300-grain Sierra Matchking can be loaded so that it does not intrude into the case where gases could flow over the heel of the boat-tail of the bullet. The cartridge is gaining a solid following and is a perfect example of how wildcatters like Jimmie Sloan can positively influence cartridge development. Currently, Black Hills (www.black-hills.com) is offering loaded ammunition.—*R.A.M.*

.338 Norma Magnum Loading Data and Factory Ballistics

Bullet (grains/type)	Powder	Grains	Velocity	Energy	Source/Comments
200 Nosler Accubond	MRP	95.0	3,211	4,578	Norma
230 Norma Oryx	MRP	90.5	2,956	4,462	Norma
300 Sierra Matchking	MRP 2	85.0	2,644	4,656	Norma

9x71mm Peterlongo

Historical Notes: This obsolete cartridge was developed by the Austrian gun maker Johann Peterlongo, of Innsbruck. His rifles have not been made for a good many years, and his products are all but unknown in the United States, except to cartridge collectors. There is also an 8x71mm Peterlongo cartridge based on this same case. A 227-grain soft-point round-nose bullet was used in this cartridge.

General Comments: 9x71 Peterlongo aficionado Victor H. Schaefferkoetter handloads this round by starting with a 9.3X74R as a parent case. He then turns the rim to .466, re-cuts the extractor groove, trims and sizes the case in a 9X71 Peterlongo full-length die, and fireforms the round. Cartridge overall length is 3.35 inches. His Johann Peterlongo Mauser Sporter has a groove diameter of .363, so he starts with a .358 bullet, a 200-grain jacketed roundnose, then swages it to .355. He puts it atop 57 grains of IMR-4064 and gets 2,501 fps muzzle velocity and 2,778 ft-lbs.

9x71mm Peterlongo Factory Ballistics

Bullet (grains/type)	Powder	Grains	Velocity	Energy	Source/Comments
184	FL	FL	2,575	2,710	German 1932 Catalog
200 RN	IMR 4064	57	2,501	2,778	Victor H. Schaefferkoetter

9x56mm Mannlicher-Schoenauer

Historical Notes: The 9x56mm Mannlicher-Schoenauer was one of the early cartridges for the Austrian-made Mannlicher-Schoenauer sporting rifle. The rifle was introduced in 1900, and most of the original cartridges for it were developed between 1900 and 1910. Catalog references indicate that the 9x56mm was added to the line of available chamberings about 1905. Remington loaded this round until the late 1930s. Modern Mannlicher-Schoenauer sporting rifles were once chambered for the 9x56. The 9x56mm is no longer loaded in Europe.

General Comments: The 9x56mm developed a moderate following, but most hunters preferred the more powerful 9x57mm Mauser. The 8x56mm Mannlicher is still loaded, and one can make 9x56mm ammunition by expanding the neck of the smaller caliber case. The 9x56mm is a notch or two above the .35 Remington, but is largely a short-range woods cartridge for deer or possibly elk. It was never very popular in the United States, because it had little to offer beyond available American cartridges. However, it is a perfectly good cartridge if you do not hunt anything larger than deer and are willing to put up with the difficulty of trying to find the now-obsolete ammunition. For handloading, use .356-inch diameter bullets. Quality Cartridge (www.qual-cart.com) currently lists brass for this round.

9x56mm Mannlicher-Schoenauer Loading Data and Factory Ballistics

Bullet (grains/type)	Powder	Grains	Velocity	Energy	Source/Comments
200 SP	IMR 3031	40.0	2,110	1,980	N/A
205 SP	FL	FL	2,114	2,234	Factory load
245 SP	FL	FL	2,100	2,400	Eley-Kynoch factory load
280 SP	FL	FL	1,850	2,128	Remington factory load

9x57mm Mauser
9x57Rmm Mauser

Historical Notes: Shortly after the 8x57mm Mauser military round was introduced in 1888, an entire family of cartridges was developed on this case length by necking it both up and down. The rimless cases were used in bolt-action repeating rifles and a rimmed version was usually made available for combination or single-shot guns. The 9x57Rmm is the rimmed twin of the pictured cartridge. This was a popular round used all over the world, and the old Remington Model 30 and Winchester Model 54 bolt-action rifles were available in 9x57mm. Most American ammunition companies loaded it until 1936-'38. It is now obsolete both in Europe and the U.S.

General Comments: The 9x57mm Mauser is in the same class as the .358 Winchester and would be suitable for all North American big game under most hunting conditions, although it is not a long-range cartridge. African hunters liked it as a meat-getter, but considered it too light for dangerous game. Velocity is moderate, but, with the proper bullet, it penetrates well on thin-skinned animals. Bullet diameter is .356-inch, but .357- to .358-inch bullets can be swaged down and used. Quality Cartridge (www.qual-cart.com) currently lists brass for both versions of this round.

9x57mm, 9x57Rmm Mauser Loading Data and Factory Ballistics

Bullet (grains/type)	Powder	Grains	Velocity	Energy	Source/Comments
245 Lead	IMR 3031	38.0	1,950	2,075	Lyman #358318GC
250 SP	IMR 3031	44.0	2,260	2,980	N/A
280 SP	IMR 3031	43.0	2,030	2,570	N/A
280 SP	IMR 4064	46.0	2,045	2,610	N/A
205 SP	FL	FL	2,423	2,682	Factory load
245 SP	FL	FL	2,150	2,520	Eley-Kynoch factory load
275 SP	FL	FL	1,850	2,090	Remington factory load
281 SP	FL	FL	1,920	2,285	RWS factory load

9x63mm

Historical Notes: At one time, there was a family of metric cartridges based on the rimless 63mm case length. However, all these German or Austrian innovations are currently obsolete. Most of these were introduced after 1905, but little information about them is available.

General Comments: The 9x63mm cartridge is interesting, because it's based on the same case length as the .30-06 and is, therefore, very similar to the .35 Whelen. It has a slightly longer body length and a more abrupt shoulder angle than the American round, otherwise, there is little difference. Each delivered practically identical ballistics. The 9x63mm would be a good choice for the heavier varieties of North American big game and many African species. Standard .357- to .358-inch bullets can be used for handloading. Factory ammunition used a 231-grain bullet.

9x63mm Loading Data and Factory Ballistics (Note: *Estimated ballistics.)

Bullet (grains/type)	Powder	Grains	Velocity	Energy	Source/Comments
231 SP	4320	57.0	2,510	3,240	N/A
250 SP	4320	56.0	2,390	3,180	N/A
231 SP	FL	FL	2,550	3,336 *	Factory load

9x70Rmm Mauser

Historical Notes: This is the same cartridge as the British .400/360 Westley Richards Nitro Express and has been obsolete for many years. It originated around 1900 and was picked up by German gunmakers for the Mauser action and other rifles intended for the African trade. It was gradually replaced by the 9.3x74Rmm.

General Comments: The Germans used a different loading than the British, with a lighter bullet at higher velocity. The German load can be fired in British double-barrel rifles, but is unsatisfactory because the barrels are not regulated for it. The .375 H&H Magnum retired the bulk of the cartridges in this class, and these cartridges are now used mostly in old rifles. The 9x70Rmm would do for any North American big game, but was not satisfactory as an all-round cartridge in Africa. This is *not* the same as the .360 No. 2 Nitro. Loading data is unavailable.

9x70Rmm Mauser Factory Ballistics

Bullet (grains/type)	Powder	Grains	Velocity	Energy	Source/Comments
217 SP	FL	FL	2,477	2,970	Factory load, German
314 SP	FL	FL	1,900	2,520	Factory load, British

.358 Norma Magnum

Historical Notes: This cartridge was developed by Norma and introduced in the United States, in 1959. At the start, no rifles were chambered for the .358 Norma Magnum. However, empty cases and loaded ammunition were available. The Schultz & Larsen Model 65 and the Husqvarna bolt-action were made available in this chambering, early in 1960. No mainstream American gun manufacturer ever chambered this cartridge.

General Comments: The .358 Norma Magnum is a short, magnum-type cartridge intended to work through standard-length actions. It is nearly identical to the wildcat .35 Ackley belted, short magnum. It is also nearly identical to the wildcat .35-338, which is the .338 Winchester necked-up to .35-caliber.

The .358 Norma Magnum delivers the same performance as the .375 H&H Magnum and would be suitable for the same range of game. It is overpowered for most North American big game, but would be an excellent choice for the big Kodiak bears. It is another good all-around number for the person who wants to be prepared for hunting anything. A-Square has reintroduced this ammunition.

.358 Norma Magnum Loading Data and Factory Ballistics

Bullet (grains/type)	Powder	Grains	Velocity	Energy	Source/Comments
180 SP	IMR 4895	69.0	3,100	3,842	Speer
200 SP	IMR 3031	66.5	2,900	3,736	Hornady
225 SP	IMR 4350	75.0	2,900	4,203	Nosler
250 SP	IMR 4320	68.0	2,800	4,353	Hornady
250 SP	IMR 4350	76.0	2,700	4,048	Speer
250 SP	Norma MRP	78.0	2,500	3,470	Speer
300 SP	IMR 4350	71.0	2,600	4,504	Barnes
250 SP	FL	FL	2,790	4,322	Norma factory load

9.3x57mm Mauser

Historical Notes: This is a rimless necked case and is another of the cartridges based on the 8x57mm Mauser expanded to take larger diameter bullets. It dates back to 1900 or earlier, and was used in both Mauser and Mannlicher sporting rifles. Except for the larger diameter bullet, it is nearly identical to the 9x57mm. The 9.3x57mm is not listed in the current RWS catalog, but Norma (www.norma-usa.com) makes cases and loaded ammunition. Apparently, no rifles are currently made for this round. A cartridge designated as the 9.3x57Rmm is not the rimmed version of this cartridge, rather that number has a straight case.

General Comments: The 9.3x57mm is in the same class as the .35 WCF and .358 Winchester. It would do for any North American big game at short to moderate ranges. It would be good for hunting in brush or heavily wooded areas. It may also be listed as the 9.2mm Mauser, and is often confused with the 9x57mm Mauser, because these cartridges differ only in bullet diameter. To further complicate matters, there is a 9.5x57mm Mannlicher, which looks similar, but is not interchangeable. Barnes (www.barnesbullets.com) and Speer (www.speer-bullets.com) make appropriate bullets for handloading this number.

9.3x57mm Mauser Loading Data and Factory Ballistics

Bullet (grains/type)	Powder	Grains	Velocity	Energy	Source/Comments
232 SP	IMR 3031	47.0	2,330	2,785	N/A
286 SP	IMR 3031	43.0	2,070	2,705	N/A
286 SP	FL	FL	2,065	2,714	Norma factory load

9.3x53mm Swiss
9.3x53Rmm Swiss

Historical Notes: These two cartridges were popular in Switzerland for target shooting. Rifles of these chamberings are rare in the United States, and the cartridge is of interest mostly to collectors. Factory ballistics place these two cartridges in the same class as the .35 Remington. Either would do for any game up to and including deer at short to medium range. Both were introduced in the mid-1920s, possibly 1925. These cartridges use .365-inch diameter bullets. Barnes (www.barnesbullets.com) and Speer (www.speer-bullets.com) make appropriate bullets.

9.3x53mm Swiss, 9.3x53Rmm Swiss Factory Ballistics

Bullet (grains/type)	Powder	Grains	Velocity	Energy	Source/Comments
200 SP	FL	FL	2,000	1,780	Factory load, Swiss 9.3x53mm
200 SP	FL	FL	2,054	1,960	Factory load, Swiss 9.3x53mm

9.3x72Rmm Sauer

Historical Notes: The 9.3x72Rmm Sauer is an obsolete cartridge developed by Sauer & Sohn for single-shot, double-barrel and combination guns. Rifles in this chambering are scarce, and it is largely a collector's cartridge. It was loaded with a 186-grain bullet. Standard ballistics and loading data are not available. Barnes (www.barnesbullets.com) and Speer (www.speer-bullets.com) make appropriate bullets for handloading.

9.3x74Rmm

Historical Notes: The 9.3x74Rmm is a popular German cartridge for single-shot, double-barrel, and combination guns. It originated in the early 1900s in answer to the .400/360 Nitro Express, which British gunmakers developed in various versions. It is quite similar to, but slightly longer than, the .400/360 Westley Richards, also loaded and chambered in various rifles by the Germans. The 9.3x74Rmm is listed in the current RWS and Norma catalog. Austrian and German combination guns are still available in this chambering, as are barrels for Thompson/Center rifles from SSK Industries.

General Comments: A popular round for heavy game, the 9.3x74Rmm is on par with the .375 Flanged Magnum Nitro Express. It gained a good reputation in Africa for general use against most game, including elephant. It would be more than adequate for North American big game. An over/under combination gun, in 9.3x74Rmm chambering and with a 12- or 16-gauge shot barrel, would be a terrific outfit for the world-wide, one-gun hunter. There is not much of anything, large or small, that such a gun could not handle. For handloading, .365-inch diameter bullets should be used. Barnes (www.barnesbullets.com) and Speer (www.speer-bullets.com) make such bullets, which should work well in most rifles. A-Square (www.a-squareco.com) and Norma (www.norma.cc; www.ruag.com/ammotec) offer ammunition and components.

9.3x74Rmm Loading Data and Factory Ballistics

Bullet (grains/type)	Powder	Grains	Velocity	Energy	Source/Comments
250 SP	H380	60.0	2,400	3,198	Barnes
270 SP	IMR 4895	55.0	2,300	3,172	Speer
286 SP	IMR 4064	55.0	2,300	3,360	Barnes
232 SP	FL	FL	2,630	3,535	Norma factory load
258 SP	FL	FL	2,460	3,465	RWS factory load
285 SP	FL	FL	2,280	3,290	RWS factory load
286 SP	FL	FL	2,360	3,530	Norma/A-Square factory load

9.3x64mm Brenneke

Historical Notes: This is the largest and most powerful of the various Brenneke cartridges. Wilhelm Brenneke was one of the best known German cartridge designers; he developed the popular and effective Brenneke-Torpedo bullets.* His career began in the late 1890s, but most of his modern cartridges were perfected in the period around 1910. He was a contemporary of Charles Newton in the development of high-velocity cartridges. There are marked similarities between the Brenneke and Newton cartridges, but it is probably a case of parallel development, rather than any influence of one by the other. Brenneke was born in 1864 and died in 1951. The 9.3x64mm is still loaded by RWS. German-made, Mauser-system bolt-action rifles are still available for the 7.8mm and 9.3mm Brenneke cartridges.

General Comments: Except in name, the 9.3x64mm has "Magnum" written all over it. This .375 H&H Magnum-class number is certainly adequate for most game worldwide. John Taylor rated it right along with the .375 H&H Magnum as an excellent all-round cartridge for African hunting. Not well known in the United States, it would probably be more of a success here if better publicized. Barnes (www.barnesbullets.com) and Speer (www.speer-bullets.com) make appropriate bullets. A-Square (www.a-squareco.com) offers ammunition and components. Quality Cartridge (www.qual-cart.com) lists this brass.

* For an account of Brenneke's life and developments, see the Gun Digest 14th Edition.

9.3x64mm Brenneke Loading Data and Factory Ballistics

Bullet (grains/type)	Powder	Grains	Velocity	Energy	Source/Comments
286 SP	IMR 4350	76.0	2,725	4,716	RWS

9.3x64mm Brenneke Loading Data and Factory Ballistics

Bullet (grains/type)	Powder	Grains	Velocity	Energy	Source/Comments
270 SP	RI-15	67.0	2,820	4,768	RWS
293 SP	IMR 4350	65.0	2,629	4,563	RWS
247 SP	FL	FL	2,760	4,178	RWS factory load
285 SP	FL	FL	2,690	4,580	RWS factory load
286 Lion	FL	FL	2,650	4,460	A-Square factory load
293 SP	FL	FL	2,570	4,298	RWS factory load

9.3x65R Collath

General Comments: This is one of a series of obsolete cartridges developed by the European gunsmith whose name appears with the cartridge. He was active in the early 1900s and well known in Europe, but his developments are recognized in the United States only by cartridge collectors. This is a rimmed, bottlenecked case with a long body and short neck. It was loaded with a 193-grain flat-nose, soft-point bullet. Standard ballistics are unknown.

9.3x74R Nimrod

Historical Notes: The Thieme & Schlegelmilch Nimrod Gewehrfabrik (Nimrod Rifle Factory) was founded in Suhl, in 1852, by Heinrich Schlegelmilch and his friend Thieme. Thieme & Schlegelmilch introduced the 9.3x75R Nimrod circa 1905 to duplicate the ballistics of older and popular black-powder 9.3 cartridges before smokeless loads were developed for them. It didn't last much past 1910. The 9.3x75R was predated by the 9.3x72R and a similar Sauer & Sohn cartridge. The 9.3x75R was too long to chamber in many older firearms, thus preventing cross-use problems, according to 9.3x75Rmm aficionado Victor H. Schaefferkoetter. An interesting piece of trivia, the word "nimrod" means a "mighty hunter."

General Comments: One characteristic that distinguishes the 9.3mm Nimrod case types is that they all have short necks, the result of a more gradual taper from the base to about 10 to 11 millimeters from the case mouth, Schaefferkoetter said. "The ring-type bullet I have goes .367 at the ring, the largest diameter on the bullet. The base mics .363 and the front driving band goes .352. As with many pre-1900 American firearm bores, groove and chamber dimensions can vary a lot," Schaefferkoetter said.

Handloads from Sherman Bell and Grahame Wright are the best resource for starting loads. Schaefferkoetter said the load below will work without a filler, and pressures will be fine. However, velocities are erratic, more than 200 fps difference shot to shot, and accuracy is poor. Schaefferkoetter forms cases from 9.3x82R brass, trimmed to length, full length size. He uses open-cell foam filler cut to fill the remaining space in the case and hold the powder against the primer.—*W.T.W.*

9.3x75Rmm Nimrod Factory Ballistics

Bullet (grains/type)	Powder	Grains	Velocity	Energy	Source
.358-caliber 200 JRN	IMR 3031	36	1,764	1,382	Victor A. Schaefferkoetter

9.1x40Rmm

Historical Notes: This is an obsolete cartridge for target and small-game shooting that was popular in the early 1900s. It was of black-powder origin and, so, probably originated before 1900. It would be all right for small to medium game, but is underpowered for anything else. Loading data not available.

9.1x40Rmm Factory Ballistics

Bullet (grains/type)	Powder	Grains	Velocity	Energy	Source/Comments
140 lead	FL	FL	1,800	1,014	Factory load

9.5x57mm Mannlicher-Schoenauer/9.5x56mm MS

Historical Notes: Introduced in 1910 for Mannlicher-Schoenauer rifles and carbines, this cartridge is also listed as the 9.5x56mm, 9.5x56.7mm, and the .375 Nitro Express Rimless. Old Eley-Kynoch catalogs listed it as the 9.5mm Mannlicher-Schoenauer. It is not listed in current RWS catalogs. No modern rifles are being chambered for it; it lacked sufficient headspace control, indicating that incautious chambering or case annealing could lead to dangerous case stretching and, potentially, case head separations.

General Comments: The 9.5 Mannlicher was popular for a number of years with those who liked the light, handy Mannlicher sporting rifles. It did not have a good reputation in Africa for heavy or dangerous game, but was liked by many as a meat-getter and performed well on thin-skinned, non-dangerous game. It is seldom seen in the United States. This is a good short-range cartridge for almost any North American big game. It is in the same class as the .358 Winchester, but uses a larger diameter bullet that is typically heavier. Quality Cartridge (www.qual-cart.com) currently lists brass for this round.

9.5x57mm Mannlicher-Schoenauer Loading Data and Factory Ballistics

Bullet (grains/type)	Powder	Grains	Velocity	Energy	Source/Comments
270 SP	IMR 3031	44.0	2,150	2,780	N/A
286 SP	IMR 3031	42.0	2,040	2,638	N/A
270 SP	FL	FL	2,150	2,780	Eley-Kynoch factory load
272 SP	FL	FL	2,148	2,791	Factory load

9.5x73mm Miller-Greiss Magnum

Historical Notes: A special and relatively little-known cartridge developed for or by Miller and Greiss, two gunsmiths of Munich, Germany, this cartridge is based on the necked down .404 Jeffery case. Rifles in this chambering were built on the Mauser bolt-action. The date of introduction isn't known, but would have been some time between 1910 and the early 1920s. The 9.5x73mm represents another German effort to bring out a cartridge competitive with the British .375 H&H Magnum. This one makes it ballistically, but never got close in popularity. Both rifles and cartridges are quite scarce and are now collector's items.

9.5x73mm Miller-Greiss Magnum Factory Ballistics

Bullet (grains/type)	Powder	Grains	Velocity	Energy	Source/Comments
271 SP	FL	FL	2,670	4,310	DWM factory load

9.5x47Rmm

Historical Notes: The 9.5x47Rmm is an obsolete, black-powder target cartridge that dates back to the 1880s. The Germans used a number of bottlenecked cartridges of 46mm to 47mm in length. These cartridges are all very similar, differing mainly in diameter of the bullet used, which varied from 9mm to 11mm. The 9.5x47Rmm (old DWM case No. 23) appears as though it would be interchangeable with the 9.5x47Rmm Martini (old DWM case No. 179), although there are slight differences in case body diameter.

General Comments: Ballistics of these old target cartridges are similar, and one wonders about the great variety. There must have been more than 40 of these at one time, with only slight differences in case length, shape, or capacity. There would be little to gain in listing these chamberings individually, because most are rare collector's gems, and rifles for these cartridges are practically nonexistent. Ballistics are in the class of the .40-60 or .44-40 Winchester. As hunting numbers, all of these would be classified as small- to medium-game numbers by today's standards.

.375 Blaser Magnum

Historical Notes: The idea for four new Blaser cartridges originated in a Las Vegas hotel. Bernhard Knöbel, who was relatively new at Blaser, wanted something fresh for the brand. Working with Christer Larsson of Norma, a man who is a very savvy ballistics engineer, they decided on a new line of cartridges based on the .404 Jeffery case without a magnum belt. The plan was to develop four cartridges—a 7mm, .30, .338, and .375—that would have a ballistic advantage over the 7mm Remington Magnum, .300 Winchester Magnum, .338 Winchester Magnum, and the famed .375 H&H. An additional requirement was that all four of these cartridges would operate at a maximum average pressure of 58,000 psi. Norma engineers, after extensive testing and evaluation, decided on barrels with four grooves, a case with more taper than the Winchester Short Magnums, a neck length that was 1.1-caliber, and a shoulder angle of 30 degrees.

General Comments: The .375 Blaser Magnum cartridge is currently available only in rifles from Blaser currently sold in Europe. Therefore, it is listed as a European Sporting Rifle cartridge. In the near future, Blaser expects to offer its rifles chambered for all four of its new magnum cartridges in the United States. Norma currently catalogs one .375 Blaser load, a 300-grain Norma Oryx bullet at 2690 fps, but ballistic reports from Norma show load development work with a 270-grain Barnes Triple Shock being driven to 2755 fps. These velocities exceed that of the most famous .375-caliber rifle cartridge of all time, the .375 H&H, by about 100 fps. Whether this cartridge will gain a following in the States remains to be seen, but that seems doubtful, unless American sporting arms manufacturers start chambering it in more affordable rifles.

.375 Blaser Magnum Factory Ballistics

Bullet (grains/type)	Powder	Grains	Velocity	Energy	Source
270 Barnes TSX	FL	FL	2,755	4,552	Norma
300 Norma Oryx	FL	FL	2,690	4,821	Norma

9.3x48Rmm/9.3x57Rmm/ 9.3x70Rmm/9.3x72Rmm/ 9.3x80Rmm

Historical Notes: These five cartridges are lumped together, because the only real difference is case length. These cartridges all date back to the 1890s, and all were originally black-powder cartridges. Most of these cartridges were still loaded until the start of World War II, but only the 9.3x72Rmm survived the war and is listed in late RWS catalogs. All are of the straight, rimmed type and were used in single-shot and combination guns.

General Comments: Old catalogs show the same bullet as suitable for all or most of these cartridges. Despite the difference in case length, there really is not much difference in ballistics or power. All are primarily medium-game cartridges fully adequate only for deer or similar animals. These cartridges can best be compared to the .38-55, although that old American cartridge has a slight edge over most of the various straight-cased 9.3s. Few modern guns are being made for any of these chamberings. Barnes (www.barnesbullets.com) makes one style of jacketed flat-point bullet for the .38-55 WCF that should work well in any of these numbers.

Various 9.3x48Rmm, 9.3x57Rmm, 9.3x70Rmm, 9.3x72Rmm, 9.3x80Rmm, 9.3x82Rmm Factory Ballistics

Bullet (grains/type)	Powder	Grains	Velocity	Energy	Source/Comments
160 SP	FL	FL	1,650	973	Factory load
190 SP	FL	FL	1,700	1,225	Factory load
300 SP	FL	FL	1,650	1,820	Factory load
193 SP	FL	FL	2,020	1,750	RWS factory load
193 SP	FL	FL	1,640	1,155	Factory load

10.25x69Rmm Hunting-Express 10.15x68Rmm Express

Historical Notes: This is a long-obsolete black-powder cartridge dating to the 1880-90 period. It was used mostly in single-shot and double-barrel rifles. The Germans had several .40-caliber cartridges that were similar to British rounds in the same class. They also loaded and chambered the various-lengthed British .450/400 cartridges popular around the turn of the century. The 10.25x69Rmm is an intermediate-length version that falls between the .450/400 23/8-inch and 3-inch. Rifles in this chambering are quite scarce.

General Comments: Cartridges of this caliber and class were developed primarily for the African gun trade. In power, these cartridges are similar to the .375 H&H Magnum, if loaded with smokeless powder to maximum performance. The 10.25 would probably do for most African game and is certainly ample for North American big game at moderate ranges. Old black-powder loads are not as effective as later smokeless versions. These cartridges are obsolete and better left to collectors. Bullet diameter is .404-inch.

10.25x69Rmm Hunting-Express Factory Ballistics

Bullet (grains/type)	Powder	Grains	Velocity	Energy	Source/Comments
235 SP	FL	FL	2,100	2,310	Factory smokeless load

10.3x60Rmm Swiss

Historical Notes: A Swiss target cartridge originally developed for single-shot Martini-action rifles, the 10.3x60Rmm is nothing more than the Swiss version of the obsolete British .450/400 (2 -inch) Blackpowder Express. Some Swiss-loaded ammunition is so marked on the box. Some modern bolt-action rifles have been made in Switzerland in this chambering. The British loaded a 255-grain lead bullet, but the Swiss use heavier bullets of soft-point or full jacketed type with smokeless powder. The Swiss loading is in the same class as the .405 Winchester and would do for any North American big game at short to medium range. This chambering is still popular in Switzerland, and guns and ammunition are still manufactured in Switzerland and in Germany by RWS. In at least one Swiss canton, the 10.3x60Rmm is the only lawful cartridge for big-game hunting. Bullet diameter is .415-inch.

10.3x60Rmm Swiss Factory Ballistics

Bullet (grains/type)	Powder	Grains	Velocity	Energy	Source/Comments
253 SP	RI-15	66.0	2,432	3,324	RWS
330 SP	FL	FL	2,070	3,143	RWS and Swiss factory loading

10.5x47Rmm

Historical Notes: One of a series of obsolete black-powder target cartridges of varying caliber based on a 47mm bottlenecked case, all of which date back to the 1880s and '90s and differ only in caliber. Some of these cartridges originated with the Austrian gunsmith Stahl. Bullet weight varied according to caliber. The 10.5x47Rmm used bullets from 260 to 298 grains. Factory ballistics are not available.

10.5x47Rmm fan Victor H. Schaefferkoetter has worked up a safe load in his rifle. To begin, he makes cast bullets of a 25-1 alloy. The result is a 270-grain .413 projectile. He uses a 50/50 beeswax/castor oil lube. The charge is 62 grains of Scheutzen Ffg black powder. Powder is dropped through a 24-inch drop tube and a .030 card wad is seated on the powder. It develops 1,379 fps muzzle velocity and 1,140 ft-lbs of energy at the muzzle.

10.5x47Rmm Loading Data

Bullet (grains/type)	Powder	Grains	Velocity	Energy	Source/Comments
270 Alloy cast (.413 diameter)	Black powder (Ffg)	62	1,379	1,140	Victor H. Schaefferkoetter

10.75x73mm (.404 Rimless Nitro Express/.404 Jeffery)

Historical Notes: This is the metric designation for the .404 Jeffery or .404 Rimless Nitro Express. One of the most popular rounds used in Africa, the .404/10.75x73mm is now back in production at RWS. The new RWS loads are assembled with Australian-made Woodleigh bullets having bonded cores and clad-steel jackets. Ruger now offers the bolt-action M77 and the No. 1 single-shot in this chambering.

General Comments: Overall length is the same as the popular .375 H&H Magnum, so rifles with magnum-length actions are suitable for this cartridge. Some say it is too powerful for North American game, but, as Elmer Keith used to say, "Too much gun always beats the alternative." Bullets for handloading are offered by Barnes (www.barnesbullets.com) and Woodleigh (www.woodleighbullets.com).

10.75x73mm (.404 Rimless Nitro Express/.404 Jeffery) Loading Data and Factory Ballistics

Bullet (grains/type)	Powder	Grains	Velocity	Energy	Source/Comments
347 SP	RI-15	80.0	2,335	4,200	RWS
400 SP	RI-15	75.5	2,220	4,379	RWS
400 SP/FMJ	FL	FL	2,315	4,761	RWS factory load

10.3x65Rmm Baenziger

Historical Notes: This was at one time a popular European target cartridge, particularly in Switzerland. It is now obsolete, but the Swiss manufactured it until after the end of World War II. Swiss Martini-action single-shot rifles were made for the 10.3x65Rmm. This cartridge is actually the brass 2.5-inch .410 (10.35mm, or 36-gauge) shotgun shell loaded with a lead or soft-point bullet. However, the rim is a bit thicker than the average .410 shotshell's. DWM case No. 164 is listed in the 1904 catalog under schrotflinten, or shotguns. Ammunition can be made from brass .410 cases, although the rim usually has to be built up to the proper thickness. A brass washer is the easiest solution to this. The equally hard-to-find .405 Winchester case can also be used, if trimmed to the right length and the rim turned down. New brass cases from Bertram Bullet Co. are being imported. Lyman #412263 (290-grain) cast bullets can be sized and used. Power is about the same as the .44 Magnum revolver cartridge fired in a rifle, so it would make a fairly satisfactory short-range deer number. There is also a 10.3x65Rmm Swiss target cartridge (old DWM case No. 237A) that is practically identical to the above except for a thin rim. This one has been obsolete for a good many years. Cases are currently made by Bertram Bullet Co. and sold through Buffalo Arms Co. (www.buffaloarms.com).

10.3x65Rmm Baenziger Loading Data and Factory Ballistics

Bullet (grains/type)	Powder	Grains	Velocity	Energy	Source/Comments
290 Lead	3031	43.0	1,625	1,705	Lyman #412263
285 SP	FL	FL	1,785	1,940	Factory load

10.75x68mm Mauser

Historical Notes: The 10.75x68mm was a Mauser development and is so listed in German ammunition catalogs. It was introduced in the early 1920s. Pre-World War II Mauser magnum-action Type A sporting rifles were chambered for this round and exported to the United States. Post-war Browning and Dumoulin bolt-action rifles were available for this cartridge in Europe. Kynoch, of England, once made the 10.75x68mm cartridge.

General Comments: This was a popular big-game cartridge with many African and Indian hunters. The 10.75x68mm has been used on all kinds of dangerous game, including elephant. However, professional ivory hunters did not consider it satisfactory for elephant. This was apparently due to bullet design. The soft-point bullet could not be depended on to hold together and, so, did not always penetrate properly. In power, it falls short of the British .404 Rimless Nitro Express. With top loads, it approaches .375 H&H Magnum energy levels— no faint praise. However, it is not considered as good a general-purpose cartridge as the .375 H&H. There is no question of it being perfectly adequate for North American big game. Bullet diameter is .424-inch. Ammunition is available from Old Western Scrounger (www.ows-ammo.com), and Barnes (www.barnesbullets.com) offers bullets. Buffalo Arms Co. also sells die sets (www.buffaloarms.com).

10.75x68mm Mauser Loading Data and Factory Ballistics

Bullet (grains/type)	Powder	Grains	Velocity	Energy	Source/Comments
347 SP	IMR 3031	59.0	2,250	3,900	N/A
347 SP	FL	FL	2,200	3,740	Eley-Kynoch factory load
347 SP	FL	FL	2,230	3,830	RWS factory load

10.75x63mm Mauser

Historical Notes: Although generally referred to in literature as a Mauser cartridge, some authorities say this is a Mannlicher development. It was introduced about 1910 and has been obsolete for a number of years. It is not listed in post-World War II German or British catalogs. Except for length, it has practically the same dimensions as the longer 10.75x68. Most samples were made by RWS, but the old DWM case No. 515 (listed as the 10.75x62) is probably the same cartridge. There was also a 10.75x62mm straight case, whereas the one listed here is bottlenecked, albeit slightly. It was loaded with a 347- or 350-grain bullet at about 2100 fps, but exact ballistics are lacking. It would probably be a little more powerful than the .405 Winchester. Barnes (www.barnesbullets.com) makes a bullet that would work in this round.

10.75x57mm (Mannlicher)

Historical Notes: This obsolete, rimless cartridge is based on the 57mm case length. It dates back to around 1900, possibly earlier. Ammunition was once made by G. Roth and RWS. It was chambered in sporting rifles based on the Model 88 German military bolt-action, and also in later Model 98 Mauser rifles. Some authorities say it originated as a Mannlicher cartridge.

General Comments: The 10.75x57mm has such a slight shoulder that one has to look closely for to realize it has one at all. The fact that it was not popular or widely used may have been due in part to headspace trouble, such as that encountered with the wildcat .400 Whelen. The Whelen cartridge was made by necking up .30-06 cases to take .405 Winchester bullets. That round had a short life and never got much beyond the experimental stage. The 10.75x57mm would be powerful enough for North American big game and most non-dangerous African game. Rifles for the cartridge are rare. Loading data is not available.

10.75x57mm (Mannlicher) Factory Ballistics

Bullet (grains/type)	Powder	Grains	Velocity	Energy	Source/Comments
350 SP	FL	FL	1,950	2,960	Factory load

10.75x65Rmm Collath

Historical Notes: The largest of the Collath-developed cartridges, this one has a straight, rimmed case. It was loaded with a 205-grain soft-point bullet, but we could find no specific data on the ballistics. The Collath cartridges are collector's items, and rifles for these are uncommon. Case dimensions are similar to the .405 Winchester. Barnes (www.barnesbullets.com) makes a bullet that would work in this cartridge.

10.8x47Rmm Martini (Target)

Historical Notes: This is an obsolete black-powder cartridge for Martini-action, single-shot target rifles. The 10.8x47Rmm was loaded with a 386-grain paper patched bullet. Ballistics are not known. There were a number of similar rounds used by target shooters during the period 1875 through the 1890s.

11.2x72mm Schüler
11.2x72mm Mauser

Historical Notes: Rifles manufactured in this chambering by H. Krieghoff, of Suhl, Germany, were exported to the United States in the early 1920s. The cartridge appears to have been developed about that time, possibly between 1920-'22. These Krieghoff-Schuler rifles were based on the Mauser Magnum action with a four-shot magazine. The case has a rebated rim (smaller than the body diameter), to fit the standard Mauser bolt face. The 11.2x72mm was used only to a limited extent by American shooters. It is now obsolete, and is not listed in the German late catalogs.

General Comments: The 11.2x72mm, often confused with the shorter and less powerful 11.2x60mm, is a powerful round, equaling the muzzle energy of the .458 Winchester Magnum and .470 Nitro Express. One does not read much about its use in Africa, although it had a small and loyal following. For some reason, the German designers never turned out the sturdy, solid bullets demanded by the professional hunters requiring deep penetration. That was the main reason many fine German cartridges were not highly regarded for shooting heavy, thick-skinned African game. This cartridge is listed in the 1911 Alpha catalog.

11.2x72mm Schüler, 11.2x72mm Mauser Loading Data and Factory Ballistics

Bullet (grains/type)	Powder	Grains	Velocity	Energy	Source/Comments
401 SP	IMR 4350	103.0	2,360	4,975	N/A
401 SP	FL	FL	2,438	5,300	Factory load

11.2x60mm Schüler
11.2x60mm Mauser

Historical Notes: This cartridge is also listed as the 11.15x59.8 Schüler. It is nothing more than a rimless, smokeless powder version of the popular German 11mm Model-71 Mauser military round. The case has a rebated rim (of smaller diameter than the body), to fit the standard 98 Mauser bolt face. This number appears to have been introduced right after World War I, but may be older. Rifles for the 11.2x60mm were exported to the U.S. in the early 1920s, but it was not popular here. It is obsolete, and late German ammunition and gun catalogs do not list it.

General Comments: The general popularity of the 11mm Mauser military round was responsible for development of the rimless version. The original cartridge could not be stepped up very much in performance, because the Models 71 and 71/84 were black-powder rifles. The rimless 11.2x60mm was chambered in the stronger Model 98 action. Although it is a considerable improvement over the old black-powder 11mm military round, it did not catch on in Africa. Most hunters there considered the bullet design unreliable for maximum penetration. In power, it is between the .405 Winchester and the .375 H&H Magnum. Bullet diameter is .440-inch.

11.2x60mm Schüler, 11.2x60mm Mauser Loading Data and Factory Ballistics

Bullet (grains/type)	Powder	Grains	Velocity	Energy	Source/Comments
332 SP	IMR 3031	60.0	2,130	3,360	NA
370 Lead	IMR 3031	45.0	1,500	1,855	Lyman #439186
332 SP	FL		2,198	3,575	Factory load

.45 Blaser

Historical Notes: Europeans have different ideas about a lot of things. For instance, while Blaser plans on eventually offering its new line of magnum cartridges in the United States, it has no intention of doing so with what might be the most marketable off all its new cartridges.

The .45 Blaser was specifically designed for driven wild boar hunts. This cartridge has a .513-inch base diameter, like the .458 Winchester Magnum, but a rim diameter of .473, like the .308 Winchester. This, in conjunction with its short overall length, makes it readily adaptable to short-action bolt rifles. Currently, it is only available in Blaser rifles, and the .45 Blaser ammunition manufactured by W. Romney isn't sold in the U.S. The round also possesses an unusually shaped case by modern standards, one having an excessively long .49-inch neck. This long case neck allows the use of heavy .458-caliber bullets, but prevents them from protruding into the powder column behind the shoulder.

General Comments: With the capability of launching a 350-grain bullet at just over 2000 fps, the .45 Blaser has very similar ballistics to .45-70 loads designed for modern rifles. However, the rimless design of the .45 Blaser makes it much more suitable to bolt and/or semi-auto rifles. It would be a great cartridge to use when hunting wild hogs or a variety of other medium and large game at short to moderate ranges.

.45 Blaser Factory Ballistics

Bullet (grains/type)	Powder	Grains	Velocity	Energy	Source
349 SJSP	FL	FL	2,034	3,205	Blaser

.460 Steyr (11.64mm)

Historical Notes: Certain European countries restrict the sale of military-caliber firearms, including those chambering cartridges of .50-caliber. Around 2004, Steyr Mannlicher GmbH developed a proprietary cartridge for the European large-caliber market by shortening the .50-caliber Browning Machine Gun cartridge case and sizing it to accept 11.64mm (.458-inch) bullets.

General Comments: This cartridge is not currently available in the United States. In the European market, it closely duplicates the performance of the .50 BMG cartridge for non-military applications. The .460 Steyr is well-suited for heavy, single-shot bolt-action target rifles that offer long range, terminal ballistic, and other performance advantages, such as the Steyr HS 50 Long Range rifle. Barrel twists used by Steyr are 1:12 and 1:14. Steyr (www.steyrarms.com) also supplies loaded ammunition.

.460 Steyr Factory Ballistics

Bullet (grains/type)	Powder	Grains	Velocity	Energy	Source/Comments
600 Steyr Brass Solid	FL	FL	3,000	11,989	Steyr

12.17x44Rmm Remington M67 (Norway & Sweden)/12x42Rmm Swedish Remington CF

Historical Notes: This is the centerfire version of the 12x42mm rimfire military cartridge. It was previously listed as a military cartridge, but was never adopted as such. It was used as sporting round in Norway and Sweden in Remington rolling-block type rifles. It originated in 1867 and was loaded by Remington and also in Germany.

General Comments: This is another large-caliber black-powder cartridge similar to the American .50-70. It would do for any North American big game. However, this cartridge is largely a collector's item, and one is not apt to have these in shooting quantities. Bullet diameter is .502-inch.

12.5x70mm Schüler

Historical Notes: Some authorities say this cartridge was an original Schüler development. Ohers claim Jeffery introduced it. John Taylor said the ammunition was loaded only in Europe, and that would indicate Schüler originated it. Krieghoff-Schüler Magnum rifles were chambered for this round and were exported from the 1920s until World War II. Earlier editions of this book stated that this cartridge is interchangeable with the .500 Jeffrey; according to custom gunsmith James Tucker, this is not the case.

General Comments: Until the introduction of the .460 Weatherby Magnum, this was the most powerful magazine-rifle cartridge in existence. It was used very successfully in Africa on some game. Bullet diameter is .510-inch. Factory loads were made in both soft-point and full metal jacket types, though German bullets had weak jackets and did not perform well. In earlier editions of this text, this cartridge was erroneously listed as the 12.7x70mm. Barnes (www.barnesbullets.com) makes an appropriate bullet.

12.5x70mm Schüler Factory Ballistics

Bullet (grains/type)	Powder	Grains	Velocity	Energy	Source/Comments
535 SP	FL		2,400	6,800	Factory load

Dimensional Data

Cartridge	Case Type	Bullet Dia.	Neck Dia.	Shoulder Dia.	Base Dia.	Rim Dia.	Rim Thck.	Case Length	Ctge. Length	Primer: Berdan Dia.	RWS Primer No.	Old DWM Case No.	Page
5.6x35Rmm Vierling (.22 WCF)	A	.222	.241	.278	.300	.297	UNK/NA	1.40	1.62	.177	1584	539	566
5.6x33mm & 5.6xR33mm Rook	C/A	.222	.248	.318	.325	.326/ .366	UNK/NA	1.31	1.62/ 1.64	.177	1584	UNK/NA	566
5.6x50mm/5.6x50Rmm Magnum	C/A	.224	.254	.355	.375	.376	.038	1 97	2.21	UNK/NA	UNK/NA	UNK/NA	567
5.6x57mm/5.6x57Rmm RWS	C/A	.224	.281	.436	.469	.470	UNK/NA	2.24	2.54	UNK/NA	UNK/NA	UNK/NA	568
5.6x61mm & 5.6x61Rmm Vom Hofe Super Express	C/A	.227	.259/ .260	.468/ .479	.476/ .470	.480/ .533	.062	2.39	3.13	.217	5603	431M	568
6x29.5Rmm Stahl	A	.243	.262	.301	.320	.370	UNK/NA	1.16	1.44	UNK/NA	.177	1584	569
6x62mm/6x62Rmm Freres	C/A	.243	.271	.451	.474	.470	UNK/NA	2.42	3.13	.217	UNK	UNK/NA	569
6x57mm Mauser/6x57mm RWS	C	.243	.284	.420	.475	.476	.045	2.23	2.95	.217	5603	494	570
6x58mm & 6x58Rmm Forster	C/A	.243	.284/ .285	.437	.470/ .471	.468/ .532	.045	2.26	3.06	UNK/NA	.217	5603	570
.244 (6mm) Halger Magnum	A	.243	.287	.435	.467	.470	UNK	2.25	3.04	.217	5603	UNK/NA	570
6.5x40Rmm	B	.250	.290	UNK/NA	.396	.451	UNK/NA	1.58	2.07	UNK/NA	UNK/NA	UNK/NA	571
6.5x52Rmm (.25-35 Winchester)	A	.257	.280	.355	.420	.500	UNK/NA	2.04	2.53	.217	5603	519	571
6.5x27Rmm	A	.257	.284	.348	.379	.428	UNK/NA	1.06	1.54	UNK/NA	.177	1584	571
6.5x48Rmm Sauer	B	.260	.284	UNK/NA	.433	.495	UNK/NA	1.88	2.43	UNK/NA	.217	5603	572
6.5x53.5mm Daudeteau	G	.263	.298	.466	.490	.524	UNK/NA	2.09	3.02	UNK/NA	UNK/NA	UNK/NA	572
6.5x54mm Mauser	C	.264	.289	.432	.468	.463	UNK/NA	2.12	2.67	.217	5603	457A	572
6.5x58Rmm Sauer	B	.264	.291	UNK/NA	.433	.501	UNK/NA	2.30	3.08	.217	5603	463	573
6.5x57mm/6.5x57Rmm Mauser & RWS	C/A	.264	.292	.430	.470/ .471	.474/ .521	UNK/NA	2.24	3.16/ 3.18	.217	5603	404A	573
6.5x58mm Portuguese	C	.264	.293	.426	.468	.465	UNK/NA	2.28	3.22	.217	5603	457	574
6.5x65mm/ 6.5x65Rmm RWS	C/A	.264	.296	.430	.474/ .475	.470/ .531	UNK/NA	2.56	3.15	UNK/NA	UNK/NA	UNK/NA	574
6.5x61mm/6.5x61Rmm Mauser	C/A	.264	.296/ .297	.452	.477	.479/ .532	UNK	2.40	3.55	.217	5603	431L-431M	574
6.5x58Rmm Krag-Jorgensen	A	.264	.300	.460	.500	.575	UNK	2.29	3.25	.217	5603	UNK/NA	575
6.5x68mm/6.5x68Rmm RWS	C/A	.265	.295	.481	.520	.510	UNK	2.66	3.27	.238	1698	UNK/NA	575
7x33mm Sako/Finnish	C	.284	.307	.365	.388	.390	UNK	1.30	1.73	UNK/NA	UNK/NA	UNK/NA	576
.270 Schuster	C	0.278	0.315	0.450	0.471	0.473	0.055	1.924	2.800	Bx			576
7x64mm/7x65Rmm Brenneke	C/A	.284	.305/ .308	.422	.463	.468/ .521	.055	2.51/ 2.53	3.21	.217	5603	557-557A	577
7mm Blaser Magnum	I	.284	.314	.515	.544	.535	.054	2.35	3.14	UNK/NA	L	UNK/NA	578
7x72Rmm	B	.284	.311	UNK/NA	.425	.482	UNK	2.84	3.48	.217	5603	573	578
7x73mm Vom Hofe (Belted)	E	.284	.315	.483	.527	.533	UNK	2.87	3.88	.217	5603	575	579
7x66mm Vom Hofe Super Express	C	.284	.316	.485	.543	.510	.048	2.58	3.25	.217	UNK/NA	603	579
7x75Rmm Vom Hofe Super Express	A	.284	.318	.416	.468	.519	.050	2.95	3.68	.217	UNK/NA	UNK/NA	580
7x57mm/7x57Rmm Mauser	C/A	.284	.320	.420	.470	.474/ .521	.035/ .056	2.24	3.06/ 3.07	.217	5603	UNK/NA	580
.300 Blaser Magnum	I	.308	.338	.511	.544	.535	.054	2.56	3.30	UNK/NA	L	UNK/NA	581
.308 Norma Magnum	E	.308	.340	.489	.514	.529	.048	2.56	3.30	UNK/NA	UNK/NA	UNK/NA	581
.300 Norma Magnum	C	.308	.341	.562	.585	.587	.059	2.50	3.68	UNK/NA	L	UNK/NA	582
.30R Blaser	I	.308	.343	.441	.480	.531	UNK	2.68	3.80	UNK/NA	UNK/NA	UNK/NA	583
8x48Rmm Sauer	B	.316	.344	UNK/NA	.432	.500	.040	1.88	2.58	.254	1775	462A	583
8x51mm Mauser 8x51RmmJ Mauser	C/A	.316	.344	.436	.467	.467/ .515	.045/ .060	1.98	2.67/ 2.68	UNK/NA	.217	5603	583
8.15x46Rmm	A	.316	.346	.378	.421	.484	UNK	1.82	2.28	.250	1794	455	584
8x57mm/8x57Rmm		.318	UNK/NA	UNK/NA	UNK/NA	UNK/NA	UNK/NA	UNK/NA	UNK/NA	UNK/NA	UNK	UNK	584
8x57Rmm 360	A	.318	.333	.375	.427	.485	UNK/NA	2.24	2.96	UNK/NA	UNK	UNK	585
8x58Rmm Sauer	B	.318	.345	UNK/NA	.438	.499	UNK/NA	2.28	3.00	.254	1775	462	585
8x42Rmm M/88	A	.318	.347	.423	.468	.525	UNK/NA	1.66	2.28	UNK/NA	.217	5603	586
8x71mm Peterlongo	C	.318	.349	.422	.462	.468	UNK/NA	2.80	3.28	UNK/NA	.216	2610	586
8x57Jmm Mauser	C	.318	.350	.435	.470	.473	UNK/NA	2.24	3.17	UNK/NA	UNK	UNK	586
8x56mm Mannlicher-Schoenauer	C	.323	.347	.424	.465	.470	.045	2.21	3.04	.217	5603	528	587
8x64mmJ or S/8x65RmmJ or S Brenneke	C/A	.323	.348	.421/ .424	.464/ .468	.469/ .520	UNK/NA	2.51/ 2.56	3.32/ 3.65	.217	5603	558-558A	587

Dimensional Data

Cartridge	Case Type	Bullet Dia.	Neck Dia.	Shoulder Dia.	Base Dia.	Rim Dia.	Rim Thck.	Case Length	Ctge. Length	Primer: Berdan Dia.	RWS Primer No.	Old DWM Case No.	Page
8x57mmJS/8x57RmmJS Mauser	C/A	.323	.350	.435	.470	.473/ .526	.043/ .048	2.24/ 2.25	3.17/ 3.55	.217	5603	366D1	588
8x54mm Krag-Jorgensen	C	.323	.351	.435	.478	.478	UNK/NA	2.12	2.85	UNK/NA	.199	1680	589
8x68mmS RWS	C	.323	.354	.473	.522	.510	UNK/NA	2.65	3.38	.238	1698	UNK/NA	589
8x60mmS Mauser	C/A	.3236	.357	.431	.471	.470	UNK/NA	2.362	3.290	UNK/NA	UNK/NA	UNK/NA	590
8x72Rmm Sauer	B	.324	.344	UNK/NA	.429	.483	UNK/NA	2.84	3.40	UNK/NA	.254	1775	591
.338 Blaser Magnum	I	.338	.368	.512	.544	.535	.054	2.507	3.34	UNK/NA	L	UNK/NA	591
.338 Norma Magnum	C	.338	.369	.570	.585	.587	.059	2.50	3.68	UNK/NA	L	UNK/NA	592
9x71mm Peterlongo	C	.350	.386	.420	.464	.466	UNK/NA	2.80	3.26	UNK/NA	.216	2610	593
9x56mm Mannlicher-Schoenauer	C	.356	.378	.408	.464	.464	UNK/NA	2.22	3.56	.217	5603	491E	593
9x57mm/9x57Rmm Mauser	C/A	.356	.380	.424/ .428	.467	.468/ .515	.045/ .050	2.24	3.10/ 3.08	.217	5603	491A-491B	594
9x63mm	C	.357	.384	.427	.467	.468	UNK/NA	2.48	3.28	UNK/NA	.217	5603	594
9x70Rmm Mauser	A	.357	.385	.418	.467	.525	UNK/NA	2.76	3.37	UNK/NA	UNK/NA	UNK/NA	595
.358 Norma Magnum	E	.358	.384	.489	.508	.526	.048	2.52	3.22	UNK/NA	L	UNK/NA	595
9.3x57mm Mauser	C	.365	.389	.428	.468	.469	UNK/NA	2.24	3.23	.217	5603	491	596
9.3x53mm Swiss	C/A	.365	.389/ .391	.453/ .455	.492/ .494	.491/ .563	.045	2.11	2.80/ 2.83	UNK/NA	UNK/NA	UNK/NA	596
9.3x72Rmm Sauer	A	.365	.390	.422	.473	.518	UNK/NA	2.83	3.34	UNK/NA	.254	1775	596
9.3x74Rmm	A	.366	.387	.414	.465	524	052	2.93	3.74	.217	5603	474A	596
9.3x64mm Brenneke	A	.366	.395	.474	.507	.496	.051	2.520	3.37	UNK/NA	L	UNK/NA	597
9.3x65Rmm Collath	A	.367	.384	.420	.443	.508	UNK/NA	2.56	3.01	UNK/NA	UNK/NA	UNK/NA	597
9.3x75Rmm Nimrod	A	.367	.395	.405	.432	.484	.044	2.93	3.523	LP	UNK/NA	UNK/NA	598
9.1x40Rmm	B	.374	.385	UNK/NA	.404	.446	UNK/NA	1.60	2.00	UNK/NA	UNK/NA	UNK/NA	599
9.5x57mm Mannlicher-Schoenauer (9.5x56mm)	C	.375	.400	.460	.471	.473	.040	2.25	2.94	.217	5603	531	598
9.5x73mm Miller-Greiss Magnum	C	.375	.402	.531	.543	.541	UNK/NA	2.86	3.50	UNK/NA	.217	5603	599
9.5x47Rmm	A	.375	.409	.497	.513	.583	UNK/NA	1.85	2.37	UNK/NA	.254	1775	600
.375 Blaser Magnum	I	.375	.405	.507	.544	.535	.054	2.822	3.622	UNK/NA	L	UNK/NA	600
9.3x48Rmm	B	.376	.382	UNK/NA	.433	.492	UNK/NA	1.89	2.35	.254	1775	246	601
9.3x72Rmm	B	.376	.385	UNK/NA	.427	.482	UNK/NA	2.84	3.27	.254	1775	77D	601
9.3x70Rmm	B	.376	.387	UNK/NA	.427	.482	UNK/NA	2.75	3.45	.254	1775	77F	601
9.3x57Rmm	B	.376	.389	UNK/NA	.428	.486	UNK/NA	2.24	2.80	.254	1775	77E	601
10.25x69Rmm Hunting-Express	A	.404	.415	.480	.549	.630	UNK/NA	2.72	3.17	UNK/NA	.254	1775	601
10.3x60Rmm Swiss	A	.415	.440	.498	.547	.619	UNK/NA	2.36	3.08	UNK/NA	UNK/NA	UNK/NA	601
10.5x47Rmm	A	.419	.445	.496	.513	.591	UNK/NA	1.85	2.40	UNK/NA	.254	1775	602
10.75x73mm/.404 Rimless Nitro/ .404 Jeffery	C	.421	.450	.520	.544	.537	.045	2.86	3.53	.217	UNK/NA	555	602
10.3x65Rmm Baenziger	B	.423	.431	UNK/NA	.462	.505	UNK/NA	2.56	3.15	UNK/NA	UNK/NA	164	603
10.75x68mm Mauser	C	.424	.445	.470	.492	.488	UNK/NA	2.67	3.16	.217	5603	515A	603
10.75x63mm Mauser	I	.424	.447	.479	.493	.467	UNK/NA	2.47	3.22	UNK/NA	UNK/NA	UNK/NA	604
10.75x57mm Mannlicher	C·	.424	.448	.465	.468	.468	UNK/NA	2.24	3.05	UNK/NA	UNK/NA	UNK/NA	604
10.75x65Rmm Collath	B	.424	.451	UNK/NA	.487	.542	UNK/NA	2.56	3.02	UNK/NA	UNK/NA	UNK/NA	604
10.8x47Rmm Martini Target	A	.441	.463	.512	.516	.591	UNK/NA	1.75	2.23	UNK/NA	UNK/NA	UNK/NA	604
11.2x72mm (Schuler/Mauser)	I	.440	.465	.510	.536	.469	UNK/NA	2.80	3.85	UNK/NA	.217	5601	605
11.2x60mm (Schuler/Mauser)	I	.440	.465	.512	.512	.465	UNK/NA	2.35	2.86	UNK/NA	.217	5601	605
.45 Blaser	I	.458	.486	.511	.513	.473	.054	2.16	2.70	UNK/NA	L	UNK/NA	606
.460 Steyr (11.64mm)	C	.458	.501	.719	.805	.805	.089	3.64	4.80	UNK/NA	Bx	UNK/NA	606
12.17x44Rmm	B		.502	.544	UNK/NA	.546	.624	.060	1.73	2.13	UNK/NA	UNK/NA	607
12.50x70mm Schüler	I	.510	.535	.615	.620	.578	UNK/NA	2.94	3.50	.254	2703	UNK/NA	607

Case Type: A = Rimmed, bottleneck. B = Rimmed, straight. C = Rimless, bottleneck. D = Rimless, straight. E = Belted, bottleneck. F = Belted, straight. G = Semi-rimmed, bottleneck. H = Semi-rimmed, straight. I = Rebated, bottleneck. J = Rebated, straight. K = Rebated, belted bottleneck. L = Rebated, belted straight.

Other codes: Unless otherwise noted, all dimensions in inches.

Primers: L = Large rifle (0.210-inch). Dimensions shown in some instances do not exactly coincide with dimensions found in *The Book of Rifles* (W.H.B. Smith, Harrisburg, Pa., 1960). Differences amount to only a few thousandths of an inch, doubtless attributable to specimen variations. Parentheses indicate maximum cartridge specifications.Ω

American Rimfire Cartridges

(Current & Obsolete – Black-Powder and Smokeless)

Rimfire cartridges differ from centerfires in that the priming compound is contained in the rim. Ignition occurs when the firing pin crushes the rim. Rimfire cartridges are of historical as well as practical interest. Although only one of a number of ignition systems leading to the modern centerfire, the rimfire was the first truly *successful* system. It's still alive and well almost 170 years later.

The common .22 rimfire had its origin with the Flobert BB Cap, in 1845, which led to the Smith & Wesson-developed .22 Short of 1857. The idea of rimfire ignition goes back to Roberts' French patent of 1831. This provided for the priming compound covering the entire head interior. The rimfire evolved by leaving the primer mix out of the center. After Smith & Wesson introduced its First Model revolver—a .22 Short chambering, in 1857—development of rimfire arms and cartridges bloomed. The New Haven Arms Co. began manufacturing .44 Henry ammunition in 1861, and .56-56 Spencer ammunition was made in quantity beginning about 1862, (although the Spencer rifle design dates back to 1860). Both of these cartridges were used by Federal troops in the Civil War. Chambering of the first successful metallic cartridge repeating arms was for rimfire cartridges. By the end of the Civil War, numerous rimfire cartridges in various calibers were available.

A great many rimfire cartridges have been developed for rifles and handguns here and in Europe. In the late 1800s, something like 75 different rimfire cartridges had been loaded by American companies, but only about 42 were still around by 1900. The decline in the number of rimfire cartridges occurred because many early types put on the market were really experimental and, so, had a very short life. These are of academic interest primarily to collectors. Space limitations rule out any effort to list all of these here. The criteria for inclusion of a cartridge is that it was loaded by American companies and survived to the turn of the century. The more obscure numbers, and those of British or Continental origin, have been covered fairly well elsewhere. The more popular rimfires lasted well past the turn of the century, and a few are still in use. The .22 Short rimfire is, in fact, the *oldest* American cartridge, having survived since 1857. It will probably still be around as long as we own and shoot firearms.

The decline in the number of rimfire cartridge types can be illustrated by a review of old catalogs. Forty-two U.S. types were in common production in 1900. By 1918, that number had dwindled to 32 and, by the 1930s, the number was down to a mere 17. After World War II, the count was less than 10. Some older rimfires are still loaded in Europe and, from time to time, imported here. Many of the cartridges listed here were available on an over-the-counter basis up through the 1920s. One or two of the obsolete rimfires would probably be useful to modern shooters, but it is unlikely ammunition manufacturers will revive these cartridges. While many shooters would welcome a return of the .25 Stevens Long, it seems unlikely this will ever happen.

Rimfire cartridges have advantages, as well as weaknesses, compared to centerfire cartridges. In smaller calibers, the rimfire is cheaper to manufacture and, within equivalent pressures, is just as good as the centerfire. One disadvantage of the rimfire is that it is not practical to reload. This was a big consideration with early buffalo hunters and pioneers of the Old West. It was also no small consideration among match shooters. The rimfire will not stand up under the pressures of modern high-velocity centerfire loads, but solid-head centerfires can be made much stronger. Large-caliber rimfire cartridges cost nearly as much as similar centerfire rounds, so there is an economic point beyond which the rimfire just is not worthwhile.

If any statements made before this give the impression that the rimfire cartridge is about to become extinct, don't worry. Nothing could be further from the truth. As recently as 1959, Winchester introduced the .22 Magnum

Rimfire and, in 1970, Remington introduced the 5mm Remington Rimfire Magnum. The .22 Magnum caught on immediately and is well into its fifth decade of popularity. The 5mm Magnum did not fare so well, despite ballistics that were somewhat superior to the .22 Magnum. It was discontinued after only a few years.

Despite the failure of the 5mm Magnum in the 1970s, Hornady introduced the .17 Hornady Magnum Rimfire, in 2002. It is similar in appearance to the earlier 5mm Magnum, but, with a 17-grain V-Max bullet at 2550 fps, its trajectory is more nearly similar to the centerfire .22 Hornet. More than a dozen rifle makers are chambering for the .17 HMR, and it seems destined for a long life.

The .22 Long Rifle has become the most accurate and highly developed sporting cartridge in existence. Its popularity for match shooting and small-game or varmint hunting remains not only undiminished, but is increasing, if anything. There are dozens of makes, models, and types of .22 rimfire arms currently manufactured, and new models appear in a steady stream. The .22 Long Rifle has established a place so secure, it will be with us as long as guns are made.

Modern rimfire cartridges are intended for target, plinking, or small-game hunting. The .22 Long Rifle does very well out to 75 yards on rabbit-sized animals, and on coyote or fox with a well-placed bullet. The .17 Hornady Magnum will extend this range to nearly 200 yards. The .22 Short is a good plinking round and is used in Olympic pistol competition. The high-velocity Long Rifle is a useful self-defense round; it will penetrate better than the .32 Smith & Wesson, when fired from a handgun. The .22 WMR develops handgun energies nearly equal to some .38 Special loads.

It would surprise many to know how many deer are killed each year by poachers using the .22 Long Rifle. However, it is *not* to be considered a deer cartridge. There is, reportedly, a case of an elephant that was killed with a .22 Long Rifle, but that hardly qualifies it as an elephant cartridge, either. Still, within their capabilities and limitations, modern rimfire cartridges are among the most useful we have.— *F.C.B., with additional text by S.S.*

15th Edition Update

There are no new rimfire entries in this edition, but it's worth noting that one round covered in the 14th Edition, the .17 Winchester Super Magnum, has begun fulfilling its promise. At the time of its introduction, Winchester called the .17 WSM "the most revolutionary rimfire cartridge in the company's almost 150-year history." The allure was that the .17 WSM would offer the downrange performance of a centerfire cartridge at only a fraction of the cost. A closer look at some specifics of the round are worth noting here in this preface.

The .17 WSM will never overtake the .22 LR in terms of loadings offered, and it likely can't catch even the popularity of the .22 Winchester Magnum Rimfire (.22 WMR). But it's not for want of trying.

The .17 WSM's downrange performance level exceeds the long-range bullet-drop capabilities of popular magnum rimfire cartridges like the .22 WMR and .17 HMR, while delivering more energy. Winchester's .17 WSM #S17W25 load firing a 25-grain bullet hits 2,600 fps at the muzzle and is still traveling at 1,893 fps 200 yards later. With a 100-yard zero, it drops only -1.8 inches at 150 yards and -5.6 inches at 200 yards. Energies at those distances are 276 and 199 ft.-lbs., respectively. A 28-grain .22 WMR generates only 120 and 60 ft.-lbs. of energy, respectively, at 100 and 200 yards. At 20 grains, the .17 WSM outclasses the .17 HMR Hornady load #83172 in ballistic terms. With 50-yard zeros, the .17 WSM drops only -1.2 inches at 150 yards and -4.7 at 200 yards, compared to the .17 HMR's flight plans of - 4.0 inches at 150 yards and -11.4 inches at 200 yards.

This is the profile of a long-term winner for varmint hunting. —*W.T.W.*

.17 Mach 2

Historical Notes: A 2004 joint rimfire cartridge development between Hornady and CCI, the .17 Mach 2 cartridge delivers higher velocities and flatter trajectories than the .22 Long Rifle cartridge. Hornady designed the .17 Mach 2 for plinking, varminting, and small-game hunting. In quality firearms, the .17 Mach 2 is capable of MOA or better accuracy.

General Comments: The .17 Mach 2 cartridge is not reloadable. It uses the rimfire .22 Stinger case as its parent. Exactly .100-inch longer that the .22 Long Rifle case, the Stinger case is necked down to accept .172-inch diameter bullets weighing 17 grains. The .17 Mach 2 is well-suited to 18/22-inch barrels with a 1:9 rifling twist. Ruger, Marlin, Thompson/Center, and other manufacturers offer rifles chambered for the .17 Mach 2. Hornady, CCI, Remington, and Eley supply loaded ammunition.

.17 Hornady Magnum Rimfire (.17 HMR)

Historical Notes: In 2002, Hornady provided shooters with serious reasons to consider a rimfire cartridge for medium-range (200-yard) varmint hunting. Its new .17 HMR is the fastest rimfire commercially available. It pushes a 17-grain bullet on trajectories very similar to the larger .22 Hornet centerfire cartridge.

General Comments: Launching a 17-grain V-Max bullet at 2550 fps, Hornady's bottleneck rimfire cartridge printed five-shot groups measuring .460-inch at 100 yards, and 1.005 inches at 200 yards, using a Wiseman-barreled Marlin rifle in factory tests. Flattening the .22 WMR's trajectory by more than 10 inches at 200 yards, the flat-shooting .17 HMR also drifts 15 inches less in a 10 mph wind. Contributing to this fine performance is the boat-tail V-Max bullet with a polymer tip engineered for dramatic expansion. Hornady achieves this performance at pressures slightly greater than the .22 WMR, which suggests existing .22 WMR rifle designs can be readily adapted to the .17 HMR. As a measure of the popularity of the new .17 HMR cartridge, rifles and pistols are available from Anschütz, Cooper, H&R 1871, Marlin, New England Arms, Remington, Ruger, Rogue River, Savage, and Thompson/Center.

.17 Winchester Super Magnum

Historical Notes: Winchester Ammunition, in conjunction with Savage, introduced the .17 Winchester Super Magnum rimfire rifle cartridge at the 2013 SHOT Show. A Winchester Ammunition announcement called this "the most revolutionary rimfire cartridge in the company's almost 150-year history." Further, the company said, "The .17 Win. Super Mag. offers the downrange performance of a centerfire cartridge at only a fraction of the cost. For the first time in history, hunters can expect pinpoint accuracy and devastating performance from a rimfire cartridge, at ranges well past 200 yards."

One of Winchester's goals with the new .17 was to keep it affordable. A box of 50 should retail for about $15, much cheaper than almost any centerfire varmint load.

"Our engineers have been developing the top-secret .17 Win Super Mag caliber for more than three years and the rimfire revolution begins now," said Brett Flaugher, Winchester Ammunition vice president of sales, marketing and strategy in 2013. "At 3,000 feet per second, it's the fastest modern rimfire cartridge on the planet. The downrange energy deposited by the .17 Win. Super Mag. will be a game-changer for varmint and predator hunters everywhere."

General Comments: This round descended from a .27-caliber nail-gun blank, which is necked down to take a .17-caliber bullet. The brass case is about half again thicker than the .17 HMR. Maximum average internal pressure is 33,000 psi, about 7,000 psi higher than the .17 HMR's. It pushes a 20-grain bullet at 3,000 fps, 625 fps faster than the .17 HMR. In a 10 mile-per-hour crosswind, the .17 WSM moves 7.3 inches at 200 yards, while the .17 HMR slides 16.6 inches.

The .17 Win Super Mag was initially offered in three bullet types: a 20-grain plastic tip in Varmint HV (High Velocity); 25-grain plastic tip in Varmint HE (High Energy); and a 20-grain jacketed hollow-point in Super-X. The .17 Win Super Mag bullet delivers more than 150 percent greater energy than the .22 Win Mag or .17 HMR. The .17 WSM first-adopter rifles included the Savage B-Mag bolt-action, Winchester 1885 Low Wall single-shot, and the semi-automatic Franklin Armory F-17.

.17 Winchester Super Magnum Factory Ballistics

Bullet (grains/type)	Powder	Grains	Velocity	Energy	Source
20 Plastic Tip Varmint HV	FL	FL	3,000	399	Winchester No. S17W20
25 Plastic Tip Varmint HE	FL	FL	2,600	375	WInchester No. S17W25
20 HP Super X	FL	FL	3,000	399	Winchester No. X17W20

.17 PMC/.17 Aguila/.17 High Standard

Historical Notes: This round was developed in 2003 by firearms maker High Standard and Mexico-based ammunition maker Aguila. It was introduced to the industry in 2004. It's formed using a .22 LR parent case necked down to accept a .172-inch-diameter bullet. As such, the .17 Aguila can be shot in rifles chambered for .17 HM2 (Hornady Mach 2), but not the reverse. The round faltered because it faced better-performing .17 rimfires from Hornady. No gun manufacturers released firearms to shoot it, so interested shooters had to re-barrel a firearm to shoot this cartridge. At one point in 2007, Natchez Shooting Supply sold .17 Aguila for $3.92 for a box of 50. Centurion Arms sold bricks of 500 for $64. Midway USA carried the .17 PMC version for $90.99 for 1,000 rounds.

General Comments: Factory loads used a 20-grain jacketed solid point to reach 1,850 fps and 152 foot-pounds in a 24-inch test barrel. Thus, the round is best used as a small-game choice that doesn't destroy a lot of edible meat. As late as 2014, Howie Glaser, owner of United Nations Ammo Company (UNammo.com.) said his company owns the remaining inventory of .17 PMC/Aguila (2 million rounds) and sold a 1000-round case for $120.

.17 PMC/.17 Aguila/.17 High Standard Factory Ballistics

Bullet (grains/type)	Powder	Grains	Velocity	Energy	Source
20 JSP	FL	FL	1,850	152	Factory load

5mm Remington Rimfire Magnum

Historical Notes: The 5mm Remington Rimfire Magnum was announced in 1969, but not actually introduced until 1970. Only the Remington bolt-action Model 591 clip-loading and Model 592 tubular magazine repeating rifles were available for the round. It was not adopted by other ammunition manufacturers. For a time, Thompson/Center furnished barrels in 5mm Remington for the Contender pistol. This was the only modern bottlenecked rimfire case. However, a number of the obsolete black-powder rimfires were necked, so it is not an entirely new development. Bullet diameter is .2045-inch with a weight of 38 grains and a muzzle velocity of 2100 fps. This round developed the highest velocity of any rimfire at the time (newer, 30-grain .22 WMR loads offer greater muzzle velocity).

General Comments: The 5mm Remington represented an interesting development, one that exceeds the performance of some of the early .22 centerfires. Its effective killing range on small, varmint-type animals is 25 to 50 yards greater than the .22 Winchester Magnum Rimfire. This is due to the better sectional density of the smaller diameter bullet combined with 150 fps higher initial velocity. Both are essentially varmint cartridges. In both, the hollow-point-type bullets ruin too much edible meat for small-game shooting. However, the .22 WMR is available with a non-expanding full jacketed bullet, or one could switch to the interchangeable .22 WRF for small-game hunting. In summary, the 5mm Remington has the edge for varmint shooting, but the .22 WMR is more versatile for small game. On the other hand, a good full metal jacket small-game bullet for the 5mm Remington might have changed that analysis. The choice would be largely a matter of use and personal preference. Remington has long since discontinued the Model 591 and 592, and no rifles are currently made in 5mm RFM. Ammunition, likewise, is no longer made by Remington. The 5mm RFM is another good idea that didn't catch on, although it had a lot to recommend it. Ammunition is available on a limited basis from Aguila (www.aguilaammo.com).

.22 BB Cap

Historical Notes: The rimfire .22 BB Cap, or Bulleted Breech Cap, is one of the oldest successful self-contained cartridges. It originated in 1845 for the Flobert indoor target rifle. These guns were also known as saloon (salon) or parlor rifles and were quite popular through the turn of the century. A great many individuals and companies have made both rifles and pistols for the .22 BB Cap. This type of social, indoor shooting has become virtually extinct. American companies loaded the .22 BB Cap up to World War II, but discontinued it after the war. The original cartridge had only a priming charge and a .22-caliber lead round ball, but American ammunition contained a small charge of powder and a conical bullet in many makes. The original case was a tapered percussion cap without a well-defined rim.

General Comments: Many insist the .22 BB Cap is completely worthless, but the original author of this book did not agree. Rainy afternoons of target practice in the basement or garage will create a certain appreciation for this little pipsqueak. These cartridges are also handy for a preliminary sighting-in of .22 rimfire rifles or pistols. Modern loads have sufficient power to kill rats, mice, sparrows, or other pests out to 40 yards or so. At close range, RWS BB Caps will penetrate an inch of soft pine board. These could seriously injure or even kill a human, so one should always be careful—these are not toys.

There is considerable variation in case length and dimensions between different makes. The CCI "Mini-Cap," loaded in .22 Short and Long Rifle cases, duplicated performance of the older .22 BB and CB cap for indoor target practice.

.22 CB Cap

Historical Notes: The .22 CB Cap, or Conical Bullet Cap, is something of a cross between the .22 BB Cap and .22 Short. It has been manufactured in various sizes. In original form, it was supposed to combine the 29-grain .22 Short bullet with the .22 BB Cap case and a light charge of black powder. In actual manufacture, some CB Cap cases have a length about halfway between the BB Cap and Short. It is not a transitional design leading to the .22 Short, but, rather, a more powerful version of the BB Cap. The earliest catalog reference appears to be about 1888, although it probably originated prior to this. American companies loaded it up to 1942, but most discontinued it after World War II. CCI occasionally catalogs this load, and RWS has offered these rounds.

General Comments: The .22 CB Cap managed to combine about all the disadvantages of the .22 BB Cap and Short into one generally useless cartridge. It was no more accurate than either of the other two and made enough noise to nullify the indoor virtues of the BB Cap. It also required a backstop almost as heavy as did the Short and was just as dangerous indoors. In killing power, it wasn't that much better than the BB Cap to make any real difference, although it might provide an additional 10 or 15 yards of effective range. In recognition of this, almost everyone quit making it, and there were few laments from the shooting public. The original charge was 1½ grains of black powder, but, after 1920, smokeless powder was used exclusively. CCI has produced loads with the 29-grain CB Cap bullet in the .22 Short case at a velocity of 710 fps. Remington offers its CBee, which is a low-velocity round based on the .22 Long case, with a 33-grain hollow-point bullet at a muzzle velocity of 700 fps. These loads are intended for indoor target practice, gallery, or pest shooting.

.22 Winchester Automatic

Historical Notes: Used only in the Winchester Model 1903 semi-auto rifle, the .22 Winchester Automatic round was dropped from standard Winchester production, in the 1970s. The rifle has been obsolete since 1932. This cartridge has a 45-grain inside-lubricated bullet and will not chamber in any standard .22 Long Rifle gun. It was designed at a time when black-powder and semi-smokeless-powder .22 rimfires were still loaded and popular. The purpose was to prevent use of anything but smokeless powder ammunition in the semi-auto rifle, so as not to foul the action. Black powder will gum up such actions and render them inoperable in short order. Remington later brought out a similar cartridge for the same reason. The two are not interchangeable.

General Comments: The .22 Winchester Automatic had little to offer over the standard Long Rifle, except smokeless powder and the semi-auto rifle in which it was fired. In killing power and range, it was on a par with the .22 Long Rifle. This cartridge is now a collector's item.

.22 Short

Historical Notes: The .22 Short is the oldest American, commercial, self-contained metallic cartridge—it has been in continuous production for more than 143 years! It was introduced in 1857 for the Smith & Wesson First Model revolver and is still widely used all over the world.

Although now popular as a short-range gallery or plinking round, the .22 Short was originally intended for self-defense. It is still used for Olympic match shooting, and heavy target pistols are built specifically for it. The initial loading was a 29-grain bullet and four grains of a fine-granulation black powder (probably similar to what we would now call FFFFg). After 1887, it was available with semi-smokeless powder and, within a short time, smokeless powder. Remington introduced non-corrosive (Kleanbore) priming for its rimfire line in 1927, and the first high-velocity type in 1930. The .22 Short can be fired in any arm chambered for the Long Rifle, but most semi-auto guns will not function properly with the .22 Short. Since the end of World War II, a number of small .22 Short pocket-automatic pistols and revolvers have appeared on the market.

General Comments: In the high-velocity loading, the Short is quite adequate for small-game or bird hunting. However, killing power declines rapidly beyond 50 yards. Hunting should be confined to animals not more than two pounds in weight.

The .22 Short can be deceiving, because it looks small and relatively harmless. When fired from a rifle, it can penetrate two inches of soft pine board and has an extreme range of almost one full mile. It can seriously wound or kill a person right up to the limit of its range—be careful! Make sure of your backstop before shooting any .22 rimfire.

The hollow-point bullet weighs 27 grains and has about 25 fps higher velocity than the solid; this is a particularly effective squirrel load. CCI is the only remaining manufacturer of the hollow-point load. Although sales today are vastly overshadowed by the less expensive .22 Long Rifle, the .22 Short cartridge was king during its first century of production.

.22 Short/40-grain

Historical Notes: We have almost no information on this interesting variation. The sample is labeled as an RWS .22 Short case loaded with a .22 Long Rifle bullet. The case appears to be pure copper, which suggests that this round is quite old. Headstamp is an RWS crest with a centered uppercase "R."

General Comments: We have included this number, because it will serve to demonstrate that rimfire ammunition is as varied and numerous in design as any other type. As we gain further information, we hope to improve the historical details included with this entry.

.22 Long

Historical Notes: The .22 Long is usually referred to as a combination of the Long Rifle case and the Short bullet. This is not true for several reasons. Foremost, the .22 Long happens to be 16 years older than the Long Rifle. It is listed in the 1871 Great Western Gun Works catalog for the seven-shot Standard revolver. A few years later, it was also listed in Remington and Stevens catalogs as a rifle cartridge. The .22 Long Rifle was not on the market until 1887. The Long was originally a black-powder number loaded with a 29-grain bullet and five grains of a fine granulation black powder (probably similar to what we now call FFFFg). Smokeless powder was available, for a time, in standard and high-velocity loads. At present, only the high-velocity load is available. A shot load was also offered.

General Comments: The original black-powder loading of the .22 Long had a slightly higher velocity than did the .22 Short or Long Rifle, but this was not true of later smokeless loads. The present high-velocity Long has a velocity between the Short and Long Rifle. The .22 Long is not as accurate as the Short or Long Rifle and has outlived any useful purpose it might have once had. We think the reason it hangs on is that a great many people still think it has a higher velocity and greater killing power than the Long Rifle.

Editor's note: Others believe that firing enough .22 Short rounds in a .22 Long Rifle-chambered gun will damage the chamber, and that the .22 Long gives similar performance to the .22 Short, but without the potential for chamber damage. Old ideas, true or not, are tenacious, because people will not readily accept concepts in opposition to what they believe. In any event, the .22 Long is strictly a small-game, short-range cartridge ballistically just a notch above the .22 Short. Only CCI still offers the .22 Long.

.22 Long Rifle

Historical Notes: Information available indicates that the .22 Long Rifle was developed by the J. Stevens Arms & Tool Co. in 1887. It is the .22 Long case with a five-grain black-powder charge (likely with a granulation similar to what we would now call FFFFg), and a 40-grain bullet instead of the original 29-grain. The Peters Cartridge Co. is supposed to have first manufactured it, specifically for Stevens. If this is true, then why does the 1888 Stevens catalog refer to a UMC .22-caliber Long rimfire rifle cartridge? This would be a gross ingratitude, at best. This 1888 catalog lists the Nos. 1, 2, 9, and 10 model break-open rifles as available in the new chambering with increased rifling twist. The New Model Pocket or Bicycle rifle also chambered it. The 1888 Marlin-Ballard catalog recommends the new .22 Long "Rifle" cartridge for its No. 3 Gallery rifle as being more accurate than the common .22 Long or Extra Long.

At one time, the .22 Long Rifle was available in black-powder, semi-smokeless, and smokeless powder loads. Remington introduced the first high-velocity type, in 1930. The 40-grain solid and 36- and 38-grain hollowpoint bullet have been available for many years. The original case was not crimped, a feature that finally appeared in 1900. Space does not permit a full discussion of the different loads and types of .22 Long Rifle cartridges or the rifles and handguns that chamber it. Suffice to say, it is the most accurate and highly developed of any rimfire cartridge ever.

General Comments: The .22 Long Rifle is the most popular match cartridge in existence, and also the most widely used small-game and varmint cartridge. The high-velocity hollowpoint is the best field load and will do a good job on rabbit-sized animals out to 75 yards. Beyond that, it is unreliable. The Long Rifle is a great favorite of poachers for killing game out of season with close-up head shots. The modest report does not alarm or alert passersby or officials. At close range, the high-velocity load with the solid-lead bullet will penetrate six inches of soft pine board and has a maximum range of nearly two miles. Maximum range is achieved at the relatively low angle of between 25 and 30 degrees, so one must be very careful. Humans shot with the .22 Long Rifle often show little immediate distress, survive without complications for several days, then die very suddenly. This is mentioned because many individuals regard .22 rimfires as play things not powerful enough to be dangerous. Careless shooting with the .22 rimfire has probably led to the closure of more areas to hunting and caused more trouble than any other cartridge. Use your head and be careful! There is also a .22 Long Rifle shot cartridge, loaded by most companies and useful mostly for rat and other pest control.

.22 Stinger, Spitfire, Viper, Yellow Jacket, Super-Max, Xpediter, etc.

Historical Notes: The .22 Stinger was the first in a series of developments aimed at improving the performance of the .22 Long Rifle. Introduced by CCI early in 1977, the concept was an immediate success and quickly copied by Winchester with its Xpediter, by Remington in its Yellow Jacket, and by Federal with the Spitfire. All of these cartridges are much the same and are based on reducing the weight of the hollow-point bullet from 36 to around 30 grains and loading it into a case full of relatively slow-burning powder. The result is a 30 percent increase in muzzle velocity and a 25 percent increase in muzzle energy, as compared to the standard .22 Long Rifle hollow-point high-velocity loading. The overall loaded length of these rounds is the same as the regular .22 Long Rifle, and so are all other dimensions, with the exception of the case length. Some use a standard-length .22 Long Rifle case and settle for a somewhat lower muzzle velocity, while others use a longer case to achieve maximum velocity. As a group, these are referred to as hyper-velocity .22s. Only Stinger, Yellow Jacket, and Viper brands are still in production.

General Comments: The original author fired all of the increased velocity .22 Long Rifle cartridges available at the time, in both rifles and handguns, comparing the performance with the standard line of .22 rimfires, as well as the .22 WMR. When fired into paraffin blocks and soap bars, the hyper-velocity hollowpoints demonstrated superior expansion and energy transfer, compared to the regular high-velocity hollowpoints.

Malfunctions can occur when firing the hyper-velocity Long Rifles in auto pistols, and Barnes didn't think they are well suited to those types of handguns. They worked fine in revolvers.

Field-testing didn't demonstrate any great advantage of one over the other in shooting jackrabbits, nor any great superiority over the .22 WMR or the standard Long Rifle high-velocity hollowpoint. The hyper-velocity cartridges do inflict greater tissue damage than does the .22 Long Rifle hollowpoint. However, dead is dead, and you can't accomplish anything beyond that.

These cartridges do provide increased velocity and energy for .22 rimfire rifles. They probably extend the effective range on varmints or small game by a few yards. These cartridges cost some 65 percent more than regular .22 Long Rifle high-velocity hollowpoint, which is a negative factor. They certainly have a place in the .22 rimfire lineup, but their increased performance is most pronounced when they are fired from a rifle, rather than a handgun. In some instances, particularly in short-barreled pistols and revolvers or any revolver with a large barrel-to-cylinder gap, these loads can generate much less energy than standard .22 Long Rifle high-velocity loads. The bullets actually exit the muzzle more slowly.

.22 Hyper-Velocities Factory Ballistics

Bullet (grains)	Powder	Grains	Velocity	Energy	Source/Comments
29	FL, Win.		1,680	182	Xpediter (obsolete)
32	FL, CCI		1,640	191	Stinger
33	FL, Fed.		1,500	164	Spitfire (obsolete)
33	FL, Rem.		1,500	164	Yellowjacket
34	FL, Win.		1,500	169	Super-Max. (obsolete)
36	FL, Fed.		1,410	158	Spitfire (obsolete)
36	FL, Rem.		1,410	158	Viper
36	FL, CCI		1,425	162	CCI, HP+V

.22 Extra Long

Historical Notes: Introduced about 1880, the .22 Extra Long was used in Ballard, Remington, Stevens, Wesson, and late (1916) versions of the 1902 and 1904 Winchester bolt-action rifles, as well as S&W revolvers. It was listed in ammunition catalogs as late as 1935. It used the same 40-grain, outside-lubricated bullet that was later adapted to the .22 Long Rifle, but the longer case held more (six grains) black powder. It was more powerful than the Long Rifle, but not noted for great accuracy. Smokeless powder loads had nearly the same velocity as the modern Long Rifle loadings.

General Comments: The .22 Extra Long will not chamber in arms made for the Long Rifle, but, since the only dimensional difference is case length, the Short, Long, or Long Rifle can be fired in the Extra Long chamber. In terms of killing power, the Extra Long is in the same class as the standard velocity Long Rifle. At one time, the .22 Extra Long was advertised as a 200-yard target cartridge, but it certainly would not qualify for this by today's standards. Case length and overall cartridge length made the Extra Long unsuitable to most repeating actions, which is another reason it became obsolete. Never fire any high-velocity or hyper-velocity .22 cartridge in any black-powder gun.

.22 Remington Automatic

Historical Notes: This cartridge was developed for the Remington Model 16 autoloading rifle (actually introduced in 1914), and was discontinued in 1928. Ammunition has not been loaded since the end of World War II. The purpose of the cartridge was the same as the Winchester .22 Automatic, to prevent use of action-gumming black-powder ammunition in a semi-auto rifle. No other gun used this round, and it is not interchangeable with the 2.2 Winchester. This is an example of senseless, jealous rivalry, if ever there was one.

General Comments: This was another .22 Long Rifle-class cartridge. It had an inside-lubricated 45-grain bullet in solid or hollow-point type, both with the same ballistics. It was neither as accurate nor as effective (generally) as the Long Rifle.

.22 Winchester Rimfire (WRF)
.22 Remington Special

Historical Notes: Introduced for the Winchester Model 1890 pump-action rifle, the original Winchester loading had a flat-nose bullet, while Remington used a round-nose type and called it the .22 Remington Special. The two are identical and interchangeable. Bullet can be either a 45-grain solid or a 40-grain hollow-point in standard or high-velocity loading. This cartridge uses a flat-base inside-lubricated bullet, rather than the "heel" type of outside-lubricated bullet of the Short, Long, Long Rifle, and Extra Long. The .22 WRF was chambered in various Remington, Stevens, and Winchester single-shot and repeating rifles and Colt's revolvers. It is no longer routinely loaded by the ammunition manufacturers, and no one makes rifles for it. However, in late 1986, Winchester made a special run of .22 WRF ammunition. This must have been aimed more at collectors than shooters. It has since been produced in limited amounts.

General Comments: The .22 WRF was the first notable improvement in the killing power of the various .22 rimfires. It is not as accurate as the Long Rifle, but in field use, this is of no consequence. Out to 75 yards, it will kill small animals more reliably than the Long Rifle. Although there is little difference in bullet diameter between the WRF and the standard .22 rimfires, the WRF has a larger case diameter to accept the bullet's full diameter. It is much too large to fit the standard .22 Long Rifle chamber. The .22 Short or Long Rifle fits the WRF chamber quite loosely and will not fire or extract in many guns. When these do fire, the case often splits, which allows particles to escape the action with possible danger to the shooter and bystanders; accuracy is extremely poor. The .22 WRF can be safely fired in any gun chambered for the .22 Winchester Magnum Rimfire. Winchester produced one batch of these cartridges in 1995.

Previous editions of this book listed this cartridge as obsolete. However, there seems to be a bit of renewed interest in the cartridge. CCI is currently loading this round as a 45-grain jacketed hollow-point with a muzzle velocity of 1300 fps and energy of 169 ft-lbs. CCI does not recommend this round for use in revolvers, noting that most revolvers have undersized bores that resist the use of copper-jacketed bullets.

.22 Winchester Magnum Rimfire (WMR)

Historical Notes: The .22 Magnum Rimfire was introduced in 1959 by Winchester, but the company didn't market a gun to shoot it until well into the following year. Ruger and Smith & Wesson, on the other hand, advertised revolvers for the new round before the end of 1959, and Savage chambered its Model 24, a .22/.410-bore over/under combination gun, for the Magnum Rimfire shortly thereafter. The discontinued slide-action Winchester Model 61 was the first rifle of that manufacture available for the new round. At present, there is a wide variety of single-shot and repeating rifles, as well as pistols and revolvers of American and European manufacture available in .22 Magnum Rimfire caliber. The standard bullet is a jacketed 40-grain type, although Federal introduced a 50-grain bullet in 1988. CCI recently introduced a hyper-velocity loading with a 30-grain bullet, and Federal soon joined the "hyper-velocity" fray with a similar loading.

General Comments: The .22 Winchester Magnum Rimfire is an elongated and more powerful version of the older .22 WRF. Case dimensions are the same except for length, and the WRF can be fired in any gun chambered for the Magnum Rimfire. It is not a safe practice to re-chamber older guns for the new round. The .22 WRF is loaded with outside-lubricated lead bullets, while the .22 WMR is loaded with jacketed bullets. With a thin-jacketed 40-grain bullet at about 1,900 fps, this is the most potent rimfire cartridge currently available. It is more powerful than the .22 Winchester Centerfire, forerunner of the .22 Hornet. Claimed ballistics in a six-inch pistol barrel exceed any other rimfire fired from a rifle, thus, it is a very effective 125-yard varmint or small-game cartridge, although overly destructive on animals intended for the pot, unless solid bullets are used. CCI also loads a shot version.

.22 ILARCO/.22 WMR Short

Historical Notes: The .22 ILARCO Rimfire originated in 1987 and was manufactured in experimental quantities by Winchester for the Illinois Arms Co. It is the .22 Winchester Magnum Rimfire shortened to the same loaded length as the .22 Long Rifle. It was chambered in the Illinois Arms Co.'s Model 180 auto/semi-auto rifle, which features a 165-round drum-type magazine. A full-auto version was available only to law-enforcement agencies. The reason for the shorter cartridge was that the Model 180 was designed for the .22 Long Rifle and the action wouldn't handle the longer .22 WMR. The Illinois Arms Co. was bought by Feather Industries, of Boulder, Colorado, and the .22 ILARCO was discontinued. The cartridge is sometimes referred to as the .22 WMR Short.

General Comments: Shortening the .22 WMR made sense, even though there was some velocity loss. For one thing, the short case used the same jacketed bullet as the parent cartridge and didn't pick up dirt and debris the way sticky, outside-lubricated .22 Long Rifle cartridges can. With a 165-round magazine and full-auto fire, this was a matter of some importance. Also, the .22 WMR is too long to function in practically any .22 semi-automatic pistol, but many of these could be adapted to fire the .22 ILARCO. Unfortunately, this cartridge never went into production, and existing specimens are now collector's items.

Bullet (grains/type)	Powder	Grains	Velocity	Energy	Source/Comments
40 FMJ	FL		1,350	160	Winchester factory load

.25 Short

Historical Notes: Originally, this pistol cartridge was developed for the F.D. Bliss revolver, also known as the .25 Bacon & Bliss. It was chambered in other cheap handguns of the period. Date of introduction was around 1860, and both Remington and Winchester listed it in catalogs up to 1920. It is a collector's item now.

General Comments: The .25 Short had a 43-grain, outside-lubricated bullet and five grains of powder. Bullet diameter is actually .245- to .246-inch, and it closely resembles the .22 Short. In power, it is similar to the black-powder .22 Long Rifle fired from a short pistol barrel. There is no record of any rifle having been chambered for the .25 Short. It should not be confused with the .25 Stevens Short.

.25 Stevens Short

Historical Notes: Introduced in 1902, this cartridge was intended as a shorter, cheaper, and less powerful version of the .25 Stevens. The original loading used 4½ to five grains of black powder, but only smokeless powder was in use, when it was discontinued in 1942. Remington, Winchester, and Stevens rifles chambered this round. It could be fired in any rifle chambered for the .25 Stevens.

General Comments: The .25 Stevens Short was not nearly as effective a field cartridge as the longer version. However, it was somewhat cheaper and certainly as good or better than the .22 Short for small game at close range. More expensive than the .22 Long Rifle and no better for hunting purposes, it was never popular.

.25 Stevens

Historical Notes: Various dates can be found for the introduction of the .25 Stevens, with most authorities agreeing on 1900. Old books and catalogs indicate an actual date of 1890, but this is uncertain. This cartridge was developed jointly by the J. Stevens Arms & Tool Co. and the Peters Cartridge Co. The Stevens Crack Shot No. 15 rifle came out in 1900, and one of its original chamberings was the .25 Stevens. However, the Stevens Favorite rifle, made from 1894 to 1935, may have been the first model available in this round. Both are under-lever single-shots. Remington and Winchester also chambered rifles for the .25 Stevens. The original load was a 67-grain bullet and 10 to 11 grains of black powder. Semi-smokeless powder was also used, but smokeless was the only propellant offered when the round was discontinued, in 1942. Remington did preliminary work on an improved, high-velocity loading prior to World War II, but the project was dropped after the war. The improved round, called the .267 Remington Rimfire, was rumored to have had a muzzle velocity of 1400 fps with the 67-grain bullet.

General Comments: The .25 Stevens had an excellent reputation on small game, especially for not ruining edible meat. Most complaints centered around the high cost, as compared to the .22 Long Rifle, as well as the high trajectory, which made hits beyond 60 to 70 yards difficult. For years, gun writers called for a high-velocity version, but the ammunition companies failed to respond. With modern powder and a longer case, a velocity of 1600 to 1800 fps might be possible.

Rifles are no longer chambered for this round and ammunition is no longer manufactured, so it appears to be a dead number. Many who used the .25 Stevens were sorry to see it go, but, with the .22 Magnum Rimfire, there isn't much need for it. It had an inside-lubricated bullet and was available with solid and hollow-point bullets.

.30 Short

Historical Notes: This old-timer originated in the early 1860s and was used mostly in low-priced handguns, such as the Sharps four-barrel, the Standard revolver, and various single-shots. Colt's New Line revolvers were also made in .30 Short and .30 Long chamberings. The .30 Short was listed in ammunition catalogs as late as 1919.

General Comments: The .30 Short had a 50- to 58-grain lead bullet and five to six grains of black powder. Not a powerful round by any standard, its use was confined to pocket or house guns. It was not as good of a cartridge as the .32 Short rimfire, and one wonders why it survived for so long. It is now a collector's item.

.30 Long

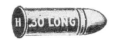

Historical Notes: This rimfire was cataloged as early as 1873, but may have originated earlier. Adapted to Colt's, Standard X.L., and Sharps handguns, it was also used in some single-shot rifles. The .30 Short survived until 1920; the .30 Long disappeared before WWI.

General Comments: The .30 Short and .30 Long were interchangeable in most guns. The bullet was actually .290- to .295-inch and of outside-lubricated type. Power of the .30 Long was about the same as the .32 Short rimfire.

.32 Long Rifle

Historical Notes: This cartridge has an inside-lubricated bullet and a longer case than the regular .32 Long rimfire. It appears on cartridge lists from 1900 into the early 1920s. Both Remington and Winchester loaded it. Some say it was a smokeless powder improvement over the older .32 Long, but the 1918-'19 Remington catalog lists it as available in the black-powder loading only. It has been obsolete for many years and is a collector's item.

General Comments: Case length of the .32 Long Rifle is between that of the .32 Long and Extra Long rimfires; other dimensions are practically identical. It could be fired in any rifle chambered for the Extra Long, and most rifles or revolvers made to handle the Long. The outside-lubricated bullet was messy to carry in the pocket or loose in a container. These bullets picked up lint and dirt, stained the pocket, etc. Inside-lubricated bullets are much cleaner to handle under any conditions, which is the reason efforts were made to produce such versions. However, this required a smaller diameter bullet, which gave unacceptable accuracy in the original barrel. That may have been why the .32 Long Rifle had a short life. No one seems to have made a gun specifically for it, or at least the author found no reference to such. The original load was an 81- or 82-grain lead bullet with 13 grains of black powder.

.32 Extra Short/.32 Protector

Historical Notes: This cartridge was made for the Remington magazine pistol and the Chicago Firearms Co.'s Protector palm pistol. The Remington pistol was manufactured from 1871 until 1888, and the odd palm pistol originated sometime in the 1880s. This fixes the date of introduction for the .32 Extra Short at 1871, though some authorities indicate a later date. The cartridge was listed in Remington catalogs until 1920. It was also known as the .32 Protector.

General Comments: The .32 was a popular chambering for both handguns and rifles for many years. The .32 Extra Short was probably designed to increase the magazine capacity of the Remington-Rider magazine pistol. Since it held five short rounds, it would have held only three of the standard .32 Short rimfires. A longer pistol would have been unhandy. Likewise, a reduced magazine capacity would not have been competitive with the five- and seven-shot revolvers of the day. Sales departments have to consider all these angles. The Remington magazine pistol had a tubular magazine below the barrel and a "lever" that protruded slightly above the hammer. Lever and hammer were drawn back together, which cocked the gun and extracted the empty shell. Release of the lever chambered a new round as it returned to the forward position. It was of limited popularity. The original load was five to 5½ grains of black powder with a 54- to 60-grain lead bullet.

.32 Short

Historical Notes: The .32 Short rimfire originated under a Smith & Wesson patent of 1860, and early cartridge boxes were so marked. It was first used in the Smith & Wesson New Model 1½ and Model 2 revolvers. It was later adapted to Colt revolvers and others with names such as Allen, Blue Jacket, Enterprise, Favorite, Whitney, X.L., and many, many others. It was also used in a variety of rifles, including models from Remington, Stevens, and Winchester. It was loaded and listed in some ammunition catalogs as late as 1972. Navy Arms had .32 rimfire ammunition made in Brazil, in 1990. Until recently, .32 Short ammunition has been available from that source.

General Comments: Rifles and pistols using the .32 Short were popular up to the early 1900s. Stevens single-shot rifles were available in this round, until 1936. There are tens of thousands of guns around for this cartridge. It actually was a good small-game cartridge out to 50 yards, killing cleanly with hits in the forward body area and not spoiling meat. Accuracy wasn't outstanding, but adequate for field use. However, ammunition costs more than .22 Long Rifle loads, which is a consideration in choosing a rimfire gun. The .32 rimfire is obsolete. The original load had an 80-grain bullet and nine grains of black powder.

.32 Long

Historical Notes: The .32 Long was originally a revolver cartridge and was later used extensively in various rifles. It was introduced for the Smith & Wesson New Model 2 revolver in 1861. It was quickly picked up by other manufacturers and offered in such makes as the Allen, Enterprise, Favorite, Forehand & Wadsworth, Harrington & Richardson, Pioneer, Webley, X.L., and many others. Colt's New Line revolvers were available in this chambering, also. Stevens single-shot pistols and rifles featured it, as did Marlin, Ballard, Maynard, Remington, and Winchester single-shot rifles. It is no longer produced in the United States. Navy Arms had .32 Long ammunition made in Brazil in 1990. Until recently, this ammunition was available from that source.

General Comments: The .32 Long rimfire has a heavier bullet and delivers more energy than the .32 Short, although velocity is about the same. The original load had an outside-lubricated 90-grain lead bullet with 12 to 13 grains of black powder. It was a good short-range small-game number because, like other cartridges in the same class, it killed cleanly without ruining edible meat. However, it was not effective beyond 50 yards, because of the relatively high trajectory, which made bullet placement difficult at long range. Single-shot Stevens rifles in this chambering were made until 1936.

.32 Extra Long

Historical Notes: The exact date of introduction of this cartridge is obscure. It is listed in various catalogs of 1876, so it probably originated in the mid-1870s. Ballard, Remington, Stevens, and Wesson single-shot rifles chambered it. It does not appear in post-World War I catalogs. Many gun companies charged extra for rifles chambered to shoot any of the extra-long rim- or centerfire cartridges. Some authorities place the date of introduction as 1866.

General Comments: The original load for this rimfire was a 90-grain, outside-lubricated lead bullet and 18 to 20 grains of black powder. The bullet is the same as that used in the ordinary .32 Long, but there were variations, depending on the ammunition maker. The .32 Extra Long was not a very accurate cartridge and never established itself as a match round. It extends the effective hunting range of the rimfire .32 out to perhaps 65 to 75 yards, but doesn't possess appreciably greater killing power than the .32 Long.

.38 Short

Historical Notes: When the Civil War ended in 1865, a number of rimfire cartridges had been developed and used successfully in battle. Most were large-caliber rifle cartridges. After the war, there was demand for smaller-caliber metallic cartridges for revolvers and sporting rifles. Both the .38 Short and Long rimfires date from this period and are listed in the 1869 Folsom Bros. & Co. gun catalog. The Remington Model 1866 revolving rifle was available in .38 rimfire. In 1871, the Remington New Model revolver was advertised as available with an extra .38 rimfire cylinder. The .38 Short rimfire was listed in the 1876 J. Brown & Son catalog for use in Ballard, Remington, and Wesson rifles and Allen, Colt's, Enterprise, Whitney, X.L., and other pistols. This is now an obsolete cartridge, but it was manufactured until 1940.

General Comments: The .38 Short rimfire is in the same class as the centerfire .38 Short Colt. The original loading was a 130-grain lead bullet and 18 grains of black powder. Like most older rimfires, the bullet is outside-lubricated. Bullet diameter is .375-inch, the same as the ball fired in .36-caliber cap-and-ball revolvers. The .38 Short probably originated as a cartridge for breech-loading conversions of these old revolvers. Many catalogs listed the .38 Short for use in pistols and revolvers, whereas the .38 Long is shown as a rifle round. The Rollin White patent covering the bored-through cylinder, held by Smith & Wesson, did not expire until 1869. This undoubtedly had an effect on the use of the rimfire .38 Short for revolvers.

.38 Long

Historical Notes: The rimfire .38 Long is an old-timer dating to before 1865 and the end of the Civil War. The Remington-Beals single-shot rifle was available in .38 Long, from 1867 until 1875. The Remington revolving rifle of 1866 was also made for it. It was used in Allen, Ballard, Remington, Stevens, and Wesson rifles of later date, and in Enterprise, Favorite, Forehand & Wadsworth, and Colt revolvers. It was a popular rifle and pistol chambering up to the turn of the century. It was replaced by similar centerfire rounds. American companies stopped loading it in the late 1920s.

General Comments: The rimfire .38 Long is in the same general class as the centerfire .38 Long Colt. The original load was a 150-grain outside-lubricated bullet and 18 grains of black powder. However, loads varied with different manufacturers, ranging from a 140- to 150-grain bullet and up to 21 grains of powder with the light bullet. In a rifle, it was a good short-range small-game load, but accuracy was only fair. No one has made rifles in this chambering since the end of World War I.

.38 Extra Long

Historical Notes: The rimfire .38 Extra Long appeared about 1870 and was chambered in Ballard, Howard, Remington, Robinson, and F. Wesson single-shot rifles. It was not a standard Ballard chambering, but a special-order item that cost 50 cents extra. It was strictly a rifle chambering, being too long for most revolvers. Because of mediocre accuracy, plus the development of similar centerfire cartridges, the .38 Extra Long rimfire did not have a long life. It was not carried in the 1918-'19 Remington catalog, but was listed in the 1916 Winchester catalog.

General Comments: The .38 Extra Long is in a class well below the centerfire .38-40 WCF black-powder loading. The original load was a 150-grain outside-lubricated bullet and 30 to 31 grains of black powder. However, some companies loaded lighter bullets down to 140 grains and with slightly more powder. It was not a bad small- to medium-game cartridge out to about 80 yards or so. It was introduced at a time when the centerfire was emerging as the dominant type, so it did not build up a following. The centerfire .38 Extra Long was developed by Ballard, in 1855-'56, and was preferred because it was reloadable.

.41 Short (Derringer)

Historical Notes: This is an old and once very popular rimfire, because of the light, handy arms that chambered it. The .41 Short was introduced with the National Arms Co. breech-loading derringer in 1863. It was originally called the .41-100 rimfire. The National derringer was patented by Daniel Moore, in 1861 and 1863. It was made by National from its introduction until 1870, when the company was purchased by Colt. From 1872 to 1890, this rotating-barrel derringer was manufactured by Colt. Colt also adapted the .41 Short to the Thuer-patented or Third Model derringer, as well as the House pistol, or Cloverleaf cylinder model, of 1871. Derringers made by Allen, Enterprise, Williamson, X.L., and others were also of .41 Short chambering. The Remington over/under or double-barrel derringer, manufactured from 1866 to 1935, was the most famous and popular of the lot. Several low-priced pocket revolvers were also chambered for the .41 Short. It has been obsolete since World War II, but special lots of ammunition have been loaded since the war.

General Comments: The .41 Short rimfire is so underpowered as to be worthless for anything but rats, mice, or sparrows at short range. Fired from the average derringer at a tree or hard object 15 to 25 yards away, the bullet will often bounce back and land at your feet. Nevertheless, it was a popular self-defense cartridge and, at point-blank range, could inflict a severe wound or kill a human being. These .41 derringer pistols were more of a threat or morale builder than anything else. The original load was a 130-grain outside-lubricated lead bullet and 13 grains of black powder. Late loads used smokeless powder.

.41 Long

Historical Notes: This is a longer and slightly more powerful version of the .41 Short. It originated in 1873, and the Colt's New Line revolvers appear to be the first to chamber it. The Enterprise No. 4, Favorite No. 4, Forehand & Wadsworth, Webley, and other revolvers were available in this chambering. A few cheap single-shot rifles also chambered it. It has been obsolete since the 1920s.

General Comments: The rimfire .41 Long is a better cartridge than the Short, but not by much. There was some variation in bullet weight and powder charge, but the original load used a 163-grain bullet and 13 to 15 grains of black powder. The centerfire .41 Short is an outgrowth of this cartridge. Guns chambered for the Long could also shoot the .41 Short rimfire. In power, this cartridge is in about the same class as the .38 S&W centerfire in the black-powder loading.

.44 Short

Historical Notes: The .44 Short was a handgun cartridge, although it could be fired in arms chambered for the .44 Long rimfire. It is well-established in old catalogs dating from 1870 and chambered in popular pistols and revolvers, including those made by Allen, Forehand & Wadsworth, and Remington. It is best noted as being the cartridge for the single-shot Hammond Bulldog pistol made by the Connecticut Arms & Mfg. Co., of Naubuc, Conn. This pistol is believed to have been marketed before the end of the Civil War, which would place the date of origin of the .44 Short about 1864-'65. It has been obsolete since the 1920s.

General Comments: The rimfire .44 Short is a better handgun cartridge than the .41 Short or Long, but wasn't generally as popular. The type and variety of guns that chambered it was rather limited. The original load was a 200- or 210-grain outside-lubricated bullet and 15 to 17 grains of black powder. While velocity was low, with the 200-grain bullet, short-range stopping power was fairly good. Performance was similar to the centerfire British .44 Webley cartridge.

.44 Henry Flat

Historical Notes: This old and particularly historic cartridge is one of the milestones in the development of modern arms and ammunition. It was developed by B. Tyler Henry for the lever-action repeating rifle bearing his name, the forerunner of the original Winchester lever-action rifle and conceptually and functionally similar to all models up to the 1876. The Henry rifle was manufactured by the New Haven Arms Co., from 1860 to 1866, at which time it was reorganized as the Winchester Repeating Arms Co.

The .44 Henry cartridge was manufactured from 1860-'61 to 1934. Two versions of the cartridge were offered. The early case was .815-inch long. Bullet and powder charge were the same. Colt's revolvers were also made in .44 Henry chambering. The Henry rifle and cartridge saw limited use in the Civil War.

General Comments: The .44 Henry, although quite successful, was not a powerful round. Barely adequate for deer and certainly no match for buffalo or grizzly bear, its principal advantage was in the 15-shot repeating rifle. This provided undreamed-of firepower, something that could be decisive in combat. In recognition of this fact, Winchester brought out an improved rifle chambered for the .44-40 cartridge, in 1873. From that date on, Winchester was in continuing competition with the makers of single-shot rifles and their big, powerful buffalo cartridges. The .44 Henry used a 200-grain bullet and 26 to 28 grains of black powder.

.44 Extra Long

Historical Notes: This Ballard-developed cartridge is a longer, more powerful version of the rimfire .44 Long. Unfortunately, it was introduced about 1869, and soon the .44-40 Winchester Center Fire was establishing a reputation in the West. This number had a very short life, becoming obsolete by the 1880s. The exact date of introduction is vague, but probably between 1870-'75. It is listed in the 1876 catalogs as adapted to Ballard, Remington, and F. Wesson rifles.

General Comments: The .44 Extra Long isn't as good a general-purpose cartridge as the .44-40 Winchester. For one, it used an outside-lubricated bullet, plus overall length was too long for many repeating actions. It was loaded with a 218-grain bullet and 46 grains of black powder. It was not noted for great accuracy. In power, it would be primarily a small-game number. Effective range was not much over 75 yards.

.44 Long

Historical Notes: The rimfire .44 Long originated with the Ethan Allen carbine, patented in 1860 and manufactured by Allen & Wheelock, of Worcester, Mass. It was later adapted to rifles made by Ballard, Howard, Remington, Robinson, and F. Wesson. It was fairly popular, but was replaced by similar centerfire types. It became obsolete in the early 1920s.

General Comments: With a 220-grain bullet and 28 grains of black powder, the .44 Long was a potent short-range cartridge for small game. The .44-40 WCF rapidly became the dominant .44-caliber cartridge after it was introduced, in 1873. It could be reloaded and was available in repeating rifles and revolvers, important factors on the western frontier. Other .44 cartridges, particularly the rimfire, gradually declined in use and popularity. The .44 Long was neither as powerful nor as accurate as the .44-40.

.46 Long

Historical Notes: The .46 Long rimfire was listed in an advertisement by Schuler, Hartley & Graham's in 1864. It is listed in the 1887 Remington catalog as a short-range chambering for the Remington rolling block single-shot Sporting Rifle No. 1, and also for Ballard rifles. The cartridge was loaded by Remington, Winchester, and others and carried in ammunition catalogs up to World War I, but did not survive the war. It originated in the early 1870s.

General Comments: The .46 Long was loaded by Remington, with a 305-grain bullet and 35 grains of black powder. Winchester listed a 300-grain bullet and 40 grains of powder. There may have been other loadings by other companies. It was a marginal short-range deer cartridge.

.46 Short

Historical Notes: The .46 Short rimfire is usually listed for the Remington Single Action Army revolver. However, the 1878 and 1891 Winchester catalogs both describe this cartridge as, "For Remington, Smith & Wesson, and other Army revolvers." Both Remington and Winchester loaded this cartridge. It was carried in their catalogs up to World War I, but did not appear after the war. Date of introduction was circa 1870.

General Comments: The .46 Short rimfire was listed in Remington catalogs as having a 227-grain bullet and 20 grains of black powder. Winchester's loading was a 230-grain bullet and 26 grains of powder. As a revolver cartridge, it would have been less powerful than the .44-40 WCF.

.46 Extra Long

Historical Notes: The .46 Extra Long rimfire was a Ballard cartridge for its single-shot rifle and may also have been used by others. It does not appear in the Remington 1871 catalog, so it originated sometime after that date. Remington appears to have been the only one that loaded this cartridge, and it was carried in later catalogs up to World War I, but did not reappear after that war.

General Comments: Remington listed the .46 Extra Long as being loaded with a 305-grain bullet and 57 grains of black powder. There was never a smokeless loading. It would have been somewhat more powerful than the .46 Long and a better short-range deer cartridge. None of the .46-caliber rifle cartridges enjoyed a reputation for great accuracy. However, since these cartridges survived for quite a few years, these evidently did have a fair following.

.56-46 Spencer

Historical Notes: This post-Civil War sporting cartridge was introduced by Spencer in 1866 for his repeating small carbine and sporting rifle. It was also listed as the No. 46 or .46/100 caliber. Spencer lever-action sporting arms were manufactured from 1866 until the firm failed, in 1868-'69. Winchester bought up the surplus guns and Spencer patents, but did not manufacture those rifles. However, the company sold off surplus rifles through its agents from 1869 to 1872. The cartridge has been obsolete since before World War I, but was cataloged until 1919.

General Comments: The .56-46 Spencer is actually a .44-caliber, bottlenecked cartridge. It was considerably more powerful than the .44-40 WCF. A 320- to 330-grain bullet and 45 grains of black powder was the standard load. It was a fairly good short-range deer cartridge, but not satisfactory for larger game. The actions of early repeating rifles weren't suited to large or long cartridges. This lack of power caused many hunters and the military to adopt the single-shot rifle, even though the repeater was well-proven. Full-powered repeating rifles, able to compete with the single-shot rifle on any basis, did not appear until 1880.

.50 Remington Navy

Historical Notes: Developed for the single-shot, rolling block, Remington Navy pistol of 1865, this load was replaced within a year by an identical, inside-primed centerfire type. The final commercial version, Boxer primed, was manufactured until World War I. The Remington Navy pistol has been obsolete since the early 1870s.

General Comments: The .50-caliber rimfire was a rather potent handgun round. Velocity was low, but the big heavy bullet would have had considerable effectiveness. However, .44- or .45-caliber handguns are more efficient, and the military eventually standardized on .45-caliber cartridge arms. The original load was a 290-grain bullet and 23 grains of black powder.

.56-50 Spencer

Historical Notes: This cartridge was actually designed by Springfield Armory late in 1861. It was used in the 1865 model Spencer repeating carbine, a seven-shot, lever-action arm with a 20- or 22-inch barrel. The magazine was in the buttstock and was loaded through a trap, as with modern .22 rimfire rifles. This particular rifle and cartridge was manufactured too late for use in the Civil War, but was issued to troops fighting Indians on the western frontier. The .56-50 cartridge was listed in ammunition catalogs until 1920. The 1918-'19 Remington catalog illustrated it as "adapted to Spencer, Remington UMC, Sharps, Peabody and other rifles and carbines." The 1865 Spencer incorporated the Stabler magazine cutoff not present on earlier models. Spencer didn't like the .56-50 cartridge, because he thought it had an excessive crimp; it is not advertised in Spencer catalogs. He designed a slightly different version, which became known as the .56-52.

General Comments: The .56-50 cartridge was loaded with a 350-grain bullet and 45 grains of black powder. It could penetrate almost a foot of soft pine at a range of 15 feet and was a potent short-range cartridge. It was adequate for deer-sized animals, but not satisfactory against larger game. Most western hunters preferred the more powerful single-shot rifles and their big, long-range cartridges. The Spencer action was not adaptable to the long centerfire cartridges that were developed in the years immediately after the Civil War.

.56-52 Spencer/.56-52 Spencer Necked

Historical Notes: Dating from 1866, this is an alteration of the Army-designed .56-50, which Spencer believed had too much crimp. His approach was to incorporate a slight bottleneck, but many manufacturers omitted this, so it is difficult to distinguish between these two rounds. However, these cartridges are interchangeable, and any arm chambered for one will fire the other. Spencer .56-52 ammunition was listed in ammunition catalogs, up until 1920.

General Comments: The .56-52 is more a sporting than a military round. Power is the same as the .56-50, but some companies loaded a heavier bullet. Remington produced a cartridge with 45 grains of powder and a two-groove, flat-point, 400-grain bullet. The .56-50 was always loaded with a 350-grain bullet. By modern standards, the .56-52 would barely qualify as a short-range deer cartridge. It was more powerful than modern smokeless factory .44-40 WCF loads.

.56-56 Spencer

Historical Notes: This is the original cartridge for the first Spencer rifle and carbine, patented March 6, 1860, and manufactured in quantity beginning in 1862. Despite great opposition from the U.S. Army Ordnance Department, these guns were finally adopted and used during the Civil War. These first appeared at the Battle of Antietam in September 1862, and later played a decisive role in other important engagements. The Spencer is credited as having provided the Union armies with an advantage in firepower that gave them a critical edge in turning back the Confederate forces at Gettysburg. President Lincoln tested the Spencer rifle in 1863 and insisted that the Army place substantial orders with Christopher M. Spencer. Many authorities insist that, if the Spencer rifle had been adopted at the onset of the war and issued in quantity, it would have shortened the Civil War by a year or more and greatly reduced the ultimate number of casualties. (Since more combatants died from dysentery than from battlefield wounds and injuries, it would seem that last contention probably has even more merit than the originators might have realized.) The .56-56 cartridge was loaded by ammunition manufacturers until 1920.

General Comments: The Spencer rifle was a seven-shot repeater of lever-action type, with the magazine located in the buttstock and loaded through a trap in the buttplate. It could be fired at the rate of seven shots in 12 seconds, faster in the hands of a real expert. Parts were interchangeable, and the gun could be disassembled with only a screwdriver. The .56-56 cartridge was loaded with a 350- to 360-grain bullet and 42 to 45 grains of black powder. Bullet diameter varies from .540- to .555-inch between various makes of ammunition. Ballard and Joslyn carbines also used this cartridge. It was a short-range number, not very effective on anything larger than deer.

.58 Miller/.58 Allin

Historical Notes: This cartridge was used in the 1867 Miller breech-loading conversion system of the muzzleloading Springfield rifled musket. It was listed in an advertisement by Schuyler, Hartley & Graham's in 1864. It came in two case lengths, 13/16 inches and 17/16 inches, and was used chiefly in first-model Allin conversions. The Miller swinging-block conversion was one of a number of experimental alterations used by the military, in an effort to salvage the million-plus .58-caliber muskets left over from the Civil War. The idea was to convert those guns to some viable breech-loading system rather than into scrap. Although some of the conversion units worked quite well, the effort was not entirely successful, and most of these guns were eventually sold off as surplus or scrap metal. There must have been a fair number of the Miller conversions around, though, because the cartridge was listed in ammunition catalogs at least as late as 1910. This cartridge is also called the .585 Springfield, .58 Musket, .58 Allen, and .58 Ball.

General Comments: The .58 Miller rimfire featured a 500-grain bullet backed by 60 grains of black powder for a muzzle velocity of approximately 1150 fps. It would have been a pretty good short-range deer cartridge. Some specimens have a heavy crimp, which affects the measurable length of the unfired case and results in variations in published figures for the case length. Remington, Winchester, and others listed this round.

Dimensional Data

Cartridge	Case	Bullet Dia.	Neck Dia.	Shoulder Dia.	Base Dia.	Rim Dia.	Rim Thick.	Case Length	Ctge. Length	Page
.17 Mach 2	A	.172	.195	.224	.225	.275	.040	.594	UNK/NA	611
.17 Mach 2	A	.172	.1900	.2046	.2260	.2780	.007	.7140	1.000	611
.17 Hornady Magnum Rimfire	A	.172	.195	.240	.241	.291	.046	1.052	UNK/NA	611
.17 Winchester Super Magnum	A	.172	UNK/NA	UNK/NA	UNK/NA	UNK/NA	UNK/NA	1.200	UNK/NA	611
.17 PMC/.17 Aguila/ .17 High Standard	A	.172	UNK/NA	UNK/NA	UNK/NA	.271	.039	.591	.9842	612
5mm Remington Magnum	A	.205	.225	.259	.259	.325	.050	1.020	UNK/NA	612
.22 BB Cap	B	.223	.224	UNK/NA	.224	.270	.040	.284	.343	613
.22 CB Cap	B	.222	.225	UNK/NA	.225	.271	.040	.420	.520	613
.22 Winchester Automatic	B	.222	.250	UNK/NA	.250	.310	.040	.665	.915	613
.22 Short	B	.223	.224	UNK/NA	.225	.273	.040	.423	.686	614
.22 Short/40-grain (RWS load)	B	.223	.224	UNK/NA	.225	.272	.042	.415	.798	614
.22 Long	B	.223	.224	UNK/NA	.225	.275	.040	.595	.880	614
.22 Long Rifle	B	.223	.224	UNK/NA	.225	.275	.040	.595	.975	615
.22 Stinger, etc. (hyper-velocities)	B	.223	.24	UNK/NA	.225	.275	.040	.694	.975	615
.22 Extra Long	B	.223	.225	UNK/NA	.225	.275	.040	.750	1.16	616
.22 Remington Automatic	B	.223	.245	UNK/NA	.245	.290	UNK/NA	.663	.920	616
.22 WRF & Remington Special	B	.224	.242	UNK/NA	.243	.295	.046	.960	1.17	616
.22 Winchester Magnum Rimfire	B	.224	.240	UNK/NA	.241	.291	.046	1.052	1.35	617
.22 ILARCO/.22 WMR Short	UNK/NA	UNK/NA	UNK/NA	UNK/NA	UNK/NA	UNK/NA	UNK/NA	UNK/NA	UNK/NA	617
.25 Short	B	.246	.245	UNK/NA	.245	.290	UNK/NA	.468	.780	618
.25 Stevens Short	B	.251	.275	UNK/NA	.276	.333	UNK/NA	.599	.877	618
.25 Stevens	B	.251	.276	UNK/NA	.276	.333	UNK/NA	1.125	1.395	618
.30 Short	B	.286	.292	UNK/NA	.292	.346	UNK/NA	.515	.822	619
.30 Long	B	.288	.288	UNK/NA	.288	.340	UNK/NA	.613	1.020	619
.32 Long Rifle	B	.312	.318	UNK/NA	.318	.377	UNK/NA	.937	1.223	619
.32 Extra Short/.32 Protector	B	.316	.318	UNK/NA	.317	.367	UNK/NA	.398	.645	619
.32 Short	B	.316	.318	UNK/NA	.318	.377	UNK/NA	.575	.948	620
.32 Long	B	.316	.318	UNK/NA	.318	.377	UNK/NA	.791	1.215	620
.32 Extra Long	B	.316	.317	UNK/NA	.318	.378	UNK/NA	1.150	1.570	620
.38 Short	B	.375	.376	UNK/NA	.376	.436	UNK/NA	.768	1.185	620
.38 Long	B	.375	.376	UNK/NA	.376	.435	UNK/NA	.873	1.380	621
.38 Extra Long	B	.375	.378	UNK/NA	.378	.435	UNK/NA	1.480	2.025	621
.41 Short	B	.405	.406	UNK/NA	.406	.468	UNK/NA	.467	.913	621
.41 Long	B	.405	.407	UNK/NA	.407	.468	UNK/NA	.635	.985	622
.44 Short	B	.446	.445	UNK/NA	.445	.519	.066	.688	1.190	622
.44 Henry Flat	B	.446	.445	UNK/NA	.446	.519	.066	.875	1.345	622
.44 Extra Long	B	.446	.456	UNK/NA	.457	.524	UNK/NA	1.250	1.843	623
.44 Long	B	.451	.455	UNK/NA	.458	.525	UNK/NA	1.094	1.842	623
.46 Long	B	.454	.456	UNK/NA	.456	.523	UNK/NA	1.25	1.876	623
.46 Short	B	.456	.458	UNK/NA	.458	.530	UNK/NA	.836	1.336	623
.46 Extra Long	B	.459	.457	UNK/NA	.457	.525	UNK/NA	1.534	2.285	624
.56-46 Spencer	A	.465	.478	.555	.558	.641	UNK/NA	1.035	1.595	624
.50 Remington Navy	B	.510	.535	UNK/NA	.562	.642	UNK/NA	.860	1.280	624
.56-50 Spencer	B	.512	.543	UNK/NA	.556	.639	.065	1.156	1.632	624
.56-52 Spencer	B	.512	.540	UNK/NA	.559	.639	.065	1.035	1.500	625
.56-52 Spencer Necked	A	.525	.547	.558	.560	.642	.065	1.020	1.660	625
.56-56 Spencer	B	.550	.560	UNK/NA	.560	.645	.065	.875	1.545	625

Codes: A = Rim, bottleneck. B = Rim, straight. Unless otherwise noted, all dimensions are in inches. These cases have slight taper at case mouth-to-neck juncture, neck diameter measurement is taken at case mouth. UNK/NA = Unknown/Not Applicable.

Note: Rimfire cartridges dimensions show considerable variation, depending upon manufacturer, specific production lot, and production era.

Current Rimfire Factory Ballistics

Load	Bullet Weight (grains)	Muzzle Velocity (fps)	Velocity 50 yards (fps)	Velocity 100 yards (fps)	Muzzle Energy (ft. lbs.)	Energy 50 yards (ft. lbs.)	Energy 100 yards (ft. lbs.)	Trajectory 50 yards (inches)	Trajectory 100 yards (inches)
.17 Mach II Hornady NTX	15.5	2,050	UNK	1,450	149	UNK	75	UNK	ZERO
.17 Mach II Hornady V-Max	17	2,100	1,884	1,677	166	134	106	ZERO	-3.0
.17 HMR CCI TNT-HP Lead Free	16	2,500	2,176	1,867	222	168	124	ZERO	-0.1
.17 HMR Federal Speer TNT	17	2,530	2,150	1,804	242	173	123	ZERO	-0.2
.17 HMR Remington Accutip-V	17	2,550	2,212	1,901	245	185	136	ZERO	-0.1
.17 HMR CCI FMJ	20	2,375	2,155	1,940	250	206	157	ZERO	-0.2
.17 HMR Hornady HP XTP	20	2,375	2,143	1,918	250	204	163	ZERO	-0.2
.17 Winchester Super Magnum Varmint HV	20	3,000	UNK/NA	UNK/NA	UNK/NA	399	UNK/NA	UNK/NA	UNK/NA
.17 Winchester Super Magnum Super-X	20	3,000	UNK/NA	UNK/NA	UNK/NA	399	UNK/NA	UNK/NA	UNK/NA
.17 Winchester Super Magnum Varmint HE	25	2,600	UNK/NA	UNK/NA	UNK/NA	375	UNK/NA	UNK/NA	UNK/NA
.17 PMC/.17 Aguila/.17 High Standard	20	1,850	UNK/NA	UNK/NA	152	UNK/NA	UNK/NA	UNK/NA	UNK/NA
.22 LR Remington Golden Bullet RN	29	1,095	982	903	72	62	52	ZERO	-7.4
.22 LR CCI LRN (Long)	29	710	673	637	32	29	26	ZERO	-17.4
.22 LR Winchester Tin RN	30	1,650	1,393	1,184	181	129	93	ZERO	-8.1
.22 LR Federal Copper Plated HP	31	1,430	1,197	1,046	141	99	75	ZERO	-4.6
.22 LR CCI Stinger HP	32	1,640	1,386	1,182	191	137	99	ZERO	-2.8
.22 LR CCI Segmented SLHP	32	1,640	1,388	1,182	191	137	99	ZERO	-8.2
.22 LR Remington CBee HP	33	740	687	638	40	35	30	ZERO	-16.9
.22 LR Remington Yellow Jacket TCHP	33	1,500	1,247	1,075	165	114	85	ZERO	-4.1
.22 LR Federal Copper Plated HP	36	1,260	1,104	1,003	127	97	80	ZERO	-5.6
.22 LR Winchester Tin RN	37	1,280	1,162	1,071	135	111	94	ZERO	-4.7
.22 LR Federal Copper Plated HP	38	1,260	1,110	1,010	134	104	86	ZERO	-5.5
.22 LR Remington Subsonic HP	38	1,050	965	901	93	79	69	ZERO	-7.7
.22 LR Federal Solid	40	1,240	1,103	1,011	137	108	91	ZERO	-5.6
.22 LR CCI Segmented SLHP	40	1,050	987	935	98	86	78	ZERO	-7.2
.22 LR CCI Velocitor CPHP	40	1,435	1,286	1,161	183	147	120	ZERO	-3.6
.22 Magnum Winchester JHP Tin	28	2,200	2,047	1,896	301	261	223	ZERO	-1.0
.22 Magnum Federal Speer TNT	30	2,200	1,777	1,419	322	210	144	ZERO	-1.3
.22 Magnum CCI Maxi- Mag TNT HP	30	2,050	1,762	1,487	280	247	149	ZERO	-1.1
.22 Magnum Hornady V-Max	30	2,200	1,911	1,639	322	243	179	ZERo	-3.0
.22 Magnum Remington Accutip-V	33	2,000	1,730	1,495	293	219	164	ZERO	-4.5
.22 Magnum Winchester JHP	34	2,120	1,861	1,617	339	251	197	ZERO	-3.0
.22 Magnum CCI Gamepoint	40	1,875	1,692	1,519	312	254	206	ZERO	-1.3
.22 Magnum Federal FMJ	40	1,880	1,570	1,311	314	219	153	ZERO	-2.1
.22 Magnum Remington PSP	40	1,910	1,610	1,340	324	227	159	ZERO	-2.0
.22 Magnum Winchester JHP	40	1,910	1,685	1,478	324	252	193	ZERO	-1.4
.22 Magnum Wildcat Dyna-Point JHP	45	1,550	1,387	1,243	240	192	154	ZERO	-2.8
.22 Magnum Federal JHP	50	1,530	1,347	1,197	260	201	159	ZERO	-3.3

Rimfire Cartridges – Factory Ballistics

Cartridge	Bullet (grs.)	Mid Range Trajectory		100 yards (inches)	Remarks
		Muzzle Velocity	Muzzle Energy		
25 Short	43	750	53	6.10	Handgun ballistics
25 Stevens Short	65	950	130	5.4	Smokeless loading
25 Stevens	65-67	1180	208	5.1	Smokeless loading
30 Long	75	750	81		8 grains blackpowder
30 Short	58	700	62		Approximate handgun ballistics
32 Extra Short	54	650	51		Approximate ballistics
32 Short	80	950	160	5.6	Late smokeless load, rifle ballistics
32 Long	90	180	5.2		Modern smokeless load
32 Long Rifle	81-82	960	186	4.9	Approximate rifle ballistics
32 Extra Long	90	1050	221	4.7	Approximate ballistics
38 Short	125-130	725	150		Handgun ballistics
38 Long	150	750	190		Handgun ballistics
	150	980	320	4.5	Rifle ballistics
38 Extra Long	150	1250	526	3.8	3-inch barrel ballistics
41 Short	130	425	52		3-inch barrel ballistics
41 Long	163	700	180		Handgun ballistics
41 Swiss	300	1325	1175	4.7	Blackpowder
	334	1345	1330	4.3	Smokeless load
44 Short	200-210	500	112		Approximate handgun ballistics
44 Long	220	825	332	4.5	Approximate rifle ballistics
44 Extra Long	218	1250	763	3.5	Approximate rifle ballistics
44 Henry Flat	200	1125	568	3.9	Approximate rifle ballistics
50 Remington Navy	290	600	234		Approximate ballistics
56-46 Spencer	330	1210	1080		Approximate ballistics
56-50 Spencer	350	1230	1175		Approximate ballistics
56-52 Spencer	340, 386, 400	1200	1300		Approximate ballistics
56-56 Spencer	350	1200	1125		Approximate ballistics
58 Miller/Allin	500	1150	1468		Approximate ballistics

The following rimfire cartridges are not included above because ballistic data could not be located; the same group, (except the 61 and 69 rimfires) is, however, listed in the Dimensional Data table: 35 Alcan, 9mm Ball, 42 Forehand & Wadsworth, 46 Ex. Short, 46 Short, 46 Remington-Carbine, 56-46 Ex. Long, 46 Hammond Carbine, 50 Ball Carbine, 50 Remington Navy, 50 Remington Pistol, 50 Warner Carbine, 50-60 Peabody, 61 rimfire and 69 rimfire.

Shotgun Shells
(Current & Obsolete – Black-Powder and Smokeless)

Shotguns, or "fowling pieces," as these guns were originally called, were among the earliest firearms to achieve sporting status. Of course, the use of a number of small pellets of varying sizes for military and hunting purposes predates what we would consider true sporting firearms made primarily for that pursuit. Originally, all guns were smooth-bored; rifling was unknown until around 1500. American colonists used shot in their flintlock muskets, because it was easier to hit small moving targets, such as birds or rabbits. Single-barrel and side-by-side double-barrel flintlock shotguns reached a high state of development in the late eighteenth and early nineteenth centuries. Indeed, in England, Joseph Manton and others turned out high-quality flintlock shotguns the equal of any made today.

In the early 1800s, percussion cap guns took hold, after the 200-plus-year reign of flintlocks. Percussion was followed in the mid-1800s by self-contained cartridges, though single- and double-barreled muzzle-loading percussion shotguns were still popular into the early twentieth century. This wasn't due to the reluctance by hunters to accept the new breechloaders, but, rather, because muzzleloaders were cheaper and didn't require expensive shotgun shells. For a largely rural population, it was a matter of economics.

The first breechloading shotguns appeared in the late 1840s, though some experimental types go back much earlier. The Lefaucheux pinfire shotshell was patented in France in 1836. In 1852, Charles Lancaster marketed an improved breechloading shotgun, which was followed by others and gradually led to our modern break-open type. The 1864 Schuyler, Hartley, and Graham catalog illustrated several breechloading shotguns. The general acceptance of the breechloading shotgun depended on the development of a gun that was affordable to middle-class hunters, rather than only the wealthy.

Flintlock, percussion lock, and pinfire designs all had external hammers. As soon as breechloaders firing self-contained centerfire ammunition became available, a number of hammerless shotguns began to appear starting in the 1870s. Sportsmen were quick to see the advantages of guns without protruding hammers. The first modern, breechloading, double-barrel gun was the Needham, patented in England in 1874. It was hammerless and had ejectors, some of the first ever seen. The Needham was the precursor of the patent by Westley Richards' workmen, Anson and Deeley, who, in 1875, developed a simple system that, like the Needham, utilized the weight of the barrels to cock the mechanism. This system has been copied ever since.

The pump-action shotgun was mostly developed in the United States in the late 1800s (though the first and not terribly functional design was actually created in England), and is, today, the most popular type in the U.S. This is also a matter of economics, because one usually can purchase a good pump-action shotgun for less than half the price of a double.

The principle of choke boring was long recognized by the late 1800s, but it wasn't widely known or used prior to that time. In 1866, Pape, in England, had a patent that permitted him to advertise as the "inventor of the choke bore," but evidence exists of recessed chokes being used as early as 1815. Then in 1868, American market hunter Fred Kimble rebored some old barrels and ended up with a 6-bore muzzleloading gun with extremely good choke, the result of lots of experimentation. Kimble made good use of his choke-bored gun in various shooting matches. As a result the success of the work done both by Kimble and by England's Greener, choke-boring became popular and accepted.

Sylvester Roper, also an American, was issued the first U.S. patent for choke-boring in 1866. However, his screw-on device was for single-barrel guns only and did not become popular. By 1990, screw-in chokes had become the practice on nearly all shotguns.

The type of shotgun used is largely a matter of personal preference. Pumps are inexpensive, but you have only one choke. The double-gun user has the instant choice of two different chokes. As to gauge, the 12-bore will cover the widest variety of game and hunting conditions and, for the man on a limited budget, the repeating 12 with an adjustable or interchangeable choke system is the way to go. The 16-gauge is almost as good, but very few guns are made today in this gauge. There is nothing wrong with the 20- or 28-gauge nor even the .410-bore, except these relatively small bore sizes impose limits on what game and ranges can be hunted effectively. At one time, smaller-gauge shells were less expensive, but, today, those shells cost the same as, or even more than, the larger gauges, so economy is no reason to pick one over the other, unless you are a handloader. Regardless the gauge, at least for the most part, the best shotgun is the one in which you have the most confidence and shoot the best.

Bore and Gauge Defined

The gauge or bore diameter of a shotgun is designated differently from that of a rifle or pistol. The system used goes back to earliest muzzleloading days. It was the custom then to give the "gauge" of muskets in terms of how many lead balls of the bore diameter weighed one pound. A 12-gauge, thus, had a bore of such diameter that a round lead ball weighing 1/12-pound would just enter the barrel. Sometimes gauge was given as a "12th-pounder" or "20th of a pounder" (20-gauge). In England, modern terminology often uses 12-bore or 20-bore, rather than "gauge," although the two mean the same thing.

The gauge system has persisted to the present. However, there are exceptions, such as with the .410-bore, which is always referred to as .410-bore, and never .410-gauge. This shell is actually a 68-gauge or .410-inch (.41-caliber). Then there's the 9mm rimfire shotshell, which is also a bore-size designation, rather than a gauge. At one time, shotguns were made in every gauge from about 1-gauge down to 32-gauge. Shotguns above 4-gauge were usually punt guns mounted on some type of support or swivel and used in boats for the market hunting of waterfowl. In addition, "gauge designations" larger than 10-gauge were often misrepresented, e.g., the bore of a 4-gauge gun would not accept a ¼-pound pure lead sphere. American manufacturers no longer load shotshells larger than 10-gauge for sporting use, but some European companies still turn out 8-gauge shells.

Shotgunning Myths

There are all sorts of odd ideas regarding shotguns. It is at least worth some effort to stamp out a few of these. For example, there is the idea that some shotguns shoot "harder" than others of the same gauge. The idea may arise in part from the fact that some shotguns have stocks poorly fitted to the user. Since apparent recoil is more severe than with other guns, the owner decides he has a harder-shooting gun. On the other hand, a shooter who has a gun that fits and handles exceptionally well may conclude he has a "hard shooter" because he does such good work with it.

Another outdated belief is that the longer the barrel, the longer the effective range. Modern smokeless powder shotshells develop maximum velocity in about 20 to 22 inches of barrel. Anything over that is just for balance and looks. If the barrel is too long, it will actually reduce velocity slightly through friction or drag. A shotgun with a 26-inch barrel will kill just as far away as one with a 40-inch barrel. In addition, the short barrel will be much faster in getting on target. In deference to those who refuse to accept this, some shotgun manufacturers provide at least one model available with extra-long tubes! If it takes a 36-inch barrel to make you happy or build your confidence, by all means, use one. However, beyond placing the muzzle 10 inches closer to the target, it does not give you any ballistic advantage over the fellow using a much shorter barrel.

The effective range of shotguns is another matter usually subject to much argument and misunderstanding. Some people believe the larger the gauge, the higher the velocity. Others believe that the smaller the gauge, the higher the velocity. Obviously, there is room for all sorts of confusion here, but both claims are wrong. The average muzzle velocity of a similar 10-, 12-, 16-, or 20-gauge load is nearly the same. Why, then, does a larger gauge have a greater effective range? It is a matter of pattern density. For example, if you fire a .410-bore at a dove flying 40 or 50 yards away, the chances are he will fly right through the pattern without being touched. If he is hit, the pellet or pellets will do as much damage as if fired from a 12-gauge. On the other hand, if you fired at this same bird with a 20-gauge, your chances of bringing him down would be greater, because you have thrown more pellets in his path. With a 12-gauge at this same range, the pattern density is great enough that the chances of the bird slipping through are even more reduced. We are, of course, assuming here the same degree of choke for all guns, because choke controls pattern size and density at a given range. There isn't much difference in the actual diameter of the pattern thrown by different gauges at the same range, if all other factors are equal. However, pattern *density* (the number of pellets in the pattern) will absolutely vary according to gauge, with the advantage going to the larger bore. This is also contrary to common belief, so, if you disagree, go out and pattern a number of guns of different gauges but similar choke (and be sure you use the same size shot and type of load in all guns.

Modern Shotshells

Shotgun shells were originally made from wound paper or drawn brass, although some have also been made from drawn aluminum, cast zinc, and molded or drawn plastic, the latter two of which are currently the most popular design. Paper shotshells (Federal Cartridge Company still makes paper-hulled shotshells), consisted of a laminated paper tube made by winding glue-impregnated paper sheets around a mandrel. The tube was then coated with paraffin wax to make it moisture-resistant, cut to proper length, and one end plugged with a tightly rolled paper or composition base wad. The final step was to add a crimped-on brass (or other metal) head, which incorporated the rim and primer pocket. Inside the shell, the height of the internal base wad determined the volumetric capacity of the hull and, therefore, loading density. Cases were divided into high-brass and low-brass types, depending upon intended loading.

In general, the low brass wad was used with black powder or bulk smokeless powder, because these powders required more volume to function correctly. The high brass wad was used with dense smokeless powders that required less volume. So, you can see, this dispells another myth, i.e., the terms "high-brass" or low-brass do not refer to the heights of the brass head. Over the years, shells with a high-brass head have become associated with high-velocity or magnum loads, and shotshells with low metal heads with target or light field loads.

Almost all modern shotgun shells are made from some variety of polyethylene plastic. Such shells were first introduced by Remington in 1958. Most plastic shells have metal heads of brass, brass-plated steel, or anodized aluminum. A few makers have marketed all-plastic shells without metal heads

Smokeless powder has completely replaced black powder for loading shotshells. Early smokeless powders were termed "bulk" powders, because these could be loaded bulk-for-bulk with black powder. However, these powders didn't all weigh the same, even though ballistics were similar with equal volume, and, so, a system of nomenclature evolved to accommodate this. Regardless the powder type, the charge is given in "drams equivalent." Thus, a shotshell marked "3¼-1¼" means the ballistics are the same as 3¼ drams of black powder and 1¼ ounces of lead shot.

Shotgun shell primers differ from rifle primers in size and type. The three- or four-piece No. 209 battery-cup primer is used in most modern shells. Until recently, some European shotshells used Gevelot-type primers, and all-brass shotshells usually take Large Rifle primers. Brass shells are shorter, but have the same volume as those of paper or plastic. These cases require larger wad diameters, as well.

There has been more meaningful development of high-performance shotshells in the past couple of decades than there has been previously in the history of arms. Shotshells now shoot payloads farther, hit game harder, and are manufactured more precisely than ever. But it has come at a price: It's not uncommon to pay $1, $2, or even more per round.

Considering what one gets in the deal, the new high-performance shotshells are well worth their prices. Yet, there is a dichotomy. Concurrently, low-tech "shootin' shells" are comparatively cheaper than ever in the history of shotshells. That's because of the global "dumping" of low-grade ammo from countries where their manufacture is subsidized. That's right, some shells sell for less in the U.S. than they can be manufactured for, even in their countries of origin. Global economy—most interesting.

The Lead Toxicity Issue

It has been recognized since the late 1800s that the ingestion of lead shot pellets by bottom-feeding waterfowl can cause a toxic reaction and lead to the death of the bird. In 1959, a wildlife biologist named Frank Bellrose completed a 15-year study on the possible affects of lead shot ingestion and the resultant lead poisoning (called "plumbism") on North American waterfowl. The results of this study were released in a bulletin known as the *Bellrose Report.* One of the conclusions in this report was that between two and three percent of the population in each waterfowl species in North America was lost each year through lead poisoning.

Truthfully, this was actually only a very rough estimate and one based upon incomplete data. The Bellrose study was based on the examination of bird gizzards furnished by hunters who had removed these from formerly live, healthy birds they had shot. In other words, *none of the wildfowl in the study were suffering from or had died from lead poisoning.*

The Bellrose Report wasn't intended to be a final conclusion on the subject, but rather an effort to point out a potential problem in a limited

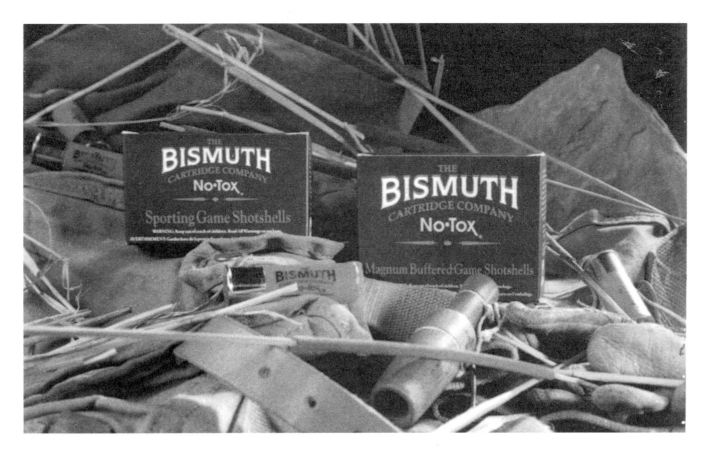

area and, at that, one possibly requiring further study. Unfortunately, this report was seized on by the U.S. Fish and Wildlife Service and the National Wildlife Federation as a *cause célèbre,* something that would demonstrate their deep concern for wildfowl and the ecology. The original study had encompassed a relatively small area in the Midwest, but this didn't stop the extrapolation of the data to cover all of North America, although there was no valid basis for such a conclusion. Whatever the merits of the argument, the fact is that Federal law now bans lead shot for virtually all waterfowl hunting (the one exception tends to be in some late-season snow goose hunting regulations, which have been instituted for some much-needed population control over the last decade or so). Furthermore, the outlook for the future has leaned towards an extension of the lead shot ban to encompass other kinds of hunting, as well, such as can now be seen on some public hunting lands frequently used for upland bird and small-game hunting.

Waterfowl Loads

To be classified as a "waterfowl" load these days, ammo must contain non-toxic shot. This means that, rather than the traditional lead, waterfowl cartridges now contain other metals such as bismuth, iron/steel, tungsten, the brands of non-toxic shot pellets known as Hevi-Shot/Hevi-Metal and NICE SHOT, and the new proprietary steel shot from Federal Cartridge Company known as FLITESTOPPER. Steel shot was the first widely used substitute for lead shot in shotshells intended for waterfowl hunting, but, as it turns out, steel shot has (or at least had, given the super-high-performance loadings available at the 2012 SHOT show), a lot of bad features, not the least of which is the ability to ruin the bores of older shotguns. It is as hard as the barrel steel of many high-grade shotguns and can dig grooves in the bores if allowed unprotected contact. Also, steel shot won't compress the way lead shot does as it passes through the choke and, so, will eventually bulge the choke area.

Steel shot also has (or again, had) poor ballistic properties, compared to lead shot of the same diameter. Lead shot of equal size is 44-percent denser. This means that steel shot doesn't carry over distance as well as lead shot, and it loses velocity and energy at a faster rate.

In descending order of actual use, today's shot payloads typically contain steel, tungsten and iron, or tungsten and polymer (in a matrix), bismuth, Hevi-Shot, or the other proprietary materials just mentioned above.

There has been relatively little, if any, actual development of late on the bismuth front. And there is good reason. Bismuth works great just as it is. It offers two major advantages. First, it acts almost exactly like traditional lead. This means it works great, since lead was/is the single finest material for shot (not withstanding the controversy over toxicity). Also, bismuth lends itself superbly to use in the older, finer shotguns that cannot handle steel or hard tungsten loads. Thanks for this product availability goes to Bob Petersen, the former publisher and general gun guru. (Incidentally, Bob's affinity for the .410-bore also has resulted in the availability of these diminutive cartridges in the Bismuth line for the waterfowler.)

Tungsten is a very heavy (heavier than lead) and extremely hard metal. This means that, to match a lead load, tungsten must be "watered down" with something else. This dilution is usually accomplished by mixing the tungsten with iron, steel, or some kind of plastic (polymer). In the tungsten/polymer shot, powdered tungsten is suspended in a plastic matrix and then formed into round pellets.

Although the Brits generally are credited with brainstorming tungsten/polymer shot, there have been a couple of North American companies that have offered such ammunition to the general trade. One was Federal, but the sales numbers and sales velocity of Federal's tungsten/polymer loading were not enough to keep that superb offering in the line. Without question, Federal's tungsten/polymer load was a great performer, and while it's not as popular as it was when it was initially introduced, the company conitnues to be an innovator in waterfowl loads, with high-performance choices like those in its Black Cloud lineup. Meanwhile, Kent Cartridge Co., headquartered in Canada, continues to offer tungsten/polymer ammunition, which work great, but this company has also recently made improvements to its steel shot loadings, with the relatively new line of super-high-velocity rounds known as SilverSteeel.

As you can see by even just the mention of the loads from Federal and Kent, most recent developments in non-toxic waterfowling ammunition has been with regular steel shot and with tungsten/other-metal combinations. The metal combo-shot used by the various companies comes in a variety of proprietary names such as Hevi-Shot (formerly a Remington product, but one now marketed independently), and the

LEAD SHOT
1. TUBE
2. SHOT
3. WAD
4. POWDER

STEEL SHOT
5. PRIMER
6. BASE WAD
7. HEAD
8. CUSHION
(lead only)

smaller company known as NICE SHOT, which offers its non-toxic pellets for handloaders. The trend for the metal combo loads has been for companies to offer payloads per volume that are heavier than lead, which, in theory, means they are ballistically superior. This trend is so evident with the heavier metal combos that, in addition to waterfowl loads, companies now are offering this kind of shot in high-density turkey hunting ammunition and upland bird loads (though this last is mostly to satisfy recent laws restricting the use of lead shot on certain public lands altogether, waterfowl habitat or not). On the steel front, most development has been a form of fine-tuning, in which velocities are increased while pattern uniformity is improved. Without question, velocity is the prime determinant in the success of steel shot load, and it doesn't hurt with the combo metal loads, either.

There are several reasons why velocity is so crucial for loads that contain super-hard payloads. With respect to steel, the higher velocity stretches the effective distance a bit. But, with all super-hard pellets, it is the way they take game that makes velocity so crucial. Because the pellets are so hard, they do not deform as lead does (even plated, hardened lead deforms a bit). This means that each individual pellet acts similarly to a full metal jacket rifle bullet; it puts a small hole in its wake, but does little other damage on the way. This was the characteristic that caused many birds hit with steel shot in the early days of steel introduction to be hit hard, yet limp off through the air, only to fall dead a mile or so away after they had bled out. Higher velocity helps preclude this kind of problem.

Years ago, really high velocities (over 1300 fps) were achieved with non-toxic loads only when the payload was relatively light for the bore diameter. In 12-gauge, this generally meant one-ounce payloads. Since then, companies have offered many heavier payloads at the higher velocities, thus removing one more negative variable from the equation. To make things even better, changes in wads and manufacturing techniques

have taken waterfowling loads to new highs in every respect. And not insignificantly, virtually all commercial non-toxic waterfowling ammunition these days is as close to being waterproof as is possible.

Turkey Loads

Developments in wild turkey hunting loads have continually focused on ways to deliver the densest patterns at ever increasing distances. This means developing ammunition that patterns superbly at high velocity. In the long ago, muzzle velocities of 1200 to 1300 fps were typical for shotshells. Now it's common to find loads, some even with quite heavy payloads, that send the shot out of the barrel at 1400 fps or faster.

Most turkey loads continue to keep muzzle velocities in the 1300 to 1400 fps range, but now deliver that speed with heavier shot charges. And what shot charges they are! Although Federal and Mossberg originally developed the 3½-inch 12-gauge shell as a way to put more of the lighter steel shot into waterfowl ammunition, the 3½-inch 12-gauge shell has found a welcome home among many turkey hunters who don't mind the recoil of a gun that shoots 2½ ounces or more of shot out of the barrel at high velocity.

Federal Cartridge Co. upped the ante a bit, in recent times, with the development of what it calls the FLITECONTROL wad. By its very design, this wad keeps the shot swarm together longer, which extends the density of the pattern downrange. This wad is used in both turkey loads and those for waterfowl.

Major breakthroughs in ammunition seem to be happening with regularity these days, and Federal's new Mag-Shok turkey hunting load, with its all-new wad design, takes patterning for big toms to a whole new level. Initial tests resulted in roughly twice as many pellets in the head/neck kill zone as was common with more traditional ammunition from the same gun/choke combination. At the heart of Federal's new turkey ammunition is an ingenious wad that keeps the pellet swarm tighter. The new wad is thick and made of a plastic that is about the same hardness as that used for steel shot loads for waterfowling. However, that's about where any similarity to most wads ends. A cross-section of the wad itself would remind one of the Nosler Partition bullet's jacket design, with the front partition area being about twice the length of the back divider. The front partition holds the buffered shot, while the rear encapsulates the top of the powder charge. Truly, it is quite different from the typical wad.

The front section of the wad is a cup that holds the shot all the way out the barrel and then some. There are no petals, slices, or slots in the front part of the wad, as is normal in most modern wad designs. Yet, at the bottom of the front part of the wad, there are three partial cutouts that, upon firing, merely relieve the bottom area of the front, shot-containing cup. These cutouts flare out, though almost not at all, during the firing process. It looks like they are there more to relieve some kind of pressure effect on the wad itself than anything else.

Most intriguing is the base, or skirt, of the long, orangish, one-piece wad. The skirt has six major petals that, upon exiting the barrel, flare out, causing major wind drag that, in turn, pulls the wad away from the shot that then continues on at normal velocity. This means the shot doesn't leave the wad until it is long gone from the barrel, and that means the pattern begins to open up much later, making it much tighter at any distance. Couple that wad with hard, copper-plated shot, and the world of turkey hunting just got a lot easier.

Upland Game Loads

There hasn't been a dramatic development in upland game loads that there has been in other arenas. About the biggest news in the past few years is that where 1300 fps was common for upland loads a decade or longer ago, 1400 fps, or even a little more, is now in vogue with the latest offerings.

Although the higher speeds work well, their primary advantage, if any, is that they mitigate, at least a bit, the amount of lead ahead of a moving target necessary to effect a hit. This probably translates into a few more pattern-edge hits for those whose timing is a little rusty. Other than that, there is an increase in felt recoil that naturally goes with the higher velocity.

Also recently, there has been a slight level of advancement in upland game loads for the smaller gauges. One must consider that, in the general shotgunning world, there are the 12- and 20-gauge, and then there's everything else, in which everything else doesn't add up to the volume of either of the top two. Nonetheless, there still is "everything else." Generally speaking, companies are now offering comparatively heavy shot charges for the 28-gauge and .410-bore guns. For example, there are 28-gauge loads with one ounce of shot (the classic shot charge weight of the 16-gauge), and Winchester, at least, now offers a three-inch .410-bore with ¾-ounce of shot (classically the shot charge weight of the 28-gauge). Although the heavier 28-gauge loading maintains velocity at slightly above 1200 fps, which is classic, the heavier .410-bore load does not. For example, the classic ½-ounce target loading for the .410-bore has a muzzle velocity of 1200 fps. The traditional three-inch .410-bore loading with 11/16-ounce of shot has a muzzle velocity of around 1135 fps, and the ¾-ounce loading goes out at 1100 fps. This data suggests that hitting relatively tough targets at relatively close ranges is where the heavier payloads shine.

Deer Hunting Loads

It was common practice with muzzleloading shotguns to load a solid roundball for big-game hunting. This worked fine, if the range was short, but accuracy beyond 40 yards was poor. It could be improved upon by using a patched ball, but the lack of proper sights limited what can be accomplished with a smooth-bored gun. When self-contained shotshells arrived, those were furnished in all gauges with a roundball loading. However, when choke-boring became common, it was necessary to use an undersized ball to prevent possible choke damage, so it became common practice to load a ball sized one or two gauges smaller than the bore. Thus, a 13-gauge ball was loaded in 12-gauge shells, a 17- or 18-gauge ball in the 16-gauge, and so on. These undersized lead balls usually were deformed when passing through the choke, so were even less accurate than bore-sized balls. Roundball loads in 12- and 16-gauge were useful in heavy cover, where they offered good short-range power on deer-size animals. In addition, 4-, 8-, and 10-gauge balls were used on dangerous game in Africa and India. Roundball loads were discontinued in 1941.

The rifled slug has an accuracy potential that will allow one to hit deer at ranges of 100 yards (and now more), provided your shotgun is equipped with a set of rifle sights or a scope and is properly sighted in. Rifled slugs were introduced by RWS in Germany, in 1898. This slug, known as the Brenneke, is still available under the Rottweil label. The American, or Foster-type, slug, was introduced by Winchester in 1936. The two differ in that the Brenneke is solid lead with a series of felt and card wads screwed to the base, whereas the Foster type has a deep, hollow base similar to the old Minié ball projectile used during the Civil War. Both have a series of angular grooves swaged into the outer circumference, and both work on the same principal as the badminton shuttlecock, in that most of the weight is forward of the center of air pressure, which causes these projectiles to fly point forward.

The newest slug design is a saboted copper solid designed to work in rifled shotgun bores, which have become common in specialized shot-guns intended only for use with slugs. When fired from these rifled barrels, these slugs (made by Remington and others) can provide rifle-like accuracy and terminal performance.

Without question, effective range for shotgun ammunition in the deer/big-game hunting world took a giant step forward with the use of rifled barrels in conjunction with saboted slugs. Briefly, this move alone doubled (even more in some instances), the effective range of the shotgun slug. Where credible distance for the more traditional shotgun slugs was somewhere around 50 yards, now 100 yards or more are common distances for successful shots.

Rifling the barrels of shotguns spins the projectile, allowing it to fly more truly to the target—as is the case with bullets in rifles and handguns. But, with modern shotgun ammunition, the maximum in accuracy and velocity for shotgun slugs has been achieved by using a sub-bore-diameter slug (bullet) cradled in a sabot (French for "shoe"). The plastic sabot engages the rifling, transferring the spin to the slug. After exiting the barrel, the sabot, due to air resistance, falls away from the slug, and the slug continues at high velocity to the target.

Advances in plastics and manufacturing techniques have allowed ammo makers to offer loads that are extremely accurate for shotguns and up the velocity several notches in the process. Some modern slug loads deliver a projectile weight and velocity similar, if not, in some cases, superior, to the black-powder express rifle cartridges used against dangerous game in Africa and India at the end of the nineteenth century.

Depending upon the gun/ammo combination, it is relatively easy to achieve groups of four inches or less at 100 yards with a projectile that delivers above the traditional minimum of 1000 ft-lbs of energy for deer-killing performance. In some combinations, groups of two inches or less at 100 yards are achievable. This was considered to be good delivered *rifle* accuracy several decades ago. This means that today's deer hunter in the woods now can use a shotgun as effectively as their ancestor did the venerable Winchester Model 1894 rifle in .30 WCF.

Fortunately, development hasn't been limited only to the saboted slug loads for rifled barrels (saboted slug loads typically do not work very well in smoothbores). There also has been some advancement in ammunition for shotgun slug hunters who continue to use smoothbore guns. Nothing smaller than the 12-gauge slug can be considered adequate for any North American big game, and the .410-bore slug is useless for anything but small game at short range. The 12-gauge Brenneke slugs have proven effective on thin-skinned African game, including some dangerous species, such as lion and leopard. Shotgun slugs can be compared to the old large-bore black-powder cartridges such as the big .45- and .50-caliber numbers. If you could only own one gun, consider a 12-gauge shotgun with an extra slug barrel. It will cover a greater range of game and hunting conditions than any other single gun.

Gauge Rifles

What I call the "gauge rifles" are those from 12- to 4-bores, though a few 2-bores have appeared (see the 2010 edition of Gun Digest). These are not shotguns, but are rifles of full weight and power, rifled through

SABOT SLUG

FOSTER TYPE RIFLED SLUG

and through. Originally, they were black-powder cartridge guns intended for use against large and dangerous game. In the 15th Edition, we added coverage of two such animals, the 12 Gauge From Hell (12 GFH) and 4 Bore Hubel.

Bore- or gauge-designated cartridges larger than 8-gauge are seldom of true implied bore size. All of these were British developments, because of the great need for powerful hunting rifles throughout the British Empire.

4-Bore: The bore designation indicates the number of bore-sized lead balls to the pound, hence, the 4-bore would nominally accept a round ball that weighed ¼-pound, or 1,750 grains. In actuality, the brass-cased 4-bore was loaded with a round ball of about 1,250 grains, or with a blunt or conical bullet that weighed about 1,880 grains. The usual propellant charge was 12 to 14 drams (325 to 380 grains) of black powder. Muzzle velocity was from 1,300 to 1,500 fps. Some 4-bore cartridges were loaded with up to 70 grains of cordite. Variances in cases length were from about 3½ inches up to a 4¼-inch version.

The 4-bore saw some use in Africa before the turn of the century, and in India for tiger shooting as recently as 1920. Typical 4-bore rifles weigh from 20 to 25 pounds. There is still quite a bit of interest in these, and at least one outfit is making new double-barrel and single-shot 4-bore rifles today.

8-Bore: The 8-bore was more popular than the 4-bore, because rifles for it could be built lighter. Typical 8-bores weighed about 15 to 16 pounds and, so, were much handier and easier to use. Its actual performance was not far behind that of the 4-bore. Typical loads are a 1,250-grain conical bullet at about 1,500 fps, or a spherical ball of 860 grains at 1,650 fps. Case length is from three to 3½ inches. Powder charge was about 10 to 12 drams (270 to 325 grains) of black powder.

There was also a Paradox-type 8-bore cartridge with lighter loadings, but it was not common. The Paradox was a Holland & Holland invention that featured rifling in the choke areas of its otherwise smooth double barrels. These were sometimes known as "ball-and-shot" guns, though some makers also used that name for smoothbores that had no rifling in the chokes. Numerous makers turned out variations on this theme and gave them highly individual names. Paradox 8-bores were a bit lighter than fully rifled guns and were, thus, somewhat handier. The 8-bore Paradox was more of a big-game gun, while the 10- and 12-bore

Paradoxes were more like heavily loaded shotguns, used only occasionally for dangerous game, but quite often on plains game.

10-Bore: Ten-bore rifles were also used against dangerous game and were, like the bigger bores, also loaded with detonating shells and/or lead-covered steel bullets for maximum penetration and performance. Here again, the Paradoxes were popular and efficient, and a common load used a 700-grain ball in front of a five-dram charge for 1,300 fps. The full rifle load would give more than 1,600 fps to the same round ball, or about 1,500 fps to a somewhat heavier conical bullet.

12-Bore: The 12-bore rifle saw lots of service against big (dangerous) game, but this size cartridge was probably most commonly seen as a Paradox load, either with a round ball or conical bullet. In this guise, it was quite popular. The 12-bore Paradox worked well on medium-size game and was useful with shot loads for filling the pot with birds and small game. Most 12-bore Paradox-types weighed from seven to eight pounds. In a fully rifled arm, the weight would be more than 10 pounds and the load significantly more powerful. Case length for fully rifled arms varies from 1.8 inches up to 2¾ inches. The author has two 12-bore double rifles, one for the shorter and one for the longer cartridge lengths. They have respective weights of 10.3 (too heavy) and 11.6 pounds (just right).

Gauge rifles were either single-shots or double rifles. These evolved from muzzleloading firearms of similar bore size and, while the rapid-fire capability of these early breechloaders must have been a boon to the early explorers and hunters, it was no panacea. The usual lead bullet's performance was such that it wasn't a good idea to take head shots on elephant. The skull of that beast consists of honeycombed cellular bone, and a lead ball could not be counted on to penetrate that, much less stay on course and find the brain. Shots to the head that missed the brain had little or no immediate effect on the animal, so the usual and much surer target was the body. A 4-bore ball through the heart would kill the elephant, but, apparently, not very quickly, as may be determined from the writings of many early African hunters.

The gauge rifles have a fascination matched by few other British or other sporting firearms. The cartridges are interesting and greatly varied, well worthy of study, collecting or, if we are lucky enough to find a suitable rifle, shooting. —F.C.B., with additional text by Steve Comus, Ray Ordorica, and Jennifer L.S. Pearsall

1- to 4-Gauge

Historical Notes: In most instances, gauges larger than 8-gauge were somewhat misnamed. Two-gauge shells are actually 4-gauge, and 4-gauge shells actually 5- or 6-gauge. Guns chambered for such cartridges were generally either punt guns, permanently or semi-permanently mounted on movable platforms, or very heavy smoothbore or fully rifled arms used by African hunters for taking the biggest and most dangerous species. In the former instance, the guns were used by market hunters, who were an important part of the expanding U.S. economy, as they provided much-needed protein for those who came to occupy new communities. The theory behind these large-bore punt guns was to launch a vast charge of shot against large flocks of birds that were on the water. In this way, the market gunner killed scores of birds with only one shot. Those used in Africa against dangerous game were also quite effective, more so when the cartridge was filled with a charge of shot. These are interesting cartridges that are well worth collecting and studying.

4 Bore Hubel — *NEW*

Historical Notes: This is another shotshell-based cartridge designed by Ed Hubel. Work on the 4 Bore began in 2009, when Hubel took brass 20mm Vulcan cannon cases (20x102mm) and straightened them, and swaged and turned the heads down to create a semi-rimmed case that will hold more than 300 grains of many smokeless powders.

General Comments: The rounds are fired in a falling-block single-shot that weighs almost 28 pounds and has a 32-inch barrel. Dimensions for the round will boggle the mind: Bullet diameter, .998 to 1 inch; mouth diameter, 1.043 inches; case length, 4.050 inches. Shooters who have fired this monster describe the recoil as manageable and more like a big push. The sound resembles that of a big-bore rifle, only twice as loud — or more. A 2 Bore with a steel 27mm Mauser cannon case is in the works.

Photo courtesy of Zachary Weighman.

4 Bore Hubel Loading Data

Bullet (grains/type)	Powder	Grains	Velocity	Energy	Source/Comments
(2) 760 Round Balls	RE-17 and Alliant Blue Dot	NA	2,500	21,088	Ed Hubel

4-Gauge

Historical Notes: The 4-gauge was popular as a long-range waterfowl chambering in unusually heavy shotguns. Toward the latter part of the nineteenth century, the 4-gauge saw significant application in market hunting, but it saw very little use in any other application in the United States. However, both smoothbore and rifled versions were made for African hunting in that same era.

General Comments: New guns in this bore size have been produced recently in both England and Belgium. It seems unlikely that any significant hunting need exists for such a gun, which suggests that the "magnum syndrome" is not limited to North America. Guns chambered for the paper-cased version are actually bored between 5- and 6-gauge size, while those chambered for the brass version can have a full 1.052-inch bore, which is truly 4-gauge. Pictured is a 3.93-inch long never-loaded casing featuring a steel head and paper body. This type of shell has no important length limitation—cutting the paper tube an inch longer adds very little cost. Therefore, in all the larger gauges (12-gauge on up), very long cases and matching chamberings were quite common. One is intrigued to speculate just how much shot might safely be fired at what velocity from such artillery-class combinations.

8-Gauge

Historical Notes: This was a very popular chambering from the late 1880s through 1917. In 1918, U.S. legislation prohibited waterfowl hunting with this or any larger gauge. In the U.S. and elsewhere, this was prized as a long-range duck and goose gun. While "8-gauge" sounds impressively huge, performance of factory loads was quite similar to that of modern 10- and 12-gauge magnums. To wit, 1¾ to 2¼ ounces of shot launched at about 1200 fps. Since those original 8-gauge loads lacked any system to protect the shot from bore abrasion, and because propellant gas sealing was not particularly effective, it is quite unlikely that the best 8-gauge loads of 100 years ago were anywhere nearly as effective as the best modern 12-gauge offerings.

General Comments: Although prohibited for waterfowl hunting in the United States, there is no prohibition against other applications. Therefore, the 8-gauge is making a significant comeback for other purposes, particularly turkey hunting, where it excels. The 8-gauge shells came in three-, 3¼-, 3¾-,and even four-inch lengths. Bore diameter is .835-inch. Gamebore Cartridge Co. of England (www.gamebore.com) currently offers 3¼-inch cased loads.

10-Gauge

Historical Notes: This is the only shotshell larger than the 12-gauge still commercially produced in the United States. Larger gauges were outlawed for sporting use in 1918. American-made single- and double-barrel guns in 10-gauge were manufactured until World War II. Then, after a short hiatus, several arms companies reintroduced the big 10- and, for a while, these guns gained popularity. However, two things have worked to nearly eliminate any sporting benefit offered by the 10-gauge for migratory bird hunting. First was the introduction of the 3½-inch 12-gauge shell, which has a higher pressure standard than the 10-gauge. Second was the adoption of mandatory non-toxic loads (originally, only steel was available) for hunting migratory species. There is nothing the 10 can do with steel shot that the higher-pressure 12-gauge loading cannot do better. However, the 10-gauge still has an advantage for turkey hunting, where large doses of lead shot are the preferred medicine and velocity isn't so important as it is with steel shot loads. The most commonly seen shell sizes are 29/16-, 2 -, 2 -, and 3½-inch. In England, Gamebore (www.gamebore.com) recently produced both the 2 - and 3½-inch shells. Bore diameter is .775-inch.

11-Gauge

Historical Notes: There is very little information on this oddball shotshell. Both Parker Brothers and UMC Co. headstamps were known producers, both listed as being in West Meridan, Conn., long ago. The Parker shell featured a large, American-type Berdan primer with three holes inside the case. The UMC loading evidently featured an internal primer, as it had no external opening to accept a primer. Best information is that two double-barrel guns and about 200 shells were made in the 1890s. Dimensions for the 11-gauge are: Rim, .835 inch; base, .790 inch; mouth, .782 inch; length, 2½ inches. 11-gauge bore diameter is .751 inch.

12/14-Gauge Martini Shotgun

Historical Notes: Our sample of this interesting shotshell is labeled as Caliber 12/14 Martini Shotgun for Police. The headstamp has lightly etched Arabic markings. The case head includes a .85-inch-wide by .95-inch-deep, square-bottomed annular groove located around the approximately .3-inch diameter primer. Outside diameter of this groove is about .540 inches.

General Comments: Previous editions of this book contained little background information on this shotshell. However, according to a gracious letter received by Glyn Jones of the Firearms Licensing Department of the Wiltshire Constabulary (UK), the 12/14-gauge Martini shotgun cartridge was made by W.W. Greener for a version of the Greener GP shotgun (a single-shot built on a Martini-type action), that was supplied to the Egyptian Police. In Mr. Jones' words:

"Greeners had supplied a large number of GPs to the Egyptian Police authorities in 1922 in 14-bore (gauge) ... . The cartridge as supplied had a conventional base, but was of a fairly unusual bore size. Some years later (1935), the authorities became concerned about widespread criminal use of the guns by corrupt policemen. The unusual ammunition for this gun was not available outside of police sources, and the authorities were easily able to keep a check on what policemen had been issued with, and make them account for any used. However, it transpired that criminals were padding out commonly available 16-bore cartridges with adhesive tape to fit the 12/14 chamber. This became apparent after an incident in which a gun was lent by a policeman to a relative to murder his mother-in-law. The gun exploded, severely injuring the would-be murderer, and the method was thus exposed when the crime scene was investigated with perpetrator and remains of gun still present."

Greener's solution was to modify the guns so that three pins attached to each other internally flew forward from the face of the block when the trigger was pulled. One of these was the central firing pin, as normal. The other two, located just each side of the central firing pin, were slightly longer, so they would strike the base of a conventional cartridge on either side of the primer and stop the central firing pin from coming into contact with the primer.

The next step was to manufacture the special cartridge with the annular base groove; the two longer pins would fall into this groove and, thus, allow the firing pin to strike the primer. The modified gun was designated Greener GP Mk III, and the first deliveries were made in 1938.

Mr. Jones adds that Leyton Greener (1903-1983) invented and designed the modification, although the patent for it was actually filed by his cousin, Jasper Hutton Howlett.

12-Gauge

Historical Notes: If there is one shotshell that holds all titles as most versatile, most popular, and most varied in loading, the 12-gauge is it. Except for the .22 rimfire, by almost any measure the 12-gauge is the most popular sporting chambering ever offered. It is commonly available loaded with shot made of lead, steel, tungsten/iron, tungsten/polymer, or bismuth. Current shot charges range from about -ounce to 2½ ounces. Common shot sizes range from No. 9 through 000 Buck. Slugs are typically one-ounce or 1¼-ounce, but other weights are available. Further, it is relatively simple to have a moderately sized batch of custom loaded 12-gauge ammunition (with either an odd-sized shot or reduced velocity), produced by a major manufacturer.

To gain a true perspective, just consider that, at one time in this country, there were literally thousands of distinct 12-gauge loadings offered. In 1995, 12-gauge commercial offerings from only the big three shotshell manufacturers totaled 435 unique manufacturer and component combinations. Further, other significant commercial manufacturers offer hundreds more loadings, especially in the various non-toxic shot offerings. In fact, commercially available, unique 12-gauge loadings exceed the total of all currently available high-powered rifle loadings for all cartridges by a significant margin.

The 12-gauge has been and is still used for police and military applications and, as recently as the Vietnam conflict, was the preferred gun of front-line troops for jungle combat. No gun is more intimidating or more effective for home-defense situations. The 12-gauge is also at home, given proper loads, hunting big-game up through whitetail deer at ranges to about 100 yards, with some shotguns and loads stretching useful range further. For sporting use, the 12-gauge performs admirably on clay pigeons. The key word here is "versatility." If any chambering offers that characteristic, this is the one.

In 1866, a rebated-rim, reloadable steel 12-gauge shell was patented by Thomas L. Sturtevant. Revolving magazine four-shot guns chambered for this shell were offered by the Roper Sporting Arms Co. until the early 1880s. Eley, in England (www.eley.co.uk/) currently produces two- and 2½-inch shells, while here in the United States, the 2¾-, three-, and 3½-inch lengths are most common and available from a variety of sources. Longer and shorter versions exist, and a rebated rim 2 -inch steel case is known to have been produced. Bore diameter for the 12-gauge is .729-inch.

12-Gauge Mi-Bullet

Historical Notes: Advanced Ballistics Concepts, LLC's Mi-Bullet is a four-segment slug, three pieces of which are joined by ballistic-grade tethers. Once in flight, the fragments expand like a web to a predetermined diameter. According to ABC, the projectile expands for the first 20 feet, reaches its "lock-out" maximum size for about four feet, then contracts for the rest of its trajectory. I.L.G Rice (1879) and H.J. Nowland (1879) previously proposed multi-segment handgun cartridges, but the Kevlar tethers make the Mi-Bullet unique. The projectiles are made of the company's zinc-based Zuerillium alloy, also called Green Lead.

General Comments: ABC, a ballistics research and development company headquartered in Greeley, Colo., has invented this shotshell and two handgun cartridges with multi-part bullets that immediately unlock and expand to a predetermined diameter and pattern of spread. Using a rifled shotgun bore, ABC says its 12-gauge round spreads three times faster than buckshot at 21 feet. With a rifled choke tube, the Mi-Bullet expands twice as fast as buckshot; with a smoothbore, the Mi-Bullet slug expands about 1.5 times faster than buckshot. The Stopper lethal round's central slug weighs 120 grains, the other three segments weigh 200.5, 202, and 205.5 grains. The whole payload, including tethers, weighs 734 grains.

The projectile construction has a "Center-Slug" sitting inside the three tethered segments, which form a nose cone. Below the cone are three fragments sitting on top of a disk, which itself sits atop a traditional powder charge. The disk effectively functions as the bottom of a shotshell wad.

If your shotgun bore or chokes aren't rifled, the company sells an accompanying rifled choke tube that fits most Remington shotguns..—W.T.W.

12-Gauge Mi-4 Stopper Bullet (Original Lethal) Loading Data and Factory Ballistics

Bullet (grains/type)	Powder	Grains	Velocity	Energy	Source
G-1 734 Zuerillium Fragments & Zuerillium Center-Slug	In-house #515 (Approximately = Win. 231)	24	1,100	1,974	Stopper Factory Load, First Generation

12-Gauge Mi-4 Stopper Bullet (Letha May 2014) Loading Data and Factory Ballistics

Bullet (grains/type)	Powder	Grains	Velocity	Energy	Source
G-2 850 Zuerillium Fragments & Lead Centr-Slug	In-house #515 (Approximately = Win. 231)	21	1,100	2,283	Stopper Factory Load, Second Generation

Bullet (grains/type)	Powder	Grains	Velocity	Energy	Source
G-2 735 Zuerillium Fragments & Lead Centr-Slug	In-house #515 (Approximately = Win. 231)	17	900	1,321	Stunner Factory Load, Second Generation

14-Gauge

Historical Notes: This chambering was generally available between 1880 and the early 1900s. Shells were domestically available until sometime after World War I, and generally available, in Europe, until the 1970s. Original loads included a three-dram (powder), one-ounce (shot charge) load. The 14-gauge was experimented with in the 1950s by Winchester, which used an aluminum casing with both roll and modified-roll crimps. There was also a modified version using a 12-gauge case head and lower body. Both brass and plastic versions of the latter are known. Most commonly seen shell lengths are 2, 2½ and 29/16 inches. The French still produce empty hulls for the 29/16-inch version. Bore diameter for the 14-gauge is .693-inch.

15-Gauge

Historical Notes: Winchester's 1877 catalog listed brass shells in this gauge, the only year these were listed. Obviously, the 15-gauge is extremely rare. Examples are found only in the best collections. The 15-gauge would have a bore diameter of .677-inch.

16-Gauge

Historical Notes: The 16-gauge lingers on in what seems to be a nearly perpetual state of surprising continued existence. Introduction of three-inch 20-gauge loadings should have sounded the 16's death knell, since the 20-gauge can launch the same shot charge at just about the same velocity and, with modern plastic shot cups, patterning is substantially equivalent. However, there are just too many perfectly good 16-gauge guns still in use, and the shells, in surprising variety, are still commonly stocked at the retail level. The 16-gauge is even available in steel shot loadings.

In 1866, a rebated-rim, reloadable-steel, 16-gauge shell was patented by Thomas L. Sturtevant. Revolving magazine four-shot guns chambered for this shell were offered by the Roper Sporting Arms Company until the early 1880s. The most common shell lengths in this gauge are 2½- and 2¾-inch, both currently produced by various European manufacturers, and the latter in U.S. production. The bore diameter for 16-gauge is .662-inch.

.64 Maynard

Historical Notes: Brass shells of this description were loaded for various models of Maynard sporting guns. The Model 1865 used a 25/16-inch shell with a Boxer primer. The Model 1873, adapted to both the No. 3 and No. 4 breechloading shotguns, used a 27/16-inch case featuring a modified Berdan primer. The Model 1882 was adapted to a reloadable case of 27/16-inch length. This gun, when equipped with interchangeable barrels, also fired the .40-40 Maynard cartridge. All Maynard shotshells were made with brass cases. This bore diameter corresponds to about 18-gauge.

18-Gauge

Historical Notes: This European gauge was loaded for use in custom shotguns. This ammunition was manufactured by Braun & Bloem, Kynoch, and Gustave Genschow. United Metallic Cartridge Co. produced a small batch for use in an experimental Browning shotgun. These UMC shells were 1 inches long and sometimes featured a 20-gauge headstamp. European pinfire versions of the 18-gauge in 29/16-inch length also exist. This gauge has a .637-inch bore.

20-Gauge

Historical Notes: Very much alive and well, the 20-gauge has always been popular, because it can be chambered in a smaller, lighter gun than the 12-gauge and offers sufficient punch for use against most sporting fowl. It is also completely at home breaking clay pigeons. Usefulness of the 20-gauge has improved dramatically, since the black-powder era, when the top loading was 2¾ drams with -ounce of shot. The comparatively recent standardization of the three-inch loading brings 20-gauge performance into a new class, with shot charges up to 1¼ ounces at higher velocity. Loaded with modern shot-protecting cups, the 20-gauge three-inch Magnum practically duplicates the performance of top 16-gauge loads. Current loadings range from one to 1¼ ounces of shot and include several buckshot combinations and the -ounce slug. Steel shot loadings up to one ounce are also gaining in utility and popularity. By a wide margin, the 20-gauge is the second most popular U.S. chambering. The 2½-inch version is currently available from various European manufacturers. Bore size is .615-inch.

24-Gauge

Historical Notes: Single-shot shotguns in this bore size were produced in the United States until the late 1930s by Stevens and Harrington & Richardson. The standard load was two-drams equivalent and ¾-ounce of shot. Shells in this gauge, and the double-barrel guns that shoot these rounds, are still manufactured in Europe. These have recently been available in the United States through American Arms Company and Beretta. Both CBC and Fiocchi have made this ammunition available domestically. Current loads launch 11/16-ounce of shot. The most common shell lengths in this gauge are two and 2½ inches. The 2½-inch version is still produced by Fiocchi. Midway USA (www.midwayusa.com) carries the Fiocchi fully loaded shells, as well as brass cases produced by Magtech. Bore size is .580-inch.

.55 Maynard

Historical Notes: Brass shells of this description were loaded for the various models of Maynard sporting guns. The Model 1865 used a 2¼-inch shell with a Boxer primer. The Model 1873, adapted to both the No. 1 and No. 2 breechloading shotguns, used a 2 -inch case featuring a modified Berdan primer. The 1882 loading used a reloadable case of 25/16-inch length and was adapted to the No. 1 and No. 2 breechloading guns. This bore size corresponds to the 28-gauge.

28-Gauge

Historical Notes: The 28-gauge 2¾-inch is currently manufactured in the United States. The original black-powder loading used a 2½-inch shell with 1¾ drams of powder and -ounce of shot. Federal Cartridge now lists a 2¾-inch, 2¼-dram, ¾-ounce load with either Nos. 6, 7½, or 8 shot at a velocity of 1295 fps. The 28-gauge is perfectly adequate for use in hunting upland birds and is at home breaking clay pigeons. However, recent innovations in shotshell technology have limited the 28-gauge's popularity since three-inch .410-bore loadings can practically duplicate 28-gauge performance. Nevertheless, light, easy handling and graceful guns still attract shotgunners, and the 28-gauge hangs on to a small but dedicated following, chiefly for these reasons. Bore size is .550-inch.

32-Gauge

Historical Notes: American manufacturers offered 32-gauge guns well into the 1930s. The Winchester Model 1886 rifle was routinely offered on a custom basis thusly chambered and barreled for the 32-gauge shotshell, which is essentially a .52-caliber bore. The standard loading was ½-ounce of shot, but a -ounce shot load and a 158-grain roundball loading were also offered. Loads in this gauge have been continuously available in Europe, and shells are domestically available through Fiocchi loaded with either No. 6 or No. 8 shot. Guns in this chambering have recently been imported through the American Arms Co. Even before World War II, the .410-bore practically duplicated 32-gauge performance. Nevertheless, light, easy-handling guns with graceful lines still attract European shotgunners, and the 32-gauge hangs on to a small but dedicated following there, chiefly for these reasons. Currently, Fiocchi offers the 2½-inch shell (available through Midway USA, www.midwayusa.com). Actual 32-gauge bore size is .526-inch.

11.15x52mm

Historical Notes: This European brass shotshell was popular in the early 1900s. It was generally loaded with shot, but was also available in a ball loading for use in rifled barrels. Performance of this loading would be quite similar to the modern .44 Magnum shot loadings offered by CCI/Speer (CCI still offers this load in the slightly shorter .44 Special configuration). The intended purpose was small-game hunting. For targets the size of rabbits and hares, the 11.15x52mm was reasonably effective. This bore size corresponds to .439-inch and would be called a 55-gauge.

.44 XL (1⁹/₁₆-inch)

Historical Notes: Made in the early 1900s, shotguns in this bore size were intended solely for use in hunting small game. This could be considered a forerunner to the .410-bore shotshell. Brass cases and paper shot containers were used. Overall length was 21/32-inch with a case length of 19/32-inch. The standard loading used No. 8 shot in a folded paper container, which protruded substantially from the brass case. Both single-barrel and double-barrel shotguns were offered in this chambering. Actual bore diameter was similar to the .44-caliber rifle cartridges (.425-inch) and would be called 61-gauge.

.410-Bore

Historical Notes: Though gun and load selection are somewhat limited, the .410-bore (12mm) is a perfectly good dove and quail chambering and can be argued to be the ideal small-game shell. A light, handy, .410-bore breech-break shotgun is a pleasure to carry on long hunts, and top three-inch loads deliver all the punch necessary to cleanly anchor rabbits and smaller species. Many use this diminutive chambering for breaking clay pigeons. Interestingly, it is possible to fire .410-bore shells in .45/70-chambered rifles. There are also a slug loading and one in 000 Buck (a three-pellet load in the three-inch shell), but their value for anything beyond their current rage as an alternate home-defense round is certainly moot. The .410-bore follows the 12- and 20-gauge in popularity. Many young shooters have learned to shoot with a .410-bore, and that tradition continues. The .410-inch bore would be called 68-gauge.

.360 Centerfire

Historical Notes: Similar to the more popular 9mm rimfire, this chiefly European chambering is strictly in the small-game and pest-control genre. Shells are found in both paper and brass and are 1¾ inches long. While it might be possible to dispatch smaller species of small game with this and others of the various diminutive shotshell chamberings, such use is ethically questionable. Nevertheless, none of these are toy cartridges. All high-velocity shot pellets are equally dangerous, regardless of source. The chief problem with these various diminutive shotshells is the lack of sufficient shot volume to achieve useful hunting pattern densit, and with shot of sufficient size, to get the job done. A.360-inch bore would be called a 99-gauge.

9.1x40mm

Historical Notes: The 9.1x40mm (.358-inch x 1.575-inch) was an early European shotshell intended for small-game hunting. It was also offered in a ball loading, for use in rifles. While it might be possible to dispatch smaller species of small game with this and others of the various diminutive shotshell chamberings, such use is ethically questionable. The chief problem with these various diminutive shotshells is lack of sufficient shot volume to achieve useful hunting pattern density, and with shot of sufficient size, to get the job done. This corresponds to a .358-inch bore and would be called a 101-gauge.

9mm Rimfire

Historical Notes: This cartridge was offered by Winchester for use in the Model 36 shotgun, which was introduced in 1920 and discontinued in 1927. Only 20,306 such shotguns were made. While that is a very small production total for a mainline arms manufacturer, this actually represents a surprising number of guns, considering the limited usefulness and market.

The only viable use for such a chambering is pest control. While it might be possible to dispatch smaller species of small game with this and others of the various diminutive shotshell chamberings, such use is ethically questionable. The chief problem with this and other diminutive shotshells is the lack of sufficient shot volume to achieve useful hunting pattern densities, and with shot of sufficient size, to get the job done. The shotshell length was 19/16-inch. This corresponds to a .354-inch bore and would be called a 105-gauge. Fiocchi again offers 9mm rimfire shotshells, available through Midway USA (www.midwayusa.com).

9mm Centerfire

Historical Notes: Recently available in Europe (by Spanish manufacture), these are found with plastic bodies and a metal head. The only viable use for such a chambering is pest control. While it might be possible to dispatch smaller species of small game with this and others of the various diminutive shotshell chamberings, such use is ethically questionable. The chief problem is the lack of sufficient shot volume to achieve useful hunting pattern densities and with shot of sufficient size, to get the job done. This corresponds to a .354-inch bore and would be called a 105-gauge.

.32 Rimfire

Historical Notes: Stevens offered its No. 20 Favorite shotgun in this chambering. Shell casings were copper or brass and shot containers were wood or paper. Case length was -inch for copper rolled rim or 25/32-inch for those with wooden shot containers. Overall length for the wooden container shotshells was 17/32-inch. Remington UMC and WRA manufactured these shells. The only viable use for such a chambering is pest control. While it might be possible to dispatch smaller species of small game with this and others of the various diminutive shotshell chamberings, such use is ethically questionable. The chief problem is lack of sufficient shot volume to achieve useful hunting pattern densities, and with shot of sufficient size, to get the job done. A .320-inch bore would be called a 142-gauge.

Note: All case length and diameter measurements include surprisingly generous tolerances, typically about .010-inch for length and about .020-inch for diameter. Numbers given for case base diameter are representative of a value somewhere near the middle of the radius of the fold where the case body blends into the rim. Generally, diameter of the cylindrical portion of the case head is somewhat smaller.

.310 Remington

Historical Notes: This brass-cased, rimfire shotshell was made by Remington for a mini-skeet shooting game. The shotgun was a bolt-action used to shoot miniature clay pigeons. Shell length was 11/16-inch.

7mm

Historical Notes: This is a European shotshell and long obsolete. It was also available in a ball loading. Shells are usually copper-based with a paper body. The only potential value of such a chambering is pest control. The 7mm shotshell corresponds to a .276-inch bore and would be called a 223-gauge. The most commonly seen length is 1¼-inch.

6mm

Historical Notes: Little is known about this diminutive chambering. The example seen here has a metal case head and paper body. The only potential value of such a chambering is pest control. The 6mm corresponds to a .236-inch bore and would be called a 353-gauge.

.20-Caliber Wingo

Historical Notes: These straight-walled rimfire shells were loaded by Winchester in the 1970s for chambering in unique, single-shot lever-action shotguns used in special indoor Wingo skeet-shooting galleries. The shells feature a .22 rimfire rim size, but have a smaller case body to prevent chambering of standard .22 rimfire ammunition in these guns. Wingo ammunition was assembled with 2.1 grains of ball powder and approximately 113 No. 12 shot pellets. Winchester-Western was the sole manufacturer of this cartridge. The .20-caliber Wingo corresponds to a .200-inch bore and would be called a 582-gauge.

Collath Gauges

Historical Notes: Available in 0-, 1-, 3-, 4-, 5-, 6-, 7-, and 8-gauge, these were an early 1900s European development. The shells used a unique gauging system. The 1-gauge is somewhat smaller than the common 12-gauge. Pinfire versions also existed. Collath ammunition was cataloged as late as 1911. The 5-gauge shell in Frank Napoli's collection has a metal band around the outer brass and paper joint. The empty shells were made in Frankfurt, Germany, and available in the Alfa Arms Catalog of 1911. Although never very popular, specimens are sometimes seen in collections and at gun shows. The unusual sizings and headstamps can cause significant confusion.

Shotshell Cartridges Dimensional Data

The following table is not exhaustive. It does not include many of the rarer, though known, case lengths and types. It should, however, provide sufficient information to help the reader identify 99 percent of those shotshells or casings he might come upon. If the example does not fit any of these data, likely it is sufficiently rare to merit advisement from a serious collector.

In many instances, data in this table represents approximations or estimates. In addition, you will note a significant number of "?" entries. We anxiously await reader input toward improving the provided dimensional data and filling in the remaining blanks. The purpose of including estimates is to help the reader make a preliminary identification of either a loaded shell or a fired casing. We believe the included estimated dimensional data will be sufficiently close to accommodate that end.

Note that loaded shell lengths can vary dramatically, especially in those shells using a folded or roll crimp. However, such variance is always toward the shorter side. In the larger gauges, current SAAMI specifications provide for a "minus" variance as great as 1/4-inch.

Gauge or Bore	Possible Sep. Shot Container	Crimp Types	Likely Case Body Material Types (not including case head)	Diameter (inch)			Closed		Open	Normal Bore Diameter (inches)	Priming Type	Comments
				Rim	Base	Mouth	Fold	Roll				
Collath 3-gauge	None	Roll w/Card	Paper	UNK/NA	UNK/NA	UNK/NA	UNK/NA	UNK/NA	2.91	UNK/NA	Pinfire	Rare
Collath 5-gauge	None	Roll w/Card	Paper	.803	.731	.666	UNK/NA	UNK/NA	2.56	?	Centerfire	Rare
.20-Caliber Wingo	None	Star(?)	Brass	.270	.21	.21	UNK/NA	UNK/NA	UNK/NA	.200	Rimfire	
6mm	None	Roll w/ Card	Paper	UNK/NA	UNK/NA	UNK/NA	UNK/NA	UNK/NA	UNK/NA	.236	UNK/NA	Rare
7mm	None	Roll w/ Card	Paper	UNK/NA	UNK/NA	UNK/NA	UNK/NA	1.20	1.25	.276	UNK/NA	
.310 Remington	None	Taper w/Card	Brass	.378	.320	.315		1.05	1.06	.310	Rimfire	
.32 Centerfire	Wood or Paper	Tape w/Card	Copper or Brass	UNK/NA	UNK/NA	UNK/NA	UNK/NA	.85	.88	.320	Rimfire	
.32 Centerfire	Wood or Paper	Taper w/Card	Copper or Brass	UNK/NA	UNK/NA	UNK/NA	UNK/NA	.78	1.22	.320	Rimfire	
9mm Centerfire	None	Roll or Taper	Paper, Plastic or Brass	.436	.391	.370	UNK/NA	1.67	1.75	.354	Centerfire	
9mm Rimfire	None	Taper w/Card	Brass	.385	.323	.320	UNK/NA	1.65	1.66	.354	Rimfire	
9mm Rimfire	None	Taper	Paper or Brass	.410	.344	.326	UNK/NA	.40	.40	.354	Rimfire	Single Ball Load
9mm Rimfire	None	Roll or Taper	Paper or Brass	.410	.344	.326	UNK/NA	1.44	1.45	.354	Rimfire	
9.1x40mm	None	Taper w/Card	Brass	UNK/NA	UNK/NA	UNK/NA		1.55	1.58	.358	Centerfire	
9.1mm Long	None	Taper w/Card	Brass	UNK/NA	UNK/NA	UNK/NA	UNK/NA	UNK/NA	UNK/NA	.358	Centerfire	

Gauge or Bore	Possible Sep. Shot Container	Crimp Types	Likely Case Body Material Types (not including case head)	Diameter (inch)			Closed		Open	Normal Bore Diameter (inches)	Priming Type	Comments
				Rim	Base	Mouth	Fold	Roll				
.360 Centerfire	None	Roll or Taper	Paper, Plastic or Brass	.474	.422	.417	UNK/NA	1.70	1.75	.360	Centerfire	
.410-Bore	UNK/NA	Star	Paper, Brass or Aluminum	.525	.470	.465	1.84	1.90	2.00	.410	Centerfire	
.410-Bore	Plastic	Star	Paper, Plastic or Brass	.525	.470	.465	2.36	2.40	2.50	.410	Centerfire	
.410-Bore	Plastic	Taper w/Card	Brass	.525	.470	.465	UNK/NA	2.85	2.88	.410	Centerfire	
.410-Bore	Plastic	Roll or Star	Paper or Plastic	.525	.470	.465	2.84	2.90	3.00	.410	Centerfire	
44 XL	Paper or Wood	Taper w/Card	Brass	.525	.471	.443	UNK/NA	1.57	2.03	.425	Centerfire	
11.15x 52mm	None	Taper w/Card	Brass	UNK/NA	UNK/NA	UNK/NA	UNK/NA	2.00	2.05	.439	Centerfire	
32-Gauge	Plastic	Roll or Taper	Paper, Plastic or Brass	.640	.580	.575	2.30	2.35	2.50	.526	Centerfire	Pinfire also
28-Gauge	None	Taper/Roll/ Star	Paper or Brass	.680	.620	.615	2.25	2.31	2.50	.550	Centerfire	Pinfire also
28-Gauge	Plastic	Roll or Taper	Paper or Plastic	.680	.620	.615	2.50	2.56	2.75	.550	Centerfire	
.55 Manard '65	None	Taper w/Card	Brass	UNK/NA	UNK/NA	UNK/NA	UNK/NA	2¼	2¼	.550	Boxer	
.55 Manard '73	None	Taper w/Card	Brass	UNK/NA	UNK/NA	UNK/NA	UNK/NA	2.375	2.375	.550	Berdan	
.55 Manard '73	None	Taper w/Card	Brass	UNK/NA	UNK/NA	UNK/NA	UNK/NA	2.3125	2.3125	.550	Berdan	Reloadable
24-Gauge	None	Roll or Star	Paper or Plastic	.725	.655	.640	1.70	1.80	2.00	.580	Centerfire	
24-Gauge	None	Taper/Roll/ Star	Paper, Plastic or Brass	.725	.655	.640	2.20	2.30	2.50	.580	Centerfire	Pinfire also
20-Gauge	Plastic	Roll or Star	Paper or Plastic	.760	.690	.675	2.20	2.30	2.50	.615	Centerfire	Pinfire also
20-Gauge	Plastic	Taper w/Card	Brass	.760	.690	.675		2.60	2.63	.615	Centerfire	
20-Gauge	Plastic	Roll or Star	Paper or Plastic	.760	.690	.675	2.45	2.55	2.75	.615	Centerfire	
20-Gauge	Plastic	Taper w/Card	Brass	.760	.690	.675		2.85	2.88	.615	Centerfire	
20-Gauge	Plastic	Roll or Star	Paper or Plastic	.760	.690	.675	2.71	2.80	3.00	.615	Centerfire	
18-Gauge	None	Roll w/Card	Paper	.782	.712	.697	UNK/NA	?	1.88	.637	Centerfire	Cases only, factory loads never seen
18-Gauge	None	Roll or Taper	Paper or Brass	.782	.712	.697	UNK/NA	?	2.56	.637	Pinfire	
18-Gauge	None	Roll or Taper	Paper or Brass	.782	.712	.697	UNK/NA	?	2.56	.637	Centerfire	
.64 Manard '65	None	Taper w/Card	Brass	UNK/NA	UNK/NA	UNK/NA	UNK/NA	2.3125	2.3125	.640	Boxer	
.64 Manard '73	None	Taper w/Card	Brass	UNK/NA	UNK/NA	UNK/NA	UNK/NA	2.4375	2.4375	.640	Berdan	
.64 Manard '82	None	Taper w/Card	Brass	UNK/NA	UNK/NA	UNK/NA	UNK/NA	2.4375	.24375	.640	Berdan	Reloadable
16-Gauge		Taper/Roll/ Star	Paper or Brass	.810	.740	.720	2.19	2.23	2.50	.662	Centerfire	
16-Gauge		Roll w/Card	Paper	.810	.740	.720	2.25	UNK/NA	2.56	.662	Centerfire	Pinfire also
16-Gauge	Plastic	Roll or Star	Paper or Plastic	.810	.740	.720	2.44	2.48	2.75	.662	Centerfire	
16-Gauge	None	Roll w/Card	Paper	.810	.740	.720	UNK/NA	2.73	3.00	.662	Centerfire	
15-Gauge	None	Roll w/Card	Paper	.813	.743	.728	UNK/NA	UNK/NA	UNK/NA	.678	Pinfire	Very Rare
15-Gauge	None	Taper w/Card	Brass	.813	.743	.728	UNK/NA	UNK/NA	UNK/NA	.678	Centerfire	Very Rare
14-Gauge	None	Roll or Star	Paper	.839	.769	.754	1.70	1.75	2.00	.693	Centerfire	
14-Gauge	None	Taper/Roll/ Star	Paper or Brass	.839	.769	.754	2.20	2.25	2.50	.693	Centerfire	
14-Gauge	None	Roll w/Card	Paper	.839	.769	.754	UNK/NA	2.31	2.56	.693	Centerfire	Pinfire also
14-Gauge	Plastic (?)	Taper w/Card	Aluminum	UNK/NA	UNK/NA	UNK/NA	UNK/NA	UNK/NA	UNK/NA	.693	Centerfire	Experimental
14-Gauge	Plastic (?)	Roll or Taper	Plastic or Brass	.875	.805	.754	UNK/NA	UNK/NA	UNK/NA	.693	Centerfire	Experimental
12/14 Martini	None	Partial Star	Brass	.892	.792	.735	2.86	UNK/NA	2.88	UNK/NA	Berdan	Police Load
12-Gauge	Plastic	Roll w/Card	Plastic	.875	.805	.790	UNK/NA	1.25	1.50	.729	Centerfire	
12-Gauge	Plastic	Roll w/Card	Plastic	.875	.805	.790	UNK/NA	1.64	1.88	.729	Centerfire	Pinfire also
12-Gauge	Plastic	Roll w/Card	Paper, Plastic	.875	.805	.790	UNK/NA	1.76	2.00	.729	Centerfire	Pinfire also
12-Gauge	None	Taper w/Card	Steel	UNK/NA	UNK/NA	UNK/NA	UNK/NA	2.35	2.38	.729	Centerfire	Pinfire also
12-Gauge	Plastic	Taper/Roll/ Star	Paper, Plastic or Brass	.875	.805	.790	2.16	2.26	2.50	.729	Centerfire	Pinfire also

Gauge or Bore	Possible Sep. Shot Container	Crimp Types	Likely Case Body Material Types (not including case head)	Diameter (inch)			Closed		Open	Normal Bore Diameter (inches)	Priming Type	Comments
				Rim	Base	Mouth	Fold	Roll				
12-Gauge		Taper w/Card	Brass	.875	.805	.790	UNK/NA	2.60	2.63	.729	Centerfire	Pinfire also
12-Gauge *	Plastic	Taper/Roll/ Star	Paper, Plastic or Brass	.875	.805	.790	2.41	2.45	2.75	.729	Centerfire	Pinfire also
12-Gauge		Taper w/Card	Brass	.875	.805	.790	UNK/NA	2.85	2.88	.729	Centerfire	Pinfire also
12-Gauge *	Plastic	Taper/Roll/ Star	Paper, Plastic or Brass	.875	.805	.790	2.66	2.76	3.00	.729	Centerfire	Pinfire also
12-Gauge *	Plastic	Roll or Star	Paper or Plastic	.875	.805	.790	3.16	UNK/NA	3.50	.729	Centerfire	
12-Gauge	None	Roll w/Card	Paper	0.875	.805	.790	UNK/NA	3.76	4.00	.729	Centerfire	
12-Gauge	None	Roll w/Card	Paper	.875	.805	.790	UNK/NA	4.76	5.00	.729	Centerfire	
12-Gauge Mi-Bullet	4-segment slug	Roll	Plastic	.875	.805	.790	UNK/NA	3.16	3.50	UNK/NA	Centerfire	Tethered Bullet
11-Gauge	None	Roll w/Card	Paper ?	.835	.790	.782	UNK/NA	2.36	2.50 ?	.751	UNK/NA	Very Rare
11-Gauge	None	Taper w/Card	Brass	.835	.790	.782	UNK/NA	2.48	2.50	.751	Berdan	Very Rare
11-Gauge	None	Taper w/Card	Brass	.835	.790	.782	UNK/NA	2.48	2.50	.751	Inside	Very Rare
10-Gauge	None	Roll w/Card	Paper	.925	.850	.830	UNK/NA	2.36	2.57	.775	Centerfire	Pinfire also
10-Gauge	None	Roll w/Card	Paper	.925	.850	.830	UNK/NA	2.42	2.63	.775	Centerfire	Pinfire also
10-Gauge *	Plastic	Taper/Roll/ Star	Paper, Plastic or Brass	.925	.850	.830	2.49	2.67	2.89	.775	Centerfire	Pinfire also
10-Gauge *	Plastic	Taper/Roll/ Star	Paper, Plastic or Brass	.925	.850	.830	3.11	3.29	3.50	.775	Centerfire	Pinfire priming is also seen
8-Gauge *	None	Roll or Taper	Paper or Brass	.998	.913	.902	UNK/NA	2.75	3.00	.835	Centerfire	
8-Gauge *	Plastic	Roll or Taper	Paper or Brass	.998	.913	.902	UNK/NA	3.00	3.25	.835	Centerfire	
8-Gauge *	None	Roll or Taper	Paper or Brass	.998	.913	.902	UNK/NA	3.13	3.38	.835	Centerfire	
8-Gauge *	None	Taper/Roll/ Star	Paper, Plastic or Brass	.998	.913	.902	UNK/NA	3.25	3.50	.835	Centerfire	
8-Gauge *	None	Roll w/Card	Paper	.998	.913	.902	UNK/NA	3.75	3.93	.835	Centerfire	
8-Gauge *	None	Roll w/Card	Paper	.998	.913	.902	UNK/NA	4.00	4.25	.835	Centerfire	
4-Gauge *	None	Roll w/Card	Paper or Plastic	1.127	1.041	1.114	2.0-4.2	Various 2.5-4.25	.918 .975 **	Berdan & Pinfire		Often a Slug
4-Gauge *	None	Roll w/Card	Paper or Plastic	1.127	1.041	1.114	2.0-4.2	Various 2.5-4.25	.918 .975 **	Berdan & Pinfire		Often a Slug
3-Gauge	None	Taper or Roll	Paper or Brass	1.515	1.388	1.350	4.12	3.875	4.125	1.157	Centerfire	
2-Gauge *	None	Taper or Roll	Paper or Brass	1.888	1.735	1.715	UNK/NA	4.500	4.875	1.325 **	Berdan	Usually a Slug

Collath/Gauge Comparisons (Collath #/Gauge #): 0 = 10; 1 = 12; 2 (not used); 3 = 14; 4 = 16; 5 = 18; 6 = 20; 7 = 24; 8 = 28

Brass shotgun shells often use Berdan primers.

* These were also used for dangerous game hunting in Africa. The larger sizes were also used for market hunting in various places. See Chapter 8 for a more complete discussion. Guns were also built with both fully rifled and "paradox" (smooth, excepting the very end, which was rifled) bores. Choking was not used.

** Bore diameters are estimates. These "gauges" were never properly described or standardized. Bore diameter measurements indicate that what various manufacturers described as a 4-gauge (bore) was closer to 5-or 6-gauge (at least three bore diameters are known). Similarly, the "2-gauge (bore)" was actually a 4-gauge (bore).

Note: 6 drams = 1 ounce = 437.5 grains

TABLE 3

Downrange Velocities and Energies
Lead and Steel Shot
12-Gauge, 2³/₄-Inch Loads

Load	Velocity @ 3 ft. Nominal ft/sec.	Velocity @ 3 ft. Measured ft/sec.	Downrange Velocity, Measured at 40 yd. ft/sec.	Energy p/Pellet at 40 yd. ft-lb.
11/8-oz. #2 Steel	1365	1350	773	4.84
11/4-oz. #2 Steel	1300	1305	761	4.69
11/4-oz. #4 Lead	1330	1319	803	4.64
11/2-oz. #4 Lead	1260	1252	778	4.35
11/2-oz. #4 Lead*	1260	1240	793	4.52

*Buffered load

TABLE 4

40-Yard Penetration
20 Percent Ordnance Gelatin
Lead and Steel Shot
12-Gauge, 2³/₄-Inch Loads

Load	Velocity At 3 ft. ft/sec.	Energy Per Pellet At 40 yd. ft-lb.	Energy Density At 40 yd. ft-lb/sq. in.	Penetration in Gelatin inches
11/8-oz. #2 Steel	1350	4.84	274	2.0
11/4-oz. #2 Steel	1305	4.69	265	1.9
11/4-oz. #4 Lead	1319	4.64	350	2.5
11/2-oz. #4 Lead	1252	4.35	328	2.4
11/2-oz. #4 Lead*	1240	4.52	341	2.5

*Buffered load

COMPARATIVE SHOTGUN SLUG PERFORMANCE

Gauge	Shell Length ins./mm	Slug Weight oz./grs.	Slug Type	Velocity (fps) MV	50 yds	100 yds	Energy (fpe) MV	50 yds	100 yds
10	31/2/89	13/4/766	Foster	1280	1080	970	2785	1980	1605
12	3/76	11/4/547	Foster	1600	1320	1130	3110	2120	1785
12	3/76	13/8/600	Brenneke	1502	1144	936	3017	1749	1240
12	3/76	1/437.5	Foster	1760	1345	1075	3009	1396	891
12	3/76	1/437.5	Sabot	1550	1410	1190	2400	1665	1220
12	23/4/70	11/4/547	Foster	1520	1260	1090	2805	1930	1450
12	23/4/70	11/10/490	Brenneke	1590	1190	975	2745	1540	1035
12	23/4/70	1/437.5	Foster	1680	1285	1045	2741	1605	1061
12	23/4/70	1/437.5	Foster	1610	1330	1140	2520	1725	1255
12	23/4/70	1/437.5	Sabot	1450	1320	1130	2100	1475	1120
12	23/4/70	1/437.5	Foster	1560	1175	977	2364	1342	927
16	23/4/70	4/5/350	Foster	1600	1180	990	1990	1075	755
16	23/4/70	9/10/415	Brenneke	1590	1190	975	2320	1300	875
20	23/4/70	3/4/328	Foster	1600	1270	1070	1865	1175	835
20	23/4/70	7/8/370	Brenneke	1590	1190	975	2080	1165	780
410	21/2/63.5	1/5/88	Foster	1830	1340	1060	650	345	215
410	3/76	1/4/110	Brenneke	1755	1162	917	780	342	213

TABLE 2

Pellet Count and Distribution in Patterns
Full, Modified and Improved Cylinder Chokes
Lead and Steel Shot
12-Gauge, $2^3/_4$-Inch Loads, 1979

Load	Choke	Approx. Number Pellets in Load	Pattern Percent 40 Yards 30" Circle	20" Circle	Annular Area, 30"-20" Circle	Pellets in Pattern 40 Yards 30" Circle	20" Circle	Annular Area, 30"-20" Circle
11/8-oz. #2 Steel	Full	135	76	47	29	103	64	39
11/8-oz. #2 Steel	Mod.	135	68	40	28	92	54	38
11/8-oz. #2 Steel	Imp. Cyl.	135	44	22	22	60	30	30
11/4-oz. #2 Steel	Full	150	76	47	29	114	71	43
11/4-oz. #2 Steel	Mod.	150	68	40	28	102	60	42
11/4-oz. #2 Steel	Imp. Cyl.	150	44	22	22	66	33	33
11/4-oz. #4 Lead*	Full	169	72	43	29	122	73	49
11/4-oz. #4 Lead*	Mod.	169	56	29	27	95	49	46
11/2-oz. #4 Lead*	Full	202	73	44	29	147	89	58
11/2-oz. #4 Lead"XX"	Full	202	87	59	28	176	119	57

*This is a standard, non-buffered load

Notes: Area of 30" Circle:707 sq. in.
Area of 20" Circle:314 sq. in.
Annular area:707 - 314:393 sq. in.

U.S. Military Ammunition (5.56 to 20mm)
(Description and Identification)

Marms and Small Arms Ammunition, Vol. 2*, Office of the Chief of Ordnance, Washington D.C., and *Small Arms Ammunition Pamphlet 23-1*, Dept. of the Army Frankford Arsenal, Philadelphia, Pa. Don't write to the author or publisher of this book asking where you can get copies of these—we don't know! Such things as industrial or manufacturing codes and drawing numbers have also been omitted, because they would not be of interest to the great majority of readers of *Cartridges of the World*.

Note: The second figure that appears with some of the data, particularly the weights and pressures, is a manufacturing tolerance and was left in so that the reader will understand that some variations can be expected between different lots and manufacture of ammunition. Also, it should be understood that, in some instances, the powder type given has been changed from tubular to ball powder in recent years. As an example, 56-2 grs. means a standard weight of 56 grains with no more than a 2-grain variation (+/-1 grain) being acceptable. The rest of the data is more or less self-explanatory.

5.56x45mm

Cartridge, Caliber 5.56mm, Ball, M193

Weapon:	Rifle, 5.56mm, M16; M16E1
Ballistic Perf.:	
Velocity:	3,250 ±40 fps at 15 feet; Std. Dev.40 fps max.
Pressure:	52,000 psi max. avg.; avg. pressure plus 3 Std. Dev. 58,000 psi max.
Port Pres.:	15,000 psi 2,000 psi
Accuracy:	2.00" mean radius max. avg. at 200 yards
Cartridge:	182 - 14 grs.
Case:	94 - 5 grs.
Bullet:	56 - 2 grs.
Primer, Perc.:	
Prim. Wt:	4.0 grs. approx.
Compos.:	Lead Styphnate
Propellant	
Brand:	IMR8208M WC846
Type:	Single Base Double Base Tubular Spheroidal
Weight:	25.5 grs. 28.5 grs.
Ident.:	Plain tip

Cartridge, Caliber 5.56mm, Ball, M855A1

Weapon:	Rifle, 5.56mm, M16A2, M249
Ballistic Perf.:	
Velocity:	3,020 ±40 fps
Pressure:	52,000 psi max. avg.; avg. pressure plus 3 Std.
Dev.:	58,000 psi max.
Port Pres.:	15,000 psi 2,000 psi
Accuracy:	2.00" mean radius max. avg. at 200 yards
Cartridge:	187 - 14 grs.
Case:	94 - 5 grs.
Bullet:	62 - 2 grs.
Primer, Perc.:	
Prim. Wt:	4.0 grs. approx.
Compos.:	Lead styphnate
Propellant	
Brand:	IMR8208M WC846
Type:	Single Base Spheroidal Tubular
Weight:	
Ident.:	Green tip

Cartridge, Caliber 5.56mm, Grenade Rifle, M195

Weapon:	Rifle, 5.56mm, XM16E1; M16
Ballistic Perf.:	
Velocity:	140 ± 165 fps at 5.5 ft. (Grenade 1.56 lbs). No individual shot below 140 fps
Cartridge:	127.5 - 4 grs.
Case:	98 - 3 grs.
Primer, Perc.:	
Prim. Wt:	4.0 grs. approx.
Compos.:	Lead Styphnate
Propellant	
Brand:	IMR4475
Type:	Single Base, Tubular
Weight:	25.0 grs.
Wad:	.5 grs. max., Cardboard, Royal Satin coated (both sides) Booklined Yellow
Ident.:	Case mouth closed with 7 petal rose crimp red tip

Cartridge, Caliber 5.56mm, Tracer, M196

Weapon:	Rifle, 5.56mm, M16; XM16E1
Ballistic Perf.:	
Velocity:	3,200 ±40 fps at 15 feet; Std. Dev. 40 fps max.
Pressure:	52,000 psi max. avg./avg. pressure plus 3 Std. Dev. 58,000 psi max.
Port Pres.:	15,000 psi 2,000 psi
Accuracy:	5.00" mean radius max. avg. at 200 yards
Trace:	The trace shall be visible from a point not greater than 75 yards from the muzzle of weapon to a point not less than 500 yards from the muzzle.
Cartridge:	177 - 11 grs.
Case:	94 - 5 grs.
Bullet:	54 - 2 grs.
Point Filler:	28 - .5 grs. - lead-antimony

Base Clos.:	Vinyl
Tracer:	2.7 grs. approx.
Ign.:	1.0 gr.
Sub Ign.:	.05 gr.
Primer, Perc.:	
Prim. Wt:	4.0 grs. approx.
Compos.:	Lead Styphnate
Propellant	
Brand:	IMR 8208M
Type:	Single Base Tubular
Weight:	25.3 grs.
Ident.:	Red Tip

Cartridge, Caliber 5.56mm, Test, High Pressure, M197

Weapon:	Used to proof test barrels and weapons (not a service cartridge)
Ballistic Perf.:	
Pressure:	70,000 3,000 psi, max. Std. Dev. 3500 psi
Cartridge:	174 - 11 grs.
Case:	94 - 5 grs.
Bullet:	C10524197 - 56 - 2 grs.
Primer:	4.0 grs. approx.
Propellant:	
Brand:	HPC 3
Type:	Double Base Flake
Weight:	20.0 grs.
Ident.:	Case Stannic Stained or Nickel Plated

Cartridge, Caliber 5.56mm, Tracer, M856A1

Weapon:	Rifle, 5.56mm, M16A2, M249
Ballistic Perf.:	
Velocity:	2,795 ±40 fps
Pressure:	52,000 psi max. avg./ avg. pressure plus 3 Std. Dev. 58,000 psi max.
Port Pres.:	15,000 psi 2,000 psi
Accuracy:	5.00" mean radius max. avg. at 200 yards
Trace:	The trace shall be visible from a point not greater than 75 yards from the muzzle of the weapon to a point not less than 500 yards from the muzzle.
Cartridge:	177 - 11 grs.
Case:	94 - 5 grs.
Bullet:	63.8 grs.
Primer, Perc.:	
Prim. Wt:	4.0 grs. approx.
Compos.:	Lead Styphnate
Propellant:	
Brand:	
Type:	
Weight:	
Ident.:	Orange tip

Dummy Cartridge, Caliber 5.56mm, M199

Weapon:	Rifle, 5.56mm, XM16E1; M16 - Training
Cartridge:	150 - 7 grs.
Case:	94 - 7 grs.
Bullet:	56 - 2 grs.
Primer:	None
Propellant:	None
Ident.:	Impressed upon the case, 6 corrugations, approx. .030-inch deep equally spaced about the periphery.

Cartridge, Caliber 5.56mm, Blank, XM200

Weapon:	Rifle, 5.56mm, M16; XM16E1 with blank firing attachment, M13
Ballistic Perf.:	
Screen perf.:	No perforations in paper screen at 15 ft.
Cyclic Rate: per minute	Min. 550 rds. per minute, max. 800 rds. per minute
Cartridge:	109.5 - 4 grs.
Case:	98 - 3 grs.
Bullet:	None, Case Mouth closed with 7-petal rose crimp
Primer, Perc.:	
Prim. Wt:	4.0 grs. approx.
Compos.:	Lead Styphnate
Propellant:	HPC 13
Type:	Double Base, Flake
Weight:	7.0 grs.

Wad:	None
Ident.:	Cannelure approx $1/22$ from head and mouth closed with 7-petal rose crimp

Dummy Cartridge, Caliber 5.56mm, Inert Loaded, M232

Weapon:	Rifle, 5.56mm, XM16E1, M16
Cartridge:	181.5 - 7.0 grs.
Case:	94 - 5 grs.
Bullet:	56 - 2 grs.
Primer:	None
Propellant:	31 grs. Sodium Carbonate Monohydrate
Ident.:	Cartridge, chemical black

Dummy Cartridge, Caliber 5.56mm, Inert Loaded, M857

Weapon:	Rifle, 5.56mm, M16A2, M249
Cartridge:	187.5 - 7.0 grs.
Case:	94 - 5 grs.
Bullet:	61 - 2 grs.
Primer:	None
Propellant:	31 grs. Sodium Carbonate Monohydrate
Ident.:	Cartridge, chemical black

.30-CALIBER CARBINE

Cartridge, Caliber .30, Carbine, Ball, M1

Weapon:	Carbine, Caliber .30, M1; Carbine., Caliber .30, M2
Ballistic Perf.:	
Velocity:	1,900 ±30 fps
Pressure:	40,000 psi, max. avg.
Accuracy:	1.5" mean radius max. avg. at 100 yards
Cartridge:	146 - 13 grs. (with gilding metal jacketed bullet) 193 - 13 grs. (with gilding metal clad steel jacketed bullet)
Case:	71 - 6 grs.
Bullet:	111 - 3 grs. (with gilding metal jacket) 108 - 3 grs. (with gilding metal clad steel jacket)
Primer, Perc.:	Lead Styphnate
Propellant:	
Brand:	WC820 HPC5
Type:	Double Base Double Base Spheroidal Flake
Weight:	13 grs. 13 grs.
Point Ident.:	Plain Tip

Cartridge, Caliber .30, Carbine, M13

Weapon:	Carbine Cal .30, M1; Carbine, Caliber .30, M2
Ballistic Perf.:	None
Cartridge:	177 grs.
Case:	66 grs.
Bullet:	111 - 3 grs. - 108 - 3 grs.
Ident.:	Drilled case, no primer

Cartridge, Caliber .30, Carbine, Rifle Grenade, M6

Weapon:	Carbine, Caliber .30, M1; Carbine, Caliber .30, M2
Ballistic Perf.:	
Velocity:	Shall propel grenade (AT, Practice, M11A3) with velocity of 145 ±15 fps at 5 feet
Cartridge:	103 grs.
Case:	77 grs.
Wad:	Pressed Paper, Commercial
Primer, Perc.:	
Propellant:	
Brand:	IMR 4809 and Black Powder
Weight:	21 grs.
Ident.:	Case Mouth closed with 5-petal rose crimp

Cartridge, Caliber .30, Carbine, Test, High Pressure, M18

Weapon:	Carbine, Caliber .30 M1; Carbine, Caliber .30, M2
Ballistic Perf.:	
Pressure:	47,500 2,500 psi max. avg.
Cartridge:	233 grs. approx.
Case:	71 - 6grs.
Bullet:	152 - 3 grs.
Primer, Perc.:	
Propellant:	

Brand: HPC-5
Type: Double Base, Flake
Weight: 14 grs.
Ident.: Case is stannic stained

Cartridge, Caliber .30, Carbine, Tracer, M27

Weapon: Carbine, Caliber .30, M1; Carbine, Caliber .30, M2

Ballistic Perf.:
Velocity: 1,800 ±30 fps
Pressure: 40,000 psi, max. avg.
Trace: Bright Trace from 100 to 400 yards
Accuracy: 3.5" mean radius max. avg. at 100 yards

Cartridge: 191 - 13 grs.
Case: B6200957, 71 - 6 grs.
Bullet: 103 - 4 grs.
Tracer: 5.5 grs. approx.
Igniter: .5 gr. approx.
Primer, Perc.:
Propellant:

Brand:	HPC-5	WC 820
Type:	Double Base Flake	Double Base Spheroidal
Weight:	13 grs.	13 grs.

Point Ident.: Orange Tip

7.62mm, NATO (.308 WIN.)

Cartridge, Caliber 7.62mm, NATO, Ball, M59

Weapon: Gun, Machine, 7.62mm, M60; M73 Rifle, 7.62mm, M14

Ballistic Perf.:
Velocity: 2,750 ±30 fps at 78 feet
Pressure: 50,000 psi, max. avg.
Accuracy: Carton or Clip Pack - 5" mean radius at 600 yards; Link Pack - 7½" mean radius at 600 yards

Cartridge: 393 - 27 grs.
Case: 190 - 20 grs.
Bullet: 150.5 - 6.5 grs. (cut cannelure)
150.5 - 5.5 grs. (knurled cannelure)
Core: 55 - 2 grs. - steel
Fill., Pt.: 24 - 1 grs. - lead-antimony
Fill., Base: 14.5 - 1 grs. - lead-antimony
Primer, Perc.:
Prim. Wt.: 5.430 - .520 grs.
Pellet Wt.: .600 - .120 grs.
Compos.: Lead Styphnate
Propellant:

Brand:	WC 846	IMR 4475
Type:	Double Base Spheroidal	Single Base Tubular
Weight:	46 grs.	41 grs.

Point Ident.: Plain tip

Cartridge, Caliber 7.62mm, NATO, Test, High Pressure, M60

Weapon: Used to proof test barrels and weapons (Not a service cartridge)

Ballistic Perf.:
Pressure: 67,500 2,500 psi, avg.

Cartridge: 412.0 - 23.5 grs.
Case: 190 - 20 grs.
Bullet: 174.5 - 3.0 grs.
Primer, Perc.:
Prim. Wt.: 5.43 - .52 grs.
Pellet Wt.: .60 - .12 grs.
Compos.: FA-956, Lead Styphnate
Propellant:
Brand: IMR 4475
Type: Single Base Tubular
Weight: 41 grs.
Ident.: Stannic Stained Case

Cartridge, 7.62mm, NATO, AP, M61

Weapon: Gun, Machine, 7.62mm, M60; M73 Rifle, 7.62mm, M14

Ballistic Perf.:
Velocity: 2,750 fps ±30 fps at 78 feet
Pressure: 50,000 psi, max. avg.

Accuracy: 7.5" mean radius at 600 yards
Cartridge: 393 - 27 grs.
Case: 190 - 20 grs.
Bullet: C7553740 - 150.5 - 6.5 grs. (cut cannelure);
150.5 - 5.5 grs. (knurled cannelure)
Core: 55 - 2 grs. - steel
Fill., Pt.: 24 - 1 grs. - Lead Antimony
Primer, Perc.:
Prim. Wt.: 5.430 - .520 grs.
Pellet Wt.: .600 - .120 grs.
Compos.: FA-956, Lead Styphnate
Propellant:

Brand:	IMR 4475	WC 846
Type:	Single Base Tubular	Double Base Spheroidal
Weight:	41 grs.	46 grs.

Point Ident.: Black Lacquer

Cartridge, Caliber 7.62mm, NATO, Tracer, M62

Weapon: Gun, Machine, 7.62mm, M60; M73 Rifle, 7.62mm, M14

Ballistic Perf.:
Velocity: 2,750 ±30 fps at 78 feet
Pressure: 50,000 psi, max. avg.
Accuracy: 15" mean radius, max. avg., at 600 yards
Trace: Visible trace between 100 and 850 yards, min.
Cartridge: 383 - 29 grs.
Case: 190 - 20 grs.
Bullet: 142 - 4 grs.
Fill., Pt.: 72.0 - 1.5 grs. - Lead Antimony
Tracer: 6.5 grs.approx.
Ign.: 1.0 grs. approx.
Sub-ign.: 1.0 grs. approx.
Primer, Perc.:
Prim. Wt.: 5.43 - .52 grs.
Pellet Wt.: .60 - .12 grs.
Compos.: FA-956, Lead Styphnate
Propellant:
Type: Double Base Spheroidal
Weight: 46 grs.
Point Ident.: Orange Lacquer

Cartridge, Caliber 7.62mm, NATO, Tracer, M62

(Overhead Fire Application)
Weapon: Gun, Machine, 7.62mm, M60; M73 Rifle, 7.62mm, M14

Ballistic Perf.:
Velocity: 2,680 ±30 fps at 78 feet
Pressure: 50,000 psi, max. avg.
Accuracy: 9" mean radius, max. avg. at 600 yards
Extreme Spread, Max. per target: 45 inches
Trace: Visible trace between 100 and 850 yards, min.
Cartridge: 387 - 29 grs.
Case: 190 - 20 grs.
Bullet: 146 - 4 grs.
Fill., Pt.: 72 - 1.5 grs. - Lead Antimony
Base Seal: None
Tracer: 6.5 grs. approx.
Igniter: 1.0 grs. approx.
Sub-ign.: 1.0 grs. approx.
Primer Perc.:
Prim. Wt.: 5.43 - .52 grs.
Pellet Wt.: .60 - .12 grs.
Compos.: FA-956, Lead Styphnate
Propellant:
Type: Double Base Spherical
Weight: 46 grs.
Ident.: Red Lacquer

Dummy Cartridge, Caliber 7.62mm, NATO, M63

Weapon: Gun, Machine, 7.62mm, M60; M73 Rifle, 7.62mm, M14
Requirements: Training and Gun Functioning
Bullet Pull: 175 lb. min.
Cartridge: 258 - 21.5 grs.
Case: 190 - 20 grs.
Bullet: 68 - 1.5 grs.
Ident.: 6 corrugations spaced equally around periphery of case

Cartridge, Caliber 7.62mm, NATO, Grenade Rifle, M64

Weapon: Rifle, 7.62mm, M14
Ballistic Perf.:
Velocity: Cartridge shall propel a grenade weighing 1.56lbs. 160 ±5 fps at 5.6 feet beyond the forward end of the grenade when fully positioned for launching.
Cartridge: 233 - 21 grs. (HPS 4 Propellant)
Case: 236 - 21 grs. (IMR8097 Propellant)
241 - 21 grs. (WC830 Propellant)
190 - 20 grs. - Copper Alloy
Primer, Perc.:
Prim. Wt.: 5.430 - .520 grs.
Pellet Wt.: .600 - .120 grs.
Compos.: FA-956, Lead Styphnate
Propellant:

Brand:	HPC4	1MR8097	WC830
Type:	Double Base Tubular	Single Base Tubular	DoubleBase Spherical
Weight:	37 grs.	40 grs.	45 grs.

Wad: Pressed Paper
Ident.: Rosette Crimp

Cartridge, Caliber 7.62mm, NATO, Ball, M80

Weapon: Gun, Machine, 7.62mm, M60; M73 Rifle, 7.62mm, M14
Ballistic Perf.:
Velocity: 2,750 ±30 fps at 78 feet
Pressure: 50,000 psi, max. avg.
Accuracy: Carton or Clip Pack - 5" mean radius, max. avg. at 600 yards; Link Pack - 7.52" mean radius, max. avg. at 600 yards
Cartridge: 392 - 31 grs.
Case: 190 - 20 grs.
Bullet: 149 - 3 grs.
Primer, Perc.:
Prim. Wt.: 5.43 - .52 grs.
Pellet Wt.: .60 - .12 grs.
Compos.: FA-956, Lead Styphnate
Propellant:

Type:	Double Base Spheroidal	Single Base Tubular	Single Base Tubular
Weight:	46 grs.	41.5 grs.	41 grs.

Ident.: Plain Tip

Cartridge, Caliber 7.62mm, NATO, Ball, M80

(Overhead Fire Application)
Weapon: Gun, Machine, 7.62mm, M60; M73 Rifle, 7.62mm, M14
Ballistic Perf.:
Velocity: 2,750 ±30 fps at 78 feet
Pressure: 50,000 psi, max. avg.
Accuracy: 5" mean radius, max. avg. at 600 yards; Extreme Spread, max. per target - 25 inches
Cartridge: 393 - 31 grs.
Case: 190 - 20 grs.
Bullet:
Primer, Perc.:
Prim. Wt.: 5.43 - .52 grs.
Pellet Wt.: .60 - .12 grs.
Compos.: FA-956, Lead Styphnate
Propellant:

Brand:	WC 846	IMR 8138M	IMR4475
Type:	Double Base Spheroidal	Single Base Tubular	Single Base Tubular
Weight:	46 grs.	41.5 grs.	41 grs.

Point Ident.: Plain Tip

Cartridge, Caliber 7.62mm, NATO, Blank, M82

Weapon: Rifle, 7.62mm, M14, Machine Gun, M60; M73 with blank-firing attachment
Ballistic Perf.:
Screen Perf.: Perforations in paper screen shall be less than .1-inch in diameter at 15 ft. from muzzle of gun
Cartridge: 222 - 225 grs. approx.
Case: 201 grs. approx.
Wad: .030-inch tagboard or chipboard
Primer, Perc.:
Prim. Wt.: 5.430 - .520 grs., 5 grs. approx.
Compos.: Lead Styphnate - FA-956; FA-1023
Propellant:

Brand:	SR4759	HPC-2	WC818
Type:	Single Base Tubular	Double Base Flake	Double Base Spheroidal
Weight:	17.5 grs.	14.5 grs.	14.5 grs.
Ident.:	No bullet, crimped mouth, double tapered neck and orifice sealed with red lacquer		

Cartridge, Caliber 7.62mm, Match, M118

Weapon:	Rifle, 7.62mm, M14 (National Match)
Ballistic Perf.:	
Velocity:	2,550 ±30 fps at 78 feet
Pressure:	50,000 psi, max. avg.
Accuracy:	3.5" mean radius, max. avg. at 600 yards
Cartridge:	390 grs. approx.
Case:	190 - 20 grs.
Bullet:	175.5 - 3.0 grs.
Primer, Perc.:	
Prim. Wt:	5.43 - .52 grs.; 5.3 grs. approx.; 5 grs. approx.
Pellet Wt:	.60 - .12 grs.; .7 - .2 grs.; .58 -.08 grs.
Compos.:	FA-956, FA-961, FA-1023
Type:	Lead Styphnate
Propellant:	
Brand:	WC 846 / IMR 4895
Type:	Double Base Spherical / Single Base Tubular
Weight:	44 grs. / 42 grs.
Ident.:	Special head stamping-Match stamped on head of case or NM stamped on head of case of cartridges for National Matches

Cartridge, Caliber 7.62mm, Match, M852

Weapon:	Rifle, 7.62mm, M14 (National Match)
Ballistic Perf.:	
Velocity:	2,550 ±30 fps at 78 feet
Pressure:	50,000 psi, max. avg.
Accuracy:	3.5" mean radius, max. avg. at 600 yards
Cartridge:	383 grs. approx.
Case:	190 - 20 grs.
Bullet:	168 grs. Hollow point boattail
Primer, Perc.:	
Prim. Wt:	5.43 - .52 grs.; 5.3 grs. approx.; 5 grs.approx.
Pellet Wt:	.60 - .12 grs.; .7 - .2 grs.; .58 -.08 grs.
Compos.:	FA-956 FA-961 FA-1023
Type:	Lead Styphnate
Propellant:	
Brand:	IMR 4895
Type:	Single Base Tubular
Weight:	42 grs.
Ident.:	Special head stamping-Match stamped on head of case or NM stamped on head of case of cartridges for National Matches

Cartridge, Caliber 7.62mm, Ball, Frangible, M160

Weapon:	Gun, Machine, 7.62mm, M73
Ballistic Perf.:	
Velocity:	1,320 ±50 fps
Accuracy:	4.0" mean radius max. avg. at 100 yards
Perf.:	The bullet of the cartridge shall not perforate a 3/162 thick plate Dural .2024 T4 (or equal) with a Brinell hardness of 105 to 125 under a 500 kilogram load at a range of 25 yards.
Cartridge:	315 - 24 grs.
Case:	190 - 20 grs.
Bullet:	108.5 - 3 grs., Bakelite, Natural and powdered lead
Primer, Perc.:	
Prim. Wt:	5.43 - .52 grs.
Compos.:	FA-956
Propellant:	
Brand:	SR8074 / HPC-8 / WC140
Type:	Single Base Tubular / Double Base Flake / Single Base Spheroidal
Weight:	10.5 grs. / 8.3 grs. / 11.4 grs.
Ident.:	Green tip; White annulus

Dummy Cartridge, Caliber 7.62mm, Inert Loaded, M172

Weapon:	Gun, Machine, M60, Testing Metallic Link Belts and Gun Function

Requirements:	Bullet Extr.: The force required to extract the bullet from the cartridge case shall not be less than 173 lbs.
Cartridge:	385 - 23 grs.
Case:	190 - 20 grs.
Bullet:	149 - 3 grs.
Filler:	Sodium Carbonate Monohydrate or equal
Ident.:	Cartridge, black oxide, no primer or primer vent hole

Cartridge, Caliber 7.62mm, NATO, Ball, Duplex, M198

Weapon:	Rifle, 7.62mm, M14
Ballistic Perf.:	
Velocity:	Front Bullet - 2,750 ±30 fps at 78 feet Rear Bullet - 2,200 fps min. indiv. at 78 feet
Pressure:	52,000 psi, max. avg.
Accuracy:	(Front Bullet) 2" mean radius, max. avg. at 100 yards
Dispersion:	(Rear Bullet) between 5 and 10 inches CEP at 100 yards
Cartridge:	411 - 31 grs.
Case:	190 - 20 grs.
Bullet:	(Front) 84 - 4 grs. (Rear) 85 - 4grs.
Primer, Perc.:	
Prim. Wt:	5.43 - .52 grs.
Compos.:	FA-956, Lead Styphnate
Propellant:	
Type:	Double Base Spheroidal
Weight:	45.5 grs.
Point Ident.:	Green Lacquer

.30 (.30-06)

Cartridge, Caliber .30, Tracer M1

Weapon:	Gun, Machine, Cal .30, M37; Gun, Machine, Cal .30 Browning M1919A4; Gun, Machine, Cal .30, M1919A6; Rifle, U.S. Cal .30, M1
Ballistic Perf.:	
Velocity:	2,700 ±30 fps at 78 feet GM Bullet 2,665 ±30 fps for GMCS Bullet
Pressure:	52,000 psi, max. avg.
Accuracy:	18" mean radius max. avg. at 600 yards
Tracer:	Visible Light from Muzzle to 900 yards
Cartridge:	408 - 27 grs. (GM Bullet) 399 - 27 grs. (GMCS Bullet)
Case:	200 – 20 grs.
Bullet:	152.5 - 3.5 grs. 143.5 - 3.5 grs.
Tracer:	13 grs. approx.
Igniter:	3 grs. approx.
Primer, Perc.:	
Prim. Wt:	5.43 - .520 grs. - Lead Styphnate
Propellant:	
Type:	Double Base, Spheroidal - IMR4895
Weight:	50 grs.
Point Ident.:	Red tip

Cartridge, Caliber .30, Test, High Pressure, M1

Weapon:	(For Proof Testing all Caliber .30 Weapons)
Ballistic Perf.:	
Pressure:	67,500 psi, max. avg.
Cartridge:	432 - 24 grs.
Bullet:	173 - 3 grs.
Primer, Perc.:	
Prim. Wt:	5.5 grs.
Compos.:	FA961 - Lead Styphnate
Propellant:	
Brand:	IMR 4198
Type:	Single Base, Tubular
Weight:	52 grs.
Ident.:	Stannic Stained (tinned) Case

Cartridge, Caliber .30, Ball, M2

Weapon:	Gun, Machine, Cal .30, M37; Gun, Machine, Cal .30 Browning M1919A4; Gun, Machine, Cal .30, M1919A6; Rifle, U.S. Cal .30, M1
Ballistic Perf.:	
Velocity:	2740 ±30 fps at 78 ft
Pressure:	50,000 psi, max. avg.

Accuracy:	7.5" mean radius max. avg. at 600 yards
Cartridge:	408 - 23 grs.
Case:	200 - 20 grs.
Bullet:	152 - 3 grs.
Primer, Perc.:	
Prim. Wt:	5.43
Compos.:	Lead Styphnate
Propellant:	
Brand:	IMR4895 / WC852 / CMR-100
Type:	Single Base Tubular / Double Base Spheroidal / Single Base Tubular
Weight:	50 grs. / 50 grs. / 45 grs.
Point Ident.:	Plain Tip

Cartridge, Caliber .30, Ball, M2

(Overhead Fire Application)

Weapon:	Guns, Machine, Caliber .30; M37, Browning M1919A4 and M1919A6
Ballistic Perf.:	
Velocity:	2,740 ±30 fps at 78 feet
Pressure:	50,000 psi maximum average
Accuracy:	5.0" mean radius maximum average at 600 yards
Cartridge:	408 - 23 grs.
Case:	200 - 20 grs.
Bullet:	152 - 3 grs.
Primer, Perc.:	
Prim. Wt:	5.43
Compos.:	FA956 - Lead Styphnate
Propellant:	
Brand:	IMR4895 / WC852 / CMR-100
Type:	Single Base Tubular / Double Base Spheroidal / Single Base Tubular
Weight:	50 grs. / 50 grs. / 45 grs.
Point Ident.:	Plain Tip

Cartridge, Caliber .30, Armor Piercing, M2

Weapon:	Gun, Machine, Cal .30, M37; Gun, Machine, Cal .30 Browning M1919A4; Gun, Machine, Cal .30, M1919A6; Rifle, U.S. Cal .30, M1
Ballistic Perf.:	
Velocity:	2,715 ±30 fps at 78 feet
Pressure:	54,000 psi, max. avg.
Accuracy:	10" mean radius max. avg. at 600 yards
Cartridge:	424 - 28 grs.
Case:	200 - 28 grs.
Bullet:	166 - 7.5 grs.
Primer, Perc.:	
Prim. Wt:	5.43
Compos.:	Lead Styphnate
Propellant:	
Brand:	WC852 / IMR 4895
Type:	Double Base Spheroidal / Single Base Tubular
Weight:	55 grs. / 55 grs.
Point Ident.:	Black tip

Cartridge, Caliber .30, Grenade Rifle, M3

Weapon:	Rifle, U.S. Caliber .30, M1
Ballistic Perf.:	
Velocity:	Shall propel Grenade (Practice, M11A2) with a velocity of 180 ±15 fps at 5.5ft
Cartridge:	246 - 20 grs.
Case:	200 - 20 grs.
Wad:	Paper
Primer, Perc.:	
Prim. Wt:	5.43 - .520 grs.
Compos.:	Lead Styphnate
Propellant:	
Type:	Single Base, IMR 4895
Weight:	40 grs. + 5.0 1.0 gr. Black powder
Ident.:	Case mouth closed with 5-petal rose crimp and sealed with red lacquered disc

Cartridge, Caliber .30, API, M14

Weapon:	Gun, Machine, Cal .30, M37 (Tank) Gun, Machine, Cal .30, Browning, M1919A4; Gun, Machine, Cal .30, 1919A6; Rifle, U.S. Cal .30, M1
Ballistic Perf.:	
Velocity:	2,780 ±30 fps at 78 feet

Pressure: 54,000 psi, max. avg.
Accuracy: 15" mean radius max. avg. at 600 yards
Incend: Shall produce flash when fired against steel target at 175 yards
Penetra: Avg. penetration depth of .422-in. when fired against steel plate at 100 yards
Cartridge: 407 - 30 grs.
Case: 200 - 20 grs.
Bullet: 151 - 6 grs.
Primer, Perc.:
Compos.: Lead Styphnate
Propellant:
Brand: WC 852   IMR 4895
Type: Double Base   Single Base
     Spheroidal   Tubular
Weight: 50 grs.   50 grs.
Point Ident.: Aluminum

Cartridge, Caliber .30, Frangible, Ball, M22

Weapon: Gun, Machine, Cal .30, M37; Gun, Machine, Cal .30, Browning, M1919A4; Rifle, U.S. Cal .30, M1

Ballistic Perf.:
Velocity: 1,320 ±30 fps at 53 feet 1500 fps, max. individual at 53 feet
Accuracy: 2.0" mean radius max. avg. at 100 yards
Perf.: Shall not perforate aluminum plate at 25 yards 3/162 Dural 2024 T4 with Brinell Hardness of 105 to 125 under 500 Kilogram load
Cartridge: 320 - 24 grs.
Case: 220 - 20 grs.
Bullet: 108.3 grs. Bakelite
Primer, Perc.:
Prim. Wt: 5.5 grs.
Compos.: Lead Styphnate
Propellant:
Brand: SR 4759
Type: Single Base, Tubular
Weight: 11 grs.
Point Ident.: Green and white tip

Cartridge, Caliber .30, Tracer, M25

Weapon: Gun, Machine, Cal .30 Browning, M1917A1 Gun, Machine, Cal .30, M37 (Tank) Gun, Machine, Cal .30 Browning, M1919A4 Gun, Machine, Cal .30 Browning, M1919A6 Rifle, U.S. Cal .30 M1

Ballistic Perf.:
Velocity: 2,665 ±30 fps at 78 feet
Pressure: 50,000 psi, max. avg.
Trace: Bright Trace, 75 to 900 yards
Cartridge: 401 - 25 grs.
Case: 200 - 20 grs.
Bullet: 145.5 - 4 grs.
Primer Perc.:
Prim. Wt: 5.430 - .520 grs.
Compos.: Lead Styphnate - FA956
Propellant:
Brand: WC 852   IMR 4895
Type: Double Base   Single Base
     Spheroidal   Tubular
Weight: 50 grs.   50 grs.
Point Ident.: Orange tip

Cartridge, Caliber .30, Tracer, M25 (Steel Case)

Same as Cartridge, Tracer, Cal .30, M25, except:
Case: Steel, 180 - 20 grs.

Cartridge, Caliber .30, Dummy, M40

Weapon: For training purposes in all caliber .30 weapons
Ballistic Perf.: None
Cartridge: 268 - 21.5 grs.
Case: 200 - 20 grs.
Bullet: 68 - 1.5 grs.
Ident.: Corrugated case - no primer

Cartridge, Caliber .30, Match, M72

Weapon: Rifle, U.S. Caliber .30, M1 National Match
Ballistic Perf.:
Velocity: 2,640 ±30 fps at 78 feet

Pressure: 50,000 psi, max. avg.
Accuracy: 3.5" mean radius max. avg. at 600 yards
Cartridge: 425 grs. approx.
Case: 200 - 20 grs.
Bullet: 175.5 - 3 grs.
Primer Perc.:
Prim. Wt: 5 to 5.6 grs.
Compos.: FA961 or FA1023 - Lead Styphnate
Propellant:
Brand: IMR 4895
Type: Single Base, Tubular
Weight: 50 grs.
Ident.: MATCH stamped on head of case, and NM stamped on head of case of cartridges for National Matches

Cartridge, Caliber 30, Blank, M1909

Weapon: Gun, Machine, Cal .30, Browning M1919A4; Gun, Machine, Cal .30 M1919A6; Rifle, U.S. Cal .30, M1
Ballistic Perf.: None
Cartridge: 218 - 20 grs.
Case: 200 - 20 grs.
Primer Perc.:
Propellant:
Brand: WC Blank   SR 4990
Type: Double Base   Single Base
     Spheroidal   Flake
Weight: 12 grs.   12 grs.
Wad: Paper 25 grs.
Ident.: No bullet, mouth sealed with red lacquered disc

Cartridge, Caliber .30, Blank, M1909 (Steel Case)

Same as Cartridge, Blank, Cal .30, M1909 except:
Case: Steel, 180 - 20 grs.

9mm

Cartridge, Caliber 9mm, Ball, NATO, M882

Weapon: Pistol, Automatic, Cal 9mm, M9, M11
Ballistic Perf.:
Velocity: 1,251 ±25 fps at 16 meters
Pressure: 27,000 psi, max. avg.
Accuracy:
Cartridge: 179 grs.
Case: 42 grs.
Bullet: 124 grs. Copper Alloy
Primer, Perc.:
Propellant:
Brand: HPC 26
Type: Double Base   Flake
Weight: 5 grs.   6 grs.
Point Ident.: Plain tip

Cartridge, Caliber 9mm, Test, High Pressure, M905

Weapon: Used to proof test barrels and weapons (Not a service cartridge)
Ballistic Perf.:
Pressure: 50,000 psi, max. avg.
Cartridge: 179 grs.
Case: 42 grs.
Bullet: 124 grs.
Primer, Perc.: Lead Styphnate
Propellant:
Brand: WC 370
Type: Double Base Ball
Weight: 7.5 grs.
Ident.: Tinned Case, HPT headstamp

Cartridge, Caliber 9mm, Practice Tracer, M939

Weapon: AT-4 Subcaliber Trainer
Ballistic Perf.:
Velocity: 885 ±25 fps at 25.5 feet
Pressure: 27,000 psi, max. avg.
Trace: Visible trace to match AT-4 rocket trajectory
Cartridge:
Case: Aluminum
Bullet: Brass
Tracer:
Ignit.:

Primer, Perc.: Lead Styphnate
Propellant:
Brand:
Type:
Weight:
Point Ident.: Red Lacquer over Blue Tip

Cartridge, Caliber 9mm, Dummy, M917

Weapon: Pistol, Automatic, Cal 9mm, M9, M11
Ballistic Perf.: Not applicable
Cartridge: 179 grs. approx.
Bullet: 124 grs.
Ident.: Hole in side wall of case

.45

Cartridge, Caliber .45, Ball, M1911

Weapon: Pistol, Automatic, Cal .45, M1911A1 Gun, Submachine, Cal. 45, M3A1
Ballistic Perf.:
Velocity: 855 ±25 fps at 25.5 feet
Pressure: 19,000 psi, max. avg.
Accuracy: 7.46" diagonal (max. avg.) at 50 yards
Cartridge: 331 - 17 grs.
Case: 87 - 10 grs.
Bullet: 234 - 6 grs. Copper Alloy
     .231 grs. Gilding Metal Clad Steel
Primer, Perc.:
Propellant:
Brand: SR 7970   HPC 1
Type: Single Base   Double Base
     Flake   Flake
Weight: 5 grs.   5 grs.
Point Ident.: Plain tip

Cartridge, Caliber .45, Ball, M1911, (Steel Case)

Weapon: Pistol, Automatic, Cal .45, M1911A1 Gun, Submachine, Cal. 45, M3A1
Ballistic Perf.:
Velocity: 855 ±25 fps at 25.5 feet
Pressure: 19,000 psi, max. avg.
Accuracy: 7.46" diagonal (max. avg.) at 50 yards
Cartridge: 321 - 20 grs.

Cartridge, Caliber .45, Ball, M1911, Match Grade

Weapon: Pistol, Automatic, Cal .45, M1911A1 National Match
Ballistic Perf:
Velocity: 855 ±25 fps at 25.5 feet
Pressure: 19,000 psi, max. avg.
Accuracy: 3" diagonal (max. avg.) at 50 yards
Cartridge: 334 - 17 grs.
Case: 87 - 10 grs.
Bullet: 234 - 6 grs.
Primer, Perc.:
Propellant:
Brand: SR 7970   HPC 1
Type: Single Base   Double Base
     Flake   Flake
Weight: 5 grs.   5grs.
Ident.: Special head stamping - Match - stamped on head of case, and NM stamped on head of case of cartridges for National Matches

Cartridge, Caliber .45, Test, High Pressure, M1

Weapon: Used to proof test barrels and weapons (Not a service cartridge)
Ballistic Perf.:
Pressure: 22,000 psi, max. avg.
Cartridge: 332-16 grs.
Case: 87 - 10 grs.
Bullet: 234 - 6 grs.
Primer, Perc.: Lead Styphnate
Propellant:
Brand: SR 7970   HPC 1
Type: Single Base   Double Base
     Flake   Flake
Weight: 7 grs.
Ident.: Stannic Stained Case

Cartridge, Caliber .45, Blank, M9

Weapon:	Pistol, Automatic, Cal .45, M1911A1
Ballistic Perf.:	
Screen Perf.:	.12 dia. max. perforations in paper screen at 15 feet
Cartridge:	104 grs. approx.
Propellant:	7 grs.

Cartridge, Caliber .45, Tracer, M26

Weapon:	Pistol, Automatic, Cal .45, M1911A1 Gun, Submachine, Cal .45, M3A1	
Ballistic Perf.:		
Velocity:	885 ±25 fps at 25.5 feet	
Pressure:	19,000 psi, max. avg.	
Trace:	Visible trace between 15 and 150 yards, min.	
Cartridge:	331 - 17 grs.	
Bullet:	203 grs. approx.	
Tracer:	3 grs. approx.	
Ignit.:	2.5 grs. approx.	
Primer, Perc.:	Lead Styphnate	
Propellant:		
Brand:	SR 7970	HPC 1
Type:	Single Base Flake	Double Base Flake
Weight:	5 grs.	5 grs.
Point Ident.:	Red Lacquer	

Cartridge, Caliber .45, Tracer, M26 (Steel Case)

Same as Cartridge, Cal .45, M26, except:	
Case:	Steel, 82 - 10 grs.

Cartridge, Caliber .45, Blank, Line Throwing M32

Case:	Brass
Primer:	Non-mercuric, non-corrosive
Propellant:	Commercial
Ballistics:	
Pressure:	20,000 psi
Ident.:	No bullet, rimmed long case, ".45 M32" stamped on head of case
Note:	This cartridge used with Lyle life-saving gun, Cal 45/70.

Cartridge, Caliber .45, Match, Wad Cutter

(Commercial)

Weapon:	Pistol Automatic Cal .45, M1911A1, National Match
Ballistics:	
Velocity:	The mean velocity of 10 rds. at 15 ft. from the muzzle of the gun shall be 765 ±45 fps
Pressure:	The mean pressure of 10 rds. shall not exceed 18,000 psi. The extreme variation shall not exceed 6,200 psi.
Accuracy:	Average extreme spread of 5-5 shot targets at 50 yards shall not exceed 3.0 inches
Cartridge:	
Case:	Brass
Bullet:	185 grains Gilding Metal
Propellant:	Commercial
Primer:	Commercial Lead Styphnate
Ident.:	Head stamp in accordance with commercial practice

Cartridge, Caliber .45, Dummy, M1921

Weapon:	Pistol, Automatic, Cal .45, M1911A1 Gun, Submachine, Cal .45, M3A1
Ballistic Perf.:	Not applicable
Cartridge:	313 grs. approx.
Bullet:	234 - 6 grs.
Ident.:	Hole in side wall of case

Cartridge, Caliber .45, Dummy, M1921 (Steel Case)

Same as Cartridge, Dummy, Cal .45, M1921, except:	
Ctg. weight:	301 grs. approx.
Case:	Steel, 82 - 10 grs.

.50

Cartridge, Caliber .50, Tracer, M1

Weapon:	Gun, Machine, Caliber .50, Browning, M2 Heavy Barrel (Turret Type); Gun, Machine, Caliber .50, Browning, M2, Heavy Barrel (Flexible); Gun, Machine, Caliber .50, Tank, M85
Ballistic Perf.:	
Velocity:	2,700 ±40 fps at 78 feet
Pressure:	52,000 psi, max. avg.
Trace:	Bright trace from 250 to 1600 yards
Cartridge:	1,785 - 68 grs.
Case:	850 - 50 grs.
Bullet:	676 - 17 grs.
Tracer	65 grs.
Ignit. Comp.	10 grs.
Primer, Perc.:	
Prim. Wt.:	18.5 grs. approx.
Propellant:	
Brand:	IMR 5010
Type:	Single Base, Tubular
Weight:	240 grs.
Point Ident.:	Red tip

Cartridge, Caliber .50, Test, High-Pressure, M1

Weapon:	For proof testing all caliber .50 weapons
Ballistic Perf.:	
Pressure:	65,000 psi, max. avg.
Cartridge:	2,108 - 62 grs.
Bullet:	999 - 11 grs.
Primer, Perc.:	
Prim. Wt:	18.5 grs. - Styphnate Cloride
Propellant:	WC 860
Type:	Double Base, Spheroidal
Weight:	240 grs.
Ident.:	Stannic stained case

Cartridge, Caliber .50, Incendiary, M1

Weapon:	Gun, Machine, Caliber .50, Browning, M2 Heavy Barrel (Turret Type); Gun, Machine, Caliber .50, Browning, M2, Heavy Barrel (Flexible); Gun, Machine, Caliber .50, Tank, M85
Ballistic Perf.:	
Velocity:	2950 ±30 fps at 78 feet
Pressure:	54,000 psi, max. avg.
Cartridge:	1,704 grs. approx.
Bullet:	633 - 26 grs.
Incend.:	34 - 2 grs.
Primer, Perc.:	
Prim. Wt:	18.5 grs.
Propellant:	
Brand:	WC860
Type:	Double Base Spheroidal
Weight:	240 grs.
Point Ident.:	Blue tip

Cartridge, Caliber .50, Blank, M1

Weapon:	Gun, Machine, Caliber .50, Browning, M2, Heavy Barrel (Flexible)
Ballistic Perf.:	None
Cartridge:	891 grs. approx.
Propellant:	
Brand:	WC-150
Weight:	46 grs.
Type:	Double Base, Spheroidal
Wad:	1.5 grs. approx.-Fiberlic No. 2 Kraftboard, or equal (commercial); 256 grs. approx. - Strawboard covered with thin red paper (commercial)
Primer, Perc.:	
Prim. Wt:	18.5 grs. approx.
Ident.:	No bullet-mouth sealed with vermilion lacquered wad

Cartridge, Caliber .50, Armor Piercing, M2

Weapon:	Gun, Machine, Caliber .50, Browning, M2, Heavy Barrel (Turret Type); Gun, Machine, Caliber .50, Browning, M2, Heavy Barrel (Flexible); Gun, Machine, Caliber .50, Tank, M85
Ballistic Perf.:	

Velocity:	2,810 ±fps at 78 feet	
Pressure:	53,000 psi, max. avg.	
Accuracy:	10.0" mean radius max. avg. at 600 yards	
Cartridge:	1,812 - 73 grs.	
Case:	850 - 80 grs.	
Bullet:	708 - 22 grs.	
Primer Perc.:		
Prim. Wt:	18.5 grs. approx.	
Propellant:		
Brand:	WC 860	IMR 5010
Type:	Double Base Spherodial	Single Base Tubular
Weight:	235 grs.	235 grs.
Point Ident.:	Black tip	

Cartridge, Caliber .50, Dummy, M2

Weapon:	All Caliber .50 Weapons - for training personnel and testing weapon mechanism
Cartridge:	1,215 - 60 grs. (GMCS Bullet Jacket); 1,248 - 60 grs. (GM Bullet Jacket)
Ident.:	Three holes in case, no primer

Cartridge, Caliber .50, Ball, M2

Weapon:	Gun, Machine, Caliber .50, Browning, M2, Heavy Barrel (Turret Type); Gun, Machine, Caliber .50, Browning, M2, Heavy Barrel (Flexible)
Ballistic Perf.:	
Velocity:	2,810 ±0 fps at 78 feet
Pressure:	55,000 psi, max. avg.
Accuracy:	9" mean radius max. avg. at 600 yards
Cartridge:	1,813 - 73 grs.
Case:	850 - 50 grs.
Bullet:	709.5 - 22 grs.
Primer Perc.:	
Prim. Wt:	18.5 grs.
Propellant:	
Brand:	WC 860
Type:	Double Base, Spheroidal
Weight:	235 grs.
Ident.:	Plain tip

Cartridge, Caliber .50, Armor Piercing Incendiary, M8

Weapon:	Gun, Machine, Caliber .50, Browning, M2 Heavy Barrel (Turret Type); Gun, Machine, Caliber .50, Browning, M2, Heavy Barrel (Flexible); Gun, Machine, Caliber .50, Tank, M85	
Ballistic Perf.:		
Velocity:	2,910 ±30 fps at 78 feet	
Pressure:	55,000 psi, max. avg.	
Accuracy:	12" mean radius max. avg. at 600 yards	
Incen. Fl.:	Incendiary flash must be capable of initiating combustion of flammable liquids	
Penetrat.:	Bullet or core must completely perforate armor plate at 100 yards	
Cartridge:	1,764.5 - 78.5 grs.	
Bullet:	662.5 - 27 grs.	
Primer, Perc.:		
Prim. Wt:	18.5 grs. approx.	
Propellant:		
Brand:	WC 860	IMR 5010
Type:	Double Base Spheroidal	Single Base Tubular
Weight:	233 grs.	233 grs.
Point Ident.:	Aluminum	

Cartridge, Caliber .50, Armor Piercing Incendiary (Same as Cartridge, Caliber .50, Armor-Piercing), M8

Cal .50, M8, Steel Case, Incendiary, M8 except:	
Case:	Steel, 800 - 50 grs.

Cartridge, Caliber .50, Tracer, M10

Weapon:	Gun, Machine, Caliber .50, Browning, M2 Heavy Barrel (Turret Type); Gun, Machine, Caliber .50, Browning, M2, Heavy Barrel (Flexible); Gun, Machine, Caliber .50, Tank, M85
Ballistic Perf.:	
Velocity:	2,860 ±40 fps at 78 feet
Pressure:	54,000 psi, max. avg.
Trace:	Bright trace from 225 to 1,600 yards

Cartridge: 1,752 - 68 grs.
Bullet: 643 - 17 grs.
Tracer: 65 grs.
Ignit.: 11 grs.
Primer Perc.:
Prim. Wt: 18.5 grs.
Propellant:
Brand: IMR 5010
Type: Single Base, Tubular
Weight: 240 grs.
Point Ident.: Orange tip

Cartridge, Caliber .50, Tracer, M17

Weapon: Gun, Machine, Caliber .50, Browning, M2 Heavy Barrel (Turret Type); Gun, Machine, Caliber .50, Browning, M2, Heavy Barrel (Flexible); Gun, Machine, Caliber .50, Tank, M85

Ballistic Perf.:
Velocity: 2,860 ±40 fps at 78 feet
Pressure: 54,000 psi, max. avg.
Trace: Bright trace from 100 to 1600 yards
Cartridge: 1,737 - 68 grs.
Bullet: 643 - 17 grs.
Ignit.: 11 grs.
Tracer: 40 grs.
Primer Perc.:
Prim. Wt: 18.5 grs.
Propellant:
Brand: IMR 5010
Type: Single Base, Tubular
Weight: 225 grs.
Point Ident.: Brown tip

Cartridge, Caliber .50, Armor-Piercing, M2/M85 Incendiary, Tracer, M20

Weapon: Gun, Machine, Caliber .50, Browning, M2 Heavy Barrel (Turret Type); Gun, Machine, Caliber .50, Browning, M2, Heavy Barrel (Flexible); Gun, Machine, Caliber .50, Tank, M85

Ballistic Perf.:
Pressure: 55,000 psi
Incend. Fl.: Incendiary flash must be capable of initiating combustion of flammable liquids
Penetra.: Bullet or core must completely penetrate 7/8" armor plate at 100 yards
Trace: Must exhibit visible trace from 100 to 1,600 yards
Cartridge: 1,718 - 76.5 grs.
Bullet: 619 - 25 grs.
Primer Perc.:
Prim. Wt: 18.5 grs.
Propellant:
Brand: IMR 5010
Type: Single Base, Tubular
Weight: 230 grs.
Point Ident.: Red tip, aluminum

Cartridge, Caliber .50, Armor Piercing Incendiary, (Same as Cartridge, Caliber .50, Armor-Piercing), M20

Tracer Cal .50, M20, Steel Case, Incindiary, Tracer, M20 except:
Case: Steel, 800 - 50 grs.

Cartridge, Caliber.50, Tracer, Headlight, M21

Weapon: Gun, Machine, Caliber .50, Browning, M2 Heavy Barrel (Turret Type); Gun, Machine, Caliber .50, Browning, M2, Heavy Barrel (Flexible); Gun, Machine, Caliber .50, Tank, M85

Ballistic Perf.:
Velocity: 2,840 ±40 fps at 78 feet
Pressure: 55,000 psi, max. avg.
Trace: Bright trace from 200 to 500 yards
Cartridge: 1,808 - 68 grs. (with gilding metal jacket bullet)

1,775 - 68 grs. (with gilding metal clad steel jacket bullet)
Case: 850-50grs.
Bullet: 699 - 17 grs. (with gilding metal jacket); 666 - 17 grs. (with gilding metal clad steel jacket)
Primer Perc.:
Prim. Wt: 18.5 grs. approx.

Propellant:
Brand: IMR 5010
Type: Single Base, Tubular
Weight: 240 grs.
Point Ident.: Red tip

Cartridge, Caliber .50, Incendiary, M23

Weapon: Gun, Machine, Caliber .50, Browning, M2 Heavy Barrel (Turret Type); Gun, Machine, Caliber .50, Browning, M2, Heavy Barrel (Flexible); Gun, Machine, Caliber .50, Tank, M85

Ballistic Perf.:
Velocity: 3,400 ±30 fps at 78 feet
Pressure: 58,000 psi, max. avg.
Incend. Fl.: Incendiary flash must be capable of initiating combustion of flammable liquids
Cartridge: 1,581 grs. approx.
Case: 850 - 50 grs.
Bullet: 512 - 24 grs.
Incen.: 90 grs. Max.
Primer Perc.:
Prim. Wt: 18.5 grs. approx.
Propellant:
Brand: IMR 4831
Type: Single Base, Tubular
Weight: 237 grs. approx.
Point Ident.: Medium blue tip, slight blue annulus

Cartridge, Caliber .50, Ball, M33

Weapon: Gun, Machine, Caliber .50, Browning, M2 Heavy Barrel (Turret Type); Gun, Machine, Caliber .50, Browning, M2, Heavy Barrel (Flexible); Gun, Machine, Caliber .50, Tank, M85

Ballistic Perf.:
Velocity: 2,910 ±30 fps at 78 feet
Pressure: 55,000 psi, max. avg.
Cartridge: 1,762.5 - 76.5 grs.
Case: 850 – 50 grs.
Bullet: 661.5 - 25 grs.
Primer Perc.:
Prim. Wt: 18.5 grs.
Propellant:

Brand:	WC860	IMR5010
Type:	Double Base Spheroidal	Single Base Tubular
Weight:	235 grs.	235 grs.

Ident.: Plain tip

Cartridge, Caliber .50, Spotter-Tracer, M48

Weapon: Rifle, Spotting, Caliber .50, M8C
Ballistic Perf.:
Velocity: 1,850 ±20 fps at 78 feet
Accuracy: 10" mean radius at 600 yards
Trace: Bright trace from 100 to 1500 yards
Pressure: 35,000 psi max. avg.
Spotting: Must flash and produce smoke upon impact
Cartridge: 1,651 grs.
Bullet: 827 - 18 grs.
Primer M26:
Primer Perc.:
Prim. Wt: 18.5 grs. approx.
Propellant:
Brand: IMR 4831
Type: Single Base, Tubular
Weight: 120 grs.
Point Ident.: Yellow tip, red annulus

Cartridge, Caliber .50, Spotter-Tracer, M48A1

Weapon: Rifle, Spotting, Caliber .50, M8C
Ballistic Perf.:
Velocity: 1,745 ±20 fps at 78 feet
Trace: Bright trace from 100 to 1500 yards
Pressure: 38,000 psi max. avg.
Impact: Must flash and produce smoke upon impact against steel plate at 175 yards
Cartridge: 1,744 - 71 grs. (with GMCS flash tube or steel flash tube), 1714 - 71 grs. (with Al - alloy flash tube)
Case: 740 - 50 grs.
Bullet: 827 - 18 grs.
Primer Perc.:

Primer Wt.: 18.5 grs. approx.
Propellant:
Type: Single Base, Tubular
Weight: 110 grs.
Point Ident.: Yellow tip, red annulus

Cartridge, Caliber .50, Spotter-Tracer, M48A2

Weapon: Rifle, Spotting, Caliber .50, M8C
Ballistic Perf.:
Velocity: 1,745 ±20 fps at 78 feet
Pressure: 38,000 psi max. avg.
Cartridge: 1,744 - 71 grs. (with GMCS flash tube or steel flash tube); 1714 - 71 grs. (with Al - alloy flash tube)
Case: 740 - 50 grs.
Bullet: 828 - 18 grs.
Primer Perc.:
Prim. Wt.: 18.5 grs. approx.
Propellant: 110 grs. approx.
Type: Single Base, Tubular
Point Ident.: Yellow tip, red annulus

Dummy Cartridge, Caliber .50, Inert Loaded, XM176

Weapon: All caliber .50 weapons
Ballistic Perf.: None
Cartridge: 1,752 - 82 grs.
Bullet: 661.5 - 27 grs.
Primer: No primer
Inert Prop.: Sodium Carbonate - Monohydrate, 5 grs.
Ident.: Cartridge coated with black chemical finish

Cartridge, Caliber .50, Target Practice, T249E2

Weapon: Rifle, Spotting, Caliber .50, M8C
Ballistic Perf.:
Velocity: 1,745 ±20 fps at 78 feet
Pressure: 38,000 max. avg.
Accuracy: 5" mean radius at 600 yards
Cartridge: 1,738 - 61 grs. (with GMCS or steel flash tube);

1,708 - 61 grs. (with Alalloy Flash Tube)
Bullet: 817 4 grs.
Primer Perc.:
Prim. Wt.: 18.5 grs. approx.
Propellant:
Brand: IMR 7383
Type: Single Base, Tubular
Weight: 110 grs. approx.
Point Ident.: Green tip

Cartridge, Caliber .50, Armor Piercing Incendiary, T49

Weapon: Gun, Machine, Caliber .50, Browning, M2 Heavy Barrel (Turret Type); Gun, Machine, Caliber .50, Browning, M2, Heavy Barrel (Flexible); Gun, Machine, Caliber .50, Tank, M85

Ballistic Perf.:
Velocity: 3,400 ±30 fps at 78 feet
Pressure: 58,000 psi, max. avg.
Accuracy: 10" mean radius at 600 yards
Cartridge: 1,597 grs. approx.
Bullet: 501 grs.
Primer Perc.:
Prim. Wt.: 18.5 grs.
Propellant:
Brand: WC 860
Weight: 252 grs.
Type: Double Base, Spheroidal
Point Ident.: Blue tip, silver annulus

Cartridge, Caliber .50, Test, High Pressure, T251

Weapon: Rifle, Spotting, Caliber .50, M8C
Ballistic Perf.:
Pressure: 55,000 psi, max. avg.
Cartridge: 1,902 - 50 grs.
Case: 740 - 50 grs.
Bullet: 999-11 grs.
Primer Perc.:
Primer Wt.: 18.5 grs. approx.
Propellant:
Brand: IMR 4831
Type: Single Base Tubular
Weight: 142 grs.

Ident.: Stannic Stained Case

20mm

Dummy Cartridge, Caliber 20mm, M51A1B1

Weapon:	Guns, Automatic, 20mm, M39, M61, XM168 and GAU-4 (XM130)
Requirements:	Projectile extraction: The cartridge assembly shall withstand a 3900 pound tension force without separation of the projectile from the cartridge case
Cartridge:	3,850 grains, min.
Bullet:	Steel, 1,520 30 grains
Ident.:	Cartridge chromate finish, marking opaque, color black

Cartridge, Caliber 20mm, Armor Piercing Incendiary Tracer, M52E1 (USAF)

Weapon:	Gun, Automatic, 20mm, M39, M61 and GAU-4 (XM130)
Ballistic Perf.:	(Single shot - test barrel)
Velocity:	3,380 ±50 fps at 78 feet
Pressure:	Not to exceed 60,500 psi
Accuracy:	15-in. mean radius - 600 yards
Cartridge:	3,900 grains approx.
Case:	M103, Brass
Prim. Elec.:	22 grs.
Propellant:	WC 870, weight to meet ballistic requirements
Projectile:	1,530 grains approx. Rotating
Blank:	133 grains approx. Gilding Metal
Ident.:	Projectile black and red - marking opaque; color orange

Cartridge, Caliber 20mm, Armor Piercing Incendiary, M53 (USAF)

Weapon:	Guns, Automatic, 20mm, M39, M61 and GAU-4 (XM 130)
Ballistic Perf.:	Single shot - test barrel
Velocity:	3,380 ±250 fps at 78 feet
Pressure:	Not to exceed 60,500 psi
Accuracy:	15-in. mean radius max. avg. at 600 yards
Cartridge:	3,980 grains approx.
Case:	2,150 grs.
Prim. Elec.:	22 grs.
Propellant:	WC 870, weight to meet ballistic requirements
Projectile:	1,540 35 grs. Rotating
Blank:	133 grains approx., Gilding Metal
Nose:	100 grains approx., Aluminum Alloy
Ident.:	Projectile black and band, red marking, opaque color red

Cartridge, Caliber 20mm, Test, High Pressure, M54A1 (USAF)

Weapon:	For use in Proofing Guns, Automatic, 20mm, M39, M61, XM168 and GAU-4 (XM130)
Ballistic Perf.:	
Pressure:	Shall equal or exceed 62,500 psi and shall not exceed 72,500 psi
Cartridge:	4,392 grains approx.
Case:	M103, Brass, 2150 grs.
Prim. Elec.:	22 grs.
Propellant:	WC 870 or IMR 7013. Weight to meet ballistic requirements
Projectile:	1,965 10 grains
Ident.:	Projectile, Purple marking, black opaque

Cartridge, Caliber 20mm, Target Practice, M55A2 (USAF)

Weapon:	Guns, Automatic, 20mm, M39, M61, and XM168 and GAU-4 (XM130)
Ballistic Perf.:	(Single shot-test barrel)
Velocity:	3,380 ±50 fps at 78 feet
Pressure:	Not to exceed 60,500 psi
Accuracy:	15-in. mean radius, max. avg. at 600 yards
Cartridge:	3,935 grains approx.
Case:	2,150 grs.
Prim. Elec.:	22 grs.
Propellant:	WC 870, weight to meet ballistic requirements
Projectile:	1,521 30 grs.

Ident.: Projectile blue, opaque black marking

Cartridge, Caliber 20mm, High Explosive Incendiary, M6A3 (USAF)

Weapon:	Guns, Automatic, 20mm, M39, M61, and GAU-4 (XM130)
Ballistic Perf.:	(Single shot - test barrel)
Velocity:	3,380 ±250 fps at 78 feet
Pressure:	Not to exceed 60,500 psi
Accuracy:	15-in. mean radius at 600 yards
Function:	The projectile shall function with high order detonation upon impact.
Cartridge:	2,965 grs. approx.
Case:	Brass, 2150 grs.
Prim. Elec.:	22 grs.
Propellant:	WC 870, weight to meet ballistic requirements
Projectile:	1,565 grs. approx.
Charged Proj.:	1230 grs.approx.
Charge:	165 grs. min.
Rotating	
Blank:	133 grs. approx. (Gilding Metal)
Ident.:	Projectile yellow, black opaque marking

Cartridge, Caliber 20mm, High Explosive Incendiary, M97A2 (USAF)

Weapon:	Guns, Automatic, 20mm, M24 and M24A1
Ballistic Perf.:	(Single shot - test barrel)
Velocity:	2,680 ±50 fps at 78 feet
Pressure:	Shall not exceed 51,000 psi
Accuracy:	15-in. mean radius at 600 yards
Function:	Projectile shall detonate high order on impact with the target plate.
Cartridge:	4,000 grs. approx.
Case:	Brass, 1520 grs.
Prim. Elec.:	22 grs.
Propellant:	IMR 7013, WC 875; Weight to meet ballistic requirements
Projectile:	HEI-2000 40 grs.
Fuze:	Point Detonating
Ident.:	Projectile yellow, marking black opaque

Cartridge, Caliber 20mm, Target Practice, M99A1 (USAF)

Weapon:	Guns, Automatic, 20mm, M24 and M24A1
Ballistic Perf.:	(Single shot - test barrel)
Velocity:	2,680 ±50 fps at 78 feet
Pressure:	Shall not exceed 51,000 psi
Accuracy:	15-in. mean radius at 600 yards
Cartridge:	4,000 grs. approx.
Case:	Brass, 1520 grs.
Prim. Elec.:	22 grs.
Projectile:	2,000 35 grs.
Ident.:	Projectile blue, marking black opaque

Cartridge, Caliber 20mm, Target Practice, M204

Weapon:	Gun, Automatic, 20mm, M3
Ballistic Perf.:	(Single shot - test barrel)
Velocity:	2,680 ±50 fps at 78 feet
Pressure:	Shall not exceed 51,000 psi
Accuracy:	15-in. mean radius at 600 yards
Cartridge:	4,000 grs. approx.
Case:	Brass, 1520 grs.
Prim. Perc.:	26 grs.
Propellant:	4814, IMR 7013 or WC 875 - Weight to meet ballistic requirements
Projectile:	TP, M99A1 - 2000 - 35 grs.
Ident.:	Projectile blue, marking black opaque

Cartridge, Caliber 20mm, Target Practice - Tracer, M206

Weapon:	Gun, 20mm, Automatic Gas Operated, Manual or Electric Fired, M139
Ballistic Perf.:	
Velocity:	3,460 ±50 fps at muzzle
Pressure:	49,500 psi max. avg.
Cartridge:	317 Grams approx.
Case:	134 5.8 Grams, Steel
Primed:	145 Grams
Primer Perc.:	10 Grams
Propellant:	50 Grams, approx.
Projectile:	120 2 Grams

Ident.: Projectile blue, red T's, black letters

Cartridge, Caliber 20mm, Target Practice - Tracer, M206E1

Weapon:	Gun, 20mm, Automatic Gas Operated, Manual or Electric Fired, M139
Ballistic Perf.:	
Velocity:	3,460 ±50 fps
Pressure:	49,500 psi max. avg.
Cartridge:	
Primer Perc.:	29 grs.
Ident.:	Projectile blue, red T's, black letters

Cartridge, Caliber 20mm, High Explosive Incendiary M210

Weapon:	Gun, Automatic, 20mm, M3
Ballistic Perf.:	
Velocity:	2,680 ±50 fps at 78 ft.
Pressure:	Shall not exceed 51,000 psi
Cartridge:	4,000 grains approx.
Case:	Brass - 1520 grs.
Primer Perc.:	26 grs.
Propellant:	IMR 7013, 4815 or WC 875; Weight to meet ballistic requirements
Projectile:	2,000 40 grains

Cartridge, Caliber 20mm, Armor Piercing Incendiary - Tracer, M601

Weapon:	Gun, 20mm, Automatic, Gas operated, Manual or Electric Fired, M139
Ballistic Perf.:	
Velocity:	3,610 ±50 fps
Pressure:	49,500 psi max. avg.
Cartridge:	310 grains
Case:	134 5.8 Grams, Steel
Primed:	145 Grams
Primer Perc.:	10 Grams
Propellant:	53 Grams, approx.
Projectile:	111 2 Grams
Ident.:	Projectile black, orange T's, red tip and white letters

Cartridge, Caliber 20mm, Armor Piercing Incendiary - Tracer, M601E1

Weapon:	Gun, 20mm, Automatic, Gas operated, Manual or Electric Fired, M139
Ballistic Perf.:	
Velocity:	3,610 ±50 fps
Pressure:	49,500 psi max. avg.
Cartridge:	
Primer Perc.:	29 grs.
Propellant:	To meet ballistic requirements
Projectile:	112.5 Grams
Ident.:	Projectile black, orange T's, red tip and white letters

Cartridge, Caliber 20mm, Test, High Pressure, MK101 Mod 0 (USN)

Weapon:	Gun, 20mm, chambered to fire MK100 series 20mm ammunition
Ballistic Perf.:	
Pressure:	Not to exceed 72,500 psi
Cartridge:	4,285 50 grs.
Case:	1880 grs. (Steel)
Prim. Elec.:	22 grs.
Propellant:	Tubular or ball, nitrocellulose, weight to meet ballistic requirements
Projectile:	1,700 grs., inert
Ident.:	Green or blue projectile with brown nose and ¼" black letters reading "High Pressure Test Round"

Cartridge, Caliber 20mm, Test, Low Pressure, MK102 Mod 0 (USN)

Weapon:	Gun, 20mm, chambered to fire MK100 series ammunition
Ballistic Perf.:	
Pressure:	
Cartridge:	4,285 50 grs.
Case:	1880 grs. (Steel)

Prim. Elec.: 22 grs.
Propellant: Tubular or ball, nitrocellulose, weight to meet ballistic requirements
Projectile: 1,700 grs., inert
Ident.: Blue or green projectile with brown nose and ¼" black letters reading "Low Pressure Test Round"

Dummy Cartridge, Caliber 20mm, MK103 Mod 0 (USN)

Inert round. Has empty primer pocket and holes in case; or when made up from rejected service case, has primer pocket plugged with brass or empty primer cup staked with three equally spaced crimps. Case may be empty or loaded with inert material. Projectile is usually brass or bronze plated.

Cartridge, Caliber 20mm, Target Practice, MK105 Mod 0 (USN)

Weapon: Guns, Automatic, 20mm, MK11 and MK12
Ballistic Perf.: (Single shot - test barrel)
Velocity: 3,350 fps at muzzle
Pressure: 60,000 psi
Accuracy: 15-in. mean radius at 600 yards
Cartridge: 4,285 50 grs.
Case: 1,880 grs. (Steel) 20mm, MK5 Mod 0
Prim. Elec.: 22 grs., MK47 Mod 0
Propellant: Tubular or ball, nitrocellulose, 650 grs. approx.
Projectile: 1,700 grs., inert
Ident.: Green or blue projectile with black lettering or blue projectile with brown nose and black lettering

Cartridge, Caliber 20mm,High Explosive Incendiary MK106 Mod 0 and 1 (USN)

Weapon: Guns, Automatic, 20mm, MK11 and MK12
Ballistic Perf.: (Single shot - test barrel)
Velocity: 3,350 fps at muzzle
Pressure: 60,000 psi
Accuracy: 15-in. mean radius at 600 yards
Cartridge: 4,285 50 grs.
Case: 1,880 grs. (Steel) 20mm, MK5 Mod 0
Prim. Elec.: 22 grs., MK47 Mod 0
Propellant: Tubular or ball, nitrocellulose, 650 grs. approx.
Projectile: 1,700 50 grs., Impact detonating
Ident.: Unpainted fuze, red and yellow projectile

Cartridge, Caliber 20mm, Armor Piercing-Incendiary, MK107 Mod 0 (USN)

Weapon: Guns, Automatic, 20mm, MK11 and MK12
Ballistic Perf.: (Single shot - test barrel)
Velocity: 3,350 fps at muzzle
Pressure: 60,000 psi
Accuracy: 15-in. mean radius at 600 yards
Cartridge: 4,285 50 grs.
Case: 1,880 grs. (Steel) 20mm, MK5 Mod 0
Prim. Elec.: 22 grs., MK47 Mod 0
Projectile: 1,700 50 grs.
Ident.: No fuze. Nose of projectile blue or brown with red band. Body of projectile black with white lettering

Cartridge, Caliber 20mm, Armor Piercing -Tracer, MK108 Mod 0 (USN)

Weapon: Guns, Automatic, 20mm, MK11 and MK12
Ballistic Perf.: (Single shot - test barrel)
Velocity: 3,350 fps at muzzle
Pressure: 60,000 psi
Accuracy: 15 inch mean radius at 600 yards
Cartridge: 4,285 50 grs.
Case: 1,880 grs. (Steel) 20mm, MK5 Mod 0
Projectile: 1,700 50 grs.
Ident.: No fuze. Hollow windshield. Brown or yellow nose, black projectile body with white lettering

Designation	Description
M1	Cartridge, Ball, Carbine, Caliber .30
M1	Cartridge, Blank, Caliber .50 (T40)
M1	Cartridge, Incendiary, Caliber .50
M1	Cartridge, Test, High Pressure, Caliber .50
M1	Cartridge, Test, High Pressure, Caliber .45
M1	Cartridge, Test, High Pressure, Caliber .30
M1	Cartridge, Tracer, Caliber .30
M1	Cartridge, Tracer, Caliber .50 (AN-MI)
M1E1	Cartridge, Incendiary, Caliber .50 (M1 loaded to 3100 f/s)
M1911	Cartridge, Ball, Caliber .45
M1911	Cartridge, Ball, Match Grade, Caliber .45
M1909	Cartridge, Blank, Caliber .30
M1921	Cartridge, Dummy, Caliber .45
M2	Cartridge, AP, Caliber .50
M2	Cartridge, AP, Caliber .30
M2	Cartridge, Ball, Caliber .50 (AN-M2)
M2	Cartridge, Ball, Caliber .30
M2	Cartridge Dummy, Caliber .50
M2	Cartridge, 12 Gauge
M3	Cartridge, Grenade, Rifle, Caliber .30
M3	Cartridge, Igniter, Caliber .38 (for Igniter, Grenade, Frangible M3
M6	Cartridge, Grenade Carbine, Caliber .30 (T6)
M7	Cartridge, Grenade, Auxiliary (T18)
M8	Cartridge, Armor-Piercing-Incendiary, Caliber .50 (T16)
M8E1	Cartridge, Armor-Piercing Incendiary, Caliber .50, Loaded with Double Base Powder to a Higher Velocity
M9	Cartridge, Blank, Caliber .45 (T31)
M10	Cartridge, Tracer, Caliber .50 (T12)
M10E1	Cartridge, Tracer, Caliber .50, Loaded to an Increased Velocity with Double Base Powder
M12	Cartridge, Shot, Caliber .45 (T23)
M13	Cartridge, Dummy, Carbine, Caliber .30
M14	Cartridge, Armor-Piercing-Incendiary, Caliber .30 (T15)
M14A1	Cartridge, Armor-Piercing-Incendiary, Caliber .30 (T15 with T1E48 Bullet)
M15	Cartridge, Shot, Caliber .45 (T29)
M16	Cartridge, Tracer, Carbine, Caliber .30 (T24)
M17	Cartridge, Tracer, Caliber .50 (T9)
M18	Cartridge, High Pressure Test, Carbine, Caliber .30 (T27)
M19	Shell, Shot Gun (All Brass), 12 Gauge - 00 Buck
M20	Cartridge, Armor-Piercing-Incendiary-Tracer, Caliber .50 (T28)
M21	Cartridge, Tracer, Headlight, Caliber .50 (T1E1)
M22	Cartridge, Ball, Frangible, Caliber .30 (T44)
M23	Cartridge, Incendiary, Caliber .50 (T48)
M24	Cartridge, Ball, Caliber .22, Long Rifle (T42)
M25	Cartridge, Tracer, Caliber .30 (T10)
M26	Cartridge, Tracer, Caliber .45 (T30)
M27	Cartridge, Tracer, Carbine, Caliber .30 (T43)
M32	Cartridge, Blank, Line Throwing, Caliber .45 (T124)
M33	Cartridge, Ball, Caliber .50 (T122)
M33E1	Cartridge, Ball, Caliber .50
M33E2	Cartridge, Ball, Caliber .50
M35	Shell, Shot Gun .410 (T135)

Designation	Description
M39	Cartridge, Ball, Caliber .22 (Hornet) (T200)
M40	Cartridge, Dummy, Caliber .30
M41	Cartridge, Ball, Caliber .38, Special
M48	Cartridge, Spotter-Tracer, Caliber .50 (T189E1)
M48A1	Cartridge, Spotter-Tracer, Caliber .50 (T189E3)
M48A1E1	Cartridge, Spotter-Tracer
M51	Cartridge, Dummy, 20mm
M51E3	Cartridge, Dummy, 20mm
M51E5	Cartridge, Dummy, 20mm (T272E4)
M51E6	Cartridge, Dummy, 20mm
M52	Cartridge, Armor-Piercing, Incendiary Tracer, 20mm (T230)
M53	Cartridge, Armor-Piercing Incendiary, 20mm (T221E3)
M54	Cartridge, High Pressure Test, 20mm
M55	Cartridge, Ball, 20mm (T199E1)
M56	Cartridge, High Explosive Incendiary, 20mm (T198E1)
M58	Cartridge, High Explosive Incendiary, 20mm (T241)
M59	Cartridge, 7.62mm, NATO, Ball (T104E2)
M60	Cartridge, 7.62mm, NATO, High Pressure Test(T17E1)
M61	Cartridge, 7.62mm, NATO, Armor-Piercing (T93E2)
M62	Cartridge, 7.62mm, NATO, Tracer (T102E2)
M62	Cartridge, 7.62mm, NATO, Tracer (Overhead Fire Application)
M63	Cartridge, 7.62mm, NATO, Dummy (T70E5)
M64	Cartridge, 7.62mm, NATO, Grenade, Rifle (T116E1)
M65	Cartridge, Ball, Caliber .22 Hornet (T200E1)
M72	Cartridge, Match, Caliber .30 (T291)
M80	Cartridge, 7.62mm, NATO, Ball, (T233)
M80	Cartridge, 7.62mm, NATO, Ball, Overhead Fire Application)
M80E1	Cartridge, 7.62mm, NATO, Ball (Canadian C1)
M82	Cartridge, 7.62mm, NATO, Blank
M95	Cartridge, Armor-Piercing Tracer, 20mm
M96	Cartridge, Incendiary, 20mm
M97E2	Cartridge, High Explosive Incendiary, 20mm
M97A1	Cartridge, High Explosive Incendiary, 20mm
M99A1	Cartridge, Target Practice, 20mm
M118	Cartridge, 7.62 Match
M160	Cartridge, 7.62mm, Ball, Frangible
M172	Cartridge, Dummy, 7.62mm (Inert Loaded)
M181	Cartridge, 14.5mm (with fuze sec) Tracer Low Charge
M182	Cartridge, 14.5mm (with fuze 6 sec) Used with M3I Field
M183	Cartridge, 14.5mm (with fuze PD) Used with M31 Field
M193	Cartridge, 5.56mm Ball
M196	Cartridge, 5.56mm Tracer
M197	Cartridge, 5.56mm High Pressure Test
M198	Cartridge, 7.62mm Ball Duplex
M199	Cartridge, Dummy 5.56mm
M200	Cartridge, 5.56mm Blank
M204	Cartridge, 20mm Target Practice
M206E1	Cartridge, 20mm Target Practice Tracer
M210	Cartridge, 20mm High Explosive Incendiary
M274	Cartridge, 12 Gauge Shotgun, No. 4, Hard Chilled Shot
M601EI	Cartridge, 20mm Armor Piercing Incendiary Tracer

Designation	Description
M855A1	Cartridge, 5.56mm, Ball
M856A1	Cartridge, 5.56mm, Tracer
M857	Cartridge, 5.56mm, Dummy
M882	Cartridge, 9mm, Ball
M905	Cartridge, 9mm, High Pressure Test
M917	Cartridge, 9mm, Dummy
M939	Cartridge, 9mm, Practice Tracer
M852	Cartridge, 7.62mm, Match

EXPERIMENTAL (XM) SERIES U.S. MILITARY CARTRIDGES

Designation	Description
XM75	Cartridge, Spotter, 10mm
XM101	Cartridge, Spotting, 20mm
XM106	Cartridge, Practice, 20mm
XM107	Cartridge, High Pressure, 20mm
XM108	Cartridge, Spotter, 15mm
XM108E1	Cartridge, Spotter, 15mm
XM115	Cartridge, 7.62mm, Ball
XM142	Cartridge, Caliber .38 Special, Ball
XM147	Dummy Cartridge, 20mm
XM156	Cartridge, Caliber .50 Spotter-Tracer
XM157	Cartridge, Spotter-Tracer, 15mm
XM162	Cartridge, 12 Gauge Shotgun; Plastic #00 Buckshot
XM170	Cartridge, Ball, 15mm
XM171	Cartridge, High Presure Test, 15mm
XM176	Dummy Cartridge, Cal. .50, Inert Loaded
XM177	Dummy Cartridge, 15mm
XM178	Cartridge, 7.62mm, Ball, Overhead Fire
XM179	Cartridge, 7.62mm, Tracer, Overhead Fire
XM180	Cartridge, 7.62mm, Tracer, Overhead Fire
XM192	Cartridge, 7.62mm Blank (Short Case)
XM195	Cartridge, 5.56mm, Grenade
XM202	Cartridge, 8.94mm Select
XM205	Cartridge, 20mm High Explosive Incendiary
XM207	Cartridge, 20mm Armor Piercing
XM220	Cartridge, 20mm Target Practice Tracer
XM232	Dummy Cartridge, 5.56mm Inert Loaded
XM239	Cartridge, 20mm High Pressure Test
XM240	Dummy Cartridge, 20mm
XM242	Cartridge, 20mm High Explosive Incendiary Tracer
XM243	Cartridge, 20mm High Explosive Incendiary Tracer
XM244	Cartridge, 20mm High Explosive Incendiary Tracer
XM246E3	Cartridge, 20mm High Explosive Incendiary Tracer
XM254	Dummy Cartridge, 20mm, Plastic
XM257	Cartridge, Shotshell, 12 Gauge No. 4B Special
XM552	Cartridge, 20mm Heat Dual Purpose
XM554	Cartridge, 30mm Practice
XM599	Cartridge, 20mm High Explosive Incendiary Tracer

EXPERIMENTAL (T) SERIES U.S. MILITARY CARTRIDGES

Designation	Description
T1	Cartridge, Explosive, Caliber .50
T1	Cartridge, Armor-Piercing, Caliber. 276
T1	Cartridge, Tracer, Caliber .30
T1E1	Cartridge, Tracer, Headlight, Caliber .50 (M21)
T1E2	Cartridge, Tracer, Headlight, Caliber .50

Designation	Description
T5	Cartridge, Armor-Piercing, Anti-Tank, Caliber .30
T6	Cartridge, Grenade, Carbine, Caliber .30 (M6)
T7	Cartridge, Grenade, Carbine, Caliber .30 (Long Case)
T8	Cartridge, Tracer, Caliber .50 - 1000 yds.
T9	Cartridge, Tracer, Caliber .50 - 2500 yds. (M17)
T10	Cartridge, Tracer, Night, Caliber .30 (Dim Igniter) (M25)
T12	Cartridge, Tracer, Caliber .50 (M10)
T13	Cartridge, Tracer, Caliber .30 Delay
T14	Cartridge, Tracer, Caliber .50
T15	Cartridge, Armor-Piercing-Incendiary, Caliber .30 (M14)
T15E1	Cartridge, Armor-Piercing-Incendiary Caliber .30
T16	Cartridge, Armor-Piercing-Incendiary, Caliber.50 (M8)
TI7	Cartridge, Tracer, Caliber .30 (Clad Steel Jacketed for Improved Accuracy)
T18	Cartridge, Auxiliary, Grenade (M7)
T19	Cartridge, Explosive, Caliber .60
T19E1	Cartridge, Explosive, Caliber .60
T19E2	Cartridge, Explosive, Caliber .60
T19E3	Cartridge, Explosive, Caliber. 60
T19E4	Cartridge, Explosive, Caliber .60
T20	Cartridge, Tracer, Caliber .50 (Spot) 500 yds.
T21	Cartridge, Tracer, Caliber .50 (Spot) 1000 yds.
T22	Cartridge, Ball, Caliber .30 with Steel Case (M2 Alternate)
T23	Cartridge, Shot, Caliber .45 (M12)
T24	Cartridge, Tracer, Carbine, Caliber .30 (M16)
T25	Cartridge, Ball, Caliber .50 with Steel Case (M2 Alternate)
T26	Cartridge, Igniter, Caliber .38 (Component for Igniter, Grenade, Frangible, M3)
T27	Cartridge, Carbine, High Pressure Test, Caliber .30 (M18)
T28	Cartridge, Armor-Piercing-Incendiary-Tracer, Caliber .50 (M20)
T28E1	Cartridge, Armor-Piercing-Incendiary-Tracer, Caliber .50 (Dim Igniter)
T29	Cartridge, Shot, Caliber .45 (M15)
T30	Cartridge, Tracer, Caliber .45 (M26)
T31	Cartridge, Blank, Caliber .45 (M9)
T32	Cartridge, Ball, Caliber .60-1196 grain bullet
T32E1	Cartridge, Ball, Caliber .60-1137 grain bullet
T32E2	Cartridge, Ball, Caliber .60
T33	Cartridge, High Pressure Test, Caliber .60
T33E1	Cartridge, High Pressure Test, Caliber .60 (T33 with M36A1 Primer)
T34	Cartridge, High Explosive Incendiary, Caliber .50
T35	Cartridge, Dummy, Caliber .60
T35E1	Cartridge, Dummy, Caliber .60
T36	Cartridge, Incendiary, Caliber .60
T36E1	Cartridge, Incendiary, Caliber .60
T36E2	Cartridge, Incendiary, Caliber .60 (With #28 Primer)
T36E3	Cartridge, Incendiary, Caliber .60 (T36E2 with M36A1 Percussion Primer)
T37	Cartridge, Tracer, Caliber .50 with trajectory to match 3.5-inch Forward Firing Rocket
T38	Cartridge, Armor-Piercing-Tracer, Caliber .50
T38E1	Cartridge, Armor-Piercing-Incendiary, Caliber .50
T39	Cartridge, Armor-Piercing-Incendiary, Caliber .60

Designation	Description
T39E1	Cartridge, Armor-Piercing-Incendiary, Caliber .60 (T39 with M36A1 Percussion Primer)
T39E2	Cartridge, Armor-Piercing-Incendiary, Caliber .60
T39E3	Cartridge, Armor-Piercing-Incendiary, Caliber .60
T39E4	Cartridge, Armor-Piercing-Incendiary, Caliber .60
T39E5	Cartridge, Armor-Piercing-Incendiary, Caliber .60
T39E6	Cartridge, Armor-Piercing-Incendiary, Caliber .60
T40	Cartridge, Blank, Caliber .50 (M1)
T41	Cartridge, Incendiary, High Velocity, Caliber .60
T41E1	Cartridge, Incendiary, High Velocity, Caliber .60
T42	Cartridge, Ball, Caliber .22, Long Rifle Jacketed Bullet (M24)
T43	Cartridge, Tracer, Carbine, Caliber .30 (M27)
T44	Cartridge, Ball, Frangible, Caliber .30 (M22)
T44E1	Cartridge, Ball, Frangible, Caliber .30
T45	Cartridge, Armor-Piercing, Caliber .60
T45E1	Cartridge, Armor-Piercing, Caliber .60
T46	Cartridge, Armor-Piercing-Tracer, Caliber .60
T46E1	Cartridge, Armor-Piercing-Tracer, Caliber .60
T47	Cartridge, High Explosive, Incendiary, Caliber .60
T48	Cartridge, Incendiary, Caliber .50 (500 grain bullet) M23
T48E1	Cartridge, Incendiary, Caliber .50 (500 grain bullet)
T48E2	Cartridge, Incendiary, Caliber .50 (500 grain bullet)
T49	Cartridge, Armor-Piercing Incendiary, Caliber .50 (500 grain bullet)
T50	Cartridge, Incendiary, Caliber .60 - .50
T51	Cartridge, Armor-Piercing-Incendiary, Caliber .60-.50
T52	Cartridge, Tracer, Caliber .60 - .50
T53	Cartridge, Tracer, Caliber .30
T54	Cartridge, Tracer, Caliber .50
T55	Cartridge, Tracer, Caliber .60
T56	Cartridge, Blank, Caliber .50 with Electric Primer
T57	Cartridge, Grenade, Auxiliary, High Pressure Test
T58	Cartridge, Incendiary, Caliber .50 (White Phosphorus Loading)
T59	Cartridge, Carbine, Spotting, Caliber .30
T60	Cartridge, Armor-Piercing-Incendiary-Tracer, Caliber .60
T60E1	Cartridge, Armor-Piercing-Incendiary-Tracer, Caliber .60 (T60 with M36A1 Percussion Primer)
T61	Cartridge, Antenna Erecting
T62	Cartridge, Armor-Piercing, Carbine, Caliber .30
T63	Cartridge, Armor-Piercing-Incendiary-Tracer, Caliber .50 (500 grain) R. V.
T64	Cartridge, Tracer, Caliber .50 (Rocket Fire Control, 2000 100 yds; Dim 500 yds bright)
T65	Cartridge, Ball, Caliber .30, Short Case (7.62mm NATO)
T65E1	Cartridge, Ball, Caliber .30, Short Case
T65E2	Cartridge, Ball, Caliber .30 (for Light Rifle)
T65E3	Cartridge, Ball, Caliber .30 (for Light Rifle)
T65E4	Cartridge, Ball, Caliber .30, Short Case, 10 Caliber, 145 grain, Minimum Boattail

Designation	Description
T66	Cartridge, Incendiary-Tracer, Caliber .60, Light Weight Bullet, High Velocity
T67	Cartridge, Grenade, Caliber .45
T68	Cartridge, High Explosive Incendiary, Caliber .60, Light Weight Bullet
T69	Cartridge, Ball, Frangible, Caliber .30 (Carbine Case, Ball Frangible Bullet) (Velocity 1300 30f/s at 78ft)
T70	Cartridge, Dummy, Caliber .30, Short Case (to match Cartridge, Ball, Caliber .30, T65)
T70E1	Cartridge, Dummy, Caliber .30 (FAT1EI Case, .030 Wall Ball Bullet)
T70E2	Cartridge, Dummy, Caliber .30 (FAT1EI Case, .020 Wall Ball Bullet)
T70E3	Cartridge, Dummy, Caliber .30 (FAT1EI Case and Based Tracer Jacket)
T70E4	Cartridge, Dummy, Caliber .30 (FAT1E3 Case, 20 Wall Ball Bullet)
T70E5	Cartridge, Dummy, Caliber .30 (M63)
T71	Cartridge, Test, High Pressure, Caliber .30, Short Case (To match Cartridge, Ball, Caliber .30, T65)
T71EI	Cartridge, Test, High Pressure, Caliber .30 (T71 with case, brass, FAT1E3; 183 grains approx.) (M60)
M72	Cartridge, Tracer, Caliber .30 (25 yds dim igniter trace)
M72E1	Cartridge, Tracer, Caliber .30
T73	Cartridge, Signal, Caliber .45
T73E1	Cartridge, Signal, Caliber .45
T73E2	Cartridge, Signal, Caliber .45
T74	Cartridge, Frangible, Caliber .30, Loaded with SR-4990 Powder (Point Identification is Green with Tan Tip)
T75	Cartridge, Armor-Piercing-Incendiary, Caliber .50/.60 Assembled w/Bullet, Armor-Piercing-Incendiary, Caliber .50, T49
T76	Cartridge, Armor-Piercing-Incendiary-Tracer, Caliber .60 with Bright Igniter
T76E1	Cartridge, Armor-Piercing-Incendiary-Tracer, Caliber .60 (T60 with Primer, Percussion, M36A1)
T77	Cartridge, Ball, Caliber .60
T77E1	Cartridge, Ball, Caliber .60 (T77 w/Primer, Percussion, M36A1)
T78	Cartridge, Incendiary, Caliber .30, Assembled with Bullet, Incendiary, Caliber .30
T79	Cartridge, Blank, Carbine, Caliber .30
T80	Cartridge, Ball, Caliber .60 (T77 Assembled with M52A3 Electric Primer)
T80E1	Cartridge, Ball, Caliber .60 (T77 Assembled with FAT38 Electric Primer)
T80E2	Cartridge, Ball, Caliber .60 (T77E1 with Cut Cannelure in Sabot)
T81	Cartridge, Incendiary, Caliber .60 (T36E2 Assembled w/Remington T41 Electric Primer)
T81EI	Cartridge, Incendiary, Caliber .60 (T36E2 with Electric Primer, M52A3 and Double Crimp)
T82	Cartridge, Armor-Piercing-Incendiary, Caliber .60 (T39 Assembled with Remington T41 Electric Primer)
T82E1	Cartridge, Armor-Piercing-Incendiary, Caliber .60 (T39E1 with Electric Primer, M52A3 and Double Crimp)
T83	Cartridge, Armor-Piercing-Incendiary-Tracer, Caliber .60 (T60 Assembled with Remington T41 Electric Primer)
T83E1	Cartridge, Armor-Piercing-Incendiary-Tracer, Caliber .60 (T60 Assembled with M52A3 Primer)
T84	Cartridge, Armor-Piercing-Incendiary-Tracer, Caliber .60 (T76 Assembled with Remington T41 Electric Primer)

Designation	Description
T84E1	Cartridge, Armor-Piercing-Incendiary-Tracer, Caliber .60 (T76 Assembled with Remington T41 Electric Primer)
T85	Cartridge, High Pressure Test, Caliber .60 (T33 Assembled with Remington T41 Electric Primer)
T85E1	Cartridge, High Pressure Test, Caliber .60 (T33 Assembled with Remington T41 Electric Primer)
T86	Cartridge, Lachrymatory, Caliber .50 (T78 Bullet Charged with LI#2)
T87	Cartridge, Incendiary, Caliber .50 (T78 Bullet Charged with White Phosphorus)
T88	Cartridge, Incendiary, Caliber .30 (Prototype of T87 Charged with White Phosphorus)
T89	Cartridge, Tracer, Caliber .30 (Headlight)
T90	Cartridge, Armor-Piercing, Caliber .30 (Short Case)
T91	Cartridge, High Explosive-Incendiary, Caliber .60
T92	Cartridge, Signal, Caliber .45 (National Fireworks)
T92E1	Cartridge, Signal, Caliber .45 (National Fireworks)
T93	Cartridge, Armor-Piercing, Caliber .30 (140-5 grains AP Bullet for Light Rifle)
T93E1	Cartridge, Armor-Piercing, Caliber .30 (T93 with Case, Brass, 183 grains approx.)
T93E2	Cartridge, Armor-Piercing, Caliber .30 (T93E1 with Bullet, AP, Caliber .30) (M61)
T94	Cartridge, Ball, Caliber .50 (Ball M2 w/aluminum case)
T96	Cartridge, Signal, Carbine, Caliber .30 (National Fireworks)
T97	Cartridge, Armor-Piercing-Incendiary, Caliber .60 (5.25 radius Ogive)
T98	Cartridge, Tracer, Smoke, Caliber .50
T99	Cartridge, Observing, Caliber .30
T100	Cartridge, Release, Life Vest
T101	Cartridge, Armor-Piercing-Incendiary, Caliber .30 (Light Rifle)
T101E1	Cartridge, Armor-Piercing-Incendiary, Caliber .30 (T101 w/Case, Brass, 183 grains approx)
T101E2	Cartridge, Armor-Piercing-Incendiary, Caliber .30 (T101E1 with 10 Caliber Ogive Bullet)
T102	Cartridge, Tracer, Caliber .30 (Light Rifle)
T102E1	Cartridge, Tracer, Caliber .30 (T102 with Case, Brass, 183 grains approx)
T102E2	Cartridge, Tracer, Caliber .30 (T102E1 with with10 Caliber Ogive Bullet) (M62)
T103	Cartridge, Observing, Caliber .30 (Light Rifle)
T103E1	Cartridge, Observing, Caliber .30 (T103 with Case, Brass, 183 grains approx)
T103E2	Cartridge, Observing, Caliber .30 (T103 with Case, Brass, 183 grains approx)
T104	Cartridge, Ball, Caliber .30 (Light Rifle)
T104E1	Cartridge, Ball, Caliber .30 (T104 with Case, Brass, 183 grains approx)
T104E2	Cartridge, Ball, Caliber .30 (T104E1 with 10 Caliber Ogive Bullet) (M59)
T106	Cartridge, Ball, Caliber .60 (High Velocity)
T107	Cartridge, Multiple Bullet, Caliber .30
T116	Cartridge, Grenade, Rifle, Caliber .30
T116E1	Cartridge, Grenade, Rifle, Caliber .30
T116E2	Cartridge, Grenade, Rifle, Caliber .30
T117	Cartridge, Ball, Caliber .35 Pistol
T117E1	Cartridge, Ball, Caliber .35 Pistol
T118	Cartridge, Tracer, Caliber .50 (Short Dim Igniter)

Designation	Description
T119	Cartridge, Armor-Piercing-Incendiary, Caliber .30 (Tungsten Carbide Core)
T119E1	Cartridge, Armor-Piercing-Incendiary, Caliber .30 (T119 w/Cast, Brass, FAT 1E2, 183 gr. approx)
T120	Cartridge, Ball, Caliber .60
T122	Cartridge, Ball, Caliber .50 (M33)
T124	Cartridge, Blank, Line Throwing, Caliber .45
T128	Cartridge, Guard, Caliber .30
T130	Cartridge, Practice, 20mm (T118 Gun)
T131	Cartridge, High Pressure Test, 20mm, (T118 Gun)
T132	Cartridge, Dummy, 20mm, Inert Loaded
T133	Cartridge, Armor-Piercing-Incendiary, 20mm (T118 Gun)
T134	Cartridge, High Explosive, 20mm (T118 Gun)
T135	Shell, Shot Gun, .410 Aluminum Case #6 Shot (M35)
T136	Shell, Shot Gun Slug, .410, 220 Grain Slug
T137	Cartridge, Spotting. Caliber .50 (Winchester Centrifugal Armed)
T138	Cartridge, Spotting, Caliber .50 (Winchester Inertia Armed)
T139	Cartridge, Tracer, Caliber .50 (BAT Rifle)
T140	Cartridge, Spotting, Caliber .30 (BAT Rifle)
T142	Cartridge, Practice, 27mm
T143	Cartridge, Dummy, 27mm
T144	Cartridge, High Explosive, 27mm
T145	Cartridge, High Pressure Test, 27mm
T147	Cartridge, Incendiary, 27mm
T148	Cartridge, High Explosive-Incendiary, 20mm (Percussion Primer; 1600 grain shell)
T148E1	Cartridge, High Explosive-Incendiary, 20mm (Percussion Primer; 1600 grain shell)
T149	Cartridge, High Explosive-Incendiary, 20mm (Electric Primer; 1600 grain shell)
T150	Cartridge, Armor-Piercing-Incendiary, 20mm (Percussion Primer; 1600 grain shell)
T150E1	Cartridge, Armor-Piercing-Incendiary, 20mm (Percussion Primer; 1600 grain shell)
T151	Cartridge, Armor-Piercing-Incendiary, 20mm (Electric Primer; 1600 grain shell)
T152	Cartridge, Dummy, 20mm (1600 grain shell)
T53	Cartridge, Practice, 20mm (Percussion Primer; 1600 grain Projectile)
T153E1	Cartridge, Practice, 20mm (Percussion Primer; 1600 grain Projectile)
T154	Cartridge, Practice, 20mm (Electric Primer; 1600 grain shell)
T155	Cartridge, High Pressure Test, 20mm (Percussion Primer; Modified M99 Projectile)
T155E1	Cartridge, High Pressure Test, 20mm (Percussion Primer; Modified M99 Projectile)
T156	Cartridge, High Pressure Test, 20mm (Electric Primer; Modified M99 Projectile)
T158	Cartridge, Practice, 30mm (Velocity 2000 f/s; 4220 grains; HF1070 grains; pressure 40,000 psi - T121 Gun)
T159	Cartridge, Dummy, 30mm
T160	Cartridge, High Explosive-Incendiary, 30mm w/Shell, T239E6
T160E1	Cartridge, High Explosive-Incendiary, 30mm with Shell, T239E7
T161	Cartridge, High Pressure Test, 30mm
T162	Cartridge, Incendiary, 30mm
T163	Cartridge, High Explosive-Incendiary, 20mm (Length 7.190 in.; T39E3 Projectile)
T164	Cartridge, Armor-Piercing-Incendiary, 20mm
T165	Cartridge, Practice, 20mm

Designation	Description
T166	Cartridge, Ball, 20mm using T114 Projectile
T167	Cartridge, Test, High Pressure, 20mm
T168	Cartridge, Dummy, 20mm
T169	Cartridge, Test, Low Pressure, 20mm
T170	Cartridge, Warning Flash
T170	Cartridge, Warning Flash
T170E1	Cartridge, Photoflash
T172	Cartridge, Ball, Caliber .30 (T65E3 with 172 grain M1 Bullet)
T173	Cartridge, Ball, Caliber .30 (T65E3 with all-steel serrated bullet)
T174	Cartridge, Ball, Caliber .30 (Standard Caliber .30 Round with all-steel serrated bullet)
T175	Cartridge, Spotting, Caliber .50 (Used with BAT weapon)
T176	Cartridge, Spotting Caliber .50 (Used with BAT weapon)
T177	Cartridge, Tracer, Caliber .50 (Used with BAT weapon)
T178	Cartridge, Practice, Caliber .50 (Used with BAT weapon)
T185	Cartridge, Bomb Release
T188	Cartridge, Tracer, Caliber .50
T189	Cartridge, Spotter-Tracer, Caliber .50
T189E1	Cartridge, Spotter-Tracer, Caliber .50 (M48)
T189E2	Cartridge, Spotter-Tracer, Caliber .50
T189E3	Cartridge, Spotter-Tracer Caliber .50 (M48A1)
T190	Cartridge, Spotting, Caliber .50
T191	Cartridge, Spotting, Caliber .50
T192	Cartridge, Tracer, Caliber .50
T193	Cartridge, Tracer, Caliber .50
T194	Cartridge, Practice, Caliber .50
T195	Cartridge, Spotter-Tracer, Caliber .50
T196	Cartridge, Spotter-Tracer, Caliber. 50
T197	Cartridge, Spotter-Tracer, Caliber .50
T198	Cartridge, High Explosive-Incendiary, 20mm
T198E1	Cartridge, High Explosive-Incendiary, 20mm (M56)
T199	Cartridge, Practice, 20mm
T199E1	Cartridge, Practice, 20mm (M55)
T200	Cartridge, Ball, Caliber .22 (M39)
T200E1	Cartridge, Ball, Caliber .22 (M65)
T201	Cartridge, Ball, Caliber .60
T202	Cartridge, Armor-Piercing-Incendiary, Caliber .60
T203	Cartridge, Incendiary, Caliber .60
T204	Cartridge, Practice, 30mm
T205	Cartridge, Dummy, 30mm
T206	Cartridge, High Explosive-Incendiary, 30mm
T206E10	Cartridge, High Explosive-Incendiary, 30mm
T206E11	Cartridge, High Explosive-Incendiary, 30mm
T206E12	Cartridge, High Explosive-Incendiary, 30mm
T206E13	Cartridge, High Explosive-Incendiary, 30mm
T206E14	Cartridge, High Explosive-Incendiary, 30mm
T207	Cartridge, Test, High Pressure, 30mm
T208	Cartridge, Incendiary, 30mm
T221	Cartridge, Armor-Piercing-Incendiary, 20mm (with anvil)
T221E1	Cartridge, Armor-Piercing-Incendiary, 20mm (without anvil)
21E2	Cartridge, Armor-Piercing-Incendiary, 20mm
T221E3	Cartridge, Armor-Piercing-Incendiary, 20mm (M53)
T222	Cartridge, High Explosive-Incendiary, 30mm
T223	Cartridge, Test, High Pressure, 30mm
T224	Cartridge, Target Practice, 30mm
T225	Cartridge, Dummy, 30mm
T228	Cartridge, Dummy, 20mm (M51)
T230	Cartridge, Armor-Piercing-Incendiary-Tracer, 20mm (M52)
T232	Cartridge, Armor-Piercing-Incendiary-Tracer, 20mm
T233	Cartridge, Ball, Caliber .30 (Light Rifle) (M80)
T239	Cartridge, Ball, 30mm
T239E1	Cartridge, Ball, 30mm
T240	Cartridge, High Explosive-Incendiary, 30mm
T241	Cartridge, High Explosive-Incendiary, 20mm (M58)
T249	Cartridge, Practice, Caliber .50 (Used w/BAT weapon)
T249E1	Cartridge, Practice, Caliber .50 (Used w/BAT weapon)
T249E2	Cartridge, Practice, Caliber .50 (Used w/BAT weapon)
T251	Cartridge, High Pressure Test, Caliber .50 (Used w/BAT weapon)
T252	Cartridge, Dummy, Caliber .50 (Used w/BAT weapon)
T252E1	Cartridge, Dummy, Caliber .50 (Used w/BAT weapon)
T252E2	Cartridge, Dummy, Caliber .50 (Used w/BAT weapon)
T253	Cartridge, Test, High Pressure, 30mm
T266	Cartridge, High Explosive-Incendiary, 30mm
T267	Cartridge, Test, High Pressure, 30mm
T268	Cartridge, Ball, 30mm
T269	Cartridge, Dummy, 30mm
T270	Cartridge, High Explosive-Incendiary, 30mm
T271	Cartridge, Ball, 9mm
T272	Cartridge, 20mm, Dummy
T272E1	Cartridge, 20mm, Dummy
T272E2	Cartridge, 20mm, Dummy
T272E3	Cartridge, 20mm, Dummy
T272E4	Cartridge, 20mm, Dummy
T275	Cartridge, 7.62mm, Ball, NATO
T275E1	Cartridge, 7.62mm, Ball, NATO
T275E2	Cartridge, 7.62mm, Ball, NATO
T276	Cartridge, Caliber .38, Special
T283	Cartridge, 20mm, Armor-Piercing-Incendiary-Tracer
T291	Cartridge, Caliber .30, Match (M72)
T334	Cartridge, Practice, 30mm
MK101 Mod 0	Cartridge, 20mm, High Pressure Test
MK102 Mod 0	Cartridge, 20mm, Low Pressure Test
MK103 Mod 0	Cartridge, 20mm, Dummy
MK105 Mod 0	Cartridge, 20mm, Target Practice
MK106, Mod 0, and Mod 1	Cartridge, 20mm. High Explosive-Incendiary
MK107 Mod 0	Cartridge, 20mm, Armor Piercing-Incendiary
MK108 Mod 0	Cartridge, 20mm, Armor Piercing-Tracer

Cartridge Identification by Measurement

The purpose of this table is to assist the cartridge collector and other interested persons in the identification of unknown cartridges or cartridge cases based upon dimensional information. The following chart contains all cartridges found in this book, organized in order of increasing bullet diameter and then increasing case length. With only minor variations, these dimensions are constant within any specific cartridge type. Once these dimensions are known, other details will allow identification of the unknown cartridge or case. Those details—rim type, neck diameter, base diameter, shoulder diameter, and cartridge length—are listed in separate columns of this table. By measuring and eliminating options, the interested party can rapidly learn the proper name of the cartridge or case in hand.

Consider a hypothetical identification:

We take the case or cartridge in hand and measure bullet diameter or case neck internal diameter (assuming a fired case that is not damaged, this will usually be no more than about .004-inch larger than bullet diameter). This measurement is easily accomplished to about .001-inch accuracy with a dial caliper. We look in the third column of this table and find the approximate bullet diameter. This limits our search to a reasonable number of cartridges.

Next, we note case length, again measured with sufficient accuracy using a dial caliper. In most instances, this will narrow our search to one or, at most, a few choices. We will then review rim type and other aspects of the cartridge in order to eliminate options. Eventually only one cartridge will remain.

As a specific example of this process, consider the following: We have a loaded cartridge, which has a military headstamp that is meaningless to us. The exposed bullet measures about .244 inch. We cannot be certain of exact bullet diameter. Nevertheless, we can narrow our search to those listings with bullets of .243-, .244-, and .245-inch diameter, and see the bullet is clearly larger than .228 inch and smaller than .249 inch. The case measures about 2.35 inches in length. This narrows our search to only two possibilities (within the specified range of bullet diameters), the 6x62mm Freres and 6mm Lee Navy. The base of the case measures about .445 inch. This eliminates the 6x62mm Freres (.474 inch). Further, the rim is about the same diameter as the base (rimless, case type C). We are satisfied with our identification, the 6mm Lee Navy.

CARTRIDGE	CASE TYPE	BULLET DIAMETER	NECK DIAMETER	SHOULDER DIAMETER	BASE DIAMETER	RIM DIAMETER	RIM THICKNESS	CASE LENGTH	CARTRIDGE LENGTH	PRIMER	PAGE
.10 Eichelberger Long Rifle	A	.1030	.122	.223	.225	.275	.043	.568	UNK/NA	RF	231
.10 Eichelberger Pup	A	.1030	.122	.247	.249	.308	.050	.767	UNK/NA	SR	232
.10 Eichelberger Squirrel	A	.1030	.122	.291	.294	.350	.065	.613	UNK/NA	SR	232
.12 Eichelberger Long Rifle	A	.1230	.140	.224	.225	.275	.043	.568	UNK/NA	RF	233
.12 Eichelberger Win Mag RF	A	.1230	.140	.238	.241	.293	.050	1.064	UNK/NA	RF	233
.12 Cooper	A	.123	.145	.247	.249	.308	.050	1.106	UNK/NA	SR	234
.12 Eichelberger Carbine	C	.123	.147	.356	.356	.360	.050	1.240	UNK/NA	SR	234
.14 Eichelberger Dart	C	.144	.164	.274	.278	.301	.043	.640	UNK/NA	SP	235
.14 Cooper	A	.144	.166	.247	.249	.3085	.051	1.104	UNK/NA	SR	236
.14 Walker Hornet	A	.144	.170	.285	.294	.350	.065	1.350	UNK/NA	SR	236
.14 Jet Junior	A	.144	.177	.366	.378	.440	.059	1.260	UNK/NA	SP	237
.14 Eichelberger Bee	A	.144	.162	.329	.349	.408	.065	1.310	UNK/NA	SR	234
.14/222	C	.144	.165	.356	.375	.375	.041	1.70	1.92	S	235
14/222 Eichelberger Mag	C	.144	.170	.356	.376	.378	.045	1.850	UNK/NA	SR	237
.17 PMC/.17 Aguila	B	.172	.172	NA		.271	.039	.591	.984		612

CARTRIDGE	CASE TYPE	BULLET DIAMETER	NECK DIAMETER	SHOULDER DIAMETER	BASE DIAMETER	RIM DIAMETER	RIM THICKNESS	CASE LENGTH	CARTRIDGE LENGTH	PRIMER	PAGE
.17 Hornet	A	.172	.194	.294	.298	.345	.050	1.35	1.72	S	66
.17 Ackley Hornet	A	.172	.195	.290	.295	.345	.060	1.39	1.47	S	238
.17 Winchester Super Magnum	B	.172	.197	.269	.333	.333	.066	1.2	1.44		611
.17-32 Magnum	A	.172	.196	.335	.335	.375	.055	.900	1.45	S	239
.17 VHA (Varmint Hunters Assn.)	C	.172	.196	.305	.316	.315	.043	1.201	1.60	S	239
.17 Remington	C	.172	.198	.355	.374	.377	.041	1.79	1.86	S	66
.17/222	C	.172	.199	.355	.375	.375	.041	1.69	1.82	S	240
.17 Mach IV/Mach III	C	.172	.199	.361	.375	.378	.041	1.40	UNK/NA	S	240
.17 Javelina	C	0.172	0.201	0.353	0.374	0.378	0.045	1.53	1.85	S	241
.17 Ackley Improved Bee	A	.172	.201	.341	.350	.408	.060	1.35	1.78	S	241
.17-357 RG	C	.172	.203	.424	.425	.424	.055	.865	1.31	SP	242
.17 Remington Fireball	C	.172	.204	.3655	.3759	.332	.045	1.41	1.83	S	67
4.5x39Rmm SPS	A	.177						1.575	5.71		417
4.6x30 HK	C	.183	.209	.305	.316	.315	.043	1.201	1.516	S	68
4.85mm British	C	.197	.220	.353	.375	.376	.041	1.925	2.455	B	487
.19 Badger	C	.198	UNK/NA	UNK/NA	UNK/NA	UNK/NA	UNK/NA	UNK/NA	1.3	S	242
.19 Calhoon	A	.198	.215	.286	.294	.350	.063	1.39	1.47	S	243
.19-223 Calhoon	C	.198	.224	.364	.373	.373	.041	1.76	2.0	S	243
.204 Ruger	C	.204	.231	.360	.375	.378	.045	1.850	2.260	SR	68
.20 Vartarg	C	.204	.232	.360	.374	.375	.048	1.40	1.90	S	294
.20 Tactical	C	.204	.233	.360	.373	.375	.041	1.755	2.1	S	294
.20 PDK	C	.204	.247	.400	.421	.417	.049	1.683	2.236	S	245
5mm Remington Magnum	A	.205	.225	.259	.259	.325	.050	1.020	UNK/NA	UNK/NA	612
5.45x18mm Soviet	C	.210	.220	UNK/NA	.300	.300	UNK/NA	.70	.98	SB	419
5x58 Sturtevant	I	0.204	0.236	0.424	0.466	0.466	0.0453	2.277	3.374		488
5.2x68 Mondragon	J	0.208	0.243	0.450	0.489	0.491	0.067	2.650	3.060		488
5.7x28mm FN P90 (Belgium)	C	.220	.249	.309	.310	.310	UNK/NA	1.13	1.71	B	488
5.45x39mm Soviet	C	.221	.246	.387	.395	.394	.053	1.56	2.22	B	489
.22 BB Cap	B	.222	.224	UNK/NA	.224	.270	.040	.284	.343	UNK/NA	613
.22 CB Cap	B	.222	.225	UNK/NA	.225	.271	.040	.420	.520	UNK/NA	613
5.6x35Rmm Vierling (.22 WCF)	A	.222	.241	.278	.300	.297	UNK/NA	1.40	1.62	.177/1584/ 539	566
.22 Winchester Automatic	B	.222	.250	UNK/NA	.250	.310	.040	.665	.915	UNK/NA	613
.22 Short	B	.223	.224	UNK/NA	.225	.273	.040	.423	.686	UNK/NA	614
.22 Short/40-grain RWS load	B	.223	.224	UNK/NA	.225	.272	.042	.415	.798	UNK/NA	614
.22 Long	B	.223	.224	UNK/NA	.225	.275	.040	.595	.880	UNK/NA	614
.22 Long Rifle	B	.223	.224	UNK/NA	.225	.275	.040	.595	.975	UNK/NA	615

CARTRIDGE	CASE TYPE	BULLET DIAMETER	NECK DIAMETER	SHOULDER DIAMETER	BASE DIAMETER	RIM DIAMETER	RIM THICKNESS	CASE LENGTH	CARTRIDGE LENGTH	PRIMER	PAGE
.22 Stinger, etc. (hyper velocities)	B	.223	.224	UNK/NA	.225	.275	.040	.694	.975	UNK/NA	615
.22 Extra Long	B	.223	.225	UNK/NA	.225	.275	.040	.750	1.16	UNK/NA	616
.297/230 Morris Extra Long	A	.223	.240	.274	.296	.248	UNK/NA	1.125	1.45	UNK/NA	532
.22 Hornet	A	.223	.242	.274	.294	.345	.060	1.40	1.72	S	69
.22 Remington Automatic	B	.223	.245	UNK/NA	.245	.290	UNK/NA	.663	.920	UNK/NA	616
5.66x39mm MPS	C	.223	.246	.364	.395	.394	.053	1.568	5.9	SR	489
.22 Remington Jet	A	.223	.247	.350	.376	.440	.055	1.28	1.58	SP	419
.22 Winchester Magnum RF	B	.224	.240	UNK/NA	.241	.291	.046	1.052	1.35	UNK/NA	617
.218 Bee	A	.224	.241	.331	.349	.408	.060	1.35	1.68	S	70
.218 Mashburn Bee	A	.224	.241	.340	.349	.408	.060	1.34	1.75	S	247
.22 Reed Express	C	.224	UNK/NA	UNK/NA	UNK/NA	UNK/NA	UNK/NA	UNK/NA	UNK/NA	UNK/NA	245
.22 WRF & Remington Special	B	.224	.242	UNK/NA	.243	.295	.046	.960	1.17	UNK/NA	617
.22 K-Hornet	A	.224	.242	.286	.294	.345	.060	1.39	1.70	S	247
.22 PPC	C	.224	.245	.430	.440	.441	.050	1.52	1.96	S	70
.22 Waldog	C	.224	.245	.431	.440	.441	.053	1.375	1.820	S	248
.22 BR Remington	C	.224	.245	.450	.466	.468	.045	1.502	2.00	S	248
.22 Eargesplitten Loudenboomer	E	.224	.246	.56	.582	.579	.063	2.913	3.35	L	249
.224 Weatherby Magnum	E	.224	.247	.405	.413	.425	.045	1.92	2.44	L	71
.223 Remington	C	.224	.249	.349	.373	.375	.041	1.76	2.10	S	72
5.56x45mm NATO	C	.224	.249	.349	.373	.375	.041	1.76	2.26	Bx	490
5.8x42mm Chinese	C	.224	UNK/NA	UNK/NA	UNK/NA	UNK/NA	UNK/NA	1.66	2.30	UNK/NA	490
.221 Remington Fireball	C	.224	.251	.355	.375	.375	.040	1.40	1.82	SP	420
.219 Donaldson Wasp	A	.224	.251	.402	.418	.497	.058	1.71	2.10	L	250
.219 Zipper	A	.224	.252	.364	.421	.497	.058	1.94	2.26	L	165
.22 Spitfire	D	.224	.253	.332	.353	.356	.05	1.2902	1.65	SR	251
.222 Remington Rimmed	A	.224	.253	.357	.375	.440	.049	1.70	2.13	S	331
.222 Remington	C	.224	.253	.355	.375	.375	.041	1.70	2.15	S	73
.222 Remington Magnum	C	.224	.253	.355	.375	.375	.041	1.85	2.21	S	166
5.6x50mm Magnum/ 5.6x50Rmm Magnum	C/A	.224	.254	.355	.375	.376/(?)	.038	1.97	2.21	UNK/NA	567
.22-243 Middlestead	C	.224	.26	.454	.47	.47	.049	2.05	2.71	L	254
.22-250 Remington	C	.224	.254	.412	.466	.470	.045	1.91	2.33	L	74
.224 Montgomery	G	.224	.254	.277	.277	.298	.064	.62	1.13	SP	251
.224-32 FA	A	.224	.255	.337	.337	.371	.05	1.2	1.6	SP	331
.22 Fawn	A	.224	.255	.430	.435	.492	.060	1.30	1.90	S	252
.22 TCM	C	.224	.255	.362	.372	.37	.049	1.025	1.265	SP	332
.226 JDJ	A	.224	.256	.410	.419	.467	.045	1.93	V	L	322

CARTRIDGE	CASE TYPE	BULLET DIAMETER	NECK DIAMETER	SHOULDER DIAMETER	BASE DIAMETER	RIM DIAMETER	RIM THICKNESS	CASE LENGTH	CARTRIDGE LENGTH	PRIMER	PAGE
.22 PDK	C	.224	.256	.400	.421	.417	.049	1.75	2.25	S	253
.22 Taranah Hornet	A	.224	UNK/NA	UNK/NA	.294	.350	.063	UNK/NA	UNK/NA	UNK/NA	246
.225 Winchester	A	.224	.260	.406	.422	.473	.045	1.93	2.50	L	76
.220 Wotkyns-Wilson Arrow	G	.224	.261	.402	.443	.472	.045	2.205	2.70	L	254
.223 WSSM	I	.244	.272	.544	.555	.535	.054	1.67	2.175 (2.360)	L	75
6mm Dasher	C	.224	.271	.462	.470	.470	.050	1.54	V	S	256
.224 Clark	C	.224 (.2249)	.275	.455	.471	.473	.045	2.237	3.075	L	251
.224 Texas Trophy Hunter	C	.224	UNK/NA	UNK/NA	UNK/NA	UNK/NA	UNK/NA	UNK/NA	UNK/NA	UNK/NA	246
5.6x57mm RWS/5.6x57Rmm RWS	C/A	.224	.281	.436	.469	.470/(?)	UNK/NA	2.24	2.54	UNK/NA	567
.25-222 Copperhead	C	.224	.285	.357	.375	.378	.045	1.850	2.485	L	256
22 Tuba II Unrimmed	C	.224	.3	.476	.476	.476	.044	.898	1.17	LP	257
22 Tuba II Rimmed	A	.224	.3	.457	.457	.514	.055	1.29	1.62	LP	257
.297/230 Morris Short	A	.225	.240	.274	.294	.347	UNK/NA	.58	.89	.177/69	532
.297/230 Morris Long	A	.225	.240	.274	.295	.345	UNK/NA	.80	1.1	.177/69	532
5.5mm Velo Dog Revolver	B	.225	.248	UNK/NA	.253	.308	UNK/NA	1.12	1.35	SPB	421
5.6x61mm & 5.6x61Rmm Vom Hofe Super Express	C/A	.227	.259/ .260	.468/ .470	.476/ .479	.480/ .533	?/.062	2.39	3.13	.217/5603/ 431M	568
.22 Winchester CF (WCF)	A	.228	.241	.278	.295	.342	.058	1.39	1.61	S	168
.22 Savage High Power	A	.228	.252	.360	.416	.500	.056	2.05	2.51	L	169
.228 Ackley Magnum	C	.228	.265	.445	.470	.473	.045	2.25	2.55	L	255
5.8x21mm DAP 92	C	.236	.259	.306	.313	.314	.044	.827	1.28	SP	421
6 Whisper	C	.243	UNK/NA	UNK/NA	.370	.375	.040	UNK/NA	UNK/NA	UNK/NA	333
6mm PPC	C	.243	.260	.430	.441	.442	.50	1.50	2.12	S	78
6mm Bench Rest Remington	C	.243	.263	.457	.466	.468	.045	1.52	2.19	S	170
6x45mm (6mm/223)	C	.243	.266	.354	.376	.378	.041	1.76	2.26	S	255
6x47mm	C	.243	.266	.357	.375	.378	.045	1.85	2.485	S	259
6mm CHeetah	C	.243	.260	.456	.470	.473	.049	2.00	UNK/NA	LR	258
.240 Weatherby Magnum	E	.243	.271	.432	.453	.473	.045	2.50	3.06	L	79
6x62mm Freres/ 6x62Rmm Freres	C/A	.243	.271	.451	.474	.470/(?)	UNK/NA	2.42	3.13	.217	569
6mm Norma BR	C	.243	.271	.458	.469	.470	.051	1.56	2.44	S	80
6XC Tubb	C	.243	.271	.450	.466	.468	.049	1.898	2.808	L	79
6mm JDJ	A	.243	.272	.415	.421	.470	.045	1.905	2.65	L	333
6mm SAW (U.S.)	C	.243	.273	.382	.410	.410		1.779	2.58	L	491
6mm-250 Walker	C	.243	.274	.420	.468	.470	.045	1.91	2.21	L	259
6mm/30-30 Ackley Improved	A	.243	.275	.392	.422	.502	.058	2.03	2.55	L	260
6.17 Spitfire	C	.243	.275	.510	.530	.530	.050	2.05	2.8	L	334
6.17 Flash	C	.243	.275	.510	.530	.530	.050	2.80	3.55	L	334

CARTRIDGE	CASE TYPE	BULLET DIAMETER	NECK DIAMETER	SHOULDER DIAMETER	BASE DIAMETER	RIM DIAMETER	RIM THICKNESS	CASE LENGTH	CARTRIDGE LENGTH	PRIMER	PAGE
.240 Hawk	C	.243	.276	.454	.4712	.473	.049	2.485	UNK/NA	L	261
.244 Remington	C	.243	.276	.429	.470	.472	.045	2.23	2.90	L	171
6mm Remington /.244 Remington	C	.243	.276	.429	.470	.472	.045	2.23	2.91 2.825	L	82
.243 Winchester	C	.243	.276	.454	.470	.470	.49	2.05	2.71	L	81
6mm-284	I	.243	.276	.475	.500	.473	.049	2.165	2.80	L	262
Spitzer 6mm-06	C	.243	.276	.441	.470	.473	.049	2.494	3.35	L	260
6x57mm Mauser/6x57mm RWS	C	.243	.284	.420	.475	.476	.045	2.23	2.95	.217/5603 494	570
.244 (6mm) Halger Magnum	A	.243	.287	.435	.467	.470	UNK/NA	2.25	3.04	.2175603	570
.244 H&H Magnum	E	.244	.263	.445	.508	.532	UNK/NA	2.78	3.58	.217/60	533
6mm Lee Navy (.236 Navy)	C	.244	.278	.402	.445	.448	.050	2.35	3.11	L	171
.240 Magnum Flanged	A	.245	.274	.402	.448	.513	UNK/NA	2.50	3.25	.217/81	532
.240 Magnum Rimless (.240 Apex)	E	.245	.274	.403	.450	467	.035	2.49	3.21	.217/81	532
.243 WSSM	I	.243	.287	.544	.555	.535	.054	1.67	2.060 (2.360)	L	83
.25 Short	B	.246	.245	UNK/NA	.245	.290	UNK/NA	.468	.780	UNK/NA	618
6x49mm "Unified"	C	.248			.444			1.92	2.736		491
.297/250 Rook	A	.250	.267	.294	.295	.343	UNK/NA	.82	1.1	.177/69	533
.25 Stevens Short	B	.251	.275	UNK/NA	.276	.333	UNK/NA	.599	.877	UNK/NA	618
.25 Automatic Colt Pistol (ACP)	D	.251	.276	UNK/NA	.277	.298	.038	.62	.91	SP	421
.25 NAA (North American Arms)	C	.251	.276	.330	.337	.337	.046	.745	.960	UNK/NA	422
.25 Stevens	B	.251	.276	UNK/NA	.276	.333	UNK/NA	1.125	1.395	UNK/NA	618
.242 Rimless Nitro Express	C	.253	.281	.405	.465	.465	UNK/NA	2.38	3.20	.217/59	534
.25-20 Marlin	A	.257	.274	.329	.349	.405	UNK/NA	1.33	UNK/NA	S	172
.25-20 Winchester	A	.257	.274	.329	.349	.405	.060	1.33	1.60	S	81
.255 Banshee	A	.257	.278	.297	.298	.345	.050	1.335	1.80	S	335
.256 Winchester Magnum (handgun)	A	.257	.277	.378	.378	.440	.055	1.30	1.53	SP	422
.257 Kimber	C	.257	.279	.365	.376	.378	.041	1.82	2.485	UNK/NA	264
.25-21 Stevens	B	.257	.280	UNK/NA	.300	.376	UNK/NA	2.05	2.30	S	173
.25-35 Winchester (WCF)/6.5x52Rmm	A	.257	.280	.355	.420	.500 (.506)	.059	2.04	2.53	L	84
.25 Remington	C	.257	.280	.355	.420	.421	.045	2.04	2.54	L	173
.25-36 Marlin	A	.257	.281	.358	.416	.499	.056	2.12	2.50	S	174
.25-25 Stevens	B	.257	.282	UNK/NA	.323	.376	UNK/NA	2.37	2.63	S	174
.257 Raptor	C	.257	.283	.370	.376	.378	.045	1.86	2.135	S	335
.25-45 Sharps	C	.257	.284	.353	.376	.378	.045	1.76	2.135	S	85
.250/3000 Ackley Improved	C	.257	.284	.445	.467	.473	.045	1.91	2.52	L	264
.256 Winchester Magnum (rifle)	A	.257	.285	.368	.381	.440	.060	1.281	1.59	S	175
.257 Weatherby Magnum	E	.257	.285	.490	.511	.530	.048	2.55	3.25	L	85

CARTRIDGE	CASE TYPE	BULLET DIAMETER	NECK DIAMETER	SHOULDER DIAMETER	BASE DIAMETER	RIM DIAMETER	RIM THICKNESS	CASE LENGTH	CARTRIDGE LENGTH	PRIMER	PAGE
.25-284	I	.257	.285	.495	.500	.473	.049	2.17	2.80	L	265
.257 STW (Shooting Times Westerner)	E	.257	.285	.487	.511	.532	.050	2.85	3.60	L	265
.25 Gibbs	C	.257	UNK/NA	UNK/NA	.440	.468	.045	UNK/NA	UNK/NA	UNK/NA	262
.250 Savage	C	.257	.286	.413	.468	.470	.045	1.91	2.52 (2.515)	L	86
.25-06 Remington	C	.257	.287	.441	.470	.471	.045	2.49	3.00	L	87
.257 Allen Xpress	C	.257	.287	.532	.544	.544	.046	2.535	3.35	Fed 215 L	266
.257 JDJ	A	.257	.288	.415	.421	.473	.045	1.905	2.81	L	336
.250-06 JDJ	C	.257	UNK/NA	UNK/NA	.440	.468	.045	UNK/NA	UNK/NA	UNK/NA	336
.257 Ackley Improved	C	.257	.288	.457	.471	.474	.045	2.23	2.78	L	266
.257 Condor	E	0.257	0.288	0.451	0.532	0.532	0.050	2.400	3.300	LRM	267
6.53 Scramjet	C	.257	.289	.510	.530	.530	.055	2.80	3.575	L	337
.257 Mini Dreadnaught	G	.257	.290	.425	.445	.467	.045	2.145	V	L	337
.257 Roberts (.257 Roberts +P)	C	.257	.290	.430	.468	.473	.045	2.23	2.74	L	87
.25-303	A	.257	.29	.412	.46	.54	.064	2.185	2.85	L	263
.257 Allen Magnum	I	.257	.29	.538	.55	.532	.05	2.75	3.655	Fed 215 L	338
.25 Hunter	A	.257	.293	.430	.435	.492	.046	1.625	2.30	L	268
.25 Ackley Krag	A	.257	.293	.442	.457	.540	.059	2.31	UNK/NA	L	268
.25 Ackley Krag Short	A	.257	.293	.442	.457	.540	.059	2.24-2.31	V	L	268
6.5mm Mannlicher-Schonauer (Greek)	C	.263	.287	.424	.447	.450	UNK/NA	2.09	3.02	B	492
6.5mm Japanese Arisaka	G	.263	.293	.425	.455	.471	.045	2.00	2.98	B	492
6.5 MPC	C	0.264	0.297	0.349	0.373	0.375	0.041	1.760	2.26	Bx	341
6.5 Mini Dreadnaught	G	.263	.296	.425	.445	.467	.045	2.150	V	L	342
6.5x53R Mannlicher (Dutch & Romanian)	A	.263	.297	.423	.450	.526	.066	2.10	3.03	B	493
6.5mm JDJx30	A	.264	.285	.409	.419	.497	.058	2.03	V	L	338
6.5mm Whisper	C	.264	.286	.357	.372	.375	.041	1.36	V	S	339
6.5x25 CBJ	C	.257	.287	.379	.390	.393	.049	.984	1.169	S	339
6.5x54mm Mauser	C	.264	.289	.432	.468	.463	UNK/NA	2.12	2.67	.217/5603/457A	572
6.5-300 Weatherby Magnum	E	0.264	0.297	0.495	0.513	0.530	0.048	2.820	3.560	L	93
.264 (6.5mm) Win. Magnum	E	.264	.289	.490	.515 (.5127)	.532	.047	2.52	3.29	L	94
.256 (6.5mm) Newton	C	.264	.290	.430	.469	.473	.045	2.44	3.40	L	175
6.5x58Rmm Sauer	B	.264	.291	UNK/NA	.433	.501	UNK/NA	2.30	3.08	.217/5603/463	573
6.5x57mm/6.5x57Rmm Mauser & RWS	C/A	.264	.292	.430	.471/ .470	.474/ .521	UNK/NA	2.23/ 2.24	3.16/ 3.18	.217/5603/404A	573
6.5mm JDJ No. 2	A	.264	.292	.450	.466	.502	.059	2.00	V	L	340
6.5mm JDJ	A	.264	.293	.410	.419	.467	.045	1.93	V	L	340
6.5/270 JDJ	C	.264	UNK/NA	UNK/NA	.440	.468	.045	UNK/NA	UNK/NA	UNK/NA	341

CARTRIDGE	CASE TYPE	BULLET DIAMETER	NECK DIAMETER	SHOULDER DIAMETER	BASE DIAMETER	RIM DIAMETER	RIM THICKNESS	CASE LENGTH	CARTRIDGE LENGTH	PRIMER	PAGE
.264 LBC-AR	C	.264	.293	.428	.439	.441	.059	1.526	2.20	S	271
6.5mm Grendel	C	.264	.293	.428	.439	.441	.059	1.526	2.26	SR	89
6.5x58mm Portuguese	C	.264	.293	.426	.468	.465	UNK/NA	2.28	3.22	.217/5603 457	574
6.508 A-Square/.260 Rem	C	.264	.294	.452	.468	.467	.045	.025	2.80	LR	90
6.5mm Leopard	C	.264	.295	.539	.551	.533	.049	2.093	UNK/NA	LR	272
6.5 Allen Xpress	C	.264	.295	.532	.544	.544	.046	2.54	3.375	Fed 215 L	272
6.5x65mm/6.5x65Rmm RWS	C/A	.264	.296	.430	.474/ .475	.470/ .531	UNK/NA	2.56	3.15	UNK/NA	574
.264 Hawk	C	.264	.296	.454	.471	.473	.049	2.485	UNK/NA	L	273
6.5x61mm/6.5x61Rmm Mauser	C/A	.264	.296/.297	.452	.477	.479/.532	UNK/NA	2.40	3.55	.217/5603 431L-431M	574
6.5 Creedmoor	C	.264	.297	.458	.467	.468	.054	1.915	2.72	L	91
6.5x47 Lapua	I	0.264	0.292	0.454	0.470	0.473	0.054	1.900	2.740	S	92
6.5x52mm American	C	.264	.297	.465	.470	.473	.054	2.024	2.735	L	269
EABCO 6.5mm BRM	A	.264	UNK/NA	UNK/NA	UNK/NA	UNK/NA	UNK/NA	UNK/NA	UNK/NA	UNK/NA	270
6.71 Phantom	C	.264	.297	.510	.530	.530	.055	2.05	2.8	L	342
6.5mm Allen Magnum	I	.264	.297	.538	.55	.532	.05	2.75	3.655	Fed 215 L	272
.260 Remington	C	0.264	0.297	0.454	0.470	0.473	0.054	2.035	2.800	L	90
6.5x55 Swedish Mauser	C	.264	.297	.435	.480 (.477)	.480 (.479)	.050	2.16	3.15	L	474
6.5-284 Norma	I	.264	.297	.475	.500	.470	.051	2.17	3.23	SR	92
6.71 Blackbird	C	.264	.297	.524	.544	.544	.055	2.80	3.575	L	343
26 Nosler	C	.264	.297	.5275	.55	.532	.05	2.59	3.34	L	93
6.5 STW (Shooting Times Westerner)	E	.264	.298	.487	.511	.532	.050	2.85	3.60	L	269
6.5x58R Krag-Jorgensen	A.	.264	.300	.460	.500	.575	UNK/NA	2.29	3.25	.217/5603 431L-431M	575
6.5-06 Ackley Improved	C	.264	.300	.455	.471	.473	.045	2.50	3.30	L	273
6.5 SAUM	I	0.264	0.295	0.534	0.550	0.534	0.050	2.015	2.226	L	274
6.5 Remington Magnum	E	.264	.300	.490	.512	.532	.047	2.17	2.80	L	176
6.5x52mm Italian Mannlicher-Carcano	C	.265	.295	.430	.445	.448	.045	2.05	3.02	B	495
6.5x68mm/6.5x68Rmm RWS	C/A	.265	.295	.481	.520	.510	UNK/NA	2.66	3.27	.238/1698	575
.270 REN	B	.277	.295	UNK/NA	.298	.350	.060	1.29	UNK/NA	S	275
.270 JDJ	A	.277	.305	.415	.419	.467	.045	1.905	2.875	L	344
.270 JDJ No. 2	C	.277	UNK/NA	UNK/NA	.440	.468	.045	UNK/NA	UNK/NA	UNK/NA	345
.270 IHMSA	C	.277	.305	.448	.471	.473	.045	1.866	2.60	L	275
.270 Gibbs	C	.277	UNK/NA	UNK/NA	.440	.468	.045	UNK/NA	UNK/NA	UNK/NA	274
.270 Weatherby Magnum	E	.277	.305	.490	.511	.530	.048	2.55	3.25	L	95
6.8 SPC (Special Purpose Cartridge)	C	.277	.306	.401	.421	.417	.049	.1.686	2.26	LR	95
.270 Winchester	C	.277	.307	.440	.468	.470	.045	2.54	3.28	L	96
.270 Hawk	C	.277	.308	.453	.471	.473	.049	2.486	UNK/NA	LR	276

CARTRIDGE	CASE TYPE	BULLET DIAMETER	NECK DIAMETER	SHOULDER DIAMETER	BASE DIAMETER	RIM DIAMETER	RIM THICKNESS	CASE LENGTH	CARTRIDGE LENGTH	PRIMER	PAGE
.270 Savage	C	.277	.308	.413	.470	.470	.045	1.88	2.62	L	276
.270 Ackley Improved	C	.277	.308	.450	.470	.470	.045	1.88	2.62	L	276
.270 Allen Xpress	C	.277	.308	.535	.544	.544	.046	2.545	3.4	Fed 215 L	277
.270 WSM	I	.277	.314	.538	.555	.535	.054	2.10	2.56 (2.860)	L	97
.270 Schuster	C	0.278	0.315	0.450	0.471	0.473	0.055	1.924	2.800	Bx	576
7mm Nambu	C	.280	.296	.337	.351	.359	UNK/NA	.78	1.06	B	423
7mm TCU	C	.284	.302	.350	.373	.375	.041	1.74	2.28	S	277
7mm Whisper	C	.284	.306	.357	.372	.375	.041	1.36	V	S	345
7mm-30 JDJ	A	.284	.306	.409	.419	.497	.058	2.03	V	L	346
7-30 Waters	A	.284	.306	.399	.422 (.4215)	.506	.058	2.04	2.52	L	98
7x33mm Sako/Finnish	C	.284	.307	.365	.388	.390	UNK/NA	1.30	1.73	UNK/NA	576
7mm GNR	A	.284	.312	.400	.420	.502	.058	2.055	2.65	L	346
28 Nosler	I	0.284	0.320	0.528	0.550	0.534	0.050	2.590	3.340	LRM	98
.280 Ackley Improved	C	.284	.311	.454	.470	.472	.049	2.525	3.33	L	99
7x72Rmm	B	.284	.311	UNK/NA	.425	.482	UNK/NA	2.84	3.48	.217/5603 573	578
7mm JDJ	A	.284	.312	.415	.421	.473	.045	1.905	V	L	347
7mm JRS	C	.284	.312	.454	.470	.467	.045	2.525	3.455	L	279
7mm Gibbs	C	.284	UNK/NA	UNK/NA	.440	.468	.045	UNK/NA	UNK/NA	UNK/NA	278
.280 JDJ	C	.284	.312	.455	.470	.467	.045	2.505	V	L	347
7mm Weatherby Magnum	E	.284	.312	.490	.511	.530	.048	2.55	3.25	L	100
7mm JDJ No. 2	A	.284	.313	.450	.466	.502	.059	2.00	V	L	348
7mm Blaser Magnum	I	.284	.314	.515	.544	.535	.054	2.35	3.14	L	578
7mm Dakota	C	.284	.314	.531	.544	.544	.042	2.50	3.33	L	348
7 STE (Shooting Tmes Easterner)	A	.284	.315	.454	.467	.502	.059	2.1	2.54	L	281
7mm-300 Weatherby Magnum	E	0.284	0.310	0.492	0.513	0.530	0.048	2.825	3.560	L	282
7mm SGLC (Simpson's Good Little Cartridge)	C	.284	.315	.465	.470	.473	.054	2.024	2.735	L	280
7mm-08 Remington	C	.284	.315	.454	.470	.473	.050	2.04 (2.035)	2.80	L	102
.280 Hawk (7mm Hawk)	C	.284	.315	.454	.471	.473	.049	2.485	UNK/NA	LR	280
.280 Remington/7mm Express Remington	C	.284	.315	.441	.470	.472	.045	2.54	3.33	L	101
.285 OKH/7mm-06	C	.284	.315	.442	.470	.472	.045	2.55	3.35	L	279
7x73mm Vom Hofe Belted	E	.284	.315	.483	.527	.533	UNK/NA	2.87	3.88	.217/5603/ 575	579
7mm Remington Magnum	E	.284	.315	.490	.511	.525	.047	2.50	3.24	L	103
.280 GNR	A	.284	.316	.448	.463	.543	.075	2.525	3.0	L	349
7x66mm Vom Hofe Super Express	C	.284	.316	.485	.543	.510	.048	2.58	3.25	.217/603	579
7mm STW (Shooting Times Western)	E	.284	.316	.487	.513	.532	.048	2.85	3.65	L	104

CARTRIDGE	CASE TYPE	BULLET DIAMETER	NECK DIAMETER	SHOULDER DIAMETER	BASE DIAMETER	RIM DIAMETER	RIM THICKNESS	CASE LENGTH	CARTRIDGE LENGTH	PRIMER	PAGE
7mm Allen Magnum	C	.284	.316	.561	.59	.59	.06	2.71	3.65	Fed 215 L	350
7.21 Tomahawk	C	.284	.318	.557	.577	.577	.060	2.05	2.80	L	350
7x75Rmm Vom Hofe Super Express	A	.284	.318	.416	.468	.519	.050	2.95	3.68	.217	580
.275 Flanged Magnum .275 No. 2 Magnum	A	.284	.318	.450	.510	.582	UNK/NA	2.50	3.26	.217	536
7.21 Firehawk	C	.284	.318	.524	.544	.544	.055	2.80	3.55	L	351
7.21 Firebird	C	.284	.318	.557	.577	.577	.060	2.80	3.6	L	351
.284 Winchester	I	.284	.320	.465 (.4748)	.495 (.500)	.470	.049	2.17	2.75	L	105
7x57mm/7x57mmR Mauser	C	.284	.320	.420 (.4294)	.470	.474	.046	2.24 (2.235)	3.06	L	104
7x57mm Mauser	C	.284	.320	.420	.470	.474	.055	2.23	3.06	B	496
7x57mm Mauser/7x57Rmm Mauser	C/A	.284	.320	.420	.470	.474/.521	.035/.056	2.24	3.06/3.07	.217/5603/ 380DM93A	496
7x61 Sharpe & Hart Super	E	.284	.320	.478	.515	.532	.048	2.40	3.27	L	176
7mm Canadian Magnum	I	.284	.322	.530	.544	.532	.046	2.83	3.60	L	352
.275 Rigby (7x57)	C	.284	.324	.428	.474	.475	UNK/NA	2.24	3.07	.217	496
.275 Belted Magnum	E	.284	.325	.454	.513	.532	UNK/NA	2.50	3.42	.217/81	536
.275 H&H Magnum	E	.284	.375	.375	.513	.532	.048	2.50	3.30	L	177
7x64mm Brenneke 7x65Rmm Brenneke	C/A	.284	.305/.308	.422	.463	.468/.521	.055	2.51, 2.53	3.21	.217/5603/ 557/557A	577
7mm Bench Rest (based on Rem. 308 BR case shortened to 1.50-inch)	C	.284	UNK/NA	SP	UNK/NA	UNK/NA	UNK/NA	1.5	UNK/NA	UNK/NA	424
.28-30-120 Stevens	B	.285	.309	UNK/NA	.357	.412	UNK/NA	2.51	2.82	L	178
.30 Short	B	.286	.292	UNK/NA	.292	.346	UNK/NA	.515	.822	UNK/NA	619
.280 Flanged (.280 Lancaster)	A	.287	.316	.423	.535	.607	UNK/NA	2.60	3.62	.217/60	536
.280 Ross (.280 Rimless)	G	.287	.317	.404	.534	.556	UNK/NA	2.59	3.50	.217/59	537
7mmRem. SAUM	I	.284	.320	.534	.550	.534	.050	2.035	2.450 (2.825)	L	106
7mm WSM	I	.284	.321	.538	.555	.535	.054	2.10	2.560 (2.860)	L	106
7mm Rem. Ultra Mag	I	.284	.322	.525	.550	.534	.050	2.85	3.450 (3.600)	L	107
.30 Long	B	.288	.288	UNK/NA	.288	.340	UNK/NA	.613	1.020	UNK/NA	619
.280 Jeffery (.33/280 Jeffery)	C	.288	.317	.504	.542	.538	UNK/NA	2.50	3.45	.217/59	537
7.62mm Russian Nagant Revolver	B	.295	.286	UNK/NA	.335	.388	UNK/NA	1.53	1.53	B	425
7.35mm Italian Carcano	C	.298	.323	.420	.445	.449	UNK/NA	2.01	2.98	B	498
7.7mm Bittner	B	.302	.319	NA	.337	.39		.665	1	B	426
.30 Remington	C	.307	.328	.402	.420	.421	.045	2.03	2.525	L	178
7.62mm Russian Tokarev	C	.307	.330	.370	.380	.390	UNK/NA	.97	1.35	B	426
.30 (7.65x21mm) Luger	C	.308	.322	.374	.388	.391	.045	.75	1.15	SPB	427
7.62 Micro-Whisper	C	.308	.328	.382	.389	.392	.045	.846	V	SP/SR	353
.30-30 Winchester	A	.308	.328	.402	.422 (.4215)	.502	.058	2.03 (2.039)	2.53	L	108
.30-30 Ackley Improved	A	.308	.328	.405	.422	.502	.058	2.04	2.54	L	282

CARTRIDGE	CASE TYPE	BULLET DIAMETER	NECK DIAMETER	SHOULDER DIAMETER	BASE DIAMETER	RIM DIAMETER	RIM THICKNESS	CASE LENGTH	CARTRIDGE LENGTH	PRIMER	PAGE
.30 ARX	C	0.308	0.330	0.428	0.439	0.441	0.059	1.526	2.26	CCI BR-4	283
.30-30 Wesson	A	.308	.329	.330	.380	.440	UNK/NA	1.66	2.50	L	179
7.63 Mini-Whisper	C	.308	.329	.375	.381	.385	.045	.985	V	SP/SR	353
.30 Herrett	A	.308	.329	.405	.421	.505	.058	1.61	2.01	L	283
.300 Whisper	C	.308	.330	.369	.375	.375	.041	1.50	2.575	S	353
.30-378 Weatherby Magnum	K	.308	.330	.560	.589	.603/.580	.060	2.90	3.865	L	109
7.63 (7.65) Mannlicher	D	.308	.331	UNK/NA	.332	.334	.030	.84	1.12	B	427
.30 (7.63mm) Mauser	C	.308	.332	.370	.381	.390	.045	.99	1.36	SPB	428
.30 USA Rimless	C	.308	.333	.417	.454	.456	.054	2.31	3.10	L	179
.308 CorBon	C	.308	.333	.532	.545	.532	.050	2.08	2.80	L	354
.303 Savage/.301 Savage	A	.308 (.311)	.334 (.3322)	.408 (.4135)	.439	.501	.058	2.0 (2.015)	2.52	L	181
.30 Kurz	C	.308	.334	.443	.470	.473	.045	1.29	1.65	L	284
.300 AAC Blackout	C	.308	.334	.361	.375	.375	.045	1.368	1.78	S	110
7.5mm Schmidt-Rubin	C	.308	.334	.452	.494	.496	.058	2.18	3.05	B	499
.300 Winchester Magnum	E	.308	.334	.4891	.5126	.530	.046	2.60 (2.62)	3.30	L	111
.30 Carbine	D	.308	.335	.355	.3567	.3598	.05	1.29	1.6799	SR	112
.309 JDJ	A	.308	.335	.453	.470	.514	.058	2.20	3.16	L	355
.30-06 JDJ	C	.308	.335	.455	.470	.467	.045	2.455	V	L	356
.307 GNR	A	.308	.336	.379	.380	.433	.055	1.55	2.0	S	355
.300 Weatherby Magnum	E	.308	.337	.495	.513 (.5117)	.530	.048	2.82 (2.825)	3.56	L	112
30 Nosler	I	0.308	0.340	0.528	0.550	0.534	0.050	2.556	3.340	LRM	113
.30 Army (.30-40 Krag)	A	.308	.338	.415 (.419)	.457 (.4577)	.540	.059	2.31	3.10 (3.089)	Bx/L	500
7.62x51mm NATO (.308 Winchester)	C	.308	.338	.447	.466	.470	UNK/NA	2.01	2.75	Bx	501
.300 Blaser Magnum	I	.308	.338	.511	.544	.535	.054	2.56	3.30	L	581
.300 Belted Rimless Magnum	E	.308	.338	.447	.513	.530	UNK/NA	2.85	3.60	.217/60	538
.300 H&H Magnum	E	.308	.338	.447	.513	.530	.048	2.85	3.60	L	115
.308x1.5Inch	C	.308	.338	.450	.466	.470	.048	1.50	2.05	L	284
.30 Flanged Magnum (H&H Super .30)	A	.308	.338	.450	.517	.572	UNK/NA	2.93	3.69	UNK/NA	538
.300 Dakota	C	.308	.338	.531	.544	.544	.046	2.55	3.33	L	356
.300 Savage	C	.308	.339	.443 (.4466)	.470	.470	.045	1.87	2.62	L	115
.300 Pegasus	C	.308	.339	.566	.580	.580	.058	2.99	3.75	L	357
7.5x54mm French MAS	C	.308	.340	.441	.480	.482	.054	2.11	2.99	B	502
7.62x63mm U.S. (.30-06)	C	.308	.340	.441	.470	.473		2.49	3.34	Bx	501
.30-06 Springfield	C	.308	.340	.441	.470	.473	.045	2.49	3.34	L	116
.30-03 Government	C	.308	.340	.441	.470	.473	.045	2.54	3.34	L	179
.30-06 Ackley Improved	C	.308	.340	.454	.470	.473	.045	2.49	3.35	L	286

CARTRIDGE	CASE TYPE	BULLET DIAMETER	NECK DIAMETER	SHOULDER DIAMETER	BASE DIAMETER	RIM DIAMETER	RIM THICKNESS	CASE LENGTH	CARTRIDGE LENGTH	PRIMER	PAGE
.30 Gibbs	C	.308	UNK/NA	UNK/NA	.440	.468	.045	UNK/NA	UNK/NA	UNK/NA	278
.308 Norma Magnum	E/C	.308	.340	.489	.514	.529	.048	2.56	3.30	L	581
.30-338 Winchester Magnum	E	.308	.340	.491	.513	.532	.048	2.50		L	286
.300 ICL Grizzly	E	0.308	0.340	0.460	0.532	0.532	0.050	2.610	3.540	LRM	287
.300 Raptor	C	0.308	0.338	0.566	0.590	0.580	0.058	3.050	4.285	Fed 215	288
.300 Allen Xpress	C	.308	.34	.56	.59	.59	.06	2.7	3.7	Fed 215 L	288
.30 Remington AR	I	.308	.341	.488	.500	.492	.054	1.525	2.260	S	118
.300 Norma Magnum	C	.308	.341	.562	.585	.587	.059	2.50	3.68	L	582
.300 Remington SAUM	I	.308	.344	.534	.550	.534	.050	2.015	2.450 (2.825)	L	124
.300 WSM	I	.308	.344	.538	.555	.535	.054 (2.860)	2.10	2.560	L	124
		.308	.340								
7.82 Patriot	C	.308	.340	.557	.577	.577	.060	2.05	2.8	L	358
7.82 Warbird	C	.308	.340	.557	.577	.577	.060	2.80	3.60	L	358
.300 Canadian Magnum	I	.308	.342	.530	.544	.532	.046	2.83	3.60	L	359
.30R Blaser	A	.308	.343	.441	.480	.531	UNK/NA	2.68	3.80	UNK/NA	583
.30 TC (Thompson/Center)	C	.308	.344	.464	.470	.473	.054	1.92	2.645	L	119
.308 Marlin Express	A	.308	.344	.448	.463	.502	.049	1.910	2.585	L	119
.307 Winchester	G	.308	.344	.454	.470	.506	.059	2.02 (2.015)	2.60 (2.56)	L	121
7.62x40 WT	C	0.308	0.325	0.365	0.376	0.375	0.041	1.565	2.260	Bx	120
.308 Winchester	C	.308	.344	.454	.470	.470	.049	2.01 (2.015)	2.75	L	121
.300 Ruger Compact Magnum (RCM)	C	.308	.344	.515	.532	.532	.040	2.1	2.825	L	122
.300 Remington Ultra Mag	I	.308	.344	.525	.550	.534	.050	2.085 (3.600)	3.450	L	123
.32-40 Remington	A	.309	.330	.358	.453	.535	UNK/NA	2.13	3.25	S	180
.32 Automatic Colt Pistol (ACP)	H	.309	.336	UNK/NA	.336	.354	.040	.68	1.03	SP	433
7.62X53Rmm (M43) Russian	C	.310	.340	.394	.443	.445	UNK/NA	1.52	2.20	B	502
7.62x39mm Soviet	C	.311	.340 (.337)	.344 (.396)	.438 (.433)	.440	.053	1.52 (1.528)	2.20	S	505
.303 British	A	.311	.337	.402	.458	.530	.062	2.21	3.05	B	503
7.7mm Japanese Arisaka	C	.311	.338	.431	.472	.474	.042	2.28	3.13	B	504
.375/303 Westley Richards	A	.311	.343	.390	.457	.505	UNK/NA	2.50	3.36	UNK/NA	539
.32 Long Rifle	B	.312	.318	UNK/NA	.318	.377	UNK/NA	.937	1.223	UNK/NA	183
.32-20 Winchester	A	.312	.326	.338 (.3424)	.353	.405	.058	1.32 (1.315)	1 59	S	127
.32-20 Marlin	A	.312	.326	.338	.353	.405	UNK/NA	1.32	UNK/NA	S	181
.32-30 Remington	A	.312	.332	.357	.378	.437	UNK/NA	1.64	2.01	S	182
.32 H&R Magnum	B	.312	.333	UNK/NA	.333	.371	.050	1.08	1.35	SP	429
.32 S&W	B	.312	.334	UNK/NA	.335	.375	.045	.61	.92	SP	430
.32 S&W Long	B	.312	.335	UNK/NA	.335	.375	.048	.93	1.27	SP	430

CARTRIDGE	CASE TYPE	BULLET DIAMETER	NECK DIAMETER	SHOULDER DIAMETER	BASE DIAMETER	RIM DIAMETER	RIM THICKNESS	CASE LENGTH	CARTRIDGE LENGTH	PRIMER	PAGE
.32 NAA (North American Arms)	C	.312	.337	.373	.374	.374	.045	.680	.984	UNK/NA	431
.327 Federal Magnum	B	.312	.337	UNK/NA	.337	.371	.050	1.20	1.46	S	432
.327 Martin Meteor	A	.312	.396	.379	.379	.440	.060	1.50	1.77	S	289
.32-35 Stevens & Maynard	B	.312	.339	UNK/NA	.402	.503	UNK/NA	1.88	2.29	S	182
.303 Magnum	C	.312	.345	.462	.530	.557	UNK/NA	2.35	3.25	UNK/NA	540
.32 Short Colt	B	.313	.313	UNK/NA	.318	.374	.045	.63	1.00	SP	433
.32 Long Colt	B	.313	.313	UNK/NA	.318	.374	.045	.92	1.26	SP	433
.32 Colt	B	UNK/NA	.313	UNK/NA	.318	.374	.052	.755	1.26	SP	434
7.65x53mm Argentine Mauser	C	.313	.338	.429	.468	.470	.040	2.09	2.95	B	505
.32-40 Bullard	A	.315	.332	.413	.453	.510	UNK/NA	1.85	2.26	S	183
8x48Rmm Sauer	B	.316	.344	UNK/NA	.432	.500	.040	1.88	2.58	.254/1775/ 462A	583
8.15x46Rmm	A	.316	.346	.378	.421	.484	UNK/NA	1.82	2.28	.250/1794/ 455	584
.32 Long, CF*	B	.317	.318	UNK/NA	.321	.369	UNK/NA	.82	1.35	S	183
.32 Ballard Extra Long*	B	.317	.318	UNK/NA	.321	.369	UNK/NA	1.24	1.80	S	183
.320 Revolver	B	.317	.320	UNK/NA	.322	.350	UNK/NA	.62	.90	B	434
7.5mm Swiss Army Revolver	B	.317	.335	UNK/NA	.345	.407	UNK/NA	.89	1.29	B	434
8x57Rmm 360	A	.318	.333	.375	.427	.485	UNK/NA	2.24	2.96	UNK/NA	585
8x75mm/8x75Rmm	C/A	.318	.345	.411	.466	.467/.522	UNK/NA	2.94	3.50/3.51	.217/5603/ 514/ A514	584
8x57Jmm Mauser	C	.318	.350	.435	.470	.473	UNK/NA	2.24	3.17	L	586
.35 S&W Auto/.35 Automatic	D	.320	UNK/NA	UNK/NA	UNK/NA	UNK/NA	UNK/NA	UNK/NA	UNK/NA	UNK/NA	435
8mm Rast-Gasser	B	.320	.332	UNK/NA	.334	.376	UNK/NA	1.037	1.391	UNK/NA	435
.32-40 Ballard & Winchester	B	.320	.338	UNK/NA	.424	.506	.058	2.13	2.59	L	184
8mm Nambu	G	.320	.338	.388	.408	.413	UNK/NA	.86	1.25	B	435
.32 Winchester Self Loading (WSL)	H	.320	.343	UNK/NA	.346	.388	UNK/NA	1.28	1.88	S	184
.32 Remington	C	.320	.344	.396	.420	.421	.045	2.04	2.57	L	185
.32 Winchester Special	A	.321	.343	.396 (.4014)	.422 (.4219)	.506	.058	2.04	2.55 (2.565)	L	128
8x50Rmm Siamese (Type 45)	A	.321	.347	.450	.480	.550	UNK/NA	1.98	2.97	B	506
8x52Rmm Siamese (Type 66)	A	.321	.347	.460	.500	.550	UNK/NA	2.04	2.96	B, Bx	507
8x58Rmm Sauer	B	.322	.345	UNK/NA	.438	.499	UNK/NA	2.28	3.00	.254/1775/ 462	585
.325 WSM	I	.323	.358	35381	.555	.535	.054	2.10	2.560	LR	130
8mm Remington Magnum	E	.323	.351 (.3541)	.485 (.4868)	.509 (.5126)	.530	.047	2.85	3.57 (3.600)	L	130
.32 Ideal	B	.323	.344	UNK/NA	.348	.411	UNK/NA	1.77	2.25	S	185
8x56mm Mannlicher-Schoenauer	C	.323	.347	.424	.465	.470	.045	2.21	3.04	.217/5603/ 528	587
8x50Rmm Lebel	A	.323	.347	.483	.536	.621	.068	1.98	2.75	B	508
8x64mmS Brenneke 8x65RmmS Brenneke	C/A	.323	.348	.424/.421	.468/.464	.469/.520	UNK/NA	2.51, 2.56	3.32/3.65	.217/5603/ 558/ 558A	587

CARTRIDGE	CASE TYPE	BULLET DIAMETER	NECK DIAMETER	SHOULDER DIAMETER	BASE DIAMETER	RIM DIAMETER	RIM THICKNESS	CASE LENGTH	CARTRIDGE LENGTH	PRIMER	PAGE
8mm Lebel Revolver	B	.323	.350	UNK/NA	.384	.400	UNK/NA	1.07	1.44	B	436
8x60mmS Mauser & RWS /8x60RmmS Mauser & RWS	C	.323	.350	.431	.470	.468/.526	.050	2.365	3.11	.217/5603/542	590
8x57mmJS Mauser/ 8x57RmmJS Mauser	C/A	.323	.350	.435	.470	.473/.526	.043/.04 8	2.24/2.25	3.17/3.55	.217/5603/366D1	588
8mm-06	C	.323	.351	.441	.470	.473	.045	2.47	3.25	L	289
8x50Rmm Austrian Mannlicher	A	.323	.351	.462	.501	.553	.040	1.98	3.00	B	508
7.92x33mm Kurz	C	.323	.352	.440	.470	.470	UNK/NA	1.30	1.88	B	509
7.9x57mmJS (8mm Mauser JS)	C	.323	.353	.443	.469	.473	UNK/NA	2.24	3.17	B	510
8x68mmS RWS	C	.323	.354	.473	.522	.510	UNK/NA	2.65	3.38	.238/1698	589
8mm JDJ	A	.323	.356	.455	.470	.514	.058	2.22	V	L	360
8x63mm Swedish	C	.323	.356	.456	.488	.479	UNK/NA	2.48	3.36	B	511
.310 Cadet	B	.324	.320	UNK/NA	.353	.405	.035	1.12	1.72	.177/69	540
7.5mm Swedish Nagant Revolver	B	.325	.328	UNK/NA	.350	.406	UNK/NA	.89	1.35	B	436
8x59mm Breda	C	.326	.357	.433	.491	.469	UNK/NA	2.33	3.17	B	512
8x56Rmm Austrian-Hungarian Mannlicher (M31)	A	.329	UNK/NA	UNK/NA	UNK/NA	UNK/NA	UNK/NA	UNK/NA	UNK/NA	UNK/NA	512
.318 Rimless Nitro Express	C	.330	.358	.445	.465	.465	UNK/NA	2.39	3.40	.217/81	540
.333 Jeffery Flanged	A	.333	.356	.484	.544	.625	UNK/NA	2.50	3.49	.317	541
.333 Jeffery Rimless	C	.333	.359	.496	.540	.538	UNK/NA	2.48	3.48	.217/59	541
.33 Winchester	A	.333	.365	.443	.508	.610	.065	2.11	2.80	L	186
8.5 Mars	C	.335	.356	.415	.505	.491	.04	1.128	1.583	B	437
.338 Spectre	C	.338	.361	.415	.425	.420	.049	1.25	2.10	L	361
.338 Whisper	C	.338	.360	.457	.463	.466	.048	1.47	V	S	361
.338 Woodswalker	A	.338	.360	.410	.420	.482	.060	1.86	2.51	L	360
.338-223 Straight	D	.338	.362	UNK/NA	.376	.378	.041	1.41	2.25	S	291
.338 Allen Magnum	C	.338	.363	.61	.637	.64	.065	3.025	4.2	Fed 215 L	362
.338 JDJ	A	.338	.365	.453	.470	.514	.058	2.20	V	L	363
.340 Weatherby Magnum	E	.338	.366	.495	.513	.530	.048	2.82	3.60	L	131
.338 Allen Xpress	C	.338	.366	.561	.59	.59	.06	2.7	3.6-3.95	Fed 215 L	291
.338 A-Square	K	.338	.367	.553	.582	.603/.580	.060	2.85	3.67	L	363
8.59 Galaxy	C	.338	.368	.557	.577	.577	.060	2.05	2.80	L	361
.338 Blaser Magnum	I	.338	.368	.512	.544	.535	.054	2.507	3.34	L	591
.338 Federal	C	.338	.369	.454	.470	.473	.049	2.01	2.75	LR	132
.338 Winchester Magnum	E	.338	.369	.480 (.491)	.515 (.5127)	.530	.047	2.49 (2.50)	3.30 (3.34)	L	132
.338 Norma Magnum	C	.338	.369	.570	.585	.587	.059	2.50	3.68	.238/1698	592
.338-06 A-Square	C	.338	.370	.441	.470	.473	.049	2.494	3.240 (3.440)	L	134
.338 Lehigh	C	.338	.369	.4268	.439	.441	.053	1.40	2.26	S	364

CARTRIDGE	CASE TYPE	BULLET DIAMETER	NECK DIAMETER	SHOULDER DIAMETER	BASE DIAMETER	RIM DIAMETER	RIM THICKNESS	CASE LENGTH	CARTRIDGE LENGTH	PRIMER	PAGE
.33 BSA (.33 Belted Rimless)	E	.338	.369	.453	.534	.534	UNK/NA	2.40	3.10	.217/59	541
.338 Canadian Magnum	I	.338	.369	.530	.544	.532	.046	2.83	3.60	L	365
8.59 Titan	C	.338	.369	.557	.577	.577	.060	2.80	3.60	L	366
.338-378 Weatherby Magnum	E	.338	.369	.561	.581	.579	.063	2.193	3.638	L	133
.338-06 JDJ	C	.338	.370	.455	.470	.467	.045	2.465	V	L	367
.338 Marlin Express	A	.338	.370	.493	.506	.553	.055	1.890	2.585	L	134
.338 Ruger Compact Magnum (RCM)	C	.338	.370	.515	.532	.532	.040	2.10	2.825	L	135
.338 GNR	A	.338	.370	.435	.463	.543	.075	2.545	3.20	L	366
.338 Lapua Magnum	C	.338	.370	.540	.590	.590	.060	2.72	3.60	L	136
.338 Remington Ultra Mag	I	.338	.371	.526	.550	.534	.050	2.76 (3.600)	3.450	L	136
.330 Dakota	C	.338	.371	.530	.544	.544	.045	2.57	3.32	L	367
.338 Excaliber	C	.338	.371	.566	.580	.580	.058	2.99	3.75	L	368
.338/50 Talbot	C	.338	.380	.748	.774	.782	.080	3.76	4.25	50 BMG	292
.348 Winchester	A	.348	.379 (.3757)	.485	.553	.610	.062	2.26 (2.255)	2.80 (2.795)	L	137
.35 Winchester Self Loading (WSL)	H	.351	.374	UNK/NA	.378	.405	.045	1.14	1.64	S	186
.351 Winchester Self Loading (WSL)	H	.351	.374	.378	.407	1.38	.045	1.91	16	UNK/NA	187
9mm Ultra	D	.355	.374	UNK/NA	.386	.366	UNK/NA	.72	I.03	SPB	437
9mm Bayard Long	D	.355	.375	UNK/NA	.390	.392	UNK/NA	.91	1.32	B	438
9mm Browning Long	D	.355	.376	UNK/NA	.384	.404	UNK/NA	.80	1.10	B	438
9mm Mauser	D	.355	.376	UNK/NA	.389	.390	.050	.981	1.38	B	439
9mm Winchester Magnum	D	.355	.379	UNK/NA	.392	.394	.046	1.16	1.545	SP	439
9mm Glisenti	D	.355	.380	UNK/NA	.392	.393	UNK/NA	.75	1.15	B	440
9mm Luger (9x19mm Parabellum)	D	.355	.380	UNK/NA	.392	.393	.042	.754	1.16	SPB	441
9x21mm	D	.355	.380	UNK/NA	.392	.393	UNK/NA	.830	1.16	SP	442
9x23mm Winchester	D	.355	.380	UNK/NA	.390	.392	.042	.900	1.245	LP	443
9mm Steyr	D	.355	.380	UNK/NA	.380	.381	UNK/NA	.90	1.30	B	443
.356 TSW (Team Smith & Wesson)	D	.355	.38	.3804	.3907	.394	.066	.85	1.16	SP	440
9mm Federal	B	.355	.382	UNK/NA	.386	.435	UNK/NA	.754	1.163	SP	444
9x25 Dillon	C	.355	.382	.423	.423	.424	.050	.99	1.26	SP	292
9mm Action Express	I	.355	.390	.433	.435	.394	.045	.866	1.152	S	293
.380 Automatic (9mm Browning Short)	D	.356	.373	UNK/NA	.373	.374	.040	.68	.98	SP	445
9x56mm Mannlicher-Schoenauer	C	.356	.378	.408	.464	.464	UNK/NA	2.22	3.56	.217/5603/491E	593
9x57mm Mauser/9x57Rmm Mauser	C/A	.356	.380	.428/.424	.467	.468/.515	.045/.05 0	2.24	3.10/3.08	.217/5603/491/A491B	593
9x21mm Russian (9x21mm Gyurza)	D	.356		.38	.39	.39	.047	.82	1.38		513
9x39mm SP-5 & SP-6	C	.356	.38	.408	.447	.447	.059	1.528	2.2	S	513
.38 AMU	H	.357	.259	.373	.376	.404	.047	1.153	1.153	SP	446

CARTRIDGE	CASE TYPE	BULLET DIAMETER	NECK DIAMETER	SHOULDER DIAMETER	BASE DIAMETER	RIM DIAMETER	RIM THICKNESS	CASE LENGTH	CARTRIDGE LENGTH	PRIMER	PAGE
.38 Short Colt	D	.357	.357	UNK/NA	.378	.433	.055	.76	1.10	SP	446
.38 Casull	C	.357	UNK/NA	UNK/NA	.476	.476	.044	UNK/NA	1.17	UNK/NA	369
.357 Remington Maximum	B	.357	.375	UNK/NA	.375	.433	.055	1.59	1.97	SP	447
.38 Long Colt	B	.357	.377	UNK/NA	.378	.433	.055	1.03	1.32	SP	446
.357 S&W Magnum	B	.357	.379	UNK/NA	.379	.440	.055	1.29	1.51	SP	449
.38 Special	B	.357	.379	UNK/NA	.379	.440	.054	1.16	1.55	SP	448
.357 SIG	C	.357	.381	.424	.425	.424	.055	.865	1.14	SP	449
.357 Auto Magnum	C	.357	.382	.461	.470	.473	.048	1.298	1.60	LP	294
.356 GNR	A	.358	.360	.433	.434	.498	.054	1.250	UNK/NA	UNK/NA	370
.358 JDJ	A	.358	.362	.453	.470	.514	.058	.220	3.065	L	370
.357 Herrett	A	.358	.375	.405	.420	.505	.058	1.75	2.10	L	294
.400/360 Nitro Exp. (2¾-inch)	A	.358	.375	.437	.470	.590	UNK/NA	2.75	3.59	.241	544
.35/30-30 (.35-30)	A	.358	.378	.401	.422	.506	.058	2.04	2.55	L	295
.35 Winchester	A	.358	.378	.412	.457	.539	UNK/NA	2.41	3.16	L	188
.400/350 Rigby	A	.358	.380	.415	.470	.520	UNK/NA	2.75	3.60	.241/34	542
.350 No. 2 Rigby	A	.358	.380	.415	.470	.520	.050	2.75	3.60	.241/34	542
.350 Rigby Magnum	C	.358	.380	.443	.519	.525	UNK/NA	2.75	3.60	.241/34	542
.38 Automatic & .38 Super Automatic	H	.358	.382	UNK/NA	.383	.405	.045	.90	1.28	SP	450
.358 BFG (1.625 Inch)	I	.358	.382	.539	.555	.535	.054	1.625	2.37	L	296
.35 Newton	C	.358	.383	.498	.523	.525	UNK/NA	2.52	3.35	L	188
.358 Gremlin	C	.358	.384	.427	.438	.440	.059	1.495	2.25	S	297
.35 Remington	C	.358	.384	.419 (.4259)	.458 (.4574)	.460	.046	1.92	2.52	L	137
.35 Indiana	C	.358	.384	.437	.458	.460	.046	1.80	2.70	L	297
.35 SuperMann	C	.358	.384	.437	.458	.460	.046	1.91	2.78	L	298
.358 Norma Magnum	E	.358	.384	.489	.508	.526	.048	2.52	3.22	L	595
.35-06 JDJ	C	.358	.385	.455	.470	.467	.045	2.445	V	L	371
.358 STA (Shooting Times Alaskan)	E	.358	.386	.502	.513	.532	.048	2.85	3.65	L	371
9.09 Eagle	C	.358	.387	.557	.577	.577	.060	2.05	2.80	L	372
.35 Whelen	C	.358	.388	.441	.470	.473	.045	2.50 (2.494)	3.34	L	138
.356 Winchester	G	.358	.388	.454	.4703	.508	.058	2.02 (2.015)	2.56	L	139
.358 Hoosier	C	.358	.388	.454	.470	.473	.048	1.80	2.70	L	299
.358 Winchester	C	.358	.388	.454	.4703	.473	.048	2.01 (2.015)	2.78	L	140
.350 Remington Magnum	E	.358	.388	.495	.5126	.532	.046	2.17	2.80	L	140
.35 Sambar	I	.358	UNK/NA	.538	.555	.535	.054	2.10	2.86	UNK/NA	300
.358/300 WSM	I	.358	.390	.538	.550	.534	.054	2.10	2.56	L	301
.358 UMT (Ultra Mag Towsley)	E	.358	.390	.525	.550	.534	.054	2.85	3.50	UNK/NA	300

CARTRIDGE	CASE TYPE	BULLET DIAMETER	NECK DIAMETER	SHOULDER DIAMETER	BASE DIAMETER	RIM DIAMETER	RIM THICKNESS	CASE LENGTH	CARTRIDGE LENGTH	PRIMER	PAGE
.360 Mars	C	.359	.37	.455	.505	.491	.04	1.045	1.414	B	451
.38 S&W/.38 Colt New Police	B	.359	.386	UNK/NA	.386	.433	.055	.78	1.20	SP	452
.35-30 Maynard (1882)	B	.359	.395	UNK/NA	.400	.494	UNK/NA	1.63	2.03	S	189
.35-40 Maynard (1873)	B	.360	.390		.400	.492		2.06	2.53	S	190
.35-40 Maynard (1882)	B	.360	.390	UNK/NA	.400	.492	UNK/NA	2.06	2.53	S	190
.360 No. 5 Rook	B	.362	.375	UNK/NA	.380	.432	UNK/NA	1.05	1.45	UNK/NA	543
9mm Russian Makarov	D	.363	.384	UNK/NA	.389	.396	UNK/NA	.71	.97	B	452
9.4mm Dutch	B	0.380	0.430		0.433	0.480	0.054	1.070	1.310	B	453
.357 Atomic GWA	B	0.357	0.379		0.379	0.440	0.055	1.29	1.51	SP	448
.375 Super Magnum	B	0.375	0.415		0.416	0.506	0.063	1.610	1.965	LP	453
.375 Atomic	B	0.375	0.400		0.415	0.502	0.063	1.4	1.62	L	454
.360 Nitro (2¼-inch)	B	.365	.384	UNK/NA	.430	.480	.040	2.25	2.80	.241/34	544
.360 Express (2¼-inch)	B	.365	.384	UNK/NA	.430	.480	.040	2.25	3.00	.241/34	543
9.3x74Rmm	A	.365	.387	.414	.465	.524	.052	2.93	3.74	.217/5603/474A	596
9.3x57mm Mauser	C	.365	.389	.428	.468	.469	UNK/NA	2.24	3.23	.217/5603/491	595
9.3x62mm Mauser	C	.365	.388	.447	.473	.470	.044	2.42	3.29	5603/474	141
9.3 Sisk	C	.366	.388	.486	.512	.532	.047	2.85	3.57	L	302
9.3mm JDJ	A	.366	.389	.455	.465	.506	.058	2.22	V	L	373
9.3 B&M	I	0.366	0.403	0.530	0.552	0.532	0.048	2.256	2.950	L	373
9.3 BS	E	.366	.390	.495	.5126	.532	.046	2.165	2.80	L	303
.366 DGW (David G. Walker)	C	.366	UNK/NA	UNK/NA	.589	.586	.058	UNK/NA	UNK/NA	UNK/NA	302
.370 Sako Magnum/7.3x66mm Sako	C	.366	.405	.450	.477	.470	.047	2.598	3.346	L	142
9.3x64mm Brenneke	C	.366	.395	.474	.507	.496	.051	2.52	3.37	L	597
.360 No. 2 Nitro Express	A	.367	.393	.517	.539	.631	.045	3.00	3.85	.254/40	544
9.3x74Rmm Nimrod	A	.367	.395	.405	.432	.484	.044	2.93	3.523	LP	598
.35-30 Maynard (1865)	B	.370	.397	UNK/NA	.408	.771/1.07	.037	1.53	1.98	Externally primed	190
.38-40 Remington Hepburn	B	.372	.395	UNK/NA	.454	.537	UNK/NA	1.77	2.32	S	190
.38 Short	B	.375	.376	UNK/NA	.376	.436	UNK/NA	.768	1.185	UNK/NA	621
.38 Long	B	.375	.376	UNK/NA	.376	.435	UNK/NA	.873	1.380	UNK/NA	621
.380 Short & Long Revolver	B	.375	.377	UNK/NA	.380	.426	.046	.70	1.10	SPB	621
.38 Long, CF*	B	.375	.378	UNK/NA	.379	.441	UNK/NA	1.03	1.45	S	191
.38 Ballard Extra Long*	B	.375	.378	UNK/NA	.379	.441	UNK/NA	1.63	2.06	S	192
.38 Extra Long	B	.375	.378	UNK/NA	.378	.435	UNK/NA	1.480	2.025	UNK/NA	621
.375 Whisper	C	.375	UNK/NA	UNK/NA	UNK/NA	UNK/NA	UNK/NA	UNK/NA	UNK/NA	UNK/NA	374
.375/454 JDJ Woodswalker	B	.375	UNK/NA	UNK/NA	UNK/NA	UNK/NA	UNK/NA	UNK/NA	UNK/NA	UNK/NA	374
.375 JDJ	A	.375	.396	.453	.470	.514	.058	2.20	3.13	L	374

CARTRIDGE	CASE TYPE	BULLET DIAMETER	NECK DIAMETER	SHOULDER DIAMETER	BASE DIAMETER	RIM DIAMETER	RIM THICKNESS	CASE LENGTH	CARTRIDGE LENGTH	PRIMER	PAGE
.375 Flanged Nitro Express (2½-inch)	B	.375	.397	UNK/NA	.456	.523	UNK/NA	2.50	3.10	.217/34	544
.400/375 Belted Nitro Express (H&H)	E	.375	.397	.435	.470	.466	UNK/NA	2.50	3.00	.217	545
.376 Steyr	I	.375	.398	.472	.501	.494	.048	2.35	3.075	L	143
.369 Nitro Express (Purdey)	A	.375	.398	.475	.543	.616	UNK/NA	2.69	3.60	.254/40	546
.378 Weatherby Magnum	E	.375	.399	.560	.582	.579	.063	2.913	3.65	L	144
.375 Winchester	B	.375	.400	UNK/NA	.415 (.4198)	.502	.063	2.02	2.56	L	144
.375 Rimless NE (9.5x57mm)	C	.375	.400	.460	.471	.473	.40	2.25	2.94	.217	545
9.5x57mm Mannlicher-Schoenauer/ 9.5x56mm Mannlicher-Schoenauer	C	.375	.400	.460	.471	.473	.040	2.25	2.94	.217/5603/ 531	598
.375 Allen Magnum	C	.375	.401	.605	.637	.64	.065	3.025	4.2	Fed 215 L	376
.38-35 Stevens	B	.375	.402	UNK/NA	.403	.492	UNK/NA	1.62	2.43	S	192
.375 H&H Magnum	E	.375	.402	.440 (.4478)	.521	.530	.046	2.85	3.60	L	145
.375 Dakota	C	.375	.402	.529	.544	.544	.046	2.57	3.32	L	376
.375 Canadian Magnum	I	.375	.402	.530	.544	.532	.046	2.83	3.60	L	377
.375 Weatherby Magnum	E	.375	.402	.492	.512	.531	.051	2.85	3.540 (3.800)	L	146
.375 Whelen & Ackley Improved Whelen	C	.375	.403	.442/.455	.470	.473	.045	2.50	3.42	L	303
.375 Allen Xpress	C	.375	.403	.56	.59	.59	.06	2.7	3173.95	Fed 215 L	304
.375 Remington Ultra Mag	I	.375	.405	.525	.550	.534	.050	2.85	3.540 (3.600)	L	147
.375 Rimless Belted Magnum	E	.375	.404	.440	.464	.530	UNK/NA	2.85	3.60	.217/60	545
.375 Flanged Magnum	A	.375	.404	.450	.515	.572	UNK/NA	2.94	3.80	.217/40	546
9.53 Hellcat	C	.375	.404	.557	.577	.577	.060	2.05	2.80	L	375
9.53 Saturn	C	.375	.404	.557	.577	.577	.060	2.80	3.60	L	378
.375-06 JDJ	C	.375	.405	.457	.470	.467	.045	2.435	V	L	375
.375 Ruger	C	.375	.405	.515	.532	.532	.050	2.58	3.34	L	146
.375 Blaser Magnum	I	.375	.405	.507	.544	.535	.054	2.822	3.622	L	599
.375 A-Square	K	.375	.405	.551	.582	.603/.580	.060	2.85	3.65	L	378
.38-50 Maynard (1882)	B	.375	.415	UNK/NA	.421	.500	.069	1.97	2.38	S	192
.375 JRS Magnum	E	.375	.498	.485	.535	UNK/NA	.048	2.84	3.69	L	379
.375 B&M	I	0.375	0.410	0.530	0.550	0.532	0.048	2.251	2.950	Fed 215	379
9.3x48Rmm	B	.376	.382	UNK/NA	.433	.492	UNK/NA	1.89	2.35	.254/1775/ 246	600
9.3x72Rmm	B	.376	.385	UNK/NA	.427	.482	UNK/NA	2.84	3.27	.254/1775/ 77D	596
9.3x57Rmm	B	.376	.389	UNK/NA	.428	.486	UNK/NA	2.24	2.80	.254/1775/ 77E	595
.38-50 Remington Hepburn	B	.376	.392	UNK/NA	.454	.535	UNK/NA	2.23	3.07	S	193
.38-50 Ballard Everlasting	B	.376	.395	UNK/NA	.425	.502	UNK/NA	2.00	2.72	S	193
.38-90 Winchester Express	A	.376	.395	.470	.477	.558	UNK/NA	3.25	3.70	L	194
.38-56 Winchester	A	.376	.403	.447	.506	.606	.065	2.10	2.50	L	194

CARTRIDGE	CASE TYPE	BULLET DIAMETER	NECK DIAMETER	SHOULDER DIAMETER	BASE DIAMETER	RIM DIAMETER	RIM THICKNESS	CASE LENGTH	CARTRIDGE LENGTH	PRIMER	PAGE
.38-72 Winchester	A	.378	.397	.427	.461	.519	UNK/NA	2.58	3.16	L	195
.38-55 Winchester/.38-55 Ballard	B	.379	.392	.3938	.422	.506	.058	2.12 (2.085)	2.51	L	148
.41 Long Colt	B	.386/4 01	.404	UNK/NA	.405	.430	.052	1.13	1.39	SP	455
.40 S&W Auto	D	.400	.423	UNK/NA	.423	.424	.050	.850	1.135	SP	455
10mm Auto	D	.400	.423	UNK/NA	.423	.424	.050	.99	1.26	LP	456
.41 Short Colt	B	.401	.404	UNK/NA	.405	.430	.052	UNK/NA	UNK/NA	SP	457
.401 Bobcat	B	0.401	0.425		0.442	0.472	0.045	1.400	1.550	L	457
.38-40 Winchester	A	.401	.416	.438 (.4543)	.465	.520	.058	1.30	1.59	LP	148
.400 A-Square DPM (400 Pondoro)	E	0.410	0.450	0.520	0.521	0.530	0.046	2.85	3.600	L	380
.400 CorBon	C	.401	.423	.469	.470	.471	.050	.898	1.20	LP	380
.40-44 Woodswalker	A	.401	.428	.455	.455	.510	.055	1.295	V	LP	381
.40-454 JDJ	A	.401	.428	.470	.470	.510	.055	1.395	V	LP	381
.40-70 Sharps (Straight)	B	.403	.420	UNK/NA	.453	.533	.078	2.50	3.18	L	195
.40-50 Sharps (Straight)	B	.403	.421	UNK/NA	.454	.554	.078	1 88	2.63	B1	196
.40-50 Sharps (Necked)	A	.403	.424	.489	.501	.580	UNK/NA	1.72	2.37	B1	196
.40-60 Marlin	B	.403	.425	UNK/NA	.504	.604	UNK/NA	2.11	2.55	S	197
.40-85 (.40-90) Ballard	B	.403	.425	UNK/NA	.477	.545	UNK/NA	2.94	3.81	S	197
.40-90 Sharps (Straight)	B	.403	.425	UNK/NA	.477	.546	UNK/NA	3.25	4.06	B1	198
.40-70 Sharps (Necked)	A	.403	.426	.500	.503	.595	UNK/NA	2.25	3.02	L	199
.40-110 Winchester Express	A	.403	.428	.485	.565	.651	UNK/NA	3.25	3.63	L	200
.40-63/.40-70 Ballard Everlasting	B	.403	.430	UNK/NA	.471	.555	UNK/NA	2.38	2.55	S	200
.40-90 Sharps (Necked)	A	.403	.435	.500	.506	.602	UNK/NA	2.63	3.44	B1	199
.40-60 Winchester	A	.404	.425	.445	.506	.630	UNK/NA	1.87	2.10	S	201
.41 Short	B	.405	.406	UNK/NA	.406	.468	UNK/NA	.467	.913	UNK/NA	622
.41 Long	B	.405	.407	UNK/NA	.407	.468	UNK/NA	.635	.985	UNK/NA	622
.40-70 Winchester	A	.405	.430	.496	.504	.604	UNK/NA	2.40	2.85	L	201
.450/400 Nitro Express (3¼-inch)	A	.405	.432	.502	.544	.615	.040	3.25	3.85	.254/40	554
.450 3¼-inch BPE	A	.405	.432	UNK/NA	UNK/NA	UNK/NA	UNK/NA	UNK/NA	UNK/NA	.254/40	552
.40-70 Remington	A	.405	.434	.500	.503	.595	UNK/NA	2.25	3.00	L	202
.400 Whelen	C	.405	.436	.462	.470	.473	.048	2.49	3.10	L	304
.40-65 Winchester	B	.406	.423	UNK/NA	.504	.604	UNK/NA	2.10	2.48	L	202
.401 Winchester Self Loading (WSL)	H	.406	.428	UNK/NA	.429	.457	.055	1.50	2.00	L	203
.40-82 Winchester Center Fire (WCF)	A	.406	.428	.448	.502	.604	.060	2.40	2.77	L	203
.40-72 Winchester	B	.406	.431	UNK/NA	.460	.518	UNK/NA	2.60	3.15	L	202
.450/400 (2 3/8-inch)	A	.407	.427	.456	.545	.616	.035	2.38	2.95	UNK/NA	548
.40-90 Peabody "What Cheer"	A	.408	.433	.546	.586	.659	UNK/NA	2.00	3.37	B1	204

CARTRIDGE	CASE TYPE	BULLET DIAMETER	NECK DIAMETER	SHOULDER DIAMETER	BASE DIAMETER	RIM DIAMETER	RIM THICKNESS	CASE LENGTH	CARTRIDGE LENGTH	PRIMER	PAGE
.41 Remington Magnum	B	.410	.432	UNK/NA	.433	.488	.054	1.28	1.58	LP	458
.41 Special	B	.410	.432	UNK/NA	.433	.488	.056	1.16	1.60	LP	305
.41 Action Express	J	.410	.434	UNK/NA	.435	.394	.045	.866	1.17	SP	459
.414 Super Magnum	B	0.410	0.434		0.435	0.492	0.059	1.610	1.965	LP	459
.41 GNR	A	.410	.436	.458	.461	.514	.055	1.24	1.60	L	382
.410 GNR	A	.410	.439	.477	.480	.512	.055	1.349	1.69	L	383
.400 Jeffery Nitro Express (.450/400 3-inch)	A	.410	.434	.518	.545	.613	UNK/NA	3.00	3.75	.254/40	548
.408 Cheytac	C	.408	.438	.601	.637	.640	.065	3.04	4.307	LR	382
.411 Express	C	.411	UNK/NA	UNK/NA	.440	.468	.045	UNK/NA	UNK/NA	UNK/NA	383
.411 JDJ	A	.411	.425	.455	.465	.506	.058	2.235	V	L	384
.411 Hawk	C	.411	UNK/NA	UNK/NA	.440	.468	.045	UNK/NA	UNK/NA	UNK/NA	384
.405 Winchester	B	.412	.436	UNK/NA	.461	.543	.075	2.58	3.18	L	205
.40-90 Bullard	A	.413	.430	.551	.569	.622	UNK/NA	2.04	2.55	L	205
.40-75 Bullard	B	.413	.432	UNK/NA	.505	.606	UNK/NA	2.09	2.54	S	206
10.4mm Swiss Vetterli	A	.415	.437	.518	.540	.630	.055	1.60	2.20	B-RF	515
10.3x60Rmm Swiss	A	.415	.440	.498	.547	.619	UNK/NA	2.36	3.08	UNK/NA	601
.40-40 Maynard (1882)	B	.415	.450	UNK/NA	.456	.532	UNK/NA	1.78	2.32	S	206
.416 Aagaard	C	.416	.441	.492	.506	.496	.049	2.35	UNK/NA	LR	307
.416 Rigby	C	.416	.445 (.4461)	.539 (.5402)	.589	.586	.058	2.90	3.75	L	551
.416 JDJ	A	.416	.430	.455	.465	.506	.058	2.22	V	L	385
.416 Barnes	A	.416	.432	.484	.505	.608	.065	2.112	2.95	L	306
.416 UMT (Ultra Mag Towsley)	C	.416	.440	.525	.550	.534	.050	2.85	3.54	L	307
.416 Dakota	C	.416	.441	.527	.544	.544	.042	2.85	3.645	L	386
.416-06 JDJ	C	.416	.443	.455	.470	.467	.045	2.415	V	L	385
.416 Weatherby Magnum	K	.416	.444	.561	.584	.603/.580	.062	2.915	3.75	L	149
.416 Ruger	C	.416	.445	.515	.532	.532	.050	2.58	3.24	L	150
.416 Rigby	C	.416	.445	.539	.589	.589	.062	2.90	3.72	Bx	150
10.57 Maverick	C	.416	.445	.557	.577	.577	.060	2.05	2.80	L	387
10.57 Meteor	C	.416	.445	.557	.577	.577	.060	2.80	3.62	L	387
.416 Rimmed	A	.416	.446	.549	.573	.665	.060	3.300	4.100	L	388
.416 BGA	C	.416	UNK/NA	UNK/NA	.504	.492	UNK/NA	UNK/NA	UNK/NA	UNK/NA	386
.416 Remington Magnum	E	.416	.447	.487	.509	.530	.046	2.85	3.60	L	151
.416 Taylor	E	.416	.447	.491	.513	.532	.048	2.50	3.34	L	388
.416 Hoffman	E	.416	.447	.491	.513	.532	.048	2.85	3.60	L	389
.416 B&M	I	0.416	0.450	0.534	0.552	0.526	0.056	2.253	3.000	Fed 215	390
.416 SM2	B	.416	.447	.538	.555	.535	.054	2.072	3.75	L	307

CARTRIDGE	CASE TYPE	BULLET DIAMETER	NECK DIAMETER	SHOULDER DIAMETER	BASE DIAMETER	RIM DIAMETER	RIM THICKNESS	CASE LENGTH	CARTRIDGE LENGTH	PRIMER	PAGE
.40-60 Maynard (1882)	B	.417	.448	UNK/NA	.454	.533	UNK/NA	2.20	2.75	S	207
.40-70 Maynard (1882)	B	.417	.450	UNK/NA	.451	.535	UNK/NA	2.42	2.88	B1	207
.44 Evans Long (.44-40 Straight)	B	.419	.434	UNK/NA	.449	.509	UNK/NA	1.54	2.00	L	207
.44 Evans Short	B	.419	.439	UNK/NA	.440	.513	UNK/NA	.99	1.44	S	208
10.75x73mm/.404 Rimless Nitro Express/.404 Jeffery	C	.421	.450	.520	.544	.537	.045	2.86	3.53	.217/555	602
10.4mm Italian Revolver	B	.422	.444	UNK/NA	.451	.505	UNK/NA	.89	1.25	B	460
.404 Jeffery (.404 Rimless Nitro Express)	C	.422	.450	.520	.544	.537	.045	2.87	3.53	.217/81	550
.425 Express	E	.423	.429	.490	.513	.532	.048	2.552	3.34	L	391
10.3x65Rmm Baenziger	B	.423	.431	UNK/NA	.462	.505	UNK/NA	2.56	3.15	UNK/NA	602
.44 Henry Center Fire Flat	B	.423	.443	UNK/NA	.445	.523	UNK/NA	.88	1.36	S	208
10.75x68mm Mauser	C	.424	.445	.470	.492	.488	UNK/NA	2.67	3.16	.217/5603/515A	602
.44 Game Getter/.44-40 Marlin/.44 Colt Lightning	A	.427	.443	.458	.471	.520	.065	1.31	Varies	L	209
.44-40 Winchester (.44 WCF)	A	.427/.429	.443	.4568	.471	.525	.058	1.31	1.92	LP	152
.44-40 Extra Long	A	.428	.442	.463	.468	.515	UNK/NA	1.58	1.96	S	209
.444 Marlin	B	.429	.453	.4549	.469	.514	.058	2.16 (2.225)	2.57	L	153
.44 S&W Russian	B	.429	.457	UNK/NA	.457	.515	.050	.97	1.43	LP	460
.44 Remington Magnum	B	.429	.457	UNK/NA	.457	.514	.055	1.29	1.61	LP	461
.44 S&W Special	B	.429	.457	UNK/NA	.457	.514	.055	1.16	1.62	LP	461
.44 Auto Mag	D	.429	.457	UNK/NA	.470	.473	.048	1.298	1.620	LP	462
.440 CorBon	I	.429	.461	.529	.538	.510	.055	1.280	1.59	LP	391
.45 Raptor	D	0.452	0.478		0.478	0.473	0.055	1.800	2.300	L	392
.44/454 JDJ Woodswalker	B	.429	UNK/NA	UNK/NA	.480	.515	.055	UNK/NA	UNK/NA	UNK/NA	391
.458 SOCOM	I	.458	.452	.530	.538	.473	.048	1.575	2.015	UNK/NA	393
10.447mm Italian M/70	A	.430	.437	.517	.540	.634	.058	1.87	2.46	B	515
10.75x58Rmm Russian Berdan	A	.430	.449	.506	.567	.637	.080	2.24	2.95	B	515
.445 Super Magnum	B	.432	.456	UNK/NA	.457	.514	.055	1.60	1.985	LP	308
.425 Westley Richards	I	.435	.456	.540	.543	.467	UNK/NA	2.64	3.30	UNK/NA	551
.416 Barrett	C	.416	.460	.730	.803	.804	.083	3.273	4.563	Bx	390
.44 Long Center Fire (Ballard)*	B	.439	.440	UNK/NA	.441	.506	UNK/NA	1.09	1.65	S	209
.44 Extra Long Center Fire (Ballard)*	B	.439	.441	UNK/NA	.441	.506	UNK/NA	1.63	2.10	S	210
.44 Wesson Extra Long*	B	.440	.441	UNK/NA	.441	.510	UNK/NA	1.63	2.19	S	210
.44 Bull Dog	B	.440	.470	UNK/NA	.473	.503	UNK/NA	.57	.95	SPB	464
10.6 German Ordnance	B	0.417	0.430	0.453	0.454	0.509	0.060	0.981	1.45	B	464
.44-90 Remington Special (Necked)	A	.442	.466	.504	.520	.628	.075	2.44	3.08	L	211
.44-95/.44-100 Peabody "What Cheer"	A	.443	.465	.550	.580	.670	UNK/NA	2.31	3.32	B1	211

CARTRIDGE	CASE TYPE	BULLET DIAMETER	NECK DIAMETER	SHOULDER DIAMETER	BASE DIAMETER	RIM DIAMETER	RIM THICKNESS	CASE LENGTH	CARTRIDGE LENGTH	PRIMER	PAGE
.44-100 Wesson	B	.445	UNK/NA	UNK/NA	.515.520	.605.610	UNK/NA	3.38	3.85	L	213
.44-70 Maynard (1882)	B	.445	.466	UNK/NA	.499	.601	UNK/NA	2.21	2.87	B1	212
11mm French Gras 11x59Rmm Vickers	A	.445	.468	.531	.544	.667	.075	2.34	3.00	B	467
.44-100 Ballard	B	.445	.485	UNK/NA	.498	.605	.080	2.81	3.25	L	212
.44-75 Ballard Everlasting	B	.445	.487	UNK/NA	.497	.603	UNK/NA	2.50	3.00	B2	213
.44 Short	B	.446	.445	UNK/NA	.445	.519	.066	.688	1.190	UNK/NA	622
.44 Henry Flat	B	.446	.445	UNK/NA	.446	.519	.066	.875	1.345	UNK/NA	623
.44 Extra Long	B	.446	.456	UNK/NA	.457	.524	UNK/NA	1.250	1.843	UNK/NA	623
11.15x60Rmm (.43) Mauser	A	.446	.465	.510	.516	.586	.075	2.37	3.00	B	519
.44-77 Sharps & Remington	A	.446	.467	.502	.516	.625	UNK/NA	2.25	3.05	LB1	214
.44-90 Sharps Necked	A	.446	.468	.504	.517	.625	.065	2.63	3.30	B1	214
.44-60 Sharps & Remington (Necked)	A	.447	.464	.502	.515	.630	UNK/NA	1.88	2.55	LB1	215
.44-60 Winchester & Peabody "Creedmoor"	A	.447	.464	.502	.518	.628	UNK/NA	1.89	2.56	B1	216
.45 Remington Thompson	D	.447	.470	UNK/NA	.472	.471	.044	1.12	1.45	LP	519
11.43mm Turkish/.45 Peabody-Martini	A	.447	.474	.560	.582	.668	UNK/NA	2.30	3.12	B	520
.45 Wildey Magnum	C	.450	UNK/NA	UNK/NA	.500	.473	.048	1.295	1.58	L	308
.44 Long	B	.451	.455	UNK/NA	.458	.525	UNK/NA	1.094	1.842	UNK/NA	623
.445 Super Magnum	B	0.429	0.456		0.457	0.514	0.055	1.610	1.965	LP	465
.45 Winchester Magnum	D	.451	.475	UNK/NA	.477	.481	.045	1.198	1.55	LP	467
.451 Detonics Magnum	D	0.451	0.475		0.477	0.481	0.045	0.944	1.294	LP	468
.460 Rowland	D	.451	.476	UNK/NA	.476	.476	.044	.955	1.27	LP	468
.45 GAP (Glock Automatic Pistol)	D	.452	.473	UNK/NA	.476	.470	.049	.760	1.137	LP	470
.45 Webley	B	.452	.471	UNK/NA	.471	.504	UNK/NA	.82	1.15	LPB	469
.45 Auto-Rim	B	.452	.472	UNK/NA	.476	.516	.085	.898	1.28	LP	469
.45 Automatic Match	D	.452	.476	NA	.476	.476	.044	.898	1.14	LP	471
45 ABC Mi-Bullet	D	.452	.476	NA	.476	.476	.044	.898	1.17	LP	472
.45 Automatic Short/.45 HP	D	.452	.476	UNK/NA	.476	.476	.044	.860	1.17	LP	471
.45 Automatic Colt Pistol (ACP)	D	.452	.476	UNK/NA	.476	.476	.044	.898	1.17	LP	472
.45 Super	D	0.452	0.476		0.476	0.476	0.044	0.898	1.17	LP	473
.450 SMC	D	0.452	0.476		0.476	0.476	0.044	0.898	1.17	SR	474
.454 Casull	B	.452	.476	UNK/NA	.480	.512	.055	1.39	1.70	S	474
.460 S&W	B	.452	.478	UNK/NA	.478	.520	.059	1.80	2.290	LP	475
11.5x57Rmm (.43) Spanish Reformado	B	.454	.466	UNK/NA	.525	.631	UNK/NA	2.26	3.06	B	521
.455 Webley Revolver MkII	B	.454	.476	UNK/NA	.480	.535	UNK/NA	.77	1.23	LPB	476
.45 Colt	B	.454	.476	UNK/NA	.480	.512	.055	1.29	1.60	LP	475
.45 S&W Schofield	B	.454	.478	UNK/NA	.478	.522	.055	1.10	1.43	LP	477

CARTRIDGE	CASE TYPE	BULLET DIAMETER	NECK DIAMETER	SHOULDER DIAMETER	BASE DIAMETER	RIM DIAMETER	RIM THICKNESS	CASE LENGTH	CARTRIDGE LENGTH	PRIMER	PAGE
.45 Colt Government	B	.454	.478	UNK/NA	.478	.506	.055	1.10	1.44	LP	476
.45-50 Peabody (Sporting)	A	.454	.478	.508	.516	.634	UNK/NA	1.54	2.08	UNK/NA	215
.45-75 Winchester (Centennial)	A	.454	.478	.547	.559	.616	UNK/NA	1.89	2.25	L	216
.45-60 Winchester	B	.454	.479	UNK/NA	.508	.629	UNK/NA	1.89	2.15(?)	L	217
.45-100 Ballard	B	.454	.487	UNK/NA	.498	.597	UNK/NA	2.81	3.25	L	217
.455 Webley Automatic	H	.455	.473	UNK/NA	.474	.500	UNK/NA	.93	1.23	B	478
.455 Enfield (.455 Colt)	B	.455	.473	UNK/NA	.478	.530	.035	.87	1.35	LPB	478
.577/450 Martini Henry	A	.455	.487	.628	.668	.746	.050	2.34	3.12	B	522
.46 Short	B	.456	.458	UNK/NA	.458	.530	UNK/NA	.836	1.336	UNK/NA	624
.45-75/.45-70 Sharps 21/10-inch	B	.457	UNK/NA	UNK/NA	UNK/NA	UNK/NA	UNK/NA	2.10	2.90	L	218
.45-82/.45-85/.45-90 Winchester & .45-90 Winchester High Velocity	B	.457	.477	UNK/NA	.501	.597	.065	2.40	2.88	L	219
.45-75 Van Choate	B	.457	Same as .45-70	UNK/NA	UNK/NA	UNK/NA	UNK/NA	2.25	2.91	L	218
.45-70 Government	B	.458	.475 (.480)	.4813	.500	.600 (.608)	.065	2.105	2.55	L	154
.450 Rigby	B	.458	.475	.539	.589	.589	UNK/NA	2.90	3.80	Bx	555
.45 Silhouette	B	.458	.477	UNK/NA	.501	.600	.065	1.51	1.97	L	309
.458 Hubel Express	F	0.458	0.481		0.527	0.532	0.050	3.400	3.950	L	309
.450 No. 2 Nitro Express (3½-inch)	A	.458	.477	.518	.564	.650	UNK/NA	3.50	4.42	.254/40	555
.458x2-inch American	F	.458	.478	UNK/NA	.508	.532	.048	2.00	2.60	L	310
.458 Winchester Magnum	F	.458	.478 (.4811)	.4825	.513	.532	.046	2.50	3.34	L	155
.450 Nitro Express (3¼-inch)	B	.458	.479	UNK/NA	.545	.624	.040	3.25	4.11	.254/40	553
.500/450 Nitro Express (3")	A	.458	.479	.500	.570	.644	UNK/NA	3.25	3.91	.254/40	554
.500/450 Magnum Express	A	.458	.479	.500	.570	.644	UNK/NA	3.25	3.91	.254/40	554
.450 Bushmaster	J	.458	.480	UNK/NA	.500	.473	.050	1.70	2.26	L	155
.457 WWG (Wild West Guns)	B	.458	.480	UNK/NA	.5039	.605	.070	2.21	2.49	L	156
.450 Marlin	F	.458	.480	UNK/NA	.511	.532	.047	2.09	2.55	L	157
.450 Alaskan	A	.458	.480	.515	.547	.605	.062	2.25	2.79	L	313
.450 Howell	C	.458	.480	.515	.545	.534	.045	2.5	3.25	L	312
.460 G&A Special	C	.458	.480	.530	.545	.545	.049	2.86	UNK/NA	L	313
.458 B&M EX	I	0.458	0.485	0.531	0.550	0.538	0.048	2.510	3.586	Fed 215	314
.458 Lott	F	.458	.481	UNK/NA	.513	.532	.050	2.80	3.400 (3.600)	L	157
.450 Watts Magnum	F	.458	.481	UNK/NA	.513	.530	.048	2.85	3.65	L	314
.450 KNR	A	.458	UNK/NA	UNK/NA	UNK/NA	UNK/NA	UNK/NA	UNK/NA	UNK/NA	UNK/NA	308
.460 A-Square Short	K	.458	.484	.560	.582	.603/.580	.060	2.50	3.50	L	395
.458 Whisper	F	.458	.485	UNK/NA	.506	.525	.048	1.75	V	L	393
.458 B&M	I	0.458	0.487	0.529	0.554	0.525	0.048	2.250	2.950	Fed 215	394
.458 B&M Super Short	I	0.458	0.490	0.534	0.554	0.534	0.052	1.648	2.245	Fed 210	394

CARTRIDGE	CASE TYPE	BULLET DIAMETER	NECK DIAMETER	SHOULDER DIAMETER	BASE DIAMETER	RIM DIAMETER	RIM THICKNESS	CASE LENGTH	CARTRIDGE LENGTH	PRIMER	PAGE
.460 Alliance	I	.458	.485	.530	.550	.534	.045	1.575	2.015	L	311
.458 Canadian Magnum	I	.458	.485	.530	.544	.532	.046	2.83	3.60	L	395
.450 Dakota	C	.458	.485	.560	.582	.580	.058	2.90	3.74	L	396
.460 Weatherby Magnum	K	.458	.485	.560	.584	.603/.580	.062	2.91	3.75	L	158
.450 Ackley Magnum	E	.458	.487	.503	.512	.532	.048	2.85	3.65	L	396
.450 Assegai	A	.458	.487	.549	.573	.665	.060	3.300	4.100	L	397
.450 Bonecrusher	A	.458	.488	.530	.535	.610	.060	1.40	1.77	L	312
.45-90/.45-100/.45-110 Sharps (24/10-inch, 26/10-inch, 2¾-inch)	B	.458	.489	UNK/NA	.500	.597	.065	2.40, 2.60, 2.75, 2.87	2.85, 3.00	B1	219
.45-120/.45-125 (3-inch) Sharps	B	.458	.490	UNK/NA	.506	.597	.065	3.25	4.16	L	220
.458x1½-inch Barnes	F	.458	.493	UNK/NA	.509	.530	UNK/NA	1.50	2.19	Bx	310
.460 Steyr (11.64mm)	C	.458	.501	.719	.805	.805	.089	3.64	4.80	Bx	605
.46 Extra Long	B	.459	.457	UNK/NA	.457	.525	UNK/NA	1.534	2.285	UNK/NA	624
11.751Rmm Danish Remington	B	.462	.486	UNK/NA	.514	.579	UNK/NA	2.01	2.45	B	523
.56-46 Spencer	A	.465	.478	.555	.558	.641	UNK/NA	1.035	1.595	UNK/NA	624
.500/465 Nitro Express	A	.466	.488	.524	.573	.650	UNK/NA	3.25	3.89	.254/40	556
.465 H&H Magnum	E/C	.468	.494	.531	.582	.579	.063	2.894	3.55	L	555
.475 Ackley & OKH Magnum	F	.474	.496	UNK/NA	.508	.528	.048	2.739	3.518	L	314
.475 Linebaugh	B	.475	.495	UNK/NA	.501	.600	.065	1.50	1.77	L	397
.475 JDJ	B	.475	.497	UNK/NA	.502	.604	.065	2.10	V	L	398
.475 Wildey Magnum	I	.475	.497	UNK/NA	.500	.473	.048	1.295	1.58	L	315
.470 Capstick	F	.475	.499	UNK/NA	.513	.532	.048	2.85	3.65	L	399
.470 Nitro Express	A	.475	.500	.528	.572	.646	.035	3.25	4.00	.254/40	556
12.04 Bibamufu	C	.475	.500	.557	.577	.577	.060	2.80	3.62	L	399
.475 B&M	I	0.474	0.506	0.533	0.553	0.526	0.056	2.244	3.040	Fed 215	316
.475 Lehigh	J	.475	.504	UNK/NA	.504	.480	.044	.950	1.17	LP	317
.499 Hubel Express No. 2	F	0.500	0.523		0.565	0.630	0.050	3.550	3.920	L	317
.480 Ruger	B	.475	.504	UNK/NA	.540	.540	.065	1.285	1.65	UNK/NA	480
.470 Nitro Express	A	.475	.504	.528 (.5322)	.5728	.655	.037	3.25	3.98	L	556
.470 Turnbull	A	.4755	.502	.5371	.5517	.61	.07	2.205	2.55	L	400
.475 B&M Super Short	I	0.474	0.506	0.538	0.557	0.535	0.052	1.650	2.318	Fed 210	400
.475 Turnbull	A	.4755	.504	.5371	.5517	.61	.07	2.205	2.78	L	400
.476 Nitro Express (Westley Richards)	A	.476	.508	.530	.570	.643	UNK/NA	3.00	3.77	.254/40	558
.475 Nitro Express (3¼-inch)	B	.483	.502	UNK/NA	.545	.621	UNK/NA	3.25	4.00	.254/40	557
.475 No. 2 Nitro and Jeffery	A	.489	.510	.547	.576	.666	UNK/NA	3.50	4.33	.254/40	557
.500 Cyrus	L	.500	.528	.580	.582	.531	.058	2.333	2.90	L	318

CARTRIDGE	CASE TYPE	BULLET DIAMETER	NECK DIAMETER	SHOULDER DIAMETER	BASE DIAMETER	RIM DIAMETER	RIM THICKNESS	CASE LENGTH	CARTRIDGE LENGTH	PRIMER	PAGE
.500 S&W	B	.500	.530	UNK/NA	.530	.560	.059	1.625	2.250	LP	481
.50 Action Express	J	.500	.540	UNK/NA	.547	.514	.055	1.285	1.610	LP	481
.500 Wyoming Express	F	.500	UNK/NA	UNK/NA	UNK/NA	UNK/NA	UNK/NA	1.37	1.765	LR	401
.510 GNR	B	.500	.514	.548	.550	.614	.070	1.19	UNK/NA	UNK/NA	402
.50 Beowulf	J	.500	.525	UNK/NA	.535	.445	.055	1.65	2.125	UNK/NA	402
.50 GI	J	.500	.526	UNK/NA	.526	.480	.048	.899	1.221	UNK/NA	403
.500 JRH	B	.500	.527	UNK/NA	.527	.545	.055	1.40	1.80	L	480
.505 Gibbs	C	.505	.530	.588	.635	.635	UNK/NA	3.15	3.85	.254/40	560
.577/500 No. 2 Express	A	.507	.538	.560	.641	.726	.055	2.83	3.40	.251/31A	558
.577/500 Nitro Express (3⅛-inch)	A	.508	.526	.585	.645	.717	.055	3.13	3.74	.251/31A	559
.50-90 Sharps	B	.509	.528	UNK/NA	.565	.663	.060	2.50	3.20	L	221
.50-140 (3¼") Sharps & Winchester	B	.509/.512	.528	UNK/NA	.565	.665	.060	3.25	3.94	L	221
.500 Phantom	I	.500	.535	UNK/NA	.620	.532	UNK/NA	1.525	2.28	UNK/NA	403
.502 Thunder Sabre	J	0.500	0.540		0.538	0.440	0.055	1.286	1.690	LP	404
.500 Express Nitro for Black (3-inch)	B	.510	.535	UNK/NA	.580	.660	.055	3.01	3.39	.251/31A	559
.500 Nitro Express (3¼-inch)	B	.510	.535	UNK/NA	.580	.660	.040	3.25	3.63	.251/31A	559
.50 Remington Navy	B	.510	.535	UNK/NA	.562	.642	UNK/NA	.860	1.280	UNK/NA	624
.500 Jeffery	I	.510	.535	.615	.620	.575	UNK/NA	2.75	3.47	.254/40	560
12.50x70mm Schüler (.500 Jeffery)	I	.510	.535	.615	.620	.578	UNK/NA	2.94	3.50	.254/2703	606
.510 Nitro Express	B	.510	.535	UNK/NA	.565	.665	UNK/NA	3.245	4.185	L	318
.500 A-Square	K	.510	.536	.568	.582	.603/.580	.060	2.90	3.74	L	404
.50 Peacekeeper	K	.510	.538	.565	.586	.603/.580	.058	2.882	V	L	405
.50 TAC	I	.510	.538	.580	.582	.531	.058	2.333	3.75	L	319
.500 Linebaugh	B	.510	.540	UNK/NA	.553	.610	.062	1.405	1.755	L	405
.500 Belted Magnum	L	.510	.540	UNK/NA	.584	.603/.580	.062	2.50	3.25	L	319
.495 A-Square	L	.510	.542	UNK/NA	.582	.603/.580	.060	2.80	3.60	L	407
50 B&M Alaskan	B	0.500	0.529	0.539	0.548	0.592	0.070	2.104	2.580	Fed 215	407
500 B&M	I	0.500	0.525	0.540	0.550	0.538	0.048	2.506	3.224	Fed 215	406
50 B&M	J	0.500	0.532		0.552	0.534	0.050	2.258	2.940	Fed 215	408
500 MDM	I	0.500	0.525	0.543	0.550	0.538	0.048	2.800	3.463	Fed 215	407
.500 Whisper	K	.510	.549	.563	.580	.603/.580	.060	2.90	V	L	408
.50 McMillan FatMac	C	.510	.550	1.111	1.152	1.158	.090	2.645	V	50 BMG	320
.510 Allen Magnum	C	.51	.552	.77	.8	.8	.08	3.9	5.75	CCI-35	409
.50 McMurdo	C	.510	.554	.725	.800	.802	.078	3.70	5.722	50 BMG	321
.50 BMG (Browning Machine Gun)	C	.510 (.511)	.555 (.560)	.708 (.714)	.800 (.804)	.800 (.804)	.080	3.90 (3.91)	5.43 (5.545)	Bx/50 BMG	159
50 B&M Super Short	I	0.500	0.535		0.555	0.536	0.055	1.645	2.258	Fed 210	409

CARTRIDGE	CASE TYPE	BULLET DIAMETER	NECK DIAMETER	SHOULDER DIAMETER	BASE DIAMETER	RIM DIAMETER	RIM THICKNESS	CASE LENGTH	CARTRIDGE LENGTH	PRIMER	PAGE
.50 American Eagle	I	.510	.560	.714	.804	.440	.053	UNK/NA	UNK/NA	UNK/NA	410
.50-100/.50-105/.50-110 Winchester/ .50-110 Winchester High Velocity	B	.512	.534	UNK/NA	.551	.607	.063	2.40	2.75	L	222
.56-52 Spencer Rifle	B	.512	.540	UNK/NA	.559	.639	.065	1.035	1.500	UNK/NA	625
.56-50 Spencer	B	.512	.543	UNK/NA	.556	.639	.065	1.156	1.632	UNK/NA	625
.50-115 Bullard	G	.512	.547	.577	.585	.619	UNK/NA	2.19	2.56	L	222
.50-95 Winchester/Winchester Express	A	.513	.533	.553	.562	.627	UNK/NA	1.94	2.26	L	223
.50 U.S. Carbine	B	.515	.535	UNK/NA	.560	.660	UNK/NA	UNK/NA	UNK/NA	B1	224
.50-70 Government Musket	B	.515	.535	UNK/NA	.565	.660	.060	1.75	2.25	L	525
.50-70 Government	B	.515	.535	UNK/NA	.565	.660	.060	1.75	2.25	Bx	526
.56-52 Spencer (Necked)	A	.525	.547	.558	.560	.642	.065	1.020	1.660	UNK/NA	625
.505/530 Woodleigh	C	.530	UNK/NA	UNK/NA	UNK/NA	UNK/NA	UNK/NA	UNK/NA	UNK/NA	UNK/NA	321
.56-56 Spencer	B	.550	.560	UNK/NA	.560	.645	.065	.875	1.545	UNK/NA	625
.577 Snider (14.7mm)	B	.570	.602	UNK/NA	.660	.747	.052	2.00	2.45	B	527
.577 Nitro Express (3-inch)	B	.584	.608	UNK/NA	.660	.748	.052	3.00	3.70	.254/40	561
.585 Nyati	I	.585	.605	.650	.660	.532/.586	UNK/NA	2.79	3.525	L	322
.585 Hubel Express	F	0.585	0.607		0.634	0.637	0.050	3.250	3.900	L	323
.700 Hubel Express	F	0.700	0.735		0.775	0.775	0.050	3.850	4.300	50 BMG	323
.577 Tyrannosaur	C	.585	.614	.673	.688	.688	.060	2.99	3.71	L	410
14.5 JDJ	C	.585	UNK/NA	UNK/NA	.804	.804	.080	UNK/NA	UNK/NA	UNK/NA	410
14.5x114mm	C	.586	.65	1.004	1.061	1.061	.098	4.5	6.134		527
.58 Carbine (Berdan)	B	.589	.625	UNK/NA	.640	.740	UNK/NA	UNK/NA	UNK/NA	B2	225
.58 U.S. Musket (Berdan)	B	.589	.625	UNK/NA	.646	.740	.062	1.75	2.15	B1	225
.600/577 JDJ	B	.620	UNK/NA	UNK/NA	.660	.748	.052	UNK/NA	UNK/NA	UNK/NA	411
.600 Nitro Express	B	.620	.648	UNK/NA	.697	.805	UNK/NA	3.00	3.68	.254/40	562
.700 Nitro Express	B	.700	.728	UNK/NA	.780	.890	UNK/NA	3.50	4.20	Bx	562
.729 Jongmans	C	.727	UNK/NA	UNK/NA	.804	.804	.080	UNK/NA	UNK/NA	UNK/NA	324
.700 JDJ	C	.727	UNK/NA	UNK/NA	.804	.804	.080	UNK/NA	UNK/NA	UNK/NA	411
.950 JDJ	C	.950	UNK/NA	UNK/NA	UNK/NA	UNK/NA	UNK/NA	UNK/NA	4.0	UNK/NA	411
12 Gauge From Hell (12 GFH)	B	0.729	0.770		0.803	0.880	0.072	3.850	4.300	Rem 209	324
4 Bore Hubel	H	1.000	1.043		1.093	1.180		4.050	4.550	Centerfire	635

Key To Abbreviations

Notes: Bullet diameter can vary by several thousandths. The sizes listed are those that are most commonly encountered or are as specified in appropriate standards.

Cartridge length is not a particularly useful measure for identifying cartridges: This often varies widely, depending upon load type and bullet weight; it can vary between manufacturers; and it can vary with time, standard length from one era might not hold in another. An example is the 45-70 cartridge: 405gr. loads from the 1870s are about 2.625" long while current standards call for a maximum length of 2.55". Similar examples abound.

Case type: (For simplicity the various common rimmed/rimless pairs are listed together but with separate dimension, where variation occurs): A = Rimmed, bottleneck. B = Rimmed, straight. C = Rimless, bottleneck. D = Rimless, straight. E = Belted, bottleneck. F = Belted, straight. G = Semi-rimmed, bottleneck. H = Semi-rimmed, straight. I = Rebated, bottleneck. J = Rebated, straight. K = Rebated, belted bottleneck. L = Rebated, belted straight.

Primer type: S = Small rifle (.175"). SP = Small pistol. (.175"). L = Large rifle (.210"). LP = Large pistol (.210"). Bx = Boxer. B = Berdan type. B-1 = Berdan #1. B-2 = Berdan #2. 50 BMG = CCI-35/VihtaVuori-110/RWS-8212.

Note on blackpowder primers: Not all companies used the same primer type or size in the same caliber or length case. For example, the 45-70 or its equivalent was usually loaded with the standard Large Rifle-diameter primers. However, Marlin's version used Small Rifle-diameter primer and Sharps Co., ammunition used Berdan primers. Primer type and size listed is what appears to have been the most general (common?) size and type used.

Finally, earliest loadings for the military and possibly other cartridges used an internal primer and were not reloadable. This practice continued until about 1877, perhaps later with some manufacturers. In some instances the earliest outside primers were .250" in diameter. Some early 30-06 military loading also used a .250" primer. It is possible other oddball primer sizes might be encountered, for example, both the 38-40 and the 45 Automatic have sometimes been loaded with small-diameter Boxer primers. Likely this is true of the 44-40 and perhaps many other chamberings, too.

Notes on handgun primers: Magnum pistol cartridges are usually loaded with special Magnum primers and the 22 Remington Jet and 256 Winchester are sometimes loaded with Small Rifle primers. The 454 Casull is always loaded with Small Rifle primers. During WWI, Frankford Arsenal made 45 Automatic cases with special #70 primers of .204" diameter instead of the standard .210". Recently, at least one foreign manufacturer produced 45 Automatic ammunition using Small Pistol primers.

* Cartridges so marked used an outside lubricated bullet when originally introduced; these bullets were heel-based. The front was about the same diameter as the outside of the case neck (shell mouth) just like a modern 22 rim fire cartridge. Later, inside-lubricated loadings used an inside case mouth diameter bullet: these bullets usually had a long, hollow base intended to expand to fill the rifling while providing a cleaner-to-handle load. (This system was never particularly successful.)

V**   Various versions exist, these differ chiefly in length of the case and loaded cartridges.

**   Original 22-10-45 Maynard case length was 1.25".

***   This is a blackpowder primer smaller than standard Small Rifle or Pistol size. It has not been used or available for decades.

****   The 8x60mm, 8x60Rmm (dimensionally similar to the 8x60mm Mauser, except for the rim) and 8x64mm Brenneke, are dimensionally the same as "S" designated series, shown, excepting use of bullets of .318" diameter.

Other codes: Belt/Rim Diameter. Twist (standard factory) is given as inches per complete revolution, e.g., 12 means 1 turn in 12 inches of barrel, etc. 25.4mm, exactly, equals 1 inch. Unless otherwise noted, all dimensions are in inches. Data in parenthesis represents SAAMI maximum specifications. UNK/NA = Unknown/Not Applicable

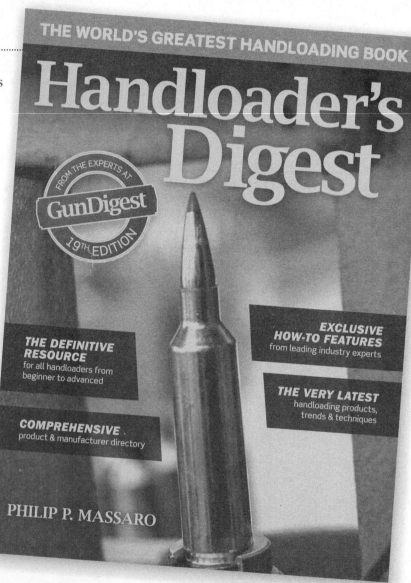